Scottis … nanac

Edited by Andy McGregor

Rel8 Media

SCOTTISH FOOTBALL ALMANAC 2021/22

Published by Rel8 Media
Unit 7, Woodend Business Centre, Cowdenbeath, Fife, KY4 8HG.

A great deal of effort has been made to ensure that the information in this book is as accurate as possible. However, in a work of this nature there will inevitably be some inaccuracies. Neither the publishers nor the author can accept responsibility for any consequences arising from using this book.

Sources used have been acknowledged where appropriate. The author has tried to clear all copyright permissions but where this has not been possible and where amendments are required, then the publisher will be pleased to make any necessary arrangements at the earliest opportunity.

British Library in Publication Data.
A catalogue record for this volume is available from the British Library.

ISBN 978-1-9164147-2-3

ARDATH CIGARETTE CARDS

In this edition of the Almanac we have used numerous Cigarette Cards from the 1936 Ardath Series. The cigarette company produced similar series covering most parts of the UK. A full list of the cards in the Scottish series is shown below.

1. Inverness Caledonians F.C.
2. Inverness Thistle F.C.
3. Clachnacuddin (Inverness) F.C.
4. Highland (Inverness) R.U.F.C
5. Forres Mechanics F.C.
6. Lossiemouth Rangers F.C.
7. Moray (Elgin) R.U.F.C
8. Elgin City F.C.
9. Keith F.C.
10. Rothes F.C.
11. Dufftown F.C.
12. Huntley Gordon Schools F.C.
13. Banff Rovers F.C.
14. Deveron Valley F.C.
15. Fraserburgh F.C.
16. Peterhead F.C.
17. Aberdeen F.C.
18. Aberdeen Abergelde F.C.
19. Aberdeen University F.C.
20. Aberdeen City Police Club
21. Aberdeen East End Juniors F.C.
22. Aberdeen Mugiemoss F.C.
23. Aberdeen School Boys
24. Aberdeen Shop Assistants Union F.C.
25. Aberdeen Wednesday Jnr. Select XI
26. Hawthorn F.C.
27. Hawthorn & East End Select
28. Rosemount F.C.
29. Mannofield F.C.
30. Inverurie Loco Works F.C.
31. Montrose F.C.
32. Montrose Roselea F.C.
33. Brechin City F.C.
34. Arbroath F.C.
35. Arbroath Victoria F.C.
36. Forfar Athletic F.C.
37. Forfarshire Jnr. Select
38. Alyth United
39. Blairgownie F.C.
40. Dundee F.C.
41. Dundee United
42. Dundee Arnott
43. Dundee East Craigie Jnrs. F.C.
44. Dundee Fairfield Jnrs. F.C.
45. Dundee Jnr. League Select
46. Dundee North End Juniors F.C.
47. Dundee St. Josephs Jnrs.FC
48. Dundee Stobswell Junrs.
49. Dundee Violet Junrs. F.C.
50. Forthill Athletic Jnrs. F.C.
51. Lochee Harp Juniors F.C.
52. Lochee United Jnrs.
53. Fair City Athletic F.C.
54. Perth Academicals F.C.
55. Perth Celtic Jnrs.
56. Perth Half Holiday Jnr. Seiect F.C.
57. Perth Roselea
58. Perthshire Jnr. Select XI
59. St Johnstone F.C.
60. Scone Thistle F.C.
61. Crieff Earngrove F.C.
62. Dunblane Rovers F.C.
63. East Stirlingshire F.C.
64. Stirlingshire Jnr. Select
65. Kings Park F.C.
66. Alloa Athletic F.C.
67. Newburgh Tayside Athletic F.C.
68. Dunfermline R.U.F.C. -
69. Dunfermline Athletic F.C.
70. Cowdenbeath F.C.
71. Raith Rovers F.C.
72. East Fife F.C.
73. Tranent Juniors F.C.
74. Spittal Council School Old Boys
75. Tweeside Co-op F.C.
76. Kelso R.U.F.C. -
77. Jedforest R.U.F.C. -
78. Hawick R.U.F.C.
79. Hawick High School R.U.F.C.
80. Selkirk R.U.F.C.
81. Gala Star R.U.F.C. -
82. Gala Red Triangle F.C.
83. Gala Red Triangle R.U.F.C
84. Walkerburn R.U.F.C
85. Peebles Rovers F.C.
86. Penicuik F.C.
87. George Heriot's School F.P. R.U.F.C. -
88. Royal High School F.P. R.U.F.C. -
89. Edinburgh Institution F.P. R.U.F.C. -
90. Edinburgh City F.C.
91. Heart of Midlothian F.C.
92. Hibernians F.C.
93. St. Bernards F.C.
94. Leith Athletic F.C.
95. Falkirk F.C.
96. Stenhousemuir F.C.
97. Kilsyth Emmet F.C.
98. Kilsyth Rangers F.C.
99. Twechar United F.C.
100. Cumbernauld Thistle F.C.
101. Belshill Athletic F.C.
102. Albion Rovers F.C.
103. Airdrieonians F.C.
104. Motherwell F.C.
105. Coltness United F.C.
106. Larkhall Thistle F.C.
107. Stonehouse Violet F.C.
108. Hamilton Academicals F.C.
109. Blantyre Victoria F.C.
110. Glasgow Rangers F.C.
111. Glasgow Celtic F.C.
112. Glasgow Academicals R.U.F.C.
113. Queens Park F.C.
114. Partick Thistle F.C.
115. Glasgow University R.U.F.C.
116. Glasgow High School F.P. R.U.F.C.
117. Glasgow Perthshire F.C.
118. West of Scotland R.U.F.C.
119. St. Anthony's Juniors F.C.
120. Shawfield Juniors F.C.
121. Kelvinside Academicals R.U.F.C.
122. Hillhead High School F.P. R.U.F.C.
123. Shettleston Juniors F.C.
124. Cambuslang Rangers F.C.
125. Pollok F.C.
126. Third Lanark F.C.
127. Petershill F.C.
128. Rutherglen Glencairn F.C.
129. Strathclyde F.C.
130. St. Rock's Jnrs.FC
131. St. Mungo F.C.
132. Parkhead Jnrs.FC
133. Bridgeton Waverley F.C.
134. Ashfield F.C.
135. Maryhill Jnrs. F.C.
136. Maryhill Hibs. F.C.
137. Clyde F.C.
138. Johnstone Jnrs. F.C.
139. Kirkintilloch Rob Roy F.C.
140. Milngavie Jnrs. F.C.
141. Renfew F.C.
142. Arthurlie F.C.
143. Clydebank Jnrs. F.C.
144. Vale of Clyde F.C.
145. Voter Athletic F.C.
146. St. Mirren F.C.
147. Dumbarton F.C.
148. Duntocher Hibs. F.C.
149. Dumbarton Harps F.C.
150. Vale Ocoba F.C.
151. Greenock Morton F.C.
152. Greenock Morton Juniors F.C.
153. Dunoon F.C.
154. Rothesay Royal Vic. F.C.
155. Androssan Winton F.C.
156. Ayr Corinthians F.C.
157. Ayr United F.C.
158. Kilmarnock F.C.
159. Maybole Amateurs F.C.
160. Girvan F.C.
161. Stranraer F.C.
162. Dalbeattie Star F.C.
163. Laurieknowe Fr
164. Queen of the South F.C.
165. Glenafton Athletic Jnrs. F.C.

CONTENTS

SOURCES / ACKNOWLEDGEMENTS

Most of the information for this book has been obtained from media sources. The websites of the SFA and SPFL have been most informative, as have some official club websites. "Unofficial" web sources, including the mine of information that is Pie and Bovril, have also been useful in clarifying certain points. Increasingly information is made available through Twitter and Facebook which are vital sources.

Club match programmes have also been useful. Those that provide a "record" of club news and events are particularly helpful when putting together a project of this nature.

Historical records have come mainly from Rothmans, Sky Sports and Sun Year Books. For football outwith the Scottish Professional Football League extensive use was made of back issues of the invaluable Scottish Non League Review, published annually by Stewart Davidson from the late 1980s until 2017.

Thanks also to John Litster who has double-checked the stats and pointed out a number of errors and omissions from the original draft.

David Stoker's website "scottishfootballfixtures.wordpress.com" has also been invaluable in keeping track of dates and scores. Jock Gardiner provided information about Scottish Cup crowds.

Others who have provided specific information are acknowledged in the body of the book.

My thanks go to everyone who takes the time to update and disseminate information about football, via websites, Twitter, Facebook and printed media.

Thanks also to the clubs and associations that responded to requests for information. Once again, those that responded were in the minority.

INTRODUCTION

Season 2020/21 must rate as the strangest in the history of Scottish football. The premise of professional and semi-professional football is that people may money to go to matches and finance the clubs. Yet virtually every game in 2020/1 was played Behind Closed Doors.

This raises some interesting questions. As far as I am aware no clubs went to the wall due to lockdown. A few clubs have gone into abeyance but no more than would be expected in any normal season. Clubs have therefore shown that it was possible to survive without fans in the ground. Of course many thousands of fans did put their hands in their pockets and purchased season tickets but had to be content with watching live streams of matches on the internet. There was some generous and welcome philanthropy from individuals to support Scottish football through difficult times and the Government played their part with funding as well. Will football lose some fans who will never return to the grounds for live action? Will football clubs continue with alternative revenue raising streams that they brought in during the lockdown? Will philanthropy continue to be evident in the Scottish game?

Team of the year were undoubtedly St Johnstone who won both major domestic Cup competitions. Successes like these have come so infrequently for the Perth side that it was desperately sad that their fans could not be present to see either win. Rangers won the Premiership title. They were worthy winners in their own right, going through the season in magnificent style, undefeated in League games, but they also benefited from a major implosion at their great rivals Celtic. It seems unlikely that the Parkhead side can make an instant recovery so Rangers will be odds on to win a second title in 2021/2.

Kilmarnock were relegated out of the top-flight for the first time in nearly 30 years, along with Hamilton Accies. Hearts and Dundee replace them meaning that the Premiership will feature Glasgow, Edinburgh and Dundee derbies this season.

Huge praise must go to Kelty Hearts for achieving SPFL status. They have managed to combine investment on the field with investment off the field – they have a decent team and excellent facilities to allow them to pursue their ambitions further. It is sad to see Brechin City drop out of the League but after four desperate seasons they cannot look beyond themselves for any blame. Perhaps Brechin and Berwick can make a concerted effort for promotion back to the SPFL – when that happens we can really say that we have a "Pyramid System" that works.

The national team's performances in the Euros were a let-down. Home defeats from Croatia and the Czech Republic were disappointing. A draw against England was regarded as a "moral victory" but the bigger picture was one of failure. The reckless behaviour of thousands of fans who travelled to London without tickets and clearly contributed to additional COVID cases in Scotland was deplorable.

So too was the behaviour of Rangers fans "celebrating" their sides League Championship win. It's a strange world – despite their being no fans allowed at games, fan behaviour continued to make the headlines for all the wrong reasons. It may not be the fault of Rangers that such a rag-tag bunch of objectionable cretins attach themselves to them but the club could do more to distance themselves from such behaviour. Celtic fans were far from blameless too with their over the top reaction to the abject failure of Neil Lennon's team. Both sets of fans ooze a sense of entitlement which is thoroughly dispiriting to the rest of Scottish football.

In a typical season I would watch 200 or more matches in the flesh. In 2020/1 I was restricted to a few trips to England at times when travel was permitted and limited numbers of fans allowed into games. I also peered through mesh fences outside a few grounds and stood on roadsides to try and see some football action. Every club at every level that managed to fulfil fixtures does deserve credit for their efforts and indefatigability in getting matches played.

Hopefully 2021/2 sees a return to some degree of normality.

Finally, an apology for the late arrival of this year's Almanac. The "bitty" nature of the season, plus major changes in the game outside the SPFL, made it more difficult and time-consuming to compile. There is also some confusion about the structure of the pages covering football outside the SPFL, reporting on an uncompleted season under old structures and previewing a new season under revised structures. If the order and lay out seems illogical to the reader then it did seem logical to me at the time of writing.

Andy McGregor
July 2021

SCOTTISH FOOTBALL ASSOCIATION

SFA STRUCTURE 2020/21 (Source SFA Handbook and Website)

CONGRESS
Created in 2015, Congress is described as the national game's first fully-representative group of stakeholders.

It was the culmination of a two-year process of evolving the traditional Scottish FA Council and making it a more functional and inclusive body to debate, discuss and make recommendations on the key issues affecting the game.

Club and affiliate representatives are now joined by recognised bodies such as PFA Scotland, Scottish Coaches' and Managers' Association, Scottish Senior Football Referees' Association, Scottish Football Writers' Association and sportscotland.

Congress meets quarterly in addition to regular consultation meetings to provide feedback and guidance on prevalent strategic topics to the Scottish FA Board.

PATRON – HER MAJESTY THE QUEEN

Office Bearers:
President: Rod Petrie, **Vice President:** Michael Mulraney
Scottish FA Chief Executive: Ian Maxwell
Scottish Professional Football League: Andrew Dickson, Neil Doncaster, Graham Peterkin, Alastair Donald, Leeann Dempster, Malcom Mackay
Scottish Highland Football League: David Dowling
Scottish Lowland Football League: Andrew Waddell
East of Scotland Football League: Alistair Wilkie
South of Scotland Football League: Richard Shaw MBE
Scottish Amateur FA: Stuart Urquhart
Scottish Junior FA: Tom Johnston
Scottish Schools' FA: Alex McMenemy
Scottish Welfare FA: Callum Shanks
Scottish Women's Football: Vivienne MacLaren
Scottish Youth FA: John McCrimmond
Scottish Para Football: Robert Craig
Scottish FA Youth Ambassador: Joshua Barrie
PFA Scotland: Fraser Wishart
Managers and Coaches Association: Walter Macadam
Scottish Senior Football Referees' Association: Kevin Clancy
sportscotland: Mel Young
Media: Lindsay Herron
Supporters Direct Scotland: Alan Russell

BOARD 2020/21
The main Board consisted of eight members: the Scottish FA Office Bearers—Rod Petrie, President; Ian Maxwell, Chief Executive; and Michael Mulraney Vice President, plus Neil Doncaster (PGB), Duncan Fraser (PGB), Thomas McKeown (NPGB) and independent non-executive directors, Ana Stewart and Michael Kpedeko.

The Board focusses on corporate strategy and top-line decision-making, with the operational Professional Game Board and Non-Professional Game Board representing their respective parts of the game. These boards were created to provide greater focus in the affairs of the Professional and Non-Professional game.

Professional Game Board

Chair: Michael Mulraney (Scottish FA)

Members: Neil Doncaster (SPFL), Ian Maxwell (SFA), Michael Nicholson (SPFL), Duncan Fraser (SPFL), Ken Ferguson (SPFL), Les Gray (SPFL), Finlay Noble (SHFL) and Tom Brown (SLFL)

Non-Professional Game Board

Chair: Rod Petrie(Scottish FA)

Members: Ian Maxwell (SFA), Tom Anderson (Scottish Youth FA), John Gold (Scottish Schools FA), John Greenhorn (East of Scotland Football League), Colin Holden (South of Scotland Football League), Tom Johnston (Scottish Junior FA), John Campbell (Scottish Welfare FA), Fiona McIntyre (Scottish Women's Football), Thomas McKeown (Scottish Amateur FA), Robert Craig (Para-Football Scotland).

Equalities & Diversity Advisory Board

Chair: Ana Stewart (Scottish FA Board Member)

Members: Ian Maxwell (Scottish FA) Helen Webster, Professor Grant Jarvie, Dr Mohammed Ishaq, David Cameron, Ebru Koksal, Fiona Lilley, Mary Galbraith, Eila Davis, Carolina De Sousa (Scottish FA Youth Ambassador), David McArdle (Scottish FA), Annika Crisp (Scottish FA)

Licensing Committee

Chair: Derek Stillie (Independent Member)
Vice Chair: Ewen Cameron (SPFL)
Members: Donald McNaught (independent member), Anne McKeown (SPFL), Richard Shaw (independent member), John McCabe (Lowland League), Roddy Morrison (independent member), Brian Urquhart (independent member)

Referee Committee
Chair: Willie Young
Vice Chair: Steve Brown (St. Johnstone), David Reid (Stenhousemuir)
Members: Kevin Toner, Kenny Clark, Martin Cryans, Alan Freeland, Ian Fyfe, Calum Murray, Brian Winter

ASSOCIATIONS AND LEAGUES 2020/21

Affiliated Associations

ABERDEENSHIRE AND DISTRICT F.A.
Secretary William Young
Email adfa7@hotmail.co.uk

EAST OF SCOTLAND F.A.
Secretary John Greenhorn
Email secretary@eastofscotlandfa.co.uk

FIFE F.A.
Secretary Robert Mullen
Email fife.fa@outlook.com

FORFARSHIRE F.A.
Secretary Ken Ferguson
Email chairman@brechincityfc.com

GLASGOW F.A.
Secretary Allison More
Email amore@celticfc.co.uk

NORTH OF SCOTLAND F.A.
Secretary Graham Wilson
Email nofasecretary@gmail.com

SOUTHERN COUNTIES F.A.
Secretary Richard Osborne
Email richard.osborne1962@googlemail.com

STIRLINGSHIRE F.A.
Secretary Alan Christie
Email alangchristie@aol.com

WEST OF SCOTLAND F.A.
Secretary Tracy McTrusty
Email tracy@ayrunitedfc.co.uk

WIGTOWNSHIRE & DISTRICT F.A.
Secretary: Richard Osborne
Email richard.osborne1962@googlemail.com

AFFILIATED NATIONAL ASSOCIATIONS

SCOTTISH AMATEUR F.A.
Secretary Thomas McKeown, Hampden Park, Glasgow G42 9DB
Telephone (B) 0141 620 4550;
Email safa@scottish-football.com
www.scottishamateurfa.co.uk

SCOTTISH JUNIOR F.A.
Executive Officer: Alex McDowell
Telephone(s) (B) 0141 620 4560;
(F) 0141 620 4561
Email scottishjuniorfa@scottish-football.com
www.scottishjuniorfa.com

SCOTTISH SCHOOLS F.A.
Secretary John Watson, Hampden Park, Glasgow G42 9AZ
Telephone(s) (B) 0141 620 4570;
Email john.watson@scottish-football.com
www.scottishschoolsfa.com

SCOTTISH WELFARE F.A.
Secretary John Campbell, 61 High Street, Rothes AB38 7AY
Email johncampbell@scottishwelfarefa.co.uk
www.scottishwelfarefa.org

SCOTTISH WOMEN'S FOOTBALL
Secretary Fiona McIntyre, Hampden Park, Glasgow G42 9DF
Telephone(s) (B) 0141 620 4580
Email swf@scottish-football.com
www.scotwomensfootball.com

SCOTTISH YOUTH FOOTBALL ASSOCIATION
Secretary Florence Witherow, Hampden Park, Glasgow, G42 9DF
Telephone(s) (B) 0141 620 4590; (F) 0141 620 4591
Email syfa@scottish-football.com
www.scottishyouthfa.co.uk

Recognised Leagues

THE SCOTTISH PROFESSIONAL FOOTBALL LEAGUE
Secretary
Iain Blair, Hampden Park, Glasgow G42 9DE
Telephone(s)
(B) 0141 620 4140; (F) 0141 620 4141
Email iainblair@spfl.co.uk www.spfl.co.uk

THE SCOTTISH HIGHLAND FOOTBALL LEAGUE
Secretary
Roderick Houston
Email secretary@highlandleague.com
www.highlandfootballleague.com

THE SCOTTISH LOWLAND FOOTBALL LEAGUE
Secretary David Baxter,
Email secretary@slfl.co.uk

THE EAST OF SCOTLAND FOOTBALL LEAGUE
Secretary David Baxter
Email leaguesecretary@eastofscotlandfa.co.uk

THE SOUTH OF SCOTLAND FOOTBALL LEAGUE
Secretary Richard Osborne
Email richard.osborne1962@googlemail.com

THE WEST OF SCOTLAND FOOTBALL LEAGUE
Secretary Dave McKenna
Email davemckenna@hotmail.co.uk

REGISTER OF COMPETITIONS 2020/2021

The following is a list of competitions approved by the Scottish Football Association.

Affiliated Associations

Aberdeenshire & District F.A.
Aberdeenshire & District F.A. Challenge Cup
Aberdeenshire & District F.A. Shield

East of Scotland F.A.
East of Scotland Cup
East of Scotland Shield
King Cup
East of Scotland Qualifying Cup
Alex Jack Cup

Fife F.A.
The Fife Cup

Forfarshire F.A.
Forfarshire F.A. Challenge Cup

Glasgow F. A .
The City of Glasgow Cup

North of Scotland F.A
North of Scotland FA Cup
North of Scotland U20 League

Southern Counties F.A.
Southern Counties FA Challenge Cup
Southern Counties FA Alba Cup
J Haig Gordon Memorial Trophy
Potts Cup
South and East Cup Winners Shield
South Region Challenge Cup

Stirlingshire F.A.
Stirlingshire Cup

West of Scotland F.A.
Renfrewshire Cup
Renfrewshire Victoria Cup

Leagues
Aberdeenshire & District League
Aberdeenshire League

East of Scotland League

East of Scotland Football League Championship Premier Division
First Division
East of Scotland Football League Cup

Scottish Highland Football League
SHFL Championship
SHFL (Morganti) Cup
SHFL Under 17 League Championship

North Caledonian League
North Caledonian League

Scottish Professional Football League
Ladbrokes Premiership
Ladbrokes Championship
Ladbrokes League 1
Ladbrokes League 2
Scottish League Cup
Scottish Challenge Cup
SPFL Reserve League
SPFL Reserve League 2
SPFL Reserve League Cup
SPFL Reserve Challenge Cup

South of Scotland Football League
South of Scotland Football League
South of Scotland Football League Cup

Scottish Lowland League
League Championship
League Cup
Lower Pyramid Play Off
Development League :
Lowland Development League Cup
Lowland Development League Championship
Lowland Development League Challenge Cup
Lowland Development League KO Cup

North Caledonian F.A.
North Caledonian Cup
Football Times Cup
Jock Mackay Cup

Wigtownshire and District FA
Cree Lodge Cup
Tweedie Cup

West of Scotland League
West of Scotland League Premier Division
Conferences A, B and C
West of Scotland League Cup

SFA REGIONAL STRUCTURE

NORTH (Shetland, Orkney, Western Isles, Highland, Moray, Aberdeenshire and Aberdeen City)
Regional Office: Forres House Community Centre, High Street, Forres, IV36 1BU
Regional Manager: Graeme Sutherland
Regional Administrator: Claire Greig
Regional Development Officer: Michael McKenzie
Girls and Womens Club Development Officer: Joanne Murphy
Club Development Manager: Mark Slater
Player & Coach Development Officer: Calum MacDonald
Football Development Officers: Peter Budge (Highland Football Academy), Gordon Duff (Ross County), Emma Hunter (Aberdeen), Scott Duncan (Aberdeen)

EAST (Fife, Perth and Kinross, Dundee, Angus)
Regional Office: Institute of Sport & Exercise, University of Dundee, Old Hawkhill, Dundee, DD1 4HN
Regional Manager: Kevin Lee
Regional Administrator: Lorna Moffat
Club Development Manager: Gavin Tinley
Girls & Womens Club Development Officer: Samantha Milne
Player & Coach Development Officer: Gavin Beith
Football Development Officer (Angus Council): Ross Smith
Football Development Officer (Dundee): Niall Nicolson
Football Development Officer (Perth & Kinross): Atholl Henderson
Football Development Officers (Fife): David Honeyman, Lee Bailey

CENTRAL (Clackmannanshire, East Dunbartonshire, North Lanarkshire, Stirling, West Dunbartonshire)
Regional Office: SFA Central Region Office, Woodlands Games Hall, Cochrane Avenue, Falkirk, FK1 1QE
Regional Manager: Alan Morgan
Regional Administrator: Emma Stevely
Girls & Womens Club Development Officer: Kerry Kennedy
Player & Coach Development Officer: Martyn Buckie
Club Development Officer: Gary Doctor
Football Development Officer (N Lanarkshire): Scott Currie
Football Development Officer (W Dunbartonshire): Kenny McComish
Football Development Officer (Clackmannanshire): vacant
Football Development Officer (E Dunbartonshire): Scott Murray
Football Development Officer (Falkirk): Dave Mackay
Football Development Officer (Active Stirling): Scott Kinross

SOUTH EAST (Borders, Lothians and Edinburgh)
Regional Office: SFA, ORIAM, Heriot Watt University, Edinburgh, EH14 4AS
Regional Manager: Jennifer Malone
Regional Administrator: Donna Forbes
Player & Coach Development Manager: Chris Smith
Club development Manager: Karen McConnell
Girls & Womens Club Development Officer: David Baird
Football Development Officer (W Lothian): Barrie Malcolm
Football Development Officer (Hearts): Alan White
Football Development Officer (Edinburgh): Jack Beesley
Football Development Officer (Borders): Drew Kelly
Football Development Officer (E Lothian) Sean McAuley
Football Development Officer (Midlothian):
Football Development Officer (Hibernian Community Foundation): Gary Hocknull

SOUTH WEST (Dumfries & Galloway, S Lanarkshire, Ayrshire)
Regional Office: SFA South West Region, 22 Quarry Road, Irvine, North Ayrshire, KA12 0TH
Regional Manager: John Brown
Regional Administrator: Kelsey Miller
Club Development Manager: David Sheldon
Girls & Womens Club Development Officer: Shirley Martin
Player & Coach Development Officer: Garry Hay
Football Development Officer (North Ayrshire) : Craig Hamilton
Football Development Officer (Dumfries & Galloway): Robbie Totten
Football Development Officer (Ayr United FC): Shaun Ferrie
Football Development Officer (S Lanarkshire): Colin McKendrick
Community Engagement Manager (Kilmarnock): Paul Di Giacomo

WEST (Glasgow, E Renfrewshire, Argyll and Bute, Renfrewshire, Inverclyde)
Regional Office: SFA West Region, Engage Renfrewshire, 10 Falcon Street, Paisley, PA3 1NS
Regional Manager: Andrew Gilchrist
Regional Administrator: Chris Schneiders
Club Development Manager: Corrie Campbell
Player & Coach Development Officer: Scott Chaplain
Girls and Womens Club Development Officer: Tina Stewart
Football Development Officer (Argyll & Bute): Martin Rae
Football Development Officer (Renfrewshire): vacant
Football Development Officer (Glasgow): Steven McGhie
Football Development Officer (Inverclyde): Stuart Rafferty
Football Development Officer (Glasgow): Liam Pattie

INTERNATIONAL FOOTBALL

UEFA Nations League 2020/21 and 2022/3

2020/21 Competition

Scotland finished in their Group B for the 2020/1 season. This means they remain in Group B. The top team are promoted and the bottom team relegated in each four team group.

The Finals of the 2020/1 competition will take place in Italy in October 2021.

The competition also served as a "back door" method of qualifying for the 2022 World Cup. The two highest-ranked Group winners from all the groups in Leagues A to D, who had not already qualified for the World Cup of the Play Offs for the World Cup, were given a Play Off spot. The two "lucky losers" are Wales and Austria.

2022/3 Competition

Dates:

Matchday 1	2-4 June 2022
Matchday 2	5-7 June 2022
Matchday 3	9-11 June 20222
Matchday 4	12-14 June 2022
Matchday 5	22-24 September 22
Matchday 6	25-27 September 22

The Semi Finals and Finals will be played in June 2023, involving the four group winners.

The Countries in Section B are ranked as follows (by 2020/1 UEFA Ranking):

13	Ukraine
14	Sweden
15	Bosnia & Herzegovina
16	Iceland
21	Finland
22	Norway
23	Scotland
24	Russia
25	Israel
26	Romania
27	Serbia
28	Republic of Ireland
33	Slovenia
34	Montenegro
35	Albania
36	Armenia

Scotland will play four of these sides.

FIFA WORLD CUP 2022—Qatar

The 2022 World Cup will take place in Qatar.

Host cities / grounds are as follows:

City	Ground	Capacity
Lusail	Lusail Iconic Stadium	80000
Al Khor	Al Bayt Stadium	60000
Doha	Ras Abu Aboud Stadium	40000
Doha	Al Thumama Stadium	40000
Al Rayyan	Education City Stadium	46350
Al Rayyan	Ahmed bin Ali Stadium	44740
Al Rayyan	Khalifa International Stadium	40,000
Al Wakrah	Al Janoub Stadium	40,000

Match Dates

Group Matches take place from November 21 –28.
The Round of 16 takes place on December 3-6.
The Quarter Finals are on December 9 and 10
The Semi Finals are on December 13-14
The Third / Fourth Place Game is on December 17
The Final is on December 18

At the time of the World Cup there is a three-hour time difference between Qatar and the UK.

Kick Off times for matches in UK time will be:

Group Games 1 and 2
10am, 1pm, 4pm, 7pm

Group Game 3
3pm and 7pm

Round of 16
3pm and 7pm

Quarter Finals
3pm and 7pm

Final and 3rd / the Placed Game
3pm

The countries taking part are allocated as follows:

Host Nation:	1	Qatar
Africa:	5	
Asia	4	
UEFA	13	
North & Central America	3	
South America	4	
Play off Winners	2	

Winners of 2 ties to be drawn between;
5th Asian side
4th from Central and North America,
5th placed South American side
Winners of the Oceania section

NB—The Holders no longer receive an automatic qualification place

Future World Cups:

2026 Canada / Mexico / USA

2030 Confirmed bids from:
Uruguay / Argentina / Chile / Paraguay
Morocco (Possibly also including Algeria & Tunisia)
Portugal / Spain
Greece / Bulgaria / Serbia / Romania

Possibly bids from:
England / Scotland / Wales / N Ireland / R of Ireland
Cameroon
Egypt

2034 None confirmed by bids considered by;
Indonesia / Malaysia / Thailand / Singapore / Vietnam
Australia / New Zealand / Papua New Guinea
Zimbabwe
Egypt
Nigeria

Mens National Team

Scotland Manager Steve Clarke in his playing days with St Mirren

MANAGER: Steve Clarke

1	4/9/20	ENL 20/1	H	Israel	Hampden Park	1 1		BCD
2	7/9/20	ENL 20/1	A	Czech Republic	Olomouc	2 1		BCD
3	8/10/20	ENL 19/20	H	Israel	Hampden Park	0 0	5-4p	BCD
4	11/10/20	ENL 20/1	H	Slovakia	Hampden Park	1 0		BCD
5	14/10/20	ENL 20/1	H	Czech Republic	Hampden Park	1 0		BCD
6	12/11/20	ENL 19/20	A	Serbia	Belgrade	1 1	5-4p	BCD
7	15/11/20	ENL 20/1	A	Slovakia	Trnava	0 1		BCD
8	18/11/20	ENL 20/1	A	Israel	Netanya	0 1		BCD
9	25/3/21	WC 22	H	Austria	Hampden Park	2 2		BCD
10	28/3/21	WC 22	A	Israel	Tel Aviv	1 1		5000
11	31/3/21	WC 22	H	Faroe Islands	Hampden Park	4 0		BCD
12	2/6/21	Fr	N	Netherlands	Faro	2 2		BCD
13	6/6/21	Fr	A	Luxembourg	Josy Bartel	1 0		2000
14	14/6/21	Euro F G	H	Czech Republic	Hampden Park	0 2		9847
15	18/6/21	Euro F G	A	England	Wembley	0 0		20306
16	22/6/21	Euro F G	H	Croatia	Hampden Park	1 3		9896

FIXTURES 2021/22

1	1/9/21	WC 22	A	Denmark
2	4/9/21	WC 22	H	Moldova
3	7/9/21	WC 22	A	Austria
4	9/10/21	WC 22	H	Israel
5	12/10/21	WC 22	A	Faroe Islands
6	12/11/21	WC 22	A	Moldova
7	15/11/21	WC 22	H	Denmark

Surname	First Name	Club	Total	1	2	3	4	5	6	7	8	9	10	11	12	13	14	15	16
Adams	Che	Southampton	7									12*	11&	10&G	W	10G	12*	10+	10&
Armstrong	Stuart	Southampton	28	14+	8&	W	W	W	Un	8+	Sq	7*	Sq	Un	8	Un	10&	12*	11+
Burke	Oliver	West Bromwich Albion / Sheffield United	13	12*	Un	W	W	W	Un	Un	16>								
Christie	Ryan	Celtic	20	9G	9G	W	W	W	11G&	4	10	9&	12*	Un	6	Sq	8*	Un	Un
Considine	Andy	Aberdeen	3				11	11	Un	11*	Un	Sq	Un	Sq					
Cooper	Liam	Leeds United	7	Un	2	6	W	W	Un	7	Un				7+	Sq	9	Un	Un
Dykes	Lyndon	QPR	15	11*	11*G	9&	7G+	7*	10*	Sq	11&	11+	15&	11*	5&	9^	7<	9	9
Fleck	John	Sheffield United	5	Un	5+	Un	9*	W				Un	Un	14+	W	Sq	Sq	Un	Un
Forrest	James	Celtic	38	6	Un										11*	17<	16>	U	Un
Fraser	Ryan	Newcastle United	20			14+	10&	9+G	W	W	W	Un	8G	7<G	12*	15&	15&	Un	14+
Gallagher	Declan	Motherwell	9	Un	Un	5	5	4	5	Un	5*	Un	Un	Un	14+	11+	Sq	Sq	Un
Gilmour	Billy	Chelsea	3												18^	12*<	Un	11*	Sq
Gordon	Craig	Hearts	57						Un	1	Un	Un	Un	1	1	Un	Un	Un	Un
Griffiths	Leigh	Celtic	22						15>	12*	14+								
Hanley	Grant	Norwich City	36						W	W	W	2G	2	2	W	5	5	5	5*
Hanlon	Paul	Hibernian	1					15&											
Hendry	Jack	AS Oostende (OL from Celtic)	7									6	6*	Un	10G	Un	11+	Un	Sq
Jack	Ryan	Rangers	10	5	Un	8+	16>	6	8	Un	8	W	W	W					
Marshall	David	Derby County	47	1	1	1	1	1	1	Un	1	1	1	Un	W	1	1	1	1
McBurnie	Oliver	Sheffield United	16	W	W	10*	14+	12*	12*	9	15&	Un	Un	15&					
McCrorie	Robby	Livingston (OL from Rangers)	0	Un	Un	Un	Un	Un											
McCrorie	Ross	Aberdeen	0				Un	Un											
McGinn	John	Aston Villa	36	8+	14+	7	6>	5>	7+	3	7+	8G	9+	8GG	W	7	6	7	Sq
McGinn	Paul	Hibernian	0				Un	Un											7
McGregor	Callum	Celtic	34	7	15&	11	12*	8	9	Un	9<	14+	7	5+	4	8*	14+	8	8G
McKenna	Scott	Aberdeen / Nottingham Forest	22	3	4	W	W	W	Un	6	12*	Un	Un	16>	17<	14+	Un	Un	12*
McLaughlin	Jon	Rangers	2	Un	Un	Un	Un	Un	Un	Un	Un	Un	Un	Un	Un	Un	Un	Un	Un
McLean	Kenny	Norwich City	20	Un	6	16>	8	14+	14+	5	17<	15&	14+	4					
McTominay	Scott	Manchester United	26	10	10	4	4	3	4	Un	4	10	10	9	Un	4	4	4	4
Nisbet	Kevin	Hibernian	6									Un	Un	12*	15&G	18^	17>	14+	15&
O'Donnell	Stephen	Motherwell	22	Un	Un	2>	2	2	2>	Un	2>	3	3	Un	W	2>	2<	2	2>
Palmer	Liam	Sheffield Wednesday	8	Un	7	W	W	W	Un	10	Un	Un	Sq	17<					
Paterson	Callum	Cardiff City	17	Un	12*	15&	15&	16>	14&	Un	Sq								
Patterson	Nathan	Rangers	2												W	16>	Un	Un	16>
Porteous	Ryan	Hibernian	0			Un	Sq	Un											
Robertson	Andy	Liverpool	48	2	3	3	3	W	3	Sq	3	4	4	3	2<	3&	3	3	3
Shankland	Lawrence	Dundee United	4	W	W	12*	Un	W	Sq	14+	Un								
Taylor	Greg	Celtic	5	Un	Un	Un	Un	10<	Sq	Un	Un	Sq	Sq	Sq	16>	Un	Un	Sq	Sq
Tierney	Kieran	Arsenal	23	4	Un	W	W	W	6	2	6	5	5	4>	3>	6	Sq	6	6
Turnbull	David	Celtic	1												9^	Un	Un	Sq	Un

Sq - Squad member,not stripped
W - Withdrawn from squad

EURO 2000 QUALIFYING	P	W	D	L	F	A	GD	PTS
Belgium	10	10	0	0	40	3	+37	30
Russia	10	8	0	2	33	8	+25	24
Scotland	10	5	0	5	16	19	-3	15
Cyprus	10	3	1	6	15	20	-5	10
Kazakhstan	10	3	1	6	13	17	-4	-4
San Marino	10	0	0	10	1	51	-50	0

EURO 2020 GROUP	P	W	D	L	F	A	GD	PTS
England	3	2	1	0	2	0	2	7
Croatia	3	1	1	1	4	3	1	4
Czech Republic	3	1	1	1	3	2	1	4
Scotland	3	0	1	2	1	5	-4	1

UEFA NATIONS LEAGUE 2020/1	P	W	D	L	F	A	GD	PTS
Czech Republic	6	4	0	2	9	5	4	12
Scotland	6	3	1	2	5	4	1	10
Israel	6	2	2	7	7	7	0	8
Slovakia	6	1	1	4	5	10	-5	4

FIFA WORLD CUP 2022 QUALIFII	P	W	D	L	F	A	GD	PTS
Denmark	3	3	0	0	14	0	14	9
Scotland	3	1	2	0	7	3	4	5
Israel	3	1	1	1	5	4	1	4
Austria	3	1	1	1	5	7	-2	4
Faroe Islands	3	0	1	2	2	8	-6	1
Moldova	3	0	1	2	2	13	-11	1

* Champions Qualify Automatically

** Runners Up go to Play Offs

***Austria guaranteed Play Off through Nations League

Scotland's World Cup Squads

1954

Scotland named a squad of 22 but only 13 players travelled. The remainder stayed at home on "stand by".

Freddie Martin (Aberdeen), Willie Cunningham (Preston North End), Jock Aird (Burnley), Bobby Evans (Celtic), Tommy Docherty (Preston North End), Jimmy Davidson (Partick Thistle), Doug Cowie (Dundee), John McKenzie (Partick Thistle), George Hamilton (Aberdeen), Allan Brown (Celtic), Neil Mochan (Celtic), Willie Fernie (Celtic), Willie Ormond (Hibernian)

Stand By: John Anderson (Leicester City), Bobby Johnstone (Hibernian), Jackie Henderson (Portsmouth), David Mathers (Partick Thistle), Alex Wilson (Portsmouth), Jimmy Binning (Queen of the South), Bobby Combe (Hibernian), Ernie Copland (Raith Rovers), Ian McMillan (Airdrieonians)

Bobby Johnstone travelled to Switzerland but was injured in training and was replaced by George Hamilton

Rangers refused to release players for the tournament as they were on a tour in North America.

1958

Tommy Younger (Liverpool), Bill Brown (Dundee), Alex Parker (Everton), Eric Caldow (Rangers), John Hewie (Charlton Athletic), Harry Haddock (Clyde), Ian McColl (Rangers), Eddie Turnbull (Hibernian), Bobby Evans (Celtic), Tommy Docherty (Preston North End), Dave Mackay (Hearts), Doug Cowie (Dundee), Sammy Baird (Rangers), Graham Leggatt (Aberdeen), Alex Scott (Rangers), Jimmy Murray (Hearts), Jackie Mudie (Blackpool), John Coyle (Clyde), Bobby Collins (Celtic), Archie Robertson (Clyde), Stewart Imlach (Nottingham Forest), Willie Fernie (Celtic)

1974

David Harvey (Leeds United), Sandy Jardine (Rangers), Danny McGrain (Celtic), Billy Bremner (Leeds United), Jim Holton (Manchester United), John Blackley (Hibernian), Jimmy Johnstone (Celtic), Kenny Dalglish (Celtic), Joe Jordan (Leeds United), David Hay (Celtic), Peter Lorimer (Leeds United), Thomson Allan (Dundee), Jim Stewart (Kilmarnock), Martin Buchan (Manchester United), Peter Cormack (Liverpool), Willie Donachie (Manchester City), Donald Ford (Hearts), Tommy Hutchison (Coventry City), Denis Law (Manchester City), Willie Morgan (Manchester United), Gordon McQueen (Leeds United), Erich Schaedler (Hibernian)

A provisional squad of 40 was named. The following players were "dropped" for the tournament: Jim Brown (Sheffield United), Jim Hermiston (Aberdeen), George Connelly (Celtic), Jackie Copland (Dundee United), Frank Munro (Wolves), Jim Smith (Newcastle United), Pat Stanton (Hibernian), Graeme Souness (Middlesbrough), Bobby Robinson (Dundee), Bobby Lennox (Celtic), Derek Parlane (Rangers), Kenny Burns (Birmingham City), Jocky Scott (Dundee), john Duncan (Dundee), Colin Stein (Coventry City), Willie Donnachie (Manchester City), Gordon McQueen (Leeds United), Derek Johnstone (Rangers)

1978

Alan Rough (Partick Thistle), Sandy Jardine (Rangers), Willie Donachie (Manchester City), Martin Buchan (Manchester United), Gordon McQueen (Manchester United), Bruce Rioch (Derby County), Don Masson (Derby County), Kenny Dalglish (Liverpool), Joe Jordan (Manchester United), Asa Hartford (Manchester City), Willie Johnston (West Bromwich Albion), Jim Blyth (Coventry City), Stuart Kennedy (Aberdeen), Tom Forsyth (Rangers), Archie Gemmill (Nottingham Forest), Lou Macari (Manchester United), Derek Johnstone (Rangers), Graeme Souness (Liverpool), john Robertson (Nottingham Forest), Bobby Clark (Aberdeen), Joe Harper (Aberdeen), Kenny Burns (Nottingham Forest)

A provisional squad of 40 was named. The following players were "dropped" for the tournament: Jim Stewart (Middlesbrough), David Stewart (Leeds United), John Blackley (Newcastle United), David Narey (Dundee United), Paul Hegarty (Dundee United), Roddie McDonald (Celtic), John Brownlie (Hibernian), Neil McNab (Tottenham Hotspur), Graeme Payne (Dundee United), Tony Fitzpatrick (St Mirren), John Wark (Ipswich Town), Roy Aitken (Celtic), Andy Gray (Aston Villa), Arthur Graham (Leeds United), Ian Wallace (Coventry City), Frank McGarvey (St Mirren)

1982

Alan Rough (Partick Thistle), Danny McGrain (Celtic), Frank Gray (Leeds United), Graeme Souness (Liverpool), Alan Hansen (Liverpool), Willie Miller (Aberdeen), Gordon Strachan (Aberdeen), Kenny Dalglish (Liverpool), Alan Brazil (Ipswich Town), John Wark (Ipswich Town), John Robertson (Nottingham Forest), George Wood (Arsenal), Alex McLeish (Aberdeen), David Narey (Dundee United), Joe Jordan (AC Milan), Asa Hartford (Manchester City), Allan Evans (Aston Villa), Steve Archibald (Tottenham Hotspur), Paul Sturrock (Dundee United), Davie Provan (Celtic), George Burley (Ipswich Town), Jim Leighton (Aberdeen)

A provisional squad of 40 was named. The following players were "dropped" for the tournament:
Billy Thomson (St Mirren), Jim Stewart (Rangers), Stuart Kennedy (Aberdeen), Ian Munro (Sunderland), Ray Stewart (West Ham United), Arthur Albiston (Manchester United), Des Bremner (Aston Villa), Paul Hegarty (Dundee United), Roy Aitken (Celtic), Tommy Burns (Celtic), Jim Bett (Rangers), Bobby Russell (Rangers), Ian McCulloch (Notts County), Andy Gray (Wolves), George McCluskey (Celtic), Derek Johnstone (Rangers), Davie Cooper (Rangers), Arthur Graham (Leeds United)

1986

Jim Leighton (Aberdeen), Richard Gough (Dundee United), Maurice Malpas (Dundee United), Graeme Souness (Rangers), Alex Mcleish (Aberdeen), Willie Miller (Aberdeen), Gordon Strachan (Manchester United), Roy Aitken (Celtic), Eamonn Bannon (Dundee United), Jim Bett (Aberdeen), Paul McStay (Celtic), Andy Goram (Oldham Athletic), Steve Nicol (Liverpool), David Narey (Dundee United), Arthur Albiston (Manchester United), Frank McAvennie (West Ham United), Steve Archibald (Barcelona), Graeme Sharp (Everton), Charlie Nicholas

(Arsenal), Paul Sturrock (Dundee United), Davie Cooper (Rangers), Alan Rough (Partick Thistle)

1990
Jim Leighton (Manchester United), Alex McLeish (Aberdeen), Roy Aitken (Newcastle United), Richard Gough (Rangers), Paul McStay (Celtic), Maurice Malpas (Dundee United), Mo Johnston (Rangers), Jim Bett (Aberdeen), Ally McCoist (Rangers), Murdo MacLeod (Borussia Dortmund), Gary Gillespie (Liverpool), Andy Goram (Hibernian), Gordon Durie (Chelsea), Alan McInally (Bayern Munich), Craig Levein (Hearts), Stuart McCall (Everton), Stewart McKimmie (Aberdeen), John Collins (Hibernian), David MacPherson (Hearts), Gary McAlister (Leicester City), Robert Fleck (Norwich City), Bryan Gunn (Norwich City)

1998
Jim Leighton (Aberdeen), Jackie McNamara (Celtic), Tom Boyd (Celtic), Colin Calderwood (Tottenham Hotspur). Colin Hendry (Blackburn Rovers), Tosh McKinlay (Celtic), Kevin Gallacher (Blackburn Rovers), Craig Burley (Celtic), Gordon Durie (Rangers), Darren Jackson (Celtic), John Collins (Monaco), Neil Sullivan (Wimbledon), Simon Donnelly (Celtic), Paul Lambert (Celtic), Scott Gemmill (Nottingham Forest), David Weir (Hearts), Billy McKinlay (Blackburn Rovers), Matt Elliot (Leicester City), Derek Whyte (Aberdeen), Scott Booth (Utrecht), Jonathan Gould (Celtic), Christian Dailly (Derby County)

Scotland's Euro Squads

1992
Andy Goram (Rangers), Richard Gough (Rangers), Paul McStay (Celtic), Maurice Malpas (Dundee United), Ally McCoist (Rangers), Brian McClair (Manchester United), Gordon Durie (Tottenham Hotspur), Dave McPherson (Hearts), Stewart McKimmie (Aberdeen), Stuart McCall (Rangers), Gary McAllister (Leeds United), Henry Smith (Hearts), Pat Nevin (Everton), Kevin Gallacher (Coventry City), Tom Boyd (Celtic), Jim McInally (Dundee United), Derek Whyte (Celtic), Dave Bowman (Dundee United), Alan McLaren (Hearts), Duncan Ferguson (Dundee United)

1996
Jim Leighton (Hibernian), Stewart McKimmie (Aberdeen), Tom Boyd (Celtic), Colin Calderwood (Tottenham Hotspur), Colin Hendry (Blackburn Rovers), Derek Whyte (Middlesbrough), John Spencer (Chelsea), Stuart McCall (Rangers), Ally McCoist (Rangers), Gary McAllister (Leeds United), John Collins (AS Monaco), Andy Goram (Rangers), Tosh McKinlay (Celtic), Gordon Durie (Rangers), Eoin Jess (Coventry City), Craig Burley (Chelsea), Billy McKinlay (Blackburn Rovers), Kevin Gallacher (Blackburn Rovers), Darren Jackson (Hibernian), Scott Booth (Aberdeen), Scott Gemmill (Nottingham Forest), Nicky Walker (Partick Thistle)

Brazil Independence Cup

1972

Brazil Independence Cup
Bobby Clark (Aberdeen), Ally Hunter (Kilmarnock), Alex Forsyth (Partick Thistle), Willie Donachie (Manchester City), John Hansen (Partick Thistle), Martin Buchan (Manchester United), Eddie Colquhoun (Sheffield United), George Graham (Arsenal), Billy Bremner (Leeds United), Asa Hartford (West Bromwich Albion), Lou Macari (Celtic), Donald Ford (Hearts), Denis Law (Manchester United), Willie Morgan (Manchester United), Jimmy Bone (Norwich City), Colin Stein Rangers), Dennis McQuade (Partick Thistle), George Anderson (Morton)

WITHDRAWN
Eddie Gray (Leeds United), Sandy Jardine (Rangers), John Brownlie (Hibernian), Charlie Cooke (Chelsea), David Hay (Celtic)

Scotland's Tour Squads

1927 Tour of USA and Canada (Not Full Caps)
Sandy Archibald (Rangers), Danny Blair (Clyde), Jock Buchanan (Morton), Willie Cook (Dundee), Tully Craig (Rangers), Andy Cunningham (Rangers), Patsy Gallacher (Falkirk), Tom Hamilton (Rangers), John Hunter (Falkirk), Adam McLean (Celtic), Jimmy McStay (Celtic), Willie McStay (Celtic), Tom Morrison (St Mirren), Tommy Muirhead (Rangers), Jimmy Munro (St Johnstone), Tom Scott (Falkirk), Jimmy Simpson (Dundee United), Andy Swallow (St Johnstone)

1935 Tour of USA and Canada Not Full Caps)
Andrew Anderson (Hearts), George Cummings (Partick Thistle), Bob Donnelly (Partick Thistle), Dally Duncan (Derby County), Alex Ferguson (St Johnstone), Bob Fraser (Aberdeen), Hughie Gallacher (Derby County), Bobby Main (Rangers), Whitey McDonald (Rangers), David Meiklejohn (Rangers), Willie Miller (Partick Thistle), Willie Mills (Aberdeen), Tom Smith (Kilmarnock), William Stevenson (Clyde), Tommy Walker (Hearts), David Wilson (Hamilton Accies), Peter Wilson (Celtic)

1939 Tour of USA and Canada (Not Full Caps)
Bobby Bolt (Falkirk), Jimmy Carabine (Third Lanark), Jimmy Caskie (St Johnstone), Jerry Dawson (Rangers), Jimmy Dykes (Hearts), Ben Ellis (Motherwell), Archie Garrett (Hearts), John Gillies (Clyde), Douglas Gray (Rangers), George Hamilton (Aberdeen), jack Jones (Third Lanark), Doug McAvoy (Kilmarnock), Willie Lyon (Celtic), Malky MacDonald (Celtic), Tommy McIntyre (Hibernian), Tommy McKenzie (Motherwell), Sandy McNab (West Bromwich Albion)

1949 Tour of USA and Canada (Not Full Caps)
George Aitken (East Fife), Jimmy Brown (Hearts), Sammy Cox (Rangers), Bobby Evans (Celtic), Jock Govan (Hibernian), Billy Houliston (Queen of the South), Johnny MacKenzie (Partick Thistle), Tommy Orr (Morton), Willie Redpath (Motherwell), Lawrie Reilly (Hibernian), Billy Steel (Derby County), Willie Telfer (St Mirren), Willie Thornton (Rangers), Willie Waddell (Rangers), Willie Woodburn (Rangers), George Young (Rangers)

1967 World Tour (Not Full Caps)
Alan Anderson (Hearts), Willie Callaghan (Dunfermline Athletic), Eddie Colquhoun (Sheffield United), Jim Cruickshank (Hearts), Alex Ferguson (Rangers), Doug Fraser (West Bromwich Albion), Joe Harper (Huddersfield Town), Harry Hood (Clyde), Bobby Hope (West Bromwich Albion), Jim McCalliog (Sheffield Wednesday), Jackie McGrory (Kilmarnock), Tommy McLean (Kilmarnock), Willie Morgan (Burnley), Andy Penman (Rangers), Harry Thomson (Burnley), Hugh Tinney (Bury), Jim Townsend (Hearts), Ian Ure (Arsenal), John Woodward (Arsenal)

June 2021 FIFA MENS WORLD RANKINGS

1 Belgium	71 Bulgaria	141 Taiwan
2 France	72 Guinea	142 Burundi
3 Brazil	73 UAE	143 Solomon Islands
4 England	74 Cabo Verde	144 Hong Kong
5 Portugal	75 South Africa	145 Yemen
6 Spain	76 Curacao	146 Lesotho
7 Italy	77 China	147 Nicaragua
8 Argentina	78 Panama	148 Kuwait
9 Uruguay	79 Syria	149 Afghanistan
10 Denmark	80 Oman	150 Botswana
11 Mexico	81 Bolivia	151 Liberia
12 Germany	82 Benin	152 Gambia
13 Switzerland	83 Haiti	153 Malausia
14 Croatia	84 Uganda	154 Eswatini
15 Colombia	85 Israel	155 Maldives
16 Netherlands	86 Uzbekistan	156 Dominican Republic
17 Wales	87 Zambia	157 New Caledonia
18 Sweden	88 Gabon	158 Andorra
19 Chile	89 Belarus	159 Singapore
20 USA	90 Armenia	160 Grenada
21 Poland	91 Georgia	161 Tahiti
22 Senegal	92 Vietnam	162 Barbados
23 Austria	93 Lebanon	163 Fiji
24 Ukraine	94 Congo	164 Vanuatu
25 Serbia	95 Jordan	165 Guyana
26 Tunisia	96 Luxembourg	166 Papua New Guinea
27 Peru	97 Cyprus	167 St Vincent & Grenadines
28 Japan	98 Bahrain	168 Bermuda
29 Turkey	99 Kyrgyz Republic	169 South Sudan
30 Venezuela	100 Madagascar	170 Belize
31 Iran	101 Mauritania	171 Nepal
32 Nigeria	102 Kenya	172 Mauritius
33 Algeria	103 Trinidad & Tobago	173 Indonesia
34 Morocco	104 Palestine	174 Cambodia
35 Paraguay	105 India	175 Malta
36 Slovakia	106 Tahiland	176 St Lucia
37 Hungary	107 Zimbabwe	177 Moldova
38 Russia	108 Guinea Bissau	178 Puerto Rico
39 South Korea	109 North Korea	179 Chad
40 Czech Republic	110 Azerbaijan	180 Montserrat
41 Austrlia	111 Namibia	181 Cuba
42 Norway	112 Niger	182 Macau
43 Romania	113 Faroe Islands	183 Djibouti
44 Scotland	114 Sierra Leone	184 Bangladesh
45 Jamiaca	115 Malawi	185 Laos
46 Egypt	116 Estonia	186 Liechtenstein
47 Republic of Ireland	117 Mozambique	187 Bhutan
48 Northern Ireland	118 Central African Republic	188 Dominican Republic
49 Ghana	119 Libya	189 Brunei
50 Costa Rica	120 Kosovo	190 Sao Tome & Principe
51 Greece	121 Tajikistan	191 American Samoa
52 Iceland	122 New Zealand	192 Mongolia
53 Ecuador	123 Sudan	193 Samoa
54 Finland	124 Kazakhstan	194 Cayman Islands
55 Cameroon	125 Philippines	195 Gibraltar
56 Bosnia & Herzegovina	126 Angola	196 Timor Leste
57 Mali	127 Guatemala	197 Somalia
58 Qatar	128 Antigua & Barbuda	198 Guam
59 Cote d'Ivoire	129 Rwanda	199 Pakistan
60 Burkina Faso	130 Turkmenistan	200 Seychelles
61 Congo DR	131 Comoros	201 Bahamas
62 North Macedonia	132 Equatorial Guinea	202 Tonga
63 Slovenia	133 Togo	203 Eritrea
64 Montenegro	134 Lithiania	204 Sri Lanka
65 Saudy Arabia	135 St Kitts & Nevis	205 Aruba
66 Albania	136 Suriname	206 Turks & Caicos Islands
67 Honduras	137 Tanzania	207 US Virgin Islands
68 Iraq	138 Latvia	208 British Virgin Islands
69 El Salvador	139 Myanmar	209 Anguilla
70 Canada	140 Ethiopia	210 San Marino

SCOTLAND'S RANKING HISTORY

	Best	Worst
1993	24	30
1994	25	33
1995	21	31
1996	26	39
1997	22	37
1998	36	44
1999	20	32
2000	20	25
2001	24	50
2002	50	63
2003	50	64
2004	51	86
2005	60	88
2006	24	62
2007	13	26
2008	14	33
2009	22	46
2010	41	57
2011	47	66
2012	41	72
2013	33	78
2014	22	37
2015	28	52
2016	40	67
2017	29	67
2018	31	42
2019	40	53
2020	45	50

SCOTLAND NATIONAL TEAM - MOST FREQUENT VENUES

262 Hampden Park, Glasgow
33 Wembley, London
31 Windsor Park, Belfast
27 Celtic Park, Glasgow
24 Racecourse Ground, Wrexham
23 Ninian Park, Cardiff
22 Ibrox, Glasgow
14 Pittodrie, Aberdeen
9 Tynecastle, Edinburgh
8 Heysel, Brussels
7 The Oval, London
7 Easter Road, Edinburgh
7 Dalymount Park, Belfast
7 Idraetsparken, Copenhagen
6 1st Hampden Park
6 Prater Stadion, Vienna
6 Ta Qali Stadium, Malta
5 Solitude, Belfast
5 Villa Park, Birmingham

SCOTLAND NATIONAL TEAM RECORDS

Most Capped Players (International Roll of Honour - 50+ Caps)
102 Kenny Dalglish; 91 Jim Leighton; 80 Darren Fletcher; 77 Alex McLeish; 76 Paul McStay; 72 Tom Boyd; 69 Kenny Miller and David Weir; 67 Christian Dailly; 65 Willie Miller; 62 Danny McGrain; 61 Ally McCoist; 58 John Collins; 57 Roy Aitken, Gary McAlister, Craig Gordon; 55 Scott Brown, Gary Caldwell, Maurice Malpas, Denis Law; 54 Billy Bremner, Graeme Souness, George Young; 53 Kevin Gallacher, Alan Rough; 52 Joe Jordan; 51 Colin Hendry, Steven Naismith; 50 Asa Hartford, Alan Hutton, Gordon Strachan.

Top Goalscorers
30 Denis Law, Kenny Dalglish; 24 Hughie Gallacher; 22 Lawrie Reilly; 19 Ally McCoist; 18 Kenny Miller; 15 Robert Hamilton, James McFadden; 14 Mo Johnston; 13 RS McColl, Andrew Wilson

Managers
1954 Andy Beattie; 1958 Dawson Walker*; 1958 Matt Busby; 1959-60 Andy Beattie; 1960-65 Ian McColl; 1965-66 Jock Stein; 1966 John Prentice; 1966-67 Malky McDonald;* 1967-71 Bobby Brown; 1971-72 Tommy Docherty; 1973-77 Willie Ormond; 1977-78 Ally MacLeod; 1978-85 Jock Stein; 1985-86 Alex Ferguson*; 1986-93 Andy Roxburgh; 1993-2002 Craig Brown; 2002-04 Berti Vogts; 2004 Tommy Burns*; 2004-07 Walter Smith; 2007 Alex McLeish; 2008-09 George Burley; 2009-12 Craig Levein; 2012 Billy Stark*; 2013-17 Gordon Strachan; 2017 Malky Mackay*; 2018-19 Alex McLeish; 2019- Steve Clarke

* Interim Managers

HAT TRICKS AGAINST SCOTLAND
7 players have scored hat tricks against Scotland. One of them, Robbie Earnshaw (Wales 2004) spent part of his career on loan at Morton. The other six are Ruud Van Nistelrooy (Netherlands 2003), Dennis Wilshaw (England 1955), Jimmy Greaves (England 1961), John Toshack (Wales 1979), Nico Claesen (Belgium 1987) and Landon Donovan (USA 2012).

SCOTLAND'S RECENT INTERNATIONAL RECORD

Date	Comp	Opponents	V	Location	Score	Res
08/10/2011	EU	Liechtenstein	A	Vaduz	1-0	Won
11/10/2011	EU	Spain	A	Alicante	1-3	Lost
11/11/2011	Fr	Cyprus	A	Larnaca	2-1	Won
29/02/2012	Fr	Slovenina	A	Koper	1-1	Drew
26/05/2012	Fr	USA	A	Jacksonville	1-5	Lost
15/08/2012	Fr	Australia	H	Easter Road	3-1	Won
08/09/2012	WC	Serbia	H	Hampden	0-0	Drew
11/09/2012	WC	FYR Macedonia	H	Hampden	1-1	Drew
12/10/2012	WC	Wales	A	Cardiff	1-2	Lost
16/10/2012	WC	Belgium	A	Brussels	0-2	Lost
14/11/2012	Fr	Luxembourg	A	Luxembourg	2-1	Won
06/02/2013	Fr	Estonia	H	Pittodrie	1-0	Won
22/03/2013	WC	Wales	H	Hampden	1-2	Lost
26/03/2013	WC	Serbia	A	Novi Sad	0-2	Lost
07/06/2013	WC	Croatia	A	Zagreb	1-0	Won
14/08/2013	WC	England	A	Wembley	2-3	Lost
06/09/2013	WC	Belgium	H	Hampden	0-2	Lost
10/09/2013	WC	FYR Macedonia	A	Skopje	2-1	Won
15/10/2013	WC	Croatia	H	Hampden	2-0	Won
15/11/2013	Fr	USA	H	Hampden	0-0	Drew
19/11/2013	Fr	Norway	A	Molde	1-0	Won
05/03/2014	Fr	Poland	A	Warsaw	1-0	Won
28/05/2014	Fr	Nigeria	N	Fulham	2-2	Drew
07/09/2014	EU	Germany	A	Dortmund	1-2	Lost
11/10/2014	EU	Georgia	H	Ibrox	1-0	Won
14/10/2014	EU	Poland	A	Warsaw	2-2	Drew
14/11/2014	EU	Republic of Ireland	H	Celtic Park	1-0	Won
18/11/2014	EU	England	H	Celtic Park	1-3	Lost
25/03/2015	Fr	Northern Ireland	H	Hampden	1-0	Won
29/03/2015	EU	Gibraltar	H	Hampden	6-1	Won
05/06/2015	Fr	Qatar	H	Easter Road	1-0	Won
13/06/2015	EU	Republic of Ireland	A	Dublin	1-1	Drew
04/09/2015	EU	Georgia	A	Tbilisi	0-1	Lost
07/09/2015	EU	Germany	H	Hampden	2-3	Lost
08/10/2015	EU	Poland	H	Hampden	2-2	Drew
11/10/2015	EU	Gibraltar	A	Faro	6-0	Won
24/03/2016	Fr	Czech Republic	A	Prague	0-1	Lost
29/03/2016	Fr	Denmark	H	Hampden	1-0	Won
29/05/2016	Fr	Italy	N	Ta Qali	0-1	Lost
04/06/2016	Fr	France	A	Metz	0-3	Lost
04/09/2016	WC	Malta	A	Ta Qali	5-1	Won
08/10/2016	WC	Lithuania	H	Hampden	1-1	Drew
11/10/2016	WC	Slovakia	A	Trnava	0-3	Lost
11/11/2016	WC	England	A	Wembley	0-3	Lost
22/03/2017	Fr	Canada	H	Easter Road	1-1	Drew
26/03/2017	WC	Slovenia	H	Hampden	1-0	Won
10/06/2017	WC	England	H	Hampden	2-2	Drew
01/09/2017	WC	Lithuania	A	Vilnius	3-0	Won
04/09/2017	WC	Malta	H	Hampden	2-0	Won
05/10/2017	WC	Slovakia	H	Hampden	1-0	Won
08/10/2017	WC	Slovenia	A	Ljubljana	2-2	Drew
09/11/2017	Fr	Netherlands	H	Pittodrie	0-1	Lost
23/03/2018	Fr	Costa Rica	H	Hampden	0-1	Lost
27/03/2018	Fr	Hungary	A	Budapest	1-0	Won
30/05/2018	Fr	Peru	A	Lima	0-2	Lost
03/06/2018	Fr	Mexico	A	Mexico City	0-1	Lost
07/08/2018	Fr	Belgium	H	Hampden	0-4	Lost
10/09/2018	ENL	Albania	H	Hampden	2-0	Won
11/10/2018	ENL	Israel	A	Haifa	1-2	Lost
14/10/2018	Fr	Portugal	H	Hampden	1-3	Lost
17/11/2018	ENL	Albania	A	Skhkoder	4-0	Won
20/11/2018	ENL	Israael	H	Hampden	3-2	Won
21/03/2019	EUROQ	Kazakhstan	A	Astana	0-3	Lost
24/03/2019	EUROQ	San Marino	A	Serraville	2-0	Won
08/06/2019	EUROQ	Cyprus	H	Hampden	2-1	Won
11/06/2019	EUROQ	Belgium	A	Brussels	0-3	Lost
06/09/2019	EUROQ	Russia	H	Hampden	1-2	Lost
09/09/2019	EUROQ	Belgium	H	Hampden	0-4	Lost
10/10/2019	EUROQ	Russia	A	Moscow	0-4	Lost
13/10/2019	EUROQ	San Marino	H	Hampden	6-0	Won
16/11/2019	EUROQ	Cyprus	A	Nicosia	2-1	Won
19/11/2019	EUROQ	Kazakhstan	H	Hampden	3-1	Won
04/09/2020	ENL	Israel	H	Hampden	1-1	Drew
07/09/2020	ENL	Czech Republic	A	Olomouc	2-1	Won
08/10/2020	EUROQ	Israel	H	Hampden	0-0	Drew
11/10/2020	ENL	Slovakia	H	Hampden	1-0	Won
14/10/2020	ENL	Czech Republic	H	Hampden	1-0	Won
12/11/2020	EUROQ	Serbia	A	Belgrade	1-1	Drew
15/11/2020	ENL	Slovakia	A	Trnava	0-1	Lost
18/11/2020	ENL	Israel	A	Netanya	0-1	Lost
25/03/2021	WC	Austria	H	Hampden	2-2	Drew
28/03/2021	WC	Israel	A	Tel Aviv	1-1	Drew
31/03/2021	WC	Faroe Islands	H	Hampden	4-0	Won
02/06/2021	Fr	Netherlands	N	Faro	2-2	Drew
06/06/2021	Fr	Luxembourg	A	Luxembourg	1-0	Won
14/06/2021	EUROF	Czech Republic	H	Hampden	0-2	Lost
18/06/2021	EUROF	England	A	Wembley	0-0	Drew
22/06/2021	EUROF	Croatia	H	Hampden	1-3	Lost

SCOTLAND'S ALL TIME RECORD

Opponent	Pld	W	D	L	%W	Opponent	Pld	W	D	L	%W
Albania	2	2	0	0	100	Lithuania	10	6	3	1	60
Argentina	4	1	1	2	25	Luxembourg	5	4	1	0	80
Australia	5	3	1	1	60	North Macedonia	4	2	1	1	50
Austria	21	6	7	8	29	Malta	7	6	1	0	85.7
Belarus	4	2	1	1	50	Mexico	1	0	0	1	0
Belgium	20	4	3	13	20	Moldova	2	1	1	0	50
Bosnia and Herzegovina	2	2	0	0	100	Morocco	1	0	0	1	0
Brazil	10	0	2	8	0	Netherlands	20	6	5	9	30
Bulgaria	6	3	3	0	50	New Zealand	2	1	1	0	50
Canada	6	5	1	0	83.3	Nigeria	2	0	1	1	0
Chile	2	2	0	0	100	Northern Ireland	40	20	11	9	50
CIS	1	1	0	0	100	Norway	18	9	6	3	50
Colombia	3	0	2	1	0	Paraguay	1	0	0	1	0
Costa Rica	2	0	0	2	0	Peru	4	1	1	2	25
Croatia	6	2	3	1	33	Poland	10	2	5	3	20
Cyprus	7	7	0	0	100	Portugal	15	4	3	8	26.7
Czech Republic	10	4	1	5	40	Qatar	1	1	0	0	100
Czechoslovakia	10	5	1	4	50	Republic of Ireland	11	4	3	4	36.4
Denmark	16	10	0	6	62.5	Romania	6	2	2	2	33.3
East Germany	6	2	1	3	33.3	Russia	4	0	2	2	0
Ecuador	1	1	0	0	100	San Marino	8	8	0	0	100
Egypt	1	0	0	1	0	Saudi Arabia	1	0	1	0	0
England	115	41	26	48	36	Serbia	2	0	1	1	0
Estonia	8	6	2	0	75	Slovakia	4	2	0	2	50
Faroe Islands	10	8	2	0	80	Slovenia	5	2	3	0	40
Finland	8	6	2	0	75	South Africa	2	1	0	1	50
France	16	8	0	8	50	South Korea	1	0	0	1	0
Georgia	4	2	0	2	50	Soviet Union	4	0	1	3	0
Germany	9	2	2	5	22.2	Spain	13	3	4	6	23.1
Gibraltar	2	2	0	0	100	Sweden	12	5	1	6	41.7
Greece	2	1	0	1	50	Switzerland	16	8	3	5	50
Hong Kong League XI	1	1	0	0	100	Trinidad and Tobago	1	1	0	0	100
Hungary	9	3	2	4	33.3	Turkey	1	0	0	1	0
Iceland	6	6	0	0	100	Ukraine	2	1	0	1	50
Iran	1	0	1	0	0	United States	7	2	3	2	28.6
Ireland	55	43	6	6	78.2	Uruguay	4	1	1	2	25
Israel	9	4	3	1	44	Wales	107	61	23	23	57
Italy	11	1	2	8	9.09	West Germany	8	2	3	3	25
Japan	3	0	2	1	0	Yugoslavia	8	2	5	1	25
Kazakhstan	2	1	0	1	50	Zaire	1	1	0	0	100
Latvia	4	4	0	0	100	**Totals**	**794**	**372**	**174**	**258**	**46.9**

Mens U21 Team

EURO QUALIFYING STANDINGS

	P	W	D	L	F	A	GD	PTS
Czech Republic	10	6	3	1	20	4	16	21
Croatia	10	6	2	2	37	7	30	20
Scotland	10	5	3	2	16	5	11	18
Greece	10	5	1	4	10	11	-1	16
Lithuania	10	3	1	6	9	15	-6	10
San Marino	10	0	0	10	0	50	-50	0

UNDER 21

Scott Gemmill

1	8/9/20	UEFA	A	Lithuania	Vilnius	1 0	BCD
2	9/10/20	UEFA	H	Czech Republic	Tynecastle	2 0	BCD
3	13/10/20	UEFA	A	San Marino	Serraville	7 0	BCD
4	12/11/20	UEFA	H	Croatia	Tynecastle	2 2	BCD
5	17/11/20	UEFA	A	Greece	Athens	0 1	BCD
6	2/6/21	Fr	H	Northern Ireland	Dumbarton	1 2	BCD
7	5/6/21	Fr	H	Northern Ireland	Dumbarton	3 2	BCD

FIXTURES

1	7/9/21	UEFA	A	Turkey
2	8/10/21	UEFA	A	Denmark
3	12/11/21	UEFA	H	Kazakhstan
4	16/11/21	UEFA	H	Belgium
5	25/3/22	UEFA	H	Turkey
6	29/3/22	UEFA	A	Kazakhstan
7	5/6/22	UEFA	A	Belgium
8	10/6/22	UEFA	H	Denmark

Surname	First Name	Club	Total	1	2	3	4	5	6	7
Anderson	Bruce	Ayr United (OL from Aberdeen)_				Un				
Ashby	Harrison	West Ham United			2+	12*G	W	W		
Banks	Scott	Crystal Palace							6&	5&
Bowie	Kieron	Fulham							14+	Un
Burroughs	Jack	Coventry City							2	2
Campbell	Allan	Motherwell		7G	6	Sq	6	6		
Campbell	Dean	Aberdeen		Un						
Chalmers	Logan	Dundee United			Un	16>			15&	9<
Clayton	Tom	Liverpool							16>	8G
Deas	Robbie	Inverness CT							5	14+
Doig	Josh	Hibernian							Sq	Sq
Doohan	Ross	Ross County (OL from Celtic)		1	1	1&	1	1		
Erhahon	Ethan	St Mirren							7>	17<
Ferguson	Lewis	Aberdeen		9	10	Sq	10+	8		
Fiorini	Lewis	NAC Breda (OL from Manchester City)		Un	W	W	Un	14+	Sq	Sq
Gilmour	Billy	Chelsea					14+			
Harper	Cameron	Inverness CT							3+	Un
Harvie	Daniel	MK Dons		2	3	2	3	2		
Hickey	Aaron	Bologna					W	W		
Hornby	Fraser	Stade de Reims		11	8G	8+GGG	8	11		
Irving	Andy					5>				
Johnston	George	SC Feyenoord Rotterdam		4	W	W	5	4		
Joseph	Kyle	Wigan Athletic							11<	Un
Kelly	Stephen	Ross County (OL from Rangers)		Un	Un	14+			9	6
Kennedy	Kai	Inverness CT (OL from Rangers)					W	W		
Kinnear	Brian	Rangers					Sq	Un	12*	12*
MacGregor	Roddy	Inverness CT							Un	18^
Mackay	Daniel	Inverness CT							16<	10
Magennis	Kyle	Hibernian					W	W		
Maguire	Barry	Motherwell			12*	7G	9	7*		
Mair	Archie	Norwich City							Un	1*
Mayo	Lewis	Dunfermline Athletic (OL from Rangers)		15&	4	3	Un	Un	Un	4
McCarron	Liam	Leeds United		Un			W	W		
McCrorie	Robbie	Livingston (OL from Rangers)		W	W	W	Un	Un		
McCrorie	Ross	Aberdeen		6	11G	Sq	11	5		
McInroy	Kerr				Un	17<				
McIntyre	Tom	Reading		Un	5	4	Un	Un		
McLennan	Connor	Aberdeen		14+	14+	11G	4&G	10		
McPake	Josh	Rangers							Un	11^
Middleton	Glenn	Rangers / St Johnstone (OL)		10+	Sq	9	12*G	9+	10G	15&G
Morrison	Peter	Motherwell			Un	Un				
Patterson	Nathan	Rangers		5&	7*	6<	7*	Un		
Porteous	Ryan	Hibernian		3	W	W	4	3		
Reading	Patrick	Ayr United			9	Sq	2&	Un		
Rudden	Zak	Partick Thistle							17^	Sq
Scott	James	Hull City		12*	W	W				
Slicker	Cieran	Manchester City							1*	Un
Smith	Lewis	Hamilton Accies		W						
Turnbull	David	Motherwell / Celtic		8*	Un	10*G	Un	12*		
Urain	Ewan	Athletic Bilbao							8^	16>
Welsh	Stephen	Celtic					Sub	Un	4	3+
Williamson	Ben	Rangers							Un	7<G
Wright	Kieran	Rangers		Un	Un	15&				

ALL TIME APPEARANCES

1	Christian Dailly	35
2	Steven Pressley	27
3	Alan Campbell	24
4	Paul Hanlon	23
5	Craig Easton	22
5	Gary Naysmith	22
7	Shaun Maloney	21
8	Stuart Armstrong	20
8	Jamie McCunnie	20
8	Jordan McGhee	20
8	Ross McCrorie	20
12	Stevie Crawford	19
12	Ryan Jack	19
12	Mark Wilson	19

ALL TIME GOALSCORERS

1	Fraser Hornby	10
2	Scott Booth	8
2	Jordan Rhodes	8
4	Jamie Muprphy	6
4	Chris Maguire	6
4	Jim Hamilton	6
4	Mark Burchill	6
8	Gerry Creaney	5
8	Christian Dailly	5
8	Steven Fletcher	5
8	Simon Lynch	5
8	Shaun Maloney	5
8	Steven Naismith	5
8	Steven Thompson	5
8	Tony Watt	5

SCOTLAND UNDER 21 MANAGERS / HEAD COACHES

1975-1982 Andy Roxburgh
1982-1986 Walter Smith
1986-1993 Craig Brown
1993-1998 Tommy Craig
1998-2002 Alex Smith
2002-2005 Rainer Bonhof
2005-2006 Maurice Malpas
2006-2007 Archie Knox
2007-2008 Maurice Malpas
2008-2014 Billy Stark
2014-2015 Ricky Sbragia
2015 Danny Lennon
2015-16 Ricky Sbragia
2016- Scott Gemmill

Scotland's first Under 21 game was in Pilsen, v Czechoslovakia, on October 12 1976. Prior to that games were at Under 23 level. The game ended 0-0 and Scotland's team was: Bobby Clark (Aberdeen)*, George Burley (Ipswich), Arthur Albiston (Man United), Pat Stanton (Celtic)*, Roy Aitken (Celtic), Tommy Burns (Celtic), Davie Cooper (Rangers), John Wark (Ipswich), David McNiven (Leeds), David Narey (Dundee Utd), Paul Sturrock (Dundee Utd). Subs Lindsay Muir (Hibs), Davie Provan (Kilmarnock)
* Over Aged Player

Mens U19 Team

All competitive matches were scrapped due to COVID. Scotland arranged to play England in two matches, under strict COVID protocols. The first of these was abandoned due to a positive test result during the game. The second was consequently postponed.

Manager: Billy Stark

Surname	First Name	Club	1	2
Anderson	Elliot	Newcastle United	10	Sq
Barron	Connor	Brechin City (OL from Aberdeen)	Un	Sq
Bowat	Ibane	Fulham	5	Sq
Bowie	Kieron	Fulham	Un	Sq
Clarke	Flynn	Peterborough United	Un	Sq
Dickson	Ciaran	Rangers	6	Sq
Dickson-Peters	Thomas	Norwich City	9	Sq
Doig	Josh	Hibernian	3	Sq
Hamilton	Jamie	Hamilton Accies	4	Sq
Henderson	Jay	Clyde (OL from St Mirren)	7	Sq
Kennedy	Kai	Rangers	11	Sq
Lo-Everton	Sonny Blu	Watford	8	Sq
Logan	Cammy	Hearts	Un	Sq
Macari	Lewis	Stoke City	2	Sq
McAvoy	Connor	Fulham	Un	Sq
McKinstry	Stuart	Leeds United	Un	Sq
Newman	Jack	Dundee United	Un	Sq
Reid	Josh	Ross County	Un	Sq
Slicker	Cieran	Manchester City	1	Sq
Winter	Andrew	Hamilton Accies	Un	Sq

1	08/10/2020	Fr	A	England	St George's Park	1 3 Abd, Half Time
2	11/10/2020	Fr	A	England	St George's Park	

Mens U17 Team

Manager - Brian McLaughlin

Surname	First Name	Club	1
Anderson	Matthew	Celtic	Sq
Awokoya-Mebude	Adedire	Rangers	Sq
Brooks	Adam	Celtic	Sq
Carse	Mackenzie	Celtic	Sq
Duncan	Ryan	Aberdeen	Sq
Ewen	Kelsey	Rangers	Sq
Hepburn	Barry	Bayern Munchen	Sq
Johnson	Murray	Hibernian	Sq
King	Leon	Rangers	Sq
Letosa	Tsonanelo	Celtic	Sq
McConnell	Jack	Rangers	Sq
McPherson	Ben	Celtic	Sq
Mullen	Jeremiah	Leeds United	Sq
Offord	Kieran	St Mirren	Sq
Reid	Dylan	St Mirren	Sq

Only one game was scheduled and it was cancelled due to COVID.

1	10/10/20	Fr	A	England	St George's Park

Mens U18 Schools Team

There was no international schools football in 2020/1.

Centenary Shield—Under 18 Schools

The **Centenary Shield** was presented to the **Schools Association Football International Board** in 1973 by the Scottish FA to mark the Association's centenary year. It is currently contested for by U18 Boys selects representing the Schoolboy Associations of the British Isles countries.

Past winners of the Centenary Shield, including occasions on which the award has been shared, have been:

1973 England & Wales
1974 England
1975 Wales
1976 Scotland & England
1977 Wales
1978 Scotland
1979 Scotland
1980 England
1981 Wales
1982 England
1983 Scotland
1984 England
1985 England
1986 England
1987 England
1988 England
1989 England
1990 Switzerland
1991 Switzerland
1992 England & Switzerland
1993 England
1994 England
1995 Switzerland
1996 N. Ireland
1997 England
1998 N Ireland
1999 N Ireland
2000 Scotland
2001 England & Scotland
2002 England
2003 Rep of Ireland
2004 Rep of Ireland
2005 N Ireland & Rep of Ireland
2006 England
2007 England
2008 Rep of Ireland
2009 England & N. Ireland
2010 Rep of Ireland
2011 Scotland & N Ireland
2012 England
2013 Northern Ireland
2014 England
2015 Republic of Ireland
2016 England
2017 Northern Ireland and England
2018 Republic of Ireland
2019 Northern Ireland

Scotland In UEFA / FIFA Under 18 / 19 Finals

1963 UEFA Youth Tournament (in England)

Group	Switzerland	Redhill	3-1
Group	W Germany	Aldershot	1-2
Group	Greece	Tooting	4-0
SF	England	White City	0-1
3/4	Bulgaria	Portsmouth	4-2

Squad: Bobby Ferguson (Kilmarnock Amateurs), John Parkes (Celtic), H Baillie (Bellfield BC), Jim Townsend (St Johnstone), Don Murray (Cardiff City), Dennis Hollywood (Southampton), Tommy McLean (Kilmarnock), Ronnie Hamilton (Kilmarnock), George Graham (Aston Villa), H Quinn, Jimmy Robertson (St Mirren)

1964 UEFA Youth Tournament (in Netherlands)

Group	Switzerland	Deventer	3-1
Group	Switzerland	Amersfoort	2-0
QF	Sweden	Amsterdam	1-0
SF	Spain	Den Bosch	2-3
3/4	Portugal	Rotterdam	2-3aet

Squad: Bobby Clark (Aberdeen), Billy Dickson (Kilmarnock), Smith (Gairdoch United), Watson (Rangers), Fraser (Dunfermline Athletic), Eric Stevenson (Hibernian), Quinn (St Mirren), Jim McCalliog (Chelsea), Joe Harper (Morton), Jimmy O'Rourke (Hibernian), Buckley (Wolves)

1965 UEFA Youth Tournament (in West Germany)

Group	Italy	Stuttgart	1-1
Group	Yugoslavia	Freiburg	0-1

Squad: G Gartshore (Hibernian), L McLean (Drumchapel Ams), P Sharpe (Hearts), D Breen (Airdrie), Anderson (Dunfermline Ath), Jim Hermiston (Aberdeen), Halpin (Hamilton Accies), Henry McLeish (East Fife), Swan (Dundee), Eddie Gray (Leeds United), Noble (Aberdeen), McLeish (Dundee United), McKay (Leicester City), Murphy (Albion Rovers), John Taylor (Queen's Park), Derek Mackay (Dundee), Walter Borthwick (Morton)

1966 UEFA Youth Tournament (in Yugoslavia)

Group	Spain	Pristina	1-1
Group	West Germany	Kos. Mitrovica	1-0
Group	Netherlands	Kos. Mitrovica	2-2

1968 UEFA Youth Tournament (in France)

Group	Portugal	Apt	0-2
Group	Switzerland	Aix en Provence	4-0
Group	Belgium	Aix en Provence	2-0

Squad: Keith McRae (Motherwell), Kerr (Morton), Mervyn Jones (Hibernian), Kerray (Leeds United), Logan (Port Vale), McCabe (Hibernian), Brown (Hearts), John Hansen (Partick Thistle), Malcolm Manley (Leicester City), John Murphy (Hibernian), Jim Steele (Dundee), Spark (Preston NE), Tommy Veitch (Hearts), Willie Watson (Manchester United), Peter Marinello (Hibernian), Goodwin (Chelsea), Tony Green (Albion Rovers), Asa Hartford (West Bromwich Albion), Hugh Reed (West Brom), Willie Waddell (Leeds Utd), Kerr (Bury), Brown (Burnley), Tommy Craig (Aberdeen)

1969 UEFA Youth Tournament (in East Germany)

Group	Poland	Jena	1-0
Group	Austria	Dresden	2-1
Group	Yugoslavia	Erfurt	1-1
SF	East Germany	Karl Marx Stadt	1-2
3/4	USSR	Halle	0-1

Squad: Keith McRae (Motherwell), Willie McEwan (Hibernian), Gray (Clydebank), Kenny Dalglish (Celtic), Eddie Kelly (Arsenal), Tommy Craig (Aberdeen), Watson, Tommy Wilson (Aberdeen), Hamilton (Aberdeen), John Whiteford (Airdrie), Asa Hartford (West Brom), Vic Davidson (Celtic), Alfie Conn (Rangers), Billy Livingstone (Celtic), Murray (Hearts), Paul Wilson (Celtic)

1970 UEFA Youth Tournament (in Scotland)

Group	Bulgaria	Ayr	2-2
Group	Italy	Motherwell	2-1
Group	Sweden	Greenock	5-0
SF	Netherlands	Ibrox	0-1
3/4	France	Firhill	0-2

Squad: Alan Rough (Partick Th), John Brownlie (Hibernian), John Gallacher (Hearts), George Anderson (Morton), Ally Robertson (West Brom), Kenny Watson (Rangers), Alfie Conn (Rangers), Graeme Souness (Spurs), Eric Carruthers (Hearts), Derek Parlane (Rangers), Ian Munro (St Mirren), McEwan (QOTS), Jim Brown (Aston Villa), Derek Renton, Arthur Graham (Aberdeen)

1972 UEFA Youth Tournament (in Spain)

Group	Hungary	Valencia	3-4
Group	West Germany	Castellon	1-0
Group	USSR	Jativa	2-0

Squad: Jim Stewart (Kilmarnock), John Shaw (Leeds Utd), Joe Filipp (Ayr Utd), Bobby McDonald (Aston Villa), George Anderson (Morton), Jim Cannon (Crystal Palace), Mike McCartney (West Brom), Brian McLaughlin (Celtic), Gordon Smith (St Johnstone), Gary Liddell (Leeds Utd), Kenny Burns (Birmingham), Steve Finnieston (Chelsea), Billy Kellock (Cardiff), Ken Mackie (Dunfermline), Jim Scott (Dunfermline), Frankie Gray (Leeds Utd)

1973 UEFA Youth Tournament (in Italy)

Group	Czechoslovakia	Lucca	0-1
Group	East German	Lucca	1-3
Group	Austria	Montecatini	2-0

Squad: Marshall Poulton (Airdrie), Jimmy Calderwood (Birmingham), Cairney (Dundee), Anderson (Dundee), George Donaldson (Rangers), Gordon Smith (Kilmarnock), McNicol (Rangers), Brian McLaughlin (Celtic), Steve Finnieston (Chelsea), Andy Ritchie (Celtic), Frank Gray (Leeds Utd), Willie Miller (Aberdeen)

1974 UEFA Youth Tournament (in Sweden)

Group	Iceland	Karlshamm	1-1
Group	Finland	Bromolla	6-0
Group	Romania	Karlshamm	3-2
SF	Bulgaria	Helsingborg	0-1
3/4	Greece	Lund	1-0

Squad included: Andy Gray (Dundee United), John Dowie (Fulham), Neil McNab (Tottenham), Graeme Payne (Dundee United), Alex O'Hara (Rangers), Steel

1978 UEFA Youth Tournament (in Poland)

Group	West Germany	Biesko Biala	1-0
Group	Portugal	Cieszyn	1-0
Group	Italy	Kety	0-0
SF	Yugoslavia	Krakow	2-2, lop
3/4	Poland	Krakow	1-3

1979 UEFA Youth Tournament (in Austria)

Group	Poland	Bruk	3-2
Group	Bulgaria	Ternitz	0-2
Group	Denmark	Modling	2-1

1980/1 UEFA Youth Tournament (in West Germany)

Group	Austria	Ludenscheid	1-0
Group	England	Aachen	1-0
Group	Spain	Duren	1-1

1981/2 UEFA Youth Tournament (in Finland)

Group	Albania	Kotka	3-0
Group	Turkey	Hamina	2-0
Group	Netherlands	Anjalankoski	1-1
SF	Poland	Lahti	2-0
F	Czechoslovakia	Helsinki	3-1

Squad: Robin Rae (Hibernian), Bruan Gunn 9Aberdeen), Andy Bruce (Rangers), Jim McInally (Celtic), Kenny Black (Rangers), Dave Beaumont (Dundee United), Dave MacPherson (Rangers), John Philliben (Stirling Albion), Jim Dobbin (Celtic), Neale Cooper (Aberdeen), Paul McStay (Celtic), Billy Davies (Rangers), Pat Nevin (Clyde), Gary Mackay (Hearts), Dave Bowman (Hearts), Ian Westwater (Hearts), Sam McGivern (Kilmarnock)

1982/3 FIFA World Youth Championship (in Mexico)

Group	South Korea	Toluca	2-0
Group	Australia	Toluca	1-2
Group	Mexico	Mexico City	1-0
QF	Poland	Mexico City	0-1

1982/3 UEFA Youth Tournament (in England)

Group	USSR	West Brom	3-0
Group	England	Birmingham	2-4*
Group	Spain	Wolves	1-1

* Scotland fielded ineligible player, awarded 0-3

1983/4 UEFA Youth Tournament (in USSR)

Group	Rep of Ireland	Leningrad	0-3
Group	Portugal	Leningrad	3-1
Group	Greece	Leningrad	1-1

1984/6 UEFA Youth Tournament (in Yugoslavia)

QF	Bulgaria	Backa Topola	1-0
SF	Italy	Backa Topola	0-1
3/4	West Germany	Subotica	0-1

Squad: Les Fridge (Chelsea), McRobb (Aberdeen), Redpath (Hearts), Derek Whyte (Celtic), David Robertson (Aberdeen), Steve Murray (Nottingham Forest), Gordon McLeod (Dundee United), John Collins (Hibernian), Joe Miller (Aberdeen), Paul Wright (Aberdeen), Scott Nisbet (Rangers), Brian Hamilton (St Mirren), Brian Ross (Airdrie), Robert Green (Aberdeen)

1987/8 FIFA World Youth Championship (in Chile)

Group	East Germany	Valparaiso	2-1
Group	Bahrain	Valparaiso	1-1
Group	Colombia	Valparaiso	2-2
QF	West Germany	Antofagasta	1-1,lop

1989 FIFA World Youth Championship (in Scotland)

Group	Ghana	Hampden	0-0
Group	Cuba	Motherwell	3-0
Group	Bahrain	Motherwell	1-1
QF	East Germany	Aberdeen	1-0
SF	Portugal	Tynecastle	1-0
F	Saudi Arabia	Hampden	2-2,lop

1991/2 UEFA Youth Tournament (in Cyprus)

Group	Cyprus	Larnaca	3-0
Group	Germany	Larnaca	0-1
Group	N Ireland	Larnaca	3-1

2005/6 UEFA Youth Tournament (in Poland)

Group	Portugal	Szamotuly	2-2
Group	Spain	Pobiedziska	0-4
Group	Turkey	Swarzedz	3-2
SF	Czech Republic	Grodzisk Wiel	1-0
F	Spain	Poznan	1-2

2006/7 FIFA World Youth Championship (in Canada)

Group	Japan	Victoria	1-3
Group	Nigeria	Victoria	0-2
Group	Costa Rica	Burnaby	1-2

Scotland have not qualified for the FInals of anu U18 / U19 Tournament since 2007.

Where are they now, Scotland Under 16 from 2015/16 ?

Over the past couple of years we have recorded that the cream of Scotland's youth talent in season 2013/14 did not seem to have fulfilled their potential. Alternatively, perhaps they weren't the cream of the talent available and the selection process was flawed? Or is it simply that the pressure for results at first team level means that 19-20 years old are not given a chance at first team level in the UK?

Did the Class of 2015/16 fare any better? Here's what has happened to Scotland's U16 players from the year, now in their early 20s. It would appear that this cohort have fared better than those from the two previous years.

Aitchison	Jack	Celtic		Joined Barnsley on a 3 year contract in October 2020, spent much of season on loan to Stevenage
Antoniazzi	Christian	Celtic		Joined Aberdeen, then Forfar Athletic and now Montrose
Church	Daniel	Celtic		Now with Alloa Athletic
Connelly	Stefan	Hamilton Accies		Freed by Hamilton in 2017, no senior clubs since
Deas	Robbie	Celtic		Now with Inverness CT
Freeman	Kieran	Dundee United		Joined Southempton in 2016. Returned to Dundee United 2020. First team squad player
Gray	Scott	Rangers		Released by Rangers in 2019, joined Dalry Thistle. With East Stirlingshire last season
Houston	Jordan	Rangers		Released by Rangers 2020, now with Ayr United
Hutchison	Lewis	Aberdeen		Released by Aberdeen 2020, now with Culter
Irving	Andrew	Rangers		Joined Hearts, made first team. Transferred to Turkgucu Munchen in 2021
Kelly	Stephen	Rangers		Signed by Rangers, seasons on loan to Ayr and Ross Co. Ibrox first team squad pre-season 2021/2
MacPherson	Joseph	Aberdeen		Released by Aberdeen in 2017, joined Formartine United. released by them 2019
Maxwell	Aidan	Forth Valley Academy		Dropped out of football 2017
Mayo	Lewis	Rangers		Still with Rangers but yet to play in first team. OL to Dunfermline 2020/1
McCracken	Jon	Hamilton Accies		Joined Norwich City in 2016, and still with them
McDonald	Anthony	Hearts		Left Hearts 2020 and joined Cordoba, returned with Inverness CT in Feb 2021
McInroy	Kerr	Celtic		Still with Celtic, OL to Dunfermline 2020/1
McLevy	Ewan	Kilmarnock		Released by Killie in 2020, then with Brechin City
Middleton	Glen	Norwich City		Joined Rangers. Spent 2020/1 OL at St Johnstone
Mullen	Ryan	Celtic		Still with Celtic, OL to Queen's Park in 2020/1
Paterson	Jack	Kilmarnock		Released by Killie 2020, now with Troon
Reid	Aaron	Hearts		Released by Hearts, gave up football and became Personal Trainer
Ross	Sebastian	Aberdeen		Released by Aberdeen 2020, joined Cove Rangers, now Falkirk
Rudden	Zak	Rangers		Released by Rangers 2020, joined Partick Thistle
Shiels	Matthew	Rangers		Released by Rangers 2021, joined Hamilton Accies
Smith	Kyle	Hearts		Released by Hearts 2018
Thomson	Jack	Rangers		Still with Rangers, OL to Orange County 2021
Watt	Elliot	Preston North End		Joined Wolves and now in first team at Bradford City
Welsh	Steven	Celtic		Still with Celtic, broke into first team 2020/1

Women's International Football

Women's National Team

Surname	First Name	Club	Total	1	2	3	4	5	6	7	8
Alexander	Lee	Glasgow City	30	1	1	1	1	1	Un	1	1
Arnot	Lizzie	Rangers	37	Un	11*	15&	Un	11G	Un	16>	14+
Arthur	Chloe	Aston Villa	22	W	W	Un	Un			5	Un
Beattie	Jen	Arsenal	131	W	W	4	4	Un	4		
Boyle	Rachael	Hibernian	36	5*	Un	5	14+	Un	Un		
Brown	Fiona	Rosengard	41			Un	Un			12*	5+
Clelland	Lana	Fiorentina	27							10*	Un
Corsie	Rachel	Birmingham City / Kansas City	123	3	4	3	3	3	3	Un	3
Crichton	Leanne	Glasgow City	72	14+	12*	8+	Un				
Cummings	Eartha	Charlton Athletic	0							Un	Un
Cunningham	Megan	Rangers	2					Un	Un		
Cuthbert	Erin	Chelsea	43	11	10	11	11	10>GG	11	Un	11&G
Docherty	Nicola	Rangers	25	Un	Un	12*	Un	7	Un	8	Un
Eddie	Leah	Hibernian	1							15&	Un
Emslie	Claire	Everton (OL from Orlando Pride)	34	9	8	Sq	Sq	15&G	9	9	10
Evans	Lisa	Arsenal	86			9	2	Sq	8		
Fife	Jenna	Rangers	6	Un	Un	Un	Un	Un	1	Un	Un
Godfrey	Hannah	Tottenham Hotspur	4	4	Un	Un	Un				
Graham	Lucy	Everton	12	10+	Un	Un	12*	4&	7	17<^	8
Grant	Abbi	Birmingham City	7	Un	Un						
Grimshaw	Christy	AC Milan	2							18^	9*
Hanson	Kirsty	Manchester United	7	7	14+	10&	Sq	9+G	12*	11>	Un
Howard	Sophie	Leicester City	21	Un	6	Un	Un	6	Un	6	Un
Kerr	Sam	Glasgow City / Rangers	2	Sq	Sq	Un	Sq	Un	5*		
Little	Kim	Arsenal	140	W	W	6	8			Un	6
Lynn	Shannon	Vittsjo GK	31	Un	Un	Un	Un				
McLauchlan	Rachel	Rangers	10	Un	Un			2	Un	2	12*
Mitchell	Emma	Reading	66	2	3	2*	Sq	Un	2		
Muir	Amy	Hibernian	1	Sq	Sq						
Murray	Christie	Birmingham City	70	Un	7&	Sq	6+			7<	15&
Ness	Zoe	Rangers	10	Un	Un	Sq	15&	17<	Un		
Robertson	Lisa	Celtic	2					12*	Un	4+	Un
Ross	Jane	Manchester United	136	8&	15&	Un	5*	16>GG	Un		
Ross	Natalie	Celtic	12					14+	Un		
Smith	Kirsty	Manchester United	44	12*	2	Sq	9			Un	2
Thomas	Martha	West Ham United	8	15&	9*	14+	10&	8<GG	10		
Weir	Caroline	Manchester City	79	6	5	7	7	5*G	6	14+G	7
Westrup	Brianna	Rangers	2							3&	4

Coach - Shelley Kerr (Games 1-4), Stuart McLaren (Games 5-8)

1	23/10/20	UEFAQ	H	Tynecastle	Albania	3	0
2	27/10/20	UEFAQ	A	Helsinki	Finland	0	1
3	27/11/20	UEFAQ	A	Lisbon	Portugal	0	1
4	1/12/20	UEFAQ	H	Easter Road	Finland	0	1
5	19/2/21	UEFAQ	A	Larnaca	Cyprus	10	0
6	23/2/21	UEFAQ	N	Larnaca	Portugal	0	2
7	10/6/21	Fr	A	Northern Ireland	Belfast (Seaview)	1	0
8	15/6/21	Fr	A	Wales	Llanelli	1	0

FIXTURES

1	17/9/21	WCQ	A	Hungary
2	21/9/21	WCQ	H	Faroe Islands
3	22/10/21	WCQ	H	Hungary
4	26/11/21	WCQ	H	Ukraine
5	30/11/21	WCQ	A	Spain
6	8/4/22	WCQ	A	Ukraine
7	12/4/22	WCQ	H	Spain
8	6/9/22	WCQ	A	Faroe Islands

No games were played by Women's National teams at other age groups in 2020/1.

UEFA QUALIFYING STANDINGS

	P	W	D	L	F	A	GD	P
Finland	8	7	1	0	24	3	22	22
Portugal	8	6	1	1	10	2	8	19
Scotland	8	4	0	4	26	5	21	12
Albania	8	2	0	6	7	21	-14	6
Cyprus	8	0	0	8	0	37	-37	0

The 2021 Women's Euros have now been moved to 2022. The tournament will run from Jul 6 -31.

Venues to be used are:

Old Trafford, Manchester (Opening Game only)
Bramall Lane, Sheffield
Brentford New Stadium, London
Falmer Stadium, Brighton
Leigh Sports Village, Leigh
Manchester City Academy Stadium
New York Stadium, Rotherham
Stadium MK, Milton Keyes
St Mary's Stadium, Southampton
Wembley Stadium (Final only)

Scotland International Womens Roll of Honour

Gemma Fay	203 caps	0 Goals
Joanna Love	191 caps	13 Goals
Pauline Hamill	141 caps	29 Goals
Kim Little	140 caps	59 Goals
Jane Ross	136 caps	62 Goals
Leanne Ross	133 caps	9 Goals
Jennifer Beattie	131 caps	23 Goals
Megan Sneddon	130 caps	4 Goals
Rachel Corsie	123 caps	17 Goals
Ifeoma Dieke	123 caps	0 Goals
Julie Fleeting	121 caps	116 Goals
Rhonda Jones	117 caps	4 Goals
Suzanne Grant	104 caps	12 Goals
Hayley Lauder	103 caps	9 Goals
Nicky Grant	98 caps	7 goals
Frankie Brown	96 caps	0 goals
Michelle Barr	87 caps	1 goal
Lisa Evans	86 caps	17 goals
Caroline Weir	79 caps	13 goals
Julie Smith	73 caps	0 goals
Leanne Crichton	72 caps	3 goals
Christie Murray	70 caps	5 goals
Stacey Cook	67 caps	10 goals
Emma Mitchell	66 caps	7 goals
Pauline McDonald	65 caps	0 goals
Shelley Kerr	59 caps	3 goals
Kirsty McBride	59 caps	2 goals
Amanda Burns	55 caps	2 goals
Linda Brown	48 caps	20 goals
Joelle Murray	48 caps	1 goal
Debbie McWhinnie	45 caps	10 goals
Kirsty Smith	44 caps	0 goals
Erin Cuthbert	43 caps	16 goals

SPFL FOOTBALL

SPFL BOARD 2020/21

The SPFL Board includes three Scottish Premiership representatives, two from the Scottish Championship and two covering Scottish League 1 and Scottish League 2.

Elected to serve on the 2020/21 SPFL Board, alongside chairman Murdoch MacLennan, SPFL chief executive Neil Doncaster and independent non-executive director Karyn McCluskey, were:

Scottish Premiership: Steve Brown (St Johnstone) Les Gray (Hamilton Academical) and Peter Lawwell (Celtic).

Scottish Championship: Ewen Cameron (Alloa Athletic) and Ross McArthur (Dunfermline Athletic)

Scottish League One and Scottish League Two: Ken Ferguson (Brechin City).

Also, Gordon Thomson (Clyde) has been elected as the alternate director for League One & League Two.

SPFL FORMAT 2020/1

Premiership
12 clubs, play each other 3 times then split into top 6 and bottom 6. Each groups plays each other once more—total 38 games.

One club relegated automatically. 11th club enters Play Off.

Championship, League One and League Two
The intention was : 10 clubs, play each other 3 times, - total 27 games.
This model was followed in the Championship. Due to COVID interruptions leagues One and Two changed to:
10 clubs, play each other twice, then split into top and bottom five. Each group plays each other once more—total 22 games.

Top Clubs promoted automatically.

In Championship club 4 plays club 3 Home and Away, with the winners playing Club 2 Home and Away, and the winners of that playing Premiership club 11 Home and Away. The winner plays in the Premiership in 2021/2.

In Leagues One and Two the 9th placed club in the higher league plays club 4 in the lower league Home and Away, and the 2nd and 4rd clubs in the lower league play Home and Away. The 2 winners contest a Home and Away final for a place in the higher league.

Club 10 in League Two plays the winner of a Play Off between the Lowland and Highland League Champions in a further Home and Away Play Off to determine if they retain SPFL membership or not.

LEAGUE STRUCTURE 2020/21

PREMIERSHIP (12)
Aberdeen
Celtic
Dundee United
Hamilton Accies
Hibernian
Kilmarnock
Livingston
Motherwell
Rangers
Ross County
St Johnstone
St Mirren

CHAMPIONSHIP (10)
Alloa Athletic
Arbroath
Ayr United
Dundee
Dunfermline Athletic
Hearts
Inverness Caledonian Thistle
Morton
Queen of the South
Raith Rovers

LEAGUE ONE (10)
Airdrieonians
Clyde
Cove Rangers
Dumbarton
East Fife
Falkirk
Forfar Athletic
Montrose
Partick Thistle
Peterhead

LEAGUE TWO (10)
Albion Rovers
Annan Athletic
Cowdenbeath
Edinburgh City
Elgin City
Peterhead
Queen's Park
Stenhousemuir
Stirling Albion
Stranraer

LEAGUE STRUCTURE 2021/2

PREMIERSHIP (12)
Aberdeen
Celtic
Dundee
Dundee United
Hearts
Hibernian
Livingston
Motherwell
Rangers
Ross County
St Johnstone
St Mirren

CHAMPIONSHIP (10)
Arbroath
Ayr United
Dunfermline Athletic
Hamilton Accies
Inverness Caledonian Thistle
Kilmarnock
Morton
Queen of the South
Raith Rovers
Partick Thistle

LEAGUE ONE (10)
Airdrieonians
Alloa Athletic
Clyde
Cove Rangers
Dumbarton
East Fife
Falkirk
Montrose
Peterhead
Queen's Park

LEAGUE TWO (10)
Albion Rovers
Annan Athletic
Cowdenbeath
Edinburgh City
Elgin City
Forfar Athletic
Kelty Hearts
Stenhousemuir
Stirling Albion
Stranraer

COVID and Scottish Football 2020/21

Season 2019/20 ended in chaos, court cases, statements, counter statements and general all round acrimony.

Scotland was in lockdown over the Summer of 2020. Elite football was given an exemption to allow players to train and play, provided they remained within bubbles and undertook the required level of COVID testing. The SPFL Premiership kicked off behind closed doors at the end of July.

The Premiership season unfolded in the normal manner - except that spectators were not allowed into games. Most clubs streamed games on demand for the benefit of home and away fans and many made home games available free for those optimists who had purchased a 2020/1 season ticket.

The Championship, League One and League Two seasons were scheduled to start in October. The clubs agreed to a League system where they played each other three times, giving a total of 27 matches. The Championship clubs continued with this model throughout the season.

A further COVID lockdown at the turn of the year 2020/2021 put paid to Leagues One and Two. They returned in March, still behind closed doors, and with rigid COVID testing protocols. The SPFL's preference was for clubs to reduce the season to 18 games. The club's themselves were unhappy with this. By that time clubs had played between 10 and 12 games and many thought that restarting after a 3 month lay off with only half a dozen games left to play was unfair. They lobbied successfully for a 22 games season - the two rounds of fixtures to be completed followed by a split, creating a further 4 matches to take the total to 22. This meant a very concentrated programme of games in April but the clubs pulled out all the stops to make it work.

Lower division clubs also streamed games live. They will be allowed to continue doing so after all COVID restrictions have been lifted.

The only matches with spectators were a very small number in December at outlying venues in Dumfries and Galloway and the North when restrictions were briefly lessened there. The Finals of the Play Offs also had small numbers of fans admitted under stringent restrictions.

The 2019/20 Scottish Cup was completed. The Semi Finals and Final were played with Celtic lifting the trophy in December.

The format of the 2020/1 Scottish Cup was altered. Initially the SFA suggested that only a small number of non-SPFL clubs should be allowed to play in it, chosen by ballot. This proved highly unpopular so a new structure came in with fewer Preliminary Rounds and no replays. The format was a success and has been adopted again for the 2021/2 season. Despite a lengthy spell with no games from January until late March, the Cup was completed on time.

The 2020/1 League Cup group games were played in two tranches in the late Autumn. Several games were unplayed due to COVID outbreaks. Clubs had agreed that if any club was unable to fulfil a fixture then the game would be awarded as a 3-0 win for their opponents. Notwithstanding this, the tournament was completed as scheduled.

The SPFL decided to scrap the Challenge Cup for 2021/2. The unplayed 2019/20 Final was also abandoned with Raith and Inverness CT declared joint winners.

There were various instances of clubs and players breaching COVID regulations that were dealt with by the SFA. These are recorded in the Disciplinary section other Almanac. At times football looked like it's own worst enemy with players ignoring the lockdown rules - high profile examples from Celtic, Rangers and Aberdeen reflected very badly on the game as a whole.

Season 2021/2 should, hopefully, run as normal. Early games were played with reduced attendances but by August the figures being admitted to grounds were starting to look more like normal.

JAMES ANDERSON'S PHILANTHROPY

James Anderson donated £3.1m to be equally shared amongst the SPFL clubs in July 2020 to help them through the COVID crisis. He also donated £300,000 to Youth football in Scotland. More recently he has funded sponsorship of the SPFL Challenge Cup for 2021/2. He has also been a long term benefactor of Hearts and has been quoted as saying that he "thinks little of Rangers and Celtic".

James Anderson (60) is based in Edinburgh and is a Fund Manager & Partner at Baillie Gifford, having joined the firm in 1983.

As co-manager of the FTSE 100 listed £11bn Scottish Mortgage Investment Trust and the US based $40bn Vanguard International Growth Fund he has helped deliver great investment success.

Mr Anderson and has family have consequently chosen to make significant donations to charities, the arts and academia.

Benefitting charities have included Médecins Sans Frontières, Save the Children, and Sistema Scotland.

In the arts the Anderson have provided multi-decade support to festivals in Edinburgh including: the Edinburgh International Festival, Edinburgh Book Festival, Edinburgh Film Festival and many others locally.

Mr Anderson funds the global Theatrum Mundi arts charity, and has provided a significant grant to the New York Public Library to help purchase the James Baldwin archive, one of the most powerful voices in 20th century American literature.

He is a trustee of and major donor to the world-renowned Johns Hopkins University (JHU) in Baltimore, Maryland, USA. Mr Anderson is also the Advisory Council Chair for the JHU School of Advanced International Studies Europe, in Bologna.

University of Oxford, University of Sussex and the London School of Economics have also received donations from Mr Anderson and his family.

Having grown up in Norfolk, Mr Anderson is still a Norwich City supporter, and having been at university there also proudly supports Bologna.

During this Covid-19 pandemic, the resilience of the assets Mr Anderson manages has enabled him to continue to offer generous support to many of these organisations. Having seen the crisis engulfing Scottish football over the last few months, he decided he wanted to offer his support.

NOTES ON THE CLUB INFORMATION SECTION

DATES OF BIRTH

The published information on player's dates of birth is very inaccurate. We have trawled many websites for information and find the same mistakes repeated over and over. In fact, the most accurate source of information has been player's own twitter feeds which frequently indicate their birthdays! Information for anyone born after 1994 is likely to be inaccurate - online databases seem to apply default birthdates to these players. Some club websites copy the inaccurate information. Presumably the SFA and SPFL are unwilling to provide this information to outside agencies. The dates printed in the Almanac contain many inaccuracies.

APPEARANCES

Information refers to Appearances (A), Used Substitute Appearances (S) and Goals (G) in League (L), Scottish Cup (SC), League Cup (LC), Challenge Cup (CC) and European Ties (UC), The UNS column refers to Unused substitute appearances in all competitions.

Most media sources use information from a single reporter at matches via an Agency. Sometimes it is clear that mistakes have been made and I have corrected these. Where possible we have cross-referenced media reports with club sources such as websites and programmes and clarified any discrepancies.

CONTRACT

The information given is for guidance only. It has been gleaned primarily from club websites and newspapers.

SCORERS

Where possible these have been double checked but there may still be disputed goals. The information on the SPFL website is sometimes updated and changed following such instances.

ATTENDANCES

Most clubs publish accurate attendances for games. In some cases, notably Celtic and Rangers, these include all tickets sold, including season tickets. Matchday attendances are, in some cases, much less than the published figure.

PLAYER NUMBERING

Numbers 1-11 refer to players who started the match but bear no relation to actual numbers worn. Used substitutes are listed as 12,14 and 15, again regardless of actual numbers worn. Press Agencies ask for teams to provided in "formation" rather than numerical order which causes problems for reporters unfamiliar with the teams. Squad numbering is mandatory in the Premiership and the Championship but is optional in the other divisions.

TRIALISTS

In most cases trialists have been identified and are entered under their correct names.

Nationalities of Players with SPFL Clubs 2020/21

ALB	Albania	**GER**	Germany	**POR**	Portugal
ALG	Algeria	**GHA**	Ghana	**ROI**	Republic of Ireland
ANG	Angola	**GRE**	Greece	**ROM**	Romania
AUS	Australia	**GUB**	Guinea Bissau	**RSA**	South Africa
AUT	Austria	**GUI**	Guinea	**SCO**	Scotland
BEL	Belgium	**HUN**	Hungary	**SEN**	Senegal
BOS	Bosnia-Herzegovina	**IRA**	Iran	**SIE**	Sierra Leone
BRA	Brazil	**ISR**	Israel	**SLO**	Slovenia
BUL	Bulgaria	**ITA**	Italy	**STL**	St Lucia
CAM	Cameroon	**JAM**	Jamaica	**SWE**	Sweden
CAN	Canada	**KOS**	Kosovo	**SWI**	Switzerland
CDI	Cote d'Ivoire	**LIT**	Lithuania	**TOG**	Togo
COL	Colombia	**MEX**	Mexico	**TUN**	Tunisia
CON	Congo	**MON**	Montenegro	**TUR**	Turkey
CRO	Croatia	**MOR**	Morocco	**UKR**	Ukraine
CYP	Cyprus	**NET**	Netherlands	**USA**	United States of America
CZE	Czech Republic	**NIG**	Nigeria	**WAL**	Wales
DRC	Democratic Republic of Congo	**NIR**	Northern Ireland	**ZIM**	Zimbabwe
ENG	England	**NOR**	Norway	**VEN**	Venezuela
FIN	Finland	**NZE**	New Zealand	**IRQ**	Iraq
FRA	France	**PHI**	Phllipinnes	**UGA**	Uganda
FRG	French Guiana	**POL**	Poland		

WORK PERMITS

Any player who is over 16 years old and is not from the European Economic Area, which covers 32 countries aside from the UK requires a work permit to play for a British club.

A Commonwealth citizen with at least one grandparent who was born in the UK does not need to apply through the points based system. Such players will still require a work permit but go through a different process.

When a club signs a player who requires a work permit, they agree to sponsor the player to be in the UK, meaning they will provide the funds for his time in the country. A certificate of sponsorship is then produced by the club, which is then submitted to the relevant FA for them to consider an endorsement.

The Scottish FA's rules on work permit endorsements follow the same guidelines as previously outlined by the UK Government. For the Scottish FA to give their approval, the player in question must have played 75 per cent of his nation's competitive games – excluding friendlies – in the two years prior to the date of application. Furthermore, the country the player is coming from must be in the top 70 of the FIFA rankings.

Failure to meet these requirements, unless it can be proven a player was unavailable for selection for a period of time, results in an automatic rejection of any application for an Scottish FA endorsement for a work permit certificate of sponsorship.

If an application is rejected, a club can then appeal to the SFA. An appeals panel will ultimately weigh up whether or not the player is, in their view, of the highest calibre and whether they would contribute significantly to the development of the game at the top level in the country. That appeals panel typically sits within three to five working days of an appeal submission, although urgent hearings can be convened.

The panel is made up of three representatives from the relevant football bodies, typically officials from the league, the association and the player's union. Up to three independent football experts, made up typically of former professionals, also sit on the panel.

The length of time a player can remain in the UK as a player depends on his grasp of the English language. There are two immigration statuses available to a player applying for a work permit: tier two and tier five.

Under tier two, a player can remain in the UK for an initial three years, with the possibility for an extension for a further two years. To qualify, the player must accrue 70 immigration points under the UK Government's system. 50 are given for getting an FA endorsement, with 10 more given for being able to prove sufficient funding to remain in the country.

The final 10 are awarded on the basis of the player's English. If the applicant comes from a predominantly English-speaking country, or has a degree from a course which was taught in English, the 10 points are subsequently awarded. Additionally, a player can sit an approved English language test upon their arrival in the UK to obtain tier two status.

Loan / Temporary Transfers—Revised for 2021/2

Loan transfers are very common these days, and the rules governing them are far from simple.

There are three types of temporary transfer:

Standard
Emergency
Development

Standard Temporary Transfers
Must be at least 28 days
Must be until the first day of the immediately succeeding transfer period

Emergency Temporary Transfers
Must be at least 28 days but no more than 93 days
Not allowed for Premiership clubs – only lower leagues

General
Maximum of 5 players plus a Goalkeeper on Standard / Emergency Temporary Transfers at any time **(down from 6)**
Maximum of ONE player on Standard / Emergency Temporary Transfer from a club in the same division at any one time **(down from 2)**
Maximum of THREE players on Standard / Emergency Temporary Transfer from a club in a different division at any one time **(down from 4)**
Maximum of FIVE players per season on Standard / Emergency Temporary Transfers

Goalkeepers
The League Management Committee can, in exceptional circumstances and on cause shown, sanction the Standard Temporary Transfer to a Premiership club, or an Emergency Temporary Transfer to a Championship, league One or League Two side, of a goalkeeper, in addition to the above.

Playing Against Own Club
Players on Temporary Transfers may not play against their parent club. No other stipulations about opponents are permitted.

Development Temporary Transfers
Players can play in Development League games and Challenge Cup ties for their parent club. If they do not play in Challenge Cup for parent club then they can play in Challenge Cup for their loan club.

There must be one clear day between a player playing for his parent club and his loan club. If there is a "clash" then the loan club takes priority unless they have agreed in writing to waive priority.

A Development Loan must terminate at the latest on the first day of the Registration Period immediately following the date on which the Player ceases to qualify as an Under 20 Player or, where such a Player will cease to so qualify during a Registration Period, the term of his Development Temporary Transfer must terminate not later than the date when he so ceases to so qualify as an Under 20 Player. Notwithstanding that a Player who is the subject of a Development Temporary Transfer has ceased to qualify as an Under 20 Player on a date which is not within a Registration Period he shall, subject to compliance with this Regulation, be deemed for all purposes to continue to qualify as an Under 20 Player until the earlier of the first day of the next Registration Period and the expiry of the term of his Development Temporary Transfer.

.

REGISTRATION PERIODS

Registration Periods will apply to Professional Players who compete in football at Scottish Professional Football League level.

To those Clubs to which Registration Periods apply, a Professional Player may only be registered to play with such a Club during one of two Registration Periods per year as determined by the Board from time to time. Notwithstanding the foregoing provision, and subject to what follows, a Professional Player who at the conclusion of a Registration Period is not registered to a Club, may sign and be registered for a Club outwith the Registration Period.

Internationally and Domestically, a Professional Player may be registered with a maximum of three Clubs to which Registration Periods apply during one Season. Notwithstanding the foregoing the Professional Player is only eligible to play Official Matches for two Clubs, to which Registration Periods apply, in any one Season.

Current Registration Periods in Scotland are:

June 9 – August 31st
January 1 – February 1

Championship, League One and League Two players can sign players On Loan during the registration periods, and the months of October and February.

Scottish Premiership Squad Numbers 2020/21

Aberdeen
1 Joe Lewis
2 Shay Logan
3 Tommie Hoban
4 Andrew Considine
5 Scott McKenna
6 Michael Devlin
7 Craig Bryson
8 Funso Ojo
9 Curtis Main
10 Niall McGinn
11 Ryan Hedges
14 Ash Taylor
15 Dylan McGeouch
16 Sam Cosgrove
17 Jonny Hayes
18 Connor McLennan
19 Lewis Ferguson
20 Tomas Cerny
21 Bruce Anderson
22 Ronald Hernandez
23 Ethan Ross
24 Dean Campbell
25 Scott Wright
26 Miko Virtanen
27 Mark Gallagher
28 Michael Ruth
29 Jack MacKenzie
30 Tom Ritchie
31 Connor Barron
32 Ryan Edmondson
33 Matthew Kennedy
34 Kevin Hanratty
38 Luke Turner
42 Michael Dangana
44 Calvin Ramsay

Celtic
1 Vasilis Barkas
2 Christopher Jullien
3 Greg Taylor
6 Nir Bitton
8 Scott Brown
9 Leigh Griffiths
10 Vakoun Bayo
11 Patryk Klimala
12 Ismaila Soro
17 Ryan Christie
18 Tom Rogic
19 Mikey Johnston
20 Marian Shved
21 Olivier Ntcham
22 Odsonne Edouard
23 Boli Bolingoli
24 Jonathan Afolabi
27 Mohamed Elyounoussi
28 Luca Connell
29 Scott Bain
30 Jeremie Frimpong
32 Lee O'Connor
35 Kristoffer Ajer
40 Barry Coffey
41 Scott Robertson
42 Callum McGregor
43 Ryan Mullen
44 Hatem Abd Elhamed
46 Daniel Church
47 Liam Hughes
48 Armstrong Oko-Flex
49 James Forrest
50 Robbie Deas
51 Paul Kennedy
52 Ewan Henderson
53 Cameron Harper
54 Adam Montgomery
55 Kerr McInroy
56 Anthony Ralston
57 Stephen Welsh
58 Connor McBride
59 Ben Wylie
61 Ewan Otoo
65 Conor Hazard
68 Brody Paterson
71 Tobi Oluwayemi
72 Leo Hjelde
73 Owen Moffat
76 Jack Aitchison
77 Karamoko Dembele

Dundee United
1 Benjamin Siegrist
2 Liam Smith
3 Adrian Sporle
4 Dillon Powers
5 Mark Connolly
6 Mark Reynolds
7 Paul McMullan
8 Peter Pawlett
10 Nicky Clark
11 Cammy Smith
15 Logan Chalmers
16 Adam King
17 Jamie Robson
18 Calum Butcher
19 Deniz Mehmet
20 Luke Bolton
21 Declan Glass
22 Kieran Freeman
23 Ian Harkes
24 Lawrence Shankland
25 Kai Fotheringham
26 Chris Mochrie
27 Louis Appere
28 Jake Davidson
29 Ross Graham
30 Lewis Neilson
31 Jack Newman
32 Archie Meekison
33 Lewis Fraser
34 Nathan Cooney
35 Mackenzie Lemon
36 Darren Watson
37 Adam Hutchison
38 Layton Bisland
39 Finn Robson
40 Flynn Duffy
41 Rhys Caves
42 Shaun Brown
43 Kerr Smith
44 Sam Lovie
45 Finlay Malcolm
46 Miller Thomson
47 Lennon Walker
48 Dominic Naglik

Hamilton Academical
2 Hakeem Odoffin
3 Scott McMann
4 Ciaran McKenna
5 Brian Easton
6 Jamie Hamilton
7 Will Collar
8 Scott Martin
9 Marios Ogkmpoe
10 David Templeton
11 Lewis Smith
12 Shaun Want
14 Charlie Trafford
15 Ronan Hughes
16 Markus Fjortoft
17 George Stanger
18 Reegan Mimnaugh
19 Andy Winter
20 David Moyo
21 Kyle Munro
22 Kyle Gourlay
23 Ryan Fulton
24 Ross Cunningham
25 Sean Slaven
31 Jamie Smith
32 Callum Smith
33 Daryl Meikle
34 Ross Callachan
36 Tunde Owolabi

Hibernian
1 Ofir Marciano
2 David Gray
4 Paul Hanlon
5 Ryan Porteous
6 Paul McGinn
7 Daryl Horgan
8 Drey Wright
9 Christian Doidge
10 Martin Boyle
11 Joe Newell
12 Fraser Murray
13 Alex Gogic
14 Stevie Mallan
15 Kevin Nisbet
16 Lewis Stevenson
17 Tom James
18 Adam Jackson
19 Jamie Gullan
20 Melker Hallberg
21 Maciej Dabrowski
22 Florian Kamberi
23 Scott Allan
24 Darren McGregor
25 Josh Doig
26 Sean Mackie
27 Ben Stirling
29 Ryan Shanley
30 Craig Samson
31 Patrick Martin
32 Josh Campbell
33 Innes Murray
34 Callum Yeats
42 Jayden Fairley
43 Steven Elder
44 Yrick Gallantes
45 Josh Currie
46 Gregor Woods
47 Jack Brydon
48 Robbie Hamilton
49 Josh O'Connor
50 Mackenzie Weir

Kilmarnock
1 Jake Eastwood
2 Aaron McGowan
3 Brandon Haunstrup
5 Kirk Broadfoot
6 Alan Power
7 Rory McKenzie
8 Gary Dicker
9 Eamonn Brophy
10 Greg Kiltie
11 Nicke Kabamba
12 Danny Whitehall
14 Zeno Rossi
15 Mohamed El Makrini
17 Stuart Findlay
18 Calum Waters
19 Mitch Pinnock
20 Innes Cameron
22 Ross Millen
23 Danny Rogers
25 Kyle Connell
27 Aaron Tshibola
29 Chris Burke
32 Tomas Brindley
33 Ally Taylor
34 Curtis Lyle
40 Harry Broun

Livingston
1 Robby McCrorie
2 Nicky Devlin
3 Ciaron Brown
4 Alan Lithgow
5 Jack Fitzwater
6 Marvin Bartley
7 Keaghan Jacobs
8 Scott Pittman
9 Lyndon Dykes
10 Craig Sibbald
11 Alan Forrest
15 Matej Poplatnik
16 Robbie Crawford
17 Scott Robinson
19 Salim Kouider-Aissa
20 Aymen Souda
21 Jack McMillan
22 Scott Tiffoney
23 Rafa De Vita
25 Efe Ambrose
27 Jon Guthrie
29 Aaron Taylor-Sinclair

30 Brian Schwake
32 Max Stryjek
33 Steve Lawson
38 Jack Hamilton
39 Carlo Pignatiello
40 Gary Maley

Motherwell

1 Trevor Carson
2 Liam Grimshaw
3 Jake Carroll
4 Ricki Lamie
5 Nathan McGinley
6 Allan Campbell
7 Mark O'Hara
8 David Turnbull
9 Jordan White
11 Jake Hastie
12 Scott Fox
14 Jermaine Hylton
15 Barry Maguire
16 Bevis Mugabi
17 Sherwin Seedorf
18 Charles Dunne
19 Liam Polworth
20 Jamie Semple
21 Harry Robinson
22 Liam Donnelly
23 Peter Morrison
24 David Devine
25 Ross MacIver
26 Dean Cornelius
27 Max Johnston
28 Yusuf Hussain
29 Callum Lang
30 Matthew Connolly
31 Declan Gallagher
32 Tony Watt
33 Sam Muir
34 Matthew McDonald
35 Cameron Williamson
36 Findlay Cook
99 Christopher Long

Rangers

1 Allan McGregor
2 James Tavernier
3 Calvin Bassey
4 George Edmundson
5 Filip Helander
6 Connor Goldson
7 Ianis Hagi
8 Ryan Jack
9 Jermain Defoe
10 Steven Davis
13 Andrew Firth
14 Ryan Kent
15 Jamie Murphy
16 Nathan Patterson
17 Joe Aribo
18 Glen Kamara
19 Nikola Katic
20 Alfredo Morelos
21 Brandon Barker
22 Jordan Jones
24 Greg Stewart
26 Leon Balogun
27 Greg Docherty
28 Ross McCrorie

30 Kai Kennedy
31 Borna Barisic
33 Jon McLaughlin
34 Lewis Mayo
36 Jamie Barjonas
37 Scott Arfield
38 Josh McPake
39 Dapo Mebude
40 Glenn Middleton

Ross County

1 Ross Laidlaw
2 Connor Randall
3 Carl Tremarco
4 Liam Fontaine
5 Callum Morris
6 Ross Draper
7 Michael Gardyne
8 Oli Shaw
9 Billy Mckay
10 Lee Erwin
11 Iain Vigurs
12 Tom Grivosti
14 Josh Mullin
15 Keith Watson
16 Alex Iacovitti
17 Regan Charles-Cook
18 Stephen Kelly
20 Blair Spittal
21 Ross Doohan
22 Jordan Tillson
23 Joe Chalmers
24 Harry Paton
25 Coll Donaldson
27 Ross Stewart
31 Ross Munro
41 Logan Ross
43 Josh Reid
44 Matthew Wright
46 Ben Williamson
47 Adam MacKinnon
48 Craig MacKenzie

St Johnstone

1 Zander Clark
2 Wallace Duffy
3 Scott Tanser
4 Jamie McCart
5 Jason Kerr
6 Liam Gordon
7 Craig Conway
8 Murray Davidson
9 Chris Kane
10 David Wotherspoon
11 Michael O'Halloran
12 Elliot Parish
14 Stevie May
15 Danny McNamara
16 Isaac Olaofe
18 Ali McCann
19 Shaun Rooney
20 John Robertson
22 Callum Hendry
23 Cammy Ballantyne
26 Liam Craig
45 Ross Sinclair

St Mirren

1 Jak Alnwick
2 Richard Tait
4 Joe Shaughnessy
5 Conor McCarthy
6 Nathan Sheron
7 Kyle Magennis
8 Ryan Flynn
9 Jon Obika
10 Kyle McAllister
11 Ilkay Durmus
14 Cammy MacPherson
15 Jack Baird
16 Sam Foley
17 Jamie McGrath
19 Junior Morias
22 Marcus Fraser
23 Isak Thorvaldsson
25 Ethan Erhahon
26 Dean Lyness
27 Peter Urminsky
30 Jay Henderson
33 Lewis Jamieson
35 Josh Jack

Pictured below is Kieran Freeman of Dundee United

Scottish Premiership Squad Numbers 2021/2

ABERDEEN

	Name	Nat
1	Joe Lewis	ENG
2	Ross McCrorie	SCO
3	Jack Mackenzie	SCO
4	Andrew Considine	SCO
5	Declan Gallagher	SCO
6	Mikey Devlin	SCO
8	Scott Brown	SCO
9	Christian Ramirez	USA
10	Niall McGinn	NIR
11	Ryan Hedges	WAL
14	Jay Emmanuel-Thomas	ENG
15	Dylan McGeouch	SCO
16	Funso Ojo	BEL
17	Jonathan Hayes	IRL
18	Connor McLennan	SCO
19	Lewis Ferguson	SCO
20	Teddy Jenks	ENG
21	Jack Gurr	ENG
22	Calvin Ramsay	SCO
24	Dean Campbell	SCO
25	Gary Woods	ENG
26	Miko Virtanen	FIN
28	Michael Ruth	SCO
31	Kieran Ngwenya	MAL
32	Ryan Duncan	SCO
33	Matthew Kennedy	SCO

CELTIC

	Name	Nat
1	Vasilios Barkas	GRE
2	Christopher Jullien	FRA
3	Greg Taylor	SCO
4	Carl Starfelt	SWE
6	Nir Bitton	ISR
8	Kyogo Furuhashi	JPN
9	Leigh Griffiths	SCO
10	Albian Ajeti	SUI
11	Liel Abada	ISR
12	Ismaila Soro	CIV
14	David Turnbull	SCO
17	Ryan Christie	SCO
18	Tomas Rogic	AUS
19	Mikey Johnston	SCO
21	Olivier Ntcham	FRA
22	Odsonne Edouard	FRA
23	Boli Bolingoli-Mbombo	BEL
24	Jonathan Afolabi	IRL
26	Osaze Urhoghide	ENG
28	Luca Connell	IRL
29	Scott Bain	SCO
30	Liam Shaw	ENG
32	Lee O'Connor	IRL
41	Scott Robertson	SCO
42	Callum McGregor	SCO
45	Ross Doohan	SCO
47	Dane Murray	SCO
49	James Forrest	SCO
52	Ewan Henderson	SCO
54	Adam Montgomery	SCO
55	Kerr McInroy	SCO
56	Anthony Ralston	SCO
57	Stephen Welsh	SCO
65	Conor Hazard	NIR
77	Karamoko Dembélé	ENG

DUNDEE

	Name	Nat
1	Adam Legzdins	ENG
2	Cammy Kerr	SCO
3	Jordan Marshall	ENG
4	Liam Fontaine	ENG
5	Ryan Sweeney	IRL
6	Jordan McGhee	SCO
7	Alex Jakubiak	SCO
8	Shaun Byrne	SCO
9	Danny Mullen	SCO
10	Paul McGowan	SCO
11	Declan McDaid	SCO
14	Lee Ashcroft	SCO
16	Christie Elliott	ENG
17	Luke McCowan	SCO
18	Paul McMullan	SCO
19	Finlay Robertson	SCO
20	Corey Panter	ENG
21	Ian Lawlor	IRL
23	Cillian Sheridan	IRL
24	Max Anderson	SCO
26	Charlie Adam	SCO
30	Harrison Sharp	SCO
35	Jason Cummings	SCO
44	Jack Wilkie	SCO

DUNDEE UNITED

	Name	Nat
1	Benjamin Siegrist	SUI
2	Liam Smith	SCO
3	Adrián Spörle	ARG
4	Charlie Mulgrew	SCO
5	Mark Connolly	IRL
6	Mark Reynolds	SCO
8	Peter Pawlett	SCO
10	Nicky Clark	SCO
11	Logan Chalmers	SCO
12	Ryan Edwards	ENG
14	Florent Hoti	KVX
16	Trevor Carson	NIR
17	Jamie Robson	SCO
18	Calum Butcher	ENG
20	Lewis Neilson	SCO
21	Declan Glass	SCO
22	Kieran Freeman	SCO
23	Ian Harkes	USA
24	Lawrence Shankland	SCO
26	Chris Mochrie	SCO
27	Louis Appéré	SCO
28	Kerr Smith	SCO
30	Darren Watson	SCO
31	Jack Newman	SCO
32	Archie Meekison	SCO
34	Nathan Cooney	SCO
35	Finn Robson	SCO
36	Rhys Caves	SCO
37	Adam Hutchinson	SCO
38	Layton Bisland	SCO
40	Flynn Duffy	SCO
41	Ruairidh Adams	SCO
42	Shaun Brown	SCO
43	Lennon Walker	SCO
44	Sam Lovie	SCO
45	Finlay Malcolm	SCO
46	Miller Thomson	SCO
47	Jacob Comerford	SCO
48	Dominik Naglik	POL
49	Stuart Heenan	SCO
50	Lewis O'Donnell	SCO
51	Bryan Mwangi	SCO
52	Craig Moore	SCO
66	Jeando Fuchs	FRA

HEARTS

	Name	Nat
1	Craig Gordon	SCO
2	Michael Smith	NIR
3	Stephen Kingsley	SCO
4	John Souttar	SCO
5	Peter Haring	AUT
6	Beni Baningime	ENG
7	Jamie Walker	SCO
8	Aaron McEneff	NIR
10	Liam Boyce	NIR
11	Gary Mackay-Steven	SCO
13	Ross Stewart	SCO
16	Andrew Halliday	SCO
17	Alex Cochrane	ENG
19	Craig Halkett	SCO
20	Jordan Roberts	ENG
21	Armand Gnanduillet	CIV
22	Euan Henderson	SCO
25	Cammy Logan	SCO
27	Connor Smith	SCO
28	Mihai Popescu	ROU
29	Loïc Damour	FRA
30	Josh Ginnelly	ENG
35	Aidan Denholm	SCO
38	Finlay Pollock	SCO

HIBERNIAN

	Name	Nat
1	Matt Macey	ENG
3	Josh Doig	SCO
4	Paul Hanlon	SCO
5	Ryan Porteous	SCO
6	Paul McGinn	SCO
7	Kyle Magennis	SCO
8	Drey Wright	ENG
9	Christian Doidge	WAL
10	Martin Boyle	SCO
11	Joe Newell	ENG
13	Alex Gogic	CYP
15	Kevin Nisbet	SCO
16	Lewis Stevenson	SCO
17	Daniel Mackay	SCO
18	Jamie Murphy	SCO
19	Jamie Gullan	SCO
20	Melker Hallberg	SWE
21	Maciej Dabrowski	POL
22	Jake Doyle-Hayes	IRL
23	Scott Allan	SCO
24	Darren McGregor	SCO
26	Sean Mackie	SCO
27	Chris Cadden	SCO
29	Steven Bradley	SCO
30	Craig Samson	SCO
32	Josh Campbell	SCO
35	Jack Brydon	SCO

LIVINGSTON

	Name	Nat
1	Daniel Barden	WAL
2	Nicky Devlin	SCO
3	Jackson Longridge	SCO
4	Tom Parkes	ENG
5	Jack Fitzwater	ENG
6	Ayo Obileye	ENG
7	Keaghan Jacobs	RSA
8	Scott Pittman	SCO
9	Bruce Anderson	SCO
10	Craig Sibbald	SCO
11	Cristian Montaño	COL
12	Ben Williamson	SCO
14	Josh Mullin	SCO
16	Adam Lewis	ENG
17	Alan Forrest	SCO
18	Jason Holt	SCO
20	Gavin Reilly	SCO
21	Jack McMillan	SCO
22	Andrew Shinnie	SCO
23	Jack Hamilton	SCO
24	Sean Kelly	SCO
29	James Penrice	SCO
32	Maksymilian Stryjek	POL
36	Gary Maley	SCO
37	Jaze Kabia	IRL
40	Marvin Bartley	ENG

MOTHERWELL

	Name	Nat
1	Liam Kelly	SCO
2	Stephen O'Donnell	SCO
3	Jake Carroll	IRL
4	Ricki Lamie	SCO
5	Bevis Mugabi	UGA
6	Barry Maguire	SCO
7	Kaiyne Woolery	ENG
8	Mark O'Hara	SCO
9	Kevin van Veen	NED
11	Steven Lawless	SCO
12	Scott Fox	SCO
14	Juhani Ojala	FIN
15	Darragh O'Connor	IRL
16	Callum Slattery	ENG
17	Justin Amaluzor	ENG
18	Dean Cornelius	SCO
19	Nathan McGinley	ENG
20	Robbie Crawford	SCO
22	Liam Donnelly	NIR
23	Liam Grimshaw	ENG
24	Max Johnston	SCO
25	David Devine	SCO
26	Mich'el Parker	ENG
29	Connor Shields	SCO
30	Sam Campbell	SCO
31	Peter Morrison	SCO
32	Tony Watt	SCO
33	Muhammad Adam	SCO
34	Corey O'Donnell	SCO
35	Adam MacDonald	SCO
36	Ali Gould	SCO
37	Cody McLeod	SCO
38	Logan Dunachie	SCO
39	Ewan Wilson	SCO
40	Kian Speirs	SCO
41	Matty Connolly	SCO

42	Daniel Hunter	SCO
43	Richard Tambwe	SCO
44	Lawton Green	NZL

RANGERS

	Name	Nat
1	Allan McGregor	SCO
2	James Tavernier	ENG
3	Calvin Bassey	ITA
4	John Lundstram	ENG
5	Filip Helander	SWE
6	Connor Goldson	ENG
7	Ianis Hagi	ROU
8	Ryan Jack	SCO
9	Jermain Defoe	ENG
10	Steven Davis	NIR
11	Cedric Itten	SUI
13	Andy Firth	ENG
14	Ryan Kent	ENG
15	Jack Simpson	ENG
16	Nathan Patterson	SCO
17	Joe Aribo	ENG
18	Glen Kamara	FIN
19	Nikola Katic	CRO
20	Alfredo Morelos	COL
21	Brandon Barker	ENG
22	Jordan Jones	NIR
23	Scott Wright	SCO
24	Nnamdi Ofoborh	NGA
25	Kemar Roofe	ENG
26	Leon Balogun	NGA
27	Stephen Kelly	SCO
28	Robby McCrorie	SCO
30	Fashion Sakala	ZAM
31	Borna Barišic	CRO
32	Jake Hastie	SCO
33	Jon McLaughlin	SCO
37	Scott Arfield	CAN
40	Glenn Middleton	SCO

ROSS COUNTY

	Name	Nat
1	Ross Laidlaw	SCO
2	Connor Randall	ENG
3	Jake Vokins	ENG
6	Harry Paton	CAN
7	Blair Spittal	SCO
8	Ross Callachan	SCO
9	Oli Shaw	SCO
10	Dominic Samuel	ENG
11	Alex Robertson	ENG
12	Tom Grivosti	ENG
15	Keith Watson	SCO
16	Alex Iacovitti	SCO
17	Regan Charles-Cook	ENG
21	Ross Munro	SCO
22	Jordan Tillson	ENG
25	Coll Donaldson	SCO
26	Jordan White	SCO
30	Matthew Wright	SCO
32	Adam MacKinnon	SCO
33	Ben Williamson	SCO
34	Ryan MacLeman	SCO

ST JOHNSTONE

	Name	Nat
1	Zander Clark	SCO
2	James Brown	ENG
3	Reece Devine	ENG
4	Jamie McCart	SCO
5	Jason Kerr	SCO
6	Liam Gordon	SCO
7	Stevie May	SCO
8	Murray Davidson	SCO
9	Chris Kane	SCO
10	David Wotherspoon	SCO
11	Michael O'Halloran	SCO
12	Elliott Parish	ENG
13	Craig Bryson	SCO
15	Charlie Gilmour	SCO
16	Hayden Muller	ENG
18	Ali McCann	NIR
19	Shaun Rooney	SCO
22	Callum Hendry	SCO
23	Cameron Ballantyne	SCO
24	Callum Booth	SCO
26	Liam Craig	SCO
45	Ross Sinclair	SCO

ST MIRREN

	Name	Nat
1	Jak Alnwick	ENG
2	Richard Tait	SCO
3	Scott Tanser	ENG
4	Joe Shaughnessy	IRL
5	Conor McCarthy	IRL
6	Alan Power	IRL
7	Jamie McGrath	IRL
8	Ryan Flynn	SCO
9	Eamonn Brophy	SCO
10	Curtis Main	ENG
11	Greg Kiltie	SCO
12	Jay Henderson	SCO
14	Cameron MacPherson	SCO
15	Dylan Reid	SCO
16	Ethan Erhahon	SCO
17	Kyle McAllister	SCO
18	Charles Dunne	ENG
19	Danny Finlayson	NIR
20	Kristian Dennis	ENG
22	Marcus Fraser	SCO
23	Lee Erwin	SCO
25	Josh Jack	SCO
26	Dean Lyness	ENG
27	Peter Urminský	SVK

Aberdeen FC 2020/21 The Dons

It's become the perennial question – how does one measure success at Aberdeen? In terms of the League third place was always the best the Dons could hope for – they achieved fourth. Occasional success in Cup competitions would be deemed a success and once again Aberdeen failed dismally on this front.

Derek McInnes parted company with the Dons towards the end of the season. He and his loyal assistant Tony Docherty had been at Pittodrie for a long time – since March 2013 – with just one League Cup to show for it. Aberdeen's League performances were consistent enough but they had seldom shown any likelihood of actually winning the title. Will the McInnes era be seen as successful? Probably not, although that is not entirely justified.

However, McInnes was probably glad the spectators were absent from Pittodrie in 2021/2. Between January and March the club played 10 competitive games, scoring just one goal. In their final 15 league games they scored just 6 times. They crashed out of the Scottish Cup losing 3-0 at home to Dundee United. They went out of the League Cup at the first hurdle, going down 2-1 to St Mirren. Results like these would have had the Pittodrie fans baying for blood.

In Europe beating Runavik was a given, defeating Viking Stavanger was a decent result, but going out to Sporting Lisbon was inevitable.

McInnes tried to solve the scoring problem in January with three loan signings. Kamberi, Hornby and Hendry looked decent on paper but, Hendry apart, rather less so on the field of play.

In the wake of the departure of McInnes Aberdeen went down a different route for his replacement. Many of the usual suspects were touted for the job but they gave it to former Dons player Stephen Glass, who was coaching in America and presumably known to Dons owner Dave Cormack. He was unable to take control immediately due to quarantine issues and the well-respected Paul Sheerin took interim charge. He has also since departed Pittodrie.

The new Manager has brought Scott Brown from Celtic as Player Coach. Brown is known to want a management career of his own and this appointment affords him the opportunity to make an impact. It remains to be seen whether he can still be an influence on the field. The arrival of Declan Gallagher in defence should be an improvement. Up front the Dons have signed Jay Emmanuel-Thomas from Livingston. He played outstandingly well against Aberdeen last season and they will he hoping he can replicate that sort of form in a red jersey.

Lewis Ferguson is a key player for Aberdeen. Despite having three years left on his contract in May 2021 he shocked the club with a transfer request. Presumably his head had been turned by some interest from elsewhere. Watford were rumoured to be interested in taking him to the English Premiership. 2021/2 will be a huge season for the player. Assuming he stays at Pittodrie then he needs to kick on and fulfil some of the enormous potential that he clearly possesses.

STAR MAN
Defender Andy Considine was rewarded for years of consistency with a call-up to the Scotland squad in October 2020. He didn't let them down and can feel slightly peeved at not being included in the group for the delayed Euros in the Summer of 2021.

PROSEPCTS 2021/2
The Dons certainly will not win the League. With Celtic seemingly in disarray, second place should be a realistic target for clubs like Aberdeen. Will they achieve it? Unlikely. As ever the fans will have high hopes of Cup success. It's certainly about time the Dons lifted some silverware and that is where their best chance will lie.

Chairman: Dave Cormack
Commercial Director: Robert Wicks
Non-Executive Directors: Stewart Milne, Zoe Ogilvie, Kevin MacIver, Darren Eales, Tom Crotty
Honorary President: Ian Donald
Football Manager: Derek McInnes, then Stephen Glass
Assistant Manager: Tony Docherty, then Alan Russell
Coach: Barry Robson, then Scott Brown
Assistant Coach: Henry Apaloo
Youth Team Coach: Paul Sheerin (until May)
Goalkeeping Coach: Gordon Marshall
Club Secretary: Roy Johnston
Communications Manager: Lisa Sheran
Director of Football Operations: Steven Gunn
Club Ambassador: Craig Brown
Pathways Manager: Neil Simpson
Academy Director: Gavin Levey
Development Phase and U18 Head Coach: Barry Robson
Head of Sports Science and Fitnes: Graham Kirk
Head of Medical Services: Adam Stokes
Team Doctors: Greg Nicol, Stuart Reary, Gary Ritchie
Physios: Tony Tompos, George Good
Kit Manager: Jim Warrender
Performance Analyst: Greig Thomson
Chaplain: Rev Barry Douglas
Programme Editor: David Bowler

Founded	1903
Ground	Pittodrie Stadium
Capacity	20961
Postcode	AB24 5QH
Tel	01224 650400
Closest Railway Station	Aberdeen
Record Attendance	45061 v Hearts, SC, 1953/4
Record Win	13-0 v Peterhead, SC, 10/2/1923
Record Defeat	0-9, v Celtic, Lge, 6/11/2010
Most League Goals in a Season	38, Benny Yorston, 1929/30
Most Goals in Career	199, Joe Harper
Colours 2020/21 Top	Red with white trim
Shorts	Red
Sponsor	Saltire Energy
Manufacturer	Adidas
Change Colours 2020/21 Top	White with Black & Gold stripe
Shorts	Black
Nicknames	Dons, Dandies, Sheep
Web	www.afc.co.uk
E Tickets	www.afc.co.uk/etickets
Match Programme 2020/21	Red Match Day £3 (Curtis Sport)

STEPHEN GLASS

Playing Career
1994-98 Aberdeen; OL to Crombie Sports 1994/5; 1998-2001 Newcastle United; 2001-3 Watford; 2003-7 Hibernian; 2007-10 Dunfermline Athletic; 2010-11 Carolina RailHawks

Coaching Career
2012-14 Shamrock Rovers (Assistant); 2019-21 Atlanta United 2; 2021- Aberdeen

International Honours
11 Scotland Under 21 Caps
3 Scotland B Caps
1 Full Scotland Cap

Date	Comp	H/A	Opponents	F	A		HT		Referee	Crowd	Scorers
01/08/2020	L	H	Rangers	0	1		0	1	B Madden	BCD	
20/08/2020	L	A	St Johnstone	1	0		0	0	W Collum	BCD	Hedges
23/08/2020	L	H	Livingston	2	1		0	0	S McLean	BCD	Ferguson pen, Wright
27/08/2020	UEL	H	NSI Runavik	6	0		2	0	I Kristjansson (ICE)	BCD	Hedges 3(1 pen), Ferguson, Main, Hayes
30/08/2020	L	A	Hibernian	1	0		1	0	N Walsh	BCD	Ferguson pen
12/09/2020	L	H	Kilmarnock	1	0		1	0	B Madden	300	McCrorie
17/09/2020	UEL	A	Viking Stavanger	2	0		1	0	F Glova (SVK)	BCD	McCrorie, Hedges
20/09/2020	L	H	Motherwell	0	3		0	3	J Beaton	BCD	
24/09/2020	UEL	A	Sporting Lisbon	0	1		0	1	N Dabanovic (MON)	BCD	
27/09/2020	L	A	Ross County	3	0		1	0	W Collum	BCD	Ferguson 2 pens, Watkins
02/10/2020	L	H	St Mirren	2	1		0	0	G Duncan	BCD	Watkins, Ferguson
17/10/2020	L	A	Dundee United	0	0		0	0	A Muir	BCD	
20/10/2020	L	H	Hamilton Accies	4	2		4	1	N Walsh	BCD	Hoban, Ferguson, Edmondson 2
25/10/2020	L	H	Celtic	3	3		1	0	W Collum	BCD	Ferguson 2 pens, Hedges
01/11/2020	SCSF	N	Celtic	0	2		0	2	D Robertson	BCD	
06/11/2020	L	H	Hibernian	2	0		2	0	E Anderson	BCD	Wright, Cosgrove
22/11/2020	L	A	Rangers	0	4		0	2	N Walsh	BCD	
25/11/2020	L	A	Hamilton Accies	1	1		1	0	G Duncan	BCD	Hedges
28/11/2020	LC	A	St Mirren	1	2		1	1	D Robertson	BCD	McGinn
05/12/2020	L	A	St Mirren	1	1		1	1	B Madden	BCD	Hayes
13/12/2020	L	H	Ross County	2	0		1	0	N Walsh	BCD	Main 2
19/12/2020	L	A	Kilmarnock	2	0		0	0	D Munro	BCD	Hedges, Cosgrove
23/12/2020	L	A	Motherwell	0	0		0	0	G Aitken	BCD	
26/12/2020	L	H	St Johnstone	2	1		1	1	A Muir	BCD	Cosgrove pen, Taylor
02/01/2021	L	H	Dundee United	0	0		0	0	K Clancy	BCD	
10/01/2021	L	H	Rangers	1	2		0	1	J Beaton	BCD	Kennedy
16/01/2021	L	A	Ross County	1	4		1	2	B Madden	BCD	Iacovitti og
23/01/2021	L	H	Motherwell	2	0		1	0	C Napier	BCD	Hoban, Considine
27/01/2021	L	A	St Johnstone	0	0		0	0	D Robertson	BCD	
30/01/2021	L	A	Livingston	0	0		0	0	S McLean	BCD	
02/02/2021	L	H	Livingston	0	2		0	2	N Walsh	BCD	
06/02/2021	L	A	Hibernian	0	2		0	1	W Collum	BCD	
13/02/2021	L	H	St Mirren	0	0		0	0	E Anderson	BCD	
17/02/2021	L	A	Celtic	0	1		0	1	A Muir	BCD	
20/02/2021	L	H	Kilmarnock	1	0		1	0	D Robertson	BCD	Hendry
27/02/2021	L	A	Celtic	0	1		0	1	W Collum	BCD	
06/03/2021	L	H	Hamilton Accies	0	0		0	0	B Madden	BCD	
20/03/2021	L	A	Dundee United	0	1		0	0	G Aitken	BCD	
03/04/2021	SC	A	Dumbarton	1	0		0	0	D Robertson	BCD	Hendry
10/04/2021	L	A	St Johnstone	1	0		0	0	J Beaton	BCD	Hayes
17/04/2021	SC	H	Livingston	2	2	AET, 5-3p	0	1	C Steven	BCD	McGinn, Kamberi
21/04/2021	L	H	Celtic	1	1		1	0	W Collum	BCD	Ferguson
25/04/2021	SC	H	Dundee United	0	3		0	2	K Clancy	BCD	
01/05/2021	L	A	Livingston	2	1		0	0	G Irvine	BCD	Hendry, Hedges
12/05/2021	L	H	Hibernian	0	1		0	1	J Beaton	BCD	
15/05/2021	L	A	Rangers	0	4		0	2	N Walsh	BCD	

Surname	First Name	Date of Birth	No	Nat	Pos	Signed	Previous	Notes	Contract	Lge A	Lge S	Lge G	SC A	SC S	SC G	LC A	LC S	LC G	UEFA A	UEFA S	UEFA G	Un
Anderson	Bruce	23/09/1988	21	SCO	F	2018	Aberdeen Youths	OL to Ayr United Sep-Jan, to Hamilton Jan-May, Released May 2021 joined Livingston		1	5									1		5
Barron	Connor	29/08/2002	31	SCO	M	2019	Aberdeen Youths	OL to Brechin City Sep-May	End 2021/2	0	0											0
Booth	Lyall	05/03/2003		SCO	D	2019	Aberdeen Youths		U20	0	0											0
Bryson	Craig	06/11/1986	7	SCO	M	2020	Derby County	Transferred to St Johnstone Sep 2020		1	1											0
Campbell	Dean	19/03/2001	24	SCO	M	2019	Aberdeen Youths		End 2022/3	12	8		3			1						10
Cerny	Tomas	10/04/1985	20	CZR	GK	2018	Partick Thistle	Retired Jan 2021		0	0											11
Considine	Andrew	01/04/1987	4	SCO	D	2005	Aberdeen Youths		End 2021/2	36	0	1	4			1			3			0
Cosgrove	Sam	02/12/1996	16	ENG	F	2018	Carlisle United	Transferred to Birmingham City Jan 2021		9	5	3	1			1						1
Dangana	Michael	29/04/2003	42	SCO	F	2019	Aberdeen Youths		U20	0	0											0
Devlin	Michael	03/10/1993	6	SCO	D	2018	Hamilton Accies		End 2021/2	0	1						1					4
Duncan	Lewis	30/01/2002		SCO	F	2018	Aberdeen Youths	Released Sep 2020, joined Fraserburgh		0	0											0
Duncan	Ryan	18/01/2004		SCO	M	2020	Aberdeen Youths		U20	0	1											10
Edmondson	Ryan	20/05/2001	32	ENG	F	2020	Leeds United (OL)	Jul-Dec		3	11	2					1			1		4
Ferguson	Lewis	24/08/1999	19	SCO	M	2018	Hamilton Accies		End 2023/4	35	0	9	4						3		1	0
Gallagher	Mark	12/02/2001	27	SCO	M	2020	Ross County	OL to Forfar Athletic for 2021/2	End 2021/2	0	0											5
Hancock	Mason	06/03/2003		ENG	D	2020	Woking		U20	0	0											0
Hanratty	Kevin	15/03/2003	34	SCO	F	2019	Aberdeen Youths	OL to Cove Rangers Mar-May	End 2023/4	0	0											1
Hayes	Jonny	09/07/1987	17	ROI	M	2020	Celtic		End 2021/2	34	0	2	3			1			3		1	0
Hedges	Ryan	08/07/1995	11	WAL	F	2019	Barnsley		End 2021/2	24	3	5	1			1			2	1	4	0
Hendry	Callum	08/12/1997		SCO	F	2021	St Johnstone (OL)	Feb-May		5	7	2	1	2	1							0
Hernandez	Ronald	04/10/1997	22	VEN	D	2020	Stabaek	OL to Atlanta United until end 2021	End 2021/2	2	2											12
Hoban	Tommie	24/01/1994	3	ROI / ENG	D	2020	Watford	Released June 2021 joined Crewe Alexandra		36	2	2	4			1			2			2
Hornby	Fraser	13/09/1999		SCO	F	2021	Stade Reims (OL)	Feb-May		5	5		1									2
Kamberi	Florian	08/03/1995		SWI / ALB	F	2021	St Gallen (OL)	Feb-May		11	0		2	1	1							0
Kennedy	Matthew	01/11/1994	33	NIR / SCO	F	2020	St Johnstone		End 2022/3	22	9	1	3	1		1			1			3
Leigh	Greg	30/09/1994	5	JAM / ENG	D	2020	NAC Breda	Released June 2021 joined Morecambe		6	2			1		1						3
Lewis	Joe	06/10/1987	1	ENG	GK	2016	Cardiff City		End 2023/4	35	0		3			1			3			1
Logan	Shay	29/01/1988	2	ENG	D	2014	Brentford	OL to Hearts Mar-May, Released June 2021		2	10								1	1		21
MacIver	Jack	10/01/2003		SCO	M	2020	Aberdeen Youths		U20	0	0											0
MacKenzie	Jack	04/07/2000	29	SCO	D	2018	Aberdeen Youths	OL to Forfar Athletic Oct-May	End 2022/3	5	1											10
Main	Curtis	20/07/1992	9	ENG	F	2019	Motherwell	Transferred to Shrewsbury Town Feb 2021		8	6	2		1			1		1	1	1	2
McCrorie	Ross	18/03/1998	40	SCO	M	2020	Rangers (OL)	Aug-Jan, Permanent from Jan	End 2023/4	28	1	1	3						3		1	0
McGeouch	Dylan	15/01/1993	15	SCO	M	2020	Sunderland		End 2021/2	7	8			1					3			12
McGinn	Niall	20/07/1987	10	NIR	F	2018	Gwangju		End 2021/2	12	13		3	1	1	1		1		1		12
McKenna	Scott	12/11/1996	5	SCO	D	2013	Aberdeen Youths	Transferred to Nottingham Forest Sep 2020		4	0								2			0
McLennan	Connor	05/10/1999	18	SCO	F	2018	Aberdeen Youths		End 2022/3	13	14		1	2						1		8
Milne	Jack	10/02/2003		SCO	M	2020	Aberdeen Youths		U20	0	0											0
Mykyta	Tyler	11/08/2002		SCO	M	2019	Aberdeen Youths	OL to Turriff United Sep-Feb	U20	0	0											0
Ngwenya	Kieran	25/09/2002	37	MAL / SCO	D	2019	Tynecastle Colts	OL to Cove Rangers Mar-May	U20	0	2											11
Ojo	Funso	28/08/1991	8	BEL / NIG	M	2019	Scunthorpe United	OL to Wigan Athletic Jan-May	End 2021/2	6	5					1				1		14
Power	Conor	15/05/2002		ROI	D	2018	St Patrick's Athletic	OL to Turriff United Sep-Feb	U20	0	0											0
Ramsay	Calvin	31/07/2003	44	SCO	D	2019	Aberdeen Youths		End 2023/4	0	4		2									11
Ritchie	Tom	27/01/2003	30	SCO	GK	2019	Aberdeen Youths		U20	0	0											7
Ross	Ethan	15/08/2001	23	SCO	M	2019	Aberdeen Youths	OL to Raith Rovers Oct-Jan, Declined new contract Jun 2021		0	2		1	2								10
Ruth	Michael	08/01/2002	28	SCO	F	2019	Queen's Park	OL to Arbroath Sep-Feb	End 2021/2	0	1			1								8
Taylor	Ash	02/09/1990	14	WAL / SCO	D	2019	Northampton Town	Released June 2021 joined Walsall		30	1	1	1						1			5
Towler	Evan	01/01/2004		SCO	D	2020	Aberdeen Youths		U20	0	0											0
Turner	Luke	20/05/2002	38	ROI	D	2018	Shamrock Rovers	OL to Turriff United Sep-Feb, Wexford Feb-May	U20	0	0											0
Virtanen	Miko	29/01/1999	26	FIN	M	2019	Aberdeen Youths	OL to Arbroath Sep-Jan	End 2021/2	0	2											13
Watkins	Marley	17/10/1990		ENG / WAL		2020	Bristol City (OL)	Aug-Jan		9	0	2	1						3			0
Woods	Gary	01/10/1990	43	ENG	GK	2020	Oldham Athletic (OL)	Oct-May		3	0		1	1								28
Wright	Scott	08/08/1997	25	SCO	F	2017	Aberdeen Youths	Transferred to Rangers Jan 2021		14	3	2	1						2	1		0
Yeats	Finn	19/04/2004		SCO	M	2020	Aberdeen Youths		U20	0	0											0
Own Goal												1										
NEW SIGNINGS																						
Brown	Scott	25/06/1985		SCO	M	2021	Celtic		End 2022/3													
Emmanuel-Thomas	Jay	27/12/1990		ENG / STL	F	2021	Livingston		End 2022/3													
Gallagher	Declan	13/02/1991		SCO	D	2021	Motherwell		End 2022/3													
Gurr	Jack	26/11/1995		ENG	D	2021	Atlanta United		End 2021/2													
Jenks	Teddy	12/03/2002		ENG	M	2021	Brighton (OL)	Jul-May	End 2021/2													
Ramirez	Christian	04/04/1991		USA	F	2021	Houston Dynamo		End 2022/3													
Woods	Gary	01/10/1990		ENG	GK	2021	Oldham Athletic		End 2022/3													

Date	Comp	H/A	Opponents	F	A		1	2	3	4	5	6	7	8	9
01/08/2020	L	H	Rangers	0	1		Lewis	Considine	Taylor	McKenna	Hernandez	Bryson+	Hayes	Ojo>	Kennedy&
20/08/2020	L	A	St Johnstone	1	0		Lewis	Hoban	Taylor	McCrorie	Hernandez*	McGinn>	Hayes	Ojo&	Campbell+
23/08/2020	L	H	Livingston	2	1		Lewis	Logan	Taylor	McKenna*	Watkins&	McCrorie	Hayes	Hedges>	Kennedy<
27/08/2020	**UEL**	**H**	**NSI Runavik**	**6**	**0**		**Lewis**	**Considine**	**McCrorie**	**McKenna**	**Watkins+**	**McGeouch**	**Hayes**	**Main***	**Kennedy**
30/08/2020	L	A	Hibernian	1	0		Lewis	Considine	McCrorie	McKenna	Watkins+	Hedges&	Hayes	Hoban	Kennedy
12/09/2020	L	H	Kilmarnock	1	0		Lewis	Considine	McCrorie&	McKenna`	Watkins	Hedges+	Hayes	Hoban	Kennedy*
17/09/2020	**UEL**	**A**	**Viking Stavanger**	**2**	**0**		**Lewis**	**Considine**	**McCrorie**	**McKenna**	**Watkins&**	**Hedges**	**Hayes**	**Hoban**	**McGeouch+**
20/09/2020	L	H	Motherwell	0	3		Lewis	Considine	McCrorie	Taylor+	Watkins<	Hedges	Hayes	Ojo&	McGinn*
24/09/2020	**UEL**	**A**	**Sporting Lisbon**	**0**	**1**		**Lewis**	**Considine**	**McCrorie**	**Taylor**	**Watkins+**	**Hedges**	**Hayes**	**Hoban**	**McGeouch***
27/09/2020	L	A	Ross County	3	0		Lewis	Considine	McCrorie	Taylor	Watkins>	Hedges<	Hayes	Hoban+	McGinn*
02/10/2020	L	H	St Mirren	2	1		Lewis	Considine	McCrorie	Taylor&	Watkins	Hedges>	Hayes	Hoban	McGinn*
17/10/2020	L	A	Dundee United	0	0		Lewis	Considine	McCrorie	Taylor	Watkins	Hedges	Hayes	Hoban	McLennan+
20/10/2020	L	H	Hamilton Accies	4	2		Lewis	Considine	Edmondson+	Taylor	Watkins	Hedges	Hayes*	Hoban	McGeouch&
25/10/2020	L	H	Celtic	3	3		Lewis	Considine	McCrorie	Taylor	Watkins+	Hedges	Hayes	Hoban	McGeouch*
01/11/2020	**SCSF**	**N**	**Celtic**	**0**	**2**		**Lewis**	**Considine**	**McCrorie**	**Taylor+**	**Watkins&**	**Hedges**	**Kennedy>**	**Hoban**	**Cosgrove***
06/11/2020	L	H	Hibernian	2	0		Lewis	Considine	McCrorie	Taylor	Kennedy+	Hedges	McLennan&	Hoban	Cosgrove*
22/11/2020	L	A	Rangers	0	4		Lewis	Considine	Logan&	Taylor	Kennedy	Hedges	Leigh>	Hoban	Cosgrove+
25/11/2020	L	A	Hamilton Accies	1	1		Lewis	Considine	Campbell	Taylor	Kennedy	Hedges	Leigh*	Hoban	Cosgrove
28/11/2020	**LC**	**A**	**St Mirren**	**1**	**2**		**Lewis**	**Considine**	**Hayes**	**McGinn***	**Kennedy**	**Hedges**	**Leigh**	**Hoban**	**Cosgrove+**
05/12/2020	L	A	St Mirren	1	1		Lewis	Considine	McCrorie	Taylor*	Kennedy>	Hedges+	Leigh	Hoban	Cosgrove&
13/12/2020	L	H	Ross County	2	0		Lewis	Considine	McCrorie	Taylor	Kennedy+	Hedges	Campbell>	Hoban	Main&
19/12/2020	L	A	Kilmarnock	2	0		Lewis	Considine	McCrorie	Taylor	Kennedy	Hedges	Hayes	Hoban*	Main&
23/12/2020	L	A	Motherwell	0	0		Lewis	Considine	McCrorie	Taylor	Kennedy	Hedges	Hayes	Hoban	Main+
26/12/2020	L	H	St Johnstone	2	1		Lewis	Considine	Campbell	Taylor	Kennedy	Hedges	Hayes	Hoban	Main*
02/01/2021	L	H	Dundee United	0	0		Lewis	Considine	McCrorie&	Taylor	Kennedy+	Hedges	Hayes	Hoban	Main>
10/01/2021	L	H	Rangers	1	2		Lewis	Considine	Campbell	Taylor&	Cosgrove	Hedges	Hayes	Hoban	Main*
16/01/2021	L	A	Ross County	1	4		Lewis	Considine	McCrorie	Taylor*	Kennedy	Wright	Hayes+	Hoban	Main&
23/01/2021	L	H	Motherwell	2	0		Lewis	Considine	Ojo*	Taylor	Kennedy&	Hedges	Hayes>	Hoban	Wright+
27/01/2021	L	A	St Johnstone	0	0		Lewis	Considine	McCrorie	Taylor	Kennedy	Hdeges	Hayes	Hoban*	Wright+
30/01/2021	L	A	Livingston	0	0		Lewis	Considine	Leigh	Taylor	Kennedy+	Hedges	Hayes	Hoban	McCrorie
02/02/2021	L	H	Livingston	0	2		Lewis	Considine	Leigh	Taylor+	McLennan&	Hedges*	Hayes	Hoban	McCrorie
06/02/2021	L	A	Hibernian	0	2		Lewis	Considine	Leigh*	Taylor>	McCrorie	McGeouch&	Hayes	Hoban	Kennedy
13/02/2021	L	H	St Mirren	0	0		Lewis	Considine	McGinn*	Campbell	McCrorie	Kamberi	Hayes	Hoban	Kennedy&
17/02/2021	L	A	Celtic	0	1		Lewis	Considine	Campbell>	Taylor	McCrorie	Kamberi	Hayes*	Hoban	Kennedy&
20/02/2021	L	H	Kilmarnock	1	0		Lewis	Considine	McGinn+	Taylor	McCrorie	Campbell&	McLennan&	Hoban	Kamberi
27/02/2021	L	A	Celtic	0	1		Lewis	Considine	McGinn&	Taylor	McCrorie	Campbell*	Hayes	Hoban	Kamberi
06/03/2021	L	H	Hamilton Accies	0	0		Lewis	Considine	McGinn&	Taylor+	McCrorie	McGeouch	Hayes	Hoban	Kamberi
20/03/2021	L	A	Dundee United	0	1		Lewis	Considine	McKenzie	Taylor	McCrorie	Campbell>	Hayes+	Hoban<	Kamberi&
03/04/2021	**SC**	**A**	**Dumbarton**	**1**	**0**		**Lewis**	**Considine**	**Ramsay+**	**McGinn**	**McCrorie**	**Campbell**	**Hayes**	**Hoban**	**Kamberi***
10/04/2021	L	A	St Johnstone	1	0		Lewis	Considine	McKenzie	McGinn&	McCrorie	Kennedy+	Hayes>	Hoban	Kamberi*
17/04/2021	**SC**	**H**	**Livingston**	**2**	**2**	**AET, 5-3p**	**Lewis***	**Considine**	**Hayes**	**McGinn>**	**McCrorie**	**Kennedy+**	**McLennan&**	**Hoban**	**Hornby+**
21/04/2021	L	H	Celtic	1	1		Woods	Considine	Hayes	McGinn&	McCrorie*	Kennedy	Hendry+	Hoban	Kamberi
25/04/2021	**SC**	**H**	**Dundee United**	**0**	**3**		**Woods**	**Considine**	**Hayes**	**McGinn***	**Ramsay**	**Kennedy**	**Hendry&**	**Hoban**	**Kamberi**
01/05/2021	L	A	Livingston	2	1		Woods	Considine	Hayes	McGinn+	McKenzie	McGeouch	Hendry*	Hoban	Kamberi
12/05/2021	L	H	Hibernian	0	1		Woods	Considine	Hayes*	Hedges+	McKenzie	McGeouch	Hendry&	Hoban	Kamberi
15/05/2021	L	A	Rangers	0	4		Lewis	Considine	Hayes&	Hedges>	McKenzie	McGeouch	Hendry*	Hoban	Kamberi+

THE GOALIES

Goalkeepers Used in League Matches, 1970-2020

Players shown in the season of their first appearance only

1970/1	Bobby Clark
1971/2	Gordon Marshall
	Andy Geoghegan
1976/7	Alistair McLean
1978/9	Jim Leighton
	John Gardiner
1980/1	Marc De Clerck
1982/3	Bryan Gunn
1988/9	Theo Snelders
1989/0	Michael Watt
	Bobby Mimms
1990/1	Andy Dibble
1993/4	Derek Stillie
1995/6	Nicky Walker
1998/9	A Warner
1999/0	David Preece
	Ryan Esson
2001/2	Peter Kjaer
	Mark Peat
2005/6	Jamie Langfield
2007/8	Derek Soutar
2009/0	Stuart Nelson
2010/1	Mark Howard
2011/2	David Gonzalez
2012/3	Jason Brown
2013/4	Nicky Weaver
2014/5	Scott Brown
2015/6	Aaron Lennox
	Danny Ward
	Adam Collin
2016/7	Joe Lewis
2017/8	Danny Rogers
	Freddie Woodman
2018/9	Tomasz Cerny

Marc De Clerck

10	11	12	13	14	15	16	17	18	19	20
Ferguson	Anderson*	Edmondson*	Campbell+	McGinn&	Hedges>	McGeouch	Hoban	McLennan	Logan	Cerny
Ferguson	Wright<	McLennan*	Kennedy+	Bryson&	Hedges>	Logan<	Ruth	McGeouch	MacKenzie	Cerny
Ferguson	Wright +	Ojo*	McGeouch+	McLennan&	Main>	Hoban<	Anderson	Hernandez	Cerny	
Ferguson	Wright&	Hedges*	Anderson+	McGinn&	Campbell	Hoban	Hernandez	Cerny		
Ferguson	Wright*	McGeouch*	Main+	McGinn&	Taylor	Logan	Hernandez	McLennan	Ojo	Cerny
Ferguson	Wright>	Logan*	McGinn+	McGeouch&	Taylor>	Main	Anderson	McLennan	Ojo	Cerny
Ferguson	Wright*	Ojo*	Logan+	Main&	Taylor	McGinn	McLennan	Cerny		
Ferguson	Wright>	Hoban*	Logan+	Edmundson&	McLennan>	Anderson<	McGeouch	Campbell	Hernandez	Cerny
Ferguson	Logan&	Wright*	Edmundson+	McLennan&	Ojo	McGinn	Hernandez	Cerny		
Ferguson	Wright&	McGeouch*	Hernandez+	McLennan&	Edmondson>	Anderson<	Logan	McKenzie	Ojo	Cerny
Ferguson	Wright+	McLennan*	Edmundson+	Anderson&	McGeouch>	Hernandez	Logan	McKenzie	Ojo	Cerny
Ferguson	Wright*	Edmondson*	McGinn+	Ramsay	McGeouch	Hernandez	Logan	Ngwenya	Ojo	Woods
Ferguson	Wright>	McLennan*	McCrorie+	Ojo&	McGinn>	Kennedy	Logan	Leigh	Cosgrove	Woods
Ferguson	Edmondson&	McLennan*	Wright+	Cosgrove&	McGinn	Kennedy	Logan	Leigh	Ojo	Woods
Ferguson	Wright	McLennan*	Leigh+	Main&	McGinn>	Edmundson	Logan	Devlin	Ojo	Woods
Ferguson	Wright	Main*	Leigh+	Logan&	McGinn	Edmundson	Hernandez	Devlin	Ojo	Woods
Ojo	Edmondson*	Main*	Campbell+	Hernandez&	Duncan>	Devlin	Ramsay	Ngwenya	Gallagher	Woods
Ojo	Main+	McGinn*	Edmondson+	Hernandez	Duncan	Devlin	Ramsay	Ngwenya	Logan	Woods
Ojo	Campbell&	Devlin*	Main+	Edmondson&	Duncan	Taylor	Ramsay	Ngwenya	Hernandez	Woods
Ferguson	Hayes<	Logan*	Ojo+	Main&	Edmondson>	Devlin<	McLennan	Campbell	Hernandez	Woods
McLennan*	Hayes<	Logan*	Cosgrove+	McGinn&	Ojo>	Ngwenya<	Edmundson	Ritchie	Hernandez	Ramsay
Ferguson	McLennan+	Campbell*	Logan+	Cosgrove&	Edmondson	Ngwenya	McGinn	Hernandez	Ojo	Woods
Ferguson	McLennan*	Cosgrove*	Edmondson+	Logan	Ramsay	Ngwenya	McGinn	Campbell	Ojo	Woods
Ferguson	Cosgrove+	Edmondson*	Ojo+	Logan	Ramsay	Ngwenya	McGinn	Duncan	Hanratty	Woods
Ferguson	McGinn*	Wright*	Cosgrove+	Campbell&	Edmondson>	Ngwenya	Logan	Duncan	Ojo	Woods
Ferguson	Wright+	Logan*	Kennedy+	Edmondson&	Virtanen	Ngwenya	McGinn	Anderson	Ojo	Woods
Ferguson	Cosgrove	Logan*	Ngwenya+	Anderson&	Virtanen	McLennan	McGinn	Campbell	Ojo	Woods
Ferguson	Cosgrove<	Campbell*	McLennan+	Virtanen&	Leigh>	Main<	McGinn	Anderson	Logan	Woods
Ferguson	Cosgrove	Campbell*	McLennan+	Virtanen	Leigh	Main	McGinn	Anderson	Logan	Woods
Ferguson	McLennan*	Wright*	Anderson+	Virtanen	Campbell	Ngwenya	McGinn	McGeouch	Logan	Woods
Ferguson	Hornby>	Kennedy*	Campbell+	Hendry&	McGinn>	MacKenzie	Virtanen	McGeouch	Logan	Woods
Ferguson	Hornby	McLennan*+	Hendry+	McGinn&	Logan>	MacKenzie	Virtanen	Ross	Campbell	Woods
Ferguson	Hornby+	McLennan*	Hendry+	Ross&	Logan	MacKenzie	Virtanen	McGeouch	Taylor	Woods
Ferguson	Hornby+	McLennan*	Hendry+	McGinn&	McGeouch>	MacKenzie	Virtanen	Logan	Ross	Woods
Ferguson	Hornby*	Hendry*	Kennedy+	Virtanen&	McGeouch	MacKenzie	Ngwenya	Logan	Ross	Woods
Ferguson	McLennan+	Hendry*	Kennedy+	McGeouch&	Virtanen	MacKenzie	Duncan	Logan	Ross	Woods
Ferguson	Hendry*	McLennan*	Kennedy+	Ruth&	Virtanen	MacKenzie	Campbell	Logan	Ross	Woods
Ferguson	McLennan*	McGinn*	Kennedy+	Hornby&	Hendry>	Ramsay<	Virtanen	McGeouch	Ross	Woods
Ferguson	Ross&	Hendry*	Kennedy+	McLennan&	Duncan	Taylor	Virtanen	McGeouch	Ruth	Woods
Ferguson	Campbell	Hornby*	McLennan+	Ramsay&	Ross>	Duncan	Virtanen	McGeouch	Ruth	Woods
Ferguson	Campbell	Woods*	Kamberi+	Hendry&	Ross>	Duncan	Ritchie	McGeouch	Ruth	Ramsay
Ferguson	Campbell	Ramsay*	McGeough+	McKenzie&	Ross	Duncan	Ritchie	Hornby	Ruth	McLennan
Ferguson	Campbell+	Ross*	McGeouch+	Ruth&	Gallagher	Duncan	Ritchie	Hornby	McLennan	Lewis
Ferguson	McLennan	Hornby*&	Hedges+	Kennedy&	Gallagher	Ramsay	Ritchie	Ross	Campbell	Ruth
Ferguson	McLennan	Kennedy*	McGinn+	Hornby&	Gallagher	Ramsay	Ritchie	Ross	Campbell	Ruth
Ferguson	McLennan	Campbell*	Hornby+	McGinn&	Ramsay>	Kennedy	Ritchie	Ross	Gallagher	Ruth

Theo Snelders

Derek Stillie

Goalkeeper turned Lawyer Derek Stillie stood as the Tory candidate in Renfrewshire South at the 2021 Scottish Parliament elections.

He finished third behind the SNP and Labour candidates.

In 2019 he had contested Central Ayrshire for the Tories at the UK General Election, finishing second.

As a lawyer he is best known for his defence of David Goodwillie and David Robertson in their rape trial.

Airdrieonians FC 2020/21 The Diamonds / The Waysiders

Chairman: Martin Ferguson
Directors: Sam Greene, Paul Hetherington, Scott Hetherington, David McArthur, Scott Russell, Gordon Watson
Honorary President: Ian McMillan
Manager: Ian Murray
Assistant Manager: Scott Agnew
First team Coach: Bryan Prunty
Coaches: Jim Low
Logistics Manager: Gordon Thomson
Academy Manager: Scott Black
Head Physio: John McMenemy
Physio: Adam Skinner

Founded	2002 (as Airdrie United)
Ground	Excelsior Stadium
Postcode	ML6 8QZ
Capacity	10101
Tel	01236 622000 (Ground)
Closest Railway Station	Drumgelloch
Record Attendance	9044, 23/8/2013 v Rangers
Ground Record	9612, 6/11/05, Chall Cup F, Hamilton v St Mirren
Record Win	11-0, v Gala Fairydean, 19/11/2011
Record Defeat	0-6, v Rangers, Lge, 23/8/2013
Most Goals in a Season	24, Andy Ryan, 2020/21
Colours 2020/21 Top	White with red diamond
Shorts	White
Sponsor	Holemasters
Manufacturer	Umbro
Change Colours 2020/21 Top	Blue and White
Shorts	Blue
Nicknames	Diamonds, Waysiders
Web	www.airdriefc.com
Match Programme 2020/21	
Theme Song	Only the Lonely

Airdrieonians operated with a mainly full-time set up in 2020/1. They were rewarded with their best season for a while, reaching the final of the promotion play offs. However, their 4-0 aggregate defeat against Morton illustrated the gap between League One and the Championship.

Their operational model allowed them to bring in a few highly-rated young players including Thomas Robert, son of French legend Laurent Robert. He earned rave reviews during the early part of the season prompting suggestions that he might sign a pre-contract with a Premiership side. Celtic were reported as being interested after he spent a week on trial with the Parkhead club. However, nothing came of it and Robert featured much less in the Airdrie side during the second half of the season.

The Cup competitions produced no joy for Airdrie. They lost three of their four League Cup section games and went out of the Scottish Cup at the first hurdle at home to League Two opponents Edinburgh City.

In terms of history and tradition Airdrie should be a Championship side. However, since they moved to the Excelsior Stadium, they have never been able to aspire to the heights of earlier times. The years they spent without a ground saw the clubs resources dwindle and many fans drifted away, never to return. The Board that presided over the sale of Broomfield and the subsequent shambles have much to answer for in the "downgrading" of what was once one of Scotland's top provincial clubs.

STAR MAN
The aforementioned Thomas Robert grabbed all the headlines but the key player for Airdrie in 2020/1 was Paul McKay. He was steady as a rock in defence or midfield for Airdrie. Son of football agent Willie McKay, Paul has a good pedigree having come through the youth system at Doncaster Rovers and then with Leeds United. Unfortunately for Airdrie his two-year spell with them came to an end during the Summer when he signed for First Division Queen of the South.

PROSPECTS 2021/2
There's no clear favourite to win League One and no clear favourites for relegation either. It promises to be a very tight League with margins of a few points making a big difference to final placings. The best Airdrie can hope for is another shot at the promotion play offs. Realistically, mid table will be where they end up.

THE GOALIES
Goalkeepers Used in League Matches, 1970-2020
Players shown in the season of their first appearance only

AIRDRIEONIANS

1970/1	Roddy McKenzie
	Tom Gourlay
1972/3	Marshall Poulton
1973/4	David McWilliams
1976/7	John Brian
1978/9	Ernie McGarr
1980/1	John Martin
	John Gardiner
	Alan Davidson
1984/5	Stuart Robertson
1988/9	Gary Walsh
1990/1	Colin Scott
1991/2	Allan McKnight
	Willie McCulloch
1995/6	Andy Rhodes
1997/8	Myles Hogarth
1998/9	Scott Thomson
1999/0	Paul Gallacher
	Stephen Wilson
2000/1	Javier Broto
	Stephen Wilson
	Tom Phillips
	Alan Ferguson
	Ramiro Gonzalez
2001/2	Neil Bennett

AIRDRIE UNITED / AIRDRIEONIANS (2)

2002/3	Mark McGeown
	Peter Cherrie
2004/5	Lee Hollis
	Stephen Robertson
2010/1	Mark Ridgers
A	dam Szpilcynski
2011/2	Paul McKane
	Connor Fairley
	Grant Adam
	Andrew Duncan
2012/3	Kenny Arthur
	Robbie Thomson
2013/4	Daniel Rogers
	Colin Stewart
2014/5	Andrew McNeill
	Rohan Ferguson
2015/6	Neil Parry
2017/8	Willie Muir
	Kyle Gourlay
	Kelbie Mason
2018/9	David Hutton
	Ben McKenzie
	Scott Gallacher
2019/0	Reece Willison

CLYDEBANK

1972/3	Mike McDonald
	S Forsyth

07/10/2020	LC	H	Alloa Athletic	0 2	0 1	S Reid	BCD	
13/10/2020	LC	A	Stenhousemuir	2 0	0 0	G Grainger	BCD	McKay, Thomson
17/10/2020	L	H	Peterhead	2 0	1 0	B Cook	BCD	Carrick pen, Fordyce
24/10/2020	L	A	Partick Thistle	1 2	1 1	G Beaton	BCD	Carrick
31/10/2020	L	H	Dumbarton	0 2	0 1	K Graham	BCD	
07/11/2020	L	H	Clyde	5 0	3 0	C Graham	BCD	Gallagher 2, Carrick 2(1 pen), Connell
11/11/2020	LC	H	Edinburgh City	0 1	0 1	K Graham	BCD	
14/11/2020	LC	A	Livingston	1 4	0 0	D Munro	BCD	Robert
21/11/2020	L	A	Forfar Athletic	3 1	3 1	G Irvine	BCD	Robert, Carrick pen, Connell
28/11/2020	L	H	Cove Rangers	1 1	0 1	G Grainger	BCD	Robert
05/12/2020	L	A	East Fife	0 2	0 1	S Lambie	BCD	
12/12/2020	L	H	Montrose	0 1	0 0	G Irvine	BCD	
20/12/2020	L	A	Falkirk	1 0	0 0	A Newlands	BCD	Connell
26/12/2020	L	A	Clyde	4 2	3 1	G Irvine	BCD	Robert, Carrick 2, Kerr
10/01/2021	SC	H	Edinburgh City	0 1	0 0	D Lowe	BCD	
20/03/2021	L	A	Peterhead	0 1	0 0	S Kirkland	BCD	
27/03/2021	L	H	Partick Thistle	2 4	1 1	C Napier	BCD	J McKay, Roy
30/03/2021	L	A	Cove Rangers	0 2	0 0	P Stuart	BCD	
01/04/2021	L	A	Dumbarton	1 0	0 0	G Ross	BCD	Roy
06/04/2021	L	H	Falkirk	2 1	1 1	C Steven	BCD	Roy, Carrick pen
10/04/2021	L	A	Montrose	2 2	0 2	P Stuart	BCD	Mclean og, Lennox og
13/04/2021	L	H	Forfar Athletic	3 1	1 1	B Cook	BCD	Thomson og, Gallagher, Connell
20/04/2021	L	H	East Fife	2 0	0 0	A Newlands	BCD	Gallagher, Carrick
24/04/2021	L	A	Partick Thistle	0 1	0 1	G Irvine	BCD	
27/04/2021	L	H	Montrose	2 1	1 0	K Graham	BCD	Connell 2
01/05/2021	L	A	Cove Rangers	2 0	0 0	C Graham	BCD	Gallagher, Ritchie
04/05/2021	L	H	Falkirk	2 0	0 0	S Lambie	BCD	Thomson, Turner
08/05/2021	PO	A	Cove Rangers	1 1	0 0	D Dickinson	BCD	Graham og
11/05/2021	PO	H	Cove Rangers	3 2 AET	1 1	C Steven	BCD	Gallagher 2, J McKay
18/05/2021	PO	H	Morton	0 1	0 0	D Munro	BCD	
21/05/2021	PO	A	Morton	0 3	0 2	A Muir	500	

Jim Gallacher
1973/4 I Matson
1975/6 Roddy McKenzie
1977/8 Colin King
1980/1 David Kenny
1982/3 Colin Brodie
1987/8 Ally Maxwell
1989/0 Hugh Stevenson
1989/0 Lindsay Hamilton
Andy Arrol
Billy Thomson
1990/1 Willie Spence
1991/2 Stephen Woods
1993/4 Alan Monaghan
Jim McQueen
Gary Matthews
1996/7 Derek Barnes
Ian McFarlane
1997/8 John Hillcoat
Neil Inglis
1998/9 Colin Scott
Ray Newland
Stevie Ross

1999/0 Andy McCondichie
Stevie Morrison
Colin Stewart
Ben Plevey
James Beggs
Steven Hutchison
2000/1 David Wylie
Jamie Campbell
2001/2 Henry Smith
David Klein
Stephen Robertson

David McWilliams

Date	Comp	H/A	Opponents	F	A	1	2	3	4	5	6	7	8	9	10	11	12	13	14	15	16	17	18	19	20
07/10/2020	LC	H	Alloa Athletic	0	2	Currie	Crighton	Fordyce	P McKay	Kerr	McCann	MacDonald+	Thomson&	Sabatini	Carrick>	Roy*	Gallagher*	Robert+	Stokes&	O'Reilly>	Murdoch	Ritchie	Walker	Hughes	Hutton
13/10/2020	LC	A	Stenhousemuir	2	0	Currie	Crighton	Fordyce	P McKay	Kerr	McCann	MacDonald	O'Reilly+	Ritchie>	Robert*	Gallagher&	Thomson*	Carrick+	Stokes&	Sabatini>	Murdoch	Mbayo	Walker	Hughes	Hutton
17/10/2020	L	H	Peterhead	2	0	Currie	Crighton	Fordyce	PMcKay&	Kerr	McCann	MacDonald	Thomson*	Sabatini	Carrick	Gallagher+	O'Reilly*	Connell+	Stokes&	Robert	Mbayo	Ritchie	Hutton		
24/10/2020	L	A	Partick Thistle	1	2	Currie	Crighton	Fordyce	P McKay	Kerr	McCann	MacDonald	Thomson	Sabatini*	Carrick+	Gallagher&	Connell*	Robert+	Stokes&	O'Reilly	Mbayo	Ritchie	Hutton		
31/10/2020	L	H	Dumbarton	0	2	Hutton	Crighton	Fordyce	P McKay	Kerr>	McCann	MacDonald+	Thomson&	Connell*	Carrick	Gallagher	Robert*	Sabatini+	Stokes&	O'Reilly>	Mbayo	Ritchie	Murdoch		
07/11/2020	L	H	Clyde	5	0	Hutton	Crighton	Fordyce	P McKay	Kerr	McCann	Robert*	Sabatini>	Connell<	Carrick&	Gallagher+	Thomson*	Stokes+	Ritchie&	MacDonald>	O'Reilly<	Mbayo	Murdoch		
11/11/2020	LC	H	Edinburgh City	0	1	Hutton	Mbayo	Fordyce	P McKay&	Kerr>	McCann	Robert	Sabatini	Connell*	Carrick	Stokes+	Thomson*	O'Reilly+	MacDonald&	Crighton>	Currie	Ritchie	Hughes		
14/11/2020	LC	A	Livingston	1	4	Hutton	Crighton	Fordyce	P McKay	Kerr	McCann	Robert&	Sabatini>	Connell+	Carrick*	MacDonald	Thomson*	O'Reilly+	Ritchie&	Stokes>	Currie	Walker	Hughes	Mbayo	Murdoch
21/11/2020	L	A	Forfar Athletic	3	1	Currie	Crighton	Fordyce	P McKay	Kerr	McCann	Robert+	Gallagher*	Connell	Carrick&	MacDonald	Sabatini*	O'Reilly+	Thomson&	Stokes	Hutton	Ritchie			
28/11/2020	L	H	Cove Rangers	1	1	Currie	Crighton	Fordyce	P McKay	Kerr	McCann	Robert>	Sabatini	Walker+	Carrick&	Gallagher*	Connell*	Thomson+	Ritchie&	Stokes>	Hutton	O'Reilly	Hughes		
05/12/2020	L	A	East Fife	0	2	Currie	Crighton	Fordyce	P McKay	Kerr	McCann	Robert	Sabatini	Connell+	Carrick*	MacDonald&	Thomson*	O'Reilly+	Gallagher&	Stokes	Hutton	Ritchie	Hughes	Walker	
12/12/2020	L	H	Montrose	0	1	Currie	Crighton	Fordyce	P McKay	Kerr	McCann	Robert*	Sabatini&	Gallagher	Carrick+	MacDonald>	Thomson*	Connell+	O'Reilly&	Stokes>	Hutton	Ritchie	Walker		
20/12/2020	L	A	Falkirk	1	0	Currie	Crighton	Fordyce	P McKay	Kerr	Connell	Robert&	Sabatini+	Gallagher*	Ritchie	MacDonald	Carrick*	Thomson+	O'Reilly&	Stokes	Hutton	Mbayo	Walker	Hughes	
26/12/2020	L	A	Clyde	4	2	Currie	Crighton	Fordyce	P McKay	Kerr	Connell&	Robert*	Thomson	Ritchie	Carrick+	MacDonald	McCann*	Sabatini+	Roy&	Stokes	Hutton	Mbayo	Walker	O'Reilly	Hughes
10/01/2021	SC	H	Edinburgh City	0	1	Currie	Crighton	Fordyce	P McKay	Kerr	Connell&	Robert	Thomson+	Stokes*	Carrick	MacDonald	Roy*	O'Reilly+	Sabatini&	McCann	Ritchie	Murdoch	Gallagher		
20/03/2021	L	A	Peterhead	0	1	Currie	Crighton	Fordyce	McCann	Turner	Connell+	Robert*	J McKay	Ritchie&	Carrick>	Gallagher	O'Reilly*	Roy+	Thomson&	Sabatini>	Walker	Mbayo	McNeil		
27/03/2021	L	H	Partick Thistle	2	4	Currie	Crighton	Fordyce	P McKay	McCann	Paton	Robert*	J McKay>	O'Reilly	Carrick+	Gallagher&	Connell*	Thomson+	Roy&	Mbayo>	Walker	Ritchie	Sabatini	McNeil	
30/03/2021	L	A	Cove Rangers	0	2	Currie	Thomson*	Fordyce	P McKay	McCann	Connell	J McKay	Sabatini&	O'Reilly<	Carrick+	Roy>	Gallagher*	Ritchie+	Robert&	Wlker>	Pyott<	Mbayo	Paton	Burke	McNeil
01/04/2021	L	A	Dumbarton	1	0	Currie	Walker&	Fordyce	P McKay	McCann	Turner	Robert*	J McKay>	O'Reilly	Ritchie	Gallagher+	Carrick*	Connell+	Roy&	Thomson>	Pyott	Mbayo	Sabatini	Burke	McNeil
06/04/2021	L	H	Falkirk	2	1	Currie	Crighton	Fordyce	P McKay	McCann	Turner	Roy>	J McKay*	O'Reilly	Ritchie+	Gallagher&	Thomson*	Carrick+	Connell&	Robert>	Walker	Mbayo	Sabatini	Stokes	McNeil
10/04/2021	L	A	Montrose	2	2	Currie	Crighton	Fordyce	P McKay	McCann	Turner	Roy*	J McKay+	O'Reilly	Carrick&	Gallagher	Connell*	Thomson+	Stokes&	Robert	Walker	Mbayo	Sabatini	Ritchie	McNeil
13/04/2021	L	H	Forfar Athletic	3	1	Currie	Crighton	Fordyce	P McKay	McCann	Turner	Roy+	J McKay*	O'Reilly	Carrick&	Gallagher	Thomson*	Connell+	Robert&	Stokes	Walker	Mbayo	Sabatini	Ritchie	McNeil
20/04/2021	L	H	East Fife	2	0	Currie	Crighton	Fordyce	P McKay	McCann	Turner	Roy*	Paton&	O'Reilly<	Carrick>	Gallagher+	Connell*	Thomson+	Ritchie&	Stokes>	Walker<	Robert	Sabatini	J McKay	McNeil
24/04/2021	L	A	Partick Thistle	0	1	Currie	Crighton	Fordyce	P McKay	McCann&	Turner	Roy+	Paton>	O'Reilly	Carrick*	Gallagher	Thomson*	Connell+	Robert&	McCann>	Walker	Ritchie	Sabatini	Stokes	McNeil
27/04/2021	L	H	Montrose	2	1	Currie	Kerr	Fordyce	P McKay	McCann	Turner	Walker	Paton	Connell&	Carrick+	Gallagher*	Stokes*	Ritchie+	Roy&	Thomson>	Pyott	Robert	Sabatini	J McKay	McNeil
01/05/2021	L	A	Cove Rangers	2	0	Currie	Kerr	Fordyce	P McKay	McCann	Turner	Walker&	Paton>	Connell<	Carrick*	Gallagher+	Robert*	Roy+	J McKay&	Ritchie>	Thomson<	Crichton	Sabatini	Stokes	McNeil
04/05/2021	L	H	Falkirk	2	0	Currie	Kerr	Fordyce	P McKay	McCann	Turner	Walker&	Paton	Connell*	Ritchie+	Gallagher>	Pyott*<	Robert+	Thomson&	Carrick>	Roy<	Stokes	Sabatini	J McKay	McNeil
08/05/2021	PO	A	Cove Rangers	1	1	Currie	Kerr	Fordyce	P McKay	McCann	Turner	Walker*	Paton	Connell	Carrick+	Gallagher&	J McKay*	Ritchie+	Roy&	Thomson	Crichton	Robert	McNeil		
11/05/2021	PO	H	Cove Rangers	3	2 AET	Currie	Kerr+	Fordyce	P McKay	McCann	Turner	Walker	Paton*	Ritchie&	Carrick<	Gallagher	Connell*>	Crichton+	Robert&	J McKay>	Thomson<	Roy	McNeil		
18/05/2021	PO	H	Morton	0	1	Currie	Crighton	Fordyce	P McKay+	McCann	Turner	Walker&	J McKay	O'Reilly	Carrick*	Gallagher	Thomson*	Robert+	Roy&	Stokes	Sabatoni	Ritchie	McNeil		
21/05/2021	PO	A	Morton	0	3	Currie	Crighton	Fordyce	Kerr*	McCann	Turner	Walker&	J McKay+	O'Reilly	Robert	Gallagher	Thomson*	Roy+	Ritchie&	Stokes	Sabatoni	McNeil			

Roddy McKenzie

Capped once for Northern Ireland against Wales in 1966/7

Career: Drumchapel Amateurs; 1963-73 Airdrieonians; 1973-75 Hibernian; 1975-1977 Clydebank; 1977-78 Brisbane Lions

John Martin

701 League appearances in total -

658	Airdrie	1980-1999
3	Albion Rovers	1997-1998
40	Cowdenbeath	2000-2002

Also played for Tranent Juniors and Preston Athletic

Surname	First Name	Date of Birth	No	Nat	Pos	Signed	Previous	Notes	Contract	Lge A	Lge S	Lge G	SC A	SC S	SC G	LC A	LC S	LC G	Un
Burke	Joshua	31/08/2001		SCO	D	2020	Airdrieonians Youths	OL to Albion Rovers Sep-Jan, Released May 2021		0	0								2
Carrick	Dale	07/01/1994	15	SCO	F	2018	Livingston	OOC May 2021 joined Stirling Albion		21	4	9				3	1		0
Connell	Kyle	19/12/2001	25	SCO	F	2020	Kilmarnock (OL)	Oct-Jan		12	12	6	1			2			0
Crighton	Sean	26/03/1990	5	SCO	D	2018	Brechin City	OOC May 2021, joined Stenhousemuir		19	1		1			3	1		2
Currie	Max	03/03/1997	20	SCO	GK	2020	Stranraer		End 2021/2	24	0		1			2			2
Fordyce	Callum	23/06/1992	6	SCO	D	2019	Queen of the South		End 2021/2	26	0	1	1			4			0
Gallagher	Calum	13/09/1994	9	SCO	F	2019	Dumbarton		End 2021/2	23	2	7				1	1		1
Hughes	James	13/03/2003	24	SCO	F	2020	Airdrieonians Youths	Released May 2021		0	0								8
Hutton	David	18/05/1985	1	SCO	GK	2018	Arbroath	released Jan 2021, joined Brechin City		2	0					2			10
Kerr	Josh	24/02/1998	4	SCO	D	2019	Brighton		End 2021/2	16	0	1	1			4			0
MacDonald	Kyle	11/01/2000	2	SCO	D	2019	Motherwell	Transferred to Dunfermline Ath Jan 2021		8	1		1			3	1		0
Mbayo	Harlain	14/03/1998	14	DRC / ENG	D	2020	Truro City	Released May 2021		0	1					1			14
McCann	Leon	16/03/2000	3	SCO	D	2020	Hamilton Accies	Released June 2021, joined Falkirk		24	2					4			1
Mckay	Paul	19/11/1996	8	ENG / SCO	M	2019	Cardiff City	OOC June 2021, joined QOTS		24	0		1			4		1	0
Mckay	Jack	19/11/1997		SCO	F	2021	Chesterfield (OL)	Feb-May		9	3	2							3
McNeil	Andy	29/03/2001		SCO	GK	2021	Berwick Rangers (OL)	Mar-May		0	0								16
Moore	Joseph	17/06/2001		SCO	F	2019	Hibernian Youth	OL to Albion Rovers Oct-Jan, Released May 2021 jo		0	0								0
Murdoch	Reece	02/03/2001	18	SCO	GK	2020	Livingston	Released May 2021		0	0								6
O'Reilly	Euan	02/05/2000	17	SCO	M	2020	St Johnstone	OOC June 2021, joined Stenhousemuir		10	8			1		1	3		3
Paton	Paul	18/04/1987		NIR / SCO	D	2021	East Kilbride (OL)	Mar-May		8	0								1
Pyott	Patrick	16/05/1999	25	SCO	F	2019	Airdrieonians Youths		End 2021/2	0	2								2
Ritchie	Dean	05/01/2001	13	SCO	M	2020	Hearts		End 2021/2	7	8	1	1			1	1		14
Robert	Thomas	31/08/2000	11	FRA	F	2020	HSC Montpellier	Son of Laurent Robert	End 2021/2	11	10	3	1			3	1	1	5
Roy	Ally	26/07/1997	10	NIR / SCO	F	2019	Partick Thistle	Released May 2021, joined QOTS		6	10	3		1		1			1
Sabatini	Griffin	23/09/1998	12	ITA / SWI	M	2020	SK Dinipro (OL)	Sep-May		8	4			1		3	1		12
Stokes	Eoghan	17/05/1996	21	ROI	M	2020	Cork City	Released May 2021, joined Dumbarton		0	9		1			1	3		11
Thomson	Craig	10/03/1995	7	SCO	M	2019	Brechin City	Released May 2021, joined Forfar Athletic		5	20	1	1			1	3	1	1
Turner	Kyle	10/11/1997		SCO	M	2021	Dunfermline Athletic (OL)	Mar-May		14	0	1							0
Walker	Scott	08/02/2001	19	SCO	D	2020	Airdrieonians Youths		End 2021/2	9	2								13
Own Goals												4							

NEW SIGNINGS

Surname	First Name	Date of Birth	Nat	Pos	Signed	Previous	Notes	Contract
Agnew	Scott	11/07/1987	SCO	M	2021	East Fife		End 2021/2
Allan	Jordan	20/10/1998	SCO	F	2021	Forfar Athletic		End 2022/3
Cantley	Jay	06/09/2002	SCO	GK	2021	Falkirk		End 2021/2
Easton	Dylan	06/04/1994	SCO	M	2021	Kelty Hearts		End 2021/2
Frizzell	Adam	22/01/1998	SCO	M	2021	Dumbarton		End 2021/2
Kouider-Assa	Salim	22/03/1996	SCO / ALG	D	2021	Livingston		End 2022/3
Lyons	Luke	29/12/2000	SCO / ENG	D	2021	Bradford Park Avenue	Ex Leeds United Youths	End 2021/2
McCabe	Rhys	24/07/1992	SCO	M	2021	QOTS		End 2021/2
McDonald	Matthew	26/08/2002	SCO	D	2021	Motherwell		End 2021/2
Quitongo	Rico	15/07/1999	SCO / ANG	D	2021	Dumbarton	Son of Jose, Brother of Jai	End 2021/2
Wardop	Sam	20/10/1997	SCO	D	2021	Dumbarton		End 2022/3
Watson	Craig	13/02/1995	SCO	D	2021	East Fife		End 2021/2

PHOTOCARDS

No. 103.

AIRDRIEONIANS FOOTBALL CLUB.

Left to right, back row :—J. M'Allister, J. Crosbie, J. M'Caffer, W. Hawthorn, T. Calder, J. Shaw (Capt.). Front row :— J. Ross, J. Law, J. Connor, T. Lyon, T. Mooney.

Members of Scottish League (Division II), have been runners-up in Division I on five occasions, and were winners of the Scottish Cup in 1923/24.

Expanding de Luxe Albums for Ardath Photocards on sale at Tobacconists Price 6d

ARDATH TOBACCO CO. LTD. Manufacturers of STATE EXPRESS and ARDATH CIGARETTES

Albion Rovers FC 2020/21 The Rovers

Founded	1882
Ground	Cliftonhill Stadium
Postcode	ML5 3RB
Tel	01236 606334
Capacity	1238
Closest Railway Station	Coatdyke
Record Attendance	27381, SC, v Rangers 8/2/36
Record Win	12-0, v Airdriehill, 3/9/1887
Record Defeat	1-11, v Partick Thistle, LC, 11/8/1993
Most League Goals in a Season	John Renwick, 41, 1932/3
Most Goals in Career	105, Bunty Weir
Colours 2020/21 Top	Yellow and Red
Shorts	Red
Sponsor	Compliance Path
Manufacturer	Joma
Change Colours 2020/21 Top	Blue and White
Shorts	Blue
Nicknames	Wee Rovers
Web	www.albionroversfc.com
Match Programme 2020/21	None

First team Manager: Brian Reid
Assistant Manager: Scott McKenzie
Coach: Alan Leslie
Fitness Coach: Davie Johnstone
Reserve Team Coach: Lewis Wilson, Graeme Liveston (Assistant), Scott Williamson (Assistant)
Chairman: Ian Benton
Secretary: Colin Woodward
Honorary Vice President: Gordon Lind
Directors: Jordan Campbell, Eddie Hagerty, Craig McKeown, Stuart Millar, Liam Nugent, Alison McGowan
Finance Director: Mark Hunter
Sports Therapist: JD Peacock
Club Chaplain: David Shaw
Kitman: Jason Bell
Club Secretary: Colin Woodward
Commercial Manager: Dianne Leslie
Club Doctor: Chris Ide
Safety Officer: Terry Gilooly
Announcer: Daniel Mossie
Programme Editors: Bill Walker, Donald Ashwood

The Cliftonhill club began the season as one of the favourites for finishing bottom. When they lost their first three games, including a home defeat from fellow strugglers Brechin City, things looked bleak for them. The long shut-down from January to March came at the right time for them. Manager Brian Reid was able to bring in numerous new signings and they proved good enough to secure vital wins in games against Cowdenbeath and Brechin City. Veteran Ryan Stevenson proved to be a steady head up front but their best arrival was young goalkeeper Harry Stone from Hearts – he looks to be a tremendous prospect.

In the League Cup Rovers featured in the highest-scoring penalty shoot out to date in Scottish football, beating Stranraer 15-14. Those were the only 2 points they gained. In the Scottish Cup Rovers were hammered 3-0 at home by Buckie Thistle.

STAR MAN
There were really only two players who featured throughout the whole season – Arron Lynas and Matty Aitken. With 12 goals in a struggling side the accolade must go to Matty Aitken. Signed from Forfar, he has returned to the Angus club for season 2021/2.

PROSPECTS 2021/2
As has become the norm Rovers will start as one of the favourites to finish bottom of League Two. There's no obvious candidate for the relegation play off this year so all teams will need to be on their mettle. Rovers should have enough quality to survive but they are unlikely to do much more than that.

Late 70s / Early 80s team group

Date	Comp	H/A	Opponents	F	A		HT	Referee	Crowd	Scorers
06/10/2020	LC	H	Ayr United	2	5		2 3	D Lowe	BCD	Aitken 2 (1 pen)
13/10/2020	LC	A	Stranraer	2	2	15-14p	2 1	C Scott	BCD	Jamieson, Fotheringham
17/10/2020	L	H	Stenhousemuir	1	3		0 1	L Wilson	BCD	Doherty
24/10/2020	L	A	Queen's Park	0	2		0 2	M McDermid	BCD	
31/10/2020	L	H	Brechin City	0	2		0 1	S Reid	BCD	
07/11/2020	L	A	Annan Athletic	3	2		0 0	K Graham	BCD	Baker pen, Aitken 2
10/11/2020	LC	H	Annan Athletic	1	5		0 4	D McFarlane	BCD	Dolan
14/11/2020	LC	A	Hamilton Accies	0	3			Awarded, Rovers unable to field team		
21/11/2020	L	H	Stirling Albion	0	1		0 1	S Lambie	BCD	
05/12/2020	L	A	Edinburgh City	2	5		1 4	S Luke	BCD	Doherty, Aitken
12/12/2020	L	H	Elgin City	3	1		0 1	C Graham	BCD	Aitken 2, Moore
19/12/2020	L	A	Stranraer	0	4		0 0	C Scott	100	
26/12/2020	SC	H	Buckie Thistle	0	3		0 2	L Watson	BCD	
20/03/2021	L	A	Stenhousemuir	0	2		0 1	L Wilson	BCD	
23/03/2021	L	H	Edinburgh City	1	2		0 1	D Williams	BCD	McGowan
27/03/2021	L	H	Annan Athletic	1	1		0 0	M McDermid	BCD	Jamieson
30/03/2021	L	H	Queen's Park	0	3		0 2	D Dickinson	BCD	
03/04/2021	L	A	Cowdenbeath	1	0		1 0	K Graham	BCD	Stevenson pen
06/04/2021	L	A	Stirling Albion	1	1		1 0	C Graham	BCD	Aitken
10/04/2021	L	A	Brechin City	4	2		2 1	G Ross	BCD	L Wilson, C Wilson, Stevenson, Gallacher
13/04/2021	L	H	Cowdenbeath	0	0		0 0	S Lambie	BCD	
17/04/2021	L	A	Elgin City	5	2		2 1	M McDermid	BCD	Aitken 2, McHale og, Doherty 2
20/04/2021	L	H	Stranraer	0	2		0 1	L Wilson	BCD	
24/04/2021	L	H	Annan Athletic	1	0		0 0	S Lambie	BCD	Leslie
29/04/2021	L	A	Stenhousemuir	1	0		1 0	S Luke	BCD	Aitken
01/05/2021	L	H	Brechin City	1	1		0 0	S Reid	BCD	Aitken pen
04/05/2021	L	A	Cowdenbeath	0	2		0 1	A Newlands	BCD	

PHOTOCARDS

No. 102.

ALBION ROVERS F.C.

Left to right, back row :—*H. Miller, A. Waddell, P. Shevlin (Capt.), R. Beath, W. Anderson, W. Bruce.* Front row :— *J. McPhee, T. Lyon, J. Rice, A. Graham, G. Grant.*

Formed 1881, this club won the Championship of the Scottish League, Division II. in 1933/34 and gained promotion to Division I. Winners of the Scottish Qualifying Cup 1913/14 and finalists Scottish Cup 1919/20.

Expanding de Luxe Albums for Ardath Photocards on sale at Tobacconists Price 6d

ARDATH TOBACCO CO. LTD. Manufacturers of STATE EXPRESS and ARDATH CIGARETTES

D

Date	Comp	H/A	Opponents	F	A		1	2	3	4	5	6	7	8	9	10	11	12	13	14	15	16	17	18	19	20
06/10/2020	LC	H	Ayr United	2	5		Goodfellow	Burke	L Wilson	Fernie	Fagan	Fotheringham>	Lynas&	C Wilson	Doherty*	Aitken	Jamieson+	Baker*	Moran+	Leslie&	Moore>	Henry	Dolan	Guy		
13/10/2020	LC	A	Stranraer	2	2	15-14p	Goodfellow	Burke	Ecrepont	Moore*	Fagan	Fotheringham	Lynas	C Wilson	Skeoch	Aitken	Jamieson+	Doherty*	Leslie+	Fernie	Moran	Henry	Dolan			
17/10/2020	L	H	Stenhousemuir	1	3		Goodfellow	Burke	Ecrepont	Moore	Fagan	Fotheringham	Lynas	C Wilson	Skeoch*	Aitken	Jamieson	Doherty*	Glover	Fernie	Moran	Henry	Dolan	L Wilson		
24/10/2020	L	A	Queen's Park	0	2		Goodfellow	L Wilson	Ecrepont	Glover	Fagan	Fotheringham+	Lynas&	C Wilson	Allan	Aitken	Doherty*	Skeoch*	Leslie+	Moore&	Burke	Henry	Dolan			
31/10/2020	L	H	Brechin City	0	2		Goodfellow	Burke	Ecrepont	Glover	Fagan	Leslie>	Lynas&	C Wilson	Allan+	Aitken	Jamieson*	Moore*	Baker+	Cairney&	Skeoch>	Henry	Dolan	Moran		
07/11/2020	L	A	Annan Athletic	3	2		Goodfellow	Baker*	Ecrepont	Glover	Fagan	Leslie	Lynas	C Wilson	Allan	Aitken	Skeoch+	Dolan*	Doherty+	Cairney	Burke	Henry	Moore	Moran		
10/11/2020	LC	H	Annan Athletic	1	5		Henry	Moran*	Ecrepont+	Glover	Fagan	Leslie	Lynas	C Wilson<	Doherty>	Baker	Skeoch&	Fotheringham*	L Wilson+	Dolan&	Moore>	Cairney<	Burke	Goodfellow		
14/11/2020	LC	A	Hamilton Accies	0	3																					
21/11/2020	L	H	Stirling Albion	0	1		Goodfellow	L Wilson	Ecrepont	Glover	Allan	Fotheringham*	Lynas	C Wilson	Doherty	Baker+	Aitken	Jamieson*	Leslie+	Dolan	Moore	Henry	Burke	Moran		
05/12/2020	L	A	Edinburgh City	2	5		Goodfellow	L Wilson	Ecrepont	Glover	Allan	Fotheringham&	Lynas	C Wilson	Doherty+	Baker*	Aitken	Jamieson*	Moore+	Leslie&	Dolan	Henry	Burke	Moran		
12/12/2020	L	H	Elgin City	3	1		Henry	L Wilson	Burke	Glover	Allan	Leslie+	Lynas	C Wilson	Doherty	Jamieson*	Aitken&	Moore*	Fotheringham+	Ecrepont&	Moran	Baker	Fagan	Goodfellow		
19/12/2020	L	A	Stranraer	0	4		Henry	Burke	Ecrepont	Glover	Allan<	Leslie	Lynas>	C Wilson+	Doherty	Jamieson&	Aitken*	Moore*	Baker+	Fotheringham&	Moran>	Fagan<	Goodfellow			
26/12/2020	SC	H	Buckie Thistle	0	3		Goodfellow	Burke	L Wilson+	Glover	Fagan*	Leslie	Lynas	C Wilson	Doherty&	Jamieson	Aitken	Fotheringham*	Ecrepont+	Moore&	Baker	Henry	Moran	Fee		
20/03/2021	L	A	Stenhousemuir	0	2		Stone	Sideserf	Robinson	Glover&	Fagan	McKernan	Lynas	C Wilson*	Cox	Stevenson>	Aitken+	Leslie*	Doherty+	Jamieson&	Baker>	Henry	McGowan	Fotheringham	Ecrepont	L Wilson
23/03/2021	L	H	Edinburgh City	1	2		Stone	Sideserf	Gallacher	McGowan	Leslie	McKernan	Lynas	C Wilson+	Cox	Stevenson	Aitken*	Doherty*	Jamieson+	Robinson	Baker	Henry	Fagan	L Wilson	Ecrepont	
27/03/2021	L	H	Annan Athletic	1	1		Stone	Sideserf	Gallacher	McGowan	Leslie	McKernan	Lynas	C Wilson*	Cox+	Stevenson	Aitken&	Jamieson*	Ecrepont+	Doherty&	Baker	Fagan	Robinson	Henry	L Wilson	
30/03/2021	L	H	Queen's Park	0	3		Stone	L Wilson	Gallacher	McGowan>	Ecrepont	McKernan&	Kidd+	Robinson	Cox*	Jamieson	Doherty	Stevenson*	Leslie+	Lynas&	Baker>	Aitken	C Wilson	Sideserf	Fagan	Henry
03/04/2021	L	A	Cowdenbeath	1	0		Stone	Sideserf	Gallacher	Robinson	Ecrepont+	McKernan&	Lynas	Kidd	Leslie	Stevenson	Jamieson*	Doherty*	C Wilson+	L Wilson&	Baker	Fagan	Moran	Aitken	Henry	
06/04/2021	L	A	Stirling Albion	1	1		Stone	Sideserf	Gallacher	Robinson	L Wilson*	McKernan	Lynas	C Wilson	Leslie	Stevenson	Aitken	Doherty*	Cox	Ecrepont	Baker	Fagan	Moran	Dolan	Henry	Kouame
10/04/2021	L	A	Brechin City	4	2		Stone	Sideserf	Gallacher	Robinson	L Wilson*	McKernan	Lynas	C Wilson+	Leslie	Stevenson&	Aitken	Kidd*	Ecrepont+	Doherty&	Baker	Fagan	Moran	Dolan	Henry	Kouame
13/04/2021	L	H	Cowdenbeath	0	0		Stone	Sideserf	Gallacher*	Robinson	L Wilson	McKernan	Lynas	C Wilson	Leslie+	Stevenson	Aitken	McGowan*	Kidd+	Doherty	Baker	Fagan	Moran	Dolan	Henry	Ecrepont
17/04/2021	L	A	Elgin City	5	2		Stone	Sideserf	McGowan	Robinson*	L Wilson	McKernan	Lynas	C Wilson>	Kidd	Stevenson+	Aitken&	Ecrepont*	Doherty+	Baker&	Leslie>	Fagan	Jamieson	Dolan	Henry	Moran
20/04/2021	L	H	Stranraer	0	2		Stone	Sideserf	McGowan	Robinson	L Wilson>	McKernan+	Lynas	C Wilson	Kidd&	Stevenson*	Aitken	Doherty*	Leslie+	Jamieson&	Ecrepont>	Baker	Kouame	Dolan	Henry	Moran
24/04/2021	L	H	Annan Athletic	1	0		Stone	Sideserf	McGowan	Robinson+	L Wilson	McKernan	Lynas	C Wilson*	Kidd>	Doherty<	Aitken&	Leslie*	Ecrepont+	Jamieson&	Cox>	Dolan<	Baker	Fagan	Henry	Moran
29/04/2021	L	A	Stenhousemuir	1	0		Stone	Sideserf	McGowan	Gallacher	L Wilson	McKernan	Lynas	Leslie	Kidd*	Doherty	Aitken	Jamieson*	Ecrepont	C Wilson	Cox	Dolan	Baker	Fagan	Henry	Moran
01/05/2021	L	H	Brechin City	1	1		Stone	Sideserf	McGowan	Ecrepont+	L Wilson*	McKernan>	Lynas	Leslie	Jamieson&	Doherty	Aitken	Fagan*	C Wilson+	Baker&	Dolan>	Moran	Kouame	Henry		
04/05/2021	L	A	Cowdenbeath	0	2		Henry	Sideserf	McGowan	C Wilson	L Wilson*	Fagan	Baker+	Leslie	Dolan&	Doherty	Aitken	Ecrepont*	Moran+	Kouame&	Smith					

THE GOALIES

Goalkeepers Used in League Matches, 1970-2020

Players shown in the season of their first appearance only

1972/3	Jim Brown
	Brian Wallace
	Ian Dick
	Patrick Dempsey
	Alexander McClory
	Richard Gray
1973/4	Hugh Graham
	Willie Duff Snr
	Willie Duff Jnr
1974/5	Steve Gryzka
1975/6	Les Hutchison
1976/7	George Thomson
	G Dodds
1977/8	Gerry Gallagher
	Neil McAdam
	Jim Orr
1978/9	Bobby Livingstone
	John Balavage
1979/0	Graham Meikle
1980/1	Michael Hill
1981/2	Ally Purdie
1983/4	Robert Russell
	Robert Burns
	N Jeffries
1984/5	Frank Houston
1985/6	John Thompson
	James McKeown
	Rab McCulloch
1986/7	Alan McKnight
1987/8	Ronnie Tracey
1988/9	David Cormack
1991/2	Steven Connelly
	M McLafferty
	Ronnie McConnachie
	Derek Jackson
	Craig Hinchcliffe
1992/3	Mark Guidi
	Joe Houston
1993/4	Darren Riley
1994/5	Alan Davidson
	John Wight
1995/6	David Moonie
	Mark Osborne
	A McEwan
	Jim Moffat
	Stuart Robertson
1996/7	Stevie Ross
	Cammy Duncan
	Tony Mitchell
1997/8	John Martin
	Barney Duffy
	Jon Connolly
1998/9	Mark McLean
	Robert McColm
1999/0	Andy McCondichie
	Derek Vennard
	T Young
2000/1	Chris Fahey
	Scott Shearer
	Neil Bennett
	Matthew Carr
2004/5	Mark Peat
2005/6	Jamie Ewings
	Alan Creer
	Gary McGlynn

Surname	First Name	Date of Birth	No	Nat	Pos	Signed	Previous	Notes	Contract	Lge A	Lge S	Lge G	SC A	SC S	SC G	LC A	LC S	LC G	Un
Aitken	Matthew	19/07/1997		SCO	F	2020	Forfar Athletic	Out of Contract June 2021, joined Forfar Ath		20		10	1			2		2	2
Allan	Paul	07/02/2000		SCO	M	2020	Dunfermline Athletic (OL)	Oct-Jan		7									0
Baker	Lewis	30/07/1994		SCO	F	2020	East Fife	Released May 2021, joined Broomhill FC		4	6	1				1	1		11
Brown	Jack	02/07/2002		SCO	D	2020	Motherwell	Released May 2021		0	0								0
Burke	Joshua	31/08/2001		SCO	D	2020	Airdrieonians (OL)	Sep-Jan		4	0		1			2			5
Cairney	Paul	29/08/1987		SCO	M	2020	Unattached	Ex Peterhead, released May 2021		0	1						1		1
Choudhry	Zadik	29/11/2000		SCO	M	2020	Albion Rovers Youths		U20	0	0								0
Cox	David	17/03/1989		SCO	M	2021	Cowdenbeath	Retired April 2021, then joined Brechin City		4	1								2
Doherty	Kyle	03/01/2001		SCO	F	2020	Albion Rovers Youths		End 2021/2	10	10	4	1			2	1		1
Dolan	Kieran	05/11/2001		SCO	F	2020	Albion Rovers Youths		U20	1	3						1		13
Doran	Mark	05/12/2000		SCO	D	2020	Albion Rovers Youths	OL to Bellshill Ath Oct-May	U20	0	0								0
Ecrepont	Finn	30/07/2002		SCO	D	2020	Ayr United (OL)	Aug-May		10	7			1		2			5
Evans	Grant	03/01/1990		SCO	D	2021	Pollok (OL)	Jan, cancelled after 3 days		0	0								0
Fagan	Sean	22/05/2000		SCO	D	2018	Alloa Athletic		End 2021/2	6	2		1			3			11
Fee	Paul	12/03/2001		SCO	M	2020	Albion Rovers Youths		U20	0	0								1
Fernie	Adam	04/02/2002		SCO	D	2020	Albion Rovers Youths		U20	0	0					1			2
Fotheringham	Gregor	19/02/1994		SCO	M	2019	Queen's Park	Released May 2021, joined BSC Glasgow		4	2			1		2	1		1
Gallacher	Paul	05/08/1991		SCO	D	2021	Pollok (OL)	Jan-May (ex Q Park)		8	0	1							0
Glover	Scott	16/11/2000		SCO	D	2020	St Mirren	Freed March 2021		8	0		1			1			1
Goodfellow	Ryan	26/05/1993		SCO	GK	2019	Cowdenbeath	Released Jan 2021, joined Edinburgh City		6	0		1			2			3
Greene	Mark	22/03/2000		SCO	F	2020	Albion Rovers Youths		U20	0	0								0
Guy	Lewis	09/01/2000		SCO	M	2020			U20	0	0								1
Henry	Chris	21/02/1999		SCO	GK	2020	Alloa Athletic	Released May 2021		3	0					1			22
Jamieson	Sam	14/03/1999		SCO	F	2020	East Kilbride	Released May 2021		7	8	1	1			2		1	1
Kidd	Lewis	30/01/1995		SCO	D	2021	East Kilbride (OL)	Mar-May		6	2								0
Kouame	Julian	09/11/2000		CDI	M	2020	Burnley Youths		U20	0	1								4
Leslie	James	19/12/1998		SCO	M	2020	Albion Rovers Youths		End 2021/2	13	8	1	1			1	2		0
Lynas	Aron	19/04/1996		SCO	D	2019	Brechin City		End 2021/2	20	1		1			3			0
McGowan	James	23/08/1992		SCO	D	2021	Troon (OL)	Mar-May, made permanent May	End 2021/2	9	1	1							1
McKernan	Jamie	01/04/1992		SCO	M	2021	Darvel		End 2021/2	13	0								0
McVey	Jamie	05/01/2002		SCO	F	2020	Albion Rovers Youths		U20	0	0								0
Moniz	Fernando	23/05/1999		POR / ANG	F	2020	Albion Rovers Youths		U20	0	0								0
Moore	Joseph	17/06/2001		SCO	F	2020	Airdrieonians (OL)	Oct-Jan		1	5	1		1		1	2		2
Moran	Daniel	12/01/2001		SCO	D	2020	Albion Rovers Youths		U20	0	2					1	1		17
Robinson	Alfie	01/01/2002		SCO	D	2020	Queen's Park Youths		End 2021/2	9	0								2
Sideserf	Mark	11/08/1988		SCO	D	2021	Pollok (OL)	Jan-May		13	0								1
Skeoch	Gabe	14/09/2000		SCO	M	2020	Ayr United (OL)	Aug-May		2	2					2			0
Smith	Chris	20/06/2001		SCO	GK	2019	Alloa Athletic		End 2021/2	0	0								1
Stevenson	Ryan	24/08/1984		SCO	F	2021	Troon (OL)		End 2021/2	9	1	2							0
Stone	Harry	20/04/2002		SCO	GK	2021	Hearts (OL)	Mar-May		13	0								0
Wilson	Lewis	01/08/1996		SCO	D	2018	Clyde		End 2021/2	14	1	1	1			1	1		4
Wilson	Callum	23/06/1999		SCO	M	2020	Dumbarton		End 2021/2	18	2	1	1			3			2
Own Goals												1							
NEW SIGNINGS																			
Binne	Cammy	08/11/1997		SCO	GK	2021	Stirling Albion		End 2021/2										
Roberts	Scott	15/03/1996		SCO	M	2021	Stirling Albion		End 2021/2										
Wilson	David	06/09/1994		SCO	M	2021	Stirling Albion		End 2021/2										
El-Zubaidi	Aldin	07/03/1995		SCO / IRQ	M	2021	Stirling Albion		End 2021/2										
Byrne	Declan	07/05/1996		SCO	M	2021	Stirling Albion		End 2021/2										
McGowan	James	23/08/1992		SCO	D	2021	Troon		End 2021/2										
Reilly	Charlie	05/12/2001		SCO	M	2021	Partick Thistle		End 2021/2										
Wright	Max	06/04/1992		SCO	F	2021	Annan Athletic		End 2021/2										

2006/7	Lee Thompson
	David Scott
2007/8	Tony Mitchell (2nd spell)
2008/9	Chris McCluskey
	Jamie Ewings
2009/0	Derek Gaston
2010/1	Thomas Flynn
2011/2	David Crawford
	Chris Fahey
2012/3	Ryan McWilliams
	Matt McGinley
	Ryan Scully
	Graeme Shepherd
2013/4	Neil Parry
2014/5	Kieran Hughes
2015/6	Ross Stewart
2016/7	Daniel Potts
2017/8	Graham Bowman
	Kieran Wright
2018/9	Gareth Halford
	PJ Morrison
2019/0	Chris Smith
	Ryan Goodfellow

Jim Brown

One full international cap for Scotland v Romania in 1975/6

1968-72	Albion Rovers	94
1972-73	Chesterfield	47
1973-78	Sheffield Utd	170
1979-80	Detroit Express	72
1981	Washington D	31
1981-82	Chicago Sting	8
1982-83	Cardiff City	3
1983	Kettering Town	10
1983-89	Chesterfield	135

Total 570 League Games

5 Scotland Under 23 caps

Alloa Athletic FC 2020/21 The Wasps

Honorary Director: Pat Lawlor
Directors: Mike Mulraney (Chairman), Martin Ross (Vice Chairman), Ewan Cameron, Steven Lynch, Dr Robert McElroy
Secretary: Ewan Cameron
Operations Manager: Carol Edgar
Manager: Peter Grant, then Barry Ferguson
Assistant: Paddy Connolly, then also Bob Malcolm
Physio: Gerry Docherty
Sports Therapist: Stuart Phinn
Goalkeeper Coach: John Gibson
Club Doctor: Andrew Deeley
Scout: Tommy Farries, Graeme Ellis
Head of Youth: Derek Nicholson
Ground Staff: John Robertson
Kit Manager: Pat Dunne, Calum Wood
Safety Officers: Robert Wilson, Carol Edgar
PA Announcer: Gerry Watson
Club Shop: June McLauchlan
Programme Editor: John Glencross

Founded	1878
Ground	Recreation Park (aka Indodrill Stadium)
Postcode	FK10 1RY
Tel	01259 722695
Capacity	3100
Closest Railway Station	Alloa
Record Attendance	15467 v Celtic, Scottish Cup, 1954/5
Record Win	9-0 v Selkirk, SC, 28/1/2005
Record Defeat	0-10 v Dundee, Lge, 8/2/47; v T Lanark, LC, 8/8/53
Most League Goals in a Season	49, Willie Crilley, 1921/2
Colours 2020/21 Top	Black and Gold Hoops
Shorts	Black
Sponsor	Northern Gas and Power
Manufacturer	Pendle
Change Colours 2020/21 Top	White
Shorts	White
Nicknames	Wasps
Web	www.alloaathletic.co.uk
Match Programme 2020/21	On line only

As one of the two part-time clubs in the League, Alloa Athletic were always going to have a tough job in maintaining their Championship place. Under the management of Peter Grant they were typically well-organised and played attractive football. However, the overall quality of the League proved too much for them and they were relegated, with Grant intimating his decision to leave at the end of the season.

An interesting stat was that Alloa scored in 21 of their 27 League games – unusual for a team that was relegated. They only really suffered one hammering – 1 0-6 defeat at Tynecastle against Hearts.

Alloa enjoyed a good run in the League Cup, winning three of their four group games. They then defeated Hearts after extra time in the ko stages before losing to Hibernian in the Quarter Final, again after extra time. The Scottish Cup was less successful with an exit at the hands of Cove Rangers, managed by former Alloa boss Paul Hartley.

For the Clackmannanshire club to have spent so many seasons at Championship level over the last ten years is remarkable. They are well run with Mike Mulraney taking a hand-on approach to the club and his enthusiasm and work-ethic rubs off on others.

STAR MAN
Neil Parry has been a stalwart in goals for Alloa since signing for the club in 2016 from Airdrie. The HMRC employee missed a few games through injury in the early part of the season but regained his place once fit. His good work kept Alloa competitive in many games and he is a fine organiser of his defence.

PROSPECTS 2021/2
With Peter Grant leaving the club Alloa were looking for a new manager. It came as a surprise when Barry Ferguson left newly-promoted Kelty Hearts to join the Recreation Park side. His previous experience as an SPFL Manager at Clyde drew a mixed response. It's a different direction for Alloa as Ferguson has been a man who brings in players and moves them on with amazing rapidity – Alloa have been known for their settled squads. It remains to be seen how it works out. If Grant had still been in charge Alloa would have been a shoo-in for a quick return to the Championship; With Ferguson anything is possible.

Alloa v Aberdeen 1976 - a game remembered more for what happened off the field than on it

Date	Comp	H/A	Opponents	F	A		HT		Referee	Crowd	Scorers
07/10/2020	LC	A	Airdrieonians	2	0		1	0	S Reid	BCD	Trouten pen, Thomson
10/10/2020	LC	A	Livingston	1	2		1	0	A Muir	BCD	Thomson
13/10/2020	LC	H	Edinburgh City	2	1		1	0	D Lowe	BCD	Scougall, Thomson
17/10/2020	L	A	Morton	0	1		0	1	A Newlands	BCD	
24/10/2020	L	H	Dunfermline Athletic	1	4		1	1	D Robertson	BCD	Cawley
06/11/2020	L	H	Dundee	3	3	BBC	1	0	A Muir	BCD	Thomson, Cawley, Trouten
11/11/2020	LC	H	Stenhousemuir	4	2		0	2	G Irvine	BCD	Buchanan 3(1 pen), Hetherington
21/11/2020	L	A	Queen of the South	0	2		0	1	J Beaton	BCD	
24/11/2020	L	A	Hearts	0	3		0	3	G Irvine	BCD	
28/11/2020	LC	H	Hearts	1	0	AET	0	0	G Duncan	BCD	Trouten pen
05/12/2020	L	H	Ayr United	0	2		0	1	B Cook	BCD	
12/12/2020	L	A	Arbroath	1	0		0	0	P Stuart	BCD	Scougall
15/12/2020	LC	H	Hibernian	1	2	AET	1	0	D Munro	BCD	Hanlon og
19/12/2020	L	H	Inverness CT	2	1		0	1	S Kirkland	BCD	Murray, Thomson
26/12/2020	L	H	Raith Rovers	2	5		0	2	S McLean	BCD	Buchanan 2 (1 pen)
29/12/2020	L	A	Dundee	1	3		1	0	S Reid	BCD	Hetherington
02/01/2021	L	H	Morton	1	1		0	0	G Irvine	BCD	Thomson
09/01/2021	SC	H	Cove Rangers	2	3		2	1	D Dickinson	BCD	Trouten, O'Donnell
16/01/2021	L	H	Hearts	1	3		0	2	A Muir	BCD	Cawley
30/01/2021	L	A	Ayr United	1	4		1	2	P Stuart	BCD	Trouten
06/02/2021	L	H	Queen of the South	2	1		1	1	G Duncan	BCD	Graham, Cawley
13/02/2021	L	H	Arbroath	1	1		0	1	S Kirkland	BCD	Cameron
20/02/2021	L	A	Dunfermline Athletic	1	2		1	1	S Reid	BCD	Cawley
23/02/2021	L	A	Inverness CT	2	2		1	0	G Irvine	BCD	Cameron, Trouten pen
27/02/2021	L	A	Raith Rovers	1	3		1	0	S Kirkland	BCD	Cameron
06/03/2021	L	H	Inverness CT	1	1		1	1	A Muir	BCD	Cameron
13/03/2021	L	A	Queen of the South	3	2		2	2	G Aitken	BCD	Murray, Connolly, Buchanan
19/03/2021	L	H	Dundee	0	3		0	1	G Irvine	BCD	
27/03/2021	L	H	Ayr United	2	2		1	1	A Muir	BCD	Cameron, Williamson
03/04/2021	L	A	Arbroath	1	2		0	0	C Graham	BCD	Trouten
09/04/2021	L	A	Hearts	0	6		0	2	S McLean	BCD	
17/04/2021	L	H	Raith Rovers	1	2		1	0	G Aitken	BCD	Cawley
24/04/2021	L	A	Morton	1	1		0	0	E Anderson	BCD	Cameron
30/04/2021	L	H	Dunfermline Athletic	1	0		0	0	P Stuart	BCD	Dick

Ronnie Lowrie

Donald Hunter

Dougie McNab

Date	Comp	H/A	Opponents	F	A		1	2	3	4	5	6	7	8	9	10	11	12	13	14	15	16	17	18	19	20
07/10/2020	LC	A	Airdrieonians	2	0		Parry	Taggart	Dick	Lynch	Trouten>	Cawley*	Robertson	Hetherington	Brown&	Grant<	Buchanan+	Thomson*	Scougall+	Connelly&	Evans>	O'Donnell<	Williamson	Malcolm	Gilhooly	Wilson
10/10/2020	LC	A	Livingston	1	2		Parry	Taggart	Dick	Lynch	Trouten	Malcolm&	Robertson	Hetherington	Murray+	Grant	Thomson*	Buchanan*	Cawley+	Scougall&	Evans	O'Donnell	Williamson	Connelly	Gilhooly	Wilson
13/10/2020	LC	H	Edinburgh City	2	1		Parry*	Taggart	Dick	Lynch>	Scougall&	Cawley*	Robertson	Connelly<	Murray	Grant+	Buchanan	Wilson*	Hetherington+	Trouten&	Graham>	Thomson<	Williamson	Malcolm	O'Donnell	Evans
17/10/2020	L	A	Morton	0	1		Willison	Taggart	Dick	Lynch	Trouten	Cawley	Robertson	Hetherington	Thomson+	Grant	Connelly*	Scougall*	Buchanan+	Malcolm	Graham	O'Donnell	Murray	Wilson		
24/10/2020	L	H	Dunfermline Athletic	1	4		Willison	Taggart	Dick	Lynch	Trouten	Cawley	Robertson	Murray+	Thomson+	Grant	Connelly*	Scougall*	Buchanan+	Malcolm	Graham	O'Donnell	Brown	Wilson		
06/11/2020	L	H	Dundee	3	3	BBC	Willison	Taggart	Dick	Brown*	Graham	Cawley	Robertson	Hetherington	Thomson+	Grant	Trouten	Connelly*	Murray+	Malcolm	Lynch	Scougall	Buchanan	Wilson		
11/11/2020	LC	H	Stenhousemuir	4	2		Willison	Jamieson	Scougall	Brown	Graham	Murray*	Malcolm	Evans+	O'Donnell	Williamson	Buchanan	Hetherington*	Grant+	Dick	Trouten	Cawley	Taggart	Thomson	Lynch	
21/11/2020	L	A	Queen of the South	0	2		Parry	Taggart	Dick	Brown*	Graham	Cawley	Robertson	Hetherington	Thomson+	Grant	Trouten	Scougall*	Buchanan+	Connelly	Jamieson	O'Donnell	Murray	Willison		
24/11/2020	L	A	Hearts	0	3		Parry	Taggart	Dick	Murray&	Graham	Cawley+	Robertson	Hetherington	Thomson*	Grant	Trouten	Buchanan*	Scougall+	Connelly&	Jamieson	Brown	Williamson	Willison		
28/11/2020	LC	H	Hearts	1	0	AET	Parry	Taggart	Dick	Jamieson	Graham	Cawley	Murray*	Hetherington	Buchanan+	Grant	Trouten	Connelly*	Thomson+	Lynch	Scougall	O'Donnell	Williamson	Malcolm	Brown	Willison
05/12/2020	L	H	Ayr United	0	2		Parry	Taggart	Dick	Robertson	Graham	Cawley+	Murray*	Hetherington	Buchanan	Grant	Trouten	Connelly*	Thomson+	Lynch	Scougall	O'Donnell	Brown	Willison		
12/12/2020	L	A	Arbroath	1	0		Parry	Taggart*	Dick	Robertson	Graham	Cawley+	Jamieson	Hetherington	Buchanan&	Scougall	Trouten	Murray*	Brown+	Thomson&	Malcom	Lynch	Connelly	Willison		
15/12/2020	LC	H	Hibernian	1	2	AET	Parry	Connelly	Dick	Robertson	Graham	Cawley	Jamieson	Hetherington	Buchanan*	Scougall+	Trouten&	Thomson*	O'Donnell+	Evans&	Malcom	Lynch	Willison			
19/12/2020	L	H	Inverness CT	2	1		Parry	O'Donnell	Dick	Robertson	Graham	Cawley	Jamieson	Hetherington	Buchanan+	Murray	Connelly*	Thomson*	Malcolm+	Evans	Lynch	Williamson	Willison			
26/12/2020	L	H	Raith Rovers	2	5		Parry*	O'Donnell	Dick	Robertson	Graham	Cawley+	Jamieson	Hetherington	Buchanan	Murray	Grant	Willison*	Thomson+	Evans	Lynch	Williamson	Malcolm	Connelly		
29/12/2020	L	A	Dundee	1	3		Willison	O'Donnell*	Dick+	Robertson	Graham	Cawley	Jamieson	Hetherington	Buchanan&	Murray	Grant	Connelly*	Malcolm+	Thomson&	Lynch	Williamson	Wilson	Evans		
02/01/2021	L	H	Morton	1	1		Parry	O'Donnell*	Dick	Robertson	Graham	Cawley	Jamieson	Hetherington	Buchanan	Murray	Grant	Thomson*	Malcolm	Connelly	Lynch	Williamson	Evans	Willison		
09/01/2021	SC	H	Cove Rangers	2	3		Parry	O'Donnell&	Dick	Robertson	Graham	Cawley	Jamieson	Hetherington	Buchanan+	Trouten*	Grant	Scougall*	Thomson+	Murray&	Lynch	Connelly	Malcolm	Willison		
16/01/2021	L	H	Hearts	1	3		Parry	Scougall+	Murray*	Robertson	Graham	Cawley	Jamieson	Hetherington	Williamson	Grant	Thomson&	Brown*	Buchanan+	Evans&	Lynch	Connelly	O'Donnell	Wright		
30/01/2021	L	A	Ayr United	1	4		Parry	Lynch	Dick	Scougall*	Graham	Cawley	Jamieson	Hetherington	Trouten	Grant	Cameron	Buchanan*	Murray+	Thomson	Robertson	Connelly	O'Donnell	Wright		
06/02/2021	L	H	Queen of the South	2	1		Parry	Taggart	Dick	Murray+	Graham	Cawley	Jamieson*	Hetherington	Trouten	Grant	Cameron	Robertson*	Buchanan+	Thomson	Scougall	Connelly	Lynch	Wright		
13/02/2021	L	H	Arbroath	1	1		Parry	Taggart	Dick	Robertson+	Graham	Cawley	Williamson*	Hetherington	Trouten	Grant	Cameron	Scougall*	Thomson+	Jamieson	Buchanan	Connelly	Murray	Wright		
20/02/2021	L	A	Dunfermline Athletic	1	2		Parry	Taggart	Dick	Robertson+	Graham	Cawley	Williamson*	Hetherington	Trouten	Scougall	Cameron	Brown*	Thomson+	Jamieson	Buchanan	Connelly	Murray	Wright		
23/02/2021	L	A	Inverness CT	2	2		Parry	Taggart	Dick	Robertson	Graham	Cawley+	Scougall*	Hetherington	Trouten&	Grant	Cameron	Murray*	Buchanan+	Jamieson&	Thomson	Connelly	Brown	Wright		
27/02/2021	L	A	Raith Rovers	1	3		Parry	Taggart	Dick	Robertson	Graham	Cawley	Scougall*	Hetherington	Trouten	Grant*	Cameron	Buchanan*	Malcolm	Jamieson	Thomson	Connelly	Murray	Wright		
06/03/2021	L	H	Inverness CT	1	1		Parry	Taggart	Dick	Robertson	Graham	Cawley	Connelly*	Hetherington	Trouten	Grant	Cameron	O'Donnell*	Buchanan	Jamieson	Malcolm	Williamson	Murray	Brown		
13/03/2021	L	A	Queen of the South	3	2		Parry	Taggart	Lynch	Robertson	Graham	Cawley	Murray&	Williamson+	Connelly*	Grant	Cameron	Buchanan*	O'Donnell+	Jamieson&	Malcolm	Brown	Evans	Willison		
19/03/2021	L	H	Dundee	0	3		Parry	Taggart	Dick	Robertson	Graham	Cawley	Murray*	Hetherington	Connelly+	Grant	Cameron	Buchanan*	Brown+	Jamieson	Lynch	Williamson	O'Donnell	Willison		
27/03/2021	L	H	Ayr United	2	2		Parry	Taggart	Dick	Robertson	Graham	Cawley	Williamson	Hetherington	Connelly*	Grant+	Cameron	Scougall*	Trouten+	Jamieson	Murray	Buchanan	Thomson	Willison		
03/04/2021	L	A	Arbroath	1	2		Parry	Taggart	Dick	Robertson	Graham	Cawley	Williamson*	Hetherington	Trouten	Grant+	Cameron	Thomson*	Scougall+	Jamieson	Connolly	Murray	Buchanan	Willison		
09/04/2021	L	A	Hearts	0	6		Parry	Taggart	Dick	Robertson	Graham	Cawley	Williamson*	Hetherington	Trouten+	Grant	Cameron	Murray*	Scougall+	Jamieson	Connolly	Thomson	Buchanan	Willison		
17/04/2021	L	H	Raith Rovers	1	2		Parry	Taggart	Dick	Robertson	Graham	Cawley	Scougall*	Hetherington	Trouten	Grant&	Cameron+	Willison*	Buchanan+	Thomson&	Connolly	Williamson	Jamieson	Murray		
24/04/2021	L	A	Morton	1	1		Parry	Taggart	Jamieson	Robertson+	Graham	Cawley	Williamson	Hetherington	Trouten*	Grant	Cameron	Buchanan*	Brown+	Thomson	Connolly	Scougall	Murray	Willison		
30/04/2021	L	H	Dunfermline Athletic	1	0		Parry	Taggart	Dick	Jamieson	Graham	Cawley	Williamson	Murray*	Scougall	Grant	Cameron	Connelly*	Buchanan	Thomson	Connolly	Brown	Lynch	Willison		

THE GOALIES

Goalkeepers Used in League Matches, 1972-2020

Players shown in the season of their first appearance only

1972/3	David McWilliams
	J Adams
	David Cooper
1973/4	Neil McNeill
	David Phillips
1974/5	Steven Anderson
	George Whisker
	Willie Whelan
	Norman Ritchie
	Sandy Thomson
1977/8	Douglas McNab
1979/0	A Fiddler
	Stan Drummond
1980/1	Gordon McBain
	A Henry
1981/2	Donald Hunter
1983/4	Hugh Stevenson
1984/5	Ronnie Lowrie
1985/6	D Kennedy
1986/7	Martin McLafferty
1989/0	Scott McGuinness
1990/1	Jim Butter
1991/2	Neil Binnie
1995/6	Paul Graham
	Willie Lamont
	Robert Balfour
1996/7	Michael Monaghan
	Justin Cameron
1997/8	Mark Cairns
	Stevie Ellison
1999/0	Colin Stewart
2000/1	Jim McQueen
	Guido Van de Kamp
2001/2	Derek Soutar
	Jim Evans
2002/3	Myles Hogarth
2004/5	Gary McGlynn
2005/6	Alan Creer
	Paul Ferguson
2006/7	Scott Findlay
	David McEwan
2007/8	Ray Jellema
2008/9	Michael White
2009/0	David Crawford
2010/1	Stephen Robertson
	Jamie Ewings
2011/2	Scott Bain
	Craig McDowall
2014/5	John Gibson
2015/6	Scott Gallacher
	David Crawford
	Andrew McNeill
2016/7	Neil Parry
	Andrew Wilson
2019/0	Jamie McDonald
	Kieran Wright

Surname	First Name	Date of Birth	No	Nat	Pos	Signed	Previous	Notes	Contract	Lge A	Lge S	Lge G	SC A	SC S	SC G	LC A	LC S	LC G	Un
Brown	Adam	09/06/1995	14	SCO	M	2018	Airdrieonians	Released May 2021, joined Stenhousemuir		2	5					2			8
Buchanan	Liam	27/03/1985	9	SCO	F	2019	Raith Rovers	Released May 2021, joined Cowdenbeath		6	13	3	1			5	1	3	8
Cameron	Innes	22/08/2000		SCO	F	2021	Kilmarnock (OL)	Jan-May		15	0	6							0
Cawley	Kevin	17/03/1989	7	SCO	F	2016	Dumbarton	Club all-time record appearance holder	End 2021/2	27	0	6	1			4	1		1
Connelly	Lee	18/10/1999	17	SCO	F	2020	Sunderland (OL)	Oct-May		7	5	1				2	2		18
Currid	Fraser	27/02/2001		SCO	GK	2020	Dundee United Youth	OL to Bo'ness United CFC Oct-May, released May 2021		0	0								0
Dick	Liam	19/08/1995	3	SCO	D	2018	Dumbarton	Released May 2021, joined Raith Rovers		24	0	1	1			5			1
Evans	Liam	17/11/2001	26	SCO	F	2020	Alloa Athletic Youth		End 2021/2	0	1					1	2		7
Gilhooly	Nathan	07/08/2001	16	SCO	D	2020	Alloa Athletic Youth	Released May 2021		0	0								2
Graham	Andrew	22/09/1983	5	SCO	D	2016	Ayr United	From Dunoon	End 2021/2	25	0	1	1			3	1		2
Grant	Ray	01/11/1996	22	SCO	M	2020	Clyde	OOC May 2021, joined Stirling Albion		24	0		1			4	1		0
Hetherington	Steven	09/02/1993	6	ENG	M	2014	Crook Town	OOC May 2021, joined Falkirk		24	0	1	1			4	2	1	0
Jamieson	Nicky	03/08/1996	15	SCO	D	2020	Queen's Park	OL to Stenhousemuir 2021/2	End 2021/2	10	2		1			3			11
Lynch	Edin	07/08/2000	25	SCO	D	2020	Kilmarnock	Released May 2021		4	0					3			15
Malcolm	Blair	03/02/1997	18	SCO	M	2019	Cowdenbeath	Released May 2021		0	2					2			14
Murray	Innes	17/02/1998	23	SCO	M	2020	Hibernian (OL)	Oct-May		12	5	2		1		4			10
O'Donnell	Cameron	29/09/2001	20	SCO	M	2019	Alloa Athletic Youth		End 2021/2	4	2		1		1	1	2		10
Parry	Neil	08/11/1985	1	SCO	GK	2016	Airdrieonians		End 2021/2	23	0		1			5			0
Robertson	Jon	25/04/1989	8	SCO	M	2016	Stenhousemuir		End 2021/2	24	1		1			4			1
Scougall	Stefan	07/12/1992	12	SCO	M	2020	Carlisle United		End 2021/2	8	8	1		1		3	2	1	5
Taggart	Scott	27/12/1991	2	SCO	D	2016	Dumbarton		End 2021/2	21	0					4			1
Thomson	Robert	28/05/1993	19	SCO	F	2019	Morton	OOC May 2021, joined Stenhousemuir		6	10	3		1		1	4	3	9
Trouten	Alan	08/11/1985	10	SCO	F	2018	Albion Rovers		End 2021/2	18	1	4	1		1	4	1	2	1
Williamson	Lucas	26/03/2003	24	SCO	D	2020	Alloa Athletic Youth	OL to Broomhill 2021/2	End 2021/2	9	0	1				1			12
Willison	Reece	27/05/1999	31	SCO	GK	2020	Airdrieonians	Released May 2021		4	2					1			16
Wilson	Andrew	22/04/1998	21	SCO	GK	2018	Alloa Athletic Youth	Released May 2021		0	0						1		6
Wright	Jordan	28/02/1999		ENG	GK	2021	Nottingham Forest (OL)	Jan-May		0	0								7
Own Goal																		1	
NEW SIGNINGS																			
Armour	Ben	17/11/2001		SCO	F	2021	Peterhead		End2021/2										
Armstrong	Jordan	02/04/1999		SCO	D	2021	East Kilbride		End2021/2										
Boyd	Steven	12/04/1997		SCO	F	2021	Peterhead		End2021/2										
Church	Daniel	21/07/2000		SCO	D	2021	Dumbarton		End2021/2										
Durnan	Mark	28/11/1992		SCO	D	2021	Falkirk		End2021/2										
Howie	Craig	02/07/1996		SCO	D	2021	Clyde		End2021/2										
King	Adam	11/10/1995		SCO	M	2021	Dundee United		End2021/2										
Lamont	Mark	25/02/1998		SCO	M	2021	Clyde		End2021/2										
McDowall	Craig	24/08/1990		SCO	GK	2021	Unattached	Ex East Fife	End2021/2										
Sammon	Conor	06/11/1986		ROI	F	2021	Falkirk		End2021/2										

PHOTOCARDS

No. 66.

ALLOA FOOTBALL CLUB.

Left to right, back row :—*D. Cadden (Trainer), J. Richardson, J. Reid (Match Sec.), J. Kerr (Capt.), R. Muir, W. Crawford (Dir.), J. Beath, J. McMullen, J. Irvine, J. Pollard, J. Mathieson (Fin. Sec.).* Front row :—*R. Shankley, T. Williamson, J. Foley, R. Duffey, J. Halliday.*

Was the first team to win the Championship of the Second Division, Scottish League, and gained promotion. Has since lost its place in the Premier Division and now plays in Second Division, in which the team occupied fourth place, 1935/36.

Expending de Luxe Albums for Ardath Photocards on sale at Tobacconists Price 6d

ARDATH TOBACCO CO. LTD. Manufacturers of STATE EXPRESS and ARDATH CIGARETTES

D

Annan Athletic FC 2020/21 The Galabankies

Chairman: Philip Jones
Vice Chairman: Russell Brown
Company Secretary: Alan Irving
President: Sam Wallace
Office Manager / Director: John Peel
Clubhouse Operations Director: Stephen Bryson
Volunteer Coordinator / Director : David Robison
Director: Susan Bryson
Entertainments Manager: Hardip Atwal
Child Wellbeing and Protection Officer: Alan Irving
Physio: Craig Bourner
Chaplain: David Wightman
Programme Editor: Neil Irving
Commercial Manager: David Carroll
Manager: Peter Murphy
Assistant Manager: Colin McMenamin
Goalkeeping Coach: Jon Connolly
Sports Scientist: Ross Banks
Kitman: Alan Casey

Founded	1942
Ground	Galabank
Postcode	DG12 5DQ
Tel	01461 204108
Capacity	2514
Closest Railway Station	Annan
Record Attendance	2517 v Rangers, Sep 2013
Record Win	Annan Athletic 6 Elgin City 0, 07.03.2009
Record Defeat	Inverness CT 8 Annan Athletic 1, 24.01.1998
Most League Goals in a Season	22, Peter Weatherston, 2014/15
Colours 2020/21 Top	Gold with Black Flashes
Shorts	Black
Sponsor	M and S Engineering
Manufacturer	Halbro
Change Colours 2020/21 Top	Red and Black
Shorts	Red and Black
Nicknames	Galabankies
Web	www.annanathleticfc.co.uk
Match Programme 2020/21	None

Peter Murphy has done a quiet but highly satisfactory job at Annan in recent years. Given how tight resources must be, they have never really looked like dropping out of the League. 2020/1 was perhaps the closest they have come but in such a short season there was absolutely no margin for error. Two vital wins in successive games in April guaranteed safety – beating Brechin 3-0 and then a 5-1 win over an extremely poor Stenhousemuir side.

Despite a 5-1 win over Brechin City, Annan made no progress in the League Cup. Their Scottish Cup hopes were ended by Highland League side Formartine United.

Perhaps it is surprising that Annan have not made more use of their links with Carlisle United. Whilst they have signed players released from Brunton Park, they have never really taken young players on loan - SPFL League Two would be an excellent level for them to develop.

STAR MAN

Formerly with Raith Rovers and St Mirren, wing man Nathan Flanagan was a threat to any defence in League Two with his pace and close control. He will be a big loss to the Galabank side having moved on to sign for Stirling Albion.

PROSPECTS 2021/2

Since stepping up to the League in 2008 Annan have come close to promotion on several occasions without ever actually achieving it. It is hard to see them pushing for promotion in 2021/2 – they will be pleased to keep themselves away from any threat of being "Club 42".

Date	Comp	H/A	Opponents	F	A		HT		Referee	Crowd	Scorers
06/10/2020	LC	H	Hamilton Accies	3	1		3	0	C Napier	BCD	Swinglehurst, Fulton, Purdue
10/10/2020	LC	H	Stranraer	1	1	4-5p	0	1	S Luke	BCD	Moxon
13/10/2020	LC	A	Ayr United	0	1		0	1	G Irvine	BCD	
17/10/2020	L	A*	Cowdenbeath	3	0		1	0	S Lambie	BCD	Flanagan, Anderson, Purdue
25/10/2020	L	H	Stranraer	1	1		1	1	B Cook	BCD	Moxon
31/10/2020	L	A	Stirling Albion	0	1		0	1	M McDermid	BCD	
07/11/2020	L	H	Albion Rovers	2	3		0	0	K Graham	BCD	Currie, Wright
10/11/2020	LC	A	Albion Rovers	5	1		4	0	D McFarlane	BCD	Wright 2, Fleming 2, Docherty pen
21/11/2020	L	A	Stenhousemuir	2	1		1	0	L Wilson	BCD	Wright 2
28/11/2020	L	H	Edinburgh City	0	4		0	2	C Scott	BCD	
05/12/2020	L	A	Elgin City	0	1		0	0	G Grainger	200	
19/12/2020	L	H	Queen's Park	1	2		0	0	L Watson	200	Currie pen
22/12/2020	L	A	Brechin City	0	0		0	0	M McDermid	BCD	
26/12/2020	SC	A	Gala Fairydean Rovers	2	1		1	0	S Luke	BCD	Smith, Lowdon
02/01/2021	L	A	Stranraer	0	2		0	0	K Graham	BCD	
20/03/2021	L	H	Cowdenbeath	0	0		0	0	G Ross	BCD	
23/03/2021	SC	A	Formartine United	1	1	AET, 1-3p	1	1	C Scott	BCD	Smith
27/03/2021	L	A	Albion Rovers	1	1		0	0	M McDermid	BCD	Anderson
03/04/2021	L	H	Elgin City	0	3		0	2	S Reid	BCD	
06/04/2021	L	A	Edinburgh City	1	1		0	0	G Ross	BCD	Wallace pen
10/04/2021	L	H	Stirling Albion	1	2		0	1	S Lambie	BCD	Wright
13/04/2021	L	A	Queen's Park	0	1		0	1	M McDermid	BCD	
17/04/2021	L	H	Brechin City	3	0		3	0	C Graham	BCD	Smith, Flanagan, Wallace
20/04/2021	L	H	Stenhousemuir	5	1		3	1	G Irvine	BCD	Flanagan, Wallace 2, Smith, Christie
24/04/2021	L	A	Albion Rovers	0	1		0	0	S Lambie	BCD	
27/04/2021	L	H	Stenhousemuir	1	1		0	0	L Wilson	BCD	Wallace
20/04/2021	L	A	Brechin City	3	0		1	0	D Lowe	BCD	Anderson, Christie, Flanagan
01/05/2021	L	H	Cowdenbeath	1	1		0	0	B Cook	BCD	Fleming

Date	Comp	H/A	Opponents	F	A		1	2	3	4	5	6	7	8	9	10	11	12	13	14	15	16	17	18	19	20
06/10/2020	LC	H	Hamilton Accies	3	1		Pettigrew	Fulton	Clark	Hunter	Douglas	Swinglehurst	Purdue+	Moxon	Anderson*	Wright	Flanagan&	Smith*	Splaine+	Currie&	*Docherty*	*Emerson*	*Fleming*	*Mitchell*		
10/10/2020	LC	H	Stranraer	1	1	4-5p	Mitchell	Fulton*	Clark	Hunter	Douglas	Swinglehurst	Purdue>	Moxon	Splaine	Smith&	Flanagan+	Docherty*	Wright+	Anderson&	Fleming>	*Emerson*	*Currie*	*Pettigrew*		
13/10/2020	LC	A	Ayr United	0	1		Mitchell	Docherty	Clark	Fleming+	Douglas<	Swinglehurst	Hunter	Anderson*	Splaine	Smith&	Flanagan>	Wright*	Purdue+	Currie&	Emerson>	P Watson<	*Pettigrew*			
17/10/2020	L	A*	Cowdenbeath	3	0		Pettigrew	Anderson&	Clark	Hunter	Douglas	Swinglehurst	Purdue+	Moxon	Splaine	Wright	Flanagan*	Smith*	Docherty+	Fleming&	*Emerson*	*P Watson*	*Currie*	*Mitchell*		
25/10/2020	L	H	Stranraer	1	1		Pettigrew	Anderson	Clark	Hunter+	Douglas	Swinglehurst	Purdue*	Moxon	Splaine	Wright	Flanagan	Smith*	Docherty+	*Fleming*	*Emerson*	*P Watson*	*Currie*	*Mitchell*		
31/10/2020	L	A	Stirling Albion	0	1		Pettigrew	Anderson*	Clark	Hunter	Douglas	Swinglehurst	Smith	Moxon	Splaine	Wright	Flanagan	Fleming*	*Docherty*	*Currie*	*Emerson*	*P Watson*	*Love*	*Mitchell*		
07/11/2020	L	H	Albion Rovers	2	3		Pettigrew	Anderson	Clark	Hunter	Douglas	Swinglehurst	Smith*	Moxon	Splaine+	Wright	Flanagan	Fleming*	Currie+	*Docherty*	*Emerson*	*P Watson*	*Love*	*Mitchell*		
10/11/2020	LC	A	Albion Rovers	5	1		Mitchell	Docherty	Clark&	Hunter	Douglas	Swinglehurst	Smith>	Moxon+	Fleming	Wright*	Love	Currie*	Emerson+	Flanagan&	Anderson>	*P Watson*	*Pettigrew*			
21/11/2020	L	A	Stenhousemuir	2	1		Mitchell	Docherty	Clark	Hunter	Douglas	Swinglehurst	Smith*	Moxon	Splaine	Wright	Fleming	Anderson*	*Emerson*	*Currie*	*Love*	*Lowdon*	*Murphy*	*Pettigrew*		
28/11/2020	L	H	Edinburgh City	0	4		Pettigrew	Docherty>	Clark	Hunter	Douglas	Swinglehurst	Smith&	Moxon	Splaine+	Wright	Fleming*	Flanagan*	Anderson+	Currie&	Fulton>	*Lowdon*	*Love*	*Emerson*		
05/12/2020	L	A	Elgin City	0	1		Mitchell	Docherty	Clark	Fulton+	Douglas	Anderson&	Love	Moxon	Splaine<	Wright>	Fleming*	Lowdon*	Smith+	Hunter&	Currie>	Emerson<	*Pettigrew*			
19/12/2020	L	H	Queen's Park	1	2		Mitchell	Docherty+	Clark	Fulton	Douglas	Anderson	Love	Moxon	Smith	Wright	Fleming*	Splaine*	Currie+	*Hunter*	*Lowdon*	*Emerson*	*Pettigrew*			
22/12/2020	L	A	Brechin City	0	0		Mitchell	Docherty	Clark	Fulton	Douglas	Anderson	Love	Moxon*	Smith	Wright	Hunter	Currie*	*Splaine*	*Fleming*	*Lowdon*	*Emerson*	*Pettigrew*			
26/12/2020	SC	A	Gala Fairydean Rovers	2	1		Mitchell	Lowdon	Clark	Fulton	Douglas	Fleming*	Love	Moxon	Smith	Wright+	Hunter	Splaine*	Anderson+	*Docherty*	*Emerson*	*Currie*	*Swinglehurst*	*Pettigrew*		
02/01/2021	L	A	Stranraer	0	2		Mitchell	Docherty	Clark	Lowdon	Douglas	Swinglehurst	Fleming*	Moxon	Smith	Wright+	Anderson&	Flanagan*	Splaine+	Love&	*Emerson*	*Currie*	*P Watson*	*Pettigrew*		
20/03/2021	L	H	Cowdenbeath	0	0		Mitchell	Docherty	Clark	Lowdon	Douglas	Fulton	Wallace	Flanagan	Smith	Hunter	Anderson*	McCaw*	Wright	*Love*	*Emerson*	*Currie*	*D Watson*	*Fleming*	*Kinnear*	
23/03/2021	SC	A	Formartine United	1	1	AET, 1-3p	Kinnear	Fleming	Clark	Lowdon*	Douglas	Fulton	Wallace>	Wright+	Smith	Hunter	McCaw&	Love*	Anderson+	Docherty&	Currie>	*Emerson*	*Mitchell*			
27/03/2021	L	A	Albion Rovers	1	1		Mitchell	Docherty+	Clark	Lowdon	Douglas	Fulton	Wallace	Anderson	Smith	Hunter	McCaw*	Fleming*	Moxon+	*Love*	*Currie*	*Emerson*	*Wright*	*D Watson*	*Kinnear*	
03/04/2021	L	H	Elgin City	0	3		Mitchell	Docherty*	Clark	Love<	Douglas	Fulton	Wallace	Anderson	Smith+	Hunter&	Flanagan>	Moxon*	Fleming+	Currie&	McCaw>	Sinnamon<	*Christie*	*Watson*	*Wright*	*Kinnear*
06/04/2021	L	A	Edinburgh City	1	1		Mitchell	Sinnamon	Clark	Lowdon	Douglas	Anderson&	Wallace	Moxon*	Smith>	Hunter	Flanagan+	Fleming*	Christie+	Wright&	D Watson>	*McCaw*	*Docherty*	*Love*	*Currie*	*Kinnear*
10/04/2021	L	H	Stirling Albion	1	2		Mitchell	Sinnamon	Clark	Lowdon	Douglas	Wright+	Wallace	Moxon	Smith	Hunter&	Christie*	Flanagan*	Anderson+	Docherty&	*D Watson*	*McCaw*	*Fleming*	*Love*	*Currie*	*Kinnear*
13/04/2021	L	A	Queen's Park	0	1		Kinnear	Sinnamon	Love	Lowdon	Douglas	Fleming+	Anderson	Moxon	Smith&	Hunter	Christie*	Flanagan*	D Watson+	Currie&	*Emerson*	*McCaw*	*Docherty*	*Mitchell*		
17/04/2021	L	H	Brechin City	3	0		Mitchell	Sinnamon*	Love	Lowdon+	Douglas	Fleming	Wallace	Moxon	Smith&	Hunter<	Flanagan>	Fulton*	Swinglehurst+	Currie&	Christie>	Docherty<	*D Watson*	*McCaw*	*Anderson*	*Kinnear*
20/04/2021	L	H	Stenhousemuir	5	1		Mitchell	Fulton	Love	Clark	Douglas	Fleming	Wallace&	Moxon<	Smith>	Hunter*	Flanagan+	Anderson*	Currie+	Christie&	Docherty>	D Watson<	*Swinglehurst*	*McCaw*	*Emerson*	*Kinnear*
24/04/2021	L	A	Albion Rovers	0	1		Mitchell	Docherty	Love>	Fulton	Douglas	Swinglehurst	Wallace*	Moxon	Smith&	Fleming	Flanagan+	Anderson*	Hunter+	Christie&	Currie>	*Sinnamon*	*D Watson*	*McCaw*	*Emerson*	*Munro*
27/04/2021	L	H	Stenhousemuir	1	1		Munro	Fulton	Love	Hunter	Douglas	Swinglehurst	Wallace	D Watson+	Smith	Fleming	Flanagan*	Christie*	Anderson+	*Docherty*	*Currie*	*Sinnamon*	*Mitchell*	*McCaw*	*Emerson*	
20/04/2021	L	A	Brechin City	3	0		Munro	Fulton*	Love	Hunter	Sinnamon>	Swinglehurst	Docherty	D Watson+	Anderson<	Fleming	Christie&	Flanagan*	Wallace+	Murphy&	McCaw>	Smith<	*Emerson*	*Currie*	*Mitchell*	
01/05/2021	L	H	Cowdenbeath	1	1		Mitchell	Docherty&	Love<	Sinnamon*	Douglas	Swinglehurst	Wallace+	Christie>	Smith	Fleming	Flanagan	Fulton*	Anderson+	Hunter&	McCaw>	Currie<	*D Watson*	*Murphy*	*Emerson*	

THE GOALIES
Goalkeepers Used in League Matches, 2008-2020
Players shown in the season of their first appearance only

2008/9	Craig Summersgill
	Doug Calder
2009/0	Greg Kelly
	Jonny Jamieson
2010/1	Alex Mitchell
2013/4	Kenny Arthur
2014/5	Jake Gemmell
	Jordan Hart
2015/6	Blair Currie
2017/8	Jim Atkinson
2018/9	Jonny Jamieson
2019/0	Chris Smith
	Aaron Taylor

Alex Mitchell

Craig Summersgill

Surname	First Name	Date of Birth	No	Nat	Pos	Signed	Previous	Notes	Contract	Lge			SC			LC			
										A	S	G	A	S	G	A	S	G	Un
Anderson	Iain	09/07/1992		SCO	F	2020	Dalbeattie Star		End 2021/2	14	7	3		2		2	2		1
Barr	Darren	17/03/1985		SCO	D	2019	Stirling Albion	Coach		0	0								0
Christie	Darren	24/11/1987		SCO	F	2021	Pollok (OL)	Apr-May		4	5	2							1
Clark	Cammy	24/10/100		SCO	D	2020	Queen's Park		End 2021/2	16	0		2			4			0
Currie	Russell	02/05/2001		ENG / SCO	F	2019	Queen of the South	Released May 2021 joined Dalbeattie Star		0	11	2		1			3		13
Docherty	Mark	15/03/1988		SCO	D	2020	Forfar Athletic	OOC Man 2021 joined Clyde		12	5			1		2	1	1	7
Douglas	Matty	17/01/1998		ENG	D	2019	Workington		End 2021/2	21	0		2			4			0
Emerson	Harry	18/10/2001		SCO	D	2020	Annan Athletic Youths	Released May 2021		0	1						2		21
Flanagan	Nathan	04/05/1997		SCO	M	2019	Raith Rovers	Out of Contract May 2021, joined Stirling Albion		12	5	4				3	1		0
Fleming	Kyle	25/02/2002		SCO	M	2020	Dundee (OL)	Sep-May		12	6	1	2			2	1	2	5
Fulton	Tyler	31/01/1996		SCO	D	2020	Eastfield Ams	OOC May 2021, joined E Stirlingshire		10	3		2			2		1	0
Hunter	Lewis	26/05/1997		SCO	M	2020	East Fife		End 2021/2	17	3		2			4			1
Kinnear	Brian	16/01/2001		SCO	GK	2021	Rangers (OL)	Mar-May		1	0		1						7
Love	Ross	11/09/2001		SCO	D	2020	Ayr United (OL)	Oct-May		11	1		1	1		1			8
Lowdon	Jordan	24/07/1992		SCO	D	2020	Stirling Albion		End 2021/2	7	1		2		1				4
McCaw	Alex	16/06/2002		SCO	M	2021	St Mirren (OL)	Jan-May		1	4		1						7
Mitchell	Alex	21/03/1991		ENG	GK	2020	Workington	OOC May 2021 joined Blyth Spartans		14	0		1			3			9
Moxon	Owen	17/01/1998		ENG	M	2017	Queen of the South		End 2021/2	16	2	1	1			3		1	0
Munro	Ross	01/04/2000		SCO	GK	2021	Ross County (OL)	Apr-May		2	0								1
Murphy	Peter	27/10/1980		ROI	D	2017	Ayr United	MANAGER	End 2022/3	0	1								2
Pettigrew	Jordan	09/10/1999		SCO	GK	2020	Dumbarton	Released Jan 2021		5	0					1			9
Purdue	Jack	20/11/1999		SCO	F	2020	Queen's Park		End 2021/2	2	0	1				2	1	1	0
Sinnamon	Ryan	22/07/1996		SCO	D	2021	East Kilbride	Relased May 2021, joined BSC Glasgow		6	1								2
Smith	Aidan	11/05/1997		SCO	F	2020	Peterhead		End 2021/2	18	4	2	2		2	3	1		0
Splaine	Aaron	13/10/1996		SCO	M	2020	FC Bruno's Magpies	Released May 2021, joined Clyde		7	2			1		2	1		1
Swinglehurst	Steven	23/10/1992		ENG	D	2012	Carlisle United		End 2021/2	11	1					4		1	2
Wallace	Tony	22/02/1991		SCO	M	2021	Gartcairn	Ex Annan		10	1	5	1						0
Watson	Peter	20/04/1986		SCO	D	2008	Albion Rovers	Retired Jan 2021									1		6
Watson	Dean	21/03/2001		SCO	F	2021	Partick Thistle (OL)	Jan-May		2	3								7
Wright	Max	06/04/1992		SCO	F	2020	Stirling Albion	OOC May 2021, joined Albion Rovers		11	1	4	2			2	2	2	3
NEW SIGNINGS																			
Adamson	Ryan	31/07/1994		SCO	GK	2021	Bo'ness United		End 2021/2										
Barnes	Charlie	08/10/2001		ENG	D	2021	Carlisle United		End 2021/2										
Birch	Charlie	23/10/2001		ENG	D	2021	Carlisle United		End 2021/2										
Docherty	Dom	22/05/1997		SCO	M	2021	Stirling Albion		End 2021/2										
Fleming	Greg	27/09/1986		SCO	GK	2021	Stranraer		End 2021/2										
Fleming	Kyle	25/02/2002		SCO	M	2021	Dundee		End 2021/2										
Goss	Tommy	14/04/1998		SCO	F	2021	Queen of the South		End 2021/2										
Johnston	Chris	03/09/1994		SCO	F	2021	Clyde		End 2021/2										
McCartney	Rob	12/05/1994		ENG	F	2021	Carlisle City		End 2021/2										
Steele	Roan	19/09/2002			D	2021	Carlisle United		End 2021/2										

Arbroath FC 2020/21 The Red Lichties

Chairman: Mike Caird
Vice Chairman: Ewen West
Treasurer: Robert Sim
Secretary: Dr Gary Callon
Directors: Gary Moir, Brian Cargill, Anne McKeown, Robert Sim, Ewen West, Jonny Booth, Douglas Bain
Safety officer: Ewen West
Head Steward: Roddy Campbell
Manager: Dick Campbell
Assistant Manager; Ian Campbell
Coach: John Young
Goalkeeper Coach: Rab Douglas
Sports Therapist: Craig Reynolds
Club Doctor: Callum Innes
Facilities & Kit Manager: Louise Walker
Facilities Coordinator: Tracy Cameron
Programme editor: Andrew Poole
Groundsman: Peter Clarke
Handyman: Gary Mann
Catering: Julie Calder

Founded	1878
Ground	Gayfield Park
Postcode	DD11 1QB
Tel	01241 872157
Capacity	6600
Closest Railway Station	Arbroath
Record Attendance	13510, v Rangers, SC, 23/2/1952
Record Win	36-0 v Bon Accord, SC, 12/9/1885
Record Defeat	1-9 v Celtic, LC, 25/8/1993
Most League Goals in a Season	45, Dave Easson, 1958/9
Most Goals in Career	120, Jimmy Jack
Colours 2020/21 Top	Maroon
Shorts	White
Sponsor	Megatech Projects
Manufacturer	Pendle
Change Colours 2020/21 Top	White with Navy trim
Shorts	Navy
Nicknames	Red Lichties
Web	www.arbroathfc.co.uk
Match Programme	The Red Lichties £2 (JJ Sports Promotions)

The Red Lichties are firmly established as the best part-time team in Scotland. At times in 2020/1 they were on the fringe of the promotion race – perhaps a lack of depth in the squad meant that they had to be content with a mid-table finish.

They failed to get any wins in their first seven games but lost just two of their next eleven. Their success was based on a very stable and strong defence of Jason Thomson, Colin Hamilton, Ricky Little and Thomas O'Brien who all had outstanding seasons. Of course they had that most wily of managers Dick Campbell pulling the strings – he motivates and organises in equal measure as well as having a great eye for a player in the loan market.

Striker Jack Hamilton from Livingston and midfielder Ben Williamson from Rangers were great temporary signings with Hamilton contributing eight goals from January onwards.

No progress was made in the Scottish Cup competition but Arbroath did qualify from their League Cup section before going out to Dunfermline Athletic.

STAR MAN
Thomas O'Brien is a Dunfermline lad who was a standout young player with Cowdenbeath. He moved to Forfar and then followed Dick Campbell to Arbroath where he has become a mainstay of their defence. He's good in the air and assured on the ground but above all has a fine temperament which means he can keep things together even when his team are under severe pressure.

PROSPECTS 2021/2
Arbroath will be the only part-time team in the Championship in 2021/2. It makes sense to think of teams who might finish below them – perhaps Morton, Queen of the South and Ayr could fall into that category. If Dick Campbell's battlers defy the odds again and stay up it will be another fantastic achievement.

Date	Comp	H/A	Opponents	F	A	HT		Referee	Crowd	Scorers
06/10/2020	LC	A	Stirling Albion	2	1	2	0	B Cook	BCD	Donnelly, O'Brien
10/10/2020	LC	H	Montrose	3	1	2	1	G Beaton	BCD	Swankie, Thomson, O'Brien
13/10/2020	LC	A	Ross County	1	2	0	0	S McLean	BCD	Hilson
17/10/2020	L	A	Raith Rovers	0	3	0	3	G Duncan	BCD	
23/10/2020	L	H	Hearts	0	1	0	0	G Aitken	BCD	
31/10/2020	L	A	Inverness CT	1	3	1	0	C Steven	BCD	Doolan
07/11/2020	L	H	Queen of the South	1	1	0	1	D Lowe	BCD	Linn
14/11/2020	LC	H	Elgin City	3	0	2	0	S McLean	BCD	Gold 2, Stewart
21/11/2020	L	H	Morton	0	0	0	0	S Reid	BCD	
28/11/2020	LC	H	Dunfermline Athletic	1	3	0	2	N Walsh	BCD	Hilson
05/12/2020	L	A	Dundee	0	1	0	1	C Graham	BCD	
12/12/2020	L	H	Alloa Athletic	0	1	0	0	P Stuart	BCD	
19/12/2020	L	H	Ayr United	2	1	2	0	D Lowe	BCD	Craigen 2
26/12/2020	L	A	Dunfermline Athletic	0	1	0	0	S Kirkland	BCD	
29/12/2020	L	A	Hearts	1	3	0	3	N Walsh	BCD	Doolan
16/01/2021	L	A	Queen of the South	2	2	0	0	S Reid	BCD	Stewart, O'Brien
22/01/2021	L	H	Dundee	1	1	0	1	G Aitken	BCD	Little
30/01/2021	L	A	Morton	1	0	0	0	D Dickinson	BCD	J Hamilton
03/02/2021	L	H	Inverness CT	1	1	1	0	A Newlands	BCD	J Hamilton
06/02/2021	L	H	Dunfermline Athletic	2	0	2	0	C Napier	BCD	O'Brien, Hilson
13/02/2021	L	A	Alloa Athletic	1	1	1	0	S Kirkland	BCD	J Hamilton
20/02/2021	L	H	Raith Rovers	1	0	0	0	G Aitken	BCD	Doolan
27/02/2021	L	A	Ayr United	1	0	0	0	G Irvine	BCD	McKenna
06/03/2021	L	H	Queen of the South	2	4	2	3	G Duncan	BCD	J Hamilton, McKenna pen
13/03/2021	L	A	Dundee	0	2	0	0	W Collum	BCD	
20/03/2021	L	H	Hearts	0	0	0	0	E Anderson	BCD	
23/03/2021	SC	H	Falkirk	1	2	1	1	D Munro	BCD	O'Brien
27/03/2021	L	A	Inverness CT	0	1	0	0	C Steven	BCD	
03/04/2021	L	H	Alloa Athletic	2	1	0	0	C Graham	BCD	J Hamilton, Gold
10/04/2021	L	A	Raith Rovers	2	2	0	1	G Duncan	BCD	J Hamilton, Little
17/04/2021	L	H	Ayr United	4	0	3	0	D Dickinson	BCD	J Hamilton, Little, Hilson, Williamson
24/04/2021	L	A	Dunfermline Athletic	3	4	2	2	S McLean	BCD	J Hamilton, Low pen, Stewart
30/04/2021	L	H	Morton	0	0	0	0	G Ross	BCD	

PHOTOCARDS

No. 34.

ARBROATH FOOTBALL CLUB.

Left to right, back row :—*J. Lowe, C. M'Nab (Capt.), J. Johnston, D. Cumming, J. A. Johnston, P. Flucker, A. Becci, G. Urquhart.* Front row :—*W. Fordyce, J. Duff, T. Connaboy, R. Grieve, A. Brand, W. Carver, W. Walker.*

Founded in 1878. Members of Scottish League (Division I). Winners of Scottish Qualifying Cup 1903/04 and are holders of the highest score (First-class Football) 36-0, recorded in Scottish Cup Tie 1885 against Bon Accord, Aberdeen. In 1935/36 they finished eleventh in League Table.

Expanding de Luxe Albums for Ardath Photocards on sale at Tobacconists Price 6d

ARDATH TOBACCO CO. LTD. Manufacturers of STATE EXPRESS and ARDATH CIGARETTES

D

Surname	First Name	Date of Birth	No	Nat	Pos	Signed	Previous	Notes	Contract	Lge A	Lge S	Lge G	SC A	SC S	SC G	LC A	LC S	LC G	Un
Craigen	James	28/03/1991	28	ENG	M	2020	AFC Fylde		End 2022/3	16	4	2	1			3	1		6
Davidson	Jake	06/10/2000		SCO	M	2021	Dundee United (OL)	Jan-May		1	0								2
Donnelly	Luke	20/01/1996	15	SCO	F	2019	Stranraer		End 2021/2	4	11					3	2	1	4
Doolan	Kris	11/12/1986	14	SCO	F	2020	Morton	Released May 2021		14	6	3				2	3		5
Douglas	Rab	24/04/1972		SCO	GK	2016	Forfar Athletic	Coach		0	0								8
Gallacher	Scott	15/07/1989	21	SCO	GK	2020	Airdrieonians	Released May 2021, joined East Fife		0	0								25
Gaston	Derek	18/04/1987	1	SCO	GK	2019	Morton		End 2021/2	27	0		1			5			0
Gold	David	01/01/1993	7	SCO	M	2015	Berwick Rangers		End 2021/2	16	7	1		1		3	1	2	4
Hamilton	Colin	07/05/1992	3	SCO	D	2016	Alloa Athletic	Brother of Jack Hamilton, Morton gk	End 2021/2	24	0		1			4			1
Hamilton	Jack	30/06/2000		SCO	F	2021	Livingston (OL)	Jan-May		14	0	8	1						1
Hilson	Dale	23/10/1992	9	SCO	F	2020	Forfar Athletic		End 2021/2	22	4	2	1			3	1	2	0
Linn	Bobby	10/10/1985	11	SCO	F	2013	Ballingry Rovers		End 2021/2	13	6	1	1			3	2		3
Little	Ricky	20/05/1989	4	SCO	D	2013	Queen's Park		End 2022/3	26	0	3	1			5			0
Low	Nicky	06/01/1992		SCO	M	2021	East Stirlingshire (OL)	Mar-May		5	1	1							0
McKenna	Michael	04/01/1991	8	SCO	M	2018	Berwick Rangers		End 2021/2	15	11	2		1		4	2		1
Moore	Lewis	04/06/1998		SCO	M	2021	Hearts (OL)	Feb-May		3	4		1						4
O'Brien	Thomas	07/08/1991	5	SCO	D	2017	Forfar Athletic		End 2023/4	26	0	2	1		1	4		2	0
Pigniatello	Carlo	16/01/2000		SCO	D	2021	Livingston (OL)	Feb-May		1	2		1						4
Ruth	Michael	08/01/2002	16	SCO	F	2020	Aberdeen (OL)	Sep-May		4	7					2	3		2
Smith	Connor	01/01/2002		SCO	M	2020	Hearts (OL)	Sep-Jan		1	2					1	3		4
Smith	Callum	11/03/1988		SCO	F	2021	Berwick Rangers (OL)	Mar-May		0	0								1
Stewart	Scott	29/04/1996	16	SCO	M	2019	Airdrieonians		End 2021/2	9	13	2	1			3	2	1	4
Swankie	Gavin	22/11/1983	10	SCO	M	2017	Forfar Athletic		End 2021/2	4	0					2	3	1	10
Thomson	Jason	26/07/1987	2	SCO	D	2018	Raith Rovers		End 2021/2	25	0					5		1	0
Virtanen	Miko	29/01/1999		FIN	M	2020	Aberdeen (OL)	Sep-Jan		8	1					3			1
Whatley	Mark	11/07/1990	6	SCO	M	2014	Spartans	Released May 2021, joined Montrose		2	3						1		18
Williamson	Ben	07/08/2001		SCO	M	2021	Rangers (OL)	Jan-May		17	0	1		1					0
NEW SIGNINGS																			
Antell	Callum	13/06/1992		WAL	GK	2021	Edinburgh City		End 2021/2										
Clark	Harrison	11/05/2003		ENG	M	2021	Livingston (OL)	Jul-May	End 2021/2										
Henderson	Liam	23/08/1996		SCO	M	2021	Edinburgh City		End 2021/2										
Low	Nicky	06/01/1992		SCO	M	2021	East Stirlingshire		End 2022/3										
Paterson	Dylan	29/04/2000		SCO	M	2021	Bo'ness Athletic		End 2021/2										
Nouble	Joel	19/01/1996		ENG	F	2021	Livingston (OL)	Jul-May	End 2021/2										

Ricky Gomes

2008-2010	FC Porto
2010-2011	Gondomar SC
2011-2012	Vitoria Guimaraes
2012-2013	SC Mindela
2013-2014	Uniao Montemor
2014-2015	RC Deportivo Fabril
2015-2016	AC Malveira
2016-2018	**Arbroath**
2018-2019	SC Olhanense
	Casa Pia AC

Gordon Marshall

Capped 3 times for England U23

1956-63	Hearts	193
1963-68	Newcastle Utd	177
1968-69	Nottm Forest	7
1969-71	Hibernian	47
1971-72	Celtic	0
1972	Aberdeen	7
1972-78	Arbroath	142

Total of 573 League games

Owned a newsagents and barbers in West Maitland Street, Edinburgh

Brian Wilson

	Arbroath Vics
1970-76	Arbroath
1976-77	Hearts
	Nairn County
1977-80	Stenhousemuir
1980-84	Dundee Violet

Date	Comp	H/A	Opponents	F	A	1	2	3	4	5	6	7	8	9	10	11	12	13	14	15	16	17	18
06/10/2020	LC	A	Stirling Albion	2	1	Gaston	Thomson	C Hamilton	Little	O'Brien	Gold>	McKenna&	Hilson+	Linn*	Donnelly<	Virtanen	Ruth*	Stewart+	Smith&	Swankie>	Doolan<	*Craigen*	*Gallacher*
10/10/2020	LC	H	Montrose	3	1	Gaston	Thomson	C Hamilton*	Little	O'Brien	Craigen+	Stewart	Smith<	Swankie	Doolan&	Ruth>	Gold*	McKenna+	Donnelly&	Linn>	Hilson<	*Virtanen*	*Gallacher*
13/10/2020	LC	A	Ross County	1	2	Gaston	Thomson	Virtanen	Little	O'Brien	Gold+	Stewart<	Hilson	McKenna&	Donnelly>	Linn*	Craigen*	Ruth+	Smith&	Doolan>	Swankie<	*Gallacher*	
17/10/2020	L	A	Raith Rovers	0	3	Gaston	Thomson	Virtanen	Little	O'Brien	Swankie	Stewart*	Hilson	McKenna+	Donnelly	Craigen&	Linn*	Smith+	Ruth&	*Gold*	*Doolan*	*Gallacher*	
23/10/2020	L	H	Hearts	0	1	Gaston	Thomson	Virtanen	Little	C Hamilton	Swankie+	Ruth	Hilson*	McKenna	Doolan&	Craigen	Linn*	Donnelly+	Gold&	*Whatley*	*Gallacher*		
31/10/2020	L	A	Inverness CT	1	3	Gaston	Thomson	Virtanen	Little	O'Brien	Hamilton	Ruth	Gold	Smith&	Doolan+	Linn*	Donnelly*	Hilson+	McKenna&	*Whatley*	*Swankie*	*Stewart*	*Douglas*
07/11/2020	L	H	Queen of the South	1	1	Gaston	Thomson	Virtanen	Little	O'Brien	Swankie+	Stewart	Hilson	McKenna	Doolan*	Linn&	Donnelly*	Gold+	Ruth&	*Craigen*	*Smith*	*C Hamilton*	*Gallacher*
14/11/2020	LC	H	Elgin City	3	0	Gaston	Thomson	C Hamilton	Little	O'Brien	Gold	Craigen>	Hilson<	McKenna+	Doolan*	Linn&	Donnelly*	Smith+	Ruth&	Swankie>	Stewart<	*Whatley*	*Douglas*
21/11/2020	L	H	Morton	0	0	Gaston	Thomson*	C Hamilton	Little	O'Brien	Gold	Craigen	Hilson&	McKenna	Doolan+	Linn	Virtanen*	Donnelly+	Stewart&	*Swankie*	*Ruth*	*Smith*	*Douglas*
28/11/2020	LC	H	Dunfermline Athletic	1	3	Gaston	Thomson	C Hamilton	Little	Stewart+	Swankie&	Craigen	Virtanen	McKenna*	Donnelly>	Ruth	Hilson*	Linn+	Whatley&	Doolan>	*Douglas*		
05/12/2020	L	A	Dundee	0	1	Gaston	Thomson	C Hamilton	Little	O'Brien	Gold	Craigen	Virtanen*	Hilson	Linn&	Ruth+	McKenna*	Stewart+	Donnelly&	*Doolan*	*Whatley*	*Swankie*	*Douglas*
12/12/2020	L	H	Alloa Athletic	0	1	Gaston	Thomson	C Hamilton	Little	O'Brien	Gold+	Craigen	Whatley&	Hilson	Doolan	Linn*	Ruth*	McKenna+	Smith&	*Swankie*	*Donnely*	*Gallacher*	*Stewart*
19/12/2020	L	H	Ayr United	2	1	Gaston	Thomson	C Hamilton	Little	O'Brien	Gold	Craigen&	Virtanen	Hilson+	Donnelly*	McKenna	Doolan*	Ruth+	Stewart&	*Swankie*	*Linn*	*Smith*	*Gallacher*
26/12/2020	L	A	Dunfermline Athletic	0	1	Gaston	Thomson	C Hamilton	Little	O'Brien	Gold	Craigen	Virtanen	Hilson&	Donnelly+	McKenna*	Stewart*	Doolan+	Ruth&	*Swankie*	*Linn*	*Smith*	*Gallacher*
29/12/2020	L	A	Hearts	1	3	Gaston	Thomson	C Hamilton	Little	O'Brien	Gold	Craigen&	Virtanen	Swankie*	Donnelly+	Doolan	Linn*	Stewart+	McKenna&	*Whatley*	*Ruth*	*Gallacher*	
16/01/2021	L	A	Queen of the South	2	2	Gaston	Thomson	C Hamilton	Davidson+	O'Brien	Gold	Craigen	Whatley*	Williamson	Doolan&	Hilson	Stewart*	Linn+	Ruth&	*Swankie*	*McKenna*	*Donnelly*	*Gallacher*
22/01/2021	L	H	Dundee	1	1	Gaston	Thomson	C Hamilton	Little	O'Brien	Gold&	Craigen*	Stewart+	Williamson	Ruth	Hilson	Linn*	McKenna+	Donnelly&	*Swankie*	*Whatley*	*Davidson*	*Gallacher*
30/01/2021	L	A	Morton	1	0	Gaston	Thomson	C Hamilton	Little	O'Brien	Gold+	McKenna	J Hamilton	Williamson	Linn&	Hilson*	Ruth*	Craigen+	Donnelly&	*Swankie*	*Stewart*	*Davidson*	*Gallacher*
03/02/2021	L	H	Inverness CT	1	1	Gaston	Thomson	C Hamilton	Little	O'Brien	McKenna	Craigen	J Hamilton+	Williamson	Linn*	Hilson&	Stewart*	Donnelly+	Doolan&	*Swankie*	*Whatley*	*Gold*	*Gallacher*
06/02/2021	L	H	Dunfermline Athletic	2	0	Gaston	Thomson	Stewart	Little	O'Brien	McKenna	Craigen	J Hamilton+	Williamson	Linn*	Hilson&	Gold*	Donnelly+	Whatley&	*Moore*	*Doolan*	*Gallacher*	
13/02/2021	L	A	Alloa Athletic	1	1	Gaston	Thomson	C Hamilton	Little	O'Brien	McKenna	Craigen	J Hamilton	Williamson+	Linn*	Hilson&	Stewart*	Gold+	Doolan&	*Moore*	*Whatley*	*Donnelly*	*Gallacher*
20/02/2021	L	H	Raith Rovers	1	0	Gaston	Thomson	C Hamilton	Little	O'Brien	McKenna+	Stewart	Doolan*	Williamson	Linn&	Hilson	Moore*	Gold+	Whatley&	*J Hamilton*	*Gallacher*		
27/02/2021	L	A	Ayr United	1	0	Gaston	Thomson	C Hamilton	Little	O'Brien	McKenna+	Stewart	J Hamilton&	Williamson	Linn*	Hilson	Moore*	Craigen+	Doolan&	*Whatley*	*Pigniatello*	*Gold*	*Gallacher*
06/03/2021	L	H	Queen of the South	2	4	Gaston	Thomson	C Hamilton	Little	O'Brien	McKenna&	Stewart+	J Hamilton	Williamson	Linn*	Hilson	Moore*	Gold+	Pigniatello&	*Whatley*	*Craigen*	*Doolan*	*Gallacher*
13/03/2021	L	A	Dundee	0	2	Gaston	Thomson	C Hamilton	Little	O'Brien	McKenna+	Stewart	J Hamilton&	Williamson*	Craigen	Hilson	Moore*	Linn+	Doolan&	*Gold*	*Pigniatello*	*Whatley*	*Gallacher*
20/03/2021	L	H	Hearts	0	0	Gaston	Pigniatello	C Hamilton	Little	O'Brien	Gold&	Doolan*	J Hamilton	Williamson	Craigen	Linn+	McKenna*	Hilson+	Stewart&	*Whatley*	*Gallacher*		
23/03/2021	SC	H	Falkirk	1	2	Gaston	Pigniatello+	C Hamilton	Little	O'Brien	Moore	Stewart&	J Hamilton	Linn*	Craigen	Hilson	Williamson*	Gold+	McKenna&	*Whatley*	*Gallacher*		
27/03/2021	L	A	Inverness CT	0	1	Gaston	Gold	C Hamilton	Little	O'Brien	McKenna&	Moore	J Hamilton	Williamson+	Craigen*	Hilson	Stewart*	Whatley+	Low&	*Pigniatello*	*Gallacher*	*Doolan*	*Smith*
03/04/2021	L	H	Alloa Athletic	2	1	Gaston	Thomson	C Hamilton	Little	O'Brien	Low&	Moore+	J Hamilton	Williamson	Gold	Doolan*	Hilson*	McKenna+	Craigen&	*Pigniatello*	*Stewart*	*Whatley*	*Gallacher*
10/04/2021	L	A	Raith Rovers	2	2	Gaston	Thomson	C Hamilton	Little	O'Brien	Low&	Moore+	J Hamilton	Williamson>	Gold	Doolan*	Hilson*	McKenna+	Stewart&	Pigniatello>	*Craigen*	*Whatley*	*Gallacher*
17/04/2021	L	H	Ayr United	4	0	Gaston	Thomson	C Hamilton	Little	O'Brien	Low+	Doolan&	J Hamilton	Williamson	Gold*	Hilson	Stewart*	McKenna+	Craigen&	*Whatley*	*Donnelly*	*Moore*	*Douglas*
24/04/2021	L	A	Dunfermline Athletic	3	4	Gaston	Thomson	C Hamilton	Little	O'Brien	Low	Doolan+	J Hamilton	Williamson	Gold*	Hilson&	Stewart*	McKenna+	Donnelly&	*Whatley*	*Craigen*	*Moore*	*Douglas*
30/04/2021	L	H	Morton	0	0	Gaston	Thomson*	C Hamilton	Little	O'Brien	Low	Doolan+	J Hamilton&	Williamson	Stewart	Hilson	Gold*	McKenna+	Donnelly&	*Whatley*	*Craigen*	*Linn*	*Douglas*

THE GOALIES

Goalkeepers Used in League Matches, 1972-2020

Players shown in the season of their first appearance only

1972/3	Gordon Marshall
1973/4	Brian Wilson
1974/5	A Campbell
1977/8	John Lister
1980/1	Eric Martin
1981/2	David Robertson
	David Larter
1983/4	Derek Jackson
1984/5	Mike McDonald
	Brian Smart
1985/6	S Jamieson
1986/7	Murray McDermott
	Eric Martin
	Brian Maxwell
1987/8	Paul Fleming
	Les Fridge
	Derek Balfour
1988/9	Hamish McAlpine
	Scott McGuinness
1991/2	Michael Harkness
1993/4	J McKeown
	Robert Duncan
1994/5	Gordon Dunn
1995/6	Craig Hinchcliffe
1996/7	Gordon Arthur
1997/8	Craig Wight
2003/4	Mark Peat
	Tony Mitchell
	Timothy Woodcock
2004/5	Neil Inglis
	Craig Coyle
2005/6	Mark Cairns
2006/7	Scott Morrison
2007/8	Darren Hill
2010/1	Darryl Burns
2011/2	Michael White
2012/3	Tony Bullock
2013/4	Sandy Wood
2014/5	David Crawford
	Mark McCallum
2015/6	Allan Fleming
2016/7	Ricky Gomes
	Robbie Mutch
2017/8	David Hutton
	Rab Douglas
2018/9	Darren Jamieson
	Darren Hill (2nd spell)
2019/0	Derek Gaston

Ayr United FC 2020/21 The Honest Men

Chairman – David Smith
Directors – Lachlan Cameron, Alan Murray, William Houston and Fraser McIntyre
Honorary Presidents – Donald R Cameron, William J Barr OBE, Andrew Charters and Alex Ingram
Company Secretary – Tracy McTrusty
General Manager – Tracy McTrusty (tracy@ayrunitedfc.co.uk)
Operations Assistant – Nicholas Provan (info@ayrunitedfc.co.uk)
Commercial Manager – Graeme Miller (commercial@ayrunitedfc.co.uk)
Safety and Stadium Manager – Roy Provan (stadium@ayrunitedfc.co.uk)
Catering Manager – Lynne Watson
Hospitality Manager – Iain Grant (hospitality@ayrunitedfc.co.uk)
First Team Manager – Mark Kerr, then David Hopkin
Assistant Manager – Michael McArdle, then Dave Timmins
Coaches: Jim Duffy, John Joyce
Physio: Steven Maguire
Goalkeeping Coach – Derek Stillie
Kit Man – Graham Steel
Grounds and Maintenance – Jason Waddell
Disability Access Officer – Roy Provan (stadium@ayrunitedfc.co.uk)
Supporter Liaison Officer – Jamie Garrett (slo@ayrunitedfc.co.uk) Twitter: @AyrSlo
Head of Youth – Davie White (david@ayrunitedfc.co.uk)
Physiotherapist – Stevie Maguire (physio@ayrunitedfc.co.uk)
Club Chaplain – Jim Smith
Programme Editor – Duncan Carmichael
Programme Team – Alistair Gemmell, David Sargent, Lisa Campbell and Jamie Stevenson
Club Photographer – David Sargent
AU Media – Calum Campbell, Iain Robb, Sunny Wyrich and Iain Martin
Club Cameraman – Willie Craig
Ayr United 5 Star Lottery – Jeanne Kerr, Janine Summers and Chris Cambers (lottery@ayrunitedfc.co.uk)
Child Welfare Officer – Stevie Maguire (physio@ayrunitedfc.co.uk)

Founded	1910
Ground	Somerset Park
Postcode	KA8 9NB
Capacity	10185
Tel	01292 263435
Closest Railway Station	Ayr
Record Attendance	25225, v Rangers, Lge, 13/9/1969
Record Win	11-1 v Dumbarton, LC 13/8/1952
Record Defeat	0-9, v Rangers 1929, v Hearts 1931, v Third Lanark 1954
Most Goals in a Season	66 Jimmy Smith, 1927/8
Most Goals in Career	213 Peter Price
Colours 2020/21 Top	White
Shorts	Black
Sponsor	Bitcoin BCH
Manufacturer	Hummell
Change Colours 2020/21 Top	Purple and Green
Shorts	Green
Nicknames	Honest Men
Web	www.ayrunitedfc.co.uk
Match Programme 2020/21	None

Ayr United reached the Semi Final of the League Cup in 1980/1. All rounds up to the Final were played over two legs with Hibs knocked out in the Quarter Finals. Ayr lost to Dundee in the Semis.

Ayr changed Manager's in mid season with Mark Kerr giving way for David Hopkirk. Kerr's tenure had not been particularly inspiring. However, Hopkirk's half season min charge also saw very mixed performances – Ayr won just one of their last ten fixtures and ended up in perilous danger of being in the relegation Play Off.

Ayr qualified from their League Cup section but were horsed 4-0 by Livingston in the first ko round. In the Scottish Cup they produced an outstanding performance to win 4-0 at Elgin before losing at home to Clyde.

The lack of a consistent goalscorer was Ayr's biggest downfall. Dario Zanatta had been signed to fill that role but was a failure. Few Ayr fans will have shed tears at the news he had moved on to Raith Rovers.

For those of us of a certain age Ayr were a top flight side in the 1870s and a very decent one at that. They qualified for the inaugural Scottish League Premier Division. Since relegation in 1978 they have seldom been close to regaining that place.

STAR MAN
Ayr benefited greatly from the services of Finnish goalkeeper Viljami Sinisalo who spent the season on loan at Somerset Park from Aston Villa. He's a Finnish Youth and Under 21 cap and has just signed a new professional contract at Villa. Great things are expected of him.

PROSPECTS 2021/2
It is difficult to see Ayr finishing above mid table in the Championship this season. They've recruited players from Morton, a team who were basically at the same level as them in 2020/1, which does not suggest a big improvement. However, this will be David Hopkirk's chance to make his own mark on the squad. Anything above mid table would be a major achievement.

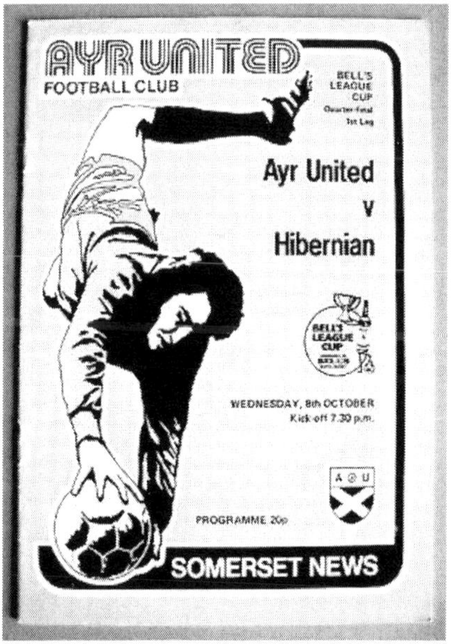

Date	Comp	H/A	Opponents	F	A		HT	Referee	Crowd	Scorers
06/10/2020	LC	A	Albion Rovers	5	2		3 2	D Lowe	BCD	Anderson 2, McCowan, Walsh, Zanatta
10/10/2020	LC	A	Hamilton Accies	1	2		0 2	C Steven	BCD	Moffat
13/10/2020	LC	H	Annan Athletic	1	0		1 0	G Irvine	BCD	Moffat pen
17/10/2020	L	H	Queen of the South	2	1		2 0	S McLean	BCD	Miller 2
24/10/2020	L	A	Inverness CT	1	1		0 0	A Muir	BCD	Cameron
31/10/2020	L	A	Morton	2	3		1 0	G Aitken	BCD	Strapp og, Smith
07/11/2020	L	H	Dunfermline Athletic	0	0		0 0	C Napier	BCD	
14/11/2020	LC	H	Stranraer	1	1	6-5p	0 1	B Cook	BCD	McCowan
21/11/2020	L	H	Dundee	2	0		2 0	G Beaton	BCD	Smith, Moffat
28/11/2020	LC	A	Livingston	0	4		0 4	D Munro	BCD	
05/12/2020	L	A	Alloa Athletic	2	0		1 0	B Cook	BCD	McCowan, Murdoch
11/12/2020	L	H	Raith Rovers	0	0		0 0	A Muir	BCD	
19/12/2020	L	A	Arbroath	1	2		0 2	D Lowe	BCD	Baird
26/12/2020	L	A	Hearts	3	5		0 1	D Munro	BCD	C Smith, McCowan, Walsh
29/12/2020	L	H	Morton	1	1		1 1	G Duncan	BCD	McCowan
02/01/2021	L	A	Queen of the South	2	3		1 2	G Aitken	BCD	Reading, Buchanan og
23/01/2021	L	A	Dunfermline Athletic	0	0		0 0	D Robertson	BCD	
30/01/2021	L	H	Alloa Athletic	4	1		2 1	P Stuart	BCD	McCowan 2, Walsh, Muirhead pen
05/02/2021	L	H	Hearts	0	1		0 0	S McLean	BCD	
20/02/2021	L	H	Inverness CT	0	2		0 1	P Stuart	BCD	
27/02/2021	L	H	Arbroath	0	1		0 0	G Irvine	BCD	
06/03/2021	L	A	Morton	2	0		0 0	M Roncone	BCD	C Smith 2
09/03/2021	L	A	Raith Rovers	0	0		0 0	S Lambie	BCD	
13/03/2021	L	A	Hearts	0	2		0 0	C Steven	BCD	
16/03/2021	L	A	Dundee	3	1		1 0	A Newlands	BCD	McKenzie 2, C Smith
20/03/2021	L	H	Raith Rovers	1	1		0 0	D Dickinson	BCD	Muirhead
23/03/2021	SC	A	Elgin City	4	0		4 0	C Napier	BCD	Chalmers, Moffat, McCowan 2
27/03/2021	L	A	Alloa Athletic	2	2		1 1	A Muir	BCD	Walsh, Robertson og
03/04/2021	SC	H	Clyde	0	1		0 1	D Munro	BCD	
06/04/2021	L	H	Dundee	0	3		0 0	S McLean	BCD	
10/04/2021	L	H	Dunfermline Athletic	1	1		1 1	G Aitken	BCD	Miller
17/04/2021	L	A	Arbroath	0	4		0 3	G Duncan	BCD	
24/04/2021	L	H	Queen of the South	0	0		0 0	N Walsh	BCD	
30/04/2021	L	A	Inverness CT	2	2		1 1	C Napier	BCD	Muirhead, Todd

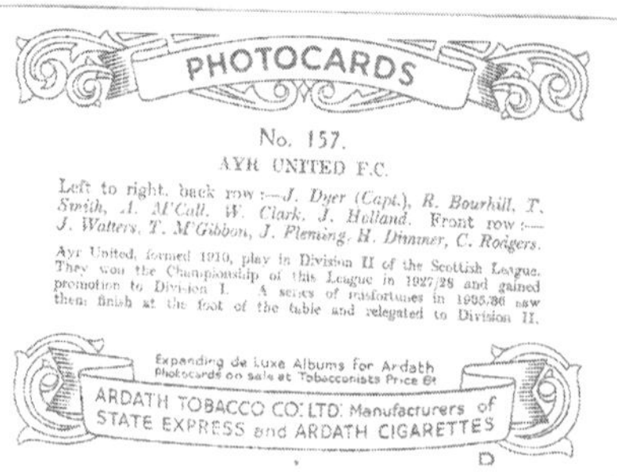

PHOTOCARDS

No. 157.

AYR UNITED F.C.

Left to right, back row:—*J. Dyer (Capt.), R. Bourhill, T. Smith, A. M'Call. W. Clark. J. Holland.* Front row:—*J. Watters, T. M'Gibbon, J. Fleming, H. Dinmer, C. Rodgers.*

Ayr United, formed 1910, play in Division II of the Scottish League. They won the Championship of this League in 1927/28 and gained promotion to Division I. A series of misfortunes in 1935/36 saw them finish at the foot of the table and relegated to Division II.

Expanding de Luxe Albums for Ardath Photocards on sale at Tobacconists Price 6d

ARDATH TOBACCO CO. LTD. Manufacturers of STATE EXPRESS and ARDATH CIGARETTES

D

Date	Comp	H/A	Opponents	F	A	1	2	3	4	5	6	7	8	9	10	11	12	13	14	15	16	17	18	19	20
06/10/2020	LC	A	Albion Rovers	5	2	Sinisalo	Muirhead	Miller	Baird	Roscoe	Chalmers	Murdoch+	Walsh*	McCowan>	Moffat&	Anderson	Zanatta*	Hewitt+	P Smith&	McKenzie>	*Kerr*	*Houston*	*Hare-Reid*		
10/10/2020	LC	A	Hamilton Accies	1	2	Sinisalo	Muirhead	Miller*	Baird	Roscoe	Chalmers	Murdoch	Zanatta	McCowan	Moffat	McKenzie+	Hewitt*	P Smith+	*Houston*	*Love*	*Kerr*	*Hare-Reid*			
13/10/2020	LC	H	Annan Athletic	1	0	Sinisalo	Muirhead	Hewitt	Baird	Roscoe	Chalmers	Murdoch+	Zanatta*	McCowan	Moffat	McKenzie	P Smith*	Houston+	*Miller*	*Love*	*Kerr*	*Hare-Reid*			
17/10/2020	L	H	Queen of the South	2	1	Sinisalo	Muirhead	Miller	Baird	Roscoe	Chalmers	Murdoch	Reading	McCowan	Moffat	Anderson*	McKenzie*	*Houston*	*P Smith*	*Love*	*Kerr*	*Hewitt*	*Hare-Reid*		
24/10/2020	L	A	Inverness CT	1	1	Sinisalo	Muirhead	Miller	Baird	Roscoe	Chalmers*	Murdoch	Reading	C Smith&	Moffat+	Anderson	Cameron*	Houston+	Hewitt&	*P Smith*	*Kerr*	*McKenzie*	*Hare-Reid*		
31/10/2020	L	A	Morton	2	3	Sinisalo	Muirhead	Reading	Baird	Roscoe	Chalmers	Murdoch	C Smith&	McCowan	Moffat*	Anderson+	Houston*	Cameron+	Miller&	*P Smith*	*Hewitt*	*McKenzie*	*Hare-Reid*		
07/11/2020	L	H	Dunfermline Athletic	0	0	Sinisalo	Houston	Reading	Baird	Roscoe	Chalmers	Murdoch&	C Smith	McCowan*	Moffat	Anderson+	Zanatta*	Cameron+	Miller&	*P Smith*	*Hewitt*	*McKenzie*	*Hare-Reid*		
14/11/2020	LC	H	Stranraer	1	1 6-5p	Sinisalo	Houston	Miller	Baird	Roscoe	Chalmers	Hewitt+	Zanatta*	McCowan	Moffat	Anderson	McKenzie*	Kerr+	*Murdoch*	*P Smith*	*Hare-Reid*				
21/11/2020	L	H	Dundee	2	0	Sinisalo	Houston	Miller	Baird	Roscoe	Chalmers	Murdoch	Reading	McCowan*	Moffat&	C Smith+	McKenzie*	Cameron+	Zanatta&	*Hewitt*	*Kerr*	*Anderson*	*Hare-Reid*		
28/11/2020	LC	A	Livingston	0	4	Sinisalo	Houston&	Reading	Baird	Roscoe	Chalmers	Murdoch*	Miller	McCowan	Moffat>	Cameron+	Zanatta*	Muirhead+	McKenzie&	*Anderson>*	*Smith*	*Hewitt*	*Hare-Reid*	*Kerr*	
05/12/2020	L	A	Alloa Athletic	2	0	Sinisalo	Muirhead	Houston	Baird	Roscoe	Chalmers	Murdoch	C Smith	McCowan	Moffat*	Anderson+	Miller*	McKenzie+	*Zanatta*	*Reading*	*Walsh*	*Cameron*	*Hare-Reid*		
11/12/2020	L	H	Raith Rovers	0	0	Sinisalo	Muirhead	Houston	Baird	Roscoe	Chalmers+	Murdoch	Miller	McCowan*	Moffat	Anderson	Zanatta*	Cameron+	*McKenzie*	*Reading*	*Kerr*	*Hewitt*	*Hare-Reid*		
19/12/2020	L	A	Arbroath	1	2	Sinisalo	Muirhead	Reading	Baird	Roscoe	Chalmers	Murdoch&	Miller*	McCowan	Moffat	Anderson+	Zanatta*	McKenzie+	Smith&	*Hewitt*	*Walsh*	*Houston*	*Hare-Reid*		
26/12/2020	L	A	Hearts	3	5	Sinisalo	Muirhead	Reading	Baird	Roscoe	Chalmers&	Murdoch	Miller	McCowan	Moffat*	C Smith+	Anderson*	Zanatta+	Walsh&	*Houston*	*McKenzie*	*Kerr*	*Hare-Reid*		
29/12/2020	L	H	Morton	1	1	Sinisalo	Muirhead	Reading	Baird	Kerr	Chalmers	Murdoch	Houston	McCowan&	Moffat*	C Smith+	Zanatta*	Walsh+	Anderson&	*McKenzie*	*Miller*	*Roscoe*	*Hare-Reid*		
02/01/2021	L	A	Queen of the South	2	3	Sinisalo	Miller	Reading	Baird	Roscoe	Chalmers	Murdoch&	Walsh*	McCowan	Zanatta+	C Smith	Moffat*	McKenzie+	Hewitt&	*Houston*	*Kerr*	*P Smith*	*Hare-Reid*		
23/01/2021	L	A	Dunfermline Athletic	0	0	Sinisalo	Muirhead	Miller	Baird	Ndaba	Chalmers	Murdoch	Walsh	McCowan	Zanatta*	C Smith	Moffat*	*McKenzie*	*Reading*	*Kerr*	*Roscoe*	*Houston*	*Hare-Reid*		
30/01/2021	L	H	Alloa Athletic	4	1	Sinisalo	Muirhead	Miller	Baird	Ndaba	Chalmers	Murdoch	Walsh+	McCowan	Wright*	C Smith&	Moffat*	Zanatta+	McKenzie&	*Hewitt*	*Roscoe*	*Reading*	*Hare-Reid*		
05/02/2021	L	H	Hearts	0	1	Sinisalo	Muirhead	Miller&	Baird	Ndaba	Chalmers+	Murdoch	Walsh*	McCowan	Wright	C Smith	Moffat*	McGavin+	McKenzie&	*Zanatta`*	*Roscoe*	*Reading*	*Hare-Reid*		
20/02/2021	L	H	Inverness CT	0	2	Sinisalo	Muirhead	Miller*	Baird	Ndaba	Chalmers	Murdoch	Walsh&	McCowan	Moffat	C Smith+	McKenzie*	Hewitt+	Zanatta&	*McGavin*	*Roscoe*	*Reading*	*Hare-Reid*		
27/02/2021	L	H	Arbroath	0	1	Urminsky	Muirhead	Reading	Baird	Ndaba	Chalmers	Houston*	Walsh+	McCowan	Zanatta	C Smith&	Murdoch*	McKenzie+	Moffat&	*McGavin*	*Roscoe*	*Miller*	*Hare-Reid*		
06/03/2021	L	A	Morton	2	0	Sinisalo	Muirhead	Reading	Baird	Ndaba	Murdoch	Houston*	Walsh&	McCowan	McKenzie+	C Smith	Miller*	Moffat+	Chalmers&	*P Smith*	*Roscoe*	*Zanatta*	*Urminsky*		
09/03/2021	L	A	Raith Rovers	0	0	Sinisalo	Muirhead	Reading	Baird	Ndaba	Murdoch	Houston*	Walsh	McCowan	Moffat+	C Smith&	Miller*	Chalmers+	McKenzie&	*P Smith*	*Roscoe*	*Zanatta*	*Sandberg*		
13/03/2021	L	A	Hearts	0	2	Sinisalo	Muirhead	Reading	Baird	Ndaba	Murdoch	Houston	Walsh*	McCowan	Moffat+	C Smith&	Chalmers*	Zanatta+	McKenzie&	*Miller*	*Roscoe*	*McGavin*	*Urminsky*		
16/03/2021	L	A	Dundee	3	1	Sinisalo	Muirhead	Reading	Baird	Ndaba	Miller+	Houston	Chalmers	McCowan&	McKenzie+	C Smith*	Murdoch*	Moffat+	Walsh&	*Zanatta`*	*Roscoe*	*McGavin*	*Urminsky*		
20/03/2021	L	H	Raith Rovers	1	1	Sinisalo	Muirhead	Reading	Baird	Ndaba	Murdoch	Houston	Chalmers*	McCowan	McKenzie+	C Smith	Moffat*	Walsh+	*Barjonas*	*Zanatta`*	*Roscoe*	*Miller*	*Urminsky*		
23/03/2021	SC	A	Elgin City	4	0	Sinisalo	Miller	Reading	Baird	Ndaba*	Walsh	Houston	Chalmers	McCowan	Moffat&	C Smith+	Roscoe*	Barjonas+	McKenzie&	*Zanatta`*	*Murdoch*	*Hewitt*	*P Smith*	*Urminsky*	
27/03/2021	L	A	Alloa Athletic	2	2	Sinisalo	Muirhead	Reading	Baird	Murdoch+	Walsh	Houston	Miller	McCowan	Moffat*	C Smith	McKenzie*	Barjonas+&	Hewitt&	*Zanatta`*	*Roscoe*	*P Smith*	*Urminsky*		
03/04/2021	SC	H	Clyde	0	1	Sinisalo	Muirhead	Reading	Baird	Roscoe	Walsh*	Chalmers	Miller&	McCowan	Moffat+	McKenzie	Todd*	Wright+	Barjonas&	*Zanatta`*	*Houston*	*P Smith*	*Murdoch*	*Hewitt*	*Urminsky*
06/04/2021	L	H	Dundee	0	3	Sinisalo	Muirhead	Reading	Baird	Chalmers+	Todd*	Houston	Murdoch&	McCowan>	Ndaba	McKenzie	Walsh*	Wright+	Barjonas&	Moffat>	*Roscoe*	*Miller*	*Urminsky*		
10/04/2021	L	H	Dunfermline Athletic	1	1	Morrison	Muirhead	Reading	Baird	Roscoe	Miller	Houston	Barjonas	McCowan*	Ndaba	McKenzie	Wright*	*Chalmers*	*Zanatta*	*Hewitt*	*Murdoch*	*Walsh*	*Urminsky*		
17/04/2021	L	A	Arbroath	0	4	Morrison	Muirhead	Reading	Baird	Roscoe*	Miller	Houston	Barjonas+	McCowan	Ndaba	Wright&	McKenzie*	Todd+	Walsh&	*Moffat*	*Chalmers*	*Murdoch*	*Urminsky*		
24/04/2021	L	H	Queen of the South	0	0	Morrison	Muirhead	Reading	Baird	Roscoe	Todd*	Houston	Chalmers+	McCowan	Moffat*	McKenzie	Zanatta*	Walsh+	*Miller*	*Wright*	*Barjonas*	*Murdoch*	*Urminsky*		
30/04/2021	L	A	Inverness CT	2	2	Morrison	Muirhead	Reading	Baird	Roscoe	Miller*	Houston	Chalmers	McCowan&	Moffat+	Todd	McKenzie*	Walsh+	Murdoch&	*Wright*	*Barjonas*	*Zanatta*	*Urminsky*		

THE GOALIES

Goalkeepers Used in League Matches, 1970-2020

Players shown in the season of their first appearance only

1970/1	David Stewart
	Jim Gilmour
1971/2	Alistair McLean
1974/5	Ian McGiffen
	Hugh Sproat
1976/7	Andy Geoghegan
1978/9	Richard Northcote
1979/0	Stuart Rennie
1981/2	Jim Brown
1982/3	Scott MacKay
1984/5	David Purdie
1987/8	George Watson
1989/0	Alan Rough
1990/1	Willie Cunningham
	Cammy Duncan
1991/2	M Robertson
1992/3	Willie Spence
1994/5	Scott McIntosh
	George Grierson
1995/6	Willie Lamont
	Kenny Barnstaple
	Henry Smith
1996/7	David Castilla
1997/8	Kevin McKeown
	Kristijan Finboggasson
1998/9	Craig Nelson
1999/0	Thomas Gill
	Jens-Martin Knudsen
	Marius Rovde
	John Dodds
2003/4	Ludovic Roy
	John Hillcoat
2004/5	Peter Cherrie
2005/6	Mark McGeown
2006/7	Ally Brown
2007/8	Barry Corr
2008/9	Stephen Grindlay
2009/0	Craig Samson
2010/1	David Crawford
	Alan Main
	Alan Martin
2011/2	Kevin Cuthbert
	R McWilliams
2012/3	Ally Brown (2nd spell)
	Darren Martin
	E Bain
	Graeme Smith
2013/4	David Hutton
2015/6	Greg Fleming
2017/8	Jordan Hart
	Jack Ruddy
2018/9	Ross Doohan

Surname	First Name	Date of Birth	No	Nat	Pos	Signed	Previous	Notes	Contract	Lge			SC			LC			
										A	S	G	A	S	G	A	S	G	Un
Anderson	Bruce	23/09/1998		SCO	F	2020	Aberdeen (OL)	Oct-Jan		7	2					2	1	2	1
Baird	Jack	07/02/1996	30	SCO	D	2020	St Mirren		End 2021/2	27	0	1	2			5			0
Baird	Nathan	24/06/1999		SCO	D	2017	Ayr United Youths	OL to Irvine M Nov-, Freed May joined Cumnock											0
Barjonas	Jamie	24/01/1999		SCO / ENG	M	2021	Rangers (OL)	Mar-May		2	2			2					3
Cameron	Innes	22/08/2000	15	SCO	F	2020	Kilmarnock (OL)	Oct-Jan		0	5	1				1			1
Chalmers	Joe	03/01/1994	18	SCO	M	2020	Ross County		End 2021/2	21	3		2		1	5			2
Ecrepont	Finn	30/07/2002		SCO	D	2019	Ayr United Youths	OL to Albion Rovers Aug-May	End 2021/2	0	0								0
Hare-Reid	Ellis	12/01/1999	21	NEZ / SCO	GK	2018	Ayr United Youths	Freed March 2021		0	0								21
Hewitt	Mikey	23/10/2000	20	SCO	D	2019	Ayr United Youths		End 2021/2	0	4					2	2		10
Houston	Jordan	28/01/2000	2	SCO	D	2020	Rangers		End 2021/2	17	2		1			2	1		8
Kerr	Mark	02/03/1982	27	SCO	M	2018	Falkirk	Left by mutual consent Feb 2021		1	0						1		11
Love	Ross	11/09/2001		SCO	D	2019	Ayr United Youths	OL to Annan Athletic Oct-May	U20	0	0								3
McCowan	Luke	09/12/1997	11	SCO	F	2017	Ayr United Youths	OOC May 2021, joined Dundee		26	0	5	2		2	5		2	0
McGavin	Brett	21/12/1999		SCO	F	2021	Ipswich Town (OL)	Feb-Mar											
McKenzie	Mark	17/08/2000	22	SCO	F	2019	Ayr United Youths		End 2021/2	6	14	2	1	1		2	2		7
Miller	Michael	31/12/1994	8	SCO	M	2020	Raith Rovers		End 2021/2	16	5	3	2			4			7
Miller	Liam	09/06/2000		SCI	M	2020	Ayr United Youths	Released May 2021											
Moffat	Michael	15/02/1985	7	SCO	F	2017	Dunfermline Athletic		End 2021/2	16	9	1	2		1	5		2	1
Moore	Craig	16/08/1994	9	SCO	F	2017	Motherwell	Released May 2021, joined Darvel		0	0								0
Morrison	PJ	27/02/1998		SCO	GK	2021	Motherwell (OL)	Apr-May		4	0								0
Muirhead	Aaron	30/08/1990	4	SCO	D	2019	Falkirk		End 2021/2	24	0	3	1			3	1		0
Murdoch	Andy	30/01/1995	6	SCO	M	2018	Morton		End 2021/2	21	3	1				4			6
Ndaba	Corrie	25/12/1999		ROI	D	2021	Ipswich Town (OL)	Jan-May		13	1		1						4
Reading	Patrick	29/03/1999	3	SCO	D	2020	Stevenage		End 2021/2	18	0	1	2			1			6
Roscoe	Sam	16/06/1998	5	ENG	D	2019	Aberdeen	OOC May 2021, joined Linfield		17	0		1	1		5			13
Sandberg	Luca	03/01/2003		SCO	GK	2020	St Mirren Youths		U20	0	0								1
Sinisalo	Viljami	11/10/2001	1	FIN	GK	2020	Aston Villa (OL)	Sep-May		22	0		2			5			0
Smith	Paul	30/03/2002		SCO	F	2019	Ayr United Youths		End 2021/2	0	0						3		12
Smith	Cammy	24/08/1995		SCO	F	2020	Dundee United (OL)	Oct-Jan		19	1	6	1						0
Todd	Josh	11/06/1994		ENG	M	2021	Falkirk (OL)	Mar-May		3	1	1		1					0
Urminsky	Peter	24/05/1999		SVK	GK	2021	St Mirren (OL)	Feb-May		1	0								12
Walsh	Tom	11/07/1996	10	SCO	M	2020	Inverness CT	OOC June 2021, joined Inverness CT		10	8	3	2			1		1	3
Wright	Andre	07/12/1996		ENG	F	2021	Bohemians Dublin	Released May 2021		3	2			1					2
Zanatta	Dario	24/05/1997	19	CAN	F	2020	Partick Thistle	OOC May 2021, joined Raith Rovers		3	10					3	2	1	11
Own Goals												3							
NEW SIGNINGS																			
Adeloye	Tomi	17/02/1996		ENG / NIG	F	2021	Barnet		End 2021/2										
Albionson	Charlie	15/10/1986		ENG	GK	2021	Warrington Town		End 2021/2										
Fjortoft	Markus	12/01/1994		NOR	D	2021	Morton		End 2021/2										
McAdams	Aidan	23/03/1999		SCO	GK	2021	Morton		End 2021/2										
McAllister	Nicky	17/01/2001		SCO	D	2021	St Mirren		End 2021/2										
McGinty	Sean	11/08/1993		ROI / ENG	D	2021	Morton		End 2021/2										
Salkeld	Cameron	06/12/1998		ENG	F	2021	Morton		End 2021/2										

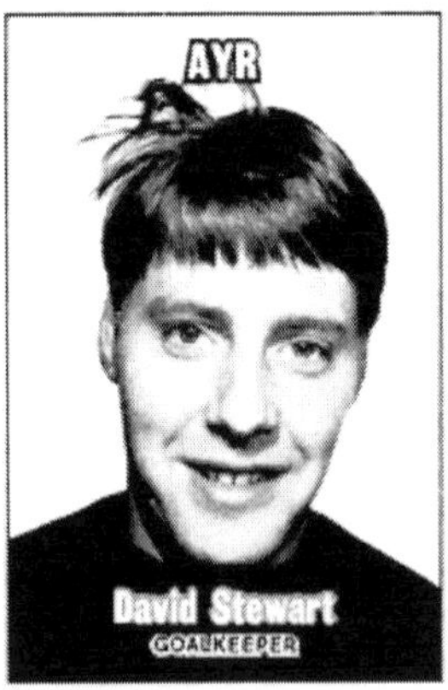

David Stewart

One Full cap for Scotland, 1977/8 v German Democratic Republic

Played for Leeds United in the 1974/5 European Cup Final against Bayern Munich in the Parc des Princes, losing 0-2

Hugh Sproat

334 Scottish League appearances for Ayr United and Motherwell, formerly with Auchinleck Talbot

Kristjan Finnbogason

Career Clubs:
KR Reykjavik, IA Akranes, **Ayr United**, KR Reykjavik, Lommel SK, Grotta, Fylkir, Hafnarfjordur

20 full caps for Iceland

Brechin City FC 2020/21 City

Founded	1906
Ground	Glebe Park
Postcode	DD9 6BJ
Tel	01356 622856
Capacity	3960
Closest Railway Station	Montrose
Record Attendance	8122 v Aberdeen, SC 3/2/1973
Record Win	12-1 v Thornhill, SC, 28/1/1926
Record Defeat	0-10, v Airdrieonians, Albion Rovers & Cowdenbeath, 1937/8
Most League Goals in a Season	26 Ronald McIntosh, 1959/60
Most Goals in Career	131 Ian Campbell
Colours 2020/21 Top	Red with white trim
Shorts	Red
Sponsor	Glencadam Distillery
Manufacturer	Pendle
Change Colours 2020/21 Top	White
Shorts	White
Nicknames	City
Web	www.brechincity.com
Match Programme 2020/21	None

Manager: Mark Wilson, then Michael Paton, then Andy Kirk
Assistant Manager: Stevie Campbell, then Stephen Simmons / Craig Nelson
Physio: Seb Panczyk
Chairman: Ken Ferguson
Vice Chairman: Martin Smith
Secretary: Grant Hood
Director: Kevan Innes, Gary Ross, Anton Gerlings, Ian Jardine, Bobby Black
At an EGM in June the club constitution was altered and a new Interim Management Committee established: Kevin Mackie, Grant Johnson, Murray Lindsay, David Taylor, Grant Turriff, Clark Renilson, Arlene Wood
Club Advisor (from June 2021): Craig Levein
Honorary President: David H Birse
Honorary Vice President: Hugh Campbell Adamson
Honorary Life Members: David Lindsay, Ian Jardine, Gus Fairlie
Media team: Media Team: Keith Johnston, Steven Mew, Graeme Youngson, Derek Watt, Corrie Robb

It is just three years since Brechin City were in the Championship. Relegated in 2017/18, and again in 2018/19, only the early termination of season 2019/20 saved them from a third successive drop. 2020/1 proved no better and after a nightmare campaign they lost home and away in the League Two play off to Lowland League Champions Brechin City.

Where did it go wrong? Brechin stuck with Manager Darren Dods through their torrid Championship and league One seasons. The appointment of Mark Wilson did not arrest their decline and he was sacked early in the season. Very surprisingly the job was given to City player Michael Paton who had no real relevant experience. After an early season win over Albion Rovers, City then went 16 games without a win including crashing out of the Scottish Cup against Linlithgow Rose. Even an influx of fresh players in February and March made little difference. When they did win a game, 2-0 at Cowdenbeath, it was already too late to give them any realistic hope of avoiding bottom place. Any hope they had in the play off evaporated early in the second leg when they were reduced to ten men – Rangers loan player Colin McKee was sent off for homophobic abuse.

Diversions were caused as Brechin canvassed support for reorganisation schemes to save their own skin. Some of their statements and attitudes lost the club a lot of long-term friends and allies.

And so ended a long history for Brechin City in the Scottish league. At times they were whipping boys but since the early 1980s they have had good spells outside the bottom division. They always seemed to be a well-run with Directors and officials who adopted a cautious and pragmatic approach. All the excellent work of guys like David Will and George Johnston has now been undone with relegation to the Highland League.

STAR MAN
Very few City players were regulars throughout the season and it impossible to pick out anyone who made an exceptional contribution.

PROSPECTS 2021/2
The club have undergone a structural change and a change of Board. Andy Kirk and Craig Levein have ben brought in to spearhead a revival of the club's fortunes. But if they expect the Highland League to be plain sailing then Brora, Buckie and Fraserburgh might have something to say about that. They need to finish above them, then beat the Lowland League Champions and then Club 42. Brechin were one of the clubs who signed up to a plan that makes it difficult to drop out of the SPFL – which by definition also means it is even harder to return if you do.

BRECHIN'S 1957 LEAGUE CUP RUN

Section		
Aug 10	H v Ayr United	5-2
Aug 14	A v Cowdenbeath	1-1
Aug 17	H v Dunfermline Ath	2-1
Aug 24	A v Ayr United	2-4
Aug 28	H v Cowdenbeath	7-1
Aug 31	A v Dunfermline Ath	1-3
QF		
Sep 11	A v Hamilton Accies	4-2
Sep 14	H v Hamilton Accies	1-0
SF		
Sep 28	N v Rangers	0-4 (at Hampden)

Date	Comp	H/A	Opponents	F	A	HT		Referee	Crowd	Scorers
07/10/2020	LC	H	Dundee United	2	6	0	3	S Kirkland	BCD	Inglis pen, Currie
10/10/2020	LC	A	St Johnstone	0	7	0	2	C Napier	BCD	
13/10/2020	LC	A	Peterhead	1	3	0	3	C Graham	BCD	Inglis
17/10/2020	L	H	Edinburgh City	1	5	0	1	G Beaton	BCD	Scott
24/10/2020	L	A	Elgin City	0	3	0	1	K Graham	BCD	
31/10/2020	L	A	Albion Rovers	2	0	1	0	S Reid	BCD	Makovora, Todd
07/11/2020	L	H	Stirling Albion	0	5	0	2	G Ross	BCD	
14/11/2020	LC	H	Kelty Hearts	0	2	0	1	G Grainger	BCD	
21/11/2020	L	A	Queen's Park	0	3	0	2	C Graham	BCD	
28/11/2020	L	H	Stranraer	1	4	1	1	S Reid	BCD	Bollan
05/12/2020	L	A	Stenhousemuir	1	2	0	2	D Williams	BCD	Motherwell
19/12/2020	L	A	Cowdenbeath	0	2	0	1	B Cook	BCD	
22/12/2020	L	H	Annan Athletic	0	0	0	0	M McDermid	BCD	
26/12/2020	SC	H	Linlithgow Rose	2	3	1	1	D Dickinson	BCD	Currie, Inglis
20/03/2021	L	A	Stirling Albion	0	1	0	0	B Cook	BCD	
23/03/2021	L	A	Stranraer	0	2	0	0	K Graham	BCD	
27/03/2021	L	H	Queen's Park	0	2	0	2	P Stuart	BCD	
30/03/2021	L	H	Elgin City	1	2	1	0	C Scott	BCD	Barron
06/04/2021	L	H	Stenhousemuir	1	1	1	1	S Lambie	BCD	Inglis
10/04/2021	L	H	Albion Rovers	2	4	1	2	G Ross	BCD	Currie, M Paton
13/04/2021	L	A	Edinburgh City	1	2	1	1	K Graham	BCD	Barr
17/04/2021	L	A	Annan Athletic	0	3	0	3	C Graham	BCD	
20/04/2021	L	H	Cowdenbeath	0	0	0	0	M McDermid	BCD	
27/04/2021	L	A	Cowdenbeath	2	0	1	0	M Roncone	BCD	McKee, Barr
29/04/2021	L	H	Annan Athletic	0	3	0	1	D Lowe	BCD	
01/05/2021	L	A	Albion Rovers	1	1	0	0	B Reid	BCD	Inglis pen
04/05/2021	L	H	Stenhousemuir	0	1	0	0	G Ross	BCD	
18/05/2021	PO	A	Kelty Hearts	1	2	1	2	G Duncan	250	Page
23/05/2021	PO	H	Kelty Hearts	0	1	0	0	C Napier	250	

PHOTOCARDS

No. 33.

BRECHIN CITY F.C.

Left to right, back row:—*D. Clark (Vice-President), E. M'Donald, D. M'Donald, P. Robertson, W. Milne, J. Morrison (Capt.), W. Cooper, H. Young (Sec.).* Front row:—*J. Taylor, J. Reid, W. Wann, P. Bolan, J. Whyte.*

Club was founded in 1906, but did not join the Second Division of the Scottish League until 1929/30. Originally members of Northern League of which they were champions 1907/08.

Expanding de Luxe Albums for Ardath Photocards on sale at Tobacconists Price 6d

ARDATH TOBACCO CO: LTD: Manufacturers of STATE EXPRESS and ARDATH CIGARETTES

D

Date	Comp	H/A	Opponents	F	A	1	2	3	4	5	6	7	8	9	10	11	12	13	14	15	16	17	18	19	20
07/10/2020	LC	H	Dundee United	2	6	McMinn	Page	Jordan	Scott+	McIntosh	Mackay	Inglis	Todd&	Cusick*	Currie	Makovora	M Paton*	Nawrocki+	Luissint&	Reekie	Brown	Bollan	O'Neill		
10/10/2020	LC	A	St Johnstone	0	7	McMinn	Brown	Jordan	Inglis	McIntosh>	Mackay+	M Paton	Todd	Cusick	Currie&	Makovora*	Scott*	Reekie+	Luissint&	Bollan>	Page	Nawrocki	O'Neill		
13/10/2020	LC	A	Peterhead	1	3	O'Neil	Page	Bollan	Reekie	McIntosh+	Mackay	M Paton	Todd*	Luissint>	Scott&	Nawrocki	Inglis*	Cusick+	Currie&	Makovora>	Brown	Jordan	McMinn		
17/10/2020	L	H	Edinburgh City	1	5	McMinn	Page+	Jordan	Inglis	McIntosh	Mackay	Currie	Todd	Cusick	Scott&	Makovora*	M Paton*	Brown+	Nawrocki&	Bollan	Luissint	Reekie	O'Neill		
24/10/2020	L	A	Elgin City	0	3	McMinn	Page	Bollan	Inglis&	McIntosh*	Mackay	Currie	Todd	Cusick+	M Paton	Barron	Reekie*	Makovora+	Scott&	Jordan	Luissint	Nawrocki	Brown	O'Neill	
31/10/2020	L	A	Albion Rovers	2	0	McMinn	Jordan	Bollan	Scott+	Brown	Mackay	Currie	Todd	Barron	M Paton+	Makovora*	Nawricki*	Inglis+	Page	McIntosh	Luissint	Reekie	O'Neill		
07/11/2020	L	H	Stirling Albion	0	5	McMinn	Jordan	Bollan	Scott	Brown	Mackay	Currie&	Todd+	Barron	M Paton	Makovora*	McIntosh*	Nawrocki+	Inglis&	Coupe	Luissint	Reekie	Trialist	Page	
14/11/2020	LC	H	Kelty Hearts	0	2	McMinn	Jordan	Bollan	Scott	Reekie	McLevy	Inglis+	Todd	Barron	M Paton	Makovora*	Currie*	Nawrocki+	Brown	Coupe	Luissint	Page			
21/11/2020	L	A	Queen's Park	0	3	McMinn	McLevy	Bollan	Scott	Reekie	Mackay	Inglis+	Todd	Barron	M Paton	Nawrocki*	Coupe*	Luissint+	Makovora	Brown	O'Neill				
28/11/2020	L	H	Stranraer	1	4	McMinn	Jordan	Bollan	McLevy	Coupe	Mackay	Inglis*	Todd+	Barron	M Paton	Currie	C Paton*	Cusick+	Nawrocki	Brown	Luissint	Reekie	O'Neill		
05/12/2020	L	A	Stenhousemuir	1	2	O'Neil	Jordan	Bollan*	McLevy	Motherwell	Mackay	C Paton+	Todd	Barron	M Paton	Currie	Reekie*	Coupe+	Nawrocki	Brown	Luissint	Inglis	Cusick	McMinn	
19/12/2020	L	A	Cowdenbeath	0	2	O'Neil	Jordan	Bollan	McLevy	Reekie	Scott	Coupe+	Todd	Barron	M Paton	Currie*	C Paton*	Luissint+	Page	Brown	Cusick	Inglis	Trialist	McMinn	
22/12/2020	L	H	Annan Athletic	0	0	O'Neil	Jordan	Page	McLevy	Reekie	Scott*	Coupe	Todd	Barron	M Paton	C Paton+	Currie*	Cusick+	Luissint&	Brown	McKay	Inglis	Trialist	McMinn	
26/12/2020	SC	H	Linlithgow Rose	2	3	O'Neil	Jordan	Page	McLevy	Reekie	Scott	Coupe	Inglis	Cusick*	M Paton	Currie	C Paton*	Mackay	Brown	Bollan	Luissint	McMinn			
20/03/2021	L	A	Stirling Albion	0	1	Hutton	McLauchlan>	Hussain	O'Connor	Osman<	Barr&	McLevy	Barron	Slaven+	M Paton*	McKee	Coupe*	C Paton+	Currie&	Jordan>	Inglis<	Page	McIntosh	Reekie	O'Neill
23/03/2021	L	A	Stranraer	0	2	Hutton	Reekie	Hussain	O'Connor	Osman*	Barr&	Devine>	Barron	Slaven	Currie	McKee	McLauchlan*+	Page+	Coupe&	Inglis>	McLevy	C Paton	McIntosh	Jordan	O'Neill
27/03/2021	L	H	Queen's Park	0	2	Hutton	Reekie	Hussain	O'Connor>	McIntosh+	Barr	Coupe	Barron	Slaven&	McLevy	Inglis*	McKee*	Jordan+	Currie&	Devine>	C Paton	O'Neil			
30/03/2021	L	H	Elgin City	1	2	Hutton	Reekie	Hussain	O'Connor	Jordan*	Currie	Devine	Barron	Slaven+	McLevy	McKee	Page*	C Paton+	McIntosh	Bollan	O'Neill				
06/04/2021	L	H	Stenhousemuir	1	1	Hutton	Reekie	McIntosh	O'Connor	Jordan	Inglis	Devine	Barron	Slaven*	McLevy	McKee	C Paton*	Bollan	McLauchlan	Osman	M Paton				
10/04/2021	L	H	Albion Rovers	2	4	Hutton	McIntosh	Hussain	O'Connor	Barr	Inglis+	Devine*	Currie	Slaven	McLevy	McKee	M Paton*	Osman+	Reekie	Coupe	C Paton	Jordan	Bollan	O'Neill	
13/04/2021	L	A	Edinburgh City	1	2	Hutton	Reekie	Hussain	O'Connor	Barr	Page	Devine	Osman&	McIntosh	M Paton+	Currie*	Slaven*	Inglis+	Coupe&	McLauchlan	C Paton	Jordan	Bollan	McLevy	O'Neill
17/04/2021	L	A	Annan Athletic	0	3	Hutton	McIntosh+	Hussain*	O'Connor	Barr	Page	Devine	Osman	Slaven>	M Paton&	McKee<	Jordan*	Reekie+	Inglis&	Coupe>	C Paton<	McLevy	Bollan	O'Neill	
20/04/2021	L	H	Cowdenbeath	0	0	Hutton	McIntosh	Hussain	O'Connor	Barr	Page	Reekie	Inglis+	Coupe*	M Paton&	McKee	Slaven*	C Paton+	McLevy&	McLauchlan	Jordan	Currie	Bollan	O'Neill	
27/04/2021	L	A	Cowdenbeath	2	0	Hutton	McIntosh	Hussain	O'Connor	Barr>	McLauchlan	Osman	Currie&	Coupe+	M Paton*	McKee	Inglis*	Slaven+	C Paton&	Devine>	Jordan	McLevy	Reekie	Page	O'Neill
29/04/2021	L	H	Annan Athletic	0	3	Hutton	McLauchlan+	Hussain	O'Connor	Barr	McIntosh	Osman	Currie&	Coupe>	M Paton*	McKee<	Inglis*	Jordan+	Slaven&	Devine>	Reekie<	C Paton	Bollan	McLevy	O'Neill
01/05/2021	L	A	Albion Rovers	1	1	O'Neil	Jordan	McLevy	O'Connor*	Reekie	Bollan	Devine	Inglis>	Slaven	C Paton&	McKee+	Hussain*	Coupe+	Barr&	Osman>	McIntosh	Currie	Hutton		
04/05/2021	L	H	Stenhousemuir	0	1	O'Neil	Jordan	Hussain&	McLevy	Reekie	Bollan+	Devine*	Inglis	Coupe	C Paton>	Currie<	Barr*	Page+	McIntosh&	Slaven>	McKee<	Osman	Hutton		
18/05/2021	PO	A	Kelty Hearts	1	2	Hutton	McIntosh	Hussain*	Barr&	Reekie	Page	Osman	Inglis	Coupe	Currie+	McKee	Jordan*	Slaven+	McLevy&	Devine>	Bollan	C Paton	O'Neill		
23/05/2021	PO	H	Kelty Hearts	0	1	Hutton	Jordan+	McIntosh	Barr&	Reekie	Page	Osman	Inglis	Coupe*	M Paton	McKee	Currie*	Paton+	McLevy&	Slaven	Bollan	O'Connor	O'Neill		

THE GOALIES

Goalkeepers Used in League Matches, 1970-2020

Players shown in the season of their first appearance only

1972/3	Andrew McEwan
	David Brown
	J Fairgrieve
	Eric Martin
1973/4	Jed Reilly
1974/5	Alan Milne
	Ian Beatson
1975/6	John Ritchie
1977/8	Sandy Thomson
1979/0	I Christie
	A Smith
1980/1	Derek Neilson
1986/7	B Stuart
1987/8	David Lawrie
	Brian Smart
1989/0	Jim Moffat
1991/2	Chris Ainslie
	Ray Allan
	Ronnie Traynor
	Stuart Garden
1993/4	Bruce Alexander
	Derek Balfour
1995/6	Bobby Brown
1997/8	Jim Butter
1999/0	Bobby Geddes
2000/1	Derek Soutar
	Martin Parkyn
2001/2	Mark Cairns
	Kevin McKeown
2002/3	David Hay
	Scott Thomson
2003/4	Kevin Budinauckas
2004/5	Craig Nelson
2005/6	John Hillcoat
2007/8	Chris McCluskey
2010/1	David Scott
2012/3	Michael Andrews
2013/4	Calum Antell
	Graeme Smith
2014/5	Patrick O'Neill
2018/9	Graham Bowman
	Connor Brennan
2019/0	Lewis McMinn
	Ross Sinclair

Surname	First Name	Date of Birth	No	Nat	Pos	Signed	Previous	Notes	Contract	Lge A	Lge S	Lge G	SC A	SC S	SC G	LC A	LC S	LC G	Un
Barr	Bobby	23/06/1988	10	SCO	M	2021	Forfar Athletic	Released June 2021 joined Cowdenbeath		11	2	2							0
Barron	Connor	29/08/2002	16	SCO	M	2020	Aberdeen (OL)	Sep-May		13		1				1			
Bollan	Luc	20/02/2000	5	SCO	D	2020	Aberdeen		End 2021/2	9		1				2	1		12
Brown	Ross	10/06/1993	4	SCO	M	2019	Berwick Rangers	Released March 2021		2	1					1			10
Coupe	Connor	29/07/1999	7	SCO	M	2020	Forfar Athletic	Released May 2021 joined Carnouistie P		10	7		1						3
Currie	Rory	20/02/1998	9	SCO	F	2020	Hearts		End 2021/2	15	4	1	1		1	2	2	1	2
Cusick	Scott	08/08/2002	11	SCO	M	2020	Dunfermline Athletic (OL)	Sep-Jan		2	2		1			2	1		2
Devine	Adam	25/03/2003		SCO	D	2021	Rangers (OL)	Mar-May		8	4								0
Hussain	Yusuf	26/04/2001		SCO	D	2021	Motherwell (OL)	Mar-May		12	1								0
Hutton	David	18/05/1985	1	SCO	GK	2021	Airdrieonians	Releaded May 2021		13	0								2
Inglis	Kieran	19/08/2000	8	SCO	M	2019	Dundee United		End 2021/2	12	8	2	1		1	3	1	2	3
Jordan	Gregor	02/12/2001	15	SCO	D	2020	Dunfermline Athletic		End 2021/2	12	5		1			3			8
Luissint	Benjamin	30/07/1998	14	FRA / GUA	M	2020	Queen of the South	Released Jan 2021		0	3					1	2		8
Mackay	Dave	07/03/2001	3	SCO	D	2020	Celtic Youths	Released April 2021		7	0					3			2
Makovora	Leeroy	05/02/2002		SCO	F	2020	Hearts (OL)	Sep-Nov		3	1	1				3	1		1
McIntosh	Sean	10/01/1997	2	SCO	D	2019	Airdrieonians	released May 2021 joined Stranraer		12	2					3			5
McKee	Chris	07/05/2002		NIR	F	2021	Rangers (OL)	Mar-May		12	2	1							0
McLauchlan	Gerry	08/03/1989	4	SCO	D	2021	Pollok	Released May 2021		3	1								3
McLevy	Ewan	02/05/2000	22	SCO	D	2020	Kilmarnock	Released May 2021		12	3		1			1			5
McMinn	Lewis	04/08/1997	1	SCO	GK	2019	Stenhousemuir	Released March 2021		6	0					3			5
Motherwell	Liam	16/02/2002		SCO	M		Trialist	Ex Morton		1	0	1							0
Nawrocki	Przemyslaw	08/04/1997	16	POL	F	2020	Warta Sieradz	Released Jan 2021		1	3					1	2		3
O'Connor	Harris	28/05/2002		SCO	D	2021	Rangers (OL)	Mar-May		12	0								1
O'Neil	Patrick	31/03/1992	19	SCO	GK	2020	Irvine Vics	Released May 2021		5	0		1			1			19
Osman	Abdul	27/02/1987	11	GHA / ENG	M	2020	Dartford	Released May 2021		8	2								2
Page	Jonathan	08/02/1990	6	ENG	D	2019	Airdrieonians	Released May 2021 joined Clyde		8	3	1	1			2			7
Paton	Michael	25/03/1989	20	SCO	F	2020	Queen of the South		End 2021/2	15	2	1	1			3	1		1
Paton	Chris	01/01/1995	17	SCO	F	2020	Unattached	Ex Stirling Albion, released May 2021		4	9			1					6
Reekie	Scott	28/01/2000	12	SCO	D	2019	Falkirk	released May 2021, joined Edinburgh City		13	4		1			2	1		8
Scott	Martin "Jimmy"	15/02/1986	10	SCO	M	2020	Cove Rangers	Released Jan 2021		6	1	1	1			3	1		0
Slaven	Sean	10/05/2001		SCO	F	2021	Hamilton Accies (OL)	Mar-May		8	6								1
Todd	Matty	14/06/2001	18	SCO	M	2020	Dunfermline Athletic (OL)	Sep-Jan		9	0	1				4			0
Trialist										0	0								3
NEW SIGNINGS 2021/2																			
Bain	Jamie	06/08/1991		SCO	D	2021	Clyde		End 2021/2										
Cox	David	17/03/1989		SCO	M	2021	Albion Rovers		End 2021/2										
Davidson	Iain	14/01/1984		SCO	D	2021	Raith Rovers		End 2021/2										
Docherty	Sean	01/09/2003		SCO	D	2021	Hearts (OL)	Jul-May	End 2021/2										
Galasso	Evan	21/03/2001		SCO	M	2021	Gretna		End 2021/2										
Mackintosh	Murray	08/08/1997		SCO	M	2021	Forfar Athletic		End 2021/2										
Scott	Marc	20/09/1996		SCo	M	2021	Broughty Athletic		End 2021/2										
Wills	Jack	16/10/2002		SCO	Gk	2021	St Johnstone (OL)	July-May	End 2021/2										
Wood	Gary	27/01/1988		SCO	F	2021	Formartine United		End 2021/2										

Derek Neilson

Mark Cairns

Graeme Smith

BRECHIN CITY'S ALL TiME SCOTTISH LEAGUIE RECORD

Season	Div	Pos	P	W	D	L	F	A	PTS
1923/4	3	16/16	30	4	6	20	28	76	14
1924/5	3	14/17	30	9	4	16	51	61	24
1925/6	3	10/16	28	12	3	13	67	73	27
1929/30	2	20/20	38	7	4	27	57	125	18
1930/1	2	16/20	38	13	7	18	52	84	33
1931/2	2	19/20	38	9	7	22	52	97	25
1932/3	2	15/18	34	11	4	19	65	95	26
1933/4	2	14/18	34	13	5	16	60	70	31
1934/5	2	15/18	34	10	6	18	51	98	26
1935/6	2	16/18	34	8	6	20	57	96	22
1936/7	2	16/18	34	8	9	17	64	98	25
1937/8	2	18/18	34	5	2	27	53	139	12
1938/9	2	10/18	34	11	9	14	82	106	31
1946/7	C	8/10	18	4	4	10	42	60	12
1947/8	C	10/12	22	6	4	12	43	54	16
1948/9	C	3/12	22	13	4	5	67	38	30
1949/50	CNE	6/16	30	14	4	12	71	53	32
1950/1	CNE	5/16	30	14	6	10	77	57	34
1951/2	CNE	11/16	30	9	7	14	57	65	25
1952/3	CNE	8/15	28	8	10	10	49	45	26
1953/4	CNE	1/13	24	13	3	8	49	24	34
1954/5	B	16/16	30	8	3	19	53	89	19
1955/6	B	6/19	36	18	6	12	60	56	42
1956/7	2	6/19	36	15	10	11	72	68	40
1957/8	2	7/19	36	16	8	12	80	81	40
1958/9	2	5/19	36	16	10	10	79	65	42
1959/60	2	12/19	36	14	6	16	66	66	34
1960/1	2	14/19	36	9	9	18	60	78	27
1961/2	2	19/19	36	5	2	29	44	123	12
1962/3	2	19/19	36	3	3	30	39	113	9
1963/4	2	15/19	36	10	8	18	61	98	28
1964/5	2	19/19	36	6	7	23	53	102	19
1965/6	2	16/19	36	10	7	19	52	92	27
1966/7	2	20/20	38	8	7	23	58	93	23
1967/8	2	16/19	36	8	12	16	45	62	28
1968/9	2	17/19	36	8	6	22	40	78	22
1969/70	2	14/19	36	11	6	19	47	74	28
1970/1	2	19/19	36	6	7	23	30	73	19
1971/2	2	15/19	36	8	7	21	41	79	23
1972/3	2	19/19	36	5	4	27	46	99	14
1973/4	2	19/19	36	5	4	27	33	99	14
1974/5	2	17/20	38	9	7	22	44	85	25
1975/6	2	13/14	26	6	5	15	28	51	17
1976/7	2	13/14	39	7	12	20	51	77	26

Season	Div	Pos	P	W	D	L	F	A	PTS
1977/8	2	14/14	39	7	6	26	45	73	20
1978/9	2	11/14	39	7	14	16	49	65	32
1979/80	2	8/14	39	15	10	14	612	59	40
1980/1	2	4/14	39	15	14	10	52	46	44
1981/2	2	5/14	39	18	10	11	61	43	46
1982/3	2	1/14	39	21	13	5	77	38	55
1983/4	1	5/14	39	14	14	11	56	58	42
1984/5	1	9/14	39	14	9	16	49	57	37
1985/6	1	10/14	39	13	9	17	58	64	35
1986/7	1	11/12	34	11	10	23	44	72	32
1987/8	2	4/14	39	20	8	11	56	40	48
1988/9	2	3/14	39	15	13	11	58	49	43
1989/90	2	1/14	39	19	11	9	59	44	49
1990/1	1	14/14	39	7	10	22	44	80	24
1991/2	2	8/14	39	13	12	14	54	55	38
1992/3	2	2/14	39	23	7	9	62	32	53
1993/4	1	12/12	44	6	7	31	30	81	19
1994/5	2	10/10	36	6	6	24	22	60	24
1995/6	3	2/10	36	18	9	9	41	21	63
1996/7	2	7/10	36	10	11	15	36	49	41
1997/8	2	10/10	36	7	11	18	42	73	32
1998/9	3	3/10	36	17	7	12	47	44	58
1999/00	3	8/10	36	10	8	18	42	51	38
2000/1	3	3/10	36	22	6	8	71	36	72
2001/2	3	1/10	36	22	7	7	67	38	73
2002/3	2	2/10	36	16	7	13	63	59	55
2003/4	1	10/10	36	6	9	21	37	73	27
2004/5	2	1/10	36	22	6	8	81	43	72
2005/6	1	10/10	36	2	11	23	28	74	17
2006/7	2	4/10	36	18	6	12	61	45	60
2007/8	2	6/10	36	13	13	10	63	48	52
2008/9	2	3/10	36	18	8	10	51	45	62
2009/10	2	4/10	36	15	9	12	47	42	54
2010/1	2	4/10	36	15	12	9	63	45	57
2011/2	2	8/10	36	10	11	15	47	62	41
2012/3	2	3/10	36	19	4	13	72	59	61
2013/4	1	8/10	36	12	6	18	57	41	42
2014/5	1	4/10	36	15	14	7	58	46	59
2015/6	1	7/10	36	12	6	18	47	59	42
2016/7	1	4/10	36	15	5	16	43	49	50
2017/8	Ch	10/10	36	0	4	32	20	90	4
2018/9	1	10/10	39	9	9	18	42	61	36
2019/20	2	10/10	27	4	5	18	31	60	17
2020/1	2	10/10	22	2	4	16	13	46	10
			3078	985	661	1436	5134	5890	2977

Celtic FC 2020/21 The Hoops

Founded	1888
Ground	Celtic Park
Postcode	G40 3RE
Tel	0871 226 1888
Capacity	60355
Closest Railway Station	Duke Street
Record Attendance	92000 v Rangers, Lge, 1/1/1938
Record Win	11-0 v Dundee, Lge, 26/10/1895
Record Defeat	0-8 v Motherwell, Lge, 30/4/1937
Most League Goals in a Season	50 Jimmy McGrory, 1935/6
Most Goals in Career	397 Jimmy McGrory
Colours 2020/21 Top	Green and White Hoops
Shorts	White
Sponsor	Dafabet
Manufacturer	Adidas
Change Colours 2020/21 Top	Mint with Dark Green trim
Shorts	Dark Green
Nicknames	Tic, Bhoys, Invincibles
Web	www.celticfc.net
Match Programme 2020/21	Occasional
E-Ticketing	www.eticketing.co.uk/celtic

Celtic PLC Directors: Ian Bankier (Chairman), Peter Lawell (Until May), Dermot Desmond, Tom Allison, Brian Wilson, Chris McKay, Sharon Brown
Chief Executive: Dom Mckay (from May)
Company Secretary: Michael Nicholson
Celtic Football & Athletic Club Directors: Peter Lawwell, Eric Riley, Michael McDonald
Manager: Neil Lennon, then John Kennedy (interim), then Ange Postecoglou
Assistant Manager: John Kennedy
First Team Coach: Damien Duff, then Gavin Strachan
Goalkeeping Coach: Steve Woods
Chief Scout: Peter Houston
Physio: Tim Williamson
Head of Pro Academy: Tommy McIntyre
Reserve Team Coach: Steven McManus
Under18s Manager: Darren O'Dea
Head of Youth: Chris McCart
Kit Controller: John Clark

The approach to Parkhead, 1979

It's not so long since "Brendan Rodgers, Here for Ten In A Row . . ." was the triumphal chant around Parkhead. That didn't age well. Celtic's rapid decline can be traced back to the day when Rodgers left to move south to Leicester City. Neil Lennon came in and early results were good – perhaps in hindsight he was simply tagging on to the good work and systems put in place by Rodgers. The decision to appoint Lennon on a permanent basis was about to come back and bite Celtic on the bum.

Maybe it isn't entirely fair to heap all the blame on him. Perhaps the club Board should also shoulder some of the responsibility for failing to invest to ensure that the dream of "ten in a row" could become reality? Whatever, a mixture of poor signings, unhappy players, underperforming players disjointed tactics became the reality. And of course Celtic, and many of their fans, seriously underestimated the challenge that would come from Rangers. Celtic had enjoyed things their own way for the best part of a decade and were ill-prepared to cope when a decent opponent came along.

Would Celtic have done better if they had removed Neil Lennon sooner? The answer to that is impossible to be sue of but my hunch is that they wouldn't have. They were stuck with the squad that they had and the mindset that head evolved. What can be said with certainty is that if crowds had been in attendance at games then Celtic would have removed Lennon more speedily. Attendances would have plummeted and those that did turn up would have been a lynching mob.

Europe is where Celtic have been judged in recent times. 2021/2 was a disaster – Celtic were outclassed by Ferencvaros in the Champions league despite having home advantage. Their Europa League group games were little better with 4-1 defeats, home and away, to Sparta Prague a special low.

The 2019/20 Scottish Cup had been secured with a win on penalties against Championship side Hearts. But Celtic's stranglehold on domestic trophies was broken when they crashed out of the League Cup at home to Ross County. In the 2020/1 version of the Scottish Cup they were well beaten by Rangers.

After so long on top elements of the Celtic support did not take 2020/1 well. They demonstrated a sense of entitlement more typical of their cross-city rivals. It really wasn't a good look. All in all, a season that they would want to forget but they really must not do that if only to ensure that there is no repeat.

STAR MAN
Mohammed Elyounoussi, on his day, was possibly Celtic's best player but he was bedevilled by inconsistency. And if estimates of his wage are to be believed, then Celtic fans were probably entitled to more. There were few Celtic players who didn't let the side down at times – Callum McGregor could never be faulted for effort, even when asked to play roles he was not suited to, so he would be choice for star man in 2020/1.

PROSPECTS 2021/2
The Eddie Howe saga sums up everything that has gone wrong at Celtic recently. Dithering, indecision and downright incompetence left Celtic having to scramble for a second choice at the last gasp. They pulled Ange Postecoglou from the hat – an Australian little known in the UK. It will either be a master-stroke or a disaster. At the time of going to press it looked like some of his want-away stars might be staying on at Parkhead – the question will be whether or not he can get the best from Edouard, Ajer, Ntcham etc if they do stay put. Last season's squad was shown to be inadequate. Early signings for 2021/2 have been underwhelming. Celtic may well have to accept second best again in 2021/2.

Date	Comp	H/A	Opponents	F	A		HT		Referee	Crowd	Scorers
02/08/2020	L	H	Hamilton Accies	5	1		2	1	W Collum	BCD	Edouard 3, Frimpong, Klimala
09/08/2020	L	A	Kilmarnock	1	1		1	1	A Muir	BCD	Christie
18/08/2020	UCL1	H	KR Reykjavik	6	0		3	0	S Gishamer (AUS)	BCD	Elyounoussi 2, Julien, Edouard, Taylor, Aoalsteinsson og
22/08/2020	L	A	Dundee United	1	0		0	0	A Dallas	BCD	Ajeti
26/08/2020	UCL2	H	Ferencvaros	1	2		1	2	A Lindhout (NET)	BCD	Christie
30/08/2020	L	H	Motherwell	3	0		1	0	D Robertson	BCD	Forrest, Ajeti, Julien
12/09/2020	L	A	Ross County	5	0		2	0	A Dallas	300	Edouard pen, Ajeti, Ajer, Duffy, Klimala
16/09/2020	L	A	St Mirren	2	1		2	1	J Beaton	BCD	Duffy, Christie
19/09/2020	L	H	Livingston	3	2		2	1	G Duncan	BCD	McGregor, Christie, Ajeti
24/09/2020	UEL	A	Riga	1	0		0	0	F Verisimmio (POR)	BCD	Elyounoussi
27/09/2020	L	H	Hibernian	3	0		2	0	S McLean	BCD	McGregor, Elyounoussi, Ajeti
01/10/2020	UEL	A	Sarajevo	1	0		0	0	B Bastien (FRA)	BCD	Edouard
04/10/2020	L	A	St Johnstone	2	0		0	0	N Walsh	BCD	Grifiths, Klimala
17/10/2020	L	H	Rangers	0	2		0	1	J Beaton	BCD	
22/10/2020	UEL	H	AC Milan	1	3		0	2	M Jug (SLOV)	BCD	Elyounoussi
25/10/2020	L	A	Aberdeen	3	3		0	1	W Collum	BCD	McGregor, Griffiths, Christie pen
29/10/2020	UEL	A	OSC Lille	2	2		2	0	A Tavrev (MAC)	BCD	Elyounoussi 2
01/11/2020	SCSF	N	Aberdeen	2	0		2	0	D Robertson	BCD	Christie, Elyounoussi
05/11/2020	UEL	H	Sparta Prague	1	4		0	2	O Kovacs (ROM)	BCD	Griffiths
08/11/2020	L	A	Motherwell	4	1		2	0	A Dallas	BCD	Elyounoussi 3, Ntcham
21/11/2020	L	A	Hibernian	2	2		0	0	B Madden	BCD	Edouard pen, Laxalt
26/11/2020	UEL	A	Sparta Prague	1	4		1	2	T Stieler (GER)	BCD	Edouard
29/11/2020	LC	H	Ross County	0	2		0	1	K Clancy	BCD	
03/12/2020	UEL	A	AC Milan	2	4		2	2	R De Burgos (SPA)	BCD	Rogic, Edouard
06/12/2020	L	H	St Johnstone	1	1		0	0	D Munro	BCD	Elyounoussi
10/12/2020	UEL	H	OSC Lille	3	2		2	1	F Verissimo (POR)	BCD	Julien, McGregor pen, Turnbull
13/12/2020	L	H	Kilmarnock	2	0		0	0	D Robertson	BCD	Elyounoussi, Duffy
20/12/2020	SCF	N	Hearts	3	3	AET, 4-3p	2	0	J Beaton	BCD	Christie, Edouard pen, Griffiths
23/12/2020	L	H	Ross County	2	0		1	0	E Anderson	BCD	Turnbull, Griffiths
26/12/2020	L	A	Hamilton Accies	3	0		0	0	D Robertson	BCD	Edouard pen, Griffiths, Turnbull
30/12/2020	L	H	Dundee United	3	0		2	0	W Collum	BCD	Soro, Turnbull, Edouard
02/01/2021	L	A	Rangers	0	1		0	0	B Madden	BCD	
11/01/2021	L	H	Hibernian	1	1		0	0	N Walsh ???	BCD	Turnbull
16/01/2021	L	H	Livingston	0	0		0	0	J Beaton	BCD	
20/01/2021	L	A	Livingston	2	2		2	1	W Collum	BCD	Elyounoussi, Bitton
27/01/2021	L	H	Hamilton Accies	2	0		1	0	C Steven	BCD	Griffiths, Edouard
30/01/2021	L	H	St Mirren	1	2		1	2	B Madden	BCD	Edouard
02/02/2021	L	A	Kilmarnock	4	0		1	0	K Clancy	BCD	Brown, Edouard 2 (1 pen), Ajeti
06/02/2021	L	H	Motherwell	2	1		1	0	N Walsh	BCD	Welsh, Edouard
10/02/2021	L	A	St Mirren	4	0		1	0	D Robertson	BCD	Rogic, Edouard pen, Christie, Turnbull
14/02/2021	L	A	St Johnstone	2	1		0	0	S McLean	BCD	Edouard 2
17/02/2021	L	H	Aberdeen	1	0		1	0	A Muir	BCD	Turnbull
21/02/2021	L	A	Ross County	0	1		0	0	D Munro	BCD	
27/02/2021	L	H	Aberdeen	1	0		1	0	W Collum	BCD	Edouard
07/03/2021	L	A	Dundee United	0	0		0	0	K Clancy	BCD	
21/03/2021	L	H	Rangers	1	1		1	1	W Collum	BCD	Elyounoussi
03/04/2021	SC	H	Falkirk	3	0		0	0	J Beaton	BCD	Forrest, Christie, Elyounoussi
10/04/2021	L	H	Livingston	6	0		2	0	N Walsh	BCD	Forrest, Turnbull, Elyounoussi 2, Christie, Fitzwater og
18/04/2021	SC	A	Rangers	0	2		0	2	B Madden	BCD	
21/04/2021	L	A	Aberdeen	1	1		0	1	W Collum	BCD	Griffiths
02/05/2021	L	A	Rangers	1	4		1	2	N Walsh	BCD	Edouard
12/05/2021	L	H	St Johnstone	4	0		2	0	B Madden	BCD	Turnbull, Edouard, Ajer, Dembele
15/05/2021	L	A	Hibernian	0	0		0	0	W Collum	BCD	

Date	Comp	H/A	Opponents	F	A		1	2	3	4	5	6	7	8	9	10
02/08/2020	L	H	Hamilton Accies	5	1		Bain	Julien	Ajer	Taylor	Frimpong+	Brown	Forrest	McGregor	Elyounoussi*	Christie&
09/08/2020	L	A	Kilmarnock	1	1		Barkas	Julien	Ajer	Taylor>	Frimpong+	Brown&	Forrest	McGregor	Elyounoussi*	Christie
18/08/2020	UCL1	H	KR Reykjavik	6	0		Barkas	Julien	Biton	Taylor	Elhamed	Brown*	Forrest	McGregor	Elyounoussi	Christie+
22/08/2020	L	A	Dundee United	1	0		Barkas	Julien	Biton	Taylor+	Frimpong	Brown	Ntcham&	McGregor	Elyounoussi*	Christie
26/08/2020	UCL2	H	Ferencvaros	1	2		Barkas	Julien	Ajer	Taylor	Elhamed+	Brown	Forrest*	McGregor	Elyounoussi	Christie
30/08/2020	L	H	Motherwell	3	0		Barkas	Julien	Ajer	Taylor+	Elhamed	Brown	Forrest	McGregor	Elyounoussi*	Christie
12/09/2020	L	A	Ross County	5	0		Barkas	Julien	Ajer	Duffy	Frimpong	Brown>	Forrest	McGregor<	Ntcham&	Ajeti*
16/09/2020	L	A	St Mirren	2	1		Barkas	Duffy	Ajer	Taylor	Elhamed	Brown	Forrest+	McGregor	Klimala*	Christie
19/09/2020	L	H	Livingston	3	2		Barkas	Duffy	Ajer	Taylor	Elhamed+	Brown	Frimpong*	McGregor	Ntcham>	Christie<
24/09/2020	UEL	A	Riga	1	0		Barkas	Duffy	Ajer	Taylor	Biton	Brown	Forrest*	McGregor	Ntcham+	Christie
27/09/2020	L	H	Hibernian	3	0		Barkas	Duffy	Ajer	Taylor	Biton	Brown&	Frimpong	McGregor<	Elyounoussi>	Christie+
01/10/2020	UEL	A	Sarajevo	1	0		Barkas	Duffy	Ajer	Taylor	Biton*	Brown	Frimpong	McGregor	Elyounoussi	Christie&
04/10/2020	L	A	St Johnstone	2	0		Barkas	Duffy	Ajer	Taylor<	Elhamed	Ntcham>	Frimpong	McGregor	Elyounoussi&	Turnbull+
17/10/2020	L	H	Rangers	0	2		Barkas	Duffy	Ajer	Laxalt<	Welsh>	Brown	Frimpong	McGregor	Elyounoussi*	Ntcham+
22/10/2020	UEL	H	AC Milan	1	3		Barkas	Duffy	Ajer	Laxalt<	Welsh*	Brown&	Frimpong	McGregor	Ajeti>	Ntcham
25/10/2020	L	A	Aberdeen	3	3		Bain	Duffy	Ajer	Laxalt	Frimpong	Rogic&	Elyounoussi	McGregor	Ajeti*	Ntcham+
29/10/2020	UEL	A	OSC Lille	2	2		Bain	Duffy	Ajer*	Laxalt	Frimpong	Brown>	Elyounoussi	McGregor	Ajeti+	Ntcham<
01/11/2020	SCSF	N	Aberdeen	2	0		Bain	Duffy	Biton	Laxalt	Frimpong	Brown	Elyounouss+	McGregor	Rogic>	Christie*
05/11/2020	UEL	H	Sparta Prague	1	4		Bain	Duffy	Biton	Laxalt&	Frimpong	Brown+	Elyounoussi*	McGregor	Rogic	Christie
08/11/2020	L	A	Motherwell	4	1		Bain	Biton	Ajer&	Laxalt	Frimpong*	Brown	Elyounoussi	McGregor	Rogic>	Christie
21/11/2020	L	A	Hibernian	2	2		Bain	Biton	Ajer	Laxalt	Frimpong	Brown+	Elyounoussi&	McGregor	Rogic>	Christie
26/11/2020	UEL	A	Sparta Prague	1	4		Bain	Elhamed	Ajer	Laxalt	Julien	Brown*	Elyounoussi	McGregor	Ntcham	Christie
29/11/2020	LC	H	Ross County	0	2		Barkas	Elhamed&	Ajer	Laxalt	Julien	Brown	Bitton*	Rogic>	Ajeti+	Christie
03/12/2020	UEL	A	AC Milan	2	4		Barkas	Elhamed	Ajer	Laxalt	Frimpong	Brown+	Bitton	McGregor	Rogic*	Christie&
06/12/2020	L	H	St Johnstone	1	1		Barkas	Julien	Ajer>	Laxalt*	Frimpong	Brown+	Bitton	McGregor	Rogic&	Christie
10/12/2020	UEL	H	OSC Lille	3	2		Hazard	Julien	Ajer&	Laxalt	Frimpong*	Soro	Duffy	McGregor	Elyounoussi	Turnbull>
13/12/2020	L	H	Kilmarnock	2	0		Hazard	Julien	Ajer	Duffy	Frimpong*	Soro	Taylor>	McGregor	Elyounoussi<	Turnbull&
20/12/2020	SCF	N	Hearts	3	3	AET, 4-3p	Hazard	Julien	Ajer	Duffy>	Taylor+	Brown	Turnbull*	McGregor	Elyounoussi&	Christie
23/12/2020	L	H	Ross County	2	0		Hazard	Julien	Ajer	Laxalt	Frimpong	Soro	Turnbull*	McGregor	Griffiths>	Christie+
26/12/2020	L	A	Hamilton Accies	3	0		Hazard	Biton	Ajer	Taylor	Frimpong	Soro	Turnbull&	McGregor	Griffiths*	Christie>
30/12/2020	L	H	Dundee United	3	0		Barkas	Julien*	Ajer	Laxalt	Frimpong	Soro<	Turnbull+	McGregor	Griffiths&	Christie
02/01/2021	L	A	Rangers	0	1		Barkas	Biton	Ajer	Laxalt	Frimpong	Soro&	Turnbull*	McGregor<	Griffiths+	Christie>
11/01/2021	L	H	Hibernian	1	1		Hazard	Duffy	Welsh	Laxalt	Frimpong	Soro	Turnbull	McGregor	Harper*	Johnston&
16/01/2021	L	H	Livingston	0	0		Hazard	Duffy	Ralston	Laxalt	Frimpong	Soro	Turnbull	McGregor	Bitton	Johnston*
20/01/2021	L	A	Livingston	2	2		Barkas	Duffy	Ajer&	Taylor	Bitton	Soro+	Turnbull>	McGregor	Elyounoussi	Christie
27/01/2021	L	H	Hamilton Accies	2	0		Bain	Duffy	Ajer	Taylor	Bitton	Soro	Turnbull*	McGregor	Elyounoussi	Griffiths+
30/01/2021	L	H	St Mirren	1	2		Bain	Duffy	Ajer	Taylor	Bitton+	Soro>	Turnbull<	McGregor	Elyounoussi&	Griffiths*
02/02/2021	L	A	Kilmarnock	4	0		Bain	Kenny	Ajer	Taylor>	Welsh	Brown	Turnbull+	McGregor	Christie*	Ajeti
06/02/2021	L	H	Motherwell	2	1		Bain	Kenny	Ajer	Taylor+	Welsh	Brown&	Turnbull>	McGregor	Rogic	Ajeti*
10/02/2021	L	A	St Mirren	4	0		Bain	Kenny	Ajer	Taylor	Welsh+	Brown	Turnbull<	McGregor	Rogic>	Ajeti*
14/02/2021	L	A	St Johnstone	2	1		Bain	Kenny	Ajer	Taylor	Duffy	Brown	Turnbull+	McGregor	Rogic*	Christie
17/02/2021	L	H	Aberdeen	1	0		Bain	Kenny	Ajer	Taylor	Welsh	Soro+	Turnbull>	McGregor	Ajeti*	Christie
21/02/2021	L	A	Ross County	0	1		Bain	Kenny	Ajer	Taylor*	Welsh	Brown	Turnbull	McGregor	Rogic+	Christie&
27/02/2021	L	H	Aberdeen	1	0		Bain	Kenny	Ajer	Laxalt	Welsh	Brown	Turnbull+	McGregor	Klimala*	Christie
07/03/2021	L	A	Dundee United	0	0		Bain	Kenny	Ajer	Laxalt	Welsh	Brown+	Turnbull*	McGregor	Elyounoussi&	Christie
21/03/2021	L	H	Rangers	1	1		Bain	Kenny	Ajer	Laxalt	Welsh	Brown&	Turnbull*	McGregor	Elyounoussi+	Christie
03/04/2021	SC	H	Falkirk	3	0		Bain	Kenny	Ajer	Laxalt	Welsh	Brown	Turnbull	Forrest&	Rogic+	Christie
10/04/2021	L	H	Livingston	6	0		Bain	Kenny	Ajer	Taylor	Welsh	Brown<	Turnbull&	McGregor	Elyounoussi>	Forrest*
18/04/2021	SC	A	Rangers	0	2		Bain	Kenny	Ajer	Laxalt*	Welsh	Brown	Turnbull	McGregor	Elyounoussi&	Christie+
21/04/2021	L	A	Aberdeen	1	1		Bain	Kenny	Biton	Taylor	Welsh	Brown&	Turnbull	McGregor	Elyounoussi	Christie*
02/05/2021	L	A	Rangers	1	4		Bain	Kenny	Ajer	Taylor	Welsh	Brown*	Turnbull	McGregor	Elyounoussi	Forrest+
12/05/2021	L	H	St Johnstone	4	0		Barkas	Kenny	Ajer	Montgomery*	Welsh	Brown+	Turnbull	Christie	Elyounoussi&	Forrest<
15/05/2021	L	A	Hibernian	0	0		Barkas	Kenny	Ajer	Taylor>	Welsh	Brown	Turnbull	McGregor	Elyounoussi&	Christie*

THE GOALIES
Goalkeepers Used in League Matches, 1970-2020
Players shown in the season of their first appearance only

1970/1	Evan Williams
	John Fallon
1971/2	Dennis Connaghan
1972/3	Ally Hunter
1974/5	Peter Latchford
1976/7	Roy Baines
1978/9	Pat Bonner
1987/8	Allan McKnight
1988/9	Ian Andrews
	Alan Rough
1991/2	Gordon Marshall
1993/4	Carl Muggleton
1996/7	Stuart Kerr
1997/8	Jonathan Gould
1998/9	Andy McCondichie
	Tony Warner
1999/0	Dhimitri Kharine
2000/1	Rab Douglas
2002/3	Marcus Hedman
	Javier Broto
2003/4	David Marshall
2005/6	Artur Boruc
2006/7	Mark Brown
2009/0	Lukasz Zaluska
2010/1	Fraser Forster
2014/5	Craig Gordon
2015/6	Logan Bailly
2016/7	Dorus De Vries
2017/8	Scott Bain
2019/0	Fraser Forster (2nd spell)

11	12	13	14	15	16	17	18	19	20	21	22	23
Edouard>	Ntcham*	Elhamed+	Dembele&	Klimala>	Bolingoli	Biton	Soro	Rogic	Barkas			
Edouard	Klimala*	Elhamed+	Ntcham&	Bolingoli>	Dembele	Biton	Soro	Robertson	Bain			
Edouard&	Ntcham*	Klimali+	Ajeti&	Rogic	Ajer	Frimpong	Bain					
Edouard>	Forrest*	Ajeti+	Ajer&	Klimala>	McInroy	Elhamed	Soro	Harper	Bain			
Ntcham	Ajeti*	Frimpong+	Klimala	Harper	Soro	Biton	Bain					
Ntcham&	Klimala*	Frimpong+	Ajeti&	Harper	Soro	Biton	McInroy	Turnbull	Bain			
Edouard+	Klimala*	Christie+	Elyounoussi&	Turnbull>	Soro<	Elhamed	Welsh	Taylor	Bain			
Edouard&	Ajeti*	Frimpong+	Ntcham&	Turnbull	Soro	Biton	Julien	Elyounoussi	Bain			
Ajeti&	Forrest*	Biton+	Klimala&	Turnbull>	Elyounoussi<	Edouard	Soro	Rogic	Bain			
Edouard&	Frimpong*	Ajeti+	Elyounoussi&	Turnbull	Klimala	Elhamed	Bain					
Ajeti*	Edouard*	Turnbull+	Ntcham&	Klimala>	Soro<	Rogic	Elhamed	Griffiths	Bain			
Edouard+	Elhamed*	Klimala+	Ntcham&	Julien	Turnbull	Griffiths	Bain					
Edouard*	Klimala*	Christie+	Griffiths&	Rogic>	Brown<	Soro	Julien	Welsh	Bain			
Klimala&	Ajeti*	Rogic+	Griffiths&	Turnbull>	Taylor<	Soro	Henderson	Ralston	Bain			
Griffiths+	Elyounoussi*	Christie+	Rogic&	Klimala>	Taylor<	Soro	Henderson	Dembele	Hazard	Turnbull	Bain	
Christie	Griffiths*	Brown+	Turnbull&	Klimala	Taylor	Soro	Ralston	Welsh	Hazard			
Christie&	Biton*	Edouard+	Rogic&	Soro>	Welsh<	Griffiths	Klimala	Dembele	Henderson	Turnbull	Taylor	Barkas
Edouard&	Elhamed*	Ajeti+	Griffiths&	Ntcham>	Soro	Taylor	Klimala	Turnbull	Barkas			
Edouard>	Griffiths*	Elhamed+	Ntcham&	Ajeti>	Soro	Taylor	Klimala	Turnbull	Henderson	Welsh	Hazard	Barkas
Ajeti+	Elhamed*	Edouard+	Duffy&	Ntcham>	Griffiths	Taylor	Klimala	Turnbull	Barkas			
Ajeti*	Edouard*	Duffy+	Griffiths&	Ntcham>	Elhamed	Taylor	Klimala	Henderson	Barkas			
Edouard+	Rogic*	Klimala+	Frimpong	Duffy	Ajeti	Taylor	Bitton	Henderson	Barkas	Hazard		
Edouard	McGregor*	Elyounoussi+	Duffy&	Klimala>	Ntcham	Taylor	Ralston	Henderson	Bain			
Edouard	Ntcham*	Soro+	Klimala&	Ajeti	Julien	Taylor	Welsh	Henderson	Bain	Hazard		
Edouard	Taylor*	Griffiths+	Turnbull&	Elyounoussi>	Klimala	Soro	Ntcham	Elhamed	Bain			
Klimala+	Henderson*	Ajeti+	Welsh&	Rogic>	Brown	Taylor	Edouard	Griffiths	Harper	Barkas	Bain	
Edouard+	Christie*	Klimala+	Rogic&	Laxalt>	Johnston<	Brown	Griffiths	Ajeti	Barkas			
Edouard<	Rogic*	Laxalt+	Frimpong&	Johnston>	Griffiths<	Soro	Klimala	Bitton	Barkas			
Edouard&	Ntcham*	Rogic+	Johnston&	Ajeti>	Bitton	Taylor	Elyounoussi	Klimala	Barkas			
Edouard+	Ajeti*	Klimala+	Johnston&	Elyounoussi>	Brown	Laxalt	Rogic	Duffy	Barkas			
Edouard>	Biton*	Rogic+	Ajeti&	Elyounoussi>	Brown&	Duffy	Johnston	Taylor	Hazard			
Edouard	Elyounoussi*	Duffy+	Brown&	Elhamed>	Rogic<	Ajeti	Ntcham	Taylor	Hazard			
Rogic+	Okoflex*	Henderson+	Dembele&	Ralston	Hjelde	Taylor	Connell	Coffey	Doohan			
Rogic+	Henderson*	Okoflex+	Dembele	Harper	Welsh<	Taylor	Connell	Robertson	Doohan			
Griffiths*	Klimala*	Brown+	Frimpong&	Johnston>	Ajeti	Welsh	Laxalt	Rogic	Bain			
Edouard&	Christie*	Ajer+	Rogic&	Johnston	Ralston	Welsh	Klimala	Laxalt	Barkas			
Edouard	Rogic*	Welsh+	Ajeti&	Christie>	Johnston<	Ralston	Klimala	Laxalt	Barkas			
Edouard&	Elyounoussi*	Johnston+	Klimala&	Laxalt>	Rogic	Duffy	Griffiths	Soro	Barkas			
Edouard	Griffiths*	Laxalt+	Soro&	Elyounoussi>	Klimala	Duffy	Johnston	Henderson	Barkas			
Edouard&	Christie*	Duffy+	Klimala&	Griffiths>	Elyounoussi<	Laxalt	Johnston	Soro	Barkas			
Edouard	Griffiths*	Elyounoussi+	Klimala	Ralston	Ajeti	Laxalt	Johnston	Soro	Barkas			
Edouard&	Rogic*	Brown+	Klimala&	Elyounoussi>	Griffiths	Laxalt	Duffy	Ralston	Barkas			
Edouard	Laxalt*	Griffiths+	Elyounoussi&	Klimala	Ajeti	Soro	Henderson	Ralston	Hazard			
Edouard	Elyounoussi*	Soro+	Duffy	Griffiths>	Ajeti	Montgomery	Henderson	Ralston	Hazard			
Edouard	Rogic*	Forrest+	Griffiths&	Soro	Ajeti	Montgomery	Klimala	Duffy	Barkas			
Edouard>	Forrest*	Rogic+	Soro&	Griffiths>	Biton	Duffy	Klimala	Taylor	Barkas			
Griffiths*	Ajeti*	Soro+	Elyounoussi&	Duffy	Ralston	Taylor	McGregor	Edouard	Barkas			
Edouard+	Christie*	Ajeti+	Rogic&	Griffiths>	Soro<	Laxalt	Duffy	Bitton	Barkas			
Edouard	Taylor*	Griffiths+	Ajeti&	Bitton	Ralston	Rogic	Soro	Montgomery	Barkas			
Edouard+	Rogic*	Griffiths+	Dembele&	Murray	Ralston	Laxalt	Soro	Montgomery	Hazard			
Edouard&	Soro*	Christie+	Johnston&	Griffiths	Biton	Ajeti	Ralston	Laxalt	Barkas			
Edouard>	Taylor*	Soro+	Johnston&	Griffiths>	Dembele<	Laxalt	Ralston	Ajeti	Hazard			
Edouard+	Forrest*	Griffiths+	Dembele&	Montgomery>	Soro	Ajeti	Murray	Ralston	Hazard			

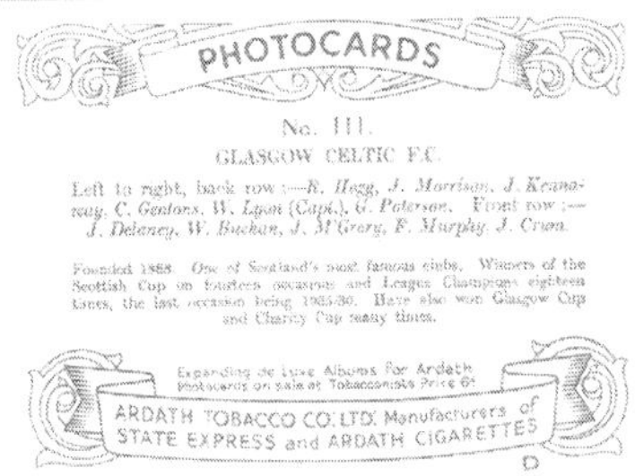
PHOTOCARDS

No. 111.

GLASGOW CELTIC F.C.

Left to right, back row :—R. Hogg, J. Morrison, J. Kennaway, C. Geatons, W. Lyon (Capt.), G. Paterson. Front row :—J. Delaney, W. Buchan, J. M'Grory, F. Murphy, J. Crum.

Founded 1888. One of Scotland's most famous clubs. Winners of the Scottish Cup on fourteen occasions and League Champions eighteen times, the last occasion being 1935/36. Have also won Glasgow Cup and Charity Cup many times.

Expanding de Luxe Albums for Ardath Photocards on sale at Tobacconists Price 6d

ARDATH TOBACCO CO. LTD. Manufacturers of STATE EXPRESS and ARDATH CIGARETTES

D

Surname	First Name	Date of Birth	No	Nat	Pos	Signed	Previous	Notes	Contract	Lge A	Lge S	Lge G	SC A	SC S	SC G	LC A	LC S	LC G	UEFA A	UEFA S	UEFA G	Un
Afolabi	Jonathan	14/01/2000		ROI / NIG	F	2019	Southampton	OL to Dundee Sep-May	End 2022/3	0	0											0
Aitchison	Jack	05/03/2000		SCO	F	2017	Celtic Youths	Freed Oct 2020, joined Barnsley		0	0											0
Ajer	Kristoffer	17/04/1998	35	NOR	D	2016	Start Kristiansand		End 2021/2	34	2	2	3			1			8			1
Ajeti	Albian	26/02/1997	10	SWI / ALB	F	2020	West Ham United		End 2023/4	10	10	6		3		1			2	5		12
Bain	Scott	22/11/1991	29	SCO	GK	2018	Dundee		End 2022/3	18	0		3						3			19
Barkas	Vasilis	30/05/1994	1	GRE	GK	2020	AEK Athens		End 2023/4	15	0					1			6			25
Bayo	Vakoun	10/01/1997		CDI	F	2019	Dunajska Streda	OL to Toulouse Aug-Jun, Transferred to Gent July 2021 £1.4m		0	0											0
Bitton	Nir	30/10/1991	6	ISR	M	2013	FC Ashdod		End 2022/3	12	2	1	1			1			5	1		12
Bolingoli	Boli	01/01/1995		BEL / DRC	D	2019	Rapid Vienna	OL to Basaksehir Sep-Jun	End 2022/3	0	1											1
Brown	Scott	25/06/1985	8	SCO	M	2007	Hibernian	OOC June 2021, joined Aberdeen		25	6	1	4			1			9			3
Christie	Ryan	22/02/1995	17	SCO	M	2015	Inverness CT		End 2021/2	26	8	6	4		3	1			8	1	1	0
Coffey	Barry	27/03/2001	40	ROI	M	2018	Celtic Youths	OL to Cliftonville Jan-May	End 2021/2	0	0											1
Connell	Luca	20/04/2001	28	ROI	M	2019	Bolton Wanderers	OL to Queen's Park Mar-May	End 2022/3	0	0											2
Deane	Frankie	19/10/2004		SCO	M	2020	Celtic Youths		End 2021/2	0	0											0
Dembele	Karamoko	22/02/2003	77	SCO / ENG	F	2019	Celtic Youths		End 2021/2	0	5	1										4
Doohan	Ross	29/03/1998		SCO	GK	2018	Celtic Youths	OL to Ross County Aug-Jan, to Dundee United Apr-May	End 2021/2	0	0											2
Duffy	Shane	01/01/1992	4	ROI	D	2020	Brighton (OL)	Sep-May		13	4	3	2				1		6			11
Edouard	Odsonne	16/01/1998	22	FRA / FRG	F	2018	Paris St Germain		End 2021/2	28	3	18	3		1	1			6	2	4	3
Elhamed	Hatem Abd	18/03/1991	44	ISR	D	2019	Hapoel Beer Sheva	Transferred to Hapoel Be'er Sheva Feb 2021		4	4			1		1			4	1		6
Elyounoussi	Mohamed	04/08/1994	27	NOR	F	2019	Southampton (OL)	Jun 2019-Jun 2021		21	13	10	3	1	2		1		7	2	6	2
Ferguson-Williams	Jaden	01/11/2002		SCO	F	2020	Celtic Youths		End 2021/2	0	0											0
Forrest	James	07/07/1991	49	SCO	M	2010	Celtic Youths		End 2022/3	8	5	2	1		1				3			0
Frimpong	Jeremie	10/12/2000		NET / GHA	D	2019	Manchester City	Transferred to Bayer Leverkusen Jan 2021		19	3	1	1	1					6	2		2
Gibb	Aiden	17/02/2001		SCO	D	2019	Celtic Youths	Freed Jul 2020		0	0											0
Goldie	Caleb	01/01/2005		SCO	D	2020	Celtic Youths		End 2022/3	0	0											0
Griffiths	Leigh	20/08/1990	9	SCO	F	2014	Wolves		End 2021/2	7	16	6	1	3	1				1	1	1	9
Gutman	Andrew	02/10/1996		USA	D	2019	Indiana Hoosiers	OL to FC Cincinnati Jun-Dec, transferred to Atlanta United Mar 2021		0	0											0
Harper	Cameron	19/11/2001	53	SCO / USA		2019	Celtic Youths	Transferred to New York Red Bulls Mar 2021		1	0											5
Hazard	Conor	05/03/1998	65	NIR	GK	2020	Celtic Youths		End 2022/3	5	0		1						1			12
Henderson	Ewan	27/03/2000	52	SCO	M	2018	Celtic Youths	OL to Dunfermline Athletic Mar-May	End 2021/2	0	2									1		11
Hendry	Jack	07/05/1995		SCO	D	2018	Dundee	OL to Oostende Jul-Jun, Made permanent July 2021		0	0											0
Hjelde	Leo	26/08/2003		NOR	D	2019	Rosenborg Trondheim	OL to Ross Couty Jan-May	End 2021/2	0	0											1
Hughes	Liam	19/08/2001		NIR	GK	2019	Celtic Youths	Released Feb 2021, joined Liverpool		0	0											0
Johnston	Mikey	19/04/1999	19	SCO	F	2019	Celtic Youths		End 2024/5	2	8			1								5
Jullien	Christopher	22/03/1993	2	FRA	D	2019	FC Toulouse		End 2022/3	9	0	1	1			1			4		2	4
Kennedy	Paul	02/03/2001	51	SCO	M	2018	Celtic Youths	Released June 2021, joined Clyde		0	0											0
Kenny	Jonjoe	15/03/1997		ENG	D	2021	Everton (OL)	Feb-Jun		14	0		2									0

Kerr	Andrew	25/04/2001		SCO	D	2019	Celtic Youths	Released July 2020		0	0									0
Klimala	Patryk	05/08/1992	11	POL	F	2020	Jagiellonia Bialystock	Transferred to New York Red Bulls Apr 2021		3	13	3				1	1	5		18
Laxalt	Diego	07/02/1993	93	URU	D	2020	AC Milan (OL)	Oct-Jun		13	4	1	3	1	1		6			11
McBride	Connor	20/03/2001		SCO	M	2019	Falkirk	Fred Sep 2020, joined Blackburn Rovers		0	0									0
McGrath	Kieran	28/03/2001		SCO	F	2015	Hibernian Youths	OL to IF Grotta Jul-Nov, Freed Jan 2021 joined E Kilbride		0	0									0
McGregor	Callum	14/06/1993	42	SCO	M	2013	Celtic Youths		End 2023/4	37	0	3	3			1	10		1	1
McInroy	Kerr	31/08/2000		SCO	D	2017	Celtic Youths	OL to Dunfermline Athletic Sep-May	End 2021/2	0	0									2
McLean	Kai	23/02/2005		SCO	GK	2020	Celtic Youths		End 2023/4	0	0									0
Moffat	Owen	06/01/2002		SCO	F	2020	Celtic Youths		End 2023/4	0	0									0
Montgomery	Adam	18/07/2002		SCO	F	2019	Celtic Youths		End 2024/5	1	1									4
Mullen	Ryan	18/05/2001		SCO	GK	2018	Celtic Youths	OL to Cove Rangers Sep-Oct	End 2022/3	0	0									0
Murray	Dane	26/06/2003		SCO	M	2021	Celtic Youths		End 2021/2	0	0									2
Ntcham	Olivier	09/02/1996	21	FRA / CAM	M	2017	Manchester City	OL to Olympique Marseille Jan-Jun	End 2021/2	7	7	1		1			5	4		3
O'Connor	Lee	28/07/2000		ROI	D	2019	Manchester United	OL to Tranmere Rovers Aug-May	End 2022/3	0	0									0
Oko-Flex	Armstrong	02/03/2002	48	ROI / ENG	F	2019	Celtic Youths	Released June 2021, joined West Ham United		0	2									0
Oluwayemi	Tobi	08/05/2003		ENG / NIG	GK	2019	Tottenham Hotspur Youths		End 2021/2	0	0									0
Otoo	Ewan	30/08/2002		SCO	M	2020	Celtic Youths	OL to Clyde Feb-May	End 2023/4	0	0									0
Paterson	Brody	24/04/2001		SCO	D	2018	Celtic Youths	OL to Queen's Park Oct-May	End 2022/3	0	0									0
Perez	Manny	19/02/1999		USA	D	2019	North Carolina State Wolfpacks	OL to North Carolina Jun- Nov, Freed Apr 2021 joined Portland Timbers		0	0									0
Ralston	Anthony	16/11/1998	56	SCO	D	2018	Celtic Youths		End 2021/2	1	0									16
Robertson	Scott	27/07/2001		SCO	M	2018	Celtic Youths	OL to Gillingham Sep-Jan, to Doncaster R Jan-May	End 2022/3	0	0									2
Rogic	Tom	16/12/1992	18	AUS	M	2013	Central Coast Mariners		End 2022/3	10	13	1	2	1	1		2	4	1	8
Savoury	Grant	07/07/2000		SCO	F	2018	Celtic Youths	Released July 2020		0	0									0
Shved	Marian	16/07/1997		UKR	F	2019	Karpaty Lviv	OL to KV Mechelen Aug-Jun	End 2022/3	0	0									0
Soro	Ismaila	07/05/1996	32	CDI	M	2020	Bnei Yehuda Tel Aviv		End 2023/4	11	8	1		1			1	2		23
Taylor	Greg	05/11/1997	3	SCO	D	2019	Kilmarnock		End 2022/3	24	3		1	1			4	1	1	18
Turnbull	David	10/07/1999	14	SCO	M	2020	Motherwell		End 2023/4	25	6	8	3				1		1	9
Welsh	Stephen	19/01/2000	57	SCO	D	2018	Celtic Youths		End 2024/5	15	2	1	2				1	2		7
Wylie	Ben	29/06/2002		NIR	M	2018	Linfield Youths	OL to Ballymena United Jan-May	End 2021/2	0	0									0
Own Goals												1							1	
NEW SIGNINGS																				
Dawson	Joey					2021	Scunthorpe United													
Shaw	Liam	12/03/2001		ENG	M	2021	Sheffield Wednesday		End 2024/5											
Urhoghide	Osaze	04/07/2000		ENG / NIG	D	2021	Sheffield Wednesday		End 2024/5											
Furuhashi	Kyogo	20/01/1995		JAP	F	2021	Vissel Kobe		End 2024/5											

Clyde FC 2020/21 The Bully Wee

Founded	1877
Ground	Broadwood Stadium
Postcode	G69 9NE
Capacity	7936
Tel	01236 451511
Closest Railway Station	Croy
Record Attendance	52000 v Rangers, 21/1/1908
Record Win	11-1 v Cowdenbeath, 6/10/1951
Record Defeat	0-11, v Dumbarton, SC 22/11/1879, v Rangers SC, 13/11/1880
Most League Goals in a Season	32 Billy Boyd, 1932/3
Most Goals in Career	124 Tommy Ring
Colours 2020/21 Top	White
Shorts	Black
Sponsor	North Lanarkshire Leisure
Manufacturer	Uhlsport
Change Colours 2020/21 Top	Red
Shorts	White
Nicknames	Bully Wee
Web	www.clydefc.co.uk
Match Programme 2020/21	None

Board of Directors
Chairman: John Taylor
Vice Chairman: Gordon Thomson
Company Secretary: Claire Thornber
Directors: Andy Allan, Ian Letham, Charlie Lowrie, David MacPherson, Gordon Nisbet
Associate Directors
Governance: Craig Downs
Operations: David Alexander

Personnel
Administration: Lynn Calder
General Manager: John Taylor
Commercial: Dougie Dewar, Dave Mackay, Leanne Sweeney
Financial Controller: Frank Meade
Club Chaplain: John MacKinnon
Community Development Manager: Tom Elliott
Supporter Liaison Officer: Kirsteen Fowell, Dean McKirdy

Matchday Personnel
Operations: John Taylor, Lynn Calder, David Alexander
Match Secretary: Gordon Thomson
Supporter Liaison: Dean McKirdy
Disability Liaison Officer: Gerard McGeachy
Reception: Allan Wilson
Matchday Announcer: Fin McKay
Match Mascot Co-ordinator: Lynne Shanks

Manager: Danny Lennon
Assistant Manager: Allan Moore
Goalkeeping Coach: James Evans
Head of Physiotherapy: Iain McKinlay
Sports Therapist: Alannah MacPherson
Sports Scientist: Matthew Fenwick
Doctor: Karen Brett
Dentist: David MacPherson
Kit: Willie Neill
Video Analyst: Andy Muir
Head of Recruitment: PJ Corr
Digital Media Manager: Sean Hart, Dominic Jack
Club Photographer: Craig Black
Video Technician: David Jamieson

Clyde gained an advantage at the end of the season with late Covid-postponement of their match against East Fife. This meant that they played the game knowing what they had to do to avoid the relegation play-off place. They won 2-1, consigning Dumbarton to the play offs.

It was disappointing for the Broadwood side to finish in such a lowly position. However, the League One table shows that most teams had little to separate them. In a short season that meant results in key games were vital. Clyde managed two wins from three against bottom side Forfar but it was a couple of shock wins, at home to Partick and away to Cove, that made the difference for them.

Three defeats from four games saw them fail to qualify in their League Cup section. Clyde did put together a good Scottish Cup run. After surviving a tricky tie at Keith, they went to First Division Ayr United and won, before succumbing to St Johnstone.

It's more than 15 years now since Clyde were on the verge of promotion to the Premier Division. Now that their differences with North Lanarkshire Council have been resolved and they seem settled at Broadwood for the long term the club needs to do all it can to foster links with the local community. Failing to include the Cumbernauld name in their title / identity after moving to the New Town in the 1990s may have been a mistake but it is still one they could rectify. CFC Cumbernauld anyone?

STAR MAN
Season after season Clyde rely on the goals of David Goodwillie. The reason why such a talented player is playing in League One are well documented. 2020/1 saw him struggling with injury at times but he still turned up trumps with some vital goals, none more so than in the delayed final match of the season against East Fife.

PROSPECTS 2021/2
As is normal these days there has been a big turnover of players during the Summer. In Clyde's case their squad looks somewhat stronger than last season's. That should mean they will not be in danger on another flirtation with the relegation play offs, but neither do they look strong enough to be title contenders.

CLYDE'S SCOTTISH CUP WINNING RUNS

1939

Jan 21	1	H	St Johnstone	2-0
Feb 4	2	A	Dundee	0-0
Feb 8	2R	H	Dundee	2-0
Feb 18	3	A	Rangers	4-1
Mar 4	QF	H	Third Lanark	1-0
Mar 25	SF	N	Hibernian	1-0
Apr 22	F	N	Motherwell	4-0

1955

Feb 5	5	H	Albion Rovers	3-0
Feb 19	6	H	Raith Rovers	3-1
Mar 5	QF	H	Falkirk	5-0
Mar 26	SF	N	Aberdeen	2-2
Apr 4	SFR	N	Aberdeen	1-0
Apr 23	F	N	Celtic	1-1
Apr 27	FR	N	Celtic	1-0

1958

Feb 1	1	A	Dumbarton	5-0
Feb 15	2	H	Arbroath	4-0
Mar 1	3	A	Celtic	2-0
Mar 15	QF	H	Falkirk	2-1
Apr 5	SF	N	Motherwell	3-2
Apr 26	F	N	Hibernian	1-0

10/10/2020 LC	H	Dumbarton	3 2	3 1	S Lambie	BCD	Cuddihy, Goodwillie pen, Cunningham
13/10/2020 LC	A	Falkirk	1 2	1	L Wilson	BCD	Goodwillie
17/10/2020 L	H	Partick Thistle	1 0	0 0	D Dickinson	BCD	Love
31/10/2020 L	H	Peterhead	0 2	0 0	G Grainger	BCD	
03/11/2020 L	A	Dumbarton	0 1	0 1	D Williams	BCD	
07/11/2020 L	A	Airdrieonians	0 5	0 3	C Graham	BCD	
10/11/2020 LC	H	Kilmarnock	0 2	0 1	G Aitken	BCD	
14/11/2020 LC	A	Dunfermline Athletic	2 3	1 0	D Dickinson	BCD	Love, Lamont
21/11/2020 L	H	Montrose	3 2	1 1	B Cook	BCD	Goodwillie 3
12/12/2020 L	H	Falkirk	0 3	0 1	C Steven	BCD	
19/12/2020 L	A	Cove Rangers	3 2	1 2	D Dickinson	BCD	Goodwillie 2 (2 pens), Lamont
26/12/2020 L	H	Airdrieonians	2 4	1 3	G Irvine	BCD	Cuddihy, Love
20/03/2021 L	H	East Fife	1 3	0 1	C Graham	BCD	Goodwillie
23/03/2021 SC	A	Keith	2 0	2 0	S Kirkland	BCD	Goodwillie, Rumsby
27/03/2021 L	A	Montrose	2 2	2 2	A Newlands	BCD	Jamieson 2
30/03/2021 L	A	Peterhead	2 0	0 0	D Williams	BCD	Howie, Cunningham
01/04/2021 L	A	East Fife	0 1	0 1	B Cook	BCD	
03/04/2021 SC	A	Ayr United	1 0	1 0	D Munro	BCD	Cuddihy
06/04/2021 L	H	Cove Rangers	1 1	0 0	M McDermid	BCD	Goodwillie
08/04/2021 L	H	Forfar Athletic	3 0	2 0	G Grainger	BCD	Goodwillie 2, Howie
10/04/2021 L	A	Falkirk	1 2	0 1	C Napier	BCD	Jack
13/04/2021 L	A	Partick Thistle	0 2	0 0	L Wilson	BCD	
15/04/2021 L	H	Dumbarton	0 1	0 1	G Irvine	BCD	
17/04/2021 SC	A	St Johnstone	0 2	0 2	S Kirkland	BCD	
20/04/2021 L	A	Forfar Athletic	3 1	1 1	K Graham	BCD	Jamieson 2, Jack
24/04/2021 L	A	Peterhead	0 3	0 0	S Reid	BCD	
29/04/2021 L	A	Forfar Athletic	1 2	1 1	D Williams	BCD	Goodwillie
01/05/2021 L	H	Dumbarton	2 0	1 0	D Lowe	BCD	Lamont, Cunningham
06/05/2021 L	H	East Fife	2 1	1 0	C Graham	BCD	Love, Goodwillie

PHOTOCARDS

No. 137.

CLYDE FOOTBALL CLUB.

Left to right, back row :—*H. Beaton, C. Ballantyne, E. Summers (Capt.), W. Stevenson, R. Murray, J. Mayes.* Front row :—*J. McCombe, J. Clark, P. McGowan, T. Hope, J. McCulloch.*

This First Division club was formed in 1877, and its record in Scottish Football is an excellent one. Although appearing twice in the final of the Scottish Cup (1909-10 and 1911-12) the club has yet to win it.

Expanding de Luxe Albums for Ardath Photocards on sale at Tobacconists Price 6d

ARDATH TOBACCO CO. LTD. Manufacturers of STATE EXPRESS and ARDATH CIGARETTES

D

Date	Comp	H/A	Opponents	F	A	1	2	3	4	5	6	7	8	9	10	11	12	13	14	15	16	17	18	19	20
10/10/2020	LC	H	Dumbarton	3	2	Mitchell	McNiff	Bain	Lang	Shiels	Johnston+	Cuddihy	Goodwillie	Love*	Cunningham	Jack&	Syvertsen*	Lamont+	Robertson&	Howie	Rumsby	Wilson			
13/10/2020	LC	A	Falkirk	1	2	Vajs	Rumsby	Howie&	Lang>	Shiels	Lamont+	Cuddihy	Goodwillie	Love*	Cunningham	Robertson<	Syvertsen*	Jack+	Johnston&	Bain>	McNiff<	Mitchell			
17/10/2020	L	H	Partick Thistle	1	0	Mitchell	McNiff	Bain	Lang	Shiels	Syvertsen*	Cuddihy	Goodwillie	Love&	Cunningham	Jack+	Howie*	Lamont+	Johnston&	Robertson	Rumsby	Vajs			
31/10/2020	L	H	Peterhead	0	2	Mitchell	McNiff	Bain	Lang	Shiels	Syvertsen&	Cuddihy	Goodwillie	Love<	Cunningham+	Jack*	Lamont*	Henderson+	Palmer&>	Johnston>	Robertson<	Rumsby	Vajs		
03/11/2020	L	A	Dumbarton	0	1	Mitchell	McNiff	Bain>	Lang	Shiels	Lamont&	Cuddihy	Goodwillie	Love	Henderson+	Jack*	Syvertsen*	Johnston+	Robertson&	Rumsby>	Vajs				
07/11/2020	L	A	Airdrieonians	0	5	Mitchell	McNiff	Bain	Lang*	Shiels	Rumsby	Cuddihy	Goodwillie	Johnston+	Syvertsen>	Robertson&	Love*	Henderson+	Lamont&	Jack>	Cunningham	Vajs			
10/11/2020	LC	H	Kilmarnock	0	2	Mitchell	McNiff	Bain	Lamont	Shiels	Rumsby	Cuddihy	Goodwillie	Love&	Cunningham*	Robertson+	Henderson*	Jack+	Syvertsen&	Vajs					
14/11/2020	LC	A	Dunfermline Athletic	2	3	Vajs	McNiff	Howie*	Lamont	Shiels	Rumsby	Cuddihy	Goodwillie	Love+	Cunningham	Robertson	Bain*	Henderson+	Syvertsen	Jack	Mitchell				
21/11/2020	L	H	Montrose	3	2	Mitchell	Lamont&	Howie+	Lang	Shiels>	Rumsby	Cuddihy	Goodwillie	Love	Cunningham	Robertson*	Syvertsen*	Bain+	Jack&	McNiff>	Henderson	Nicoll	Vajs		
12/12/2020	L	H	Falkirk	0	3	Vajs	Lamont*	Bain&	Lang	Shiels	Rumsby	Cuddihy	Goodwillie	Love+	Cunningham<	Syvertsen>	Jack*	Nicoll+	Howie&	Robertson>	Henderson<	Trialist	Magee		
19/12/2020	L	A	Cove Rangers	3	2	Mitchell	Howie	Bain	Lang	Jack*	Rumsby	Cuddihy	Goodwillie	Love	Cunningham+	Syvertsen	Palmer*	Lamont+	Trialist	Robertson	Henderson	Vajs			
26/12/2020	L	H	Airdrieonians	2	4	Mitchell	McNiff	Bain	Lang	Nicoll+	Rumsby	Cuddihy	Goodwillie	Love	Cunningham*	Palmer	Lamont*	Howie+	Trialist	Robertson	Henderson	Vajs			
20/03/2021	L	H	East Fife	1	3	Mitchell	McNiff	Howie	Lang	McGlinchey	Thomson&	Cuddihy>	Goodwillie	Lamont+	Cunningham	Jamieson*	Munro*	Jack+	Ritchie-Hosler&	Robertson>	Butterworth	Bain	Wilson		
23/03/2021	SC	A	Keith	2	0	Mitchell	Howie	Bain&	Nicoll	Otoo	Rumsby	Cuddihy	Goodwillie	Lamont+	Cunningham	Love*	Thomson*	Jamieson+	Jack&	Robertson	Munro	McNiff	Vajs		
27/03/2021	L	A	Montrose	2	2	Mitchell	McNiff	Munro	Lang&	McGlinchey	Nicoll	Cuddihy*	Goodwillie>	Thomson	Otoo	Jamieson+	Love*	Cunningham+	Rumsby&	Jack>	Bain	Wilson	Robertson		
30/03/2021	L	A	Peterhead	2	0	Mitchell	McNiff	Munro	Nicoll	McGlinchey+	Rumsby	Love<	Cunningham&	Thomson*	Otoo	Jamieson>	Howie*	Lamont+	Jack&	Cuddihy>	Ritchie-Hosler<	Wilson	Robertson	Bain	Butterworth
01/04/2021	L	A	East Fife	0	1	Mitchell	McNiff&	Bain+	Howie	McLinchey	Rumsby	Cuddihy<	Cunningham	Lamont*	Otoo	Jack>	Nicoll*	Thomson+	Love&	Jamieson>	Ritchie-Hosler<	Wilson	Robertson	Munro	Butterworth
03/04/2021	SC	A	Ayr United	1	0	Mitchell	Nicoll	Munro	Howie	Robertson*	Rumsby	Cuddihy	Cunningham&	Thomson	Love	Jamieson+	McNiff*	Goodwillie+	Bain&	Jack	Ritchie-Hosler	Lamont	Butterworth	Vajs	
06/04/2021	L	H	Cove Rangers	1	1	Mitchell	Nicoll*	Munro	Howie	McGlinchey>	Rumsby	Love&	Cunningham	Thomson	Otoo	Jamieson+	Cuddihy*	Goodwillie+	Lang&	Lamont>	Ritchie-Hosler	McNiff	Wilson	Bain	Jack
08/04/2021	L	H	Forfar Athletic	3	0	Mitchell	Nicoll&	Munro	Howie	Lang	Rumsby	Cuddihy>	Cunningham*	Love+	Otoo	Goodwillie<	Robertson*	McNiff+	McGlinchey&	Lamont>	Jamieson<	Thomson	Wilson	Bain	Jack
10/04/2021	L	A	Falkirk	1	2	Mitchell	Nicoll+	Munro	Howie	Lang	Rumsby	Cuddihy>	Cunningham*	Jamieson&	Otoo<	Goodwillie	Love*	Thomson+	Jack&	Lamont>	McNiff<	Robertson	Wilson	Bain	Butterworth
13/04/2021	L	A	Partick Thistle	0	2	Wilson	McNiff	Bain	Jack&	Lang	Rumsby	Love>	McGlinchey*	Thomson<	Robertson+	Goodwillie	Otoo*	Cuddihy+	Ritchie-Hosler&	Jamieson>	Lamont<	Munro	Butterworth	Vajs	Cunningham
15/04/2021	L	H	Dumbarton	0	1	Wilson	Nicoll+	Munro&	Howie	Lang	Rumsby	Cuddihy	Jamieson*	Love>	Otoo	Goodwillie	Lamont*	Thomson+	Jack&	Butterworth>	Ritchie-Hosler	Robertson	McNiff	Vajs	Bain
17/04/2021	SC	A	St Johnstone	0	2	Vajs	McNiff	Bain	Howie	Munro*	Thomson	Lamont&	Cunningham+	Jack	Otoo	Robertson	Butterworth*	Ritchie-Hosler+	Jamieson&	Rumsby	Love	Goodwillie	Nicoll	Mitchell	
20/04/2021	L	A	Forfar Athletic	3	1	Mitchell	Nicoll	Cuddihy	Howie	Munro*	Rumsby	Love>	Cunningham+	Jamieson&	Otoo*	Goodwillie	McNiff*	Butterworth+	Jack&	Thomson>	Ritchie-Hosler	Robertson	Bain	Lamont	Wilson
24/04/2021	L	A	Peterhead	0	3	Mitchell	Nicoll+	Cuddihy*	Howie	Munro	Rumsby	Love<	Cunningham	Jamieson	Otoo&	Goodwillie>	Robertson*	Thomson+	Ritchie-Hosler&	Jack>	McNiff<	Lamont	Bain	Wilson	Butterworth
29/04/2021	L	A	Forfar Athletic	1	2	Wilson	Nicoll	Cuddihy	Howie	McGlinchey+	Rumsby	Love>	Cunningham&	Thomson*	Otoo	Goodwillie	Munro*	Lamont+	Butterworth&	McNiff>	Bain	Robertson	Vajs		
01/05/2021	L	H	Dumbarton	2	0	Wilson	McNiff	Cuddihy	Howie*	Bain	Rumsby	Love&	Cunningham	Robertson+	Lamont>	Goodwillie	Otoo*	McGlinchey+	Thomson&	Butterworth>	Vajs				
06/05/2021	L	H	East Fife	2	1	Mitchell	McNiff	Cuddihy&	Lamont+	Bain	Rumsby	Love>	Cunningham<	Robertson*	Otoo	Goodwillie	McGlinchey*	Jamieson+	Jack&	Munro>	Thomson<	Butterworth	Wilson	Ritchie-Hosler	

THE GOALIES
Goalkeepers Used in League Matches, 1970-2020
Players shown in the season of their first appearance only

1970/1	Tommy McCulloch
	Brian Wallace
1971/2	Phil Cairney
1972/3	Neil Carr
1974/5	Evan Williams
1975/6	Ken Ross
1976/7	John Arrol
1978/9	Greg Young
1979/0	Dennis Connaghan
	David McWilliams
1980/1	Allan Campbell
1982/3	Bobby Clark
1984/5	Derek Atkins
1984/5	Scott Mackay
	Ronnie Tracey
	Jack Steele
1987/8	Peter Latchford
1988/9	Stevie Ross
1989/0	Stuart Robertson
1990/1	Steve O'Hanlon
1991/2	Hugh Stevenson
	Scott Howie
1993/4	Les Fridge
	John Hillcoat
1995/6	Jim McQueen
1996/7	Mark McLean
	Robert Balfour
1998/9	Gordon McIntyre
	Dean Sexton
	David Wylie
2000/1	Bryn Halliwell
	Danny Hanley
2001/2	Kevin Budinauckas
	Marc Graham
2002/3	David McEwan
	Allan Morrison
2005/6	Paul Jarvie
	Peter Cherrie
2006/7	David Hutton
2009/0	Callum Reidford
	Jordan Allan
	Scott Findlay
2020/1	JC Hutchison
	Bryn Halliwell
2011/2	Filip Mentel
	Alan Combe
	David Crawford
	Nick Feely
2012/3	Jamie Barclay
2013/4	Joe McGovern
	Nick Rajovic
2014/5	Alan Martin
2015/6	John Gibson
	Marc Waters
2016/7	Kyle Gourlay
	Mark McMillan
	Brett Long
	Craig Quinn
2017/8	Blair Currie
	David Crawford
2019/0	David Mitchell

Surname	First Name	Date of Birth	No	Nat	Pos	Signed	Previous	Notes	Contract	Lge			SC			LC			
										A	S	G	A	S	G	A	S	G	Un
Bain	Jamie	06/08/1991		SCO	D	2020	Forfar Athletic	Released May 2021		11	1		2	1		2	2		10
Butterworth	Zac	24/03/2001		SCO	M	2021	Rangers (OL)	Mar-May		0	4			1					8
Cassidy	Aidan	22/11/2002		SCO	D	2020	Forth Wanderers		End 2021/2										
Cuddihy	Barry	19/12/1996		SCO	D	2017	Annan Athletic		End 2021/2	19	3	1	2		1	4		1	0
Cunningham	Ross	23/05/1998		SCO	M	2020	Hamilton Accies		End 2021/2	17	1	2	3			4		1	2
Goodwillie	David	28/03/1989		SCO	F	2017	Doune Castle Ams	ex Dundee United, Blackburn Rovers	End 2021/2	19	1	11	1	1	1	4		2	1
Henderson	Jay	07/03/2002		SCO	M	2020	St Mirren (OL)	Oct-May		1	3						2		3
Howie	Craig	02/07/1996		SCO	D	2019	East Kilbride	OOC May 2021, joined Alloa Athletic		12	4	2	3			2			1
Jack	Josh	04/02/2001		SCO	F	2020	St Mirren (OL)	Oct-May		6	11	2	1	1		1	?		4
Jamieson	Lewis	17/04/2002		SCO	F	2021	St Mirren (OL)	Mar-May		8	4	4	1	2					0
Johnston	Chris	03/09/1994		SCO	M	2019	Annan Athletic	Released June 2021, joined Annan Athletic		1	3					1	1		0
Lamont	Mark	25/02/1998		SCO	M	2018	Partick Thistle	Released May 2021, joined Alloa Athletic		7	12	2	2			3	1	1	3
Lang	Tom	12/06/1997		SCO	D	2020	Dunfermline Athletic	Joined Raith Rovers May 2021		14	1					2			0
Love	Ally	22/08/1991		SCO	M	2018	Brechin City		End 2021/2	17	4	3	2			4		1	1
McGee	Michael	06/09/2000		SCO	GK	2018	Airdrie Youths	OL to Forth W Sep-Oct, to Cumbernauld Utd Oct-May , Freed May Joined Cumbernauld Utd		0	0								1
McCormack	Kai	23/09/2002		SCO	M	2020	Clyde Youths	OOC	End 2021/2	0	0								0
McGlinchey	Michael	07/01/1987		NEZ	M	2021	Queen's Park	Released May 2021		7	3								0
McNiff	Martin	23/08/1991		SCO	D	2016	Annan Athletic	Released May 2021, joined Stirling Albion		12	6		1	1		3	1		3
Mitchell	David	04/04/1990		SCO	GK	2019	Falkirk		End 2021/2	17	0		2			2			3
Munro	Marky	10/03/2001		SCO	D	2021	St Johnstone	Released May 2021		8	3		2						3
Nicoll	Kevin	16/06/1986		SCO	M	2020	Cumbernauld United	ex Clyde, Stirling Albion etc	End 2021/2	10	2		2						2
Otoo	Ewan	30/08/2002		SCO / GHA	D	2021	Celtic (OL)	Mar-May		11	?		2						0
Palmer	Cammy	15/05/2000		NIR / CAN	M	2020	Rangers (OL)	Oct-May		1	2								0
Ritchie-Hosler	Kane	13/09/2002		ENG	F	2021	Rangers (OL)	Mar-May		0	5			1					5
Robertson	Lloyd	13/01/2001		SCO	D	2020	Aberdeen	Released May 2021 joined Inverurie Locos		5	6		2			3	1		11
Rumsby	Scott	01/01/1994		SCO	D	2018	Cowdenbeath		End 2021/2	17	2		2		1	3			4
Shiels	Matthew	13/09/2000		ROI / SCO	D	2020	Rangers (OL)	Oct-May		6	0					4			0
Syvertsen	Kristoffer	21/06/1998		NOR	F	2018	CD Almunecar	Released May 2021 joined Dumbarton		5	2						3		1
Thomson	Jack	20/01/2000		SCO	M	2021	Rangers (OL)	Jan-May		6	7		2	1					1
Vajs	Matej	29/06/2000		SVK	GK	2020	MSK Zilina B		End 2021/2	1	0		1			2			14
Wilson	David	05/03/2001		SCO	GK	2020	St Mirren	OL to BSC Glasgow Oct-Jan, Refused New Contract May 2021 joined Stenhousemuir		4	0								11
Trialist										0	0								3
NEW SIGNINGS																			
Andrew	Owen	23/10/2001		SCO	F	2021	St Andrew's United	Sonny of Benny Andrew (E Fife)	End 2021/2										
Balatoni	Conrad	27/01/1991		ENG / SCO	D	2021	Edinburgh City		End 2021/2										
Bradley-Hurst	Joshua	10/01/2002		SCO	GK	2021	Dumbartin		End 2021/2										
Docherty	Mark	15/05/1988		SCO	D	2021	Annan Athletic		End 2021/2										
Gomis	Morgaro	14/07/1985		FRA / SEN		2021	Falkirk		End 2021/2										
Jones	Robert	22/09/1995		SCO	F	2021	Dumbarton		End 2021/2										
Kennedy	Paul	02/03/2001		SCO	M	2021	Celtic		End 2022/3										
Livingstone	Adam	22/02/1998		SCO	D	2021	Cove Rangers		End 2021/2										
McGrath	Kieran	28/03/2001		SCO	F	2021	East Kilbride	Ex Celtic	End 2021/2										
Mortimer	Willie	09/01/1997		SCO	M	2021	Cumbernauld Colts	ex Q Park	End 2021/2										
Page	Jonathan	08/02/1990		ENG	D	2021	Brechin City		End 2021/2										
Robinson	Harry	26/09/2000		NIR	F	2021	Motherwell	Son of Stephen Robinson, ex Motherwell manager, Contract terminated July 2021											
Splaine	Aaron	13/10/1996		SCO	M	2021	Annan Athletic		End 2021/2										

Tommy McCulloch

Dennis Connaghan

John Gibson

Cove Rangers FC 2021/21 Cove

Founded	1922
Ground	Balmoral Stadium,
Postcode	AB12 3JG
Tel	01224 392111
Capacity	2322
Closest Railway Station	Aberdeen
Record Attendance	1955 v Berwick Rangers, May 2019 (Ground Record)
Record League Win	7-1, A v Stirling Albion, 10/3/2020
Record League Defeat	1-6, A v Annan Ath, 30/11/2019
Most League Goals in a Season	76, 2020/21
Colours 2020/21 Top	Blue
Shorts	Blue
Sponsor	ACE Group
Manufacturer	Adidas
Change Colours 2020/21 Top	White
Shorts	White
Nicknames	Cove
Web	www.coverangersfc.com
Match Programme 2020/21	None

Honorary President: Alan McRae
Chairman: Keith Moorhouse
Vice Chairman: Graeme Reid
Secretary/Stadium Manager: Duncan Little
Financial Controller: Graeme Reid
Director Of Football: John Sheran
Commercial Manager: Angela Bruce
Media Officer: Charlie Allan
Child Wellbeing & Protection Officer: Kate Dean
Board Of Directors: Keith Moorhouse, Graeme Reid, Duncan Little, Darren Anderson, Grant Moorhouse, John Sheran
General Committee: Michael Coull, Mike Pirie, Richard Forbes, Bill Ogilvie
Football Manager: Paul Hartley
Assistant Manager: Gordon Young
Fitness Coach: Tam Ritchie
Goalkeeping Coach: John Mccafferty
Head Of Youth Development: Gary Hake
Performance Analyst: Ryan Docherty
Head Of Medical Services: Donal Gallagher
Physiotherapist: Eilidh McGregor
Club Doctor: David Fowler
Kit Manager: Adrian Thomson

THE GOALIES
Goalkeepers Used in League Matches, 1970-2020
Players shown in the season of their first appearance only

2019/0 Stuart McKenzie

Having won the Highland League and then the League Two title at a canter, Cove were expected to make a decent impact in League One. For most clubs in their position reaching the promotion play offs would be regarded as a success. However, such is the expectation and ambition at Cove that falling at the first play-off stage against Airdrie seemed more like failure.

Mitch Megginson continued his prolific scoring record against League One defences. Cove had options up front with Rory McAllister also chipping in with his fair share of goals. Their defence was also tight and goalkeeper McKenzie was regarded as one of the best in the division. They didn't lose in three games against Champions Partick (one win and two draws). Defeats against Clyde and Dumbarton can be picked out as the results that cost Cove most dearly.

Cove have put together a squad that is not far from Championship level. They are sometimes accused of being bank-rolled to success by a wealthy owner – that is not entirely true. They have several generous backers and sponsors who have helped the club make the transition from Highland League to League One and are willing to support them in their bid to go further.

They didn't qualify from their League Cup section despite some good performances, including a narrow 1-2 defeat to Hibernian. In the Scottish Cup a win at Alloa was rewarded with an away tie at Ibrox. In normal times that would have been a bumper pay day but not in this strange season.

STAR MAN
Striker Mitch Megginson would be the obvious choice. However, goalkeeper Stuart McKenzie was a colossus between the sticks for Cove in 2020/1. The former Montrose man has been with the club every inch of their journey from the Highland League and has played a vital part on that road. His vital saves and calm organisation of the defence make him a real unsung hero at the Balmoral Stadium.

PROSPECTS 2021/2
Cove will not rest until they achieve Championship status. Looking at their opponents in League One for the coming season and at their own squad, then they will be amongst the favourites for the automatic promotion spot.

Date	Comp	H/A	Opponents	F	A		HT		Referee	Crowd	Scorers
10/10/2020	LC	H	Hibernian	1	2		1	0	E Anderson	BCD	Higgins
13/10/2020	LC	A	Brora Rangers	2	2	6-5p	2	1	D Williams	BCD	McAllister, Semple
17/10/2020	L	H	East Fife	3	1		1	0	G Ross	BCD	Megginson 2, McIntosh
24/10/2020	L	A	Peterhead	2	0		1	0	A Newlands	BCD	Megginson, Milne
31/10/2020	L	H	Partick Thistle	1	0		0	0	S Lambie	BCD	McAllister
07/11/2020	L	H	Forfar Athletic	3	0		2	0	S Lambie	BCD	McAllister, Megginson 2(1 pen)
10/11/2020	LC	A	Dundee	0	3		0	1	C Napier	BCD	
14/11/2020	LC	H	Forfar Athletic	1	0		0	0	D Williams	BCD	McAllister pen
21/11/2020	L	A	Falkirk	0	1		0	0	D Dickinson	BCD	
28/11/2020	L	A	Airdrieonians	1	1		1	0	G Grainger	BCD	Masson
05/12/2020	L	H	Montrose	1	2		1	0	L Wilson	BCD	Milne
12/12/2020	L	A	Dumbarton	0	1		0	0	G Aitken	BCD	
19/12/2020	L	H	Clyde	2	3		2	1	D Dickinson	BCD	Megginson 2
26/12/2020	L	A	Forfar Athletic	1	0		0	0	D Lowe	BCD	Megginson
02/01/2021	L	H	Peterhead	1	0		1	0	P Stuart	BCD	McAllister
09/01/2021	SC	A	Alloa Athletic	3	2		1	2	D Dickinson	BCD	Strachan, McAllister, Masson
20/03/2021	L	A	Partick Thistle	1	1		0	0	S Reid	BCD	Megginson
27/03/2021	L	A	East Fife	0	0		0	0	M Roncone	BCD	
30/03/2021	L	H	Airdrieonians	2	0		0	0	P Stuart	BCD	Masson 2
04/04/2021	SC	A	Rangers	0	4		0	4	K Clancy	BCD	
06/04/2021	L	A	Clyde	1	1		0	0	M McDermid	BCD	Scully
10/04/2021	L	H	Dumbarton	1	0		0	0	D Lowe	BCD	McAllister
17/04/2021	L	H	Falkirk	2	0		1	0	D Dickinson	BCD	Megginson 2
20/04/2021	L	A	Montrose	0	1		0	1	S Lambie	BCD	
24/04/2021	L	A	Falkirk	2	2		1	1	G Duncan	BCD	McIntosh, Megginson
27/04/2021	L	H	Partick Thistle	2	2		1	1	C Napier	BCD	McAllister pen, Strachan
29/04/2021	L	A	Montrose	2	0		1	0	A Newlands	BCD	Megginson 2
01/05/2021	L	H	Airdrieonians	0	2		0	0	C Graham	BCD	
08/05/2021	L	PO	Airdrieonians	1	1		0	0	D Dickinson	BCD	McIntosh
11/05/2021	L	PO	Airdrieonians	2	3	AET	1	1	C Steven	BCD	Megginson, McAllister

Progress?

Cove's old ground at Allan Park had character and charm. Unfortunately for Cove the dimensions of the playing surface and their proximity to solid walls made it impossible for the club to get a licence there. After a spell of nomadic existence, Cove moved into their new home at the Balmoral Stadium. It may not have charm or character but it's functionality has allowed Cove to win two rapid promotions from the Highland League to the SPFL League One.

Date	Comp	H/A	Opponents	F	A	1	2	3	4	5	6	7	8	9	10	11	12	13	14	15	16	17	18	19	20
10/10/2020	LC	H	Hibernian	1	2	McKenzie	Scott Ross	Higgins	Milne	Livingstone*	Graham	Masson	Yule	Scully	Megginson	McIntosh	Semple*	*Watson*	*Leighton*	*Brown*	*McAllister*	*Demus*			
13/10/2020	LC	A	Brora Rangers	2	2 6-5p	McKenzie	Leighton+	Higgins	Milne	Livingstone	Graham	Watson	Brown&	Scully	Semple	McAllister*	McIntosh*	Seb Ross+	Yule&	*Demus*					
17/10/2020	L	H	East Fife	3	1	McKenzie	Scott Ross	Higgins	Milne	Strachan	Semple*	Masson	Yule	Scully+	Megginson&	McIntosh	Watson*	Seb Ross+	McAllister&	*Livingstone*	*Graham*	*Brown*	*Demus*		
24/10/2020	L	A	Peterhead	2	0	McKenzie	Scott Ross	Higgins	Milne	Strachan	Semple*	Masson	Yule	Scully	Megginson&	McIntosh+	Seb Ross*	Watson+	McAllister&	*Livingstone*	*Graham*	*Brown*	*Demus*		
31/10/2020	L	H	Partick Thistle	1	0	McKenzie	Scott Ross	Higgins+	Milne	Strachan	Livingstone*	Masson	Yule	Scully	Megginson&	McIntosh	McAllister*	Graham+	Seb Ross&	*Ritchie*	*Semple*	*Brown*	*Watson*	*Demus*	
07/11/2020	L	H	Forfar Athletic	3	0	McKenzie	Scott Ross	Graham	Milne	Strachan	McAllister*	Masson	Yule	Scully	Megginson	McIntosh	Watson*	*Livingstone*	*Seb Ross*	*Ritchie*	*Semple*	*Brown*	*Demus*		
10/11/2020	LC	A	Dundee	0	3	McKenzie	Scott Ross	Livingstone	Brown+	Strachan	Seb Ross&	Masson	Yule	Semple*	Megginson<	McIntosh>	Graham*	Scully+	Ritchie&	Watson>	McAllister<	*Demus*			
14/11/2020	LC	H	Forfar Athletic	1	0	McKenzie	Scott Ross	Livingstone	Graham	Strachan	Fyvie*	Scully	Watson+	Seb Ross	Megginson	McAllister	Brown*	Semple+	*Milne*	*Demus*					
21/11/2020	L	A	Falkirk	0	1	McKenzie	Scott Ross	Livingstone+	Milne	Strachan	Fyvie	Scully	Yule	McAllister*	Megginson	McIntosh	Watson*	Semple+	*Graham*	*Brown*	*Seb Ross*	*Demus*			
28/11/2020	L	A	Airdrieonians	1	1	McKenzie	Scott Ross	Graham	Milne	Strachan	Fyvie	Scully	Yule	Masson	Megginson	McIntosh	*Seb Ross*	*Watson*	*Semple*	*Livingstone*	*Brown*	*McAllister*	*Demus*		
05/12/2020	L	H	Montrose	1	2	McKenzie	Scott Ross	Higgins	Milne*	Strachan	Fyvie	Scully+	Yule	Masson&	McAllister>	McIntosh	Livingstone*	Seb Ross+	Watson&	*Semple>*	*Brown*	*Graham*	*Demus*		
12/12/2020	L	A	Dumbarton	0	1	McKenzie	Scott Ross	Higgins	Milne	Strachan	Fyvie	Scully+	Yule	Masson	Watson*	McIntosh	Semple*	Seb Ross+	Brown	*Livingstone*	*Graham*	*Demus*			
19/12/2020	L	H	Clyde	2	3	McKenzie	Masson	Higgins	Milne	Strachan	Fyvie	Scully	Yule	Seb Ross*	Megginson	McIntosh	McAllister*	*Semple*	*Brown*	*Livingstone*	*Graham*	*Watson*	*Demus*		
26/12/2020	L	A	Forfar Athletic	1	0	McKenzie	Scott Ross	Graham	Milne	Strachan	Fyvie	McAllister	Yule	Masson	Megginson	McIntosh	*Scully*	*Semple*	*Seb Ross*	*Livingstone*	*Higgins*	*Watson*	*Demus*		
02/01/2021	L	H	Peterhead	1	0	McKenzie	Scott Ross	Graham	Milne	Strachan	Fyvie	McAllister	Yule	Masson	Megginson	McIntosh	*Higgins*	*Demus*	*Seb Ross*	*Scully*					
09/01/2021	SC	A	Alloa Athletic	3	2	McKenzie	Scott Ross	Graham	Milne	Strachan	Fyvie	McAllister+	Yule	Masson	Megginson	Scully	McIntosh*	Demus	*Seb Ross*	*Smith*	*Logan*				
20/03/2021	L	A	Partick Thistle	1	1	McKenzie	Logan*	Graham	Livingstone	Strachan	Fyvie	McIntosh&	Yule	Masson	Megginson	Scully+	Smith*	Watson+	McAllister&	*Seb Ross*	*Demus*	*Higgins*			
27/03/2021	L	A	East Fife	0	0	McKenzie	Scott Ross>	Graham	Livingstone<	Strachan	Fyvie	McIntosh&	Yule	Masson*	Megginson	Smith+	Watson*	Hanratty+	*Seb Ross&*	*McAllister>*	Ngwenya<	*Logan*	*Scully*	*Higgins*	*Demus*
30/03/2021	L	H	Airdrieonians	2	0	McKenzie	Scott Ross	Graham	Ngwenya&	Strachan	Fyvie	McIntosh*	Yule<	Scully	Megginson>	Seb Ross+	McAllister*	Masson+	*Logan&*	*Watson>*	Smith<	*Higgins*	*Hanratty*	*Livingstone*	*Demus*
04/04/2021	SC	A	Rangers	0	4	McKenzie	Scott Ross	Graham	Livingstone	Higgins	Fyvie	Scully	Watson+	Masson&	Megginson*	Smith	McAllister*	McIntosh+	Hanratty&	*Ngwenya*	*Logan*	*Yule*	*Strachan*	*Durmus*	
06/04/2021	L	A	Clyde	1	1	McKenzie	Logan	Graham	Ngwenya	Strachan	Fyvie	Scully	Yule	Watson*	McAllister	Seb Ross+	Hanratty*	Smith+	*Higgins*	*Livingstone*	*Scott Ross*	*Demus*			
10/04/2021	L	H	Dumbarton	1	0	McKenzie	Scott Ross	Graham	Livingstone	Strachan	Fyvie	Scully	Yule	McAllister	Megginson	McIntosh*	Smith*	*Watson*	*Hanratty*	*Ngwenya*	*Seb Ross*	*Logan*	*Higgins*	*Demus*	
17/04/2021	L	H	Falkirk	2	0	McKenzie	Scott Ross	Graham	Ngwenya*	Strachan	Fyvie	Scully	Yule	McAllister&	Megginson	Smith+	Logan*	McIntosh+	Seb Ross&	*Livingstone*	*Higgins*	*Hanratty*	*Watson*	*Demus*	
20/04/2021	L	A	Montrose	0	1	McKenzie	Scott Ross>	Graham	Logan&	Strachan	Fyvie	Scully	Yule	McAllister*	Megginson<	Smith+	McIntosh*	Seb Ross+	Livingstone&	Watson>	Hanratty<	*Ngwenya*	*Higgins*	*Demus*	
24/04/2021	L	A	Falkirk	2	2	McKenzie	Scott Ross	Graham	Livingstone	Higgins	Fyvie	Scully	Yule	McIntosh	Megginson	Seb Ross*	McAllister*	*Logan*	*Smith*	*Watson*	*Hanratty*	*Ngwenya*	*Demus*		
27/04/2021	L	H	Partick Thistle	2	2	McKenzie	Scott Ross	Graham	Livingstone	Strachan	Fyvie	Scully	Yule	McIntosh	Megginson	McAllister*	Smith*	*Higgins*	*Seb Ross*	*Watson*	*Hanratty*	*Ngwenya*	*Logan*	*Demus*	
29/04/2021	L	A	Montrose	2	0	McKenzie	Scott Ross	Higgins	Ngwenya+	Strachan	Fyvie>	Watson	Yule	McIntosh&	Megginson*	Smith<	McAllister*	Livingstone+	Seb Ross&	Scully>	Hanratty<	*Graham*	*Logan*	*Demus*	
01/05/2021	L	H	Airdrieonians	0	2	McKenzie	Higgins	Graham&	Livingstone<	Strachan	Logan*	Scully+	Yule	Seb Ross>	Megginson	McAllister	Scott Ross*	Watson+	Smith&	Fyvie>	McIntosh<	*Hanratty*	*Demus*		
08/05/2021	L	PO	Airdrieonians	1	1	McKenzie	Scott Ross	Graham	Ngwenya	Strachan	Fyvie	Scully	Yule	McIntosh	Megginson	McAllister	Logan*	*Watson*	*Smith*	*Seb Ross*	*Higgins*	*Livingstone*	*Demus*		
11/05/2021	L	PO	Airdrieonians	2	3 AET	McKenzie	Scott Ross	Graham	Ngwenya	Strachan	Fyvie	Scully	Yule	McIntosh+	Megginson*	McAllister	Smith*	Watson+	*Logan*	*Seb Ross*	*Higgins*	*Livingstone*	*Demus*		

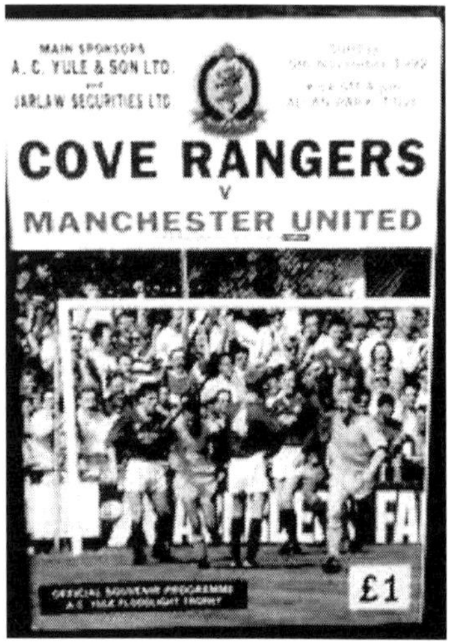

TEAM LINES

COVE RANGERS
Archie Maclean
K McKenzie
David Whyte
David Morland
Andy Paterson
Mike Cormack (1 goal)
Michael Megginson (1 goal)
Raymond Yule
Ray Stephen
Douglas Baxter
Derek Nicol

Subs
R Collins
Tommy Forbes
Andy Lavelle
Mark Murphy

MANCHESTER UNITED
Fraser Digby
John O'Kane
Lee Martin
Steve Bruce (2 goals, 1 pen)
Brian Carey
Michael Phelan
Bryan Robson
Andrei Kanchelskis
Brian McClair
Danny Wallace
Lee Sharpe (4 goals)

Subs
George Switzer
Beardsmore
Keith Gillespie

Ref: Sandy Roy

Match played Sunday November 15th 1992

Surname	First Name	Date of Birth	No	Nat	Pos	Signed	Previous	Notes	Contract	Lge A	Lge S	Lge G	SC A	SC S	SC G	LC A	LC S	LC G	Un
Brown	Jordon	28/11/1992	18	SCO	M	2018	Peterhead	Released Dec 20, joined Peterhead		0	0					2	1		10
Demus	Balint	29/03/2002	21	HUN / SCO	GK	2020	Cove Rangers Youth	June 2021 joined Formartine Utd on loan		0	0								30
Fyvie	Fraser	27/03/1993	24	SCO	M	2019	Dundee United		End 2022/3	19	1		2			1			0
Graham	Ross	20/02/2001	20	SCO	D	2020	Dundee United (OL)	Oct-May		16	1		2			3	1		7
Hanratty	Kevin	15/03/2003		SCO	M	2021	Aberdeen (OL)	Mar-May		0	4			1					6
Higgins	Daniel	08/04/1998	12	SCO	D	2019	Kilmarnock		End 2021/2	9	0		1			2		1	12
Leighton	Tom	25/01/2000		SCO	D	2019	Watford	OL to East Kilbride Oct-May, Released June 2021		0	0					1			1
Livingstone	Adam	22/02/1998	14	SCO	D	2020	Motherwell	Trensferred to Clyde June 2021		8	3		1			4			12
Logan	Cammy	28/01/2002		SCO	D	2021	Hearts (OL)	Jan-May		4	3								8
Masson	Jamie	05/04/1993	10	SCO	F	2017	Formartine United		End 2021/2	13	1	3	2		1	2			0
McAllister	Rory	13/05/1987	13	SCO	F	2020	Peterhead		End 2022/3	12	9	6	1	1	1	2	1	2	2
McIntosh	Leighton	06/02/1993	11	SCO	F	2020	Wrexham	ex Dundee, Peterhead	End 2021/2	20	3	3		2		2	1		0
McKenzie	Stuart	06/01/1988	1	SCO	GK	2015	Montrose		End 2022/3	24	0		2			3			0
Megginson	Mitch	27/07/1992	9	SCO	F	2016	Alloa Athletic		End 2023/4	21	0	15	2			3			0
Milne	Harry	29/10/1996	3	SCO	D	2014	Banchory St Ternan		End 2021/2	11	0	2	1			2			1
Mullen	Ryan	18/05/2001		SCO	GK	2020	Celtic (OL)	Sep-Oct		0	0								0
Ngwenya	Kieran	25/09/2002		SCO	D	2021	Aberdeen (OL)	Mar-May		6	1								5
Redman	Jamie	13/08/1986	17	SCO	D	2019	Montrose			0	0								0
Ritchie	Hamish	01/01/1998	17	SCO	F	2020	Inverurie Locos (OL)	Oct-Jan		0	0						1		2
Ross	Scott	19/04/1991	5	SCO	D	2017	Peterhead		End 2022/3	20	1		2			4			1
Ross	Seb	20/01/2000	16	SCO	F	2020	Aberdeen	Transferred to Falkirk July 2021		5	9					2	1		11
Scully	Connor	13/10/1992	4	SCO	M	2012	Dee Boys Club		End 2022/3	20	1	1	2			3	1		3
Semple	Jamie	17/05/2001	15	SCO	M	2020	Motherwell (OL)	Oct-May		2	3					2	2	1	5
Smith	Connor	01/02/2002		SCO	F	2021	Hearts (OL)	Jan-May		4	7		1						3
Strachan	Ryan	01/08/1990	6	SCO	D	2017	Peterhead		End 2021/2	23	0	1	1		1	2			1
Watson	Broque	05/02/1999	7	SCO	F	2020	Annan Athletic	ex Celtic youth	End 2021/2	3	11		1			2	1		10
Yule	Blair	23/08/1992	8	SCO	M	2018	Arbroath		End 2022/3	24	0		1			2	1		1
NEW SIGNINGS																			
Draper	Ross	20/10/1988		ENG	M	2021	Ross County		End 2023/4										
Gourlay	Kyle	24/09/1998		SCO	GK	2021	Hamilton Accies		End 2022/3										
Leitch	Robbie	01/04/1998		SCO	M	2021	Falkirk		End 2022/3										
Neill	Morgyn	10/03/1996		SCO	D	2021	Dumbarton		End 2023/4										
Vigurs	Iain	07/03/1988		SCO	M	2021	Ross County		End 2023/4										

The glass fronted stand at Allan Park was unique in modern Scottish football. It also posed great problems of steaming up during games.

Cowdenbeath FC 2020/21 The Miners / Blue Brazil

Founded	1882
Ground	Central Park
Postcode	KY4 9QQ
Tel	01383 610166
Capacity	4309
Closest Railway Station	Cowdenbeath
Record Attendance	25586 v Rangers, LC, 21/9/49
Record Win	12-0 v Johnstone, SC, 21/1/1928
Record Defeat	1-11, v Clyde, Lge, 6/10/51
Most League Goals in a Season	54, Rab Walls, 1938/9
Most Goals in Career	127 Willie Devlin
Colours 2020/21 Top	Blue with White Candy Stripe
Shorts	White
Sponsor	Collier Haulage
Manufacturer	Errea
Change Colours 2020/21 Top	Yellow
Shorts	Blue
Nicknames	Blue Brasil, Miners
Web	www.cowdenbeathfc.com
Match Programme 2020/21	Monthly

Chairman: Donald Findlay QC
Presidents: Sandy Ferguson (Hon), Dr Robert Brownlie, Alex Anderson (Hon)
Directors: David Allan, John Cameron, Tom Ewing, Neil Fentie, Alan Smart, Yolamda Hilton, Margaret Steven, Malcolm Slora, Craig Scott
Secretary: David Allan
Hon Secretary: Tom Ogilvie
Office Manager: Dianne Blair
Manager: Gary Bollan
Assistant: Craig Easton
Coach: Ian Flaherty, David McGurn
Club Doctor: Lucy Fraser
Physio: Sophie Marr, Neil Bryson
Kit Manager: Robert McKinlay
Community Coordinator: Alex Haddow
Community Coach: Dean Ewing
Groundsman: Craig Surgeon

For most of the season Cowden were looking over their shoulder at the dreaded 42nd spot in the League. In the end they finished some distance clear of it but only die to the even more dismal season suffered by Brechin City. Cowden managed just five League wins with two of them coming in the closing weeks of the season. On the plus side they didn't really take any hammerings other than a home game with Stirling Albion which finished 1-5 and could have been much worse.

Their biggest problem was scoring goals. In seven games they scored just once and in eleven they failed to score at all – and that was in a 22 game season. Cowdenbeath's cause was not helped by running with a very small squad. Injuries and suspensions meant that they frequently had only one or two substitutes who manager Bollan was prepared to use – the remainder being young lads.

In the League Cup Cowden failed to score in their four fixtures. In the Scottish Cup they defeated Wick Academy 2-0 before going down to Partick Thistle.

STAR MAN
Defender and skipper Craig Barr was a beacon of light in an otherwise disappointing season. He also popped up to score 3 goals making him joint top scorer for Cowden.

PROSPECTS 2021/2
With money tight things are going to be tough for Cowdenbeath. Some clubs can afford the luxury of spending cash to try and make sure they stay away from the foot of the league and push for the promotion play offs. Cowden have to be prudent and rely on picking up bargains. Their acquisitions for 2021/2 do look to be an improvement on last season's squad so it may be the first season for a while that Cowden fans haven't had to worry too much about relegation.

Cowdenbeath 1979

Date	Comp	H/A	Opponents	F	A		HT		Referee	Crowd	Scorers
06/10/2020	LC	A	East Fife	0	2		0	0	C Graham	BCD	
10/10/2020	LC	H*	Hearts	0	1		0	0	A Newlands	BCD	
13/10/2020	LC	A	Inverness CT	0	0	2-4p	0	0	G Beaton	BCD	
17/10/2020	L	H*	Annan Athletic	0	3		0	1	S Lambie	BCD	
24/10/2020	L	A	Edinburgh City	1	0		0	0	C Graham	BCD	Smith
31/10/2020	L	H	Stenhousemuir	1	1		0	0	C Scott	BCD	Smith
07/11/2020	L	A	Cowdenbeath	0	2		0	1	G Grainger	BCD	
14/11/2020	LC	H	Raith Rovers	0	1		0	1	D Lowe	BCD	
28/11/2020	L	A	Elgin City	2	5		0	2	G Ross	220	Miller, Kavanagh
05/12/2020	L	H	Queen's Park	0	3		0	1	C Scott	BCD	
12/12/2020	L	A	Stirling Albion	0	1		0	0	D Dickinson	BCD	
19/12/2020	L	H	Brechin City	2	0		1	0	B Cook	BCD	Barr, Russell
26/12/2020	SC	H	Wick Academy	2	0		1	0	C Napier	BCD	Barr, Renton
20/03/2021	L	A	Annan Athletic	0	0		0	0	G Ross	BCD	
23/03/2021	SC	A	Partick Thistle	0	3		0	1	G Grainger	BCD	
27/03/2021	L	H	Stranraer	1	1		1	0	D Williams	BCD	Morrison
30/03/2021	L	H	Edinburgh City	1	3		1	2	M McDermid	BCD	Swann
03/04/2021	L	H	Albion Rovers	0	1		0	1	K Graham	BCD	
06/04/2021	L	A**	Queen's Park	0	3		0	1	S Luke	BCD	
08/04/2021	L	A	Stenhousemuir	0	1		0	1	L Watson	BCD	
10/04/2021	L	H	Elgin City	1	0		1	0	D Dickinson	BCD	Renton
13/04/2021	L	A	Albion Rovers	0	0		0	0	S Lambie	BCD	
17/04/2021	L	H	Stirling Albion	1	5		1	3	C Scott	BCD	Barr
20/04/2021	L	A	Brechin City	0	0		0	0	M McDermid	BCD	
24/04/2021	L	A	Stenhousemuir	2	0		0	0	D Williams	BCD	Renton, Todd
27/04/2021	L	H	Brechin City	0	2		0	1	M Roncone	BCD	
01/05/2021	L	A	Annan Athletic	1	1		0	0	B Cook	BCD	Buchanan
04/05/2021	L	H	Albion Rovers	2	0		1	0	A Newlands	BCD	K Miller, Russell pen

* at New Bayview
** at Falkirk

Stephan Gollasch

Career Details

1993/4	Arminia Bielefeld
1994/5	SC Gottingen
1995/6	Gottingen 05
1996/7	SC Herford
1997/8	SV Babelsberg 03
1998/00	FC St Pauli
2000/2	FC Schaffhausen
2002/3	FC Schonberg 95
2002/3	SV Rochling Volkingen
2003/4	**Cowdenbeath**

Ross Sinclair

Date	Comp	H/A	Opponents	F	A	1	2	3	4	5	6	7	8	9	10	11	12	13	14	15	16	17	18	19	20
06/10/2020	LC	A	East Fife	0	2	Sinclair	Barr	Mullen	Todd	Clarke	K Miller	Herd+	Taylor	Renton*	Buchanan	Hamilton	Kavanagh*	Swann+	*Owens*	*Pollock*	*Sneddon*	*Glass*	*Whyte*		
10/10/2020	LC	H*	Hearts	0	1	Sinclair	Barr	Pollock	Todd	Clarke	K Miller	Herd	Taylor	Renton*	Kavanagh	Hamilton	Cox*	*Swann*	*Owens*	*Easton*	*Sneddon*	*Glass*	*Whyte*		
13/10/2020	LC	A	Inverness CT	0	0 2-4p	Sinclair	Glass	Pollock	Todd	Clarke	K Miller	Herd*	Taylor	Cox+	Kavanagh	Hamilton	Swann*	Renton+	*Owens*	*Easton*	*Sneddon*	*Whyte*			
17/10/2020	L	H*	Annan Athletic	0	3	Sinclair	Barr	Pollock	Hay	Clarke	K Miller	Smith	Taylor	Cox	Kavanagh	Hamilton*	Swann*	*Glass*	*Owens*	*Easton*	*Herd*	*Whyte*			
24/10/2020	L	A	Edinburgh City	1	0	Whyte	Barr	Mullen	Hay	Clarke	K Miller	Smith	Taylor	Cox	Buchanan	Todd	Glass	*Easton*	*Owens*	*Swann*	*Hamilton*				
31/10/2020	L	H	Stenhousemuir	1	1	Sinclair	Barr	Mullen	Hay	Clarke	K Miller	Smith	Taylor	Todd	Buchanan	Kavanagh*	Hamilton*	*Easton*	*Owens*	*Swann*	*Herd*	*Glass*	*Whyte*		
07/11/2020	L	A	Cowdenbeath	0	2	Sinclair	Barr	Mullen	Swann	Clarke	K Miller	Todd	Taylor	Herd	Buchanan	Hamilton	*Pyper*	*Kavanagh*	*Glass*	*Easton*	*Whyte*				
14/11/2020	LC	H	Raith Rovers	0	1	Sinclair	Barr	Mullen	Glass	Clarke+	Smith	Todd*	Russell	Herd>	Kavanagh	Hamilton&	Miller*	Pyper+	Taylor&	Swann>	*Easton*	*Owens*	*Whyte*		
28/11/2020	L	A	Elgin City	2	5	McGurn	Barr	Mullen	Glass	Clarke>	K Miller	Todd*	Taylor	Herd&	Russell	Hamilton+	Swann*	Kavanagh+	Renton&	Pollock>	*Easton*	*Owens*	*Whyte*		
05/12/2020	L	H	Queen's Park	0	3	Sinclair	Barr	Mullen	Herd	Swann	K Miller	Todd	Taylor	Buchanan	Russell*	Renton	Hamilton*	*Kavanagh*	*Pyper*	*Morrison*	*Pollock*	*Glass*	*Whyte*		
12/12/2020	L	A	Stirling Albion	0	1	Munro	Barr	Mullen	Herd	Swann	K Miller*	Todd	Taylor	Buchanan	Morrison	Renton	Russell*	*Hamilton*	*Easton*	*Glass*	*Whyte*				
19/12/2020	L	H	Brechin City	2	0	Munro	Barr	Mullen	Morrison	Swann	K Miller	Todd	Taylor	Buchanan	Russell*	Renton	Kavanagh*	*Herd*	*Glass*	*Pollock*	*Easton*	*Owens*	*Hamilton*	*Watson*	*Whyte*
26/12/2020	SC	H	Wick Academy	2	0	Hogarth	Barr	Mullen	Morrison	Swann	K Miller	Todd	Taylor+	Buchanan	Russell*	Renton	Kavanagh*	Hamilton+	*Glass*	*Pollock*	*Herd*	*Watson*	*Whyte*		
20/03/2021	L	A	Annan Athletic	0	0	Hogarth	Barr	Mullen	Finnie	Swann*	K Miller	Todd	Taylor	Buchanan	Morrison	Renton	Russell*	*Hamilton*	*Glass*	*Pollock*	*Herd*	*Watson*	*Whyte*	*Easton*	*Owens*
23/03/2021	SC	A	Partick Thistle	0	3	Hogarth	Barr*	Mullen	Pollock	Swann+	Glass	Herd	Taylor<	Buchanan&	Russell	Hamilton>	Todd*	Morrison+	Miller&	Renton>	Watson<	*Owens*	*Pyper*		
27/03/2021	L	H	Stranraer	1	1	Hogarth	Barr	Morrison	Finnie	Swann	K Miller	Todd	Taylor	Buchanan	Z Miller+	Renton*	Hutton*	Russell+	*Glass*	*Hamilton*	*Pyper*	*Mullen*	*Herd*	*Pollock*	*Adamson*
30/03/2021	L	H	Edinburgh City	1	3	Hogarth	Barr	Morrison	Finnie	Swann	K Miller	Todd	Taylor&	Buchanan*	Z Miller+	Hutton	Renton*	Russell+	Glass&	*Hamilton*	*Pyper*	*Watson*	*Herd*	*Pollock*	*Adamson*
03/04/2021	L	H	Albion Rovers	0	1	Hogarth	Barr>	Morrison*	Finnie	Swann	K Miller	Todd	Taylor&	Renton	Z Miller+	Hutton	Buchanan*	Russell+	Glass&	*Herd>*	*Pyper*	*Hamilton*	*Sandison*	*Pollock*	*Adamson*
06/04/2021	L	A**	Queen's Park	0	3	Hogarth	Mullen	Morrison&	Finnie	Swann	Sandison*	Todd	Taylor+	Renton	Buchanan	Hutton	Glass*	Russell+	K Miller&	*Herd*	*Pyper*	*Hamilton*	*Pollock*	*Z Miller*	*Adamson*
08/04/2021	L	A	Stenhousemuir	0	1	Hogarth	Barr	Mullen	Finnie	Swann	K Miller	Todd	Z Miller	Russell*	Buchanan	Hutton+	Taylor*	Morrison+	*Watson*	*Herd*	*Pyper*	*Hamilton*	*Pollock*	*Renton*	*Adamson*
10/04/2021	L	H	Elgin City	1	0	Hogarth	Barr	Mullen	Finnie	Swann	K Miller	Todd	Morrison	Renton	Buchanan*	Hutton	Taylor*	*Z Miller*	*Sandison*	*Herd*	*Pyper*	*Hamilton*	*Pollock*	*Russell*	*Whyte*
13/04/2021	L	A	Albion Rovers	0	0	Hogarth	Barr	Mullen	Finnie	Swann+	K Miller	Todd	Morrison	Renton	Buchanan*	Hutton	Taylor*	Z Miller+	*Sandison*	*Herd*	*Pyper*	*Hamilton*	*Pollock*	*Russell*	*Whyte*
17/04/2021	L	H	Stirling Albion	1	5	Hogarth	Barr	Mullen	Finnie	Swann+	K Miller	Todd	Morrison*	Renton<	Buchanan>	Hutton&	Z Miller*	Taylor+	Herd&	Hamilton>	Russell<	*Sandison*	*Pollock*	*Pyper*	*Whyte*
20/04/2021	L	A	Brechin City	0	0	Hogarth	Barr	Mullen	Finnie	Taylor+	K Miller	Todd	Russell*	Renton	Buchanan	Hutton	Z Miller*	Swann+	*Herd*	*Morrison*	*Pyper*	*Sandison*	*Pollock*	*Hamilton*	*Whyte*
24/04/2021	L	A	Stenhousemuir	2	0	Hogarth	Barr	Morrison	Finnie	Swann	K Miller	Todd	Taylor*	Renton	Buchanan	Hutton	Herd*	*Glass*	*Z Miller*	*Russell*	*Pyper*	*Sandison*	*Pollock*	*Hamilton*	*Whyte*
27/04/2021	L	H	Brechin City	0	2	Hogarth	Barr	Morrison	Finnie	Swann	K Miller	Todd	Taylor+	Renton	Buchanan	Hutton*	Z Miller*	Hutton+	*Herd*	*Russell*	*Pyper*	*Glass*	*Pollock*	*Hamilton*	*Whyte*
01/05/2021	L	A	Annan Athletic	1	1	Hogarth	Pyper	Mullen	Finnie	Swann*	Morrison	Todd	Russell&	Renton+	Buchanan	Hutton	Taylor*	Z Miller+	Barr&	*K Miller*	*Herd*	*Glass*	*Pollock*	*Hamilton*	*Whyte*
04/05/2021	L	H	Albion Rovers	2	0	Hogarth	Barr>	Mullen	Finnie	Swann&	K Miller	Todd	Pyper*	Renton<	Buchanan	Morrison+	Herd*	Z Miller+	Watson&	Glass>	Russell<	*Taylor*	*Pollock*	*Hamilton*	*Whyte*

THE GOALIES

Goalkeepers Used in League Matches, 1970-2020

Players shown in the season of their first appearance only

1970/1	Alan Wyllie
	Billy McGann
	Jim McArthur
1972/3	Ray Allan
1973/4	Ronnie Danks
	David Eccles
1974/5	Willie Wilson
1975/6	Ted McFeat
	Frank Connor
1976/7	Peter McBain
	W Lawson
	Mike Mallin
1977/8	Ernie McGarr
1978/9	J Meikle
	Anton Putka
	David Cooper
	John Anderson
1981/2	John Doyle
1983/4	David Westwood
1985/6	John Thomson
1988/9	Allan Main
1989/0	Willie Lamont
1990/1	John Dodds
	C Wilson
	Frank Houston
1991/2	C Robertson
	Stephen O'Hanlon
1992/3	Alan Combe
1993/4	Stewart Filshill
	James Maloney
	Jim Moffat
1994/5	Neil Russell
	D Wilson
1995/6	Steve Oliver
1996/7	Ross Godfrey
1997/8	Steven Hutchison
2000/1	John Martin
2001/2	Craig Gordon
	Gary O'Connor
2002/3	Marc Graham
2003/4	Andy Carlin
	Allan Fleming
2004/5	Stephan Gollasch
	Scott Findlay
2005/6	David Hay
2006/7	David Orr
	Kyle Allison
2007/8	Scott Gallacher
2009/0	Artut Veiculus
	Cameron McKay
2010/1	Ludovic Roy
2011/2	Youssef Bejaoui
	Thomas Flynn
	Lee Wilson
2012/3	Colin Stewart
2013/4	Grant Adam
	Sebastian Usai
2014/5	Robbie Thomson
2015/6	Michael Andrews
	Alin Roman
	Jamie Sneddon
2016/7	David McGurn
2017/8	Joe McGovern
	Blair Penman
2018/9	Aaron Lennox
2019/0	Kevin Dabrowski
	PJ Morrison
	Josh Rae

Surname	First Name	Date of Birth	No	Nat	Pos	Signed	Previous	Notes	Contract	Lge A	Lge S	Lge G	SC A	SC S	SC G	LC A	LC S	LC G	Un
Adamson	Ryan	31/07/1994		SCO	GK	2021	Bo'ness United (OL)	Mar-Apr		0	0								5
Barr	Craig	29/03/1987		SCO	D	2019	Dumbarton		End 2021/2	20	1	2	2		1	3			
Buchanan	Robbie	23/02/1996		SCO	F	2017	Hearts		End 2021/2	19	1	1	2			1			
Clarke	Ross	21/12/1995		SCO	D	2020	Albion Rovers		End 2021/2	5	0					4			
Cox	David	17/03/1989		SCO	F	2018	Forfar Athletic	Released Jan 2021, joined Albion Rovers		2	0					1	1		
Easton	Craig	26/02/1979		SCO	D	2019	Dundee United	Assistant Manager		0	0								11
Finnie	Ryan	19/02/1995		SCO	D	2021	Berwick Rangers (OL)	Mar-May		14	0								0
Glass	Jacob	17/05/2003		SCO	D	2020	Cowdenbeath Youths	Released June 2021		1	5		1			2			14
Hamilton	Olly	13/12/2001		SCO	F	2020	St Johnstone (OL)	Sep-May		3	3		1	1		4			16
Hay	Graham	11/06/1987		SCO	D	2020	Broughty Athletic (OL)	Oct-Nov		3	0								0
Herd	Michael	29/04/1989		SCO	M	2019	Spartans	Released May 2021, joined Spartans		4	4		1			4			14
Hogarth	Nicky	04/07/2001		SCO	GK	2020	Rangers (OL)	Dec-Jan		14	0		2						0
Hutton	Kyle	15/02/1991		SCO	M	2021	East Kilbride (OL)	Mar-May		11	2								0
Kavanagh	Cian	03/01/2003		ROI	F	2020	Hearts	Released Feb 2021 joined Waterford		2	2	1		1		3	1		2
McGurn	David	14/09/1980		SCO	GK	2020	Raith Rovers (OL)	Nov-Dec		1	0								0
Miller	Kyle	08/08/1992		SCO	M	2011	Cowdenbeath Youths		End 2021/2	20	1	2	1	1		3	1		1
Miller	Zander	14/12/1992		SCO	F	2021	Bo'ness United (OL)	Mar-May		4	6								3
Morrison	Gavin	03/01/1990		SCO	M	2020	Brora Rangers		End 2021/2	14	1	1	1	1					2
Mullen	Fraser	08/11/1993		SCO	D	2016	East Fife		End 2021/2	16	0		2			2			1
Munro	Ross	01/04/2000		SCO	GK	2020	Ross County (OL)	Dec		2	0								0
Owens	Lewis	25/05/2003		SCO	M	2020	Cowdenbeath Youths	Released June 2021		0	0								11
Pollock	Ross	28/02/2003		SCO	D	2020	Cowdenbeath Youths		End 2021/2	1	1		1			2			18
Pyper	Jamie	22/08/1993		SCO	D	2017	Gallivare FF	Released June 2021, joined Berwick Rangers		2	0						1		14
Renton	Kris	12/07/1990		SCO	F	2018	Alloa Athletic		End 2021/2	15	2	2	1	1	1	2	1		1
Russell	Iain	14/11/1982		SCO	F	2020	Pollok (OL)	Oct-May		6	8	2	2			1			4
Sandison	Jay	05/03/2001		SCO	D	2021	Hearts	Released May 2021, joined Camelon		1	0								6
Sinclair	Ross	07/05/2001		SCO	GK	2020	St Johnstone (OL)	Sep-May		4	0	2				4			0
Smith	Brad	23/04/1997		SCO	M	2020	Broughty Athletic (OL)	Oct-Nov		3	0					1			3
Sneddon	Kyle	19/12/2002		SCO	D	2017	Fife Elite FA	OL to St Andrews U, Nov-Jan, Freed Mar 2021		0	0								3
Swann	Harvey	12/08/1997		ENG / SCO	D	2016	Cowdenbeath Youths		End 2021/2	17	3	1	2				3		0
Taylor	Graham	19/03/1998		SCO	M	2019	Edinburgh City	OOC May 2021, joined Berwick Rangers		16	5		2			3	1		1
Todd	Jamie	01/01/1995		SCO	D	2019	Berwick Rangers		End 2021/2	21	0	1	1	1		4			0
Watson	Lennon	01/01/2003		SCO	D	2020	Dunfermline Athletic		End 2021/2	0	1			1					5
Whyte	Mac	26/05/2001		SCO	GK	2019	Kirrie Thistle	Released June 2021		1	0								21

NEW SIGNINGS

Surname	First Name	Date of Birth	No	Nat	Pos	Signed	Previous	Notes	Contract
Barr	Bobby	23/06/1988		SCO	M	2021	Brechin City		End 2021/2
Buchanan	Liam	27/03/1995		SCO	F	2021	Alloa Athletic		End 2021/2
Collins	James	26/04/2000		SCO	F	2021	Kennoway Star Hearts		End 2021/2
Coulson	Quinn	01/09/2003		SCO	F	2021	Raith Rovers (OL)	Jul-Jan	End 2021
Gill	Cammy	07/04/1998		SCO	GK	2021	Dunfermline Athletic		End 2021/2
Hutton	Kyle	15/02/1991		SCO	M	2021	East Kilbride		End 2021/2
Mahady	Luke	26/02/2004		SCO	F	2021	Raith Rovers (OL)	Jul-Jan	End 2021
McGurn	David	14/09/1980		SCO	GK	2021	Raith Rovers		End 2021/2
Thomson	Craig	17/04/1991		SCO	D	2021	Edinburgh City		End 2021/2

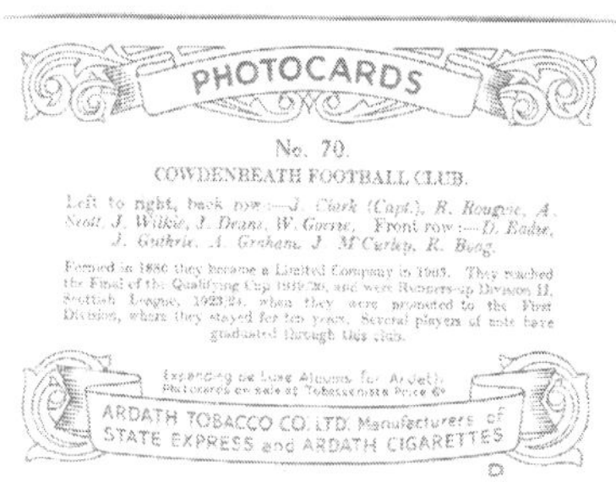

Dumbarton FC 2020/21 The Sons

Founded	1872
Ground	Dumbarton Stadium
Postcode	G82 1JJ
Tel	01389 762569
Capacity	2020
Closest Railway Station	Dumbarton East
Record Attendance	18000 v Raith Rovers, SC, 2/3/57
Record Win	13-1 v Kirkintilloch Central, SC, 1/1/1888
Record Defeat	1-11 v Albion Rovers, Lge, 30/1/1926; v Ayr United, LC, 13/8/52
Most League Goals in a Season	38 Kenny Wilson, 1971/2
Most Goals in Career	202 Hughie Gallacher
Colours 2020/21 Top	Yellow with Black across yop
Shorts	Black
Sponsor	C and G Systems
Manufacturer	Joma
Change Colours 2020/21 Top	Black and White Halves
Shorts	White
Nicknames	Sons
Web	www.dumbartonfootballclub.com
Match Programme 2020/21	Sons View £2.50

Manager : Jim Duffy, then Stevie Farrell
Assistant Manager: Barry Smith, then Frank McKeown
Goalkeeping Coach: Jamie Ewings, then Eric Phillips
Physio: Kirsten Murray
Team Chaplain: The Rev Grant Hamilton
Kit Man: David Richardson

Directors
Chairman: John Steele
Vice-Chairman : Colin Hosie
Dr Neil MacKay
Stephanie Park (Sonstrust Director)
Graham Casey (Associate Director)
Andy Gordon (Associate Director)
Honorary President: Ian MacFarlane
General Manager: Antonia Love
Company Secretary : Stephen Lynch
Disability Access and Safety Officer: Jacqui Sibbald

Supporter Liaison Officer: Robbi Docherty
Deputy Supporter Liaison Officer: Jack Brough
Marketing and Digital Promotions Executive : Angela Pounder
Programme: Graeme Robertson

Thirteen goals in twenty-two regular season League matches says much about Dumbarton's season. Few of their supporters were confident as they went into the play offs. They squeezed past Stranraer but many felt that Edinburgh City would see them off in the Final. Thankfully from Dumbarton's point of view they reserved their best performance of the season for the first leg at Ainslie Park, winning 3-1. The jitters returned for the second game as they lost 0-1 but they had done enough to secure their League One place.

In recent seasons the Sons always seem to have been scratching around for a team at the start of the season. For early games they had just two outfield subs to choose from. Loan players were required to fill spaces in the team and they seemed to lurch from one selection crisis to another.

Four straight defeats saw them finish bottom of their League Cup section. In the Scottish Cup they had a comfortable home win over Huntly. That set up a home match versus Aberdeen in which Dumbarton played well but lost 0-1.

STAR MAN
It would be difficult to pick a star player for Dumbarton in 2020/1. Jaime Wilson was top scorer with five goals and won himself a move to Falkirk. In the early part of the season loan goalkeeper Dabrowski from Hibs was outstanding. The experienced Ross Forbes came onto a game at the vital stage of the season after looking out of sorts at times. However, defender Morgyn Neill was a pillar of consistency and an ever-present in League games, demonstrating the sort of attitude that Dumbarton needed to survive.

PROSPECTS 2021/2
Manager Jim Duffy has left the club. It looks like Dumbarton have recruited a slightly larger squad this time round which should improve things for them. New Manager Stevie Farrell, arriving from Stranraer, is no stranger to the club having been Assistant there when they were a Championship side. Farrell's appointment came shortly after the majority shareholding in the club was bought by Cognitive Capital Ltd, led by architect Matthew Atkinson and sales director Henning Kristoffersen.
The new owners hope to bring full-time football back to Dumbarton, to get the club back to the Championship, and to revive plans to build a new stadium at Young's Farm to the west of the town. In the meantime, reaching the promotion play offs would be a great achievement for Dumbarton next season.

Boggy Boghead

06/10/2020	LC	H	Dunfermline Athletic	0 1	0 1	G Ross	BCD	
10/10/2020	LC	A	Clyde	2 3	1 3	S Lambie	BCD	Hamilton, Jones
17/10/2020	L	A	Forfar Athletic	0 0	0 0	P Stuart	BCD	
31/10/2020	L	A	Airdrieonians	2 0	1 0	K Graham	BCD	Wilson, McCann og
03/11/2020	L	H	Clyde	1 0	1 0	D Williams	BCD	Frizzell
07/11/2020	L	A	East Fife	1 2	0 1	S Reid	BCD	Wilson
10/11/2020	LC	H	Falkirk	0 4	0 1	S Lambie	BCD	
14/11/2020	LC	A	Kilmarnock	0 2	0 2	G Duncan	BCD	
21/11/2020	L	A	Peterhead	0 1	0 1	C Scott	BCD	
24/11/2020	L	H	Falkirk	0 3	0 2	S Kirkland	BCD	
05/12/2020	L	A	Partick Thistle	0 0	0 0	D Lowe	BCD	
12/12/2020	L	H	Cove Rangers	1 0	0 0	G Aitken	BCD	Wedderburn
19/12/2020	L	A	Montrose	0 4	0 3	M McDermid	BCD	
20/03/2021	L	H	Forfar Athletic	0 1	0 0	K Graham	BCD	
23/03/2021	SC	H	Huntly	4 0	2 0	M McDermid	BCD	Wilson 2, McGeever, Forbes
27/03/2021	L	H	Peterhead	0 1	0 0	C Graham	BCD	
30/03/2021	L	A	Falkirk	1 1	0 0	S Kirkland	BCD	Omar
01/04/2021	L	H	Airdrieonians	0 1	0 0	G Ross	BCD	
03/04/2021	SC	H	Aberdeen	0 1	0 0	D Robertson	BCD	
06/04/2021	L	H	Montrose	0 0	0 0	C Scott	BCD	
08/04/2021	L	H	East Fife	2 1	1 0	B Cook	BCD	McGeever, Frizzell
10/04/2021	L	A	Cove Rangers	0 1	0 0	D Lowe	BCD	
15/04/2021	L	A	Clyde	1 0	1 0	G Irvine	BCD	Wedderburn
20/04/2021	L	H	Partick Thistle	0 2	0 0	B Cook	BCD	
24/04/2021	L	A	East Fife	1 2	0 1	G Ross	BCD	Crossan
27/04/2021	L	H	Forfar Athletic	1 0	0 0	M McDermid	BCD	Duthie
01/05/2021	L	A	Clyde	0 2	0 1	D Lowe	BCD	
04/05/2021	L	H	Peterhead	3 2	1 1	D Dickinson	BCD	Wilson 2, Neill
08/05/2021	PO	A	Stranraer	0 0	0 0	C Graham	BCD	
11/05/2021	PO	H	Stranraer	1 0	1 0	G Duncan	BCD	Wilson
17/05/2021	PO	A	Edinburgh City	3 1	0 1	C Steven	BCD	McGeever, Brindley, Neill
20/05/2021	PO	H	Edinburgh City	0 1	0 0	A Newlands	500	

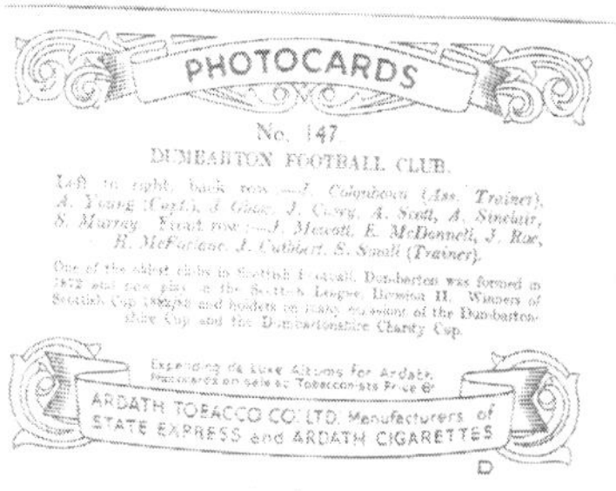

Date	Comp	H/A	Opponents	F	A	1	2	3	4	5	6	7	8	9	10	11	12	13	14	15	16	17	18	19
06/10/2020	LC	H	Dunfermline Athletic	0	1	Dabrowski	McGeever	Neill	Wardrop	R Quitongo	Wedderburn	Carswell	Langan+	McCluskey*	Johnstone	Crossan	Hamilton*	Jones+	Smith					
10/10/2020	LC	A	Clyde	2	3	Dabrowski	McGeever	Neill	Wardrop*	R Quitongo	Wedderburn	Carswell	Forbes+	Hamilton	Jones	Crossan	Johnstone*	Langan+	Smith					
17/10/2020	L	A	Forfar Athletic	0	0	Dabrowski	McGeever	Neill	Wardrop	R Quitongo	Wedderburn	Carswell	Forbes	Johnstone	Jones+	Reilly*	Wilson*	Langan+	Morrison	Smith				
31/10/2020	L	A	Airdrieonians	2	0	Smith	McGeever	Neill	Wardrop	R Quitongo	Wedderburn	Carswell	Forbes	Hamilton+	Jones	Wilson*	Langan*	Reilly+	Frizzell					
03/11/2020	L	H	Clyde	1	0	Dabrowski	McGeever	Neill	Wardrop	R Quitongo	Wedderburn	Carswell	Forbes	Hamilton&	Frizzell+	Wilson*	Jones*	Reilly+	Langan&	Calder				
07/11/2020	L	A	East Fife	1	2	Dabrowski	McGeever	Neill	Wardrop	R Quitongo*	Wedderburn	Carswell+	Forbes	Hamilton	Frizzell	Wilson	Johnstone*	Jones+	Morrison	Calder	*Reilly*	*Langan*		
10/11/2020	LC	H	Falkirk	0	4	Dabrowski+	McGeever	Morrison	Wardrop	R Quitongo*	Langan	Reilly	Forbes	Jones	Johnstone	Wilson	Frizzell*	Calder+						
14/11/2020	LC	A	Kilmarnock	0	2	Dabrowski	McGeever*	Neill	Wardrop	Church	Wedderburn	Hamilton	Forbes	Langan+	Frizzell&	Wilson	Johnstone*	Reilly+	Morrison&	Jones	*Calder*			
21/11/2020	L	A	Peterhead	0	1	Dabrowski	McGeever	Neill	Wardrop	Church	Wedderburn+	Hamilton	Forbes&	Carswell	Frizzell	Wilson*	Jones*	Johnstone+	*Reilly&*	*Langan*	*Morrison*			
24/11/2020	L	H	Falkirk	0	3	Dabrowski	McGeever*	Neill	Wardrop	R Quitongo&	Wedderburn>	Church	Langan	Carswell	Frizzell+	Wilson	Johnstone*	Crossan+	Jones&	*Morrison>*				
05/12/2020	L	A	Partick Thistle	0	0	Dabrowski	Church	Neill	Wardrop	R Quitongo	Wedderburn	Hamilton	Forbes*	Carswell	Frizzell&	Jones+	Crossan*	Johnstone+	*Langan&*	*Wilson*	*Morrison*	*McCluskey*	*Trialist*	
12/12/2020	L	H	Cove Rangers	1	0	Dabrowski	Church*	Neill	Wardrop	R Quitongo	Wedderburn	Hamilton>	Forbes	Carswell	Frizzell&	Wilson+	Crossan*	Johnstone+	McCluskey&	*Jones>*	*Morrison*	*Langan*	*Trialist*	
19/12/2020	L	A	Montrose	0	4	Dabrowski	Church&	Neill	Wardrop	R Quitongo	Wedderburn	Hamilton	Forbes>	Carswell*	Frizzell<	Johnstone+	Wilson*	Jones+	McCluskey&	*Langan>*	*Morrison<*	*Smith*		
20/03/2021	L	H	Forfar Athletic	0	1	Ramsbottom	McGeever	Neill	Wardrop	Brindley	Wedderburn&	Wilson+	Forbes	Carswell	Frizzell	Jones*	Crossan*	McCluskey+	Duthie&	*McAllister*	*Langan*	*Smith*		
23/03/2021	SC	H	Huntly	4	0	Smith	McGeever	Neill	Wardrop	McAllister*	Wedderburn+	Wilson	Forbes	Carswell	Frizzell	Crossan&	Brindley*	Langan+	Duthie&	*Jones*	*Ramsbottom*			
27/03/2021	L	H	Peterhead	0	1	Smith	McGeever	Neill	Wardrop	McAllister*	Brindley	Wilson>	Forbes	Carswell<	Frizzell+	Omar&	Wallace*	Crossan+	Jones&	*Duthie>*	*Langan<*	*Wedderburn*	*Ramsbottom*	
30/03/2021	L	A	Falkirk	1	1	Ramsbottom	McGeever	Neill	Wardrop	McAllister*	Wedderburn	Brindley*	Crossan&	Jones>	Frizzell+	Omar	Carswell*	Forbes+	Wilson&	*Layne>*	*Duthie*	*Wallace*	*Langan*	*Smith*
01/04/2021	L	H	Airdrieonians	0	1	Ramsbottom	Carswell	Neill	Wardrop	McAllister*	Duthie&	Brindley	Forbes	Langan>	Wallace*	Wilson+	Crossan*	Jones+	Omar&	*Wedderburn>*	*McGeever*	*Quitongo*	*Frizzell*	*Smith*
03/04/2021	SC	H	Aberdeen	0	1	Ramsbottom	McGeever	Neill	Wardrop	McAllister	Wedderburn	Brindley*	Jones+	Carswell	Frizzell&	Wilson	Omar*	Crossan+	Quitongo&	*Langan*	*Duthie*	*Wallace*	*Smith*	
06/04/2021	L	H	Montrose	0	0	Ramsbottom	McGeever	Neill	Quitongo	McAllister	Wedderburn	Brindley+	Omar	Carswell	Crossan	Wilson*	Jones*	Wallace+	Duthie	*Langan*	*Frizzell*	*Wardrop*		
08/04/2021	L	H	East Fife	2	1	Ramsbottom	McGeever	Neill	Wardrop	Quitongo	Wedderburn+	Frizzell	Forbes	Langan*	Wallace>	Jones&	Omar*	Carswell+	Wilson&	*Crossan>*	*Brindley*	*McAllister*	*Duthie*	*Barclay*
10/04/2021	L	A	Cove Rangers	0	1	Ramsbottom	McGeever	Neill	Wardrop>	Quitongo	McAllister	Brindley&	Forbes	Omar+	Crossan*	Wilson<	Frizzell*	Jones+	Wedderburn&	*Wattace>*	*Duthie<*	*Barclay*		
15/04/2021	L	A	Clyde	1	0	Ramsbottom	McGeever	Neill	Wardrop	Quitongo*	Wedderburn	McAllister	Forbes	Frizzell+	Crossan&	Jones>	Brindley*	Wilson+	Duthie&	*Wallace>*	*Omar*	*Barclay*		
20/04/2021	L	H	Partick Thistle	0	2	Ramsbottom	McGeever	Neill	Wardrop+	Quitongo	Wedderburn*	McAllister	Forbes	Omar	Brindley	Jones&	Frizzell*	Wilson+	Duthie&	*Langan*	*Wallace*	*Barclay*		
24/04/2021	L	A	East Fife	1	2	Ramsbottom	McGeever	Neill	Brindley+	Quitongo>	Wilson	McAllister	Forbes	Frizzell&	Crossan	Jones*	Omar*	Wallace+	Duthie&	*Langan>*	*Barclay*			
27/04/2021	L	H	Forfar Athletic	1	0	Ramsbottom	McGeever	Neill	Brindley&	Quitongo	Langan+	McAllister*	Forbes	Frizzell<	Wallace	Layne>	Carswell*	Omar+	Crossan&	*Jones>*	*Duthie<*	*Barclay*	*Wilson*	
01/05/2021	L	A	Clyde	0	2	Ramsbottom	McGeever	Neill	Brindley+	Quitongo	Carswell>	Omar*	Forbes	Frizzell	Wallace	Jones&	Crossan*	Langan+	Wilson&	*Duthie>*	*Barclay*			
04/05/2021	L	H	Peterhead	3	2	Ramsbottom	McGeever*	Neill	Omar<	Quitongo&	Carswell	McAllister	Forbes	Frizzell>	Wallace+	Wilson	Wedderburn*	Brindley+	Jones&	*Duthie>*	*Langan<*	*Barclay*		
08/05/2021	PO	A	Stranraer	0	0	Ramsbottom	Wedderburn	Neill	Omar	Quitongo	Carswell	McAllister	Forbes	Frizzell&	Langan*	Wilson+	Wallace*	Duthie+	Jones&	*Brindley*	*Barclay*			
11/05/2021	PO	H	Stranraer	1	0	Ramsbottom	Wedderburn	Neill	Brindley	Quitongo	Carswell	McAllister	Forbes	Jones	Wallace+	Wilson*	Omar*	Duthie+	Langan	*Frizzell*	*Barclay*			
17/05/2021	PO	A	Edinburgh City	3	1	Ramsbottom	McGeever	Neill	Brindley	Quitongo	Carswell	McAllister	Forbes	Jones+	Frizzell*	Wedderburn	Wallace*	Omar+	Langan	*Duthie*	*Barclay*			
20/05/2021	PO	H	Edinburgh City	0	1	Ramsbottom	McGeever	Neill	Brindley	Quitongo	Carswell	McAllister	Forbes	Jones	Frizzell+	Wedderburn*	Omar*	Duthie+	Langan	*Layne*	*Wallace*	*Barclay*		

THE GOALIES

Goalkeepers Used in League Matches, 1972-2020

Players shown in the season of their first appearance only

1972/3	Lawrie Williams
	Willie Whigham
1973/4	John Taylor
1974/5	Ian McGregor
1977/8	Jim Cruickshank
1978/9	Donald Hunter
1979/0	Tom Carson
1982/3	Murray Bowman
1983/4	Jim Stewart
1984/5	Dougie McNab
	Gordon Arthur
1985/6	Hugh Stevenson
1988/9	Boyd Strachan
1990/1	Paul Graham
1991/2	Ian McFarlane
1992/3	Michael Monaghan
1993/4	Kenny Meechan
1994/5	John Burridge
1995/6	Peter Dennison
1996/7	Derek Barnes
2000/1	John Hillcoat
	John Wight
2001/2	Jon Connolly
2002/3	Stephen Grindlay
2003/4	K Robertson
2004/5	Craig Wight
2007/8	Anton Nugent
	Peter Shaw
	David Crawford
2008/9	David McEwan
	Mark McGeown
2009/0	Michael White
	Jan Vojacek
2011/2	Jamie Ewings
	Arnaud Gastal
2012/3	C Turner
2013/4	Jamie Ewings
2014/5	Danny Rogers
2015/6	Mark Brown
2016/7	Alan Martin
2017/8	Scott Gallacher
2018/9	Jamie McGowan
	Robbie Mutch
	Grant Adam
	Connor Brennan
	Chris Smith

DUMBARTON'S SCOTTISH CUP WINNING RUN - 1882/3

Sep 9	1	H v Kilmarnock Thistle	walkover
Sep 30	2	H v King's Park (Stirling)	8-1
Oct 21	3	H v Jamestown	8-1
Nov 11	4	A v Thornliebank	3-0
	5	Bye	
Feb 3	QF	H v Queen's Park	3-1
Feb 24	SF	A v Pollokshields Athletic	1-0 Protested
Mar 17	SFR	H v Pollokshields Athletic	5-0
Mar 31	F	N v Vale of Leven	2-2
Apr 7	FR	N v Vale of Leven	2-1

Surname	First Name	Date of Birth	No	Nat	Pos	Signed	Previous	Notes	Contract	Lge A	Lge S	Lge G	SC A	SC S	SC G	LC A	LC S	LC G	Un
Barclay	Jamie	29/09/1989		SCO	GK	2021	Kilwinning Ranger	Apr-May		0	0								12
Brindley	Tomas	13/10/2001		SCO	M	2021	Kilmarnock (OL)	Mar-May		13	2	1	1	1					2
Calder	Chris	12/08/1990	21	SCO	GK	2020	St Rochs (OL)	Oct-Jan		0	0						1		3
Carswell	Stuart	09/09/1992	6	SCO	M	2017	Keflavik		End 2022/3	19	3		2			2			0
Church	Daniel	21/07/2000	19	SCO	D	2020	Celtic	Joined Alloa Athletic June 2021		5	0					1			0
Crossan	PJ	09/10/1998	24	SCO	F	2019	Celtic	Released May 2021, joined Forfar Athletic		5	9	1	1	1		2			0
Dabrowski	Maciej	09/06/1998	1	POL	GK	2020	Hibernian (OL)	Sep-May		8	0					4			0
Duthie	Conner	02/02/1997		SCO	M	2021	Ex Stenhousemuir		End 2021/2	1	12	1		1					0
Forbes	Ross	03/03/1989	8	SCO	M	2020	Forfar Athletic	Released May 2021, joined Stenhousemuir		23	1		1		1	3			5
Frizzell	Adam	22/01/1998	11	SCO	M	2020	Kilmarnock	OOC June 2021, joined Airdrieonians		19	2	2	2			1	1		4
Hamilton	Chris	13/07/2001	18	SCO	D	2020	Hearts (OL)	Sep-Jan		7	0					2	1	1	0
Johnstone	Denny	09/01/1995	9	SCO	F	2020	Falkirk	Released Jan 2021 joined Benburb		2	5					2	2		0
Jones	Robert	22/09/1995	10	SCO	F	2020	Stranraer	Joined Clyde June 2021		13	13		1			2	1	1	2
Langan	Ruaridh	15/06/1998	4	SCO	M	2019	Morton	Joined Stranraer June 2021		5	9			1		3	1		11
Layne	Isaac	16/05/1995		ENG	F	2021	Peterhead (OL)	Mar-May		1	1								1
McAllister	Nicky	17/01/2001		SCO	D	2021	St Mirren (OL)	Mar-May		14	0		2						2
McCluskey	Stefan	22/08/1990	7	SCO	F	2019	Pollok	Joined Forfar Athletic June 2021		0	3					1			1
McGeever	Ryan	30/04/1994	2	SCO	D	2019	Brechin City		End 2022/3	20	0	2	2		1	4			1
Morrison	Donald	01/08/2001	15	SCO	D	2020	Inverness CT	Released Jan 2021		0	2					1	1		5
Neill	Morgyn	10/03/1996	5	SCO	D	2019	Stenhousemuir	OOC June 2021, joined Cove Rangers		26	0	2	2			3			0
Omar	Rabin	21/07/1997		NET / IRQ	M	2021	Morton (OL)	Mar-May		8	7	1		1					1
Quitongo	Rico	15/07/1999	3	ANG / SCO	D	2019	Hearts	OOC June 2021, joined Airdrieonians		21	0			1		3			1
Ramsbottom	Sam	03/04/1996		ENG	GK	2020	Ex Morton		End 2021/2	16	0		1						2
Reilly	Matthew	05/07/2000	17	SCO	M	2020	St Mirren	Freed March 2021		1	3					1	1		1
Smith	Chris	05/03/1986	21	SCO	GK	2020	Annan Athletic	Freed April 2021		2	0		1						8
Trialist										0	0								2
Wallace	James	29/08/2000		SCO	F	2021	Morton (OL)	Mar-May		6	7								4
Wardrop	Sam	20/10/1997	12	SCO	D	2020	Dundee United	OOC June 2021, joined Airdrieonians		17	0		2			4			1
Wedderburn	Nathaniel	30/06/1991	16	ENG	M	2020	Airdrieonians	Released May 2021, joined Stenhousemuir		19	3	2	2			3			1
Wilson	Jaime	13/12/1997	14	SCO	F	2020	Northcote City SC	Joined Falkirk July 2021		15	7	5	2		2	2			2
Own Goals												1							
NEW SIGNINGS																			
Boyle	Paddy	20/03/1987		SCO	D	2021	Kelty Hearts		End 2021/2										
Buchanan	Gregor	31/03/1990		SCO	D	2021	Queen of the South		End 2022/3										
Erskine	Callum	24/04/2001		SCO	GK	2021	Stenhousemuir		End 2021/2										
Geggan	Andy	08/05/1987		SCO	M	2021	BSC Glasgow		End 2021/2										
Hopkirk	David	17/01/1993		SCO	F	2021	Stenhousemuir		End 2021/2										
Lynch	Edin	07/08/2000		SCO	D	2021	Alloa Athletic		End 2021/2										
MacLean	Ross	13/03/1997		SCO	F	2021	Queen's Park		End 2022/3										
Maley	Evan	09/06/1998		SCO	F	2021	St Cadocs		End 2021/2										
McKee	Joe	31/10/1992		SCO	M	2021	QOTS		End 2022/3										
McKnight	Kirk			SCO	M	2021	Kilmarnock (OL)	Jul-Jan	End 2021										
Muir	Sam	10/07/2002		SCO	D	2021	Motherwell		End 2021/2										
Orsi	Kalvin	15/04/1997		SCO	F	2021	Morton		End 2021/2										
Paton	Paul	18/04/1987		NIR	M	2021	East Kilbride		End 2021/2										
Pigniatello	Carlo	16/01/2000		SCO	M	2021	Livingston (OL)	July-May	End 2021/2										
Stokes	Eoghan	17/05/1996		ROI	M	2021	Airdrieonians		End 2021/2										
Syvertsen	Kristoffer	21/06/1998		NOR	F	2021	Clyde		End 2021/2										
Wilson	Calum	24/07/2003		SCO	M	2021	Hibernian		End 2021/2										

Murray Bowman

Michael Monaghan

Alan Martin

Dundee FC 2020/21 The Dee

Founded	1893
Ground	Kilmac Stadium at Dens Park
Postcode	DD3 7JY
Tel	01382 889966
Capacity	11506
Closest Railway Station	Dundee
Record Attendance	43024, SC, v Rangers 7/2/1953
Record Win	10-0 v Alloa, Lge 9/3/47; v Dunfermline 22/3/47
Record Defeat	0-11 v Celtic, Lge, 26/10/1895
Assistant Manager	Jimmy Nicholl
Colours 2020/21 Top	Navy Blue with white sleeves
Shorts	White
Sponsor	Crown Engineering Services
Manufacturer	Macron
Change Colours 2020/21 Top	White
Shorts	Dark Blue
Nicknames	Dee, Dark Blues
Web	www.dundeefconline.co.uk
Match Programme 2020/21	The Dee £3 (Curtis Sport)

Chairman: Tim Keyes
Managing Director: John Nelms
Company Secretary: Lindsay Darroch
Club Secretary: Eric Drysdale
Directors: David Gray, R W Hynd
Honorary L:ife President: Pat Liney
Manager: James McPake
Assistant Manager: Dave Mackay
First team Coach: Martin Harty
Goalkeeping Coach: Bobby Geddes
Technical Director: Gordon Strachan
Head of Academy: Stephen Wright
Head of Professional Programme: Scott Robertson
Physio: Gerry Docherty
First team Sports Scientist: Cameron McDermid
Video Analysis: Matty Castle
Club Doctor: Angela Duncan
Kit Coordinator: Lorraine Noble
Head Groundsman: Brian Robertson
Programme Editor: Tommy Young

If ever there was a case of a team hitting form at the right time then it was Dundee. Early in the season they were desperately inconsistent. Speculation abounded that James McPake's jaiket was on a shoogly peg. To the club's credit they persevered with him, weathered the storm and towards the end of the season they were hitting good form.

Dundee lost just one of their last ten League games allowing them to make it into the play-offs behind Hearts . Overtaking Raith Rovers and Dunfermline was probably crucial as it gave them more time to prepare for the vital games. Raith were dispatched on the back of a fine away performance but there was a lot of money on Kilmarnock to survive in the Final. It turned out to be money wasted as Dundee won both legs.

Dundee's cause in the League Cup was helped with a 3-0 default win over Forfar who called off for COVID reasons. The bizarre format of the competition saw them qualify alongside Hibs, then play the Edinburgh side again in the first ko round, losing 1-0. In the Scottish Cup Dundee featured in a thrilling televised match against Bonnyrigg Rose and went through after looking like losing. St Johnstone knocked them out in the next round.

STAR MAN
Eyebrows were raised when the veteran Charlie Adam was recruited at the start of the season. Adam had never hid the fact that he was a Dundee fan and playing for them meant a lot to him. At the start of the season he looked unfit but his touch was sublime. He was then missing for along spell due to a bout of COVID. He actually returned looking fitter and quicker and was instrumental in the good run OF form at the end of the season.

PROSPECTS 2021/2
Survival will be the immediate aim for Dundee. The financial bonus of being back in the top flight cannot be underestimated but Dundee need a season of consolidation. They will be looking around and perhaps view Ross County as a club they could finish above. Otherwise, it will be about taking their share of the points against the Motherwell's, Livingstons and St Mirren's to ensure that they don't find themselves at the wrong end of the table. Derbies against United will look after themselves – expect Dundee to take their scalp at some point in the season.

Albert Kidd scores THAT goal

Date	Comp	H/A	Opponents	F	A		HT	Referee	Crowd	Scorers
06/10/2020	LC	H	Forfar Athletic	3	0*					FORFAR ATHLETIC FORFEITED GAME DUE TO COVID
10/10/2020	LC	A	Brora Rangers	2	0		2 0	B Cook	BCD	Dorrans, Mullen
16/10/2020	L	A	Hearts	2	6		1 4	D Munro	BCD	Adam, Mullen
24/10/2020	L	H	Morton	1	0		1 0	G Ross	BCD	Afolabi
31/10/2020	L	H	Raith Rovers	1	1		1 0	A Newlands	BCD	Adam
06/11/2020	L	A	Alloa Athletic	3	3		0 1	A Muir	BCD	McDaid, Adam 2 (1 pen)
10/11/2020	LC	H	Cove Rangers	3	0		1 0	C Napier	BCD	McGowan, Mullen, Adam pen
15/11/2020	LC	A	Hibernian	1	4		0 1	J Beaton	BCD	Elliot
21/11/2020	L	A	Ayr United	0	2		0 2	G Beaton	BCD	
28/11/2020	LC	A	Hibernian	0	1		0 1	W Collum	BCD	
05/02/2020	L	H	Arbroath	1	0		1 0	C Graham	BCD	McGowan
12/12/2020	L	A	Inverness CT	2	2		1 0	C Napier	250	Fontaine, McGhee
19/12/2020	L	H	Dunfermline Athletic	3	3		1 0	G Irvine	BCD	Adam, Sow, Fontaine
26/12/2020	L	A	Queen of the South	3	1		2 0	A Newlands	BCD	Sow 3
29/12/2020	L	H	Alloa Athletic	3	1		0 1	S Reid	BCD	Sow 2, Fontaine
02/01/2021	L	H	Hearts	3	1		2 0	D Robertson	BCD	McGee, Mullen, Afolabi pen
09/01/2021	SC	H	Bonnyrigg Rose	3	2	AET	0 1	G Duncan	BCD	Afolabi pen, Ashcroft, Sow
22/01/2021	L	A	Arbroath	1	1		1 0	G Aitken	BCD	Adam pen
30/01/2021	L	A	Raith Rovers	1	3		1 1	C Napier	BCD	Sow
20/02/2021	L	H	Queen of the South	2	3		0 2	B Cook	BCD	Cummings, Marshall
27/02/2021	L	A	Morton	2	2		0 1	C Napier	BCD	Cummings, Mullin
02/03/2021	L	H	Inverness CT	2	1		2 0	S Kirkland	BCD	Anderson, Cummings
06/03/2021	L	A	Hearts	1	2		0 1	D Robertson	BCD	Cummings pen
13/03/2021	L	H	Arbroath	2	0		0 0	W Collum	BCD	Mullen, Anderson
16/03/2021	L	H	Ayr United	1	3		0 1	A Newlands	BCD	Sow
19/03/2021	L	A	Alloa Athletic	3	0		1 0	G Irvine	BCD	Ashcroft 2, Anderson
27/03/2021	L	H	Dunfermline Athletic	3	2		1 2	B Madden	BCD	Cummings, Mullen, Ashcroft
03/04/2021	SC	H	St Johnstone	0	1		0 1	C Napier	BCD	
06/04/2021	L	A	Ayr United	3	0		0 0	S McLean	BCD	Anderson, Afolabi, McGowan
10/04/2021	L	H	Morton	1	1		0 0	A Newlands	BCD	Ashcroft
13/04/2021	L	A	Dunfermline Athletic	0	0		0 0	K Clancy	BCD	
20/04/2021	L	A	Inverness CT	1	1		0 0	M Roncone	BCD	Ashcroft
24/04/2021	L	H	Raith Rovers	2	1		2 0	W Collum	BCD	Cummings pen, Fontaine
30/04/2021	L	A	Queen of the South	2	0		2 0	D Robertson	BCD	Cummings 2
12/05/2021	PO	A	Raith Rovers	3	0		1 0	N Walsh	BCD	McGhee 2, Sow
15/05/2021	PO	H	Raith Rovers	0	1		0 1	D Robertson	BCD	
20/05/2021	PO	H	Kilmarnock	2	1		1 0	J Beaton	500	McGhee, Adam
24/05/2021	PO	A	Kilmarnock	2	1		2 0	B Madden	500	Mullen, Ashcroft

Julian Speroni

Thomson Allan

Ally Donaldson

Date	Comp	H/A	Opponents	F	A	1	2	3	4	5	6	7	8	9	10	11	12	13	14	15	16	17	18	19	20
06/10/2020	LC	H	Forfar Athletic	3	0*																				
10/10/2020	LC	A	Brora Rangers	2	0	J Hamilton	Forster	Elliot&	Ashcroft	McGhee	Marshall	Adam<	Dorrans	McGowan>	Anderson+	Mullen*	Sow*	Robertson+	Kerr&	*McDaid>*	*Byrne<*	*Blacklock*	*D Strachan*	*Cunningham*	*Ferrie*
16/10/2020	L	A	Hearts	2	6	J Hamilton	Forster*	Kerr	Ashcroft	McGhee	Marshall	Adam	Dorrans	McGowan	Robertson&	Sow+	Afolabi*	Mullen+	Anderson&	*Elliot*	*Byrne*	*McDaid*	*Ferrie*		
24/10/2020	L	H	Morton	1	0	Ferrie	Byrne	Kerr	Ashcroft	McGhee	Marshall	Adam*	Dorrans	McDaid	Afolabi	Mullen+	Elliot*	McGowan+	*Anderson*	*Robertson*	*D Strachan*	*Blacklock*	*J Hamilton*		
31/10/2020	L	H	Raith Rovers	1	1	Ferrie	Byrne	Kerr	Ashcroft	McGhee	Marshall	Adam+	Dorrans	McDaid&	Afolabi	Mullen*	Elliot*	McGowan+	Anderson&	*Robertson*	*L Strachan*	*Blacklock*	*J Hamilton*		
06/11/2020	L	A	Alloa Athletic	3	3	Ferrie	Byrne+	Kerr	Elliot	McGhee	Marshall	Adam	McGowan	McDaid	Afolabi*	Mullen	Sow*&	Anderson+	Robertson&	*N Hamilton*	*L Strachan*	*Wilkie*	*J Hamilton*		
10/11/2020	LC	H	Cove Rangers	3	0	J Hamilton	Byrne*	Kerr	Elliot	McGhee>	Marshall	Adam	McGowan	McDaid	Anderson&	Mullen+	Robertson*	Wilkie+	Blacklock&	N Hamilton>	*L Strachan*	*D Strachan*	*Ferrie*		
15/11/2020	LC	A	Hibernian	1	4	J Hamilton	Byrne	Kerr	Elliot	McGhee	Marshall	Adam	McGowan	McDaid	Robertson	Mullen	*Legzdins*	*L Strachan*	*Wilkie*	*Blacklock*	*N Hamilton*				
21/11/2020	L	A	Ayr United	0	2	Legzdins	Ashcroft	Kerr+	Elliot	McGhee&	Marshall	Adam	McGowan	Byrne	Anderson	Sow*	Jakubiak*	McDaid+	Fontaine&	*N Hamilton*	*Wilkie*	*Robertson*	*J Hamilton*		
28/11/2020	LC	A	Hibernian	0	1	J Hamilton	Ashcroft	Fontaine	Elliot	Jakubiak	Marshall	Adam	McGowan	Byrne	Anderson*	Afolabi+	McDaid*	Sow+	*Murray*	*N Hamilton*	*Kerr*	*Robertson*	*Forster*	*McGhee*	*Ferrie*
05/02/2020	L	H	Arbroath	1	0	J Hamilton	Ashcroft	Fontaine	Elliot	Jakubiak*	Marshall	Adam	McGowan	Byrne	Anderson+	Mullen	McDaid*	Sow+	*Robertson*	*Forster*	*Kerr*	*McGhee*	*Ferrie*		
12/12/2020	L	A	Inverness CT	2	2	J Hamilton	Ashcroft	Fontaine	Elliot	McGhee	Marshall	Adam	McGowan+	Byrne	Jakubiak&	Mullen*	Sow*	McDaid+	Anderson&	*Forster*	*Kerr*	*Robertson*	*Ferrie*		
19/12/2020	L	H	Dunfermline Athletic	3	3	J Hamilton	Ashcroft	Fontaine	Elliot	McGhee	Marshall	Adam+	McGowan	Byrne	Sow*	Mullen&	Afolabi*	Anderson+	Forster&	*McDaid*	*Kerr*	*Robertson*	*Ferrie*		
26/12/2020	L	A	Queen of the South	3	1	J Hamilton	Ashcroft	Fontaine	Elliot	McGhee	Marshall	Adam&	McGowan	Byrne	Sow+	Mullen*	McDaid*	Afolabi+	Robertson&	*Forster*	*Kerr*	*Anderson*	*Ferrie*		
29/12/2020	L	H	Alloa Athletic	3	1	J Hamilton	Ashcroft	Fontaine	Elliot	McGhee	Marshall	Adam&	McGowan+	Byrne	Sow	McDaid*	Mullen*	Afolabi+	*Robertson*	*Forster*	*Kerr*	*Anderson*	*Ferrie*		
02/01/2021	L	H	Hearts	3	1	J Hamilton	Ashcroft	Fontaine	Elliot	McGhee	Marshall	Adam+	McGowan	Byrne	Sow&	Mullen*	Afolabi*	Robertson+	Kerr&	*Forster*	*McDaid*	*Anderson*	*Ferrie*		
09/01/2021	SC	H	Bonnyrigg Rose	3	2 AET	J Hamilton	Ashcroft	Fontaine	Forster	Robertson*	Marshall	Adam	McGowan	Byrne+	Sow	Mullen&	Afolabi*	Anderson+	Moore&	*N Hamilton*	*Murray*	*D Strachan*	*Ferrie*		
22/01/2021	L	A	Arbroath	1	1	J Hamilton	Ashcroft	Fontaine&	Elliot	McGhee*	Marshall	Adam	McGowan	Byrne	Sow	Mullen+	Kerr*	Afolabi+	Forster&	*Robertson*	*Anderson*	*Cameron*	*Legzdins*		
30/01/2021	L	A	Raith Rovers	1	3	J Hamilton	Fagan-Walcott	Fisher	Elliot	McMullan*	Marshall	Adam	McGowan	Byrne	Sow	Moore+	Cummings*	Mullen+	*Anderson*	*Robertson*	*Cameron*	*Kerr*	*Ferrie*		
20/02/2021	L	H	Queen of the South	2	3	J Hamilton	Ashcroft	Fontaine	Kerr	McMullan	Marshall	Adam	McGowan	Byrne*	Sow+	Cummings	Mullen*	Afolabi+	*Anderson*	*Robertson*	*Elliot*	*Fagan-Wallcott*	*Legzdins*		
27/02/2021	L	A	Morton	2	2	J Hamilton	Ashcroft	Fontaine	Elliot	McMullan	Marshall	Robertson*	McGowan	Byrne&	Sow+	Cummings	Anderson*	Mullen+	McDaid&	*Afolabi*	*Kerr*	*Fagan-Wallcott*	*Legzdins*		
02/03/2021	L	H	Inverness CT	2	1	J Hamilton	Ashcroft	Fontaine	Elliot	McMullan	Marshall	McDaid	McGowan	Anderson+	Mullen*	Cummings&	Sow*	Byrne+	Afolabi&	*Robertson*	*Kerr*	*Fagan-Wallcott*	*Legzdins*		
06/03/2021	L	A	Hearts	1	2	J Hamilton	Ashcroft	Fontaine	Elliot	McMullan	Marshall	McDaid	McGowan	Anderson+	Mullen*	Cummings	Sow*	Afolabi+	*Byrne*	*Robertson*	*Kerr*	*Fagan-Wallcott*	*Legzdins*		
13/03/2021	L	H	Arbroath	2	0	Legzdins	Ashcroft	Fagan-Walcott+	Elliot	McMullan	Marshall	McDaid	McGowan	Anderson	Mullen*	Cummings&	Adam*	Fisher+	Sow&	*Afolabi*	*Byrne*	*Kerr*	*J Hamilton*		
16/03/2021	L	H	Ayr United	1	3	Legzdins	Ashcroft	Fisher	Elliot	McMullan	Marshall	Adam	McGowan+	Anderson	Mullen*	Cummings&	McDaid*	Sow+	Afolabi&	*Cameron*	*Byrne*	*Kerr*	*J Hamilton*		
19/03/2021	L	A	Alloa Athletic	3	0	Legzdins	Ashcroft	Fisher	Elliot	McMullan	Marshall	McDaid	McGowan*	Anderson	Mullen&	Cummings+	Byrne*	Adam+	Afolabi&	*Cameron*	*L Strachan*	*Kerr*	*J Hamilton*		
27/03/2021	L	H	Dunfermline Athletic	3	2	Legzdins	Ashcroft	Fontaine	Elliot	McMullan	Marshall	McDaid	McGowan	Anderson+	Sow*	Cummings&	Mullen*	Byrne+	Afolabi&	*Cameron*	*Fisher*	*Kerr*	*Ferrie*		
03/04/2021	SC	H	St Johnstone	0	1	Legzdins	Ashcroft*	Fontaine	Kerr	McMullan	Marshall	McDaid	Adam&	Anderson+	Mullen	Byrne	McGowan*	Cummings+	Afolabi&	*Elliot*	*Fisher*	*Murray*	*L Strachan*	*Cameron*	*Ferrie*
06/04/2021	L	A	Ayr United	3	0	Legzdins	Ashcroft	Fontaine	Elliot	McMullan>	Marshall	McDaid	McGowan&	Anderson+	Mullen	Cummings*	Afolabi*	Byrne+	Cameron&	*Adam>*	*Fisher*	*Kerr*	*Ferrie*		
10/04/2021	L	H	Morton	1	1	Legzdins	Ashcroft	Fontaine	Elliot	McMullan	Marshall	McDaid	McGowan	Anderson&	Mullen+	Cummings*	Afolabi*	Sow+	Adam&	*Byrne*	*Fisher*	*Kerr*	*Ferrie*		
13/04/2021	L	A	Dunfermline Athletic	0	0	Legzdins	Ashcroft	Fontaine	Kerr	McMullan	Marshall*	McDaid&	McGhee	Byrne	Mullen	Cummings+	Elliot*	Sow+	Afolabi&	*Adam*	*Fisher*	*Jakubiak*	*Ferrie*		
20/04/2021	L	A	Inverness CT	1	1	Legzdins	Ashcroft	Fontaine	Elliot	McMullan	Kerr	McDaid	McGhee	Byrne&	Mullen+	Afolabi*	Adam*	Cummings+	Anderson&	*Sow*	*Fisher*	*Jakubiak*	*Ferrie*		
24/04/2021	L	H	Raith Rovers	2	1	Legzdins	Ashcroft	Fontaine*	Ellot	McMullan&	Kerr	Adam	McGowan	Byrne	McGhee	Cummings+	Anderson*	Mullen+	Jakubiak&	*Sow*	*Fisher*	*Afolabi*	*Ferrie*		
30/04/2021	L	A	Queen of the South	2	0	Legzdins	Ashcroft	Anderson	Elliot	McMullan*	Kerr	Adam	McGowan	Byrne	McGhee	Cummings+	McDaid*	Sow+	*Jakubiak*	*Mullen*	*Fisher*	*Afolabi*	*Ferrie*		
12/05/2021	PO	A	Raith Rovers	3	0	Legzdins	Ashcroft	Fontaine+	Elliot	McMullan&	Kerr	Adam	McGowan	Byrne	McGhee	Cummings*	Mullen*	Anderson+	Sow&	*Jakubiak*	*McDaid*	*Marshall*	*Ferrie*		
15/05/2021	PO	H	Raith Rovers	0	1	Legzdins	Ashcroft	Anderson	Elliot	McMullan+	Kerr	Adam&	McGowan	Byrne	McGhee	Cummings*	Sow*	McDaid+	Mullen&	*Jakubiak*	*Fisher*	*Afolabi*	*Ferrie*		
20/05/2021	PO	H	Kilmarnock	2	1	Legzdins	Ashcroft	Fontaine	Elliot*	McMullan+	Kerr	Adam	McGowan	Byrne	McGhee	Mullen&	Marshall*	Sow+	McDaid&	*Jakubiak*	*Cummings*	*Anderson*	*Ferrie*		
24/05/2021	PO	A	Kilmarnock	2	1	Legzdins	Ashcroft	Fontaine	Marshall	McMullan	Kerr	Adam	McGowan+	Byrne	McGhee	Mullen*	Sow*	McDaid+	*Anderson*	*Jakubiak*	*Cummings*	*Fisher*	*Ferrie*		

THE GOALIES

Goalkeepers Used in League Matches, 1970-2020

Players shown in the season of their first appearance only

1970/1	Ally Donaldson
	Mike Hewitt
1972/3	Thomson Allan
1980/1	Bobby Geddes
	Lawrie Williams
	Alan Blair
1982/3	Colin Kelly
1984/5	Tom Carson
1989/0	Paul Mathers
1991/2	Jim Leighton
1993/4	Michel Pageaud
1996/7	Billy Thomson
	Gary McGlynn
1997/8	Rab Douglas
1998/9	Jamie Langfield
2000/1	Marco Roccati
2001/2	Julian Speroni
2003/4	Derek Soutar
2004/5	Kelvin Jack
2005/6	Scott Murray
2006/7	Ludovic Roy
	Chad Harpur
	Callum Reidford
2007/8	Craig Samson
	Michael White
2009/0	Tony Bullock
2010/1	Scott Fox
	John Gibson
2012/3	Steve Simonsen
2013/4	Kyle Letheren
	Dan Twardzik
2014/5	Scott Bain
	Arvid Schenk
2015/6	David Mitchell
2017/8	Elliot Parish
	Callum Ferrie
2018/9	Senny Dieng
	Jack Hamilton
2019/0	Connor Hazard

DUNDEE'S SCOTTISH CUP WINNING RUN - 1909/10

Jan 22	1	H v Beith	1-1*
Jan 29	1R	H v Beith	1-0
Feb 5	2	H v Falkirk	3-0
Feb 26	3	A v Motherwell	3-1
Mar 12	SF	A v Hibernian	0-0
Mar 19	SFR	H v Hibernian	0-0
Mar 23	SFR	N v Hibernian (at Celtic Park)	1-0
Apr 9	F	N v Clyde (at Ibrox)	2-2
Apr 16	FR	N v Clyde (at Ibrox)	0-0
Apr 20	FR	N v Clyde (at Ibrox)	2-1

* This tie was originally scheduled to be played at Beith. Dundee offered the Ayrshire side £120 to reverse the match, which they accepted.

Surname	First Name	Date of Birth	No	Nat	Pos	Signed	Previous	Notes	Contract	Lge A	Lge S	Lge G	SC A	SC S	SC G	LC A	LC S	LC G	Un
Adam	Charlie	10/12/1985	26	SCO	M	2020	Reading	Son of ex St Johnstone player, brother of Grant	End 2021/2	21	4	7	2			4		1	1
Afolabi	Jonathan	14/01/2000	17	ROI / NIG	F	2020	Celtic (OL)	Sep-May		4	15	3		2	1	1			5
Anderson	Max	10/10/2002	24	SCO	M	2019	Dundee Youths		End 2022/3	12	9	4	1	1		3			9
Ashcroft	Lee	29/08/1993	14	SCO	D	2020	Dunfermline Athletic		End 2021/2	29	0	6	2		1	2			0
Blacklock	Cammy	01/01/2002		SCO	M	2020	Dundee Youths		End 2021/2	0	0						1		4
Byrne	Shaun	09/06/1993	8	SCO	M	2019	Livingston		End 2021/2	22	4		2			3	1		5
Cameron	Lyall	10/10/2002	25	SCO	M	2020	Dundee Youths	OL to Peterhead Oct-Jan, Ol to Peterhead for 2021/2	End 2022/3	0	1								6
Cummings	Jason	01/08/1995		SCO	F	2021	Shrewsbury Town		End 2021/2	15	2	8		1					2
Cunningham	Michael	10/03/2001	31	SCO	F	2020	Dundee Youths	Released June 2021		0	0								1
Dorrans	Graham	05/05/1987		SCO	M	2019	Rangers	Transferred to Western Sydney Wanderers, Nov 2020		3	0					1		1	0
Elliot	Christie	26/05/1991	16	ENG	D	2020	Carlisle United		End 2021/2	25	3					4		1	3
Fagan-Walcott	Malachi	11/03/2002		ENG	D	2021	Tottenham Hotspur (OL)	Jan-Mar		2	0								4
Ferrie	Callum	19/06/1998	12	ENG	GK	2018	Dundee Youths	Released June 2021		3	0								24
Fisher	Sam	26/07/2001	29	SCO	D	2020	Dundee Youths	OL to Forfar Athletic Oct-Jan	End 2022/3	3	1								10
Fleming	Kyle	25/02/2002		SCO	M	2018	Celtic Youths	OL to Annan Athletic Sep-May, Released June 2021		0	0								0
Fontaine	Liam	07/01/1986	4	ENG	D	2020	Ross County		End 2021/2	20	1	4	2			1			0
Forster	Jordan	23/09/1993	5	SCO	D	2019	Cheltenham Town	Released May 2021, joined Kelty Hearts		1	2		1			1			6
Hamilton	Nicholas	16/03/1996	39	JAM	F	2020	York United (CAN) (OL)	Sep-Jun		0	0						1		5
Hamilton	Jack	22/03/1994	1	SCO	GK	2018	Hearts	Released June 2021		13	0		1			4			7
Jakubiak	Alex	27/08/1996	7	SCO	M	2020	Watford		End 2021/2	2	2					1			7
Joyce	Louis	20/03/2003		SCO	D	2020	Dundee Youths	Released June 2021											
Kemlo	Finn	17/05/2003		SCO	D	2020	Dundee Youths	Released June 2021											
Kerr	Cammy	10/09/1995	2	SCO	D	2014	Dundee Youths		End 2022/3	14	2		1			2	1		16
Legzdins	Adam	28/11/1986	13	LAT / ENG	GK	2020	Burnley		End 2022/3	15	0		1						6
Mansouri	Adam	10/01/2003		SCO	F	2019	Rangers Youth	OL to Kennoway SH Aug-Jan, Released June 2021											
Marshall	Jordan	27/10/1996	23	ENG	D	2019	Queen of the South		End 2022/3	25	1	1	2			4			1
McDaid	Declan	22/11/1995	11	SCO	M	2019	Ayr United		End 2021/2	13	10	1	1			2	2		4
McGhee	Jordan	24/07/1996	3	SCO	D	2019	Falkirk		End 2022/3	19	0	5				3			2
McGowan	Paul	07/10/1987	10	SCO	M	2014	St Mirren		End 2021/2	27	2	2	1	1		4		1	0
McGrath	Grady	06/04/2002		SCO	M	2019	Dundee United Youths	Released June 2021											
McMullan	Paul	25/02/1996		SCO	M	2021	Dundee United (OL)	Jan-May		19	0		1						0
Moore	Callum	22/03/2000	22	SCO	M	2019	Dundee Youths	Rejected new contract and left, June 2021		1	0			1					0
Mullen	Danny	01/03/1995	9	SCO	F	2020	St Mirren		End 2021/2	20	9	6	2			3		2	1
Mulligan	Josh	12/11/2002		SCO	M	2019	Dundee Youths	OL to Peterhead, Oct 5-11, OL to Peterhead for 2021/2	End 2022/3										
Murray	Ewan	25/11/2004		SCO	D	2020	Dundee Youths		U20	0	0								3
Robertson	Finlay	12/11/2002	19	SCO	M	2019	Dundee Youths		End 2022/3	2	3		1			1	2		13
Sharp	Harry	04/04/2001		SCO	GK	2019	Dundee Youths	OL to Edinburgh City Oct-Jan	End 2022/3										
Sow	Osman	22/04/1990	21	SWE / SEN	F	2020	Dundee United	Released June 2021		11	14	9	1		1		2		2
Strachan	Luke	01/05/2001	27	ENG / SCO	F	2019	Peterborough United		End 2021/2	0	0								6
Strachan	Danny	17/07/2002		SCO	D	2019	Aberdeen Youths	OL to Peterhead for 2021/2	End 2021/2	0	0								4
Wilkie	Jack	20/12/2002	20	SCO	D	2020	Dundee United Youths			0	0						1		3
NEW SIGNINGS																			
McCowan	Luke	09/12/1997		SCO	F	2021	Ayr United		End 2022/3										
McMullan	Paul	25/02/1996		SCO	M	2021	Dundee United		End 2022/3										
Sweeney	Ryan	15/04/1997		ROI / ENG	D	2021	Mansfield Town		End 2022/3										
Panter	Corey	19/10/2000		ENG	D	2021	Luton Town (OL)	Jul-May	End 2021/2										

PHOTOCARDS

No. 40.

DUNDEE FOOTBALL CLUB.

Left to right, back row :—*J. Quskley (Trainer), L. Morgan, L. Richards, W. Marsh, J. Guthrie (Capt.), T. Wemuss, T. Smith, W. M'Candless (Sec. Manager).* Front row :—*J. Gilmour, T. Robertson, G. M'Naughton, A. Coats, W. Phillips, N. Kirby, J. Evans.*

Founded 1893, and won Scottish Cup 1909/10, and were Runners-up in First Division of the Scottish League 1902/03, 1906/07, 1908/09, and finished thirteenth in 1935/36.

Expanding de Luxe Albums for Ardath Photocards on sale at Tobacconists Price 6d

ARDATH TOBACCO CO. LTD. Manufacturers of STATE EXPRESS and ARDATH CIGARETTES

D

Dundee United FC 2020/21 The Arabs

Founded	1909
Ground	Tannadice Park
Capacity	14229
Postcode	DD3 7JW
Tel	01382 833166
Closest Railway Station	Dundee
Record Attendance	28000 v Barcelona, Fairs Cup, 16/11/1966
Record Win	14-0 v Nithsdale Wanderers, SC, 17/1/1931
Record Defeat	1-12 v Motherwell, Lge, 23/1/1954
Most League Goals in a Season	40 John Coyle, 1955/6
Colours 2020/21 Top	Tangerine
Shorts	Black
Sponsor	Utilita
Manufacturer	Macron
Change Colours 2020/21 Top	Purple
Shorts	Purple
Nicknames	United, Terrors, Arabs
Web	www.dundeeunitedfc.co.uk
Match Programme 2020/21	Occasional

Chairman: Mark J Ogren
Vice Chairman: Scott Ogren
Directors: David Dorward, Jimmy Fyffe
Associate Directors: Colin Stewart, Stuart Campbell
Managing Director: Malachy Brannigan
Head of Football Administration: Laura McCallum
Sporting Director: Tony Asghar
Finance Director: Derek Bond
Club Ambassadors: David Dodds, Hamish McAlpine, Paul Hegarty, John Holy, Maurice Malpas
Head Coach: Mickey Mellon, then Tom Courts
Assistant Manager: Liam Fox
Goalkeeping Coach: Neil Alexander (until July 2021)
Player Transition Coach: David Bowman
Academy Director: Andrew Goldie
Head Professional Development Coach: Adam Asghar
Academy Operations Manager: Michael McPake
Head of Player Pathway & Loans: Brian Grant
Scouting Operations Manager: Sean McGhee
Head of Medical: Marcin Szostak
Physios: Jordan Clelland, Jeff Clarke
Kit Man: Andy Bryan
Football Operations Manager: Ross Starke
Head of Business Partnerships: Paul Reid
Head of Finance: Katie Paton
Business Development Manager: David Rennie
Partnerships Manager: Declan Montgomery
Events Manager: Kerri Taylor
Head of Communications and Media: Joe Rice
Facilities Manager: Dean Milne
Operations and Safety Officer: Ian Low
Head Groundsman: Billy Milton
Ticket Office Manager: Fran Ritchie
Head of Retail: Grant Blue
Support Liaison: Moira Hughes

Nobody quite knew what to expect when Mickey Mellon took over as United Manager for 2021/2. Newly promoted sides usually enjoy a honeymoon period before being ground down by the reality of the Premiership. That wasn't really the case with United. They were inconsistent from the off and never really hit any run of sustained form.

Rumours suggested that budgets were tight so new signings were mainly of the speculative nature. Some worked well and some were disappointing. As the season progressed United looked increasingly to their own youth academy for first team players, recalling the glory days of the 1980s.

United got to the Semi Final of the Scottish Cup before folding at the hands of Hibernian. Their League form led to a lower mid-table position – they were not seriously troubled by relegation but nor did they shown any likelihood of qualifying for Europe. Their best result was a 3-0 win at Aberdeen in the Cup; Their worst a 5-1 home defeat from St Mirren or a home loss to Peterhead in the League Cup.

STAR MAN
Goalkeeper Benjamin Siegrist once again demonstrated abilities that make him one of the best keepers in the League. He was linked with moves away from Tannadice and if me maintains the same level of performance in 2021/2 he will surely be off.

PROSPECTS 2021/2
When Mellon left al the usual suspects were tipped for the United job. The successful candidate came from so far out in left field that nobody saw him coming. The job went to Tam Courts, part of the United Technical Analysis Department, whose only previous Managerial experience was with Kelty Hearts in the Juniors, East of Scotland Lowland Leagues. His sudden departure from Kelty a few years ago raised some eyebrows as he seemed to be "in with the bricks" at the club. Clearly that was not the case. Early reaction from some noisy United fans was not favourable. However, the more measured supporters will give him the opportunity to prove himself. However, if things are not going quite well by the late Autumn the pressure will really be on him.

DUNDEE UNITED'S SCOTTISH CUP WINNING RUNS - 1993/4 AND 2009/10

1993/4

Jan 29	3	A v Arbroath	3-2
Feb 19	4	H v Motherwell	2-2
Mar 1	4R	A v Motherwell	1-0
Mar 12	QF	A v Airdrie	0-0
Mar 15	QFR	H v Airdrie	2-0
Apr 9	SF	N v Aberdeen	1-1
Apr 12	SFR	N v Aberdeen	1-0
May 21	F	N v Rangers	1-0

2009/10

Jan 9	4	A v Partick Thistle	2-0
Feb 6	5	A v St Johnstone	1-0
Mar 14	6	A v Rangers	3-3
Mar 24	6R	H v Rangers	1-0
Apr 11	SF	N v Raith Rovers	2-0
May 15	F	N v Ross County	3-0

Date	Comp	H/A	Opponents	F	A		HT		Referee	Crowd	Scorers
01/08/2020	L	H	St Johnstone	1	1		1	0	K Clancy	BCD	Clark pen
08/08/2020	L	A	Motherwell	1	0		0	0	S McLean	BCD	Reynolds
11/08/2020	L	H	Hibernian	0	1		0	0	D Robertson	BCD	
15/08/2020	L	A	Ross County	2	1		1	1	C Napier	BCD	Pawlett, Clark
22/08/2020	L	H	Celtic	0	1		0	0	A Dallas	BCD	
29/08/2020	L	A	Kilmarnock	0	4		0	2	D Munro	BCD	
12/09/2020	L	A	Rangers	0	4		0	2	K Clancy	BCD	
19/09/2020	L	H	St Mirren	2	1		1	0	C Steven	BCD	Shankland, Sporle
26/09/2020	L	A	Hamilton Accies	1	1		0	1	A Muir	BCD	Shankland
02/10/2020	L	H	Livingston	1	2		1	0	J Beaton	BCD	Clark
07/10/2020	LC	A	Brechin City	6	2		3	0	A Newlands	BCD	Clark 2, C Smith 2, Butcher, Harkes
10/10/2020	LC	H	Peterhead	0	1		0	0	B Madden	BCD	
13/10/2020	LC	H	Kelty Hearts	1	0		1	0	D Robertson	BCD	Edwards
17/10/2020	L	H	Aberdeen	0	0		0	0	A Muir	BCD	
24/10/2020	L	A	St Johnstone	0	0		0	0	A Dallas	BCD	
31/10/2020	L	H	Ross County	2	1		1	0	S Kirkland	BCD	Clark 2 (1 pen)
06/11/2020	L	A	St Mirren	0	0		0	0	D Munro	BCD	
10/11/2020	LC	A	St Johnstone	0	0	4-3p	0	0	D Robertson	BCD	
21/11/2020	L	H	Hamilton Accies	2	1		0	0	C Napier	BCD	Clark 2
05/12/2020	L	A	Livingston	0	2		0	0	D Robertson	BCD	
13/12/2020	L	H	Rangers	1	2		1	2	S McLean	BCD	L Smith
19/12/2020	L	A	Hibernian	1	1		0	1	G Duncan	BCD	Bolton
23/12/2020	L	H	Kilmarnock	2	0		2	0	S McLean	BCD	McNulty, Shankland
26/12/2020	L	H	Motherwell	1	1		0	1	B Madden	BCD	Clark
30/12/2020	L	A	Celtic	0	3		0	2	W Collum	BCD	
02/01/2021	L	A	Aberdeen	0	0		0	0	K Clancy	BCD	
12/01/2021	L	H	St Johnstone	2	2		1	2	C Steven	BCD	Appere, Shankland
16/01/2021	L	A	Hamilton Accies	0	0		0	0	G Aitken	BCD	
27/01/2021	l	H	St Mirren	1	5		0	3	J Beaton	BCD	Harkes
30/01/2021	L	H	Hibernian	0	2		0	1	G Duncan	BCD	
03/02/2021	L	A	Motherwell	1	2		0	2	D Robertson	BCD	Edwards
06/02/2021	L	A	Ross County	2	0		0	0	G Irvine	BCD	Edwards, Shankland
13/02/2021	L	H	Livingston	3	0		2	0	N Walsh	BCD	Sporle, Shankland 2
21/02/2021	L	A	Rangers	1	4		0	2	N Walsh	BCD	McNulty
27/02/2021	L	A	Kilmarnock	1	1		1	0	D Munro	BCD	Sporle
07/03/2021	L	H	Celtic	0	0		0	0	K Clancy	BCD	
20/03/2021	L	H	Aberdeen	1	0		0	0	G Aitken	BCD	Sporle
03/04/2021	SC	H	Partick Thistle	2	1		0	1	S McLean	BCD	Shankland, Clark
10/04/2021	L	A	Hamilton Accies	1	0		1	0	B Madden	BCD	McNulty
16/04/2021	SC	A	Forfar Athletic	1	0		0	0	D Robertson	BCD	Pawlett
21/04/2021	L	A	Kilmarnock	0	3		0	3	A Muir	BCD	
25/04/2021	SC	A	Aberdeen	3	0		2	0	K Clancy	BCD	McNulty 2, Edwards
01/05/2021	L	H	Ross County	0	2		0	2	K Clancy	BCD	
08/05/2021	SC	N	Hibernian	0	2		0	1	B Madden	BCD	
12/05/2021	L	H	Motherwell	2	2		2	0	D Dickonson	BCD	Shankland, Meekison
16/05/2021	L	A	St Mirren	0	0		0	0	E Anderson	BCD	

Date	Comp	H/A	Opponents	F	A		1	2	3	4	5	6	7	8	9	10
01/08/2020	L	H	St Johnstone	1	1		Siegrist	Reynolds	Connolly	L Smith	Robson&	Pawlett	Butcher	Harkes	Neilson*	Clark+
08/08/2020	L	A	Motherwell	1	0		Siegrist	Reynolds	Connolly	L Smith	Robson	Pawlett&	Butcher	Harkes>	Appere	Bolton*
11/08/2020	L	H	Hibernian	0	1		Siegrist	Reynolds	Connolly	Edwards+	Robson*	Pawlett	Butcher	Harkes	Appere	Bolton&
15/08/2020	L	A	Ross County	2	1		Siegrist	Reynolds	Connolly	Sporle	Freeman*	Pawlett	Butcher>	Harkes	Appere+	Bolton&
22/08/2020	L	H	Celtic	0	1		Siegrist	Reynolds	Connolly	Neilson*	Robson	Pawlett	Butcher	Harkes	Clark&	Bolton>
29/08/2020	L	A	Kilmarnock	0	4		Siegrist	Reynolds	Connolly	Neilson+	Robson	Pawlett*	Butcher	Harkes	Clark	Bolton
12/09/2020	L	A	Rangers	0	4		Siegrist	Reynolds	Powers	Neilson>	Robson*	Pawlett	Butcher	Harkes	Clark+	Bolton&
19/09/2020	L	H	St Mirren	2	1		Siegrist	Reynolds	Sporle	Edwards	Robson	Chalmers*	Butcher	Harkes	Clark+	Bolton
26/09/2020	L	A	Hamilton Accies	1	1		Siegrist	Reynolds	Sporle*	Edwards	Robson	Chalmers+	Butcher&	Harkes	Clark	Bolton
02/10/2020	L	H	Livingston	1	2		Mehmet	Connolly	Sporle+	Edwards	Robson	Chalmers*	Butcher	Harkes	Clark	Bolton
07/10/2020	LC	A	Brechin City	6	2		Mehmet	Reynolds	Neilson>	Edwards&	Robson	McMullan	Butcher*	Harkes<	Clark+	Bolton
10/10/2020	LC	H	Peterhead	0	1		Mehmet	Connolly	L Smith*	Edwards	Robson	McMullan+	Butcher&	Harkes	Pawlett	Bolton
13/10/2020	LC	H	Kelty Hearts	1	0		Mehmet	Reynolds	Connolly+	Edwards	Robson	Pawlett&	Butcher	Harkes	Clark	Bolton
17/10/2020	L	H	Aberdeen	0	0		Siegrist	Reynolds+	Connolly	Edwards	Robson	Pawlett&	Butcher>	Harkes	Clark*	Bolton
24/10/2020	L	A	St Johnstone	0	0		Siegrist	Reynolds	Connolly	Edwards	Robson	Powers	McNulty*	Harkes	Clark	Bolton
31/10/2020	L	H	Ross County	2	1		Siegrist	Reynolds	L Smith	Edwards	Robson	Pawlett*	Butcher	Harkes+	Clark&	Bolton
06/11/2020	L	A	St Mirren	0	0		Siegrist	Reynolds	L Smith	Edwards	Robson	Pawlett*	Butcher	Harkes+	Clark	Bolton&
10/11/2020	LC	A	St Johnstone	0	0	4-3p	Mehmet	Reynolds	Connolly	Edwards	L Smith	Sporle&	Butcher	McMullan+	Clark	Fuchs*
21/11/2020	L	H	Hamilton Accies	2	1		Siegrist	Reynolds>	Connolly	Edwards	L Smith	Sporle+	Butcher	McMullan*	Clark	Fuchs&
05/12/2020	L	A	Livingston	0	2		Siegrist	Reynolds	Connolly	Edwards	L Smith	Sporle	Powers*	Harkes	Shankland	Fuchs
13/12/2020	L	H	Rangers	1	2		Siegrist	Reynolds	Connolly	Edwards	L Smith	Sporle*	Robson	Harkes	Shankland	Fuchs
19/12/2020	L	A	Hibernian	1	1		Siegrist	Reynolds	Connolly	Edwards+	L Smith	Clark*	Robson	Butcher	Shankland	Fuchs&
23/12/2020	L	H	Kilmarnock	2	0		Siegrist	Reynolds	Connolly	McMullan	L Smith	Bolton&	Robson	Butcher*	Shankland	Fuchs
26/12/2020	L	H	Motherwell	1	1		Siegrist	Reynolds	Connolly	McMullan+	L Smith	Bolton	Robson*	Butcher&	Shankland	Fuchs
30/12/2020	L	A	Celtic	0	3		Siegrist	Reynolds	Connolly	Edwards	L Smith>	Pawlett+	Robson&	Harkes	Shankland*	Clark
02/01/2021	L	A	Aberdeen	0	0		Siegrist	Reynolds	Connolly	Neilson	L Smith	Pawlett*	Robson	Harkes	Shankland	Clark
12/01/2021	L	H	St Johnstone	2	2		Siegrist	Reynolds	Connolly	Neilson*	L Smith	Powers	Robson	Harkes	Shankland	Clark
16/01/2021	L	A	Hamilton Accies	0	0		Siegrist	Reynolds	Connolly	Neilson	L Smith	Powers	Robson	Harkes	Shankland	Clark
27/01/2021	l	H	St Mirren	1	5		Mehmet	Reynolds	Connolly	Bolton+	L Smith	Powers*	Robson	Harkes	Shankland	Clark
30/01/2021	L	H	Hibernian	0	2		Siegrist	Reynolds	Connolly	Bolton*	L Smith	Fuchs+	Robson	Butcher	Shankland	Clark
03/02/2021	L	A	Motherwell	1	2		Siegrist	Edwards	Sporle	Butcher	L Smith	Fuchs	Robson	Harkes	Shankland	Clark*
06/02/2021	L	A	Ross County	2	0		Siegrist	Reynolds	Sporle*	Butcher&	L Smith	Fuchs+	Robson	Edwards	Shankland	Pawlett
13/02/2021	L	H	Livingston	3	0		Siegrist	Reynolds	Sporle*	Butcher	L Smith	Fuchs	Robson	Edwards	Shankland	Pawlett
21/02/2021	L	A	Rangers	1	4		Siegrist	Reynolds	Robson	Butcher	L Smith	Fuchs	Harkes+	Edwards	Shankland	Clark
27/02/2021	L	A	Kilmarnock	1	1		Siegrist	Reynolds	Robson	Butcher	L Smith	Fuchs+	Harles	Edwards	Shankland	Sporle*
07/03/2021	L	H	Celtic	0	0		Siegrist	Reynolds	Robson	Butcher	L Smith	Fuchs	Harkes&	Edwards	Shankland	Clark*
20/03/2021	L	H	Aberdeen	1	0		Siegrist	Reynolds	Robson	Butcher+	L Smith	Fuchs	Harkes	Edwards	Shankland	Sporle*
03/04/2021	SC	H	Partick Thistle	2	1		Mehmet	Reynolds	Robson*	Butcher	Sporle	Fuchs+	Harkes	Edwards	Shankland	Bolton
10/04/2021	L	A	Hamilton Accies	1	0		Siegrist	Reynolds	Robson	Butcher	L Smith	Fuchs&	Harkes+	Edwards	Shankland>	Sporle*
16/04/2021	SC	A	Forfar Athletic	1	0		Mehmet	Reynolds	Robson	Butcher+	L Smith	Pawlett&	Clark	Edwards	Shankland*	Sporle
21/04/2021	L	A	Kilmarnock	0	3		Mehmet	Connolly	Robson	Sporle	L Smith	Fuchs	Harkes	Bolton	Hoti*	K Smith
25/04/2021	SC	A	Aberdeen	3	0		Mehmet	Reynolds	Robson	Butcher*	L Smith	Fuchs	Harkes	Edwards	Shankland+	Clark&
01/05/2021	L	H	Ross County	0	2		Mehmet	Reynolds>	Robson	Butcher	L Smith	Fuchs<	Harkes*	Edwards	Shankland&	Clark
08/05/2021	SC	N	Hibernian	0	2		Mehmet	Reynolds	Robson	Butcher	L Smith	Fuchs	Harkes+	Edwards	Shankland	Clark*
12/05/2021	L	H	Motherwell	2	2		Doohan	Connolly	Sporle	Pawlett*	L Smith	Fuchs	Meekison+	K Smith	Shankland	Chalmers&
16/05/2021	L	A	St Mirren	0	0		Doohan	Edwards	Robson	Harkes+	L Smith	Fuchs	Meekison*	K Smith>	Shankland	Chalmers&

THE GOALIES

Goalkeepers Used in League Matches, 1970-2020
Players shown in the season of their first appearance only

1970/1	Donald Mackay
	Hamish McAlpine
1972/3	Sandy Davie
1977/8	Andy Graham
1979/0	Peter Bonetti
1984/5	Billy Thomson
1986/7	Allan Main
1989/0	Scott Thomson
1991/2	Guido Van De Kamp
1993/4	Brian Flies
1994/5	Henrik Jorgensen
	Kelham O'Hanlon
1995/6	Ally Maxwell
1996/7	Lance Key
	Sieb Dykstra
1998/9	Alan Combe
1999/0	Paul Gallacher
2003/4	Tony Bullock
2004/5	Lars Hirschfeld
	Paul Jarvie
	Nick Colgan
2005/6	Derek Stillie
	Craig Samson
2006/7	Euan McLean
2007/8	Gregorz Szamotulski
	Lukasz Zaluska
2009/0	Nicky Weaver
	Dusan Pernis
	Stephen Banks
2012/3	Radiszlaw Cierzniak
2013/4	Mark McCallum
2014/5	Michael Szromnik
2015/6	Luis Zwick
	Eliji Kawashima
2016/7	Cammy Bell
2017/8	Deniz Mehmet
	Harry Lewis
2018/9	Ross Laidlaw
	Benjamin Siegrist
	Matej Rakovan

Donald Mackay

11	12	13	14	15	16	17	18	19	20
Shankland	Bolton*	C Smith+	Chalmers&	Glass	Mochrie	Powers	Appere	Sporle	Mehmet
Chalmers+	C Smith*	Sporle+	Clark&	Powers>	Neilson	Freeman	Edwards	Glass	Mehmet
Clark>	Sporle*	Neilson+	Chalmers&	C Smith>	King	Powers	Freeman	Glass	Mehmet
Chalmers	Neilson*	Clark+	C Smith&	Powers>	King	Mochrie	Graham	Glass	Mehmet
Chalmers+	Freeman*	Sporle+	Appere&	McMullan>	King	Powers	C Smith	Glass	Mehmet
Chalmers	Appere*	McMullan+	Sporle	Edwards	Freeman	Powers	C Smith	Glass	Mehmet
Edwards	Chalmers*	Shankland+	Sporle&	Freeman>	McMullan	Graham	C Smith	Appere	Mehmet
Shankland	Pawlett*	Glass+	Powers	Freeman	McMullan	Neilson	C Smith	Appere	Mehmet
Shankland	Connolly*	Pawlett+	Powers&	Mochrie	McMullan	Neilson	C Smith	Appere	Mehmet
Shankland	Pawlett*	Appere+	Powers	Mochrie	McMullan	Neilson	Newman	Reynolds	
Appere	Powers*	C Smith+	Connolly&	Fotheringham>	Pawlett<	Hoti	King	Mochrie	Alexander
C Smith	Appere*	Fotheringham+	Powers&	King	Reynolds	Hoti	Neilson	Mochrie	Alexander
Appere*	C Smith*	Powers+	Mochrie&	King	McMullan	Hoti	Neilson	Fotheringham	Alexander
Shankland	McNulty*	L Smith+	Chalmers&	Powers>	Appere	C Smith	Neilson	Fotheringham	Mehmet
Shankland	L Smith*	King	Hutchinson	McMullan	Watson	Appere	Neilson	Fotheringham	Mehmet
Shankland	Sporle*	Fuchs+	Appere&	McMullan	Powers	King	Neilson	Fotheringham	Mehmet
Shankland	McNulty*	Powers+	McMullan&	Fuchs	Appere	Sporle	Neilson	Fotheringham	Mehmet
McNulty	Harkes*	Appere+	Bolton&	Robson	Powers	King	Neilson	Fotheringham	Siegrist
McNulty	Shankland*	Bolton+	Harkes&	Robson>	Powers	Appere	Neilson	Fotheringham	Mehmet
McNulty	Appere*	Hutchison	Watson	Duffy	Robson	Caves	Neilson	Malcolm	Mehmet
McNulty	Watson*	Hutchison	Powers	Duffy	K Smith	Appere	Neilson	Malcolm	Mehmet
McNulty	McMullan*	Bolton+	Pawlett&	Sporle	Powers	Appere	Neilson	Harkes	Mehmet
McNulty+	Pawlett*	Clark+	Sporle&	Edwards	Powers	Appere	Neilson	Harkes	Mehmet
McNulty	Pawlett*	Sporle+	Clark&	Edwards	Powers	Appere	Neilson	Harkes	Mehmet
McNulty	McMullan*	Powers+	Sporle&	Bolton>	Hutchison	Appere	Neilson	Fotheringham	Mehmet
Appere	Powers*	McMullan	Sporle	Bolton	Hutchison	Davidson	Smith	Fotheringham	Mehmet
Appere+	Bolton*	McNulty+	Sporle	K Smith	Hutchison	Watson	Pawlett	Fotheringham	Mehmet
Appere*	McNulty*	Bolton	Sporle	K Smith	Edwards	Mochrie	Pawlett	Fotheringham	Mehmet
McNulty	Fotheringham*	Appere+	Sporle	Pawlett	Edwards	Mochrie	Neilson	Edwards	Siegrist
McNulty	Pawlett*	Harkes+	Sporle	Appere	Edwards	Powers	Neilson	Fotheringham	Mehmet
McNulty	Pawlett*	Hoti	Mochrie	Appere	Bolton	Powers	Neilson	Reynolds	Mehmet
McNulty	Bolton*	Harkes+	Powers&	Appere	Clark	Mochrie	K Smith	Fotheringham	Mehmet
Appere+	Harkes*	McNulty+	Neilson	Connolly	Clark	Mochrie	Hoti	Bolton	Mehmet
Appere*	McNulty*	K Smith+	Neilson	Connolly	Sporle	Chalmers	Hoti	Bolton	Mehmet
McNulty	Appere*&	Connolly+	Clark&	K Smith	Neilson	Chalmers	Hoti	Bolton	Mehmet
McNulty+	Pawlett*	Appere+	Chalmers&	Connolly	Sporle	Neilson	Hoti	Bolton	Mehmet
McNulty	Appere*	Clark+	Hoti	Connolly	K Smith	Chalmers	Meekinson	Bolton	Mehmet
McNulty&	Chalmers*	Clark+	Pawlett&	Connolly	Appere	Bisland	Walker	Smith	Siegrist
McNulty	Clark*	Pawlett+	Hoti&	Appere>	K Smith	Chalmers	Connolly	Bolton	Mehmet
McNulty	Appere*	Harkes+	Fuchs&	Connolly	Bolton	Watson	Smith	Hutchison	Alexander
Appere	Meekison*	Clark	McNulty	Edwards	Davidson	Reynolds	Shankland	Butcher	Alexander
McNulty	Pawlett*	Appere+	Bolton&	Connolly	Davidson	Watson	Chalmers	Smith	Doohan
McNulty+	Pawlett*	Chalmers+	Appere&	K Smith>	Hoti<	Sporle	Connolly	Bolton	Doohan
McNulty	Sporle*	Pawlett+	Appere&	Connolly	Davidson	Watson	Chalmers	K Smith	Doohan
Appere>	Harkes*	Butcher+	McNulty&	Robson>	Davidson	Edwards	Reynolds	Clark	Mehmet
Appere	Hoti*	McNulty+	Sporle&	Reynolds>	Davidson	Butcher	Watson	Clark	Mehmet

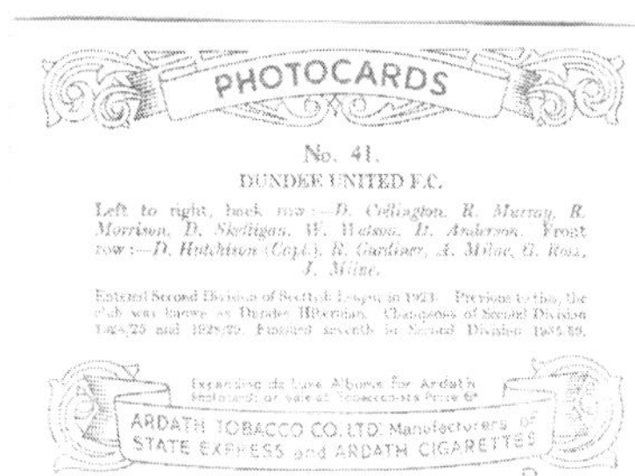

Surname	First Name	Date of Birth	No	Nat	Pos	Signed	Previous	Notes	Contract	Lge			SC			LC			
										A	S	G	A	S	G	A	S	G	Un
Adams	Ruairidh			SCO	GK	2021	Hutchison Vale		End 2022/3		1								7
Alexander	Neil	10/03/1978		SCO	GK	2020	Ex Livingston	GK Coach											
Appere	Louis	26/03/1999	27	SCO / FRA	F	2019	Dundee United Youths		End 2021/2	11	0	1		3		2	2		5
Bisland	Layton	02/02/2004	38	SCO	D	2020	Dundee United Youths		End 2022/3	0	11								17
Bolton	Luke	07/10/1999	20	ENG	M	2020	Manchester City (OL)	Jul-May		18	0	1	1	1		3	1		1
Brown	Shaun	18/09/2003	42	SCO	F	2019	Forth Valley Elite Acad		End 2021/2	0	6								11
Butcher	Calum	26/02/1991	18	ENG	M	2019	Mansfield Town		End 2022/3	27	0		4			4		1	0
Caves	Rhys	23/11/2003	41	SCO	M	2020	Dundee United Youths		End 2021/2	0	1								2
Chalmers	Logan	24/03/2000	15	SCO	F	2019	Dundee United Youths		End 2021/2	9	0			1					1
Clark	Nicky	03/06/1991	10	SCO	F	2018	Dunfermline Athletic		End 2022/3	24	6	8	3	1	1	3		2	6
Comerford	Jacob	22/02/2004		SCO	D	2020	Hutchison Vale			0	7								5
Comerford	Jacob			SCO	D	2020	Hutchison Vale		End 2022/3										
Connolly	Mark	16/12/1991	5	ROI	D	2019	Crawley Town		End 2022/3	23	0					3	1		0
Cooney	Nathan	21/02/2002	34	SCO	D	2011	Dundee United SC	OL to Kelty Hearts Nov-Jan, to Raith Rovers Mar-May	End 2021/2	0	2								10
Davidson	Jake	06/10/2000	28	SCO	D	2018	Dundee United Youths	OLto Waterford Jul-Jan, to Arbroath Jan-May, Transferred to Q Park June 2021		0	0								0
Doohan	Ross	29/03/1998		SCO	GK	2021	Celtic (OL)	Apr-May		2	0								6
Duffy	Flynn	13/08/2003	40	SCO	D	2020	Dundee United Youths		End 2022/3	0	0								3
Edwards	Ryan	07/10/1993	12	ENG	D	2020	Blackpool	OOC June 2021		24	0	2	4		1	4		1	2
Fotheringham	Kai	18/04/2003	25	SCO	M	2017	Forth Valley Elite Acad	OL to Falkirk Mar-May	End 2022/3	0	0						2		10
Fraser	Lewis	31/03/2002	33	SCO	M	2019	Dundee United Youths	OL to East Craigie Nov-Jan, Released June 2021		0	1								13
Freeman	Kieran	30/03/2000	22	SCO	D	2020	Southampton	OL to Peterhead Sep-Jan	End 2021/2	1	0								0
Fuchs	Jeando	11/10/1997	66	CAM / GER	M	2020	Deportivo Alaves		End 2021/2	19	2		3	1		1			4
Glass	Declan	07/06/2000	21	SCO	M	2014	Hutchison Vale		End 2021/2	0	1								1
Graham	Ross	20/02/2001	29	SCO	D	2012	Dundee West BC	OL to Cove Rangers Oct-Jan, to Dunfermline for 2021/2	End 2021/2	0	1								6
Harkes	Ian	30/03/1995	23	USA / ENG	M	2019	DC United		End 2021/2	30	0	1	3	1		3	1	1	2
Hoti	Florent	11/12/2000	14	KOS / ENG	M	2019	Rochdale	OL to Forfar Athletic Sep-Jan	End 2021/2	1	5								3
Hutchison	Adam	15/02/2003	37	SCO	D	2020	Dundee United Youths		End 2022/3	0	3								9
King	Adam	11/10/1995	16	SCO	M	2019	Swansea City	OL to Raith Rovers Jan-May, Released June 2021 joined Alloa		0	0								7
Lemon	Mackenzie	19/11/2002	35	SCO	D	2019	Dundee United Youths	OL to Dundee NE Nov-Jan, Released June 2021		0	0								9
Lovie	Sam	26/03/2004	44	SCO	D	2020	Dundee United Youths		End 2021/2	0	0								0
Malcolm	Finlay	04/02/2004	45	SCO	F	2018	Forth Valley Elite Acad		End 2021/2	0	0								0
McInnes	Ryan	01/01/2001		SCO	M					0	0								2
McMullan	Paul	25/02/1996	7	SCO	M	2017	Celtic	OL to Dundee Jan-May, Permanent from June 2021		3	0					3			0
McNulty	Marc	14/09/1992	9	SCO	F	2020	Reading (OL)	Oct-May		17	5	3	4		2	1			8
Meekison	Archie	04/05/2002	32	SCO	F	2019	Dundee United Youths	OL to Spartans Sep-Jan	End 2021/2	2	8	1							1
Mehmet	Deniz	19/09/1992	19	TUR / ENG	GK	2019	Queen of the South	Joined Dunfermline Athletic July 2021		4	1		4			4			1
Mochrie	Chris	07/04/2003	26	SCO	M	2019	Dundee United Youths	OL to Montrose Oct-Jan	End 2021/2	0	0						1		34
Naglik	Dominic	14/03/2004	48	POL	F	2020	Dundee United Youths		End 2021/2	0	0								11
Neilson	Lewis	15/05/2003	30	SCO	D	2019	Dundee United Youths	OL to Falkirk Mar-May	End 2021/2	7	0					1			0
Newman	Jack	12/02/2002	31	SCO	GK	2020	Sunderland		End 2022/3	0	2								25
O'Donnell	Lewis	01/01/2001		SCO	M	2020	Dundee United Youths		End 2022/3	0	0								1
Pawlett	Peter	03/02/1991	8	SCO	M	2019	MK Dons		End 2022/3	15	0	1	1	3	1	2	1		0
Powers	Dillon	14/02/1991	4	USA /ITA	M	2020	Orlando City SC	Released June 2021		6	11						3		3
Reynolds	Mark	07/05/1987	6	SCO	D	2019	Aberdeen		End 2021/2	33	8	1	4			3			15
Robson	Finn	29/07/2003	39	SCO	M	2020	Dundee United Youths		End 2021/2	13	1								5
Robson	Jamie	19/12/1997	17	SCO	D	2016	Dundee United Youths		End 2021/2	21	0		4			3			0
Shankland	Lawrence	10/08/1995	24	SCO	F	2019	Ayr United		End 2021/2	30	2	8	4		1				2
Siegrist	Benjamin	31/01/1992	1	SWI	GK	2018	Vejle BK		End 2021/2	32	2								1
Smith	Kerr	12/12/2004	43	SCO	D				End 2022/3	3	0								3
Smith	Liam	10/04/1996	2	SCO	D	2019	Ayr United		End 2022/3	28	2	1	3			2			12
Smith	Cammy	24/08/1995	11	SCO	F	2019	St Mirren	OL to Ayr U Oct-Jan, Freed Feb joined Ayr United		0	2					1	2	2	0
Sporle	Adrian	13/07/1995	3	ARG / GER	D	2019	CA Banfield		End 2021/2	15	4	4	2	1		1			6
Thomson	Miller	20/07/2004	46	SCO	F	2020	Dundee United Youths		End 2021/2	0	9								12
Walker	Lennon	01/01/2001	47	SCO	M	2020	Dundee United Youths		End 2022/3	0	0								0
Watson	Darren	10/08/2003	36	SCO	F	2015	Fife Elite Academy		End 2022/3	0	0								1
NEW SIGNINGS																			
Carson	Trevor	05/03/1988		NIR	GK	2021	Motherwell		End 2022/3										
Mulgrew	Charlie	06/03/1986		SCO	D	2021	Blackburn Rovers		End 2022/3										

Dunfermline Athletic FC 2020/21 The Pars

Founded	1885
Ground	East End Park
Postcode	KY12 7RB
Tel	01383 724295
Capacity	11480
Closest Railway Station	Dunfermline Town
Record Attendance	27816, v Celtic, Lge, 30/4/68
Record Win	11-2 v Stenhousemuir, Lge 27/9/1930
Record Defeat	1-13 v St Bernards, SC, 15/9/1883
Most League Goals in a Season	53, Bobby Skinner, 1925/6
Colours 2020/21 Top	White with Black stripes
Shorts	White with Black stripes
Sponsor	SRJ Windows
Manufacturer	Joma
Change Colours 2020/21 Top	Red
Shorts	Red
Nicknames	Pars
Web	www.dafc.co.uk
Match Programme 2020/21	None

Chairman: Ross McArthur
Vice Chairman: William Braisby
Directors: Bob Garmary, Ian Hunter, Jim Leishman MBE, Christpher McBay, Drew Main
Financial Controller: David McMorrone
Head Coach: Stephen Crawford, then Peter Grant
First team Coaches: Greg Shields, Steven Whittaker
Head Physio: Kevin Bain
Physio: John Porteous
Sports Scientist: Paul Green
Kit Coordinator: Sammi Connell
Kit Man: Mo Hutton
Match Analyst: David Honeyman
Kit Coordinators: Sammi Connell, Iain Kirk
Club Doctor: James Parris
Chaplain: Rev Rae McKenzie
Club Secretary: Shirley Forrester
Media and PR Officer: Craig brown
Operations Manager: Margaret Miller
Club Shop / Ticket Office: Matthew Ford
Ground Staff: Willie Davis, Kevin

Being realistic a play off place was the best Dunfermline could have hoped for in 2020/1. Hearts were always likely to run away with the League so it was a case of playing for second. What was disappointing was the Pars abject performance in the play offs against Raith Rovers. They surrendered very tamely and manager Stevie Crawford left shortly afterwards.

The Pars had made a great start to the season. They won all four League Cup group games and then beat Arbroath before losing to St Johnstone in the Quarter Final on penalties. They also unbeaten in lost just one of their first twelve League games and looked every inch title contenders. They then won just two from ten and slipped way off the pace. A 5-1 defeat from Raith was depressing as was a home defeat from Queen of the South. The goals just dried up and a previously tight looking defence began to look like they couldn't keep hens out of a close.

The appointment of Peter Grant to replace Crawford was not what the fans expected. However, he needs to be given the chance to stamp his impression on the team in the coming season.

STAR MAN
Defender Euan Murray was man marvel in the opening weeks of the season – excellent in defence and seemingly coring at will from set pieces. He maintained the defensive consistency although his goalscoring exploits soon dried up – 7 before the end of November and none after that.

PROSPECTS 2021/2
Dunfermline must be viewed as one of the potential promotion candidates in the Championship this season. Peter Grant will be working with a different type of player compared to those he had at Alloa, but he has experience of coaching at the highest level in England. Dunfermline ned to maintain consistency and also start to take more points against their fellow challengers.

1985/6 DAFC

1985/6 was the season that saw the Pars turn things around. They had been relegated from the top flight in 1975, and again to the bottom flight in 1976. Promoted in 78/9, they went back down again in 1982/3. With Jim Leishman at the helm they won promotion in 195/6 and 1986/7 to reclaim a place in the top level of Scottish football for 1987/8.

Date	Comp	H/A	Opponents	F	A		HT	Referee	Crowd	Scorers
06/10/2020	LC	A	Dumbarton	1	0		1 0	G Ross	BCD	O'Hara pen
09/10/2020	LC	H	Falkirk	2	0		0 0	G Irvine	BCD	E Murray 2
13/10/2020	LC	A	Kilmarnock	3	0		0 0	A Dallas	BCD	E Murray, F Murray 2
17/10/2020	L	H	Inverness CT	3	1		1 1	W Collum	BCD	E Murray, Dow, McManus
24/10/2020	L	A	Alloa Athletic	4	1		1 1	D Robertson	BCD	Dow, O'Hara 3(1 pen)
31/10/2020	L	H	Queen of the South	3	2		2 0	G irvine	BCD	E Murray, McManus pen, Watson
07/11/2020	L	A	Ayr United	0	0		0 0	C Napier	BCD	
14/11/2020	LC	H	Clyde	3	2		0 1	D Dickinson	BCD	O'Hara pen, McManus, Watson
20/11/2020	L	H	Hearts	2	1		0 0	D Robertson	BCD	Thomas, E Murray
28/11/2020	LC	A	Arbroath	3	1		2 0	N Walsh	BCD	Dow, E Murray, O'Hara pen
05/12/2020	L	A	Raith Rovers	2	2		0 1	E Anderson	BCD	F Murray, McManus
12/12/2020	L	H	Morton	1	2		0 1	D Munro	BCD	McManus pen
15/12/2020	LC	H	St Johnstone	1	1	AET, 3-4p	0 0	D Eobertson	BCD	Wilson
19/12/2020	L	A	Dundee	3	3		0 1	G Irvine	BCD	Watson, McManus 2 (1 pen)
26/12/2020	L	H	Arbroath	1	0		0 0	S Kirkland	BCD	O'Hara
29/12/2020	L	A	Inverness CT	1	1		1 0	E Anderson	BCD	Turner
15/01/2021	L	A	Morton	0	0		0 0	S Kirkland	BCD	
23/01/2021	L	H	Ayr United	0	0		0 0	D Robertson	BCD	
30/01/2021	L	A	Hearts	0	1		0 0	W Collum	BCD	
03/02/2021	L	H	Raith Rovers	4	1		1 0	C Steven	BCD	McManus, Comrie, F Murray 2
06/02/2021	L	A	Arbroath	0	2		0 2	C Napier	BCD	
20/02/2021	L	H	Alloa Athletic	2	1		1 1	S Reid	BCD	Wighton 2
27/02/2021	L	A	Queen of the South	0	1		0 0	M Roncone	BCD	
13/03/2021	L	H	Morton	1	0		1 0	S Kirkland	BCD	Wighton
20/03/2021	L	H	Inverness CT	0	1		0 0	P Stuart	BCD	
23/03/2021	SC	A	Morton	0	0	AET, 5-6p	0 0	D Robertson	BCD	
27/03/2021	L	A	Dundee	2	3		2 1	B Madden	BCD	O'Hara, Wighton
30/03/2021	L	A	Raith Rovers	1	5		1 3	E Anderson	BCD	O'Hara
03/04/2021	L	H	Hearts	0	0		0 0	C Steven	BCD	
10/04/2021	L	A	Ayr United	1	1		1 1	G Aitken	BCD	McManus
13/04/2021	L	H	Dundee	0	0		0 0	K Clancy	BCD	
17/04/2021	L	H	Queen of the South	3	1		1 0	D Lowe	BCD	O'Hara, F Murray, Henderson
24/04/2021	L	H	Arbroath	4	3		2 2	S McLean	BCD	McManus pen, O'Hara, Wighton 2
30/04/2021	L	A	Alloa Athletic	0	1		0 0	P Stuart	BCD	
04/05/2021	PO	H	Raith Rovers	0	0		0 0	S Kirkland	BCD	
08/05/2021	PO	A	Raith Rovers	0	2		0 0	G Aitken	BCD	

Hugh Whyte

Lindsay Hamilton

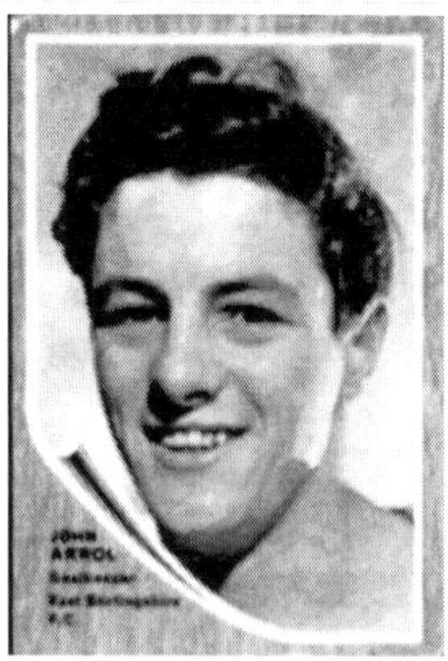

John Arrol

Date	Comp	H/A	Opponents	F	A		1	2	3	4	5	6	7	8	9	10	11	12	13	14	15	16	17	18	19	20
06/10/2020	LC	A	Dumbarton	1	0		Fon Williams	Whittaker	Watson	E Murray	Comrie	Edwards	Dow*	Thomas	Turner+	McInroy	O'Hara&	F Murray*	McManus+	Wilson&	*Fenton*	*Swinton*	*Allan*	*McCann*	*Gill*	
09/10/2020	LC	H	Falkirk	2	0		Fon Williams	Whittaker+	Watson	E Murray	Comrie	Edwards	Dow&	Thomas	F Murray*	McManus	O'Hara	Turner*	Wilson+	*McCann&*	*Fenton*	*Swinton*	*Allan*	*Gill*		
13/10/2020	LC	A	Kilmarnock	3	0		Gill	Whittaker	Watson	E Murray	Wilson	Edwards	Turner+	Thomas&	F Murray	McManus<	O'Hara*	Dow*	Allan–	McCann&	McGill>	*Swinton*	*Fenton*	*Martin*	*Fon Williams*	
17/10/2020	L	H	Inverness CT	3	1		Fon Williams	Wilson	Watson	E Murray	Comrie	Edwards	Dow	Thomas	Turner+	McManus	O'Hara*	F Murray*	McInroy+	*McCann*	*Mayo*	*Martin*	*Allan*	*Gill*		
24/10/2020	L	A	Alloa Athletic	4	1		Fon Williams	Whittaker	Watson*	E Murray	Comrie	Edwards	Dow+	Thomas	Wilson&	McManus	F Murray	Mayo*	O'Hara+	Turner&	*Fenton*	*McInroy*	*McCann*	*Gill*		
31/10/2020	L	H	Queen of the South	3	2		Fon Williams	Whittaker	Watson	E Murray	Comrie*	Edwards	Turner+	Thomas	McInroy	McManus	O'Hara+	Wilson*	F Murray+	*Mayo*	*Fenton*	*Berry*	*McCann*	*Gill*		
07/11/2020	L	A	Ayr United	0	0		Fon Williams	Whittaker	Watson	E Murray	Mayo	Edwards	Turner+	Thomas	McInroy	McManus&	F Murray*	Dow*	Wilson+	O'Hara&	*Fenton*	*Berry*	*McCann*	*Gill*		
14/11/2020	LC	H	Clyde	3	2		Gill	Dow	Watson	E Murray	Wilson*	Edwards	F Murray+	Bowman&	McInroy	McManus	O'Hara	Turner*	Thomas+	McCann&	*Fenton*	*Swinton*	*Whittaker*	*Berry*		
20/11/2020	L	H	Hearts	2	1		Fon Williams	Whittaker	Watson	E Murray	Mayo	Edwards	Dow	Thomas+	McInroy	McManus*	Turner	O'Hara*	F Murray+	*McCann*	*Bowman*	*Comrie*	*Wilson*	*Gill*		
28/11/2020	LC	A	Arbroath	3	1		Fon Williams	Dow	Watson	E Murray	Mayo	Edwards	Wilson	Thomas&	McInroy	McManus*	Turner+	O'Hara*	Comrie+	*F Murray&*	*Bowman*	*Berry*	*McCann*	*Whittaker*	*Fenton*	*Gill*
05/12/2020	L	A	Raith Rovers	2	2		Fon Williams	Dow	Watson	E Murray	Mayo*	Edwards	Wilson+	Thomas	McInroy&	McManus	Turner	Comrie*	F Murray+	*O'Hara&*	*Bowman*	*Fenton*	*McCann*	*Gill*		
12/12/2020	L	H	Morton	1	2		Fon Williams	Dow	Watson	E Murray	Comrie	Edwards	O'Hara*	Thomas	McInroy+	McManus	Turner	F Murray*	McCann+	*Mayo*	*Bowman*	*Fenton*	*Wilson*	*Gill*		
15/12/2020	LC	H	St Johnstone	1	1	AET, 3-4p	Fon Williams	Dow	Watson	E Murray	Comrie*	Edwards	F Murray>	Thomas&	McInroy	McManus+	Turner	Mayo*	O'Hara+	McCann&	Wilson>	*Fenton*	*Whittaker*	*Gill*	*Bowman*	*Berry*
19/12/2020	L	A	Dundee	3	3		Fon Williams	Whittaker&	Watson	E Murray	Mayo	Edwards	Dow	Thomas+	McInroy*	McManus	Turner	Wilson*	O'Hara+	McCann&	*Bowman*	*Fenton*	*Berry*	*Gill*		
26/12/2020	L	H	Arbroath	1	0		Fon Williams	Whittaker+	Watson	E Murray	Mayo*	Edwards	Dow	Thomas	Wilson&	McManus	Turner	Comrie*	McInroy+	O'Hara&	*Bowman*	*McCann*	*Berry*	*Gill*		
29/12/2020	L	A	Inverness CT	1	1		Fon Williams	Comrie	Watson	E Murray	Mayo	Edwards	McInroy*	McCann+	Wilson	O'Hara&	Turner	Dow*	McManus+	Thomas&	*F Murray*	*Berry*	*Whittaker*	*Gill*		
15/01/2021	L	A	Morton	0	0		Fon Williams	Comrie	Watson	E Murray	Whittaker	Edwards	Dow	Thomas+	Wilson*	McManus	McCann&	Turner*	F Murray+	O'Hara&	*Todd*	*McInroy*	*Mayo*	*Gill*		
23/01/2021	L	H	Ayr United	0	0		Fon Williams	Comrie	Watson	E Murray	Whittaker+	Edwards	Dow	Thomas&	Wilson	McManus	Turner*	McCann*	Mayo+	F Murray&	*McDonald*	*McInroy*	*O'Hara*	*Gill*		
30/01/2021	L	A	Hearts	0	1		Fon Williams	Comrie	Watson	E Murray	Whittaker&	Edwards	Dow	Mayo	Wilson	McManus+	F Murray*	Banks*	O'Hara+	McCann&	*McDonald*	*McInroy*	*Todd*	*Gill*		
03/02/2021	L	H	Raith Rovers	4	1		Fon Williams	Comrie	Watson	E Murray&	F Murray	Edwards	Dow*	Mayo	Wilson	McManus	Banks+	O'Hara*	McInroy+	Whittaker&	*McDonald*	*McCann*	*Turner*	*Gill*		
06/02/2021	L	A	Arbroath	0	2		Fon Williams	Comrie+	Watson	E Murray	F Murray	Edwards	McInroy	Mayo*	Wilson&	McManus	O'Hara	McCann*	Banks+	Todd&	*McDonald*	*Turner*	*Allan*	*Gill*		
20/02/2021	L	H	Alloa Athletic	2	1		Fon Williams	Comrie*	Watson	E Murray	F Murray	Edwards	Banks+	Mayo	Wilson	McManus&	Wighton	McDonald*	Whittaker+	O'Hara&	*McCann*	*McInroy*	*Thomas*	*Gill*		
27/02/2021	L	A	Queen of the South	0	1		Fon Williams	Whittaker*	Watson	McDonald	F Murray	Edwards	McInroy	Mayo	Thomas&	McManus+	Wighton	Wilson*	O'Hara+	Banks&	*Yurner*	*McCann*	*Gaspuitis*	*Gill*		
13/03/2021	L	H	Morton	1	0		Fon Williams	Comrie	Watson	E Murray	Whittaker	Wilson	F Murray	Banks&	Thomas*	McDonald	Wighton+	Turner*	McManus+	Gaspuitis&	*O'Hara*	*McCann*	*Todd*	*Gill*		
20/03/2021	L	H	Inverness CT	0	1		Fon Williams	Comrie	Watson&	E Murray	Whittaker	Wilson*	F Murray	Banks+	Thomas	McDonald	Wighton	Mayo*	McManus+	Gaspuitis&	*O'Hara*	*McCann*	*Edwards*	*Gill*		
23/03/2021	SC	A	Morton	0	0	AET, 5-6p	Fon Williams	Comrie	Mayo	E Murray	Whittaker&	Edwards	McInroy+	Todd*	O'Hara	McManus>	McCann	F Murray*	Wilson+	Thomas&	*Wighton>*	*Banks*	*Allan*	*Gill*		
27/03/2021	L	A	Dundee	2	3		Fon Williams	Comrie	Watson*	E Murray	Mayo	Edwards	Thomas&	Wilson	O'Hara+	F Murray	Wighton	Henderson*	McManus+	*Banks&*	*McInroy*	*McCann*	*McDonald*	*Gill*		
30/03/2021	L	A	Raith Rovers	1	5		Fon Williams	Comrie	McInroy+	E Murray	Mayo	Edwards	F Murray	Henderson&	O'Hara	Banks*	Wighton	McCann*	Wilson+	McManus&	*Allan*	*Thomas*	*McDonald*	*Gill*		
03/04/2021	L	H	Hearts	0	0		Fon Williams	Comrie	Gaspuitis	E Murray	Mayo	Wilson	Thomas	Banks*	O'Hara+	McManus&	Edwards	F Murray*	Henderson+	*McCann&*	*Allan*	*McInroy*	*McDonald*	*Gill*		
10/04/2021	L	A	Ayr United	1	1		Fon Williams	Comrie	Gaspuitis	E Murray&	Mayo	F Murray*	Thomas+	Henderson	O'Hara	McManus	Edwards	Watson*	Wighton+	Whittaker&	*McCann*	*McInroy*	*McDonald*	*Gill*		
13/04/2021	L	H	Dundee	0	0		Fon Williams	Comrie	Gaspuitis	E Murray	Whittaker*	Edwards	Thomas	Henderson	O'Hara+	McManus	Wighton&	Mayo*	F Murray+	*McCann&*	*Watson*	*McInroy*	*McDonald*	*Gill*		
17/04/2021	L	H	Queen of the South	3	1		Fon Williams	Comrie	Gaspuitis	Mayo	Whittaker	Edwards	Thomas	Henderson	O'Hara	McManus*	Wighton+	F Murray*	McInroy+	McCann	*Allan*	*Todd*	*McDonald*	*Gill*		
24/04/2021	L	H	Arbroath	4	3		Fon Williams	Comrie	Gaspuitis+	Mayo	Whittaker	Edwards	Thomas	Henderson&	O'Hara	McManus*	Wighton	McInroy*	Watson+	*F Murray&*	*Allan*	*McCann*	*McDonald*	*Gill*		
30/04/2021	L	A	Alloa Athletic	0	1		Gill	McDonald	Watson	E Murray*	McInroy	Edwards	Allan	Henderson+	O'Hara	McManus&	McCann	Mayo*	Banks+	McGill&	*Comrie*	*Gaspuitis*	*Todd*	*Fon Williams*		
04/05/2021	PO	H	Raith Rovers	0	0		Fon Williams	Comrie	Watson	E Murray	Whittaker	Edwards	Thomas+	Henderson	O'Hara	McManus*	Wighton	McInroy*	Banks+	*McCann*	*Mayo*	*Gaspuitis*	*McDonald*	*Gill*		
08/05/2021	PO	A	Raith Rovers	0	2		Fon Williams	Comrie	Watson	E Murray&	Whittaker	Edwards	Thomas	Henderson	O'Hara	Mayo+	Wighton*	Banks*	McManus+	F Murray&	*McInroy*	*Gaspuitis*	*McDonald*	*Gill*		

THE GOALIES

Goalkeepers Used in League Matches, 1970-2020

Players shown in the season of their first appearance only

1970/1	John Arrol
	Ernie McGarr
1973/4	George Thomson
	Geir Karlsen
1975/6	Graham Barclay
1976/7	Hugh Whyte
1978/9	Kevin Gallagher
1981/2	George Young
1982/3	Jim Moffat
1984/5	David Westwood
	Ian Westwater
1985/6	Hamish McAlpine
1987/8	Tom Carson
	Nicky Walker
	David McKellar
	Hans Segers
1990/1	Andy Rhodes
1992/3	Lindsay Hamilton
	John Hillcoat
1994/5	Jim Will
	Jim McQueen
	Guido Van de Kamp
1996/7	Zoran Lamajic
1998/9	Lee Butler
1999/0	Kris Mampaey
2000/1	Marco Ruitenbeek
	Scott Thomson
2002/3	Derek Stillie
2005/6	Bryn Halliwell
	Allan McGregor
2006/7	Roddy McKenzie
	Dorus De Vries
2007/8	Sean Murdoch
	Paul Gallacher
2009/0	Greg Fleming
	Chris Smith
	Greg Paterson
2011/2	Iain Turner
2012/3	Martin Hrivnak
2013/4	Ryan Goodfellow
	Ryan Scully
2014/5	Jamie Wilson
2015/6	Sean Murdoch
	David Hutton
2017/8	Lee Robinson
2018/9	Cammy Gill
2019/0	Owain Fon Williams

DUNFERMLINE'S SCOTTISH CUP WINNING RUNS

1960/1

Jan 28	1	A v Berwick Rangers	4-1
Feb 11	2	A v Stranraer	3-1
Feb 25	3	A v Aberdeen	6-3
Mar 11	QF	H v Alloa	4-0
Apr 1	SF	N v St Mirren	0-0
Apr 5	SFR	N v St Mirren	1-0
Apr 22	F	N v Celtic	0-0
Apr 26	FR	N v Celtic	2-0

1967/8

Jan 27	1	A v Celtic	2-0
Feb 17	2	H v Aberdeen	2-1
Mar 9	QF	H v Partick Thistle	1-0
Mar 30	SF	N v St Johnstone	1-1
Apr 2	SFR	N v St Johnstone	2-1
Apr 27	F	N v Hearts	3-1

Surname	First Name	Date of Birth	No	Nat	Pos	Signed	Previous	Notes	Contract	Lge A	Lge S	Lge G	SC A	SC S	SC G	LC A	LC S	LC G	Un
Allan	Paul	07/02/2002		SCO	M	2018	Dunfermline Athletic Youths	OL to Albion Rovers Oct-Jan	End 2021/2	1							1		9
Banks	Scott	26/09/2001		SCO	F	2021	Crystal Palace (OL)	Jan-May		6	7								1
Berry	Lucas	23/03/2002	27	SCO	M	2019	Fife Elite Academy	Released June 2021		0									8
Bowman	Matty	26/11/2000	17	ENG	M	2019	Hull City	Released Feb 2021		0						1			7
Bragg	Thomas	28/07/2002		ENG	D	2019	Southampton Youths	Freed Oct 2020, joined Eastleigh		0	0								0
Comrie	Aaron	03/02/1997	2	SCO	D	2019	St Johnstone		End 2022/3	22	2	1	1			3	1		2
Cusick	Scott	08/08/2002		SCO	M	2020	Celtic Youths	OL to Brechin City Sep-Jan, Released June 2021		0	0								0
Dow	Ryan	07/06/1991	11	SCO	M	2019	Peterhead		End 2021/2	11	2	2				5	1	1	0
Edwards	Josh	27/03/2000	3	SCO	D	2019	Airdrieonians		End 2022/3	27	0		1			6			1
Fenton	Miller	16/10/2003	19	SCO	D	2019	Fife Elite Academy	OL to East Fife Mar-May	End 2021/2	0	0								12
Fon Williams	Owain	17/03/1987	1	WAL	GK	2020	Hamilton Accies	Welsh International	End 2021/2	28	0		1			4			2
Gaspuitis	Vytas	04/03/1994		LIT	D	2021	FK Panevezys		End 2022/3	5	2								4
Gill	Cammy	07/04/1998	20	SCO	GK	2018	Dunfermline Athletic Youths	Released June 2021, joined Cowdenbeath		1	0					2			33
Henderson	Ewan	27/03/2000		SCO	M	2021	Celtic (OL)	Mar-May		8	2	1							0
Martin	Lewis	08/04/1996	4	SCO	D	2013	Dunfermline Athletic Youths		Dec-21	0	0								2
Mayo	Lewis	19/03/2000	22	SCO	D	2020	Ranghers (OL)	Sep-May		18	5		1			1	1		5
McCann	Lewis	07/06/2001	14	ENG / NIR	F	2019	Dunfermline Athletic Youths		End 2021/2	3	8		1				4		19
McDonald	Kyle	11/01/2000		SCO	D	2021	Airdrieonians		End 2022/3	4	1								13
McGill	Gabby	04/09/2000		ENG	F	2019	Middlesbrough	OL to York City Jan-May, Released May 2021		0	1						1		0
McInroy	Kerr	31/08/2000	24	SCO	M	2020	Celtic (OL)	Sep-May		11	6		1			4			10
McManus	Declan	03/08/1994	10	SCO	F	2020	Ross County	Tranjsferred to TNS June 2021, £60,000		23	6	9	1			5	1	1	0
Murray	Euan	20/01/1994	5	SCO	D	2019	Raith Rovers	Out of Contract June 2021, joined Kilmarnock		26	0	3	1			6		4	0
Murray	Fraser	07/05/1999	21	SCO	M	2020	Hibernian (OL)	Sep-May		12	12	4		1		4	2	2	1
O'Hara	Kevin	11/08/1998	7	SCO	F	2020	Alloa Athletic		End 2022/3	15	11	8	1			4	2	3	3
Swinton	Ben	06/06/2001	30	SCO	GK	2019	AM Soccer	Released June 2021		0	0								4
Thomas	Dom	14/02/1996	23	SCO	M	2020	Kilmarnock		End 2021/2	22	1	1		1		5	1		2
Todd	Matty	14/06/2001		SCO	N	2018	Dunfermline Athletic Youths	OL to Brechin City Sep-Jan	End 2021/2	0	1		1						5
Turner	Kyle	10/11/1997	8	SCO	M	2019	Stranraer	Released May 2021, joined Partick Thistle		10	3	1				4	2		3
Watson	Paul	20/12/1990	44	SCO	D	2020	Dundee United		End 2021/2	23	2	2				6		1	1
Whittaker	Steven	16/06/1984	16	SCO	D	2020	Hibernian	Retired June 2021		17	3		1			3			4
Wighton	Craig	27/07/1997		SCO	F	2021	Hearts (OL)	Feb-May		11	1	6		1					0
Wilson	Iain	15/12/1998	15	SCO	M	2020	Kilmarnock		End 2021/2	15	5			1		3	3	1	2
NEW SIGNINGS																			
Graham	Ross	20/02/2001		SCO	M	2021	Dundee United (OL)	Jul-May	End 2021/2										
Mehmet	Deniz	19/09/1992		ENG / TUR	GK	2021	Dundee United		End 2022/3										
Pybus	Dan	12/12/1997		ENG	M	2021	Queen of the South		End 2022/3										
Todorov	Nikolay	24/08/1996		BUL	F	2021	Bulgaria		End 2022/3										
Wighton	Craig	27/07/1997		SCO	F	2021	Hearts		End 2022/3										

PHOTOCARDS

No. 69.

DUNFERMLINE ATHLETIC F.C.

Left to right, back row :– E. Dencie (Trainer), J. Johnman, J. Warden, P. Steele, R. Bolt, J. Crawford, R. Donald. Front row :—J. Thomson, R. Syme, R. M'Gowan, A. Thomson (Capt.), J. Dobson.

Joined Scottish League, Second Division, in 1921 and gained promotion to First Division in 1925-26 by winning the Second Division Championship. Winners of the Scottish Qualifying Cup 1911-12 and in 1935-36 finished twelfth in the League Table.

Expanding de Luxe Albums for Ardath Photocards on sale at Tobacconists Price 6d

ARDATH TOBACCO CO. LTD. Manufacturers of STATE EXPRESS and ARDATH CIGARETTES

D

East Fife FC 2020/21 The Fifers

Founded	1903
Ground	Bayview Stadium
Postcode	KY8 3RW
Tel	01333 426323
Capacity	1980
Closest Railway Station	Kirkcaldy
Record Attendance	22515 v Raith Rovers, 2/1/1950
Record Win	13-2 v Edinburgh City, Lge, 11/12/1937
Record Defeat	0-9, v Hearts, Lge, 5/10/1957
Most League Goals in a Season	41 Jock Wood 1926/7; Henry Morris 1947/8
Colours 2020/21 Top	Gold and Black Stripes
Shorts	White
Sponsor	BW Technology
Manufacturer	Joma
Change Colours 2020/21 Top	White with Red Trim
Shorts	Red
Nicknames	Fifers
Web	www.eastfifefc.info
Match Programme	None

Chairman: Jim Stevenson
Vice Chairman: David Marshall
Company Secretary: Douglas Briggs
Directors: John Barclay, John Donaldson, Ken Henderson, Stephen Mill (Supporters Trust Rep), Liam Anderson
Associate Directors: Liam Anderson, , Elizabeth Anderson, Leona Guidi, Robert Cargill, Denis Nicol, David Stevenson, Harry Blyth
Honorary Directors: Jim Stewart
Security Manager: John Donaldson
Manager: Darren Young
Assistant Manager: Tony McMinn
Goalkeeping Coach: Lindsay Hamilton
Physio: Lauren Wilson
Admin: Carolyn Graham
Announcer: Caroline Maxwell

Methil Power Station, No More

The Methil side retained their League One place for the fifth consecutive season. They won ten games and lost nine – just lacking the consistency to achieve a promotion play off spot. Their best run of results was a three-game winning streak spanning the long January / February COVID shutdown. Perhaps that came at the wrong time as just beforehand they had won three from four and cruised past Tranent in the Scottish Cup with a 5-1 win.

In the next round of the Scottish Cup the Fifers were beaten by Morton after extra time. No progress was made in the League Cup although East Fife gained admiration for a good performance against Hearts when they lost 2-3.

League One sems to be the natural home for East Fife these days – a far cry from the late 1940s and early 1950s when they won the League Cup twice and finished third in the top flight. Those days will never return but their fans can always dream!

STAR MAN
Midfielder Ross Davidson had a very consistent season. The player was lauded for his honesty following an incident with Peterhead's Gary Fraser in December. The Blue Toon midfielder was given a straight red card by referee Graham Beaton during the 2-1 win against the Fifers for an alleged headbutt on Davidson after 65 minutes. But the Buchan outfit were adamant there was no headbutt and Fraser and Davidson had only squared up to each other. A Scottish FA judicial panel downgraded Fraser's red card to a yellow with Davidson helping Peterhead's appeal by writing to the SFA to say he hadn't been headbutted.

PROSPECTS 2021/2
There have been the usual comings and goings at East Fife. Last season they relied heavily on loan signing Jack Hamilton for goals. They had hoped to replace him by signing Mark McGuigan from Stenhousemuir but the player decided to retire shortly after signing for the club. Another regular scorer is necessary and would ensure another mid-table finish for the Fifers.

EAST FIFE'S SCOTTISH CUP WINNING RUN - 1937/8

Jan 22	1	A v Airdrie	2-1
Feb 12	2	H v Dundee United	5-0
Mar 5	3	H v Aberdeen	1-1
Mar 9	3R	A v Aberdeen	2-1
Mar 19	QF	H v Raith Rovers	2-2
Mar 23	QFR	A v Raith Rovers	3-2
Apr 2	SF	N v St Bernards	1-1
Apr 6	SFR	N v St Bernards	1-1
Apr 13	SFR	N v St Bernards	2-1
Apr 23	F	N v Kilmarnock	1-1
Apr 27	FR	N v Kilmarnock	4-2

11 Games to win the Cup

Date	Comp	H/A	Opponents	F	A		HT		Referee	Crowd	Scorers
06/10/2020	LC	H	Cowdenbeath	2	0		0	0	C Graham	BCD	Hamilton, Wallace
10/10/2020	LC	A	Raith Rovers	1	2		1	1	D Lowe	BCD	Newton
17/10/2020	L	A	Cove Rangers	1	3		0	1	G Ross	BCD	Hamilton
24/10/2020	L	H	Montrose	2	2		2	1	D Lowe	BCD	Hamilton, Smith
31/10/2020	L	A	Falkirk	0	2		0	1	G Beaton	BCD	
07/11/2020	L	H	Dumbarton	2	1		1	0	S Reid	BCD	Hamilton, Wallace
10/11/2020	LC	H	Hearts	2	3		1	2	E Anderson	BCD	Hamilton, Wallace
14/11/2020	LC	A	Inverness CT	0	1		0	0	C Graham	BCD	
21/11/2020	L	A	Partick Thistle	0	2		0	1	D Williams	BCD	
05/12/2020	L	H	Airdrieonians	2	0		1	0	S Lambie	BCD	Hamilton 2
12/12/2020	L	A	Peterhead	1	2		1	1	G Beaton	BCD	Denholm
19/12/2020	L	H	Forfar Athletic	2	0		1	0	P Stuart	BCD	Hamilton, Denholm
02/01/2021	L	H	Falkirk	2	1		1	0	G Beaton	BCD	Smith, Hamilton
09/01/2021	SC	H	Tranent	5	1		2	1	B Cook	BCD	Agnew 3, Watson, Smith
20/03/2021	L	A	Clyde	3	1		1	0	C Graham	BCD	Austin, Denholm, Wallace
27/03/2021	L	H	Cove Rangers	0	0		0	0	M Roncone	BCD	
30/03/2021	L	A	Montrose	0	3		0	2	S Lambie	BCD	
01/04/2021	L	H	Clyde	1	0		1	0	B Cook	BCD	Denholm
03/04/2021	SC	H	Morton	1	2	AET	0	0	A Muir	BCD	Smith
06/04/2021	L	H	Partick Thistle	2	2		2	0	D Dickinson	BCD	Wallace pen, Smith
08/04/2021	L	A	Dumbarton	1	2		0	1	B Cook	BCD	Dunlop
10/04/2021	L	A	Forfar Athletic	2	1		1	0	D Williams	BCD	Wallace, Smith
17/04/2021	L	H	Peterhead	2	1		0	1	L Wilson	BCD	Denholm, Agnew
20/04/2021	L	A	Airdrieonians	0	2		0	0	A Newlands	BCD	
24/04/2021	L	H	Dumbarton	2	1		1	0	G Ross	BCD	Dunsmore, Steele
29/04/2021	L	H	Peterhead	1	3		1	1	G Grainger	BCD	Dunsmore
04/05/2021	L	A	Forfar Athletic	3	2		1	1	B Cook	BCD	Davidson, Murdoch, Brown
06/05/2021	L	A	Clyde	1	2		0	1	C Graham	BCD	Agnew pen

Ernie McGarr

Gordon Marshall

David Gorman

Date	Comp	H/A	Opponents	F	A	1	2	3	4	5	6	7	8	9	10	11	12	13	14	15	16	17	18	19	20
06/10/2020	LC	H	Cowdenbeath	2	0	Long	Higgins	Dunlop	Murdoch<	Dunsmore*	Swanson&	Agnew>	Davidson	Slattery	Wallace	Hamilton+	Denholm*	Watt+	Smith&	Watson>	Newton<	*Collins*	*Hart*		
10/10/2020	LC	A	Raith Rovers	1	2	Hart	Higgins	Dunlop	Watson	Denholm+	Watt*	Agnew	Davidson	Slattery	Wallace	Newton&	Collins*	Dunsmore+	Hamilton&	*Murdoch*	*Smith*	*Long*	*McConville*	*Bell*	*McLaughlin*
17/10/2020	L	A	Cove Rangers	1	3	Long	Higgins	Dunlop*	Murdoch	Dunsmore	Denholm	Agnew	Newton+	Slattery	Wallace>	Hamilton&	Watson*	Collins+	Smith&	Watt>	*Swanson*	*McLaughlin*	*Hart*		
24/10/2020	L	H	Montrose	2	2	Long	Higgins	Watson	Murdoch	Swanson*	Watt	Agnew	Davidson	Slattery	Smith+	Hamilton	Collins*	McKenzie+	*Healy*	*Dow*	*McConville*	*McLaughlin*	*Newton*	*Hart*	
31/10/2020	L	A	Falkirk	0	2	Long	Higgins	Dunlop	Murdoch	Wallace	Watt*	Agnew	Davidson	Slattery	Smith+	Hamilton	Collins*	Watson+	*Newton*	*Dunsmore*	*McConville*	*McLaughlin*	*Hart*		
07/11/2020	L	H	Dumbarton	2	1	Hart	Higgins	Dunlop	Murdoch	Dunsmore+	Wallace	Agnew	Davidson	Slattery	Smith*	Hamilton	Denholm*	Watson+	*Newton*	*Watt*	*McConville*	*McLaughlin*	*Long*		
10/11/2020	LC	H	Hearts	2	3	Hart	Higgins	Dunlop	Murdoch	Dunsmore&	Wallace	Agnew	Davidson	Slattery	Denholm*	Hamilton+	Collins*	Smith+	Watt&	*Newton*	*McConville*	*McLaughlin*	*Watson*	*Dow*	*Long*
14/11/2020	LC	A	Inverness CT	0	1	Hart	Higgins	Dunlop	Murdoch>	Smith&	Wallace*	Agnew<	Davidson	Slattery	Denholm+	Hamilton	Collins*	Dunsmore+	Watt&	Watson>	Newton<	*McLaughlin*	*Long*		
21/11/2020	L	A	Partick Thistle	0	2	Hart	Higgins	Dunlop	Murdoch	Dunsmore&	Smith>	Agnew+	Davidson	Slattery	Denholm*	Hamilton	Watt*	Newton+	Swanson&	Collins>	*McConville*	*McLaughlin*	*Watson*	*Long*	
05/12/2020	L	H	Airdrieonians	2	0	Long	Higgins	Watson	Murdoch	Dunsmore*	Wallace&	Agnew	Davidson	Slattery	Newton+	Hamilton	Denholm*	Watt+	Smith&	*Swanson*	*Dunlop*	*McLaughlin*	*Collins*	*Scoon*	
12/12/2020	L	A	Peterhead	1	2	Long	Higgins	Watson	Murdoch	Denholm&	Wallace	Agnew	Davidson	Slattery+	Newton*	Hamilton	Swanson*	Smith+	Collins&	*Dunsmore*	*Dunlop*	*McLaughlin*	*Watt*	*Hart*	
19/12/2020	L	H	Forfar Athletic	2	0	Long	Higgins	Watson	Murdoch	Denholm*	Wallace	Agnew+	Davidson	Slattery	Watt	Hamilton	Smith*	Newton+	*Collins*	Dunsmore	*Dunlop*	*McLaughlin*	*Swanson*	*Hart*	
02/01/2021	L	H	Falkirk	2	1	Long	Higgins	Watson	Murdoch	Denholm*	Smith	Agnew	Davidson	Slattery	Watt	Hamilton	Dunlop*	*Newton*	*Swanson*	*Dunsmore*	*Collins*	*Hart*			
09/01/2021	SC	H	Tranent	5	1	Long	Higgins	Watson	Murdoch	Denholm*	Smith+	Agnew	Davidson	Slattery	Watt&	Wallace	Dunsmore*	Swanson+	Newton&	*Dunlop*	*Matheson*	*McLaughlin*	*Hart*		
20/03/2021	L	A	Clyde	3	1	Long	Higgins	Watson	Murdoch	Denholm+	Austin*	Agnew<	Davidson	Slattery	Watt&	Wallace>	Smith*	Dunsmore+	Swanson&	Brown>	McKinnon<	*Fenton*	*Newton*	*Dunlop*	*Hart*
27/03/2021	L	H	Cove Rangers	0	0	Long	Higgins	Watson	Murdoch	Denholm*	Austin>	Agnew+	Davidson	Slattery	Watt&	Wallace	Smith*	Swanson+	Newton&	Dunsmore>	*McKinnon*	*Fenton*	*Brown*	*Dunlop*	*Hart*
30/03/2021	L	A	Montrose	0	3	Long	Higgins	Watson	Murdoch	Dunsmore*	Austin>	Agnew	Davidson	Slattery+	Smith&	Wallace	Fenton*	Dunlop+	Swanson&	Brown>	*McKinnon*	*Denholm*	*Newton*	*Watt*	*Hart*
01/04/2021	L	H	Clyde	1	0	Hart	Higgins*	Dunlop	Swanson+	Dunsmore	Denholm&	Watt<	McKinnon	Fenton	Newton	Brown>	Watson*	Davidson+	Spence&	Wallace>	Slattery<	*McConville*	*Smith*	*Agnew*	*Adams*
03/04/2021	SC	H	Morton	1	2 AET	Long	Dunlop	Watson	Murdoch	Dunsmore+	Watt	Agnew	Davidson	Slattery>	Newton*	Smith&	McKinnon*	Swanson+	Denholm&	Fenton>	*Steele*	*McConville*	*Higgins*	*Hart*	
06/04/2021	L	H	Partick Thistle	2	2	Long	Higgins	Watson<	Murdoch	Swanson&	Denholm*	McKinnon	Davidson	Slattery	Smith+	Wallace>	Dunsmore*	Spence+	Newton&	Watt>	Dunlop<	*Fenton*	*Brown*	*Agnew*	*Hart*
08/04/2021	L	A	Dumbarton	1	2	Hart	Higgins	Dunlop	Fenton&	Dunsmore	McKinnon	Agnew	Watt<	Newton+	Spence>	Brown*	Wallace*	Smith+	Watson&	Denholm>	Swanson<	*Steele*	*Davidson*	*Murdoch*	*Adams*
10/04/2021	L	A	Forfar Athletic	2	1	Long	Higgins	Dunlop	Murdoch	Dunsmore	Swanson+	Agnew	Davidson	Denholm&	Smith*	Wallace	Watt*	Brown+	Dunsmore&	Fenton>	*Spence*	*Steele*	*Newton*	*Slattery*	*Hart*
17/04/2021	L	H	Peterhead	2	1	Long	Higgins	Dunmop	Murdoch	Watson	Swanson+	Agnew	Davidson	Denholm&	Smith*	Wallace	Spence*	McKinnon+	Dunsmore&	*Brown*	*Watt*	*Fenton*	*Newton*	*Slattery*	*Hart*
20/04/2021	L	A	Airdrieonians	0	2	Long	Higgins&	Dunlop	Slattery*	Dunsmore	Swanson	Agnew	McKinnon	Denholm	Brown	Wallace+	Spence*	Watt+	Steele&	*Newton*	*Smith*	*Fenton*	*Hart*		
24/04/2021	L	H	Dumbarton	2	1	Hart	Watson	Dunlop	Slattery*	Dunsmore	Swanson+	Steele	Davidson	Newton&	Watt	Spence	Fenton*	Brown+	McKinnon&	*Agnew*	*Long*				
29/04/2021	L	H	Peterhead	1	3	Hart	Watson	Dunlop	Fenton	Dunsmore*	Swanson<	Steele+	Davidson	Agnew>	McKinnon	Spence&	Murdoch*	Brown+	Smith&	Watt>	Denholm<	*Dow*	*Allan*	*Newton*	*Long*
04/05/2021	L	A	Forfar Athletic	3	2	Long	Newton>	Dunlop	Murdoch	Watson	Swanson	Steele	Davidson	Denholm&	Watt*	Spence+	Dow*	Brown+	Dunsmore&	Healy>	*Allan*	*McConville*	*Fenton*	*Hart*	
06/05/2021	L	A	Clyde	1	2	Hart	Dunsmore	Dunlop	Fenton*	Watson	Agnew	Steele&	Davidson	Brown>	Watt	Spence+	Denholm*	Healy+	McKinnon&	McKenzie>	*Newton*	*Dow*	*Allan*		

THE GOALIES

Goalkeepers Used in League Matches, 1971-2020

Players shown in the season of their first appearance only

1971/2	Gerry Gallagher
	Dave Gorman
1972/3	Ernie McGarr
1974/5	Steven Anderson
1976/7	Alan Blair
1978/9	Gordon Heaney
1980/1	David Huggins
1981/2	Peter Christensen
1982/3	Gordon Marshall
1986/7	Ray Charles
1987/8	Alan Banner
1989/0	Jim Moffat
	Derek Atkins
1992/3	Ewan Wilson
1994/5	D Robertson
1995/6	Lindsay Hamilton
1996/7	Calum Rushford
1997/8	Willie McCulloch
	Barry Thompson
	Andy Stewart
1998/9	Jim Butter
2001/2	Ross Godfrey
2003/4	Gary O'Connor
	Marc Graham
2004/5	John Dodds
	Scott Morrison
	John McCafferty
2006/7	Ian Ross
2007/8	Craig Wight
2008/9	Michael Brown
	Stewart Baillie
	Mark Ridgers
2012/3	Andy Collier
	Callum Antell
2013/4	Jack Hamilton
	Dylan Rooney
	Greg Paterson
2014/5	Allan Fleming
	Jordan Miller
2015/6	Darren Hill
	Ryan Goodfellow
	Liam Kelly
2016/7	Willie Muir
	Mark Hurst
2017/8	Ben McKenzie
2018/9	Brett Long
	Craig McDowell
	Daniel Terry
2019/0	Jordan Hart

Surname	First Name	Date of Birth	No	Nat	Pos	Signed	Previous	Notes	Contract	Lge A	Lge S	Lge G	SC A	SC S	SC G	LC A	LC S	LC G	Un
Adams	Ally	01/11/1991		SCO	GK	2021	Tranent (OL)	Jan-May		0	0								2
Agnew	Scott	11/07/1987	11	SCO	M	2018	Stranraer	OOC May 2021, joined Airdrieonians		18	0	2	2		3	4			3
Allan	Jamie	11/12/2001		SCO	M	2020	East Fife Youths	OL to Dundonald Bluebell Dec-Jan	U20	0	0								3
Austin	Nathan	15/02/1994		SCO	F	2021	Kelty Hearts (OL)	Mar-21		3	0	1							0
Bell	Kyle	17/10/1999		SCO	M	2018	Raith Rovers Youth	OL to Bo'ness United Sep-Jan, Freed May 2021 joined Glenrothes		0	0								1
Brown	Sean	14/06/1997		SCO	F	2021	East Stirlingshire (OL)	Mar-May		4	6	1							3
Collins	Thomas	27/08/1996	19	SCO	F	2020	BSC Glasgow	Released June 2021, joined Kilwinning Rangers		0	5						3		4
Davidson	Ross	28/10/1993	16	SCO	M	2018	Albion Rovers		End 2021/2	18	1	1	2			4			1
Denholm	Danny	26/08/1990	7	SCO	M	2019	Arbroath		End 2021/2	13	5	5	1	1		3	1		1
Dow	Cameron	14/03/2002		SCO	M	2020	Dundee	OL to Carnoustie Panmure Nov-Jan	U20	0	1								4
Dunlop	Ross	03/08/1989	5	SCO	D	2018	Stenhousemuir		End 2021/2	13	3	1	1			4			6
Dunsmore	Aaron	24/07/1996	2	SCO	D	2017	Hibernian		End 2021/2	12	6	2	1	1		2	2		4
Fenton	Miller	16/10/2003		SCO	D	2021	Dunfermline Athletic (OL)	Mar-May		4	3			1					6
Hamilton	Jack	30/06/2000	15	SCO	F	2020	Livingston (OL)	Oct-May		9	0	7				3	1	2	0
Hart	Jordan	22/01/1996	21	SCO	GK	2019	Queen's Park	Released May 2021		7	0					3			17
Healy	Jack	16/12/2002		SCO	F	2020	East Fife Youths	OL to St Andrews United Nov-Jan	U20	0	2								1
Higgins	Chris	04/07/1985	3	SCO	D	2019	Ayr United		End 2021/2	18	0		1			4			1
Laird	Nathan	27/06/2000		SCO	D	2020	East Fife Youths	OL to Burntisland Shipyard Nov-Jan	U20	0	0								0
Long	Brett	11/04/1997	1	NIR	GK	2018	Dundee United	Released May 2021, joined Peterhead		15	0		2			1			7
Matheson	Jack	01/05/2001		SCO	D	2021	East Fife Youths		U20	0	0								1
McConville	Josh	08/09/2002	17	SCO	M	2020	East Fife Youths	OL to Lochee United Nov-Jan, Freed May 2021 joined Lochee U		0	0								9
McKenzie	Jordan	15/02/2002		SCO	F	2020	East Fife Youths	OL to Burntisland Shipyard Nov-Jan	U20	0	2								0
McKinnon	Cole	29/01/2003		SCO	M	2021	Rangers (OL)	Mar-May		5	4			1					2
McLaughlin	Aiden	01/02/2002	20	SCO	M	2020	Fife Elite Academy		U20	0	0								11
Murdoch	Stewart	17/12/1990	4	SCO	M	2019	Dundee United		End 2022/3	16	1	1	2			3			2
Newton	Liam	08/05/2000	18	SCO	M	2020	East Fife Youths		End 2021/2	7	5		1	1		1	2	1	12
Scoon	Josh	01/01/2002		SCO	GK	2020	East Fife Youths		U20	0	0								1
Slattery	Pat	03/06/1993	8	SCO	D	2015	Queen of the South		End 2022/3	15	1		2			4			2
Smith	Kevin	20/03/1987	10	SCO	F	2014	Dumbarton		End 2021/2	9	8	4	2		2	1	2		3
Spence	Greig	06/07/1992		SCO	F	2021	Stenhousemuir (OL)	Mar-May		5	4								1
Steele	Aaron	12/04/2002		SCO	D	2021	St Johnstone (OL)	Mar-May		4	1	1							3
Swanson	Danny	28/12/1986	12	SCO	M	2020	St Johnstone		End 2021/2	9	6			2		1			4
Wallace	Ryan	30/07/1990	9	SCO	F	2019	Arbroath		End 2022/3	13	2	4	1			4		2	0
Watson	Craig	13/02/1995	6	SCO	D	2017	Hamilton Accies	Released May 2021, joined Airdrieonians		14	5		2		1	1	2		2
Watt	Liam	21/06/1994	14	SCO	M	2018	Brechin City		End 2022/3	11	7		2			1	3		4
Wilkinson	Ali	09/01/2001		SCO	D	2020	East Fife Youths	OL to St Andrews United Nov-Jan	U20	0	0								0
NEW SIGNINGS																			
Brown	Sean	14/06/1997		SCO	F	2021	East Stirlingshire		End 2021/2										
Gallagher	Scott	15/07/1989		SCO	GK	2021	Arbroath		End 2022/3										
McGuigan	Mark					2021	Stenhousemuir	Retired July 2021											
McManus	Connor	29/02/1996		SCO	M	2021	Stranraer		End 2022/3										
Mercer	Scott	18/06/1995		SCO	D	2021	Falkirk		End 2022/3										
Steele	Aaron	12/04/2002		SCO	D	2021	St Johnstone		End 2021/2										
Anderson	Lewis			SCO	M	2021	Fife Elite Academy		End 2021/2										
Campbell	Liam			SCO	GK	2021	Fife Elite Academy		End 2021/2										
Cunningham	Michael	10/03/2001		SCO	F	2021	Dundee		End 2021/2										

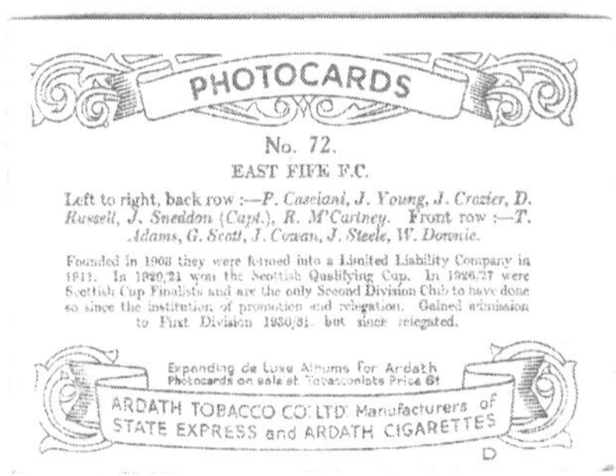

Edinburgh City FC 2020/21 The Citizens

Founded	1928 (Old Club)
Ground	Ainslie Park (Spartans FC)
Postcode	EH5 2HF
Tel	
Capacity	2000
Closest Railway Station	Edinburgh Haymarket
Record Attendance	6000, H v St Bernards, Scottish Cup 1931/2
Record League Win	6-1 v Brechin City, 18/9/37
Record League Defeat	2-13, v East Fife, 11/12/37
Most League Goals in a Season	78, 1931/2
Colours 2020/21 Top	White
Shorts	Black
Sponsor	Forth Capital
Manufacturer	Macron
Change Colours 2020/21 Top	Red and Black
Shorts	White
Nicknames	City, Lilywhites, Citizens
Web	www.edinburghcityfc.com
Match Programme 2020/21	The Citizen, £2.50

Chairman: Jim Brown
Club Secretary: Colin Campbell
Company Secretary: Paul McIntosh
Directors: Colin Campbell, Gordon Kneebone, Calum Smith, Tom Tracey
Sporting Director: James McDonaugh
Manager: James McDonaugh, then Gary Naysmith
Coach: Alex Connon
Physio: Scott Anderson
Sports Therapist: Ryan Elliot
Strength & Conditioning: Andrew Wilson
Kit Man: Ian McIntyre
Under 20 Coaches: Callum Jeffrey, Stevie Thomson, Jamie Hawkins
Matchday Operations: James Lumsden, Andrew McDonald, Alick Milne
Safety Officer: Sam Bryce
Chaplain: Russell McCarty

THE GOALIES

Goalkeepers Used in League Matches, 2016- 2020

Players shown in the season of their first appearance only

2016/7	Calum Antell
	Andrew Stobie
2017/8	Fraser Morton
2019/0	Ryan Adamson
	Aidan McAdams
	Josh Rae
	Alan Martin
	Kelbie Mason

With Queen's Park spending big the League Two season was always about who would make it into the play offs and could they overcome the 9th placed side in League One. City achieved their play off spot reasonably comfortably and then took on Elgin City. They were dismissed leaving a show down between City and Dumbarton for the League One place.

City gave an insipid performance in the home game, losing 3-1. Despite winning the second leg 1-0 they had to content themselves with another season in League Two. They made no progress in the League Cup but got through two rounds of the Scottish before losing on penalty kicks to Forfar Athletic.

STAR MAN

Josh Campbell, on loan from Hibernian for the season, was a stand out performer for City.

PROSPECTS 2021/2

City announced that they would be returning to Meadowbank for 2021/2 after their exile at Ainslie Park. Unfortunately their announcement was premature – Meadowbank will not be ready until at least October. In the meantime Spartans accepted new tenants on Lothian Thistle HV. City now face the prospect of playing all their home games on Friday evenings at Ainslie Park until Meadowbank opens. On the field, Manager Gary Naysmith opted to get rid of several stalwarts to stamp his own mark on the side. Whether or not the newcomers match the likes of Antell, Thomson, Laird, Black and Henderson remains to be seen. A play off spot is as much as they can hope for.

City hope to move to their new Meadowbank home sometime this season

Date	Comp	H/A	Opponents	F	A		HT		Referee	Crowd	Scorers
06/10/2020	LC	H	Livingston	1	5		0	3	W Collum	BCD	Handling pen
10/10/2020	LC	H	Stenhousemuir	2	2	2-4p	1	1	M McDermid	BCD	B Henderson, De Vita
13/10/2020	LC	A	Alloa Athletic	1	2		0	1	D Lowe	BCD	B Henderson
17/10/2020	L	A	Brechin City	5	1		1	0	G Beaton	BCD	Balatoni, Brown, B Henderson, Campbell, Jardine
24/10/2020	L	H	Cowdenbeath	0	1		0	0	C Graham	BCD	
31/10/2020	L	H	Elgin City	1	0		1	0	P Stuart	BCD	McGill
07/11/2020	L	A	Stenhousemuir	0	2		0	0	D Williams	BCD	
11/11/2020	LC	A	Airdrieonians	1	0		1	0	K Graham	BCD	B Henderson
21/11/2020	L	H	Stranraer	0	1		0	1	G Ross	BCD	
28/11/2020	L	A	Annan Athletic	4	0		2	0	C Scott	BCD	L Henderson, B Henderson 2, Campbell
05/12/2020	L	H	Albion Rovers	5	2		4	1	S Luke	BCD	L Henderson 3, Thomson 2
12/12/2020	L	A	Queen's Park	3	3		1	0	L Wilson	BCD	Campbell 2, McGill
19/12/2020	L	H	Stirling Albion	2	3		0	3	D Williams	BCD	McIntyre, Brown
26/12/2020	SC	H	Caledonian Braves	3	1		1	1	B Cook	BCD	Reid og, McIntyre, Campbell
10/01/2021	SC	A	Airdrieonians	1	0		0	0	D Lowe	BCD	See
20/03/2021	L	A	Elgin City	2	1		2	1	D Lowe	BCD	Campbell, McIntyre
23/03/2021	L	A	Albion Rovers	2	1		1	0	D Williams	BCD	See 2
27/03/2021	L	H	Stenhousemuir	3	1		1	0	G Grainger	BCD	De Vita 2, Handling
30/03/2021	L	A	Cowdenbeath	3	1		2	1	M McDermid	BCD	Brown, B Henderson 2
03/04/2021	SC	A	Forfar Athletic	2	2	AET, 3-5p	2	1	S Kirkland	BCD	See, Hamilton
06/04/2021	L	H	Annan Athletic	1	1		0	0	G Ross	BCD	See
10/04/2021	L	A	Stranraer	1	0		1	0	M Roncone	BCD	Brown
13/04/2021	L	H	Brechin City	2	1		1	1	K Graham	BCD	Handling, De Vita
17/04/2021	L	H	Queen's Park	2	3		0	1	G Grainger	BCD	L Henderson, Campbell
20/04/2021	L	A	Stirling Albion	1	0		1	0	D Lowe	BCD	See
24/04/2021	L	H	Stirling Albion	0	1		0	1	L Watson	BCD	
29/2/21	L	A	Queen's Park	0	2		0	1	L Wilson	BCD	
01/05/2021	L	H	Elgin City	2	0		2	0	M McDermind	BCD	Campbell, Brown
04/05/2021	L	A	Stranraer	1	2		1	1	G Grainger	BCD	Robertson og
08/05/2021	PO	A	Elgin City	1	0		1	0	A Newlands	BCD	Campbell
11/05/2021	PO	H	Elgin City	2	2		1	2	C Napier	BCD	Handling, Campbell
17/05/2021	PO	H	Dumbarton	1	3		1	0	C Steven	BCD	McIntyre
20/05/2021	PO	A	Dumbarton	1	0		0	0	A Newlands	500	See

Josh Rae

Aidan McAdams

Kelby Mason

Date	Comp	H/A	Opponents	F	A		1	2	3	4	5	6	7	8	9	10	11	12	13	14	15	16	17	18	19	20
06/10/2020	LC	H	Livingston	1	5		Antell	Thomson	Balatoni	Crane	L Henderson	Handling>	Harris*	Black+	Brown	Campbell	See&	Butterworth*	Jardine+	B Henderson&	Hamilton>	Quate	Jarron	Newman		
10/10/2020	LC	H	Stenhousemuir	2	2	2-4p	Antell	Thomson	Balatoni	Crane*	L Henderson	Handling>	Jardine&	Black+	Brown	Campbell	B Henderson	Hamilton*	De Vita+	Butterworth&	See>	Quate	Jarron	Sharp	Newman	
13/10/2020	LC	A	Alloa Athletic	1	2		Antell	Thomson	Balatoni	Newman	L Henderson	De Vita&	Jardine*	Black+	Brown	Campbell	See	Handling*	B Henderson+	Hamilton&	Quate	Jarron	Butterworth	Sharp		
17/10/2020	L	A	Brechin City	5	1		Antell	Thomson	Balatoni	Newman	L Henderson	Handling*	De Vita+	Black	Brown	Campbell>	B Henderson&	See*	Jardine+	McGill&	Cunningham>	Quate	Laird	Butterworth	Sharp	Hamilton
24/10/2020	L	H	Cowdenbeath	0	1		Antell	Thomson	Balatoni	Newman	L Henderson	Handling>	De Vita&	Black*	Brown+	Campbell	B Henderson	Laird*	See+	McGill&	Jardine>	Cunningham	Quate	Butterworth	Sharp	Hamilton
31/10/2020	L	H	Elgin City	1	0		Antell	Thomson	Balatoni	Newman	L Henderson	Handling	De Vita+	Laird	McGill*	Campbell	See	Harris*	Brown+	B Henderson&	Jardine	Cunningham	Black	Butterworth	Sharp	Hamilton
07/11/2020	L	A	Stenhousemuir	0	2		Antell	Thomson	Balatoni	Newman	L Henderson	Handling	De Vita+	Laird>	McGill&	Campbell	See*	B Henderson*	Cunningham+	Brown&	Butterworth>	Quate	Black	Hamilton	Sharp	
11/11/2020	LC	A	Airdrieonians	1	0		Antell	Thomson	Balatoni	Newman+	L Henderson	Black	Brown	Hamilton	Cunningham*	Campbell	B Henderson	Handling*	De Vita+	Jarron	Sharp	See	Butterworth	Quate		
21/11/2020	L	H	Stranraer	0	1		Antell	Thomson	Balatoni	Newman*	L Henderson	Handling+	Brown>	Hamilton	Black&	Campbell	B Henderson	McGill*	De Vita+	Jardine&	See>	Sharpe	Butterworth	Quate		
28/11/2020	L	A	Annan Athletic	4	0		Antell	Thomson	Balatoni	Laird&	L Henderson	McGill+	Brown>	Hamilton	Black*	Campbell	B Henderson<	Crane*	See+	De Vita&	Jardine>	Newman<	Cunningham	Harris	Sharp	Quate
05/12/2020	L	H	Albion Rovers	5	2		Antell	Thomson	Balatoni	De Vita<	L Henderson	McGill+	Brown>	Hamilton*	Black	Campbell	B Henderson&	Crane*	Harris+	See&	Jardine>	Cunningham<	Laird	Newman	Sharp	Quate
12/12/2020	L	A	Queen's Park	3	3		Antell	Hamilton	Balatoni	Crane*	L Henderson	Harris&	Brown>	Laird	Black<	Campbell	See+	McIntyre*	B Henderson+	McGill&	Jardine>	Newman<	Sharp	Quate		
19/12/2020	L	H	Stirling Albion	2	3		Antell	Thomson	Balatoni	Hamilton&	L Henderson	Harris+	Brown	Laird>	Black*	Campbell	B Henderson	De Vita*	See+	McIntyre&	Jardine>	McGill	Sharp	Newman	Quate	
26/12/2020	SC	H	Caledonian Braves	3	1		Antell	Thomson	De Vita+	Hamilton	L Henderson	McIntyre	Brown	Laird	See*	Campbell&	B Henderson	Jardine*	Black+	Newman&	Jarron	Beveridge				
10/01/2021	SC	A	Airdrieonians	1	0		Antell	Thomson	De Vita+	Hamilton	L Henderson	McIntyre	Brown	Laird	See	Campbell	Black*	Crane*	Balatoni+	Harris	Jarron	Newman	Jardine	Quate		
20/03/2021	L	A	Elgin City	2	1		Antell	Thomson	Crane	Hamilton	L Henderson	McIntyre	Brown>	Laird	See*	Campbell&	De Vita+	Henderson*	Black+	Smith&	Harris>	Jardine	Denham	Handling	Newman	Goodfellow
23/03/2021	L	A	Albion Rovers	2	1		Antell	Thomson	Crane	Hamilton	L Henderson	McIntyre	Brown&	Handling*	Black	Harris+	See	De Vita*	Smith+	Jardine&	B Henderson	Beveridge	Denham	Newman	Goodfellow	
27/03/2021	L	H	Stenhousemuir	3	1		Antell	Thomson	Crane	Hamilton*	L Henderson	McIntyre	Brown>	Jardine	Black	De Vita+	See&	Denham*	Harris+	B Henderson&	Handling>	Smith	Beveridge	Newman	Goodfellow	
30/03/2021	L	A	Cowdenbeath	3	1		Antell	Thomson	Campbell	Hamilton	L Henderson	McIntyre	Brown&	Jardine	Black	De Vita+	B Henderson*	See*	Laird+	Newman&	Handling	Smith	Beveridge	Harris	Denham	Goodfellow
03/04/2021	SC	A	Forfar Athletic	2	2	AET, 3-5p	Antell	Denham+	Crane	Hamilton	L Henderson	Harris*	Handling&	Jardine>	Laird	Campbell	See	De Vita*	Thomson+	Black&	Brown>	Newman	Beveridge	Quate		
06/04/2021	L	H	Annan Athletic	1	1		Antell	Thomson	Tapping	Hamilton	Campbell	McIntyre	Handling+	Jardine	Laird&	De Vita*	See	Brown*	Dishington+	Black&	Crane	Newman	Beveridge	L Henderson	Goodfellow	
10/04/2021	L	A	Stranraer	1	0		Antell	Thomson	Tapping	Hamilton	Crane	McIntyre	Brown*	Jardine+	Black	Campbell&	See	Laird*	De Vita+	Handling&	Dishington	Newman	Beveridge	Goodfellow		
13/04/2021	L	H	Brechin City	2	1		Antell	Thomson	Tapping*	Hamilton	Crane	Handling&	Brown+	Laird>	Black	Campbell	De Vita<	McIntyre*	See+	Jardine&	Dishington>	Newman<	Beveridge	Goodfellow		
17/04/2021	L	H	Queen's Park	2	3		Antell	Thomson	Crane	Denham	L Henderson+	McIntyre	Handling*	Jardine	Black&	Campbell	See	Brown*	Laird+	Dishington&	De Vita	Newman	Beveridge	Goodfellow		
20/04/2021	L	A	Stirling Albion	1	0		Antell	Balatoni	Crane*	Denham	Laird	McIntyre	Handling+	Jardine	Brown&	De Vita	See	Newman*	Campbell+	Black&	Dishington	Thomson	Beveridge	Goodfellow		
24/04/2021	L	H	Stirling Albion	0	1		Antell	Thomson	Balatoni	Newman	Campbell	McIntyre	Handling	Jardine+	Black	De Vita*	See	Brown*	Dishington+	Laird	Crane	Denham	Beveridge	Goodfellow	Jarron	
29/2/21	L	A	Queen's Park	0	2		Antell	Thomson	Balatoni	Laird&	Crane	McIntyre	Brown	Jardine	De Vita*	Campbell	See+	Handling*	Dishington+	Smith	Newman	Denham	Black	Goodfellow	Jarron	
01/05/2021	L	H	Elgin City	2	0		Antell	Thomson	Crane	Hamilton	Brown	McIntyre	Handling*	Jardine	Black	Campbell	See+	Laird*	Henderson+	De Vita&	Balatoni	Denham	Dishington	Goodfellow	Jarron	Newman
04/05/2021	L	A	Stranraer	1	2		Goodfellow	Balatoni	Denham	Campbell	Laird<	Dishington>	Brown	Newman+	Black	De Vita&	B Henderson*	See*	McIntyre+	Jardine&	Handling>	Jarron<	Beveridge			
08/05/2021	PO	A	Elgin City	1	0		Antell	Thomson	Crane	Hamilton	Brown	McIntyre	Handling*	Jardine	Black	Campbell	See+	De Vita*	Henderson+	Denham	Harris	Balatoni	Dishington	Goodfellow		
11/05/2021	PO	H	Elgin City	2	2		Antell	Thomson	Crane+	Hamilton	Brown	McIntyre	Handling	Jardine	Black*	Campbell	See	Dishington*	Balatoni+	Denham	Harris	De Vita	B Henderson	Goodfellow		
17/05/2021	PO	H	Dumbarton	1	3		Antell	Thomson	Brown	Hamilton	L Henderson	McIntyre	Handling+	Jardine	Black*	Campbell	See	De Vita*	B Henderson+	Denham	Harris	Balatoni	Dishington	Goodfellow		
20/05/2021	PO	A	Dumbarton	1	0		Antell	Thomson	Balatoni	Hamilton+	L Henderson	McIntyre	Handling*	Jardine	Brown	Campbell&	See	B Henderson*	Harris+	Dishington&	Black	Denham	Tapping	Goodfellow		

THE ORIGINAL EDINBURGH CITY'S LEAGUE RECORD

1931/2
Finished bottom of the Second Division with 17 points.
Five games won - at home to Arbroath, Dunfermline, Dumbarton and Hibs, and away to Montrose
Beaten 8-4 at home by Queen of the South

1932/3
Finished bottom of the Second Division with 12 points
Four games won - at home to Leith, Forfar and Brechin, and away to Albion Rovers
Beaten 8-1 away by St Bernards in a local derby

1933/4
Finished bottom of the Second Division with 14 points
Four games won - all at home, v Brechin, Dumbarton, Dundee United and King's Park
Went down 8-1 away to Albion Rovers

1934/5
Finished bottom of the Second Division with 8 points
Three games won - at home to Dumbarton and Montrose, and away to East Stirlingshire
Managed to lose 6-9 at Tannadice, and 4-9 at King's Park

1935/6
Finished 15th out of 18 in Second Division with 25 points
Eight games won - at home to Alloa, Brechin, King's Park, Montrose and St Mirren, and away to Brechin, Dumbarton and Leith
Managed a 5-0 home win over King's Park

1936/7
Finished bottom of the Second Division with 7 points
Two games won, at home to Airdrie and King's Park
Beaten 8-2 at home by East Fife

1937/8
Finished 17th out of 18 in the Second Division with 17 points
Seven games won - at home to Brechin, Cowdenbeath, Dumbarton, King's Park, Montrose and Stenhousemuir, and away to Brechin
Lost 2-13 away to East Fife

1938/9
Finished bottom of the Second Division with 16 points
Six games won, at home to Alloa, Dundee United, Montrose and Morton, and away to Dundee United and East Stirlingshire
Lost all four derby games, losing home and away to Leith and St Bernards

Surname	First Name	Date of Birth	No	Nat	Pos	Signed	Previous	Notes	Contract	Lge A	Lge S	Lge G	SC A	SC S	SC G	LC A	LC S	LC G	Un
Antell	Calum	13/06/1992	1	WAL	GK	2016	Nairn County	Released May 2021, joined Arbroath		25			3			4			
Balatoni	Conrad	27/01/1991	5	ENG / SCO	D	2018	Torquay United	On Transfer List May 2021, joined Clyde		14	1	1		1		4			3
Beveridge	Dean	04/05/2002		SCO	GK	2019	Edinburgh City Youths	OL to LT HV Sep-Dec, Freed May 2021 joined Gala FR		0	0								12
Black	Andy	20/09/1995	4	SCO	M	2018	Stirling Albion	Released May 2021, joined Kelty Hearts		19	3		1	2		4			4
Brown	Liam	06/04/1999	8	SCO	M	2019	Motherwell	Transferred to Queen's Park June 2021		22	5	5	2	1		4			0
Butterworth	Zac	24/03/2001	18	SCO	M	2020	Rangers (OL)	Sep-May		0	1						2		6
Campbell	Josh	06/05/2000	16	SCO	M	2020	Hibernian (OL)	Sep-May		23	1	9	3		1	4			0
Crane	Callum	08/03/1996	14	SCO	D	2019	Livingston		End 2021/2	12	2		1	1		2			2
Cunningham	Michael	10/03/2001		SCO	F	2020	Dundee (OL)	Oct-Jan		0	3					1			3
De Vita	Rafa	23/09/1987	26	ITA	F	2020	Livingston (OL)	Sep-May		14	8	3	2	1		1	2	1	2
Denham	Sam	25/10/2002		SCO	D	2021	St Johnstone (OL)	Mar-May		3	1								10
Dishington	Jamie	12/12/1996		SCO	M	2021	East Stirlingshire (OL)	Mar-May		1	7								5
Goodfellow	Ryan	26/05/1993	21	SCO	GK	2021	Albion Rovers		End 2021/2	1	0								16
Hamilton	Lee	15/09/1995	15	SCO	D	2020	Stranraer		End 2021/2	17	0		3		1	1	3		4
Handling	Danny	06/02/1994	10	SCO	F	2018	Dumbarton		End 2021/2	15	4	3	1			2	2	1	2
Harris	Alex	31/08/1994	33	SCO	M	2019	York City	Released May 2021, joined Berwick Rangers		3	5		1			1			6
Henderson	Liam	23/08/1996	22	SCO	D	2018	Stirling Lions (AUS)	Out of Contract May 2021, joined Arbroath		16	0	5	3			4			1
Henderson	Blair	10/08/1994	9	SCO	F	2018	Annan Athletic	Transferred to Spartans June 2021		8	9	5	1			2	2	3	2
Jardine	Danny	17/01/1996	11	SCO	M	2020	Stirling Albion		End 2021/2	13	10	1	1	1		2	1		3
Jarron	Jonny			SCO	M	2020	Spartans Youths		U20	0	1								9
Laird	Marc	23/01/1986	6	SCO	M	2016	Yeovil Town	Released May 2021, joined Stirling Albion		11	5		3						3
Mason	Kelby	16/10/1998	21	SCO	GK	2020	Hearts	Released May 2021		0	0								0
McGill	Gabby	04/09/2000		ENG	F	2020	Dunfermline Athletic (OL)	Oct-Jan		4	4	2							1
McIntyre	Robbie	17/04/1994	3	SCO	D	2018	Tynecastle		End 2021/2	15	4	3	2		1				0
Newman	Sam	08/06/2001	20	SCO	M	2020	Edinburgh City Youths	Released May 2021		7	5			1		2			14
Quate	Cammy	14/03/2001		SCO	GK	2020	Edinburgh City Youths		U20	0	0								14
See	Ouzy	25/08/1994	19	SCO	F	2020	Albion Rovers		End 2021/2	17	9	5	3		2	2	1		1
Sharp	Harry	04/04/2001	21	SCO	GK	2020	Dundee (OL)	Oct-May		0	0								12
Smith	Allan	25/01/1994	7	SCO	F	2018	Peterhead		End 2021/2	0	2								3
Smith	Darren	27/03/1988		SCO	F	2021	East Kilbride (OL)	Mar-May											0
Tapping	Jordan	04/07/1996		ENG	D	2021	East Stirlingshire (OL)	Mar-May		3	0								1
Thomson	Craig	17/04/1991	2	SCO	D	2017	Kelty Hearts	Released May 2021, joined Cowdenbeath		23	0	2	3	1		4			1
Own Goal												1			1				
NEW SIGNINGS																			
Bronsky	Stephen	16/06/1994		SCO	D	2021	Elgin City		End 2021/2										
Ferguson	Alex	10/09/2003		SCO	M	2021	St Johnstone (OL)	Jul-May	End 2021/2										
Hilton	James	02/11/1997		SCO	M	2021	Stranraer		End 2021/2										
Kane	Chris	31/05/1993		SCO	D	2021	Stenhousemuir		End 2021/2										
Kidd	Lewis	30/01/1995		SCO	D	2021	East Kilbride		End 2021/2										
McFarlane	Michael	18/09/2002		SCO	F	2021	St Johnstone		End 2021/2										
Reekie	Scott	28/01/2000		SCO	D	2021	Brechin City		End 2021/2										
Schwake	Brian	24/08/2001		USA	GK	2021	Livingston (OL)	Jul-May	End 2021/2										
Shanley	Ryan	16/01/2001		SCO	F	2021	Hibernian (OL)	Jul-May	End 2021/2										
Tapping	Callum	05/06/1993		SCO / ENG	D	2021	Stenhousemuir		End 2021/2										
Toshney	Lewis	26/04/1992		SCO	D	2021	Downfield		End 2021/2										

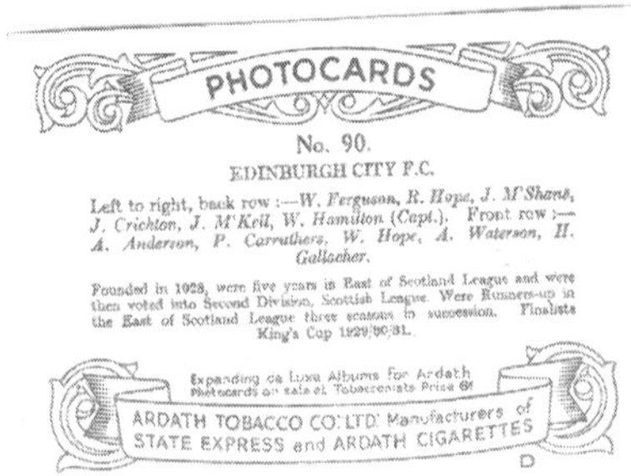
PHOTOCARDS

No. 90.

EDINBURGH CITY F.C.

Left to right, back row :—*W. Ferguson, R. Hope, J. M'Shane, J. Crichton, J. M'Kell, W. Hamilton (Capt.).* Front row :—*A. Anderson, P. Carruthers, W. Hope, A. Waterson, H. Gallacher.*

Founded in 1928, were five years in East of Scotland League and were then voted into Second Division, Scottish League. Were Runners-up in the East of Scotland League three seasons in succession. Finalists King's Cup 1929/30/31.

Expanding de Luxe Albums for Ardath Photocards on sale at Tobacconists Price 6d

ARDATH TOBACCO CO. LTD. Manufacturers of STATE EXPRESS and ARDATH CIGARETTES

D

Elgin City FC 2020/21 City

Founded	1893
Ground	Boroughbriggs
Postcode	IV30 1AP
Tel	01343 551114
Capacity	4520
Closest Railway Station	Elgin
Record Attendance	12608 v Arbroath, SC, 17/2/1968
Record Win	18-1 v Brora Rangers, NOS Cup, 6/2/1960
Record Defeat	1-14 v Hearts, SC, 4/2/1939
Most League Goals in a Season	19 Martin Johnston 2005/6
Colours 2020/21 Top	Black and White Stripes
Shorts	Black
Sponsor	McDonald and Munro
Manufacturer	Joma
Change Colours 2020/21 Top	Red with Black Detail
Shorts	Red
Nicknames	City
Web	www.elgincity.com
Match Programme 2020/21	On line only

Chairman: Graham Tatters
Directors: Isla Benzie, Cecil Jack, Graham Mutch, Stephen Scott, Grant Shewan
Secretary: Keiran Carty
Manager: Gavin Price MBE
Assistant Manager: Keith Gibson
Goalkeeping Coach: Stevie Dunn
Club Doctors: James Jack, Alan Rodger
Physiotherapists: Andy Jones, Grace Bibby, Catherine Graham
Kit Controller: John Jack
Under 20s and Academy Manager: Robbie Hope
Community Football Co-ordinator: Craigh Stewart
Programme Editor: Mike Whelan
Club Photographer: Bob Crombie
Social Media: Aimee Walker

FROM THE NORTHERN SCOT . . .

ELGIN City manager Gavin Price has been made a Member of the British Empire in the Queen's birthday honours.

Aberfeldy-based Mr Price has been given the honour for his work in establishing the Feldy Roo project to support vulnerable and elderly residents of the Perthshire community at the peak of coronavirus lockdown.

The hotelier was among a group of volunteers in the community who supplied regular hot meals and social contact for people living alone or less able to get out of the house.

Reacting to his award on social media, Mr Price said: "People that know me will understand that I was a bit bewildered on hearing the news about the MBE. To be honest, slightly embarrassed as the FeldyRoo project involved so many people and businesses across the Aberfeldy community.

"However after a bit of soul searching, I accepted the honour. My understanding, and I hope that of everyone else is, that this is not an individual award.

"I have accepted the MBE on behalf of FeldyRoo, Aberfeldy and all the volunteers and businesses that were involved in the fantastic project. Our community pulled together like never before and that was down to a team, not an individual."

Season after season "inconsistency" seems to be the watchword for Elgin City. On their day they can produce fantastic football and starting results but they are also capable of surprising defeats. For much of the season they hovered between 3rd and 5th and they assured themselves of a play off spot with a last day win over Champions Queen's Park. However, hopes of a first ever promotion were thwarted when they went down to Edinburgh City at the semi final stage.

Neither Cup competition brought much joy. Two wins and two defeats saw them knocked out of the League Cup at the group stage. In the Scottish they had a good win over Civil Service Strollers but lost heavily to Ayr United.

Scoring goals was not a problem for City with a very sharp strike force available to them.

STAR MAN
Striker Kane Hester was once again top scorer and possibly the best striker in League Two. The club will be waiting anxiously for the outcome of a forthcoming court case to see what the future holds for him.

PROSPECTS 2021/2
Elgin look capable of replicating last season's performance in reaching the play offs. They are unlikely to win the League but perhaps this will be their year to go up through the back door.

THE GOALIES
Goalkeepers Used in League Matches, 2000- 2020
Players shown in the season of their first appearance only

2000/1	Martin Pirie
	Michael Rae
2001/2	Gary Hamilton
2002/3	Robert Taylor
	Peter Hamilton
2003/4	Andy Goram
2004/5	Kieran Renton
2006/7	Charlie Fox
2007/8	Joe Malin
	Stephen Dunn
	Ally Ridgers
	Mark Bowden
2008/9	Andy McNulty
2009/0	John Gibson
2010/1	Scott Baln
	Peter Donnelly
	Jim Calder
2011/2	Zander Clark
2013/4	Stewart Black
	John Gibson (2nd spell)
	Ray Jellema
2014/5	Michael Fraser
	Ross Laidlaw
2015/6	Mark Hurst
2016/7	Cammy Mackay
	David Crawford
	Marc Waters
2017/8	Iain Ross
	Brett Long
2018/9	Kyle Gourlay
	Tom McHale

Date	Comp	H/A	Opponents	F	A	HT		Referee	Crowd	Scorers
10/10/2020	LC	H	Stirling Albion	2	0	0	0	D McFarlane	BCD	Hester, R Dingwall pen
13/10/2020	LC	A	Montrose	2	0	2	0	D Dickinson	BCD	O'Keefe, Peters
17/10/2020	L	A	Stranraer	4	1	1	0	G Irvine	BCD	R Dingwall 2 (1 pen), Hester, O'Keefe
24/10/2020	L	H	Brechin City	3	0	1	0	K Graham	BCD	Cameron, Hester 2
31/10/2020	L	A	Edinburgh City	0	1	0	1	P Stuart	BCD	
07/11/2020	L	H	Queen's Park	0	1	0	1	B Cook	BCD	
10/11/2020	LC	H	Ross County	1	4	0	2	G Duncan	BCD	Cameron
14/11/2020	LC	A	Arbroath	0	3	0	2	S McLean	BCD	
21/11/2020	L	A	Stirling Albion	2	1	1	0	D Lowe	BCD	Bronsky, Sopel
28/11/2020	L	H	Cowdenbeath	5	2	2	0	G Ross	220	Sopel, Hester 3, O'Keefe
05/12/2020	L	H	Annan Athletic	1	0	0	0	G Grainger	200	R Dingwall
12/12/2020	L	A	Albion Rovers	1	3	1	0	C Graham	BCD	Cooper
19/12/2020	L	H	Stenhousemuir	2	0	2	0	S Reid	BCD	Hester, Cameron
26/12/2020	SC	H	Civil Service Strollers	4	0	1	0	D McFarlane	BCD	Hester 3, R Dingwall
20/03/2021	L	H	Edinburgh City	1	2	1	2	D Lowe	BCD	Peters
23/03/2021	SC	H	Ayr United	0	4	0	4	C Napier	BCD	
27/03/2021	L	H	Stirling Albion	1	1	0	0	G Irvine	BCD	McHardy
30/03/2021	L	A	Brechin City	2	1	0	1	C Scott	BCD	Hester pen, McHardy
03/04/2021	L	A	Annan Athletic	3	0	2	0	S Reid	BCD	T Dingwall, Cameron, Osadolor
06/04/2021	L	H	Stranraer	2	1	0	0	P Stuart	BCD	R Dingwall, Hester
10/04/2021	L	A	Cowdenbeath	0	1	0	1	D Dickinson	BCD	
13/04/2021	L	A	Stenhousemuir	0	2	0	0	C Scott	BCD	
17/04/2021	L	H	Albion Rovers	2	5	1	2	M McDermid	BCD	Hester, O'Keefe
20/04/2021	L	A	Queen's Park	0	0	0	0	S Reid	BCD	
27/04/2021	L	A	Stranraer	4	1	4	0	C Scott	BCD	Hester 2, Sopel, Cameron
29/04/2021	L	H	Stirling Albion	3	1	2	0	S Lambie	BCD	Sopel, R Dingwall, Cameron
01/05/2021	L	A	Edinburgh City	0	2	0	2	M McDermid	BCD	
04/05/2021	L	H	Queen's Park	3	2	0	0	D Williams	BCD	Hester 3
08/05/2021	PO	H	Edinburgh City	0	1	0	1	A Newlands	BCD	
11/05/2021	PO	A	Edinburgh City	2	2	2	1	C Napier	BCD	McHardy 2

Andy Goram

Mark Hurst

Ray Jellema

Date	Comp	H/A	Opponents	F	A	1	2	3	4	5	6	7	8	9	10	11	12	13	14	15	16	17	18	19	20
10/10/2020	LC	H	Stirling Albion	2	0	McHale	Cooper	Bronsky	Spark	Wilson*	Cameron	O'Keefe>	R Dingwall	Sopel+	Hester	Osadolor&	McDonald*	Macbeath+	Mailer&	Jamieson>	*Thomson*	*MacEwan*	*Peters*	*Hay*	*Kelly*
13/10/2020	LC	A	Montrose	2	0	McHale	Cooper	Bronsky	Spark+	Mailer	Cameron	O'Keefe&	R Dingwall	McDonald	Peters*	Osadolor	Macbeath*	Wilson+	Sopel&	Jamieson>	*Thomson*	*MacEwan*	*Hay*	*Kelly*	
17/10/2020	L	A	Stranraer	4	1	McHale	Cooper	Bronsky	Spark	Mailer*	Cameron	O'Keefe&	R Dingwall	McDonald	Hester>	Osadolor+	Macewan*	Sopel+	Wilson&	Peters>	*Loveland*	*McHardy`*	*Macbeath*	*Kelly*	
24/10/2020	L	H	Brechin City	3	0	McHale	Cooper	Bronsky	Spark+	MacEwan>	Cameron	O'Keefe&	R Dingwall	McDonald	Hester	Osadolor*	Sopel*	McHardy+	Peters&	Mcbeath>	*Loveland*	*Jamieson*	*Wilson*	*Mailer*	*Kelly*
31/10/2020	L	A	Edinburgh City	0	1	McHale	Cooper	Bronsky	Spark+	MacEwan>	Cameron	O'Keefe	R Dingwall	McDonald&	Hester	Osadolor*	Sopel*	Peters+	McHardy&	Mailer>	*Wilson*	*Macbeath*	*Kelly*		
07/11/2020	L	H	Queen's Park	0	1	McHale	Cooper	Bronsky	Spark	MacEwan*	Cameron	O'Keefe+	R Dingwall	McDonald	Hester	Sopel&	Osadolor*	Peters+	Macbeath&	*Mailer*	*Loveland*	*McHardy`*	*Kelly*	*Wilson*	*Hay*
10/11/2020	LC	H	Ross County	1	4	McHale	Cooper	Bronsky	Spark&	MacEwan>	Cameron	O'Keefe+	R Dingwall	McDonald	Hester*	Osadolor<	Peters*	Sopel+	McHardy&	Mailer>	Macbeath<	*Wilson*	*Kelly*	*Loveland*	*Hay*
14/11/2020	LC	A	Arbroath	0	3	McHale	Cooper	Bronsky	Spark<	Wilson*	Cameron	O'Keefe&	R Dingwall>	McDonald	Hester	Osadolor+	MacEwan*	Sopel+	Peters&	Macbeath>	McHardy<	*Mailer*	*Kelly*		
21/11/2020	L	A	Stirling Albion	2	1	McHale	Cooper	Bronsky	Spark	MacEwan+	Cameron	Sopel&	R Dingwall	McDonald	Peters*	Macbeath	Osadolor*	Mailer+	McHardy&	*O'Keefe*	*Wilson*	*Allan*	*Kelly*	*Loveland*	*Hay*
28/11/2020	L	H	Cowdenbeath	5	2	McHale	Cooper	Bronsky	Spark	MacEwan*	Cameron	Sopel&	R Dingwall	McDonald	Hester>	Peters+	Osadolor*	Mailer+	O'Keefe&	Macbeath>	*Loveland*	*Allan*	*McHardy*	*Wilson*	*Kelly*
05/12/2020	L	H	Annan Athletic	1	0	McHale	Cooper	Bronsky+	Spark	MacEwan*	Cameron	Sopel	R Dingwall>	McDonald	Hester	Peters&	O'Keefe*	McHardy+	Osadolor&	Mailer>	*Macbeath*	*Wilson*	*Loveland*	*Allan*	*Kelly*
12/12/2020	L	A	Albion Rovers	1	3	McHale	Cooper	Bronsky	Spark	MacEwan*	Cameron	Sopel<	R Dingwall>	McDonald&	Hester	Peters+	Macbeath*	Mailer+	McHardy&	O'Keefe>	Osadolor<	*Wilson*	*Loveland*	*Hay*	*Kelly*
19/12/2020	L	H	Stenhousemuir	2	0	McHale	Cooper	Bronsky	Spark	MacEwan+	Cameron	O'Keefe&	R Dingwall	McDonald	Hester>	Peters*	Sopel*	Mailer+	T Dingwall&	Macbeath>	*Allan*	*Osadolor*	*Loveland*	*McHardy*	*Kelly*
26/12/2020	SC	H	Civil Service Strollers	4	0	McHale	Cooper	Bronsky	Spark	MacEwan+	Cameron&	O'Keefe	R Dingwall	McHardy	Hester	Peters*	Sopel*	Mailer+	Macbeath&	*T Dingwall*	*McDonald*	*Osadolor*	*Kelly*		
20/03/2021	L	H	Edinburgh City	1	2	McHale	Cooper	Bronsky>	Spark	MacPhee	Cameron	T Dingwall&	R Dingwall<	Sopel+	Hester	Peters*	O'Keefe*	Osadolor+	Brown&	McHardy>	MacEwan<	*Wilson*	*Mailer*	*Macbeath*	*Kelly*
23/03/2021	SC	H	Ayr United	0	4	McHale	Cooper	Bronsky	Spark	MacPhee*	Cameron	T Dingwall&	R Dingwall	Mailer+	MacEwan	Osadolor	McHardy*	Sopel+	Peters&	*Mcbeath*	*Loveland*	*Wilson*	*Jamieson*	*Kelly*	
27/03/2021	L	H	Stirling Albion	1	1	McHale	Cooper	Brosnky	Spark	McHardy	Cameron	MacEwan	R Dingwall	Sopel+	Peters*	Osadolor&	Hester*	O'Keefe+	Brown&	*Mcbeath*	*Loveland*	*Wilson*	*T Dingwall*	*Mailer*	*Kelly*
30/03/2021	L	A	Brechin City	2	1	McHale	Cooper	Bronsky	Spark	McHardy	Cameron	MacEwan*	R Dingwall&	O'Keefe<	Brown+	Hester>	Osadolor*	T Dingwall+	McPhee&	Peters>	Mailer<	*Macbeath*	*Sopel*	*Wilson*	
03/04/2021	L	A	Annan Athletic	3	0	McHale	Cooper	Bronsky	Spark	McHardy	Cameron	McPhee	R Dingwall&	O'Keefe>	T Dingwall*	Hester+	Osadolor*	Peters+	Mailer&	Sopel>	*Wilson*	*Dalling*	*Miller*	*Brown*	*Kelly*
06/04/2021	L	H	Stranraer	2	1	McHale	Cooper	Bronsky	Spark	McHardy+	Cameron	McPhee	R Dingwall&	O'Keefe>	T Dingwall*	Hester	Osadolor*	Wilson+	Mailer&	Sopel>	*Peters*	*Dalling*	*Miller*	*Brown*	*Kelly*
10/04/2021	L	A	Cowdenbeath	0	1	McHale	Cooper	Bronsky	Spark&	McHardy	Cameron	McPhee>	R Dingwall+	O'Keefe	Osadolor*	Hester	Peters*	Sopel+	Mailer&	Mcbeath>	*Wilson*	*Dalling*	*Miller*	*Brown*	*Kelly*
13/04/2021	L	A	Stenhousemuir	0	2	McHale	Cooper	Bronsky	Spark	McHardy>	Cameron	McPhee*	R Dingwall	O'Keefe&	T Dingwall+	Hester	Peters*	Osadolor+	Sopel&	Brown>	*Wilson*	*Dalling*	*Miller*	*Mailer*	*Kelly*
17/04/2021	L	H	Albion Rovers	2	5	McHale	MacEwan*	Bronsky	Spark&	McHardy	Cameron	McPhee	R Dingwall<	Sopel>	Peters+	Hester	O'Keefe*	Osadolor+	T Dingwall&	Brown>	Mailer<	*Dalling*	*Miller*	*Wilson*	*Kelly*
20/04/2021	L	A	Queen's Park	0	0	McHale	Mailer	Bronsky	Spark	McHardy	Cameron	Wilson	R Dingwall+	Sopel*	Brown&	Hester>	O'Keefe*	MacEwan+	Peters&	T Dingwall>	*Osadolor*	*Dalling*	*Miller*	*Macbeath*	*Kelly*
27/04/2021	L	A	Stranraer	4	1	McHale	Cooper	Mailer	Spark	McHardy	Cameron<	Wilson	R Dingwall+	Sopel*	Brown&	Hester>	T Dingwall*	Miller+	Osadolor&	Peters>	MacEwan<	*Dalling*	*O'Keefe*	*Macbeath*	*Kelly*
29/04/2021	L	H	Stirling Albion	3	1	McHale	Cooper	Mailer	Spark	McHardy*	Cameron&	Wilson	R Dingwall	Sopel>	Brown+	Hester	Bronsky*	MacEwan+	Osadolor&	O'Keefe>	*T Dingwall*	*Miller*	*McPhee*	*Peters*	*Kelly*
01/05/2021	L	A	Edinburgh City	0	2	McHale	Cooper	Mailer&	Spark	McHardy	Cameron	Wilson	R Dingwall+	Sopel>	Brown*	Hester	MacPhee*	O'Keefe+	T Dingwall&	Peters>	*Osadolor*	*Dalling*	*Miller*	*MacEwan*	*Kelly*
04/05/2021	L	H	Queen's Park	3	2	McHale	Cooper	Mailer	Spark	McHardy	Cameron	McPhee*	R Dingwall&	Sopel+	Bronsky	Hester>	Brown*	MacEwan+	O'Keefe&	Peters>	*T Dingwall*	*Wilson*	*Miller*	*Osadolor*	*Kelly*
08/05/2021	PO	H	Edinburgh City	0	1	McHale	Cooper	Mailer*	Spark	McHardy	Cameron	McPhee	R Dingwall&	Sopel+	Bronsky	Hester	Brown*	O'Keefe+	Peters&	*Wilson*	*MacEwan*	*Osadolor*	*Kelly*		
11/05/2021	PO	A	Edinburgh City	2	2	McHale	Cooper	Brosnky	Spark	McHardy	Cameron	McPhee&	R Dinfwall	O'Keefe+	MacEwan*	Hester	Brown*	Sopel+	Peters&	*Wilson*	*Mailer<*	*Osadolor*	*Kelly*		

Elgin City's Scottish Cup Record as a Non League Team

Elgin City	1907/8	25-Jan	1	A	Dunblane	3-8		1500
Elgin City	1908/9	23-Jan	1	A	Motherwell	1-6		2000
Elgin City	1909/10	22-Jan	1	A	St Mirren	0-8		4000
Elgin City	1920/21	05-Feb	2	A	Dumbarton	0-3		4000
Elgin City	1922/23	13-Jan	1	H	St Mirren	0-3		4700
Elgin City	1926/27	22-Jan	1	H	Albion Rovers	1-0		3400
Elgin City	1926/27	05-Feb	2	H	Clyde	2-4		4500
Elgin City	1927/28	21-Jan	1	A	Forres Mechanics	1-2		1100
Elgin City	1930/31	17-Jan	1	A	Queen's Park	0-5		8675
Elgin City	1935/36	01-Feb	1	H	Chimside United	2-2		3000
Elgin City	1935/36	08-Feb	2	H	Queen of the South	0-3		7000
Elgin City	1935/36	05-Feb	1R	A	Chimside United	4-3	aet	2000
Elgin City	1936/37	06-Feb	1	A	King's Park	1-1		2000
Elgin City	1936/37	10-Feb	1R	H	King's Park	3-4	aet	2029
Elgin City	1937/38	22-Jan	1	H	Aberdeen	1-6		8403
Elgin City	1938/39	21-Jan	1	A	Falkirk Amateurs	4-2		250
Elgin City	1938/39	04-Feb	2	A	Hearts	1-14		7857
Elgin City	1948/49	22-Jan	1	A	Rangers	1-6		29000
Elgin City	1950/51	27-Jan	1	A	Hamilton Academical	2-2		5000
Elgin City	1950/51	31-Jan	1R	H	Hamilton Academical	0-3		6198
Elgin City	1951/52	09-Feb	2	A	Rangers	1-6		36000
Elgin City	1952/53	24-Jan	1	H	Third Lanark	2-3		9200
Elgin City	1954/55	11-Sep	1	A	Newton Stewart	5-3		
Elgin City	1954/55	25-Sep	2	H	Clachnacuddin	1-1		
Elgin City	1954/55	02-Oct	2R	A	Clachnacuddin	1-7		
Elgin City	1955/56	10-Sep	1	A	Chimside United	9-1		
Elgin City	1955/56	24-Sep	2	A	Keith	0-2		
Elgin City	1956/57	08-Sep	1	H	Shawfield Amateurs	5-1		
Elgin City	1956/57	22-Sep	2	H	Clachnacuddin	2-2		
Elgin City	1956/57	29-Sep	2R	A	Clachnacuddin	2-3		
Elgin City	1959/60	13-Feb	2	H	Forfar Athletic	5-1		3560
Elgin City	1959/60	05-Mar	3	H	Celtic	1-2		11200
Elgin City	1960/61	28-Jan	1	H	Airdrieonians	2-2		7690
Elgin City	1960/61	01-Feb	1R	A	Airdrieonians	0-2		6215
Elgin City	1961/62	09-Dec	1	A	Hamilton Academical	1-3		2000
Elgin City	1964/65	06-Feb	2	A	Stenhousemuir	1-4		581
Elgin City	1965/66	22-Jan	2	A	East Fife	0-1		2855
Elgin City	1966/67	17-Dec	1	A	Chimside United	7-1		700
Elgin City	1966/67	14-Jan	2	A	Hawick Royal Albert	1-1		1294
Elgin City	1966/67	01-Feb	3	H	Ayr United	2-0		9000
Elgin City	1966/67	18-Feb	4	A	Celtic	0-7		34000
Elgin City	1966/67	23-Jan	2R	H	Hawick Royal Albert	2-0		
Elgin City	1967/68	16-Dec	1	H	Albion Rovers	3-1		
Elgin City	1967/68	06-Jan	2	A	Tarff Rovers	3-2		500
Elgin City	1967/68	27-Jan	3	H	Forfar Athletic	3-1		6608
Elgin City	1967/68	17-Feb	4	H	Arbroath	2-0		12650
Elgin City	1967/68	09-Mar	5	A	Morton	1-2		10759
Elgin City	1968/69	04-Jan	2	A	Stranraer	0-2		1545
Elgin City	1970/71	05-Dec	1	A	Stenhousemuir	1-0		
Elgin City	1970/71	19-Dec	2	H	Berwick Rangers	2-0		
Elgin City	1970/71	25-Jan	3	A	Aberdeen	0-5		24136
Elgin City	1971/72	08-Dec	1	H	Stenhousemuir	2-0		3603
Elgin City	1971/72	15-Jan	2	A	Burntisland Shipyard	4-1		500
Elgin City	1971/72	05-Feb	3	H	Inverness Caledonian	3-1		5598
Elgin City	1971/72	26-Feb	4	H	Kilmarnock	1-4		10506
Elgin City	1972/73	13-Jan	2	A	Ferranti Thistle	2-2		2100
Elgin City	1972/73	03-Feb	3	H	Hamilton Academical	0-1		4977
Elgin City	1972/73	20-Jan	2R	H	Ferranti Thistle	2-1		2712
Elgin City	1975/76	13-Dec	1	H	Forres Mechanics	0-1		2000
Elgin City	1975/76		Q		QUALIFYING CUP			
Elgin City	1976/77	28-Dec	1	H	Vale of Leithen	4-0		2000
Elgin City	1976/77	08-Jan	2	A	Forfar Athletic	2-0		950
Elgin City	1976/77	29-Jan	3	A	Stirling Albion	1-1		2970
Elgin City	1976/77	26-Feb	4	A	Rangers	0-3		18000
Elgin City	1976/77	02-Feb	3R	H	Stirling Albion	3-2		2500
Elgin City	1981/82	20-Jan	2	A	Montrose	0-0		450
Elgin City	1981/82	25-Jan	2R	H	Montrose	0-0	aet	300
Elgin City	1981/82	01-Feb	2R2	N	Montrose	1-2	aet	1252
Elgin City	1982/83	11-Dec	1	A	Meadowbank Thistle	2-1		650
Elgin City	1982/83	08-Jan	2	H	Gala Fairydean	5-2		1180
Elgin City	1982/83	29-Jan	3	A	Dunfermline Athletic	0-5		1817
Elgin City	1983/84	10-Dec	1	H	Queen's Park	0-2		905
Elgin City	1988/89	07-Jan	2	H	Dumbarton	2-2		2074
Elgin City	1988/89	14-Jan	2R	A	Dumbarton	0-4		1000
Elgin City	1989/90	09-Dec	1	H	Arbroath	2-1		1542
Elgin City	1989/90	30-Dec	2	H	Brechin City	2-2		3370
Elgin City	1989/90	06-Jan	2R	A	Brechin City	0-8		1500
Elgin City	1996/97	07-Dec	1	H	Whitehill Welfare	0-3		1011

Surname	First Name	Date of Birth	No	Nat	Pos	Signed	Previous	Notes	Contract	Lge			SC			LC			
										A	S	G	A	S	G	A	S	G	Un
Allan	Finn	01/01/2004		SCO	M	2020	Elgin City Youths		End 2021/2										4
Bronsky	Stephen	16/06/1994		SCO	D	2017	Annan Athletic	Joined Edinburgh City June 2021		21	1	1	2			4			0
Brown	Craig	18/02/1999		SCO	M	2021	Stirling University (OL)	Mar-May, permanent from Jun	End 2021/2	5	7								3
Cameron	Brian	19/12/1990		SCO	M	2008	Elgin City Youths		End 2023/4	24	0	5	2			4		1	0
Cooper	Matthew	01/07/1994		SCO	D	2014	Inverness CT		End 2023/4	22	0	1	2			4			0
Dalling	Kyle	27/03/2002		SCO	D	2021	Forfar Athletic (OL)	Mar-May		0	0								8
Dingwall	Russell	26/06/1997		SCO	M	2019	Ross County		End 2022/3	24	0	5	2		1	4		1	0
Dingwall	Tony	25/07/1994		SCO	M	2020	Raith Rovers		End 2021/2	4	6	1	1						4
Hay	Charlie	15/10/2003		SCO	M	2020	Elgin City Youths		End 2021/2#	0	0								6
Hester	Kane	12/07/1995		SCO	F	2019	Arbroath		End 2022/3	22	1	15	1		3	3		1	0
Jamieson	Matt	01/01/2003		SCO	F	2020	Elgin City Youths	OL to Deveronvale for 2021/2	End 2021/2	0	0						2		2
Kelly	Oliver	06/06/2001		SCO	GK	2020	Elgin City Youths	OL to Lossiemouth for 2021/2	End 2021/2	0	0								29
Loveland	Owen	01/11/2002		SCO	F	2019	Elgin City Youths	OL to Forres Mechanics for 2021/2	End 2021/2	0	0								11
MacEwan	Rory	23/11/1997		SCO	M	2019	Stirling University		End 2021/2	12	7		2			1	1		4
Mailer	Angus	04/07/1998		SCO	D	2020	Stirling University		End 2022/3	7	12		1	1		1	2		6
McBeath	Joel	18/05/2001		SCO	F	2020	Ross County		End 2021/2	1	6			1			4		9
McDonald	Andy	11/05/1998		SCO	D	2020	St Cadoc's (OL)	Oct-May		9	0					3	1		1
McHale	Tom	08/09/1995		ENG	GK	2018	Truro City		End 2022/3	24	0		2			4			0
McHardy	Darryl	22/05/1995		SCO	D	2014	Elgin City Youths		End 2022/3	14	6	4	1	1			2		4
McPhee	Archie	20/03/1993		SCO	D	2021	Formartine United (OL)	Mar-May, permanent from Jun	End 2021/2	9	2		1						1
Miller	Murray	29/01/2002		SCO / AUS	M	2021	Rangers (OL)	Mar-May		0	1								9
O'Keefe	Conor	21/07/1998		SCO	F	2019	Stranraer		End 2021/2	11	10	3	1			4		1	2
Osadolor	Smart	26/03/1991		SCO	F	2020	Albion Rovers	Released May 2021, joined Cumnock		5	13	1	1			4			7
Peters	Josh	04/09/1996		SCO	F	2020	Stirling Albion		End 2022/3	8	14	1	1	1		1	2	1	3
Sopel	Aidan	18/10/1999		SCO	F	2019	Elgin City Youths		End 2022/3	14	9	4		2		1	3		1
Spark	Ewan	29/11/1996		SCO	D	2019	Brechin City		End 2021/2	24	0		2			4			0
Thomson	Jake	17/09/2001		SCO	M	2020	Elgin City Youths		U20	0	0								2
Wilson	David	18/03/2000		SCO	D	2018	Elgin City Youths	Freed May 2021		4	2					2	1		19
NEW SIGNINGS																			
Hoban	Daniel	05/04/1998		SCO	GK	2021	Forfar Athletic		End 2021/2										
Lawrence	Dylan					2021	Elgin City Youths		End 2021/2										
Little	Creag	16/04/1993		SCO	D	2021	Stenhousemuir		End 2022/3										
McPhee	Archie	20/03/1993		SCO	D	2021	Formartine United		End 2021/2										
Tinnock	Jamie					2021	Elgin City Youths		End 2021/2										

Falkirk FC 2020/21 The Bairns

Founded	1876
Ground	Falkirk Stadium
Postcode	FK2 9DX
Tel	01324 624121
Capacity	8750
Closest Railway Station	Falkirk Grahamston
Record Attendance	23100 v Celtic, SC, 21/2/1953
Record Win	11-1 v Tillicoultry, SC, 7/9/1889
Record Defeat	1-1 v Airdrieonians, Lge, 28/4/51
Most League Goals in a Season	43 Evelyn Morrison, 1928/9
Colours 2020/21 Top	Navy Blue
Shorts	White
Sponsor	Central Demolition
Manufacturer	Puma
Change Colours 2020/21 Top	Red
Shorts	Navy Blue
Nicknames	Bairns
Web	www.falkirkfc.co.uk
Match Programme 2020/21	On line

Chairman: Gary Deans
Directors: Peter Duncan, Lex Miler, Kieran Koszary, Craig Campbell, Gordon Wright, Colin McFarlane, Gordon Colborn
Head Coaches: Lee Miller, David McCracken, replaced by Gary Holt (interim) then by Paul Sheerin
Assistant: Danny Grainger (from June 2021)
Goalkeeping Coach: Derek Jackson then Tony Caig
Head of Performance: Graeme Henderson
Head of Youth Development: Ian Fergus
Kit Manager: Robert Lochhead
Assistant Kitman: Bobby Wilson
Director of Commercial Operations: Kieran Koszary
Commercial Co-Ordinator: Sharon McGuire,
Football Operations Manager: Liam Corr
Operations Manager/Match Safety Officer: Keith Hogg,
Disability Access Officer: Andy Thomson
Safeguarding Officer: Alan Dick

Most observers rated Falkirk as favourites to win the Championship last season. To be fair many of their own fans had serious reservations and they were to be proved correct. Co-Managers Lee Miller and David McCracken survived until late in the season – if fans had been allowed inside the Falkirk Stadium then their departure might have been hastened somewhat. Things deteriorated after the re-start in March – they began ok with two wins from three but then results deteriorated.

It became apparent that the automatic promotion place was beyond their reach but a play off spot still seemed certain. But one draw and five defeats in their last six games put paid to that and Falkirk finished fifth. A 0-5 defeat at Partick was apparently an especially inept display.

Falkirk progressed from their League Cup section helped by getting three points on the nod when Killie forfeited their game due to COVID. Rangers dispatched the Bairns 4-0 at the first knock out stage. In the Scottish Cup Falkirk defeated Championship side Arbroath and were drawn away to Celtic. Given that Celtic were in meltdown at the time and there for the taking it was surprising that Falkirk opted to field a shadow side and lost 0 -3.

The goodwill of the Falkirk fans has now been stretched to breaking point. Most remember the club as a Premiership side and a season when finished below Montrose and Cove Rangers does not sit well with their hopes and expectations.

STAR MAN
Bairns fans would say there weren't any. That would be slightly harsh of forward Callumn Morrison, signed from Hearts in 2020. He was the best of a bad bunch and one of the few players to be retained for the new season,

PROSPECTS 2021/2
Between 1977 and 1980 Falkirk were in the bottom flight of Scottish football. It was a long road to redemption before they re-established themselves as one of the stronger provincial sides. Failure to win promotion from League One in 2021/2 would be a disaster for the club and could see them reverting to part-time football. New Manager Paul Sheerin, in his first managerial post, will have a tough task with sides like Cove Rangers to compete with.

Date	Comp	H/A	Opponents	F	A	HT		Referee	Crowd	Scorers
06/10/2020	LC	H	Kilmarnock	3	0					KILMARNOCK FORFEITED TIE DUE TO COVID
09/10/2020	LC	A	Dunfermline Athletic	0	2	0	0	G irvine	BCD	
13/10/2020	LC	H	Clyde	2	1	1	1	L Wilson	BCD	Keena, Morrison pen
17/10/2020	L	A	Montrose	3	1	0	1	C Napier	BCD	Francis, Morrison pen, Leitch
24/10/2020	L	H	Forfar Athletic	1	1	1	0	S Kirkland	BCD	Dowds
31/10/2020	L	H	East Fife	2	0	1	0	G Beaton	BCD	Leitch, Francis
07/11/2020	L	A	Partick Thistle	2	2	1	0	G irvine	BCD	Morrison, Telfer
10/11/2020	LC	A	Dumbarton	4	0	1	0	S Lambie	BCD	Morrison 2, Sammon, Dowds
21/11/2020	L	H	Cove Rangers	1	0	0	0	D Dickinson	BCD	Morrison
24/11/2020	L	A	Dumbarton	3	0	2	0	S Kirkland	BCD	Morrison, Alston, Connolly
29/11/2020	LC	H	Rangers	0	4	0	3	B Madden	BCD	
05/12/2020	L	H	Peterhead	2	1	2	0	P Stuart	BCD	Alston, Sammon
12/12/2020	L	A	Clyde	3	0	1	0	C Steven	BCD	Telfer, Mercer, Hall
20/12/2020	L	H	Airdrieonians	0	1	0	0	A Newlands	BCD	
26/12/2020	L	H	Partick Thistle	0	0	0	0	D Williams	BCD	
02/01/2021	L	A	East Fife	1	2	0	1	G Beaton	BCD	Morrison
20/03/2021	L	H	Montrose	2	0	1	0	G Duncan	BCD	Durnan, Morrison
23/03/2021	SC	A	Arbroath	2	1	1	1	D Munro	BCD	Telfer, Fotheringham
27/03/2021	L	A	Forfar Athletic	2	0	1	0	S Reid	BCD	Telfer, Alston
30/03/2021	L	H	Dumbarton	1	1	0	0	S Kirkland	BCD	Dowds
03/04/2021	SC	A	Celtic	0	3	0	0	J Beaton	BCD	
06/04/2021	L	A	Airdrieonians	1	2	1	1	C Steven	BCD	Telfer
10/04/2021	L	H	Clyde	2	1	1	0	C Napier	BCD	Hall, Keena
17/04/2021	L	A	Cove Rangers	0	2	0	1	D Dickinson	BCD	
20/04/2021	L	A	Peterhead	0	1	0	0	D Williams	BCD	
24/04/2021	L	H	Cove Rangers	2	2	1	1	G Duncan	BCD	Morrison pen, Sammon
29/04/2021	L	A	Partick Thistle	0	5	0	3	D Dickinson	BCD	
01/05/2021	L	H	Montrose	1	2	1	1	S Kirkland	BCD	Sammon
04/05/2021	L	A	Airdrieonians	0	2	0	0	S Lambie	BCD	

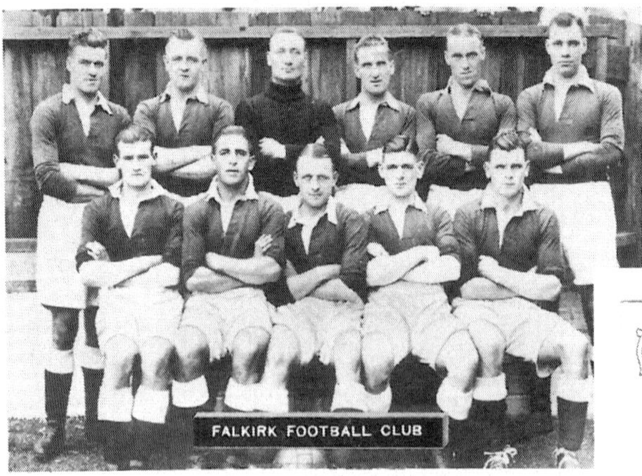

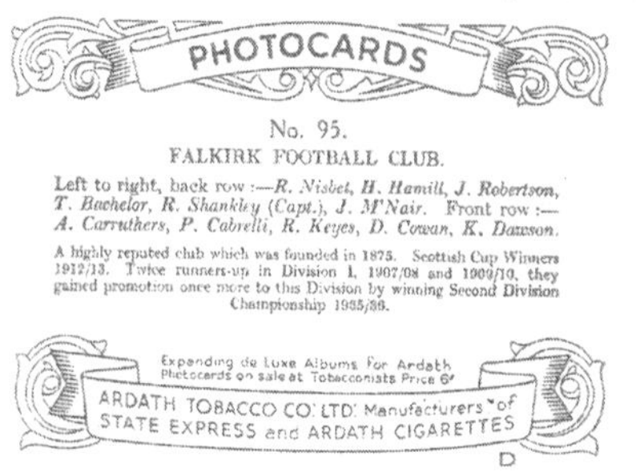
PHOTOCARDS

No. 95.

FALKIRK FOOTBALL CLUB.

Left to right, back row :—*R. Nisbet, H. Hamill, J. Robertson, T. Bachelor, R. Shankley (Capt.), J. M'Nair.* Front row :—*A. Carruthers, P. Cabrelli, R. Keyes, D. Cowan, K. Dawson.*

A highly reputed club which was founded in 1875. Scottish Cup Winners 1912/13. Twice runners-up in Division 1, 1907/08 and 1909/10, they gained promotion once more to this Division by winning Second Division Championship 1935/36.

Expanding de Luxe Albums for Ardath Photocards on sale at Tobacconists Price 6d

ARDATH TOBACCO CO. LTD. Manufacturers of STATE EXPRESS and ARDATH CIGARETTES

D

Date	Comp	H/A	Opponents	F	A	1	2	3	4	5	6	7	8	9	10	11	12	13	14	15	16	17	18	19	20
06/10/2020	LC	H	Kilmarnock	3	0																				
09/10/2020	LC	A	Dunfermline Athletic	0	2	Mutch	Dixon	Durnan	Hall	Mercer	Gomis	G Miller	C Morrison	Leitch*	Keena+	Dowds&	Todd*	Francis+	Sammon&	L Miller	Connolly	Sneddon			
13/10/2020	LC	H	Clyde	2	1	Mutch	Dixon	Durnan	Hall	Mercer	Gomis	Todd&	C Morrison	Leitch+	Keena*	Dowds	Francis*	Alston+	Sammon&	L Miller	Connolly	Sneddon			
17/10/2020	L	A	Montrose	3	1	Mutch	Dixon	Durnan	Hall	Mercer	G Miller	Todd>	C Morrison	Alston*	Francis&	Dowds+	Leitch*	Sammon+	L Miller&	Gomis>	Laverty	Sneddon	Telfer	Trialist	PJ Morrison
24/10/2020	L	H	Forfar Athletic	1	1	Mutch	Dixon	Durnan	Hall	Mercer	Gomis+	G Miller	C Morrison	Alston&	Francis*	Dowds>	PJ Morrison*	Leitch+	Sammon&	Deveney&	Laverty	L Miller	Telfer		
31/10/2020	L	H	East Fife	2	0	PJ Morrison	Dixon	Durnan	Hall	Mercer	Leitch+	G Miller	C Morrison	Alston	Francis*	Dowds	Todd*	Kelly+	Sammon	Deveney	Laverty	Cantley	Telfer	Sneddon	
07/11/2020	L	A	Partick Thistle	2	2	PJ Morrison	Dixon	Durnan	Hall	Mercer	Leitch+	G Miller	C Morrison	Alston&	Francis>	Dowds*	Todd*	Kelly+	Telfer&	Sammon>	Laverty	Cantley	Deveney	Sneddon	
10/11/2020	LC	A	Dumbarton	4	0	PJ Morrison	Dixon	Kelly	Hall	Todd	Leitch&	G Miller	C Morrison>	Alston*	Francis+	Sammon	Gomis*	Dowds+	Telfer&	Laverty>	Durnan	Sneddon	Mutch		
21/11/2020	L	H	Cove Rangers	1	0	PJ Morrison	Dixon	Kelly	Hall	Gomis	Leitch+	G Miller	C Morrison>	Alston	Sammon*	Dowds&	L Miller*	Telfer+	Francis&	Connolly>	Durnan	Laverty	Deveney	Sneddon	Mutch
24/11/2020	L	A	Dumbarton	3	0	PJ Morrison	Dixon	Kelly	Hall	Gomis>	Leitch*	G Miller	C Morrison&	Alston	Sammon	Dowds+	Telfer*	Francis+	Connolly&	Todd>	Durnan	Laverty	Deveney	L Miller	Mutch
29/11/2020	LC	H	Rangers	0	4	PJ Morrison	Dixon	Kelly	Hall	Gomis	Durnan	Todd>	C Morrison+	Alston	Sammon*	Telfer&	Dowds*	Connolly+	Leitch&	Deveney>	Mercer	Laverty	G Miller	Francis	Cantley
05/12/2020	L	H	Peterhead	2	1	PJ Morrison	Dixon	Kelly	Hall	Gomis*	Mercer	Telfer+	C Morrison	Alston	Sammon	Dowds&	Todd*	Connolly+	Leitch&	Deveney	Francis	L Miller	Durnan	Laverty	Cantley
12/12/2020	L	A	Clyde	3	0	Mutch	Dixon	Kelly	Hall	Gomis	Mercer	Telfer&	C Morrison*	Connolly>	Sammon+	Dowds<	Leitch*	Francis+	Todd&	G Miller>	Deveney<	L Miller	Durnan	Laverty	PJ Morrison
20/12/2020	L	H	Airdrieonians	0	1	Mutch	Dixon	Kelly	Hall	Gomis	Mercer	Telfer+	Leitch*	Connolly	Sammon&	Dowds>	C Morrison*	Alston+	Francis&	L Miller>	Deveney<	Durnan	Todd	G Miller	PJ Morrison
26/12/2020	L	H	Partick Thistle	0	0	Mutch	Dixon	Kelly	Hall	Gomis	Mercer	G Miller*	C Morrison	Alston&	Sammon>	Todd+	Dowds*	Leitch+	Telfer&	Francis>	Laverty	L Miller	Deveney	PJ Morrison	
02/01/2021	L	A	East Fife	1	2	Mutch	Dixon	Kelly	Hall	Gomis>	Mercer	Todd+	C Morrison	Alston<	Sammon&	Dowds*	Keena*	Leitch+	L Miller&	Telfer>	G Miller<	Laverty	Durnan	Deveney	Cantley
20/03/2021	L	H	Montrose	2	0	Mutch	Dixon	Durnan	Hall	Gomis	G Miller	Leitch&	C Morrison	Alston	Keena+	Fotheringham*	Francis*	Dowds+	Telfer&	Neilson	Sammon	L Miller	McClelland	Deveney	Cantley
23/03/2021	SC	A	Arbroath	2	1	Mutch	McClelland+	Deveney	Hall	Gomis*	Neilson	Leitch&	Telfer	Francis	Sammon	Dowds	Fotheringham*	Dixon+	C Morrison	Laverty	Keena	Sneddon	Cantley		
27/03/2021	L	A	Forfar Athletic	2	0	Mutch	Dixon	Durnan	Hall	Gomis&	G Miller	Telfer	C Morrison	Alston	Keena+	Fotheringham*	Dowds*	Francis+	Leitch&	Neilson	Deveney	Mercer	McClelland	Sammon	Cantley
30/03/2021	L	H	Dumbarton	1	1	Mutch	Dixon	Durnan	Hall	Gomis>	G Miller	Telfer<	C Morrison&	Alston	Keena+	Leitch*	Fotheringham*	Dowds+	Sammon&	Francis>	Neilson<	Mercer	Connolly	Deveney	Cantley
03/04/2021	SC	A	Celtic	0	3	Mutch	Mercer	McClelland	Deveney	Neilson	G Miller	Sammon	Francis	Leitch&	Dowds*	Fotheringham+	Keena*	Telfer+	Alston&	Laverty	Dixon	L Miller	Hall	Gomis	Cantley
06/04/2021	L	A	Airdrieonians	1	2	Mutch	Dixon	Mercer*	Hall	Gomis	Neilson	Telfer	C Morrison	Alston	Keena+	Fotheringham&	Francis*	L Miller+	Sammon&	Laverty	Leitch	McClelland	G Miller	Deveney	Cantley
10/04/2021	L	H	Clyde	2	1	Mutch	Dixon>	Durnan	Hall*	Alston	Neilson	Telfer<	C Morrison	Sammon	Keena&	Fotheringham+	McClelland*	Leitch+	Francis&	G Miller>	Deveney<	L Miller	Gomis	Mercer	Cantley
17/04/2021	L	A	Cove Rangers	0	2	Mutch	McClelland	Durnan	G Miller	Gomis	Neilson+	Alston	C Morrison	Sammon&	Keena	Fotheringham*	Leitch*	Mercer+	L Miller&	Laverty	Deveney	Francis	Kelly	Cantley	
20/04/2021	L	A	Peterhead	0	1	Mutch	McClelland	Durnan>	Deveney*	Gomis	Mercer	Alston	C Morrison	Sammon	Keena&	Fotheringham+	Kelly*	Leitch+	Francis&	G Miller>	Neilson	L Miller	Laverty	Cantley	
24/04/2021	L	H	Cove Rangers	2	2	Mutch	McClelland	Kelly	Neilson	G Miller	Mercer	Alston	C Morrison	Sammon	Leitch+	Fotheringham*	Keena*	Francis+	Laverty	Sneddon	Cantley				
29/04/2021	L	A	Partick Thistle	0	5	Mutch	McClelland	Kelly	Neilson&	G Miller	Mercer+	Alston	C Morrison<	Sammon>	Leitch*	Fotheringham	Dowds*	Durnan+	Gomis&	Keena>	Francis<	Laverty	Sneddon	Cantley	
01/05/2021	L	H	Montrose	1	2	Mutch	McClelland	Kelly	Neilson	Gomis	Mercer	Alston	C Morrison	Sammon	Leitch*	Fotheringham+	Dowds*	Keena+	Laverty	Sneddon	Francis	Durnan	G Miller	Cantley	
04/05/2021	L	A	Airdrieonians	0	2	Mutch	Durnan	Kelly	Neilson	Gomis	Mercer*	Alston	C Morrison	Sammon	Miller	Fotheringham+	Leitch*	Dowds+	Laverty	Sneddon	Francis	Keena	Cantley		

THE GOALIES

Goalkeepers Used in League Matches, 1970- 2020

Players shown in the season of their first appearance only

1970/1	Stewart Rennie
	Douglas Devlin
1971/2	Ally Donaldson
1975/6	George Watson
1977/8	Ted McFeat
1978/9	Bobby McKell
1980/1	Thomson Allan
1981/2	Kenny Cowan
1986/7	Nicky Walker
	Gordon Marshall
1991/2	Ian Westwater
	Gordon McDougall
1992/3	Tony Parks
1994/5	Willie Lamont
	John Burridge
1995/6	Neil Inglis
1996/7	Paul Mathers
	Craig Nelson
1998/9	Myles Hogarth
2001/2	Darren Hill
2002/3	Alan Ferguson
2005/6	Matt Glennon
	Mark Howard
2006/7	Scott Higgins
	Jeroen Lambers
	Kasper Schmeichel
2007/8	Tim Krul
	Robert Olejnik
	Shane Supple
2008/9	Scott Flinders
	Dani Mallo
2011/2	Michael McGovern
	Graham Bowman
2014/5	Jamie McDonald
2015/6	Danny Rodgers
	Denez Mehmet
2016/7	Robbie Thomson
2017/8	David Mitchell
	Robbie Mutch
	Conor Hazard
2018/9	Leo Fasan
	Harry Burgoyne
2019/0	Cammy Bell

Surname	First Name	Date of Birth	No	Nat	Pos	Signed	Previous	Notes	Contract	Lge A	Lge S	Lge G	SC A	SC S	SC G	LC A	LC S	LC G	Un
Alston	Blair	23/03/1992	8	SCO	M	2020	Hamilton Accies	Released May 2021, joined Kilmarnock		20	1	3		1		2	1		18
Cantley	Jay	06/09/2002	25	SCO	GK	2020	Hibernian Youths	Released May 2021, joined Airdrie		0	0								0
Connelly	Matthew	02/03/2003	30	SCO	GK	2020	Motherwell (OL)	Sep-Jan		0	0								3
Connolly	Aidan	15/08/1995	11	SCO	F	2019	Dunfermline Athletic	Released June 2021, joined Raith Rovers		2	3	1					1		12
Deveney	Euan	16/11/2002	19	SCO	D	2020	Kilmarnock (OL)	Oct-May		1	4		2				1		1
Dixon	Paul	22/11/1986	3	SCO	D	2019	Grimsby Town		End 2021/2	16	0			1		4			0
Dowds	Anton	16/11/1996	10	SCO	F	2020	East Fife		End 2021/2	10	7	2	2			2	2	1	8
Durnan	Mark	28/11/1992	5	SCO	D	2019	Dunfermline Athletic	Released May 2021, joined Alloa Athletic		10	1	1				3			0
Fotheringham	Kai	18/04/2003		SCO	F	2021	Dundee United (OL)	Mar-May		10	1		1	1	1				5
Francis	Akeel	30/03/1999	16	ENG / JAM	F	2020	Grantham Town	Released May 2021		4	13	2	2			1	2		2
Gomis	Morgaro	14/07/1985	14	FRA / SEN	M	2019	Dundee United	Released May 2021, joined Clyde		16	2		1			3	1		1
Hall	Ben	16/01/1997	4	NIR	D	2020	Partick Thistle		End 2021/2	16	0	2	1			4			2
Keena	Aidan	25/04/1999	9	ROI	F	2020	Hartlepool United		End 2021/2	7	4	1		1		2		1	1
Kelly	Sean	01/11/1993	33	SCO	D	2020	Ross County	Released June 2021		11	3					2			20
Laverty	Aidan	23/03/2000	20	SCO	M	2017	Hamilton Accies	Released May 2021		0	0						1		1
Leitch	Robbie	01/04/1998	17	SCO	M	2019	NK Novigrad	Released May 2021, joined Cove Rangers		10	11	2	2			3	1		3
McClelland	David Kyle	10/02/2002		SCO	D	2021	Rangers (OL)	Mar-May		6	1		2						4
Mercer	Scott	18/06/1995	2	SCO	D	2020	Queen of the South	Released May 2021, joined East Fife		14	1	1	1			2			4
Miller	Gary	15/04/1987	6	SCO	D	2019	Carlisle United		End 2021/2	15	4		1			2			11
Miller	Lee	18/05/1983	99	SCO	F	2019	Livingston	Co-Manager, Released Apr 2021		0	6								4
Morrison	PJ	27/02/1998	23	SCO	GK	2020	Motherwell (OL)	Oct-May		5	1					2			1
Morrison	Callumn	05/07/1999	38	SCO	M	2020	Hearts		End 2021/2	21	1	7				4		3	3
Mutch	Robbie	20/08/1998	1	SCO	GK	2017	Aberdeen		End 2021/2	17	0		2			2			3
Neilson	Lewis	15/05/2003		SCO	D	2021	Dundee United (OL)	Mar-May		7	1		2						3
Sammon	Conor	06/11/1986	19	ROI	F	2019	Hearts	Released May 2021, joined Alloa Athletic		14	5	3	2			2	2	1	12
Sneddon	Blair	27/04/2002	22	SCO	D	2020	Camelon Juniors		End 2022/3	0	0								3
Telfer	Charlie	04/07/1995	21	SCO	M	2019	Morton		End 2021/2	7	6	4	1	1	1	1	1		1
Todd	Josh	17/01/2020	7	SCO	M	2020	Dundee	Released May 2021, joined QOTS		3	5					3	1		1
Trialist										0	0								

NEW SIGNINGS

Surname	First Name	Date of Birth	No	Nat	Pos	Signed	Previous	Notes	Contract
Hetherington	Steven	09/02/1993		SCO	M	2021	Alloa Athletic		End 2022/3
Holt	Luke	21/08/1997		SCO	GK	2021	Metro State Roadrunners	Son of Gary Holt	End 2022/3
Martin	Paddy	21/06/1999		SCO	GK	2021	Hibernian		End 2021/2
McCann	Leon	16/03/2000		SCO	D	2021	Airdrieonians		End 2023/4
McGuffie	Craig	15/12/1997		SCO	M	2021	Morton		End 2022/3
McKay	Brad	26/03/1993		SCO	D	2021	Inverness CT		End 2023/4
Nesbitt	Aiden	05/02/1997		SCO	F	2021	Morton		End 2021/2
Ross	Seb	20/01/2000		SCO	F	2021	Cove Rangers		End 2022/3
Weekes	Ben			SCO	F	2021	Leith Athletic		End 2021/2
Williamson	Ryan	14/03/1996		SCO	D	2021	Partick Thistle		End 2022/3
Williamson	Cameron	05/03/2003		SCO	D	2021	Motherwell		End 2021/2
Wilson	Jaime	13/12/1997		SCO	F	2021	Dumbarton		End 2022/3

Kasper Schmeichel

Jeroen Lambers

George Watson

Forfar Athletic FC 2020/21 The Loons

Founded	1885
Ground	Station Park
Postcode	DD8 3BT
Tel	01307 463576
Capacity	6777
Closest Railway Station	Dundee
Record Attendance	19780 v Rangers, SC, 2/2/1970
Record Win	14-1 v Lindertis, SC, 1/9/1888
Record Defeat	2-12 v King's Park, Lge, 2/1/1930
Most League Goals in a Season	46 David Kilgour, 1929/30
Colours 2020/21 Top	Sky Blue
Shorts	Navy Blue
Sponsor	Orchard Timber Products
Manufacturer	Pendle
Change Colours 2020/21 Top	Gold
Shorts	Navy Blue
Nicknames	Loons
Web	www.forfarathletic.co.uk
Match Programme 2020/21	None issued

Chairman: Scott Murdie
Vice-Chairman: Alastair Donald
Secretary: David McGregor
Treasurer: Raymond Hutt
Directors: Alastair Donald, Raymond Hutt, David McGregor, John Milne, Scott Murdie, Alan Shepherd, & Louise Taylor (Company Secretary)
Honorary Vice President: Neill Wilson
Club Doctor: Jane Crawford
Manager: Stuart Malcolm, then Gary Irvine
Assistant Manager:
Goalkeeping Coach: Wayne Henderson
Sports Scientist: Martin Farrell
Club Therapists: Lara Jordan
Groundsman/Kit Man: Martin Gray
Safety Officer & Disability Access Officer: Iain Reid
Housekeeper: Jane Fyfe
Club Photographer: Christopher Coutts
Club Videographer: Joshua Grimes

Forfar's season got off to a bad start as they had to forfeit a League Cup game against Dundee due to COVID issues. Their only points in their group came from a penalty shoot out win over Brora Rangers. Their League campaign also began badly with just one win from their first ten games and just five goals scored. Manager Stuart Malcolm chopped and changed his side but just couldn't find a winning combination.

He parted company with the club in March and player Gary Irvine took over, with former Aberdeen Assistant Manager Tony Docherty coming on board to help him. Things barely improved – after the restart of fixtures Forfar won their first match at Dumbarton then failed to win in the next eight. Two wins in the last week of the season were too little, too late.

Forfar's Scottish Cup performances were better – defeating Linlithgow Rose and Edinburgh City then putting up a brave show against Dundee United.

STAR MAN
There is some pre-Christmas cheer for 'Loons' supporters with the news that Ross Meechan, undoubtedly the club's most consistent performer of the season had agreed a new deal which will keep him at Station Park till the end of the 2022/23 season. Ross had been a model of consistency and a fans favourite since joining the club from Stenhousemuir in the summer of 2018.

PROSPECTS 2021/2
In recent seasons Cowdenbeath and Brechin City have shown that relegation from League One to League Two can lead to a battle at the wrong end of the League. Forfar need to arrest their decline and get off to a good start – basically they must win the matches against the teams who are likely to be near the bottom of the table. A mid-table of play off position would be a success for Gary Irvine in his first full season in charge of the club.

Date	Comp	H/A	Opponents	F	A		HT	Referee	Crowd	Scorers
06/10/2020	LC	A	Dundee	0	3					FORFAR ATHLETIC FORFEIRTED TIE DUE TO COVID
13/10/2020	LC	H	Hibernian	0	1		0 0	D Munro	BCD	
17/10/2020	L	H	Dumbarton	0	0		0 0	P Stuart	BCD	
24/10/2020	L	A	Falkirk	1	1		0 1	S Kirkland	BCD	Allan pen
31/10/2020	L	H	Montrose	2	3		0 1	L Wilson	BCD	Allan, Antoniazzi
07/11/2020	L	A	Cove Rangers	0	3		0 2	S Lambie	BCD	
10/11/2020	LC	H	Brora Rangers	3	3	4-3p	1 1	G Irvine	BCD	MacKintosh 2, Allan pen
14/11/2020	LC	A	Cove Rangers	0	1		0 0	D Williams	BCD	
21/11/2020	L	H	Airdrieonians	1	3		1 3	G Irvine	BCD	Antoniazzi
28/11/2020	L	A	Peterhead	1	0		1 0	C Graham	BCD	Barr
12/12/2020	L	H	Partick Thistle	0	2		0 0	G Ross	BCD	
19/12/2020	L	A	East Fife	0	2		0 1	P Stuart	BCD	
26/12/2020	L	H	Cove Rangers	0	1		0 0	D Lowe	BCD	
02/01/2021	L	A	Montrose	0	0		0 0	S Lambie	BCD	
09/01/2021	SC	H	Linlithgow Rose	4	1	AET	1 1	K Graham	BCD	MacKintosh, Fotheringham, Allan 2
20/03/2021	L	A	Dumbarton	1	0		0 0	K Graham	BCD	McGeever og
27/03/2021	L	H	Falkirk	0	2		0 1	S Reid	BCD	
30/03/2021	L	A	Partick Thistle	2	2		2 1	D Lowe	BCD	Fenwick 2
03/04/2021	SC	H	Edinburgh City	2	2	AET, 5-3p	1 2	S Kirkland	BCD	Allan, Nditi
06/04/2021	L	H	Peterhead	1	1		0 0	A Newlands	BCD	Scott
08/04/2021	L	A	Clyde	0	3		0 2	G Grainger	BCD	
10/04/2021	L	H	East Fife	1	2		0 1	D Williams	BCD	Allan
13/04/2021	L	A	Airdrieonians	1	3		1 1	B Cook	BCD	G Anderson
16/04/2021	SC	H	Dundee United	0	1		0 0	D Robertson	BCD	
20/04/2021	L	H	Clyde	1	3		1 1	K Graham	BCD	Fenwick
27/04/2021	L	A	Dumbarton	0	1		0 0	M McDermind	BCD	
29/04/2021	L	H	Clyde	2	1		1 1	D Williams	BCD	Scally 2
01/05/2021	L	A	Peterhead	2	1		0 0	M Roncone	BCD	Strachan og, Shepherd
04/05/2021	L	H	East Fife	2	3		1 1	B Cook	BCD	Fenwick, Scally

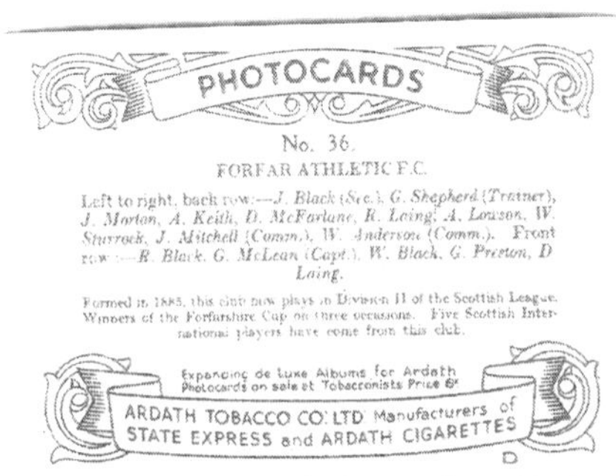
PHOTOCARDS

No. 36.

FORFAR ATHLETIC F.C.

Left to right, back row:—*J. Black (Sec.), G. Shepherd (Trainer), J. Morton, A. Keith, D. McFarlane, R. Laing, A. Lowson, W. Sturrock, J. Mitchell (Comm.), W. Anderson (Comm.).* Front row:—*R. Black, G. McLean (Capt.), W. Black, G. Preston, D Laing.*

Formed in 1885, this club now plays in Division II of the Scottish League. Winners of the Forfarshire Cup on three occasions. Five Scottish International players have come from this club.

Expanding de Luxe Albums for Ardath Photocards on sale at Tobacconists Price 6d

ARDATH TOBACCO CO. LTD Manufacturers of STATE EXPRESS and ARDATH CIGARETTES

Date	Comp	H/A	Opponents	F A	1	2	3	4	5	6	7	8	9	10	11	12	13	14	15	16	17	18	19	20
06/10/2020	LC	A	Dundee	0 3																				
13/10/2020	LC	H	Hibernian	0 1	McCallum	Meechan	Whyte*	MacKenzie	Fisher&	Irvine	Barr	MacKintosh	Scally	Shepherd	Robertson+	Thomas*	Allan+	Coll&	*Breadner*	*Starrs*	*Fotheringham*	*Hoban*		
17/10/2020	L	H	Dumbarton	0 0	McCallum	Meechan	Thomas&	MacKenzie	Fisher	Irvine	Barr*	MacKintosh	Scally	Shepherd+	Robertson>	Antoniazzi*	Allan+	Hoti&	Doris>	*Starrs*	*Fotheringham*	*Breadner*	*Coll*	*Hoban*
24/10/2020	L	A	Falkirk	1 1	McCallum	Meechan	Thomas*	MacKenzie	Fisher	Irvine	Barr	MacKintosh	Hoti	Shepherd&	Robertson+	Allan*	Breadner+	Doris&	*Hill*	*Starrs*	*Fotheringham*	*Anotniazzi*	*Scally*	*Hoban*
31/10/2020	L	H	Montrose	2 3	McCallum*	Meechan	Thomas+	MacKenzie	Fisher	Irvine	Barr	MacKintosh	Allan	Shepherd&	Robertson>	Hoban*	Doris+	Antoniazzi&	Breadner>	*Starrs*	*Fotheringham*	*Hill*		
07/11/2020	L	A	Cove Rangers	0 3	Hoban	Meechan	Barr	MacKenzie	Fisher	Irvine	Doris*	MacKintosh	Allan+	Shepherd	Robertson	Breadner*	Antoniazzi+	*Dalling*	*Hill*	*Thomas*	*Diamond*	*Starrs*	*Coll*	
10/11/2020	LC	H	Brora Rangers	3 3 4-3p	Hoban	Coll>	Hill*	MacKenzie	Fisher	Irvine	Barr	MacKintosh	Hoti&	Antoniazzi	Robertson+	Thomas*	Allan+	Shepherd&	Breadner>	*Starrs*	*Fotheringham*	*Diamond*	*Dalling*	
14/11/2020	LC	A	Cove Rangers	0 1	Hoban	Coll	Thomas	MacKenzie	Fisher	Irvine	Barr+	MacKintosh	Hoti	Antoniazzi	Shepherd*	Allan*	Starrs+	*Robertson*	*Breadner*	*Hill*	*Fotheringham*	*Diamond*	*Dalling*	
21/11/2020	L	H	Airdrieonians	1 3	McCallum	Coll+	Meechan	MacKenzie	Fisher	Irvine	Barr	Thomas	Hoti*	Antoniazzi&	Allan	MacKintosh*	Shepherd+	Scally&	*Breadner*	*Hill*	*Robertson*	*Starrs*	*Dalling*	
28/11/2020	L	A	Peterhead	1 0	McCallum	Coll	Meechan	MacKenzie	Hill*	Irvine	Barr	MacKintosh	Scally+	Shepherd	Allan	Thomas*	Antoniazzi+	*Hoti*	*Breadner*	*Diamond*	*Fotheringham*	*Starrs*	*Dalling*	
12/12/2020	L	H	Partick Thistle	0 2	McCallum	Coll	Meechan	MacKenzie	S Anderson*	Thomas	Barr	MacKintosh	Scally	Shepherd>	Allan+	Breadner*&	Robertson+	Antoniazzi&	Fotheringham>	*Dalling*	*Hill*	*Starrs*	*Hoban*	
19/12/2020	L	A	East Fife	0 2	McCallum	Coll	Meechan	MacKenzie	Hill*	Dalling	Barr	MacKintosh	Scally	Shepherd	Robertson+	Hoti*	Allan+	*Antoniazzi*	*Fotheringham*	*Thomas*	*Breadner*	*Starrs*	*Hoban*	
26/12/2020	L	H	Cove Rangers	0 1	McCallum	Coll*	Meechan	MacKenzie	Thomas	Irvine	Barr	MacKintosh	Hoti	Antoniazzi	Robertson+	Allan*	Shepherd+	*Breadner*	*Hill*	*Dalling*	*Starrs*	*Hoban*		
02/01/2021	L	A	Montrose	0 0	McCallum	Coll	Meechan	MacKenzie	Fisher	Irvine	Barr	MacKintosh	Hoti	Shepherd	Thomas*	Antoniazzi*	*Doris*	*Allan*	*Hill*	*Dalling*	*Fotheringham*	*Starrs*	*Watson*	Hoban
09/01/2021	SC	H	Linlithgow Rose	4 1 AET	McCallum	Coll&	Meechan	MacKenzie	Doris+	Irvine	Barr	MacKintosh	Hoti	Shepherd	Thomas*	Scally*	Fotheringham+>	Allan&	Antoniazzi>	*Dalling*	*Hill*	*Hoban*		
20/03/2021	L	A	Dumbarton	1 0	McCallum	Coll	Meechan	Munro	Scott	Irvine	G Anderson&	MacKintosh	Nditi+	Moore	Northcott*	Shepherd*	Holmes+	Allan&	*Antoniazzi*	*Dalling*	*Scally*	*Thomson*	*Hoban*	
27/03/2021	L	H	Falkirk	0 2	McCallum	Coll>	Meechan	Munro	Scott+	Irvine*	Holmes&	MacKintosh	Nditi	Moore	Fenwick	G Anderson*	Shepherd+	Thomson&	Northcott>	*Dalling*	*Scally*	*Antoniazzi*	*Allan*	*Hoban*
30/03/2021	L	A	Partick Thistle	2 2	Hoban	Coll	Meechan	Munro	Scally*	Shepherd+	G Anderson&	MacKintosh	Nditi	Moore	Fenwick>	Northcott*	Allan+	Holmes&	Scott>	*Dalling*	*Irvine*	*Antoniazzi*	*Diamond*	*Thomson*
03/04/2021	SC	H	Edinburgh City	2 2 AET, 5-3p	Hoban	Thomson	Meechan	Allan*	Scally	Irvine	Holmes&	MacKintosh	Nditi	Northcott+	Fenwick	Shepherd*	Doris+	Coll&	*Hill*	*McCallum*				
06/04/2021	L	H	Peterhead	1 1	McCallum	Coll	Meechan	G Anderson+	Scally&	Irvine	Moore	MacKintosh	Nditi	Shepherd*	Fenwick>	Scott*	Holmes+	M Anderson&	Doris>	*Allan*	*Hill*	*Northcott*	*Hoban*	
08/04/2021	L	A	Clyde	0 3	McCallum	Coll	Meechan	Munro	Holmes	Scott	Moore	MacKintosh>	Fenwick+	M Anderson	G Anderson*	Allan*	Scally+&	Doris&	Northcott>	*Irvine*	*Hill*	*Shepherd*	*Thomson*	*Hoban*
10/04/2021	L	H	East Fife	1 2	McCallum	Coll	Meechan	Munro	Thomson	Scally+	Moore	MacKintosh	Fenwick	Allan*	G Anderson&	Doris*	M Anderson+	Shepherd&	*Northcott*	*Irvine*	*Holmes*	*Scott*	*Nditi*	*Hoban*
13/04/2021	L	A	Airdrieonians	1 3	McCallum	Holmes	Meechan	Munro	Thomson	Irvine	Moore*	MacKintosh&	Fenwick+	Scally	G Anderson>	Scott*	Doris+	Shepherd&	M Anderson>	*Nditi*	*Hill*	*Northcott*	*Allan*	*Hoban*
16/04/2021	SC	H	Dundee United	0 1	McCallum	Coll	Meechan	Nditi	Holmes	Irvine	Allan	MacKintosh	Doris*	Scally	Shepherd+	Fenwick*	Northcott+	Hill	*Hoban*					
20/04/2021	L	H	Clyde	1 3	McCallum	Coll	Meechan	Nditi	Holmes	Irvine<	Allan*	MacKintosh&	Fenwick+	Scally	G Anderson>	Scott*	Doris+	Moore&	Shepherd>	Munro<	*M Anderson*	*Northcott*	*Hoban*	
27/04/2021	L	A	Dumbarton	0 1	McCallum	Coll	Meechan	Nditi	Scott+	Irvine	G Anderson	MacKintosh>	Fenwick*	Scally&	Moore	Allan*	Doris	Northcott&	Shepherd>	*Hill*	*M Anderson*	*Thomson*	*Holmes*	*Hoban*
29/04/2021	L	H	Clyde	2 1	Hoban	Coll	Meechan	Nditi	Holmes	Irvine	Scally	Moore	Doris+	Allan*	Shepherd	Fenwick*	G Anderson+	MacKintosh	*Munro*	*Northcott*	*M Anderson*	*Thomson*	*Scott*	*McCallum*
01/05/2021	L	A	Peterhead	2 1	McCallum	Coll	Meechan	Nditi	Shepherd&	Irvine	G Anderson+	MacKintosh	Fenwick	Scally*	Moore	Holmes*	Allan+	Northcott&	*Munro*	*Doris*	*M Anderson*	*Thomson*	*Scott*	*Hoban*
04/05/2021	L	H	East Fife	2 3	McCallum	Coll	Meechan	Nditi	Holmes+	Irvine	G Anderson	Shepherd&	Fenwick*	Scally	Moore	MacKintosh*	Allan+	Doris&	*Munro*	*Northcott*	*M Anderson*	*Thomson*	*Scott*	*Hoban*

THE GOALIES

Goalkeepers Used in League Matches, 1972- 2020

Players shown in the season of their first appearance only

1972/3	Jimmy Milne
	Billy McGann
1973/4	Alistair Thorne
1974/5	Tony Milkinski
1976/7	Ian Beatson
1977/8	David Nicol
	Gordon Archibald
	David Gillies
1978/9	David McWilliams
	Ian Boardley
1980/1	Stewart Kennedy
1981/2	John Gardiner
1982/3	Andy Graham
1983/4	Jim Moffat
1989/0	Ray Allan
1991/2	Scott Thomson
1993/4	Gordon Arthur
	Neil Russell
1994/5	Craig Stephen
1995/6	John Donegan
	Dean Robertson
1999/0	Stuart Garden
2000/1	Neal Ferrie
2001/2	Michael Brown
2004/5	Alan Creer
2005/6	Colin Meldrum
	Mark Peat
	Francois Dubordeau
	Sean Murdoch
2006/7	Sandy Wood
2007/8	Andy Reid
2008/9	Ally Brown
	John Gibson
2009/0	Conor Grant
	Euan McLean
2010/1	Scott Gallacher
	Neil Duffy
2011/2	Greg Paterson
	Adam McHugh
	Jamie Langfield
	Marc McCallum
2012/3	Derek Soutar
	David Scott
	Jack Hamilton
	Darren Hill
2013/4	Rab Douglas
2015/6	Scott Gallacher
2016/7	Grant Adam
	Bryn Halliwell
2017/8	Marc McCallum (2nd spell)

Surname	First Name	Date of Birth	No	Nat	Pos	Signed	Previous	Notes	Contract	Lge			SC			LC			
										A	S	G	A	S	G	A	S	G	Un
Allan	Jordan	20/10/1998		SCO	F	2020	Cowdenbeath	Released May 2021, joined Airdrieonians		8	10	3	2	1	3		3	1	4
Anderson	Steven	19/12/1985		SCO	D	2020	St Johnstone		End 2021/2	1	0								0
Anderson	Grant	20/08/1986		SCO	M	2021	Kelty Hearts		End 2021/2	10	2	1							0
Anderson	Michael	07/02/2000		SCO	M	2021	BSC Glasgow (OL)	Mar-May		1	3								5
Antnoniazzi	Chris	01/05/2000		SCO	M	2020	Aberdeen	OL to Montrose Mar-May, Premanent from May		2	6	2		1		2			5
Barr	Bobby	23/06/1988		SCO	M	2020	East Stirlingshire	Transferred to Brechin City Jan 2021		10	0	1	1			3			0
Breadner	Cammy	13/10/2000		SCO	F	2020	St Mirren (OL)	Oct-Jan		0	4						1		7
Coll	Bernard	07/09/1994		SCO	D	2020	East Kilbride	Released May 2021, joined Stenhousemuir		17	0		2	1		2	1		2
Dalling	Kyle	27/03/2002		SCO	D	2020	Aberdeen	Releaded May 2021 joined Huntly		1	0								12
Diamond	Sean	27/01/1993		SCO	GK	2020	Broughty Athletic (OL)	Nov		0	0								5
Doris	Steven	09/08/1988		SCO	F	2020	Arbroath		End 2021/2	2	9		2	1					3
Fenwick	Scott	09/04/1990		ENG	F	2020	Cork City	Released May 2021		10	1	4	1	1					0
Fisher	Sam	26/07/2001		SCO	D	2020	Dundee (OL)	Oct-Jan		6	0					3			0
Fotheringham	Martyn	23/03/1983		SCO	D	2019	Montrose	Released April 2021		0	1			1	1				9
Hill	Mark	10/07/1998		SCO	M	2020	Celtic	Released May 2021		2	0					1			15
Hoban	Daniel	05/04/1998		SCO	GK	2020	Inverness CT	Released May 2021, joined Elgin City		3	1		1			2			19
Holmes	Graeme	26/03/1984		SCO	M	2021	Edinburgh City	Released May 2021 joined Cumbernauld Colts		6	4		2						2
Hoti	Florent	11/12/2000		KOS / SCO	M	2020	Dundee United (OL)	Oct-Jan		4	2		1			2			1
Irvine	Gary	17/03/1985		SCO	D	2019	St Mirren	Appointed Manager April 2021		17	0		3			3			3
MacKenzie	Jack	04/07/2000		SCO	D	2020	Aberdeen (OL)	Oct-May		10	0		1			3			0
MacKintosh	Murray	08/08/1997		SCO	M	2017	Forfar Athletic Youths	Released May 2021 joined Brechin City		19	2		3		1	3		2	1
McCallum	Marc	27/03/1993		SCO	GK	2017	Plymouth Argyle		End 2023/4	19	0		2			1			2
Meechan	Ross	10/11/1994		SCO	D	2018	Stenhousemuir		End 2022/3	22	0		3			1			0
Moore	Callum	22/03/2000		SCO	M	2021	Dundee (OL)	Mar-May		11	1								0
Munro	Andy	15/11/1992		SCO	D	2021	Stenhousemuir		End 2022/3	6	1								3
Nditi	Roberto	01/10/2000		ENG / NIG	D	2021	Bracknell Town	OOC June 2021, joined QOTS		9	0		2		1				2
Northcott	Jordan	09/02/2002		SCO	F	2021	St Johnstone (OL)	Mar-May		1	5		1	1					6
Robertson	John	26/08/2001		SCO	F	2020	St Johnstone (OL)	Oct-Jan		6	1					2			2
Scally	Daniel	20/12/1999		SCO	M	2020	Albion Rovers	Released May 2021		13	2	3	2	1		1			3
Scott	Martin "Jimmy"	15/02/1986		SCO	F	2021	Brechin City	Contract Terminated June 2021, joined Gala FR		4	4	1							4
Shepherd	Scott	29/05/1996		SCO	F	2020	Edinburgh City		End 2021/2	13	8	1	2	1		2	1		1
Starrs	Cole	25/04/2002		SCO	F	2020	Motherwell	Released Feb 2021 joined Caley Braves		0	0						1		12
Thomas	Archie	12/11/1999		ENG	M	2020	Cowdenbeath		End 2021/2	7	1		1			1	2		2
Thomson	Hamish	15/05/1998		SCO	D	2021	Tindastoll (ICE)	Released May 2021 joined Tranent Juniors		2	1		1						7
Travis	Michael	06/05/1993		RSA / SCO	D	2015	Arbroath		End 2021/2	0	0								0
Watson	Eric						Trialist			0	0								1
Whyte	Darren	16/03/1997		SCO	D	2018	St Mirren		End 2021/2	0	0					1			0
Own Goals												2							
NEW SIGNINGS																			
Aitken	Matthew	19/07/1997		SCO		2021	Albion Rovers		End 2022/3										
Crossan	PJ	09/10/1998		SCO	F	2021	Dumbarton		End 2022/3										
Fisher	Sam	26/07/2001		SCO	D	2021	Dundee (OL)	Jul-May	End 2021/2										
Gallagher	Mark	12/02/2001		SCO	M	2021	Aberdeen (OL)	Jul-May	End 2021/2										
Hussain	Yussuf	26/04/2001		SCO	D	2021	Motherwell		End 2022/3										
McCluskey	Stefan	22/08/1990		SCO	F	2021	Dumbarton		End 2021/2										
Sanderson	Lewis	31/07/2000		SCO	GK	2021	Cumbernauld United		End 2021/2										
Slater	Craig	26/04/1994		SCO	M	2021	Queen's Park		End 2022/3										
Strachan	Luke	22/03/2001		SCO / ENG	D	2021	Dundee (OL)	Jul-May	End 2021/2										
Thomson	Craig	10/03/1995		SCO	M	2021	Airdrieonians		End 2022/3										

Gordon Arthur

Scott Thomson

Scott Gallacher

Hamilton Accies FC 2020/21 The Accies

Founded	1874
Ground	New Douglas Park
Postcode	ML3 0FT
Tel	01698 368652
Capacity	6078
Closest Railway Station	Hamilton West
Record Attendance	28690 v Hearts, SC, 3/3/1937
Ground Record	5895 v Rangers, Lge, 28/2/2009
Record Win	9-0 v Gala Fairydean, SC, 28/1/1922
Record Defeat	1-1 v Hibernian, Lge, 6/11/1965
Most League Goals in a Season	35 David Wilson, 1936/7
Colours 2020/21 Top	Red and White Hoops
Shorts	White
Sponsor	EMH
Manufacturer	Adidas
Change Colours 2020/21 Top	Cyan Blue
Shorts	Cyan Blue
Nicknames	Accies, Acas
Web	www.acciesfc.co.uk
Match Programme 2020/21	None

Chairman and Director of Youth – Allan Maitland
Vice Chairman – Les Gray
Directors – Colin McGowan (CEO), David McDonald (Recruitment), Daniel Doherty (Secretary), John Brown, Seref Zengin, Bob Hay
Associate Directors – Ken Blake, Arthur Lynch
Head Coach – Brian Rice
First Team Coach – Guillaume Beuzelin
Academy Director – George Cairns
Head of Youth: Gary Hocknull
Kit Manager – Tom Robertson
Physiotherapist – Rob Crimin, Calum McAskill
Sports Scientist – Ruaridh Cuthbertson & Sunan Shah
Technical Analyst: Keith Glendinning

Goalkeeper Coach – Brian Potter
U18s Coach – Dougie Imrie
Hon Medical Officers – Dr Simon Gibson & Dr Josh Thompson
Stadium Manager – Jimmy Thompson
Safety & Security Officer – Colin Murphy
Head Groundsman – William Watson
Communications Officer – Marcus Nash
Supporters Liaison Officer – Sean McHugh

After years of hanging on to their Premiership status Accies finally found it too tough in 2020/1. They recorded just two wins from their first fourteen League fixtures, leaving them too much ground to make up. One win from their final seventeen games ensured that they did not do so. The only plus from a difficult season was decent performances from some of their locally-reared young players. Otherwise their squad of bargain-basement signings and journeymen proved inadequate for this level of football.

There was no bonus of enjoying a Cup run. St Mirren handed them a 3-0 defeat in the Scottish Cup and they failed to qualify from their League Cup group despite being handed a 3-0 win against Albion Rovers who couldn't fulfil their fixture.

STAR MAN
Ross Callachan was the outstanding player at Accies in 2020/1. He proved a scoring threat from midfield and a genuine quality player, finally fulfilling potential that had seen him move from Raith to Hearts in the past.

PROSPECTS 2021/2
It is hard to see Accies bouncing back at the first time of asking. However, they might still have a chance of getting into the promotion play offs.

Douglas Park

Date	Comp	H/A	Opponents	F	A	HT		Referee	Crowd	Scorers
02/08/2020	L	A	Celtic	1	5	1	2	W Collum	BCD	S Martin
08/08/2020	L	H	Ross County	0	1	0	0	B Madden	BCD	
15/08/2020	L	H	St Mirren	0	1	0	1	S Kirkland	BCD	
22/08/2020	L	A	Motherwell	1	0	0	0	A Muir	BCD	Odofin
29/08/2020	L	H	Rangers	0	2	0	2	W Collum	BCD	
12/09/2020	L	A	Livingston	2	1	0	1	D Robertson	BCD	Templeton, Munro
19/09/2020	L	A	Kilmarnock	1	2	1	1	N Walsh	BCD	Odofin
26/09/2020	L	H	Dundee United	1	1	0	1	A Muir	BCD	Odofin
02/10/2020	L	A	Hibernian	2	3	0	2	B Madden	BCD	Callachan pen, Porteous og
06/10/2020	LC	A	Annan Athletic	1	3	0	3	C Napier	BCD	McMann
10/10/2020	LC	H	Ayr United	2	1	2	0	C Steven	BCD	Ogkmpoe, Trafford
17/10/2020	L	H	St Johnstone	3	5	2	3	K Clancy	BCD	Hughes 2, Ogkmpoe
20/10/2020	L	A	Aberdeen	2	4	1	4	N Walsh	BCD	Moyo, Callachan pen
08/11/2020	L	A	Rangers	0	8	0	4	S McLean	BCD	
10/11/2020	LC	A	Stranraer	1	2	0	1	W Collum	BCD	Odofin
14/11/2020	LC	H	Albion Rovers	3	0					Awarded, Albion Rovers unable to field team
21/11/2020	L	A	Dundee United	1	2	0	0	C Napier	BCD	Callachan
25/11/2020	L	H	Aberdeen	1	1	0	1	G Duncan	BCD	Ogkmpoe
05/12/2020	L	H	Kilmarnock	1	0	0	0	W Collum	BCD	Callachan pen
12/12/2020	L	H	Hibernian	0	4	0	2	K Clancy	BCD	
19/12/2020	L	A	Ross County	2	0	1	0	W Collum		Callachan, S Martin
23/12/2020	L	H	Livingston	0	2	0	0	G Duncan	BCD	
26/12/2020	L	H	Celtic	0	3	0	0	D Robertson	BCD	
30/12/2020	L	A	St Johnstone	0	0	0	0	D Munro	BCD	
02/01/2021	L	H	Motherwell	3	0	1	0	C Steven	BCD	Hodson, Callachan, C Smith
09/01/2021	L	A	Kilmarnock	0	2	0	1	G Irvine	BCD	
16/01/2021	L	H	Dundee United	0	0	0	0	G Aitken	BCD	
27/01/2021	L	A	Celtic	0	2	0	1	C Steven	BCD	
03/02/2021	L	H	Ross County	1	2	1	0	W Collum	BCD	Kelly og
06/02/2021	L	H	Rangers	1	1	0	0	B Madden	BCD	Callachan
13/02/2021	L	A	Motherwell	4	1	3	0	D Munro	BCD	Anderson, Callachan pen, Ogkmpoe, Moyo
17/02/2021	L	A	St Mirren	1	1	0	0	S McLean	BCD	Anderson
20/02/2021	L	A	Hibernian	0	2	0	1	C Napier	BCD	
03/03/2021	L	H	St Johnstone	1	1	1	0	G Irvine	BCD	Callachan
06/03/2021	L	A	Aberdeen	0	0	0	0	B Madden	BCD	
13/03/2021	L	A	Livingston	1	2	1	2	K Clancy	BCD	C Smith
20/03/2021	L	H	St Mirren	1	1	0	1	D Robertson	BCD	Munro
03/04/2021	SC	H	St Mirren	0	3	0	1	E Anderson	BCD	
10/04/2021	L	H	Dundee United	0	1	0	1	B Madden	BCD	
21/04/2021	L	H	Motherwell	0	1	0	1	K Clancy	BCD	
01/05/2021	L	A	St Mirren	2	1	1	0	J Beaton	BCD	Callachan, Moyo
12/05/2021	L	A	Ross County	1	2	1	1	W Collum	BCD	McMann
16/05/2021	L	H	Kilmarnock	0	2	0	2	K Clancy	BCD	

Surname	First Name	Date of Birth	No	Nat	Pos	Signed	Previous	Notes	Contract	Lge A	Lge S	Lge G	SC A	SC S	SC G	LC A	LC S	LC G	Un
Anderson	Bruce	23/09/1997	7	SCO	F	2021	Aberdeen (OL)	Feb-May		13		2	1						
Callachan	Ross	04/09/1993	34	SCO	M	2020	St Johnstone	June 2021, joined Ross County		32	1	10	1			3			
Collar	Will	03/02/1997	7	ENG	M	2019	Brighton	Freed Feb 2021, joined Stockport County		5	1								3
Cunningham	Ross	23/05/1998	24	SCO	M	2018	Hamilton Accies Youths	Freed Sep 2020 joined Clyde		0	0								0
Easton	Brian	05/03/1988	5	SCO	D	2019	St Johnstone		End 2021/2	24	0		1			1			2
Fjortoft	Markus	12/01/1994	16	ENG	D	2019	Southern United	Freed Sep 2020, joined Morton		1	1								5
Fulton	Ryan	23/05/1996	23	SCO	GK	2017	Liverpool	OOC June 2021		28	0		1			2			1
Garrad	Jack	24/05/2003	29	SCO	M	2020	Hamilton Accies Youths		End 2021/2	0	0								0
Gourlay	Kyle	24/09/1998	22	SCO	GK	2019	Dundee	OOC June 2021, joined Cove Rangers		9	1					1			30
Hamilton	Jamie	01/03/2001	6	SCO	D	2019	Hamilton Accies Youths		End 2021/2	21	6			1					6
Harris	Liam	19/12/2002		SCO	F	2020	Hamilton Accies Youths	OL to Clydebank Aug-Jan		0	0								0
Hodson	Lee	02/10/1991	27	NIR	D	2020	Gillingham (OL)	Aug-May		33	0	1	1			2			2
Hughes	Ronan	15/12/1998	15	SCO	M	2018	Hamilton Accies Youths		End 2021/2	7	9	2	1				1		13
Johnson	Justin	27/08/1996	37	NET / GHA	F	2020	Othelios Athienou	Freed Feb 2021, joined Morton		1	4						2		12
Martin	Scott	01/04/1997	8	SCO	M	2018	Hibernian		End 2021/2	21	3	2	1			1	1		1
Martin	Aaron	29/09/1989	16	ENG	D	2020	Exeter City	OOC June 2021, joined Port Vale		24	0		1			1			1
McKenna	Ciaran	25/03/1998	4	SCO	D	2019	Falkirk	Freed Aug 2020, joined Partick Thistle		0	1								1
McMann	Scott	09/07/1996	3	SCO	D	2014	Hamilton Accies Youths		End 2021/2	36	0	1	1			3		1	0
Meikle	Daryl	14/01/2001	33	SCO	M	2018	Hamilton Accies Youths	OL to Blackburn Utd Oct-Jan, to Linlithgow R Jan-May	End 2021/2	0	0								1
Mimnaugh	Reegan	18/12/2001	18	SCO	M	2019	Hamilton Accies Youths		End 2021/2	8	9					1	1		21
Moyo	David	17/12/1994	20	SCO	F	2019	St Albans City		End 2022/3	23	10	3	1				2		5
Munro	Kyle	29/11/2001	21	SCO	F	2017	Dumbarton Youths		End 2021/2	9	7	2		1		1	2		18
Odoffin	Hakeem	13/04/1998	2	ENG / NIG	D	2020	Livingston		End 2021/2	37	0	3	1			3		1	0
Ogkmpoe	Marios	10/10/1994	9	GRE / NIG	F	2018	OFI Crete	Released June 2021		15	5	3				2		1	0
Owolabi	Tunde	26/07/1996	36	NIG / BEL	F	2020	FC United of Manchester	Freed Feb 2021		1	6					1	1		13
Redfern	Marley	27/08/2002		SCO	M	2020	Hamilton Accies Youths	OL to Blackburn United Oct-Jan	End 2022/3	0	1								6
Scully	Ryan	29/10/1992		ROI	GK	2020	Dunfermline Athletic	Freed Jan 2021		0	0								14
Slaven	Sean	10/05/2001	25	SCI	F	2020	Hamilton Accies Youths	OL to Linlithgow Rose Sep-Jan, to Brechin City Jan-May, Freed Jul 2021		0	0								3
Smith	Lewis	16/03/2000	11	SCO	M	2019	Hamilton Accies Youths		End 2021/2	4	5					1			0
Smith	Jamie	08/05/2002	31	SCO	GK	2019	Hamilton Accies Youths	OL to Rossvale Oct-May	End 2021/2	1	0								0
Smith	Callum	13/11/1999	32	SCO	F	2020	Dunfermline Athletic		End 2021/2	8	15	2				3			14
Stanger	George	15/08/2000	17	SCO /NEZ	D	2019	Hamilton Accies Youths		End 2021/2	1	4								23
Stirling	Ben	16/08/1998	4	SCO	D	2020	Hibernian		End 2021/2	16	4					2			11
Templeton	David	07/01/1989	10	SCO	F	2020	Burton Albion		End 2021/2	7	1	1				2			1
Thomas	Nathan	27/09/1994	24	ENG	F	2020	Sheffield United	Released June 2021		3	7					1		1	4
Trafford	Charlie	24/05/1992	14	CAN	M	2020	Inverness CT	Released June 2021		9	7					1			16
Want	Shaun	09/02/1997	12	SCO	D	2017	Hamilton Accies Youths		End 2021/2	11	0								1
Winter	Andy	10/03/2002	19	SCO	F	2018	Hamilton Accies Youths		End 2021/2	10	12					1			6
Own Goals												2							
NEW SIGNINGS																			
Hilton	Joe	11/10/1999		ENG	GK	2021	Blackburn Rovers (OL)		End 2021/2										
MacDonald	Kieran	31/07/1993		SCO	D	2021	Raith Rovers		End 2021/2										
Ryan	Andy	29/09/1994		SCO	F	2021	Stirling Albion		End 2022/3										
Shiels	Matthew	13/09/2000		SCO / ROI	D	2021	Rangers		End 2021/2										
Spence	Lewis	28/01/1996		SCO	M	2021	Scunthorpe United		End 2022/3										

Date	Comp	H/A	Opponents	F	A	1	2	3	4	5	6	7	8	9	10
02/08/2020	L	A	Celtic	1	5	Fulton	McMann	Odofin&	Want	Hamilton	Callachan+	S Martin	Hughes*	L Smith	Moyo
08/08/2020	L	H	Ross County	0	1	Fulton	McMann	Odofin	Want&	Fjortoft	Callachan<	S Martin	C Smith*	L Smith>	Moyo
15/08/2020	L	H	St Mirren	0	1	Fulton	McMann	Odofin	Want	Hodson	Callachan&	S Martin	Templeton	L Smith+	Moyo*
22/08/2020	L	A	Motherwell	1	0	Fulton	McMann	Odofin	Want	Hodson	Callachan	S Martin<	Templeton+	Johnson*	Moyo>
29/08/2020	L	H	Rangers	0	2	Fulton	McMann	Odofin	Want	Hodson	Callachan	S Martin	Trafford*	Mimnaugh+	Ogkmpoe&
12/09/2020	L	A	Livingston	2	1	Fulton	Collar+	Odofin	Want	Munro	Callachan	S Martin	Templeton&	Mimnaugh	Moyo
19/09/2020	L	A	Kilmarnock	1	2	Fulton	McMann	Odofin	Want	Hamilton+	Collar>	S Martin*	Templeton	Mimnaugh	Moyo
26/09/2020	L	H	Dundee United	1	1	Fulton	McMann	Odofin	Want	Hodson&	Munro<	S Martin	Templeton	Mimnaugh*	Owolabi>
02/10/2020	L	A	Hibernian	2	3	Gourlay	McMann	Odofin	Want*	Hodson	Collar	S Martin&	Templeton>	Hamilton	Callachan
06/10/2020	LC	A	Annan Athletic	1	3	Gourlay	McMann	Odofin	Stirling	Hodson	Munro	C Smith	Templeton*	Owolabi+	Callachan
10/10/2020	LC	H	Ayr United	2	1	Fulton	McMann	Odofin	Stirling	Hodson	Trafford	C Smith+	Templeton&	Mimnaugh	Callachan*
17/10/2020	L	H	St Johnstone	3	5	Fulton	McMann	Odofin	Want	Hodson&	Munro+	S Martin	Templeton*	Moyo	Callachan
20/10/2020	L	A	Aberdeen	2	4	Fulton	McMann	Odofin	Want	Hodson	Hughes>	S Martin*	Collar+	Moyo	Callachan&
08/11/2020	L	A	Rangers	0	8	Fulton	McMann	Odofin	Easton	Hodson	Hughes*	Stirling	Collar	Moyo	Callachan&
10/11/2020	LC	A	Stranraer	1	2	Fulton	McMann	Odofin	Easton	A Martin	Thomas*	S Martin>	Winter&	C Smith	Callachan+
14/11/2020	LC	H	Albion Rovers	3	0										
21/11/2020	L	A	Dundee United	1	2	Fulton	McMann	Odofin	Easton*	A Martin	Stirling	S Martin	Hodson	C Smith	Callachan
25/11/2020	L	H	Aberdeen	1	1	Fulton	McMann	Odofin	Easton	A Martin	Stirling	S Martin	Hodson	C Smith+	Callachan
05/12/2020	L	H	Kilmarnock	1	0	Fulton	McMann	Odofin	Easton	A Martin	Stirling	S Martin	Hodson*	C Smith+	Callachan
12/12/2020	L	H	Hibernian	0	4	Fulton	McMann	Trafford+	Easton	A Martin	Stirling	S Martin	Hodson&	C Smith*	Callachan
19/12/2020	L	A	Ross County	2	0	Fulton	McMann	Odofin	Easton	A Martin	Stirling>	S Martin+	Hodson	Thomas*	Callachan
23/12/2020	L	H	Livingston	0	2	Fulton+	McMann	Odofin	Easton>	A Martin	Stirling	Hughes*	Hodson	Mimnaugh	Munro
26/12/2020	L	H	Celtic	0	3	Gourlay	McMann	Odofin	Easton	A Martin	Stirling+	Hamilton	Hodson	Trafford	Winter*
30/12/2020	L	A	St Johnstone	0	0	Gourlay	McMann	Odofin	Easton*	A Martin	Stirling	Hamilton	Hodson	Thomas+	Winter
02/01/2021	L	H	Motherwell	3	0	Gourlay	McMann	Odofin	Easton*	A Martin	Stirling	Hamilton	Hodson	Winter&	Callachan>
09/01/2021	L	A	Kilmarnock	0	2	Gourlay	McMann	Odofin	Trafford	Stanger	Stirling	Hamilton	Hodson	Winter	Callachan
16/01/2021	L	H	Dundee United	0	0	Fulton	McMann	Odofin	Easton	A Martin	Stirling	Hamilton	Hodson	C Smith+	Callachan
27/01/2021	L	A	Celtic	0	2	Fulton	McMann	Odofin	Easton	A Martin	Stirling+	Hamilton	Hodson	Ogkmpoe*	Callachan&
03/02/2021	L	H	Ross County	1	2	Fulton	McMann	Odofin	Easton>	A Martin	Stirling*	Hamilton	Hodson	Ogkmpoe&	Callachan
06/02/2021	L	H	Rangers	1	1	Fulton	McMann	Odofin	Easton	A Martin	Trafford*	Hamilton	Hodson	Ogkmpoe	Callachan
13/02/2021	L	A	Motherwell	4	1	Fulton	McMann	Odofin	Easton&	A Martin	Trafford*	Hamilton	Hodson	Ogkmpoe+	Callachan
17/02/2021	L	A	St Mirren	1	1	Fulton	McMann	Odofin	Easton	A Martin*	Trafford+	Hamilton	Hodson	Ogkmpoe	Callachan
20/02/2021	L	A	Hibernian	0	2	Fulton	McMann	Odofin	Easton	S Martin>	Trafford&	Hamilton	Hodson	Ogkmpoe*	Callachan
03/03/2021	L	H	St Johnstone	1	1	Fulton	McMann	Odofin	Easton	A Martin	Trafford+	S Martin*	Hodson	Moyo	Callachan
06/03/2021	L	A	Aberdeen	0	0	Fulton	McMann	Odofin	Easton+	A Martin	Thomas*	Hamilton	Hodson	Moyo&	Callachan
13/03/2021	L	A	Livingston	1	2	Fulton	Munro	Odofin	Easton	A Martin	C Smith+	Hamilton	Hodson*	Anderson	Callachan
20/03/2021	L	H	St Mirren	1	1	Fulton	McMann	Odofin	Easton	A Martin+	Stirling*	C Smith&	Hodson	Anderson	Callachan
03/04/2021	SC	H	St Mirren	0	3	Fulton	McMann	Odofin	Easton	A Martin	Hughes+	Moyo	Hodson	Anderson	Callachan
10/04/2021	L	H	Dundee United	0	1	Gourlay	McMann	Odofin	Easton*	A Martin	Hamilton	Munro	Hodson	Anderson	Callachan
21/04/2021	L	H	Motherwell	0	1	Gourlay	McMann	Odofin	Easton+	A Martin	Hamilton	Munro	Hodson&	Anderson	Callachan*
01/05/2021	L	A	St Mirren	2	1	Gourlay	McMann	Odofin	Mimnaugh&	A Martin	Hamilton	Munro*	Hodson	Anderson+	Callachan>
12/05/2021	L	A	Ross County	1	2	Gourlay	McMann	Odofin	Easton*	A Martin	Hamilton	Mimnaugh&	Hodson	Anderson+	Callachan
16/05/2021	L	H	Kilmarnock	0	2	J Smith	McMann	Odofin	Stirling*	A Martin	Hamilton	Munro&	Hughes	Anderson+	Mimnaugh<

THE GOALIES

Goalkeepers Used in League Matches, 1970-2020

Players shown in the season of their first appearance only

1972/3	Tommy McCulloch
	Graham MacLean
	Billy McGann
	David Archer
1973/4	Billy Whiteside
	Peter McBain
1974/5	Rikki Ferguson
	Bobby McKell
	Ronnie Lowrie
1977/8	David McWilliams
1979/0	Jim Muir
1981/2	Jim Moffat
1982/3	Howard Sammeroff
1983/4	Dougie McNab
1985/6	Robin Rae
1986/7	Dave McKellar
1987/8	Alan Ferguson
1988/9	Alan Rough
1989/0	Andy Murdoch
	Ian McFarlane
1991/2	Michael Monaghan
	Rab McCulloch
1993/4	David Cormack
1996/7	Colin Scott
	Steve Paris
	John Hillcoat
1997/8	Andy McCondichie
	Myles Hogarth
1998/9	Chris Reid
	Stephen Robertson
2000/1	Graham Potter
2001/2	Andy Goram
	Colin Stewart
	Michael Herbert
2003/4	David McEwan
2004/5	Ray Jellema
2006/7	Sean Murdoch
2007/8	Bryn Halliwell
	Tomas Cerny
2011/2	David Hutton
	Scott Christie
	Alan Combe
	Blair Currie
2012/3	Kevin Cuthbert
2014/5	Michael McGovern
2015/6	Alan Martin
2016/7	Remi Matthews
	Gary Woods
2017/8	Darren Jamieson
	Ryan Fulton
2018/9	Jan Mucha
2019/0	Owain Fon Williams
	Luke Southwood

11	12	13	14	15	16	17	18	19	20
Winter	Ogkmpoe*	Trafford+	McKenna&	C Smith	Owolabi	Fjortoft	Munro	Mimnaugh	Gourlay
Winter+	Trafford*	Templeton+	Hamilton&	Johnson>	Owolabi<	McKenna	Munro	Mimnaugh	Gourlay
Winter	Ogkmpoe*	Johnson+	Mimnaugh&	C Smith	Hamilton	Fjortoft	Munro	Trafford	Gourlay
Ogkmpoe&	L Smith*	Trafford+	Winter&	C Smith>	Mimnaugh<	Fjortoft	Hamilton	Owolabi	Gourlay
Winter>	Hamilton*	Munro+	Moyo&	C Smith>	Templeton	Fjortoft	Johnson	Owolabi	Gourlay
Ogkmpoe*	Winter*	Trafford+	Fjortoft&	C Smith	Hamilton	Meikle	Johnson	Owolabi	Gourlay
Ogkmpoe&	C Smith*	Johnson+	Winter&	Trafford&	Fjortoft	Stanger	Hughes	Owolabi	Gourlay
Winter+	Callachan*	Ogkmpoe+	Hamilton&	C Smith>	Collar<	Moyo	Johnson	Trafford	Gourlay
Winter+	Munro*	Ogkmpoe+	Owolabi&	C Smith>	Stirling	Moyo	Mimnaugh	Trafford	Scully
Ogkmpoe	Johnson*	Moyo+	Stanger	Mimnaugh	S Martin	Hughes	Scully		
Ogkmpoe	S Martin*	Moyo+	Munro&	Collar	Stanger	Hughes	Johnson	Owolabi	Scully
Ogkmpoe	Hughes*	C Smith+	Stirling&	Collar	Trafford	Mimnaugh	Johnson	Owolabi	Gourlay
Ogkmpoe	Trafford*	Mimnaugh+	Strachan&	C Smith>	Stanger	Easton	Johnson	Owolabi	Gourlay
Ogkmpoe+	L Smith*	Winter+	Mimnaugh&	C Smith	Stanger	A Martin	Johnson	Thomas	Gourlay
L Smith<	Munro*	Hughes+	Owolabi&	Mimnaugh>	Johnson<	Stirling	Hodson	Stanger	Gourlay
Ogkmpoe	Moyo*	Hughes	Hamilton	Munro	Stanger	Mimnaugh	Thomas	Gourlay	
Ogkmpoe*	Moyo*	Winter+	Hamilton	Munro	Stanger	Mimnaugh	Thomas	Hughes	Gourlay
Moyo	Thomas*	Owolabi+	Hamilton	Munro	Trafford	Mimnaugh	Winter	Hughes	Gourlay
Moyo>	Owolabi*	Thomas+	Winter&	Hamilton>	Stanger	Mimnaugh	Munro	Hughes	Gourlay
Moyo&	Munro*	Hughes+	Winter&	Hamilton>	Trafford	Mimnaugh	C Smith	Owolabi	Gourlay
Moyo&	Johnson*	Gourlay+	Winter&	Hamilton>	Stanger	Owolabi	Trafford	Scully	
Moyo&	Owolabi*	Mimnaugh+	Munro&	Hughes	Stanger	Johnson	Scully		
Moyo	Stanger*	Owolabi+	Mimnaugh	Hughes	C Smith	Johnson	Trafford	Munro	Scully
Moyo+	Stanger*	C Smith+	Munro&	Trafford>	Hughes	Johnson	Mimnaugh	Owolabi	Scully
Moyo*	C Smith*	Scully	Slaven	Munro	Hughes	Johnson	Mimnaugh	Owolabi	Fulton
Moyo*	Ogkmpoe*	Winter+	Trafford	Munro	Stanger	Johnson	Mimnaugh	Owolabi	Gourlay
Moyo	S Martin*	Winter+	Mimnaugh&	Munro	Stanger	C Smith	Trafford	Collar	Gourlay
Anderson+	Mimnaugh*	Winter+	Moyo&	Thomas>	Stanger	C Smith	Hughes	Munro	Gourlay
Anderson	Hughes*	Munro	Moyo	Slaven	Stanger	C Smith	Mimnaugh	Winter	Gourlay
Anderson>	S Martin*	Moyo+	Stirling&	Winter>	Hughes	C Smith	Mimnaugh	Munro	Gourlay
Anderson&	S Martin*	Hughes+	Moyo&	Stirling	Munro	C Smith	Mimnaugh	Winter	Gourlay
Anderson+	Moyo*	Mimnaugh+	Hughes&	C Smith>	Munro	Stirling	Want	Winter	Gourlay
Anderson	Hughes*	Stirling+	Mimnaugh	Stanger	Munro	C Smith	Thomas	Winter	Gourlay
S Martin	C Smith*	Munro+	Hughes&	Stanger	Mimnaugh	Stirling	Trafford	Winter	Gourlay
S Martin	Hughes*	Moyo+	Slaven	Stanger	Mimnaugh	Stirling	Trafford	Redfern	Gourlay
S Martin	Moyo*	Hughes+	Munro&	Stanger	Mimnaugh	Scully	Trafford	Redfern	Gourlay
S Martin*	Hamilton*	Munro+	C Smith	Stanger	Stirling	Scully	Gourlay		
Hughes	C Smith*	Stirling	Stanger	Redfern	Moyo	Scully			
Hughes	L Smith*	Mimnaugh+	Thomas&	Redfern	C Smith	Stirling	Stanger	Moyo	Scully
Moyo	L Smith*	C Smith+	Stanger&	Thomas>	Redfern	Stirling	Trafford	Scully	
Moyo	Thomas*	C Smith+	L Smith&	Redfern	Trafford	Stirling	Stanger	Scully	Munro
L Smith>	Stanger*	C Smith+	Thomas&	Moyo>	Redfern<	Easton	Trafford	Hodson	Gourlay

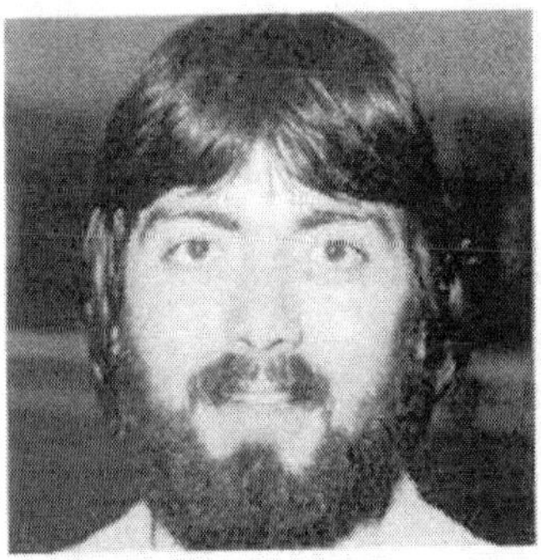

Rikki Ferguson

Howard Sammeroff

Colin Stewart

Heart of Midlothian FC 2020/21 The Jam Tarts

Founded	1874
Ground	Tynecastle Park
Postcode	EH11 2NL
Tel	0131 200 7207
Capacity	17529
Closest Railway Station	Haymarket
Record Attendance	57857 v Barcelona, Friendly, 28/7/2007
Ground Record	53396 v Rangers, SC, 13/2/1932
Record Win	21-0 v Anchor, East of Scotland Cup, 30/10/1880
Record Defeat	1-8, v Vale of Leven, Scottish Cup, 1882
Most League Goals in a Season	44 Barney Battles, 1930/1
Most League Goals in Career	214 John Robertson
Colours 2020/21 Top	Maroon
Shorts	White
Sponsor	Save the Children
Manufacturer	Umbro
Change Colours 2020/21 Top	Blue
Shorts	Maroon
Nicknames	Jam Tarts, Jambos
Web	www.heartsfc.co.uk
Match Programme 2020/21	Curtis Sport

Board of Directors
Owner and Chair : Ann Budge
CEO: Andrew McKinlay
Non Executive Director: Eric Hogg, Donald Cumming, Kevin Windram
Foundation of Hearts Chair: Stuart Wallace
Finance Director: Jacqui Duncan
Marketing & Comms Director: Catriona McCallum
Sporting Director: Joe Savage (ex Stenhousemuir player)
Head of Recruitment: William Lancefield
Principal Ambassador: Gary Locke
Foundation of Hearts Chairman: Stuart Wallace
Manager: Robbie Neilson
Assistant Managers: Gordon Forrest and Lee McCulloch
Football Staff
Goalkeeper Coach: Paul Gallacher
Football Development Manager: Steven Naismith
Medic: Karen Gibson
U18 Coach: John Rankin
Youth Coach: Angus Beith
Head of Coach Education: Darren Murray
Loans Manager: Gary Naysmith
Club Doctor: Ivan Brenkel
Physio: Craig Maitland
Sports Scientists: Mike Williams
Academy Manager: Roger Arnott

Despite winning promotion from the Championship in a canter, an element amongst the Hearts support were still calling for the head of Manager Robbie Neilson. Part of the reason was their two stunning Cup exits at the hands of Alloa Athletic and Brora Rangers. Losing to Brora must count as the worst Cup result in Hearts history and one of the biggest upsets in the long story of the Scottish Cup. There were some unconvincing League performances as well, especially away from home. Some Hearts fans also remember Neilson's last stint as Manager when he also got them promoted, then struggled in the Premier League. Why did he leave Dundee United when he got them promoted rather than staying and trying again in the Premiership? Was it devotion to Hearts, or was it a preference to continue managing at Championship level? Nobody knows.

IT certainly wasn't the most inspiring title winning campaign of all time. A run of ten league games from January to March saw Hearts win four, draw five and lose one, scoring just eleven goals in the process. It was turgid stuff but enough to get Hearts back to where they feel they always should have been, the Premiership. Only once promotion had been achieved did they open up and start winning games convincingly.

Early season saw Hearts get through their League Cup section before going out to Alloa. They also had the held-over Scottish Cup to play in. Victory over Hibs in the Semi Final was as sweet as it was surprising. Defat to Celtic in the Final, on penalty kicks after a 3-3 draw was hard to take. Brora was just incomprehensible.

STAR MAN
Liam Boyce was by far Hearts most consistent forward player. His goals, including from the penalty spot, earned Hearts a high proportion of their points, especially in those low-scoring games in mid season.

PROSPECTS 2021/2
Hearts seem to be going with much the same squad as the guys that got them promoted so the question is will they be good enough for the Premiership? Clearly they have a few outstanding individuals – Craig Gordon and Liam Boyce stand out. Much will depend on how players like Gary Mackay-Steven and Stephen Kingsley perform. Both were inconsistent after joining Hearts during the season but they must step up now and show that they have what it takes to play at the top level.

Away up in Gorgie at Tynecastle Park,
There's a wee fitba team that can aye makes it's mark,
They've won all the honours for footballing arts,
Aye there's nae other team tae compare with the Hearts

Hearts, Hearts, Glorious Hearts
It's down at Tynecastle they bide,
The boys in maroon are the talk o' the toon,
And Auld Reekie Supports them with Pride.

This is my story, This is my song,
Follow the Hearts and you can't go wrong,
Some say the Celtic and Rangers are grand,
But the Boys in Maroon are the best in the land.

Date	Comp	H/A	Opponents	F	A		HT		Referee	Crowd	Scorers
06/10/2020	LC	H	Inverness CT	1	0		0	0	S McLean	BCD	Walker pen
10/10/2020	LC	A*	Cowdenbeath	1	0		0	0	A Newlands	BCD	Halkett
13/10/2020	LC	H	Raith Rovers	3	1		2	0	C Napier	BCD	Wighton 3 (2 pens)
16/10/2020	L	H	Dundee	6	2		4	1	D Munro	BCD	Smith, Ginnelly, Boyce pen, Kingsley 2, Halliday
23/10/2020	L	A	Arbroath	1	0		0	0	G Aitken	BCD	Wighton
31/10/2020	SCSF	N	Hibernian	2	1	AET	0	0	W Collum	BCD	Wighton, Boyce pen
07/11/2020	L	H	Inverness CT	2	1		0	0	B Madden	BCD	Naismith, Boyce
10/11/2020	LC	A	East Fife	3	2		2	1	E Anderson	BCD	Lee 2, Irving
20/11/2020	L	A	Dunfermline Athletic	1	2		0	0	D Robertson	BCD	Kingsley
24/11/2020	L	H	Alloa Athletic	3	0		3	0	G Irvine	BCD	Smith, Halliday, Haring
28/11/2020	LC	A	Alloa Athletic	0	1	AET	0	0	G Duncan	BCD	
05/12/2020	L	A	Morton	2	0		1	0	G Aitken	BCD	Walker 2
12/12/2020	L	H	Queen of the South	6	1		2	0	W Collum	BCD	Naismith, Boyce 2, Walker, Frear, Gonelly
20/12/2020	SCF	N	Celtic	3	3	AET,3-4p	0	2	J Beaton	BCD	Boyce, Kingsley, Ginnelly
26/12/2020	L	H	Ayr United	5	3		1	0	D Munro	BCD	Kingsley, Wighton 2, Lee, Boyce
29/12/2020	L	H	Arbroath	3	1		3	0	N Walsh	BCD	Naismith 3 (1 pen)
02/01/2021	L	A	Dundee	1	3		0	2	D Robertson	BCD	Irving
16/01/2021	L	A	Alloa Athletic	3	1		2	0	A Muir	BCD	Irving, Frear, Ginnelly
23/01/2021	L	H	Raith Rovers	2	3		0	1	J Beaton	BCD	Boyce 2
26/01/2021	L	A	Raith Rovers	4	0		2	0	E Anderson	BCD	Boyce, Henderson, Gnanduileet 2
30/01/2020	L	H	Dunfermline Athletic	1	0		0	0	W Collum	BCD	Walker
05/02/2021	L	A	Ayr United	1	0		0	0	S McLean	BCD	Boyce pen
12/02/2021	L	A	Queen of the South	1	1		0	1	C Steven	BCD	Boyce pen
20/02/2021	L	H	Morton	1	1		0	0	D Dickinson	BCD	Walker
26/02/2021	L	A	Inverness CT	1	1		1	1	N Walsh	BCD	Boyce
06/03/2021	L	H	Dundee	2	1		1	0	D Robertson	BCD	Halliday, Gnanduillet
13/03/2021	L	H	Ayr United	2	0		0	0	C Steven	BCD	Gnanduillet, Walker
20/03/2021	L	A	Arbroath	0	0		0	0	E Anderson	BCD	
23/03/2021	SC	A	Brora Rangers	1	2		0	1	P Stuart	BCD	Berra
27/03/2021	L	H	Queen of the South	2	3		1	2	G Duncan	BCD	Popescu, Gnanduillet
03/04/2021	L	A	Dunfermline Athletic	0	0		0	0	C Steven	BCD	
19/04/2021	L	H	Alloa Athletic	6	0		2	0	S McLean	BCD	Boyce 3(1 pen), Henderson, McEneff, Walker
20/04/2021	L	A	Morton	0	0		0	0	J Beaton	BCD	
24/04/2021	L	H	Inverness CT	3	0		3	0	B Madden	BCD	Mackay-Steven 2, McEneff
30/04/2021	L	A	Raith Rovers	4	0		1	0	D Munro	BCD	Mackay-Steven 2, Henderson, Naismith

* at New Bayview

Jim Cruickshank

Henry Smith

Victor Noring

Date	Comp	H/A	Opponents	F	A		1	2	3	4	5	6	7	8	9	10	11	12	13	14	15	16	17	18	19	20
06/10/2020	LC	H	Inverness CT	1	0		Gordon	White	Halkett	Popescu	Brandon	Lee>	Walker	Ginnelly<	Irving+	Naismith&	Wighton*	Roberts*	Halliday+	Kingsley&	Haring>	Henderson<	Frear	Stewart		
10/10/2020	LC	A*	Cowdenbeath	1	0		Gordon	White	Halkett	Popescu	Brandon	Lee&	Walker	Ginnelly	Roberts	Naismith*	McGill+	Wighton*	Frear+	Haring&	Moore	Henderson	Cochrane	Zlamal		
13/10/2020	LC	H	Raith Rovers	3	1		Stewart	White*	Kingsley	Haring	Brandon	Frear>	Moore<	Cochrane	McGill+	Henderson&	Wighton	Roberts*	Lee+	Popescu&	Walker>	Ginnelly<	Halkett	Gordon		
16/10/2020	L	H	Dundee	6	2		Gordon	Smith	Kingsley	Popescu	Halkett	Lee	Walker	Ginnelly+	Roberts	Irving*	Boyce&	Haring*	Halliday+	Wighton&	Frear	White	Naismith	Stewart		
23/10/2020	L	A	Arbroath	1	0		Gordon	Smith	Kingsley	Popescu	Halkett	Lee	Walker&	Ginnelly*	Frear+	Halliday	Boyce&	Wighton*	White+	Haring&	Brandon	Irving	Naismith	Stewart		
31/10/2020	SCSF	N	Hibernian	2	1	AET	Gordon	Smith	Kingsley	Popescu	Halkett	Lee>	Walker*	Wighton&	Roberts+	Halliday<	Boyce	Naismith*	Haring+	White&	Henderson>	Irving<	Moore	Brandon	McGill	Stewart
07/11/2020	L	H	Inverness CT	2	1		Gordon	Smith	Kingsley	Popescu	Halkett	Lee	Haring*	Wighton	Naismith+	Halliday	Boyce&	Irving*	White+	Frear&	Henderson	Berra	Brandon	Stewart		
10/11/2020	LC	A	East Fife	3	2		Stewart	Berra+	White	Popescu	Brandon	Lee*	Frear	Wighton	Irving	Henderson	McGill	Naismith*	Kingsley+	Moore	Darge	Denholm	C Logan	Zlamal		
20/11/2020	L	A	Dunfermline Athletic	1	2		Gordon	Smith	Kingsley	Popescu	Halkett	Lee&	Frear*	Wighton+	Halliday	Naismith	Boyce	Walker*	Roberts+	Irving&	Brandon	Berra	White	Stewart		
24/11/2020	L	H	Alloa Athletic	3	0		Gordon	Smith+	Kingsley	Berra	Halkett	Haring	Walker	Roberts*	Halliday&	Naismith	Boyce	White*	Popescu+	Lee&	Wighton	Henderson	McGill	Stewart		
28/11/2020	LC	A	Alloa Athletic	0	1	AET	Gordon	Smith	Kingsley	Berra	Popescu	Lee>	Walker	Haring<	Halliday&	White*	Boyce+	Wighton*	Naismith+	Roberts&	Irving>	Henderson<	Brandon	Stewart	McGill	
05/12/2020	L	A	Morton	2	0		Gordon	Smith	Kingsley	Berra	Halkett	Lee	Walker	Irving*	Halliday	Naismith	Wighton+	Haring*	Roberts+	White	Henderson	Boyce	Popescu	Stewart		
12/12/2020	L	H	Queen of the South	6	1		Gordon	Smith	Kingsley	Berra	Halkett	Lee+	Walker	Irving	White*	Naismith&	Boyce	Frear*	Ginelly+	Halliday&	Popescu	Haring	Wighton	Stewart		
20/12/2020	SCF	N	Celtic	3	3	AET,3-4p	Gordon	Smith	Kingsley	Berra	Halkett	White&	Walker*	Irving<	Halliday>	Naismith	Boyce+	Ginnelly*	Wighton+	Lee&	Haring>	Frear<	Popescu	Roberts	Henderson	Stewart
26/12/2020	L	H	Ayr United	5	3		Gordon	Smith	Kingsley&	Berra	Halkett	Lee	Frear+	Irving	Halliday	Roberts*	Boyce	Naismith*	Wighton+	Haring&	Henderson	Walker	Popescu	Stewart		
29/12/2020	L	H	Arbroath	3	1		Gordon	Smith	Haring	Berra+	Halkett	Lee&	Wighton	Irving	Halliday	Naismith	Boyce*	Walker*	Frear+	Popescu&	Brandon	Roberts	Henderson	Stewart		
02/01/2021	L	A	Dundee	1	3		Gordon	Haring*	Kingsley	Berra	Halkett	Lee	Walker	Brandon	Halliday	Naismith	Wighton+	Irving*	Henderson+	Popescu	Moore	Roberts	Frear	Stewart		
16/01/2021	L	A	Alloa Athletic	3	1		Gordon	Smith	Kingsley	Berra	Halkett	Frear&	Walker	Roberts*	Halliday	Irving	Henderson+	Mackay-Steven*	Boyce+	Ginnelly&	Naismith	Popescu	Haring	Stewart		
23/01/2021	L	H	Raith Rovers	2	3		Gordon	Smith	Kingsley	Berra*	Halkett	Frear+	Mackay-Steven	Irving	Halliday&	Naismith	Boyce	Popescu*	Ginnelly+	Walker&	Henderson	Wighton	Haring	Stewart		
26/01/2021	L	A	Raith Rovers	4	0		Gordon	Smith	Kingsley	Popescu	Halkett	Ginnelly*	Walker	Irving	Halliday	Mackay-Steven&	Boyce+	Henderson*	Gnanduillet+	Naismith&	Frear	White	Haring	Stewart		
30/01/2020	L	H	Dunfermline Athletic	1	0		Gordon	Smith	Kingsley	Popescu	Halkett	Henderson+	Mackay-Steven*	Irving	Halliday	Naismith&	Boyce	White*	Gnanduillet+	Walker&	Frear	Berra	Haring	Stewart		
05/02/2021	L	A	Ayr United	1	0		Gordon	Smith	Kingsley	Popescu	Halkett	Walker	Mackay-Steven+	Irving&	Halliday	Gnanduillet*	Boyce	McEneff*	Kasteneer+	Naismith&	White	Berra	Haring	Stewart		
12/02/2021	L	A	Queen of the South	1	1		Gordon	Smith	Kingsley	Popescu	Halkett	Walker	Mackay-Steven	Irving+	Halliday&	Kastaneer*	Boyce	McEneff*	Henderson+	Naismith&	Frear	Berra	Haring	Stewart		
20/02/2021	L	H	Morton	1	1		Gordon	Smith	Kingsley	Popescu	Halkett	McEneff	Mackay-Steven&	Naismith	Halliday+	Kasteneer*	Boyce	Gnanduillet*	Walker+	Irving&	Henderson	Berra	Haring	Stewart		
26/02/2021	L	A	Inverness CT	1	1		Gordon	Smith&	Kingsley	Popescu	Halkett	McEneff	Mackay-Steven	Naismith+	Halliday	Kasteneer*	Boyce	Gnanduillet*	Walker+	Irving&	Henderson	Berra	Haring	Stewart		
06/03/2021	L	H	Dundee	2	1		Gordon	Smith	Kingsley	Popescu	Halkett	McEneff	Mackay-Steven*	Irving&	Halliday	Gnanduillet+	Boyce	Walker*	White+	Haring&	Henderson	Berra	Kasteneer	Stewart		
13/03/2021	L	H	Ayr United	2	0		Gordon	Smith	Kingsley	Popescu	Halkett	McEneff*	Mackay-Steven+	Irving	Halliday	Gnanduillet&	Boyce	Kasteneer*	Walker+	White&	Henderson	Berra	Frear	Stewart		
20/03/2021	L	A	Arbroath	0	0		Gordon	Smith	Kingsley&	Popescu	Halkett	McEneff*	Mackay-Steven+	Irving	Halliday	Gnanduillet	Boyce	White*	Kasteneer+	Walker&	Henderson	Berra	Frear	Stewart		
23/03/2021	SC	A	Brora Rangers	1	2		Stewart	Berra	White	Haring	Halkett	McEneff+	Mackay-Steven	Irving	Walker	Gnanduillet	Kasteneer*	Boyce*	Henderson+	Popescu	Frear	McGill	Souttar	Zlamal		
27/03/2021	L	H	Queen of the South	2	3		Stewart	Berra	White	Popescu	Halkett	McEneff+	Mackay-Steven*	Irving	Halliday	Gnanduillet	Boyce	Walker*	Henderson+	McGill	Frear	Kasteneer	Haring	Zlamal		
03/04/2021	L	A	Dunfermline Athletic	0	0		Gordon	Smith	White*	S Logan	Halkett	McEneff&	Mackay-Steven	Irving	Haring	Henderson+	Boyce	Popescu*	Naismith+	Gnanduillet&	Walker>	Souttar	McGill	Stewart		
19/04/2021	L	H	Alloa Athletic	6	0		Gordon	Smith	Souttar&	S Logan	Halkett	McEneff	Haring	Henderson*	Halliday	Gnanduillet	Boyce+	Naismith*	Mackay-Steven+	Walker&	Frear	Popescu	Irving	Stewart		
20/04/2021	L	A	Morton	0	0		Gordon	Smith	Souttar	S Logan*	Halkett	McEneff&	Haring	Henderson+	Halliday	Gnanduillet	Boyce	Mackay-Steven*	Naismith+	McGill&	Frear	Popescu	Irving	Stewart		
24/04/2021	L	H	Inverness CT	3	0		Gordon	Smith	Souttar	S Logan	Halkett	McEneff	Mackay-Steven&	Haring*	Halliday	Gnanduillet+	Boyce	Irving*	Naismith+	Pollock&	Popescu	McGill	Henderson	Stewart		
30/04/2021	L	A	Raith Rovers	4	0		Gordon	Smith*	Souttar	S Logan	Halkett	McEneff&	Mackay-Steven	Haring	Halliday	Henderson+	Boyce	Irving*	Naismith+	Pollock&	Popescu	Kasteneer	McGill	Stewart		

THE GOALIES

Goalkeepers Used in League Matches, 1970-2020

Players shown in the season of their first appearance only

1970/1	Jim Cruickshank
	Kenny Garland
1973/4	David Graham
1976/7	Brian Wilson
1977/8	Ray Dunlop
	John Brough
1978/9	Thomson Allan
1980/1	Ian Westwater
1981/2	Henry Smith
1986/7	Andy Bruce
1990/1	Nicky Walker
1992/3	Ian Baird
1994/5	Craig Nelson
1995/6	Gary O'Connor
	Gilles Rousset
	Myles Hogarth
1996/7	Roddy McKenzie
1999/0	Antii Niemi
2002/3	Teuvo Moilanen
2003/4	Craig Gordon
2005/6	Steven Banks
2007/8	Anthony Basso
	Eduardas Kurskis
2008/9	Marian Kello
	Janos Balogh
	Jamie MacDonald
2011/2	Mark Ridgers
2014/5	Neil Alexander
	Scott Gallacher
	Jack Hamilton
2016/7	Victor Noring
2017/8	Jon McLaughlin
2018/9	Zdenek Zlamal
	Colin Doyle
2019/0	Joel Pereira

Surname	First Name	Date of Birth	No	Nat	Pos	Signed	Previous		Contract	Lge			SC			LC			
										A	S	G	A	S	G	A	S	G	Un
Berra	Christophe	31/01/1985	6	SCO	D	2017	Ipswich Town	Released June 2021, joined Raith Rovers		9	0		2		1	2			10
Boyce	Liam	08/04/1991	10	NIR	F	2020	Burton Albion		End 2022/3	24	1	14	2	1	2	1			1
Brandon	Jamie	05/02/1998	25	SCO	D	2018	Hearts Youths		End 2021/2	1	0					4			6
Charleston-King	Jay	06/03/2003		SCO	F	2019	Hearts Youths		End 2021/2	0	0								0
Cochrane	Harry	24/04/2001		SCO	M	2014	Rangers Youths	OL to Montrose Oct-Jan, Released June 2021		0	0					1			1
Damour	Loic	08/01/1991	22	FRA	M	2019	Cardiff City		End 2022/3	0	0								0
Darge	Arron	26/04/2003		SCO	D	2019	Hearts Youths		End 2021/2	0	0								1
Denholm	Aidan	09/11/2003	49	SCO	M	2019	Hearts Youths		End 2021/2	0	0								1
Docherty	Sean	01/09/2003		ROI	D	2019	Hearts Youths	OL to Brechin City for 2021/2	End 2021/2	0	0								0
Doyle	Colin	12/06/1985		ROI	GK	2018	Bradford City	OL to Kilmarnock Aug-Jan, Released June 2021 joined Kilmarnock		0	0								0
Frear	Elliot	11/09/1990	24	ENG	M	2020	Forest Green Rovers	Released June 2021		5	3	2		1		2	1		12
Ginnelly	Josh	24/04/1997	30	ENG	F	2020	Preston North End (OL)	Sep-May		3	3	3		1	1	2	1		0
Gnanduillet	Armand	13/02/1992		FRA / CDI	F	2021	Altay SK (TUR)		End 2021/2	8	5	5	1						0
Gordon	Craig	31/12/1982	1	SCO	GK	2020	Celtic		End 2021/2	26	0		2			3			1
Haikett	Craig	29/05/1995	26	SCO	D	2019	Livingston		End 2021/2	27	0		3			2		1	1
Halliday	Andy	11/10/1991	16	SCO	M	2020	Rangers		End 2021/2	24	2	3	2			1	1		0
Hamilton	Christopher	13/07/2001		SCO	D	2009	Crossgates Primrose	OL to Dumbarton Sep-Jan, to Stirling Albion Jan-May	End 2021/2	0	0								0
Haring	Peter	02/06/1993	5	AUS	M	2018	SV Ried		End 2021/2	9	5	1	1	2		2	2		10
Henderson	Euan	29/06/2000	31	SCO	F	2020	Hearts Youths		End 2021/2	6	4	3		2		2	2		14
Irving	Andy	13/05/2000	19	SCO	M	2019	Hearts Youths	OOC June , joined Turkgucu Munchen		16	7	2	2	1		2	1	1	3
Kasteneer	Gervane	09/06/1996		NET / CUR	F	2021	Coventry City (OL)	Feb-May		3	3		1						3
Kingsley	Stephen	23/07/1994	21	SCO	D	2020	Hull City		End 2021/2	20	0	4	2		1	2	2		0
Lawler	Mckenzie	01/12/2002	54	SCO	F	2018	Hearts Youths	Released June 2021		0	0								0
Lee	Olly	11/07/1991	8	ENG	M	2018	Luton Town	OL to Gillingham Jan-May, Released June 2021 joined Gillingham		9	1	1	1	1		4	1	2	0
Logan	Cammy	28/01/2002	37	SCO	D	2020	Hearts Youths		End 2021/2	0	0								1
Logan	Shay	29/01/1988		ENG	D	2021	Aberdeen (OL)	Mar-May		5	0								0
Mackay-Steven	Gary	31/08/1990		SCO	M	2021	New York City		End 2022/3	14	3	4	1						0
Makovora	Leeroy	05/02/2002		SCO	F	2018	Hearts Youths	OL to Brechin City Sep-Nov, to Gala FR Dec-Jan, Released June 2021		0	0								0
McEneff	Aaron	09/07/1995		NIR	M	2021	Shamrock Rovers		End 2022/3	11	2	2	1						0
McGill	Scott	27/01/2002	36	SCO	M	2020	Hearts Youths			0	1					3			8
Moore	Lewis	04/06/1998	27	SCO	M	2018	Hearts Youths	OL to Arbroath Feb-May, Released June 2021 joined Queen's Park		0	0					1			4
Naismith	Steven	14/09/1986	14	SCO	F	2019	Norwich City	Retired July 2021		11	9	6	1	1		2	2		3
Pollock	Finlay	01/01/2005	54	SCO	M	2021	Hearts Youths		End 2021/2	0	2								0
Popescu	Mihail	07/05/1993	28	ROM	D	2020	Dinamo Bucharest	ex St Mirren	End 2021/2	14	4	1	1			4	1		11
Roberts	Jordan	05/01/1994	11	ENG	M	2020	Ipswich Town	OL to Motherwell Feb-May	End 2021/2	4	2		1			1	3		3
Sandison	Jay	05/03/2001		SCO	D	2016	Hearts Youths	Freed Jan 2021 joined Cowdenbeath		0	0								0
Schiavone	Ryan	07/05/2003		SCO	F	2019	Hearts Youths		End 2021/2	0	0								0
Smith	Michael	04/09/1988	2	NIR	D	2017	Peterborough United		End 2021/2	25	0	2	2			1			0
Smith	Connor	01/01/2002		SCO	F	2018	Hearts Youths	OL to Arbroath Sep-Jan, to Cove R Jan-May	End 2021/2	0	0								0
Souttar	John	25/09/1996	4	SCO	D	2016	Dundee United		End 2021/2	4	0								2
Spratt	Harris	13/11/2003		SCO	GK	2019	Hearts Youths		End 2021/2	0	0								0
Stewart	Ross	16/04/1995	13	SCO	GK	2020	Livingston (OL)	Sep-Jan		1	0		1			2			30
Stone	Harry	20/04/2002		SCO	GK	2015	Spartans	OL to Stirling Alb Oct, to Spartans Oct-Jan, to Albion Rov Mar-May, OL to Partick Th for 2021/2	End 2021/2	0	0								0
Walker	Jamie	25/06/1993	7	SCO	M	2019	Wigan Athletic		End 2021/2	10	12	7	3			3	1	1	1
White	Aidy	10/10/1991	3	ROI / ENG	D	2019	Barnsley	Released June 2021		3	7		2	1		5			5
Wighton	Craig	27/07/1997	15	SCO	F	2018	Dundee	OL to Dunfermline Ath Feb-May, Made Permanent June 2021		5	3	3	1	1	1	3	2	3	3
Zlamal	Zdenek	05/11/1985	23	CZR	GK	2018	FC Zlin	OL to St Mirren Sep 12-20, to St Johnstone May, released June 2021		0	0								4
NEW SIGNINGS																			
Cochrane	Alex					2021	Brighton (OL)	Jul-Jun	End 2021/2										
Ginnelly	Josh	24/04/1997		ENG	F	2021	Preston North End		End 2022/3										
Stewart	Ross	16/04/1995		SCO	GK	2021	Livingston		End 2022/3										

PHOTOCARDS

No. 91.

HEART OF MIDLOTHIAN F.C.

Left to right, back row:—W. Russell, W. Reid (Capt.), Andrew Anderson, J. Harkness, A. Herd, J. Harvey, J. Kerr (Trainer). Front row:—R. Murray, T. Walker, Alex. Anderson, G. Robson, A. Black.

Also known as "Edinboro' Darlings," this club can be said to have introduced football into the capital of Scotland. Formed in 1873, the team has always provided first-class football. They have won the Scottish Cup on four occasions; first in 1895-96, and last in season 1905-06, and won the League Championship twice.

Expanding de Luxe Albums for Ardath Photocards on sale at Tobacconists Price 6d

ARDATH TOBACCO CO. LTD. Manufacturers of STATE EXPRESS and ARDATH CIGARETTES

D

Hibernian FC 2020/21 The Hibees

Founded	1875
Ground	Easter Road Stadium
Postcode	EH7 5QG
Tel	0131 661 2159
Capacity	20421
Closest Railway Station	Edinburgh Waverley
Record Attendance	65860 v Hearts, Lge, 2/1/1950
Record Win	15-1 v Peebles Rovers, SC, 11/2/1961
Record Defeat	0-10 v Rangers, Lge, 24/12/1898
Most League Goals in a Season	42 Joe Baker, 1959/60
Colours 2020/21 Top	Green
Shorts	White
Sponsor	Thank You NHS
Manufacturer	Macron
Change Colours 2020/21 Top	Black
Shorts	Black
Nicknames	Hibees
Web	www.hibernianfc.co.uk
Match Programme 2020/21	Curtis Sport

Board of Directors
Executive Chairman: Ronald Gordon
Directors: David Davies, Jemma Goba, Kathrin Hamilton, Brian Houston, Gillian Hutchison. Bruce Langham, Malcolm MacPherson, Archie Paton
Secretary: Christopher Gaunt

Football Staff
Head Coach: Jack Ross
Assistant Head Coach: John Potter
Coach: David Gray
Goalkeeper Coach: Craig Samson
Head of Football Operations: Finlay Stark
Head of Academy Coaching; Eddie May
Head of Sports Medicine & Science: Nathan Ring
Strength & Conditioning Coach: Colin Clancy
Sporting Director: Graeme Mathie

Despite finishing third in the Premiership there are some Hibs fans who feel that season 2020/1 was a disappointment. That notion is largely based on Cup performances. Hibs started with a delayed Semi Final from the 2019/20 season, against local rivals and now Championship side Hearts. They lost 2-1 in extra time. Next, after cruising through their League Cup section they progressed to the Semi Final, coming up against St Johnstone. Hibs were strong favourites – and lost 3-0. Finally it was the current season's version of the Scottish Cup. Hibs went through the rounds to reach the Final where they came up against St Johnstone for the second time – and lost 1-0.

So, third place in the League plus a Cup Final and two Semi Finals equates to failure? Of course not, but it was the manner of the defeats in the Cups, especially in the Scottish Cup Final, that upset the Hibernian support. They felt that their side hadn't turned up on such an important day.

Being "best of the rest" in the premiership table is all very well but critics would say that the opposition was fairly feeble. Aberdeen had a dismal season and nobody else came close to them. Hibs failed to get any wins in eight meetings with the two teams above them emphasising the gap that they must aim to narrow.

STAR MAN
Kevin Nisbet came in from Dunfermline and demonstrated that he could carry his goalscoring form from the lower leagues into the Premiership. Indeed, he performed well enough to earn a call-up to the Scotland squad and appearances in the delayed Euro 2020 Finals.

PROSPECTS 2021/2
It will be hard for Hibs to match their performances from 2020/1. The support will expect them to challenge for third place again and to perform much better if they do get to the later stages of any of the Cup competitions. With Hearts back in the League it will be harder for Hibs – their city rivals potentially taking points off them and pushing them hard.

Date	Comp	H/A	Opponents	F	A		HT		Referee	Crowd	Scorers
01/08/2020	L	H	Kilmarnock	2	1		2	1	J Beaton	BCD	Boyle 2
08/08/2020	L	A	Livingston	4	1		3	0	E Anderson	BCD	Nisbet 3 (1 pen), Doidge
11/08/2020	L	A	Dundee United	1	0		0	0	D Robertson	BCD	Doidge
15/08/2020	L	H	Motherwell	0	0		0	0	G Aitken	BCD	
23/08/2020	L	A	St Johnstone	1	0		0	0	J Beaton	BCD	Mallan pen
30/08/2020	L	H	Aberdeen	0	1		0	1	N Walsh	BCD	
12/09/2020	L	A	St Mirren	3	0		2	0	W Collum	BCD	Nisbet, Newell, Boyle
20/09/2020	L	H	Rangers	2	2		1	1	D Robertson	BCD	Wright, Doidge
27/09/2020	L	A	Celtic	0	3		0	2	S McLean	BCD	
02/10/2020	L	H	Hamilton Accies	3	2		2	0	B Madden	BCD	Nisbet 2, Hanlon
07/10/2020	**LC**	**H**	**Brora Rangers**	**3**	**1**		**2**	**0**	**A Muir**	**BCD**	**Mallan 2, Hanlon**
10/10/2020	**LC**	**A**	**Cove Rangers**	**2**	**1**		**0**	**1**	**E Anderson**	**BCD**	**Gullan, Doidge**
13/10/2020	**LC**	**A**	**Forfar Athletic**	**1**	**0**		**0**	**0**	**D Munro**	**BCD**	**Gray**
17/10/2020	L	A	Ross County	0	0		0	0	N Walsh	BCD	
24/10/2020	L	A	Kilmarnock	1	0		1	0	C Steven	BCD	Nisbet pen
31/10/2020	**SCSF**	**N**	**Hearts**	**1**	**2**	**AET**	**0**	**0**	**W Collum**	**BCD**	**Doidge**
06/11/2020	L	A	Aberdeen	0	2		0	2	E Anderson	BCD	
15/11/2020	**LC**	**H**	**Dundee**	**4**	**1**		**1**	**0**	**J Beaton**	**BCD**	**Mallan, Nisbet, Gullan, Hallberg**
21/11/2020	L	H	Celtic	2	2		0	0	B Madden	BCD	Murphy, Nisbet
24/11/2020	L	H	St Johnstone	2	2		1	1	K Clancy	BCD	P McGinn 2
28/11/2020	**LC**	**H**	**Dundee**	**1**	**0**		**1**	**0**	**W Collum**	**BCD**	**Murphy**
05/12/2020	L	A	Motherwell	3	0		0	0	A Dallas	BCD	Boyle, Doidge, S McGinn
12/12/2020	L	A	Hamilton Accies	4	0		2	0	K Clancy	BCD	Boyle pen, Doidge, P McGinn, Nisbet
15/12/2020	**LC**	**A**	**Alloa Athletic**	**2**	**1**	**AET**	**0**	**1**	**D Munro**	**BCD**	**Doidge, Jamieson og**
19/12/2020	L	H	Dundee United	1	1		1	0	G Duncan	BCD	Magennis
23/12/2020	L	H	St Mirren	1	0		1	0	S Kirkland	BCD	Nisbet
26/12/2020	L	A	Rangers	0	1		0	1	W Collum	BCD	
30/12/2020	L	H	Ross County	0	2		0	1	D Robertson	BCD	
02/01/2021	L	H	Livingston	0	3		0	2	D Munro	BCD	
11/01/2021	L	A	Celtic	1	1		0	0	N Walsh ???	BCD	Nisbet
16/01/2021	L	H	Kilmarnock	2	0		0	0	W Collum	BCD	Power og, Gogic
23/01/2021	**LC**	**N**	**St Johnstone**	**0**	**3**		**0**	**1**	**N Walsh**	**BCD**	
27/01/2021	L	H	Rangers	0	1		0	1	K Clancy	BCD	
30/01/2021	L	A	Dundee United	2	0		1	0	G Duncan	BCD	McGregor, Boyle
02/02/2021	L	A	St Mirren	2	1		0	0	A Muir	BCD	Porteous, Boyle pen
06/02/2021	L	H	Aberdeen	2	0		1	0	W Collum	BCD	Boyle 2 (1 pen)
20/02/2021	L	H	Hamilton Accies	2	0		1	0	C Napier	BCD	Boyle, Doig
27/02/2021	L	H	Motherwell	0	2		0	1	A Muir	BCD	
06/03/2021	L	A	St Johnstone	0	1		0	1	D Dickinson	BCD	
13/03/2021	L	A	Ross County	2	1		0	0	J Beaton	BCD	Boyle pen, Nisbet
20/03/2021	L	A	Livingston	1	1		1	1	N Walsh	BCD	Doidge
05/04/2021	**SC**	**A**	**Queen of the South**	**3**	**1**		**1**	**0**	**W Collum**	**BCD**	**Doidge 2, Boyle**
11/04/2021	L	A	Rangers	1	2		0	1	D Robertson	BCD	Nisbet
18/04/2021	**SC**	**A**	**Stranraer**	**4**	**0**		**1**	**0**	**D Munro**	**BCD**	**Boyle 2 (1 pen), Nisbet, Doidge**
21/04/2021	L	H	Livingston	2	1		2	0	C Napier	BCD	Nisbet, Boyle pen
24/04/2021	**SC**	**H**	**Motherwell**	**2**	**2**	**AET, 4-2p**	**0**	**0**	**J Beaton**	**BCD**	**Doidge, Irvine**
01/05/2021	L	H	St Johnstone	0	1		0	1	G Aitken	BCD	
08/05/2021	**SC**	**N**	**Dundee United**	**2**	**0**		**1**	**0**	**B Madden**	**BCD**	**Nisbet, Doidge**
12/05/2021	L	A	Aberdeen	1	0		1	0	J Beaton	BCD	Doidge
15/05/2021	L	H	Celtic	0	0		0	0	W Collum	BCD	
22/05/2021	**SC**	**N**	**St Johnstone**	**0**	**1**		**0**	**1**	**N Walsh**	**BCD**	

Date	Comp	H/A	Opponents	F	A		1	2	3	4	5	6	7	8	9
01/08/2020	L	H	Kilmarnock	2	1		Marciano	Hanlon	P McGinn	Gogic	Porteous	Doig+	Boyle	Allan*	Newell
08/08/2020	L	A	Livingston	4	1		Marciano	Hanlon	P McGinn	Gogic	Porteous	Doig	Boyle	Horgan*	Newell
11/08/2020	L	A	Dundee United	1	0		Marciano	Hanlon	P McGinn	Gogic	Porteous	Doig	Boyle	Horgan*	Newell+
15/08/2020	L	H	Motherwell	0	0		Marciano	Hanlon	P McGinn	Gogic	Porteous	Doig&	Boyle	Horgan*	Newell+
23/08/2020	L	A	St Johnstone	1	0		Marciano	Hanlon	P McGinn	Gogic	Porteous	Doig&	Boyle	Horgan*	Newell>
30/08/2020	L	H	Aberdeen	0	1		Marciano	Hanlon	P McGinn	Hallberg&	Porteous	Doig+	Boyle	Wright	Newell
12/09/2020	L	A	St Mirren	3	0		Marciano	Hanlon	P McGinn	Gogic	Porteous	Doig	Boyle>	Murphy+	Newell&
20/09/2020	L	H	Rangers	2	2		Marciano	Hanlon	P McGinn	Gogic	Porteous	Doig*	Boyle	Wright+	Newell
27/09/2020	L	A	Celtic	0	3		Marciano	Hanlon	P McGinn	Gogic	Porteous	Doig*	Boyle	Wright+	Newell
02/10/2020	L	H	Hamilton Accies	3	2		Marciano	Hanlon	P McGinn	Gogic	Porteous	Stevenson	Boyle	Murphy+	Newell*
07/10/2020	LC	H	Brora Rangers	3	1		Barnes	Hanlon	Gray	S McGinn+	McGregor	Stevenson	Mallan	Murphy*	Hallberg>
10/10/2020	LC	A	Cove Rangers	2	1		Barnes	Wright*	Gray	S McGinn+	McGregor	Stevenson	Mallan	Boyle	Hallberg
13/10/2020	LC	A	Forfar Athletic	1	0		Barnes	Mackie	Gray	S McGinn	McGregor	Magennis*	Mallan	Shanley+	Hallberg
17/10/2020	L	A	Ross County	0	0		Marciano	Hanlon	P McGinn	Gogic	Porteous	Stevenson+	Boyle	Magennis*	Newell
24/10/2020	L	A	Kilmarnock	1	0		Marciano	Hanlon	P McGinn	Gogic	Porteous	Stevenson*	Boyle	Mallan&	Newell
31/10/2020	SCSF	N	Hearts	1	2	AET	Marciano	Hanlon	P McGinn	Gogic&	Porteous	Doig+	Boyle	Magennis*	Newell
06/11/2020	L	A	Aberdeen	0	2		Marciano	Hanlon	P McGinn	Gogic	Porteous	Doig	Boyle	Murphy+	Newell*
15/11/2020	LC	H	Dundee	4	1		Barnes	Hanlon	P McGinn	McGregor	Wright	Doig	Boyle	Murphy	Newell
21/11/2020	L	H	Celtic	2	2		Marciano	Hanlon	P McGinn	Gogic	Porteous	Mackie	Boyle	Murphy*	Newell&
24/11/2020	L	H	St Johnstone	2	2		Marciano	Hanlon*	P McGinn	Gogic+	Porteous	Mackie	Boyle	Murphy	Newell
28/11/2020	LC	H	Dundee	1	0		Marciano	Murphy&	P McGinn	McGregor	Porteous	Mackie	Boyle	Doidge	Newell
05/12/2020	L	A	Motherwell	3	0		Marciano	Hanlon	P McGinn	Stevenson	Porteous	Hallberg+	Boyle	Murphy&	Newell
12/12/2020	L	A	Hamilton Accies	4	0		Marciano	Hanlon	P McGinn	Stevenson	Porteous	Hallberg+	Boyle<	Wright&	Newell>
15/12/2020	LC	A	Alloa Athletic	2	1	AET	Marciano	Hanlon	P McGinn	Stevenson	Porteous	Hallberg*	Boyle	Wright+	Newell
19/12/2020	L	H	Dundee United	1	1		Marciano	Hanlon	P McGinn	Stevenson	Porteous	Hallberg+	Boyle	Magennis*	Newell
23/12/2020	L	H	St Mirren	1	0		Marciano+	Hanlon	P McGinn	Stevenson	Porteous	Hallberg>	Boyle	Magennis*	Newell
26/12/2020	L	A	Rangers	0	1		Barnes	Hanlon	P McGinn	Gogic	Porteous	Doig	Boyle	Hallberg	Newell
30/12/2020	L	H	Ross County	0	2		Barnes	Hanlon	P McGinn	Hallberg&	Porteous	Doig*	Boyle	Wright+	Newell
02/01/2021	L	H	Livingston	0	3		Barnes	Hanlon	P McGinn	Stevenson&	Porteous	Gogic*	Boyle	Mallan	Newell
11/01/2021	L	A	Celtic	1	1		Macey	Hanlon	P McGinn	Doig*	Porteous	Gogic	Wright+	Hallberg>	Newell&
16/01/2021	L	H	Kilmarnock	2	0		Macey	Hanlon	P McGinn	Doig	Porteous	Gogic	Boyle+	Hallberg	Irvine*
23/01/2021	LC	N	St Johnstone	0	3		Marciano	Hanlon	P McGinn	Doig	Porteous	Gogic+	Boyle	Cadden*	Irvine
27/01/2021	L	H	Rangers	0	1		Marciano	McGregor	P McGinn	Doig+	Porteous*	Gogic>	Hallberg&	Cadden	Irvine
30/01/2021	L	A	Dundee United	2	0		Marciano	Hanlon	P McGinn	Doig	McGregor	Gogic	Boyle+	Cadden	Irvine
02/02/2021	L	A	St Mirren	2	1		Marciano	Hanlon	P McGinn	Doig	McGregor*	Gogic	Boyle	Cadden+	Irvine
06/02/2021	L	H	Aberdeen	2	0		Marciano	Hanlon	P McGinn	Doig*	McGregor	Gogic	Boyle	Cadden	Irvine+
20/02/2021	L	H	Hamilton Accies	2	0		Marciano	Hanlon	P McGinn	Doig>	McGregor	Newell&	Boyle	Cadden	Irvine
27/02/2021	L	H	Motherwell	0	2		Marciano	Halon	P McGinn	Stevenson+	McGregor&	Newell&	Boyle	Cadden	Irvine>
06/03/2021	L	A	St Johnstone	0	1		Marciano	Hanlon	P McGinn	Doig	Porteous	Gogic	Boyle	Cadden*	Irvine+
13/03/2021	L	A	Ross County	2	1		Marciano	Hanlon	P McGinn	Doig+	Porteous	Gogic	Boyle	Cadden*	Irvine
20/03/2021	L	A	Livingston	1	1		Marciano	Hanlon	P McGinn	Doig	Porteous	Gogic	Boyle	Doidge	Irvine
05/04/2021	SC	A	Queen of the South	3	1		Macey	Hanlon	P McGinn	Doig	Porteous	Gogic	Boyle+	Doidge&	Irvine*
11/04/2021	L	A	Rangers	1	2		Marciano	Hanlon	P McGinn	Doig	Porteous	Gogic&	Boyle	Doidge*	Irvine+
18/04/2021	SC	A	Stranraer	4	0		Macey	Hanlon	P McGinn	Doig+	Porteous	Magennis*	Boyle	Doidge	Irvine
21/04/2021	L	H	Livingston	2	1		Marciano	Hanlon	P McGinn	Stevenson	Porteous	Gogic	Boyle	Doidge*	Irvine
24/04/2021	SC	H	Motherwell	2	2	AET, 4-2p	Macey	Hanlon	P McGinn	Doig&	Porteous	Gogic	Boyle	Doidge*	Irvine
01/05/2021	L	H	St Johnstone	0	1		Marciano	Hanlon	P McGinn	Doig>	Porteous	Gogic+	Boyle	Doidge	Irvine
08/05/2021	SC	N	Dundee United	2	0		Macey	Hanlon	P McGinn	Doig	Porteous+	Hallberg	Boyle	Doidge	Irvine
12/05/2021	L	A	Aberdeen	1	0		Macey	Hanlon	P McGinn	Doig&	McGregor	Gogic	Boyle	Doidge	Irvine
15/05/2021	L	H	Celtic	0	0		Marciano	Gray>	Stevenson	McGregor	Porteous	Gogic	Murphy+	Hallberg*	Wright&
22/05/2021	SC	N	St Johnstone	0	1		Macey	Hanlon	P McGinn	Doig&	Porteous	Gogic*	Boyle	Doidge	Irvine

THE GOALIES

Goalkeepers Used in League Matches, 1970-2020

Players shown in the season of their first appearance only

1970/1	Gordon Marshall
	Roy Baines
1971/2	Jim Herriot
1972/3	Jim McArthur
1973/4	Roddy McKenzie
1974/5	Hugh Whyte
1975/6	Mike McDonald
1979/0	David Huggins
1980/1	Colin Kelly
1981/2	Robin Rae
1982/3	Alan Rough
1986/7	Tom Carson
1987/8	Andy Goram
1989/0	Chris Reid
1991/2	John Burridge
1993/4	Jim Leighton
1997/8	Ole Gottskalsson
	Bryan Gunn
1999/0	Nick Colgan
2000/1	Mike Franks
2001/2	Tony Caig
2002/3	Daniel Anderson
2004/5	Simon Brown
2005/6	Zbigniew Malkowski
2006/7	Andy McNeil
2007/8	Yves Ma'kalambay
2008/9	Grzegorz Szamotulski
2009/0	Graham Stack
	Graeme Smith
2010/1	Mark Brown
	Jakub Divis
2011/2	Paul Grant
2012/3	Ben Williams
	Sean Murdoch
2014/5	Mark Oxley
	Kleton Pemtreou
2015/6	Conrad Logan
2016/7	Ofir Marciano
	Ross Laidlaw
2017/8	Cammy Bell
2018/9	Adam Bogdan
2019/0	Chris Maxwell

10	11	12	13	14	15	16	17	18	19	20
Wright&	Nisbet>	Horgan*	Doidge+	Stevenson&	Hallberg>	F Murray	Gray	McGregor	Gullan	Dabrowski
Doidge	Nisbet+	Hallberg*	Gullan+	Stevenson	Allan	F Murray	Gray	McGregor	Stirling	Dabrowski
Doidge	Nisbet	Allan*	Hallberg+	Stevenson	Gullan	F Murray	Gray	McGregor	Stirling	Dabrowski
Doidge	Nisbet	Allan*	Hallberg+	Stevenson&	Gullan	Mallan	Gray	McGregor	Stirling	Dabrowski
Doidge	Allan+	Wright*	Mallan+	Gullan&	Hallberg>	F Murray	Gray	McGregor	Stevenson	Dabrowski
Doidge	Allan*	Murphy*	Mallan+	Gullan&	Stevenson	F Murray	Gray	McGregor	Stirling	Dabrowski
Doidge	Nisbet*	Gullan*	Wright+	Mallan&	Shanley>	Hallberg	Gray	McGregor	Stevenson	Barnes
Doidge	Nisbet	Stevenson*	Hallberg+	Mallan	Shanley	Gullan	Gray	McGregor	S McGinn	Barnes
Doidge&	Nisbet	Stevenson*	Murphy+	Mallan&	Shanley	Gullan	Gray	McGregor	Hallberg	Barnes
Doidge	Nisbet&	Hallberg*	Wright+	Mallan&	Shanley	Gullan	Gray	McGregor	Doig	Barnes
Wright&	Gullan	Boyle*	Magennis+	Doidge&	Nisbet>	P McGinn	Mackie	Bradley	Shanley	Samson
Doidge	Nisbet	Gullan*	Magennis+	Bradley	Mackie	Shanley	Samson			
Doidge&	Gullan	Boyle*	Nisbet+	Bradley&	Samson					
Doidge	Nisbet	Mallan*	Gullan+	Hallberg	Shanley	S McGinn	Gray	McGregor	Mackie	Barnes
Doidge	Nisbet+	Doig*	Magennis+	Hallberg&	Bradley	S McGinn	Gray	McGregor	Gullan	Barnes
Doidge	Nisbet	Murphy*	Mackie+	Mallan&	Wright	Hallberg	Gray	McGregor	Gullan	Barnes
Doidge	Nisbet&	Mallan*	Wright+	Gullan&	S McGinn	Hallberg	Gray	McGregor	Mackie	Barnes
Mallan	Nisbet	Gullan*	Mackie+	Hallberg&	S McGinn>	Bradley<	Gray	Shanley	Samson	
Mallan+	Nisbet	Gray*	Hallberg+	S McGinn&	Wright	Gullan	Bradley	McGregor	Doig	Barnes
Mallan	Nisbet&	McGregor*	Doidge+	Gullan&	S McGinn	Hallberg	Gray	Wright	Doig	Barnes
Mallan*	Nisbet+	Hallberg*	Gullan+	Wright&	S McGinn	Gogic	Gray	Bradley	Doig	Barnes
Wright*	Nisbet	Doidge*	S McGinn+	Gullan&	Mallan	Doig	Gray	Bradley	McGregor	Barnes
Doidge	Nisbet*	Gullan*	Magennis+	Mallan&	S McGinn>	Bradley<	Gray	McGregor	Doig	Barnes
Doidge	Gullan	Magennis*	Mallan+	S McGinn	Bradley	Doig	Gray	McGregor	Barnes	
Doidge	Nisbet	Wright*	Gogic+	S McGinn	Bradley	Doig	Gray	McGregor	Gullan	Barnes
Doidge	Nisbet&	Wright*	Barnes+	Gullan&	Gogic>	Doig	Gray	McGregor	S McGinn	Bradley
Wright*	Nisbet	Gullan*	McGregor	S McGinn	Stevenson	Bradley	Gray	Samson		
Doidge	Nisbet	Stevenson*	Gullan+	S McGinn&	Gogic	Bradley	Gray	McGregor	Samson	
Doidge+	Nisbet	Murphy*	Gullan+>	Doig&	Wright>	S McGinn	Gray	McGregor	Hallberg	Samson
Murphy	Nisbet	Stevenson*	Doidge+	Mallan&	S McGinn>	Gullan	Gray	McGregor	Bradley	Dabrowski
Murphy>	Nisbet&	Doidge*	Cadden+	Mallan&	Gullan>	Wright	Gray	McGregor	Stevenson	Dabrowski
Murphy&	Nisbet	Doidge*	Magennis+	Allan&	Hallberg	Wright	Gullan	McGregor	Stevenson	Macey
Doidge	Nisbet	Hanlon*	Boyle+	Magennis&	Allan>	Wright	Gullan	Mallan	Stevenson	Macey
Doidge	Murphy*	Magennis*	Wright+	Hallberg	Allan	Nisbet	Gullan	Porteous	Stevenson	Macey
Doidge	Murphy&	Porteous*	Nisbet+	Magennis&	Allan	Hallberg	Wright	Bradley	Stevenson	Macey
Doidge&	Murphy&	Stevenson*	Magennis+	Hallberg&	Nisbet>	Porteous	Gray	Wright	Allan	Macey
Doidge+	Murphy*	Nisbet*	Allan+	Gogic&	Stevenson>	Porteous	Gray	Wright	Hallberg	Macey
Doidge	Murphy*	Nisbet*	Gogic+	Porteous&	Allan>	Bradley	Gray	Wright	Hallberg	Macey
Newell&	Nisbet	Doidge*	Murphy+	Hallberg&	Allan	McGregor	Gray	Wright	Stevenson	Macey
Newell	Doidge&	Nisbet*	Stevenson+	McGregor&	Allan	Magennis	Gray	Wright	Hallberg	Macey
Newell	Nisbet	Cadden	Stevenson	McGregor	Allan	Magennis	Gray	Wright	Hallberg	Macey
Newell	Nisbet	Magennis*	Cadden+	Wright&	Bradley	McGregor	Gray	Stevenson	Hallberg	Dabrowski
Newell	Nisbet	Cadden*	Magennis+	Hallberg&	Stevenson	McGregor	Gray	Wright	Laidlaw	Macey
Newell&	Nisbet	Wright*	Stevenson+	Hallberg&	Gogic	McGregor	Gray	Laidlaw	Marciano	
Newell+	Nisbet	Wright*	Magennis+	Hallberg	Bradley	McGregor	Gray	Macey		
Newell+	Nisbet	Wright*	Hallberg+	Stevenson&	Bradley	McGregor	Gray	Magennis	Marciano	
Newell&	Wright*	Magennis*	Hallberg+	Bradley&	Stevenson>	McGregor	Gray	Macey		
Newell*	Nisbet&	Magennis*	McGregor+	Murphy&	Stevenson	Laidlaw	Gray	Wright	Marciano	
Hallberg*	Nisbet+	Magennis*	Stevenson+	Murphy&	Porteous	Wright	Gray	Newell	Dabrowski	
Newell	Magennis	Doidge*	Irvine+	Doig&	P McGinn>	Nisbet	Hanlon	Boyle	Macey	Dabrowski
Newell+	Nisbet	Murphy*	Hallberg+	Stevenson&	Magennis	Wright	GRay	McGregor	Marciano	

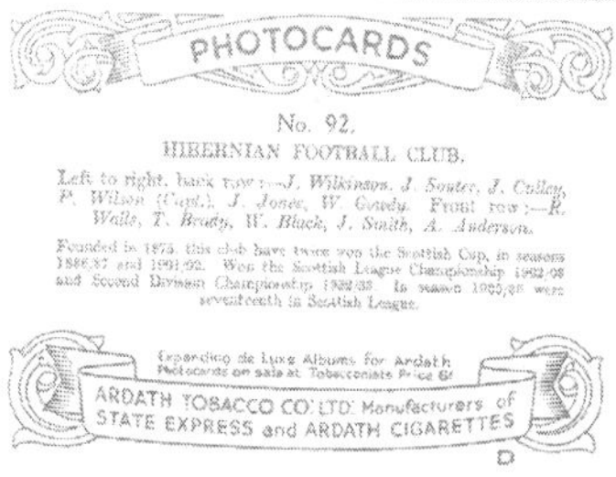
PHOTOCARDS

No. 92.

HIBERNIAN FOOTBALL CLUB.

Left to right, back row:—J. Wilkinson, J. Souter, J. Culley, P. Wilson (Capt.), J. Jones, W. Goody. Front row:—R. Walls, T. Brady, W. Black, J. Smith, A. Anderson.

Founded in 1875, this club have twice won the Scottish Cup, in seasons 1886/87 and 1901/02. Won the Scottish League Championship 1902/03 and Second Division Championship 1932/33. In season 1935/36 were seventeenth in Scottish League.

Expanding de Luxe Albums for Ardath Photocards on sale at Tobacconists Price 6

ARDATH TOBACCO CO. LTD. Manufacturers of STATE EXPRESS and ARDATH CIGARETTES

D

Surname	First Name	Date of Birth	No	Nat	Pos	Signed	Previous	Notes	Contract	Lge A	Lge S	Lge G	SC A	SC S	SC G	LC A	LC S	LC G	Un
Aitken	Murray		52	SCO	M	2020	Hibernian Youths		End 2021/2										
Allan	Scott	28/11/1991	23	SCO	M	2019	Celtic	OL to Inverness CT Apr-May	End 2021/2	3	5						1		7
Barnes	Dillon	08/04/1996		ENG	GK	2020	QPR (OL)	Sep-Jan		3	1					4			15
Blaney	Jacob	08/09/2004	46	SCO	M	2020	Hibernian Youths		End 2021/2	0	0								0
Block	Tommy	23/12/1999		ENG	D	2019	Bognor Regis Town	Freed Sep 2020, joined Woking		0	0								0
Boyle	Martin	25/04/1993	10	AUS	F	2015	Dundee		End 2022/3	35	1	12	6		3	5	2		1
Bradley	Steven	17/03/2002	43	SCO	F	2020	Hibernian Youths		End 2021/2	0	2						2		17
Brydon	Jack	01/01/2004	47	SCO	D	2020	Hibernian Youths	OL to CSS Oct-Jan, then Stenhousemuir Mar-May	End 2021/2	0	0								0
Cadden	Chris	19/09/1996	27	SCO	M	2021	Columbus Crew		End 2022/3	8	2			1		1			1
Campbell	Josh	06/05/2000	32	SCO	M	2018	Hibernian Youths	IL to Edinburgh City Sep-May	End 2021/2	0	0								0
Currie	Josh	07/01/2003	45	SCO	F	2020	Hibernian Youths	OL to CSStrollers 2021/2	End 2021/2	0	0								0
Dabrowski	Maciej	09/01/1998	21	POL	GK	2018	Hibernian Youths	OL to Dumbarton Aug-Jan	End 2022/3	0	0								11
Doidge	Christian	25/08/1992	9	WAL	F	2019	Forest Green Rovers		End 2021/2	29	7	7	6		6	4	2	2	0
Doig	Josh	18/05/2002	25	SCO	D	2019	Hibernian Youths		End 2024/5	25	3	1	6			2			9
Elder	Steven		43					Freed July 2020		0	0								0
Fairley	Jayden	22/09/2003	42	SCO	M	2019	Hibernian Youths	OL to Stenhousemuir Oct-May	End 2021/2	0	0								0
Gallantes	Yrick	14/01/2001	44	PHI / SCO	M	2018	Hibernian Youths	OL to Azkals DT (Philippines) Oct-Jun, OL to CSStrollers 2021/2	End 2021/2	0	0								0
Gogic	Alex	13/04/1994	13	CYP / SER	M	2020	Hamilton Accies		End 2021/2	30	4	1	4			1			3
Gray	David	04/05/1988	2	SCO	D	2014	Burton Albion	Retired July 2021		1	1					3		1	42
Gullan	Jamie	02/07/1999	19	SCO	F	2015	Hearts Youths	OL to Raith Rovers Feb-May	End 2021/2	0	14					3	3	2	14
Hallberg	Melker	20/10/1995	20	SWE	M	2019	Vejle BK		End 2021/2	12	13		1	3		4	2	1	16
Hamilton	Robbie		48	SCO	M	2020	Hibernian Youths		End 2021/2	0	0								0
Hanlon	Paul	20/01/1990	4	SCO	D	2008	Hibernian Youths		End 2021/2	36	1	1	6			4		1	1
Horgan	Daryl	10/08/1992	7	ROI	M	2018	Preston North End	Transferred to Wycombe Wanderers Sep 2020		4	1								0
Irvine	Jackson	07/05/1993	36	AUS	M	2021	Hull City	OOC June 2021, joined FC St Pauli		14	1		5		1	1			0
Jackson	Adam	18/05/1994	18	ENG	D	2019	Barnsley	Freed Aug 2020 joined Lincoln City		0	0								0
James	Tom	15/04/1996	17	WAL	D	2019	Yeovil Town	OL Wigan Ath Sep-Jan, to Salford City Jan-May	End 2021/2	0	0								0
Johnson	Murray	13/11/2004	41	SCO	GK	2020	Hibernian Youths		End 2021/2	0	0								0
Kamberi	Florian	08/03/1995	22	SWI / ALB	F	2018	Grasshoppers Zurich	Transferred to St Gallen Aug 2020		0	0								0
Laidlaw	Ethan	02/01/2005		SCO	F	2020	Hibernian Youths			0	0								3
Leddie	Dino	27/08/2001	61	SCO	D	2019	Ytterhogdals IF	OL to CD Almenucar Aug-Jan, OL to CSStrollers 2021/2	End 2021/2	0	0								0
Macey	Matt	09/09/1994	33	ENG	GK	2021	Arsenal		End 2022/3	3	0		5						14
Mackie	Sean	04/11/1998	26	SCO	D	2018	Hibernian Youths		End 2021/2	2	0			1		2	1		4
Magennis	Kyle	26/08/1998	7	SCO	M	2020	St Mirren		End 2024/5	4	10	1	2	2		1	4		4
Mallan	Stevie	25/03/1996	14	SCO	M	2018	Barnsley	OL to Yeni Malatyaspor Feb-Jun	End 2021/2	4	10	1		1		5	1	3	4
Marciano	Ofir	07/10/1989	1	ISR	GK	2017	FC Ashdod	Released June 2021, joined Feyenoord		32	0		1			3			4
Martin	Patrick	21/06/1999	31	SCO	GK	2016	St Johnstone Youths	OL to Stenhousemuir Oct-May, Transferred to Falkirk July 2021		0	0								0
McGinn	Paul	22/10/1990	6	SCO	D	2020	St Mirren		End 2021/2	37	1	3	6			4			1
McGinn	Stephen	02/12/1988	22	SCO	M	2020	St Mirren	OL to Morton Mar-May, Released June joined Kilmarnock		0	5	1				3	1		11
McGregor	Darren	07/08/1985	24	SCO	D	2015	Rangers		End 2022/3	8	3	1		1		5			34
Murphy	Jamie	28/08/1989	18	SCO	F	2020	Rangers (OL)	Jan-May		14	5	1		3		4		1	0
Murray	Fraser	07/05/1999	12	SCO	M	2018	Hibernian Youths	OL to Dunfermline Ath Sep-May, Transferred to Kilmarnock July 2021		0	0								5
Murray	Innes	17/02/1998	33	SCO	M	2016	Celtic Youths	OL to Alloa Ath Sep-May		0	0								0
Newell	Joe	15/03/1993	11	ENG	M	2019	Rotherham United		End 2022/3	32	0	1	6			3			1
Nisbet	Kevin	08/03/1997	15	SCO	F	2020	Dunfermline Athletic		End 2023/4	28	5	14	6		2	4	2	1	2
O'Connor	Josh	01/01/2004	49	SCO	F	2020	Hibernian Youths		End 2021/2	0	0								0
Porteous	Ryan	25/03/1999	5	SCO	D	2018	Hibernian Youths		End 2022/3	32	2	1	6			3			4
Sadiki	Kosovar	27/01/1998		CAN / KOS	D	2019	Lokomotiva Zagren	Freed Jul 2020 joined Finn Harps		0	0								0
Samson	Craig	24/08/1984	30	SCO	GK	2020	St Mirren	Coach		0	0								7
Shanley	Ryan	16/01/2001	29	SCO	F	2019	Hibernian Youths	OL to Kelty Hearts Nov-Jan, Finn Harps Jan-May, OL to Edinburgh City for 2021/2	End 2021/2	0	1					1			7
Stevenson	Lewis	05/01/1988	16	SCO	D	2007	Hibernian Youths		End 2021/2	11	11			3		3			16
Stirling	Ben	16/08/1998	27	SCO	D	2015	Hibernian Youths	Transferred to Hamilton Acc Sep 2020		0	0								4
Weir	Mackenzie		50							0	0								0
Woods	Gregor	19/06/2001	46	SCO	M	2019	Hibernian Youths	Freed Oct 2020, joined Spartans		0	0								0
Wright	Drey	30/04/1995	8	ENG	M	2020	St Johnstone		End 2021/2	11	9	1		3		4	1		17
Yeats	Callum	04/10/2001	34	SCO	D	2019	Hibernian Youths	OL to Stenhousemuir Oct-May	End 2021/2	0	0								0
Young	Connor	01/01/2004		SCO	F	2019	Leith Athletic	OL to Civil Service S, Oct-Jan	End 2021/2										
												1						1	
NEW SIGNINGS																			
Doyle-Hayes	Jake	30/12/1998		ROI	M	2021	St Mirren		End 2022/3										
Mackay	Daniel	20/04/2001		SCO	F	2021	Inverness CT		End 2024/5										
Murphy	Jamie	28/08/1989		SCO	M	2021	Rangers		End 2021/2										

Ally Brown

Daniel Andersson

Grzegorz Szamotulski

Inverness Caledonian Thistle FC 2020/21 Caley Jags

Founded 1994
Ground Caledonian Stadium
Postcode IV1 1FF
Tel 01463 222880
Capacity 7800
Closest Railway Station Inverness
Record Attendance 7753 v Rangers, Lge, 20/1/2008
Record Win 8-1 v Annan Athletic, SC 24/1/88
Record Defeat 0-6 v Airdrie Lge 21/9/2000; v Celtic LC 22/9/2010
Most League Goals in a Season 27 Iain Stewart 1996/7, Dennis Wyness 2002/3
Colours 2020/21 Top Royal Blue / Red Stripes
Shorts Royal Blue
Sponsor ILI Group
Manufacturer Puma
Change Colours 2020/21 Top Pink
Shorts Black
Nicknames Caley
Web www.ictfc.co.uk
Match Programme 2020/21 None issued, Online only

Hon. Club President: Roddy Ross
Chairman: Ross Morrison
Director: Gordon Fyfe, Liam Dalgarno, Allan Munro, David Cameron
Company Secretary: Ian Macdonald
Sporting Director: John Robertson
Manager: Billy Dodds
Assistant Manager: Scott Kellacher
Coach: Barry Wilson
Goalkeeping Coach: Ryan Esson
Head of Youth Development: Charlie Christie
Youth Academy Coach: Ross Tokeley
Physio: Dougie Sim
Sports Therapist: Becky Mussell
Club Doctor: Paul McMullan
Groundsman: Dale Stephen
Kit Man: Jack Davis

If the season wasn't disrupted enough through COVID, Inverness also had to deal with disruption top their management team. With Assistant Manager Scot Kellacher already on leave due to a long term illness, Manager John Robertson was granted compassionate leave in February due to family issues. The club approached former Dundee boss Neil McCann to take over on a temporary basis. He did so from February until the end of the season. Robertson ultimately returned but in an "upstairs" role with Billy Dodds becoming Manager for 2021/2.

Given all that upheaval ICT will be content to have finished in mid-table. They also reached the Quarter Finals of the Scottish Cup, losing to St Mirren. In the League Cup they did not manage to progress from their group.

Young Daniel Mackay showed great promise in the second half of the season. He was snapped up by Hibs for a £200k fee – huge money to change hands for a player these days. ICT shop in the bargain basement but again managed to bring in some good signings. Deas at the back and Todorov up front proved to be excellent captures showing a good level of consistency.

STAR MAN
Nikolay Todorov proved to be a good striker for ICT last season. The former Hearts and Queen of the South player hit top form. For 2021/2 the Bulgarian has moved on to Dunfermline Athletic.

PROSPECTS 2021/2
Billy Dodds is untried as a manager having only ever been an Assistant in the past. From his punditry on BBC Radio Scotland he is apparently the next Mourinho – an expert on every aspect of football, so ICT should be in for a fine season. Maybe. Being realistic another season of mid-table obscurity would probably suit them. Hopefully the public gets out and supports the club in greater numbers than they have in the past. Maintaining full-time football must be very difficult on the sort of attendances ICT can rely upon.

Telford Street Main Gates 1926 and 1990

Date	Comp	H/A	Opponents	F	A		HT		Referee	Crowd	Scorers
06/10/2020	LC	A	Hearts	0	1		0	0	S McLean	BCD	
13/10/2020	LC	H	Cowdenbeath	0	0	4-2p	0	0	G Beaton	BCD	
17/10/2020	L	A	Dunfermline Athletic	1	3		1	1	W Collum	BCD	Todorov
24/10/2020	L	H	Ayr United	1	1		0	0	A Muir	BCD	Todorov
31/10/2020	L	H	Arbroath	3	1		0	1	C Steven	BCD	Todorov, Allardice, D Mackay
07/11/2020	L	A	Hearts	1	2		0	0	B Madden	BCD	Doran
10/11/2020	LC	A	Raith Rovers	3	3	2-3p	1	1	S Reid	BCD	Sutherland, Keatings pen, MacGregor
14/11/2020	LC	H	East Fife	1	0		0	0	C Graham	BCD	Sutherland
21/11/2020	L	H	Raith Rovers	2	0		1	0	A Newlands	250	Keatings, Allardice
04/12/2020	L	A	Queen of the South	3	0		1	0	S McLean	BCD	Kennedy, MacGregor, Storey
12/12/2020	L	H	Dundee	2	2		0	1	C Napier	250	Deas, Keatings
19/12/2020	L	A	Alloa Athletic	1	2		1	0	S Kirkland	BCD	B McKay
29/12/2020	L	H	Dunfermline Athletic	1	1		0	1	E Anderson	BCD	Storey
27/01/2021	L	A	Morton	2	2		2	1	P Stuart	BCD	Sutherland, D Mackay
03/02/2021	L	A	Arbroath	1	1		0	1	A Newlands	BCD	Sutherland
17/02/2021	L	H	Queen of the South	0	1		0	0	D Lowe	BCD	
20/02/2021	L	A	Ayr United	2	0		1	0	P Stuart	BCD	D Mackay, Sutherland
23/02/2021	L	H	Alloa Athletic	2	2		0	1	G Irvine	BCD	Duffy, Keatings
26/02/2021	L	H	Hearts	1	1		1	1	N Walsh	BCD	Storey
02/03/2021	L	A	Dundee	1	2		0	2	S Kirkland	BCD	Todorov
06/03/2021	L	A	Alloa Athletic	1	1		1	1	A Muir	BCD	Todorov
09/03/2021	L	H	Morton	0	1		0	0	G Ross	BCD	
12/03/2021	L	H	Raith Rovers	0	0		0	0	S McLean	BCD	
16/03/2021	L	A	Raith Rovers	1	0		0	0	C Steven	BCD	D Mackay
20/03/2021	L	A	Dunfermline Athletic	1	0		0	0	P Stuart	BCD	Carson
23/03/2021	SC	A	Buckie Thistle	3	2		2	1	S Reid	BCD	Keatings, Welsh, Mackay
27/03/2021	L	H	Arbroath	1	0		0	0	C Steven	BCD	Todorov
02/04/2021	SC	A	Ross County	3	1		1	1	N Walsh	BCD	Todorov, McKay, Sutherland
06/04/2021	L	A	Morton	4	1		2	0	S Reid	BCD	Allardice, Todorov 2, D McKay
10/04/2021	L	A	Queen of the South	1	1		0	0	G Irvine	BCD	Todorov
16/04/2021	SC	A	St Mirren	1	2		0	0	J Beaton	BCD	Todorov
20/04/2021	L	H	Dundee	1	1		0	0	M Roncone	BCD	D McKay
24/04/2021	L	A	Hearts	0	3		0	3	B Madden	BCD	
30/04/2021	L	H	Ayr United	2	2		1	1	C Napier	BCD	D McKay, Welsh pen

Dean Brill

Jim Calder

Nicky Walker

Date	Comp	H/A	Opponents	F	A		1	2	3	4	5	6	7	8	9	10	11	12	13	14	15	16	17	18	19
06/10/2020	LC	A	Hearts	0	1		Ridgers	Duffy+	B McKay	Deas	Harper	Welsh	Allardice	MacGregor	D Mackay&	Sutherland*	Storey	Todorov*	Hyde+	Keatings&	Harkness	Fyffe	C Mackay		
13/10/2020	LC	H	Cowdenbeath	0	0	4-2p	C Mackay	Duffy>	B McKay	Deas	McHattie+	Welsh	Vincent&	MacGregor	Keatings	D Mackay	Storey*	Todorov*	Harper+	Allardice&	Devine>	Fyffe	Hyde	Harkness	Ridgers
17/10/2020	L	A	Dunfermline Athletic	1	3		Ridgers	Duffy	B McKay	Deas	McHattie	Welsh	Allardice	MacGregor+	Keatings	D Mackay	Todorov*	Vincent*	Harper+	Harkness	Devine	Fyffe	Hyde	C Mackay	
24/10/2020	L	H	Ayr United	1	1		Ridgers	Duffy	B McKay+	Deas	Duffy	Harper	Allardice	MacGregor	Keatings*	D Mackay	Todorov	Kennedy*	Fyffe+	Harkness	Hyde	C Mackay			
31/10/2020	L	H	Arbroath	3	1		Ridgers	Duffy	B McKay	Deas	Welsh	Harper	Allardice	MacGregor+	Kennedy*	D Mackay	Todorov&	Keatings*	Doran+	Devine&	Hyde	Fyffe	Nicolson	C Mackay	
07/11/2020	L	A	Hearts	1	2		Ridgers	Duffy	B McKay	Deas	Welsh	Harper	Allardice	MacGregor*	Kennedy&	D Mackay+	Todorov	Sutherland*	Keatings+	Doran&	Vincent	Fyffe	Devine	C Mackay	
10/11/2020	LC	A	Raith Rovers	3	3	2-3p	Ridgers	Duffy	B McKay+	Devine	Vincent*	Harper	Allardice	Doran&	Kennedy	Sutherland	Keatings	MacFregor*	Deas+	Todorov&	Hyde	Fyffe	Nicolson	C Mackay	
14/11/2020	LC	H	East Fife	1	0		C Mackay	Devine	Doran+	Deas	Nicolson	Harper	Allardice	MacGregor	Kennedy&	Sutherland	Todorov*	Storey*	D Mackay+	Keatings&	Hyde	Fyffe	Ridgers		
21/11/2020	L	H	Raith Rovers	2	0		Ridgers	Devine	B McKay	Deas	Storey*	Harper	Allardice	MacGregor	Kennedy&	Sutherland	Keatings+	D Mackay*	Welsh+	Doran&	Todorov	Nicolson	Vincent	C Mackay	
04/12/2020	L	A	Queen of the South	3	0		Ridgers	Devine	B McKay	Deas	Storey	Harper	Allardice	MacGregor	Kennedy+	Sutherland&	Keatings*	Welsh*	Doran+	Todorov&	Vincent	D Mackay	Duffy	C Mackay	
12/12/2020	L	H	Dundee	2	2		Ridgers	Devine	B McKay	Deas	Storey	Harper	Allardice	MacGregor	Kennedy*	Sutherland+	Keatings	Doran*	Todorov+	Welsh	Vincent	D Mackay	Duffy	C Mackay	
19/12/2020	L	A	Alloa Athletic	1	2		Ridgers	Devine	B McKay	Deas	Storey	Harper	Allardice	MacGregor	Kennedy+	Sutherland&	Keatings*	Welsh*	Doran+	Todorov&	Vincent	D Mackay	Carson	C Mackay	
29/12/2020	L	H	Dunfermline Athletic	1	1		Ridgers	Devine	B McKay	Deas	Storey+	Harper	Allardice	Vincent	Doran*	Sutherland&	Welsh	Kennedy*	Todorov+	D MacKay&	Duffy	Carson	MacGregor	C Mackay	
27/01/2021	L	A	Morton	2	2		Ridgers	Devine	Duffy	Deas	Doran+	Harper	Allardice*	Vincent	D Mackay&	Sutherland	Welsh	Todorov*	Keatings+	MacGregor&	Hyde	Carson	Nicolson	C Mackay	
03/02/2021	L	A	Arbroath	1	1		Ridgers	Duffy	B McKay	D Mackay+	Todorov	Harper	Storey	Vincent	Keatings*	Sutherland	Welsh	Allardice*	Doran+	MacGregor	Fyffe	Carson	Nicolson	C Mackay	
17/02/2021	L	H	Queen of the South	0	1		Ridgers	Duffy	B McKay	Deas	D Mackay+	Harper	Allardice	Storey	Keatings*	Sutherland	Welsh&	Todorov*	MacGregor+	Carson&	Hyde	Devine	Nicolson	C Mackay	
20/02/2021	L	A	Ayr United	2	0		Ridgers	Duffy	Devine	Deas	D Mackay&	Harper	Allardice	MacGregor+	Carson	Sutherland	Todorov*	Storey*	Welsh+	B McKay&	Keatings	Hyde	Nicolson	C Mackay	
23/02/2021	L	H	Alloa Athletic	2	2		Ridgers	Duffy	Devine	Deas	D Mackay*	Harper	Allardice	MacGregor+	Carson	Sutherland	Todorov	Storey*	Keatings+	B McKay	Harkness	Hyde	Nicolson	C Mackay	
26/02/2021	L	H	Hearts	1	1		Ridgers	Duffy	Devine	Deas	Welsh	Harper	Storey	MacGregor*	Carson+	Sutherland	Keatings&	D Mackay*	Allardice+	Todorov&	B McKay	Hyde	Nicolson	C Mackay	
02/03/2021	L	A	Dundee	1	2		Ridgers	Duffy	Devine&	Deas	Welsh	Harper	Allardice*	Storey	D Mackay+	Sutherland	Keatings	Carson*	Todorov+	B McKay&	Vincent	Fyffe	Nicolson	C Mackay	
06/03/2021	L	A	Alloa Athletic	1	1		Ridgers	Duffy	B McKay	Deas	Welsh	Harper*	Storey+	MacGregor	Carson	Sutherland	Todorov&	Devine*	D Mackay+	Keatings&	Toshney	Vincent	Allardice	C Mackay	
09/03/2021	L	H	Morton	0	1		Ridgers	Duffy	B McKay	Deas	Devine	Keatings*	Allardice	MacGregor	Carson+	Sutherland	Todorov	Doran*	D Mackay+	Nicolson	McHattie	Welsh	Fyffe	C Mackay	
12/03/2021	L	H	Raith Rovers	0	0		Ridgers	Welsh	B McKay	Deas	Devine	D Mackay	Allardice	MacGregor	Carson	Sutherland	Todorov	Hyde	Duffy	Nicolson	McHattie	Harkness	Keatings	C Mackay	
16/03/2021	L	A	Raith Rovers	1	0		Ridgers	Welsh+	B McKay	Deas	Devine	D Mackay	Allardice	MacGregor	Carson	Sutherland*	Todorov	Storey*	Keatings+&	McHattie&	Duffy	Hyde	Nicolson	C Mackay	
20/03/2021	L	A	Dunfermline Athletic	1	0		Ridgers	Welsh	B McKay	Deas	Devine	D Mackay+	Allardice	MacGregor	Carson	Sutherland	Todorov*	Storey*	McHattie+	Harkness	Duffy	Hyde	Nicolson	C Mackay	
23/03/2021	SC	A	Buckie Thistle	3	2		C Mackay	Welsh	McHattie*	Deas	Fyffe	D Mackay&	Allardice	MacGregor	Keatings+	Storey	Nicolson	Harper*	Sutherland+	Lyall&	Riddle	Davies	Ridgers		
27/03/2021	L	H	Arbroath	1	0		Ridgers	Welsh	Devine	Deas	Harper	D Mackay	Allardice	MacGregor+	Carson	Sutherland*	Todorov&	Allan*	Storey+	McHattie&	Keatings	Vincent	Lyall	C Mackay	
02/04/2021	SC	A	Ross County	3	1		Ridgers	Welsh	Devine	Deas	B McKay	D Mackay&	Allardice	Allan*	Carson	Storey	Todorov+	Sutherlanc*	MacGregor+	Harper&	Keatings	Duffy	Lyall	McHattie	C Mackay
06/04/2021	L	A	Morton	4	1		Ridgers	MacGregor	Devine	Deas	B McKay	D Mackay&	Allardice	Allan*	Carson	Storey+	Todorov	Sutherland*	Vincent+	Harper&	Lyall	McHattie	C Mackay		
10/04/2021	L	A	Queen of the South	1	1		Ridgers	MacGregor*	Devine	Deas	B McKay	D Mackay	Allardice	Allan+	Carson	Storey	Todorov&	Vincent*	Sutherland+	Harper&	McHattie	Lyall	Duffy	C Mackay	
16/04/2021	SC	A	St Mirren	1	2		Ridgers	Welsh+	Devine	Deas	B McKay	D Mackay	Allardice	Allan	Carson	Storey	Todorov*	Sutherland*	Lyall+	Harper	McHattie	Doran	Vincent	MacGregor	C Mackay
20/04/2021	L	H	Dundee	1	1		Ridgers	Welsh	Devine	Deas	B McKay	D Mackay	Allardice	Allan*	Carson	Sutherland+	Todorov&	MacGregor*	Storey+	Harper&	McHattie	Lyall	Vincent	C Mackay	
24/04/2021	L	A	Hearts	0	3		Ridgers	Welsh	Devine	Deas	Harper	D Mackay	Allardice*	Allan	Carson	Storey&	Todorov+	MacGregor*	Lyall+	Sutherland&	McHattie	Duffy	Vincent	C Mackay	
30/04/2021	L	H	Ayr United	2	2		Ridgers	Welsh	Devine	Deas	Harper	D Mackay+	MacGregor	Allan	Carson	Sutherland*	Todorov&	Lyall*	Doran+	Storey&	McHattie	Allardice	Vincent	C Mackay	

THE GOALIES
Goalkeepers Used in League Matches, 1970-2020
Players shown in the season of their first appearance only

1994/5	Mark McRitchie
	Jim Calder
1996/7	Norman McMillan
1997/8	Les Fridge
2001/2	Nicky Walker
2002/3	Mark Brown
2005/6	Michael Fraser
2007/8	Zbigniew Malkowski
2008/9	Ryan Esson
2010/1	Jonny Tuffey
2012/3	Antonio Reguero
2013/4	Dean Brill
2015/6	Owain Fon Wiliams
2016/7	Cammy Mackay
2017/8	Mark Ridgers

Antonio Reguero

ICT'S SCOTTISH CUP WINNING RUN 2014/15

Nov 29	4	A v St Mirren	1-1
Dec 2	4R	H v St Mirren	4-0
Feb 7	5	A v Partick Thistle	2-1
Mar 10	QF	H v Raith Rovers	1-0
Apr 19	SF	N v Celtic	3-2 aet
May 30	F	N v Falkirk	2-1

Surname	First Name	Date of Birth	No	Nat	Pos	Signed	Previous	Notes	Contract	Lge A	Lge S	Lge G	SC A	SC S	SC G	LC A	LC S	LC G	Un
Allan	Scott	28/11/1991		SCO	M	2021	Hibernian (OL)	Mar-May		5	1		2						
Allardice	Scott	31/03/1998	18	SCO	M	2020	Waterford		End 2022/3	23	2	3	3			3	1		2
Carson	David	20/09/1995	8	ENG	M	2019	Morpeth Town		End 2023/4	14	2	1	2						4
Davies	Kane	11/03/2003	42	SCO	F	2020	ICT Youths			0	0								1
Deas	Robbie	27/02/2000	24	SCO	D	2020	Celtic	Son of Bruce Deas, Nephew of Paul Deas	End 2022/3	26	0	1	3			3	1		0
Devine	Danny	07/09/1992	6	SCO	D	2020	Dunfermline Athletic		End 2021/2	20	2		2			2	1		3
Doran	Aaron	13/05/1991	10	ROI	M	2013	Blackburn Rovers			2	9	1				2			1
Duffy	Wallace	12/04/1999	2	SCO	D	2020	St Johnstone		End 2021/2	14	0	1				3			9
Fyffe	Ryan	21/05/2001		SCO	D	2020	ICT Youths	OL to Clach Oct-Jan	End 2021/2	0	1		1						10
Harkness	Shane	06/01/2001	29	SCO	F	2020	ICT Youths	OL to Rothes Oct-Jan		0	0								7
Harper	Cameron	10/11/2001	16	SCO	D	2020	ICT Youths		End 2021/2	19	4			2		3	1		1
Hyde	Lewis	15/07/2002		SCO	M	2020	ICT Youths	OL to Rothes Oct-Jan	End 2021/2	0	0						1		14
Keatings	James	20/01/1992	7	SCO	F	2019	Hamilton Accies	Released May 2021, joined Raith Rovers		11	6	3	1		1	2	2	1	4
Kennedy	Kai	28/03/2002		SCO	F	2020	Rangers (OL)	Oct-Jan		6	2	1				2			0
Lyall	Arron	27/09/2003		SCO	F	2021	Rangers (OL)	Mar-May		0	2			2					5
MacGregor	Roddy	21/12/2001	12	SCO	M	2020	ICT Youths	Son of Bruce MacGregor of BBC Radio Scotland	End 2021/2	20	4	1	1	1		3	1	1	3
Mackay	Cammy	09/12/1996	21	SCO	GK	2016	ICT Youths			0	0		1			2			31
Mackay	Daniel	20/04/2001	27	SCO	F	2019	ICT Youths	Transferred to Hibernian May 2021 £200k		19	5	7	3		2	2	1		3
McDonald	Anthony	17/03/2001		SCO	M	2021	Cordoba CF "B"	ex Hearts	End 2021/2										
McHattie	Kevin	15/07/1993	3	SCO	D	2019	Derry City	Released June 2021		1	3		1			1			9
McKay	Brad	26/03/1993	22	SCO	D	2016	St Johnstone	Released June 2021, joined Falkirk		19	2	1	2			3			2
McKinnon	Martin	03/05/2000		SCO	GK	2018	ICT Youths	OL to Buckie Thistle Dec-Jan		0	0								0
Nicolson	Harry	11/09/2020	20	SCO	D	2020	ICT Youths		End 2021/2	0	0		1			1			14
Riddle	Ally	22/02/2004	32	SCO	M	2020	ICT Youths			0	0								1
Ridgers	Mark	09/08/1990	1	SCO	GK	2017	Partick Thistle		End 2021/2	27	0		2			2			3
Storey	Miles	04/01/1994	17	ENG	F	2019	Partick Thistle	Released June 2021, joined Hereford		13	7	3	3			2	1		0
Sutherland	Shane	23/10/1990	11	SCO	F	2020	Elgin City		End 2021/2	20	4	3		3	1	3		2	0
Todorov	Nikolay	24/08/1996	77	BUL	F	2019	Falkirk	OOC June 2021, joined Dunfermline Ath		18	8	9	2		2	1	3		1
Toshney	Lewis	26/04/1992	5	SCO	D	2020	Falkirk	Released May 2021, became Downfield Manager		0	0								1
Vincent	James	27/09/1989	14	ENG	M	2019	Dundee	Released June 2021, joined Hereford		3	3					2			12
Welsh	Sean	15/03/1990	4	SCO	M	2018	Falkirk		End 2021/2	17	4	1	3		1	2			2
NEW SIGNINGS																			
Broadfoot	Kirk	08/08/1984		SCO	D	2021	Kilmarnock		End 2021/2										
Duku	Manny	28/12/1992		NET / GHA	F	2021	Raith Rovers		End 2021/2										
Gardyne	Michael	23/01/1986		SCO	M	2021	Ross County		End 2021/2										
Mackay	Billy	22/10/1999		NIR	F	2021	Ross County		End 2022/3										
McAlear	Reece	12/02/2002		SCO	M	2021	Norwich City (OL)	Jul-May	End 2021/2										
Walsh	Tom	11/07/1996		SCO	M	2021	Ayr United		End 2022/3										

PHOTOCARDS

No. 1.

INVERNESS CALEDONIAN F.C.

Left to right, back row :—*W. Anderson, A. Munro, J. McKenzie, C. Stewart, D. McDonald, R. Reid.* Front Row :—*W. Stewart, A. McKenzie, J. Main, J. McIntosh, J. Paterson.*

Formed 1885, this Club has won the championship of the Highland League, in which it plays, on eight occasions. Owners of their ground, other successes include the North of Scotland Cup on twelve occasions, the Inverness Cup on thirteen occasions, and the Inverness Charity Cup on fourteen occasions.

Kelty Hearts FC 2020/21 Maroon Machine

Hon Chairman: Gus Eaglesham
Chairman: Ian Thomson
Vice Chairman: Derek Hodgson
General Manager: Dean McKenzie
Secretary: Gary Grandison
Treasurer: Stuart Mill
Matchday manager: Gus Anderson
Committee: Shug Wells, Ivor Edwards, Scott Dow, Sandy White, Paddy Feeney, Ross Cormack, Kieran Brannan
Manager: Kevin Thomson
Assistant: Kevin MacDonald
Goalkeeping Coach: Andy Forbes
Coach: Mac Kenney
Physio: Gordon Edwards
Kitman: John Cantley

Founded	1975 (as Marian United)
Ground	New Central Park
Postcode	KY4 0AG
Tel	
Capacity	2181
Closest Railway Station	Cowdenbeath
Record Attendance	2500 v Rangers (Testimonial)
Record League Win	N/A
Record League Defeat	N/A
Most League Goals in a Season	N/A
Colours 2020/21 Top	Maroon
Shorts	White
Sponsor	Conservatory Converters
Manufacturer	Joma
Change Colours 2020/21 Top	
Shorts	
Nicknames	
Web	www.keltyhearts.co.uk
Match Programme 2020/21	£2, occasional

Date	Comp	H/A	Opponents	F	A		HT	Referee	Crowd	Scorers
07/10/2020	LC	H	St Johnstone	1	2		0 1	A Newlands	BCD	Tidser
10/10/2020	L	H	Edinburgh University	4	0		2 0	David Dickinson	BCD	Higginbotham 2, Flynn, Philp
13/10/2020	LC	A	Dundee United	0	1		0 1	D Robertson	BCD	
17/10/2020	L	A	Civil Service Strollers	3	2		1 1	Chris Newman		Tidser, Higginbotham, Philp
24/10/2020	L	H	Dalbeattie Star	2	0		2 0	Chris Fordyce		Anderson, Stevenson
27/10/2020	L	H	Vale of Leithen	4	0		2 0			Anderson, Higginbotham, Easton, Philp
31/10/2020	L	A	Caledonian Braves	1	0		1 0	Ross Anderson		Hooper
07/11/2020	L	H	East Kilbride	0	1		0 0	Dan McFarlane		
10/11/2020	LC	H	Peterhead	1	1	3-5p	0 0	G Ross	BCD	Stevenson
14/11/2020	LC	A	Brechin City	2	0		1 0	G Grainger	BCD	Easton, McNab
21/11/2020	L	H	Cumbernauld Colts	5	0		2 0	Lorraine Watson		Tidser, Stevenson, Easton 2, Austin
25/11/2020	L	A	Cumbernauld Colts	2	0			Gavin Ross		Austin 2
28/11/2020	L	A	Gala Fairydean Rovers	2	1		2 1	John McKendrick		Hill,Easton
05/12/2020	L	A	Berwick Rangers	4	0		2 0	Iain Snedden		Austin 2, Easton, Ferguson og
12/12/2020	L	H	Gretna	7	0		3 0	Scott Lambie		Higginbotham 2 , Austin 2, Shanley, Flynn, Easton
15/12/2020	L	A	Spartans	4	0		2 0	Alex Shepherd		Philp, Higgonbotham, Austin, Shanley
19/12/2020	L	H	Stirling University	2	0			Barry Dickson		Shanley, Austin
26/12/2020	SC	H	Jeanfield Swifts	2	1		1 0	Iain Snedden		Shanley, Easton
09/01/2021	SC	H	Stranraer	2	3		2 0	Lorraine Watson		
04/05/2021	PO	A	Brora Rangers	2	0		1 0	Grant Irvine		Easton, Higginbotham pen
08/05/2021	PO	H	Brora Rangers	4	1		1 1			Austin 3, Easton
18/05/2021	PO	H	Brechin City	2	1		2 1	Gavin Duncan		HIgginbotham, Russell
23/05/2021	PO	A	Brechin City	1	0		0 0	Craig Napier		Tidser

Date	Comp	H/A	Opponents	F	A	1	2	3	4	5	6	7	8	9	10	11	12	13	14	15	16	17	18
07/10/2020	LC	H	St Johnstone	1	2	Darren Jamieson	Paddy Boyle	Craig Reid	Scott Hooper	Jamie Stevens	Michael Tidser	Ross Philp	Thomas Reilly	Kallum Higginbotham	Dylan Easton+	Cammy Russell*	Matty Flynn*	Robbie McNab+	*Tom Scobbie*	*Tyler McKenzie*	*Josh Donaldson*	*Arnault Bembo*	
10/10/2020	L	H	Edinburgh University	4	0	Darren Jamieson	Scott Hooper	Paddy Boyle	Craig Reid<	Thomas Reilly	Michael Tidser	Robbie McNab	Ross Philp*	Dylan Easton&	Kallum Higginbotham	Matty Flynn+	Nathan Austin*>	Cammy Russell+	Jamie Stevenson&	Tyler McKenzie>	Tom Scobbie<	*Arnauld Bembo*	*Josh Donaldson*
13/10/2020	LC	A	Dundee United	0	1	Darren Jamieson	Paddy Boyle	Craig Reid*	Scott Hooper	Jamie Stevens	Michael Tidser	Philp&	Thomas Reilly	Kallum Higginbotham	Dylan Easton	Robbie McNab+	Tom Scobbie*	Matty Flynn+	Cammy Russell&	*Tyler McKenzie*	*Arnault Bembo*	*Josh Donaldson*	
17/10/2020	L	A	Civil Service Strollers	3	2	Darren Jamieson	Scott Hooper	Paddy Boyle	Jamie Stevenson	Thomas Reilly	Michael Tidser	Tom Scobbie	Cammy Russell	Dylan Easton	Kallum Higginbotham	Matty Flynn	*Ross Philp*	*Robbie McNab*	*Dougie Hill*	*Arnault Bembo*	*Jay Bridgeford*	*Tyler McKenzie*	*Josh Donaldson*
24/10/2020	L	H	Dalbeattie Star	2	0	Darren Jamieson	Scott Hooper	Dougie Hill&	Jamie Stevenson	Thomas Reilly	Michael Tidser	Tom Scobbie	Ross Philp	Dylan Easton	Kallum Higginbotham*	Grant Anderson+	Robbie McNab*	Matty Flynn+	Cammy Russell&	*Arnault Bembo*	*Josh Donaldson*		
27/10/2020	L	H	Vale of Leithen	4	0	Darren Jamieson	Scott Hooper	Dougie Hill	Jamie Stevenson	Thomas Reilly	Michael Tidser	Tom Scobbie	Ross Philp	Dylan Easton>	Kallum Higginbotham	Grant Anderson	Matty Flynn*	Robbie McNab+	Craig Reid&	Cammy Russell>	*Arnault Bembo*	*Josh Donaldson*	
31/10/2020	L	A	Caledonian Braves	1	0	Darren Jamieson	Scott Hooper	Dougie Hill	Jamie Stevenson	Thomas Reilly	Michael Tidser	Paddy Boyle	Ross Philp	Dylan Easton	Kallum Higginbotham	Grant Anderson*	Matty Flynn*	Tom Scobbie	Craig Reid&	*Robbie McNab*	*Cammy Russell*	*Arnault Bembo*	*Josh Donaldson*
07/11/2020	L	H	East Kilbride	0	1	Darren Jamieson	Craig Reid	Dougie Hill	Jamie Stevenson+	Thomas Reilly	Michael Tidser	Paddy Boyle	Ross Philp	Dylan Easton	Kallum Higginbotham	Cammy Russell*	Robbie McNab*	Grant Anderson+	*Tom Scobbie*	*Matty Flynn*	*Arnault Bembo*	*Cooney*	*Josh Donaldson*
10/11/2020	LC	H	Peterhead	1	1	Darren Jamieson	Paddy Boyle	Dougie Hill	Scott Hooper	Jamie Stevens	Michael Tidser	Ross Philp	Thomas Reilly	Kallum Higginbotham	Dylan Easton	Matty Flynn*	Robbie McNab*	*Craig Reid*	*Tom Scobbie*	*Arnault Bembo*	*Nathan Cooney*	*Josh Donaldson*	
14/11/2020	LC	A	Brechin City	2	0	Darren Jamieson	Boyle	Dougie Hill*	Scott Hooper	Jamie Stevens	Michael Tidser	Ross Philp+	Craig Reid>	Kallum Higginbotham	Dylan Easton	Matty Flynn&	Nathan Cooney*	Robbie McNab+	Austin&	Scobbie>	*Arnault Bembo*	*Josh Donaldson*	
21/11/2020	L	H	Cumbernauld Colts	5	0	Darren Jamieson	Scott Hooper	Dougie Hill	Jamie Stevenson	Thomas Reilly	Michael Tidser	Paddy Boyle	Robbie McNab+	Dylan Easton	Kallum Higginbotham	Nathan Austin*	Matty Flynn*	Grant Anderson+	*Ross Philp*	*Arnault Bembo*	*Nathan Cooney*	*Josh Donaldson*	
25/11/2020	L	A	Cumbernauld Colts	2	0	Darren Jamieson	Scott Hooper	Dougie Hill	Jamie Stevenson*	Thomas Reilly	Michael Tidser	Paddy Boyle	Robbie McNab	Dylan Easton	Kallum Higginbotham	Nathan Austin+	Ross Philp*	Grant Anderson+	Craig Reid&	*Matty Flynn*	*Nathan Cooney*	*Josh Donaldson*	
28/11/2020	L	A	Gala Fairydean Rovers	2	1	Darren Jamieson	Scott Hooper	Dougie Hill	Jamie Stevenson*	Thomas Reilly	Michael Tidser	Paddy Boyle	Ross Philp	Dylan Easton	Kallum Higginbotham	Nathan Austin	Craig Reid*	*Grant Anderson*	*Robbie McNab*	*Matty Flynn*	*Nathan Cooney*	*Josh Donaldson*	
05/12/2020	L	A	Berwick Rangers	4	0	Darren Jamieson	Scott Hooper	Dougie Hill*	Craig Reid<	Thomas Reilly	Grant Anderson	Paddy Boyle	Ross Philp	Dylan Easton	Kallum Higginbotham	Nathan Austin	Robbie McNab*	*Matty Flynn+*	*Michael Tidser*	*Josh Donaldson*			
12/12/2020	L	H	Gretna	7	0	Darren Jamieson	Scott Hooper	Dougie Hill*	Jamie Stevenson+	Thomas Reilly	Michael Tidser	Paddy Boyle	Ryan Shanley	Dylan Easton	Kallum Higginbotham&	Nathan Austin>	Craig Reid*	Ross Philp+	Matty Flynn&<	Steven Anderson	*Nathan Cooney<*	*Josh Donaldson*	
15/12/2020	L	A	Spartans	4	0	Darren Jamieson	Scott Hooper	Dougie Hill+	Jamie Stevenson>	Thomas Reilly	Michael Tidser	Paddy Boyle	Ryan Shanley*	Dylan Easton	Kallum Higginbotham	Nathan Austin&	Ross Philp*	Grant Anderson+	Craig Reid&	Nathan Cooney>	*Josh Donaldson*		
19/12/2020	L	H	Stirling University	2	0	Darren Jamieson	Scott Hooper	Dougie Hill	Jamie Stevenson	Thomas Reilly	Michael Tidser	Paddy Boyle	Ryan Shanley*	Dylan Easton+	Kallum Higginbotham	Nathan Austin	Ross Philp*	Craig Reid+	*Grant Anderson*	*Nathan Cooney*	*Josh Donaldson*		
26/12/2020	SC	H	Jeanfield Swifts	2	1	Darren Jamieson	Scott Hooper	Dougie Hill+	Jamie Stevenson	Thomas Reilly	Michael Tidser	Paddy Boyle	Ryan Shanley*	Dylan Easton	Kallum Higginbotham	Nathan Austin	Ross Philp*	Craig Reid+	*Grant Anderson*	*Nathan Cooney*	*Josh Donaldson*		
09/01/2021	SC	H	Stranraer	2	3	Darren Jamieson	Scott Hooper	Dougie Hill	Jamie Stevenson	Thomas Reilly	Michael Tidser	Paddy Boyle	Ross Philp*	Dylan Easton	Kallum Higginbotham	Nathan Austin	Grant Anderson*	*Ryan Shanley*	*Craig Reid*	*Nathan Cooney*	*Josh Donaldson*		
04/05/2021	PO	A	Brora Rangers	2	0	Darren Jamieson	Scott Hooper	Dougie Hill	Jamie Stevenson	Thomas Reilly	Michael Tidser	Paddy Boyle	Ross Philp*	Dylan Easton	Kallum Higginbotham	Nathan Austin	Craig Reid*	*Tom Scobbie*	*Matty Flynn*	*Robbie McNab*	*Cammy Russell*	*Andy Rodgers*	*Josh Donaldson*
08/05/2021	PO	H	Brora Rangers	4	1	Darren Jamieson	Scott Hooper	Dougie Hill*	Jamie Stevenson	Thomas Reilly	Michael Tidser	Paddy Boyle	Ross Philp	Dylan Easton	Kallum Higginbotham&	Nathan Austin+	Craig Reid*	Cammy Russell+	Andy Rodgers&	*Robbie McNab*	*Matty Flynn*	*Josh Donaldson*	
18/05/2021	PO	H	Brechin City	2	1	Darren Jamieson	Scott Hooper	Craig Reid	Jamie Stevenson*	Thomas Reilly	Michael Tidser	Paddy Boyle	Ross Philp	Dylan Easton	Kallum Higginbotham	Nathan Austin	Cammy Russell*	*Dougie Hill*	*Tom Scobbie*	*Robbie McNab*	*Matty Flynn*	Andy Rodgers	*Josh Donaldson*
23/05/2021	PO	A	Brechin City	1	0	Darren Jamieson	Scott Hooper	Dougie Hill	Craig Reid	Thomas Reilly	Michael Tidser	Paddy Boyle	Ross Philp	Dylan Easton&	Kallum Higginbotham	Nathan Austin*	Cammy Russell*+	Robbie McNab+	Andy Rodgers&	*Tom Scobbie*	*Matty Flynn*	*Jamie Stevenson*	*Josh Donaldson*

CLUB EARLY HISTORY - ADAPTED FROM CLUB WEBSITE

In 1975 the committee members of the newly formed Kelty Hearts Amateur Football Club (then known as Marian United) made a pledge that they wanted to reach the top in 'Amateur' football circles and then attempt to bring 'Junior' football back to the village. Their record over the ensuing seasons certainly put them on the right path to achieve their goal. They worked their way up from the bottom of the Kirkcaldy & District Amateur Football Association to the top in four seasons and along the way added several local trophies as well as some decent runs in the national competition.

During season 1978/79 Kelty Hearts Amateurs played a friendly against top junior side Halbeath Juniors as preparation for Halbeath's Scottish Junior Cup quarter final against Pollok. Kelty Hearts won 3-1 and at the end of the season Halbeath signed five of Kelty's team. This in effect nearly finished the club as the existing management team quit and other players left or retired. The remaining committee resolved to address the challenge head on by turning Junior themselves.

During season 1979/80 the newly extended committee spent all their efforts on keeping the club alive, fund raising and improving the facilities at Central Park to meet the Scottish Junior F.A. requirements. Planning permission was received to build a six foot high wooden perimeter fence around the ground with access for supporters to pay admission. The local council had been renovating many of the houses in the village and the club purchased the old flooring from a local scrap merchant. All the old nails were removed and then the wood was cut into six feet lengths, this was all done by the committee and volunteers, the fence was erected and then painted. Wooden poles and a rope to keep spectators off the pitch was also installed and new removable steel goalposts were manufactured by local firm Kingdom Engineering and fitted. A separate changing room and shower for match officials was built in the old pavilion and existing home and away changing rooms were extended, refurbished and new showers installed. After match refreshments were also a pre-requisite in the 'Juniors' and this was supplied by the clubs main sponsor, Peter Wright at the No 1 Inn.

The club still managed to field a team mainly of local players and fulfilled all their fixtures that season. Ian Hutchinson became treasurer and Danny Wells was elected as club secretary. Former Dunfermline Athletic & Scotland defender Willie Callaghan Snr became team manager for a short period and Eric McMillan was recruited as his assistant. Things went very well off the field unfortunately the team finished well down the league but everyone who was involved during that trying time felt they had achieved something very special.

After an inspection of the park and facilities by two Scottish Junior F.A. officials (Davie Roy and Frank Fraser) the dream became reality when the clubs application to the Fife Region of the Scottish Junior Football Association was accepted at their AGM in June 1980. The upgrade of the facilities at Central Park was passed to allow participation in the Fife Junior League the coming 1980/81 season.

KELTY HEARTS HONOURS LIST

Senior Club Lowland League Winners
2019-20, 2020-21
East Of Scotland League Winners
2017-18
King Cup Winners
2017-18

Junior Club East Super League Winners:
2014-15, 2016-17
East Super League Runners Up:
2015-16
Fife League Winners:
1990–91, 1991–92, 1992–93, 1996–97,1998–99, 2002–03
Scottish Junior Cup Runners-up:
1998–99, 2006–07
East Region Premier League Runners-up:
2006–07
Fife & Tayside (Taycars) Trophy Winners:
1997–98
Fife Junior (PSM) Cup Winners:
1982–83, 1983–84, 1984–85, 1986–87, 1992–93, 2007–08, 2008–09
Cowdenbeath (Interbrew) Cup Winners:
1981–82, 1984–85, 1985–86, 1986–87, 1992–93, 1999–00
Laidlaw Shield Winners:
1983–84, 1984–85, 1986–87
Clark Beckett Cup Winners:
1993–94
ACA Sports League Cup Winners:
2006–07
Rosslyn Trophy Winners:
1991–92, 1996–97

Adapted from an article in The Scotsman, by Barry Anderson, May 15 2021

The contrast between the two most recent points on his football career map is not lost on Kallum Higginbotham He gives a wry chortle comparing them. Swapping David Robertson's Real Kashmir for Barry Ferguson's Kelty Hearts last summer was both sensible and necessary. He has gone from fighting to Fife, from crazy insurgents to the cusp of history. There are potential programme names all over the place and Higginbotham might feel he is living in a fly-on-the-wall show. Kelty's surge towards the Scottish Professional Football League would certainly do any TV director justice.

They meet Brechin City this Tuesday in the first leg of a long-awaited play-off for the right to a place in next season's SPFL. The Lowland League winners have been on a constant upward trajectory for the last 30 months. Higginbotham arrived last July to join the upsurge having had enough of the uprising in India. Real Kashmir were profiled in recent BBC Scotland documentaries which became as watchable for manager Robertson's colourful language and broad Scottish brogue as the area's civil tensions.

The fight for control of the region – officially known as the Princely State of Kashmir and Jammu – intensified the day Salford-born Higginbotham arrived two years ago as the first Englishman ever to join Real. Article 370 was revoked by India the same afternoon, removing Kashmir's special political status. The battle between India and Pakistan continues to rage and Higginbotham is well out of it. Kelty is something of a tranquil paradise by comparison.

The forward is revelling in a push for the senior leagues, where he previously played with Dunfermline, Kilmarnock, Partick Thistle and Falkirk. His everyday life is also back to normal. He now works full-time as a tiler, plays part-time with Kelty, plus gets quality time with wife Nicola and young children Mia and Alfie. No longer need he contend with riots and armed guards. Well, not unless the next derby with Hill of Beath gets out of hand.

"I knew I'd never earn enough money in football to sit back on my sun lounger. I wanted a career behind me," he explains. "It was the best decision I've made coming home because I'm still playing at a good level with an ambitious club. Kashmir was an amazing experience and I did enjoy it. If I hadn't gone, I probably would have kicked myself for the rest of my life. I can say I've been and experienced it but there's no place like home. I love football but family means a lot more to me than chasing the money.

"There was a documentary on Kashmir but that didn't even scratch the surface. You have no idea what went on over there. It's an amazing club with an amazing owner. The management team there were magnificent. If people knew what the management had to contend with just to get games on and training sessions, it would shock them. We were in lockdown for ten weeks. I was stuck in the hotel for those ten weeks so I had a lot of time to think. That's when I decided I had to start thinking about life after football. I'm 31 years of age now. If I get a trade, I can always make money and provide for my family."

"Sampling a different lifestyle and way of football was good. Every away game with Kashmir was a plane journey, something I wasn't used to. Then when you're in Kashmir you see all the army personnel. It took quite a few weeks to get used to. Some mornings we'd have to train at 5.30am or 6am because there had been trouble the night before. There was so much to contend with. I knew all of that before I went out there because I'd watched documentaries about the place, but I don't think you can really prepare yourself for what actually went on. I really missed my family and my two kids. I'm at my best mentally and physically when I'm at home with my family around me."

Kashmir is no place to risk taking your wife and young children so Higginbotham was alone in India. Cinemas and shopping malls are a no-no unless you travel to larger cities like Mumbai. It was in every way a solitary existence. Armed guards were at times stationed outside his hotel or at Real Kashmir's matches to ensure public safety. Not exactly what he imagined when dreaming of a football career as a kid on the outskirts of Manchester. Yet the entire experience served a purpose, and not only from a professional perspective.

"We were never in danger. There was never any trouble towards us," Higginbotham adds. "It was right on the border between Pakistan and India and there is a lot of conflict between them. There was always that danger of insurgents coming into the state and causing trouble, which happened quite regularly when I was there. "Sometimes you would be warned that you couldn't leave the hotel because something had happened. The internet would be turned off quite often and you would lose your phone signal a lot. The Government would switch all that off so people couldn't organise large groups to cause trouble."

"That sort of stuff was tough. There were weeks where you wouldn't be able to Facetime home or see the kids. Mentally, it made me a lot stronger. It made me realise what I've got at home. When you think life is tough here, I can reflect back to how people get by over there. I'm very fortunate for the things I have in life today."

Going from Kashmir to Kelty meant trading in one former Rangers stalwart for another as manager. Robertson and Ferguson both share some similar traits. Again, Higginbotham laughs when the comparison is put to him. "They're both born winners. They just want the best for the players and that's the biggest similarity. They want to win every single game, whether they are playing or managing. Every single day in training that's what the gaffer demands from us. It's a great attribute to have."

Kelty's board will agree. They sit just two games from a historic passage to the SPFL after a 6-1 aggregate mauling of Brora Rangers in last week's pyramid play-off. That teed up another two-legged meeting with Club 42, the bottom side in the last tier of the professional league system. Brechin have been dreading this tie for more than a year.

The rest, of course, is history. Kelty defeated Brechin City home and away, and took their place in the SPFL for 2021/2. Manager Barry Ferguson departed a couple of days later to be replaced by another former Rangers player, Kevin Thomson.

			A	S	G	Signed	From	Notes
Anderson	Grant	M	4	5	2	2020	Raith Rovers	OL to Forfar Athletic Mar-May, Made permanent May 2021
Austin	Nathan	F	7	1	9	2019	Inverness CT	OL to East Fife Mar 2021
Bembo	Arnault	M				2019	Cumbernauld Colts	Transferred to Linlithgow Rose Nov 2020
Boyle	Paddy	D	11			2020	Peterhead	Joined Dumbarton June 2021
Bridgeford	Jay					2020	Kelty Hearts Youths	Ol to Burntisland Shipyard Oct-Jan
Cooney	Nathan			2		2020	Dundee United (OL)	Nov-Jan
Donaldson	Josh	GK				2020	Dundee United	
Easton	Dylan	F	13		6	2019	Forfar Athletic	Joined Airdrieonians June 2021
Flynn	Matty	F	2	6	2	2020	East Stirlingshire	Released June 2021
Higginbotham	Kallum	F	13		7	2020	Real Kashmir	
Hill	Dougie	D	11		1	2020	Brechin City	
Hooper	Scott	D	12		1	2020	Peterhead	
Jamieson	Darren	GK	13			2020	Arbroath	
McKenzie	Tyler	M		1		2020	Kelty Hearts Youths	OL to Burntisland Shipyard Oct-Jan
McNab	Robbie		3	4		2020	BSC Glasgow	
Own Goal					1			
Philp	Ross	M	7	4	4	2017	Bo'ness United	
Reid	Craig	D	3	7		2020	East Kilbride	Released May 2021
Reilly	Thomas	M	13			2019	Forfar Athletic	
Rodgers	Andy	F				2021	East Stirlingshire	Released June 2021, joined Syngenta
Russell	Cammy	F	2	3		2019	Airdrieonians	
Scobbie	Tom	D	3	1		2019	Dundee United	Released May 2021
Shanley	Ryan	M	3		3	2020	Hibernian (OL)	Nov-Jan
Stevenson	Jamie	M	11	1	2	2020	Peterhead	Joined East Kilbride June 2021
Tidser	Michael	M	12		2	2020	Falkirk	

Manager Barry Ferguson (until May 2021), then Kevin Thomson
Assistant Manager Bob Malcolm (until May 2021), then Kevin McDonald

NEW SIGNINGS

			Signed	From
Forster	Jordan	D	2021	Dundee
Cardle	Joe	F	2021	Partick Thistle
Barjonas	Jamie	M	2021	Rangers
Black	Andy	M	2021	Edinburgh City
Peggie	Reis	D	2021	East Stirlingshire
Agyeman	Alfie	F	2021	BSC Glasgow
Biabi	Botti	F	2021	Stenhousemuir
O'Ware	Thomas	D	2021	Partick Thistle

KELTY HEARTS - MANAGERS

1980s

JOHN FORRESTER | AUG 1980 – OCT 1980
JIM LEISHMAN | OCT 1980 – OCT 1981
BILLY GILLIES | OCT 1981 – NOV 1983
JOHN SHORT | NOV 1983 – FEB 1984
WALTER LOGIE | FEB 1984 – MAY 1987
IAN DAIR | JULY 1987 – MAY 1988
JIM McARTHUR | JUNE 1988 – MAR 1989
ANDY CAMPBELL | MAR 1989 – SEPT 1989
PETER McQUADE | SEPT 1989 – MAY 1990

1990s

LES McLELLAN | MAY 1990 – AUG 1991
ANDY HARROW | AUG 1991 – JULY 1992
DANNY HENDRY | AUG 1992 – DEC 1993
ANDY HARROW | DEC 1993 – OCT 1994
BRIAN INGLIS & ERIC McMILLAN | OCT 1994 – NOV 1994
RAB MORRIS & BRIAN MARR | NOV 1994 – AUG 2000

2000s

COLIN HARRIS | SEPT 2000 – APRIL 2001
CRAIG ROBERTSON | JUNE 2001 – APRIL 2002
DAVIE STEWART | APRIL 2002 – JUNE 2002
JOHN STEEL | JUNE 2002 – MAY 2004
DAVIE WILCOX | MAY 2004 – SEPT 2005
STEVIE LEIGHTON | SEPT 2005 – OCT 2010

2010s

KEITH BURGESS | OCT 2010 – MAY 2013
WILLIE NEWBIGGING | JUNE 2013 – SEP 2013
THOMAS COURTS | OCT 2013 – OCT 2018
BARRY FERGUSON | NOV 2018 – MAY 2021
KEVIN THOMSON | MAY2021-date

Kilmarnock FC 2020/21 Killie

Founded	1869
Ground	Rugby Park
Postcode	KA1 2DP
Tel	01563 545300
Capacity	18128
Closest Railway Station	Kilmarnock
Record Attendance	35995 v Rangers, SC, 10/3/1962
Record Win	11-1 v Paisley Academical, SC, 18/1/1930
Record Defeat	1-9 v Celtic, Lge 13/8/1938
Most League Goals in a Season	34 Harry Cunningham 1927/8, Andy Kerr 1960/1
Colours 2020/21 Top	Blue with white stripe
Shorts	White
Sponsor	Brownings The Bakers
Manufacturer	Hummell
Change Colours 2020/21 Top	White with yellow chevrons
Shorts	Blue
Nicknames	Killie
Web	www.kilmarnockfc.co.uk
Match Programme 2020/21	Curtis Sport

Head of Football Operations: James Fowler
Manager: Alex Dyer, then Tommy Wright
Assistant Manager: Andy Millen, then Paul Stephenson
Goalkeeping Coach: Billy Thomson, then Colin Doyle
Coach / Analyst: Alan Maybury
Head Physio: Ryan Barr
Head of Medical: Alex McQueen
Sports Scientist: Stuart McFarlane
Club Doctor: Hamish Simpson
Head of Academy Recruitment: Alan Mahood
Academy Director: Paul McDonald
Chairman: Billy Bowie
Company Secretary: Graeme Bryson
Directors: Cathy Jamieson, Phyllis McLeish

The Johnnie Walker Enclosure at Rugby Park - stylistically unique

Nearly two generations of Killie fans have grown up knowing nothing other than Premiership football at Rugby Park. Killie were promoted to the top flight in 1993 and have maintained their seat at the top table since then. Relegation will be a huge blow but in many respects they only have themselves to blame for the mess they found themselves in.

It's only two short years since Steve Clark's Killie side finished third in the Premiership and qualified for Europe. That's when things began to unravel. Many people thought Clarke's assistant Alex Dyer would get the job. He was not selected and in came Alessandro Alessio, an Italian who had coached at Chelsea. His tenure was a disaster and he was binned, with Dyer given the task. That raises the question that if Dyer was not deemed suitable in the first place, why turn to him then? Rumours that player power had contributed to Alessio's departure may also have been true. Certainly the team spirit and togetherness fostered under Clarke evaporated overnight.

Dyer took the team into 2020/1. Scoring goals was a huge problem. In a run of eight games Killie scored in just one of them. Dyer was replaced by the affable Tommy Wright but the squad he inherited was lacking in confidence and organisation. He brought in Kyle Lafferty who rewarded him with a barrowload of goals. But defensive frailties saw Killie finish second bottom. Still, they had the safety net of the play offs to avoid relegation – but the fragility of the Killie team was hammered home by a double defeat at the hands of Dundee.

STAR MAN
Kyle Lafferty deserves credit for his efforts in attempting to keep Killie away from the drop zone. But as he scored the goals his defence conceded them – ultimately his sterling efforts were to no avail.

PROSPECTS 2021/2
Tommy Wright has gutted the squad that he inherited and brought in almost a whole new team. On paper they look good enough to challenge for promotion and anything less than that will be a failure. Will they win the League? Possibly not, so the play offs might be their means of reclaiming a top division spot.

Date	Comp	H/A	Opponents	F	A	HT	Referee	Crowd	Scorers
01/08/2020	L	A	Hibernian	1	2	1 2	J Beaton	BCD	Burke
09/08/2020	L	H	Celtic	1	1	1 1	A Muir	BCD	Burke
12/08/2020	L	A	Ross County	2	2	0 1	G Duncan	BCD	Power, Burke
15/08/2020	L	H	St Johnstone	1	2	0 0	A Dallas	BCD	Tshibola
22/08/2020	L	A	Rangers	0	0	0 0	K Clancy	BCD	
29/08/2020	L	H	Dundee United	4	0	2 0	D Munro	BCD	Kabamba 2, Brophy, McKenzie
12/09/2020	L	A	Aberdeen	0	1	0 1	B Madden	300	
19/09/2020	L	H	Hamilton Accies	2	1	1 1	N Walsh	BCD	Kiltie, Kabamba
26/09/2020	L	A	St Mirren	1	0	1 0	D Munro	BCD	Kabamba
06/10/2020	LC	A	Falkirk	0	3		KILMARNOCK FORFEITED TIE DUE TO COVID		
13/10/2020	LC	H	Dunfermline Athletic	0	3	0 0	A Dallas	BCD	
17/10/2020	L	A	Livingston	3	1	2 1	G Aitken	BCD	Tshibola, Burke pen, Kiltie
24/10/2020	L	H	Hibernian	0	1	0 1	C Steven	BCD	
01/11/2020	L	H	Rangers	0	1	0 1	A Dallas	BCD	
06/11/2020	L	A	St Johnstone	0	1	0 0	G Duncan	BCD	
10/11/2020	LC	A	Clyde	2	0	1 0	G Aitken	BCD	Whitehall 2
14/11/2020	LC	H	Dumbarton	2	0	2 0	G Duncan	BCD	Brophy, Pinnock
21/11/2020	L	H	Ross County	3	1	1 1	C Steven	BCD	Brophy, Kabamba pen, Burke
05/12/2020	L	A	Hamilton Accies	0	1	0 0	W Collum	BCD	
13/12/2020	L	A	Celtic	0	2	0 0	D Robertson	BCD	
19/12/2020	L	H	Aberdeen	0	2	0 0	D Munro	BCD	
23/12/2020	L	A	Dundee United	0	2	0 2	S McLean	BCD	
26/12/2020	L	H	Livingston	1	2	0 0	K Clancy	BCD	Burke pen
30/12/2020	L	A	Motherwell	2	0	1 0	J Beaton	BCD	Kiltie, Whitehall pen
02/01/2021	L	H	St Mirren	1	1	1 0	C Napier	BCD	Whitehall
09/01/2021	L	H	Hamilton Accies	2	0	1 0	G Irvine	BCD	Kiltie 2
16/01/2021	L	A	Hibernian	0	2	0 0	W Collum	BCD	
27/01/2021	L	A	Livingston	0	2	0 0	S Kirkland	BCD	
30/01/2021	L	H	St Johnstone	2	3	2 0	G Aitken	BCD	Burke, Tshibola
02/02/2021	L	H	Celtic	0	4	0 1	K Clancy	BCD	
06/02/2021	L	A	St Mirren	0	2	0 1	J Beaton	BCD	
10/02/2021	L	H	Motherwell	0	1	0 0	W Collum	BCD	
13/02/2021	L	A	Rangers	0	1	0 1	D Robertson	BCD	
20/02/2021	L	A	Aberdeen	0	1	0 1	D Robertson	BCD	
27/02/2021	L	H	Dundee United	1	1	0 1	D Munro	BCD	Medley
06/03/2021	L	A	Ross County	2	3	1 1	E Anderson	BCD	Lafferty 2 (1 pen)
20/03/2021	L	H	Motherwell	4	1	1 1	A Muir	BCD	Lafferty, Mckenzie, Pinnock, Burke
03/04/2021	SC	A	Stenhousemuir	4	0	2 0	G Aitken	BCD	Lafferty 3 (1 pen), Oakley
10/04/2021	L	H	Ross County	2	2	2 1	W Collum	BCD	Burke, Pinnock
17/04/2021	SC	H	Montrose	3	1	2 0	N Walsh	BCD	Lafferty, Steeves og, Kiltie
21/04/2021	L	H	Dundee United	3	0	3 0	A Muir	BCD	Lafferty 3 (1 pen)
26/04/2021	SC	H	St Mirren	3	3	2 1	D Robertson	BCD	Kiltie, Rossi, Millen pen
01/05/2021	L	A	Motherwell	0	2	0 0	B Madden	BCD	
12/05/2021	L	H	St Mirren	3	3	1 0	D Munro	BCD	Lafferty 2, Kiltie
16/05/2021	L	A	Hamilton Accies	2	0	2 0	K Clancy	BCD	Pinnock 2
20/05/2021	PO	A	Dundee	1	2	0 1	J Beaton		Haunstrup
24/05/2021	PO	H	Dundee	1	1	0 2	B Madden	500	Lafferty pen

Surname	First Name	Date of Birth	No	Nat	Pos	Signed	Previous	Notes	Contract	Lge A	Lge S	Lge G	SC A	SC S	SC G	LC A	LC S	LC G	Un
Abed	Tarek	19/04/2002		SCO / EGY	D	2020	Kilmarnock Youths	Released July 2021											1
Brindley	Tomas	13/10/2001	32	SCO	M	2020	Kilmarnock Youths	OL to Dumbarton Mar-May	End 2021/2		1					1			11
Broadfoot	Kirk	08/08/1984	5	SCO	D	2020	St Mirren	Rel;eased June 2021, joined Inverness CT		33	0		3			1			1
Brophy	Eamonn	10/03/1996	9	SCO	F	2017	Hamilton Accies	OL to St Mirren Jan-May, then permanent		8	7	2				2		1	3
Broun	Harry	16/08/2003	40	SCO	GK	2021	Kilmarnock Youths		End 2021/2	0	0								2
Burke	Chris	02/12/1983	29	SCO	M	2017	Ross County		End 2021/2	30	9	9	3			1			2
Cameron	Innes	22/08/2000	20	SCO	F	2018	Kilmarnock Youths	OL to Ayr Utd Oct-Jan, to Alloa Ath Jan-May	End 2022/3	0	0					1			10
Connell	Kyle	19/12/2001	25	SCO	F	2020	Kilmarnock Youths	OL to Airdrieonians Oct-May	End 2021/2	0	0								0
Dabo	Diaguely	26/08/1992	26	SEN / FRA	M	2021	Stevenage	Released June 2021		1	5								8
Dee	Fergus	21/10/2003		SCO	M	2021	Kilmarnock Youths		End 2021/2	0	0						1		0
Deveney	Euan	16/11/2002		NIR	D	2018	Rangers Youths	OL to Falkirk Oct-May	End 2021/2	0	0					1			0
Devenney	Justin	11/10/2003		SCO	M	2021	Kilmarnock Youths		End 2021/2	0	0								1
Dicker	Gary	31/07/1986	8	ROI	M	2016	Carlisle United	Released June 2021, joined Brighton		27	0		1	1		1			3
Dikamona	Clevid	23/06/1990	4	CON / FRA	D	2020	Hearts	Released June 2021, joined AG Caen		10	2								12
Doyle	Colin	12/06/1985	16	ROI	GK	2020	Hearts (OL)	Aug-May		13	0		3			2			23
Eastwood	Jake	03/10/1996	1	ENG	GK	2020	Sheffield United (OL)	Jul-Jan		1	0					1			2
El Makrini	Mohamed	06/07/1987	15	NET	M	2019	Roda JC	Transferred to Start Kristiansand Sep 2020		0	0								4
Findlay	Stuart	14/09/1995	17	SCO	D	2018	Kilmarnock Youths	Transferred to Philadelphia Union Feb 2021		21	1					1			1
Haunstrup	Brandon	26/10/1996	3	ENG	D	2020	Portsmouth		End 2021/2	23	6	1	2			3			10
Kabamba	Nicke	01/02/1993	11	DRC / ENG	F	2020	Hartlepool United	Released June 2021, joined Northampton Town		21	12	5		1		1			3
Kiltie	Greg	18/01/1997	10	SCO	M	2014	Kilmarnock Youths	OOC June 2021 joined St Mirren		24	7	6	2		2				7
Lafferty	Kyle	16/09/1987	28	NIR	F	2021	Reggina	OO June 2021 joined Anorthosis Famagusta		10	1	9	2		4				0
Lyle	Curtis	08/09/1999	34	SCO	GK	2020	Kilmarnock Youths	OL to Stranraer for 2021/2	End 2021/2	0	0								4
McGowan	Aaron	24/07/1996	2	SCO	D	2020	Hamilton Accies	Released June 2021 joined Northampton Town	End 2021/2	15	3					2			21
McKenzie	Rory	07/10/1993	7	SCO	F	2012	Kilmarnock Youths		End 2021/2	24	7	2	1	2		3			5
Medley	Zech	09/07/2000	24	ENG	D	2021	Arsenal (OL)	Feb-May		7	1	1	2						7
Millen	Ross	28/09/1994	22	SCO	D	2018	Queen's Park	Released June 2021, joined Scunthorpe United		20	1		3		1				3
Mullen	Michael	02/05/2003	60	SCO	F	2020	Kilmarnock Youths		End 2021/2	0	0						1		0
Mulumbu	Youssuf	25/01/1987	21	DRC / FRA	M	2020	Celtic	Released June 2021		6	11		2			2			9
Oakley	George	18/11/1995	9	ENG	F	2021	Pirin Blavoegrad	Released June 2021, joied Woking		3	3		1	2	1				8
Pierrick	Brandon	10/12/2001	15	CAM / ENG	F	2021	Crystal Palace (OL)	Feb-May		1	2								2
Pinnock	Mitch	12/12/1994	19	ENG	F	2020	AFC Wimbledon	OOC June 2021, joined Northampton Town		19	13	4	3			2		1	7
Power	Alan	23/01/1988	6	ROI	M	2017	Lincoln City	Joined St Mirren July 2021		34	0	1	3			1			1
Rennicks	Craig	30/07/2002		SCO	M	2020	Kilmarnock Youths	Released July 2021		0	0								0
Rennie	Josh	28/05/2002		SCO	F	2020		OL to Hurlford U Oct-May, Freed June joined Stranraer		0	0						1		0
Rogers	Danny	23/03/1994	23	ROI / USA	GK	2020	Aberdeen	Released June 2021		26	1								13
Ross	Craig	09/06/2002		SCO	M	2020	Kilmarnock Youths	OL to Kilwinning R Oct-May, Freed June joined Stranraer		0	0					1			0
Rossi	Zeno	28/10/2000	14	ITA / ENG	F	2020	AFC Bournemouth (OL)	Jul-May		13	3		1	1	1	2			14
Russell	Keir	12/01/2002		SCO	D	2020	Kilmarnock Youths	OL to Spartans Sep-Jan, released July 2021		0	0						1		0
Sloan	Kenny	17/06/2003	58	SCO	D	2020	Kilmarnock Youths		End 2021/2	0	0					1			0
Smith	Ross	14/10/2003		SCO	M	2020	Kilmarnock Youths		End 2021/2	0	0						1		0
Taylor	Ally	12/09/2001	33	SCO	M	2020	Kilmarnock Youths	OL to Stranraer Mar-May, Released May 2021		0	0	3							13
Tshibola	Aaron	02/01/1995	27	DRC / ENG	M	2020	Desportivo Aves	Released June 2021 joined Genclerbirligi		27	5			3					9
Warnock	Steven	12/06/2003	63	SCO	F	2020	Kilmarnock Youths		End 2021/2	0	0			1		1			0
Waters	Calum	10/03/1996	18	SCO	D	2017	Alloa Athletic		End 2021/2	18	0		1						17
Whitehall	Danny	08/10/1995	12	ENG	F	2020	Maidenhead United	Released June 2021		5	13	2				2		2	22
Willis	Jake	13/08/2002		SCO	D	2020	Kilmarnock Youths	Released July 2021		0	0								0
Own Goal															1				
NEW SIGNINGS																			
Alston	Blair	23/03/1992		SCO	M	2021	Falkirk		End 2022/3										
Armstrong	Daniel	11/10/1997		SCO	F	2021	Raith Rovers		End 2022/3										
Doyle	Colin	12/06/1985		ROI	GK	2021	Hearts		End 2021/2										
Hemming	Zach	07/03/2000		ENG	GK	2021	Middlesbrough (OL)	Jul-Jun	End 2021/2										
Lyons	Brad	26/05/1997		NIR	N	2021	Blackburn Rovers		End 2022/3										
McGinn	Stephen	02/12/1988		SCO	M	2021	Hibernian		End 2021/2										
McGowan	Dylan	06/08/1991		SCO / AUS	M	2021	Sydney Wanderers		End 2022/3										
Murray	Euan	20/01/1994		SCO	D	2021	Dunfermline Athletic		End 2022/3										
Murray	Fraser	07/05/1999		SCO	M	2021	Hibernian		End 2022/3										
Naismith	Jason	25/06/1994		SCO	D	2021	Ross County		End 2021/2										
Polworth	Liam	12/10/1994		SCO	M	2021	Motherwell		End 2022/3										
Robinson	Scott	11/03/1992		SCO	F	2021	Livingston		End 2022/3										
Sanders	Jack	18/03/1999		ENG	D	2021	Wigan Athletic		End 2022/3										
Stokes	Chris	08/03/1991		ENG	D	2021	Forest Green Rovers		End 2022/3										
Walker	Sam	02/10/1991		ENG	GK	2021	Reading		End 2022/3										

Date	Comp	H/A	Opponents	F	A	1	2	3	4	5	6	7	8	9	10
01/08/2020	L	A	Hibernian	1	2	Eastwood*	Broadfoot	Findlay	Waters	Millen	Burke	Power	Tshibola&	McKenzie	Kiltie+
09/08/2020	L	H	Celtic	1	1	Rogers	Broadfoot	Findlay	Waters	Millen	Burke+	Power	Tshibola	McKenzie*	Dicker
12/08/2020	L	A	Ross County	2	2	Rogers	Broadfoot	Findlay	Waters	Millen	Burke	Power	Tshibola	Pinnock*	Dicker
15/08/2020	L	H	St Johnstone	1	2	Rogers	Broadfoot	Findlay	Waters	Millen	Burke&	Power	Tshibola	Pinnock*	Dicker
22/08/2020	L	A	Rangers	0	0	Rogers	Broadfoot	Findlay	Waters	McGowan	Burke	Power>	Tshibola	Haunstrup&	Dicker+
29/08/2020	L	H	Dundee United	4	0	Rogers	Broadfoot	Findlay*	Waters<	Rossi	Burke>	Kiltie	Tshibola&	Brophy+	Dicker
12/09/2020	L	A	Aberdeen	0	1	Rogers	Broadfoot*	Findlay	Waters>	Millen	Burke&	Kiltie	Tshibola	Brophy+	Dicker
19/09/2020	L	H	Hamilton Accies	2	1	Rogers	Broadfoot	Findlay	Waters	Millen	Burke*	Kiltie+	Tshibola	Brophy	Dicker
26/09/2020	L	A	St Mirren	1	0	Rogers	Broadfoot	Findlay	Waters	Millen+	Burke*	Power	Tshibola	Kiltie	Dicker
06/10/2020	LC	A	Falkirk	0	3										
13/10/2020	LC	H	Dunfermline Athletic	0	3	Doyle	Haunstrup+	E Deveney	Ross	McKenzie	Burke>	Sloan	Warnock<	Cameron*	Dicker
17/10/2020	L	A	Livingston	3	1	Rogers	Broadfoot	Dikamona	Waters	Rossi	Burke+	Power	Tshibola<	Kiltie>	Dicker
24/10/2020	L	H	Hibernian	0	1	Rogers	Broadfoot	Dikamona*	Waters	Rossi	Burke	Power	Tshibola>	Kiltie&	Dicker+
01/11/2020	L	H	Rangers	0	1	Rogers	Broadfoot	Findlay	Waters	Millen	Burke+	Power	Tshibola&	McKenzie	Dicker
06/11/2020	L	A	St Johnstone	0	1	Rogers	Broadfoot	Findlay	Waters&	Millen	Burke	Power	Tshibola+	Kiltie*	Dicker
10/11/2020	LC	A	Clyde	2	0	Doyle	Haunstrup	Findlay	Rossi	McGowan	Mulumbu	McKenzie	Pinnock	Brophy	Brindley
14/11/2020	LC	H	Dumbarton	2	0	Eastwood	Broadfoot	Haunstrup	Rossi	McGowan	Mulumbu	Power	Pinnock	Brophy	McKenzie
21/11/2020	L	H	Ross County	3	1	Rogers	Broadfoot	Findlay	Haunstrup	McGowan	Tshibola	McKenzie	Pinnock&	Brophy*	Dicker
05/12/2020	L	A	Hamilton Accies	0	1	Rogers	Broadfoot	Dikamona	Haunstrup	McGowan	Tshibola	Power	Pinnock	Brophy	Kiltie*
13/12/2020	L	A	Celtic	0	2	Rogers	Broadfoot	Findlay	Haunstrup	McGowan	Tshibola	Power	Pinnock+	McKenzie	Kiltie*
19/12/2020	L	H	Aberdeen	0	2	Rogers	Broadfoot	Findlay&	Waters	McGowan*	Tshibola	Power	Burke	McKenzie	Brophy
23/12/2020	L	A	Dundee United	0	2	Rogers	Broadfoot	Findlay	Waters	Dikamona+	Tshibola	Power>	Burke	McKenzie	Brophy&
26/12/2020	L	H	Livingston	1	2	Rogers	Broadfoot	Findlay	Waters	McGowan	Tshibola	Power	Burke	McKenzie	Mulumbu
30/12/2020	L	A	Motherwell	2	0	Rogers	Broadfoot	Findlay	Waters*	McGowan	Tshibola+	Power	Pinnock	McKenzie>	Kiltie
02/01/2021	L	H	St Mirren	1	1	Rogers	Broadfoot	Findlay	Haunstrup	McGowan	Mulumbu	Power	Burke	McKenzie	Kiltie
09/01/2021	L	H	Hamilton Accies	2	0	Rogers	Broadfoot	Findlay	Haunstrup	McGowan	Mulumbu*	Power>	Burke+	McKenzie	Kiltie
16/01/2021	L	A	Hibernian	0	2	Rogers	Dikamona	Findlay	Haunstrup	McGowan&	Mulumbu	Power	Pinnock	Tshibola*	Kiltie
27/01/2021	L	A	Livingston	0	2	Rogers	Rossi	Findlay*	Haunstrup	McGowan	Burke+	Power	Pinnock	Tshibola	Oakley&
30/01/2021	L	H	St Johnstone	2	3	Rogers	Dikamona	Millen	Haunstrip	Rossi	Burke	Power	Kabamba	Tshibola	Oakley*
02/02/2021	L	H	Celtic	0	4	Doyle	Dikamona	Millen	Haunstrup	Rossi	Burke&	Power	Dicker+	Tshibola	Oakley*
06/02/2021	L	A	St Mirren	0	2	Doyle	Medley	Pierrick+	Haunstrup	Rossi	Whitehall&	Power	Dicker	Tshibola*	Kiltie>
10/02/2021	L	H	Motherwell	0	1	Doyle	Dikamona	Medley	Haunstrup	McGowan	Burke	Power&	Dicker	Kamamba	Kiltie*
13/02/2021	L	A	Rangers	0	1	Doyle	Dikamona	Medley	Haunstrup	McGowan	Mulumbi	Tshibola&	Dicker*	Kabamba	Kiltie
20/02/2021	L	A	Aberdeen	0	1	Doyle	Broadfoot	Dikamona*	Haunstrup>	Millen	Burke+	Mulumbu	Dicker	Dabo&	Pinnock
27/02/2021	L	H	Dundee United	1	1	Doyle	Broadfoot	Medley	Haunstrup	Millen	Kiltie	Power	Ficker	Lafferty	Pinnock+
06/03/2021	L	A	Ross County	2	3	Doyle	Broadfoot	Medley&	Haunstrup	Millen	Kiltie<	Power	Dicker>	Lafferty	Pinnock*
20/03/2021	L	H	Motherwell	4	1	Doyle	Broadfoot	McGowan	Haunstrup	Medley	Burke*	Power	Dicker	Lafferty&	Pinnock+
03/04/2021	SC	A	Stenhousemuir	4	0	Doyle	Broadfoot	Millen	Haunstrup	Medley*	Burke&	Power	Dicker	Lafferty+	Pinnock
10/04/2021	L	H	Ross County	2	2	Doyle	Broadfoot	McGowan	Haunstrup	Medley	Burke	Power	Dicker	Lafferty	Pinnock
17/04/2021	SC	H	Montrose	3	1	Doyle	Broadfoot	Millen	Waters	Medley	Burke+	Power*	Mulumbu	Lafferty&	Pinnock
21/04/2021	L	H	Dundee United	3	0	Doyle	Broadfoot	Millen	Haunstrup	Rossi	Burke*	Power	Dicker	Lafferty+	Pinnock
26/04/2021	SC	H	St Mirren	3	3	Doyle	Broadfoor	Millen	Haunstrup	Rossi	Burke>	Power	Mulumbu*	Oakley+	Pinnock
01/05/2021	L	A	Motherwell	0	2	Rogers	Broadfoot	Millen	Haunstrup	Rossi	Kiltie+	Power*	Dicker	Lafferty	Pinnock
12/05/2021	L	H	St Mirren	3	3	Rogers	Broadfoot	Millen	Waters*	Rossi	Burke	Power	Dicker	Lafferty	Pinnock
16/05/2021	L	A	Hamilton Accies	2	0	Doyle	Broadfoot	Millen	Haunstrup	Rossi	Burke*	Power	Dicker>	Lafferty&	Pinnock
20/05/2021	PO	A	Dundee	1	2	Doyle	Broadfoot	Millen	Haunstrup	Rossi	Burke	Power	Dicker	Lafferty	Pinnock
24/05/2021	PO	H	Dundee	1	1	Doyle	Broadfoot	Millen	Haunstrup*	Rossi	Burke+	Power	Tshibola	Lafferty	Pinnock

THE GOALIES

Goalkeepers Used in League Matches, 1970-2020

Players shown in the season of their first appearance only

1970/1 Ally Hunter
Sandy McLaughlin
1972/3 Jim Stewart
1973/4 Ally McCulloch
1980/1 James Brown
Alistair Wilson
1984/5 Cammy Melville
1985/6 Barry Holland
1989/0 Bobby Geddes
Dave McKellar
1991/2 Andy Graham
1994/5 Colin Meldrum
Dragan Lekovic
1997/8 Gordon Marshall
1999/0 Michael Watt
2002/3 Colin Stewart
2003/4 Francois Dubordeau
Craig Samson
Graham Smith
2004/5 Alan Combe
2007/8 Chad Harpur
2008/9 Damien Rascle
Cammy Bell
2009/0 Mark Brown
2010/1 Anssi Jaakola
2011/2 Kyle Letheren
2014/5 Connor Brennan
2015/6 Jamie McDonald
2016/7 Freddy Woodman
2017/8 Leo Fasan
2018/9 Daniel Bachmann
2019/0 Laurentiu Branescu
Jan Koprivec

11	12	13	14	15	16	17	18	19	20
Kabamba	Rogers*	Brophy+	Whitehall&	McGowan	Cameron	El Makrini	Dicker	Rossi	Brindley
Kabamba	Haunstrup*	Kiltie+	Whitehall	McGowan	Brophy	El Makrini	Dikamona	Pinnock	Lyle
Kabamba	Haunstrup*	Kiltie	Whitehall	McGowan	Cameron	El Makrini	Dikamona	Brindley	Doyle
Kabamba+	McGowan*	Brophy+	Kiltie&	Whitehall	Cameron	El Makrini	Dikamona	Haunstrup	Doyle
Brophy*	Kabamba*	Kiltie+	Pinnock&	Brindley>	Cameron	Rossi	Dikamona	Whitehall	Doyle
Kabamba	Dikamona*	McKenzie+	Mulumbu&	Pinnock>	Haunstrup<	McGowan	Cameron	Whitehall	Doyle
Kabamba	Dikamona*<	Pinnock+	McKenzie&	Whitehall>	Rossi<	McGowan	Cameron	Haunstrup	Doyle
Kabamba	McKenzie*	Pinnock+	Dikamona	Whitehall	Rossi	McGowan	Cameron	Haunstrup	Doyle
Kabamba	McKenzie*	Rossi+	Dikamona	Whitehall	Pinnock	McGowan	Cameron	Haunstrup	Doyle
Kabamba&	Rennie*	Russell+	Mullen&	Dee>	Smith<	Broun	Abed	J Devenny	
Kabamba*	Brophy*	McKenzie+	Pinnock&	Mulumbu>	Brindley	Whitehall	Cameron	Haunstrup	Doyle
Kabamba	Findlay*	Brophy+	Pinnock&	Mulumbu>	Brindley	Whitehall	McKenzie	Haunstrup	Doyle
Kabamba*	Brophy*	Pinnock+	Mulumbu&	Kiltie	McGowan	Whitehall	Rossi	Haunstrup	Doyle
Kabamba	Brophy*	Pinnock+	Whitehall&	Eastwood	McGowan	McKenzie	Mulumbu	Haunstrup	Rossi
Whitehall	Kiltie	Burke	Kabamba	Broadfoot	Eastwood	Tshibola	Power	Waters	
Whitehall	Kiltie	Findlay	Kabamba	Waters	Brindley	Tshibola	Taylor	Burke	Doyle
Kabamba+	Rossi*	Whitehall+	Burke&	Waters	Kiltie	Taylor	Doyle		
Kabamba	Whitehall*	Taylor	McKenzie	Waters	Mulumbu	Doyle			
Kabamba&	Burke*	Mulumbu+	Brophy&	Waters	Rossi	Taylor	Whitehall	Doyle	
Kabamba+	Kiltie*	Whitehall+	Haunstrup&	Taylor	Mulumbu	Pinnock	Doyle		
Kiltie*	Pinnock*	Kabamba+	Whitehall&	Mulumbu>	Taylor	Doyle			
Kabamba	Dikamona	Pinnock	Kiltie	Taylor	Brophy	Whitehall	Haunstrup	Doyle	
Whitehall&	Haunstrup*	Mulumbu+	Kabamba&	Burke>	Brophy	Taylor	Dikamona	Doyle	
Whitehall*	Kabamba*	Pinnock	Daba	Tshibola	Dikamona	Taylor			
Whitehall&	Dabo*	Pinnock+	Kabamba&	Tshibola>	Broun	Taylor	Waters	Dikamona	Brindley
Whitehall+	Burke*	Kabamba+	Dabo&	Brindley	Waters	Taylor	Cameron	Doyle	
McKenzie	Millen*	Dabo+	Kabamba&	Brindley	Whitehall	Taylor	Doyle		
McKenzie	Whitehall*	Dabo	McGowan	Brindley	Dicker	Taylor	Pinnock	Doyle	
McKenzie	Kabamba*	Pierrick+	Pinnock&	McGowan	Dabo	Medley	Whitehall	Brindley	Lyle
Mckenzie	Mulumbu*	Burke+	Pinnock&	Kabamba>	Dabo	Millen	McGowan	Brindley	Lyle
McKenzie+	Oakley*	Pinnock+	Mulumbu&	Pierrick	Whitehall	Millen	Rossi	Tshibola	Lyle
McKenzie+	Burke*	Whitehall+	Dabo&	Pierrick	Pinnock	Millen	Rossi	Oakley	Rogers
Kabamba<	Medley*	McGowan+	Lafferty&	Kiltie>	Whitehall<	Tshibola	Rossi	McKenzie	Rogers
McKenzie*	Kabamba*	Burke+	McGowan	Oakley	Mulumbu	Tshibola	Rossi	Waters	Rogers
McKenzie+	Kabamba*	McGowan+	Burke&	Dabo>	Tshibola<	Waters	Rossi	Whitehall	Rogers
McKenzie	Mulumbu*	Pierrick+	Whitehall&	Dabo	Tshibola	Oakley	Rossi	Waters	Rogers
McKenzie>	Rossi*	Oakley+	Tshibola&	Warnock>	Whitehall	Mulumbu	Waters	Kabamba	Rogers
McKenzie*	Kiltie*	Oakley	Rossi	Dabo	Whitehall	Mulumbu	Waters	Dikamona	Rogers
Kiltie	Tshibola*	McKenzie+	Oakley&	Haunstrup	Rossi	McGowan	Whitehall	Dicker	Rogers
McKenzie	Tshibola*	Kabamba+	Oakley	Medley	Waters	McGowan	Mulumbu	Kiltie	Rogers
Kiltie&	Tshibola*	Kabamba+	McKenzie&	Dicker>	Waters	McGowan	Dikamona	Whitehall	Rogers
McKenzie&	Tshibola*	Oakley+	Burke&	Whitehall	Waters	McGowan	Mulumbu	Medley	Doyle
Kiltie+	Haunstrup*	Whitehall+	Oakley	Tshibola	Medley	McGowan	Mulumbu	Mckenzie	Doyle
Kiltie+	McKenzie*	Tshibola+	Oakley&	Mulumbu>	Medley	McGowan	Whitehall	Waters	Rogers
Kiltie*	McKenzie*	Tshibola	Oakley	Dabo	Medley	McGowan	Waters	Rogers	
McKenzie	Whitehall*	Kiltie+	Oakley	Dabo	Medley	McGowan	Rogers		

Ally Hunter

Jim Brown

Chad Harpur

Livingston FC 2020/21 Livi / The Lions

Founded	1943
Ground	Almondvale Stadium
Postcode	EH54 7DN
Tel	01506 417000
Capacity	9865
Closest Railway Station	Livingston North / Livingston South
Record Attendance	10024, Lge v Celtic, 18/8/2001
Record Win	8-0 v Stranraer, LC, 4/8/12
Record Defeat	0-8 v Hamilton Accies, Lge, 14/12/74
Most League Goals in a Season	22 Leigh Griffiths 2008/9 / Iain Russell 2010/11
Colours 2020/21 Top	Yellow
Shorts	Amber
Sponsor	Phoenix Drilling
Manufacturer	Nike
Change Colours 2020/21 Top	Amber
Shorts	Black / Grey
Nicknames	Black
Web	www.livingstonfc.co.uk
Match Programme 2020/21	None issued

Chief Executive: John Ward
Chairman: Robert Wilson
Secretary: Derek White
Hon. President: Gordon Ford
Manager: Gary Holt, then David Martindale
Assistant Manager: David Martindale, then Marvin Bartley
Coach and Head of Academy: Dougie Imrie
First Team Analyst: Euan Blondin
Sports Scientist: Colin Ritchie
Sports Therapist: Andy MacKenzie
Kit Manager: Stephen Sproule
Goalkeeping Coach: Stuart Garden

Below

Ferranti Thistle take on Elgin City at a packed City Park in the Scottish Cup in January 1973. The game ended 2-2. This game, plus a match against Partick the following season, put the previously little-known Edinburgh side "on the map" and was a big factor in their election to the Scottish League in 1974.

City Park was demolished a few years ago although the name lives on with the "City Park" housing development.

In the early part of the season Livingston were managed by Gary Holt but he unexpectedly quit in November. The club installed his Assistant David Martindale as Caretaker. They wanted to appoint him on a permanent basis but had to apply to the SFA for permission to see if he was deemed "fit and proper" for the job. Martindale was sentenced to six and a half years in prison in 2006 for drug trafficking and money laundering. He also had £100,000 of assets seized under proceed of crime legislation. The club argued that he had been rehabilitated, worked hard to turn his life around, and deserved the opportunity to take charge. After lengthy deliberation the SFA concurred and Martindale was given the job.

The club had performed brilliantly during his interim spell. As often happens they struggled more once he had been given the job permanently. Still, he guided them through to the League Cup Final where they met St Johnstone. Perhaps the Cup run saw them lose focus in the League but results in the closing third of the season were disappointing.

STAR MAN

Scott Pittman continues to impress in Livingston's midfield. Plucked from Junior football, he has adjusted to the SPFL and looks every inch a Premiership player. It is surprising that bigger clubs haven't been hovering around looking to sign him.

PROSPECTS 2021/2

Given their poor end to the season Livi need to turn things around quickly. They will start as one of the club's tipped for relegation but the West Lothian side, and their Manager, have a habit of defying the odds.

Date	Comp	H/A	Opponents	F	A		HT		Referee	Crowd	Scorers
01/08/2020	L	A	St Mirren	0	1		0	1	D Robertson	BCD	
08/08/2020	L	H	Hibernian	1	4		0	3	E Anderson	BCD	Dykes pen
12/08/2020	L	A	Motherwell	2	2		1	2	C Steven	BCD	Dykes pen, Forrest
16/08/2020	L	H	Rangers	0	0		0	0	N Walsh	BCD	
23/08/2020	L	A	Aberdeen	1	2		0	0	S McLean	BCD	Pittman
29/08/2020	L	H	Ross County	1	0		0	0	J Beaton	BCD	Guthrie
12/09/2020	L	H	Hamilton Accies	1	2		1	0	D Robertson	BCD	Pittman
19/09/2020	L	A	Celtic	2	3		1	2	G Duncan	BCD	Holt pen, Serrano
26/09/2020	L	H	St Johnstone	2	0		2	0	C Napier	BCD	Tiffoney, Forrest
02/10/2020	L	A	Dundee United	2	1		0	1	J Beaton	BCD	Guthrie, Forrest
06/10/2020	LC	A	Edinburgh City	5	1		3	0	W Collum	BCD	Robinson, Mullin 2, Poplatnik, Lokotsch
10/10/2020	LC	H	Alloa Athletic	2	1		0	1	A Muir	BCD	Forrest, Mullin
17/10/2020	L	H	Kilmarnock	1	3		1	2	G Aitken	BCD	Pittman
25/10/2020	L	A	Rangers	0	2		0	2	N Walsh	BCD	
31/10/2020	L	H	Motherwell	0	2		0	2	J Beaton	BCD	
06/11/2020	L	A	Ross County	1	1		0	1	K Clancy		Devlin
10/11/2020	LC	A	Stenhousemuir	4	0		3	0	C Steven	BCD	Forrest 2, Poplatnik, Taylor-Sinclair
14/11/2020	LC	H	Airdrieonians	4	1		0	0	D Munro	BCD	Forrest 2, Emmanuel-Thomas 2(1 pen)
21/11/2020	L	H	St Mirren	0	1		0	0	W Collum	BCD	
28/11/2020	LC	H	Ayr United	4	0		4	0	D Munro	BCD	Chalmers og, Fitzwater 2, Forrest
05/12/2020	L	H	Dundee United	2	0		0	0	D Robertson	BCD	Pittman, Bartley
12/12/2020	L	A	St Johnstone	2	1		0	0	J Beaton	BCD	Guthrie, Robinson
16/12/2020	LC	H	Ross County	2	0		2	0	S McLean	BCD	Sibbald, Forrest
23/12/2020	L	A	Hamilton Accies	2	0		0	0	G Duncan	BCD	Guthrie, Mullin
26/12/2020	L	A	Kilmarnock	2	1		0	0	K Clancy	BCD	Emmanuel-Thomas, Robinson
02/01/2021	L	A	Hibernian	3	0		2	0	D Munro	BCD	Mullin, Guthrie, Robinson
10/01/2021	L	H	Ross County	3	1		1	1	A Muir	BCD	Robinson, Forrest, Hamilton
16/01/2021	L	A	Celtic	0	0		0	0	J Beaton	BCD	
20/01/2021	L	H	Celtic	2	2		1	2	W Collum	BCD	Brown, Emmanuel-Thomas
24/01/2021	LC	N	St Mirren	1	0		1	0	D Munro	BCD	Robinson
27/01/2021	L	H	Kilmarnock	2	0		0	0	S Kirkland	BCD	Kabia, Pittman
30/01/2021	L	H	Aberdeen	0	0		0	0	S McLean	BCD	
02/02/2021	L	A	Aberdeen	2	0		2	0	N Walsh	BCD	Lewis og, Devlin
06/02/2021	L	H	St Johnstone	1	2		0	1	E Anderson	BCD	Pittman
13/02/2021	L	A	Dundee United	0	3		0	2	N Walsh	BCD	
20/02/2021	L	A	St Mirren	1	1		1	1	W Collum	BCD	McCarthy og
28/02/2021	LC	N	St Johnstone	0	1		0	1	D Robertson	BCD	
03/03/2021	L	H	Rangers	0	1		0	0	J Beaton	BCD	
06/03/2021	L	A	Motherwell	1	3		0	1	C Steven	BCD	Fitzwater
13/03/2021	L	H	Hamilton Accies	2	1		2	1	K Clancy	BCD	Emmanuel-Thomas, Pittman
20/03/2021	L	H	Hibernian	1	1		1	1	N Walsh	BCD	Sibbald
03/04/2021	SC	H	Raith Rovers	2	1	AET	0	1	B Madden	BCD	Poplatnik, Fitzwater
10/04/2021	L	A	Celtic	0	6		0	2	N Walsh	BCD	
17/04/2021	SC	A	Aberdeen	2	2	AET, 3-5p	1	0	C Steven	BCD	Emmanuel-Thomas 2 (1 pen)
21/04/2021	L	A	Hibernian	1	2		0	2	C Napier	BCD	Emmanuel-Thomas
01/05/2021	L	H	Aberdeen	1	2		0	0	G Irvine	BCD	Emmauel-Thomas
12/05/2021	L	H	Rangers	0	3		0	0	D Robertson	BCD	
15/05/2021	L	A	St Johnstone	0	0		0	0	C Napier	BCD	

Date	Comp	H/A	Opponents	F	A	1	2	3	4	5	6	7	8	9	10
01/08/2020	L	A	St Mirren	0	1	McCrorie	Ambrose	Taylor-Sinclair&	Devlin	Guthrie	Fitzwater	Bartley	Sibbald+	Forrest*	Pittman
08/08/2020	L	H	Hibernian	1	4	McCrorie	Ambrose	Robinson&	Devlin*	Guthrie	Fitzwater>	Bartley	Sibbald+	Brown	Pittman
12/08/2020	L	A	Motherwell	2	2	McCrorie	Brown*	Taylor-Sinclair&	Robinson+	Guthrie	Fitzwater	Bartley	Sibbald	Forrest	Pittman
16/08/2020	L	H	Rangers	0	0	Stryjek	Devlin	McMillan	Holt	Guthrie	Fitzwater	Bartley*	Sibbald	Forrest&	Pittman
23/08/2020	L	A	Aberdeen	1	2	McCrorie	Devlin	McMillan*	Holt	Guthrie	Fitzwater+	Bartley	Sibbald&	Forrest>	Pittman
29/08/2020	L	H	Ross County	1	0	McCrorie	Devlin	Ambrose	Robinson	Guthrie	Serrano	Bartley	Sibbald*	Forrest	Pittman
12/09/2020	L	H	Hamilton Accies	1	2	McCrorie	Devlin	Ambrose	Robinson&	Guthrie	Serrano	Bartley	Holt+	Forrest	Pittman
19/09/2020	L	A	Celtic	2	3	McCrorie	Devlin	Ambrose	Brown&	Guthrie	Serrano	Bartley>	Sibbald*	Holt	Pittman
26/09/2020	L	H	St Johnstone	2	0	McCrorie	Devlin	Ambrose	Robinson&	Guthrie	Serrano	Bartley	Holt	Forrest*	Pittman
02/10/2020	L	A	Dundee United	2	1	McCrorie	Devlin	Ambrose	Robinson	Guthrie	Serrano	Bartley	Holt	Forrest+	Pittman
06/10/2020	**LC**	**A**	**Edinburgh City**	**5**	**1**	**Stryjek**	**Fitzwater<**	**McMillan>**	**Robinson**	**Guthrie**	**Serrano+**	**Mullin**	**Holt**	**Forrest&**	**Pittman**
10/10/2020	**LC**	**H**	**Alloa Athletic**	**2**	**1**	**Stryjek**	**Devlin**	**Ambrose**	**Taylor-Sinclair**	**Emmanuel-Thomas**	**Serrano**	**Bartley**	**Mullin***	**Forrest**	**Pittman**
17/10/2020	L	H	Kilmarnock	1	3	McCrorie	Devlin	Ambrose	Robinson+	Guthrie	Serrano	Bartley	Holt	Forrest&	Pittman
25/10/2020	L	A	Rangers	0	2	Stryjek	Devlin	Ambrose*	Emmanuel-Thomas&	Guthrie	Serrano	Bartley	Holt	Brown	Pittman
31/10/2020	L	H	Motherwell	0	2	Stryjek	Devlin	Brown	Emmanuel-Thomas	Guthrie	Serrano	Bartley	Holt&	Mullin*	Pittman
06/11/2020	L	A	Ross County	1	1	Stryjek	Devlin	Brown+	Emmanuel-Thomas	Guthrie	Robinson	Bartley	Lawson	Forrest	Pittman
10/11/2020	**LC**	**A**	**Stenhousemuir**	**4**	**0**	**Maley**	**Devlin***	**Ambrose**	**Emmanuel-Thomas**	**McMillan&**	**Fitzwater**	**Mullin**	**Holt**	**Forrest**	**Pittman+**
14/11/2020	**LC**	**H**	**Airdrieonians**	**4**	**1**	**Maley**	**Devlin**	**Taylor-Sinclair+**	**Emmanuel-Thomas**	**Guthrie**	**Serrano&**	**Bartley**	**Robinson**	**Forrest**	**Mullin***
21/11/2020	L	H	St Mirren	0	1	Stryjek	Devlin	Brown	Emmanuel-Thomas	Guthrie	Lawson+	Bartley	Holt	Forrest	Pittman&
28/11/2020	**LC**	**H**	**Ayr United**	**4**	**0**	**Stryjek**	**Devlin>**	**Bartley&**	**Poplatnik***	**Guthrie<**	**Lawson**	**Fitzwater**	**Mullin+**	**Forrest**	**Pittman**
05/12/2020	L	H	Dundee United	2	0	Stryjek	Devlin	Bartley	Poplatnik*	Guthrie	Serrano	Fitzwater	Mullin	Forrest&	Pittman
12/12/2020	L	A	St Johnstone	2	1	Stryjek	Devlin	Bartley	Poplatnik*	Guthrie	Serrano	Fitzwater	Mullin>	Forrest&	Pittman
16/12/2020	**LC**	**H**	**Ross County**	**2**	**0**	**Stryjek**	**Devlin**	**Bartley**	**Robinson&**	**Guthrie**	**Serrano**	**Fitzwater**	**Mullin+**	**Forrest***	**Pittman**
23/12/2020	L	A	Hamilton Accies	2	0	Stryjek	Devlin	Holt	Robinson	Guthrie	Serrano	Fitzwater	Mullin	Forrest*	Pittman
26/12/2020	L	A	Kilmarnock	2	1	Stryjek	Devlin	Bartley	Emmanuel-Thomas*	Guthrie	Serrano	Fitzwater	Mullin	Holt	Pittman
02/01/2021	L	A	Hibernian	3	0	Stryjek	Devlin	Bartley	Ambrose	Guthrie	Brown	Robinson&	Mullin*	Holt	Pittman
10/01/2021	L	H	Ross County	3	1	Stryjek	Devlin	Bartley	Ambrose	Guthrie	Brown	Robinson+	Mullin*	Holt	Pittman
16/01/2021	L	A	Celtic	0	0	Stryjek	Devlin	Bartley	Ambrose	Guthrie	Brown	Robinson+	Mullin	Lawson	Pittman
20/01/2021	L	H	Celtic	2	2	McCrorie	Serrano	Fitzwater	Emmanuel-Thomas&	Guthrie	Brown	McMillan>	Forrest*	Lawson	Pittman
24/01/2021	**LC**	**N**	**St Mirren**	**1**	**0**	**Stryjek**	**Devlin**	**Bartley**	**Ambrose**	**Guthrie**	**Serrano**	**Robinson+**	**Mullin***	**Holt**	**Pittman**
27/01/2021	L	H	Kilmarnock	2	0	Stryjek	Devlin	Bartley&	Fitzwater	Guthrie	Brown	Forrest>	Mullin+	Holt	Pittman
30/01/2021	L	H	Aberdeen	0	0	Stryjek	Devlin	Bartley	Ambrose	Guthrie	Brown	Robinson&	Serrano+	Holt	Pittman
02/02/2021	L	A	Aberdeen	2	0	Stryjek	Devlin	Taylor-Sinclair	Ambrose	Emmanuel-Thomas*	Serrano	Longridge	Mullin+	Holt	Pittman
06/02/2021	L	H	St Johnstone	1	2	Stryjek	Devlin	Taylor-Sinclair	Ambrose	Bartley	Robinson	Longridge	Forrest*	Holt	Pittman
13/02/2021	L	A	Dundee United	0	3	Stryjek	Devlin	Bartley>	Fitzwater	Guthrie	Serrano	Robinson*	Mullin	Holt	Pittman&
20/02/2021	L	A	St Mirren	1	1	McCrorie	Devlin	Forrest*	Ambrose	Guthrie	Serrano	Reilly+	Mullin>	Holt	Pittman
28/02/2021	**LC**	**N**	**St Johnstone**	**0**	**1**	**McCrorie**	**Devlin**	**Bartley**	**Ambrose**	**Guthrie**	**Serrano**	**Robinson**	**Mullin+**	**Holt>**	**Pittman&**
03/03/2021	L	H	Rangers	0	1	Styjek	Devlin	Bartley	Fitzwater	Guthrie	Serrano	Reilly*	Mullin	Holt+	Pittman
06/03/2021	L	A	Motherwell	1	3	McCrorie	Devlin	Bartley&	Fitzwater	Guthrie	Serrano	Taylor-Sinclair+	Mullin	Lawson*	Poplatnik
13/03/2021	L	H	Hamilton Accies	2	1	McCrorie	Devlin	Bartley	Fitzwater	Guthrie	Longridge	Emmanuel-Thomas&	Forrest*	Holt	Pittman
20/03/2021	L	H	Hibernian	1	1	McCrorie	Devlin	Bartley	Fitzwater	Guthrie	Longridge*	Emmanuel-Thomas&	Forrest+	Holt	Pittman
03/04/2021	**SC**	**H**	**Raith Rovers**	**2**	**1 AET**	**McCrorie**	**Devlin**	**Bartley**	**Fitzwater**	**Guthrie**	**Longridge**	**Emmanuel-Thomas+**	**Forrest***	**Holt**	**Pittman>**
10/04/2021	L	A	Celtic	0	6	McCrorie	Devlin	Bartley&	Fitzwater<	Guthrie	Longridge	Emmanuel-Thomas+	Forrest>	Holt	Pittman
17/04/2021	**SC**	**A**	**Aberdeen**	**2**	**2 AET, 3-5p**	**Stryjek**	**Devlin**	**Bartley**	**Fitzwater>**	**Guthrie**	**Longridge&**	**Emmanuel-Thomas**	**Forrest***	**Holt**	**Pittman**
21/04/2021	L	A	Hibernian	1	2	Stryjek	Devlin	Lithgow	Ambrose+	Guthrie	Longridge*	Emmanuel-Thomas	Mullin&	Holt	Pittman
01/05/2021	L	H	Aberdeen	1	2	Stryjek	Devlin	Bartley	Fitzwater	Guthrie	Longridge	Emmanuel-Thomas	Poplatnik+	Holt	Pittman
12/05/2021	L	H	Rangers	0	3	Stryjek	Devlin	Diani	Fitzwater<	Guthrie	Longridge	Emmanuel-Thomas>	Mullin*	Holt+	Pittman
15/05/2021	L	A	St Johnstone	0	0	Stryjek	Bartley+	Diani	Fitzwater	Githrie	Longridge	Emmanuel-Thomas	McMillan	Kabia&	Pittman

THE GOALIES

Goalkeepers Used in League Matches, 1970-2020

Players shown in the season of their first appearance only

1974/5 Derek Gray
I Graham
Tom Cooper
Allan Wilson
1976/7 David Graham
Steve Denholm
1977/8 Ian McLaren
1978/9 Charlie Sinclair
Thomson Allan
Conrad Johnston
Alex Porwol
1979/0 Derek Neilson
1980/1 Bobby McKell
1981/2 Jim McQueen
1982/3 Jim McArthur
1984/5 Dougie McNab
1985/6 Alan Carswell
1986/7 Murray McDermott
1992/3 Steve Ellison
1993/4 Rab Douglas
1994/5 Horace Stoute
1997/8 Ian McCaldon
1998/9 Neil Alexander
2000/1 Javier Broto
2001/2 Nick Culkin
2002/3 David McEwan
Alan Main
2003/4 Roddy McKenzie
2004/5 Colin Meldrum
2005/6 Ludovic Roy
2006/7 Craig Wight
Colin Stewart
2007/8 Mariusz Liberda
Mark Lunn
2008/9 Pierre-Antoine Martini
Roddy McKenzie
2009/0 Andy McNeil
Craig McDowall
2010/1 Tony Bullock
Darren Jamieson
2013/4 Kevin Walker
2015/6 Marc McCallum
2016/7 Liam Kelly
Gary Maley
2017/8 Neil Alexander (2nd spell)
2018/9 Ross Stewart
2019/0 Martija Sarkic
Ross McCrorie
Ryan Schofield

11	12	13	14	15	16	17	18	19	20
Dykes	Kouider-Aissa*	Robinson+	Souda&	McMillan	Tiffoney	Crawford	Hamilton	Pigniatello	Stryjek
Dykes	Forrest*	Poplatnik+	Tiffoney&	Kouider-Aissa>	McMillan	Crawford	Souda	Taylor-Sinclair	Stryjek
Dykes	Ambrose*	Souda+	McMillan&	Devlin	Hamilton	Tiffoney	Poplatnik	Holt	Stryjek
Hamilton+	Crawford*	Poplatnik+>	Robinson&	Kouider-Aissa>	Ambrose	Tiffoney	Pigniatello	Taylor-Sinclair	Schwake
Robinson	Serrano*	Ambrose+	Hamilton&	Tiffoney>	Kouider-Assa	Crawford	Strykek	Taylor-Sinclair	
Lokotsch+	Holt*	Tiffoney+	Hamilton	McMillan	Kouider-Assa	Crawford	Poplatnik	Taylor-Sinclair	Stryjek
Lokotsch*	Tiffoney*	Sibbald+	Koider-Aissa&	McMillan	Lawson	Crawford	Poplatnik	Taylor-Sinclair	Stryjek
Tiffoney+	Robinson*	Lokotsch+	Forrest&	Pigniatello>	Lawson	McMillan	Poplatnik	Taylor-Sinclair	Stryjek
Tiffoney+	Lawson*	Lokotsch+	Brown&	Fitzwater	Sibbald	McMillan	Poplatnik	Taylor-Sinclair	Stryjek
Tiffoney*	Popiatnik*	McMillan+	Brown	Fitzwater	Sibbald	Lawson	Lokotsch	Taylor-Sinclair	Stryjek
Tiffoney*	Poplatnik*	Taylor-Sinclair+	Lokotsch&	Devlin>	Ambrose<	Sibbald	Bartley	Maley	
Sibbald	Holt*	Tiffoney	Fitzwater	Guthrie	McMillan	Lokotsch	Poplatnik	Robinson	Maley
Tiffoney*	Emmanuel-Thomas*	Poplatnik+	Sibbald&	Fitzwater	Brown	Lokotsch	Lawson	Taylor-Sinclair	Stryjek
Sibbald+	Mullin*	Forrest+	Poplatnik&	Fitzwater	Robinson	Lokotsch	Lawson	Taylor-Sinclair	Pigniatello
Sibbald+	Forrest*	Lawson+	Tiffoney&	Fitzwater	Robinson	Ambrose	Poplatnik	Taylor-Sinclair	McCrorie
Sibbald*	Poplatnik*	Ambrose+	Tiffoney	Fitzwater	McMillan	Mullin	Holt	Taylor-Sinclair	McCrorie
Poplatnik	Taylor-Sinclair*	Sibbald+	Pigniatello&	Guthrie	Serrano	Brown	Bartley	Robinson	
Sibbald	Holt*	Ambrose+	Pigniatello&	Fitzwater	McMillan	Poplatnik	Pittman		
Sibbald*	Serrano*	Mullin+	Poplatnik&	Fitzwater	Robinson	Ambrose	McMillan	Taylor-Sinclair	Maley
Sibbald	Tiffoney*	Emmanuel-Thomas+	Serrano&	McMillan>	Brown<	Ambrose	Robinson	Taylor-Sinclair	Maley
Sibbald+	Emmanuel-Thomas*	Robinson+	Brown&	McMillan	Ambrose	Tiffoney	Lawson	Taylor-Sinclair	McCrorie
Sibbald	Tiffoney*+	Robinson+	Brown&	Holt>	Ambrose	McMillan	Emmanuel-Thomas	Taylor-Sinclair	McCrorie
Sibbald	Brown*	Holt+	Poplatnik&	McMillan	Ambrose	Lawson	Emmanuel-Thomas	Taylor-Sinclair	McCrorie
Sibbald	Emmanuel-Thomas*	Pigniatello	Poplatnik	McMillan	Ambrose	Lawson	Brown	Taylor-Sinclair	McCrorie
Sibbald+	Robinson*	Poplatnik	Forrest	McMillan	Ambrose	Lawson	Brown	Taylor-Sinclair	McCrorie
Sibbald+	Lawson*	Serrano+	Emmanuel-Thomas&	McMillan	Forrest	Taylor-Sinclair	Pigniatello	McCrorie	
Sibbald&	Forrest*	Hamilton+	Emmanuel-Thomas&	McMillan	Serrano	Lawson	Tiffoney	Taylor-Sinclair	McCrorie
Sibbald*	Forrest*	Hamilton+	Emmanuel-Thomas	McMillan	Serrano	Fitzwater	Tiffoney	Taylor-Sinclair	McCrorie
Hamilton+	Kabia*	Reilly+	Devlin&	Robinson>	Sibbald	Pigniatello	Taylor-Sinclair	Mullin	Maley
Sibbald&	Reilly*	Fitzwater+	Longridge&	McMillan	Forrest	Lawson	Emmanuel-Thomas	Kabia	McCrorie
Reilly*	Emmanuel-Thomas*	Robinson+	Sibbald&	Kabia>	Serrano	Lawson	McMillan	Longridge	McCrorie
Sibbald*	Emmanuel-Thomas*	Longridge+	Lawson&	Kabia	Forrest	Reilly	McMillan	Mullin	McCrorie
Lawson	Reilly*	Robinson+	McMillan	Kabia	Forrest	Bartley	McCrorie		
Lawson+	Emmanuel-Thomas*	Kabia+	McMillan	Tifoney	Poplatnik	Sibbald	Pigniatello	Fitzwater	McCrorie
Sibbald+	Emmanuel-Thomas*	Kabia+	Poplatnik&	Lawson>	Ambrose	McMillan	Forrest	Taylor-Sinclair	McCrorie
Sibbald&	Taylor-Sinclair*	Kabia+	Lawson&	Emmanuel-Thomas>	Poplatnik	Tiffoney	McMillan	Pigniatello	Stryjek
Lawson*	Sibbald*	Forrest+	Reilly&	Emmanual-Thomas>	Fitzwater	Kabia	McMillan	Taylor-Sinclair	Stryjek
Sibbald	Robinson*&	Lawson+	Tiffoney&	Forrest	Ambrose	Kabia	McMillan	Taylor-Sinclair	Maley
Sibbald	Forrest*	Pittman+	Tiffoney&	Holt>	Ambrose	Kabia	McMillan	Longridge	Stryjek
Sibbald+	Mullin*	Serrano+	Poplatnik&	Lawson	Ambrose	Kabia	McMillan	Tiffoney	Maley
Sibbald	Serrano*	Lawson+	Poplatnik&	Mullin	Ambrose	Kabia	McMillan	Tiffoney	Stryjek
Sibbald&	Mullin*	Poplatnik+	Kabia&	Diani>	Ambrose	Lawson	McMillan	Lithgow	Stryjek
Sibbald*	Mullin*	Poplatrnik+	Diani&	Ambrose>	Lithgow<	Lawson	McMillan	Kabia	Stryjek
Sibbald+	Poplatnik*	Lithgow+	McMillan&	Taylor-Sinclair>	Ambrose	Kabia	Diani	Mullin	McCrorie
Sibbald>	McMillan*	Forrest+	Poplatnik&	Diani>	Bartley	Kabia	Fitzwater	Taylor-Sinclair	McCrorie
Sibbald*	Kabia*	Mullin+	McMillan	Lithgow	Ambrose	Forrest	Diani	Serrano	Maley
Sibbald&	Kabia*	Bartley+	McMillan&	Poplatnik>	Ambrose<	Fitzwater	Serano	Lithgow	Maley
Poplatnik*	Forrest*	Holt+	Mullin&	Lithgow	Ambrose	Serrano	Maley		

Mariusz Liberda

Rab Douglas

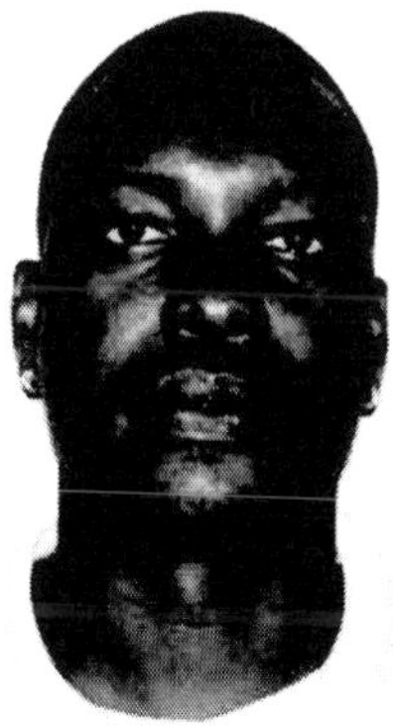

Horace Stoute

Surname	First Name	Date of Birth	No	Nat	Pos	Signed	Previous	Notes	Contract	Lge A	Lge S	Lge G	SC A	SC S	SC G	LC A	LC S	LC G	Un
Ambrose	Efe	18/10/1988	25	NIG	D	2020	Derby County	Released May 2021		17	5					4	2		18
Balde	Joao	21/05/2001		SCO / POR	M	2020	Rangers	OL to Bonnyrigg Rose Nov-Jan		0	0								0
Barr	Kenny	16/06/2000		SCO	D	2020	Kilmarnock	OL to Linlithgow Rose Nov-Jan, Released July joined E Stirling		0	0								0
Bartley	Marvin	04/07/1986	6	JAM / ENG	M	2019	Hibernian		End 2021/2	32	1	1	2			6			4
Boubekri	Kieran	23/07/1999		SCO	F	2020	Livingston Youths	OL to Linlithgow Rose Nov-May											
Brown	Ciaron	14/01/1998	3	ENG	D	2020	Cardiff City (OL)	Jul-Jan		13	3	1					2		5
Crawford	Robbie	22/06/1994	16	SCO	M	2019	Ayr United	OL to Motherwell Sep-Jan, permanent from Feb		0	1								5
De Vita	Rafa	23/09/1987	23	ITA	F	2016	Ross County	OL to Edinburgh City Oct-May, Released May 2021		0	0								0
Devlin	Nicky	17/10/1993	2	SCO	D	2019	Walsall		End 2021/2	35	1	2	2			7	1		1
Diani	Djibril	11/02/1998		FRA	M	2021	Grasshoppers Zurich (OL)	Feb-May		2	2			1					2
Donald	Gregor	27/04/2001		SCO	D	2020	St Johnstone	OL to Jeanfield Swifts Dec-May, Released June		0	0								0
Duncan	Jack	04/03/2001		SCO	D	2019	Hibernian Youths	OL to Dunbar United Oct-Jan		0	0								0
Dykes	Lyndon	07/10/1995	9	AUS / SCO	F	2019	Queen of the South	Transferred to QPR Aug 2020		3	0	2							0
Emmanuel-Thomas	Jay	27/12/1990	9	ENG / STL	F	2020	PTT Rayong	OOC May 2021, joined Aberdeen		14	10	5	2		2	3	2	2	4
Fitzwater	Jack	23/09/1997	5	ENG	D	2020	West Bromwich Albion		End 2021/2	20	0	1	2		1	4	1	2	14
Forrest	Alan	09/09/1996	11	SCO	M	2020	Ayr United		End 2021/2	21	9	4	2			6	1	7	8
Gregory	Jason	01/01/2001		SCO	D	2019	Livingston Youths	Released July 2020 joined Livingston United		0	0								0
Guthrie	Jon	29/07/1992	27	ENG	D	2019	Walsall	OOC June 2021, joined Northampton Town		36	0	5	2			6			2
Hamilton	Jack	30/06/2000	38	SCO	F	2016	Leith Athletic	OL to East Fife Sep-Jan, to Arbroath Jan-May	End 2021/2	2	3	1							3
Holt	Jason	19/02/1993	18	SCO	M	2020	Rangers		End 2021/2	27	4	1	2			4	3		2
Irving	Ross	09/10/2001		SCO	F	2020	Queen of the South	OL to Dalbeattie S Oct-Jan, Freed June 2021 joined Stranraer		0	0								0
Jacobs	Keaghan	09/09/1989	7	RSA / SCO	M	2017	Bidvest Vits		End 2021/2	0	0								0
Jones	Alassan	23/02/2001		SCO / SWE	F	2020	Dundee United	OL to Bonnyrigg Rose Nov-Jan		0	0								0
Kabia	Jaze	08/07/2000	37	ROI / ENG	F	2021	Shelbourne		End 2022/3	1	7	1		1					11
Kouider-Aissa	Salim	22/03/1996	19	SCO / ALG	F	2020	Queen's Park	OL to Partick Thistle Aug-Jan, to Q Park Mar-May, Transferred to Airdrie July 2021		0	4								2
Lawson	Steve	08/08/1994	33	FRA / TOG	M	2018	Neuchatel Xamax	Released May 2021		7	8					2			15
Lithgow	Alan	12/03/1988	4	SCO	D	2016	Airdrieonians	Released May 2021 joined Morton		1	1			1					4
Lokotsch	Lars	17/05/1996		GER	F	2020	SV Rodinghausen	OL to Raith Rovers Oct-Jan, Released Jan joined FSV Zwickau		2	2						1	1	5
Longridge	Jackson	12/04/1995	23	SCO	D	2021	Bradford City		End 2022/3	9	1		2				1		2
Mack	Jay	28/07/2001		SCO	D	2019	Rangers	Released July 2020		0	0								0
Maley	Gary	03/08/1982	40	SCO	GK	2016	Broxburn Athletic	OL to QOS Jan 2020	End 2021/2	0	0					2			10
McCrorie	Robby	18/03/1998	1	SCO	GK	2020	Rangers (OL)	Jul-May		16	0		1			1			18
McMillan	Jack	18/12/1997	21	SCO	D	2018	Motherwell		End 2021/2	4	4			1		2	1		33
Moffat	Jonathan	08/09/2002		SCO	D	2020	Livingston Youths	OL to Civil Service S Oct-Mar, Released June joined CSS											
Mullin	Josh	23/09/1992	14	SCO	F	2020	Ross County		End 2022/3	16	6	2		1		8		3	5
Pignatiello	Carlo	16/01/2000	39	SCO	M	2018	St Mirren Youths	OL to Arbroath Jan-May, OL to Dumbarton for 2021/2	End 2021/2	0	1						2		8
Pittman	Scott	09/07/1992	8	USA / SCO	M	2015	Bo'ness United		End 2022/3	37	1	7	2			7			1
Popiatnik	Matej	15/07/1992	15	SVN	F	2020	Kerala Blasters	OL to Raith Rovers for 2021/2	End 2021/2	5	13			2	1	2	2	2	12
Reilly	Gavin	10/05/1993	20	SCO	F	2021	Carlisle United		End 2021/2	3	2						2		1
Robinson	Scott	11/03/1992	17	SCO	M	2017	East Fife	Released May 2021 joined Kilmarnock		16	10	4				5		2	6
Schwake	Brian	24/08/2001	30	USA	GK	2020	De Paule Blue Demons	OL to Linlithgow Rose Sep-Jan, OL to Edinburgh City 2021/2	End 2021/2	0	0								1
Serrano	Julian	13/02/1998	12	FRA	D	2020	AS Monaco (OL)	Aug-May		19	5	1				6	1		7
Sibbald	Craig	18/05/1995	10	SCO	M	2018	Falkirk		End 2021/2	29	3	1	2			5	2	1	5
Smith	Marc	05/01/2001		SCO	M	2019	St Mirren Youths	OL to Blackburn U Oct-Mar, Released June joined Carluke R											
Souda	Aymen	28/02/1993	20	FRA / TUN	F	2019	2019 Dunarea Calarasi	Released Oct 2020 joined FC Sete		0	2								1
Stewart	Ross	16/04/1995		SCO	GK	2018	St Mirren	OL to Hearts Aug-May, Permanent from June 2021		0	0								0
Stokes	Anthony	25/07/1988		ROI	F	2020	Persepolis	Released Sep 2020		0	0								0
Strang	Brodie	11/11/2002		SCO	M	2020	Hearts	OL to Linlithgow Rose Nov-Jan		0	0								0
Stryjek	Max	18/07/1996	32	POL	GK	2020	Eastleigh		End 2022/3	22	0		1			5			16
Taylor-Sinclair	Aaron	08/04/1991	29	SCO	D	2019	Motherwell	Released May 2021		5	1			1		2	2	1	26
Tiffoney	Scott	26/08/1998	22	SCO	M	2018	Morton	OL to Partick Thistle Mar-May, permanent from June 2021		4	8	1				1	1		12
Wilson	David	17/01/2001		SCO	D	2019	Airdrieonians			0	0								0
Own Goals												2						1	
NEW SIGNINGS																			
Anderson	Bruce	23/09/1988		SCO	F	2021	Aberdeen		End 2023/4										
Barden	Daniel	02/01/2000		WAL	GK	2021	Norwich City (OL)	Jul-May	End 2021/2										
Clark	Harrison	11/05/2003		ENG	M	2021	Chester le Street Town	OL to Arbroath for 2021/2	End 2021/2										
Lewis	Adam	08/11/1999		ENG	D	2021	Liverpool (OL)	Jul-May	End 2021/2										
Montano	Christian	11/12/1991		COL / ENG	M	2021	Port Vale		End 2022/3										
Nouble	Jon	19/01/1996		ENG / CDI	F	2021	Aldershot Town	OL to Arbroath for 2021/2	End 2021/2										
Obileye	Abo	02/09/1994		ENG / NIG	D	2021	Queen of the South		End 2022/3										
Parkes	Tom	15/01/1992		ENG	D	2021	Exeter City		End 2021/2										
Penrice	James	22/12/1998		SCO	D	2021	Partick Thistle		End 2023/4										
Williamson	Ben	07/08/2001		SCO	M	2021	Rangers (OL)	Jul-May	End 2021/2										

Montrose FC 2020/21 The Gable Endies

Founded	1879
Ground	Links Park
Postcode	DD10 8QD
Tel	01674 673200
Capacity	3292
Closest Railway Station	Montrose
Record Attendance	8983 v Dundee, SC, 17/3/1973
Record Win	12-0 v Vale of Leithen, SC, 4/1/1975
Record Defeat	0-13 v Aberdeen, 17/3/1951
Most League Goals in a Season	28 Brian Third, 1972/3
Colours 2020/21 Top	Blue with White Sleeves
Shorts	Blue
Sponsor	Carnegie Fuels
Manufacturer	Hummell
Change Colours 2020/21 Top	White
Shorts	White
Nicknames	Gable Endies
Web	www.montrosefc.co.uk
Match Programme 2020/21	£2.50

Chairman: John Crawford
Vice Chairman: Dabid Laing
Vice Chairman: Peter Stuart
Hon President: John Paton
Financial Director: Tom Murray
Hon Vice President: Malcolm Watters
Secretary: Brian Petrie
Safety Officer: Alan Kenny
Assistant Secretary: Andrew Stephen
Director: Peter Davidson
Director: Tracy Park, Barry O'Neill, Michael Fotheringham
Manager: Stewart Petrie
Assistant Manager: Ross Campbell
Coach: Sean Dillon, Iain Campbell
Physio: Gemma Collier
Sports Scientist: Stuart McFarlane
Goalkeeping Coach: Tony Bullock
Physio: Scott Shepherd
Groundsman /Kitman: Ron Marquis
Assistant Kitman: Robert Ogg

Manager Stewart Petrie keeps defying the odds at Montrose and has now established them as a League One side. It's important to remember that they were the first SPFL club to contest the Pyramid Play Off, beating Brora Rangers a few years ago.

Petrie's secret is a fairly tight squad with players who can fill a variety of positions. His defence is always rock solid but he can adapt the midfield and forwards from game to game according to requirements. Reaching the promotion play off was probably more than most people expected and it looked unlikely after a slump in results in early April. However, Montrose recovered to defeat Falkirk and Partick in their last two games and pipped the Bairns for the final place. After beating Morton at Links Park in the first leg they went down in extra time at Cappielow.

The Scottish Cup saw convincing wins over Highland League opponents Nairn County and Fraserburgh before a defeat to Kilmarnock. They failed to qualify from their League Cup section.

STAR MAN
Montrose did their best to confuse with two Cammy Ballantyne's in their side. Cammy Ballantyne I is a defender who signed for the Gable Endies from Dumbarton after being a young player at Dundee United. Cammy Ballantyne II was on loan from St Johnstone for a second season. Both had excellent seasons so it would seem apt to say that Montrose's star man was definitely Cammy Ballantyne.

PROSPECTS 2021/2
Every time a Managerial vacancy crops up in the Championship the name of Petrie is linked with it. This Summer he was tipped for both the Dundee United and Dunfermline jobs. However, Petrie has a well-paid full-time job with the Bank of Scotland and has said that he doesn't want a full-time football post – not now at least. That's great news for the Links Park club. His target will be to repeat last season's performance and push them back into the promotion play off zone.

Montrose v Hearts, Scottish Cup QF, 1975/6

Montrose score. The match ended 2-2. The Replay at Tynecastle was also draw, with Hearts going through following a third game staged at Muirton Park in Perth.

Date	Comp	H/A	Opponents	F	A		HT		Referee	Crowd	Scorers
07/10/2020	LC	H	Ross County	3	3	4-5p	0	2	G Duncan	BCD	Webster, Ballantyne 1, Steeves
10/10/2020	LC	A	Arbroath	1	3		1	2	G Beaton	BCD	Webster
13/10/2020	LC	H	Elgin City	0	2		0	2	D Dickinson	BCD	
17/10/2020	L	H	Falkirk	1	3		0	1	C Napier	BCD	Quinn
24/10/2020	L	A	East Fife	2	2		1	2	D Lowe	BCD	Milne, Webster pen
31/10/2020	L	A	Forfar Athletic	3	2		1	0	L Wilson	BCD	Watson 2, Callaghan
07/11/2020	L	H	Peterhead	3	2		1	1	M McDermid	BCD	Mclean 2, Webster pen
10/11/2020	LC	A	Stirling Albion	1	2		1	2	P Stuart	BCD	Hawke
21/11/2020	L	A	Clyde	2	3		1	1	B Cook	BCD	McLean, Mochrie
28/11/2020	L	H	Partick Thistle	0	1		0	1	K Graham	BCD	
05/12/2020	L	A	Cove Rangers	2	1		0	1	L Wilson	BCD	Webster pen, McLean
12/12/2020	L	A	Airdrieonians	1	0		0	0	G Irvine	BCD	McLean
19/12/2020	L	H	Dumbarton	4	0		3	0	M McDermid	BCD	Ballantyne I (2), Steeves, McLean
22/12/2020	L	A	Peterhead	1	1		0	1	G Grainger	BCD	Webster pen
02/01/2021	L	H	Forfar Athletic	0	0		0	0	S Lambie	BCD	
20/03/2021	L	A	Falkirk	0	2		0	1	G Duncan	BCD	
23/03/2021	SC	A	Nairn County	7	1		4	0	G Ross	BCD	Johnston 3, Quinn 2, McLean, Hawke
27/03/2021	L	H	Clyde	2	2		2	2	A Newlands	BCD	Webster 2(1 pen)
30/03/2021	L	H	East Fife	3	0		2	0	S Lambie	BCD	Webster, Steeves, Milne
03/04/2021	SC	A	Fraserburgh	4	2		2	2	G Irvine	BCD	Mochrie, Webster, McLean, Milne
06/04/2021	L	A	Dumbarton	0	0		0	0	C Scott	BCD	
10/04/2021	L	H	Airdrieonians	2	2		2	0	P Stuart	BCD	Ballantyne II, Crighton og
15/04/2021	L	A	Partick Thistle	0	5		0	2	A Muir	BCD	
17/04/2021	SC	A	Kilmarnock	1	3		0	2	N Walsh	BCD	Ballantyne I
20/04/2021	L	H	Cove Rangers	1	0		1	0	S Lambie	BCD	Fyvie og
27/04/2021	L	A	Airdrieonians	1	2		0	1	K Graham	BCD	Webster
29/04/2021	L	H	Cove Rangers	0	2		0	1	A Newlands	BCD	
01/05/2021	L	A	Falkirk	2	1		1	1	S Kirkland	BCD	Ballantyne II, Milne
04/05/2021	L	H	Partick Thistle	3	2		2	1	P Stuart	BCD	Ballatyne II, Rennie, McLean
08/05/2021	PO	H	Morton	2	1		0	1	G Irvine	BCD	McLean, Webster
11/05/2021	PO	A	Morton	1	3	AET	0	2	E Anderson	BCD	McLean

Ray Charles

David Larter

Scott Bennett

Date	Comp	H/A	Opponents	F	A		1	2	3	4	5	6	7	8	9	10	11	12	13	14	15	16	17	18	19	20
07/10/2020	LC	H	Ross County	3	3	4-5p	Fleming	Dillon	Steeves	Allan>	Ballantyne I	Waddell&	Watson	Webster	Ballantyne II	Hawke+	Johnston*	Quinn*	R Campbell+	Rennie&	Milne>	*I Campbell*	*Lennox*			
10/10/2020	LC	A	Arbroath	1	3		Lennox	Quinn	Steeves	Allan+	Ballantyne I	Waddell	Milne	Webster	Ballantyne II	Rennie&	Johnston*	Hawke*	Watson+	R Campbell&	*Dillon*	*I Campbell*	*Fleming*			
13/10/2020	LC	H	Elgin City	0	2		Fleming	Dillon<	Steeves	Allan	Ballantyne I&	Quinn+	Watson>	Webster	Ballantyne II	Rennie	Hawke*	Johnston*	Milne+	Waddell&	R Campbell>	I Campbell<	*Lennox*			
17/10/2020	L	H	Falkirk	1	3		Lennox	Dillon	Steeves	Quinn	Milne	Waddell	Watson&	Webster	Ballantyne II	Mochrie+	Johnston*	Rennie*	R Campbell+	Hawke&	*Allan*	*I Campbell*	*Fleming*			
24/10/2020	L	A	East Fife	2	2		Lennox	I Campbell	Watson+	Quinn	Milne	Waddell*	Rennie&	Webster	Ballantyne II	Mochrie>	Johnston	Callaghan*	R Campbell+	Hawke&	McLean>	*Rollo*	*Clark*	*McCormick*	*Fleming*	
31/10/2020	L	A	Forfar Athletic	3	2		Lennox	I Campbell	Steeves	Quinn	Ballantyne I	Watson+	Milne&	Webster	Cochrane*	Mochrie	Johnston>	McLean*	Rennie+	Callaghan&	Hawke>	*Rollo*	*Clark*	*R Campbell*	*McCormick*	*Fleming*
07/11/2020	L	H	Peterhead	3	2		Lennox	I Campbell	Steeves	Quinn	Cochrane&	Watson>	Milne+	Webster	Ballantyne II	Mochrie	McLean*	Rennie*	Johnston+	R Campbell&	Callaghan>	*Hawke*	*Waddell*	*McCormick*	*Clark*	*Fleming*
10/11/2020	LC	A	Stirling Albion	1	2		Fleming	I Campbell	McCormick>	Quinn	Milne*	Callaghan+	Leslie	R Campbell	Hawke&	Rennie	Johnston	Ballantyne II*	Watson+	McLean&	Rollo>	*Ballantyne I*	*Steeves*	*Webster*	*Clark*	*Lennox*
21/11/2020	L	A	Clyde	2	3		Lennox	I Campbell	Steeves	Cochrane+	Ballantyne I	Callaghan&	Milne	Webster<	Ballantyne II	Mochrie>	McLean*	Johnston*	Watson+	Dillon&	R Campbell>	Rennie<	*Rollo*	*Leslie*	*McCormick*	*Fleming*
28/11/2020	L	H	Partick Thistle	0	1		Fleming	Dillon	Steeves	Waddell&	Ballantyne I	Watson*	Milne>	Webster	Ballantyne II	Mochrie	McLean+	Cochrane*	Johnston+	Campbell&	Callaghan>	*Allan*	*Quinn*	*Rennie*	*I Campbell*	*Lennox*
05/12/2020	L	A	Cove Rangers	2	1		Fleming	Dillon	Steeves	Waddell	Ballantyne I	Watson+	Milne	Webster>	Ballantyne II*	Cochrane	McLean&	Callaghan*	Mochrie+	Johnston&	R Campbell>	*Allan*	*Quinn*	*I Campbell*	*Lennox*	
12/12/2020	L	A	Airdrieonians	1	0		Fleming	Dillon	Steeves	Waddell	Ballantyne I	Mochrie*	Milne+	Webster	Ballantyne II&	Cochrane	McLean>	Johnston*	Callaghan+	Watson&	R Campbell>	*Allan*	*Quinn*	*I Campbell*	*Lennox*	
19/12/2020	L	H	Dumbarton	4	0		Fleming	Dillon&	Steeves	Waddell<	Ballantyne I	Mochrie	Milne+	Webster>	Ballantyne II	Cochrane*	McLean	Watson*	Callaghan+	Allan&	Johnston>	Quinn<	*R Campbell*	*I Campbell*	*Lennox*	*Hawke*
22/12/2020	L	A	Peterhead	1	1		Fleming	Dillon	Steeves	Waddell	Ballantyne I	Johnston	Milne	Webster	Ballantyne II+	Cochrane*	McLean	Callaghan*	Watson+	*Allan*	*Hawke*	*Quinn*	*R Campbell*	*I Campbell*	*Lennox*	
02/01/2021	L	H	Forfar Athletic	0	0		Fleming	Dillon	Steeves	Waddell	Ballantyne I	Johnston	Milne	Webster	Ballantyne II+	Cochrane*	Mochrie&	Watson*	Callaghan+	Campbell&	*Allan*	*Masson*	*Hawke*	*I Campbell*	*Lennox*	*Quinn*
20/03/2021	L	A	Falkirk	0	2		Lennox	Dillon	Steeves	Waddell<	Ballantyne I	Masson	Milne+	Webster&	Ballantyne II>	McLean	Mochrie*	Quinn*	Johnston+	Cochrane&	Watson>	Rennie<	*Hawke*	*Callaghan*	*R Campbell*	*Fleming*
23/03/2021	SC	A	Nairn County	7	1		Fleming	Dillon	Steeves	Quinn	Ballantyne I+	Masson&	Milne	Cochrane	Johnston	McLean*	Mochrie	Hawke*	Callaghan+	Rennie&	*Allan*	*Webster*	*Watson*	*Ballantyne II*	*R Campbell*	*Lennox*
27/03/2021	L	H	Clyde	2	2		Lennox	Dillon*	Steeves	Waddell	Ballantyne I	Watson>	Webster<	Cochrane&	Ballantyne II	McLean+	Johnston	Quinn*	Mochrie+	Masson&	Milne>	Rennie<	*Hawke*	*Callaghan*	*R Campbell*	*Fleming*
30/03/2021	L	H	East Fife	3	0		Lennox	Dillon	Steeves	Waddell<	Quinn	Masson*	Webster	Callaghan&	Ballantyne II	McLean>	Johnston+	Milne*	Rennie+	Mochrie&	Watson>	McGale<	*Hawke*	*McFarlane*	*R Campbell*	*Fleming*
03/04/2021	SC	A	Fraserburgh	4	2		Lennox	Dillon	Steeves	Waddell*	Ballantyne I	Masson	Webster	Milne	Watson	McLean	Mochrie&	Quinn*	Johnston*	Ballantyne II&	*Callaghan*	*Allan*	*Hawke*	*Rennie*	*R Campbell*	*Fleming*
06/04/2021	L	A	Dumbarton	0	0		Lennox	Dillon	Steeves	Quinn	Ballantyne I	Callaghan+	Webster	Milne	Ballantyne II*	Rennie>	Johnston&	McLean*	Mochrie+	Masson&	Antoniazzi>	*Watson*	*Hawke*	*McFarlane*	*McGale*	*Fleming*
10/04/2021	L	H	Airdrieonians	2	2		Lennox	Dillon	Steeves	Quinn	Ballantyne I	Masson+	Webster*	Milne>	Ballantyne II	McLean<	Mochrie&	Johnston*	Watson+	Rennie&	Callaghan>	McFarlane<	*Hawke*	*Antoniazzi*	*McGale*	*Fleming*
15/04/2021	L	A	Partick Thistle	0	5		Fleming	Dillon<	Steeves	Quinn	Ballantyne I	Masson+	Webster&	Milne*	Ballantyne II	McLean>	Antoniazzi	Johnston*	Callaghan+	McGale&	Campbell>	Watson<	*Hawke*	*Mochrie*	*Waddell*	*Lennox*
17/04/2021	SC	A	Kilmarnock	1	3		Fleming	Dillon	Steeves	Quinn	Ballantyne I	Watson*	Callaghan	Milne	Cochrane&	McLean	Mochrie+	Ballantyne II*	Masson+	Hawke&	*Rennie*	*I Campbell*	*Webster*	*Johnston*	*R Campbell*	*Lennox*
20/04/2021	L	H	Cove Rangers	1	0		Fleming	Dillon	Steeves	Quinn	Ballantyne I	Cochrane&	Callaghan+	Milne	Ballantyne II	McLean>	Mochrie*	Masson*	Webster+	Antoniazzi&	R Campbell>	*Rennie*	*Allan*	*Johnston*	*McGale*	*Lennox*
27/04/2021	L	A	Airdrieonians	1	2		Fleming	Dillon	Steeves<	Quinn	Ballantyne I	Masson	Callaghan+	Milne	Ballantyne II>	Cochrane*	R Campbell&	Allan*	Webster+	Mochrie&	Antoniazzi>	Johnston<	*Rennie*	*Waddell*	*McGale*	*Lennox*
29/04/2021	L	H	Cove Rangers	0	2		Fleming	Dillon	Steeves	Quinn&	Ballantyne I<	Masson	Callaghan+	Milne	Mochrie*	McLean	Webster>	Antoniazzi*	Ballantyne II+	McGale&	Rennie>	McFarlane<	*Allan*	*Johnston*	*R Campbell*	*Lennox*
01/05/2021	L	A	Falkirk	2	1		Fleming	Dillon	Steeves	Quinn*	Ballantyne I	Masson	Allan	Milne	Ballantyne II>	McLean+	Webster&	Mochrie*	Johnston+	Rennie&	R Campbell>	*McFarlane*	*Hawke*	*Antoniazzi*	*McGale*	*Lennox*
04/05/2021	L	H	Partick Thistle	3	2		Fleming	Dillon	Johnston*	Quinn	Ballantyne I	Masson	Rennie+	Milne&	Ballantyne II	McLean	Webster	Mochrie*	Antoniazzi+	R Campbell&	*McGale*	*McFarlane*	*Hawke*	*I Campbell*	*Lennox*	
08/05/2021	PO	H	Morton	2	1		Fleming	Dillon	Steeves	Waddell	Ballantyne I	Masson	Rennie*	Milne	Ballantyne II	McLean	Webster	Antoniazzi*	*Callaghan*	*R Campbell*	*Quinn*	*Mochrie*	*Johnston*	*Lennox*		
11/05/2021	PO	A	Morton	1	3	AET	Fleming	Dillon	Steeves	Waddell	Ballantyne I	Masson	Rennie*	Milne	Ballantyne II+	McLean	Webster&	Mochrie*	Johnston+	Callaghan&	*Antoniazzi*	*Quinn*	*R Campbell*	*Lennox*		

THE GOALIES

Goalkeepers Used in League Matches, 1970-2020

Players shown in the season of their first appearance only

1972/3	George Whisker
	Dave Gollan
1973/4	M Thomson
	J Robertson
	C Bell
	David Nicoll
	C MacKenzie
1974/5	Dave Gorman
1977/8	Jim Moffat
1979/0	Ray Charles
1980/1	David Nicol
1981/2	Colin Kelly
1983/4	Neil Connell
1984/5	David Larter
1986/7	Grant Clark
	Ian Christie
	Jim Buchan
1987/8	John Gardiner
1991/2	Andy Locke
1993/4	Ronnie Massie
1996/7	Jim Butter
1997/8	Neil Russell
	Mark Murray
	Barry Thompson
1998/9	Fraser Fitzpatrick
1999/0	Gary McGlynn
2002/3	Jamie Campbell
	Michael Hankinson
2005/6	Andy Reid
	Sandy Wood
2006/7	John Farquhar
	Cammy Bell
	Stuart McKenzie
2007/8	Mark Peat
2008/9	Greg Kelly
	Fraser Stark
	Tony Bullock
2009/0	Steven Coutts
	Andy McNeil
2010/1	Scott Bennett
	Michael Fraser
	Daniele Giordano
	Ramiro Gonzalez
2011/2	Michael Andrews
2012/3	David Crawford
	John Gibson
2014/5	Lucas Birnstingl
	Joe McGovern
	John McCafferty
2015/6	Jordan Miller
	Ross Salmon
	Alex Tokarczyk
2016/7	Allan Fleming
2019/0	Aaron Lennox

Surname	First Name	Date of Birth	No	Nat	Pos	Signed	Previous	Notes	Contract	Lge A	Lge S	Lge G	SC A	SC S	SC G	LC A	LC S	LC G	Un
Allan	Matty	17/01/1996	4	SCO	D	2017	Dundee		End 2022/3	1	2					3			10
Antoniazzi	Chris	01/05/2000		SCO	M	2021	Forfar Athletic (OL)	Mar-May		1	6								3
Ballantyne I	Cammy	13/04/1997	2	SCO	D	2019	Dumbarton			20	0	2	3		1	3		1	1
Ballantyne II	Cammy	22/04/2000	22	SCO	M	2020	St Johnstone (OL)	Sep-May		22	1	3		2		3	1		1
Callaghan	Liam	10/10/1994	19	SCO	M	2017	Arbroath		End 2021/2	5	12	1	1	1		1			4
Campbell	Iain	28/06/1985	18	SCO	D	2016	Forfar Athletic			4	0					1	1		11
Campbell	Ross	11/07/1983	15	SCO	F	2015	East Fife			1	12					1	3		12
Clark	Rhys	25/02/2002		SCO	D	2020	Montrose Youths		U20	0	0								4
Cochrane	Harry	24/04/2001	12	SCO	M	2020	Hearts (OL)	Oct-Jan		12	2		2						0
Dillon	Sean	30/07/1983	14	ROI	D	2017	Dundee United			20	1		3			2			1
Fleming	Allan	06/05/1984	1	SCO	GK	2016	Arbroath		End 2021/2	14	0		2			3			12
Hawke	Lewis	22/10/1993	9	SCO	F	2020	Stirling Albion	Released May 2021		0	3			2	1	3	1	1	13
Johnston	Craig	22/12/1994	16	SCO	F	2017	Cowdenbeath		End 2022/3	9	12		1	1	3	3	1		4
Lennox	Aaron	19/02/1993	21	AUS	GK	2019	Partick Thistle		End 2021/2	10	0		1			1			19
Leslie	Theo			SCO	M	2020	Montrose Youths		End 2021/2	0	0					1			1
Masson	Terry	03/07/1988	6	SCO	M	2010	Brechin City		End 2022/3	10	3		2	1					1
Matthews	Ross			SCO	D	2020	Montrose Youths	OL to Forfar WE Sep-Mau	End 2021/2										
McCormick	Jack	02/02/2003		SCO	D	2020	Montrose Youths		U20	0	0					1			4
McFarlane	Stuart	28/07/1989		SCO	D	2021	Bo'ness United (OL)	Mar-May		0	2								4
McGale	Robbie	30/01/2000		SCO	F	2021	Stirling University (OL)	Mar-May		0	3								6
McLean	Russell	16/06/1996	10	SCO	F	2019	Peterhead	released May 2021 joined Peterhead		18	3	9	3		2		1		0
Milne	Lewis	26/04/1994	11	SCO	M	2019	Raith Rovers		End 2022/3	22	2	3	3		1	2	2		0
Mochrie	Chris	07/04/2003	20	SCO	M	2020	Dundee United (OL)	Oct-May		13	8	1	3		1				2
Own Goal												2							
Quinn	Aidan	01/08/1998	17	SCO	D	2019	Stirling University		End 2022/3	13	3	1	2	1	2	3	1		7
Rennie	Martin	09/05/1994	23	SCO	F	2020	St Patrick's Athletic		End 2021/2	5	10	1		1		3	1		5
Rollo	Jack	01/01/2002		SCO	M	2020	Dundee Youths		U20	0	0						1		3
Steeves	Andrew	25/07/1994	3	SCO	D	2015	Forfar Athletic		End 2022/3	22	0	2	3			3		1	1
Waddell	Kerr	14/06/1998	5	SCO	D	2019	Dundee		End 2022/3	13	0		1			2	1		3
Watson	Paul	22/11/1985	8	SCO	M	2012	Peterhead		End 2021/2	7	9	2	2			2	2		2
Webster	Graham	15/05/1992	7	SCO	M	2013	Dundee		End 2022/3	22	2	9	1		1	3		2	3
NEW SIGNINGS																			
Antoniazzi	Chris	01/05/2000		SCO	M	2021	Forfar Athletic		End 2021/2										
Brown	Craig	18/02/1999		SCO	M	2021	Stirling University	Grandson of Scotland Manager Craig Brown	End 2022/3										
Garnham	Sam	17/02/2003		SCO	F	2021	Montrose Youths		End 2021/2										
Lyons	Blair	23/09/1996		SCO	F	2021	Partick Thistle (OL)	Jul-May	End 2021/2										
Whatley	Mark	11/07/1990		SCO	M	2021	Arbroath		End 2022/3										

PHOTOCARDS

No. 31.

MONTROSE FOOTBALL CLUB.

Left to right, back row :—*R. Craigen, J. Osborne, E. Mackay, W. Duncan, G. Reid (Capt.), J. Herbert.* Front row :—*J. Allan, F. Jamieson, J. Malloy, G. Smith, A. Pinkerton.*

This is an old established club although they did not enter the Second Division until the season 1929/30. In 1935/36 they finished twelfth in the League. In season 1921/22 they won the Scottish Qualifying Cup.

Expanding de Luxe Albums for Ardath Photocards on sale at Tobacconists Price 6d

ARDATH TOBACCO CO. LTD. Manufacturers of STATE EXPRESS and ARDATH CIGARETTES

D

Morton FC 2020/21 Ton

Founded	1874
Ground	Cappielow Park
Postcode	PA15 2TY
Tel	01475 723571
Capacity	11589
Closest Railway Station	Cartsdyke
Record Attendance	23500 v Celtic, 29/4/1922
Record Win	11-0 v Carfin Shamrock, SC, 13/11/1886
Record Defeat	1-10 v Port Glasgow, Lge, 5/5/1894 / v St Bernards Lge 14/10/1933
Most League Goals in a Season	58 Allan McGraw, 1963/4
Colours 2020/21 Top	Blue and White Hoops
Shorts	White
Sponsor	Millions
Manufacturer	est 1874
Change Colours 2020/21 Top	Yellow
Shorts	Blue
Nicknames	Ton
Web	www.gmfc.net
Match Programme 2020/21	Curtis Sport

Directors (from July 2021)
Graham McLennan, Gordon Ritchie, Graham Barr, Stewart Farmer, Alex Gray, Nick Robinson

Season 2021/1:
Chairman: Crawford Rae
Board of Directors: Nick Robinson, Alex Gray, Brian Clements, Derek Anderson, Graham McLennan

Chief Executive: David McKinnon
Club Secretary: Brendan McEleny
Manager: David Hopkin, then Gus MacPherson
Assistant Manager: Anton McElhone, then Andy Millen
Goalkeeping Coach: David Timmins
Head of Youth Pathway: David Garrett
Club Physio:
Kit Manager:
Media Assistant: Ewan Boyle
Club Doctors: Craig Spiers, Fraser Gray, Alan Mclaughlin
Groundsman: Mark Farrell
Commercial Manager: Lesley Ann Webb
Health & Safety officer: Elliot Brown
Club Chaplain: Rev. Ian Arthur
Programme Editor: Niall McGilp

Problems behind the scenes were an issue for Morton in the early part of the season. Aspects of the ownership of the club were uncertain. The club belonged to Golden casket, the company owned by former Chairman Douglas Rae. Following his death it looked like his family wanted to sell the club and recoup the money that had been loaned to Morton. By April things had moved on and a new proposal was on the table. Under the proposal, the full debt owed by Greenock Morton to Golden Casket would be written off. A new company would be set up and ownership of Cappielow stadium, as well as Golden Casket's 75 per cent ownership of Greenock Morton, would be transferred to it. The new company would be owned by Morton Club Together, ensuring Cappielow is in the control of the fans. Morton Club Together would own approximately 90 per cent of Greenock Morton — Golden Casket's 75 per cent stake and the current 15 per cent held already by Morton Club Together. Ownership of the Sinclair Street car park would remain with Golden Casket and the club would be permitted to use the land for parking when required. Funds currently held by Greenock Morton would remain with the club for community ownership, including a significant proportion of the government covid pandemic grant.

In the circumstances Morton will just be glad to have survived in the Championship, even if they needed the play offs to do so. Their victories over Montrose and especially Airdrie were achieved with some style

STAR MAN
Lewis Strapp performed consistently in defence for the Cappielow side. The Dunoon-lad was one of the few bright lights in a team that struggled for any sort of consistent form.

PROSPECTS 2021/2
Morton will hope to improve on last year's performance and avoid relegation or the play offs. Still expect them to be in the lower half of the table.

Date	Comp	H/A	Opponents	F	A		HT		Referee	Crowd	Scorers
06/10/2020	LC	H	Queen of the South	2	2	2-4p	1	0	D Robertson	BCD	McGinty, Nesbitt
13/10/2020	LC	H	Queen's Park	1	0		0	0	G Ross	BCD	Blues
17/10/2020	L	H	Alloa Athletic	1	0		1	0	A Newlands	BCD	Salkeld
24/10/2020	L	A	Dundee	0	1		0	1	G Ross	BCD	
31/10/2020	L	H	Ayr United	3	2		0	1	G Aitken	BCD	Oliver, Blues, Strapp
07/11/2020	L	A	Raith Rovers	0	5		0	2	W Collum	BCD	
11/11/2020	LC	A	St Mirren	1	1	5-6p	0	1	B Madden	BCD	MacIver
14/11/2020	LC	A	Partick Thistle	0	0	2-4p	0	0	S Kirkland	BCD	
21/11/2020	L	A	Arbroath	0	0		0	0	S Reid	BCD	
05/12/2020	L	H	Hearts	0	2		0	1	G Aitken	BCD	
12/12/2020	L	A	Dunfermline Athletic	2	1		1	0	D Munro	BCD	McAlister, McGuffie
19/12/2020	L	H	Queen of the South	2	0		1	0	C Steven	BCD	Orsi 2
29/12/2020	L	A	Ayr United	1	1		1	1	G Duncan	BCD	Nesbitt (pen)
02/01/2021	L	A	Alloa Athletic	1	1		0	0	G Irvine	BCD	Fjortoft
15/01/2021	L	H	Dunfermline Athletic	0	0		0	0	S Kirkland	BCD	
23/01/2021	L	A	Queen of the South	1	2		0	2	A Newlands	BCD	Orsi
27/01/2021	L	H	Inverness CT	2	2		1	2	P Stuart	BCD	McGinty, Blues
30/01/2021	L	H	Arbroath	0	1		0	0	D Dickinson	BCD	
02/02/2021	L	H	Raith Rovers	0	1		0	1	C Graham	BCD	
20/02/2021	L	A	Hearts	1	1		0	0	D Dickinson	BCD	McGuffie
27/02/2021	L	H	Dundee	2	2		1	0	C Napier	BCD	McGuffie, Colville
06/03/2021	L	H	Ayr United	0	2		0	0	M Roncone	BCD	
09/03/2021	L	A	Inverness CT	1	0		0	0	G Ross	BCD	Nesbitt
13/03/2021	L	A	Dunfermline Athletic	0	1		0	1	S Kirkland	BCD	
20/03/2021	L	H	Queen of the South	2	1		1	1	D Munro	BCD	Nesbitt, Oliver
23/03/2021	SC	H	Dunfermline Athletic	0	0	AET, 6-5p	0	0	D Robertson	BCD	
27/03/2021	L	A	Raith Rovers	0	1		0	0	J Beaton	BCD	
03/04/2021	SC	A	East Fife	2	1	AET	0	0	A Muir	BCD	McGinty pen, Muirhead
06/04/2021	L	H	Inverness CT	1	4		0	2	S Reid	BCD	Muirhead
10/04/2021	L	A	Dundee	1	1		0	0	A Newlands	BCD	Nesbitt
16/04/2021	SC	A	Motherwell	1	1	AET, 3-5p	0	0	W Collum	BCD	Fjortoft
20/04/2021	L	H	Hearts	0	0		0	0	J Beaton	BCD	
24/04/2021	L	H	Alloa Athletic	1	1		0	0	E Anderson	BCD	Fjortoft
30/04/2021	L	A	Arbroath	0	0		0	0	G Ross	BCD	
08/05/2021	PO	A	Montrose	1	2		1	0	G Irvine	BCD	Oliver
11/05/2021	PO	H	Montrose	3	1	AET	2	0	E Anderson	BCD	Oliver, Salkeld, McGuffie
18/05/2021	PO	A	Airdrieonians	1	0		0	0	D Munro	BCD	Muirhead
21/05/2021	PO	H	Airdrieonians	3	0		2	0	A Muir	500	Muirhead 2, Oliver

Erik Sorensen

Dave Brcic

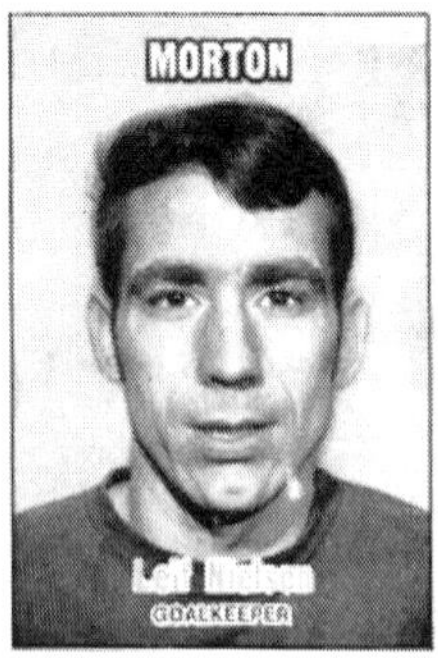

Leif Neilsen

Date	Comp	H/A	Opponents	F	A		1	2	3	4	5	6	7	8	9	10	11	12	13	14	15	16	17	18	19	20
06/10/2020	LC	H	Queen of the South	2	2	2-4p	McAdams	McLean	McGinty	Jacobs	McAlister	Nesbit	Orsi	Strapp	Omar	MacIver	McPake	Salkeld*	Muirhead+	Colville&	Fjortoft	McGuffie	Lyon	Blues	Oliver	Wallace
13/10/2020	LC	H	Queen's Park	1	0		McAdams	Fjortoft	McGinty	Ledger	Blues<	McGuffie+	Lyon*	Colville	Muirhead	Oliver&	Salkeld>	Jacobs*	Wallace+	Orsi&	McPake>	Nesbitt<	Omar	McLean	MacIver	McAlister
17/10/2020	L	H	Alloa Athletic	1	0		McAdams	McLean	McGinty	Jacobs	McAlister	Fjortoft	Orsi*	Nesbitt&	Muirhead	McCabe	Salkeld+	MacIver*	Blues+	McGuffie&	Ledger	Oliver	Colville	Wallace		
24/10/2020	L	A	Dundee	0	1		McAdams	McLean	McGinty	Jacobs*	McAlister	Fjortoft	Orsi+	Ledger	Muirhead	Blues	Salkeld&	Nesbit*	MacIver+	Oliver&	McGuffie	Omar	Colville	Strapp		
31/10/2020	L	H	Ayr United	3	2		McAdams	McLean	McGinty	Strapp	McAlister	Fjortoft	Orsi+	Nesbitt&	McPake	Blues	Salkeld*	McGuffie*	MacIver+	Oliver&	Jacobs	Omar	Colville	Ledger		
07/11/2020	L	A	Raith Rovers	0	5		McAdams	McLean	McGinty	Strapp	McAlister	Fjortoft	Orsi+	Jacobs&	McPake*	Blues	Oliver	Salkeld*	Omar+	Lyon&	McGuffie	Nesbitt	MacIver	Muirhead		
11/11/2020	LC	A	St Mirren	1	1	5-6p	McAdams	McLean<	McGinty	Strapp	Ledger	Fjortoft	Nesbitt+	Omar	Muirhead>	Blues*	Salkeld&	Jacobs*	MacIver+	McPake&	Oliver>	McGuffie<	Lyon	Orsi	Colville	Wallace
14/11/2020	LC	A	Partick Thistle	0	0	2-4p	McAdams	McLean<	McGinty	Strapp	Ledger	Fjortoft	McGuffie*	Jacobs	Lyon+	Colville&	MacIver>	Salkeld*	Omar+	Muirhead&	McPake>	Wallace<	Nesbitt	Orsi	Blues	Millar
21/11/2020	L	A	Arbroath	0	0		McAdams	McLean*	McGinty	Strapp	Ledger	Fjortoft	McAlister	Jacobs	Lyon+	Colville	MacIver&	Omar*	Salkeld+	Oliver&	Muirhead	Orsi	Nesbitt	Blues		
05/12/2020	L	H	Hearts	0	2		McAdams	McLean*	McGinty	Strapp	McAlister	Fjortoft	Omar	Jacobs	Muirhead&	McPake	MacIver+	Salkeld*	Oliver+	Nesbit&	Orsi	Colville	Lyon	Millar		
12/12/2020	L	A	Dunfermline Athletic	2	1		McAdams	McLean	McGinty	Strapp	McAlister	Muirhead&	Orsi	Jacobs*	Lyon	McPake+	Salkeld	Omar*	Nesbit+	McGuffie&	Millar	Oliver	MacIver	Fjortoft		
19/12/2020	L	H	Queen of the South	2	0		McAdams	McLean	McGinty	Strapp	Ledger	Muirhead	Orsi	McAlister+	Lyon	McPake&	Salkeld*	Nesbitt	Omar+	Oliver&	Fjortoft	McGuffie	Colville	MacIver		
29/12/2020	L	A	Ayr United	1	1		McAdams	McLean	McGinty	Strapp	Ledger	Muirhead+	Orsi	McAlister	Lyon	Nesbitt&	Salkeld*	Oliver*	McGuffie+	MacIver&	Fjortoft	Millar	Wallace	Omar		
02/01/2021	L	A	Alloa Athletic	1	1		McAdams	Fjortoft	McGinty	Strapp	Ledger	Colville*	Orsi	McAlister	Lyon&	Nesbitt	Salkeld+	Oliver*	Omar+	Miller&	Easdale	Wallace	Blues			
15/01/2021	L	H	Dunfermline Athletic	0	0		McAdams	Fjortoft	McGinty	Strapp	Ledger	Colville	Orsi*	Omar+	Lyon&	Nesbitt	Salkeld	Oliver*	McGuffie+	Jacobs&	Easdale	McAlister	McGrattan	Hynes		
23/01/2021	L	A	Queen of the South	1	2		McAdams	Fjortoft	McGinty	Strapp&	Ledger	Colville	Orsi	McAlister	Lyon*	Nesbitt	Salkeld+	McGuffie*	Omar+	Oliver&	Muirhead	Wallace	Blues	McLean		
27/01/2021	L	H	Inverness CT	2	2		McAdams	Fjortoft	McGinty	Strapp	Ledger	Colville	Blues+	McGuffie*	Omar	Nesbitt	Oliver&	Millar*	Lyon+	Salkeld&	Muirhead	Orsi	McAlister	McLean		
30/01/2021	L	H	Arbroath	0	1		McAdams	McLean	McGinty	Strapp	Ledger	Millar*	Blues+	McGuffie+	Muirhead	Nesbitt	Oliver&	Lyon*	Orsi+	McAlister&	Fjortoft	Colville	Salkeld	Wallace		
02/02/2021	L	H	Raith Rovers	0	1		McAdams	McLean	McGinty	Strapp	Ledger	Millar*	Blues&	McGuffie+	Colville	Nesbitt	Oliver	Omar*	Sterling+	Salkeld&	Fjortoft	Muirhead	Orsi	Jacobs		
20/02/2021	L	A	Hearts	1	1		McAdams	McLean	McGinty	Strapp	Ledger	Jacobs	Blues	McGuffie*	Colville&	Nesbitt	Salkeld+	Muirhead*	Orsi+	Lyon&	Fjortoft	Johnson	Sterling	Oliver		
27/02/2021	L	H	Dundee	2	2		McAdams	McLean	McGinty	Strapp	Ledger	Jacobs	Blues	McGuffie+	Colville&	Nesbitt	Salkeld*	Orsi*	Johnson+	Lyon&	Fjortoft	Muirhead	Sterling	Oliver		
06/03/2021	L	H	Ayr United	0	2		McAdams	McLean	McGinty	Strapp*	Ledger	Jacobs	Blues	McGuffie+	Colville&	Nesbitt	Salkeld	Muirhead*	Johnson+	Sterling&	Fjortoft	Lyon	Oliver	Millar		
09/03/2021	L	A	Inverness CT	1	0		McAdams	Mclean	McGinty	Fjortoft	Ledger	Jacobs	Lyon*	McGuffie	Colville&	Nesbitt+	Sterling	Blues*	Salkeld+	Omar&	Johnston	Hynes	Oliver	Millar		
13/03/2021	L	A	Dunfermline Athletic	0	1		McAdams	McLean	McGinty	Fjortoft	Ledger	McGinn	Lyon*	McGuffie+	Colville	Nesbitt	Sterling&	Oliver*	Salkeld+	Orsi&	Omar	Blues	Muirhead			
20/03/2021	L	H	Queen of the South	2	1		McAdams	McLean	McGinty	Fjortoft*	Strapp	McGinn	Hynes	Oliver+	Colville	Nesbitt	Orsi&	Ledger*	Sterling+	Lyon&	McGuffie	Blues	Muirhead	Salkeld		
23/03/2021	SC	H	Dunfermline Athletic	0	0	AET, 6-5p	McAdams	McLean	McGinty	Strapp	Ledger	Jacobs&	Hynes	McGuffie+	Lyon	Nesbitt>	Sterling*	Orsi*	Oliver+	Blues&	Muirhead>	McGrattan	Easdale	Fjortoft	Colville	Wylie
27/03/2021	L	A	Raith Rovers	0	1		McAdams	McLean	McGinty	Strapp	Ledger	McGinn	Hynes	Colville&	Lyon*	Nesbitt	Oliver+	Jacobs*	Orsi+	McGuffie&	Sterling	Blues	Muirhead	Fjortoft		
03/04/2021	SC	A	East Fife	2	1	AET	McAdams	McLean	McGinty	Strapp	Ledger+	Jacobs	Hynes	Blues&	Lyon	McGuffie*	Orsi >	Nesbitt*	Muirhead+	Oliver&	Sterling>	McGrattan	Easdale	Colville	Fjortoft	Wylie
06/04/2021	L	H	Inverness CT	1	4		McAdams	McLean	McGinty	Strapp	Ledger*	McGinn	Hynes	Colville	Muirhead+	Nesbitt	Oliver&	Orsi*	Sterling+	McGuffie&	Lyon	Jacobs	Fjortoft	Blues		
10/04/2021	L	A	Dundee	1	1		McAdams	McLean	McGinty	Strapp	Ledger	McGinn&	Fjortoft	Colville*	Muirhead+	Nesbitt	Jacobs	Lyon*	Sterling+	Blues&	McGuffie	Hynes	Orsi	Oliver		
16/04/2021	SC	A	Motherwell	1	1	AET, 3-5p	McAdams	McLean	McGinty	Fjortfot	Ledger	McGinn	Lyon+	McGuffie>	Muirhead*	Nesbitt&	Jacobs	Orsi*	McGrattan+	Strapp&	Easdale>	Hynes	Colville	Blues	Oliver	Wylie
20/04/2021	L	H	Hearts	0	0		McAdams	McLean	McGinty	Fjortoft	Ledger	McGinn	Lyon*	Strapp	Orsi&	Nesbitt	Jacobs+	Colville*	Oliver+	Easdale&	McGrattan	Hynes	Muirhead	McGuffie		
24/04/2021	L	H	Alloa Athletic	1	1		McAdams	McLean	McGinty	Fjortoft	Ledger	McGinn	Muirhead+	Strapp*	Orsi&	Nesbitt	Jacobs	McGuffie*	Oliver+	Hynes&	McGrattan	Lyon	Colville	Easdale		
30/04/2021	L	A	Arbroath	0	0		McAdams	McLean	McGinty	Fjortoft	Ledger	McGinn	Colville*	McGuffie+	Oliver	Nesbitt&	Jacobs	Strapp*	Lyon+	Muirhead&	Orsi	Hynes	McGrattan	Easdale		
08/05/2021	PO	A	Montrose	1	2		McAdams	McLean	Strapp	Fjortoft	Ledger	McGinn	Orsi*	McGuffie	Oliver	Nesbitt+	Jacobs	Muirhead*	Blues+	Colville	Lyon	Hynes	McGrattan	Easdale		
11/05/2021	PO	H	Montrose	3	1	AET	McAdams	Mclean	Strapp	Fjortoft	Miller>	McGinn	Blues*	Muirhead&	Oliver+	Salkeld	Jacobs	Lyon*	Nesbitt+	McGuffie&	Ledger>	Hynes	Colville	Wylie		
18/05/2021	PO	A	Airdrieonians	1	0		Fox	McLean	Strapp	Fjortoft	Ledger	McGinn	Blues	Muirhead	Oliver	Salkeld+	Jacobs*	Lyon*	Nesbitt+	McGuffie	McGinty	Hynes	Colville	Wylie		
21/05/2021	PO	H	Airdrieonians	3	0		Fox	McLean	Strapp	Fjortoft	Ledger	McGinn	Blues	Muirhead	Oliver+	Salkeld*	Lyon&	Nesbitt*	McGuffie+	Colville&	McGinty	Hayes	Orsi	Wylie		

THE GOALIES

Goalkeepers Used in League Matches, 1970-2020

Players shown in the season of their first appearance only

1970/1	Eric Sorensen
	Leif Neilson
1972/3	Roy Baines
1974/5	Ray Goddard
1975/6	Jim Herriot
1976/7	Jim Liddell
1977/8	Dennis Connaghan
1978/9	Dave Brcic
1982/3	Graham Kyle
1983/4	Murray McDermott
1983/4	Jim McArthur
1984/5	Craig Adams
1985/6	Robin Rae
	David Wylie
	Robert Turner
1986/7	Rikki Ferguson
	Andy Bruce
	David Harvey
1990/1	Paul Graham
1995/6	Andre Boe
1996/7	Neil Inglis
1997/8	John Hillcoat
1998/9	Ally Maxwell
1999/0	Andy Carlin
2000/1	Matthew Boswell
	Stuart Webster
2001/2	Craig Coyle
	Keith Ross
2004/5	David McGurn
2005/6	Stefan Gonet
2006/7	Paul Mathers
2007/8	Lee Robinson
2008/9	Colin Stewart
	Kevin Cuthbert
2009/0	Bryn Halliwell
	Ryan McWilliams
2011/2	Matthew McGinley
	Dominic Cervi
	Alan Combe
2012/3	Derek Gaston
	David Hutton
2013/4	Nicolas Caraux
2014/5	Grant Adam
2015/6	Derek Gaston
	Jamie McGowan
	Andy McNeill
2016/7	Bryn Halliwell
2017/8	Connor Brennan
2018/9	Robbie McCrorie
	Ryan Scully
2019/0	Sam Ramsbottom
	Danny Rogers

Date	Comp	H/A	Opponents	F	A		HT		Referee	Crowd	Scorers
03/08/2020	L	A	Ross County	0	1		0	1	M Walsh	BCD	
08/08/2020	L	H	Dundee United	0	1		0	0	S McLean	BCD	
12/08/2020	L	H	Livingston	2	2		2	1	C Steven	BCD	Turnbull, Campbell
15/08/2020	L	A	Hibernian	0	0		0	0	G Aitken	BCD	
22/08/2020	L	H	Hamilton Accies	0	1		0	0	A Muir	BCD	
27/08/2020	**UEL**	**H**	**Glentoran**	**5**	**1**		**0**	**0**	**B Van Driessche (BEL)**	**BCD**	**Lang, Long, O'Donnell, Polworth, Watt**
30/08/2020	L	A	Celtic	0	3		0	1	D Robertson	BCD	
12/09/2020	L	H	St Johnstone	1	0		1	0	E Anderson	BCD	Campbell
17/09/2020	**UEL**	**A**	**Coleraine**	**2**	**2**	**3-0p**	**2**	**0**	**A Munukka (FIN)**	**BCD**	**Lang, Watt**
20/09/2020	L	A	Aberdeen	3	0		3	0	J Beaton	BCD	O'Hara pen, Long, Mugabi
24/09/2020	**UEL**	**A**	**Hapoel Bee Sheva**	**0**	**3**		**0**	**1**	**S Boyko (UKR)**	**BCD**	
27/09/2020	L	H	Rangers	1	5		0	3	R Madden	BCD	Edmundson og
24/10/2020	L	H	Ross County	4	0		1	0	C Napier	BCD	Watt, O'Hara pen, Lang, Cole
31/10/2020	L	A	Livingston	2	0		2	0	J Beaton	BCD	Lang, Watt
08/11/2020	L	H	Celtic	1	4		0	2	A Dallas	BCD	Gallagher
21/11/2020	L	A	St Johnstone	1	1		1	1	S Kirkland	BCD	O'Hara
28/11/2020	**LC**	**H**	**St Johnstone**	**1**	**2**		**0**	**0**	**A Muir**	**BCD**	**Watt**
05/12/2020	L	H	Hibernian	0	3		0	0	A Dallas	BCD	
12/12/2020	L	H	St Mirren	0	1		0	1	E Anderson	BCD	
19/12/2020	L	A	Rangers	1	3		3	1	D Robertson	BCD	Lang
23/12/2020	L	h	Aberdeen	0	0		0	0	G Aitken	BCD	
26/12/2020	L	A	Dundee United	1	1		1	0	B Madden	BCD	Watt
30/12/2020	L	H	Kilmarnock	0	2		0	1	J Beaton	BCD	
02/01/2021	L	A	Hamilton Accies	0	3		0	1	C Steven	BCD	
09/01/2021	L	A	St Mirren	1	1		1	0	B Madden	BCD	Cole
17/01/2021	L	H	Rangers	1	1		1	0	D Robertson	BCD	Cole
23/01/2021	L	A	Aberdeen	0	2		0	1	C Napier	BCD	
27/01/2021	L	A	Ross County	2	1		0	1	N Walsh	BCD	Cole, Mugabi
03/02/2021	L	H	Dundee United	2	1		2	0	D Robertson	BCD	Cole, Long
06/02/2021	L	A	Celtic	1	2		0	1	N Walsh	BCD	Campbell
10/02/2021	L	A	Kilmarnock	1	0		0	0	W Collum	BCD	Campbell
13/02/2021	L	H	Hamilton Accies	1	4		0	3	D Munro	BCD	O'Hara pen
20/02/2021	L	H	St Johnstone	0	3		0	2	J Beaton	BCD	
24/02/2021	L	A	St Mirren	0	0		0	0	K Clancy	BCD	
27/02/2021	L	A	Hibernian	2	0		1	0	A Muir	BCD	Cole, Roberts
06/03/2021	L	H	Livingston	3	1		1	0	C Steven	BCD	Cole 2(1 pen), Long
20/03/2021	L	A	Kilmarnock	1	4		1	1	A Muir	BCD	Maguire
03/04/2021	**SC**	**A**	**Formartine United**	**5**	**0**		**2**	**0**	**M Roncone**	**BCD**	**Long, Roberts 2, Cole, Campbell**
10/04/2021	L	H	St Mirren	1	0		0	0	K Clancy	BCD	Cole
16/04/2021	**SC**	**H**	**Morton**	**1**	**1**	**AET, 5-3p**	**0**	**0**	**W Collum**	**BCD**	**O'Donnell**
21/04/2021	L	A	Hamilton Accies	1	0		1	0	K Clancy	BCD	O'Hara
24/04/2021	**SC**	**A**	**Hibernian**	**2**	**2**	**AET, 2-4p**	**0**	**0**	**J Beaton**	**BCD**	**Lamie, Watt**
01/05/2021	L	H	Kilmarnock	2	0		0	0	B Madden	BCD	Cole, O'Donnell
12/05/2021	L	A	Dundee United	2	2		0	2	D Dickinson	BCD	Long, Cole
16/05/2021	L	H	Ross County	1	2		1	0	S McLean	BCD	Foley

Surname	First Name	Date of Birth	No	Nat	Pos	Signed	Previous	Notes	Contract	Lge			SC			LC			UEFA			
										A	S	G	A	S	G	A	S	G	A	S	G	Un
Archer	Jordan	12/04/1993		SCO / ENG	GK	2020	Fulham	Transferred to Middlesbrough Jan 2021		4												4
Campbell	Allan	04/07/1998	6	SCO	M	2018	Motherwell Youths	OOC June 2021 joined Luton Town		34		4	3		1				3			1
Carroll	Jake	11/08/1991	3	ROI / ENG	D	2019	Cambridge United		End 2022/3	14	1											10
Carson	Trevor	05/03/1988	1	NIR	GK	2017	Hartlepool United	Transferred to Dundee United July 2021		12	0								3			0
Chapman	Aaron	29/05/1990	34	ENG	GK	2020	Peterborough United	Released June 2021 joined Gillingham		4	2					1						11
Cole	Devante	10/05/1995	44	JAM / ENG	F	2020	Doncaster Rovers	OOC June 2021 joined Barnsley		24	3	11	3		1	1						1
Connolly	Matthew	02/03/2003	30	SCO	GK	2019	Motherwell Youths	OL to Falkirk Oct-Jan	End 2021/2	0	0											0
Cook	Findlay	31/05/2002	36	SCO	F	2019	Motherwell Youths	Released July 2021		0	0											0
Cornelius	Dean	11/04/2001	26	SCO	M	2019	Motherwell Youths		End 2022/3	0	1											30
Crawford	Robbie	22/06/1994	8	SCO	M	2021	Livingston		End 2021/2	19	3		3			1						8
Devine	David	20/06/2001	24	SCO	D	2020	Motherwell Youths		End 2022/3	0	0											14
Donnelly	Liam	07/03/1996	22	ENG	M	2018	Hartlepool United		End 2021/2	1	0											0
Dunne	Charles	13/02/1993	18	ROI / ENG	D	2017	Oldham Athletic	Released June 2021, joined St Mirren		0	0											7
Foley	Sam	17/10/1986	37	ROI / ENG	M	2021	St Mirren	Released June 2021		3	1	1		1								4
Fox	Scott	28/01/1987	12	SCO	GK	2020	Partick Thistle	OL to Morton May 2021	End 2021/2	0	0											5
Gallagher	Declan	13/02/1991	31	SCO	D	2019	Livingston	Out of Contract May 2021, joined Aberdeen		27	2	1	3			1			3			3
Grimshaw	Liam	02/02/1995	2	ENG	D	2018	Preston North End		End 2021/2	12	2						1		2			6
Hale	Paul	26/01/2003	40	SCO	M	2019	Motherwell Youths	Released July 2021		0	0											0
Hastie	Jake	18/03/1998	11	SCO	F	2020	Rangers (OL)	Jul-Jun		7	7			2						1		25
Hussain	Yusuf	26/04/2001	28	SCO	D	2020	Motherwell Youths	OL to Brechin C Mar-May, Freed June 2021 joined Forfar A		0	0											3
Hylton	Jermaine	28/06/1993	14	ENG	F	2019	Solihull Moors	Transferred to Ross County Oct 2020		0	5											3
Johnston	Max	26/12/2003	27	SCO	D	2020	Motherwell Youths		End 2021/2	1	1											17
Kelly	Liam	23/01/1996	13	SCO	GK	2021	QPR (OL)	Jan-Jun		18	0		3									0
Lamie	Ricki	20/06/1993	4	SCO	D	2020	Livingston		End 2021/2	27	4		2	1	1	1			3			2
Lang	Callum	08/09/1988	29	ENG	F	2020	Wigan Athletic (OL)	Jul-Jan		12	4	3				1			2	1	2	0
Lawless	Steven	12/04/1991	14	SCO	F	2021	Burton Albion		End 2021/2	3	4		2	1								4
Long	Christopher	25/02/1995	99	ENG	F	2019	Blackpool	Released June 2021 joined Crewe Alexandra		19	11	4	3		1				2	1	1	3
MacIver	Ross	28/02/1999	25	SCO	F	2020	Motherwell Youths	OL to Morton Sep-Jan, Partick Th Mar-May, OOC May joined Partick Th		0	1											6
Magliore	Tyler	21/12/1998	40	ENG	D	2021	Blackburn Rovers (OL)	Feb-Jun		8	2		2									4
Maguire	Barry	27/04/1998	15	SCO	M	2019	Motherwell Youths		End 2021/2	14	10	1	1	1						2		15
McDonald	Matthew	26/08/2002	34	SCO	D	2019	Motherwell Youths	Released July 2021, joined Airdrieonians		0	0											1
McGinley	Nathan	15/09/1996	5	ENG	D	2020	Forest Green Rovers		End 2021/2	12	7		3						2			10
Morrison	Peter "PJ"	27/02/1999	23	SCO	GK	2018	Motherwell Youths	OL to Falkirk Oct-Jan, to Ayr Utd Apr-May	End 2021/2	0	0											23
Mugabi	Bevis	01/05/1995	16	UGA / ENG	D	2019	Yeovil Town		End 2021/2	21	2	2		1		1			2			8
Muir	Sam	10/07/2002	33	SCO	D	2019	Motherwell Youths	OL to Gretna Oct-Jan, Released July 2021		0	0											0
Nolan	Eddie	05/08/1988	38	ROI	D	2021	Crewe Alexandra (OL)	Feb-May		0	0											0
O'Donnell	Stephen	11/05/1992	33	SCO	D	2020	Kilmarnock		End 2022/3	34	0	1	3		1	1			3		1	0
O'Hara	Mark	12/12/1995	7	SCO	M	2020	Peterborough United		End 2021/2	23	4	5	1	1		1			3			0
Polworth	Liam	12/10/1994	19	SCO	M	2019	Inverness CT	Released June 2021 joined Kilmarnock		18	3					1			3		1	12
Roberts	Jordan	05/01/1994	39	ENG	M	2021	Hearts (OL)	Feb-Jun		5	2	1	1		2							3
Robertson	Lewis	01/01/2003	42	SCO	M	2019	Rangers Youths	Released July 2021		0	0											0
Robinson	Harry	26/09/2000	21	NIR	F	2020	Motherwell Youths	OL to QOS Sep-Feb, Released June 2021 joined Clyde		0	1									1		4
Seedorf	Sherwin	17/05/1998	17	NET / SUR	F	2019	Wolves	Released June 2021		6	4						1			2		10
Semple	Jamie	17/05/2001	20	SCO	M	2019	Motherwell Youths	OL to Cove Rangers Sep-Feb, Released June 2021		0	0											0
Smith	Harry	18/05/1995	29	ENG	F	2021	West Ham United (OL)	Jan-Jun		0	5											0
Turnbull	David	10/07/1999	8	SCO	M	2018	Motherwell Youths	Transferred to Celtic Aug 2020		5	0	1										0
Watt	Tony	29/12/1993	32	SCO	F	2020	CSKA Sofia		End 2021/2	28	7	3		1	1	1		1	2	1	2	1
White	Jordan	04/02/1992	9	SCO	F	2020	Inverness CT	Transferred to Ross Co Jan 2021		3	15						1			1		3
Williamson	Cameron	05/03/2003	35	SCO	D	2019	Motherwell Youths	Released July 2021		0	0											0
												1										
NEW SIGNINGS																						
Amaluzor	Justin	17/10/1996		ENG / NIG	F	2021	Maidstone United		End 2021/2													
Kelly	Liam	23/01/1996		SCO	GK	2021	QPR		End 2023/4													
O'Connor	Darragh	05/08/1999		ROI	D	2021	Leicester City		End 2021/2													
Parker	Mich'el	22/10/1998		ENG	D	2021	Millwall		End 2021/2													
Shields	Connor	29/07/1997		SCO	F	2021	Queen of the South		End 2023/4													
Van Veen	Kevin	01/01/1991		NET	F	2021	Scunthorpe United		End 2022/3													
Woolery	Kaiyne	11/01/1995		ENG	D	2021	Tranmere Rovers		End 2023/4													

PHOTOCARDS

No. 104.

MOTHERWELL FOOTBALL CLUB.

Left to right, back row:—H. Wales, J. Blair, A. McClory, B. Ellis (Capt.), P. McArthur, C. Johnston, T. McKenzie. Front row:—D. Ogilvie, T. Wylie, J. McMenemy, G. Stevenson, W. McFadyen, R. Ferrier, T. Crawley.

Celebrating its Jubilee last year Motherwell, the famous First Division Scottish Team, is looked upon as an institution in Scottish Football. Nearly every football honour has been held by the club, and Motherwell players often appear in the Scottish International Team.

Date	Comp	H/A	Opponents	F	A		1	2	3	4	5	6	7	8
03/08/2020	L	A	Ross County	0	1		Carson	Gallagher	Donnelly	Lamie	Grimshaw	Polworth	O'Hara*	McGinley
08/08/2020	L	H	Dundee United	0	1		Carson	Gallagher	Mugabi	Lamie	Grimshaw	Campbell&	O'Hara	Seedorf>
12/08/2020	L	H	Livingston	2	2		Carson	Gallagher	Mugabi	Lamie	Grimshaw	Campbell	O'Hara	Seedorf*
15/08/2020	L	A	Hibernian	0	0		Carson	Gallagher	Mugabi	Lamie	O'Donnell>	Campbell	O'Hara	Seedorf*
22/08/2020	L	H	Hamilton Accies	0	1		Carson	Gallagher	Mugabi	Lamie	O'Donnell	Campbell&	O'Hara	Seedorf>
27/08/2020	**UEL**	**H**	**Glentoran**	**5**	**1**		**Carson**	**Gallagher**	**Mugabi**	**Lamie**	**O'Donnell&**	**Campbell**	**O'Hara**	**Grimshaw***
30/08/2020	L	A	Celtic	0	3		Carson	Gallagher	Mugabi	Lamie+	O'Donnell	Campbell	O'Hara	Grimshaw
12/09/2020	L	H	St Johnstone	1	0		Carson	Gallagher	Mugabi	Lamie	O'Donnell	Campbell	O'Hara	McGinley+
17/09/2020	**UEL**	**A**	**Coleraine**	**2**	**2**	**3-0p**	**Carson**	**Gallagher**	**Mugabi**	**Lamie**	**O'Donnell**	**Campbell>**	**O'Hara**	**McGinley***
20/09/2020	L	A	Aberdeen	3	0		Carson	Gallagher	Mugabi	Lamie	O'Donnell	Campbell	O'Hara	Grimshaw
24/09/2020	**UEL**	**A**	**Hapoel Bee Sheva**	**0**	**3**		**Carson**	**Gallagher**	**McGinley**	**Lamie**	**O'Donnell**	**Campbell**	**O'Hara**	**Grimshaw**
27/09/2020	L	H	Rangers	1	5		Carson	Gallagher	Mugabi	Lamie	O'Donnell*	Campbell	O'Hara	Grimshaw
24/10/2020	L	H	Ross County	4	0		Carson*	Gallagher	McGinley	Maguire	O'Donnell	Campbell	O'Hara	Cole>
31/10/2020	L	A	Livingston	2	0		Chapman	Gallagher	McGinley	Maguire	O'Donnell	Campbell	O'Hara	Cole*
08/11/2020	L	H	Celtic	1	4		Chapman	Gallagher	McGinley	Maguire*	O'Donnell	Campbell	O'Hara	Cole+
21/11/2020	L	A	St Johnstone	1	1		Chapman	Gallagher	McGinley	Mugabi	O'Donnell	Crawford	O'Hara	Cole*
28/11/2020	**LC**	**H**	**St Johnstone**	**1**	**2**		**Chapman**	**Gallagher**	**Mugabi**	**Lamie+**	**O'Donnell**	**Crawford**	**O'Hara**	**Cole***
05/12/2020	L	H	Hibernian	0	3		Archer	Gallagher	McGinley	Mugabi	O'Donnell	Campbell	O'Hara	Watt
12/12/2020	L	H	St Mirren	0	1		Archer	Gallagher	Grimshaw	Mugabi&	O'Donnell	Campbell	O'Hara>	Watt
19/12/2020	L	A	Rangers	1	3		Archer	Gallagher	Grimshaw>	Mugabi	O'Donnell	Campbell	O'Hara	Watt*
23/12/2020	L	h	Aberdeen	0	0		Archer	Gallagher	Grimshaw	Lamie	O'Donnell	Campbell	O'Hara	Watt&
26/12/2020	L	A	Dundee United	1	1		Carson	Gallagher	Grimshaw	Lamie	O'Donnell	Campbell	O'Hara	Watt
30/12/2020	L	H	Kilmarnock	0	2		Carson*	Gallagher	Grimshaw+	Lamie	O'Donnell	Campbell	O'Hara	Watt
02/01/2021	L	A	Hamilton Accies	0	3		Chapman	Gallagher	Grimshaw	Carroll	O'Donnell	Campbell	Mugabi	Watt
09/01/2021	L	A	St Mirren	1	1		Kelly	Gallagher	Mugabi	Carroll	O'Donnell	Campbell	O'Hara	Watt
17/01/2021	L	H	Rangers	1	1		Kelly	Gallagher	Mugabi	Carroll	O'Donnell	Campbell	Crawford>	Watt+
23/01/2021	L	A	Aberdeen	0	2		Kelly	Gallagher	Mugabi	Carroll&	O'Donnell	Campbell	Crawford<	Watt+
27/01/2021	L	A	Ross County	2	1		Kelly	Gallagher	Mugabi	Carroll	O'Donnell	Campbell	Crawford	Watt&
03/02/2021	L	H	Dundee United	2	1		Kelly	Lamie	Mugabi	Carroll	O'Donnell	Campbell	Crawford	Watt+
06/02/2021	L	A	Celtic	1	2		Kelly	Lamie	Mugabi	Carroll	O'Donnell	Campbell	Crawford+	Watt*
10/02/2021	L	A	Kilmarnock	1	0		Kelly	Lamie	Mugabi	Carroll	O'Donnell	Campbell	Crawford*	Watt
13/02/2021	L	H	Hamilton Accies	1	4		Kelly	Lamie	Mugabi+	Carroll	O'Donnell	Campbell	O'Hara	Watt
20/02/2021	L	H	St Johnstone	0	3		Kelly	Lamie	Magliore	Carroll+	Polworth	Johnston	Crawford	Watt
24/02/2021	L	A	St Mirren	0	0		Kelly	Lamie	Magliore	Carroll	O'Donnell	Campbell	Crawford	Watt
27/02/2021	L	A	Hibernian	2	0		Kelly	Lamie	Magliore	Carroll*	O'Donnell	Campbell	Crawford	Watt+
06/03/2021	L	H	Livingston	3	1		Kelly	Lamie	Magliore	Carroll	O'Donnell	Campbell	Crawford	Watt*
20/03/2021	L	A	Kilmarnock	1	4		Kelly	Lamie	Magliore	Carroll	O'Donnell	Campbell	Crawford	Watt
03/04/2021	**SC**	**A**	**Formartine United**	**5**	**0**		**Kelly**	**Gallagher**	**Magiore**	**McGinley**	**O'Donnell**	**Campbell&**	**Crawford***	**Lawless**
10/04/2021	L	H	St Mirren	1	0		Kelly	Gallagher	Lamie	McGinley	O'Donnell	Campbell	Crawford	Lawless*
16/04/2021	**SC**	**H**	**Morton**	**1**	**1**	**AET, 5-3p**	**Kelly**	**Gallagher**	**Lamie**	**McGinley**	**O'Donnell**	**Campbell+**	**Crawford**	**Lawless&**
21/04/2021	L	A	Hamilton Accies	1	0		Kelly	Gallagher	Lamie	McGinley	O'Donnell	Campbell	Crawford	O'Hara
24/04/2021	**SC**	**A**	**Hibernian**	**2**	**2**	**AET, 2-4p**	**Kelly**	**Gallagher**	**Lamie**	**McGinley**	**O'Donnell**	**Campbell&**	**Crawford+**	**O'Hara**
01/05/2021	L	H	Kilmarnock	2	0		Kelly	Gallagher	Lamie	McGinley	O'Donnell	Campbell	Foley	Lawless+
12/05/2021	L	A	Dundee United	2	2		Kelly	Magliore	Lamie	McGinley	O'Donnell	Campbell*	Foley&	Lawless+
16/05/2021	L	H	Ross County	1	2		Kelly	Magliore	Lamie	McGinley	O'Donnell	Foley	Crawford+	O'Hara

THE GOALIES

Goalkeepers Used in League Matches, 1970-2020

Players shown in the season of their first appearance only

1970/1	Keith McRae
	Billy Ritchie
1971/2	Thomas Burns
	John Fallon
1973/4	Stewart Rennie
1974/5	Graham Lloyd
1976/7	Ally Hunter
	Jim Muir
1978/9	Dave Latchford
1979/0	Hugh Sproat
1980/1	Alistair McLean
	Lawrie Williams
1981/2	Howard Sammeroff
1982/3	Nicky Walker
1983/4	Ally Maxwell
1984/5	John Gardiner
1986/7	Kevin McKeown
1987/8	Cammy Duncan
1991/2	Billy Thomson
	Sieb Dykstra
1994/5	Stevie Woods
	Scott Howie
1997/8	Scott Thomson
1998/9	Mikko Kaven
	Andy Goram
2000/1	Jon Connolly
2001/2	Mark Brown
	Francois Dubordeau
2003/4	Gordon Marshall
	Barry Corr
2005/6	Graham Smith
	Colin Meldrum
2007/8	Luke Daniels
2008/9	Artur Krysiak
2009/0	Jon Ruddy
	Michael Fraser
2010/1	Darren Randolph
	Lee Hollis
2013/4	Gunnar Neilsen
	Dan Twardzik
2014/5	George Long
2015/6	Connor Ripley
	Craig Samson
2016/7	Russell Griffiths
2017/8	Trevor Carson
2018/9	Mark Gillespie

Dat
07/
10/
13/
17/
24/
31/
07/
14/
21/
28/
05/
12/
19/
26/
20/(
23/(
27/(
30/(
03/(
06/(
10/(
13/(
15/(
20/(
24/(
27/(
29/(
04/(

9	10	11	12	13	14	15	16	17	18	19	20
Turnbull>	Long&	Hastie+	Lang*	Seedorf+	White&	Watt>	Campbell	Maguire	Hylton	Robinson	Fox
Turnbull	Long+	Hastie*	Watt*	White+	Hylton&	Robinson>	Hussain	Johnston	Polworth	Maguire	Fox
Turnbull+	Long&	White	Hylton*	Polworth+	Hastie&	Robinson	Watt	Johnston	Cornelius	Maguire	Fox
Lang+	Turnbull	White&	Hylton*	Long+	Watt&	Grimshaw>	Hastie	Robinson	Polworth	Maguire	Morrison
Lang*	Turnbull	White+	Hylton*	Long+	Watt&	Hastie>	Grimshaw	Robinson	Polworth	Maguire	Morrison
Lang+	Long	Polworth	Seedorf*	Watt+	Robinson&	Hastie	White	Maguire	Morrison		
Watt*	Long&	Polworth	Lang*	White+	Hylton&	Hastie	Seedorf	Maguire	Cornelius	Robinson	Morrison
Lang	Watt*	Polworth	White*&	Grimshaw+	Long&	Hastie	Seedorf	Maguire	MacIver	Johnston	Morrison
Lang&	Watt	Polworth+	Seedorf*	Maguire+	Hastie&	Long>	MacIver	Grimshaw	Morrison		
Watt+	Long*	Polworth&	White*&	Lang+	McGuire&	Seedorf	Hastie	Hylton	McGinley	Crawford	Morrison
Watt+	Long*	Polworth&	Lang*	White+	Maguire&	Seedorf	Hastie	Cornelius	Morrison		
Lang&	Watt>	Polworth+	Maguire*	Long+	Seedorf&	White>	Crawford	Cornelius	McGinley	Hylton	Morrison
Watt	Long+	Polworth&	Chapman*	Long+	Crawford&	Hastie>	Devine	Cornelius	Johnston	White	Hussain
Lang+	Watt	Polworth	White*	Long+	Hussain	Hastie	Devine	Cornelius	Johnston	McDonald	Archer
Lang	Watt&	Polworth	Crawford*	Long+	White&	Hastie	Devine	Cornelius	Johnston	Grimshaw	Archer
Lang&	Watt	Polworth	Long*+	Lamie+	White&	Hastie	Devine	Cornelius	Seedorf	Grimshaw	Archer
Lang	Watt	Polworth&	Seedorf*	Grimshaw+	White&	Hastie	Devine	Cornelius	Long	McGinley	Archer
Lang	Long*	Polworth+	Seedorf*	Hastie+	Crawford	Grimshaw	Lamie	Cornelius	Devine	Maguire	Chapman
Lang+	Long*	Maguire	Hastie*	Cole+	Polworth&	Lamie>	Johnston	McGinley	Devine	Crawford	Chapman
Lang+	Crawford<	Lamie&	McGinley*	White+	Seedorf&	Polworth>	Cole<	Cornelius	Maguire	Johnston	Chapman
Lang*	Crawford+	Polworth	Cole*	Maguire+	White&	Seedorf	Cornelius	Hastie	Mugabi	Carroll	Chapman
Lang*	Crawford+	Polworth	White*	Cornelius+	McGuire	Cole	McGinley	Hastie	Mugabi	Carroll	Chapman
Cole>	Crawford&	Polworth	Chapman*	Carroll+	Lang&	White>	Seedorf	Hastie	Mugabi	Maguire	Cornelius
Cole*	Hastie+	Polworth	White*	Maguire+	Johnson	Devine	Seedorf	Cornelius	Crawford	McGinley	Morrison
Cole+	Hastie*	Polworth	White*	Maguire+	Grimshaw	Devine	Seedorf	Cornelius	Crawford	McGinley	Morrison
Cole	Seedorf*	Polworth&	MacIver*	Lawless+	Lamie&	Maguire>	Devine	White	Johnston	McGinley	Morrison
Cole>	Seedorf*	Polworth	Long*	Smith+	McGinley&	Hastie>	Maguire<	MacIver	Johnston	Lamie	Morrison
Cole+	Long*	Maguire	Smith*	Lamie+	McGinley&	Hastie	Lawless	MacIver	Johnston	Seedorf	Morrison
Cole	Long*	Maguire	Smith*	McGinley+&	Foley&	Hastie	Roberts	Polworth	Johnston	Magloire	Morrison
Cole	Long	Maguire&	Roberts*	O'Hara+	Smith&	Hastie	Polworth	Cornelius	Johnston	Magloire	Morrison
Cole+	Long&	Maguire	O'Hara*	Magliore+	Smith&	Hastie	Polworth	Cornelius	Johnston	Roberts	Morrison
Cole	Long*	Maguire	Magloire*	Johnston+	Crawford	Hastie	Polworth	Cornelius	MacIver	Roberts	Morrison
Cole	Long&	Maguire*	Roberts*	McGinley+&	Hastie&	MacIver	Devine	Cornelius	Morrison		
Cole	Roberts	Maguire	Polworth	Lawless	Hastie	Long	Devine	Cornelius	Johnston	McGinley	Morrison
Cole	Roberts&	Maguire	McGinley*	Gallagher+	Lawless&	Hastie	Devine	Cornelius	Long	Polworth	Morrison
Cole	Roberts&	Maguire	Long*+	Gallagher+	McGinley&	Hastie	Devine	Cornelius	Lawless	Polworth	Morrison
Cole+	Roberts	Maguire*	Lawless*	Long+	McGinley	Hastie	Gallagher	Cornelius	Mugabi	Polworth	Morrison
Cole	Long	Roberts+	Foley*	Hastie+	Lamie&	Maguire	Polworth	Cornelius	Mugabi	Carroll	Chapman
Cole	Long&	Roberts+	Maguire*	O'Hara+	Mugabi&	Hastie	Foley	Cornelius	Dunne	Carroll	Chapman
Cole	Long	Maguire*	Hastie*	O'Hara+	Mugabi&	Magliore	Foley	Cornelius	Dunne	Carroll	Chapman
Cole	Long*	Magliore	Maguire*	Lawless	Mugabi	Hastie	Foley	Cornelius	Dunne	Carroll	Chapman
Cole	Long	Magliore*	Watt*	Lawless+	Maguire&	Hastie	Foley	Mugabi	Dunne	Carroll	Chapman
Cole	Long&	Hastie*	Watt*	Mugabi+	Maguire&	Crawford	Magliore	Cornelius	Dunne	Carroll	Chapman
Cole	Long	Hastie	Crawford*	Watt+	O'Hara&	Maguire	Gallagher	Cornelius	Dunne	Carroll	Fox
Cole	Long	Hastie*	Lawless*	Watt+	Johnston	Maguire	Gallagher	Cornelius	Dunne	Carroll	Fox

Stewart Rennie

Keith MacRae

Sieb Dykstra

Date	Comp	H/A	Opponents	F	A		1	2	3	4	5	6	7	8	9	10	11	12	13	14	15	16	17	18	19	20
07/10/2020	LC	A	St Mirren	1	4		Sneddon	Brownlie	Williamson+	Penrice	Breen	Cardle*	Bannigan	Docherty	Gordon	Graham>	Murray&	Spittal*	McKenna+	Lyons&	Kouider-Assa>	*Rodden*	*Reilly*	*Niang*	*Rudden*	*Scullion*
10/10/2020	LC	H	Queen's Park	2	0		Sneddon	Brownlie	Foster+	Penrice	McKenna	Spittal&	Bannigan	Docherty	Gordon>	Graham	Rudden*	Cardle*	Williamson+	Murray&	Niang>	*Kouider-Assa*	*Reilly*	*Breen*	*Lyons*	*Scullion*
13/10/2020	LC	A	Queen of the South	0	0	3-2p	Sneddon	Brownlie	Foster	Penrice	McKenna	Cardle+	Bannigan>	Docherty	Gordon&	Graham	Murray*	Rudden*	Niang+	Spittal&	Kouider-Assa>	*Williamson*	*Reilly*	*Breen*	*Lyons*	*Scullion*
17/10/2020	L	A	Clyde	0	1		Sneddon	Brownlie	Foster<	Penrice	McKenna	Cardle+	Bannigan>	Docherty	Gordon*	Kouider-Assa&	Murray	Spittal*	Lyons+	Niang&	Williamson>	*Reilly<*	*Wright*	*Breen*	*Rodden*	
24/10/2020	L	H	Airdrieonians	2	1		Wright	Brownlie	Foster	Penrice	Breen	Spittal*	Bannigan	Docherty	Gordon	Graham	Murray+	Lyons*	Niang+	*Cardle*	*Williamson*	*Kouider-Assa*	*Reilly*	*Scullion*	*Rodden*	
31/10/2020	L	A	Cove Rangers	0	1		Wright	Brownlie	Foster	Penrice	Breen	Spittal	Bannigan	Docherty	Gordon	Graham	Niang	*Lyons*	*Murray*	*Cardle*	*Williamson*	*Kouider-Assa*	*Reilly*	*McCready*		
07/11/2020	L	H	Falkirk	2	2		Wright	Brownlie	Williamson+	Penrice	Breen	Spittal	Bannigan	Docherty	Cardle+	Graham	Murray*	Lyons*	Gordon+	*Reilly*	*Foster*	*Niang*	*McCready*			
14/11/2020	LC	H	Morton	0	0	4-2p	Wright	Brownlie	Williamson+	Penrice	Breen	Foster	Bannigan	Spittal*	Cardle	Gordon+	Murray&	Lyons*	Niang+	Reilly&	*McCready*					
21/11/2020	L	H	East Fife	2	0		Wright	Brownlie	Williamson	Penrice	Foster	Cardle	Bannigan	Docherty	Niang	Graham	Murray*	Gordon*	*Lyons*	*Scullion*	*Reilly*					
28/11/2020	L	A	Montrose	1	0		Wright	Brownlie	Williamson	Penrice	Foster	Cardle	Bannigan	Docherty	Niang	Graham	Murray*	Gordon*	*Reilly*	*Lyons*	*Scullion*					
05/12/2020	L	H	Dumbarton	0	0		Wright	Brownlie	Williamson	Penrice+	Foster	Cardle	Bannigan	Docherty	Niang	Graham	Murray*	Gordon*	Lyons+	*Reilly*	*Scullion*					
12/12/2020	L	A	Forfar Athletic	2	0		Wright	Brownlie	Williamson	Penrice&	Foster	Cardle+	Bannigan	Docherty	Niang	Graham	Murray*	Gordon*	Lyons+	Lyon&	*Reilly*	*Breen*	*Owens*	*Scullion*		
19/12/2020	L	H	Peterhead	0	1		Wright	Brownlie	Williamson	Penrice&	Foster	Cardle	Bannigan+	Docherty	Niang	Graham>	Murray*	Gordon*	Rudden+	Lyons&	Breen>	*McKenna*	*Owens*	*Scullion*	*Reilly*	*Lyon*
26/12/2020	L	A	Falkirk	0	0		Wright	Brownlie	McKenna	Penrice	Foster	Cardle+	Bannigan	Docherty*	Niang	Rudden	Murray	Gordon*	Lyons+	*Breen*	*Reilly*	*Scullion*	*Ocholi*			
20/03/2021	L	H	Cove Rangers	1	1		Wright	Brownlie	McKenna	Penrice	Foster	Gordon	Bannigan	MacIver+	Niang	Graham	Murray*	Cardle*	Erskine+	*Rodden*	*Geggan*	*Devine*	*Bell*	*Lyon*	*Ocholi*	*Sneddon*
23/03/2021	SC	H	Cowdenbeath	3	0		Wright	Brownlie	Williamson+	Penrice	Cardle*	Gordon	Bannigan	MacIver&	Niang	Rudden>	Tiffoney	Murray*	McKenna+	Graham&	Lyon>	*Foster*	*Rodden*	*Ocholi*	*Sneddon*	
27/03/2021	L	A	Airdrieonians	4	2		Wright	Brownlie<	Williamson&	Cardle*	Foster	Gordon	Bannigan>	Murray	Niang	Graham	Tiffoney+	Penrice*	Rudden+	McKenna&	Geggan>	Bell<	*Lyon*	*MacIver*	*Erskine*	*Sneddon*
30/03/2021	L	H	Forfar Athletic	2	2		Sneddon	Bell	Williamson	Penrice	Cardle<	Docherty+	Bannigan	Murray	Niang&	Rudden*	MacIver>	Graham*	Gordon+	Brownlie&	Tiffoney>	Erskine<	*Foster*	*McKenna*	*Geggan*	*Wright*
03/04/2021	SC	A	Dundee United	1	2		Wright	Brownlie	McKenna	Cardle*	Foster	Docherty	Bannigan	Gordon	Niang	Graham&	Tiffoney+	Murray*	Penrice+	Rudden&	*Williamson*	*MacIver*	*Rodden*	*Lyon*	*Ocholi*	*Sneddon*
06/04/2021	L	A	East Fife	2	2		Sneddon	Brownlie	Williamson+	Gordon*	Foster>	Docherty	Bannigan	Murray<	Niang&	Graham	Tiffoney	Rudden*	McKenna+	Bell&	Penrice>	Cardle<	*McCready*	*Lyon*	*Geggan*	*MacIver*
10/04/2021	L	A	Peterhead	3	0		Sneddon	Brownlie	McKenna	Cardle>	Foster	Docherty&	Bannigan	Murray<	Bell	Graham*	Tiffoney+	MacIver*	Geggan+	Penrice&	Lyons>	Rudden<	*McCready*	*Williamson*	*Gordon*	*Niang*
13/04/2021	L	H	Clyde	2	0		Sneddon	Brownlie	McKenna*	Cardle&	Foster	Docherty	Bannigan	Murray+	Bell	Graham	Tiffoney	Williamson*	Rudden+	Gordon&	*MacIver*	*Geggan*	*McCready*	*Lyons*	*Rodden*	*Niang*
15/04/2021	L	H	Montrose	5	0		Sneddon	Brownlie	Williamson	Bell	Foster	Docherty&	Bannigan	Gordon<	Rudden>	Graham*	Tiffoney+	MacIver*	Cardle+	Geggan&	Murray>	Lyons<	*McCready*	*McKenna*	*Reilly*	*Niang*
20/04/2021	L	A	Dumbarton	2	0		Sneddon	Brownlie	McKenna	Bell	Foster	Docherty	Bannigan	Gordon+	Rudden	Graham*	Tiffoney	MacIver*	Cardle+	*Williamson*	*Murray*	*Geggan*	*McCready*	*Lyons*	*Penrice*	*Niang*
24/04/2021	L	H	Airdrieonians	1	0		Sneddon	Brownlie	McKenna	Bell	Foster	Docherty	Cardle*	Gordon	Rudden+	Graham	Tiffoney&	Murray*	*Niang+*	Geggan&	*MacIver*	*Reilly*	*McCready*	*Lyons*	*Williamson*	*Lyon*
27/04/2021	L	A	Cove Rangers	2	2		Sneddon	Brownlie	McKenna	Bell	Foster	Docherty	Murray*	Gordon	Rudden&	Graham+	Tiffoney>	Cardle*	Penrice+	MacIver&	Niang>	*Geggan*	*Wright*	*Reilly*	*Williamson*	*Lyons*
29/04/2021	L	H	Falkirk	5	0		Sneddon	Brownlie	Williamson	Bell>	Foster	Docherty*	Bannigan&	Penrice	Rudden<	Graham	Tiffoney+	Gordon*	Cardle+	Niang&	Geggan>	Murray<	*Wright*	*Lyons*	*MacIver*	*McKenna*
04/05/2021	L	A	Montrose	2	3		Wright	Williamson	McKenna	Penrice	Foster	Reiily+	Cardle&	Gordon<	Niang	MacIver>	Lyons*	Lyon*	Rudden+	Tiffoney&	Murray>	Owens<	*McCready*	*Rodden*	*Ocholi*	*Sneddon*

THE GOALIES

Goalkeepers Used in League Matches, 1970-2020
Players shown in the season of their first appearance only

1971/2	Allan Rough
1974/5	John Arrol
1978/9	Alistair McLean
1979/0	Dougie McNab
1983/4	John Brough
	Gordon Arthur
	Andy Bruce
1984/5	Andy Smyth
	John Wilson
	David Harvey
1985/6	Graham Kyle
	Nelson Still
1986/7	Jim Stewart
	Colin Brodie
1987/8	Tom Carson
	Rikki Ferguson
	Murray McDermott
	Hugh Stevenson
	Fred Jackson
	David Haxton
	Archie McLean
1988/9	Andy Murdoch
1989/0	Cammy Duncan
	Paul Graham
1990/1	Craig Nelson
1994/5	Nicky Walker
1995/6	Mark Cairns
1996/7	John Hillcoat
1997/8	Gary O'Connor
	Andy Stewart
	Kenny Arthur
	Lindsay Hamilton
1998/9	Stevie Ross
1999/0	Kevin Budinauckas
2000/1	Michael Brown
2001/2	Gary Gow
	David Klein
2003/4	Jakup Mikkelsen
	Jamie Langfield
	Steven Pinkowski
2004/5	Neil Bennett
2005/6	Colin Stewart
2006/7	Jonny Tuffey
2007/8	Craig Hinchcliffe
2009/0	Bryn Halliwell
2010/1	Scott Fox
	Graeme Shepherd
	Ryan Scully
2012/3	Graeme Smith
	Glenn Daniels
2013/4	Paul Gallacher
2015/6	Tomas Czerny
2016/7	Thomas Stuckmann
	Mark Ridgers
2018/9	Connor Hazard
	Cammy Bell
	Jamie Sneddon
2019/0	Scott Fox

Surname	First Name	Date of Birth	No	Nat	Pos	Signed	Previous	Notes	Contract	Lge A	Lge S	Lge G	SC A	SC S	SC G	LC A	LC S	LC G	Un
Bannigan	Stuart	17/09/1992	8	SCO	M	2009	Partick Thistle Youths		End 2022/3	19		1	2			4			
Bell	Chris					2020	Thistle Weir Academy		U20	2									
Bell	Steven	24/02/1985		SCO	D	2021	East Kilbride (OL)	Mar-May		6	2								1
Black	Oliver			SCO	D	2020	Thistle Weir Academy		U20	0									
Breen	Rhys	06/01/2000	15	SCO	D	2020	Rangers (OL)	Aug-May		3	1					2			5
Brownlie	Darren	10/04/1994	5	SCO	D	2020	Queen of the South		End 2021/2	20	1		2			4			0
Cameron	Ewan					2020	Thistle Weir Academy		U20	0	0								0
Cardle	Joe	07/02/1987	7	ENG	M	2019	AFC Fylde	Released May 2021, joined Kelty Hearts		14	6	5	2			3	1	2	2
Collins	Matthew				F	2020	Thistle Weir Academy		U20	0	0								0
Devine	Adam	25/03/2003		SCO	D	2021	Rangers (OL)	Mar-21		0	0								1
Docherty	Ross	23/01/1993	23	SCO	M	2020	Ayr United		End 2022/3	19	0	1	1			3			0
Erskine	Chris	08/02/1987		SCO	M	2021	East Kilbride (OL)	Mar-May		0	2								1
Foster	Ricky	31/07/1985	22	SCO	D	2020	Ross County		End 2021/2	20	0		1			3			3
Geggan	Andy	08/05/1987		SCO	M	2021	BSC Glasgow (OL)	Mar-May		0	5								7
Giovanazzi	Lorenzo				M	2019	Rangers Youths		U20	0	0								0
Gordon	Shea	16/05/1998	14	NIR	M	2019	Motherwell		End 2021/2	11	10	2	2		1	4			0
Graham	Brian	23/11/1987	9	SCO	F	2020	Ross County		End 2022/3	18	1	11	1	1		3			0
Kouider-Assa	Salim	22/03/1996	19	ALG / SCO	F	2020	Livingston (OL)	Sep-May		1	0						2		3
Lyon	James	25/06/2003		SCO	M	2020	Thistle Weir Academy	OL to Stenhousemuir for 2021/2	U20	0	2			1					6
Lyons	Blair	23/09/1996	11	SCO	F	2020	Montrose	OL to Montrose for 2021/2	End 2021/2	1	9						2		10
MacIver	Ross	28/02/1999		SCO	F	2021	Motherwell (OL)	Mar-May		3	4	2	1						6
McCready	Mason	01/01/2003		SCO	GK	2020	Partick Thistle Youths		U20	0	0								10
McDonald	Joe			SCO	D	2020	Thistle Weir Academy		U20	0	0								0
McKenna	Ciaran	25/03/1998	16	SCO	D	2020	Hamilton Accies		End 2021/2	9	2		1	1		2	1		4
Murray	Connor	24/04/1997	17	SCO	F	2020	Queen of the South		End 2021/2	16	4	3		2	1	3	1		2
Niang	Mouhammed	08/10/1999	21	SEN	M	2020	Partick Thistle Youths		End 2022/3	12	5		2				3		6
Ocholi	Gospel	20/01/2003		SCO	F	2021	Thistle Weir Academy		U20	0	0								5
O'Ware	Thomas	20/03/1993	4	SCO	D	2018	Morton		End 2021/2	0	0								0
Owens	Billy	01/01/2002		SCO	M	2020	Thistle Weir Academy		U20	0	1								2
Penrice	James	22/12/1998	3	SCO	D	2016	Partick Thistle Youths	OOC June 2021, joined Livingston		14	4		1	1		4			1
Reilly	Charlie	05/12/2001	18	SCO	M	2020	Hamilton Accies	Released May 2021, joined Albion Rovers		1	1						1		15
Renfrew	Bradley	16/03/2002		SCO	D	2019	Thistle Weir Academy	OL to Cumbernauld Colts Oct-May, Released May 2021		0	0								0
Rodden	Andy	01/10/2001	28	SCO	D	2019	Partick Thistle Youths	Released May 2021		0	0								8
Rudden	Zak	06/02/2000	10	SCO	F	2020	Rangers		End 2021/2	7	6	7	1	1	1	1	1		1
Scullion	Luke	17/01/2002	27	SCO	GK	2019	Thistle Weir Academy	Released May 2021		0	0								10
Sneddon	Jamie	06/09/1997	1	SCO	GK	2017	Cowdenbeath		End 2021/2	10	0					3			5
Spittal	Blair	19/12/1995	6	SCO	M	2020	Ross County (OL)	Oct-Jan		3	1	1				2	2	1	0
Tiffoney	Scott	26/08/1998		SCO	F	2021	Livingston (OL)	Mar-May		9	2	7	2		1				0
Watson	Dean	21/03/2001		SCO	F	2019	Thistle Weir Academy	OL to East Stirlingshire Oct-Dec, to Annan Ath Jan-May, Released May 2021 joined E Stirling		0	0								0
Williamson	Ryan	14/03/1996	2	SCO	D	2019	Dunfermline Athletic	Released May 2021, joined Falkirk		12	2		1			2	1		8
Wright	Kieran	01/04/2000	12	SCO	GK	2020	Rangers (OL)	Aug-May		12	0		2			1			4

NEW SIGNINGS

Surname	First Name	Date of Birth	No	Nat	Pos	Signed	Previous	Notes	Contract
Bell	Steven	24/02/1985		SCO	D	2021	East Kilbride		End 2021/2
Holt	Kevin	25/01/1993		SCO	D	2021	Ermis Aradippou		End 2022/3
MacIver	Ross	28/02/1999		SCO	F	2021	Motherwell		End 2021/2
Stone	Harry	20/04/2002		SCO	GK	2021	Hearts (OL)	Jul-May	End 2021/2
Tiffoney	Scott	26/08/1998		SCO	F	2021	Livingston		End 2022/3
Turner	Kyle	10/11/1997		SCO	M	2021	Dunfermline Athletic	Son of Tommy Turner	End 2022/3

PHOTOCARDS

No. 114.

PARTICK THISTLE F.C.

Left to right, back row :—*S. Calderwood (Capt.), G. Cummings, R. Johnstone, A. Elliot, G. Sutherland, E. M'Leod.* Front row :—*R. Regan, P. M'Kennan, G. Wylie, A. Hastie, A. M'Lennan.*

This team, which was founded in 1876, are members of the First Division, Scottish League. In 1920/21 season they won the Scottish Cup and were finalists in 1929/30. They finished tenth in the League 1935/36.

Expanding de Luxe Albums for Ardath Photocards on sale at Tobacconists Price 6d

ARDATH TOBACCO CO. LTD. Manufacturers of STATE EXPRESS and ARDATH CIGARETTES

D

Peterhead FC 2020/21 The Blue Toon

Founded	1891
Ground	Balmoor Stadium
Postcode	AB42 1EU
Tel	01779 478256
Capacity	3150
Closest Railway Station	Aberdeen
Record Attendance	8643 v Raith Rovers, SC, 25/2/1987
Ground Record	4855 v Rangers, Lge, 19/1/2013
Record Win	8-0 v Forfar Athletic, Lge, 30/9/2006
Record Defeat	0-13 v Aberdeen, SC, 10/2/1923
Most League Goals in a Season	21 Iain Stewart 2002/3,
	Scott Michie 2004/5, Rory McAllister 2012/13
Colours 2020/21 Top	Blue
Shorts	Blue
Sponsor	The Score Group
Manufacturer	Adidas
Change Colours 2020/21 Top	Pink
Shorts	Pink
Nicknames	Blue Toon
Web	www.peterheadfc.co.uk
Match Programme 2020/21	On line only

Chairman: Rodger Morrison
Director: Michael Duncan
Director: Leslie Hill
Director: Charlie Watt
General Manager: Martin Johnston
Youth and Community Liaison: Nat Porter
Manager: Jim McInally
Assistant Manager: David Nicholls
Coach: Simon Ferry
Goalkeeping Coach: Jim Butters
Fitness Coach: Stuart Hogg
Club Scout and Match Analyst: Mick Murphy
Physiotherapist: Greig Smith
Goalkeeping Coach: Scott Tait

THE GOALIES
Goalkeepers Used in League Matches, 2000-2020
Players shown in the season of their first appearance only

2000/1	Ivor Pirie
	Ross Buchanan
2001/2	Paul Mathers
2004/5	Barry Thompson
2005/6	John McCafferty
2006/7	Greg Kelly
	Ian McCaldon
	John Farquhar
2007/8	Jim Will
	Michael Kula
	Paul Leask
2008/9	Paul Jarvie
2009/0	John Bateman
2011/2	Raymond Jellema
	Neil Duffy
2012/3	Mark McCallum
	Graeme Smith
2016/7	Fraser Hobday
2017/8	Greg Fleming

It was another season of mid-table football for Peterhead and they will be pleased to have retained their League One place. In a short season any bad run could have proved disastrous but Jim McInally's team were consistently hard to beat. A run of three wins against East Fife, Falkirk and Clyde late on made sure of survival after a rather iffy period after the resumption of matches in March.

No joy in either Cup for the Blue Toon – they started brilliantly in the League Cup by winning away to Dundee United and beating Brechin City but failed to qualify after losing to St Johnstone and drawing with Kelty. The Scottish Cup brought a defeat from Stenhousemuir – perhaps no bad thing as it allowed them to concentrate on the League in a season when there was no prospect of a big gate from a favourable Cup draw.

STAR MAN
Peterhead fielded three different Brown's in 2020/1, hence Sky Sports Jeff Stelling referring to the club as "Mrs Brown's Boys". Top man was midfielder Scott Brown, a midfielder who has now played almost 150 games for the Balmoor side. He started out with Clyde, moved to Bradford City, returned to Scotland with St Johnstone, and then joined Peterhead in 2016.

PROSPECTS 2021/2
With Jim McInally at the helm Peterhead will always be well-organised and hard to beat. He sets up his teams to give nothing away and to strike quickly on the break. Attracting players to the club is always different - he has again gone for mainly Central Belt signings. Expect them to finish in mid table again.

Greg Fleming

Date	Comp	H/A	Opponents	F	A		HT		Referee	Crowd	Scorers
10/10/2020	LC	A	Dundee United	1	0		0	0	B Madden	BCD	Boyd
13/10/2020	LC	H	Brechin City	3	1		3	0	C Graham	BCD	Layne 2, Boyd
17/10/2020	L	A	Airdrieonians	0	2		0	1	B Cook	BCD	
24/10/2020	L	H	Cove Rangers	0	2		0	1	A Newlands	BCD	
31/10/2020	L	A	Clyde	2	0		0	0	G Grainger	BCD	Cameron, S Brown
07/11/2020	L	A	Montrose	2	3		1	1	M McDermid	BCD	Armour 2
10/11/2020	LC	A	Kelty Hearts	1	1	5-3p	0	0	G Ross	BCD	Fraser
14/11/2020	LC	H	St Johnstone	1	3		0	0	E Anderson	BCD	Rooney og
21/11/2020	L	H	Dumbarton	1	0		1	0	C Scott	BCD	Armour
28/11/2020	L	H	Forfar Athletic	0	1		0	1	C Graham	BCD	
05/12/2020	L	A	Falkirk	1	2		0	2	P Stuart	BCD	Cameron
12/12/2020	L	H	East Fife	2	1		1	1	G Beaton	BCD	Cameron, S Brown
19/12/2020	L	A	Partick Thistle	1	0		1	0	K Graham	BCD	S Brown
22/12/2020	L	H	Montrose	1	1		1	0	G Grainger	BCD	Layne pen
02/01/2021	L	A	Cove Rangers	0	1		0	1	P Stuart	BCD	
20/03/2021	L	H	Airdrieonians	1	0		0	0	S Kirkland	BCD	Jordan Brown
23/03/2021	SC	H	Stenhousemuir	0	1		0	1	M Roncone	BCD	
27/03/2021	L	A	Dumbarton	1	0		0	0	C Graham	BCD	Armour
30/03/2021	L	H	Clyde	0	2		0	0	D Williams	BCD	
06/04/2021	L	A	Forfar Athletic	1	1		0	0	A Newlands	BCD	Ritchie
10/04/2021	L	H	Partick Thistle	0	3		0	1	K Graham	BCD	
17/04/2021	L	A	East Fife	1	2		1	0	Wilson	BCD	Ritchie
20/04/2021	L	H	Falkirk	1	0		0	0	D Williams	BCD	Jason Brown
24/04/2021	L	H	Clyde	3	0		0	0	S Reod	BCD	S Brown pen, Ritchie 2
29/04/2021	L	A	East Fife	3	1		1	1	G Grainger	BCD	Lyle, McDonald, Strachan
01/05/2021	L	H	Forfar Athletic	1	2		0	0	M Roncone	BCD	S Brown
04/05/2021	L	A	Dumbarton	2	3		1	1	D Dickinson	BCD	Boyd, Lyle

Surname	First Name	Date of Birth	No	Nat	Pos	Signed	Previous	Notes	Contract	Lge			SC			LC			
										A	S	G	A	S	G	A	S	G	Un
Armour	Ben	17/04/1998	15	SCO	F	2019	Morton	Released May 2021		7	5	4		1		4			3
Bailey	Kyle	14/10/1993	32	ENG	D	2020	Nybergsund	Released May 2021		15	3		1			4			3
Bakar	Hashim	11/10/1994	18	GHA / ENG	F	2020	Civil Service Strollers	Released Jan 2021		0	1						1		6
Boyd	Steven	12/04/1997	10	SCO	F	2020	East Fife	Ooc July 20021, joined Alloa Athletic		18	2	1				3	1	2	1
Brown	Jason	07/07/1996	4	SCO	D	2017	Inverness CT		End 2022/3	20	0	1	1			4			0
Brown	Scott	25/11/1994	8	SCO	M	2016	St Johnstone		End 2021/2	22	0	5	1			4			0
Brown	Jordon	28/11/1992		SCO	M	2021	Cove Rangers		End 2021/2	5	6	1							2
Cameron	Lyall	10/10/2002	17	SCO	M	2020	Dundee (OL)	Oct-May		7	4	3				1	3		0
Conroy	Ryan	28/04/1987	3	SCO	M	2019	Airdrieonians		End 2021/2	16	0		1			4			0
Cook	Alan	25/04/1992	11	SCO	M	2020	Stenhousemuir		End 2021/2	6	6					1	3		0
Ferry	Simon	11/01/1988	6	SCO	M	2015	Dundee		End 2021/2	13	0					3	1		3
Fraser	Gary	02/07/1994	14	SCO	M	2019	Cowdenbeath		End 2021/2	8	0					2	1	1	0
Freeman	Kieran	30/03/2000	2	SCO	D	2020	Dundee United (OL)	Sep-May		22	0		1			2	1		0
Kesson	Derryn	02/06/1998	16	SCO	F	2020	Broughty Athletic		End 2021/2	1	13		1				1		11
Layne	Isaac	16/05/1995	9	UGA / ENG	F	2020	Dumbarton	OL to Dumbarton Mat-May, Released May 2021		3	3	1	1			2		2	2
Lyle	Derek	13/02/1981	99	SCO	F	2018	Queen of the South		End 2021/2	3	13	2					3		6
McCarthy	Andy	20/10/1998	12	SCO	M	2020	Queen of the South		End 2021/2	19	0		1			4			1
McDonald	Andy	11/05/1998		SCO	D	2021	St Cadocs		End 2021/2	7	1	1	1						0
McGrath	Kieran	28/03/2001		SCO	F	2021	East Kilbride (OL)	Mar-May		0	7			1					3
McKenzie	Gary	15/10/1985	5	SCO	D	2020	St Mirren	Retired May 2021		5	1					1			2
Mulligan	Josh	12/11/2002	7	SCO	M	2020	Dundee (OL)	Oct-May		0	0					1			0
Payne	Niah	25/09/1998		ENG / JAM	F	2021	Bridlington Town		End 2021/2	7	3		1						1
Rae	Josh	17/10/2000	1	SCO	GK	2020	Cowdenbeath	OOC June 2021, joined QOTS		18	0		1			2			4
Ritchie	Hamish	07/05/1997		SCO	F	2021	Inverurie Locos (OL)	Mar-May		10	1	4							0
Strachan	Danny	17/07/2002		SCO	D	2021	Dundee (OL)	Mar-May		6	2	1		1					3
Trialist										0	2								4
Wilson	Lenny	29/12/1996	21	SCO	GK	2019	St John's Red Storm		End 2021/2	4	0					2			21
Own Goal																		1	

NEW SIGNINGS

Surname	First Name	Date of Birth	No	Nat	Pos	Signed	Previous	Notes	Contract
Cameron	Lyall	10/10/2002		SCO	M	2021	Dundee (OL)	Jul-May	End 2021/2
Long	Brett	11/04/1997		NIR	GK	2021	East Fife		End 2021/2
McLean	Russell	16/06/1998		SCO	F	2021	Montrose		End 2021/2
Mulligan	Josh	12/11/2002		SCO	M	2021	Dundee (OL)	Jul-May	End 2021/2
Musanhu	Jadel	29/10/2002		ZIM / EBG	D	2021	City of Liverpool FC		End 2021/2
Ritchie	Hamish	07/05/1997		SCO	F	2021	Inverurie Locos		End 2022/3
Strachan	Danny	17/07/2002		SCO	D	2021	Dundee (OL)	Jul-May	End 2021/2

Date	Comp	H/A	Opponents	F	A	1	2	3	4	5	6	7	8	9	10	11	12	13	14	15	16	17	18	19	20
10/10/2020	LC	A	Dundee United	1	0	Rae	Jason Brown	Bailey	Ferry	Conroy	S Brown	McCarthy	Mulligan*	Boyd	Armour&	Layne+	Fraser*	Cook+	Cameron&	*MacKenzie*	*Lyle*	*Kesson*	*Wilson*		
13/10/2020	LC	H	Brechin City	3	1	Rae	Jason Brown	Bailey	Ferry	Conroy	S Brown	McCarthy<	McKenzie&	Boyd>	Armour*	Layne+	Cook*	Lyle+	Freeman&	Kesson>	Cameron<	*Wilson*			
17/10/2020	L	A	Airdrieonians	0	2	Rae	Jason Brown	Bailey	Ferry*	Conroy	S Brown	McCarthy	McKenzie>	Boyd&	Freeman	Layne+	Cook*	Lyle+	Cameron&	Kesson>	*Wilson*				
24/10/2020	L	H	Cove Rangers	0	2	Rae	Jason Brown	Bailey	Cook	Conroy	S Brown	McCarthy	Cameron	Boyd	Freeman	Lyle*	Kesson*	*Trialist*	*Trialist*	*Layne*	*Wilson*				
31/10/2020	L	A	Clyde	2	0	Rae	Jason Brown	Bailey	Cook*	Conroy	S Brown	McCarthy	Cameron&	Boyd+	Freeman	Fraser	Lyle*	Trialist+	Kesson&	*Armour*	*Wilson*				
07/11/2020	L	A	Montrose	2	3	Rae	Jason Brown	Bailey	Cook	Conroy&	S Brown	McCarthy+	Cameron	Armour*	Freeman	Fraser	Lyle*	Trialist+	Kesson&	*Wilson*	*Ferry*	*Trialist*	*Boyd*		
10/11/2020	LC	A	Kelty Hearts	1	1 5-3p	Wilson	Jason Brown	Bailey	Cook*	Conroy	S Brown	McCarthy>	Cameron+	Armour&	Freeman	Fraser	Lyle*	Boyd+	Ferry&	Bakar>	*Kesson*				
14/11/2020	LC	H	St Johnstone	1	3	Wilson	Jason Brown+	Bailey	Ferry	Conroy	S Brown	McCarthy	Boyd	Armour*	Freeman	Fraser&	Cook*	Lyle+	Cameron&	*Bakar*	*Kesson*				
21/11/2020	L	H	Dumbarton	1	0	Rae	Cook&	Bailey	Ferry*	Conroy	S Brown	McCarthy	Boyd	Armour+	Freeman	Fraser	Cameron*	Layne+>	Lyle&	Bakar>	*Trialist*	*Wilson*	*Kesson*		
28/11/2020	L	H	Forfar Athletic	0	1	Rae	Jason Brown	Bailey*	Boyd	Conroy	S Brown	McCarthy&	Cameron	Armour	Freeman	Fraser+	McKenzie*	Cook+	Lyle&	*Bakar*	*Wilson*	*Kesson*			
05/12/2020	L	A	Falkirk	1	2	Rae	Jason Brown	Bailey	Cook	Conroy	S Brown	McCarthy+	McKenzie*	Boyd	Freeman	Fraser	Lyle*	Cameron+	*Bakar*	*Wilson*	*Kesson*				
12/12/2020	L	H	East Fife	2	1	Rae	Jason Brown	Bailey	Cameron+	Conroy	S Brown	McCarthy*	McKenzie	Boyd&	Freeman	Fraser	Cook*	Layne+	Lyle&	*Bakar*	*Wilson*	*Kesson*			
19/12/2020	L	A	Partick Thistle	1	0	Rae	Jason Brown	Bailey	Ferry	Conroy	S Brown	Layne*	McKenzie+	Boyd	Freeman	Fraser&	Cook*	Cameron+	Lyle&	*Bakar*	*Wilson*	*Kesson*	*McCarthy*		
22/12/2020	L	H	Montrose	1	1	Rae	Jason Brown	Bailey	Ferry	Cook	S Brown	Cameron	McKenzie&	Boyd	Freeman	Fraser*	Layne*+	Lyle+	Kesson&	*Bakar*	*Wilson*				
02/01/2021	L	A	Cove Rangers	0	1	Rae	Jason Brown	Jordan Brown	Ferry	Conroy	S Brown	Cameron	McCarthy	Boyd	Freeman	Cook	Kesson*	*Bakar*	*McKenzie*	*Wilson*					
20/03/2021	L	H	Airdrieonians	1	0	Rae	Jason Brown	Jordan Brown+	Freeman	Conroy	S Brown	Bailey	McCarthy	Payne*	Ritchie	Layne&	Armour*	Kesson+	Strachan&	*Lyle*	*Wilson*				
23/03/2021	SC	H	Stenhousemuir	0	1	Rae	Jason Brown	McDonald	Freeman	Conroy	S Brown*	Bailey&	McCarthy	Payne	Kesson	Layne+	Armour*	McGrath+	Strachan&	*Jordan Brown*	*Wilson*				
27/03/2021	L	A	Dumbarton	1	0	Rae	Jason Brown	McDonald	Freeman	Conroy	S Brown	Ferry>	McCarthy<	Payne+	Ritchie&	Armour*	Boyd*	McGrath+	Kesson&	Jordan Brown>	*Strachan<*	*Lyle*	*Layne*	*Bailey*	*Wilson*
30/03/2021	L	H	Clyde	0	2	Rae	Jason Brown	McDonald	Freeman&	Conroy	S Brown	Ferry	McCarthy	Boyd*	Ritchie>	Armour+	Jordan Brown*	Payne+	Lyle&	Kesson>	*Strachan*	*Bailey*	*McGrath*	*Wilson*	
06/04/2021	L	A	Forfar Athletic	1	1	Rae	Jason Brown	McDonald	Freeman	Conroy	S Brown	Ferry	McCarthy	Boyd&	Ritchie+	Armour*	Payne*	Jordan Brown+	McGrath&	*Kesson*	*Wilson*	*Bailey*	*Lyle*	*Strachan*	
10/04/2021	L	H	Partick Thistle	0	3	Rae	Jason Brown	McDonald	Freeman	Conroy*	S Brown	Ferry+	Jordan Brown>	Boyd<	Ritchie	Payne&	Bailey*	McGrath+	Lyle&	Armour>	Kesson<	*Wilson*	*Strachan*		
17/04/2021	L	A	East Fife	1	2	Rae	Jason Brown	McDonald	Freeman	Strachan	S Brown	Ferry&	McCarthy	Boyd+	Ritchie	Lyle*	Armour*	Bailey+	McGrath&	*Jordan Brown*	*Payne*	*Kesson*	*Wilson*		
20/04/2021	L	H	Falkirk	1	0	Wilson	Jason Brown	Bailey	Freeman	Strachan	S Brown	Jordan Brown*	McCarthy	Boyd	Ritchie	Payne+	Kesson*	McGrath+	*Armour*	*Lyle*	*Ferry*	*Rae*			
24/04/2021	L	H	Clyde	3	0	Wilson	Jason Brown	Bailey	Freeman	Strachan	S Brown	Ferry	McCarthy*	Boyd+	Ritchie	Payne&	McDonald*	Jordan Brown+	Lyle&	*Kesson*	*Armour*	*McGrath*	*Rae*		
29/04/2021	L	A	East Fife	3	1	Wilson	McDonald	Bailey	Freeman	Strachan	S Brown	Jordan Brown>	McCarthy	Armour*	Kesson&	Lyle+	Payne*	McGrath+	Ritchie&	Boyd>	*Ferry*	*Rae*			
01/05/2021	L	H	Forfar Athletic	1	2	Rae	Jason Brown	Bailey<	Freeman	Strachan	S Brown	Ferry	McCarthy&	Boyd*	Ritchie+	Payne>	Kesson*	Jordan Brown+	Armour&	McGrath>	Cook<	*Wilson*	*Lyle*		
04/05/2021	L	A	Dumbarton	2	3	Wilson	Jason Brown&	McDonald	Frreman	Strachan	S Brown	Ferry*	McCarthy	Boyd+	Ritchie>	Payne<	Lyle*	Cook+	Bailey&	Armour>	Kesson<	*McGrath*	*Rae*		

PETERHEAD FC HONOURS

SPFL League Two Winners:
2013-14, 2018-19

Petrofac Cup Finalists:
2016

Highland League Winners:
1946–47, 1948–49, 1949–50, 1988–89, 1998–99

Highland League Cup Winners:
1962–63, 1965–66, 1967–68, 1980–81, 1988–89

Scottish Qualifying Cup (North) Winners:
1946–47, 1975–76, 1977–78, 1978–79, 1985–86, 1997–98

Aberdeenshire Cup Winners:

1905–06,	1934–35,	1935–36,
1946–47,	1948–49,	1949–50,
1958–59,	1962–63,	1964–65,
1967–68,	1968–69,	1969–70,
1970–71,	1974–75,	1976–77,
1978–79,	1984–85,	1987–88,
1988–89,	1998–99	

Aberdeenshire Shield Winners:
1998–99, 2009-10

EARLY HISTORY (from Club Website)

Football had been played in the town of Peterhead as far back as the 1870's, but in 1890 Peterhead Football club was formed within the hopes and aspirations of a number of enthusiastic football fans in 1890, those men forming the first committee of the Club. The newly formed committee decided it was time for a properly organised team playing within the rules set down by the Scottish FA.

Within a year, the ambitions plans of those men were partly realised by the towns Feuars Managers who gifted to the newly formed Peterhead FC a piece of land within the town's Raemoss Park. Named Recreation Park, it was opened by the town's Provost Smith, who was accompanied by philanthropist Andrew Carnegie in August of 1891 and became Peterhead's home for over 100 years.

Andrew Carnegie - Spectator at Peterhead's first game at Recreation Park

Queen of the South FC 2020/21 The Doonhamers

Founded	1919
Ground	Palmerston Park
Postcode	DG2 9BA
Tel	01387 254853
Capacity	7620
Closest Railway Station	Dumfries
Record Attendance	26552 v Hearts, SC, 23/2/1952
Record Win	11-1 v Stranraer, SC, 16/1/1932
Record Defeat	2-10 v Dundee, Lge 1/12/1962
Most League Goals in a Season	37 Jimmy Gray 1927/8
Colours 2020/21 Top	Blue
Shorts	Blue
Sponsor	BPs Taxis
Manufacturer	Macron
Change Colours 2020/21 Top	Yellow with Navy sleeves
Shorts	Navy blue
Nicknames	Doonhamers
Web	www.qosfc.com
Match Programme 2020/21	None

Chairman: Billy Hewitson
Vice Chairman: Craig Paterson
Directors: Mark Blount,), Norman Blount (Honorary), David Rae (Honorary)
Supporter Liaison Officers: Simon Clingan, Nathan Maxwell, Iain Wright
Disability Access Officer: Keith Thon
Football Admin: Ewan Lithgow
Kitman: Graeme Dalgleish
Safety Officer: Phil Stewart
Groundsman / Kitman: Kevin McCormick
Club Doctor: Guy Beaumont
Community Development Coach: Daniel Armstrong
Manager: Allan Johnston
Assistant Manager: Sandy Clark
Goalkeeping Coach: Ross Ballantyne
Coach: George Paterson
Physio: Gavin Lee
Reserve Team Manager: Willie Gibson

Queens fans were very pessimistic about their teams chances pre-season. Early form did little to cheer them. They went eight games before recording a win in a League Cup game and they lost six of their first nine League fixtures. A relegation battle looked to be on the cards. However, they gradually turned things around as improved from the turn of the year. They had a run of ten games with just one defeat and at one point looked like promotion play-off contenders. Their form shaded off towards the end and they failed to win another game after defeating Hearts 3-2 at Tynecastle.

Injuries hit the club hard. The absence of their talisman striker Stephen Dobbie for a large part of the season was a big blow. They relied heavily on the vast experience of Willie Gibson to see them through – he had joined the club as a reserve team coach and ended up playing virtually every game for them.

No progress was made in the League Cup and their Scottish Cup run came unstuck at the second hurdle, losing to Hibs.

STAR MAN
The aforementioned Willie Gibson deserves the accolade. 36 years of age, he rolled back the years to recollect his first spell with the club between 2001 and 2007. His journey took him via Kilmarnock, Dunfermline, Crawley, St Johnstone, Falkirk, Queens (again), Celtic Nation, Stranraer (twice), Dumbarton, Peterhead and Stenhousemuir. He moved from an attack minded wide player to full back and proved to be a massive asset for Queens in 2020/1.

PROSPECTS 2021/2
Once again Queens have been faced with a rebuilding job with several players moving on. In particular they have to face the prospect of A.D., after Dobbie. The striker has decided to retire and he will be a big loss to the club. They are more likely to be embroiled in the relegation dog fight than any contest for promotion.

The Finest Floodlight Pylons in the Land

Date	Comp	H/A	Opponents	F	A		HT		Referee	Crowd	Scorers
06/10/2020	LC	A	Morton	2	2	4-2p	0	1	D Robertson	BCD	Dobbie, Shields
10/10/2020	LC	H	St Mirren	2	2	2-4p	2	0	W Collum	BCD	Shields, Fitzpatrick
13/10/2020	LC	H	Partick Thistle	0	0	2-3p	0	0	P Stuart	BCD	
17/10/2020	L	A	Ayr United	1	2		0	2	S McLean	BCD	Dobbie pen
24/10/2020	L	H	Raith Rovers	2	5		1	3	E Anderson	BCD	Dobbie pen, Obileye
31/10/2020	L	A	Dunfermline Athletic	2	3		0	2	G Irvine	BCD	McKee, Dobbie pen
07/11/2020	L	A	Arbroath	1	1		1	0	D Lowe	BCD	Maxwell
10/11/2020	LC	A	Queen's Park	3	1		2	1	A Newlands	BCD	East, Joseph, Maxwell
21/11/2020	L	H	Alloa Athletic	2	0		1	0	J Beaton	BCD	Buchanan, McKee
04/12/2020	L	H	Inverness CT	0	3		0	1	S McLean	BCD	
12/12/2020	L	A	Hearts	1	6		0	2	W Collum	BCD	Obileye
19/12/2020	L	A	Morton	0	2		0	1	C Steven	BCD	
26/12/2020	L	H	Dundee	1	3		0	2	A Newlands	BCD	Shields
29/12/2020	L	A	Raith Rovers	2	0		1	0	B Cook	BCD	Shields, Goss
02/01/2021	L	H	Ayr United	3	2		2	1	G Aitken	BCD	Obileye pen, Shields 2
08/01/2021	SC	A	Queen's Park	3	0		1	0	E Anderson	BCD	Gibson, Fitzpatrick, Shields
16/01/2021	L	H	Arbroath	2	2		0	0	S Reid	BCD	Shields 2
23/01/2021	L	H	Morton	2	1		2	0	A Newlands	BCD	Obileye, Fitzpatrick
06/02/2021	L	A	Alloa Athletic	1	2		1	1	G Duncan	BCD	Jones
12/02/2021	L	H	Hearts	1	1		1	0	C Steven	BCD	Obileye pen
17/02/2021	L	A	Inverness CT	1	0		0	0	D Lowe	BCD	Nortley
20/02/2021	L	A	Dundee	3	2		2	0	B Cook	BCD	Obileye pen, Breen, Gibson
27/01/2021	L	H	Dunfermline Athletic	1	0		0	0	M Roncone	BCD	Gibson
06/03/2021	L	A	Arbroath	4	2		3	2	G Duncan	BCD	Obileye 2, Shields, Mebude
13/03/2021	L	H	Alloa Athletic	2	3		2	2	G Aitken	BCD	Mebude, East
20/03/2021	L	A	Morton	1	2		1	1	D Munro	BCD	Obileye
27/03/2021	L	A	Hearts	3	2		2	1	G Duncan	BCD	Shields 2, Irving og
05/04/2021	SC	H	Hibernian	1	3		0	1	W Collum	BCD	Maxwell
10/04/2021	L	H	Inverness CT	1	1		0	0	G Irvine	BCD	Fitzpatrick
13/04/2021	L	H	Raith Rovers	0	1		0	1	D Dickinson	BCD	
17/04/2021	L	A	Dunfermline Athletic	1	3		0	1	D Lowe	BCD	Maxwell
24/04/2021	L	A	Ayr United	0	0		0	0	N Walsh	BCD	
30/04/2021	L	H	Dundee	0	2		0	2	D Robertson	BCD	

Matthew 12:42

The Queen of the South will rise at the judgment with this generation and condemn it; for she came from the ends of the earth to listen to Solomon's wisdom, and now something greater than Solomon is here.

Who was the Queen of the South?
Jesus identifies the Queen of the South as a Queen who visited King Solomon to benefit from his wisdom. From this, we can deduce that she is the Queen of Sheba who came to test Solomon with difficult questions (1 Kings 10:1).

Most biblical scholars believe that Sheba was a city in modern-day Ethiopia or Yemen, and that the Queen of the South was the ruler of that city, a woman of amazing wealth and power. Having heard reports of King Solomon's wisdom, the Queen of Sheba wanted to find out if what she had heard was true, if there really could be a king that wise. So she travelled to Jerusalem to quiz Solomon with riddles. She also brought a wealth of gifts and spices and jewels from her own land to give to him (1 Kings 10:10; 2 Chronicles 9:9). Solomon answered all her questions (1 Kings 10:3) and repaid her in gifts of equal value. The Queen of the South then returned home (2 Chronicles 9:12).

Date	Comp	H/A	Opponents	F	A		1	2	3	4	5	6	7	8	9	10	11	12	13	14	15	16	17	18	19	20
06/10/2020	LC	A	Morton	2	2	4-2p	Ferguson	Maxwell	Buchanan	Obileye	McKee	Pybus*	Shields	Dobbie+	McCabe	East&	Gibson	Fitzpatrick*	Robinson+	Joseph&	Goss	McGrory	Nortley	McKechnie	Crooks	Leighfield
10/10/2020	LC	H	St Mirren	2	2	2-4p	Ferguson	Maxwell	Buchanan	Obileye	McKee	Pybus	Shields	Dobbie+	Fitzpatrick	East*	Gibson	Goss*	McGrory+	Joseph	McCabe	Sylla	Nortley	McKechnie	Robinson	Leighfield
13/10/2020	LC	H	Partick Thistle	0	0	2-3p	Ferguson	Maxwell	Buchanan	Obileye	Nortley	McCabe	Shields	McGrory	Fitzpatrick	Robinson+	Joseph*	Goss*	Gibson+	East	Crooks	Sylla	Douglas	Leighfield		
17/10/2020	L	A	Ayr United	1	2		Ferguson	Maxwell	Buchanan	Obileye	Nortley	McCabe	McKee	Dobbie	Fitzpatrick	Robinson	East*	Goss*	Gibson	McGrory	Shields	Sylla	McMahon	Leighfield		
24/10/2020	L	H	Raith Rovers	2	5		Ferguson	Gibson	Buchanan	Obileye	Nortley	McCabe	McKee*	Dobbie	Fitzpatrick	Shields&	East+	McGrory*	Pybus+	Goss&	Robinson	Sylla	Joseph	Leighfield		
31/10/2020	L	A	Dunfermline Athletic	2	3		Ferguson	Gibson	Buchanan+	Obileye	Maxwell	Pybus	McKee	Dobbie	Fitzpatrick	Shields&	McGrory*	East*	Nortley+	Robinson&	Goss	Sylla	Joseph	Leighfield		
07/11/2020	L	A	Arbroath	1	1		Leighfield	Gibson	Buchanan	Obileye	Maxwell	Pybus	McKee	Dobbie	Fitzpatrick	Shields+	East*	Joseph*	Goss+	McMahon	Nortley	Sylla	McKechnie	Cowie		
10/11/2020	LC	A	Queen's Park	3	1		Leighfield	Nortley	Buchanan	Obileye	Maxwell	Pybus	McKee	Joseph	Fitzpatrick	Shields	East	McMahon	Goss	Dobbie	Gibson	Sylla	McKechnie	Cowie		
21/11/2020	L	H	Alloa Athletic	2	0		Leighfield	Gibson	Buchanan	Obileye	Maxwell	Pybus	McKee	Dobbie*	Fitzpatrick	Shields	Joseph	East*	Goss	Ferguson	McCabe	Sylla	McKechnie	McKechnie		
04/12/2020	L	H	Inverness CT	0	3		Leighfield	Gibson+	Buchanan	Obileye	Maxwell	Pybus	McKee	Dobbie	Fitzpatrick&	Shields	Joseph*	East*	Nortley+	McCabe&	McGrory	Goss	Ferguson	McKechnie		
12/12/2020	L	A	Hearts	1	6		Leighfield	Gibson	Buchanan	Obileye	Maxwell	Pybus	Nortley	Dobbie+	Fitzpatrick*	Shields	McCabe&	East*	McKechnie+	McGrory&	Joseph	Goss	McMahon	Ferguson		
19/12/2020	L	A	Morton	0	2		Ferguson	Gibson	Buchanan	Obileye	Maxwell	McCabe	Nortley	Dobbie*	Goss+	Shields	East	Fitzpatrick*	Pybus+	McKechnie	Joseph	McKee	Robinson	Leighfield		
26/12/2020	L	H	Dundee	1	3		Ferguson	Gibson	Buchanan	Obileye	Maxwell	Pybus	McKee*	McCabe	Fitzpatrick+	Shields	East	Goss*	Robinson+	McMahon	Sylla	McGrory	Leighfield			
29/12/2020	L	A	Raith Rovers	2	0		Cowie	Gibson	Buchanan	Obileye	Maxwell	Pybus	McKee	McCabe	Fitzpatrick	Shields*	East	Goss*	McGrory+	McMahon	Sylla	Leighfield				
02/01/2021	L	H	Ayr United	3	2		Ferguson	Gibson	Buchanan	Obileye	Maxwell	Pybus	Mckee	McCabe	Fitzpatrick*	Shields	East	Goss*	McGrory	McMahon	Sylla	Cowie				
08/01/2021	SC	A	Queen's Park	3	0		Ferguson	Gibson	Buchanan	Obileye	Maxwell	Pybus+	McKee	McCabe	Fitzpatrick	Shields*	East	Goss*	McGrory+	McMahon	Breen	McKechnie	Joseph	Armstrong		
16/01/2021	L	H	Arbroath	2	2		Ferguson	Gibson	Buchanan	Obileye	Maxwell	Pybus	McKee*	McCabe	Fitzpatrick	Shields	East	Dobbie*	McGrory	Goss	Robinson	Joseph	Breen	Cowie		
23/01/2021	L	H	Morton	2	1		Ferguson	Gibson	Breen	Obileye	Maxwell	Pybus	McGrory	McCabe	Fitzpatrick*	Shields	East	Mebude*	McKechnie	McMahon	Sylla	Joseph	Goss	Maley		
06/02/2021	L	A	Alloa Athletic	1	2		Ferguson	Gibson	Breen	Obileye	Maxwell&	Pybus	Jones	McCabe	Fitzpatrick+	Shields*	East	Mebude*	Joseph+	Goss&	Buchanan	Nortley	McKechnie	Rae		
12/02/2021	L	H	Hearts	1	1		Ferguson	Gibson	Buchanan	Obileye	Maxwell	Pybus*	Jones+	Nortley	Breen	Mebude&	East	McGrory*	Joseph+	Goss&	McMahon	McKechnie	Dobbie	Rae		
17/02/2021	L	A	Inverness CT	1	0		Ferguson	Gibson	Buchanan	Obileye	Maxwell	McGrory&	Jones+	Nortley	Breen	Dobbie*	East	Joseph*	Goss+	McMahon&	Sylla	McKechnie	Rae			
20/02/2021	L	A	Dundee	3	2		Ferguson	Gibson	Buchanan	Obileye	Maxwell	McGrory*	Jones	Nortley	Breen	Joseph+	East	McCabe*	Dobbie+	McMahon	McKechnie	Rae				
27/01/2021	L	H	Dunfermline Athletic	1	0		Ferguson	Gibson	Buchanan	Obileye	Maxwell	McGrory	Jones	McCabe	Breen	Joseph*	East	Mebude*	Dobbie	McMahon	McKechnie	Goss	Fitzpatrick	Rae		
06/03/2021	L	A	Arbroath	4	2		Ferguson	Gibson	Buchanan	Obileye	Maxwell	Dickson*	Jones+	McCabe	Breen	Shields&	East	Mebude*	Fitzpatrick+	Dobbie&	McGrory	Goss	Joseph	Rae		
13/03/2021	L	H	Alloa Athletic	2	3		Ferguson	Gibson	Buchanan	Obileye	Maxwell	Fitzpatrick*	Mebude	McCabe	Breen	Shields	East+	McGrory*	Goss+	Joseph	Dickson	McKechnie	McMahon	Leighfield		
20/03/2021	L	A	Morton	1	2		Ferguson	Gibson	Buchanan	Obileye	Maxwell	McGrory+	Mebude*	McCabe	Breen	Shields	East&	Dobbie*	Joseph+	Fitzpatrick&	Dickson	McKechnie	Goss	Leighfield		
27/03/2021	L	A	Hearts	3	2		Ferguson	Gibson	Buchanan	Obileye	Maxwell	Dickson*	Dobbie*	McCabe	Breen	Shields+	Joseph	Mebude*	East+	Fitzpatrick	Goss	McKee	McGrory	Leighfield		
05/04/2021	SC	H	Hibernian	1	3		Ferguson	Gibson	Buchanan	Obileye	Maxwell	Dickson	Dobbie&	McCabe	Breen	Shields+	Joseph*	Jones*	Mebude+	McKee&	Goss	McMahon	East	McGrory	Fitzpatrick	Leighfield
10/04/2021	L	H	Inverness CT	1	1		Ferguson	Gibson	Buchanan	Obileye	Maxwell	Dickson	Mebude	McCabe	Breen	Shields	Jones*	Fitzpatrick*	Joseph	McKee&	Dobbie	Pybus	East	Leighfield		
13/04/2021	L	H	Raith Rovers	0	1		Ferguson	Gibson	Buchanan	Obileye	Maxwell	Dickson+	Mebude	McCabe	Breen	Shields	Fitzpatrick*	Jones*	Joseph+	Nortley	McKee	Pybus	East	Leighfield		
17/04/2021	L	A	Dunfermline Athletic	1	3		Ferguson	Gibson	Buchanan	Obileye&	Maxwell	Dickson+	Mebude	McCabe	Breen	Shields	Jones*	Dobbie*	Fitzpatrick+	Pybus&	Joseph	Nortley	East	Leighfield		
24/04/2021	L	A	Ayr United	0	0		Ferguson	Gibson	Buchanan	Obileye	Maxwell	Pybus	Dobbie+	McCabe	Breen	Shields	East*	Fitzpatrick*	Jones+	McKee&	Joseph	Nortley	Goss	Leighfield		
30/04/2021	L	H	Dundee	0	2		Leighfield	Gibson	Buchanan	Obileye	Maxwell	Fitzpatrick	Dobbie&	McCabe	Breen*	Goss+	Jones	Nortley*	Shields+	Joseph&	Pybus	McMahon	East	Ferguson		

THE GOALIES

Goalkeepers Used in League Matches, 1970-2020

Players shown in the season of their first appearance only

1972/3	Alan Ball
	John Lyle
1975/6	Graham MacLean
1978/9	David Clark
	Marshall Poulton
1979/0	Ray Dunlop
	David Kelly
1981/2	Alan Boles
1982/3	Alan Davidson
1984/5	Graham Kyle
	Brian Noonan
1986/7	Alex Williams
1987/8	Tom Carson
	Willie Cunningham
1988/9	Rikki Ferguson
	Barry Holland
1989/0	Archie McLean
1990/1	Martin Thomson
1992/3	Derrick Hoy
	Phil Hair
1993/4	Robert McColm
	David Purdie
1994/5	Jim McQueen
1995/6	Jim Butter
	John Burridge
1996/7	David Mathieson
1999/0	John Hillcoat
2000/1	Colin Scott
	Jamie Campbell
2002/3	Andy Goram
2003/4	John Dodds
	Kris Robertson
	Craig Samson
2004/5	Richie Barnard
2006/7	Barry Corr
	Craig Hinchcliffe
	Jamie MacDonald
2007/8	Stephen Grindlay
2008/9	Bryn Halliwell
	Cammy Bell
2009/0	David Hutton
	Ludovic Roy
	Scott Fox
2010/1	Lee Robinson
	Roddy McKenzie
2013/4	Calum Antell
	Jim Atkinson
	Zander Clark
2015/6	Robbie Thomson
2016/7	Lee Robinson
2017/8	Alan Martin
	Jack Leighfield
2018/9	Deniz Mehmet
2019/0	Robbie McCrorie
	Ross Stewart

Surname	First Name	Date of Birth	No	Nat	Pos	Signed	Previous	Notes	Contract	Lge A	Lge S	Lge G	SC A	SC S	SC G	LC A	LC S	LC G	Un
Armstrong	Daniel	18/03/1997		ENG	GK	2021	Gretna	Released June 2021		0									1
Bell	Kai	02/12/2003		SCO	D	2020	Queen of the South Youths	OL to Kello Rovers Sep-Jan, Released Jan 2021											0
Breen	Rhys	06/01/2000	19	SCO	D	2021	Rangers (OL)	Sep-May		15		1	1						2
Buchanan	Gregor	31/03/1990	4	SCO	D	2020	Falkirk	Released May 2021		25		1	2			4			1
Cowie	Charlie	29/02/2004		SCO	GK	2020	Queen of the South Youths	Ol to Dalbeattie Star Sep-Dec	End 2022/3	1									4
Crooks	Cameron	15/03/2002		SCO	D	2020	Partick Thistle Youths	OL to Cumbernauld United Sep-Jan, Released July 2021		0									2
Dickson	Ciaran	21/05/2002		SCO	M	2021	Rangers (OL)	Mar-May		5			1						2
Dobbie	Stephen	05/12/1982	11	SCO	F	2016	Bolton Wanderers	Retired May 2021		12	5	3	1			2		1	4
Douglas	Liam	07/01/2001		SCO	D	2018	Queen of the South Youths	OL to Dalbeattie Star Sep-Jan, released Jul 2021 joined Cumnock		0	0								1
Dunn	Scott	21/02/2002		SCO	D	2020	Airdrieonians	OL to St Cuthbert W	End 2021/2	0	0								0
East	Euan	05/07/2000	16	SCO	F	2020	Albion Rovers		End 2021/2	18	5	1	1			3		1	6
Ferguson	Rohan	06/12/1997	20	SCO	GK	2020	Motherwell	OOC June 2021, joined Larne		21	0		2			3			4
Fitzpatrick	Aidan	20/03/2001	7	SCO	M	2020	Norwich City (OL)	Aug-May		16	6	2	1		1	3	1	1	3
Gibson	Willie	06/08/1984	33	SCO	M	2019	Stenhousemuir	Also Reserve Team Manager	End 2021/2	26	0	2	2		1	2	1		2
Goss	Tommy	14/04/1998	9	SCO	F	2020	Queen of the South Youths	OOC June 2021, joined Annan Ath		2	10	1		1			2		14
Jones	Isaiah	26/06/1999		ENG	M	2021	Middlesbrough (OL)	Jan-May		9	2	1		1					0
Joseph	Niyah	12/05/2001	17	SCO	D	2020	Hamilton Accies		End 2021/2	5	7		1			2	1	1	13
Leighield	Jack	01/01/2016	1	SCO	GK	2016	Queen of the South Youths	Released July 2021		5	0					1			17
Maley	Gary	03/08/1982	31	SCO	GK	2021	Livingston (OL)	Jan 23-28		0	0								1
Maxwell	James	09/12/2001	3	SCO	D	2020	Rangers (OL)	Sep-May		26	0	2	2		1	4		1	0
McCabe	Rhys	24/07/1992	12	SCO	M	2020	Brechin City	OOC June 2021, joined Airdrieonians		20	2		2			2			2
McGrory	Calvin	09/08/1999	15	SCO	M	2020	Queen's Park		End 2021/2	6	5			1		1	1		9
McKechnie	Kieran	04/04/2001	18	SCO	F	2020	Rangers		End 2021/2	0	1								17
McKee	Joe	31/10/1992	6	SCO	M	2020	Dumbarton	Released May 2021		10	2	2	1	1		3			3
McKie	Arran	28/03/2002		SCO	M	2019	Queen of the South Youths	OL to Newton Stewart Sep-Jan, Released July 2021		0	0								0
McMahon	Dom	24/05/2001		SCO	M	2018	Queen of the South Youths		End 2021/2	0	1								15
Mebude	Dapo	29/07/2001	29	SCO / NIG	F	2021	Rangers (OL)	Jan-May		6	5	2		1					0
Moffat	Aidan	03/01/2002		SCO	D	2019	Ayr United Youths	OL to Abbey Vale Sep-Jan	End 2021/2	0	0								0
Newbould	Christopher	23/03/2003		SCO	D	2019	Queen of the South Youths	OL to Lochmaben Sep-Jan, Released May 2021		0	0								0
Nortley	Nortei	29/10/1994	2	ENG / GHA	M	2020	Chorley	Released May 2021		7	3	1				2			7
Obileye	Ayo	02/09/1994	5	ENG / NIG	D	2020	Ebbsfleet United	OOC May 2021, joined Livingston		27	0	9	2			4			0
Paton	Kane	14/05/2002		SCO	F	2020	Queen of the South Youths		End 2021/2	0	0								0
Potts	Connor	08/10/2002		SCO	F	2019	Queen of the South Youths	OL to Dalbeattie Star Sep-Jan	End 2021/2	0	0								0
Pybus	Dan	12/12/1997	8	ENG	M	2019	FK Tonsberg	Released May 2021		13	3		1			3			3
Rae	Josh	17/10/2000		SCO	GK	2021	Peterhead (OL)	Jan-Mar		0	0								6
Robinson	Harry	26/09/2000	14	NIR	F	2020	Motherwell (OL)	Sep-May		1	2					1	1		4
Service	Jake	25/02/2002		SCO	D	2018	Stranraer Youths	OL to Newton Stewart Sep-May, Released June 2021		0	0								0
Shaw	Cameron	04/07/2002		SCO	M	2019	Lochar Thistle	OL to Heston Rovers Sep-Jan	End 2021/2	0	0								0
Shields	Connor	29/07/1997	10	SCO	F	2020	Aldershot Town	OOC May 2021, joined Motherwell		21	1	9	2		1	4		2	1
Sylla	Diste	23/01/2001		GUI / SPA	D	2020	Lochgelly Albert	Released June 2021		0	0								13
Wiggett	Owen	30/12/2003		ENG	M	2020	Queen of the South Youths		End 2021/2	0	0								0
Young	Campbell	24/02/2002		SCO	M	2019	Dunipace	Released Jan 2021		0	0								0
Own Goal												1							
NEW SIGNINGS																			
Connelly	Lee	18/10/1999		SCO	F	2021	Sunderland		End 2021/2										
Cooper	Alex	04/11/1991		SCO	M	2021	Sligo Rovers		End 2021/2										
McKay	Paul	19/11/1996		ENG / SCOT	D	2021	Airdrieonians		End 2021/2										
Nditi	Robert	01/10/2000		ENG / NIG	D	2021	Forfar Athletic		End 2021/2										
Paton	Ruari	09/08/2000		ROI	F	2021	Stranraer		End 2022/3										
Rae	Josh	17/10/2000		SCO	GK	2021	Peterhead		End 2021/2										
Roy	Ally	26/07/1997		NIR	F	2021	Airdrieonians		End 2021/2										
Soares Junior	Ruben	18/01/2000		POR	F	2021	Billericay Town		End 2021/2										
Todd	Josh	11/06/1995		ENG	M	2021	Falkirk		End 2021/2										

Alan Ball

Alan Davidson

David Mathieson

Queen's Park FC 2020/21 The Spiders

Founded	1867
Ground	New Lesser Hampden
Postcode	G42 9BA
Tel	0141 620 4000
Capacity	2000
Closest Railway Station	Mount Florida
Record Attendance	95772 v Rangers, SC, 18/1/1930
Ground Record	149547, Scotland v England, 1937
Record Win	16-0 v St Peters, SC, 12/9/1885
Record Defeat	0-9 v Motherwell, Lge, 26/4/1930
Most League Goals in a Season	30 William Martin, 1937/8
Colours 2020/21 Top	Black and White Hoops
Shorts	White
Sponsor	Irn Bru
Manufacturer	Admiral
Change Colours 2020/21 Top	Red
Shorts	Red
Nicknames	Spiders
Web	www.queensparkfc.co.uk
Match Programme 2020/21	None issued

President: David Hunter
Treasurer: David Gordon
Immediate Past President: Gerry Crawley
Directors: Alan Hutchison, , Jim Nicholson, Graeme Shields, Gregor Hall, Gary Templeman, Damiano Agostini, Keith McKenzie, Alistair Marr
Chief Executive: Leanne Dempster
Company Secretary: Christine Wright
Head Coach: Ray McKinnon (until May), then Laurie Ellis
Assistant Head Coach: Laurie Ellis, then Grant Murray
Goalkeeping Coach: Glen Johnson
Assistant Coach: Tony Quinn
Physio: Euan Duffy
Club Doctor: Sandesh Gulhane

Considering the money they spent on establishing a full-time set up it would have been unthinkable for the Spiders not to have won League Two. Of course in such a short season there was always the possibility of a slip up but Ray McKinnon's team performed well. They lost just twice and both were after promotion had been secured.

They lost all four of their League Cup ties and went out of the Scottish Cup at the second hurdle. However, the League was clearly their focus of attention. From April they were forced to play home games at Falkirk. Their lease at Hampden had expired and work on upgrading Lesser Hampden had ground to a halt.

At the end of the season they surprisingly parted company with Manager Ray McKinnon. The reasons were unclear but one can only assume there was some disagreement on the future direction of the playing side of things.

STAR MAN
The Spiders were a team without any outstanding individual – everyone contributed on equal measure to their success. However, their unsung hero was often goalkeeper Willie Muir, outstanding in his second spell with the Glasgow side.

PROSPECTS 2021/2
Laurie Ellis is the man tasked with the next stage in Queen's Park plan to climb the Leagues. They will be based at Firhill this season as work on Lesser Hampden is on hold. League One will be a far tougher proposition and it may be that the play offs will be their best hope of a second successive promotion.

Unscheduled Horse of the Year Show at Hampden, 1980

Date	Comp	H/A	Opponents	F	A		HT		Referee	Crowd	Scorers
10/10/2020	LC	A	Partick Thistle	0	2		0	0	K Graham	BCD	
13/10/2020	LC	A	Morton	0	1		0	0	G Ross	BCD	
17/10/2020	L	A	Stirling Albion	0	0		0	0	G Grainger	BCD	
24/10/2020	L	H	Albion Rovers	2	0		2	0	M McDermid	BCD	Baynham 2
31/10/2020	L	A	Stranraer	1	0		0	0	D Williams	BCD	MacLean
07/11/2020	L	A	Elgin City	1	0		1	0	B Cook	BCD	Lyon
10/11/2020	LC	H	Queen of the South	1	3		1	2	A Newlands	BCD	Quitongo
14/11/2020	LC	H	St Mirren	0	1		0	0	G Aitken	BCD	
21/11/2020	L	H	Brechin City	3	0		2	0	C Graham	BCD	Quitongo, McHugh, Lyon
28/11/2020	L	H	Stenhousemuir	3	1		1	1	D Lowe	BCD	Kilday, McHugh, Murray
05/12/2020	L	A	Cowdenbeath	3	0		1	0	C Scott	BCD	Grant, Gillespie, Murray
12/12/2020	L	H	Edinburgh City	3	3		0	1	L Wilson	BCD	MacLean, McHugh, Baynham
19/12/2020	L	A	Annan Athletic	2	1		0	0	L Watson	200	McHugh, Slater
28/12/2020	SC	A	Dundonald Bluebell	3	1	AET	0	0	S Lambie	BCD	Quitongo, Murray, Longridge
08/01/2021	SC	H	Queen of the South	0	3		0	1	E Anderson	BCD	
20/03/2021	L	H	Stranraer	3	0		2	0	D Williams	BCD	Doyle, Kilday, McHugh pen
27/03/2021	L	A	Brechin City	2	0		2	0	P Stuart	BCD	McHugh, Longridge
30/03/2021	L	A	Albion Rovers	3	0		2	0	D Dickinson	BCD	Lyon, Connell, Kouider-Assa
03/04/2021	L	H*	Stirling Albion	1	0		1	0	D McFarlane	BCD	Meggatt og
06/04/2021	L	H*	Cowdenbeath	3	0		1	0	S Luke	BCD	Quitongo, Lyon, Baynham
10/04/2021	L	A	Stenhousemuir	3	1		2	0	C Graham	BCD	Murray, McHugh, Longridge
13/04/2021	L	H*	Annan Athletic	1	0		1	0	M McDermid	BCD	Murray
17/04/2021	L	A	Edinburgh City	3	2		1	0	G Grainger	BCD	Grant, Murray 2
20/04/2021	L	H*	Elgin City	0	0		0	0	S Reid	BCD	
23/04/2021	L	H*	Stranraer	0	1		0	1	B Cook	BCD	
27/04/2021	L	A	Stirling Albion	2	1		1	0	D McFarlane	BCD	Kouider-Assa 2
29/04/2021	L	H*	Edinburgh City	2	0		1	0	L Wilson	BCD	Longridge, Connell
04/05/2021	L	A	Elgin City	2	3		0	0	D Williams	BCD	Baynham, Connell

* at Falkirk Stadium

David Crawford

Adam Strain

Willie Muir

Date	Comp	H/A	Opponents	F	A	1	2	3	4	5	6	7	8	9	10	11	12	13	14	15	16	17	18	19	20
10/10/2020	LC	A	Partick Thistle	0	2	Muir	Doyle&	Grant	Robson	Morrison	Gillespie	Longridge	Lyon	MacLean+	McHugh	Paterson*	Galt*	Baynham+	Kilday&	Biggar	Gillies	Heraghty			
13/10/2020	LC	A	Morton	0	1	Muir	Doyle	Grant	Robson*	Kilday	Gillespie	Longridge	Lyon	Galt&	McHugh	Baynham+	Paterson*	MacLean+	Biggar&	Morrison	Gillies	Heraghty			
17/10/2020	L	A	Stirling Albion	0	0	Muir	Doyle	Grant	Robson	Kilday	Gillespie	Longridge	Lyon	MacLean*	McHugh+	Baynham	Galt*	J Quitongo+	Biggar	Morrison	Gillies	Paterson	Heraghty		
24/10/2020	L	H	Albion Rovers	2	0	Muir	Doyle	Grant	Robson>	Kilday*	Gillespie	Longridge	Lyon+	Galt&	McHugh<	Baynham	Morrison*	Slater+	MacLean&	Paterson>	Quitongo<	Biggar	Bell		
31/10/2020	L	A	Stranraer	1	0	Muir	Doyle	Grant	Robson	Kilday	Gillespie	Longridge&	Slater	Galt*	McHugh+	Baynham	Quitongo*	MacLean+	Morrison&	Paterson	McGlinchey	Lyon	Bell		
07/11/2020	L	A	Elgin City	1	0	Muir	Doyle	Grant	Robson	Kilday	McGlinchey*	Slater	Lyon&	Galt+	McHugh>	MacLean	Longridge*<	Carroll+	Quitongo&	Baynham>	Gillespie<	Morrison	Paterson	Bell	
10/11/2020	LC	H	Queen of the South	1	3	Muir	Doyle	Morrison	Carroll	Kilday+	Gillespie>	Slater*	Lyon <	Quitongo&	Paterson	Baynham	McGlinchey*	Grant+	Galt&	McHugh>	Biggar<	Gillies	Heraghty		
14/11/2020	LC	H	St Mirren	0	1	Muir	Doyle	Grant	Robson	Kilday>	Morrison	Carroll	Lyon&	Galt*	McHugh<	Baynham+	MacLean*	Quitongo+	Gillespie&	Biggar>	McGlinchey<	Gillies	Paterson	Heraghty	
21/11/2020	L	H	Brechin City	3	0	Muir	Doyle	Quitongo&	Robson>	Kilday	Morrison	Carroll	Lyon	Galt+	McHugh	Baynham*	MacLean*	McGlinchey+	Biggar&	Paterson>	Gillespie	Gillies	Bell		
28/11/2020	L	H	Stenhousemuir	3	1	Muir	Doyle	Gillespie	Robson	Kilday	Morrison	Quitongo+	Lyon	Galt	McHugh	Baynham*	MacLean*	Murray+	Gillies	McGlinchey	Biggar	Bell			
05/12/2020	L	A	Cowdenbeath	3	0	Muir	Doyle	Grant	Robson	Kilday	Gillespie	Quitongo*	Lyon	Galt	McHugh	MacLean	Murray*	Morrison	Slater	McGlinchey	Paterson	Longridge	Baynham	Heraghty	
12/12/2020	L	H	Edinburgh City	3	3	Muir	Doyle	Grant>	Robson	Kilday	Gillespie	Quitongo+	Carroll	Galt*	McHugh	Murray&	Longridge*	MacLean+	Baynham&	Morrison>	Paterson	Lyon	Slater	McGlinchey	Heraghty
19/12/2020	L	A	Annan Athletic	2	1	Muir	Doyle	Grant	Robson	Kilday	Slater>	Longridge&	Carroll	MacLean*	McHugh+	Baynham	Galt*	Murray+	McGlinchey&	Lyon>	Paterson	Morrison	Gillespie	Quitongo	Heraghty
28/12/2020	SC	A	Dundonald Bluebell	3	1 AET	Muir	Paterson	Grant	Morrison	McGlinchey&	Gillespie	Quitongo+	Lyon	MacLean	Murray	Baynham*	McHugh*	Longridge+	Slater&	Kilday	Galt	Biggar	Heraghty		
08/01/2021	SC	H	Queen of the South	0	3	Muir	Doyle	Grant	Robson	Kilday	Gillespie&	Carroll	Longridge*	MacLean+	Murray	McHugh	Galt*	Quitongo+	Baynham&	Morrison	Paterson	Gillies	Heraghty		
20/03/2021	L	H	Stranraer	3	0	Muir	Doyle	Grant	Robson	Kilday	Connell&	Carroll*	Galt>	MacLean<	Murray	McHugh+	Lyon*	Kouider-Assa+	Gillespie&	Longridge>	Quitongo<	Gillies	Paterson	Morrison	Mullen
27/03/2021	L	A	Brechin City	2	0	Muir	Doyle	Grant	Gillespie	Kilday+	Quitongo*	Longridge	Lyon	McHugh>	Kouider-Assa&	Paterson*	MacLean*	Morrison+	Baynham&	Galt>	Mullen	Gillies	Heraghty		
30/03/2021	L	A	Albion Rovers	3	0	Muir	Doyle	Grant	Connell	Kilday>	Quitongo*	Longridge+	Lyon&	McHugh>	Kouider-Assa<	Paterson	Galt*	MacLean+	Gillespie&	Morrison>	Baynham<	Biggar	Mullen	Gillies	Heraghty
03/04/2021	L	H*	Stirling Albion	1	0	Muir	Doyle	Grant	Connell	Kilday	MacLean*	Longridge	Lyon<	McHugh+	Kouider-Assa>	Paterson	Quitongo*	Galt+	Baynham&	Gillespie>	Morrison	Biggar	Mullen	Gillies	Heraghty
06/04/2021	L	H*	Cowdenbeath	3	0	Muir	Doyle<	Grant	Connell*	Kilday	Gillespie	Longridge+	Quitongo&	Baynham>	Galt	Paterson	Lyon*	Murray+	MacLean&	Kouider-Assa>	Morrison>	McHugh	Mullen	Carroll	Robson
10/04/2021	L	A	Stenhousemuir	3	1	Muir	Doyle	Grant	Quitongo+	Kilday	Gillespie	Longridge<	Lyon>	McHugh*	Murray&	Paterson	Morrison*	MacLean+	Kouider-Assa&	Carroll>	Galt<	Gillies	Mullen	Baynham	Robson
13/04/2021	L	H*	Annan Athletic	1	0	Muir	Doyle	Robson	Connell&	Kilday	Carroll<	Longridge*	Quitongo>	Murray	Kouider-Assa+	Morrison	Galt*	McHugh+	Lyon&	MacLean>	Gillespie<	Gillies	Mullen	Baynham	Paterson
17/04/2021	L	A	Edinburgh City	3	2	Muir	Doyle	Grant	Connell	Kilday	Gillespie	Longridge	Lyon+	Murray&	McHugh*	Paterson	Baynham*	MacLean+	Kouider-Assa&	Carroll	Robson	Biggar	Mullen	Galt	Morrison
20/04/2021	L	H*	Elgin City	0	0	Muir	Doyle	Grant*	Connell	Kilday	Gillespie	Longridge	MacLean&	Murray+	McHugh>	Paterson	Morrison*	Baynham+	Galt&	Kouider-Assa>	Robson	Lyon	Mullen	Carroll	Gillies
23/04/2021	L	H*	Stranraer	0	1	Mullen*	Doyle	Robson	Morrison	Kilday	Galt&	Longridge	Lyon	Carroll<	Biggar>	Baynham+	Heraghty*	Kouider-Assa+	MacLean&	Connell>	McHugh<	Gillies	Paterson	Gillespie	
27/04/2021	L	A	Stirling Albion	2	1	Muir	Doyle	Connell+	Morrison	Kilday	Gillespie	Longridge*	MacLean&	Carroll	Kouider-Assa>	Paterson	McHugh*	Galt+	Gillies&	Biggar>	Baynham<	Robson	Lyon	Mullen	
29/04/2021	L	H*	Edinburgh City	2	0	Muir	Doyle	Robson	Morrison	Kilday	Connell*	Longridge<	Gillies+	Carroll>	McHugh	Baynham&	Gillespie*	MacLean+	Galt&	Kouider-Assa>	Lyon<	Biggar	Paterson	Collumbine	
04/05/2021	L	A	Elgin City	2	3	Muir	Doyle	Lyon&	Morrison	Kilday	Gillespie*	Kouider-Assa>	MacLean	Galt<	McHugh	Paterson+	Connell*	Paterson+	Carroll&	Baynham>	Longridge<	Biggar	Heragthy	Gillies	

THE GOALIES

Goalkeepers Used in League Matches, 1970-2020

Players shown in the season of their first appearance only

1972/3	John Taylor
	A Black
	George Rowan
1973/4	Ronnie Lowrie
	Robert Cameron
1975/6	David Gillespie
1978/9	Jim Preston
	Derek Atkins
	Gordon Wilson
1979/0	Ron Cant
1981/2	Graham Storrie
1983/4	Stevie Ross
1984/5	Willie Spence
1987/8	Michael Monaghan
1991/2	Joe Houston
	David Moonie
	Jim Chalmers
1995/6	Gordon Bruce
1996/7	Scott Starr
1997/8	Lindsay Hamilton
1998/9	Barry Cook
	Neil Inglis
2000/1	Colin Stewart
	Allan Smith
	Barry Corr
2001/2	Graham Smith
	Tony Mitchell
2002/3	Mark Cairns
2003/4	Derek Scrimgeour
	David Crawford
2004/5	Brian McCue
	Steve McGovern
2007/8	Scott Murray
	Zander Cowie
	Z Terry
2009/0	Scott Black
	Peter Hamilton
	Mark McGeown
2010/1	Adam Strain
	Gordon MacPherson
2011/2	Neil Parry
2012/3	Blair Lochhead
2013/4	Lucas Birnstingl
	Michael Brown
2014/5	Willie Muir
2016/7	Andrew Murphy
2017/8	Michael White
2018/9	Jordan Hart
	Kieran McDougall
2019/0	Josh Rae

Surname	First Name	Date of Birth	No	Nat	Pos	Signed	Previous	Notes	Contract	Lge			SC			LC			
										A	S	G	A	S	G	A	S	G	Un
Baynham	Will	13/06/1997	20	CAN	F	2020	UCSB Gauchos		End 2021/2	9	9	5	1	1		3	1		3
Bell	Cammy	18/09/1986		SCO	GK	2020	Falklirk	Retired Dec 2020		0	0								5
Biggar	Calum	01/01/2002	18	SCO	M	2020	Queen's Park Youths		End 2021/2	1	2						3		10
Carroll	Canice	26/01/1999	28	ROI / ENG	D	2020	Stevenage	Released June 2021		8	3		1			2			3
Collumbine	Evan			SCO	GK	2021	Queen's Park Youths			0	0								1
Connell	Luca	20/04/2001		EBG / ROI	M	2021	Celtic (OL)	Mar-May		9	2	3							0
Doyle	Michael	01/08/1991	24	SCO	D	2020	Falkirk		End 2021/2	22	0	1	1			4			0
Galt	David	07/11/1990	10	SCO	F	2019	Cambuslang Rangers	Released June 2021		11	10			1		2	2		2
Gillespie	Grant	02/01/1991	21	SCO	M	2020	Ayr United		End 2021/2	13	6	1	2			3	1		3
Gillies	Max	01/01/2002	15	SCO	D	2020	Queen's Park Youths		End 2021/2	1	1								17
Grant	Peter	11/03/1994	5	SCO	D	2020	Morton		End 2021/2	15	0	2	2			3	1		0
Heraghty	Jacques	15/09/2002	17	FRA / SCO	GK	2020	Queen's Park Youths		End 2021/2	0	1								14
Kilday	Lee	04/02/1992	4	SCO	D	2020	Queen of the South		End 2021/2	22	0	2	1			3	1		1
Kouider-Assa	Salim	22/03/1996		SCO / ALG	F	2021	Livingston (OL)	Mar-May		6	7	3							0
Longridge	Louis	05/07/1991	7	SCO	F	2020	Falkirk		End 2021/2	15	4	3	1	1	1	2			1
Lyon	Darren	08/01/1995	12	SCO	M	2020	Queen of the South		End 2021/2	13	5	4	1			4			4
MacLean	Ross	13/03/1997	11	SCO	F	2020	Falkirk	Released June 2021, joined Dumbarton		9	13	2	2			1	2		0
McGlinchey	Michael	07/01/1987	18	NEZ / SCO	M	2020	Central Coast Mariners	Fred Jan 2021 joined Clyde		1	2		1				2		4
McHugh	Bob	16/07/1991	9	SCO	F	2020	Morton		End 2021/2	18	3	7	1	1		3	1		1
Morrison	Stuart	18/04/1999	6	SCO	D	2020	Dunfermline Athletic		End 2021/2	7	8		1			3			9
Muir	William	16/03/2003	1	SCO	GK	2019	East Kilbride		End 2021/2	21	0		2			4			0
Mullen	Ryan	18/05/2001		SCO	GK	2021	Celtic (OL)	Mar-May		1	0								10
Murray	Simon	15/03/1992	23	SCO	F	2020	Bidvest Wits		End 2021/2	6	4	6	2		1				0
Paterson	Brody	24/04/2001	14	SCO	F	2020	Celtic (OL)	Oct-May		9	3		1			2	1		12
Quitongo	Jai	14/09/1997	19	ANG / SCO	F	2020	Dumbarton		End 2021/2	9	6	2	1	1	1	1	1	1	1
Robson	Tommy	11/09/1995	3	ENG	D	2020	Partick Thistle		End 2021/2	13	0		1			3			5
Slater	Craig	26/04/1994	8	SCO	M	2020	Partick Thistle	Released May 2021, joined Forfar Ath		3	1	1		1		1			2
Own Goals												1							
NEW SIGNINGS																			
Brown	Liam	06/04/1999		SCO	M	2021	Edinburgh City		End 2023/4										
Davidson	Jake	06/10/2000		SCO	D	2021	Dundee United		End 2021/2										
Ferrie	Calum	19/06/1998		ENG	GK	2021	Dundee		End 2022/3										
Fox	Charlie	26/11/1998		ENg	D	2021	Bromley		End 2021/2										
Moore	Lewis	04/06/1998		SCO	M	2021	Hearts		End 2022/3										
Yeats	Callum	04/10/2001		SCO	D	2021	Hibernian		End 2021/2										

PHOTOCARDS

No. 113.

QUEEN'S PARK F.C.

Left to right, back row :—*T. Campbell (Capt.), H. Dickson, T. Smith, A. Hosie, R. Cross, R. Grant.* Front row :—*J. Crawford, J. Kyle, J. Dodds, W. Martin, T. Soutar.*

This remarkable team was founded in 1867 and play in Division I of the Scottish League. During the first seven years of their existence they did not lose a game. They were winners of the Scottish Cup 1873/74/75/76, 1879/80/81/82, 1883/84, 1885/86, 1889/90 and 1892/93, and finalists in the English Cup 1882/84/85. In 1922/23 they won the Scottish League Second Division Championship. They still retain their amateur status.

Expanding de Luxe Albums for Ardath Photocards on sale at Tobacconists Price 6d

ARDATH TOBACCO CO. LTD. Manufacturers of STATE EXPRESS and ARDATH CIGARETTES

D

THE QUEEN'S PARK FOOTBALL CLUB LTD.

1ST TEAM — SEASON 1976-77

T. & R. ANNAN & SONS GLASGOW

Back Row:—Jas. Gillies (*Ground Secretary*), S. McNaughton (*Assistant Trainer*), F. C. Thomson, A. M. Bowie, I. McWilliams, R. Cameron, A. J. Mackin, J. Nicholson, R. McSkimming, J. Gilroy (*Trainer/Coach*) Jas. Logan, C.A. (*Secretary*).
Front Row:—R. Dickson, J. Rooney, A. McNaughton, G. Colgan, R. L. Cromar (*President*). A. Glavin, J. Sinclair, B. Donnelly, D. Wilkie.

Raith Rovers FC 2020/21 Rovers

Founded	1883
Ground	Stark's Park, Pratt Street
Postcode	KY1 1SA
Tel	01592 263514
Capacity	8473
Closest Railway Station	Kirkcaldy
Record Attendance	31306 v Hearts, SC, 7/2/1953
Record Win	10-1 v Coldstream, SC, 13/2/1954
Record Defeat	2-11 v Morton, Lge, 18/3/1936
Most League Goals in a Season	38 Norman Haywood, 1937/8
Colours 2020/21 Top	Navy Blue with sky design
Shorts	Navy Blue with sky design
Sponsor	valmcdermid.com
Manufacturer	Joma
Change Colours 2020/21 Top	White with sky blue design
Shorts	White
Nicknames	Rovers
Web	www.raithrovers.net
Match Programme 2020/21	Season ticket holders only

Honorary President: Alex Penman
Chairman: John Sim
Vice Chairman: Steven MacDonald, David Sinton
Directors: John Sim, Bill Clark, Tom Morgan, Andy Mill,
Manager: John McGlynn
Assistant Manager: Paul Smith
Club Doctor: Katy Green
Kit Manager: Simon Pollock
Physio: Stewart Duff
Kit: Simon Pollock
Strength & Conditioning Coach: Cameron Ross
Sport Scientist: Blair Doughty
Football Analyst: Andrew Tannahill
Commercial Manager: Laura Andreucci
Laundry Supervisor: June McArdle
Administration Manager: Lynn Lamont
Hospitality Assistant: Linda Patrick
Facilities Administrator: Margaret Shanley
Stadium Maintenance: Eric Swinley, Tony Coventry

Having just come up from League One, any Raith fans would have bitten your hand off for a place in the promotion play offs. That place was seldom in doubt from early in the season as Raith were the team who did most to stick in behind Hearts at the top of the table. In the end they were overhauled by Dundee which meant they had to play in the First Round of the play offs. Having beaten local rivals Dunfermline, they were well beaten by Dundee after a horror-show performance in the home leg.

Still, getting that far was a decent achievement for a club with a small squad and what looked like a scattergun signing policy. Players like Duku and Ugwu were unknown but proved to be reasonable signings. John McGlynn used his good name and good contacts to bring in decent loan signings.

The Cups were disappointing with no progress in the League Cup and a second game exit from the Scottish at the hands of Livingston.

STAR MAN
Regan Hendry was the stand out player for Rovers. The former Celtic midfielder oozed quality and it became apparent that would be off at the end of the season. The surprise was that he opted for Forest Green Rovers rather than joining a bigger club in Scotland – both Hibs and Hearts were reported to be keen on him.

PROSPECTS 2021/2
Lewis Vaughan returned to something approaching full fitness towards the of last season. If he can remain injury-free than that will be important for Rovers. John McGlynn is a pragmatic manager who will set his team up in whatever way is required to get results – expect them to be back up challenging for a play off place again this season.

Stark's Park in the 1980s

Date	Comp	H/A	Opponents	F	A		HT		Referee	Crowd	Scorers
10/10/2020	LC	H	East Fife	2	1		1	1	D Lowe	BCD	Hendry pen, Duku
13/10/2020	LC	A	Hearts	1	3		0	2	C Napier	BCD	Duku
17/10/2020	L	H	Arbroath	3	0		3	0	G Duncan	BCD	Armstrong, Tumilty, Hendry pen
24/10/2020	L	A	Queen of the South	5	2		3	1	E Anderson	BCD	Duku 2, Tait, Armstrong, Matthews
31/10/2020	L	A	Dundee	1	1		0	1	A Newlands	BCD	Musonda
07/11/2020	L	H	Morton	5	0		2	0	W Collum	BCD	Armstrong pen, Musonda, Matthews 2, Mendy
10/11/2020	LC	H	Inverness CT	3	3	3-2p	1	1	S Reid	BCD	Duku 2, Devine og
14/11/2020	LC	A	Cowdenbeath	1	0		1	0	D Lowe	BCD	Duku
21/11/2020	L	A	Inverness CT	0	2		0	1	A Newlands	250	
05/12/2020	L	H	Dunfermline Athletic	2	2		1	0	E Anderson	BCD	Duku, Musonda
11/12/2020	L	A	Ayr United	0	0		0	0	A Muir	BCD	
26/12/2020	L	A	Alloa Athletic	5	2		2	0	S McLean	BCD	Duku, Armstrong, Lokotsch, Ross 2
29/12/2020	L	H	Queen of the South	0	2		0	1	B Cook	BCD	
23/01/2021	L	A	Hearts	3	2		1	0	J Beaton	BCD	Ugwu, Duku pen, Tumilty
26/01/2021	L	H	Hearts	0	4		0	2	E Anderson	BCD	
30/01/2021	L	H	Dundee	3	1		1	1	C Napier	BCD	Benedictus, Tumilty, Kennedy
03/02/2021	L	A	Dunfermline Athletic	1	4		0	1	C Steven	BCD	Spencer
06/02/2021	L	A	Morton	1	0		1	0	C Graham	BCD	Davidson
20/02/2021	L	A	Arbroath	0	1		0	0	G Aitken	BCD	
27/02/2021	L	H	Alloa Athletic	3	1		0	1	S Kirkland	BCD	Davidson, Hendry, Gullan
09/03/2021	L	H	Ayr United	0	0		0	0	S Lambie	BCD	
12/03/2021	L	A	Inverness CT	0	0		0	0	S McLean	BCD	
16/03/2021	L	H	Inverness CT	0	1		0	0	C Steven	BCD	
20/03/2021	L	A	Ayr United	1	1		0	0	D Dickinson	BCD	Benedictus
23/03/2021	SC	A	Stirling Albion	2	0		1	0	A Newlands	BCD	Ugwu, Tait
27/03/2021	L	H	Morton	1	0		0	0	J Beaton	BCD	Gullan
30/03/2021	L	H	Dunfermline Athletic	5	1		3	1	E Anderson	BCD	Hendry, Vaughan 2, Gullan 2
03/04/2021	SC	A	Livingston	1	2	AET	1	0	B Madden	BCD	Vaughan
10/04/2021	L	H	Arbroath	2	2		1	0	G Duncan	BCD	Armstrong 2
13/04/2021	L	A	Queen of the South	1	0		1	0	D Dickinson	BCD	Ugwu
17/04/2021	L	A	Alloa Athletic	2	1		0	1	G Aitken	BCD	Ugwu pen, Tait
24/04/2021	L	A	Dundee	1	2		0	2	W Collum	BCD	Benedictus
30/04/2021	L	H	Hearts	0	4		0	1	D Munro	BCD	
04/05/2021	PO	A	Dunfermline Athletic	0	0		0	0	S Kirkland	BCD	
08/05/2021	PO	H	Dunfermline Athletic	2	0		0	0	G Aitken	BCD	Vaughan, Ugwu
12/05/2021	PO	H	Dundee	0	3		0	1	N Walsh	BCD	
15/05/2021	PO	A	Dundee	1	0		1	0	D Robertson	BCD	Vaughan

Ramiro Gonzalez

Tom Carson

Bobby Reid

Date	Comp	H/A	Opponents	F	A		1	2	3	4	5	6	7	8	9	10	11	12	13	14	15	16	17	18	19
10/10/2020	LC	H	East Fife	2	1		J MacDonald	Davidson	Benedictus	K MacDonald	Tumilty	Matthews	Hendry	Armstrong	Ross*	Tait	Duku	Anderson*	*Mendy*	*Spencer*	*Coulson*	*Smith*	*Arnott*	*Mahady*	*Thomson*
13/10/2020	LC	A	Hearts	1	3		J MacDonald	Davidson	Benedictus	K MacDonald	Tumilty	Matthews	Hendry	Mendy*	Spencer+	Tait>	Duku&	Ross*	Vaughan+	Armstrong&	Anderson>	*Mahady*	*Coulson*	*Thomson*	
17/10/2020	L	H	Arbroath	3	0		J MacDonald	Davidson	Benedictus	K MacDonald	Tumilty*	Matthews	Hendry	Armstrong	Ross	Tait	Duku+	Musonda*	Anderson+	*Spencer*	*Coulson*	*Thomson*	*Vaughan*	*Mendy*	
24/10/2020	L	A	Queen of the South	5	2		J MacDonald	Davidson	Benedictus&	K MacDonald+	Tumilty	Matthews	Hendry	Armstrong	Ross*	Tait	Duku	Spencer*	Musonda+	Mendy&	*Coulson*	*Thomson*	*Mahady*	*Smith*	
31/10/2020	L	A	Dundee	1	1		J MacDonald	Davidson&	Benedictus	K MacDonald*	Tumilty	Matthews	Hendry	Armstrong	Ross+	Tait	Lokotsch	Musonda*	Spencer+	Mendy&	*Coulson*	*Thomson*	*Mahady*	*Arnott*	
07/11/2020	L	H	Morton	5	0		J MacDonald	Davidson*	Benedictus	Musonda	Tumilty	Matthews+	Hendry	Armstrong	Ross&	Tait	Lokotsch	Mendy*	Spencer+	Coulson&	*Duku*	*Arnott*	*Mahady*	*Thomson*	
10/11/2020	LC	H	Inverness CT	3	3	3-2p	Thomson	Mendy	Benedictus	Musonda	Tumilty	Matthews	Hendry	Armstrong	Ross	Spencer	Duku	Arnott	Coulson	*Mahady*	*J MacDonald*				
14/11/2020	LC	A	Cowdenbeath	1	0		Thomson	Mendy	Spencer	Musonda	Tumilty	Matthews	Hendry	Armstrong	Ross*	Tait	Duku	Coulson*	Arnott	*Mahady*	*J MacDonald*				
21/11/2020	L	A	Inverness CT	0	2		J MacDonald	Musonda	Benedictus	K MacDonald	Tumilty	Matthews	Hendry	Armstrong	Ross*	Tait+	Duku	Lokotsch*	Spencer+	*Ugwu*	*Coulson*	*Arnott*	*Mendy*	*Thomson*	
05/12/2020	L	H	Dunfermline Athletic	2	2		J MacDonald	Musonda	Benedictus	K MacDonald	Tumilty	Matthews	Hendry	Armstrong	Ross*	Tait	Duku+	Spencer*	Lokotsch+	*Ugwu*	*Coulson*	*Mendy*	*Mahady*	*Thomson*	
11/12/2020	L	A	Ayr United	0	0		J MacDonald	Musonda	Benedictus	K MacDonald	Tumilty	Matthews	Hendry	Armstrong	Ross+	Tait	Duku*	Lokotsch*	Spencer+	*Ugwu*	*Coulson*	*Mendy*	*Arnott*	*Thomson*	
26/12/2020	L	A	Alloa Athletic	5	2		J MacDonald*	Musonda	Benedictus	Mendy	Tumilty	Matthews	Hendry	Armstrong	Ross	Tait&	Duku+	Thomson*	Lokotsch+	Spencer&	*Coulson*	*Arnott*	*Ugwu*	*Mahady*	
29/12/2020	L	H	Queen of the South	0	2		Thomson	Musonda	Benedictus	Mendy	Tumilty	Matthews	Hendry	Armstrong+	Ross*	Tait&	Duku	Lokotsch*	Spencer+	Ugwu&	*Coulson*	*Arnott*	*Smith*	*McGurn*	
23/01/2021	L	A	Hearts	3	2		J MacDonald	Musonda	Benecictus	K MacDonald	Tumilty	Matthews+	Hendry	Armstrong	Spencer	Kennedy&	Ugwu*	Duku*	Tait+	Ross&	*Mendy*	*Davidson*	*Smith*	*Thomson*	
26/01/2021	L	H	Hearts	0	4		J MacDonald	Musonda	Benedictus	K MacDonald	Tumilty	Vaughan*	Hendry	Armstrong&	Spencer	Kennedy&	Duku+	Tait*	Davidson+	Ross&	*Mendy*	*Coulson*	*Arnott*	*Thomson*	
30/01/2021	L	H	Dundee	3	1		J MacDonald	Musonda	Benedictus*	K MacDonald	Tumilty	Vaughan	Tait	Armstrong+	Spencer	Kennedy	Abraham&	Davidson*	King+	Duku&	*Coulson*	*Smith*	*Mendy*	*Thomson*	
03/02/2021	L	A	Dunfermline Athletic	1	4		J MacDonald	Musonda	Davidson	K MacDonald	Tumilty	Vaughan*	Tait+	Armstrong&	Spencer	Kennedy	Abraham	Gullan*	King+	*Duku&*	*Coulson*	*Smith*	*Mendy*	*Thomson*	
06/02/2021	L	A	Morton	1	0		J MacDonald*	Musonda	Davidson	K MacDonald	Tumilty	Mendy	Hendry	Armstrong	Spencer	Ugwu&	Gullan+	Thomson*	Abraham+	Kennedy&	*Coulson*	*Smith*	*Duku*	*King*	
20/02/2021	L	A	Arbroath	0	1		J MacDonald	Benedictus	Davidson	K MacDonald	Tumilty	Tait*	Hendry	Armstrong	Ugwu+	Kennedy	Gullan&	King*	*Duku+*	*Abraham&*	*Coulson*	*Mendy*	*Thomson*		
27/02/2021	L	H	Alloa Athletic	3	1		J MacDonald	Benedictus	Davidson	K MacDonald	Tumilty&	Matthews	Hendry	Armstrong	Spencer	Kennedy+	Duku*	Ugwu*	Gullan+	Musonda&	*Tait*	*Mendy*	*Thomson*	*King*	
09/03/2021	L	H	Ayr United	0	0		J MacDonald	Benedictus	Davidson	K MacDonald	Tumilty	Matthews	Hendry	Armstrong&	Spencer+	Kennedy	Duku*	Ugwu*	Tait+	*Gullan&*	*Musonda*	*Abraham*	*King*	*Thomson*	
12/03/2021	L	A	Inverness CT	0	0		J MacDonald	Benedictus	Musonda	K MacDonald	Tumilty	King*	Hendry	Tait	Ugwu&	Kennedy	Gullan+	Armstrong*	Matthews+	Duku&	*Spencer*	*Abraham*	*Davidson*	*Thomson*	
16/03/2021	L	H	Inverness CT	0	1		J MacDonald	Benedictus	Davidson	K MacDonald	Tumilty	Matthews	Hendry	Armstrong*	Ugwu	Kennedy+	Spencer&	Musonda*	Gullan+	*Vaughan&*	*Duku*	*Abraham*	*Tait*	*Thomson*	
20/03/2021	L	A	Ayr United	1	1		J MacDonald	Benedictus	Musonda	K MacDonald	Tumilty	Matthews	Hendry	Armstrong&	Vaughan*	Duku+	Gullan	Kennedy*	Abraham+	Tait&	*King*	*Spencer*	*Ugwu*	*Thomson*	
23/03/2021	SC	A	Stirling Albion	2	0		J MacDonald	Benedictus	Musonda	K MacDonald	Tumilty	King	Spencer	Kennedy+	Tait	Ugwu*	Gullan&	Vaughan*	Armstrong+	*Abraham&*	*Matthews*	*Hendry*	*Duku*	*Thomson*	
27/03/2021	L	H	Morton	1	0		J MacDonald	Benedictus	Musonda	K MacDonald	Tumilty	King&	Hendry	Armstrong*	Tait	Ugwu+	Duku	Vaughan*	Gullan+	Matthews&	*Spencer*	*Kennedy*	*Abraham*	*Thomson*	
30/03/2021	L	H	Dunfermline Athletic	5	1		J MacDonald	Benedictus	Musonda	K MacDonald*	Tumilty	Matthews	Hendry	Spencer	Kennedy+	Vaughan&	Gullan	Armstrong*	Tait+	*Duku&*	*Abraham*	*Ugwu*	*King*	*Thomson*	
03/04/2021	SC	A	Livingston	1	2	AET	J MacDonald	Benedictus	Musonda	Davidson	Tumilty	Tait>	Hendry	Spencer	Kennedy&	Vaughan+	Gullan*	Duku*	Ugwu+	Armstrong&	*King>*	*Smith*	*Abraham*	*Cooney*	*Thomson*
10/04/2021	L	H	Arbroath	2	2		J MacDonald	Benedictus	Musonda	K MacDonald	Tumilty	Tait*	Hendry	Spencer	Kennedy	Vaughan	Armstrong+	Cooney*	*King+*	*Smith*	*Ugwu*	*Duku*	*Abraham*	*Thomson*	
13/04/2021	L	A	Queen of the South	1	0		J MacDonald	Benedictus	Musonda	Davidson	Tumilty	King	Hendry	Spencer	Kennedy*	Ugwu&	Armstrong+	Tait*	Duku+	Abraham&	*Coulson*	*Smith*	*Cooney*	*Thomson*	
17/04/2021	L	A	Alloa Athletic	2	1		J MacDonald	Benedictus	Tait	Davidson	Tumilty	King*	Hendry	Spencer	Kennedy+	Ugwu&	Armstrong	Duku*	Smith+	*Abraham&*	*Cooney*	*Mendy*	*K MacDonald*	*Thomson*	
24/04/2021	L	A	Dundee	1	2		J MacDonald	Benedictus	Davidson	K MacDonald	Tumilty	Tait	Hendry	Spencer	Kennedy*	Ugwu+	Gullan	Vaughan*	King+	Duku	*Cooney*	*Mendy*	*Armstrong*	*Thomson*	
30/04/2021	L	H	Hearts	0	4		J MacDonald	Benedictus	Davidson	K MacDonald	Tumilty	King	Hendry	Spencer	Mendy*	Vaughan+	Gullan&	Armstrong*	*Cooney+*	*Ugwu&*	*Kennedy*	*Abraham*	*Duku*	*Thomson*	
04/05/2021	PO	A	Dunfermline Athletic	0	0		J MacDonald	Benedictus	Davidson	K MacDonald	Tumilty	Matthews*	Hendry	Spencer	Kennedy	Vaughan+	Gullan&	King*	Duku+	Ugwu&	*Cooney*	*Mendy*	*Armstrong*	*Thomson*	
08/05/2021	PO	H	Dunfermline Athletic	2	0		J MacDonald	Benedictus	Davidson&	K MacDonald	Tumilty	Matthews*	Hendry	Armstrong	Spencer	Vaughan	Gullan+	Tait*	Ugwu+	*Mendy&*	*Cooney*	*Abraham*	*King*	*Thomson*	
12/05/2021	PO	H	Dundee	0	3		J MacDonald	Benedictus	Davidson	K MacDonald	Tumilty	Matthews+	Hendry	Armstrong&	Spencer*	Vaughan	Gullan	Ugwu*	Tait+	Duku&	*Cooney*	*Mendy*	*King*	*Thomson*	
15/05/2021	PO	A	Dundee	1	0		J MacDonald	Benedictus	Mendy	K MacDonald	Tumilty	Matthews&	Hendry	Armstrong+	Ugwu	Vaughan	Gullan*	Duku*	Tait+	*Spencer&*	*Cooney*	*Coulson*	*King*	*Thomson*	

THE GOALIES

Goalkeepers Used in League Matches, 1972-2020

Players shown in the season of their first appearance only

1972/3	Bobby Reid
	Murray McDermott
1973/4	Alan Blair
1977/8	Callum Frame
1981/2	Tom Walker
	Ally Donaldson
1982/3	Peter Cramb
1983/4	Andy Graham
	Jim McArthur
1984/5	Alex Inglis
	Mark Glynn
	Ronnie McLafferty
1985/6	Scott Thomson
1986/7	Hamish McAlpine
1988/9	Gordon Arthur
1990/1	Alan Banner
1991/2	Gordon Arthur
1992/3	Tom Carson
1993/4	Brian Potter
1994/5	Ray Allan
1995/6	Les Fridge
	Bobby Geddes
1996/7	Colin Scott
1997/8	Guido Van De Kamp
1998/9	Mark McGeown
1999/0	Andy McCondichie
	Craig Coyle
2000/1	Samuel Monin
2001/2	Simon Miotto
2002/3	Raul Ojeda
	Jamie Sweeney
	Ramiro Gonzalez
2003/4	Jamie Langfield
	David Berthelot
2004/5	Rudy Pounousammy
	Stuart Hall
2005/6	Ally Brown
2006/7	Michel Brown
	Chris Fahey
2007/8	Kieran Renton
2008/9	David McGurn
	Gary O'Connor
2010/1	Andy McNeil
2011/2	Ross Laidlaw
2013/4	Lee Robinson
2014/5	Kevin Cuthbert
2015/6	Pavol Penska
	Connor Brennan
	Aaron Lennox
2017/8	Rory Brian
	Graeme Smith
2018/9	Robbie Thomson
	Dean Lyness
	Kieran Wright
2019/0	Ross Munro

Surname	First Name	Date of Birth	No	Nat	Pos	Signed	Previous	Notes	Contract	Lge A	Lge S	Lge G	SC A	SC S	SC G	LC A	LC S	LC G	Un
Abraham	Timmy	28/12/2000		ENG	F	2021	Fulham (OL)	Jan-May		2	5			1					9
Anderson	Grant	20/08/1986		SCO	M	2019	Stranraer	Transferred to Kelty Hearts Oct 2020		0	1						2		0
Armstrong	Danny	11/10/1997	7	SCO	F	2019	Ross County	Turned down contract May 2021, joined Kilmarnock		#	3	6		2		3	1		2
Arnott	Aaron	19/11/2003	25	SCO	M	2020	Fife Elite Academy		End 2021/2	0	0								10
Benedictus	Kyle	07/12/1991	6	SCO	D	2015	Dundee		End 2021/2	#	0	3	2			3			0
Bow	Kyle	02/11/2003	28	SCO	GK	2020	Inverkeithing Hillfield S	OL to Inverkeithing HS Nov-Jan	End 2021/2	0	0								0
Cooney	Nathan	21/02/2002		SCO	D	2021	Dundee United (OL)	Mar-May		0	2								8
Coulson	Quinn	01/09/2003	27	SCO	F	2020	Raith Rovers Youths	OL to Cowdenbeath Jul-Dec 2021	End 2021/2	0	1						1		18
Davidson	Iain	14/01/1984	4	SCO	D	2015	Dundee	Released May 2021, joined Brechin City		#	2	2	1			2			2
Duku	Manny	28/12/1992	9	NET / GHA	F	2020	Hayes & Yeading	Released May 2021, joined Inverness CT		#	#	5		1		4		5	7
Gullan	Jamie	02/07/1999		SCO	F	2021	Hibernian	Feb-May		#	5	4	2						0
Hendry	Regan	21/01/1998	8	SCO	M	2019	Celtic	Refused new contract May 2021, joined Forest Green R		#	0	3	1			4		1	1
Kennedy	Kai	28/03/2002	21	SCO	F	2021	Rangers (OL)	Jan-May		#	2	1	2						2
King	Adam	11/10/1995		SCO	M	2021	Dundee United (OL)	Feb-May		5	6		1	1					8
Lokotsch	Lars	17/05/1996		GER	F	2020	Livingston (OL)	Oct-Jan		2	5	1							0
MacDonald	Jamie	17/04/1986	1	SCO	GK	2020	Kilmarnock		End 2021/2	#	0		2			2			2
MacDonald	Kieran	21/07/1993	3	SCO	D	2019	Airdrieonians	Joined Hamilton Accies June 2021		#	0		1			2			1
Mackay	David	17/06/1998	15	SCO	D	2017	Raith Rovers Youths		End 2021/2	0	0								0
Mahady	Luke	26/02/2004	19	SCO	F	2020	Celtic Youths	OL to Cowdenbeath Jul-Dec 2021	End 2021/2	0	0								9
Matthews	Ross	23/01/1996	12	SCO	M	2015	Raith Rovers Youths		End 2023/4	#	2	3				4			1
McGurn	David	14/09/1980	20	SCO	GK	2019	Cowdenbeath	Released May 2021, joined Cowdenbeath		0	0								1
Mendy	Fernandy	16/01/1994	5	FRA / GUB	D	2019	RC La Fleche	Released May 2021, Capped by Guinea Bissau 2020/1		5	4	1				3			15
Musonda	Frankie	12/12/1997	14	ZAM / ENG	D	2020	Luton Town		End 2021/2	#	5	3	2			2			1
Ross	Ethan	15/08/2001	22	SCO	M	2020	Aberdeen (OL)	Oct-May		9	2	2				3	1		0
Smith	Jack	18/02/2000	16	SCO	F	2018	Raith Rovers Youths	Released May 2021, joined Dundonald Bluebell		0	1								10
Spencer	Brad	16/05/1998	13	SCO	M	2019	Forfar Athletic	Offered new contract May 2021	End 2021/2	#	9	1	2			3			5
Tait	Dylan	01/12/2001	18	SCO	M	2019	Fife Elite Academy		End 2023/4	#	9	2	2		1	3			2
Thomson	Robbie	07/03/1993	17	SCO	GK	2018	Falkirk		End 2022/3	1	2					2			32
Tumilty	Reghan	26/02/1997	2	SCO	D	2020	Morton		End 2021/2	#	0	3	2			4			0
Ugwu	Gozie	22/04/1993	23	NIG / ENG	F	2020	Ebbsfleet United	Released May 2021, joined Morton		#	7	4	1	1	1				7
Vaughan	Lewis	19/12/1995	10	SCO	F	2012	Raith Rovers Youths		End 2023/4	#	3	4	1	1	1		1		1
Own Goal																		1	

NEW SIGNINGS

Surname	First Name	Date of Birth	No	Nat	Pos	Signed	Previous	Notes	Contract
Berra	Christophe	31/01/1985		SCO	D	2021	Hearts		End 2022/3
Connolly	Aidan	15/08/1995		SCO	F	2021	Falkirk		End 2022/3
Dick	Liam	19/08/1995		SCO	D	2021	Alloa Athletic		End 2022/3
Keatings	James	20/01/1992		SCO	F	2021	Inverness CT		End 2022/3
Lang	Tom	12/06/1997		SCO	D	2021	Clyde		End 2022/3
Poplatnik	Matej	15/07/1992		SLN	F	2021`	Livingston (OL)	Jul-May	End 2021/2
Zanatta	Dario	24/05/1997		CAN	F	2021	Ayr United		End 2021/2

PHOTOCARDS

No. 71.

RAITH ROVERS F.C.

Left to right, back row :— *R. Allan (Capt.), J. Sneddon, J. Paterson, M. M'Neil, W. Crichton, J. Gilbert.* Front row :— *J. Wilson, G. Denholm, G. Fulton, H. Philp, W. Dobbie.*

Founded 1898. Winners of the Scottish Qualifying Cup 1906/07, and were finalists in the Scottish Cup 1912/13. In 1935/36 finished rather low in Scottish League, Division II, but the start of the 1936/37 season saw the team determined to improve their position.

Expanding de Luxe Albums for Ardath Photocards on sale at Tobacconists Price 6d

ARDATH TOBACCO CO. LTD. Manufacturers of STATE EXPRESS and ARDATH CIGARETTES

D

Rangers FC 2020/21 The Gers

Founded	1872
Ground	Ibrox Stadium
Postcode	G51 2XD
Tel	0141 580 8647
Capacity	50987
Closest Railway Station	Ibrox (Subway)
Record Attendance	118567 v Celtic, Lge, 2/1/1939
Record Win	14-2 v Blairgowrie, SC, 20/1/1934
Record Defeat	1-7 v Celtic, LC Final, 19/10/1957
Most League Goals in a Season	44 Sam English, 1931/2
Colours 2020/21 Top	Blue
Shorts	White
Sponsor	32 Red
Manufacturer	Castore
Change Colours 2020/21 Top	White
Shorts	Blue
Nicknames	Gers, Teddy Bears
Web	www.rangers.co.uk
Match Programme 2020/21	£3.50

Chairman: Douglas Park
Deputy Chairman: John Bennett
Company Secretary: James Blair
Non-Executive Director: Alastair Johnston
Non-Executive Director: Graeme Park
Non-Executive Director: Barry Scott
Non-Executive Director: Julian Wolhardt
Managing Director: Stewart Robertson
Commercial and Marketing Director: James Bisgrove
Company Secretary: James Blair
Director of Finance and Administration: Andrew Dickson
Accountant: George Letham
Sporting Director: Ross Wilson
Manager: Steven Gerrard
Assistant Manager: Gary McAllister
First Team Coach: Michael Beale
Coach: Jermaine Defoe
Technical Coach : Tom Culshaw
Goalkeeping Coach: Colin Stewart
Head of Scouting: Andy Scoulding
Club Scouts: John Brown, Mervyn Day, Billy McLaren, Piotr Kasprzak
Scouting Coordinator: Rob Clarkson
Lead Technical Scout: Steve Doyle
Loans Manager: Billy Kirkwood
Head of Performance: Jordan Milsom
Head of Performance Analysis: Scott Mason
First Team Analyst: Graeme Stevenson
Head of Preparation: Craig Flannigan
Head of Strength and Conditioning: Paraskevas Polychronopoulos
Sports Scientist: Kevin Symon
Club Doctor: Dr Mark Waller
Head of Medical: Matt Konopinski
Head Physiotherapist: Steve Walker
Physio: Adam Roberts
Rehabilitation Physiotherapist: Eamon Swift
Masseur: David Lavery
Kit Executive: Jimmy Bell
Kit Man: Jim McAlister
Honorary Life President: John Greig
Head of Comms: David Graham
Head of Ambassadors and Business Development: Mark Hateley
Global Ambassador: Richard Gough

Since the broken and battered club re-started their life in the Third Division in 2012, it has been a long road back for them. There have been hurdles along the way. Ally McCoist's spell as Manager saw them promoted twice but meanwhile contriving to lose some highly unlikely fixtures. Throwing away a 2-goal lead with ten minutes left in a Challenge Cup Semi Final at Alloa stands out as a particular low. They failed to get promoted from the Championship at the first attempt. Back in the Premiership they struggled initially to match a Celtic side that was firing on all cylinders. Little wonder then that 2020/1 brought wild celebrations from Rangers supporters. How ironic that their return to success should happen at a time when spectators were not permitted to attend games.

Steven Gerrard's team did almost everything right in 2020/1. They never took their foot off the pedal in the L:eague campaign, ending up undefeated. It was only in the domestic Cups that they came slightly unstuck – losing to St Mirren in the League Cup and St Johnstone in the Scottish Cup. Their European run exceeded expectations and Rangers defeated teams they would previously have lost to. It was only ended by a high quality Slavia Prague side. One of the best aspects for Rangers was that they no longer elide so heavily on Morelos for goals. This season was a team without real stars – every player contributed in equal measure to their success. With less pressure on him, Morelos also calmed down his temperament and was more of a consistent asset to the club rather than an occasional liability. McGregor, Goldson, Kamara and Kent were stalwarts and youngster Patterson emerged as an exciting home-grown talent. Hopefully the club can give him and others the platform they need rather than relying so heavily on imports.

The sad thing is that stopping "ten in a row" was as much a mantra for some Rangers fans as winning the league in their own right. Schadenfreude is what it is all about. Will Rangers go on to dominate for years to come? With Celtic in disarray the immediate future looks bright for them.

STAR MAN
Glen Kamara must rate as one of the bargain signings of all time. His performances at the Euros for Finland drew admiring glances from the wealthier leagues of Europe. It's a win-win for Rangers. They wither continue to benefit from his midfield abilities or they can cash in and make a huge profit on the man they signed from Dundee for buttons.

PROSPECTS FOR 2021/2
It is inconceivable that rangers will not win the League again in 2021/2. They are starting from such a position of a strength compared to all their opponents and that includes Celtic. As happened when Celtic were dominant, the question will be to see if rangers can compete at the highest levels in European football. Qualification for the Champions league group stages is more difficult than ever thanks to UEFA favouring the "big leagues", so the Europa League might be their best hope. It's a Catch 22 situation – the money from the Champions League is a huge carrot but Rangers would struggle against Europe's top clubs. Winning the Europa league, or at least reaching the final stages, is a realistic hope but much less lucrative.

Date	Comp	H/A	Opponents	F	A		HT		Referee	Crowd	Scorers
01/08/2020	L	A	Aberdeen	1	0		1	0	B Madden	BCD	Kent
06/08/2020	UEL	A	Bayer Leverkusen	0	1		0	1	D Makkelie	BCD	
09/08/2020	L	H	St Mirren	3	0		1	0	A Dallas	BCD	McCarthy og, Morelos 2
12/08/2020	L	H	St Johnstone	3	0		2	0	E Anderson	BCD	Barisic, Kent, Aribo
16/08/2020	L	A	Livingston	0	0		0	0	N Walsh	BCD	
22/08/2020	L	H	Kilmarnock	2	0		0	0	K Clancy	BCD	Roofe, Kent
29/08/2020	L	A	Hamilton Accies	2	0		2	0	W Collum	BCD	Hagi, Tavernier
12/09/2020	L	H	Dundee United	4	0		2	0	K Clancy	BCD	Kent, Tavernier, Roofe, Arfield
17/09/2020	UEL	A	Lincoln Red Imps	5	0		2	0	I Griffith (WAL)	BCD	Tavernier, Goldson, Defoe, Morelos (2)
20/09/2020	L	A	Hibernian	2	2		1	1	D Robertson	BCD	Morelos, Arfield
24/09/2020	UEL	A	Willem II Tilburg	4	0		2	0	M Mariani (ITA)	BCD	Taverner pen, Kent, Goldson, Helander
27/09/2020	L	A	Motherwell	5	1		3	0	B Madden	BCD	Tavernier 2 pens, Itten 2, Jones
01/10/2020	UEL	H	Galatasaray	2	1		0	0	A Treimanis (AUS)	BCD	Arfield, Tavernier
04/10/2020	L	H	Ross County	2	0		1	0	G Aitken	BCD	Tavernier pen, Barker
17/10/2020	L	A	Celtic	2	0		2	0	J Beaton	BCD	Goldson 2
22/10/2020	UEL	A	Standard Liege	2	0		1	0	J Kehlet (DEN)	3750	Tavernier pen, Roofe
25/10/2020	L	H	Livingston	2	0		2	0	N Walsh	BCD	Aribo, Defoe
29/10/2020	UEL	H	Lech Poznan	1	0		0	0	K Tohver (EST)	BCD	Morelos
01/11/2020	L	A	Kilmarnock	1	0		1	0	A Dallas	BCD	Tavernier pen
05/11/2020	UEL	A	Benfica	3	3		2	1	J Gil (SPA)	BCD	Goncalves og, Kamara, Morelos
08/11/2020	L	H	Hamilton Accies	8	0		4	0	S McLean	BCD	Arfield, Roofe 2, Aribo 2, Barker, Tavernier 2 (1 pen)
22/11/2020	L	H	Aberdeen	4	0		2	0	N Walsh	BCD	Kent, Roofe, Arfield, Tavernier pen
26/11/2020	UEL	H	Benfica	2	2		1	0	R Petrescu (ROM)	BCD	Arfield, Roofe
29/11/2020	LC	A	Falkirk	4	0		3	0	B Madden	BCD	Defoe, Bassey, Barisic, Tavernier
03/12/2020	UEL	H	Standard Liege	3	2		2	2	B Pandzic (SWE)	BCD	Goldson, Tavernier pen, Arfield
06/12/2020	L	A	Ross County	4	0		1	0	B Madden	BCD	Roofe, Tavernier, Morris og, Defoe
10/12/2020	UEL	A	Lech Poznan	2	0		1	0	J Sanchez (SPA)	BCD	Itten, Hagi
13/12/2020	L	A	Dundee United	2	1		2	1	S McLean	BCD	Tavernier, Goldson
16/12/2020	LC	A	St Mirren	2	3		1	1	A Dallas	BCD	Goldson, Davis
19/12/2020	L	H	Motherwell	3	1		0	1	D Robertson	BCD	Roofe 2, Itten
23/12/2020	L	A	St Johnstone	3	0		2	0	N Walsh	BCD	Roofe, Kamara, Hagi
26/12/2020	L	H	Hibernian	1	0		1	0	W Collum	BCD	Hagi
30/12/2020	L	A	St Mirren	2	0		2	0	A Muir	BCD	Roofe, Morelos
02/01/2021	L	H	Celtic	1	0		0	0	B Madden	BCD	McGregor og
10/01/2021	L	A	Aberdeen	2	1		1	0	J Beaton	BCD	Morelos 2
17/01/2021	L	A	Motherwell	1	1		0	1	D Robertson	BCD	Itten
23/01/2021	L	H	Ross County	5	0		3	0	E Anderson	BCD	Kent, Helander, Aribo, Jack, Goldson
27/01/2021	L	A	Hibernian	1	0		1	0	K Clancy	BCD	Morelos
03/02/2021	L	H	St Johnstone	1	0		0	0	D Munro	BCD	Hagi
06/02/2021	L	A	Hamilton Accies	1	1		0	0	B Madden	BCD	Easton og
13/02/2021	L	H	Kilmarnock	1	0		1	0	D Robertson	BCD	Jack
18/02/2021	UEL	A	Royal Antwerp	4	3		1	2	G Kabakov (LIT)	BCD	Barisic 2 pens, Kent, Aribo
21/02/2021	L	H	Dundee United	4	1		2	0	N Walsh	BCD	Hagi, Kent, Aribo, Morelos
25/02/2021	UEL	H	Royal Antwerp	5	2		1	1	P Rczkowski (POL)	BCD	Morelos, Patterson, Kent, Barisic pen, Itten pen
03/03/2021	L	A	Livingston	1	0		0	0	J Beaton	BCD	Morelos
06/03/2021	L	H	St Mirren	3	0		2	0	S McLean	BCD	Kent, Morelos, Hagi
11/03/2021	UEL	A	Slavia Prague	1	1		1	1	O Hategan (ROM)	300	Helander
18/03/2021	UEL	H	Slavia Prague	0	2		0	1	O Grinfeld (ISR)	BCD	
21/03/2021	L	A	Celtic	1	1		1	1	W Collum	BCD	Morelos
04/03/2021	SC	H	Cove Rangers	4	0		4	0	K Clancy	BCD	Defoe, Roofe 2, Patterson
11/04/2021	L	H	Hibernian	2	1		1	0	D Robertson	BCD	Aribo, Kent
18/04/2021	SC	H	Celtic	2	0		2	0	B Madden	BCD	Davis, Kenny og
21/04/2021	L	A	St Johnstone	1	1		0	0	E Anderson	BCD	Wright
25/04/2021	SC	H	St Johnstone	1	1	AET, 2-4p	0	0	A Muir	BCD	Tavernier
02/05/2021	L	H	Celtic	4	1		2	1	N Walsh	BCD	Roofe 2, Morelos, Defoe
12/05/2021	L	A	Livingston	3	0		0	0	D Robertson	BCD	Tavernier pen, Kent, Hagi
15/05/2021	L	H	Aberdeen	4	0		2	0	N Walsh	BCD	Lewis og, Roofe 2, Defoe

Date	Comp	H/A	Opponents	F	A		1	2	3	4	5	6	7	8	9	10
01/08/2020	L	A	Aberdeen	1	0		McGregor	Balogun	Tavernier	Goldson	Barisic	Jack	Kamara	Aribo	Hagi*	Morelos
06/08/2020	UEL	A	Bayer Leverkusen	0	1		McGregor	Helander	Tavernier<	Goldson	Barisic	Jack	Davis+	Aribo	Barker*	Morelos>
09/08/2020	L	H	St Mirren	3	0		McLaughlin	Balogun	Tavernier	Goldson	Barisic>	Jack+	Kamara	Aribo*	Hagi	Morelos&
12/08/2020	L	H	St Johnstone	3	0		McLaughlin	Balogun*	Tavernier	Goldson	Barisic	Jack+	Kamara	Aribo&	Hagi	Morelos<
16/08/2020	L	A	Livingston	0	0		McLaughlin	Helander	Tavernier	Goldson	Barisic	Jack	Kamara	Arfield+	Hagi*	Morelos&
22/08/2020	L	H	Kilmarnock	2	0		McLaughlin	Helander	Tavernier<	Goldson	Barisic	Jack	Davis+	Roofe*	Itten	Barker&
29/08/2020	L	A	Hamilton Accies	2	0		McLaughlin	Helander	Tavernier	Goldson	Barisic	Jack	Davis	Roofe+	Hagi*	Barker
12/09/2020	L	H	Dundee United	4	0		McLaughlin	Helander	Tavernier	Goldson	Barisic&	Jack*	Davis	Roofe	Hagi	Barker+
17/09/2020	UEL	A	Lincoln Red Imps	5	0		McGregor	Edmundson	Tavernier+	Goldson	Barisic	Arfield	Kamara	Roofe*	Hagi	Stewart
20/09/2020	L	A	Hibernian	2	2		McLaughlin	Helander	Tavernier	Goldson	Barisic	Arfield	Kamara+	Davis	Hagi*	Morelos
24/09/2020	UEL	A	Willem II Tilburg	4	0		McGregor	Helander	Tavernier	Goldson	Barisic+	Arfield	Kamara	Davis	Hagi	Morelos&
27/09/2020	L	A	Motherwell	5	1		McGregor	Helander*	Tavernier	Goldson	Bassey	Arfield	Kamara	Davis<	Jones>	Morelos&
01/10/2020	UEL	H	Galatasaray	2	1		McGregor	Helander	Tavernier	Goldson	Barisic	Arfield	Kamara	Davis	Hagi*	Morelos+
04/10/2020	L	H	Ross County	2	0		McLaughlin	Balogan	Tavernier	Goldson	Barisic+	Arfield	Kamara	Jack*	Jones&	Morelos
17/10/2020	L	A	Celtic	2	0		McGregor	Helander	Tavernier	Goldson	Barisic	Arfield&	Kamara	Davis	Barker*	Morelos+
22/10/2020	UEL	A	Standard Liege	2	0		McGregor	Balogan	Tavernier	Goldson	Barisic*	Arfield	Kamara	Jack*	Hagi+	Morelos&
25/10/2020	L	H	Livingston	2	0		McGregor	Helander	Tavernier	Goldson	Bassey	Davis	Aribo&	Jack	Hagi>	Defoe*
29/10/2020	UEL	H	Lech Poznan	1	0		McGregor	Balogan	Tavernier	Goldson	Barisic	Davis	Kamara	Arfield&	Hagi+	Roofe*
01/11/2020	L	A	Kilmarnock	1	0		McGregor	Helander	Tavernier	Goldson	Barisic	Arfield	Aribo*	Jack	Itten	Morelos+
05/11/2020	UEL	A	Benfica	3	3		McGregor	Helander	Tavernier	Goldson	Barisic	Davis	Kamara	Jack	Aribo*	Morelos
08/11/2020	L	H	Hamilton Accies	8	0		McLaughlin	Balogan	Tavernier	Goldson	Barisic+	Arfield<	Roofe	Jack*	Aribo>	Defoe
22/11/2020	L	H	Aberdeen	4	0		McGregor	Balogan	Tavernier	Goldson	Barisic	Arfield	Roofe<	Jack*	Aribo>	Morelos+
26/11/2020	UEL	H	Benfica	2	2		McGregor	Balogan	Tavernier	Goldson	Barisic	Arfield	Roofe	Davis	Kamara	Morelos
29/11/2020	LC	A	Falkirk	4	0		McLaughlin	Bassey	Tavernier>	Goldson	Barisic+	Arfield&	Zungu<	Hagi	Barker*	Defoe
03/12/2020	UEL	H	Standard Liege	3	2		McGregor	Balogan	Tavernier	Goldson	Barisic&	Arfield+	Kamara	Davis	Roofe>	Morelos*
06/12/2020	L	A	Ross County	4	0		McGregor	Balogan	Tavernier	Goldson	Bassey	Aribo*	Kamara<	Davis	Roofe>	Morelos+
10/12/2020	UEL	A	Lech Poznan	2	0		McLaughlin	Balogan<	Patterson*	Goldson	Barisic	Aribo	Kamara	Zungu+	Arfield	Itten>
13/12/2020	L	A	Dundee United	2	1		McGregor	Balogan	Tavernier	Goldson	Barisic	Davis	Kamara+	Roofe	Arfield	Morelos*
16/12/2020	LC	A	St Mirren	2	3		McGregor	Balogan<	Tavernier	Goldson	Bassey*	Aribo	Zungu>	Roofe	Arfield+	Itten&
19/12/2020	L	H	Motherwell	3	1		McGregor	Helander	Tavernier	Goldson	Barisic	Davis	Kamara*	Roofe	Arfield+	Defoe&
23/12/2020	L	A	St Johnstone	3	0		McGregor	Helander	Tavernier	Goldson	Barisic	Davis+	Kamara	Roofe*	Aribo	Hagi>
26/12/2020	L	H	Hibernian	1	0		McGregor	Balogan	Tavernier	Goldson	Barisic	Davis	Kamara	Roofe+	Aribo	Hagi*
30/12/2020	L	A	St Mirren	2	0		McGregor	Helander	Tavernier&	Goldson	Barisic	Davis	Kamara	Roofe*	Aribo	Hagi+
02/01/2021	L	H	Celtic	1	0		McGregor	Balogan	Tavernier	Goldson	Barisic	Davis	Kamara	Roofe*	Aribo>	Morelos+
10/01/2021	L	A	Aberdeen	2	1		McGregor	Balogan	Tavernier	Goldson	Barisic	Davis	Kamara	Hagi*	Aribo	Morelos
17/01/2021	L	A	Motherwell	1	1		McGregor	Balogan	Tavernier	Goldson	Barisic	Davis	Kamara	Hagi*	Aribo	Morelos+
23/01/2021	L	H	Ross County	5	0		McGregor	Helander	Tavernier<	Goldson	Barisic	Davis+	Kamara*	Hagi	Aribo>	Morelos&
27/01/2021	L	A	Hibernian	1	0		McGregor	Helander	Tavernier	Goldson	Barisic	Davis	Kamara	Jack+	Aribo&	Morelos*
03/02/2021	L	H	St Johnstone	1	0		McGregor	Helander	Tavernier	Goldson	Barisic	Davis	Hagi+	Jack	Aribo	Roofe*
06/02/2021	L	A	Hamilton Accies	1	1		McGregor	Helander	Tavernier	Goldson	Barisic	Zungu*	Kamara>	Hagi&	Aribo	Itten+
13/02/2021	L	H	Kilmarnock	1	0		McGregor	Balogan	Tavernier	Goldson	Barisic	Davis	Hagi*	Jack	Aribo	Itten
18/02/2021	UEL	A	Royal Antwerp	4	3		McGregor	Helander	Tavernier*	Goldson	Barisic	Davis	Kamara>	Arfield&	Aribo	Morelos
21/02/2021	L	H	Dundee United	4	1		McGregor	Helander<	Balogan	Goldson	Barisic	Davis+	Hagi&	Jack*	Aribo	Morelos>
25/02/2021	UEL	H	Royal Antwerp	5	2		McGregor	Helander	Balogan*	Goldson	Barisic	Davis>	Kamara	Hagi+	Arobo	Morelos<
03/03/2021	L	A	Livingston	1	0		McGregor	Helander	Patterson*	Goldson	Barisic	Davis	Kamara	Arfield*	Aribo	Morelos
06/03/2021	L	H	St Mirren	3	0		McGregor	Helander*	Patterson	Goldson	Barisic	Davis+	Kamara	Hagi>	Aribo	Morelos&
11/03/2021	UEL	A	Slavia Prague	1	1		McGregor	Helander	Patterson	Goldson	Barisic	Davis	Kamara&	Hagi*	Aribo+	Morelos
18/03/2021	UEL	H	Slavia Prague	0	2		McGregor	Balogan	Patterson+	Goldson	Barisic	Davis<	Kamara	Arfield*	Aribo	Morelos>
21/03/2021	L	A	Celtic	1	1		McGregor	Balogan*	Helander	Goldson	Barisic	Davis	Kamara	Hagi+	Aribo&	Morelos>
04/03/2021	SC	H	Cove Rangers	4	0		McLaughlin	Bassey	Patterson	Goldson	Bassey	Davis*	Kamara	Arfield	Wright	Defoe&
11/04/2021	L	H	Hibernian	2	1		McGregor	Helander	Patterson	Goldson	Barisic	Davis&	Kamara	Roofe>	Aribo*	Morelos+
18/04/2021	SC	H	Celtic	2	0		McGregor	Helander	Patterson	Goldson	Barisic	Davis	Kamara	Arfield	Aribo	Morelos*
21/04/2021	L	A	St Johnstone	1	1		McLaughlin	Simpson	Tavernier*	Goldson	Barisic<	Davis&	Kamara	Wright+	Hagi>	Itten
25/04/2021	SC	H	St Johnstone	1	1	AET, 2-4p	McGregor	Helander&	Tavernier	Goldson	Barisic	Davis>	Kamara	Hagi*	Aribo	Morelos+
02/05/2021	L	H	Celtic	4	1		McGregor	Simpson	Tavernier	Goldson	Barisic*	Davis	Kamara	Roofe&	Aribo	Morelos+
12/05/2021	L	A	Livingston	3	0		McLaughlin	Simpson	Tavernier	Goldson	Hagi<	Davis	Kamara	Roofe+	Aribo>	Morelos*
15/05/2021	L	H	Aberdeen	4	0		McGregor	Simpson	Tavernier	Goldon	Hagi*	Davis	Kamara	Roofe>	Aribo<	Morelos+

11	12	13	14	15	16	17	18	19	20	21	22	23
Kent	Arfield*	Stewart	Murphy	Bassey	Helander	Patterson	Edmundson	Barker	McLaughlin			
Kent&	Hagi*	Arfield+	Jones&	Stewart>	Patterson<	McCrorie	Edmundson	Mayo	Barjonas	Firth		
Kent<	Arfield*	Davis+	Itten&	Bassey>	Barker<	Patterson	Helander	Jones	Firth			
Kent>	Helander*	Roofe+	Arfield&	Davies>	Itten<	Patterson	Bassey	Barker	Firth			
Kent	Roofe*	Barker+	Itten&	Stewart	Edmundson	Patterson	Bassey	Davis	Firth			
Kent>	Arfield*	Kamara+	Stewart&	Hagi>	Patterson<	Murphy	Bassey	Edmundson	McGregor			
Kent	Arfield*	Stewart+	Kamara	Balogun	Patterson	Morelos	Bassey	Jones	McGregor			
Kent	Kamara*	Morelos+>	Bassey&	Arfield>	Patterson	Itten	Stewart	Edmundson	Firth			
Itten&	Patterson*	Morelos+>	Defoe&	Helander	Kent	Davis	McLaughlin					
Kent	Defoe*	Itten+	Bassey	Patterson	Edmundson	Belogan	Jones	Barjonas	McGregor			
Kent*	Jones*	Bassey+	Itten&	Patterson	Defoe	Belogan	McLaughlin					
Kent+	Balogan*	Itten+	Hagi&	Edmundson>	Defoe<	Patterson	Stewart	Barisic	McLaughlin			
Kent	Jack*	Itten+	Jones	Belogan	Defoe	Bassey	McLaughlin					
Kent>	Hagi*	Bassey+	Barker&	Davis>	Defoe	Patterson	Edmundson	Barjonas	McGregor			
Kent	Jack*	Itten+	Aribo&	Balogan	Defoe	Bassey	Hagi	Jones	McLaughlin			
Kent	Bassey*	Aribo+	Roofe&	Barker	Itten	King	Patterson	Henander	Stewart	Davis	Barjonas	McLaughlin
Kent+	Roofe*	Itten+	Arfield&	Jones>	Barisic	Morelos	Balogan	Kamara	McLaughlin			
Kent>	Morelos*	Aribo+	Jack&	Barker>	Itten	Stewart	Patterson	Barjonas	Zungu	Bassey	Helander	McLaughlin
Kent	Davis*	Balogan+	Barker	Kamara	Defoe	Bassey	Hagi	Roofe	McLaughlin			
Kent	Arfield*	Balogan	Barker	Dickson	Barjonas	Bassey	Stewart	Roofe	Patterson	Hagi	Itten	McLaughlin
Kent&	Zungu*	Bassey+	Barker&	Hagi>	Itten<	Morelos	Helander	Kamara	McGregor			
Kent&	Davis*	Defoe+	Kamara&	Itten>	Hagi<	Barker	Helander	Bassey	McLaughlin			
Kent	Hagi	Dickson	King	Itten	Helander	Barker	Stewart	Barjonas	Bassey	McLaughlin		
Itten	Kamara*	Middleton+	Dickson&	King>	Stewart<	Kent	Balogan	Morelos	Firth			
Kent	Aribo*	Zungu+	Bassey&	Itten>	Hagi	Dickson	Patterson	Barjonas	Barker	King	Stewart	McLaughlin
Kent&	Arfield*	Defoe+	Hagi&	Itten>	Zungu<	Barisic	Patterson	Barker	McLaughlin			
Hagi&	Tavernier*	Barker+	Kent&	Morelos>	Bassey<	Dickson	Stewart	Barjonas	Kinnear	McGregor		
Kent&	Itten*	Zungu+	Aribo&	Hagi	Defoe	Helander	Patterson	Bassey	McLaughlin			
Kent	Barisic*	Davis+	Defoe&	Kamara>	Hagi<	Helander	Patterson	Barker	McLaughlin			
Kent>	Aribo*	Hagi+	Itten&	Zungu>	Stewart	Bassey	Patterson	Barker	McLaughlin			
Kent&	Morelos*	Zungu+	Arfield&	Itten>	Balogan	Defoe	Patterson	Bassey	McLaughlin			
Kent	Arfield*&	Morelos+	Zungu&	Itten	Helander	Bassey	Defoe	Barker	McLaughlin			
Morelos	Kent*	Zungu+	Balogan&	Itten	Patterson	Bassey	Defoe	Barker	McLaughlin			
Kent&	Hagi*	Itten+	Zungu&	Barker>	Helander	Bassey	Defoe	Patterson	McLaughlin			
Kent	Zungu*	Itten	Helander	Barker	Patterson	Bassey	Defoe	Stewart	McLaughlin			
Kent&	Itten*	Defoe+	Barker&	Helander	Patterson	Bassey	Zungu	Stewart	McLaughlin			
Kent	Zungu*	Jack+	Defoe&	Itten>	Patterson>	Bassey	Roofe	Balogan	McLaughlin			
Kent	Roofe*	Zungu+	Itten&	Hagi	Patterson	Bassey	Barker	Balogan	McLaughlin			
Kent	Itten*	Kamara+	Zungu&	Wright	Patterson	Bassey	Stewart	Balogan	McLaughlin			
Kent	Jack*	Roofe+	Wright&	Davis>	Patterson	Bassey	Simpson	Balogan	McLaughlin			
Kent+	Wright*	Arfield+	Defoe	Stewart	Patterson	Bassey	Helander	Kamara	McLaughlin			
Roofe+	Balogan*	Kent+	Jack&	Hagi>	Stewart	Itten	Simpson	Wright	McLaughlin			
Kent	Kamara*	Wright+	Arfield&	Defoe>	Simpson<	Itten	King	Stewart	McLaughlin			
Kent&	Patterson*	Arfield+	Wright&	Zungu>	Itten<	Simpson	King	Stewart	Bassey	McLaughlin		
Kent+	itten*	Zungu+	Simpson	Hagi	Defoe	Bassey	Wright	Stewart	McLaughlin			
Kent<	Balogan*	Arfield+	Defoe&	Wright>	Stewart<	Bassey	Itten	Simpson	McLaughlin			
Kent	Arfield*	Roofe+	Zungu&	King	Stewart	Bassey	Itten	Simpson	Wright	McLaughlin		
Kent&	Roofe*	Simpson+	Zungu&	Wright>	Itten<	Bassey	King	Stewart	Hagi	Helander	McLaughlin	
Kent	Patterson*	Arfield+	Wright&	Roofe>	Itten	Bassey	Zungu	Defoe	McLaughlin			
Roofe+	Hagi*	Itten+	Stewart&	Kent	Morelos	Simpson	Aribo	Balogan	McGregor			
Kent	Arfield*	Hagi+	Zungu&	Itten>	Wright	Simpson	Stewart	Bassey	McLaughlin			
Kent	Roofe*	Bassey	Zungu	Tavernier	Wright	Simpson	Hagi	Itten	McLaughlin			
Roofe	Patterson*	Arfield+	Aribo&	Defoe>	Bassey<	Helander	Kent	Morelos	McGregor			
Kent	Wright*	Roofe+	Simpson&	Defoe>	Stewart	Itten	King	McLaughlin				
Kent	Wright*	Hagi+	Defoe&	Itten	Stewart	King	McLaughlin					
Kent&	Defoe*	Itten+	Wright&	King>	Stewart<	McGregor						
Kent&	Arfield*	Defoe+	Stewart&	Wright>	Itten<	King	Firth	McLaughlin				

Surname	First Name	Date of Birth	No	Nat	Pos	Signed	Previous	Notes	Contract	Lge			SC			LC			UEFA			
										A	S	G	A	S	G	A	S	G	A	S	G	Un
Arfield	Scott	01/11/1988	37	CAN / SCO	M	2018	Burnley		End 2021/2	11	17	4	2			2			10	4	3	
Aribo	Joe	21/07/1996	17	ENG / NIG	M	2019	Charlton Athletic		End 2022/3	27	4	7	2			1			7	3	1	1
Balogun	Leon	28/06/1988	26	NIG / GER	D	2020	Wigan Athletic		End 2021/2	15	4					1			7	1		14
Barisic	Borna	10/11/1992	31	CRO	D	2018	NK Osijek		End 2023/4	34	0	1	2			1	1	1	14		3	3
Barjonas	Jamie	24/01/1999	36	SCO	M	2017	Rangers Youths	OL to Ayr Utd Mar-May, Released June 2021 joined Kelty Hearts		0	0											9
Barker	Brandon	04/10/1996		ENG	F	2019	Manchester City	OL to Oxford United Feb-May	End 2021/2	4	6	2				1			1	2		15
Bassey	Calvin	31/12/1999	3	ENG / NIG	D	2020	Leicester City		End 2023/4	2	5		2			2		1		4		34
Breen	Rhys	06/01/2000		SCO	D	2017	Rangers Youths	OL to QOTS Jan-May, OL to Orange County May - Nov 2021	End 2021/2	0	0											0
Budinauckas	Lewis	19/06/2002	64	SCO	GK	2018	Rangers Youths	OL to Civil Service Strollers Oct-Jan	End 2021/2	0	0											0
Butterworth	Zak	24/03/2001	47	SCO	M	2013	Alloa Athletic Youths	OL to Clyde Mar-May, Released July 2021		0	0											0
Cervantes	Aaron	20/03/2002	67	USA	GK	2020	Orange County		End 2021/2	0	0											0
Davis	Steven	01/01/1985	10	NIR	M	2019	Southampton		End 2021/2	29	6		3		1		1	1	11			3
Defoe	Jermain	07/10/1982	9	ENG	F	2020	AFC Bournemouth		End 2021/2	3	12	4	1	1	1	1	1	1		1	1	14
Devine	Adam	25/03/2003	65	SCO	D	2020	Rangers Youths	OL to Partick Th Mar 2021, to Brechin City Mar-May	End 2021/2	0	0											0
Dickson	Ciaran	21/05/2002	55	SCO	M	2018	Rangers Youths	OL to Queen of the South Mar-May	End 2022/3	0	0						1					4
Docherty	Greg	10/09/1996		SCO	M	2018	Hamilton Accies	Transferred to Hull City Aug 2020		0	0											0
Edmundson	George	31/08/1997		ENG	D	2019	Oldham Athletic	OL to Derby County Feb-May	End 2022/3	0	1								1			7
Finlayson	Danny	19/01/2001		SCO / NIR	D	2018	Rangers Youths	OL to St Mirren Oct-May, Released May joined St Mirren		0	0											0
Firth	Andrew	26/09/1996	13	ENG	GK	2019	Barrow		End 2021/2	0	0											7
Goldson	Connor	18/12/1992	6	ENG	D	2018	Brighton		End 2021/2	38	0	4	3			2		1	14		3	0
Hagi	Ianis	22/10/1998	7	ROM / BEL	M	2020	KRC Genk		End 2023/4	23	10	7	1	1		1	1		8	2	1	10
Hastie	Jake	18/03/1998		SCO	F	2019	Motherwell	OL to Motherwell Jul-May	End 2022/3	0	0											0
Helander	Filip	22/04/1993	5	SWE	D	2019	Bologna		End 2022/3	21	1	1	2						7		2	17
Hogarth	Nicky	04/07/2001	48	SCO	GK	2018	Rangers Youths	OL to Cowden Dec-May, Released June 2021 joined Nottingham F		0	0											0
Itten	Cedric	27/12/1996	11	SWI	F	2020	St Gallen		End 2023/4	5	22	4		1		2			2	5	2	16
Jack	Ryan	27/02/1992	8	SCO	M	2017	Aberdeen		End 2022/3	16	3	2							3	3		0
Jones	Jordan	24/10/1994		NIR / ENG	F	2019	Kilmarnock	OL to Sunderland Jan-May	End 2022/3	2	1	1								2		5
Kamara	Glen	28/10/1995	18	FIN	M	2019	Dundee		End 2022/3	28	5	1	3				2		13		1	5
Katic	Nikola	10/10/1996	19	CRO	D	2018	Slaven Belupo Koprivnica		End 2022/3	0	0											0
Kelly	Stephen	13/04/2000		SCO	M	2017	Rangers Youths	OL to Ross County Jul-May	End 2022/3	0	0											0
Kennedy	Kai	28/03/2002	30	SCO	F	2018	Rangers Youths	OL to Inverness CT Oct-Jan, to Raith Rovers Jan-May	End 2022/3	0	0											0
Kent	Ryan	11/11/1996	14	ENG	F	2019	Liverpool		End 2022/3	36	1	10	2			1			11	2	3	4
King	Leon	14/01/2004	61	SCO	D	2020	Rangers Youths		End 2021/2	0	1						1					10
Kinnear	Brian	16/01/2001	49	SCO	GK	2018	Rangers Youths	OL to Annan Athletic Mar-May, Released July 2021		0	0											1
Lyall	Arron	27/09/2003	68	SCO	F	2019	St Peters FC	OL to Inverness CT Mar-May	End 2021/2	0	0											0
Maxwell	James	09/12/2001	51	SCO	D	2018	Falkirk Youths	OL to Queen of the South Sep-May	End 2021/2	0	0											0

Mayo	Lewis	19/03/2000	34	SCO	D	2017	Rangers Youths	OL to Dunfermline Athletic Sep-May	End 2022/3	0	0											1
McCrorie	Ross	18/03/1998		SCO	M	2015	Rangers Youths	OL to Aberdeem Jul-Jan, permanent from Jan		0	0											1
McCrorie	Robbie	18/03/1998		SCO	GK	2015	Rangers Youths	OL to Livingston Jul-May	End 2022/3	0	0											0
McGregor	Allan	31/01/1982	1	SCO	GK	2018	Hull City		End 2021/2	27	0		2			1			13			9
McKee	Chris	07/05/2002	58	NIR	F	2018	Linfield	OL to Brechin City Mar-May	End 2021/2	0	0											0
McLaughlin	Jon	09/09/1987	33	SCO	GK	2020	Sunderland		End 2021/2	11	0		1			1			1			42
McLelland	Kyle	10/02/2002	56	SCO / NIR	D	2018	Rangers Youths	OL to Falkirk Mar-May	End 2021/2	0	0											0
McPake	Josh	31/08/2001		SCO / ROI	F	2013	Hibernian Youths	OL to Morton Sep-Dec, to Harrogate T Jan-May, OL to Morecambe for 2021/2	End 2021/2	0	0											0
Mebude	Dapo	29/07/2001	39	SCO / NIG	F	2018	Rangers Youths	OL to QOTS Jan-May, Released June 2021 joined Watford		0	0											0
Middleton	Glenn	01/01/2000		SCO	M	2018	Norwich City	OL to St Johnstone Jan-May	End 2022/3	0	0						1					0
Miller	Murray	29/01/2002	57	AUS / SCO	M	2017	Motherwell Youths	OL to Elgin City Mar-May		0	0											0
Morelos	Alfredo	21/06/1996	20	COL	F	2017	HJK Helsinki		End 2022/3	26	3	12	2						11	3	5	6
Murphy	Jamie	28/08/1989		SCO	M	2018	Brighton	OL to Hibernian Aug-May, Released June joined Hibernian		0	0											2
O'Connor	Harris	28/03/2002		SCO	D	2018	Kilmarnock Youths	OL to Brechin City Mar-May, Released July 2021		0	0											0
Palmer	Cammy	15/05/2000		SCO / NIR	M	2017	Rangers Youths	OL to Clyde Oct-Jan, Freed Jan joined Linfield		0	0											0
Patterson	Nathan	16/10/2001	16	SCO	D	2020	Rangers Youths		End 2023/4	3	4		2		1				3	3	1	27
Ritchie-Hosler	Kane	13/09/2002		ENG	F	2019	Manchester City Youths	OL to Clyde Mar-May		0	0											0
Roofe	Kemar	06/01/1993	25	JAM / ENG	F	2020	RSC Anderlecht		End 2023/4	18	6	14	1	2	2	1			5	3	2	3
Shiels	Matthew	13/09/2000		SCO	D	2017	Rangers Youths	OL to Clyde Aug-Mar, released Jul 2021 joined Hamilton Accies		0	0											0
Simpson	Jack	18/12/1996	4	ENG	D	2021	AFC Bournemouth		End 2024/5	4	1			1						1		9
Stewart	Greg	17/03/1990	24	SCO	F	2019	Birmingham City	Released June 2021		0	5			1			1		1	1		24
Tavernier	James	31/10/1991	2	ENG	D	2015	Wigan Athletic		End 2023/4	33	0	12	1		1	2		1	10	1	5	1
Thomson	Jack	20/01/2000	46	SCO	M	2017	Rangers Youths	OL to Clyde Jan-May, OL to Orange County May-Nov	End 2021/2	0	0											0
Weston	Tony	17/09/2003	88	ENG	F	2020	Blackpool		End 2022/3	0	0											0
Williamson	Ben	07/08/2001	54	SCO	M	2018	Rangers Youths	OL to Arbroath Jan-May	End 2021/2	0	0											0
Wright	Scott	08/08/1997	23	SCO	F	2021	Aberdeen		End 2024/5	1	8	1	1	1						2		6
Wright	Kieran	01/04/2000		SCO	GK	2016	Garnkirk United BC	OL to Partick Thistle Aug-May	End 2022/3	0	0											0
Young-Coombes	Nathan	15/01/2003		ENG	F	2019	Chelsea Youths	Transferred to Brentford B June 2021		0	0											0
Zungu	Bongani	09/10/1992	15	RSA	M	2020	Amiens SC (OL)	Oct-Jun		1	14					2			1	4		4
Own Goals												5			1						1	
NEW SIGNINGS																						
Lundstram	John	18/02/1994		ENG	D	2021	Sheffield United		End 2023/4													
Ofoborh	Nnamdi	07/11/1999		ENG / NIG	M	2021	AFC Bournemouth		End 2024/5													
Sakala	Fashion	14/03/1997		ZAM	F	2021	KV Oostende		End 2024/5													

PHOTOCARDS

No. 110.

GLASGOW RANGERS F.C.

Left to right, back row :—*J. Dawson, J. Smith, D. Wallace, J. Simpson, J. Drysdale, W. Cheyne, R. Campbell, W. Thornton, G. Jenkins.* Second row :—*Mr. W. Struth (Manager), J. Stewart, R. McPhail, J. Galloway, T. Soutar, T. McKillop, J. Reid, G. McKenzie, J. Fiddis, J. Turnbull, R. McDonald, A. Dixon (Trainer).* Front row :—*J. Kennedy, D. Gray, D. McLatchie, A. Venters, T. Hart, D. Meiklejohn (Capt.), R. Main, G. Brown, D. Kinnear, A. Winning, A. McAulay.*

Expanding de Luxe Albums for Ardath Photocards on sale at Tobacconists Price 6d

ARDATH TOBACCO CO: LTD: Manufacturers of STATE EXPRESS and ARDATH CIGARETTES

D

THE GOALIES

Goalkeepers Used in League Matches, 1972-2020

Players shown in the season of their first appearance only

1970/1	Peter McCloy
	Gerhard Neef
1973/4	Stewart Kennedy
	Donald Hunter
1979/0	George Young
1980/1	Jim Stewart
1982/3	Andy Bruce
1983/4	Nicky Walker
1986/7	Chris Woods
1989/0	Bonni Ginzburg
1991/2	Andy Goram
1992/3	Ally Maxwell
1993/4	Colin Scott
1994/5	Billy Thomson
1995/6	Theo Snelders
1996/7	Andy Dibble
1997/8	Antii Niemi
1998/9	Lionel Charbonnier
	Stefan Klos
1999/0	Mark Brown
	Thomas Myrhe
2000/1	Jesper Christiansen
2001/2	Allan McGregor
2004/5	Ronald Wattereus
2006/7	Lionel Letizi
2007/8	Neil Alexander
2013/4	Cammy Bell
	Steve Simonsen
	Scott Gallacher
2014/5	Lee Robinson
2015/6	Wes Foderingham
2016/7	Jak Alnwick
2018/9	Allan McGregor (2nd spell)

Gerry Neef

Andy Bruce

Lionel Letizi

Ross County FC 2020/21 The Staggies

Founded	1929
Ground	Victoria Park
Postcode	IN15 9QZ
Tel	01349 860860
Capacity	6541
Closest Railway Station	Dingwall
Record Attendance	6110 v Celtic, Lge, 18/8/2012
Record Win	11-0 v St Cuthbert Wanderers, SC, 1/12/1993
Record Defeat	0-7 v Kilmarnock, SC, 17/2/1962
Most League Goals in a Season	24 Andy Barrowman, 2007/8
Colours 2020/21 Top	Navy Blue / Dark Blue
Shorts	Navy Blue
Sponsor	Ross-shire Engineering
Manufacturer	Macron
Change Colours 2020/21 Top	Columbia Blue and White
Shorts	White
Nicknames	Staggies
Web	www.rosscountyfootballclub.co.uk
Match Programme 2020/21	None issued

Chief Executive Officer: Steven Ferguson
Manager: Stuart Kettlewell, then John Hughes, then Malky Mackay
Assistant Manager: Don Cowie
First Team Coach: Stuart Taylor
Goalkeeping Coach: Scott Thomson
Performance and Recruitment Analysis: Enda Barron
Head of Physiotherapy: Willie Nolan
Sports Scientists: Liam Jukes
Secretary: Fiona McBean
Head of Youth Academy: Richard Hastings
Head of Academy Operations: Jim Kelly
Managing Director: Roderick MacGregor
Directors: John W McGregor, Ronald Fraser, Michael Kydd, James Macdonald, Leo Daly, Peter Swanson, Alistair Kelly

When things were looking bleak for County in mid season they turned to that old war-horse John Hughes to dig them out of trouble. He added a few new signings and managed to get more out of the players already there – and County ended up clear of the relegation and play off positions. Realistically, for a club of their size, that is as much as can be expected and anything better than that would be a huge bonus.

Hughes's managerial skills were very evident in the vital five matches that took place after the split. County won three and drew one of them to ensure their survival. It was certainly a massive improvement form a bleak spell at the tail end of 2020 when the club went five straight League games without scoring.

Scotland's obsession with the Old Firm means that County's 2-0 win over Celtic in the League Cup is the result that most people will remember. Winning 2-0 at Parkhead was unexpected but County deserved their success on the day. It wasn't all down to Celtic being in a sorry state. The Scottish Cup was somewhat less successful with a home defeat from neighbours Inverness – but it did leave County free to concentrate on the more pressing business of staying in the Premiership.

STAR MAN
Hughes turned to a player he was familiar with to help get the goals to keep County up. Jordan White had spent the first half of the season with Motherwell without scoring. His total with County in the second half of the campaign may have been just four but they were all vital goals. His presence and ability to stretch defences also created chances for others.

PROSPECTS 2021/2
As always County will start amongst the favourites to go down. It is highly likely that, as usual, they will do enough to avoid the drop.

ROSS COUNTY 1979/80

Date	Comp	H/A	Opponents	F	A		HT		Referee	Crowd	Scorers
03/08/2020	L	H	Motherwell	1	0		1	0	N Walsh	BCD	Stewart pen
08/08/2020	L	A	Hamilton Accies	1	0		0	0	B Madden	BCD	Mckay
12/08/2020	L	H	Kilmarnock	2	2		1	0	G Duncan	BCD	Draper, Stewart pen
15/08/2020	L	H	Dundee United	1	2		1	1	C Napier	BCD	Donaldson
22/08/2020	L	A	St Mirren	1	1		0	1	M Roncone	BCD	Sheron og
29/08/2020	L	A	Livingston	0	1		0	0	J Beaton	BCD	
12/09/2020	L	H	Celtic	0	5		0	2	A Dallas	300	
19/09/2020	L	A	St Johnstone	1	0		1	0	D Munro	BCD	Vigurs
27/02/2020	L	H	Aberdeen	0	3		0	1	W Collum	BCD	
04/10/2020	L	A	Rangers	0	2		0	1	G Aitken	BCD	
07/10/2020	LC	A	Montrose	3	3	5-4p	2	0	G Duncan	BCD	Shaw, Mackay, Charles-Cook
13/10/2020	LC	H	Arbroath	2	1		0	0	S McLean	BCD	Stewart 2 (1 pen)
17/10/2020	L	H	Hibernian	0	0		0	0	N Walsh	BCD	
24/10/2020	L	A	Motherwell	0	4		0	1	C Napier	BCD	
31/10/2020	L	A	Dundee United	1	2		0	1	S Kirkland	BCD	Shaw
06/11/2020	L	H	Livingston	1	1		1	0	K Clancy	300	Shaw
10/11/2020	LC	A	Elgin City	4	1		2	0	G Duncan	BCD	Shaw, Iacovitti, Paton, Lakin
14/11/2020	LC	H	Stirling Albion	3	0		1	0	A Muir	300	Shaw, Stewart (pen), Charles-Cook
21/11/2020	L	A	Kilmarnock	1	3		1	1	C Steven	BCD	Grivosti
29/11/2020	LC	A	Celtic	2	0		1	0	K Clancy	BCD	Stewart, Iacoivitti
06/12/2020	L	H	Rangers	0	4		0	1	J Beaton	300	
12/12/2020	L	A	Aberdeen	0	2		0	1	N Walsh	BCD	
16/12/2020	LC	A	Livingston	0	2		0	2	S McLean	BCD	
19/12/2020	L	H	Hamilton Accies	0	2		0	1	W Collum	300	
22/12/2020	L	A	Celtic	0	2		0	1	E Anderson	BCD	
26/12/2020	L	H	St Mirren	0	2		0	0	C Steven	BCD	
30/12/2020	L	A	Hibernian	2	0		1	0	D Robertson	BCD	Paton, Shaw
02/01/2021	L	H	St Johnstone	1	1		1	1	W Collum	BCD	Draper
10/01/2021	L	A	Livingston	1	3		1	1	A Muir	BCD	Lakin
16/01/2021	L	H	Aberdeen	4	1		2	1	B Madden	BCD	Shaw 2, Lakin, Hylton
23/01/2021	L	A	Rangers	0	5		0	3	E Anderson	BCD	
27/01/2021	L	H	Motherwell	1	2		1	0	N Walsh	BCD	Shaw
03/02/2021	L	A	Hamilton Accies	2	1		0	1	W Collum	BCD	White, McKay
06/02/2021	L	H	Dundee United	0	2		0	0	G Irvine	BCD	
21/02/2021	L	H	Celtic	1	0		0	0	D Munro	BCD	White
27/02/2021	L	A	St Mirren	0	1		0	0	G Aitken	BCD	
06/03/2021	L	H	Kilmarnock	3	2		1	1	E Anderson	BCD	McKay 2, Hjelde
13/03/2021	L	H	Hibernian	1	2		0	0	J Beaton	BCD	McKay
20/03/2021	L	A	St Johnstone	0	1		0	0	C Napier	BCD	
02/04/2021	SC	H	Inverness CT	1	3		1	1	N Walsh	BCD	McKay
10/04/2021	L	A	Kilmarnock	2	2		1	2	W Collum	BCD	Gardyne, Iacovitti
21/04/2021	L	H	St Mirren	1	3		1	0	B Madden	BCD	White
01/05/2021	L	A	Dundee United	2	0		2	0	K Clancy	BCD	White, Iacovitti
12/05/2021	L	H	Hamilton Accies	2	1		1	1	W Collum	BCD	Spittal, Lakin
16/05/2021	L	A	Motherwell	2	1		0	1	S McLean	BCD	Vigurs, Gardyne

Surname	First Name	Date of Birth	No	Nat	Pos	Signed	Previous	Notes	Contract	Lge A	Lge S	Lge G	SC A	SC S	SC G	LC A	LC S	LC G	Un
Andreu	Tony	22/05/1988	28	FRA	M	2021	St Mirren	Released June 2021	[redacted]	4	2								5
Chalmers	Joe	03/01/1994	23	SCO	M	2019	Inverness CT	Transferred to Ayr Utd Sep 2020	[redacted]	0	0								0
Charles-Cook	Regan	14/02/1997	17	ENG / JAM	F	2020	Gillingham		End 2021/2	9	17			1		5		2	5
Donaldson	Coll	09/04/1995	25	SCO	D	2020	Inverness CT		End 2021/2	26	2	1	1			4	1		5
Doohan	Ross	29/03/1998	21	SCO	GK	2020	Celtic (OL)	Aug-Jan	[redacted]	5	0								17
Draper	Ross	20/10/1988	6	ENG	M	2017	Inverness CT	Released June 2021 joined Cove Rangers	[redacted]	13	9	2					1		8
Erwin	Lee	19/05/1994	10	SCO	F	2019	Tractor FC	Transferred to St Mirren Sep 2020	[redacted]	2	2								0
Fontaine	Liam	07/01/1986	4	ENG	D	2018	Hibernian	Freed Oct 2020 joined Dundee	[redacted]	0	0								0
Gardyne	Michael	23/01/1986	7	SCO	F	2015	Dundee United	Released June 2021 joined Inverness CT	[redacted]	21	10	2	1			1	2		6
Grivosti	Tom	15/06/1999	12	ENG	D	2018	Ross County Youths		End 2021/2	3	2	1				2			3
Hilton	Joe	11/10/1999	21	ENG	GK	2021	Blackburn Rovers (OL)	Jan-May	[redacted]	0	0								14
Hjelde	Leo Fuhr	26/08/2003	4	NOR	D	2021	Celtic (OL)	Jan-May	[redacted]	10	1	1	1						0
Hylton	Jermaine	28/06/1993	14	ENG	F	2020	Motherwell	Released June 2021 joined Newport County	[redacted]	7	11	1		1		4			10
Iacovitti	Alex	02/09/1997	16	SCO	D	2020	Oldham Athletic		End 2021/2	34	2	2				5	1	2	0
Kelly	Stephen	13/04/2000	18	SCO	M	2020	Rangers (OL)	Jul-May	[redacted]	16	9		1			3			11
Laidlaw	Ross	12/07/1992	1	SCO	GK	2019	Hibernian		End 2022/3	33	0		1			6			5
Lakin	Charlie	08/05/1999	19	ENG	M	2020	Birmingham City (OL)	Oct-May	[redacted]	14	5	3	1			2	2	1	5
MacKenzie	Craig	15/06/2003	48	SCO	M	2020	Ross County Youths	Freed Oct 2020 joined Strathspey Thistle	[redacted]	0	0								0
MacKinnon	Adam	30/04/2003	47	SCO	F	2017	Back FC	OL to Brora Rangers Nov-May	End 2021/2	0	0						1		7
Maouche	Mohamed	10/01/1993	32	FRA / ALG	M	2021	Oldham Athletic	Released June 2021	[redacted]	0	0								2
Mckay	Billy	22/10/1988	9	NIR	F	2017	Wigan Athletic	Released June 2021 joined Inverness CT	[redacted]	14	14	5	1		1	4	2	1	7
Morris	Callum	03/02/2001	5	ROI / NIR	D	2018	Dunfermline Athletic	Released June 2021	[redacted]	12	0					4	1		8
Mullin	Josh	23/09/1992	14	SCO	M	2018	Livingston	Released Oct joined Livingston	[redacted]	1	4								2
Munro	Ross	01/04/2000	31	SCO	GK	2018	Ross County Youths	OL to Cowdenbeath Dec, to Annan Ath Apr-May	End 2021/2	0	0								8
Naismith	Jason	25/06/1994	23	SCO	D	2020	Peterborough United	Released June 2021 joined Kilmarnock	[redacted]	17	0		1						0
O'Connor	Michael	31/07/1998		ROI / NIR	F	2020	Waterford	Released Jan joined Shelbourne	[redacted]	0	0						1		8
Paton	Harry	23/05/1998	24	CAN	M	2018	Hearts		End 2021/2	25	10	1				4	1	1	5
Randall	Connor	21/10/1995	2	ENG	D	2020	FK Arda Kardzhali			13	2					1	1		2
Reid	Josh	03/05/2002	43	SCO	D	2018	Ross County Youths	Transferred to Coventry City Jan 2021	[redacted]	17	3					3	1		2
Ross	Logan	12/05/2004	41	SCO	GK	2020	Ross County Youths	OL to Lossiemouth Nov-Jan		0	0								1
Shaw	Oli	12/09/1998	8	SCO	F	2020	Hibernian		End 2021/2	12	13	6	1			3	2	3	10
Spittal	Blair	19/12/1995	20	SCO	M	2019	Partick Thistle	OL to Partick Thistle Oct-Jan	End 2021/2	7	2	1							1
Stewart	Ross	01/09/1996	27	SCO	F	2018	St Mirren	Transferred to Sunderland Jan 2021	[redacted]	19	0	2				4	1	4	1
Tillson	Jordan	05/03/1993	22	ENG	M	2020	Exeter City			20	12					2	2		9
Tremarco	Carl	11/10/1985	3	ENG	D	2020	Inverness CT	Released June 2021, Retired	[redacted]	8	4					3			10
Vigurs	Iain	07/05/1988	11	SCO	M	2018	Inverness CT	Released June 2021 joined Cove Rangers	[redacted]	28	2	2	1			4			4
Watson	Keith	14/11/1989	15	SCO	D	2018	St Johnstone		End 2021/2	17	6		1			2			14
White	Jordan	04/02/1992	26	SCO	F	2021	Motherwell		End 2021/2	11	1	4		1					0
Williamson	Ben	17/03/2003	46	SCO	D	2020	Ross County Youths		End 2021/2	0	0						2		12
Wright	Matthew	16/10/2002	44	SCO	F	2020	Ross County Youths		End 2021/2	0	1						1		15
												1							
NEW SIGNINGS																			
Callachan	Ross	04/09/1993		SCO	M	2021	Hamilton Accies		End 2022/3										
Robertson	Alex	17/04/2003		ENG / AUS	M	2021	Manchester City (OL)	Jul-Jun	End 2021/2										
Samuel	Dominic	01/04/1994		ENG / A&B	F	2021	Gillingham		End 2022/3										
Vokins	Jake	17/03/2000		ENG	D	2021	Southampton (OL)	Jul-Jun	End 2021/2										
MacLeman	Ryan	01/01/2004		SCO	M	2021	Ross County Youths		End 2022/3										

RCFC left to right v Inverness Caledonian at Telford Street, 1966. RCFC 7 I.Caley 3
Back Row :Angus Fraser,Alex Sutherland,Derri Garrow,Hamish Faser,Nick McCallum,Jock MacKay,Sandy Wallace
Front:Denis Laughton, Denis Pryde,Calum Grant,Dusty Vass.
ICFC
Back :
John Jolly,Alla Patience,Rod Mackie,Charlie Nairne,Denis Mcintosh,David Lazenby.
Front : Sany Anderson,Roshie Fraser,Wilie McDougall,Rod Clyne, Ian Taylor

Date	Comp	H/A	Opponents	F	A		1	2	3	4	5	6	7	8	9
03/08/2020	L	H	Motherwell	1	0		Laidlaw	Randall	Donaldson	Iacovitti	Reid	Vigurs	Tillson&	Paton*	McKay>
08/08/2020	L	A	Hamilton Accies	1	0		Laidlaw	Randall	Donaldson	Iacovitti	Reid	Vigurs	Tillson+	Paton>	McKay&
12/08/2020	L	H	Kilmarnock	2	2		Laidlaw	Randall	Donaldson	Iacovitti	Reid	Vigurs	Gardyne&	Draper<	Mullin+
15/08/2020	L	H	Dundee United	1	2		Laidlaw	Randall	Donaldson	Iacovitti	Reid>	Vigurs	Gardyne*	Draper&	McKay<
22/08/2020	L	A	St Mirren	1	1		Laidlaw	Randall<	Donaldson*	Iacovitti	Reid&	Vigurs>	Gardyne	Draper	McKay
29/08/2020	L	A	Livingston	0	1		Laidlaw	Randall+	Donaldson	Iacovitti	Tremarco	Vigurs>	Gardyne<	Draper&	McKay*
12/09/2020	L	H	Celtic	0	5		Laidlaw	Randall	Donaldson	Iacovitti	Reid	Vigurs>	Gardyne&	Paton	McKay*
19/09/2020	L	A	St Johnstone	1	0		Laidlaw	Randall*	Donaldson	Iacovitti	Reid	Vigurs	Gardyne+	Paton&	Shaw
27/02/2020	L	H	Aberdeen	0	3		Laidlaw	Watson	Donaldson	Iacovitti	Reid	Vigurs	Gardyne&	Paton	Shaw+
04/10/2020	L	A	Rangers	0	2		Laidlaw	Morrison	Donaldson	Iacovitti	Reid	Draper*	Gardyne+	Paton	Charles-Cook&
07/10/2020	LC	A	Montrose	3	3	5-4p	Laidlaw	Watson	Tremarco	Iacoviiti	Morris	Vigurs&	Shaw+	Paton	Charles-Cook
13/10/2020	LC	H	Arbroath	2	1		Laidlaw	Randall	Donaldson	Tremarco	Morris*	Lakin	Tillison+	Stewart	Charles-Cook
17/10/2020	L	H	Hibernian	0	0		Doohan	Randall	Donaldson*	Iacovitti	Watson	Vigurs	Gardyne&	Paton>	Charles-Cook
24/10/2020	L	A	Motherwell	0	4		Doohan	Reid	Donaldson	Iacovitti	Grivosti&	Vigurs>	Gardyne*	Paton+	Charles-Cook
31/10/2020	L	A	Dundee United	1	2		Doohan	Randall*	Donaldson	Iacovitti	Reid	Vigurs+	Kelly	McKay>	Charles-Cook&
06/11/2020	L	H	Livingston	1	1		Doohan	Grivosti	Donaldson	Iacovitti	Reid	Gardyne*	Kelly	Paton	Shaw
10/11/2020	LC	A	Elgin City	4	1		Laidlaw	Tremarco*	Donaldson	Iacovitti	Grivosti>	Hylton	Kelly&	Paton<	Charles-Cook
14/11/2020	LC	H	Stirling Albion	3	0		Laidlaw	Reid	Donaldson+	Iacovitti&	Grivosti	Hylton	Tillison	Vigurs	Charles-Cook>
21/11/2020	L	A	Kilmarnock	1	3		Doohan	Reid	Donaldson	Iacovitti	Grivosti+	Kelly	Tillison*	Paton&	Charles-Cook
29/11/2020	LC	A	Celtic	2	0		Laidlaw	Reid+	Donaldson	Iacovitti	Morris	Kelly	Watson	Paton&	Vigurs
06/12/2020	L	H	Rangers	0	4		Laidlaw	Reid+	Donaldson	Iacoviiti	Morris	Gardyne&	Watson*	Paton	Vigurs
12/12/2020	L	A	Aberdeen	0	2		Laidlaw	Randall+	Donaldson	Iacovitti*	Morris	Kelly	Vigurs	Paton>	Charles-Cook
16/12/2020	LC	A	Livingston	0	2		Laidlaw	Reid	Gardyne	Iacovitti	Morris	Kelly+	Vigurs	Paton&	Charles-Cook*
19/12/2020	L	H	Hamilton Accies	0	2		Laidlaw	Reid	Watson	Iacovitti	Morris	Gardyne	Vigurs	Tillson*	Shaw
22/12/2020	L	A	Celtic	0	2		Laidlaw	Reid	Watson	Iacovitti	Morris	Gardyne+	Vigurs>	Paton	Draper&
26/12/2020	L	H	St Mirren	0	2		Laidlaw	Reid	Watson&	Iacovitti	Morris	Hylton+	Vigurs*	Paton	Draper
30/12/2020	L	A	Hibernian	2	0		Laidlaw	Tremarco*	Watson	Iacovitti	Donaldson	Hylton	Vigurs*	Paton	Tillson
02/01/2021	L	H	St Johnstone	1	1		Laidlaw	Naismith	Watson	Draper	Donaldson	Hylton&	Vigurs*	Paton+	Lakin
10/01/2021	L	A	Livingston	1	3		Laidlaw	Naismith	Watson	Iacovitti	Donaldson	Tillson+	Draper	Paton*	Lakin>
16/01/2021	L	H	Aberdeen	4	1		Laidlaw	Naismith	Morris	Iacovitti	Randall	Hylton	Vigurs	Paton	Lakin
23/01/2021	L	A	Rangers	0	5		Laidlaw	Naismith	Morris	Iacovitti	Randall*	Hjelde	Vigurs>	Paton+	Lakin&
27/01/2021	L	H	Motherwell	1	2		Laidlaw	Naismith	Morris	Iacovitti	Hylton	Hjelde	Vigurs&	Paton	Charles-Cook+
03/02/2021	L	A	Hamilton Accies	2	1		Laidlaw	Naismith	Morris	Iacovitti&	Hylton>	Hjelde	Vigurs*	Paton+	Andreu
06/02/2021	L	H	Dundee United	0	2		Laidlaw	Naismith	Morris	Tremarco&	Hylton+	Hjelde	Andreu	Paton*	McKay&
21/02/2021	L	H	Celtic	1	0		Laidlaw	Naismith	Morris*	Iacovitti	Tremarco	Gardyne>	Andreu<	Spittal+	Lakin
27/02/2021	L	A	St Mirren	0	1		Laidlaw	Naismith	Watson	Gardyne&	Tremarco+	Hjelde	Andreu*	Spittal>	Lakin<
06/03/2021	L	H	Kilmarnock	3	2		Laidlaw	Naismith	Donaldson	Iacovitti	Tremarco*	Tillson>	Watson	Spittal+	Lakin&
13/03/2021	L	H	Hibernian	1	2		Laidlaw	Naismith	Donaldson>	Iacovitti<	Watson	Tillson+	Hjelde	Spittal*	Lakin&
20/03/2021	L	A	St Johnstone	0	1		Laidlaw	Naismith	Donaldson>	Iacovitti	Watson	Tillson	Hjelde	Paton+	Lakin&
02/04/2021	SC	H	Inverness CT	1	3		Laidlaw	Naismith	Donaldson	Gardyne+	Watson	Kelly	Hjelde	Vigurs*	Lakin
10/04/2021	L	A	Kilmarnock	2	2		Laidlaw	Naismith	Tremarco	Iacovitti	Watson	Tillson*	Gardyne&	Vigurs+	Draper
21/04/2021	L	H	St Mirren	1	3		Laidlaw	Naismith>	Vigurs*	Iacovitti	Watson	Tillson	Hjelde	Gardyne+	Draper<
01/05/2021	L	A	Dundee United	2	0		Laidlaw	Naismith	Donaldson	Iacovitti	Vigurs	Tillson	Hjelde	Gardyne+	Spittal*
12/05/2021	L	H	Hamilton Accies	2	1		Laidlaw	Naismith	Donaldson	Iacovitti*	Vigurs	Tillson	Hjelde+	Gardyne>	Spittal&
16/05/2021	L	A	Motherwell	2	1		Laidlaw	Naismith	Donaldson	Tremarco*	Watson	Tillson	Vigurs	Gardyne+	Spittal

THE GOALIES

Goalkeepers Used in League Matches, 1994-2020

Players shown in the season of their first appearance only

1994/5	Steve Hutchison
	Don McMillan
1996/7	Dave Cormack
	Kevin Morgan
1997/8	Nicky Walker
1998/9	Colin Meldrum
	David Ross
	Garry Stewart
	Craig Tully
1999/0	Gary Hamilton
	Barry Thompson
2001/2	Tony Bullock
	Ramiro Gonzalez
	Les Fridge
2003/4	Colin Stewart
	Graham Smith
2004/5	Stuart Garden
2005/6	Ian McCaldon
	Joe Malin
2006/7	Craig Samson
	Matteo Tomei
2007/8	Tony Bullock (2nd spell)
	Alan Creer
2008/9	Derek Souter
2009/0	Michael McGovern
2011/2	Michael Fraser
2012/3	Mark Brown
2014/5	Antonio Reguero
2015/6	Scott Fox
	Gary Woods
2016/7	Aaron McCarey
2019/0	Ross Laidlaw
	Nathan Baxter

10	11	12	13	14	15	16	17	18	19	20
Erwin+	Stewart	Gardyne*	Charles-Cook+	Shaw&	Draper>	Mullin	Kelly	Watson	Morris	Doohan
Erwin*	Stewart	Mullin*	Gardyne+	Charles-Cook&	Draper>	Shaw	Kelly	Watson	Morris	Doohan
Charles-Cook*	Stewart>	Mckay*	Erwin+	Paton&	Shaw>	Tillson<	Kelly	Watson	Morris	Doohan
Paton+	Stewart	Erwin*	Tillson+	Mullin&	Tremarco>	Charles-Cook<	Kelly	Watson	Shaw	Doohan
Paton+	Stewart	Watson*	Charles-Cook+	Tremarco&	Kelly>	Mullin<	Spitall	Tillison	Shaw	Doohan
Watson	Stewart	Reid*	Mullin+	Tillson&	Shaw>	Kelly<	Paton	Charles-Cook	Morris	Doohan
Tillison+	Stewart	Shaw*	Draper+	Charles-Cook&	Kelly>	Wright	McKinnon	Watson	Morris	Munro
Tillison	Stewart	Watson*	Charles-Cook+	Kelly&	Tremarco	Wright	McKinnon	Mullin	Morris	Doohan
Tillison*	Stewart	Charles-Cook*	Kelly+	Mackay&	Tremarco	Wright	McKinnon	O'Connor	Morris	Doohan
Tillison	Stewart	Hylton*	McKay+	Shaw&	Tremarco	Watson	McKinnon	O'Connor	Grivosti	Doohan
McKay	Hylton*	Lakin*	Stewart+	Gardyne&	Tillison	Williamson	McKinnon	O'Connor	Grivosti	Ross
McKay>	Hylton&	Iacovitti*	Paton+	Gardyne&	Shaw>	Vigurs	Watson	O'Connor	Grivosti	Munro
Lakin+	Stewart	Grivosti*	Kelly+	McKay&	Tillison>	Shaw	Tremarco	O'Connor	Hylton	Laidlaw
Lakin	Stewart	McKay*	Kelly+	Hylton&	Tillison>	Shaw	Tremarco	O'Connor	Williamson	Laidlaw
Lakin	Stewart	Grivosti*	Paton+	Gardyne&	Shaw>	Tillison	Tremarco	O'Connor	Hylton	Laidlaw
Lakin+	Stewart	Charles-Cook*	Tillson+	Hylton	Vigurs	B McKay	Tremarco	O'Connor	Williamson	Laidlaw
McKay	Shaw+	Reid*	Lakin+	Tillson&	Williamson>	O'Connor<	Wright	Vigurs	Stewart	Munro
Stewart<	Shaw*	Mckay*	Morris+	Williamson&	Wright>	Mackinnon<	Lakin	Kelly	Paton	Munro
Lakin	Stewart	McKay*	Watson+	Hylton&	Williamson	Morris	Wright	Laidlaw		
Lakin*	Stewart	Tillson*	Randall+	McKay&	Williamson	Gardyne	Wright	Hylton	Munro	
Tillson>	Stewart	Randall*	Charles-Cook+	Hylton&	Wright>	Williamson	Mackay	Doohan		
Tillson&	Stewart	Reid*	McKay+	Gardyne&	Hylton>	Williamson	Wright	Doohan		
McKay	Stewart	Donaldson*	Draper+	Shaw&	Hylton	Watson	Wright	Doohan	Tremarco	Tillson
McKay+	Stewart	Paton*	Wright+	Kelly	Hylton	Tremarco	Draper	Doohan	Williamson	Donaldson
Kelly	Stewart*	Shaw*	Hylton+	Tillson&	McKay>	Tremarco	Wright	Donaldson	Williamson	Munro
Kelly	Shaw	Tremarco*>	Tillson+	McKay&	Donaldson>	Williamson	Wright	Doohan		
Kelly	Shaw	Randall*	Wright	McKay	Williamson	Gardyne	Lakin	Doohan		
Kelly	Shaw>	Gardyne*	Reid+	Tillson&	Mckay>	Williamson	Wright	MacKinnon	Randall	Doohan
Kelly&	Shaw	Charles-Cook*	McKay+	Andreu&	Vigurs>	Randall	Hylton	Doohan	Gardyne	Reid
Charles-Cook*	Shaw+	Draper*	McKay+	Andreu	Watson	Gardyne	Tillison	Kelly	Reid	Munro
Draper<	Shaw	Watson*	Hylton+	Charles-Cook&	Andreu>	Tillson<	Gardyne	Donaldson	Mackay	Munro
Draper<	Shaw*	Gardyne*	Spittal+	McKay&	Andreu	Tillson	Kelly	Lakin	Hilton	Watson
Kelly	Shaw<	White*	McKay+	Tremarco&	Lakin>	Gardyne<	Watson	Tillison	Hilton	Draper
Kelly>	White	Lakin*	Shaw+	Gardyne&	Draper>	Iacovitti>	Watson	Tillison	Hilton	Charles-Cook
Kelly&	White	Watson*	Tillson+	Paton&	Draper>	Charles-Cook<	McKay	Shaw	Hilton	Hylton
Kelly	White	Donaldson*	Iacovviti+	Shaw&	Tillson>	Paton<	McKay	Draper	Hilton	Hylton
McKay<	White	Hjelde*	Paton+	Shaw&	Kelly>	Draper<	Gardyne	Charles-Cook	Hilton	Hylton
McKay	White	Hylton*	Paton+	Draper&	Gardyne>	Shaw<	Kelly	Charles-Cook	Hilton	Vigurs
McKay*	White	Vigurs*	Gardyne+	Shaw&	Hylton>	Wright	Kelly	Charles-Cook	Hilton	Draper
McKay	Shaw&	Hylton*	Charles-Cook+	White&	Tillson	McKinnon	Maouche	Paton	Hilton	Draper
McKay>	White	Paton*	Kelly+	Charles-Cook&	Hylton>	Shaw	Donaldson	Lakin	Hilton	Wright
McKay&	White	Hylton*	Charles-Cook+	Paton&	Spittal>	Shaw<	Donaldson	Lakin	Hilton	Kelly
Kelly	White	Charles-Cook*	Lakin+	Paton	Watson	Shaw	Draper	Hylton	Hilton	McKay
Kelly	White	Watson*	Lakin+	Paton&	Charles-Cook>	Shaw	Draper	Hylton	Hilton	Andreu
Kelly	White	Lakin*	Charles-Cook+	Paton	Maouche	Shaw	Draper	Wright	Hilton	Andreu

Scott Fox

Tony Bullock

St Johnstone FC 2020/21 The Sainties

Founded	1884
Ground	McDiarmid Park
Postcode	PH1 2SJ
Tel	01738 459096
Capacity	10696
Closest Railway Station	Perth
Record Attendance	29972 v Dundee, SC, 10/2/1951
Ground Record	10545 v Dundee, Lge, 23/5/99
Record Win	9-0 v Albion Rovers, LC, 9/3/1946
Record Defeat	1-10 v Third Lanark, SC, 24/1/1903
Most League Goals in a Season	36 Jimmy Benson, 1931/2
Colours 2020/21 Top	Blue
Shorts	White
Sponsor	Binn Group
Manufacturer	Macron
Change Colours 2015/146Top	Yellow
Shorts	Blue
Nicknames	Saints, Sainties
Web	www.perthstjohnstonefc.co.uk
Match Programme 2020/21	Curtis Sport

Chair-
man:
Steve
Brown
Vice

Chairman: Charlie Fraser
Directors: Stan Harris, Roddy Grant, Peter Loudon, Alan Storrar
Business Development Executive: Paul Hebbourn
SLO and Disabled Access: Beverley Mayer
Operations Supervisor: Adam Omeish
Head Groundsman: Chris Smith
Buyer and Auditor: Dougie Tait
Manager: Callum Davidson
Coaches: Alec Cleland, Steven MacLean
Goalkeeping Coach Paul Mathers
Head of Football Operations: Scott Boyd
Head of Youth Development: Alastair Stevenson
Club Doctor: Peter Davies
Physiotherapist: Melanie Stewart
Sports Scientist Alex Headrick
Kitman: Graeme Robertson

The fact that St Johnstone FC have been awarded the Freedom of the City of Perth for their achievements in 2020/1 says it all. Manager Callum Davidson, in his first season in charge, led them to victory in both domestic Cups. Achieved with a small squad, Saints success is testimony to the prudent and pragmatic approach taken by the Perth club over many years and shows what can be achieved through stability, realism and hard work. They were one of only two teams to get the better of Rangers, beating them on penalties in the Scottish Cup at Ibrox.

Both Cup Finals were won by single goals, both scored by Shaun Rooney. He wasn't a regular in the team during the first half of the season. If Millwall hadn't recalled McNamara at the turn of the year, Rooney might not have been involved in either game. Now he has emerged as a name that will be illuminated for ever in Saints' history. The sad thing was that the club's fans were unable to attend either Final. In turn that meant that Saints were unable to fully capitalise on the financial opportunities normally presented by such success. Hopefully the Perth public will get behind them in 2021/2 as they return to European football.

STAR MAN
Saints success was a real team effort so it is difficult to single out any individual. However, the talents of young Ali McCann shone bright and he clearly has the potential for a big future at the highest levels of the game.

PROSPECTS 2021/2
It will be difficult to match the highs of last season. Improving their League position and challenging for third place will be their aim. Callum Davidson must surely be a candidate for a move to a bigger club – Saints fans will be hoping to hold on to him for another year at least.

Walking Up the Dunkeld Road, To See the Ormond Aces

Date	Comp	H/A	Opponents	F	A		HT		Referee	Crowd	Scorers
01/08/2020	L	A	Dundee United	1	1		0	1	K Clancy	BCD	Craig
12/08/2020	L	A	Rangers	0	3		0	2	E Anderson	BCD	
15/08/2020	L	A	Kilmarnock	2	1		0	0	A Dallas	BCD	Wotherspoon, O'Halloran
20/08/2020	L	H	Aberdeen	0	1		0	0	W Collum	BCD	
23/08/2020	L	H	Hibernian	0	1		0	0	J Beaton	BCD	
29/08/2020	L	H	St Mirren	1	0		0	0	K Clancy	BCD	May
12/09/2020	L	A	Motherwell	0	1		0	1	E Anderson	BCD	
19/09/2020	L	H	Ross County	0	1		0	1	D Munro	BCD	
26/09/2020	L	A	Livingston	0	2		0	2	C Napier	BCD	
04/10/2020	L	H	Celtic	0	2		0	0	N Walsh	BCD	
07/10/2020	**LC**	**A**	**Kelty Hearts**	**2**	**1**		**1**	**0**	**A Newlands**	**BCD**	**Kerr, Kane**
10/10/2020	**LC**	**H**	**Brechin City**	**7**	**0**		**2**	**0**	**C Napier**	**BCD**	**May 3, Wotherspoon 2, Hendry pen, Davidson**
17/10/2020	L	A	Hamilton Accies	5	3		3	2	K Clancy	BCD	Conway 2, May 2, Wotherspoon
24/10/2020	L	H	Dundee United	0	0		0	0	A Dallas	BCD	
06/11/2020	L	H	Kilmarnock	1	0		0	0	G Duncan	BCD	McNamara
10/11/2020	**LC**	**H**	**Dundee United**	**0**	**0**	**3-4p**	**0**	**0**	**D Robertson**	**BCD**	
14/11/2020	**LC**	**A**	**Peterhead**	**3**	**1**		**0**	**0**	**E Anderson**	**BCD**	**May 2 (2 pens), Kane**
21/11/2020	L	H	Motherwell	1	1		1	1	S Kirkland	BCD	May pen
24/11/2020	L	A	Hibernian	2	2		1	1	K Clancy	BCD	McCann, Wotherspoon
28/11/2020	**LC**	**A**	**Motherwell**	**2**	**1**		**0**	**0**	**A Muir**	**BCD**	**Hendry, Wotherspoon**
06/12/2020	L	A	Celtic	1	1		0	0	D Munro	BCD	Kane
12/12/2020	L	H	Livingston	1	2		0	0	J Beaton	BCD	Kane
15/12/2020	**LC**	**A**	**Dunfermline Athletic**	**1**	**1**	**AET, 4-3p**	**0**	**0**	**D Robertson**	**BCD**	**Rooney**
19/12/2020	L	A	St Johnstone	2	3		2	1	S McLean	BCD	May pen, Tanser
23/12/2020	L	H	Rangers	0	3		0	2	N Walsh	BCD	
26/12/2020	L	A	Aberdeen	1	2		1	1	A Muir	BCD	Gordon
30/12/2020	L	H	Hamilton Accies	0	0		0	0	D Munro	BCD	
02/01/2021	L	A	Ross County	1	1		1	1	W Collum	BCD	Conway pen
12/01/2021	L	A	Dundee United	2	2		2	1	C Steven	BCD	Melamed, Kane
16/01/2021	L	H	St Mirren	1	0		0	0	S McLean	BCD	Kane
23/01/2021	**LC**	**N**	**Hibernian**	**3**	**0**		**1**	**0**	**N Walsh**	**BCD**	**Kerr, Rooney, Conway**
27/01/2021	L	H	Aberdeen	0	0		0	0	D Robertson	BCD	
30/01/2021	L	A	Kilmarnock	3	2		0	2	G Aitken	BCD	Melamed, Davidson, McCann
03/02/2021	L	A	Rangers	0	1		0	0	D Munro	BCD	
06/02/2021	L	A	Livingston	2	1		1	0	E Anderson	BCD	Tanser, Rooney
14/02/2021	L	H	Celtic	1	2		0	0	S McLean	BCD	Rooney
20/02/2021	L	A	Motherwell	3	0		2	0	J Beaton	BCD	Melamed 2 (1 pen), Kerr
28/02/2021	**LC**	**N**	**Livingston**	**1**	**0**		**1**	**0**	**D Robertson**	**BCD**	**Rooney**
03/03/2021	L	A	Hamilton Accies	1	1		0	1	G Irvine	BCD	Melamed
06/03/2021	L	H	Hibernian	1	0		1	0	D Dickinson	BCD	Craig
20/03/2021	L	H	Ross County	1	0		0	0	C Napier	BCD	Middleton
03/04/2021	**SC**	**A**	**Dundee**	**1**	**0**		**1**	**0**	**C Napier**	**BCD**	**Melamed**
10/04/2021	L	H	Aberdeen	0	1		0	0	J Beaton	BCD	
17/04/2021	**SC**	**H**	**Clyde**	**2**	**0**		**2**	**0**	**S Kirkland**	**BCD**	**Melamed, O'Halloran**
21/04/2021	L	H	Rangers	1	1		0	0	E Anderson	BCD	Craig pen
25/04/2021	**SC**	**A**	**Rangers**	**1**	**1**	**AET, 4-2p**	**0**	**0**	**A Muir**	**BCD**	**Kane**
01/05/2021	L	A	Hibernian	1	0		1	0	G Aitken	BCD	Middleton
09/05/2021	**SC**	**N**	**St Mirren**	**2**	**1**		**0**	**0**	**W Collum**	**BCD**	**Kane, Middleton**
12/05/2021	L	A	Celtic	0	4		0	2	B Madden	BCD	
15/05/2021	L	H	Livingston	0	0		0	0	C Napier	BCD	
22/05/2021	**SC**	**N**	**Hibernian**	**1**	**0**		**1**	**0**	**N Walsh**	**BCD**	**Rooney**

Date	Comp	H/A	Opponents	F	A		1	2	3	4	5	6	7	8	9
01/08/2020	L	A	Dundee United	1	1		Parish	Booth&	Gordon	McCart	Kerr	McNamara	Craig	Wotherspoon+	McCann
12/08/2020	L	A	Rangers	0	3		Parish	Booth>	Gordon	McCart	Kerr	McNamara	Craig+	Wotherspoon	McCann
15/08/2020	L	A	Kilmarnock	2	1		Parish	Tanser+	Gordon	Rooney*	Kerr	McNamara	Craig	O'Halloran	McCann
20/08/2020	L	H	Aberdeen	0	1		Parish	Tanser	Gordon>	McCart	Kerr	McNamara&	Craig	Wotherspoon+	McCann
23/08/2020	L	H	Hibernian	0	1		Parish	Tanser	Gordon	McCart	Kerr	McNamara	Craig	Conway*	McCann
29/08/2020	L	H	St Mirren	1	0		Parish	Tanser	Gordon	McCart	Kerr	McNamara	Wotherspoon	Conway&	McCann
12/09/2020	L	A	Motherwell	0	1		Parish	Tanser	Gordon&	McCart	Kerr	McNamara	Wotherspoon>	Conway	McCann
19/09/2020	L	H	Ross County	0	1		Parish	Tanser	Gordon	McCart	Kerr	McNamara&	Craig+	Wotherspoon>	McCann
26/09/2020	L	A	Livingston	0	2		Clark	Tanser	Davidson	McCart	Kerr>	McNamara*	Craig+	Conway&	McCann
04/10/2020	L	H	Celtic	0	2		Clark	Tanser	Gordon	McCart	Kerr+	McNamara	Davidson	Conway	McCann
07/10/2020	**LC**	**A**	**Kelty Hearts**	**2**	**1**		**Parish**	**Tanser**	**Gordon**	**Booth**	**Kerr**	**Rooney**	**Craig***	**Conway+**	**Kane**
10/10/2020	**LC**	**H**	**Brechin City**	**7**	**0**		**Clark**	**Booth**	**Gordon**	**McCart**	**Davidson**	**Rooney**	**Craig**	**Conway&**	**Bryson***
17/10/2020	L	A	Hamilton Accies	5	3		Clark	Tanser	Gordon	McCart	Kerr	McNamara	Davidson	Conway	McCann*
24/10/2020	L	H	Dundee United	0	0		Clark	Tanser	Gordon	McCart	Kerr	McNamara	Davidson	Conway+	Bryson&
06/11/2020	L	H	Kilmarnock	1	0		Clark	Tanser	Gordon	McCart	Kerr	McNamara	Davidson	Conway	McCann
10/11/2020	**LC**	**H**	**Dundee United**	**0**	**0**	**3-4p**	**Clark**	**Tanser**	**Gordon**	**Booth**	**Kerr**	**Rooney**	**Craig**	**Bryson>**	**Kane+**
14/11/2020	**LC**	**A**	**Peterhead**	**3**	**1**		**Clark**	**Booth**	**Rooney**	**McCart**	**Kerr**	**Davidson**	**Craig**	**Conway***	**Melamed+**
21/11/2020	L	H	Motherwell	1	1		Clark	Tanser	Gordon	McCart	Kerr	McNamara	Davidson*	Conway+	McCann
24/11/2020	L	A	Hibernian	2	2		Clark	Tanser	Gordon	McCart	Rooney	McNamara	Craig	Melamed*	McCann
28/11/2020	**LC**	**A**	**Motherwell**	**2**	**1**		**Clark**	**Booth**	**Gordon**	**McCart**	**Rooney**	**Hendry***	**Craig**	**O'Halloran**	**McCann**
06/12/2020	L	A	Celtic	1	1		Clark	Tanser	Gordon	McCart	Rooney	McNamara	Bryson+	O'Halloran*	McCann
12/12/2020	L	H	Livingston	1	2		Clark	Tanser	Gordon	McCart	Kerr&	McNamara	Bryson>	Kane+	McCann
15/12/2020	**LC**	**A**	**Dunfermline Athletic**	**1**	**1**	**AET, 4-3p**	**Clark**	**Tanser>**	**Gordon**	**Booth**	**Kerr**	**Rooney**	**Craig**	**Kane***	**McCann**
19/12/2020	L	A	St Johnstone	2	3		Clark	Tanser	Gordon	McCart	Kerr	McNamara	Conway*	Davidson>	McCann
23/12/2020	L	H	Rangers	0	3		Clark	Booth	Gordon	McCart	Rooney	McNamara^	Conway*	Davidson+	Bryson<
26/12/2020	L	A	Aberdeen	1	2		Clark	Tanser*	Gordon	McCart	Rooney	McNamara	Craig&	Kane+	McCann
30/12/2020	L	H	Hamilton Accies	0	0		Clark	Booth	Gordon	McCart	Rooney	McNamara	Craig&	Kane	McCann
02/01/2021	L	A	Ross County	1	1		Clark	Booth	Gordon	McCart	Rooney	McNamara	Conway&	Kane+	McCann
12/01/2021	L	A	Dundee United	2	2		Clark	Booth*	Gordon	McCart	Rooney	Davidson	Craig	Kane+	McCann
16/01/2021	L	H	St Mirren	1	0		Clark	Tanser	Gordon	McCart	Rooney	Kerr	Bryson>	Kane&	McCann
23/01/2021	**LC**	**N**	**Hibernian**	**3**	**0**		**Clark**	**Tanser**	**Gordon**	**McCart**	**Rooney**	**Kerr**	**Conway**	**Kane***	**McCann**
27/01/2021	L	H	Aberdeen	0	0		Clark	Tanser	Gordon	McCart	Rooney	Kerr	Conway&	Kane+	Bryson
30/01/2021	L	A	Kilmarnock	3	2		Clark	Tanser	Gordon	McCart	Rooney	Kerr	Melamed+	Kane*	McCann
03/02/2021	L	A	Rangers	0	1		Clark	Tanser	Gordon	McCart	Brown&	Kerr	Conway>	Bryson>	McCann
06/02/2021	L	A	Livingston	2	1		Clark	Tanser	Gordon	McCart	Rooney	Kerr	Craig	Kane+	McCann
14/02/2021	L	H	Celtic	1	2		Clark	Booth	Gordon	McCart	Rooney	Kerr&	Conway*	Kane+	McCann
20/02/2021	L	A	Motherwell	3	0		Clark	Booth	Gordon	McCart	Rooney	Kerr	Craig	Kane+	McCann>
28/02/2021	**LC**	**N**	**Livingston**	**1**	**0**		**Clark**	**Booth**	**Gordon**	**McCart**	**Rooney**	**Kerr**	**Craig**	**Kane**	**McCann**
03/03/2021	L	A	Hamilton Accies	1	1		Clark	Tanser	Gordon	McCart	Rooney*	Kerr	Craig	Bryson+	May&
06/03/2021	L	H	Hibernian	1	0		Clark	Booth	Gordon	McCart	O'Halloran	Kerr	Craig	Kane+	McCann
20/03/2021	L	H	Ross County	1	0		Clark	Booth&	Gordon	McCart	Rooney	Kerr	Craig	Kane*	McCann
03/04/2021	**SC**	**A**	**Dundee**	**1**	**0**		**Clark**	**Booth**	**Gordon**	**McCart**	**Rooney**	**Kerr**	**Craig***	**May&**	**McCann**
10/04/2021	L	H	Aberdeen	0	1		Clark	Booth>	Gordon	McCart	Rooney	Kerr	Conway<	Bryson&	McCann
17/04/2021	**SC**	**H**	**Clyde**	**2**	**0**		**Parish**	**Tanser**	**Gordon**	**McCart**	**Brown&**	**Kerr**	**Craig&**	**O'Halloran**	**Melamed+**
21/04/2021	L	H	Rangers	1	1		Clark	Booth+	Gordon	McCart	Rooney	Kerr	Craig	Melamed*	McCann
25/04/2021	**SC**	**A**	**Rangers**	**1**	**1**	**AET, 4-2p**	**Clark**	**Tanser>**	**Gordon**	**McCart**	**Rooney**	**Kerr**	**Craig**	**Melamed***	**McCann**
01/05/2021	L	A	Hibernian	1	0		Parish	Booth	Gordon	McCart	Brown>	Kerr	Bryson<	Kane&	McCann
09/05/2021	**SC**	**N**	**St Mirren**	**2**	**1**		**Clark**	**Booth**	**Gordon**	**McCart**	**Rooney**	**Kerr**	**Bryson**	**Kane+**	**McCann**
12/05/2021	L	A	Celtic	0	4		Zlamal	Booth	Brown	McCart	Rooney	Kerr	Bryson	Kane>	Conway*
15/05/2021	L	H	Livingston	0	0		Zlamal	Booth>	Brown	McCart	Rooney	Kerr	Craig	Davidson	May+
22/05/2021	**SC**	**N**	**Hibernian**	**1**	**0**		**Clark**	**Booth**	**Gordon**	**McCart**	**Rooney+**	**Kerr**	**Bryson***	**Kane**	**McCann**

THE GOALIES

Goalkeepers Used in League Matches, 1994-2020

Players shown in the season of their first appearance only

1970/1	Jim Donaldson
1971/2	Derek Robertson
1974/5	David Nicoll
1977/8	Andy Geoghegan
1979/0	George Tulloch
	John Arrol
	Hamish Morrison
1980/1	Ally Jenkins
1981/2	Robert McGregor
1982/3	Gordon Drummond
	Mike McDonald
1983/4	Roy Baines
1984/5	John Balavage
1985/6	G Henderson
1986/7	George Watson
1987/8	Jim Butter
1990/1	Lindsay Hamilton
1991/2	Stewart Kennedy
1992/3	Andy Rhodes
1994/5	Allan Main
1995/6	Stephen Robertson
1998/9	Alan Ferguson
2001/2	Kevin Cuthbert
	Alan Miller
	Ludovic Roy
2003/4	Craig Nelson
2004/5	Allan McGregor
	Craig Samson
2005/6	Mark Paston
	Matt Glennan
2006/7	Bryn Halliwell
	Michael McGovern
2008/9	Euan McLean
2009/0	Graeme Smith
2010/1	Peter Enckelman
2011/2	Allan Mannus
2013/4	Steven Banks
2015/6	Zander Clark
2018/9	Cammy Bell

10	11	12	13	14	15	16	17	18	19	20
O'Halloran	Hendry*	May*	Conway+	Tanser&	Duffy	Olaofe	Ballantyne	Rooney	Sinclair	
Conway*	Hendry&	Olaofe*	Rooney+	Robertson&	Tanser>	Duffy	Ballantyne	Sinclair		
Conway&	Hendry	Wotherspoon*	Booth+	Robertson&	Duffy	Olaofe	Ballantyne	Sinclair		
O'Halloran	Hendry*	Conway*	Olaofe+	Robertson&	Rooney>	Duffy	Ballantyne	Sinclair		
O'Halloran&	Hendry+	Wotherspoon*	May+	Robertson&	Olaofe	Duffy	Ballantyne	Rooney	Booth	Sinclair
O'Halloran*	Hendry+	May*	Davidson+	Kane&	Olaofe	Duffy	Robertson	Rooney	Booth	Sinclair
O'Halloran*	Hendry+	May*	Kane+	Craig&	Davidson>	Duffy	Robertson	Rooney	Olaofe	Clark
May	Hendry*	Kane*	Conway+	O'Halloran&	Davidson>	Olaofe	Robertson	Rooney	Clark	
O'Halloran	May	Gordon*	Hendry+	Wotherspoon&	Rooney>	Olaofe	Robertson	Parish		
Wotherspoon*	May	O'Halloran*	Hendry+	Booth	Rooney	Olaofe	Robertson	Bryson	Craig	Parish
Wotherspoon	Hendry&	Bryson*	Davidson+	May&	Denham	McCart	Ferguson	Clark		
Wotherspoon	May+	Hendry*	Kane+	Ferguson&	Denham	Kerr	Tanser	Parish		
Wotherspoon&	May+	Bryson*	Kane+	Booth&	Craig	Rooney	O'Halloran	Hendry	Parish	
Wotherspoon	May*	Hendry*	O'Halloran+	McCann&	Craig	Rooney	Kane	Booth	Parish	
Wotherspoon*	May+	O'Halloran*	Kane+	Hendry	Craig	Bryson	Melamed	Booth	Rooney	Parish
Wotherspoon&	Hendry*	May*	Conway+	O'Halloran&	Davidson>	Ferguson	Melamed	McCart	Parish	
O'Halloran	May&	Bryson*	Hendry+	Kane&	Tanser	Ferguson	Gordon	Wotherspoon	Parish	
Wotherspoon	May&	Bryson*	O'Halloran+	Kane&	Hendry	Craig	Melamed	Booth	Rooney	Parish
O'Halloran	May+	Wotherspoon*	Kane+	Ferguson	Hendry	Booth	Parish			
Wotherspoon	May	Kane*	Tanser	Ferguson	McFarlane	Bryson	Melamed	Parish		
Wotherspoon	May	Kane*	Craig+	Ferguson	Kerr	Denham	Hendry	Melamed	McFarlane	Parish
Wotherspoon	May*	Melamed*	Hendry+	Rooney&	Davidson>	Craig	Conway	Booth	Parish	
Wotherspoon&	Davidson+	May*	Conway+	Hendry&	McCart>	Bryson	Ferguson	McNamara	Melamed	Parish
Wotherspoon+	May&	Rooney*	Bryson+	Henry&	Melamed>	Kane	Ferguson	Booth	Craig	Parish
Wotherspoon	Kane>	May*	McCann+	O'Halloran&	Melamed>	Craig<	Ferguson	Hendry	Parish	
Wotherspoon	May	Booth*	Hendry+	Melamed&	Davidson	Conway	Ferguson	Denham	Bryson	Parish
Wotherspoon+	May*	Conway*	Davidson+	O'Halloran&	Bryson	Melamed	Parish			
Davidson	O'Halloran*	Wotherspoon*	May+	Bryson&	Tanser	Melamed	Hendry	Craig	Parish	
Wotherspoon&	Melamed>	Tanser*	May+	Conway&	Hendry>	Bryson	Ferguson	Denham	Parish	
Wotherspoon*	Melamed+	Davidson*	May+	Hendry&	Craig>	Booth	Conway	Parish		
Wotherspoon	Davidson	May*	Craig	Hendry	O'Halloran	Booth	Bryson	Melamed	Brown	
O'Halloran*	Davidson	Wotherspoon*	May+	Middleton&	McCann	Booth	Craig	Brown	Melamed	Parish
Wotherspoon&	Davidson	May*	Conway+	Bryson&	O'Halloran	Booth	Craig	Brown	Middleton	Parish
May+	Davidson*	Craig*	Kane+	Rooney&	Melamed>	Booth	Gilmour	O'Halloran	Parish	
Wotherspoon	Melamed*	May*	O'Halloran+	Bryson	Middleton	Booth	Gilmour	Conway	Brown	Parish
Wotherspoon	Bryson	Middleton*	May+	O'Halloran&	Craig	Brown	Gilmour	Melamed	Parish	
Wotherspoon*	Melamed&	Bryson*	May+	Middleton&	Gilmour>	Brown	Tanser	O'Halloran	Conway	Parish
Wotherspoon	Conway*	May*	Melamed	Bryson	Gilmour	Brown	Tanser	O'Halloran	Parish	
Wotherspoon	Melamed	Brown*	O'Halloran+	Middleton&	Ferguson	Booth	Gilmour	McCann	Conway	Parish
Wotherspoon&	Melamed*	Conway*	May+	Tanser&	Ferguson	Brown	Gilmour	Middleston	Denham	Parish
Wotherspoon	Melamed+	May*	Middleston+	Tanser&	Conway	Bryson	Gilmour	O'Halloran	Brown	Parish
Wotherspoon	Melamed+	Bryson*	Kane+	Middleton&	COnway	Tanser	Gilmour	O'Halloran	Brown	Parish
Kane+	Middleton*	May*	Wotherspoon+	Melamed&	Tanser>	O'Halloran<	Gilmour	Craig	Brown	Parish
Wotherspoon*	May	Gilmour*	Middleton+	McCann&	Rooney	Bryson	Booth	Kane	Ferguson	Clark
Wotherspoon>	May&	Kane*	Tanser+	O'Halloran&	Bryson>	Gilmour	Brown	Ferguson	Parish	
Wotherspoon+	May&	Kane*	Bryson+	O'Halloran&	Booth>	Gilmour	Brown	Ferguson	Conway	Parish
O'Halloran+	Middleton*	Conway*	Wotherspoon+	May&	Rooney>	Davidson<	Gilmour	Melamed	Wills	
Wotherspoon	Melamed*	Middleton*	O'Halloran+	Ferguson	Robertson	Brown	Gilmour	Conway	Zlamal	
Gilmour&	Middleton+	Wotherspoon*	Melamed+	Ferguson>	Robertson<	Wills				
Wotherspoon&	Melamed*	Middleton*	Kane+	Conway&	Bryson>	Gilmour	Ferguson	Robertson	Wills	
Wotherspoon	Middleton&	Davidson*	Brown+	O'Halloran&	Craig	May	Melamed	Tanser	Conway	Parish

PHOTOCARDS

No. 59.

ST. JOHNSTONE FOOTBALL CLUB.

Left to right, back row:— J. Welsh, W. Clark, R. Wylie, D. Baxter, J. Littlejohn, J. Smeaton. Front row:— J. Tennant, H. Moon, H. Lyle, H. Ferguson (Capt.), W. Nicholson.

Founded in 1884. Members of Scottish League since 1921. Champions of Division II. 1923/24. In [illegible] were relegated from Division I to Division II. but returned to Division I in [illegible]. In [illegible] finished seventh in League table.

Expanding de luxe Albums for Ardath Photocards on sale at Tobacconists Price 6d

ARDATH TOBACCO CO. LTD. Manufacturers of STATE EXPRESS and ARDATH CIGARETTES

D

Surname	First Name	Date of Birth	No	Nat	Pos	Signed	Previous	Notes	Contract	Lge A	Lge S	Lge G	SC A	SC S	SC G	LC A	LC S	LC G	Un
Ballantyne	Cammy	22/04/2000	23	SCO	M	2018	St Johnstone Youth	OL to Montrose Sep-May											5
Booth	Callum	30/05/1991	24	SCO	D	2019	Dundee United		End 2021/2	15	3		3	1		7			17
Bou	Rudy	16/08/2003		SCO	F	2020	St Johnstone Youth		End 2022/3	0	0								0
Brown	James	12/01/1998	2	ENG	D	2021	Millwall (OL)	Jan-May		4	1		1	1					14
Bryson	Craig	06/11/1986	13	SCO	M	2020	Aberdeen		End 2021/2	12	8		2	2		2	2		12
Clark	Zander	26/06/1992	1	SCO	GK	2011	St Johnstone Youth		End 2021/2	27	0		4			7			4
Conway	Craig	02/05/1985	7	SCO	F	2020	Salford City	Released June 2021		19	9	3				5	2	1	11
Craig	Liam	27/12/1986	26	SCO	M	2015	Hibernian		End 2021/2	18	5	3	3			7			14
Davidson	Murray	07/03/1988	8	SCO	M	2009	Livingston		End 2021/2	14	7	1		1		4	2	1	1
Denham	Sam	25/10/2002	40	SCO	D	2019	Celtic	OL to Edinburgh City Mar-May	End 2021/2	0	0								6
Duffy	Wallace	12/04/1999	2	SCO	D	2019	Celtic	Freed Oct 2020, joined Invernes CT		0	0								7
Ferguson	Alex	10/09/2003		SCO	M	2020	St Johnstone Youth	OL to Edinburgh City for 2021/2	End 2022/3	0	1						1		18
Gilmour	Charlie	11/02/1999	15	SCO	M	2021	Norwich City		End 2022/3	1	1			1					14
Gordon	Liam	26/01/1996	6	SCO	D	2016	St Johnstone Youth		End 2021/2	35	1	1	5			7			1
Hamilton	Olly	13/12/2001		SCO	F	2019	St Johnstone Youth	OL to Cowdenbeath Sep-May, released May 2021		0	0								0
Hendry	Callum	08/12/1997	22	SCO	F	2017	St Johnstone Youth	Ol to Aberdeen Feb-May	End 2021/2	8	8					3	3	2	8
Johnstone	Max	18/08/1998		ENG	GK	2019	Sunderland Youth	Freed Sep 2020, joined AFC Fylde		0	0								0
Kane	Chris	05/09/1994	9	SCO	F	2014	St Johnstone Youth		End 2022/3	17	11	4	2	2	2	5	3	2	3
Kerr	Jason	06/02/1997	5	SCO	D	2017	St Johnstone Youth		End 2021/2	31	0	1	5			6		2	2
MacFarlane	Aidan	22/02/2002		SCO	M	2020	St Johnstone Youth			0	0								0
May	Stevie	02/11/1992	14	SCO	F	2019	Aberdeen		End 2022/3	17	17	5	3			3	5	5	1
McCann	Ali	04/12/1999	18	NIR	M	2017	St Johnstone Youth		End 2022/3	32	2	2	4	1		4			2
McCart	Jamie	20/06/1997	4	SCO	D	2020	Inverness CT		End 2021/2	37	0		5			5	1		2
McFarlane	Michael	18/09/2002		SCO	M	2020	St Johnstone Youth	OL to Edinburgh City 2021/2	End 2021/2	0	0								2
McNamara	Danny	27/12/1998	15	ROI / ENG	D	2020	Millwall (OL)	Jul-Jan		22	0	1							1
Melamed	Guy	21/12/1992	17	ISR	F	2020	Maccabi Netanya	Released June 2021		11	7	5	4		2	1			14
Middleton	Glenn	01/01/2000	16	SCO	M	2021	Ranmgers (OL)		Jan-May	3	6	2	1	3	1				3
Northcott	Jordan	09/02/2002	50	SCO	F	2019	St Johnstone Youth	OL to Forfar Athletic Mar-May		0	0								0
O'Halloran	Michael	06/01/1991	11	SCO	F	2019	Melbourne City		End 2022/3	13	12	1	1	3	1	2	1		8
Olaofe	Isaac	21/11/1999	16	ENG	F	2020	Millwall (OL)	Jul-Oct		0	2								8
Parish	Elliot	20/05/1990	12	ENG / WAL	GK	2019	Dundee		End 2021/2	9	0		1			1			36
Robertson	John	26/08/2001	20	SCO	F	2020	St Johnstone Youth	OL to Forfar Athletic Oct-Jan, released May 2021		0	5								7
Rooney	Shaun	26/07/1996	19	SCO	D	2020	Inverness CT		End 2021/2	20	7	2	4		1	8		3	11
Sinclair	Ross	07/05/2001	45	SCO	GK	2019	St Johnstone Youth	OL to Cowdenbeath Sep-Feb	End 2023/4	0	0								6
Smith	Lennon	01/01/2002		SCO	D	2019	St Johnstone Youth			0	0								0
Steele	Aaron	12/04/2002		SCO	D	2020	St Johnstone Youth	OL to East Fife Mar-May, released May joined E Fife		0	0								0
Tanser	Scott	23/10/1994	3	SCO	D	2017	Port Vale	OOC June 2021 joined St Mirren		23	7	2	2			4			8
Wills	Jack	16/10/2002	48	SCO	GK	2020	St Johnstone Youth		End 2021/2	0	0								3
Wotherspoon	David	16/01/1990	10	SCO / CAN	M	2013	Hibernian		End 2022/3	28	9	3	5			7		3	1
Zlamal	Zdenek	05/11/1985		CZR	GK	2021	Hearts (OL)	May-21		2	0								1
NEW SIGNINGS																			
Brown	James	12/01/1998		ENG	D	2021	Millwall		End 2022/3										
Devine	Reece	18/12/2001		ENG	D	2021	Manches[illegible]		End 2021/2										
Muller	Hayden	07/02/2002		ENG	D	2021	Millwall		End 2021/2										

Derek Robertson

Jim Donaldson

George Tulloch

St Mirren FC 2020/21 The Buddies

Founded	1876
Ground	St Mirren Park, Greenhill Road
Postcode	PA3 1RU
Tel	0141 889 2558
Capacity	8023
Closest Railway Station	Paisley St James
Record Attendance	47438 v Celtic, LC, 20/8/49
Ground Record	7542 v Kilmarnock, 31/1/09
Record Win	15-0 v Glasgow University, SC, 30/1/1960
Record Defeat	0-9 v Rangersd, Lge, 4/12/1897
Most League Goals in a Season	45 Dunky Walker, 1921/2
Colours 2020/21 Top	Black and White Stripes
Shorts	Black
Sponsor	Sky View Capital
Manufacturer	Joma
Change Colours 2020/21 Top	Black and Red stripes
Shorts	Black
Nicknames	Buddies
Web	www.saintmirren.net
Match Programme 2020/21	Curtis Sport

Chairman: Gordon Scott
CEO: Tony Fitzpatrick
Vice Chairman: Jim Gillespie
Directors: Mark MacMillan, John Needham, David Riley, Chris Stewart, Tony Fitzpatrick, Alan Wardrop, Gavin Whyte, John Melrose
Director / Secretary: Chris Stewart
Team Manager: Jim Goodwin
Assistant Manager: Lee Sharp
Goalkeeping Coach: Jamie Langfield
Head of Youth development: Allan McManus
Physio: Kevin Bain
Sports Scientist: Junior Mendes
Kit Manager: Joe Hayes
Club Doctors: Gerry Canning, David Wong
Commercial / Marketing Manager: Campbell Kennedy
Conference / Functions: Kate Wallace
Club Secretary: Lynn Watson
Academy Secretary: Susan McLellan
Groundsman: Tommy Docherty
Programme Editor: Norrie Jamieson

Overall 2020/1 must have been a more than satisfactory season for St Mirren. They stayed clear of the relegation zone and reached the Semi Finals of both major Cups, playing some entertaining football along the way. They were the only club to inflict a domestic defeat on Rangers, beating them in the League Cup.

Credit must go to manager Jim Goodwin for the job he did. Saints had a sticky patch with six straight defeats early in the season but he worked through it and turned things around. Clearly Goodwin has a good eye in the transfer market, picking up some bargains from down south and Ireland. His teams are able to mix the "dirty work" with some very entertaining football. He is another Manager who could be cherry-picked to go further in the game.

STAR MAN
Saints made a good signing when they picked up Rangers free Jak Alnwick in goals. He was very consistent throughout the season and was responsible for saving a considerable number of points for the Paisley side.

PROSPECTS 2021/2
How do Saints improve for next season? A top six place and a Cup Final appearance will be their targets. Nobody should bet against them achieving at least one of those goals.

St Mirren 1973/4

Date	Comp	H/A	Opponents	F	A		HT		Referee	Crowd	Scorers
01/08/2020	L	H	Livingston	1	0		1	0	D Robertson	BCD	Tait
09/08/2020	L	A	Rangers	0	3		0	1	A Dallas	BCD	
15/08/2020	L	A	Hamilton Accies	1	0		1	0	S Kirkland	BCD	Obika
22/08/2020	L	H	Ross County	1	1		1	0	M Roncone	BCD	Obika
29/08/2020	L	A	St Johnstone	0	1		0	0	K Clancy	BCD	
12/09/2020	L	H	Hibernian	0	3		0	2	W Collum	BCD	
16/09/2020	L	H	Celtic	1	2		1	2	J Beaton	BCD	Erwin
19/09/2020	L	A	Dundee United	1	2		0	1	C Steven	BCD	Connolly
26/09/2020	L	H	Kilmarnock	0	1		0	1	D Munro	BCD	
02/10/2020	L	A	Aberdeen	1	2		0	0	G Duncan	BCD	Erhahon
07/10/2020	LC	H	Partick Thistle	4	1		1	0	C Steven	BCD	Tait, Obika, Breen og, Connolly
10/10/2020	LC	A	Queen of the South	2	2	4-2p	0	2	W Collum	BCD	McGrath, Fraser
06/11/2020	L	H	Dundee United	0	0		0	0	D Munro	BCD	
11/11/2020	LC	H	Morton	1	1	6-5p	1	0	B Madden	BCD	Obika
14/11/2020	LC	A	Queen's Park	1	0		0	0	G Aitken	BCD	Obika
21/11/2020	L	A	Livingston	1	0		0	0	W Collum	BCD	Doyle-Hayes
28/11/2020	LC	H	Aberdeen	2	1		1	1	D Robertson	BCD	Durmus, McGrath
05/12/2020	L	H	Aberdeen	1	1		1	1	B Madden	BCD	McGrath pen
12/12/2020	L	A	Motherwell	1	0		1	0	E Anderson	BCD	McGrath
16/12/2020	LC	H	Rangers	3	2		1	1	A Dallas	BCD	McGrath 2(1 pen), McCarthy
19/12/2020	L	H	St Johnstone	3	2		1	2	S McLean	BCD	Erhahon, Erwin, Obika
23/12/2020	L	A	Hibernian	0	1		0	1	S Kirkland	BCD	
26/12/2020	L	A	Ross County	2	0		0	0	C Steven	BCD	Fraser, Dennis
30/12/2020	L	H	Rangers	0	2		0	2	A Muir	BCD	
02/01/2021	L	A	Kilmarnock	1	1		0	1	C Napier	BCD	Rogers og
09/01/2021	L	H	Motherwell	1	1		0	1	B Madden	BCD	McGrath pen
16/01/2021	L	A	St Johnstone	0	1		0	0	S McLean	BCD	
24/01/2021	LC	N	Livingston	0	1		0	1	D Munro	BCD	
27/01/2021	L	A	Dundee United	5	1		3	0	J Beaton	BCD	Shaughnessy, McGrath 2 pens, Connolly, Dennis
30/01/2021	L	A	Celtic	2	1		2	1	B Madden	BCD	Dennis, Durmus
02/02/2021	L	H	Hibernian	1	2		0	0	A Muir	BCD	Obika
06/02/2021	L	H	Kilmarnock	2	0		1	0	J Beaton	BCD	McAllister, Obika
10/02/2021	L	H	Celtic	0	4		0	1	D Robertson	BCD	
13/02/2021	K	A	Aberdeen	0	0		0	0	E Anderson	BCD	
17/02/2021	L	H	Hamilton Accies	1	1		0	0	S McLean	BCD	Durmus
20/02/2021	L	H	Livingston	1	1		1	1	W Collum	BCD	MacPherson
24/02/2021	L	H	Motherwell	0	0		0	0	K Clancy	BCD	
27/02/2021	L	H	Ross County	1	0		0	0	G Aitken	BCD	McGrath pen
06/03/2021	L	A	Rangers	0	3		0	2	S McLean	BCD	
20/03/2021	L	A	Hamilton Accies	1	1		1	0	D Robertson	BCD	McGrath pen
03/04/2021	SC	A	Hamilton Accies	3	0		1	0	E Anderson	BCD	McGrath 2 (1 pen), Dennis
10/04/2021	L	A	Motherwell	0	1		0	0	K Clancy	BCD	
16/04/2021	SC	H	Inverness CT	2	1		0	0	J Beaton	BCD	Dennis, Fraser
21/04/2021	L	A	Ross County	3	1		0	1	B Madden	BCD	Erwin, Durmus, McGrath pen
26/04/2021	SC	A	Kilmarnock	3	3	AET, 5-4p	1	2	D Robertson	BCD	Doyle og, Shaugnessy, McGrath
01/05/2021	L	H	Hamilton Accies	1	2		0	1	J Beaton	BCD	McGrath
09/05/2021	SC	N	St Johnstone	1	2		0	0	W Collum	BCD	McCarthy
12/05/2021	L	A	Kilmarnock	3	3		0	1	D Munro	BCD	McGrath, McPherson, Quaner
16/05/2021	L	H	Dundee United	0	0		0	0	E Anderson	BCD	

Surname	First Name	Date of Birth	No	Nat	Pos	Signed	Previous	Notes	Contract	lge A	lge S	lge G	SC A	SC S	SC G	LC A	LC S	LC G	Un
Alnwick	Jak	17/06/1993	1	ENG	GK	2020	Rangers		End 2021/2	34			4			7			
Baird	Jack	07/02/1996	15	SCO	D	2014	St Mirren Youths	Transferred to Ayr United Sep 2020		0									5
Baker	Danny				D	2019	St Mirren Youths	Released June 2020		0									0
Breadner	Cameron	13/10/2000		SCO	F	2018	St Mirren Youths	OL to Forfar Ath Sep-Jan		0									0
Brophy	Eamonn	10/03/1996	29	SCO	F	2021	Kilmarnock		End 2021/2	4	2			1		1			0
Connolly	Dylan	02/05/1995	21	ROI	M	2020	AFC Wimbledon	Released June 2021, joined Northampton Town		18	11	2	2	1		4	3	1	2
Dennis	Kristian	12/03/1990	20	ENG	F	2020	Notts County		End 2021/2	6	11	3	3	1	2	1	2		5
Doyle-Hayes	Jake	30/12/1998	7	ROI	M	2020	Aston Villa	OOC June 2021 joined Hibernian		21	1	1	4			3	1		0
Durmus	Ilkay	01/05/1994	11	TUR / GER	M	2019	Wacker Innsbruck	OOC June 2021 joined Lechia Gdansk		23	8	3	4			2	2	1	4
Ellis	Sam	02/10/2002		SCO	D	2019	St Mirren Youths			0	0								0
Erhahon	Ethan	09/05/2001	25	SCO	M	2019	St Mirren Youths		End 2022/3	28	3	2	2	1		6			6
Erwin	Lee	19/03/1994	23	SCO	F	2020	Ross County		End 2021/2	17	10	3	3			2	3		7
Finlayson	Danny	19/01/2001	15	NIR / SCO	M	2020	Rangers (OL)	Oct-May		2	1								25
Flynn	Ryan	04/09/1988	8	SCO	M	2018	Oldham Athletic		End 2021/2	8	6			1			1		16
Foley	Sam	17/10/1986	16	ENG	M	2019	Northampton Town	Transferred to Motherwell Jan 2021		10	1					3	1		12
Fraser	Marcus	23/06/1994	22	SCO	D	2020	Ross County		End 2022/3	37	0	1	4		1	7		1	0
Frew	Carter	08/04/2002		SCO	M	2019	St Mirren Youths	Released July 2021 joined Hurlford United		0	0								0
Gray	Findlay	28/02/2002		SCO	M	2019	St Mirren Youths	Released July 2021 joined Broomhill		0	0								0
Henderson	Jay	07/03/2002	30	SCO	M	2020	St Mirren Youths	OL to Clyde Sep-Jan	End 2022/3	4	1		1	1					18
Jack	Josh	04/02/2001	35	SCO	F	2020	St Mirren Youths	OL to Clyde Sep-May	End 2021/2	0	0								5
Jamieson	Lewis	17/04/2002	33	SCO	F	2020	St Mirren Youths	OL to Clyde Sep-May	End 2021/2	0	3						1		23
Langfield	Jamie	22/12/1979		SCO	GK	2015	Aberdeen	GK Coach		0	0								1
Lyness	Dean	20/07/1991	26	ENG	GK	2019	Raith Rovers		End 2022/3	1	1								43
MacPherson	Cammy	29/12/1998	14	SCO	M	2018	St Mirren Youths		End 2021/2	14	18	2		2		4	2		7
Magennis	Kyle	26/08/1998	7	SCO	M	2016	St Mirren Youths	Transferred to Hibernian Oct 2020		0	0								0
Mason	Brendan	20/09/1997	3	ENG	D	2020	Coventry City (OL)	Oct-May		9	2			1		3	1		10
McAllister	Kyle	21/06/1999	10	SCO	F	2019	Derby County		End 2021/2	8	23	1	1	1		2	4		6
McAllister	Nicholas	17/01/2001		SCO	D	2019	Queen's Park	OL to Dumbarton Mar-May, released May 2021 joined Ayr United		0	0								0
McCarthy	Conor	11/04/1998	5	ROI	D	2020	Cork City		End 2021/2	37	0		4		1	5		1	0
McCaw	Alex	16/06/2002		SCO	M	2020	St Mirren Youths	OL to Annan Ath Jan-May		0	0								0
McGrath	Jamie	30/09/1996	17	ROI	M	2020	Dundalk		End 2021/2	34	1	10	4		3	6	1	4	0
McMaster	Dean	24/09/2002		SCO	M	2020	St Mirren Youths	Released July 2020		0	0								0
Miller	Liam	09/06/2000		SCO	M	2020	St Mirren Youths	Released July 2020		0	0								0
Morias	Junior	04/07/1995	19	JAM	F	2019	Northampton Town	OL to Boreham Wood Jan-May, Released May 2021 joined King's Lynn T		7	7					2	2		5
Obika	Jonathan	12/09/1990	9	ENG / NIG	F	2019	Oxford United	Released May 2021 joined Morecambe		21	13	5	2			4	3	3	1
Quaner	Collin	18/06/1991	45	GER / GHA	F	2021	Huddersfield Town	Released May 2021		2	4	1		2					1
Reid	Dylan	01/03/2005		SCO	M	2020	St Mirren Youths		End 2022/3	0	1								6
Shaughnessy	Joe	06/07/1992	4	ROI / ENG	D	2020	Southend United		End 2022/3	33	0	1	4		1	6			0
Sheron	Nathan	04/10/1997	6	ENG	D	2020	Fleetwood Town (OL)	Jul-Jan		6	1					2			8
Tait	Richard	02/12/1989	2	SCO	D	2020	Motherwell		End 2021/2	31	2	1	2	1		7		1	4
Thorvaldsson	Isak	01/05/2001	23	NOR	M	2020	Norwich City (OL)	Jul-Aug		0	2								1
Urminsky	Peter	24/05/1999	27	SVK	GK	2020	Spartak Trnava	OL to Ayr United Feb-May	End 2021/2	0	0								13
Zlamal	Zdenek	05/11/1985		CZE	GK	2020	Hearts (OL)	Sep-20		3	0								0
Own Goals												1			1			1	
NEW SIGNINGS																			
Dunne	Charlie	13/02/1993		ROI / NIR	D	2021	Motherwell		End 2022/3										
Finlayson	Daniel	19/01/2001		NIR / SCO	D	2021	Rangers		End 2022/3										
Kiltie	Greg	18/01/1997		SCO	M	2021	Kilmarnock		End 2022/3										
Main	Curtis	20/06/1992		ENg	F	2021	Shrewsbury Town		End 2022/3										
Power	Alan	23/01/1988		ROI	M	2021	Kilmarnock		End 2021/2										
Tanser	Scott	23/10/1994		ENG	D	2021	St Johnstone		End 2021/2										

Donald Hunter

Billy Thomson

Billy Bald

Date	Comp	H/A	Opponents	F	A		1	2	3	4	5	6	7	8	9
01/08/2020	L	H	Livingston	1	0		Alnwick	Tait	Shaughnessy	Fraser	McCarthy	Foley	Durmus+	McGrath	McAllister*
09/08/2020	L	A	Rangers	0	3		Alnwick	Tait	Shaughnessy	Fraser	McCarthy	Foley>	Durmus+	McGrath	Sheron*
15/08/2020	L	A	Hamilton Accies	1	0		Alnwick	Tait	Shaughnessy	Fraser	Sheron	Foley	Morais	McGrath	McAllister*
22/08/2020	L	H	Ross County	1	1		Alnwick	Tait	Shaughnessy	Fraser	Sheron	Foley	McCarthy	McGrath	McAllister*
29/08/2020	L	A	St Johnstone	0	1		Alnwick	Tait	Durmus	Fraser&	Sheron>	Foley	McCarthy	McGrath	McAllister*
12/09/2020	L	H	Hibernian	0	3		Zlamal	Tait	Durmus&	Fraser	Sheron+	Foley	McCarthy	McGrath>	Erhahon
16/09/2020	L	H	Celtic	1	2		Zlamal	Tait	Shaughnessy	Fraser	McCarthy	Foley&	Connolly*	McGrath	Erhahon
19/09/2020	L	A	Dundee United	1	2		Zlamal	Tait	Shaughnessy	Fraser	McCarthy	Foley	McAllister*	McGrath+	Erhahon>
26/09/2020	L	H	Kilmarnock	0	1		Alnwick	Durmus&	Shaughnessy	Fraser	McCarthy	Foley*	MacPherson	McGrath+	Erhahon>
02/10/2020	L	A	Aberdeen	1	2		Alnwick	Sheron	Shaughnessy	Fraser	McCarthy	Obika	MacPherson	McGrath	Erhahon
07/10/2020	LC	H	Partick Thistle	4	1		Alnwick	Tait	Shaughnessy	Fraser	Sheron+	Obika<	MacPherson>	McGrath	Erhahon
10/10/2020	LC	A	Queen of the South	2	2	4-2p	Alnwick	Tait	Shaughnessy	Fraser	Sheron*	Foley	Durmus&	McGrath	Erhahon
06/11/2020	L	H	Dundee United	0	0		Alnwick	Tait	Shaughnessy	Fraser	McCarthy	Mason&	Doyle-Hayes	McGrath>	Erhahon
11/11/2020	LC	H	Morton	1	1	6-5p	Alnwick	Tait	Shaughnessy	Fraser	McCarthy<	Mason	Foley	McAllister&	Erhahon*
14/11/2020	LC	A	Queen's Park	1	0		Alnwick	Tait	Shaughnessy	Fraser	McCarthy	Connolly>	Doyle-Hayes	McGrath&	Erhahon
21/11/2020	L	A	Livingston	1	0		Alnwick	Tait	Mason	Fraser	McCarthy	Connolly*	Doyle-Hayes	McGrath&	Erhahon
28/11/2020	LC	H	Aberdeen	2	1		Alnwick	Tait	Durmus*	Fraser	McCarthy	Connolly&	Doyle-Hayes	McGrath	MacPherson
05/12/2020	L	H	Aberdeen	1	1		Alnwick	Tait	Shaughnessy	Fraser	McCarthy	Connolly&	Doyle-Hayes	McGrath	Erhahon+
12/12/2020	L	A	Motherwell	1	0		Alnwick	Tait+	Shaughnessy	Fraser	McCarthy	Connolly&	Doyle-Hayes	McGrath	Erhahon
16/12/2020	LC	H	Rangers	3	2		Alnwick	Tait	Shaughnessy	Fraser	McCarthy	Connolly*	Doyle-Hayes	McGrath	Erhahon
19/12/2020	L	H	St Johnstone	3	2		Alnwick	Tait	Shaughnessy	Fraser&	McCarthy	Connolly*	Doyle-Hayes	McGrath	Erhahon+
23/12/2020	L	A	Hibernian	0	1		Alnwick	Tait*	Shaughnessy	Fraser	McCarthy	Connolly>	Mason	McGrath&	Erhahon
26/12/2020	L	A	Ross County	2	0		Alnwick	Tait	Shaughnessy	Fraser<	McCarthy	McAllister*	Doyle-Hayes	McGrath>	Erhahon&
30/12/2020	L	H	Rangers	0	2		Alnwick	Tait	Shaughnessy	Fraser	McCarthy	Connolly&	Doyle-Hayes	McGrath*	Erhahon>
02/01/2021	L	A	Kilmarnock	1	1		Alnwick	Tait*	Shaugnessy	Fraser	McCarthy	Connolly>	Doyle-Hayes	McGrath	Erhahon&
09/01/2021	L	H	Motherwell	1	1		Alnwick	Tait	Shaughnessy	Fraser	McCarthy	Connolly	Doyle-Hayes	McGrath	Erhahon+
16/01/2021	L	A	St Johnstone	0	1		Alnwick	Tait	Shaughnessy	Fraser	McCarthy	Connolly*	Doyle-Hayes	McGrath	MacPherson
24/01/2021	LC	N	Livingston	0	1		Alnwick	Tait	Shaughnessy	Fraser	McCarthy	Connolly*	Mason+	McGrath	MacPherson&
27/01/2021	L	A	Dundee United	5	1		Alnwick	Tait	Shaughnessy	Fraser	McCarthy	Flynn	Durmus&	McGrath	Erhahon
30/01/2021	L	A	Celtic	2	1		Alnwick	MacPherson&	Shaughnessy	Fraser	McCarthy	Connolly>	Durmus	McGrath	Erhahon
02/02/2021	L	H	Hibernian	1	2		Alnwick	Tait>	Shaughnessy	Fraser	McCarthy	Flynn	Durmus+	McGrath	Brophy&
06/02/2021	L	H	Kilmarnock	2	0		Lyness	Tait	Shaughnessy	Fraser	McCarthy	McAllister*	Durmus+	McGrath	Erhahon
10/02/2021	L	H	Celtic	0	4		Alnwick	Connolly+	Shaughnessy	Fraser	McCarthy	Flynn&	Durmus	McGrath*	Erhahon
13/02/2021	K	A	Aberdeen	0	0		Alnwick	Tait	Shaughnessy	Fraser	McCarthy	Flynn	Durmus	Connolly&	Erhahon
17/02/2021	L	H	Hamilton Accies	1	1		Alnwick	Tait+	Shaughnessy	Fraser	McCarthy	McAllister	Durmus	MacPherson	Erhahon
20/02/2021	L	H	Livingston	1	1		Alnwick	Tait	Shaugnessy	Fraser	McCarthy	Flynn	Durmus	Connolly*	Erhahon
24/02/2021	L	H	Motherwell	0	0		Alnwick	Tait+	Shaughnessy	Fraser	McCarthy	Doyle-Hayes	Durmus	McGrath	Erhahon
27/02/2021	L	H	Ross County	1	0		Alnwick	McAllister	Shaughnessy*	Fraser	McCarthy	McGrath	Durmus<	Connolly>	Erhahon&
06/03/2021	L	A	Rangers	0	3		Alnwick	Tait	Shaughnessy	Fraser	McCarthy	Doyle-Hayes	Durmus*	Connolly&	Erhahon>
20/03/2021	L	A	Hamilton Accies	1	1		Alnwick	Tait	Shaughnessy	Fraser	McCarthy	Doyle-Hayes	Durmus	McAllister *	Erwin+
03/04/2021	SC	A	Hamilton Accies	3	0		Alnwick	Erahahon	Shaughnessy	Fraser	McCarthy	Doyle-Hayes	Durmus&	Connolly+	Erwin*
10/04/2021	L	A	Motherwell	0	1		Alnwick	Erahahon+	Shaughnessy>	Fraser	McCarthy	Doyle-Hayes	Durmus	Connolly	Erwin&
16/04/2021	SC	H	Inverness CT	2	1		Alnwick	Dennis&	Shaughnessy	Fraser	McCarthy	Doyle-Hayes*	Durmus	Connolly	McAllister+
21/04/2021	L	A	Ross County	3	1		Alnwick	Tait&	Shaughnessy	Fraser	McCarthy	Dennis*	Durmus	MacPherson	Erwin
26/04/2021	SC	A	Kilmarnock	3	3	AET, 5-4p	Alnwick	Tait	Shaughnessy	Fraser>	McCarthy	Doyle-Hayes	Durmus&	McGrath	Erwin+
01/05/2021	L	H	Hamilton Accies	1	2		Alnwick	Tait&	Shaughnessy	Finlayson	McCarthy	Doyle-Hayes	MacPherson*	Quaner+	Erhahon
09/05/2021	SC	N	St Johnstone	1	2		Alnwick	Tait+	Shaughnessy	Fraser	McCarthy	Doyle-Hayes	Durmus	McGrath	Erhahon&
12/05/2021	L	A	Kilmarnock	3	3		Alnwick	Finlayson<	Flynn	Fraser	McCarthy	Doyle-Hayes>	Durmus*	McGrath	Henderson
16/05/2021	L	H	Dundee United	0	0		Alnwick	Tait	Flynn*	Fraser	McCarthy	Connolly>	Erhahon	McGrath	Henderson

THE GOALIES

Goalkeepers Used in League Matches, 1994-2020

Players shown in the season of their first appearance only

1970/1	Dennis Connaghan
	Billy McGann
1972/3	Danny Stevenson
	Alex Morrison
1973/4	Jim Herriot
	Ian Dick
	Gordon Knowles
1975/6	John Hunt
1976/7	Donald Hunter
1977/8	Ally Hunter
	Alan McCulloch
1978/9	Alistair McLean
	Billy Thomson
1981/2	Campbell Money
1984/5	Jim Stewart
1986/7	Barney Duffy
	Les Fridge
1993/4	Alan Combe
1994/5	Derek Scrimgeour
1997/8	Gordon Marshall
1998/9	Ludovic Roy
2000/1	Ian McCaldon
2001/2	Kris Robertson
	John HIllcoat
	Scott Strang
2002/3	Billy Bald
2003/4	Craig Hinchcliffe
	Stephen Woods
2004/5	Chris Smith
2005/6	Tony Bullock
2007/8	Mark Howard
2009/0	Paul Gallacher
2010/1	Craig Samson
2013/4	David Cornell
	Christopher Dilo
	Marian Kello
2014/5	Mark Ridgers
2015/6	Jamie Langfield
2016/7	Scott Gallacher
	Billy O'Brien
2017/8	Craig Samson
2018/9	Vaclav Hladky
	Danny Rogers
	Dean Lyness

10	11	12	13	14	15	16	17	18	19	20
MacPherson	Obika	Morais*	Thorvaldsson+	*Erhahon*	*Baird*	*Jack*	*Urminsky*	*Henderson*	*Jamieson*	*Lyness*
MacPherson<	Obika&	Morais*	McAllister+	Thorvaldsson&	Erhahon>	Jamieson<	*Baird*	*Henderson*	*Jack*	*Lyness*
MacPherson	Obika	Durmus*	*Urminsky*	*Thorvaldsson*	*Erhahon*	*Jamieson*	*Baird*	*Henderson*	*Jack*	*Lyness*
Morais	Obika+	MacPherson*	Dennis+	*Urmisnky*	*Erhahon*	*Jamieson*	*Baird*	*Henderson*	*Jack*	*Lyness*
Morais+	Obika	MacPherson*	Connolly+	Dennis&	Jamieson>	*Erhahon*	*Baird*	*Henderson*	*Jack*	*Lyness*
Dennis*	Obika<	Erwin*	McAllister+	Connolly&	MacPherson>	Morais<	*Jamieson*	*Langfield*		
Morais+	Erwin	McAllister*	Obika+	Durmus&	*MacPherson*	*Sheron*	*Jamieson*	*Urminsky*		
Erwin	Obika&	Durmus*	Connolly+	MacPherson&	Morais>	*Sheron*	*Jamieson*	*Urminsky*		
Erwin	Morais	Sheron*	Obika+	Connolly&	McAllister>	*Jamieson*	*Urminsky*			
Erwin	Morais	*Durmus*	*McAllister*	*Jamieson*	*Lyness*					
Erwin&	Morais*	McAllister*	Connolly+	Durmus&	Foley>	Jamieson<	*Urminsky*	*Lyness*		
Erwin+	McAllister+	Obika*	Morais+	Connelly&	MacPherson>	*Jamieson*	*Urminsky*	*Lyness*		
MacPherson+	Dennis*	Erwin*	Obika+	Foley&	Morais>	*Sheron*	*Finlayson*	*Connolly*	*McAllister*	*Lyness*
Morais+	Obika>	Doyle-Hayes*	Dennis+	Erwin&	Connolly>	McGrath<	*Finlayson*	*Flynn*	*MacPherson*	*Lyness*
MacPherson*	Dennis+	Mason*	Obika+	Flynn&	McAllister>	*Erwin*	*Morais*	*Foley*	*Sheron*	*Lyness*
Foley	Obika+	McAllister*	Erwin+	MacPherson&	*Flynn*	*Morais*	*Dennis*	*Durmus*	*Sheron*	*Lyness*
Foley	Obika+	McAllister*	Erwin+	Morais&	*Finlayson*	*Sheron*	*Dennis*	*Flynn*	*Jamieson*	*Lyness*
Durmus<	Obika*	Erwin*	MacPherson+	McAllister&	Dennis>	*Morais*	*Foley*	*Mason*	*Flynn*	*Lyness*
Durmus	Obika*	Erwin*	Mason+	MacPherson&	*Dennis*	*Morais*	*Foley*	*McAllister*	*Flynn*	*Lyness*
Mason	Obika+	MacPherson*	Erwin+	*Durmus*	*Dennis*	*Jamieson*	*Foley*	*McAllister*	*Flynn*	*Lyness*
Durmus>	Erwin<	Obika*	McAllister	MacPherson&	Mason>	*Morais<*	*Foley*	*Finlayson*	*Flynn*	*Lyness*
MacPherson<	Erwin+	Durmus*	Obika+	Dennis&	Morais>	*McAllister<*	*Foley*	*Finlayson*	*Flynn*	*Lyness*
Morais	Erwin+	Durmus*	Obika+	Dennis&	MacPherson>	*Flynn<*	*Foley*	*Jamieson*	*Connolly*	*Lyness*
Mason+	Obika	Dennis*	Durmus+	McAllister&	MacPherson>	*Flynn*	*Foley*	*Erwin*	*Morais*	*Lyness*
Mason	Obika+	McAllister*	*Erwin+*	Dennis&	MacPherson>	*Flynn*	*Foley*	*Jamieson*	*Finlayson*	*Lyness*
McAllister*	Erwin	Brophy*	Durmus+	*Sheron*	*MacPherson*	*Flynn*	*Foley*	*Jamieson*	*Finlayson*	*Lyness*
Brophy+	Erwin&	Erhahon*	Quaner+>	Obika&	McAllister>	*Flynn*	*Foley*	*Dennis*	*Durmus*	*Lyness*
Brophy>	Erhahon	McAllister*	Durmus+	Obika&	Dennis>	*Flynn*	*Foley*	*Finlayson*	*Erwin*	*Lyness*
Brophy*	Obika+	Dennis*	Connolly+	*McAllister&*	*Sheron*	*Jamieson*	*Henderson*	*Finlayson*	*Lyness*	
McAllister*	Dennis+	Doyle-Hayes*	Brophy+	Obika&	Tait>	*Jamieson*	*Henderson*	*Finlayson*	*Flynn*	*Lyness*
Doyle-Hayes	Dennis*	Lyness*	Obika+	Connolly&	McAllister>	*Mason*	*Erhahon*	*Finlayson*	*MacPherson*	*Erwin*
Doyle-Hayes	Obika	Connolly*	Flynn+	*Jamieson*	*Erwin*	*Mason*	*Henderson*	*Finlayson*	*MacPherson*	*Urminsky*
Doyle-Hayes	Obika	McAllister*	MacPherson+	Erwin&	Jamieson	*Mason*	*Henderson*	*Finlayson*	*Tait*	*Lyness*
Doyle-Hayes*	Erwin+	MacPherson*	Obika+	McAllister&	Jamieson>	*Mason*	*Henderson*	*Finlayson*	*Urminsky*	*Lyness*
Obika	Erwin*	Flynn*	Connolly+	*Finlayson*	*Jamieson*	*Urminsky*	*Henderson*	*Lyness*		
MacPherson+	Obika	McAllister*	Erwin+	*Finlayson*	*Jamieson*	*Urminsky*	*Henderson*	*Lyness*		
MacPherson*	Obika&	Erwin*	McAllister+	*Connolly&*	*Jamieson*	*Flynn*	*Henderson*	*Finlayson*	*Urminsky*	*Lyness*
Doyle-Hayes	Erwin+	Tait*	Obika+	MacPherson&	Quaner>	Flynn<	*Henderson*	*Finlayson*	*Jamieson*	*Lyness*
Quaner+	McGrath<	McAllister*	Obika+	MacPherson&	Flynn>	Reid<	*Henderson*	*Erwin*	*Jamieson*	*Lyness*
Obika&	McGrath	Erhahon*	Connolly+	Flynn&	*MacPherson*	*Reid*	*Henderson*	*Mason*	*Finlayson*	*Lyness*
Obika	McGrath	Flynn*	Dennis+	Henderson&	*Reid*	*McAllister*	*Tait*	*MacPherson*	*Finlayson*	*Lyness*
Flynn*	McGrath	MacPherson*	McAllister+	Dennis&	*Henderson>*	*Reid*	*Tait*	*Lyness*	*Finlayson*	
Obika	McGrath	Tait*	MacPherson+	Mason&	*Henderson*	*Reid*	*Erwin*	*Lyness*	*Finlayson*	
Henderson+	McGrath	Quaner*	McAllister+	Finlayson&	*Mason*	*Lyness*				
Henderson	Dennis*	Quaner*	Erhahon+	McAllister&	*MacPherson>*	*Reid*	*Mason*	*Finlayson*	*Lyness*	
Henderson	Dennis>	McGrath*	Erwin+	*Durmus&*	*McAllister>*	*Mason*	*Lyness*			
Erwin	Dennis*	Quaner*	Connolly+	Brophy&	*Finlayson*	*Obika*	*Henderson*	*Flynn*	*McAllister*	*Lyness*
Erwin&	Obika+	Connolly*	Quaner+	Dennis&	*MacPherson>*	*McAllister<*	*Mason*	*Tait*	*Erhahin*	*Lyness*
Erwin&	Brophy+	MacPherson*	Dennis+	Obika&	*McAllister>*	*Reid*	*Quaner*	*Finlayson*	*Lyness*	

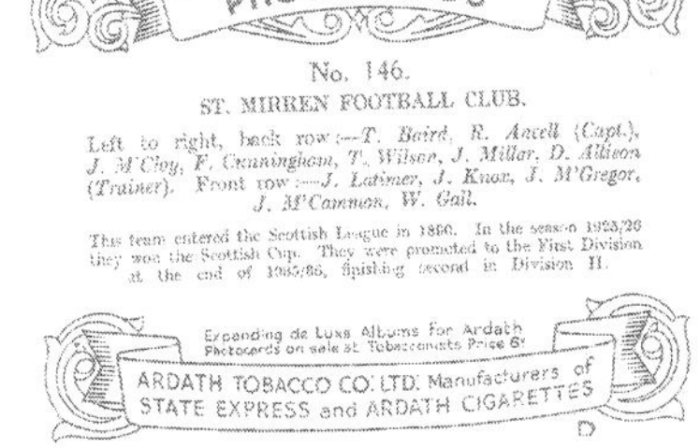
PHOTOCARDS

No. 146.

ST. MIRREN FOOTBALL CLUB.

Left to right, back row:—*T. Baird, R. Ancell (Capt.), J. M'Cloy, F. Cunningham, T. Wilson, J. Millar, D. Allison (Trainer).* Front row:—*J. Latimer, J. Knox, J. M'Gregor, J. M'Cannon, W. Gall.*

This team entered the Scottish League in 1890. In the season 1925/26 they won the Scottish Cup. They were promoted to the First Division at the end of 1935/36, finishing second in Division II.

Expanding de Luxe Albums for Ardath Photocards on sale at Tobacconists Price 6d

ARDATH TOBACCO CO. LTD. Manufacturers of STATE EXPRESS and ARDATH CIGARETTES

D

Stenhousemuir FC 2020/21 The Warriors

Founded	1884
Ground	Ochilview Park
Postcode	FK5 4QL
Tel	01324 562 992
Capacity	3746
Closest Railway Station	Larbert
Record Attendance	12500 v East Fife, SC, 11/3/1950
Ground Record	01324 562992
Record Win	Ochilview
Record Defeat	2-11 v Dunfermline Athletic, 27/9/1930
Most League Goals in a Season	32 Robert Taylor, 1925/6
Colours 2020/21 Top	Maroon
Shorts	White
Sponsor	LOC Hire
Manufacturer	uhlsport
Change Colours 2020/21 Top	White
Shorts	Maroon
Nicknames	Warriors
Web	www.stenhousemuirfc.com
Match Programme 2020/21	None

Chairman: Iain McMenemy
Vice Chair: David Reid
Hon President & Director: Terry Bulloch
Directors: Robert Beagley, Gordon Cook, Martin McNairney
Supporters Rep: Andy McPhate
Chief Executive: Jamie Swinney
General Admin and Football Secretary: Margaret Kilpatrick
Commercial Coordinator: Fiona Smith
Football Development Officer: Daniel Newbigging
Community Coach: Declan Kidd
Chaplain: Michael Rollo
Football Development Officer: Andrew Thomson
Manager: David Irons, then Stephen Swift
Assistant: Kevin McGoldrick, then Frazer Wright & Michael Moore
Coach: Stephen Bryceland
Physio: Jenna Orr
Kitman: Stuart Orr
Doctor: Andy Little

The season started relatively brightly for the Warriors with two wins and two draws but after the restart in March their form dipped badly. Manager Davie Irons stepped down in the wake of heavy defeats to Stranraer and Annan Athletic.

It is hard to pinpoint what went wrong because on paper Stenhousemuir had a decent squad. Perhaps they just didn't respond to Irons' methods?

In the course of the season the club announced a partnership with Hibernian. They took several young Hibbies on loan and that policy will continue next season. Stennie themselves have a partnership with Syngenta who now ground share at Ochilview with some young Stenhosuemuir players joining them on loan.

STAR MAN
Goalkeeper Paddy Martin, on loan from, Hibs, looks like he could be a decent prospect. He was released by the Easter Road side at the end of the season but quickly signed for Falkirk.

PROPSECTS 2021/2
New Manager Stephen Swift has released almost the entire squad and recruited a new one. Many of these came from BSC Glasgow, the Lowland League side he managed successfully for several years. However, the question must eb asked – if they weren't good enough to win the Lowland League, will they be good enough to do well in League Two?

Date	Comp	H/A	Opponents	F	A		HT		Referee	Crowd	Scorers
10/10/2020	LC	A	Edinburgh City	2	2	4-2p	1	1	M McDermid	BCD	Biabi, Tapping
13/10/2020	LC	H	Airdrieonians	0	2		0	0	G Grainger	BCD	
17/10/2020	L	A	Albion Rovers	3	1		1	0	L Wilson	BCD	Spence, Little, Biabi
24/10/2020	L	H	Stirling Albion	2	2		0	1	S Luke	BCD	Biabi, Spence pen
31/10/2020	L	A	Cowdenbeath	1	1		0	0	C Scott	BCD	Graham
07/11/2020	L	H	Edinburgh City	2	0		0	0	D Williams	BCD	Spence 2 (1 pen)
10/11/2020	LC	H	Livingston	0	4		0	3	C Steven	BCD	
14/11/2020	LC	A	Alloa Athletic	2	4		2	0	G Irvine	BCD	Graham, Spence pen
21/11/2020	L	H	Annan Athletic	1	2		0	1	L Wilson	BCD	McGuigan
28/11/2020	L	A	Queen's Park	1	3		1	1	D Lowe	BCD	Biabi
05/12/2020	L	H	Brechin City	2	1		2	0	D Williams	BCD	Munro, McGuigan
12/12/2020	L	H	Stranraer	2	2		0	2	D McFarlane	BCD	Biabi, Graham
19/12/2020	L	A	Elgin City	0	2		0	2	S Reid	BCD	
26/12/2020	SC	H	Preston Athletic	4	1		2	0	K Graham	BCD	McGuigan 2, Tiffoney, Hodge
20/03/2021	L	H	Albion Rovers	2	0		1	0	L Wilson	BCD	Biabi, McGuigan
23/03/2021	SC	A	Peterhead	1	0		1	0	M Roncone	BCD	McGuigan
27/03/2021	L	A	Edinburgh City	1	3		0	1	G Grainger	BCD	McGuigan
30/03/2021	L	A	Stirling Albion	0	1		0	0	G Grainger	BCD	
03/04/2021	SC	H	Kilmarnock	0	4		0	2	G Aitken	BCD	
06/04/2021	L	A	Brechin City	1	1		1	1	S Lambie	BCD	Hodge
08/04/2021	L	H	Cowdenbeath	1	0		1	0	L Watson	BCD	Yeats
10/04/2021	L	H	Queen's Park	1	3		0	2	C Graham	BCD	Muir pen
13/04/2021	L	H	Elgin City	2	0		0	0	C Scott	BCD	Muir, Biabi
15/04/2021	L	A	Stranraer	0	4		0	3	P Stuart	BCD	
20/04/2021	L	A	Annan Athletic	1	5		1	3	G Irvine	BCD	McGuigan
24/04/2021	L	H	Cowdenbeath	0	2		0	0	D Williams	BCD	
27/04/2021	L	A	Annan Athletic	1	1		0	0	L Wilson	BCD	Hopkirk
29/04/2021	L	H	Albion Rovers	0	1		0	1	S Luke	BCD	
04/05/2021	L	A	Brechin City	1	0		0	0	G Ross	BCD	McGuigan
ABANDONED											
02/01/2021	L	H	Stirling Albion	0	1				C Graham		
30 mins, ice											

Jon Connolly

Roddy McKenzie

Stewart Kennedy

Date	Comp	H/A	Opponents	F	A		1	2	3	4	5	6	7	8	9	10	11	12	13	14	15	16	17	18	19	20
10/10/2020	LC	A	Edinburgh City	2	2	4-2p	Erskine	Tiffoney	Little	Munro	Yeats	Tapping	Blair	Spence	McGuigan	Hopkirk	Biabi*	Hodge*	Brown	Watters	Halleran	Smith	Fairley	Grigor	McQueen	
13/10/2020	LC	H	Airdrieonians	0	2		Erskine	Tiffoney	Little	Munro	Yeats	Tapping	McQueen*	Spence&	Hodge<	Hopkirk+	Muir>	Brown*	Biabi+	Fairley&	McGuigan>	Watters<	Halleran	Grigor	Smith	
17/10/2020	L	A	Albion Rovers	3	1		Smith	Tiffoney*	Little	Munro	Yeats	Tapping	McGuigan	Biabi	Hodge	Hopkirk	Muir+	Fairley*	Grigor+	McQueen	Graham	Watters	Halleran	Erskine		
24/10/2020	L	H	Stirling Albion	2	2		Smith*	Tiffoney	Little	Munro	Yeats	Tapping	Blair	Spence	Brown+	Hopkirk&	Muir>	Erskine*	Biabi+	Hodge&	McGuigan>	Watters	Fairley	Grigor	Graham	McQueen
31/10/2020	L	A	Cowdenbeath	1	1		Martin	Tiffoney	Little	Munro	Yeats	Tapping	Blair	Spence&	Halleran+	Biabi	Muir*	McGuigan*	Graham+	Hodge&	Brown	Watters	Erskine	Grigor	McQueen	
07/11/2020	L	H	Edinburgh City	2	0		Martin	Tiffoney	Little	Munro	Yeats	Tapping	Blair	Spence&	Hodge+	Biabi*	Muir	McGuigan*	Brown+	Graham&	Fairley	Watters	Erskine	Grigor	McQueen	Halleran
10/11/2020	LC	H	Livingston	0	4		Martin	Tiffoney	McQueen	Munro	Yeats	Tapping	Blair	McGuigan	Brown*	Fairley+	Graham&	Muir*	Hodge+	Biabl&	Spence	Watters	Erskine	Grigor	Halleran	
14/11/2020	LC	A	Alloa Athletic	2	4		Martin	Grigor	McQueen	Hodge	Yeats+	Tapping	Blair	McGuigan	Spence	Muir	Graham*	Halleran*	Watters+	Shiels	Erskine	Fairley	Biabi	Brown		
21/11/2020	L	H	Annan Athletic	1	2		Martin	Graham*	Hodge	Munro	Yeats	Tapping	Blair	McGuigan	Spence	Muir	Biabi*	Grigor*	Watters	Brown	Erskine	Fairley	Halleran	McQueen	Shiels	
28/11/2020	L	A	Queen's Park	1	3		Martin	Tiffoney&	Hodge	Munro	Little	Tapping	Blair	Watters	Spence	Muir*	Biabi+	McGuigan*	Graham+	Grigor&	Erskine	McQueen	Shiels	Halleran		
05/12/2020	L	H	Brechin City	2	1		Martin	Tiffoney	Hodge*	Munro	Little	Tapping	Blair	Watters	McGuigan	Grigor	Biabi+	Halleran*	Spence+	Graham	Erskine	McQueen	Shiels	Kane	Fairley	
12/12/2020	L	H	Stranraer	2	2		Martin	Grigor	Hodge	Munro	Little	Tapping	Blair	Watters	McGuigan	Spence+	Biabi*	Graham*	Fairley+	Halleran	Tiffoney	McQueen	Shiels	Kane	Erskine	McCracken
19/12/2020	L	A	Elgin City	0	2		Martin	Tiffoney>	Hodge+	Munro	Little*	Grigor	Blair	Watters<	McGuigan	Spence	Biabi&	McQueen*	Graham+	Halleran&	Fairley>	McCracken<	Erskine			
26/12/2020	SC	H	Preston Athletic	4	1		Martin	Tiffoney	Hodge	Munro	Little	Halleran+	Blair	McCracken	McGuigan	Spence*	Graham	Biabi*	Fairley+	Erskine	McQueen	Brown				
20/03/2021	L	H	Albion Rovers	2	0		Martin	Tiffoney	Corbett	Brown	Little	Tapping	Blair	Hopkirk	McGuigan	Muir*	Biabi+	Spence*	Collins+	Erskine	McQueen	Kane	Fairley	McCracken	Hodge	Halleran
23/03/2021	SC	A	Peterhead	1	0		Martin	Tiffoney	Kane	Brown	Little	Tapping	Blair	Hopkirk	McGuigan+	Muir*	Biabi	Spence*	Collins+	Erskine	Hodge	Grigor	Fairley	Halleran	McQueen	
27/03/2021	L	A	Edinburgh City	1	3		Martin	Tiffoney	Kane	Brown+	Little	Tapping	Blair	Hopkirk&	McGuigan	Muir*	Biabi	Docherty*	Corbett+	Fairley&	Erskine	Grigor	Spence	Halleran	Collins	Hodge
30/03/2021	L	A	Stirling Albion	0	1		Martin	Tiffoney	Kane	Corbett*	Yeats	Tapping	Blair&	Brydon	McGuigan	Collins+	Biabi	Muir*	Hopkirk+	Spence&	Erskine	Brown	Docherty	Halleran	Fairley	Hodge
03/04/2021	SC	H	Kilmarnock	0	4		Martin	Tiffoney	Kane>	Yeats	Hodge	Tapping	Blair&	Hopkirk	McGuigan*	Collins	Biabi+	McQueen*	Fairley+	Grigor&	Halleran>	Shiels	Watters	McCracken	Erskine	
06/04/2021	L	A	Brechin City	1	1		Martin	Tiffoney+	Corbett	Yeats	Little	Tapping	Blair	Docherty>	McGuigan*	Brydon	Hodge&	Hopkirk*	Biabi+	Halleran&	Collins>	Kane	Watters	Grigor	Fairley	Erskine
08/04/2021	L	H	Cowdenbeath	1	0		Martin	Tiffoney	Corbett	Yeats	Little	Brydon	Blair	Docherty+	Biabi&	Muir*	Hodge>	McGuigan*	Collins+	Hopkirk&	Halleran>	Kane	Fairley	Grigor	Tapping	Erskine
10/04/2021	L	H	Queen's Park	1	3		Martin	Tiffoney*	Corbett	Tapping	Little	Brydon	Blair+	McGuigan	Biabi>	Muir<	Hodge&	Fairley*	Brown+	Hopkirk&	Halleran>	Collins<	Watters	Grigor	Kane	Erskine
13/04/2021	L	H	Elgin City	2	0		Martin	Docherty+	Corbett	Yeats	Little	Brydon	Blair	Tapping	Brown*	Muir	Hodge	Kane*	Biabi+	Fairley	Halleran	Collins	Watters	Grigor	McGuigan	Erskine
15/04/2021	L	A	Stranraer	0	4		Martin	Kane+	Corbett<	Yeats	Little	Brydon	Blair>	Tapping	Docherty*	Muir&	Hodge	McGuigan*	Biabi+	Hopkirk&	Fairley>	Grigor<	Watters	Halleran	Collins	Erskine
20/04/2021	L	A	Annan Athletic	1	5		Martin	Kane*	Corbett	Yeats	Little	Brydon	Hopkirk	Tapping	McGuigan>	Collins+	Hodge&	Biabi*	Muir+	Blair&	Halleran>	Grigor	Watters	Shields	Erskine	
24/04/2021	L	H	Cowdenbeath	0	2		Martin	Kane	Corbett+	Yeats>	Biabi&	Brydon	Hopkirk	Tapping	McGuigan	Muir	Hodge*	Blair*	Little+	Collins&	Halleran>	Grigor	Watters	Shields	McCracken	Erskine
27/04/2021	L	A	Annan Athletic	1	1		Martin	Kane	Tiffoney+	Grigor	Little	Brydon	Hopkirk	Blair	Watters*	Biabi&	Hodge	Collins*	Halleran+	Muir&	McQueen	McGuigan	McCracken	Shields	Erskine	
29/04/2021	L	H	Albion Rovers	0	1		Martin	Kane&	Tiffoney	Grigor	Corbett*	Halleran	Hopkirk	Blair	McGuigan	Collins+	Muir	Hodge*	Biabi+	McQueen&	Shiels	McCracken	Erskine			
04/05/2021	L	A	Brechin City	1	0		Martin	McCracken	McQueen*	Grigor	Little	Halleran	Hopkirk	Blair	McGuigan	Collins	Hodge+	Kane*	Shiels+	Biabl&	Erskine					
ABANDONED																										
02/01/2021	L	H	Stirling Albion	0	1		Martin	Tiffoney	Graham	Munro	Little	Tapping	Blair	McCracken	McGuigan	Spence	Biabi	Erskine	McQueen	Hodge	Brown	Hopkirk	Halleran			

THE GOALIES

Goalkeepers Used in League Matches, 1972-2020
Players shown in the season of their first appearance only

1972/3	Stewart Kennedy
	Gerry Grzybowski
	Ray Dunlop
	Neil McNeill
1975/6	Alex Porwol
1976/7	Norrie McDonald
1977/8	Ian McGregor
	Brian Wilson
1978/9	Brian Howie
	Stan Drummond
1980/1	R Mulholland
	Ian McLaren
1982/3	Lindsay Hamilton
1985/6	Gary McPhail
	Ian Spalding
	David Kenny
	Graham Kyle
1986/7	Brian Cassidy
	Kevin McKeown
	Alan Carswell
	Ally Jenkins
	Andy Arrol
1987/8	Stuart Robertson
	Andy Keith
1989/0	Kevin McKeown
	John Paterno
	Charlie Kelly
1990/1	Alan Joyce
1991/2	Kenny Barnstaple
1993/4	Michael Harkness
1995/6	Roddy McKenzie
1996/7	Stevie Ellison
	Neil Alexander
1998/9	Kevin Budinauckas
1999/0	Ryan McGurk
	Jon Connolly
2000/1	Gary Gow
2001/2	Marc Graham
	Paul Jarvie
	Andy Carlin
2002/3	Aaron Gillespie
	Graham Smith
2003/4	Willie McCulloch
	Alex Hardie
2004/5	James Kirkham
	David Orr
2005/6	Chris Fahey
2006/7	Andy Carlin
	Scott Johnstone
2007/8	John Hillcoat
	Ally Brown
2008/9	Kieran Renton
	C Rankin
	Scott Bennett
2009/0	Chris McCluskey
2011/2	Dean Shaw
2012/3	Callum Reidford
	Robbie Thomson
	Chris Smith
2014/5	Greg Fleming
	Jack Hamilton
2015/6	Matthew Gould
	Jamie Barclay
	Graham Bowman
	Colin McCabe
	Sean Robertson
2016/7	David Crawford
2017/8	Chris Smith Lewis McMinn
2018/9	Graeme Smith
2019/0	Daniel Terry

Surname	First Name	Date of Birth	No	Nat	Pos	Signed	Previous	Notes	Contract	Lge A	Lge S	Lge G	SC A	SC S	SC G	LC A	LC S	LC G	Un
Biabi	Botti	08/03/1996	12	ROI / SCO	F	2019	Ebbsfleet United	Released May 2021, joined Kelty Hearts		15	7	6	2	1		1	2	1	1
Blair	Ryan	23/02/1996	6	SCO	M	2020	Swansea City	Released May 2021		19	2		3			3			0
Brown	Paul	22/03/2001	3	SCO	M	2020	Dunfermline Athletic	Released June 2021		4	2		1			1	1		6
Brydon	Jack	01/01/2004		SCO	D	2021	Hibernian (OL)	Mar-May		9	0								0
Collins	Thomas	27/08/1996		SCO	F	2021	East Fife (OL)	Jan-May		4	6		1	1					3
Corbett	Adam	29/10/1997		SCO	D	2021	Spartans		End 2021/2	10	1								0
Docherty	Alan	25/10/1996		SCO	F	2021	Camelon (OL)	Mar-May		4	1								1
Erskine	Calum	24/04/2001	17	SCO	GK	2020	Bury	Released June 2021, joined Dumbarton		0	1					2			26
Fairley	Jayden	22/09/2003	20	SCO	M	2020	Hibernian (OL)	Oct-May		0	6			2		1	1		12
Graham	Cammy	23/03/2002		SCO	M	2020	Dunfermline Athletic		End 2021/2	1	5	2	1			2		1	3
Grigor	Josh	14/08/2002	9	SCO	D	2020	Hamilton Accies	OL to Syngetna 2021/2	End 2021/2	6	4			1		1			14
Halleran	Thomas	21/03/2000	8	SCO	M	2017	Forth Valley Elite Acad	Released May 2021, joined Linlithgow Rose		3	8		1	1			1		14
Hodge	Jack	25/04/2001	21	SCO	M	2020	Hibernian	Released May 2021, joined Broomhill FC		16	3	1	2		1	2	2		4
Hopkirk	David	17/01/1993	10	SCO	F	2019	Clyde	Transferred to Dumbarton June 2021		9	5	1	2			2			0
Kane	Chris	31/05/1993	5	SCO	M	2020	Edinburgh City	Released May 2021		7	2		2						6
Little	Creag	16/04/1993	4	SCO	D	2020	Queen's Park	Released May 2021, joined Elgin City		18	2	1	2			2			0
Martin	Paddy	21/06/1999	1	SCO	GK	2020	Hibernian (OL)	Oct-May		20	0		3			2			0
McCracken	Adam	21/11/1998	23	NIR	D	2020	Broughty Athletic	Freed June 2021		1	1		1						6
McGuigan	Mark	07/11/1988	25	SCO	F	2017	Stranraer	Released May 2021, joined East Fife		14	6	6	3		3	3	1		2
McQueen	Chris	20/02/2002	24	SCO	D	2020	Celtic	Released May 2021		1	2			1		3			13
Muir	Tommy	21/04/1997	22	SCO	F	2020	Annan Athletic	Released May 2021, joined Stranraer		14	3	2	1			2	1		0
Munro	Andy	15/11/1992	19	SCO	D	2019	Forfar Athletic	Transferred to Forfar Ath, Feb 2021		9	0	1	1			3			0
Shiels	Martin	21/07/1994	15	SCO	M	2020	Gartcairn	Released May 2021, joined Shotts BA		0	1								10
Smith	Graeme	08/01/1983	1	SCO	GK	2018	Brechin City		End 2021/2	2	0								2
Spence	Greig	06/07/1992	11	SCO	F	2020	Arbroath	OL to East Fife, Mar-May, Released May 2021		7	3	4	1	1		3		1	2
Tapping	Callum	05/06/1993	7	ENG / SCO	M	2020	Forfar Athletic	Transferred to Edinburgh City June 2021		17	0		2			4		1	1
Tiffoney	Jonathan	07/05/1991	2	SCO	D	2019	Ashington	Released May 2021		15	0		3		1	3			1
Watters	Ryan	12/05/1998	14	SCO	F	2019	Albion Rovers	Released May 2021		5	0						2		13
Yeats	Callum	04/10/2001	16	SCO	D	2020	Hibernian (OL)	Oct-May		12	0	1	1			4			0
NEW SIGNINGS																			
Anderson	Michael	07/02/2000		SCO	M	2021	BSC Glasgow		End 2021/2										
Brown	Adam	09/06/1995		SCO	M	2021	Alloa Athletic		End 2021/2										
Christie	Darren	24/11/1987		SCO	F	2021	Pollok		End 2021/2										
Coll	Bernard	07/09/1994		SCO	D	2021	Forfar Athletic		End 2021/2										
Crighton	Sean	26/03/1990		SCO	D	2021	Airdrieonians		End 2021/2										
Forbes	Ross	03/03/1989		SCO	M	2021	Dumbarton		End 2021/2										
Hughes	Declan	17/05/1995		SCO	M	2021	BSC Glasgow		End 2021/2										
Jamieson	Nicky	03/08/1996		SCO	D	2021	Alloa Athletic (OL)												
Lyon	Ross	26/03/1998		SCO	M	2021	BSC Glasgow		End 2021/2										
Lyon	James	25/01/2003		SCO	M	2021	Partick Thistle (OL)	Jul-May	End 2021/2										
Marshall	Ryan	24/09/1990		SCO	GK	2021	BSC Glasgow		End 2021/2										
Mills	Jamie	01/03/1996		SCO	D	2021	BSC Glasgow		End 2021/2										
O'Reilly	Euan	02/05/2000		SCO	M	2021	Airdrieonians		End 2021/2										
Orr	Thomas	13/03/1997		SCO	F	2021	Stranraer		End 2021/2										
Reid	Craig	26/02/1986		SCO	D	2021	Kelty Hearts		End 2021/2										
Tapping	Jordan	04/07/1996		SENG / SCO	D	2021	East Stirlingshire		End 2021/2										
Thomson	Robert	28/05/1993		SCO	F	2021	Alloa Athletic		End 2021/2										
Tierney	Ryan	30/01/1998		SCO	F	2021	BSC Glasgow		End 2021/2										
Wedderburn	Nat	30/06/1991		ENG	M	2021	Dumbarton		End 2021/2										
Wilson	David	05/03/2001		SCO	GK	2021	Clyde		End 2021/2										

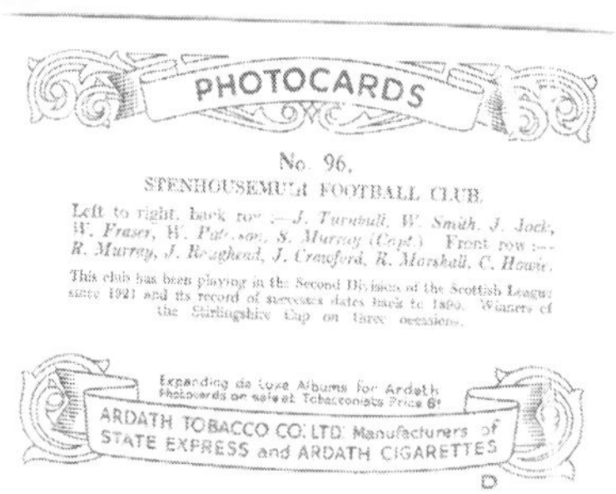
PHOTOCARDS

No. 96.

STENHOUSEMUIR FOOTBALL CLUB.

Left to right, back row :— *J. Turnbull, W. Smith, J. Jock, W. Fraser, W. Paterson, S. Murray (Capt.)* Front row :— *R. Murray, J. Roughead, J. Crawford, R. Marshall, C. Howie.*

This club has been playing in the Second Division of the Scottish League since 1921 and its record of successes dates back to 1890. Winners of the Stirlingshire Cup on three occasions.

Expanding de Luxe Albums for Ardath Photocards on sale at Tobacconists Price 6d

ARDATH TOBACCO CO. LTD. Manufacturers of STATE EXPRESS and ARDATH CIGARETTES

D

Stirling Albion FC 2020/21 The Binos

Founded	1945
Ground	Forthbank Stadium
Postcode	FK7 7UJ
Tel	01786 450399
Capacity	3808
Closest Railway Station	Stirling
Record Attendance	26400 v Celtic, SC, 14/3/1959
Ground Record	3808 v Aberdeen, SC, 15/2/1996
Record Win	20-0 v Selkirk, SC, 8/12/1984
Record Defeat	0-9 v Dundee Utd, L, 30/12/1967; v Ross Co, SC, 6/2/2010
Most League Goals in a Season	27 Joe Hughes, 1969/70
Colours 2020/21 Top	Red with white sleeves
Shorts	Red
Sponsor	Prudential
Manufacturer	Macron
Change Colours 2014/15 Top	Purple
Shorts	Purple
Nicknames	Binos
Web	www.stirlingalbionfc.co.uk
Match Programme 2020/21	£2

Chairman and Operations Director: Stuart Brown
Finance Director: Alan Christie
Commercial Director: Colin Rowley
Club Secretary and Director: Graham Douglas
Community Engagement Director: Grant Morrice
Supporter and Media Director: John Daly
Child Wellbeing and Protection Managers
Stirling Albion Junior Academy: Jim McAllister
Community and Youth Development: Duncan Strathdee
Manager: Kevin Rutkiewicz
Goalkeeping Coach: Kevin Budinauckas
Physio: Kenny Crichton
Head Of Performance Analysis: Bill Orr
Head of Scouting: David Peat
Kit Man: John Knox
Head of Youth (Coaching): Niall Marshall
Head of Youth (Admin): David Brown
Under 18s Coaches: Aurelien Mazel and Shaun Conlon
Under 16s Coaches: Jamie Baxter, Mark Pincombe
Goalkeeping Coach: Graham Hamilton
Physio: Stephanie Wells
Club Doctor: Dr Veronica McBurnie
Club Chaplain: Duncan Strathdee
Community Engagement Manager: Callum Parry
Disability Access Officer: Stevie Peebles

2020/1 can only be regarded a spectacular failure for Stirling Albion. Given the squad that they had a play off place should have been assured but they failed at the last kick and finished fifth. They had some of the best platers in the League – notably striker Andy Ryan – but their home performances let them down badly. They won just four home league games all season – against Annan, Cowden, Brechin and Stenhousemuir, all teams that finished well below them in the table.

They failed to qualify from their League Cup group and went out of the Scottish Cup at the second hurdle, losing at home to Raith Rovers.

STAR MAN

Andy Ryan was their top scorer and key player. His contract included a clause allowing him to leave if he was offered full time football so he left in the Summer to join Hamilton Accies.

PROSPECTS 2021/2

Manager Kevin Rutkiewicz looks to have recruited well. He will need to get off to a good start or else his job could be in jeopardy. Clearly Stirling have spent good money to mount a promotion challenge and anything less will not be acceptable.

The Original Forthbank

Crowds gather at the original Forthbank, circa 1900. The ground was closer to the city centre, adjacent to the railway and what is now Kerse Road. The ground was destroyed by a German bomb during World War Two.

A competition was held to name Stirling Albion's new ground when they left Annfield in 1992. Forthbank was the name chosen for their return to the town in 1993 after a year in exile at Stenhousemuir.

Date	Comp	H/A	Opponents	F	A	HT		Referee	Crowd	Scorers
06/10/2020	LC	H	Arbroath	1	2	0	2	B Cook	BCD	Ryan
10/10/2020	LC	A	Elgin City	0	2	0	0	D McFarlane	BCD	
17/10/2020	L	H	Queen's Park	0	0	0	0	G Grainger	BCD	
24/10/2020	L	A	Stenhousemuir	2	2	1	0	S Luke	BCD	Wilson, Leitch
31/10/2020	L	H	Annan Athletic	1	0	1	0	M McDermind	BCD	Ryan
07/11/2020	L	A	Brechin City	5	0	2	0	G Ross	BCD	Ryan, S Roberts, Byrne, Wilson, Leitch
10/11/2020	LC	H	Montrose	2	1	2	1	P Stuart	BCD	Heaver, Mackin
14/11/2020	LC	A	Ross County	0	3	0	1	A Muir		
21/11/2020	L	H	Elgin City	1	2	0	1	D Lowe	BCD	K Roberts
28/11/2020	L	A	Albion Rovers	1	0	1	0	S Lambie	BCD	Ryan
05/12/2020	L	A	Stranraer	2	2	2	1	D Williams	BCD	Ryan pen, McManus og
12/12/2020	L	H	Cowdenbeath	1	0	0	0	D Dickinson	BCD	Byrne
19/12/2020	L	A	Edinburgh City	3	2	3	0	D Williams	BCD	Leitch, Byrne, Ryan
26/12/2020	SC	A	Berwick Rangers	3	0	2	0	M Roncone	BCD	K Roberts, Byrne, Ryan
20/03/2021	L	H	Brechin City	1	0	0	0	B Cook	BCD	Moore
23/03/2021	SC	H	Raith Rovers	0	2	0	1	A Newlands	BCD	
27/03/2021	L	A	Elgin City	1	1	0	0	G Irvine	BCD	Ryan
30/03/2021	L	H	Stenhousemuir	1	0	0	0	G Grainger	BCD	Leitch
03/04/2021	L	A	Queen's Park	0	1	0	1	D McFarlane	BCD	
06/04/2021	L	H	Albion Rovers	1	1	0	1	C Graham	BCD	Ryan pen
10/04/2021	L	A	Annan Athletic	2	1	1	0	S Lambie	BCD	Mackin, Ryan pen
13/04/2021	L	H	Stranraer	0	1	0	0	D Williams	BCD	
17/04/2021	L	A	Cowdenbeath	5	1	3	1	C Scott	BCD	Ryan 2(1 pen), Banner, Hamilton, Mackin
20/04/2021	L	H	Edinburgh City	0	1	0	1	D Lowe	BCD	
24/04/2021	L	A	Edinburgh City	1	0	1	0	L Watson	BCD	Mackin
27/04/2021	L	H	Queen's Park	1	2	0	1	D McFarlane	BCD	Heaver
29/04/2021	L	A	Elgin City	1	3	0	2	S Lambie	BCD	Bikey
01/05/2021	L	H	Stranraer	2	2	1	1	C Scott	BCD	McGeachie, Byrne
ABANDONED										
02/01/2021	l	A	Stenhousemuir	1	0			C Graham	BCD	Docherty
30 mins, ice										

Henry Heighton

Mark McGeown

Date	Comp	H/A	Opponents	F	A	1	2	3	4	5	6	7	8	9	10	11	12	13	14	15	16	17	18	19	20
06/10/2020	LC	H	Arbroath	1	2	Binnie	Banner	Creaney	McLean	McGregor	K Roberts*	Ryan	Wilson	Leitch	Moore+	Mackin&	S Roberts*	Thomson+	Byrne&	*Greenhorn*	*Heaver*	*El-Zubaidi*	*France*	*Law*	
10/10/2020	LC	A	Elgin City	0	2	Binnie	Banner	Creaney>	McLean	McGregor	K Roberts*	Ryan	Wilson&	Leitch	S Roberts+	Byrne	Thomson*	Moore+	Docherty&	Heaver>	*Greenhorn*	*Magee*	*Carey*	*Law*	
17/10/2020	L	H	Queen's Park	0	0	Stone	Banner	McGeachie	McLean	McGregor	K Roberts	Ryan	Wilson	Leitch	Moore+	Mackin*	Byrne*	S Roberts+	*Docherty*	*Heaver*	*El-Zubaidi*	*Magee*	*Thomson*	*Law*	
24/10/2020	L	A	Stenhousemuir	2	2	Binnie	Banner	McGeachie	McLean*	McGregor	K Roberts+	Ryan	Wilson	Leitch	S Roberts	Byrne	El-Zubaidi*	Heaver+	*Creaney*	Magee	*Olly McDonald*	*Docherty*	*Thomson*	*Law*	
31/10/2020	L	H	Annan Athletic	1	0	Binnie	Banner	McGeachie	El-Zubaidi	McGregor	K Roberts	Ryan	Wilson	Leitch	S Roberts	Byrne	*Thomson*	*Docherty*	*Creaney*	Magee	*Olly McDonald*	*Heaver*	*Law*		
07/11/2020	L	A	Brechin City	5	0	Binnie	Banner	McGeachie<	El-Zubaidi>	McGregor	K Roberts	Ryan+	Wilson&	Leitch*	S Roberts	Byrne	Heaver*	Docherty+	Mackin&	Magee>	Thomson<	*Moore*	*Creaney*	*Law*	
10/11/2020	LC	H	Montrose	2	1	Binnie	Banner	McGeachie	El-Zubaidi	McGregor	Docherty	Heaver	Wilson	Leitch	S Roberts	Mackin	Magee*	Creaney+	Byrne&	K Roberts>	Mitchell<	*Ryan*	*Thomson*	*Law*	*Moore*
14/11/2020	LC	A	Ross County	0	3	Binnie	Banner	McGeachie	El-Zubaidi	McGregor	K Roberts	Docherty+	Wilson&	Leitch>	Byrne<	Creaney*	Moore*	Mackin+	Magee&	Heaver>	Ryan<	*Thomson*	*Law*		
21/11/2020	L	H	Elgin City	1	2	Binnie	Banner	McGeachie	El-Zubaidi	McGregor	K Roberts	Ryan	Wilson	Leitch	S Roberts+	Byrne*	Mackin*	Moore+	*Magee*	*McLean*	*Creaney*	*Thomson*	*Johnston*	*Currie*	
28/11/2020	L	A	Albion Rovers	1	0	Binnie	Banner	McLean	El Zubaidi	McGregor	K Roberts	Ryan	Mackin+	Leitch	S Roberts*	Moore&	McGeachie*	Byrne+	Creaney&	*Heaver*	*Thomson*	*Magee*	*Johnston*	*Currie*	
05/12/2020	L	A	Stranraer	2	2	Binnie	Banner	McLean	Creaney*	McGregor+	K Roberts	Ryan	Wilson	Leitch	Byrne&	Moore	S Roberts*	El-Zubaidi+	Mackin&	*Heaver*	*Thomson*	*Magee*	*Docherty*	*Currie*	
12/12/2020	L	H	Cowdenbeath	1	0	Binnie	Banner	McLean	McGeachie	McGregor	K Roberts	Ryan	Wilson*	Docherty>	Heaver+	Moore&	Leitch*	Byrne+	S Roberts&	Magee>	*El-Zubaidi*	*Mackin*	*Mitchell*	*Thomson*	*Currie*
19/12/2020	L	A	Edinburgh City	3	2	Binnie	Banner	McLean	McGeachie	McGregor	K Roberts	Ryan&	El-Zubaidi	Leitch>	S Roberts*	Byrne+	Docherty*	Moore+	Mackin&	Mitchell>	*Thomson*	*Heaver*	*Johnston*	*Currie*	
26/12/2020	SC	A	Berwick Rangers	3	0	Currie	El-Zubaidi	McLean	McGeachie	McGregor	K Roberts	Ryan*	Docherty	Leitch	S Roberts+	Byrne&	Mackin*	Thomson+	Heaver&	*Banner*	*Mitchell*	*Moore*	*Binnie*		
20/03/2021	L	H	Brechin City	1	0	Binnie	El-Zubaidi	McLean*	McGeachie	McGregor	K Roberts	Ryan	Docherty&	Banner	S Roberts+	Byrne	Wilson*	Moore+	Hamilton&	*Heaver*	*Creaney*	*Mackin*	*Greenhorn*	*Currie*	
23/03/2021	SC	H	Raith Rovers	0	2	Currie	El-Zubaidi	Hamilton	McGeachie+	Meggatt	Wilson*	Heaver	Banner	Leitch	Moore&	Mackin	Kirkpatrick*	Allan+	S Roberts&	*Byrne*	*McGregor*	*Ryan*	*K Roberts*	*Docherty*	*Binnie*
27/03/2021	L	A	Elgin City	1	1	Binnie	El-Zubaidi&	Banner	McGeachie	McGregor	K Roberts>	Ryan	Byrne<	Leitch+	Moore*	Wilson	Allan*	Kirkpatrick+	Meggatt&	Hamilton>	*Heaver<*	*Docherty*	*Mackin*	*S Roberts*	*Currie*
30/03/2021	L	H	Stenhousemuir	1	0	Binnie	Meggatt	Banner	Allan	McGregor*	K Roberts	Ryan&	Byrne+	Leitch	Moore	Wilson	Eadie*	Mackin+	Heaver&	*Hamilton*	*Thomson*	*Docherty*	*Kirkpatrick*	*S Roberts*	*Currie*
03/04/2021	L	A	Queen's Park	0	1	Binnie	Meggatt	Banner	McGeachie	Hamilton>	K Roberts	Allan	Heaver*	Leitch	S Roberts+	Mackin&	Kirkpatrick*	Moore+	Byrne&	Ryan>	*Thomson*	*Docherty*	*Eadie*	*Wilson*	*Currie*
06/04/2021	L	H	Albion Rovers	1	1	Currie	Meggatt+	Banner	McGeachie&	McGregor	Kirkpatrick	Ryan	Byrne*	Leitch	Moore	Wilson>	Mackin*	Eadie+	S Roberts&	K Roberts>	*Thomson*	*Docherty*	*Hamilton*	*Heaver*	*Binnie*
10/04/2021	L	A	Annan Athletic	2	1	Currie	Eadie	Banner	McGeachie	McGregor	K Roberts>	Ryan	Wilson	Leitch*	S Roberts+	Mackin&	Allan*	Hamilton+	Byrne&	Kirkpatrick>	*Bikey*	*Docherty*	*Moore*	*Heaver*	*Binnie*
13/04/2021	L	H	Stranraer	0	1	Currie	Eadie	Banner	McGeachie<	McGregor	K Roberts	Kirkpatrick+	Wilson>	Byrne*	S Roberts&	Mackin	Moore*	Leitch+	Heaver&	Bikey>	Allan<	*Docherty*	*Hamilton*	*Meggatt*	*Binnie*
17/04/2021	L	A	Cowdenbeath	5	1	Binnie	Eadie	Banner	McGeachie	Allan*	Hamilton	Ryan>	Moore<	Leitch&	Docherty	Mackin+	Thomson*	Kirkpatrick+	Bikey&	Heaver>	S Roberts<	*Byrne*	*Wilson*	*Currie*	
20/04/2021	L	H	Edinburgh City	0	1	Binnie	Eadie	Banner	McGeachie	Allan*	Hamilton	Ryan>	Moore+	Leitch	Docherty&	Mackin	S Roberts*	Kirkpatrick+	Byrne&	Bikey>	*Wilson*	*K Roberts*	*McGregor*	*Heaver*	*Currie*
24/04/2021	L	A	Edinburgh City	1	0	Currie	Eadie	Banner	McGeachie	McGregor	Hamilton	Ryan	Allan+	Leitch&	K Roberts	Mackin*	Byrne*	Moore+	Wilson&>	Docherty>	*Bikey*	*Heaver*	*Thomson*	*S Roberts*	*Binnie*
27/04/2021	L	H	Queen's Park	1	2	Currie	Eadie*	Thomson	McGeachie>	McGregor	K Roberts&	Docherty	Moore<	Byrne+	S Roberts	Bikey	Hamilton*	Wilson+	Heaver&	Creaney>	Greenhorn<	*Ryan*	*Binnie*		
29/04/2021	L	A	Elgin City	1	3	Currie	El Zubaidi	Allan	McGeachie	Banner	Hamilton	Ryan+	Moore*	Leitch&	K Roberts	Mackin	S Roberts*>	Bikey+	Byrne&	Thomson>	*Greenhorn*	*Docherty*	*Creaney*	*Binnie*	
01/05/2021	L	H	Stranraer	2	2	Currie	El Zubaidi	Allan	McGeachie	McGregor	Hamilton	Wilson+	Heaver*	Leitch*	K Roberts	Bikey&	Docherty*	Mackin+	Byrne&	*Thomson*	*Greenhorn*	*Banner*	*Creaney*	*S Roberts*	*Binnie*
ABANDONED																									
02/01/2021	I	A	Stenhousemuir	1	0	Binnie	El-Zubaidi	McLean	McGeachie	McGregor	K Roberts	Ryan	Docherty	Banner	S Roberts	Byrne	*Mitchell*	*Thomson*	*Heaver*	*Bikey*	*Moore*	*Johnston*	*Mackin*	*Currie*	
30 mins, ice																									

THE GOALIES

Goalkeepers Used in League Matches, 1972-2020

Players shown in the season of their first appearance only

1972/3	George Young
1975/6	Brian Howie
1977/8	Gordon Arthur
1981/2	David Gordon
1982/3	Andy Graham
1984/5	Craig Anderson
1987/8	David Mills
	Les Fridge
1988/9	Mark McGeown
	Kevin McKeown
1989/0	Lindsay Hamilton
1991/2	Jamie Picken
1993/4	Michael Monaghan
1998/9	Gary Gow
1999/0	Jason Gardiner
	Graeme Donald
2000/1	Chris Reid
2001/2	Henry Heighton
2002/3	Iain Turner
	Anton Nugent
	Myles Hogarth
2003/4	Scott Morrison
2004/5	Scott Christie
2005/6	Robert Giacomi
2010/1	Callum Reidford
2011/2	Sam Filler
	Jamie Cleland
2012/3	Mark Peat
	David Crawford
2013/4	Cammy Binnie
	Greg Paterson
2015/6	Chris Smith
2017/8	Craig Wight
	Mark Foden
2018/9	Callum Ferrie
2019/0	Nicky Hogarth

Surname	First Name	Date of Birth	No	Nat	Pos	Signed	Previous	Notes	Contract	Lge A	Lge S	Lge G	SC A	SC S	SC G	LC A	LC S	LC G	Un
Allan	Jordan	07/02/1995		SCO	D	2021	Darvel (OL)	Mar-May		7	3			1					0
Banner	Kyle	13/07/1999		SCO	D	2018	Stirling Albion Youths		End 2021/2	20	0	1	1			4			2
Bikey	Dylan	18/02/1995		FRA / CAM	F	2019	Doxo Katokopias		End 2021/2	2	4	1							2
Binnie	Cammy	08/11/1997		SCO	GK	2015	Stirling Albion Youths	Released May 2021, joined Albion Rovers		14	0					4			9
Byrne	Declan	07/05/1996		SCO	F	2020	Albion Rovers	Released May 2021, joined Albion Rovers		12	9	4	1		1	2	2		2
Carey	Sandy	26/04/2002		SCO	F	2020	Stirling Albion Youths	OL to Cumbernauld Utd Oct-May	U20	0	0								1
Creaney	James	19/10/1988		SCO	D	2019	Annan Athletic		End 2021/2	1	2					3	1		7
Currie	Blair	25/05/1993		SCO	GK	2019	Clyde		End 2021/2	7	0		2						11
Docherty	Dom	22/05/1997		SCO	M	2018	Queen's Park	Released May 2021, joined Annan Ath		5	4		1			2	1		12
Eadie	Cameron	27/02/1998		SCO	D	2021	Darvel (OL)	Mar-May		6	2								1
El Zubaidi	Aldin	07/03/1995		IRQ / SCO	D	2020	Caledonian Braves	Released May 2021, joined Albion Rovers		9	2		2			2			3
France	Martin	10/05/2002		SCO	F	2020	Stirling Albion Youths	OL to Dunipace Oct-May	U20	0	0								1
Greenhorn	Will	24/07/2002		SCO	D	2019	Stirling Albion Youths	OL to Cumbernauld Utd Oct-May	U20	0	1								5
Hamilton	Chris	13/07/2001		SCO	D	2021	Hearts (OL)	Jan-May		6	4	1	1						3
Heaver	Sean	05/06/1992		SCO	F	2019	Bannockburn Amateurs		End 2021/2	3	7	1	1	1		1	2	1	11
Johnston	Kyle	01/01/2003		SCO	M	2020	Stirling Albion Youths		U20	0	0								3
Kirkpatrick	Jordan	06/03/1992		SCO	M	2021	Darvel (OL)	Mar-May		2	5			1					1
Law	Callum	28/05/2001		SCO	GK	2020	St Mirren		End 2021/2	0	0								8
Leitch	Jack	17/07/1995		SCO	M	2020	Peterhead		End 2021/2	18	2	4	2			4			0
Mackin	Dylan	15/01/1997		SCO	F	2018	Falkirk		End 2021/2	9	7	3	1	1		2	1	1	3
Magee	Lewis	19/05/2000		SCO	D	2020	Queen's Park	Released May 2021, joined Hurlford United		0	2						2		7
McDonald	Olly						Trialist, ex Kilmarnock			0	0								2
McGeachie	Ross	04/05/1994		SCO	D	2012	Stirling Albion Youths		End 2021/2	19	1	1	2			2			0
McGregor	Jordan	18/03/1997		SCO	D	2019	Aberdeen		End 2021/2	18	0		1			4			2
McLean	Paul	02/02/1990		SCO	D	2019	Brechin City		End 2021/2	7	0		1			2			1
Meggatt	Daryll	20/1090		SCO	D	2021	Darvel (OL)	Mar-May		3	1		1						1
Mitchell	Jonny	16/03/2000		SCO	M	2020	Brentford	Released May 2021, joined Bo'ness Utd		0	1						1		2
Moore	Kieran	11/09/1999		SCO	F	2020	Queen's Park		End 2021/2	11	6	1	1			1	2		4
Roberts	Kurtis	06/09/1994		SCO	M	2020	Airdrieonians		End 2021/2	19	1	1	1		1	3	1		2
Roberts	Scott	15/03/1996		SCO	M	2020	Albion Rovers	Released May 2021, joined Albion Rovers		11	7	1	1	1		2	1		4
Ryan	Andy	29/09/1994		SCO	F	2020	Dunfermline Athletic	Transferred to Hamilton Accies June 2021		18	1	10	1		1	2	1	1	3
Stone	Harry	20/04/2002		SCO	GK	2020	Hearts (OL)	Oct-20		1	0								0
Thomson	Cammy	28/11/1999		SCO	M	2018	St Johnstone	Released June 2021, joined Linlithgow Rose*		1	3			1			2		15
Wilson	David	06/03/1994		SCO	M	2019	Annan Athletic	Released May 2021, joined Albion Rovers		13	3	2	1			4			3
Own Goals												1							

* Stirling Albion have a "first option" on player at end of 2021/2

NEW SIGNINGS

Surname	First Name	Date of Birth	Nat	Pos	Signed	Previous	Contract
Carrick	Dale	07/01/1994	SCO	F	2021	Airdrieonians	End 2021/2
Cummins	Adam	03/03/1993	ENG	D	2021	Stranraer	End 2021/2
Flanagan	Nathan	04/05/2007	SCO	F	2021	Annan Athletic	End 2021/2
Grant	Ray	01/11/1996	SCO	M	2021	Alloa Athletic	End 2021/2
Laird	Mark	23/01/1986	SCO	M	2021	Edinburgh City	End 2021/2
McNiff	Martin	23/08/1991	SCO	D	2021	Clyde	End 2021/2
Omar	Rabin	21/07/1997	SCO	M	2021	Morton	End 2021/2

Stranraer FC 2019/20 The Blues

Founded	1870
Ground	Stair Park
Postcode	DG9 8BS
Tel	01776 703271
Capacity	2988
Closest Railway Station	Stranraer
Record Attendance	6500 v Rangers, 24/1/1948
Record Win	9-0 v St Cuthbert W, SC, 23/10/2010, v Wigtown & Bladnoch, SC, 22/10/2011
Record Defeat	1-11 v QOS, SC, 16/1/1932
Most League Goals in a Season	27 Derek Frye, 1977/8
Colours 2020/21 Top	Blue
Shorts	White
Sponsor	Stena Line
Manufacturer	Joma
Change Colours 2020/21 Top	White
Shorts	White
Nicknames	Blues
Web	www.stranraerfc.org
Match Programme 2020/21	On line

Manager: Stevie Farrell, then Jamie Hamill
Assistant: Frank McKeown, then Darryl Duffy
First Team Coach: Scott Robertson
Goalkeeping Coach: Billy Thomson
Head of Youth: Allan Jenkins
Chairman:
Vice-Chairman: Shaun Niven
Secretary: Shaun Niven
Committee: Ian Alldred, Stewart Marshall, Sandy Sutherland
Treasurer: Alex Thomson
Chief Scout: Stuart Wild
Club Doctor: Dr Simon Reid
Physiotherapist: Jamie Donnachie
Groundsman: Colin Agnew
Kit Man: Jamie Dougan

Over recent decades Stranraer have punched above their weight with lengthy spells out of the bottom division. After relegation in 2020 they would have hoped for a quick return to League One but it never really looked likely. They did manage to squeeze into the play offs but were beaten at the semi-final stage by Dumbarton.

Stranraer did have a fine Scottish Cup run. Most notably they defeated both Kelty Hearts and Brora Rangers, Champions of the Lowland and Highland Leagues, suggesting that the gap between the SPFL and the rest may be bigger than some people think.

STAR MAN
Goalkeeper Greg Fleming was a consistent performer for Stranraer. It will be disappointing for their fans that he has moved to Annan for next season.

PROSPECTS 2021/2
It was a Summer of upheaval for Stranraer with their Manager and Assistant leaving, then the Chairman and Vice Chairman resigning. Given all that and with a new manager in Jamie Hamill in charge, Stranraer should be happy if they can replicate last season's upper mid-table finish.

Date	Comp	H/A	Opponents	F	A		HT		Referee	Crowd	Scorers
10/10/2020	LC	A	Annan Athletic	1	1	5-4p	1	0	S Luke	BCD	Paton
13/10/2020	LC	H	Albion Rovers	2	2	14-15p	1	2	C Scott	BCD	Sonkur, Paton
17/10/2020	L	H	Elgin City	1	4		0	1	G Irvine	BCD	Devitt
24/10/2020	L	A	Annan Athletic	1	1		1	1	B Cook	BCD	Stirling
31/10/2020	L	H	Queen's Park	0	1		0	0	D Williams	BCD	
07/11/2020	L	H	Cowdenbeath	2	0		1	0	G Grainger	BCD	Orr, Victoria
11/11/2020	LC	H	Hamilton Accies	2	1		1	0	W Collum	BCD	Orr, Duffy
14/11/2020	LC	A	Ayr United	1	1	5-6p	1	0	B Cook	BCD	Duffy
21/11/2020	L	A	Edinburgh City	1	0		1	0	G Ross	BCD	Duffy
28/11/2020	L	A	Brechin City	4	1		1	1	S Reid	BCD	Paton, Orr, Duffy, Hilton
05/12/2020	L	H	Stirling Albion	2	2		1	2	M McDermid	BCD	Orr, Duffy
12/12/2020	L	A	Stenhousemuir	2	2		2	0	D McFarlane	BCD	Cummings, Paton pen
19/12/2020	L	H	Albion Rovers	4	0		0	0	C Scott	100	Paton, Orr, Duffy, Elliot
26/12/2020	SC	H	Spartans	5	0		3	0	L Wilson	BCD	Duffy, Paton, Cummins, Yates 2
02/01/2021	L	K	Annan Athletic	2	0		0	0	K Graham	BCD	Orr, Paton pen
09/01/2021	SC	A*	Kelty Hearts	3	2		0	2	L Watson	BCD	Robertson, Paton, Orr
20/03/2021	L	A	Queen's Park	0	3		0	2	D Williams	BCD	
23/03/2021	L	H	Brechin City	2	0		0	0	K Graham	BCD	Stirling, Orr
27/03/2021	L	A	Cowdenbeath	1	1		0	1	D Williams	BCD	Sonkur, Paton
03/04/2021	SC	A	Brora Rangers	3	1	AET	0	1	S Lambie	BCD	Malon og, Yates. Orr
06/04/2021	L	A	Elgin City	1	2		0	0	P Stuart	BCD	Yates pen
10/04/2021	L	H	Edinburgh City	0	1		0	1	M Roncone	BCD	
13/04/2021	L	A	Stirling Albion	1	0		0	0	D Williams	BCD	Stirling
15/04/2021	L	H	Stenhousemuir	4	0		3	0	P Stuart	BCD	Hilton, Orr, Paton 2
18/04/2021	SC	H	Hibernian	0	4		0	1	D Munro	BCD	
20/04/2021	L	A	Albion Rovers	2	0		1	0	L Wilson	BCD	Hilton, Victoria
23/04/2021	L	A	Queen's Park	1	0		1	0	B Cook	BCD	Yates
27/04/2021	L	H	Elgin City	1	4		0	4	C Scott	BCD	Elliot
01/05/2021	L	A	Stirling Albion	2	2		1	1	C Scott	BCD	Allan og, Duffy
04/05/2021	L	H	Edinburgh City	2	1		2	1	G Grainger	BCD	Stirling, Orr
08/05/2021	PO	H	Dumbarton	0	0		0	0	C Graham	BCD	
11/05/2021	PO	A	Dumbarton	0	1		0	1	G Duncan	BCD	

Jon Kapuscziak

Barney Duffy

John Hillcoat

Date	Comp	H/A	Opponents	F	A		1	2	3	4	5	6	7	8	9	10	11	12	13	14	15	16	17	18	19	20
10/10/2020	LC	A	Annan Athletic	1	1	5-4p	Fleming	Robertson	Burns	Devitt	Sonkur	Stirling	Gallagher	Millar	Duffy&	Victoria*	Paton+	Elliot*	McManus+	Orr&	Hilton	Jamie Walker	Cummins	Hamill		
13/10/2020	LC	H	Albion Rovers	2	2	14-15p	Fleming	Robertson	Burns	Devitt	Sonkur*	Stirling	McManus	Millar	Duffy&	Hilton+	Paton	Cummins*	Elliot+	Orr&	McIntyre	Jamie Walker	Gallagher	Hamill		
17/10/2020	L	H	Elgin City	1	4		Fleming	Robertson	Burns	Devitt	Cummins&	Stirling	McManus	Millar	Duffy+	Gallagher	Paton*	Elliot*	Orr+	Victoria&	McIntyre	Jamie Walker	Hamill			
24/10/2020	L	A	Annan Athletic	1	1		Fleming	Robertson	Burns	Devitt	Hamill	Stirling	McManus	Orr	Duffy*	Gallagher	Paton	Cummins*	Yates	Josh Walker	McIntyre	Jamie Walker				
31/10/2020	L	H	Queen's Park	0	1		Fleming	Robertson	Burns	Devitt	Hamill	Stirling	McManus&	Millar	Duffy*	Orr	Paton+	Hilton*	Yates+	Cummins&	McIntyre	Jamie Walker	Josh Walker			
07/11/2020	L	H	Cowdenbeath	2	0		Fleming	Robertson	Burns	Cummins	Hamill	Stirling	McManus	Millar	Victoria	Orr+	Paton*	Duffy*	Hilton+	Sonkur	McIntyre	Jamie Walker	Josh Walker	Yates		
11/11/2020	LC	H	Hamilton Accies	2	1		Fleming	Robertson	Sonkur	Cummins	Gallagher	Stirling*	McManus	Millar	Victoria	Orr+	Paton	Hilton*	Duffy+	Jamie Walker	McIntyre					
14/11/2020	LC	A	Ayr United	1	1	5-6p	Fleming	Robertson	Sonkur	Cummins	Gallagher	McIntyre	Duffy	Hilton	Victoria	Orr	Paton	Adair	Jamie Walker	Hamill	Mitchell	Wilde				
21/11/2020	L	A	Edinburgh City	1	0		Fleming	Robertson	Sonkur	Cummins	Gallagher	Miller	McManus	Duffy*	Victoria+	Orr	Paton&	Yates*	Hilton+	Josh Walker&	McIntyre	Jamie Walker	Hamill	Devitt		
28/11/2020	L	A	Brechin City	4	1		Fleming	Robertson	Sonkur	Cummins	Gallagher	Miller	McManus	Duffy+	Victoria*	Orr	Paton&	Hilton*	Yates+	Josh Walker&	Hamill	McIntyre	Devitt	Jamie Walker		
05/12/2020	L	H	Stirling Albion	2	2		Fleming	Robertson	Sonkur	Cummins	Gallagher	Miller	McManus	Duffy*	Victoria	Orr	Paton+	Stirling*	Yates+	Devitt	Hilton	Burns	Jamie Walker	Hamill		
12/12/2020	L	A	Stenhousemuir	2	2		Fleming	Robertson	Sonkur	Cummins	Gallagher*	Miller	McManus	Duffy+	Victoria	Orr	Paton&	Hamill*	Stirling+	Hilton&	Yates	Devitt	Elliot	Jamie Walker	Burns	
19/12/2020	L	H	Albion Rovers	4	0		Fleming	Robertson	Sonkur	Cummins<	Hamill	Miller	McManus	Duffy+	Victoria*	Orr&	Paton>	Stirling*	Hilton+	Elliot&	Yates>	Burns<	Devitt	Jamie Walker		
26/12/2020	SC	H	Spartans	5	0		Fleming	Robertson	Sonkur	Cummins	Hamill	Miller	McManus	Duffy*	Stirling	Orr+	Paton&	Yates*	Hilton+	Elliot&	Victoria	Gallagher	Devitt	Jamie Walker		
02/01/2021	L	K	Annan Athletic	2	0		Fleming	Robertson	Sonkur	Cummins	Gallagher	Miller	McManus	Duffy*	Stirling	Orr&	Paton+	Yates*	Elliot+	Victoria&	Hilton	Hamill	Devitt	McIntyre	Burns	Jamie Walker
09/01/2021	SC	A*	Kelty Hearts	3	2		Fleming	Robertson	Sonkur	Cummins	Gallagher	Miller	McManus+	Duffy*	Stirling	Orr	Paton	Victoria*	Hilton+	Burns	Elliot	Devitt	Yates	Jamie Walker		
20/03/2021	L	A	Queen's Park	0	3		Fleming	Robertson	Sonkur	Cummins	Gallagher	Miller	McManus>	Duffy*	Stirling<	Orr&	Paton+	Victoria*	Hilton+	Taylor&	Elliot>	Yates<	Devitt	McIntyre	Burns	Jamie Walker
23/03/2021	L	H	Brechin City	2	0		Fleming	Robertson*	Sonkur	Cummins	Gallagher	Hamill	McManus	Duffy&	Stirling<	Orr>	Victoria+	Devitt*	Paton+	Hilton&	Yates>	Elliot<	Taylor	Jamie Walker	Burns	McIntyre
27/03/2021	L	A	Cowdenbeath	1	1		Fleming	Robertson	Sonkur	Burns	Gallagher	Miller	McManus	Elliot*	Hilton+	Orr	Paton	Duffy*	Victoria+	Devitt	Hamill	Taylor	Yates	Jamie Walker	Cummins	
03/04/2021	SC	A	Brora Rangers	3	1	AET	Fleming	Robertson>	Sonkur	Cummins	Gallagher	Miller	McManus+	Duffy*	Stirling	Orr	Paton&	Yates*	Hilton+	Victoria&	Devitt>	Taylor	Hamill	Jamie Walker	Elliot	Burns
06/04/2021	L	A	Elgin City	1	2		Fleming	Robertson	Sonkur	Cummins	Gallagher	Burns&	Taylor*	Hilton+	Stirling	Orr	Yates	Paton*	Victoria+	Duffy&	Devitt	McManus	Hamill	Jamie Walker	Elliot	Josh Walker
10/04/2021	L	H	Edinburgh City	0	1		Fleming	Robertson	Devitt	Cummins<	Gallagher	Burns	Victoria+	Miller&	Stirling>	Orr	Yates*	Elliot*	Duffy+	Hilton&	McManus>	Paton<	Sonkur	Jamie Walker	Taylor	Josh Walker
13/04/2021	L	A	Stirling Albion	1	0		Fleming	Robertson	Sonkur	Cummins	Paton+	Burns	McManus	Miller	Stirling	Duffy*	Hilton	Orr*	Elliot+	Victoria	Devitt	Yates	Hamill	Jamie Walker	Taylor	Josh Walker
15/04/2021	L	H	Stenhousemuir	4	0		Fleming	Robertson	Sonkur	Cummins	Paton	Burns>	McManus	Miller	Stirling+	Orr*	Hilton&	Yates*	Victoria+	Josh Walker&	Taylor>	Duffy	Hamill	Jamie Walker	Elliot	Devitt
18/04/2021	SC	H	Hibernian	0	4		Fleming	Robertson	Sonkur	Miller	Gallagher	Burns*	McManus	Duffy+	Stirling	Orr&	Hilton	Hamill*	Paton+	Yates&	Taylor	Victoria	Devitt	Jamie Walker	Elliot	Josh Walker
20/04/2021	L	A	Albion Rovers	2	0		Fleming	Robertson	Sonkur	Miller<	Gallagher	Hamill	McManus	Paton>	Stirling+	Orr&	Hilton*	Yates*	Victoria+	Duffy&	Elliot>	Josh Walker<	Devitt	Jamie Walker	Taylor	
23/04/2021	L	A	Queen's Park	1	0		Fleming	Robertson	Sonkur	Miller	Gallagher*	Hamill	McManus	Paton>	Victoria	Yates+	Hilton&	Devitt*	Orr+	Stirling&	Elliot>	Josh Walker	Duffy	Jamie Walker	Taylor	
27/04/2021	L	H	Elgin City	1	4		Fleming	Robertson	Sonkur	Miller>	Burns	Hamill+	McManus	Paton	Stirling<	Orr&	Hilton*	Yates*	Duffy+	Elliot&	Taylor>	Josh Walker<	Devitt	Jamie Walker		
01/05/2021	L	A	Stirling Albion	2	2		Fleming	Robertson	Sonkur	Miller	Burns	Hamill	McManus	Elliot	Stirling	Orr+	Hilton*	Duffy*	Devitt+	Josh Walker	Taylor	Jamie Walker				
04/05/2021	L	H	Edinburgh City	2	1		Fleming	Robertson	Sonkur	Miller	Burns	Hamill	McManus	Elliot+	Stirling	Orr&	Duffy*	Hilton*	Paton+	Victoria&	Taylor	Josh Walker	Devitt	Jamie Walker	McIntyre	Gallagher
08/05/2021	PO	H	Dumbarton	0	0		Fleming	Robertson	Sonkur	Miller	Burns	Hamill	McManus	Elliot+	Stirling&	Orr	Duffy*	Paton*	Hilton+	Victoria&	Taylor	Josh Walker	Devitt	Jamie Walker		
11/05/2021	PO	A	Dumbarton	0	1		Fleming	Robertson	Sonjur	Miller	Burns	Gallagher	McManus	Elliot&	Stirling*	Orr	Paton+	Hilton*	Yates+	Duffy&	Victoria	Josh Walker	Devitt	Jamie Walker		

THE GOALIES

Goalkeepers Used in League Matches, 1972-2020

Players shown in the season of their first appearance only

1972/3	Billy Whiteside
1973/4	Gerry Gallagher
1974/5	Ronnie Lowrie
1975/6	Billy Ritchie
1976/7	John Taylor
1977/8	Douglas McClintock
	John Boyd
1978/9	J Stewart
	Billy Greenhorn
1979/0	Billy Bentley
	Ian Hildersley
1981/2	Ronnie McFall
	Colin Traynor
	J Allan
	Andy Robinson
	Boyd Strachan
1983/4	Barney Duffy
	J Docherty
1984/5	R Hamilton
	Craig Lawson
1985/6	Brian Noonan
	Barry Holland
	John Thompson
1987/8	Tony Bryden
	John Kapuscziak
	Ally MacLean
	Ian McFarlane
	Martin McLafferty
	M Graham
1990/1	Derek Atkins
1992/3	Stevie Ross
1996/7	Gary Matthews
1998/9	Colin Meldrum
	Gordon Bruce
1999/0	Mark McGeown
2000/1	Stephen O'Neill
2001/2	Colin Stewart
2002/3	Willie McCulloch
	John Hillcoat
2003/4	Andy McCondichie
2004/5	Kenny Meechan
	Michael McGovern
2005/6	Barry Corr
2006/7	Allan Morrison
	Scott Black
	Allan Ferguson
2008/9	Fraser Cantley
	Duncan Crossthwaite
2009/0	David Mitchell
	Ryan Marshall
2012/3	R Caldwell
	Colin Stewart (2nd spell)
2014/5	Chris Fahey
2015/6	Cammy Belford
	Connor Brennan
	Max Currie
	David McGurn
2018/9	Lyle Avci
2019/0	Dale Burgess

Surname	First Name	Date of Birth	No	Nat	Pos	Signed	Previous	Notes	Contract	Lge A	Lge S	Lge G	SC A	SC S	SC G	LC A	LC S	LC G	Un
Adair	Robert	19/01/2000		SCO	D	2021	Stranraer Reserves		U20	0	0								1
Burns	Sean	06/10/1991	3	SCO	D	2020	Stenhousemuir		End 2021/2	14	1		1			2			7
Cummins	Adam	03/03/1993	4	ENG	D	2018	Queen's Park	OOC May 2021, joined Stirling Albion		14	2	1	3		1	2	1		2
Devitt	Tom	14/06/1996	18	ENG	D	2020	Blyth Spartans	Released May 2021		4	3	1		1		2			19
Duffy	Darryl	16/04/1984	9	SCO	F	2020	Stirling Albion	Offered New Contract May 2021		14	8	5	4		1	3	1	2	2
Elliot	Cameron	27/05/1999	14	SCO	F	2018	Stranraer Youths	Offered New Contract May 2021, joined East Kilbride		5	10	2		1	2		2		6
Fleming	Greg	27/09/1986	1	SCO	GK	2020	Peterhead	Trenaferred to Annan Ath June 2021		24	0		4			4			0
Gallagher	Grant	11/01/1991	8	SCO	M	2019	Airdrieonians		End 2021/2	15	0		3			3			3
Hamill	Jamie	29/07/1986	22	SCO	D	2017	Queen of the South		End 2021/2	11	1		1	1					13
Hilton	James	02/11/1997	7	SCO	F	2019	Ayr United	Offered New Contract May 2021, joined Edinburgh City		8	12	3	1	3		2	1		3
McIntyre	Lewis	16/08/1996	16	SCO	D	2019	Wigtown & Bladnoch	Released May 2021		0	0					1			12
McManus	Connor	29/02/1996	6	SCO	M	2018	East Fife	Released May 2021, joined East Fife		22	1		4			2	1		1
Millar	Kieran	14/10/1993	15	SCO	M	2020	Airdrieonians		End 2021/2	21	0		4			3			0
Mitchell	Harry	25/12/2001		SCO	F	2021	Stranraer Reserves		U20	0	0								1
Orr	Thomas	13/03/1997	19	SCO	F	2020	BSC Glasgow	Released May 2021, joined Stenhousemuir		21	3	8	4		2	2	2	1	0
Paton	Ruari	09/08/2000	17	ROI	F	2020	East Kilbride	Refused New Contract May 2021 joined QOTS		18	5	7	3	1	2	4		2	0
Robertson	Scott	26/11/1987	2	SCO	D	2019	Airdrieonians		End 2021/2	24	0		4			4			0
Sonkur	Ayrton	02/06/1998	5	SCO	D	2020	Annan Athletic		End 2021/2	19	0	1	4		1	4		1	2
Stirling	Andy	05/03/1990	10	SCO	M	2019	Alloa Athletic	Released May 2021, joined Darvel		17	4	4	4			3			0
Taylor	Ally	12/09/2001		SCO	M	2021	Kilmarnock (OL)	Mar-May		1	3								12
Victoria	Joao	21/04/1989	11	POR / ANG	F	2020	Raith Rovers	Rleased May 2021, joined East Kilbride		9	9	2		2		3			4
Walker	Jamie	07/09/2001	21	SCO	GK	2020	Kilmarnock		End 2021/2	0	0								32
Walker	Josh	21/06/2001	23	SCO	F	2020	Kilmarnock		End 2021/2	0	5								12
Wilde	Danny				D		Ex Newton Stewart		U20	0	0								1
Yates	Matty	14/06/2002	20	SCO	F	2020	Hibernian Youths		End 2021/2	3	12	2		3	2				5
Own Goal												1			1				
NEW SIGNINGS																			
Hawkshaw	Dean	24/04/1997		SCO	M	2021	Glenafton Athletic		End 2021/2										
Irving	Ross	09/10/2001		SCO	F	2021	Livingston		End 2021/2										
Langan	Ruaridh	15/06/1998		SCO	M	2021	Dumbarton		End 2021/2										
Lyle	Curtis	08/09/1999		SCO	GK	2021	Kilmarnock (OL)	Jul-Jan	End 2021										
McIntosh	Sean	10/01/1997		SCO	D	2021	Brechin City		End 2021/2										
Moore	Joe	17/06/2001		SCO	F	2021	Airdrieonians		End 2021/2										
Muir	Tommy	21/04/1997		SCO	F	2021	Stenhousemuir		End 2021/2										
Rennie	Josh	28/05/2002		SCO	F	2021	Kilmarnock		End 2021/2										
Ross	Craig	09/06/2002		SCO	M	2021	Kilmarnock		End 2021/2										
Scullion	Luke	17/01/2002		SCO	GK	2021	Partick Thistle		End 2021/2										
Woods	Paul	18/09/1986		SCO	M	2021	East Kilbride		End 2021/2										

PHOTOCARDS

No. 161.

STRANRAER FOOTBALL CLUB.

Left to right, back row :—*W. McDonald, J. Dixon, W. Docherty.* Middle row :—*J. Murray (Treasurer), J. Currie, D. Leslie, A. Hill, J. McCrea (Sec.).* Front row :—*G. Forbes, W. Beattie, J. Brannan (Capt.), C. Black, J. Britton.*

Founded in 1870, is one of the oldest clubs in South Scotland. In 1927/28 was successful in winning seven cups. 1933/34 saw the team winners of the Cree Lodge Cup.

CLUBS NO LONGER IN THE SPFL -

THE GOALIES

Goalkeepers Used in League Matches, 1972-2020
Players shown in the season of their first appearance only

BERWICK RANGERS

1972/3 Willie Wilson
Dave Archer
1973/4 John Lyle
1975/6 Ronnie Tolmie
1976/7 David McConnell
David Graham
1978/9 Callum Frame
Alistair Skilling
Ian McLaren
1979/0 Doug Berwick
Keith Davidson
1980/1 Ernie McGarr
Mike McDonald
Mark Glynn
1981/2 Murray McDermott
1982/3 Kenny Redpath
1983/4 Kevin Baldwin
Ian Watson
1984/5 M Stanton
John Wilson
1985/6 John Thomson
George Tulloch
1987/8 Doug Sanderson
Brian Donaldson
1988/9 Mark Cairns
Steve Watson
Derek Neilson
Neil Kerr
1991/2 John Egan
1992/3 Kevin Massie
Gary O'Connor
1993/4 Gavin Kirkwood
Paolo Ceccarelli
Owen Lawson
Mark Osborne
Neil Young
1995/6 Jim McQueen
1996/7 Willie Lamont
Darren Collier
Michael Burgess
1997/8 Gary O'Connor (2nd spell)
1999/0 Derek Scrimgeour
2000/1 Mark McLean
Willie McCulloch
2001/2 Paul Mathers
2002/3 Ross Godfrey
Neil Inglis
Henry Smith
Gary O'Connor (3rd spell)
Gavin McCann
2005/6 Craig Coyle
2006/7 Chris Flockhart
2007/8 Peter Logan
Gary McGlynn
2008/9 Ryan McGurk
Mark Lunn
Jamie Barclay
2009/0 Mark Peat
Ian McCaldon
2011/2 Jamie Barclay
Youssef Bejaoui
2012/3 Mark McCallum
2013/4 Michael Andrews
Billy Bald
Paul Grant
2015/6 Kevin Walker
Mark Walters
2016/7 Sean Brennan
Devlin Mackay
2017/8 Robbie McCrorie
2018/9 Ally Adams
Ryan Goodfellow
Kyle Allison

EAST STIRLINGSHIRE

1972/3 Gerry Gallacher
Bert Archibald
1973/4 Tony Macis
Ted McFeat
1974/5 Tom Gourlay
1975/6 Rab Taylor
1976/7 Alex Morrison
1977/8 Fred Jackson
Phil Cairney
1978/9 Derek Neilson
Kevin Gallagher
1979/0 Charlie Kelly
1981/2 Brian Pearce
1982/3 Gordon Marshall
George Young
Trialist
1983/4 George Tulloch
1985/6 Gordon Drummond
Andy Bowie
1987/8 Gavin Kirkwood
1988/9 Lindsay Hamilton
Allan Main
1989/0 Mark Cairns
David Love
George Watson
1990/1 Owen Lawson
1992/3 Paul Imrie
1993/4 Gordon McDougall
1994/5 Jim Moffat
1996/7 Ewan Wilson
Willie Lamont
Willie Devine
1997/8 Robert Balfour
1998/9 Gordon Bruce
Barry Thompson
1999/0 Jim Butter
2001/2 David Hay
Stuart Robertson
Chris Todd
2002/3 Scott Findlay
2003/4 Jon Connolly
Ross Gilpin
2004/5 Tony Mitchell
Derek Jackson
2005/6 Aaron Gillespie
Euan Wilson (2nd spell)
Matthew Carr
2006/7 Robert Tiropolous
Anton Nugent
2007/8 Darren Hill
Michel Brown
Gary O'Connor
Norrie McIntyre
2008/9 John Hillcoat
Greig Mitchell
Jamie Barclay
Kemoko Camara
Barry Corr
Mark Peat
2009/0 Gavin Sorley
2010/1 Michael Andrews
2011/2 Callum Antell
Grant Hay
2012/3 R McWilliams
Craig Gordon
2014/5 Richie Barnard
2015/6 Darren Dolan

GRETNA

2002/3 David Mathieson
David Wylie
2003/4 Craig Summersgill
2004/5 Alan Main
2006/7 Greg Fleming
Zbigniew Malkowski
2007/8 Tony Caig
Artur Krysiak

Murray McDermott

Alan Main

Scottish Professional Football League Tables 2020/1

	PREMIERSHIP	P	W	D	L	F	A	GD	PTS
1	**Rangers**	38	32	6	0	92	13	79	102
2	Celtic (C)	38	22	11	5	78	29	49	77
3	Hibernian	38	18	9	11	48	35	13	63
4	Aberdeen	38	15	11	12	36	38	-2	56
5	St Johnstone	38	11	12	15	36	46	-10	45
6	Livingston	38	12	9	17	42	54	-12	45
7	St Mirren	38	11	12	15	37	45	-8	45
8	Motherwell	38	12	9	17	39	55	-16	45
9	Dundee United (P)	38	10	14	14	32	50	-18	44
10	Ross County	38	11	6	21	35	66	-31	39
11	**Kilmarnock**	38	10	6	22	43	54	-11	36
12	**Hamilton Accies**	38	7	9	22	34	67	-33	30

	CHAMPIONSHIP	P	W	D	L	F	A	GD	PTS
1	**Hearts (R)**	27	17	6	4	63	24	39	57
2	**Dundee**	27	12	9	6	49	40	9	45
3	Raith Rovers (P)	27	12	7	8	45	36	9	43
4	Dunfermline Athletic	27	10	9	8	38	34	4	39
5	Inverness CT	27	8	12	7	36	31	5	36
6	Queen of the South	27	9	5	13	38	51	-13	32
7	Arbroath	27	7	9	11	28	34	-6	30
8	Ayr United	27	6	11	10	31	37	-6	29
9	Morton	27	6	11	10	22	33	-11	29
10	**Alloa Athletic**	27	5	7	15	30	60	-30	22

	LEAGUE ONE	P	W	D	L	F	A	GD	PTS
1	**Partick Thistle (R)**	22	11	7	4	40	18	22	40
2	Airdrieonians	22	12	2	8	35	24	11	38
3	Cove Rangers (P)	22	10	6	6	28	18	10	36
4	Montrose	22	9	6	7	33	33	0	33
5	Falkirk	22	9	5	8	29	26	3	32
6	East Fife	22	10	3	9	30	33	-3	33
7	Peterhead	22	9	2	11	24	27	-3	29
8	Clyde	22	8	2	12	27	38	-11	26
9	Dumbarton	22	7	4	11	14	24	-10	25
10	**Forfar Athletic**	22	4	5	13	18	37	-19	17

	LEAGUE TWO	P	W	D	L	F	A	GD	PTS
1	**Queen's Park**	22	17	3	2	43	13	30	54
2	Edinburgh City	22	12	2	8	40	27	13	38
3	Elgin City	22	12	2	8	39	28	11	38
4	Stranraer (R)	22	11	5	6	36	25	11	38
5	Stirling Albion	22	10	6	6	32	22	10	36
6	Stenhousemuir	22	7	5	10	25	35	-10	26
7	Albion Rovers	22	7	4	11	25	38	-13	25
8	Annan Athletic	22	5	7	10	25	27	-2	22
9	Cowdenbeath	22	5	6	11	15	32	-17	21
10	**Brechin City**	22	2	4	16	13	46	-33	10

C = Champions 2019/20
R = relegated 209/20
P = Promoted 2019/20

SPFL PRIZE MONEY 2020/21

	Premiership	%	£
1	**Rangers**	13.4	4.2m
2	Celtic	9.6	2.88m
3	Hibernian	8.25	2.475m
4	Aberdeen	7.25	2.175m
5	St Johnstone	6.75	2.025m
6	Livingston	6.25	1.875m
7	St Mirren	5.75	1.725m
8	Motherwell	5.5	1.65m
9	Dundee United	5.25	1.575m
10	Ross County	5	1.5m
11	**Kilmarnock**	4.75	1.425m
12	**Hamilton Accies**	4.5	1.35m

	Championship	%	£
1	**Hearts**	2.25	675k
2	**Dundee**	1.9	570k
3	Raith Rovers	1.6	480k
4	Dunfermline Athletic	1.3	390k
5	Inverness CT	1	300k
6	Queen of the South	0.9	270k
7	Arbroath	0.85	255k
8	Ayr United	0.8	240k
9	Morton	0.75	225k
10	**Alloa Athletic**	0.7	210k

	League One	%	£
1	**Partick Thistle**	0.5	150k
2	Airdrieonians	0.43	129k
3	Cove Rangers	0.35	105k
4	Montrose	0.34	102k
5	Falkirk	0.33	99k
6	East Fife	0.32	96k
7	Peterhead	0.31	93k
8	Clyde	0.3	90k
9	Dumbarton	0.29	87k
10	**Forfar Athletic**	0.28	84k

	League Two	%	£
1	**Queen's Park**	0.27	81k
2	Edinburgh City	0.26	78k
3	Elgin City	0.25	75k
4	Stranraer	0.24	72k
5	Stirling Albion	0.23	69k
6	Stenhousemuir	0.22	66k
7	Albion Rovers	0.21	63k
8	Annan Athletic	0.2	60k
9	Cowdenbeath	0.19	57k
10	**Brechin City**	0.18	54k

These figures are based on the published distribution model and the projected prize pool.
In addition all 42 clubs received a donation of £50k from the funding donated to the SPFL by James Anderson.

In the English Premiership every club receives an "equal share" payment of £79 million. This is augmented with prize money ranging from approximately £40 million for the winners, to £2 million for the last-placed club.

Putting that into perspective the bottom placed Premiership club receives considerably more prize money than all 42 SPFL clubs put together.

PREMIER SHIP PLAY OFF

QF	04/05/2021	Dunfermline Athletic	Raith Rovers	0 0	BCD
QF	08/05/2021	Raith Rovers	Dunfermline Athletic	2 0	BCD
SF	12/05/2021	Raith Rovers	Dundee	0 3	BCD
SF	15/05/2021	Dundee	Raith Rovers	0 1	BCD
F	20/05/2021	Dundee	Kilmarnock	2 1	500
F	24/05/2021	Kilmarnock	Dundee	1 2	500
		AET, 2-0 on pens			

CHAMPIONSHIP PLAY OFF

SF	08/05/2021	Montrose	Morton	2 1	BCD
SF	08/05/2021	Cove Rangers	Airdrieonians	1 1	BCD
SF	01/05/2021	Morton	Montrose	3 1 AET	BCD
SF	11/05/2019	Airdrieonians	Cove Rangers	3 2 AET	BCD
F	18/05/2021	Airdrieonians	Morton	0 1	500
F	21/05/2021	Morton	Airdrieonians	3 0	500

LEAGUE ONE PLAY OFF

SF	08/05/2021	Stranraer	Dumbarton	0 0	BCD
SF	08/05/2021	Elgin City	Edinburgh City	0 1	BCD
SF	11/05/2021	Dumbarton	Stranraer	1 0	BCD
SF	11/05/2019	Edinburgh City	Elgin City	2 2	BCD
F	17/05/2021	Edinburgh City	Dumbarton	1 3	BCD
F	20/05/2021	Dumbarton	Edinburgh City	0 1	500

LEAGUE TWO PLAY OFF

F	18/05/2021	Kelty Hearts	Brechin City	2 1	250
F	23/05/2021	Brechin City	Kelty Hearts	0 1	500

PYRAMID PLAY OFF

F	04/05/2021	Brora Rangers	Kelty Hearts	0 2	BCD
F	08/05/2021	Kelty Hearts	Brora Rangers	4 1	BCD

May 4 2021, Pyramid Play off 1st Leg
Brora Rangers v Kelty Hearts 0-2, H.T. 0-1
BR: Malin, A McDonald, Williamson, Nicolson, Gillespie, Morrison, MacLean, J MacRae, A MacRae, Kelly, Wagenaar. Subs Sutherland for Wagenaar, Pickles for MacRae, Brindle for Kelly
KH: Jamieson, Hooper, Hill, Boyle, Stevenson, Reilly, Tidser, Philp, Easton, Higginbotham, Austin. Subs Reid (for Philp), Scobbie, McNab, Flynn, Russell, Rodgers, Donaldson
Scorers: Easton, Higginbotham pen

May 8th 2021, Pyramid Play Off 2nd Leg
Kelty Hearts v Brora Rangers, 4-1, H.T.1-1
KH: Jamieson, Hooper, Hill, Boyle, Stevenson, Reilly, Tidser, Philp, Easton, Higginbotham, Austin.
Subs Reid (for Hill), Scobbie, McNab, Flynn, Russell (for Austin), Rodgers (for Higginbotham), Donaldson
Scorers: Austin 3, Easton
BR: BR: Malin, A McDonald, Williamson, Nicolson, Gillespie, Morrison, MacLean, Pickles, A MacRae, Sutherland, Wagenaar.
Subs Kelly, J MacRae, G McDonald, Gamble, Stephen
Scorer: Morrison

May 18th 2021, League 2 Play Off 1st Leg,
Kelty Hearts v Brechin City, 2-1, H.T. 2-1
KH: KH: Jamieson, Hooper, Reid, Boyle, Stevenson, Reilly, Tidser, Philp, Easton, Higginbotham, Austin.
Subs Hill, Scobbie, McNab, Flynn, Russell (for Stevenson), Rodgers, Donaldson
Scorers: Higginbotham, Russell
BC: Hutton, McIntosh, Page, Coupe, Inglis, Currie, Barr, Osman, Reekie, Hussain, McKee. Subs Bollan, Jordan (for Hussain), Paton, O'Neil, McLevy (For Barr), Slaven (For Currie), Devine

May 23rd 2021, League 2 Play Off 2nd Leg,
Brechin City v Kelty Hearts, 0-1, H.T. 0-0
BC: Hutton, McIntosh, Page, Coupe, Inglis, Jordan, Barr, Osman, Reekie, M Paton, McKee. Subs Bollan, Currie (for Coupe), C Paton (for Jordan), O'Neil, O'Connor, McLevy, Slaven
KH: KH: Jamieson, Hooper, Hill, Boyle, Reid, Reilly, Tidser, Philp, Easton, Higginbotham, Austin.
Subs Scobbie, McNab (for Russell), Flynn, Russell (for Austin), Stevenson, Rodgers (for Easton), Donaldson
Scorer: Tidser

Fash's Goals Helped Kelty to Promotion

LEAGUE POSITIONS SINCE 1994 (creation of the 4 Division structure)

	94/5	95/6	96/7	97/8	98/9	99/0	00/1	01/2	02/3	03/4	04/5	05/6	06/7	07/8	08/9	09/10	10/1	11/2	12/3	13/4	14/5	15/6	16/7	17/8	18/9	19/0	20/1
Aberdeen	A9	A3	A6	A6	A8	A10	A7	A4	A8	A11	A4	A6	A3	A4	A4	A9	A9	A9	A8	A3	A2	A2	A2	A2	A4	A4	A4
Airdrieonians (1)	B4	B8	B2	B4	B4	B9	B8	B2																			
Albion Rovers	D10	D10	D5	D5	D7	D10	D7	D3	D3	D8	D9	D8	D6	D7	D8	D5	D2+	C9	C10-	D7	D1+	C6	C8	C10-	D9	D9	D7
Alloa	D5	D9	D4	D1+	C5	C2+	B10-	C2+	B9-	C7	C6	C9	C7	C4	C8	C2	C9-	D1+	C2+	B8	B9	B10-	C2	C3+	B8	B8	B10-
Annan Athleic															D7	D8	D4	D6	D8	D2	D5	D5	D3	D7	D4	D7	D8
Arbroath	D7	D5	D10	D2+	C7	C4	C2+	B7	B10-	C8	C9-	D4	D2	D4+	C7	C9-	D1+	C2	C5	C10-	D3	D9	D1+	C4	C1+	B5	B7
Ayr United	B9-	C6	C1+	B7	B3	B7	B2	B3	B6	B9-	C8	C6	C5	C7	C2+	B10-	C2+	B9-	C7	C4	C8	C2+	B10-	C1+	B4	B4	B8
Berwick Rangers	C5	C3	C10-	D6	D5	D2+	C3	C6	C5	C5	C10-	D2	D1+	C10-	D9	D6	D6	D7	D4	D5	D8	D6	D8	D8	D10-		
Brechin City	C10-	D2+	C7	C10-	D3	D8	D3	D1+	C2+	B10-	C1+	B10-	C4	C6	C3	C4	C4	C8	C3	C8	C4	C7	C4+	B10-	C10-	D10	D10-
Celtic	A4	A2	A2	A1	A2	A2	A1	A1	A2	A1	A2	A1	A1	A1	A2	A2	A2	A1	A1	A1	A1	A1	A1	A1	A1	A1	A2
Clyde	C6	C5	C4	C8	C3	C1+	B5	B5	B2	B2	B3	B5	B5	B9	B10-	C10-	D10	D9	D9	D4		D3	D9	D5	D2+	C7	C8
Clydebank / Airdrie(2)	B8	B7	B9-	C2+	B7	B10-	C5	C4	C3	C1+	B5	B6	B9-	C2+	B9	B9-	C6	C4+	B10-	C6	D6	C5	C3	C7	C5	C3	C2
Cowdenbeath	D9	D8	D7	D8	D9	D5	D2+	C8	C10-	D5	D3	D1+	C6	C9-	D2+	C3+	B9-	C1+	B8	B9	B10-	C9-	D10	D10	D6	D4	D9
Cove Rangers																										D1+	C3
Dumbarton	C2+	B10-	C9-	D10	D4	D6	D6	D2+	C6	C3	C7	C10-	D5	D8	D1+	C6	C7	C3+	B7	B5	B7	B8	B8	B9-	C6	C6	C9
Dundee	B3	B5	B3	B1+	A5	A7	A6	A9	A6	A7	A12-	B7	B3	B2	B4	B2	B6	B2+	A12-	B1+	A6	A8	A10	A9	A12-	B3	B2+
Dundee United	A10-	B2+	A3	A7	A9	A8	A11	A8	A11	A5	A9	A9	A9	A5	A5	A3	A4	A4	A6	A4	A5	A12-	B3	B3	B2	B1+	A9
Dunfermline Ath	B2	B1+	A5	A8	A10-	B2+	A9	A6	A5	A4	A11	A11	A12-	B5	B3	B3	B1+	A12-	B9-	C2	C7	C1+	B5	B4	B7	B6	B4
East Fife	C8	C2+	B10-	C6	C9-	D4	D4	D8	D2+	C9-	D8	D7	D4	D1+	C6	C7	C5	C6	C9	C9-	D4	D1+	C5	C6	C7	C5	C6
East Stirlingshire	D4	D7	D9	D4	D8	D7	D8	D7	D10	D10	D10	D10	D10	D9	D3	D3	D9	D10	D10	D8	D9	D10-					
Edinburgh City																							D7	D9	D3	D2	D2
Elgin City							D10	D6	D9	D9	D6	D5	D9	D6	D10	D9	D7	D4	D5	D9	D7	D2	D5	D6	D8	D3	D3
Falkirk	A5	A10-	B5	B2	B2	B3	B3	B9	B1	B4	B1+	A10	A7	A7	A10	A12-	B3	B3	B3	B3	B5	B2	B2	B8	B10-	C2	C5
Forfar Athletic	D1+	C9-	D2+	C7	C10-	D3+	C8	C3	C4	C6	C5	C8	C10-	D10	D6	D2+	C3	C7	C4	C7	C3	C10	D2+	C8	C2	C9	C10-
Gretna									D6	D3	D1+	C1+	B1+	A12-													
Hamilton Accies	B6	B9-	C2+	B8	B9-	C10-	D1+	C5	C8	C2+	B7	B3	B4	B1+	A9	A7	A12-	B4	B5	B2+	A7	A10	A11	A10	A10	A11	A12-
Hearts	A6	A4	A4	A3	A6	A3	A5	A5	A3	A3	A5	A2	A4	A8	A3	A6	A3	A5	A10	A12-	B1+	A3	A5	A6	A6	A12-	B1+
Hibernian	A3	A5	A9	A10-	B1+	A6	A3	A10	A7	A8	A3	A4	A6	A6	A6	A4	A10	A11	A7	A11-	B2	B3	B1+	A4	A5	A7	A3
Inverness CT	D6	D3	D1+	C5	C2+	B6	B4	B6	B4	B1+	A8	A7	A8	A9	A12-	B1+	A7	A10	A4	A5	A3	A7	A12-	B5	B3	B2	B5
Kilmarnock	A7	A7	A7	A4	A4	A9	A4	A7	A4	A10	A7	A5	A5	A1	A8	A11	A5	A7	A9	A9	A10	A11	A8	A5	A3	A8	A11-
Livingston	C9-	D1+	C3	C3	C1+	B4	B1+	A3	A9	A9	A10	A12-	B6	B7	B7-	D1+	C1+	B5	B4	B6	B8	B9-	C1	B2+	A9	A5	A6
Montrose	D2+	C10-	D6	D9	D10	D9	D9	D5	D7	D6	D5	D9	D8	D3	D5	D10	D8	D8	D6	D6	D10	D8	D4	D1+	C4	C4	C4
Morton	C1+	B3	B8	B5	B6	B8	B9-	C10-	D1+	C4	C3	C2	C1+	B8	B6	B8	B7	B8	B2	B10-	C1+	B5	B4	B7	B5	B7	B9
Motherwell	A2	A8	A8	A9	A7	A4	A8	A11	A12	A6	A6	A8	A10	A3	A7	A5	A6	A3	A2	A2	A11	A5	A9	A7	A8	A3	A8
Partick Thistle	A8	A9-	B6	B9-	C8	C5	C1+	B1+	A10	A12-	B9-	C4+	B7	B6	B2	B6	B5	B6	B1+	A10	A8	A9	A6	A11-	B6	B10-	C1+
Peterhead							D5	D4	D4	D4	D2+	C3	C8	C5	C4	C5	C10-	D5	D2	D1+	C6	C3	C9-	D2	D1+	C8	C7
Queen of the S	C7	C7	C5	C4	C4	C9	C6	C1+	B5	B5	B4	B8	B8	B4	B5	B4	B4	B10-	C1+	B4	B4	B7	B6	B6	B9	B9	B6
Queen's Park	D8	D6	D8	D7	D6	D1+	C9-	D10	D8	D7	D4	D6	D3+	C8	C9-	D4	D3	D2	D3	D10	D2	D4+	C6	C9-	D7	D5	D1+
Raith Rovers	B1+	A6	A10-	B3	B8	B5	B7	B10-	C1+	B8	B10-	C7	C3	C3	C1+	B7	B2	B7	B6	B7	B6	B4	B9-	C2	C3	C1+	B3
Rangers	A1	A1	A1	A2	A1	A1	A2	A2	A1	A2	A1	A3	A2	A2	A1	A1	A1	A2-	D1+	C1+	B3	B1+	A3	A3	A2	A2	A1
Ross County	D3	D4	D3	D3	D1+	C3+	B6	B4	B8	B6	B6	B4	B10-	C1+	B8	B5	B8	B1+	A5	A7	A9	A6	A7	A12-	B1+	A10	A10
St Johnstone	B5	B4	B1+	A5	A3	A5	A10	A12-	B3	B3	B8	B2	B2	B3	B1+	A8	A8	A6	A3	A6	A4	A4	A4	A8	A7	A6	A5
St Mirren	B7	B6	B4	B6	B5	B1+	A12-	B8	B7	B7	B2	B1+	A11	A10	A11	A10	A11	A8	A11	A8	A12-	B6	B7	B1+	A11	A9	A7
Stenhousemuir	C4	C4	C6	C9-	D2+	C8	C7	C9	C7	C10-	D7	D3	D7	D5	D4+	C8	C8	C5	C6	C5	C9	C8	C10-	D4+	C9-	D8	D6
Stirling Albion	C3	C1+	B7	B10-	C6	C7	C10-	D9	D5	D2+	C4	C5	C2+	B10-	C5	C1+	B10-	C10-	D7	D3+	C10-	D7	D6	D3	D5	D6	D5
Stranraer	B10-	C8	C8	C1+	B10-	C6	C4	C7	C9-	D1+	C2+	B9-	C9-	D2+	C10-	D7	D5	D3+	C8	C3	C2	C4	C7	C5	C8	C10-	D4

A Premier Division / Premiership
B Division One / Championship
C Division Two / League One
D Division Three / League Two

*** Clydebank changed their name to Airdrie United in 2002, then to Airdrieonians in 2013**

1994-2021

TEAMS NEVER OUT OF TOP DIVISION
Aberdeen, Celtic, Kilmarnock (relegated 2021), Motherwell, Rangers

TEAMS NEVER OUT OF BOTTOM DIVISION
Annan Athletic, East Stirlingshire, Elgin City

TEAMS PLAYED IN ALL FOUR DIVISIONS
Hamilton Accies, Inverness CT, Livingston, Ross County

TEAMS PLAYED IN THREE DIVISIONS
Alloa, Brechin City, Clyde, Cowdenbeath, Dumbarton, Dunfermline Athletic, East Fife, Falkirk, Partick Thistle, Raith Rovers, Stirling Albion, Stranraer

Scottish Football Play Offs—All Time Records

Season	Lev	Rd	Home	Away	F	A	Agg	Att
1890/1	C	F	Dumbarton	Rangers	2	2		
			at Cathkin Park (1)					
1899/00	1	F	St Mirren	St Bernards	2	1		
			at Dens Park (2)					
1904/5	C	F	Celtic	Rangers	2	1		30000
			at Hampden (3)					
1905/6	1	F	Port Glasgow	Kilmarnock	6	0		500
			at Cathkin Park (4)					
1906/7	2	F	Raith Rovers	East Stirlingshire	3	2		
			at Logie Green (4)					
1994/5	1	F	Aberdeen	Dunfermline Athletic	3	1		21000
1994/5	1	F	Dunfermline Athletic	Aberdeen	1	3	2-6	16000
1995/6	1	F	Partick Thistle	Dundee United	1	1		10414
1995/6	1	F	Dundee United	Partick Thistle	2	1	3-2aet	12120
1996/7	1	F	Hibernian	Airdrieonians	1	0		15308
1996/7	1	F	Airdrieonians	Hibernian	2	4		7500
2005/6	2	SF	Stranraer	Partick Thistle	1	3		1100
2005/6	2	SF	Partick Thistle	Stranraer	1	2	3-4	3596
2005/6	2	SF	Morton	Peterhead	0	0		3995
2005/6	2	SF	Peterhead	Morton	1	0	1-0	3717
2005/6	2	F	Partick Thistle	Peterhead	1	2		3400
2005/6	2	F	Peterhead	Partick Thistle	1	2	3-3, 2-4p	3700
2006/7	2	SF	Brechin City	Airdrie United	1	3		954
2006/7	2	SF	Airdrie United	Brechin City	3	0	6-1	1298
2006/7	2	SF	Raith Rovers	Stirling Albion	0	0		3043
2006/7	2	SF	Stirling Albion	Raith Rovers	3	1	3-1	2656
2006/7	2	F	Stirling Albion	Airdrie United	2	2		2118
2006/7	2	F	Airdrie United	Stirling Albion	2	3	4-5	3465
2007/8	2	SF	Alloa Athletic	Clyde	2	1		1026
2007/8	2	SF	Clyde	Alloa Athletic	5	3	6-5 aet	1548
2007/8	2	SF	Raith Rovers	Airdrie United	0	2		2841
2007/8	2	SF	Airdrie United	Raith Rovers	2	2	2-4	2077
2007/8	2	F	Airdrie United	Clyde	0	1		1878
2007/8	2	F	Clyde	Airdrie United	2	0	3-0	2548
2008/9	2	SF	Brechin City	Ayr United	0	2		902
2008/9	2	SF	Ayr United	Brechin City	3	2	5-2	1974
2008/9	2	SF	Peterhead	Airdrie United	0	2		1364
2008/9	2	SF	Airdrie United	Peterhead	2	1	4-1	1008
2008/9	2	F	Ayr United	Airdrie United	2	2		3378
2008/9	2	F	Airdrie United	Ayr United	0	1	2-3	3303
2009/10	2	SF	Brechin City	Airdrie United	2	1		583
2009/10	2	SF	Airdrie United	Brechin City	0	1	1-3	1156
2009/10	2	SF	Cowdenbeath	Alloa Athletic	1	1		578
2009/10	2	SF	Alloa Athletic	Cowdenbeath	0	2	1-3	1234
2009/10	2	F	Cowdenbeath	Brechin City	0	0		1119
2009/10	2	F	Brechin City	Cowdenbeath	0	3	0-3	1627
2010/11	2	SF	Brechin City	Cowdenbeath	2	2		596
2010/11	2	SF	Cowdenbeath	Brechin City	0	2	2-4	645
2010/11	2	SF	Forfar Athletic	Ayr United	1	4		924
2010/11	2	SF	Ayr United	Forfar Athletic	3	3	7-4	1198
2010/11	2	F	Ayr United	Brechin City	1	1		2020
2010/11	2	F	Brechin City	Ayr United	1	2	2-3	2404
2011/12	2	SF	Dumbarton	Arbroath	2	1		911
2011/12	2	SF	Arbroath	Dumbarton	0	0	1-2	1454
2011/12	2	SF	Airdrie United	Ayr United	0	0		1971
2011/12	2	SF	Ayr United	Airdrie United	1	3	1-3	2782
2011/12	2	F	Dumbarton	Airdrie United	2	1		1746
2011/12	2	F	Airdrie United	Dumbarton	1	4		2914
2012/13	2	SF	Forfar Athletic	Dunfermline Athletic	3	1		1562
2012/13	2	SF	Dunfermline Athletic	Forfar Athletic	6	1	7-4 aet	4252
2012/13	2	SF	Brechin City	Alloa Athletic	0	2		582
2012/13	2	SF	Alloa Athletic	Brechin City	2	3	4-3	856
2012/13	2	F	Alloa Athletic	Dunfermline Athletic	3	0		2765
2012/13	2	F	Dunfermline Athletic	Alloa Athletic	1	0	1-3	5110
2013/14	2	SF	Ayr United	Cowdenbeath	1	2		1495
2013/14	2	SF	Cowdenbeath	Ayr United	3	1	5-2	933
2013/14	2	SF	Stranraer	Dunfermline Athletic	2	1		867
2013/14	2	SF	Dunfermline Athletic	Stranraer	3	0	4-2 aet	4525
2013/14	2	F	Cowdenbeath	Dunfermline Athletic	1	1		3379
2013/14	2	F	Dunfermline Athletic	Cowdenbeath	0	3	1-4	8288
2014/15	2	SF	Brechin City	Alloa Athletic	0	2		505
2014/15	2	SF	Alloa Athletic	Brechin City	0	1	2-1	606
2014/15	2	SF	Forfar Athletic	Stranraer	3	0		717
2014/15	2	SF	Stranraer	Forfar Athletic	1	1	1-4	519
2014/15	2	F	Forfar Athletic	Alloa Athletic	3	1		1212
2014/15	2	F	Alloa Athletic	Forfar Athletic	3	0	4-3	1423
2015/16	2	SF	Peterhead	Ayr United	1	4		807
2015/16	2	SF	Ayr United	Peterhead	2	1	6-2	1848
2015/16	2	SF	Stranraer	Livingston	5	2		589
2015/16	2	SF	Livingston	Stranraer	4	3	6-8 aet	1018
2015/16	2	F	Stranraer	Ayr United	1	1		1652
2015/16	2	F	Ayr United	Stranraer	0	0	1-1, 3-1p	4581
2016/17	2	SF	Brechin City	Raith Rovers	1	1		1022
2016/17	2	SF	Raith Rovers	Brechin City	3	3	4-4, 3-4p	2932
2016/17	2	SF	Airdrieonians	Alloa Athletic	1	0		1199
2016/17	2	SF	Alloa Athletic	Airdrieonians	1	0	1-1, 4-3p	1181
2016/17	2	F	Brechin City	Alloa Athletic	1	0		702
2016/17	2	F	Alloa Athletic	Brechin City	4	3	4-4, 4-5p	1204
2017/18	2	SF	Arbroath	Dumbarton	1	2		892
2017/18	2	SF	Dumbarton	Arbroath	1	1	3-2	872
2017/18	2	SF	Alloa Athletic	Raith Rovers	2	0		1123
2017/18	2	SF	Raith Rovers	Alloa Athletic	1	2	1-4	1831
2017/18	2	F	Alloa Athletic	Dumbarton	0	1		811
2017/18	2	F	Dumbarton	Alloa Athletic	0	2	1-2aet	1115
2018/19	2	SF	Montrose	Queen of the South	2	1		1124
2018/19	2	SF	Queen of the South	Montrose	5	0	6-2	2001
2018/19	2	SF	Raith Rovers	Forfar Athletic	2	1		2007
2018/19	2	SF	Forfar Athletic	Raith Rovers	1	1	3-2	2512
2018/19	2	F	Raith Rovers	Queen of the South	1	3		2471
2018/19	2	F	Queen of the South	Raith Rovers	0	0	3-1	2420
2020/1	2	SF	Montrose	Morton	2	1		BCD
2020/1	2	SF	Morton	Montrose	3	1	4-3	BCD
2020/1	2	SF	Cove Rangers	Airdrieonians	1	1		BCD
2020/1	2	SF	Airdrieonians	Cove Rangers	3	2	3-3	BCD
2020/1	2	F	Airdrieonians	Morton	0	1		500
2020/1	2	F	Morton	Airdrieonians	3	0	4-0	500
2005/6	3	SF	Arbroath	Alloa Athletic	1	1		1163
2005/6	3	SF	Alloa Athletic	Arbroath	1	0	2-1	1318
2005/6	3	SF	Stehousemuir	Berwick Rangers	0	1		593
2005/6	3	SF	Berwick Rangers	Stenhhousemuir	0	0	1-0	913
2005/6	3	F	Alloa Athletic	Berwick Rangers	4	0		975
2005/6	3	F	Berwick Rangers	Alloa Athletic	2	1	2-5	866
2006/7	3	SF	East Fife	Stranraer	4	1		742
2006/7	3	SF	Stranraer	East Fife	1	0	2-4	426
2006/7	3	SF	Queen's Park	Arbroath	2	0		974
2006/7	3	SF	Arbroath	Queen's Park	1	2	1-4	1114
2006/7	3	F	Queen's Park	East Fife	4	2		1027
			at Firhill					
2006/7	3	F	East Fife	Queen's Park	0	3	2-7	1625
2007/8	3	SF	Arbroath	Cowdenbeath	1	1		638
2007/8	3	SF	Cowdenbeath	Arbroath	1	2	2-3 aet	778
2007/8	3	SF	Montrose	Stranraer	1	1		706
2007/8	3	SF	Stranraer	Montrose	3	0	4-1	451
2007/8	3	F	Arbroath	Stranraer	2	0		1016
2007/8	3	F	Stranraer	Arbroath	1	0	1-2	836
2008/9	3	SF	East Stirlingshire	Cowdenbeath	1	2		605
2008/9	3	SF	Cowdenbeath	East Stirlingshire	1	1	3-2	633
2008/9	3	SF	Stenhousemuir	Queen's Park	2	1		617
2008/9	3	SF	Queen's Park	Stenhousemuir	0	0	1-2	854
2008/9	3	F	Cowdenbeath	Stenhousemuir	0	0		775
2008/9	3	F	Stenhousemuir	Cowdenbeath	0	0	0-0, 5-4p	1530
2009/10	3	SF	Queen's Park	Arbroath	0	4		651
2009/10	3	SF	Arbroath	Queen's Park	2	2	6-2	588
2009/10	3	SF	East Stirlingshire	Forfar Athletic	0	1		487
2009/10	3	SF	Forfar Athletic	East Stirlingshire	2	2	3-2	745
2009/10	3	F	Arbroath	Forfar Athletic	0	0		1027
2009/10	3	F	Forfar Athletic	Arbroath	2	0	2-0	2207
2010/11	3	SF	Annan Athletic	Alloa Athletic	2	1		621
2010/11	3	SF	Alloa Athletic	Annan Athletic	0	0	1-2	622
2010/11	3	SF	Queen's Park	Albion Rovers	1	1		789
2010/11	3	SF	Albion Rovers	Queen's Park	2	0	3-1	859
2010/11	3	F	Albion Rovers	Annan Athletic	3	1		1014
2010/11	3	F	Annan Athletic	Albion Rovers	2	1	3-4	1165
2011/12	3	SF	Elgin City	Albion Rovers	1	0		1258
2011/12	3	SF	Albion Rovers	Elgin City	2	0	2-1	827
2011/12	3	SF	Stranraer	Queen's Park	3	1		481

2011/12	3	SF	Queen's Park	Stranraer	0 2 1-5	1188
2011/12	3	F	Stranraer	Albion Rovers	2 0	506
2011/12	3	F	Albion Rovers	Stranraer	3 1 3-3, 5-3p	1008
2012/13	3	SF	Berwick Rangers	East Fife	1 1	732
2012/13	3	SF	East Fife	Berwick Rangers	2 1 3-2 aet	856
2012/13	3	SF	Queen's Park	Peterhead	0 1	651
2012/13	3	SF	Peterhead	Queen's Park	3 1 4-1	954
2012/13	3	F	East Fife	Peterhead	0 0	825
2012/13	3	F	Peterhead	East Fife	0 1 0-1	1855
2013/14	3	SF	Clyde	East Fife	1 0	1005
2013/14	3	SF	East Fife	Clyde	2 1 2-2, 7-6p	1018
2013/14	3	SF	Stirling Albion	Annan Athletic	3 1	972
2013/14	3	SF	Annan Athletic	Stirling Albion	3 5 4-8	912
2013/14	3	F	Stirling Albion	East Fife	1 2	1501
2013/14	3	F	East Fife	Stirling Albion	0 2 2-3	1516
2014/15	3	SF	Arbroath	Queen's Park	2 2	837
2014/15	3	SF	Queen's Park	Arbroath	1 0 3-2 aet	1026
2014/15	3	SF	East Fife	Stenhousemuir	1 1	679
2014/15	3	SF	Stenhousemuir	East Fife	3 1 4-2 aet	799
2014/15	3	F	Queen's Park	Stenhousemuir	0 1	811
2014/15	3	F	Stenhousemuir	Queen's Park	1 1 2-1	1165
2015/16	3	SF	Clyde	Elgin City	3 1	804
2015/16	3	SF	Elgin City	Clyde	0 2 1-5	1371
2015/16	3	SF	Queen's Park	Cowdenbeath	2 0	572
2015/16	3	SF	Cowdenbeath	Queen's Park	1 0 1-2	585
2015/16	3	F	Clyde	Queen's Park	1 3	1312
2015/16	3	F	Queen's Park	Clyde	0 1 3-2	2107
2016/17	3	SF	Montrose	Peterhead	1 1	1251
2016/17	3	SF	Peterhead	Montrose	3 0 4-1	1096
2016/17	3	SF	Annan Athletic	Forfar Athletic	2 2	629
2016/17	3	SF	Forfar Athletic	Annan Athletic	4 2 6-4	629
2016/17	3	F	Forfar Athletic	Peterhead	2 1	958
2016/17	3	F	Peterhead	Forfar Athletic	1 5 2-7	1084
2017/18	3	SF	Stehousemuir	Queen's Park	1 1	657
2017/18	3	SF	Queen's Park	Stenhousemuir	1 2 2-3	948
2017/18	3	SF	Stirling Albion	Peterhead	0 1	729
2017/18	3	SF	Peterhead	Stirling Albion	3 0 4-0	861
2017/18	3	F	Stenhousemuir	Peterhead	2 0	796
2017/18	3	F	Peterhead	Stenhousemuir	1 0 1-2	880
2018/19	3	SF	Annan Athletic	Stenhousemuir	2 0	637
2018/19	3	SF	Stenhousemuir	Annan Athletic	1 2 1-4	794
2018/19	3	SF	Edinburgh City	Clyde	0 1	617
2018/19	3	SF	Clyde	Edinburgh City	3 0 4-0	1204
2018/19	3	F	Annan Athletic	Clyde	1 0	1006
2018/19	3	F	Clyde	Annan Athletic	2 0 2-1	2725
2020/1	3	SF	Elgin City	Edinburgh City	0 1	BCD
2020/1	3	SF	Edinburgh City	Elgin City	2 2 3-2	BCD
2020/1	3	SF	Stranraer	Dumbarton	0 0	BCD
2020/1	3	SF	Dumbarton	Stranraer	1 0 1-0	BCD
2020/1	3	F	Edinburgh City	Dumbarton	1 3	BCD
2020/1	3	F	Dumbarton	Edinburgh City	0 1 3-2	500
2014/15	4	SF	Edinburgh City	Brora Rangers	1 1	908
2014/15	4	SF	Brora Rangers	Edinburgh City	1 1 2-2, 4-2p	400
2014/15	4	F	Brora Rangers	Montrose	1 0	525
2014/15	4	F	Montrose	Brora Rangers	3 1 3-2	2132
2015/16	4	SF	Cove Rangers	Edinburgh City	0 3	500
2015/16	4	SF	Edinburgh City	Cove Rangers	1 1 4-1	839
2015/16	4	F	Edinburgh City	East Stirlingshire	1 1	1090
2015/16	4	F	East Stirlingshire	Edinburgh City	0 1 1-2	1286
2016/17	4	SF	Buckie Thistle	East Kilbride	2 2	1000
2016/17	4	SF	East Kilbride	Buckie Thistle	2 1 4-3	6000
2016/17	4	F	East Kilbride	Cowdenbeath	0 0	548
2016/17	4	F	Cowdenbeath	East Kilbride	1 1 1-1, 5-3p	1676
2017/18	4	SF	Cove Rangers	Spartans	4 0	500
2017/18	4	SF	Spartans	Cove Rangers	2 1 2-5	655
2017/18	4	F	Cove Rangers	Cowdenbeath	0 0	650
2017/18	4	F	Cowdenbeath	Cove Rangers	3 2 3-2	1762
2018/19	4	SF	East Kilbride	Cove Rangers	1 2	700
2018/19	4	SF	Cove Rangers	East Kilbride	3 0 5-1	1152
2018/19	4	F	Cove Rangers	Berwick Rangers	4 0	1955
2018/19	4	F	Berwick Rangers	Cove Rangers	0 3 0-7	1314
2020/1	4	SF	Brora Rangers	Kelty Hearts	0 2	BCD
2020/1	4	SF	Kelty Hearts	Brora Rangers	4 1 6-1	BCD
2020/1	4	F	Kelty Hearts	Brechin City	2 1	250
2020/1	4	F	Brechin City	Kelty Hearts	0 1 1-3	500

2013/14	1	QF	Queen of the South	Falkirk	2 1	1996
2013/14	1	QF	Falkirk	Queen of the South	3 1 4-3 aet	4427
2013/14	1	SF	Falkirk	Hamilton Accies	1 1	4194
2013/14	1	SF	Hamilton Accies	Falkirk	1 0 2-1	4678
2013/14	1	F	Hamilton Accies	Hibernian	0 2	5322
2013/14	1	F	Hibernian	Hamilton Accies	0 2 2-2, 3-4p	18031
2014/15	1	QF	Queen of the South	Rangers	1 2	5224
2014/15	1	QF	Rangers	Queen of the South	1 1 3-2	48035
2014/15	1	SF	Rangers	Hibernian	2 0	41236
2014/15	1	SF	Hibernian	Rangers	1 0 1-2	14742
2014/15	1	F	Rangers	Motherwell	1 3	49200
2014/15	1	F	Motherwell	Rangers	3 0 6-1	9220
2015/16	1	QF	Raith Rovers	Hibernian	1 0	5330
2015/16	1	QF	Hibernian	Raith Rovers	2 0 2-1	11133
2015/16	1	SF	Hibernian	Falkirk	2 2	11830
2015/16	1	SF	Falkirk	Hibernian	3 2 5-4	7851
2015/16	1	F	Falkirk	Kilmarnock	1 0	7636
2015/16	1	F	Kilmarnock	Falkirk	4 0 4-1	11013
2016/17	1	QF	Morton	Dundee United	1 2	3306
2016/17	1	QF	Dundee United	Morton	3 0 5-1	6506
2016/17	1	SF	Dundee United	Falkirk	2 2	7034
2016/17	1	SF	Falkirk	Dundee United	1 2 3-4	7926
2016/17	1	F	Dundee United	Hamilton Accies	0 0	9386
2016/17	1	F	Hamilton Accies	Dundee United	1 0 1-0	5027
2017/18	1	QF	Dunfermline Athletic	Dundee United	0 0	6474
2017/18	1	QF	Dundee United	Dunfermline Athletic	2 1 2-1	7994
2017/18	1	SF	Dundee United	Livingston	2 3	5610
2017/18	1	SF	Livingston	Dundee United	1 1 4-3	4508
2017/18	1	F	Livingston	Partick Thistle	2 1	5469
2017/18	1	F	Partick Thistle	Livingston	0 1 1-3	7122
2018/19	1	QF	Ayr United	Inverness CT	1 3	2171
2018/19	1	QF	Inverness CT	Ayr United	1 1 4-2	2323
2018/19	1	SF	Inverness CT	Dundee United	0 1	2604
2018/19	1	SF	Dundee United	Inverness CT	3 0 4-0	8504
2018/19	1	F	Dundee United	St Mirren	0 0	11082
2018/19	1	F	St Mirren	Dundee United	1 1 1-1	7732
			AET, 2-0 on pens			
2020/1	1	QF	Dunfermline Athletic	Raith Rovers	0 0	BCD
2020/1	1	QF	Raith Rovers	Dunfermline Athletic	2 0 2-0	BCD
2020/1	1	SF	Raith Rovers	Dundee	0 3	BCD
2020/1	1	SF	Dundee	Raith Rovers	0 1 3-1	BCD
2020/1	1	F	Dundee	Kilmarnock	2 1	500
2020/1	1	F	Kilmarnock	Dundee	1 2 2-4	500

(1) Championship Decider ,teams tied on points, title shared
(2) Relegation Play off, teams tied on points
(3) Championship play off, teams tied on points
(4) Play Off to determine team requiring re-election

NORTHERN LEAGUE.
North, 2; South, 0. Inter-County match. At Aberdeen.
Arbroath, 3; Lochee United, 1. At Lochee.

FORFARSHIRE LEAGUE.
Forfar Athletic, 4; Wanderers, 4. At Forfar.

SCOTTISH LEAGUE—FIRST DIVISION. TEST MATCH.
St Mirren, 2; St Bernard, 1. At Dundee.

SCOTTISH LEAGUE SECOND DIVISION.
Morton, 3; Motherwell, 0. At Greenock.

PERTHSHIRE 2D XI. FINAL.
St Johnstone Strollers, 2; Tulloch, 2. At Perth.

WESTERN LEAGUE.
Port-Glasgow Athletic, 3; Clyde, 0. At Port-Glasgow.

Play Offs were known as Test Matches in the early days of Scottish League football

Scottish League Championship Winners 1890-date

Season	Level 1 Champions	Level 2 Champions	Level 3 Champions
1890/1	Dumbarton / Rangers		
1891/2	Dumbarton		
1892/3	Celtic		
1893/4	Celtic	Hibernian	
1894/5	Hearts	Hibernian	
1895/6	Celtic	Abercorn	
1896/7	Hearts	Partick Thistle	
1897/8	Celtic	Kilmarnock	
1898/9	Rangers	Kilmarnock	
1899/00	Rangers	Partick Thistle	
1900/1	Rangers	St Bernards	
1901/2	Rangers	Port Glasgow	
1902/3	Hibernian	Airdrieonians	
1903/4	Third Lanark	Hamilton Accies	
1904/5	Celtic	Clyde	
1905/6	Celtic	Leith Athletic	
1906/7	Celtic	St Bernards	
1907/8	Celtic	Raith Rovers	
1908/9	Celtic	Abercorn	
1909/10	Celtic	Leith Athletic	
1910/1	Rangers	Dumbarton	
1911/2	Rangers	Ayr United	
1912/3	Rangers	Ayr United	
1913/4	Celtic	Cowdenbeath	
1914/5	Celtic	Cowdenbeath	
1915/6	Celtic		
1916/7	Celtic		
1917/8	Rangers		
1918/9	Celtic		
1919/20	Rangers		
1920/1	Rangers		
1921/2	Celtic	Alloa Athletic	
1922/3	Rangers	Queen's Park	
1923/4	Rangers	St Johnstone	Arthurlie
1924/5	Rangers	Dundee United	Nithsdale Wanderers
1935/6	Celtic	Dunfermline Athletic	Not awarded
1926/7	Rangers	Bo'ness	
1927/8	Rangers	Ayr United	
1928/9	Rangers	Dundee United	
1929/30	Rangers	Leith Athletic	
1930/1	Rangers	Third Lanark	
1931/2	Motherwell	East Stirlingshire	
1932/3	Rangers	Hibernian	
1933/4	Rangers	Albion Rovers	
1934/5	Rangers	Third Lanark	
1935/6	Celtic	Falkirk	
1936/7	Rangers	Ayr United	
1937/8	Celtic	Raith Rovers	
1938/9	Rangers	Cowdenbeath	
1946/7	Rangers	Dundee	
1947/8	Hibernian	East Fife	
1048/9	Rangers	Raith Rovers	
1949/50	Rangers	Morton	
1950/1	Hibernian	Queen of the South	
1951/2	Hibernian	Clyde	
1952/3	Rangers	Stirling Albion	
1953/4	Celtic	Motherwell	
1954/5	Aberdeen	Airdrieonians	
1955/6	Rangers	Queen's Park	
1956/7	Rangers	Clyde	
1957/8	Hearts	Stirling Albion	
1958/9	Rangers	Ayr United	
1959/60	Hearts	St Johnstone	
1960/1	Rangers	Stirling Albion	
1961/2	Dundee	Clyde	
1962/3	Rangers	St Johnstone	
1963/4	Rangers	Morton	

Scottish Football Leagues—Changing Structure

1890 (April 30th) Scottish Football League formed with 11 clubs

1893 Second Division formed. Promotion / relegation was on the basis of ballot.

1915 Second Division suspended

1921 Second Division re-started with automatic promotion / relegation

1923 Third Division Formed with automatic promotion / relegation

1926 Third Division Scrapped

1939 SFL League competitions suspended

1946 League competitions re-started with 3 Divisions, Division A, B and C. Automatic promotion / relegation but promoted clubs from Division C could not be Reserve sides

1949 C Division divided into two Sections, North East and South West

1955 C Division scrapped. Reserve teams formed Reserve League, others added to expanded Division B

1956 A Division and B Division renamed Divisions 1 and 2

1975 Three Division structure introduced, Premier, First and Second

1994 Four Division structure introduced, Premier, First, Second and Third

1998 Premier Division clubs broke away to form SPL, separate from SFL

2013 SPL and SFL merged to form Scottish Professional Football League. No change to Divisional structures. Names changed to SPFL Premiership, Championship, League One and League Two

SCOTTISH LEAGUE SECOND DIVISION.

Decisions At Last Night's Meeting.

A private meeting of the Scottish League was held in Glasgow last night to discuss the question of the formation of a Second Division and automatic promotion, and at the end of a two-hours sitting it was announced that no official communication was to be made.

We understand, however, that the decisions arrived at were:—That the First Division remain as at present, consisting of 22 clubs, and that the Central League be asked to form a Second Division consisting of 16 clubs, with automatic promotion for the leading club at the end of season 1921-22.

Season	Level 1 Champions	Level 2 Champions	Level 3 Champions	Level 4 Champions
1964/5	Kilmarnock	Stirling Albion		
1965/6	Celtic	Ayr United		
1966/7	Celtic	Morton		
1967/8	Celtic	St Mirren		
1968/9	Celtic	Motherwell		
1969/70	Celtic	Falkirk		
1970/1	Celtic	Partick Thistle		
1971/2	Celtic	Dumbarton		
1972/3	Celtic	Clyde		
1973/4	Celtic	Airdrieonians		
1974/5	Rangers	Falkirk		
1975/6	Rangers	Partick Thistle	Clydebank	
1976/7	Celtic	St Mirren	Stirling Albion	
1977/8	Rangers	Morton	Clyde	
1978/9	Celtic	Dundee	Berwick Rangers	
1979/80	Aberdeen	Hearts	Falkirk	
1980/1	Celtic	Hibernian	Queen's Park	
1981/2	Celtic	Motherwell	Clyde	
1982/3	Dundee United	St Johnstone	Brechin City	
1983/4	Aberdeen	Morton	Forfar Athletic	
1984/5	Aberdeen	Motherwell	Montrose	
1985/6	Celtic	Hamilton Accies	Dunfermline Athletic	
1986/7	Rangers	Morton	Meadowbank Thistle	
1987/8	Celtic	Hamilton Accies	Ayr United	
1988/9	Rangers	Dunfermline Athletic	Albion Rovers	
1989/90	Rangers	St Johnstone	Brechin City	
1990/1	Rangers	Falkirk	Stirling Albion	
1991/2	Rangers	Dundee	Dumbarton	
1992/3	Rangers	Raith Rovers	Clyde	
1993/4	Rangers	Falkirk	Stranraer	
1994/5	Rangers	Raith Rovers	Morton	Forfar Athletic
1995/6	Rangers	Dunfermline Athletic	Stirling Albion	Livingston
1996/7	Rangers	St Johnstone	Ayr United	Inverness CT
1997/8	Celtic	Dundee	Stranraer	Alloa Athletic
1998/9	Rangers	Hibernian	Livingston	Ross County
1999/0	Rangers	St Mirren	Clyde	Queen's Park
2000/1	Celtic	Livingston	Partick Thistle	Hamilton Accies
2001/2	Celtic	Partick Thistle	Queen of the South	Brechin City
2002/3	Rangers	Falkirk	Raith Rovers	Morton
2003/4	Celtic	Inverness CT	Airdrie United	Stranraer
2004/5	Rangers	Falkirk	Brechin City	Gretna
2005/6	Celtic	St Mirren	Gretna	Cowdenbeath
2006/7	Celtic	Gretna	Morton	Berwick Rangers
2007/8	Celtic	Hamilton Accies	Ross County	East Fife
2008/9	Rangers	St Johnstone	Raith Rovers	Dumbarton
2009/10	Rangers	Inverness CT	Stirling Albion	Livingston
2010/11	Rangers	Dunfermline Athletic	Livingston	Arbroath
2011/2	Celtic	Ross County	Cowdenbeath	Alloa Athletic
2012/3	Celtic	Partick Thistle	Queen of the South	Rangers
2013/4	Celtic	Dundee	Rangers	Peterhead
2014/5	Celtic	Hearts	Morton	Albion Rovers
2015/6	Celtic	Rangers	Dunfermline Athletic	East Fife
2016/7	Celtic	Hibernian	Livingston	Arbroath
2017/8	Celtic	St Mirren	Ayr United	Monttrose
2018/9	Celtic	Ross County	Arbroath	Peterhead
2019/20	Celtic	Dundee United	Raith Rovers	Cove Rangers
2020/1	Rangers	Hearts	Partick Thistle	Queen's Park

SPFL MONTHLY AWARDS 2020/21

	Premiership Player	Championship Player	League One Player	League Two Player
August	Ryan Kent (Rangers)			
September	James Tavernier (Rangers)			
October	Connor Goldson (Rangers)	Euan Murray (Dunfermline Athletic)	Stuart McKenzie (Cove Rangers)	Willie Muir (Queen's Park)
November	James Tavernier (Rangers)	Kyle Turner (Dunfermline Athletic)	Thomas Robert (Airdrieonians)	Darryl Duffy (Stranraer)
December	David Turnbull (Celtic)	Charlie Adam (Dundee)	Jack Hamilton (East Fife)	Andy Ryan (Stirling Albion)
January	Scott Robinson (Livingston)	Connor Shields (QOTS)		
February	Odsonne Edouard (Celtic)	Willie Gibson (QOTS)		
March	Alfredo Morelos (Rangers)	David Carson (Inverness CT)	Graham Webster (Montrose)	Raffaele De Vita (Edinburgh City)
April	Kyle Lafferty (Kilmarnock)	Jack Hamilton (Arbroath)	Scott Tiffoney (Partick Thistle)	Matthew Aitken (Albion Rovers)

	Premiership Manager	Championship Manager	League One Manager	League Two Manager
August	Steven Gerrard (Rangers)			
September	Neil Lennon (Celtic)			
October	Steven Gerrard (Rangers)	Stevie Crawford (Dunfermline Athletic)	Paul Hartley (Cove Rangers)	Ray McKinnon (Queen's Park)
November	Steven Gerrard (Rangers)	Stevie Crawford (Dunfermline Athletic)	Lee Miller / David McCracken (Falkirk)	Stephen Farrell (Stranraer)
December	David Martindale (Livingston)	Robbie Neilson (Hearts)	Stewart Petrie (Montrose)	Kevin Rutkiewicz (Stirling Albion)
January	David Martindale (Livingston)	Allan Johnston (QOTS)		
February	Steven Gerrard (Rangers)	Dick Campbell (Arbroath)		
March	Callum Davidson (St Johnstone)	James McPake (Dundee)	Lee Miller / David McCracken (Falkirk)	Gary Naysmith (Edinburgh City)
April	Graham Alexander (Motherwell)	Robbie Neilson (Hearts)	Ian McCall (Partick Thistle)	Brian Reid (Albion Rovers

SPFL TEAM OF THE SEASON 2020/1

Premiership

Allan McGregor (Rangers), James Tavernier (Rangers), Connor Goldson (Rangers), Jason Kerr (St Johnstone), Josh Doig (Hibernian), Martin Boyle (Hibernian), Steven Davis (Rangers), David Turnbull (Celtic), Ryan Kent (Rangers), Odsonne Edouard (Celtic), Alfredo Morelos (Rangers)

Championship

Craig Gordon (Hearts), Reghan Tumilty (Raith Rovers), Lee Ashcroft (Dundee), Ayo Obileye (QOTS), Kieran MacDonald (Raith Rovers), Paul McMullan (Dundee), Regan Hendry (Raith Rovers), Charlie Adam (Dundee), Daniel Mackay (ICT), Liam Boyce (Hearts), Connor Shields (QOTS)

League One

Stuart McKenzie (Cove Rangers), Cammy Ballantyne (Montrose), Darren Brownlie (Partick Thistle), Callum Fordyce (Airdrie), Leon McCann (Airdrie), Graham Webster (Montrose), Scott Brown (Peterhead), Stuart Bannigan (Partick Thistle), Scott Tiffoney (Partick Thistle), Mitch Megginson (Cove Rangers), Brian Graham (Partick Thistle)

League Two

Willie Muir (Queen's Park), Michael Doyle (Queen's Park), Lee Kilday (Queen's Park), Liam Henderson (Edinburgh City), Andy Stirling (Stranraer), Brian Cameron (Elgin City), Grant Gillespie (Queen's Park), Josh Campbell (Edinburgh City), Andy Ryan (Stirling Albion), Kane Hester (Elgin City), Thomas Orr (Stranraer)

PFA SCOTLAND AWARDS 2020/1

Due to Covid 19 the Scottish PFA cancelled their awards for 2019/20.

SPFA PLAYER OF THE YEAR AWARDS

Season	Premier			Division One			Division Two			Division Three			Young Player		
1977/8	Johnstone	Derek	Rangers	Pirie	Billy	Dundee	Smith	David	Berwick Rangers				Payne	Graeme	Dundee United
1978/9	Hegarty	Paul	Dundee United	McLaughlin	Brian	Ayr United	Leonard	Mike	Dunfermline Athletic				Stewart	Raymond	Dundee United
1979/80	Provan	Davie	Celtic	Clark	Sandy	Airdrieonians	Leetion	Paul	Falkirk				MacDonald	John	Rangers
1980/1	McGhee	Mark	Aberdeen	Sinclair	Eric	Dundee	Robertson	Jimmy	Queen of the South				Nicholas	Charlie	Celtic
1981/2	Clark	Sandy	Airdrieonians	McLaughlin	Brian	Motherwell	Nevin	Pat	Clyde				McAvennie	Frank	St Mirren
1982/3	Nicholas	Charlie	Celtic	McCabe	Gerry	Clydebank	Colquhoun	John	Stirling Albion				McStay	Paul	Celtic
1983/4	Miller	Willie	Aberdeen	McCabe	Gerry	Clydebank	Liddle	Jim	Forfar Athletic				Robertson	John	Hearts
1984/5	Duffy	Jim	Morton	McCabe	Gerry	Clydebank	Slaven	Bernie	Albion Rovers				Levein	Craig	Hearts
1985/6	Gough	Richard	Dundee United	Brogan	John	Hamilton Accies	Smith	Mark	Queen's Park				Levein	Craig	Hearts
1986/7	McClair	Brian	Celtic	Holmes	Jim	Morton	Sludden	John	Ayr United				Fleck	Robert	Rangers
1987/8	McStay	Paul	Celtic	Taylor	Alex	Hamilton Accies	Templeton	Henry	Ayr United				Collins	John	Hibernian
1988/9	Sneiders	Theo	Aberdeen	Jack	Ross	Dunfermline Athletic	Hunter	Paul	East Fife				McKinlay	Billy	Dundee United
1989/90	Bett	Jim	Aberdeen	Eadie	Ken	Clydebank	Watters	Willie	Kilmarnock				Crabbe	Scott	Hearts
1990/1	Elliot	Paul	Celtic	Stainrod	Simon	Falkirk	Todd	Kevin	Berwick Rangers				Jess	Eoin	Aberdeen
1991/2	McCoist	Ally	Rangers	Dalziel	Gordon	Raith Rovers	Thomson	Andy	Queen of the South				O'Donnell	Phil	Motherwell
1992/3	Goram	Andy	Rangers	Dalziel	Gordon	Raith Rovers	Ross	Sandy	Brechin City				Jess	Eoin	Aberdeen
1993/4	Hateley	Mark	Rangers	Cadette	Richard	Falkirk	Thomson	Andy	Queen of the South				O'Donnell	Phil	Motherwell
1994/5	Laudrup	Brian	Rangers	Crawford	Steven	Raith Rovers	McInnes	Derek	Morton	Bingham	David	Forfar Athletic	Miller	Charlie	Rangers
1995/6	Gascoigne	Paul	Rangers	O'Boyle	George	St Johnstone	McCormick	Steve	Stirling Albion	Young	Jason	Livingston	McNamara	Jackie	Celtic
1996/7	Di Canio	Paulo	Celtic	Grant	Roddy	St Johnstone	Ritchie	Paul	Hamilton Accies	Stewart	Iain	Inverness CT	Winters	Robbie	Dundee United
1997/8	McNamara	Jackie	Celtic	Grady	James	Dundee	Lovering	Paul	Clydebank	Irvine	Willie	Alloa	Naysmith	Gary	Hearts
1998/9	Larsson	Henrik	Celtic	Latapy	Russell	Hibernian	Bingham	David	Livingston	Tarrant	Neil	Ross County	Ferguson	Barry	Rangers
1999/00	Viduka	Mark	Celtic	Crawford	Steven	Dunfermline Athletic	Carrigan	Brian	Clyde	Milne	Steven	Forfar Athletic	Miller	Kenny	Hibernian
2000/1	Larsson	Henrik	Celtic	Bingham	David	Livingston	McLean	Scott	Partick Thistle	Hislop	Steven	East Stirlingshire	Petrov	Stilian	Celtic
2001/2	Amoruso	Lorenzo	Rangers	Coyle	Owen	Airdrieonians	O'Neil	John	Queen of the South	McManus	Paul	East Fife	McNaughton	Kevin	Aberdeen
2002/3	Ferguson	Barry	Rangers	Wyness	Dennis	Inverness CT	Templeman	Chris	Brechin City	Williams	Alex	Morton	McFadden	James	Motherwell
2003/4	Sutton	Chris	Celtic	Harty	Ian	Clyde	Tosh	Paul	Forfar Athletic	Moore	Michael	Stranraer	Pearson	Steven	Celtic
2004/5	*Ricksen	Fernando	Rangers	Latapy	Russell	Falkirk	Hampshire	Steven	Brechin City	Bingham	David	Gretna	Riordan	Derek	Hibernian
	*Hartson	John	Celtic												

SCOTTISH FOOTBALL WRITERS AWARDS PLAYER OF THE YEAR 2020/1

Player of the Year:
Steven Davis (Rangers)

Young Player of the Year:
Josh Doig (Hibernian)

Manager of the Year:
Steven Gerrard (Rangers)

SCOTTISH FOOTBALL WRITERS AWARDS—PREVIOUS WINNERS

	Player of the Year			Young Player of the Year			Manager of the Year	
1986/7	Brian McClair	Celtic				1986/7	Jim McLean	Dundee United
1987/8	Paul McStay	Celtic				1987/8	Billy McNeill	Celtic
1988/9	Richard Gough	Rangers				1988/9	Graeme Souness	Rangers
1989/90	Alex McLeish	Aberdeen				1989/90	Andy Roxburgh	Scotland
1990/1	Maurice Malpas	Dundee United				1990/1	Alex Totten	St Johnstone
1991/2	Ally McCoist	Rangers				1991/2	Walter Smith	Rangers
1992/3	Andy Goram	Rangers				1992/3	Walter Smith	Rangers
1993/4	Mark Hateley	Rangers				1993/4	Walter Smith	Rangers
1994/5	Brian Laudrup	Rangers				1994/5	Jimmy Nicholl	Raith Rovers
1995/6	Paul Gascoigne	Rangers				1995/6	Walter Smith	Rangers
1996/7	Brian Laudrup	Rangers				1996/7	Walter Smith	Rangers
1997/8	Craig Burley	Celtic				1997/8	Wim Jansen	Celtic
1998/9	Henrik Larsson	Celtic				1998/9	Dick Advocaat	Rangers
1999/00	Barry Ferguson	Rangers				1999/00	Dick Advocaat	Rangers
2000/1	Henrik Larsson	Celtic				2000/1	Martin O'Neill	Celtic
2001/2	Paul Lambert	Celtic	2001/2	James McFadden	Motherwell	2001/2	Martin O'Neill	Celtic
2002/3	Barry Ferguson	Rangers	2002/3	Zurab Khizanishvili	Dundee	2002/3	Alex McLeish	Rangers
2003/4	Jackie McNamara	Celtic	2003/4	Craig Gordon	Hearts	2003/4	Martin O'Neill	Celtic
2004/5	John Hartson	Celtic	2004/5	Derek Riordan	Hibernian	2004/5	Tony Mowbray	Hibernian
2005/6	Craig Gordon	Hearts	2005/6	Steven Naismith	Kilmarnock	2005/6	Gordon Strachan	Celtic
2006/7	Shunsuke Nakamura	Celtic	2006/7	Scott Brown	Hibernian	2006/7	Gordon Strachan	Celtic
2007/8	Carlos Cuellar	Rangers	2007/8	Steven Fletcher	Hibernian	2007/8	Walter Smith	Rangers
2008/9	Gary Caldwell	Celtic	2008/9	Steven Fletcher	Hibernian	2008/9	Csaba Laszlo	Hearts
2009/10	David Weir	Rangers	2009/10	Danny Wilson	Rangers	2009/10	Walter Smith	Rangers
2010/1	Emilio Izaguirre	Celtic	2010/1	David Goodwillie	Dundee United	2010/1	Mixu Paatelainen	Kilmarnock
2011/2	Charlie Mulgrew	Celtic	2011/2	James Forrest	Celtic	2011/2	Neil Lennon	Celtic
2012/3	Leigh Griffiths	Hibernian	2012/3	Stuart Armstrong	Dundee United	2012/3	Neil Lennon	Celtic
2013/4	Kris Commons	Celtic	2013/4	Stevie May	St Johnstone	2013/4	Derek McInnes	Aberdeen
2014/5	Craig Gordon	Celtic	2014/5	Ryan Christie	ICT	2014/5	John Hughes	ICT
2015/6	Leigh Griffiths	Celtic	2015/6	Kieran Tierney	Celtic	2015/6	Jim McIntyre	Ross County
2016/7	Scott Sinclair	Celtic	2016/7	Kieran Tierney	Celtic	2016/7	Brendan Rodgers	Celtic
2017/8	Scott Brown	Celtic	2017/8	Kieran Tierney	Celtic	2017/8	Steve Clarke	Kilmarnock
2018/9	James Forrest	Celtic	2018/9	David Turnbull	Motherwell	2018/9	Steve Clarke	Kilmarnock
2019/20	Odsonne Edouard	Celtic	2019/20	Lewis Ferguson	Aberdeen	2019/20	Neil Lennon	Celtic
2020/1	Steven Davis	Rangers	2020/1	Josh Doig	Hibernian	2020/1	Steven Gerrard	Rangers

SPFL CLUB TOP LEAGUE SCORERS 1975/6-2020/1

ABERDEEN

Season	Player	Goals
1975/6	Jocky Scott	14
1976/7	Joe Harper	18
1977/8	Joe Harper	17
1978/9	Joe Harper	19
1979/80	Steve Archibald / Drew Jarvie	12
1980/1	Mark McGhee	18
1981/2	John Hewitt	11
1982/3	Mark McGhee	17
1983/4	Mark McGhee / Gordon Strachan	13
1984/5	Frank McDougall	22
1985/6	Frank McDougall	14
1986/7	Billy Stark	12
1987/8	Jim Bett	10
1988/9	Charlie Nicholas	16
1989/90	Charlie Nicholas	11
1990/1	Hans Gillhaus	14
1991/2	Eoin Jess	12
1992/3	Duncan Shearer	22
1993/4	Duncan Shearer	17
1994/5	Billy Dodds	15
1995/6	Scott Booth / Joe Miller	9
1996/7	Billy Dodds	15
1997/8	Billy Dodds	10
1998/9	Eoin Jess	14
1999/00	Arild Stavrum	9
2000/1	Arild Stavrum	17
2001/2	Robbie Winters	13
2002/3	Paul Sheerin	8
2003/4	Scott Booth	8
2004/5	Darren Mackie	12
2005/6	Stephen Lovell / Jamie Smith	8
2006/7	Darren Mackie	13
2007/8	Lee Miller	12
2008/9	Lee Miller	10
2009/10	Steven McLean	5
2010/1	Scott Vernon	10
2011/2	Scott Vernon	11
2012/3	Niall McGinn	20
2013/4	Niall McGinn	13
2014/5	Adam Rooney	18
2015/6	Adam Rooney	20
2016/7	Adam Rooney	12
2017/18	Kenny McLean / Adam Rooney	8
2018/19	Sam Cosgrove	17
2019/20	Sam Cosgrove	11
2020/21	Lewis Ferguson	9

AIRDRIE

Season	Player	Goals
1975/6	Derek Whiteford	8
1976/7	Derek Whiteford	15
1977/8	Joe Cairney	22
1978/9	Sandy Clark	23
1979/80	Sandy Clark	22
1980/1	Sandy Clark	10
1981/2	Sandy Clark	15
1982/3	Blair Millar	12
1983/4	John Flood	11
1984/5	David McCabe	21
1985/6	John Flood	11
1986/7	David McCabe	13
1987/8	David McCabe	20
1988/9	Kenny MacDonald	22
1989/90	Owen Coyle	10
1990/1	Owen Coyle	20
1991/2	Owen Coyle	11
1992/3	Owen Coyle	9
1993/4	David Kirkwood	10
1994/5	Andy Smith	12
1995/6	Jim McIntyre	9
1996/7	Paddy Connolly / Steve Cooper / Brian McPhee	8
1997/8	Brian McPhee	12
1998/9	Steve Cooper	8
1999/00	Alex Neil / Neil Thompson	5
2000/1	Davide Fernandez	7
2001/2	Owen Coyle	23
2002/3		
2003/4		
2004/5		
2005/6		
2006/7		
2007/8		
2008/9		
2009/10		
2010/1		
2011/2		
2012/3		
2013/4		
2014/5		
2015/6		

ALBION ROVERS

Season	Player	Goals
1975/6	John Brogan	7
1976/7	Donnie McLean	20
1977/8	Donnie McLean	23
1978/9	Bruce Cleland	24
1979/80	Peter Houston	18
1980/1	Ian Campbell	12
1981/2	Steve Evans	16
1982/3	Steve Evans	12
1983/4	Tommy McGorm	11
1984/5	Bernie Slaven	27
1985/6	Sammy Conn / Vic Kasule / Alan Rodgers	6
1986/7	Chris Wilson	11
1987/8	Ally Graham	10
1988/9	Jim Chapman	15
1989/90	Mike McAnenay	10
1990/1	Mike McAnenay	12
1991/2	Gerry McCoy	11
1992/3	Martin Scott	16
1993/4	Martin Scott	17
1994/5	Martin Scott	7
1995/6	Gordon Young	12
1996/7	Willie Watters	11
1997/8	Willie Watters	13
1998/9	David Lorimer	10
1999/00	Ian Diack	7
2000/1	Mark Booth	6
2001/2	Colin McLean	11
2002/3	Jim Mercer	10
2003/4	Paul McManus	18
2004/5	John Bradford	7
2005/6	Scott Chaplain	8
2006/7	Scott Chaplain	18
2007/8	John Gemmell	11
2008/9	Bobby Barr	11
2009/10	Marc McCusker	6
2010/1	Robert Love	10
2011/2	John Gemmell	9
2012/3	David Crawford	10
2013/4	Scott Chaplain	9
2014/5	Mark McGuigan	11
2015/6	Ally Love	13
2016/7	Ross Stewart	12
2017/18	Alan Trouten	20
2018/19	Lewis McLear / Gregor Fotheringham	4
2019/20	Declan Byrne	11
2020/21	Matthew Aitken	10

ALLOA

Season	Player	Goals
1975/6	Billy Morrison	15
1976/7	Gordon Forrest	19
1977/8	Donnie Wilson	7
1978/9	Willie Irvine	13
1979/80	Colin McIntosh	14
1980/1	Alan Holt	14
1981/2	Scott Murray	14
1982/3	Lennie McComb	12
1983/4	David Lloyd	10
1984/5	David Lloyd	16
1985/6	Mike Jamieson / Stuart Sorbie	11
1986/7	Stuart Sorbie	14
1987/8	Paul Rutherford	14
1988/9	Charlie Lytwyn	23
1989/90	Peter Lamont	9
1990/1	John Irvine	11
1991/2	Mike Hendry	12
1992/3	Barrie Moffat	19
1993/4	Willie Newbigging	7
1994/5	Barrie Moffat	13
1995/6	Barrie Moffat / Steve Rixon	5
1996/7	Willie Irvine	12
1997/8	Willie Irvine	18
1998/9	Martin Cameron / Willie Irvine	15
1999/00	Martin Cameron	15
2000/1	Ross Hamilton	9
2001/2	Gareth Hutchison	14
2002/3	Robert Sloan	8
2003/4	Ross Hamilton	13
2004/5	Andy Brown	8
2005/6	Jamie Stevenson	9
2006/7	Graeme Brown	6
2007/8	Graeme Brown	11
2008/9	Andy Scott	7
2009/10	Steven Noble	10
2010/1	Brian Prunty	8
2011/2	Stevie May	19
2012/3	Kevin Cawley	13
2013/4	Kevin Cawley	8
2014/5	Liam Buchanan	14
2015/6	Michael Duffy / Ian Flannigan	3
2016/7	Greg Spence	16
2017/18	Ross Stewart	10
2018/19	Alan Trouten	10
2019/20	Kevin O'Hara / Alan Trouten	10
2020/21	Kevin Cawley	6

ANNAN ATHLETIC

Season	Player	Goals
1975/6		
1976/7		
1977/8		
1978/9		
1979/80		
1980/1		
1981/2		
1982/3		
1983/4		
1984/5		
1985/6		
1986/7		
1987/8		
1988/9		
1989/90		
1990/1		
1991/2		
1992/3		
1993/4		
1994/5		
1995/6		
1996/7		
1997/8		
1998/9		
1999/00		
2000/1		
2001/2		
2002/3		
2003/4		
2004/5		
2005/6		
2006/7		
2007/8		
2008/9	Michael Jack	15
2009/10	Graham Bell	9
2010/1	Ian Harty	14
2011/2	S Gibson / A Muirhead / S O'Connor	7
2012/3	Alistair Love	12
2013/4	Kenny Mackay	13
2014/5	Peter Weatherson	22
2015/6	Peter Weatherson	16
2016/7	David McKenna	11
2017/18	Blair Henderson	16
2018/19	Tommy Muir	13
2019/20	Tommy Muir	7
2020/21	Tony Wallace	5

ARBROATH

Season	Player	Goals
1975/6	Jimmy Bone	13
1976/7	Jimmy Bone	15
1977/8	John Fletcher	9
1978/9	Steve Mylles / Tommy Yule	9
1979/80	Tommy Yule	10
1980/1	Ian Harley	15
1981/2	Dougie Robb	21
1982/3	Billy Steele	15
1983/4	Ian Harley	18
1984/5	Rod Brown	6
1985/6	Mark McWalter	14
1986/7	Jim Fotheringham	14
1987/8	Alan McKenna	13
1988/9	Jim Fotheringham	11
1989/90	Jim Marshall	12
1990/1	Martin Bennett / Stuart Sorbie	10
1991/2	Stuart Sorbie	12
1992/3	Stuart Sorbie	19
1993/4	Danny Diver	10
1994/5	Steven Tosh	11
1995/6	Stephen McCormick / David Pew	8
1996/7	Brian Grant	5
1997/8	Billy Spence	16
1998/9	Colin McGlashan	12
1999/00	Colin McGlashan	16
2000/1	Steven Mallan	10
2001/2	Graeme Bayne / Colin McGlashan	6
2002/3	Murray McDowell / John Cusick	4
2003/4	John McGlashan	10
2004/5	Greg Henslee	11
2005/6	Jay Stein	9
2006/7	Willie Martin	9
2007/8	Barry Scott	11
2008/9	Barry Scott / Barry Sellars	6
2009/10	Stephen Hislop	8
2010/1	Gavin Swankie	22
2011/2	Steven Doris	21
2012/3	Steven Doris	11
2013/4	Alan Cook	12
2014/5	Simon Murray	19
2015/6	Bobby Linn	11
2016/7	Ryan McCord	13
2017/18	Danny Denholm	10
2018/19	Bobby Linn	21
2019/20	Bobby Linn	6
2020/21	Jack Hamilton	8

AYR UNITED

Season	Player	Goals
1975/6	Johnny Graham	16
1976/7	Walker McCall	16
1977/8	Walker McCall	12
1978/9	Brian McLaughlin	19
1979/80	Derek Frye	16
1980/1	Derek Frye / Eric Morris	10
1981/2	Derek Frye	13
1982/3	Mike Larnach / Derek Frye / Alan McInally	7
1983/4	Alan McInally	15
1984/5	Gerry Collins	8
1985/6	David Irons	6
1986/7	John Sludden	26
1987/8	John Sludden	31
1988/9	Henry Templeton	17
1989/90	Tommy Bryce	10
1990/1	Tommy Bryce	11
1991/2	Ally Graham	14
1992/3	Ally Graham	9
1993/4	Sammy McGivern	12
1994/5	Justin Jackson	4
1995/6	Brian Bilsland / Isaac English	5
1996/7	Stevn J Kerrigan	14
1997/8	Laurent D'Jaffo	10
1998/9	Greg Hurst	18
1999/00	Greg Hurst	14
2000/1	Eddie Annand	18
2001/2	Eddie Annand	14
2002/3	Stuart Kean	7
2003/4	Stuart Kean	9
2004/5	Stuart Kean	10
2005/6	Jerome Vareille	13
2006/7	Gareth Wardlaw	7
2007/8	Alex Williams	16
2008/9	Brian Prunty	15
2009/10	Mark Roberts	8
2010/1	Mark Roberts	21
2011/2	Michael Moffat / Mark Roberts	8
2012/3	Michael Moffat	16
2013/4	Michael Moffat	26
2014/5	Alan Forrest	9
2015/6	Craig Moore	14
2016/7	Alan Forrest	6
2017/18	Lawrence Shankland	26
2018/19	Lawrence Shankland	24
2019/20	Alan Forrest	10
2020/21	Cammy Smith	6

BERWICK RANGERS

Season	Player	Goals
1975/6	Ian Smith	10
1976/7	Billy Laing	8
1977/8	Eric Tait / Billy Laing	14
1978/9	Jim Morton	20
1979/80	Eric Tait	13
1980/1	Eric Tait	8
1981/2	Mickey Lawson	16
1982/3	Stuart Romaines / Ian Cashmore	8
1983/4	Peter Davidson	9
1984/5	Peter Davidson	9
1985/6	John Sokuluk	12
1986/7	Eric Tait	8
1987/8	Mark Cameron / Hugh Douglas / Tom Graham	3
1988/9	John Hughes	10
1989/90	Scott Sloan	16
1990/1	Kevin Todd	14
1991/2	Steve Bickmore	12
1992/3	David Scott	11
1993/4	Willie Irvine	15
1994/5	Warren Hawke	16
1995/6	Willie Irvine	13
1996/7	Paul Forrester	6
1997/8	Paul Forrester	10
1998/9	Moray Ieask	12
1999/00	Marc Anthony	9
2000/1	Gary Wood	14
2001/2	Gary Wood	9
2002/3	Alex Burke / Gary Wood	12
2003/4	Gareth Hutchison	22
2004/5	Gareth Hutchison /Darren Smith	8
2005/6	Kevin Haynes	15
2006/7	Gary Wood	10
2007/8	Ian Diack	9
2008/9	Darren Gribben	14
2009/10	Damon Gray	11
2010/1	Darren Gribben	17
2011/2	Darren Gribben	10
2012/3	Darren Lavery	17
2013/4	Lee Currie	17
2014/5	Darren Lavery	10
2015/6	Blair Henderson	17
2016/7	Steven Thomson	13
2017/18	Jack Hamilton	8
2018/19	Lewis Barr	6
2019/20		
2020/21		

BRECHIN CITY

Season	Player	Goals
1975/6	Albert Rice	7
1976/7	Ronnie Robb	16
1977/8	Jim Morton	10
1978/9	Ian Campbell	16
1979/80	Ian Campbell	25
1980/1	Ian Campbell	11
1981/2	Ian Campbell	16
1982/3	Ian Campbell	24
1983/4	Ian Campbell	19
1984/5	Ken Eadie	17
1985/6	Ken Eadie	22
1986/7	Charlie Adam	12
1987/8	Graham Buckley	15
1988/9	Charlie Adam	15
1989/90	Gordon Lees	12
1990/1	Paul Ritchie	14
1991/2	Paul Ritchie	12
1992/3	Sandy Ross	23
1993/4	Marc Miller	10
1994/5	Gavin Price / Ray Smith	6
1995/6	Sandy Ross	8
1996/7	Stephen P Kerrigan	7
1997/8	Craig Feroz	7
1998/9	John Dickson	15
1999/00	Ben Honeyman	11
2000/1	Roddy Grant	22
2001/2	Chris Templeman	15
2002/3	Chris Templeman	21
2003/4	Chris Templeman	5
2004/5	Steve Hampshire	17
2005/6	Kevin Byers	6
2006/7	Ian Russell	21
2007/8	Charlie King	10
2008/9	Gary Twigg	12
2009/10	Rory McAllister	21
2010/1	Rory McAllister	19
2011/2	Paul McManus	15
2012/3	Alan Trouten	17
2013/4	Andy Jackson	12
2014/5	Alan Trouten	15
2015/6	Robbie Thomson	15
2016/7	Andy Jackson	13
2017/18	Jordan Sinclair	5
2018/19	Andy Jackson	11
2019/20	Paul McManus	7
2020/21	Kieran Inglis / Bobby Bar	2

CELTIC

Season	Player	Goals
1975/6	Kenny Dalglish	24
1976/7	Ronnie Glavin	19
1977/8	Johannes Edvaldsson	10
1978/9	Andy Lynch / Tom McAdam	7
1979/80	George McCluskey	10
1980/1	Frank McGarvey	23
1981/2	George McCluskey	21
1982/3	Charlie Nicholas	29
1983/4	Brian McClair	23
1984/5	Brian McClair	19
1985/6	Brian McClair	22
1986/7	Brian McClair	35
1987/8	Andy Walker	26
1988/9	Mark McGhee	16
1989/90	Dariusz Dziekanowski	8
1990/1	Tommy Coyne	18
1991/2	Charlie Nicholas	21
1992/3	Andy Payton	13
1993/4	Pat McGinlay	10
1994/5	John Collins	8
1995/6	Pierre Van Hooijdonk	26
1996/7	Jorge Cadete	25
1997/8	Henrik Larsson	16
1998/9	Henrik Larsson	29
1999/00	Mark Viduka	25
2000/1	Henrik Larsson	35
2001/2	Henrik Larsson	29
2002/3	Henrik Larsson	28
2003/4	Henrik Larsson	30
2004/5	John Hartson	23
2005/6	John Hartson	18
2006/7	Jan Vennegoor of Hesselink	13
2007/8	Scott McDonald	25
2008/9	Scott McDonald	16
2009/10	Robbie Keane	12
2010/1	Gary Hooper	20
2011/2	Gary Hooper	24
2012/3	Gary Hooper	19
2013/4	Kris Commons	27
2014/5	Leigh Griffiths	14
2015/6	Leigh Griffiths	31
2016/7	Scott Sinclair	21
2017/18	Scott Sinclair	10
2018/19	Odsonne Edouard	15
2019/20	Odsonne Edouard	22
2020/21	Odsonne Edouard	18

CLYDE

Season	Player	Goals
1975/6	Neil Hood	14
1976/7	Neil Hood	16
1977/8	Neil Hood	21
1978/9	Joe Ward	10
1979/80	Neil Hood	11
1980/1	Danny Masterton	19
1981/2	Danny Masterton	23
1982/3	Danny Masterton	14
1983/4	Derek Frye	17
1984/5	Derek Frye	19
1985/6	Derek Frye	12
1986/7	Jim Murphy	12
1987/8	Colin McGlashan	16
1988/9	Colin McGlashan	16
1989/90	Colin McGlashan	11
1990/1	Steve Mallan	8
1991/2	David Thompson	16
1992/3	Frank McGarvey	16
1993/4	Ian McConnell / Gordon Parks	5
1994/5	John Dickson	10
1995/6	Eddie Annand	21
1996/7	Eddie Annand	21
1997/8	Paul Brownlie	8
1998/9	Steve Convery	12
1999/00	Brian Carrigan	18
2000/1	Andrew Kane	7
2001/2	Leigh Hinds	11
2002/3	Pat Keogh	12
2003/4	Ian Harty	25
2004/5	Ian Harty	15
2005/6	Alex Williams	13
2006/7	Gary Arbuckle	11
2007/8	Pat Clarke	6
2008/9	Pat Clarke	11
2009/10	Willie Sawyers	10
2010/1	Marc McCusker	11
2011/2	John Neill	7
2012/3	John Sweeney / Kevin Watt	9
2013/4	Stefan McCluskey	11
2014/5	Scott McManus	7
2015/6	Sean Higgins / Scott Linton	9
2016/7	Peter MacDonald	17
2017/18	David Goodwillie	25
2018/19	David Goodwillie	18
2019/20	David Goodwillie	20
2020/21	David Goodwillie	11

CLYDEBANK / AIRDRIE UNITED / AIRDRIEONI/

1975/6	Davie Cooper
1976/7	Joe McCallan
1977/8	John McCormack
1978/9	Blair Miller
1979/80	Blair Miller
1980/1	Blair Miller
1981/2	Blair Miller
1982/3	Bobby Williamson
1983/4	Tommy Coyne
1984/5	Michael Conroy
1985/6	Michael Conroy / David Lloyd
1986/7	Michael Conroy / Stuart Gordon
1987/8	Michael Conroy
1988/9	Ken Eadie
1989/90	Ken Eadie
1990/1	Ken Eadie
1991/2	Ken Eadie
1992/3	Craig Flannigan
1993/4	Ken Eadie / Craig Flannigan
1994/5	Ken Eadie
1995/6	James Grady
1996/7	James Grady
1997/8	Colin McDonald
1998/9	Colin McDonald
1999/00	Ian Cameron
2000/1	Alex Burke
2001/2	Alex Burke
2002/3	Jerome Vareille
2003/4	Owen Coyle / Alan Gow
2004/5	Owen Coyle
2005/6	Brian Prunty
2006/7	Gary Twigg
2007/8	Allan Russell
2008/9	Simon Lynch
2009/10	John Baird
2010/1	Scott Gemmill
2011/2	Ryan Donnelly
2012/3	John Boyle
2013/4	Jim Lister
2014/5	Brian Prunty
2015/6	Jim Lister
2016/7	Andy Ryan
2017/18	Ryan Conroy / Willis Furtado
2018/19	Leighton McIntosh
2019/20	Dale Carrick
2020/21	Dale Carrick

COVE RANGERS

Season	Player	Goals
2019/20	Mitch Megginson	23
2020/21	Mitch Megginson	15

COWDENBEATH

Season	Player	Goals
1975/6	John Murphy	10
1976/7	George Hunter	17
1977/8	Billy Steele	20
1978/9	Billy Steele	20
1979/80	Billy Steele	13
1980/1	Jim Liddle	18
1981/2	Gordon Forrest	16
1982/3	Willie Gibson	13
1983/4	Ian Paterson	7
1984/5	Kenny Ward	16
1985/6	Colin McGlashan	15
1986/7	Billy Blackie / Roddy Grant	14
1987/8	Roddy Grant	11
1988/9	Alan McGonnigal	8
1989/90	Sandy Ross	16
1990/1	Alan McKenzie	15
1991/2	Graham Buckley	21
1992/3	Willie Callaghan	9
1993/4	Willie Callaghan	11
1994/5	Mark Yardley	23
1995/6	David Scott	11
1996/7	Gary Wood	6
1997/8	Willie Stewart	6
1998/9	Willie Stewart	7
1999/00	Murray McDowell	13
2000/1	Murray McDowell	10
2001/2	Graeme Brown	17
2002/3	Graeme Brown / Kevin Gordon	10
2003/4	Dene Shields	12
2004/5	Darren Gribben	12
2005/6	Liam Buchanan	17
2006/7	Liam Buchanan	20
2007/8	Pat Clarke	6
2008/9	John Gemmell	12
2009/10	Gareth Wardlaw	16
2010/1	Greg Stewart	9
2011/2	Marc McKenzie	18
2012/3	Jamie Stevenson	8
2013/4	Kane Hemmings	18
2014/5	Kudus Oyenuga	6
2015/6	Greg Spence	17
2016/7	Kris Renton	10
2017/18	Robbie Buchanan	7
2018/19	Jordan Allan / David Cox	9
2019/20	Fraser Mullen / David Cox	6
2020/21	5 players 2 each	2

DUMBARTON

Season	Player	Goals
1975/6	John Bourke	17
1976/7	John Bourke	19
1977/8	Derek Whiteford / John Whiteford	15
1978/9	Raymond Blair	9
1979/80	Graeme Sharp	16
1980/1	Brian Gallagher	14
1981/2	Raymond Blair	9
1982/3	Raymond Blair	10
1983/4	Joe Coyle	15
1984/5	Joe Coyle	7
1985/6	Gerry McCoy	13
1986/7	Gerry McCoy	21
1987/8	Owen Coyle	14
1988/9	Stuart MacIver	13
1989/90	Charlie Gibson	20
1990/1	John McQuade	14
1991/2	Jimmy Gilmour	19
1992/3	John McQuade	15
1993/4	Charlie Gibson	13
1994/5	Martin Mooney	17
1995/6	Martin Mooney	5
1996/7	Hugh Ward	7
1997/8	Colin McKinnon	10
1998/9	Paddy Flannery	17
1999/00	Paddy Flannery	14
2000/1	Paddy Flannery	17
2001/2	Paddy Flannery	18
2002/3	Paddy Flannery / Gary McCutcheon	8
2003/4	Ian Russell	10
2004/5	Ian Russell	11
2005/6	Andy Rodgers	12
2006/7	Stephen Dobbie	10
2007/8	Fergus Tiernan	6
2008/9	Ross Clark	14
2009/10	Scott Chaplain	10
2010/1	Jon McShane	13
2011/2	Bryan Prunty	14
2012/3	Jim Lister	12
2013/4	Chris Kane / Mitch Megginson	1o
2014/5	Gary Fleming	6
2015/6	Gary Fleming / Christian Nade	7
2016/7	Robert Thomson	11
2017/18	Calum Gallagher / Dmytrios Froxylias / OG	4
2018/19	Dom Thomas	14
2019/20	Isaac Layne	8
2020/21	Jaime Wilson	5

DUNDEE

Season	Player	Goals
1975/6	Gordon Wallace	12
1976/7	Billy Pirie	36
1977/8	Billy Pirie	35
1978/9	Billy Pirie	16
1979/80	Ian Redford	9
1980/1	Eric Sinclair	19
1981/2	Ian Ferguson	12
1982/3	Ian Ferguson	9
1983/4	Walker McCall	13
1984/5	Ray Stephen	8
1985/6	Ray Stephen	14
1986/7	Graham Harvey	12
1987/8	Tommy Coyne	33
1988/9	Tommy Coyne	9
1989/90	Billy Dodds	13
1990/1	Keith Wright	15
1991/2	Billy Dodds	19
1992/3	Billy Dodds	16
1993/4	Dragutin Ristic / George Haw	6
1994/5	George Shaw / Gerry Britton / Jim Hamilton	12
1995/6	Jim Hamilton	14
1996/7	Jerry O'Driscoll	10
1997/8	James Grady	15
1998/9	Eddie Annand	9
1999/00	Willie Falconer	13
2000/1	Juan Sara	14
2001/2	Juan Sara	11
2002/3	Stephen Lovell	13
2003/4	Nacho Novo	20
2004/5	Stephen Lovell	14
2005/6	Simon Lynch	12
2006/7	Derek Lyle	12
2007/8	Kevin McDonald	9
2008/9	Mickael Antoine-Curier	14
2009/10	Gary Harkins	14
2010/1	Stephen Higgins	9
2011/2	Ryan Conroy / Steven Milne	11
2012/3	Ryan Conroy	6
2013/4	Peter MacDonald	17
2014/5	Greg Stewart	13
2015/6	Kane Hemmings	21
2016/7	Marcus Haber	9
2017/18	Sofien Moussa	7
2018/19	Kenny Miller	8
2019/20	Danny Johnson	5
2020/21	Osman Sow	9

DUNDEE UNITED

Season	Player	Goals
1975/6	Tom McAdam	12
1976/7	Paul Sturrock	15
1977/8	George Fleming	9
1978/9	David Dodds	10
1979/80	Willie Pettigrew	14
1980/1	David Dodds	14
1981/2	Paul Sturrock	15
1982/3	David Dodds	22
1983/4	David Dodds	15
1984/5	Paul Sturrock	14
1985/6	David Dodds	12
1986/7	Ian Ferguson	16
1987/8	Ian Ferguson	11
1988/9	Mixu Paatelainen	10
1989/90	Darren Jackson / Mixu Paatelainen	7
1990/1	Darren Jackson	12
1991/2	Duncan Ferguson	15
1992/3	Paddy Connolly	16
1993/4	Craig Brewster	16
1994/5	Craig Brewster	7
1995/6	Craig Brewster / Gary McSwegan	17
1996/7	Kjell Olofsson	12
1997/8	Kjell Olofsson	18
1998/9	Billy Dodds	17
1999/00	Billy Dodds	9
2000/1	Derek Lilley	6
2001/2	Derek Lilley / Jim McIntyre / Stephen Thompson	6
2002/3	Jim McIntyre	9
2003/4	Billy Dodds / Jim McIntyre	10
2004/5	Jim McIntyre	11
2005/6	Lee Miller	8
2006/7	Barry Robson	11
2007/8	Noel Hunt	13
2008/9	Fran Sandaza	10
2009/10	John Daly	13
2010/1	David Goodwillie	17
2011/2	John Daly	19
2012/3	Jonny Russell	13
2013/4	Nadir Ciftci	11
2014/5	Nadir Ciftci	14
2015/6	Billy McKay	12
2016/7	Tony Andreu	13
2017/18	Scott McDonald	16
2018/19	Pavol Safranko	13
2019/20	Lawrence Shankland	24
2020/21	Nicky Clark / Lawrence Shankland	8

DUNFERMLINE ATH

Season	Player	Goals
1975/6	Ken Mackie	10
1976/7	Alan Evans	13
1977/8	Bobby Morrison	11
1978/9	Mike Leonard	20
1979/80	Sandy McNaughton	17
1980/1	Sandy McNaughton	20
1981/2	Sandy McNaughton	13
1982/3	Steve Morrison	8
1983/4	Steve Morrison	9
1984/5	John Watson	15
1985/6	John Watson	24
1986/7	John Watson	13
1987/8	Craig Robertson	13
1988/9	Ross Jack	18
1989/90	Ross Jack	16
1990/1	Ross Jack	8
1991/2	David Moyes	5
1992/3	Hamish French	12
1993/4	George O'Boyle	17
1994/5	Stewart Petrie	14
1995/6	Stewart Petrie	13
1996/7	Gerry Britton	13
1997/8	Andy Smith	16
1998/9	Andy Smith	8
1999/00	Steven Crawford	16
2000/1	Steven Crawford	9
2001/2	Barry Nicholson	7
2002/3	Steven Crawford	19
2003/4	Steven Crawford	13
2004/5	Andy Tod	6
2005/6	Mark Burchill	12
2006/7	Steven Crawford	5
2007/8	Mark Burchill	11
2008/9	Andy Kirk	12
2009/10	Willie Gibson	9
2010/1	Andy Kirk	12
2011/2	Andy Kirk	11
2012/3	Andy Barrowman	10
2013/4	Ryan Wallace	10
2014/5	Faisal El Bakhtoui / Gozie Ugwu	7
2015/6	Faisal El Bakhtoui	22
2016/7	Nicky Clark	15
2017/18	Nicky Clark	14
2018/19	Jackson Longridge / Bruce Anderson	5
2019/20	Kevin Nisbet	18
2020/21	Kevin O'Hara	8

EAST FIFE

Season	Player	Goals
1975/6	Drew Rutherford / Kevin Hegarty	8
1976/7	Willie Gillies / Kevin Hegarty	7
1977/8	Ken Mackie	11
1978/9	Ken Mackie	17
1979/80	John Lumsden / Ken Mackie	7
1980/1	Robin Thomson	10
1981/2	Gordon Scott	16
1982/3	Robin Thomson	13
1983/4	Gordon Durie	16
1984/5	Gavin Murray	12
1985/6	Steve Kirk	14
1986/7	Brian McNaughton	15
1987/8	Paul Hunter	17
1988/9	Paul Hunter	9
1989/90	Paul Hunter	14
1990/1	Willie Brown / Ronnie Scott	10
1991/2	John Sludden	21
1992/3	Robert Scott	16
1993/4	Robert Scott	10
1994/5	Robert Scott	14
1995/6	Robert Scott	11
1996/7	Matt Dyer / Paul Ronald	4
1997/8	Matt Dyer	11
1998/9	Barrie Moffat	13
1999/00	Barrie Moffat	11
2000/1	Steven P Kerrigan	8
2001/2	Paul McManus	11
2002/3	Kenny Deuchar	20
2003/4	Kenny Deuchar	11
2004/5	Steven Nicholas	9
2005/6	John Bradford / Greg McDonald	7
2006/7	Craig O'Reilly	13
2007/8	Paul McManus	17
2008/9	Paul McManus	12
2009/10	Paul McManus	15
2010/1	Bobby Linn	13
2011/2	Ryan Wallace	20
2012/3	Scott McBride	11
2013/4	Liam Buchanan	11
2014/5	Kevin Smith	12
2015/6	Nathan Austin	22
2016/7	Jason Kerr	8
2017/18	Chris Duggan	14
2018/19	Kevin Smith	8
2019/20	Scott Agnew	10
2020/21	Jack Hamilton	7

EAST STIRLINGSHIRE

Season	Player	Goals
1975/6	Jim Mullin	8
1976/7	Ian Cochrane	11
1977/8	Jim Docherty	14
1978/9	Jim Docherty	14
1979/80	Ally Grant	14
1980/1	Paul Lamont	7
1981/2	Jim Blair / Paul Lamont / Raymond Edgar	4
1982/3	Charlie Gibson	6
1983/4	Charlie Gibson	13
1984/5	Steve Maskrey	12
1985/6	Steve Maskrey	12
1986/7	Alan McGonnigal / John Paisley / David Strange	5
1987/8	Gary Murray	9
1988/9	Billy McNeill	16
1989/90	Billy McNeill / Colin Wilson / David Wilcox	4
1990/1	Charlie Lytwyn / Derek Walker	10
1991/2	Danny Diver	18
1992/3	Paul Roberts	9
1993/4	Mungo McCallum	12
1994/5	Michael Geraghty	16
1995/6	Peter Dwyer	21
1996/7	Grant Inglis	9
1997/8	David Watt	13
1998/9	Billy McNeill	8
1999/00	Gary Higgins / Steven Laidlaw	9
2000/1	Steven Hislop	16
2001/2	Kevin Gordon	11
2002/3	Jordan Leishman / Derek Ure	5
2003/4	Derek Ure	9
2004/5	Joe Robertson	7
2005/6	Ian Diack	8
2006/7	Marc McKenzie	5
2007/8	Andy Brand	11
2008/9	Brian Graham	15
2009/10	Simon Lynch	13
2010/1	Kevin Cawley	8
2011/2	Kevin Turner	6
2012/3	Paul Quinn	11
2013/4	Paul Quinn	7
2014/5	David McKenna	12
2015/6	David McKenna	8
2016/7		
2017/18		
2018/19		
2019/20		
2020/21		

EDINBURGH CITY

Season	Player	Goals
2016/7	Dougie Gair	9
2017/18	Scott Shepherd	8
2018/19	Blair Henderson	30
2019/20	Danny Handling	10
2020/21	Josh Campbell	9

ELGIN CITY

Season	Player	Goals
1975/6		
1976/7		
1977/8		
1978/9		
1979/80		
1980/1		
1981/2		
1982/3		
1983/4		
1984/5		
1985/6		
1986/7		
1987/8		
1988/9		
1989/90		
1990/1		
1991/2		
1992/3		
1993/4		
1994/5		
1995/6		
1996/7		
1997/8		
1998/9		
1999/00		
2000/1	Colin Milne / David Ross	6
2001/2	Ian Gilzean	12
2002/3	Kevin Steele	6
2003/4	Alex Bone	15
2004/5	Willie Martin	9
2005/6	Martin Johnston	20
2006/7	Martin Johnston	19
2007/8	Darren Shallicker	12
2008/9	Darren Shallicker	7
2009/10	Craig Gunn	17
2010/1	Jason Crooks	13
2011/2	Craig Gunn	18
2012/3	Stuart Leslie	15
2013/4	Craig Gunn	15
2014/5	Craig Gunn	13
2015/6	Craig Gunn	21
2016/7	Shane Sutherland	18
2017/18	Brian Cameron	10
2018/19	Shane Sutherland	11
2019/20	Shane Sutherland	16
2020/21	Kane Hester	15

FALKIRK

Season	Player	Goals
1975/6	John Whiteford	17
1976/7	Bobby Ford	5
1977/8	Ally McRoberts	13
1978/9	Ally McRoberts	11
1979/80	Paul Leetion	13
1980/1	Colin Spence	5
1981/2	Willie Herd	10
1982/3	Peter Houston	8
1983/4	Kevin McAllister	11
1984/5	Gerry McCoy	22
1985/6	Jimmy Gilmour	15
1986/7	Ken Eadie	6
1987/8	Crawford Baptie	9
1988/9	Alex Rae	12
1989/90	Derek McWilliams	17
1990/1	Simon Stainrod	16
1991/2	Kevin McAllister / Eddie May	9
1992/3	Richard Cadette	8
1993/4	Richard Cadette	18
1994/5	Colin McDonald	9
1995/6	Paul McGrillen	6
1996/7	Mark McGraw	8
1997/8	David Moss	12
1998/9	Marino Keith	17
1999/00	Scott Crabbe	14
2000/1	Gareth Hutchison	11
2001/2	Lee Miller	11
2002/3	Owen Coyle	20
2003/4	Jason Lee	8
2004/5	Darrell Duffy	17
2005/6	Darrell Duffy	9
2006/7	Anthony Stokes	14
2007/8	Michael Higdon / Pedro Moutinho	8
2008/9	Stephen Lovell	8
2009/10	P Moutinho / Flynn / C Finnegan	
2010/1	Mark Stewart	15
2011/2	Faroud El Alagui	18
2012/3	Lyle Taylor	24
2013/4	Rory Loy	20
2014/5	Rory Loy	9
2015/6	John Baird	17
2016/7	Craig Sibbald	10
2017/18	Louis Longridge	7
2018/19	Zak Rudden	12
2019/20	Declan McManus	19
2020/21	Callumn Morrison	7

FORFAR ATHLETIC

Season	Player	Goals
1975/6	Sandy White	10
1976/7	Sandy White	10
1977/8	Alex Rae	11
1978/9	Alex Rae	11
1979/80	John Clark	20
1980/1	Neil Watt	13
1981/2	John Clark / Steve Hancock	9
1982/3	Kenny MacDonald	16
1983/4	Jim Liddle	22
1984/5	Kenny MacDonald	14
1985/6	John Clark	10
1986/7	Kenny MacDonald	17
1987/8	Kenny MacDonald	20
1988/9	Kenny Ward	12
1989/90	Craig Brewster	8
1990/1	Gary Whyte	12
1991/2	Gordon Winter	8
1992/3	Stewart Petrie	21
1993/4	David Bingham	13
1994/5	David Bingham	22
1995/6	Gary Higgins	12
1996/7	Ben Honeyman	17
1997/8	Martin McLauchlan	14
1998/9	Ralph Brand	10
1999/00	Steven Milne	16
2000/1	Willie Stewart	9
2001/2	Paul Tosh	19
2002/3	Martin Bavidge	15
2003/4	Paul Tosh	18
2004/5	Paul Shields	20
2005/6	Darren Gribben	10
2006/7	Darren Gribben	11
2007/8	John Ovenstone / Michael Stuart	4
2008/9	Ross Campbell	13
2009/10	Ross Campbell	16
2010/1	Ross Campbell	11
2011/2	Chris Templeman	16
2012/3	Gavin Swankie / Chris Templeman	10
2013/4	Dale Hilson	12
2014/5	Gavin Swankie	11
2015/6	Andy Ryan	9
2016/7	Danny Denholm	12
2017/18	Matthew Aitken	7
2018/19	John Baird	18
2019/20	Dale Hilson	4
2020/21	Scott Fenwick	4

GRETNA

Season	Player	Goals
1975/6		
1976/7		
1977/8		
1978/9		
1979/80		
1980/1		
1981/2		
1982/3		
1983/4		
1984/5		
1985/6		
1986/7		
1987/8		
1988/9		
1989/90		
1990/1		
1991/2		
1992/3		
1993/4		
1994/5		
1995/6		
1996/7		
1997/8		
1998/9		
1999/00		
2000/1		
2001/2		
2002/3	Mark Dobie	10
2003/4	Martin Cameron	17
2004/5	Kenny Deuchar	38
2005/6	Kenny Deuchar	18
2006/7	Colin McMenamin	24
2007/8	Kenny Deuchar	6
2008/9		
2009/10		
2010/1		
2011/2		
2012/3		
2013/4		
2014/5		
2015/6		
2016/7		

HAMILTON ACCIES

Season	Player	Goals
1975/6	Billy Thomas	14
1976/7	Joe McGrogan	7
1977/8	Joe McGrogan	16
1978/9	Bobby Graham	18
1979/80	Jaimie Fairlie / Bobby Graham	11
1980/1	Jamie Fairlie	13
1981/2	Jamie Fairlie	10
1982/3	Jamie Fairlie	15
1983/4	Doug Somner	9
1984/5	John McGachie	8
1985/6	John Brogan	23
1986/7	John Brogan	6
1987/8	Mark Caughey	10
1988/9	Stuart Gordon / Colin Harris	5
1989/90	Colin Harris	9
1990/1	George McCluskey	14
1991/2	Gary Clark	14
1992/3	Paul McDonald	11
1993/4	Peter Duffield	19
1994/5	Peter Duffield	20
1995/6	Paul Hartley	11
1996/7	Paul Ritchie	31
1997/8	Paul Ritchie	7
1998/9	Gary Wales	11
1999/00	Darren Henderson / Nicky Henderson	6
2000/1	David McFarlane	24
2001/2	Michael Moore	12
2002/3	Brian McPhee	11
2003/4	Brian McPhee	19
2004/5	Scott Tunbridge	5
2005/6	Brown Ferguson	7
2006/7	Richard Offiong	14
2007/8	Richard Offiong	19
2008/9	James McCarthy / Simon Mensing/ Richard Offiong	6
2009/10	Simon Mensing	8
2010/1	Dougie Imrie / Mickael Antoine-Curier	4
2011/2	Jon McShane	9
2012/3	Stevie May	25
2013/4	Tony Andreu / James Keatings	13
2014/5	Tony Andreu	12
2015/6	Carlton Morris	8
2016/7	Ali Crawford	8
2017/18	David Templeton	9
2018/19	Mikael Miller	5
2019/20	Marios Ogkampoe	6
2020/21	Ross Callachan	10

HEARTS

Season	Player	Goals
1975/6	Drew Busby / Willie Gibson	8
1976/7	Willie Gibson	15
1977/8	Willie Gibson	20
1978/9	Derek O'Connor	8
1979/80	Willie Gibson	17
1980/1	Willie Gibson / Derek O'Connor	4
1981/2	Willie Pettigrew	16
1982/3	John Robertson	21
1983/4	John Robertson	13
1984/5	Sandy Clark / John Robertson	8
1985/6	John Robertson	20
1986/7	John Robertson	16
1987/8	John Robertson	26
1988/9	John Colquhoun / Ian Ferguson	5
1989/90	John Robertson	17
1990/1	John Robertson	12
1991/2	Scott Crabbe	15
1992/3	John Robertson	11
1993/4	John Robertson	10
1994/5	John Robertson	10
1995/6	John Robertson	11
1996/7	John Robertson	14
1997/8	Jim Hamilton	14
1998/9	Stephane Adam	10
1999/00	Gary McSwegan	13
2000/1	Colin Cameron / Andy Kirk	12
2001/2	Kevin McKenna	9
2002/3	Mark De Vries	15
2003/4	Mark De Vries	12
2004/5	Paul Hartley	11
2005/6	Rudi Skacel	16
2006/7	Andrius Velicka	10
2007/8	Andrius Velicka	11
2008/9	Bruno Aguiar	7
2009/10	Suso Santana	6
2010/1	Rudi Skacel	13
2011/2	Rudi Skacel	11
2012/3	John Sutton	8
2013/4	Callum Paterson	11
2014/5	Genero Zeefuik	12
2015/6	Juanma Delgado	12
2016/7	Jamie Walker	12
2017/18	Kyle Lafferty	12
2018/19	Steven Naismith	10
2019/20	Sean Clare / Steven Naismith	4
2020/21	Liam Boyce	14

HIBERNIAN

Season	Player	Goals
1975/6	Arthur Duncan	13
1976/7	Bobby Smith	8
1977/8	Ally MacLeod	16
1978/9	Ralph Callachan	9
1979/80	Ally MacLeod	8
1980/1	Ally MacLeod	15
1981/2	Gordon Rae	11
1982/3	Gordon Rae / Gary Murray	6
1983/4	Willie Irvine	18
1984/5	Gordon Durie / Paul Kane	8
1985/6	Steve Cowan	19
1986/7	George McCluskey	9
1987/8	Paul Kane	10
1988/9	Steve Archibald	13
1989/90	Keith Houchen	8
1990/1	Paul Wright	6
1991/2	Mickey Weir	11
1992/3	Darren Jackson	13
1993/4	Keith Wright	16
1994/5	Darren Jackson / Michael O'Neill	10
1995/6	Darren Jackson / Keith Wright	9
1996/7	Darren Jackson	11
1997/8	Steve Crawford	9
1998/9	Steve Crawford	14
1999/00	Kenny Miller	11
2000/1	Mixu Paatelainen	11
2001/2	Gary O'Connor	10
2002/3	Tom McManus	12
2003/4	Derek Riordan	15
2004/5	Derek Riordan	20
2005/6	Derek Riordan	17
2006/7	Chris Killen	13
2007/8	Steven Fletcher	13
2008/9	Steven Fletcher / Derek Riordan	12
2009/10	Anthony Stokes	22
2010/1	Derek Riordan	11
2011/2	Gary O'Connor	12
2012/3	Leigh Griffiths	23
2013/4	James Collins / Liam Craig	6
2014/5	Jason Cummings	18
2015/6	Jason Cummings	18
2016/7	Jason Cummings	19
2017/18	Florian Kamberi	9
2018/19	Florian Kamberi	8
2019/20	Christian Doidge	12
2020/21	Kevin Nisbet	14

INVERNESS CT

Season	Player	Goals
1975/6		
1976/7		
1977/8		
1978/9		
1979/80		
1980/1		
1981/2		
1982/3		
1983/4		
1984/5		
1985/6		
1986/7		
1987/8		
1988/9		
1989/90		
1990/1		
1991/2		
1992/3		
1993/4		
1994/5	Charlie Christie / Alan Hercher	6
1995/6	Ian Stewart	23
1996/7	Ian Stewart	27
1997/8	Ian Stewart	16
1998/9	Scott McLean	19
1999/00	Barry Wilson	13
2000/1	Dennis Wyness	24
2001/2	Dennis Wyness	18
2002/3	Dennis Wyness	19
2003/4	Paul Ritchie	14
2004/5	Barry Wilson	11
2005/6	Craig Dargo	17
2006/7	Craig Dargo	10
2007/8	Don Cowie	9
2008/9	Adam Rooney	5
2009/10	Adam Rooney	24
2010/1	Adam Rooney	15
2011/2	Gregory Tade	9
2012/3	Billy McKay	23
2013/4	Billy McKay	18
2014/5	Billy McKay	10
2015/6	Miles Storey	11
2016/7	Alex Fisher	8
2017/18	George Oakley / Ian Vigurs	8
2018/19	Jordan White	9
2019/20	Jordan White	7
2020/21	Nikolay Todorov	9

KILMARNOCK

Season	Player	Goals
1975/6	Ian Fallis	10
1976/7	Ian Fallis	10
1977/8	Donny McDowell	13
1978/9	John Bourke	21
1979/80	Bobby Street	9
1980/1	John Bourke	5
1981/2	John Bourke	14
1982/3	Brian Gallagher	9
1983/4	Robert Clark	11
1984/5	Blair Millar	12
1985/6	Ian Bryson	14
1986/7	Ian Bryson	10
1987/8	Colin Harkness	16
1988/9	Willie Watters	12
1989/90	Willie Watters	23
1990/1	Bobby Williamson	14
1991/2	Callum Campbell / Ally Mitchell	10
1992/3	George McCluskey	11
1993/4	Bobby Williamson	7
1994/5	Colin McKee	6
1995/6	Paul Wright	13
1996/7	Paul Wright	15
1997/8	Paul Wright	10
1998/9	Ally McCoist	7
1999/00	Christophe Cocard	8
2000/1	Paul Wright	8
2001/2	Alan Johnson	7
2002/3	Kris Boyd	12
2003/4	Kris Boyd	15
2004/5	Kris Boyd	17
2005/6	Kris Boyd	15
2006/7	Steven Naismith	16
2007/8	Colin Nish	7
2008/9	Kevin Kyle	8
2009/10	Kevin Kyle	8
2010/1	Connor Sammon	15
2011/2	Dene Shiels	13
2012/3	Paul Heffernan / Cillian Sheridan	9
2013/4	Kris Boyd	22
2014/5	Topi Obadeyi	9
2015/6	Josh Magennis	10
2016/7	Kris Boyd / Solameyn Coulibaly	8
2017/18	Kris Boyd	18
2018/19	Eamonn Brophy	11
2019/20	Eamonn Brophy	9
2020/21	Kyle Lafferty / Chris Burke	9

LIVINGSTON / MEADOWBANK

Season	Player	Goals
1975/6	Kenny Davidson	7
1976/7	Kenny Davidson / Jimmy Hancock	8
1977/8	Kenny Davidson / Jimmy Hancock / Tom Downie	6
1978/9	Gerry Adair	7
1979/80	John Jobson	17
1980/1	John Jobson	12
1981/2	John Jobson	15
1982/3	Tom Hendrie	13
1983/4	Chris Robertson	10
1984/5	Adrian Sprott	14
1985/6	Darren Jackson	17
1986/7	John McGachie	21
1987/8	John McGachie	14
1988/9	David Roseburgh	6
1989/90	Brian McNaughton	8
1990/1	David Roseburgh	15
1991/2	David Roseburgh	8
1992/3	Paul Rutherford	9
1993/4	Ian Little	12
1994/5	Lee Bailey	6
1995/6	Jason Young	18
1996/7	Graham Harvey	15
1997/8	Graham Harvey	15
1998/9	John Robertson	12
1999/00	David Bingham	15
2000/1	David Bingham	14
2001/2	Barry Wilson	9
2002/3	Rolando Zarate	9
2003/4	Derek Lilley	12
2004/5	Burton O'Brien	8
2005/6	Richard Brittain / Robert Snodgrass	4
2006/7	Stephen Craig	7
2007/8	Graham Dorrans	11
2008/9	Leigh Griffiths	17
2009/10	Andy Halliday	14
2010/1	Ian Russell	22
2011/2	Rory Boulding / Mark McNulty	11
2012/3	Ian Russell	15
2013/4	Marc McNulty	17
2014/5	Jordan White	11
2015/6	Liam Buchanan	11
2016/7	Liam Buchanan	23
2017/18	Ryan Hardie	8
2018/19	Craig Halkett / Ryan Hardie	7
2019/20	Lyndon Dykes	9
2020/21	Scott Pittman	7

MONTROSE

Season	Player	Goals
1975/6	Bobby Livingstone	12
1976/7	Dougie Robb	13
1977/8	Bobby Livingstone	10
1978/9	Gary Murray	12
1979/80	Gary Murray	15
1980/1	Gary Murray / Dougie Robb	12
1981/2	Ian Campbell	9
1982/3	Eddie Copeland	12
1983/4	Neil Burke	7
1984/5	Doug Somner	12
1985/6	Martin Allan	6
1986/7	Ian Paterson	10
1987/8	Hamish Mackay	11
1988/9	Gary Murray	21
1989/90	Danny Powell	11
1990/1	Gary Murray	11
1991/2	John McGachie	9
1992/3	Derek Grant	10
1993/4	Derek Grant	12
1994/5	Colin McGlashan	19
1995/6	Colin McGlashan	16
1996/7	Colin McGlashan	11
1997/8	Colin McGlashan	20
1998/9	Scott Taylor	7
1999/00	Scott Taylor	12
2000/1	John Mitchell	7
2001/2	Steven Laidlaw	13
2002/3	Steven P Kerrigan	8
2003/4	Scott Michie	14
2004/5	Craig Smart	14
2005/6	Greg Henslee	10
2006/7	Andy Rodgers	10
2007/8	John Baird	18
2008/9	Roddy Hunter	9
2009/10	Paul Tosh	9
2010/1	Paul Tosh	12
2011/2	Martin Boyle	22
2012/3	Martin Boyle	9
2013/4	Bryan Deasley	10
2014/5	Gary Wood	10
2015/6	Gary Fraser	19
2016/7	Gary Fraser	11
2017/18	Lewis Milne / Chris Templeman	11
2018/19	Martin Rennie	12
2019/20	Blair Lyons	10
2020/21	Russell Mclean	9

MORTON

Season	Player	Goals
1975/6	Rikki Sharp / John Goldthorp / Ian Harley	5
1976/7	Andy Ritchie	22
1977/8	John Goldthorp / Andy Ritchie	20
1978/9	Andy Ritchie	22
1979/80	Andy Ritchie	19
1980/1	Andy Ritchie	8
1981/2	Andy Ritchie	6
1982/3	Jim Rooney	6
1983/4	John McNeil	17
1984/5	Jim Gillespie	5
1985/6	John McNeil	14
1986/7	Rowan Alexander	23
1987/8	Jim Boag	8
1988/9	Rowan Alexander	11
1989/90	Rowan Alexander	11
1990/1	David McCabe	21
1991/2	Alex Mathie	18
1992/3	Alex Mathie	13
1993/4	Rowan Alexander	11
1994/5	Derek Lilley	16
1995/6	Derek Lilley	14
1996/7	Derek Lilley	15
1997/8	Warren Hawke	10
1998/9	Kevin Thomas	9
1999/00	Harry Curran	9
2000/1	Ross Matheson	9
2001/2	Scott Bannerman / Sean O'Connor	8
2002/3	Alex Williams	23
2003/4	Alex Williams	15
2004/5	Chris Millar / Peter Weatherson`	11
2005/6	Derek Lilley	12
2006/7	Peter Weatherson	15
2007/8	Peter Weatherson	9
2008/9	Brian Wake	9
2009/10	Peter Weatherson	10
2010/1	Allan Jenkins	8
2011/2	Peter MacDonald	10
2012/3	Peter MacDonald	14
2013/4	Dougie Imrie	9
2014/5	Declan McManus	20
2015/6	Denny Johnstone	14
2016/7	Ross Forbes	9
2017/18	Gary Harkins	8
2018/19	Bob McHugh / Greg Kiltie	6
2019/20	Bob McHugh	8
2020/21	Gary Oliver	5

MOTHERWELL

Season	Player	Goals
1975/6	Willie Pettigrew	22
1976/7	Willie Pettigrew	21
1977/8	Vic Davidson	8
1978/9	Willie Pettigrew	6
1979/80	Willie Irvine	13
1980/1	Albert Kidd	13
1981/2	Willie Irvine	20
1982/3	Brian McClair	11
1983/4	John Gahagan	7
1984/5	Andy Harrow	9
1985/6	John Reilly	9
1986/7	Steve Kirk / Andy Walker	10
1987/8	Steve Cowan	9
1988/9	Steve Kirk	14
1989/90	Nick Cusack	11
1990/1	Dougie Arnott	14
1991/2	Dougie Arnott	8
1992/3	Steve Kirk	10
1993/4	Tommy Coyne	12
1994/5	Tommy Coyne	16
1995/6	Willie Falconer	5
1996/7	Tommy Coyne	11
1997/8	Tommy Coyne	15
1998/9	Owen Coyle /John Spencer	7
1999/00	John Spencer	11
2000/1	Stuart Elliott	10
2001/2	Stuart Elliott / James McFadden	10
2002/3	James McFadden	13
2003/4	David Clarkson	11
2004/5	Scott McDonald	15
2005/6	Richie Foran	11
2006/7	Scott McDonald	15
2007/8	Chris Porter	14
2008/9	David Clarkson	14
2009/10	Lucas Jutkiewicz / John Sutton	12
2010/1	Nick Blackman / John Sutton	10
2011/2	Michael Higdon	14
2012/3	Michael Higdon	26
2013/4	John Sutton	22
2014/5	John Sutton	12
2015/6	Louis Moult	15
2016/7	Louis Moult	15
2017/18	Louis Moult	8
2018/19	David Turnbull	15
2019/20	Chris Long / Liam Donnelly	7
2020/21	Devante Cole	11

PARTICK THISTLE

Season	Player	Goals
1975/6	Doug Somner	16
1976/7	Doug Somner	11
1977/8	Doug Somner	15
1978/9	Doug Somner	11
1979/80	Colin McAdam	17
1980/1	Tony Higgins / Alex O'Hara	7
1981/2	Maurice Johnston	9
1982/3	Maurice Johnston	21
1983/4	Kenny McDowall	13
1984/5	Alan Logan	12
1985/6	Gordon Smith	11
1986/7	Colin West	10
1987/8	Eddie Gallagher	13
1988/9	Gerry McCoy	19
1989/90	Calum Campbell	18
1990/1	David Elliot	13
1991/2	Colin McGlashan	18
1992/3	Gerry Britton	12
1993/4	Albert Craig	14
1994/5	Wayne Foster	7
1995/6	Andy Lyons / Rod McDonald	5
1996/7	David Moss	11
1997/8	Jered Stirling	6
1998/9	Robert Dunn	10
1999/00	Robert Dunn	5
2000/1	Scott McLean	16
2001/2	Gerry Britton	12
2002/3	Alex Burns	16
2003/4	James Grady	15
2004/5	Juan Escalas	10
2005/6	Mark Roberts	10
2006/7	Mark Roberts	16
2007/8	Liam Buchanan	11
2008/9	Gary Harkins	9
2009/10	Liam Buchanan	10
2010/1	Kris Doolan	15
2011/2	Kris Doolan	13
2012/3	Steven Lawless	13
2013/4	Kris Doolan	11
2014/5	Kris Doolan	9
2015/6	Kris Doolan	14
2016/7	Kris Doolan	14
2017/18	Kris Doolan / Connor Sammon	7
2018/19	Blair Spittal	7
2019/20	Kenny Miller	5
2020/21	Brian Graham	11

PETERHEAD

Season	Player	Goals
1975/6		
1976/7		
1977/8		
1978/9		
1979/80		
1980/1		
1981/2		
1982/3		
1983/4		
1984/5		
1985/6		
1986/7		
1987/8		
1988/9		
1989/90		
1990/1		
1991/2		
1992/3		
1993/4		
1994/5		
1995/6		
1996/7		
1997/8		
1998/9		
1999/00		
2000/1	Craig Yeats	11
2001/2	Ian Stewart	19
2002/3	Ian Stewart	21
2003/4	Martin Johnston	18
2004/5	Scott Michie	21
2005/6	Bobby Linn	11
2006/7	Martin Bavidge	11
2007/8	Martin Bavidge	15
2008/9	Martin Bavidge	9
2009/10	Martin Bavidge	11
2010/1	Dennis Wyness	8
2011/2	Rory McAllister	20
2012/3	Rory McAllister	21
2013/4	Rory McAllister	32
2014/5	Rory McAllister	8
2015/6	Rory McAllister	22
2016/7	Rory McAllister	16
2017/18	Rory McAllister	21
2018/19	Rory McAllister	15
2019/20	Scott Brown	9
2020/21	Scott Brown	5

QOS

Season	Player	Goals
1975/6	Peter Dickson / Ian Reid	11
1976/7	Peter Dickson	15
1977/8	Tommy Bryce	8
1978/9	Tommy Bryce	12
1979/80	Rowan Alexander	21
1980/1	Jim Robertson	19
1981/2	Gerry Phillips	12
1982/3	Rowan Alexander	23
1983/4	John Robertson	9
1984/5	George Cloy	9
1985/6	Tommy Bryce / Stewart Cochrane	15
1986/7	Tommy Bryce	20
1987/8	Jim Hughes	17
1988/9	Gary Fraser	7
1989/90	Stuart Gor 'on	8
1990/1	Andy Thomson	11
1991/2	Andy Thomson	26
1992/3	Andy Thomson	21
1993/4	Andy Thomson	29
1994/5	Duncan Campbell / Steve Mallan	9
1995/6	Steve Mallan	12
1996/7	Steve Mallan	13
1997/8	Steve Mallan	10
1998/9	Steve Mallan	15
1999/00	Steve Mallan	13
2000/1	Peter Weatherson	16
2001/2	John O'Neil	19
2002/3	John O'Neil	9
2003/4	Alex Burke	13
2004/5	David McNiven	12
2005/6	John O'Neil	10
2006/7	John O'Neil	8
2007/8	Stephen Dobbie	16
2008/9	Stephen Dobbie	23
2009/10	Derek Holmes	12
2010/1	Colin McMenamin	11
2011/2	Sam Parkin	6
2012/3	Nicky Clark	23
2013/4	Ian Russell	13
2014/5	Derek Lyle	15
2015/6	Derek Lyle	13
2016/7	Stephen Dobbie	19
2017/18	Stephen Dobbie	21
2018/19	Stephen Dobbie	24
2019/20	Stephen Dobbie	8
2020/21	Connor Shields / Ayo Obileye	9

QUEEN'S PARK

Season	Player	Goals
1975/6	Sandy McNaughton / Hugh McGill	8
1976/7	Bernie Donnelly	15
1977/8	Bernie Donnelly	8
1978/9	Ian Ballantyne	13
1979/80	Jim Gillespie	21
1980/1	Gerry McCoy	17
1981/2	Gerry Crawley	10
1982/3	Jimmy Gilmour	10
1983/4	Lex Grant	17
1984/5	Jim Nicholson	18
1985/6	Gary Fraser	11
1986/7	Ross Caven	13
1987/8	Paul O'Brien	17
1988/9	Mike Hendry	9
1989/90	Mike Hendry	10
1990/1	Mike Hendry	17
1991/2	Steve McCormick	17
1992/3	Ross Caven	11
1993/4	John O'Neil	18
1994/5	Steve McCormick	8
1995/6	Scott Edgar / Kevin McGoldrick	6
1996/7	Danny Ferry	7
1997/8	Scott Edgar	8
1998/9	Scott Edgar	7
1999/00	Mark Gallagher	13
2000/1	Mark Gallagher	7
2001/2	Steven Canning / Ross Jackson	5
2002/3	John Gemmell	8
2003/4	Stephen Reilly	7
2004/5	Frank Carroll	14
2005/6	Mark Ferry	8
2006/7	David Weatherston	16
2007/8	Alan Trouten	12
2008/9	Paul Cairney	8
2009/10	Barry Douglas	8
2010/1	Jamie Longworth	12
2011/2	Jamie Longworth	20
2012/3	Lawrence Shankland	11
2013/4	Blair Spittal	8
2014/5	Paul Woods	9
2015/6	Paul Woods	11
2016/7	Ross Millen	7
2017/18	Aidan Keena / Adam Cummins / Luke Donnelly	8
2018/19	Scott McLean	7
2019/20	Salim Kouider-Aissa	13
2020/21	Bob McHugh	7

RAITH ROVERS

Season	Player	Goals
1975/6	Malcolm Robertson / Gordon Wallace	9
1976/7	Gordon Wallace	8
1977/8	Ronnie Duncan	11
1978/9	Gordon Wallace	14
1979/80	Ian Ballantyne	13
1980/1	Ian Ballantyne	12
1981/2	Ian Ballantyne	12
1982/3	Colin Harris	18
1983/4	Jim Kerr	16
1984/5	Keith Wright	22
1985/6	Paul Smith / Keith Wright	21
1986/7	Colin Harris	22
1987/8	Gordon Dalziel	25
1988/9	Gordon Dalziel	11
1989/90	Gordon Dalziel	20
1990/1	Gordon Dalziel	25
1991/2	Gordon Dalziel	26
1992/3	Gordon Dalziel	32
1993/4	Gordon Dalziel	8
1994/5	Gordon Dalziel	15
1995/6	Colin Cameron	9
1996/7	Peter Duffield / Danny Lennon	5
1997/8	Paul Hartley / Keith Wright	10
1998/9	Craig Dargo	8
1999/00	Craig Dargo	12
2000/1	Paul Tosh	9
2001/2	Nacho Novo	19
2002/3	Karl Hawley	7
2003/4	John Sutton	13
2004/5	Pat Clarke / John Martin	4
2005/6	Paul McManus	15
2006/7	Paul McManus	7
2007/8	Graham Weir	10
2008/9	Kevin Smith	18
2009/10	Gregory Tade	5
2010/1	John Baird	13
2011/2	Brian Graham	11
2012/3	Brian Graham	18
2013/4	Greg Spence	9
2014/5	Mark Stewart	10
2015/6	Mark Stewart	10
2016/7	Ryan Hardie	6
2017/18	Lewis Vaughan	15
2018/19	Kevin Nisbet	31
2019/20	Jamie Gullan	9
2020/21	Danny Armstrong	6

RANGERS

Season	Player	Goals
1975/6	Derek Johnstone	15
1976/7	Derek Parlane	16
1977/8	Derek Johnstone	25
1978/9	Gordon Smith	11
1979/80	Derek Johnstone	14
1980/1	Colin McAdam	12
1981/2	John MacDonald	14
1982/3	John MacDonald	10
1983/4	Sandy Clark / Ally McCoist	9
1984/5	Ally McCoist	12
1985/6	Ally McCoist	24
1986/7	Ally McCoist	33
1987/8	Ally McCoist	31
1988/9	Kevin Drinkell	12
1989/90	Maurice Johnston	15
1990/1	Mark Walters	11
1991/2	Ally McCoist	34
1992/3	Ally McCoist	34
1993/4	Mark Hateley	22
1994/5	Mark Hateley	13
1995/6	Gordon Durie	17
1996/7	Brian Laudrup	16
1997/8	Marco Negri	32
1998/9	Rod Wallace	18
1999/00	Jorg Albertz	17
2000/1	Tore Andree Flo	11
2001/2	Tore Andree Flo	17
2002/3	Ronald de Boer / Barry Ferguson	16
2003/4	Shota Arveladze	12
2004/5	Nacho Novo	19
2005/6	Kris Boyd	17
2006/7	Kris Boyd	20
2007/8	Kris Boyd	14
2008/9	Kris Boyd	27
2009/10	Kris Boyd	23
2010/1	Kenny Miller	21
2011/2	Nikica Jelavic	15
2012/3	Andy Little	22
2013/4	John Daly	20
2014/5	Nicky Law	10
2015/6	Martin Waghorn	20
2016/7	Kenny Miller	11
2017/18	Alfredo Morelos	14
2018/19	Alfredo Morelos	18
2019/20	Jermaine Defoe	13
2020/21	Kemar Roofe	14

ROSS COUNTY

Season	Player	Goals
1975/6		
1976/7		
1977/8		
1978/9		
1979/80		
1980/1		
1981/2		
1982/3		
1983/4		
1984/5		
1985/6		
1986/7		
1987/8		
1988/9		
1989/90		
1990/1		
1991/2		
1992/3		
1993/4		
1994/5	Brian Grant	12
1995/6	Colin Milne	5
1996/7	Derek Adams	22
1997/8	Derek Adams	16
1998/9	Steven Ferguson / Neil Tarrant	17
1999/00	George Shaw	13
2000/1	Alex Bone	14
2001/2	Steven Hislop	14
2002/3	Graham Bayne	6
2003/4	David Winters	10
2004/5	Alex Burke / David Winters	6
2005/6	John Rankin	12
2006/7	Don Cowie	7
2007/8	Andy Barrowman	24
2008/9	Stephen Craig / Sean Higgins	10
2009/10	Richard Brittain	9
2010/1	Andy Barrowman	5
2011/2	Colin McMenamin	19
2012/3	Richard Brittain	9
2013/4	Melvin De Leeuw	9
2014/5	Liam Boyce	10
2015/6	Liam Boyce	15
2016/7	Liam Boyce	23
2017/18	Alex Schalk	11
2018/19	Billy Mckay	17
2019/20	Billy Mckay / Ross Stewart	7
2020/21	Oli Shaw	6

ST JOHNSTONE

1975/6	Jim O'Rourke	8
1976/7	Ian Anderson	8
1977/8	Derek O'Connor	19
1978/9	John Brogan	14
1979/80	John Brogan	22
1980/1	Ally McCoist	22
1981/2	Jim Morton	17
1982/3	John Brogan	26
1983/4	John Brogan	9
1984/5	Joe Reid	9
1985/6	Willie Brown	11
1986/7	Willie Brown	25
1987/8	Willie Watters	16
1988/9	Steve Maskrey	12
1989/90	Roddy Grant	19
1990/1	Harry Curran	9
1991/2	Paul Wright	18
1992/3	Paul Wright	14
1993/4	Paul Wright	7
1994/5	George O'Boyle	19
1995/6	George O'Boyle	21
1996/7	Roddy Grant	19
1997/8	George O'Boyle	10
1998/9	Gary Bollan / Roddy Grant / Miguel Simao	4
1999/00	Nathan Lowndes	10
2000/1	Keigan Parker	9
2001/2	Paul Hartley	5
2002/3	Chris Hay	9
2003/4	Mixu Paatelainen	11
2004/5	Peter MacDonald	11
2005/6	Jason Scotland	15
2006/7	Jason Scotland	18
2007/8	Andy Jackson	14
2008/9	Steven Milne	14
2009/10	Liam Craig	9
2010/1	Liam Craig	5
2011/2	Fran Sandaza	14
2012/3	Liam Craig / Mrray davidson	7
2013/4	Stevie May	20
2014/5	Brian Graham	9
2015/6	Steven MacLean	14
2016/7	Danny Swanson	10
2017/18	Steven MacLean	9
2018/19	Matty Kennedy	6
2019/20	Callum Hendry	7
2020/21	Stevie May / Guy Melamed	5

ST MIRREN

1975/6	Donnie McDowell	12
1976/7	Derek Hyslop / Frank McGarvey	17
1977/8	Frank McGarvey	17
1978/9	Frank McGarvey	13
1979/80	Doug Somner	25
1980/1	Doug Somner	13
1981/2	Frank McAvennie	13
1982/3	Frank McDougall	9
1983/4	Frank McDougall	13
1984/5	Frank McAvennie	16
1985/6	Gardner Speirs	7
1986/7	Frank McGarvey	10
1987/8	Paul Chalmers	10
1988/9	Paul Chalmers	11
1989/90	Gudmundur Torfason	12
1990/1	Paul Kinnaird / Kenny McDowall / Gudmundur Torfason	4
1991/2	Gudmundur Torfason	8
1992/3	Barry Lavety	18
1993/4	Barry Lavety	10
1994/5	Barry Lavety	7
1995/6	Barry Lavety	11
1996/7	Mark Yardley	15
1997/8	Junior Mendes	9
1998/9	Mark Yardley	11
1999/00	Mark Yardley	19
2000/1	Ricky Gillies	10
2001/2	Ricky Gillies / Brian McGinty	6
2002/3	Martin Cameron	12
2003/4	Ricky Gillies	8
2004/5	John O'Neil	7
2005/6	John Sutton	14
2006/7	John Sutton	12
2007/8	Billy Mehmet	6
2008/9	Andy Dorman	10
2009/10	Andy Dorman	6
2010/1	Michael Higdon	14
2011/2	Steven Thompson	13
2012/3	Steven Thompson	13
2013/4	Steven Thompson	13
2014/5	Kenny McLean	7
2015/6	Steven Mallan	11
2016/7	Steven Mallan / John Sutton	7
2017/18	Lewis Morgan	14
2018/19	Danny Mullen	6
2019/20	Jonathan Obika	8
2020/21	Jamie McGrath	10

STENHOUSEMUIR

1975/6	Jim Wight	14
1976/7	Frank Coulston	7
1977/8	Frank Wilson	14
1978/9	Sandy McNaughton	16
1979/80	David Jack	12
1980/1	Stevie Hancock	20
1981/2	Brian Jenkins	8
1982/3	Gavin Murray	15
1983/4	Gordon Forrest	14
1984/5	Harry Erwin / Sandy McNaughton	6
1985/6	Jim Sinnet	11
1986/7	Alan Bateman / Peter Russell /John Waddell	5
1987/8	Tom Condie	10
1988/9	Colin Walker	9
1989/90	Stephen McCormick	15
1990/1	Tony Speirs	17
1991/2	Miller Mathieson	9
1992/3	Miller Mathieson	26
1993/4	Miller Mathieson	14
1994/5	Gareth Hutchison	10
1995/6	Miller Mathieson	10
1996/7	Ian Little	14
1997/8	Ian Little	15
1998/9	Ross Hamilton	11
1999/00	Martin Mooney	8
2000/1	Isaac English	18
2001/2	Willie Irvine	7
2002/3	Mark Booth	9
2003/4	Andy Brown	5
2004/5	Paul McGrillen	18
2005/6	Colin Cramb	16
2006/7	John Dempster	10
2007/8	Scott Dalziel	9
2008/9	Scott Dalziel	14
2009/10	Kevin Motion	7
2010/1	Grant Anderson	7
2011/2	Andy Rodgers	14
2012/3	John Gemmell	18
2013/4	John Gemmell	11
2014/5	Colin McMenamin	15
2015/6	Alan Cook	8
2016/7	Colin McMenamin / Oli Shaw	7
2017/18	Mark McGuigan	22
2018/19	Mark McGuigan	16
2019/20	Mark McGuigan	5
2020/21	Mark McGuigan / Botti Biabi	6

STIRLING ALBION

1975/6	Mickey Lawson	18
1976/7	Bobby Gray	13
1977/8	Billy Steele	13
1978/9	Billy Steele	7
1979/80	Andy Kennedy	11
1980/1	Graeme Armstrong / Billy Steele	4
1981/2	John Colquhoun	13
1982/3	John Colquhoun	21
1983/4	Willie Irvine	12
1984/5	Willie Irvine	21
1985/6	Willie Irvine	17
1986/7	Steve Gavin / Charlie Gibson	7
1987/8	John Brogan	23
1988/9	Charlie Gibson	18
1989/90	Joe Reid	16
1990/1	David Lloyd	14
1991/2	Willie Watters	17
1992/3	Willie Watters	11
1993/4	Willie Watters	13
1994/5	Willie Watters	15
1995/6	Steve McCormick	25
1996/7	Alex Bone	9
1997/8	Alex Bone	13
1998/9	Alex Bone	21
1999/00	Ally Graham	17
2000/1	Craig Feroz / Ally Graham	5
2001/2	Alex Williams	17
2002/3	Steven Nicholas	11
2003/4	Scott McLean	21
2004/5	Scott McLean	9
2005/6	Paddy Connolly	14
2006/7	Colin Cramb	14
2007/8	Chris Aitken	8
2008/9	Martin Grehan / David McKenna	12
2009/10	Martin Grehan	8
2010/1	Gordon Smith	11
2011/2	Alan Cook	8
2012/3	Jordan White	13
2013/4	Jordan White	15
2014/5	Gordon Smith	8
2015/6	Steven Doris / Darren Smith	9
2016/7	Darren Smith	11
2017/18	Darren Smith	22
2018/19	Darren Smith	11
2019/20	Darryl Duffy	10
2020/21	Andy Ryan	10

STRANRAER

1975/6	J Traynor	12
1976/7	Derek Frye	24
1977/8	Derek Frye	27
1978/9	Drew Harvey	11
1979/80	Ian Gibb	15
1980/1	Hugh Hay	7
1981/2	Sean Sweeney	11
1982/3	Sean Sweeney	11
1983/4	Jim McGuire	11
1984/5	Sean Sweeney	10
1985/6	Jim McGuire / Stuart Mauchlen	8
1986/7	Bruce Cleland	13
1987/8	Bruce Cleland	8
1988/9	David Lloyd	11
1989/90	Colin Harkness	13
1990/1	Colin Harkness	14
1991/2	Tommy Sloan	14
1992/3	Tommy Sloan	19
1993/4	Tommy Sloan	16
1994/5	Darren Henderson / Tommy Sloan	4
1995/6	Lex Grant	6
1996/7	Paul McIntyre	7
1997/8	Graham Young	11
1998/9	Paul Ronald / Graham Young	5
1999/00	Paul Ronald	12
2000/1	Ian Harty	13
2001/2	Ian Harty	16
2002/3	Ian Harty	12
2003/4	Michael Moore	24
2004/5	David Graham	14
2005/6	David Hamilton	9
2006/7	Michael Moore	12
2007/8	Michael Mullen	13
2008/9	Gregory Tade	7
2009/10	Michael Moore / Armand One	8
2010/1	Armand One	17
2011/2	Craig Malcolm	15
2012/3	Craig Malcolm	18
2013/4	Jamie Longworth	14
2014/5	Jamie Longworth	11
2015/6	Craig Malcolm	12
2016/7	Craig Malcolm	13
2017/18	Scott Agnew	10
2018/19	Innes Cameron	10
2019/20	James Hilton	5
2020/21	Thomas Orr	8

SPFL Individual Stats 2020/21

PREMIERSHIP

TOP SCORERS

18	O Edouard	Celtic
14	K Nisbet	Hibernian
14	K Roofe	Rangers
12	M Boyle	Hibernian
12	A Morelos	Rangers
12	J Tavernier	Rangers
11	D Cole	Motherwell
10	M Elyounoussi	Celtic
10	R Kent	Rangers
10	J McGrath	St Mirren
9	C Burke	Kilmarnock
9	R Callachan	Hamilton Accies
9	L Ferguson	Aberdeen
9	D Turnbull	Celtic
8	N Clark	Dundee United
8	K Lafferty	Kilmarnock

MOST BOOKINGS

17	I Vigurs	Ross County
16	A Power	Kilmarnock
12	M Bartley	Livingston
11	R Callachan	Hamilton Accies
10	C Butcher	Dundee United
10	L Ferguson	Aberdeen
9	J Newell	Hibernian
9	A Tshibola	Kilmarnock
8	L Craig	St Johnstone
8	A Gogic	Hibernian
8	J Guthrie	Livingston
8	A Morelos	Rangers
8	H Odofin	Hamilton Accies
8	T Watt	Motherwell

MOST RED CARDS

2	A Millen	Kilmarnock
2	M O'Halloran	St Johnstone

ASSISTS

11	I Hagi	Rangers
9	J Tavernier	Rangers
9	R Kent	Rangers
9	R Christie	Celtic
7	C McGregor	Celtic
6	M Boyle	Hibernian
6	D Turnbull	Celtic / Mwell
6	B Barisic	Rangers
5	D Cole	Motherwell
5	S Arfield	Rangers
5	J White	Ross Co / Mwell
5	T Watt	Motherwell
5	F Taylor	Motherwell

CHAMPIONSHIP

TOP SCORERS

14	L Boyce	Hearts
9	D McManus	Dunfermline
9	A Obileye	QOS
9	N Todorov	ICT
9	C Wighton	Dunfermline
8	J Cummings	Dundee
8	J Hamilton	Arbroath
8	K O'Hara	Dunfermline
8	C Shields	QOS
8	O Sow	Dundee
7	I Cameron	Alloa
7	D McKay	ICT
7	J Walker	Hearts
6	D Armstrong	Raith Rovers
6	S Naismith	Hearts
6	C Smith	Ayr

MOST BOOKINGS

11	S Hetherington	Alloa Athletic
8	W Gibson	QOS
8	C Hamilton	Arbroath
8	S Welsh	ICT
7	C Adam	Dundee
7	S Allardice	ICT
7	D Armstrong	Raith Rovers
7	B McKay	ICT
7	D Tait	Raith Rovers
6	R Grant	Alloa Athletic
6	R Matthews	Raith Rovers
6	R Tumilty	Raith Rovers
6	S Whittaker	Dunfermline Ath
6	I Wilson	Dunfermline Ath

MOST RED CARDS

2	I Davidson	Raith Rovers

ASSISTS

7	C Adam	Dundee
7	A Irving	Hearts
7	P McMullan	Dundee
6	L Boyce	Hearts
6	D Thomas	Dunfermline Ath
5	J Walker	Hearts
5	S Sutherland	ICT
5	R Hendry	Raith Rovers
5	O Lee	Hearts

LEAGUE ONE

TOP SCORERS

14	M Megginson	Cove Rangers
11	D Goodwillie	Clyde
11	B Graham	Partick Thiste
e	D Carrick	Airdrieonians
8	G Webster	Montrose
7	J Hamilton	East Fife
7	R Mclean	Montrose
7	S Tiffoney	Partick Thiste
6	K Connell	Airdrieonians
6	C Gallagher	Airdrieonians
6	C Morrison	Falkirk
6	Z Rudden	Partick Thiste

MOST BOOKINGS

8	A McCarthy	Peterhead
7	B Coll	Forfar Athletic
7	J Penrice	Partick Thistle
6	C Ballantyne	Montrose
6	S Brown	Peterhead
6	J Brown	Peterhead
6	A Dunsmore	East Fife
6	R McLean	Montrose
6	A Steeves	Montrose
5	K Connell	Airdrieonians
5	R Davidson	East Fife
5	R Meechan	Forfar Athletic
5	M Megginson	Cove Rangers

MOST RED CARDS

2	J Brown	Peterhead

ASSISTS

6	J Cardle	Partick Thistle
6	R Forbes	Dumbarton
4	C Ballantyne II	Montrose
4	H Ritchie	Peterhead
4	R Wallace	East Fife

LEAGUE TWO

TOP SCORERS

15	Kane Hester	Elgin City
10	M Aitken	Albion Rovers
10	A Ryan	Stirling Albion
8	T Orr	Stranraer
7	J Campbell	Edinburgh City
6	B Iabi	Stenhousemuir
6	M McGuigan	Stenhousemuir
6	R McHugh	Queen's Park
6	S Murray	Queen's Park
6	R Paton	Stranraer
5	W Baynham	Queen's Park
5	B Cameron	Elgin City
5	R Dingwall	Elgin City
5	D Duffy	Stranraer
5	L Henderson	Edinburgh City
5	B Henderson	Edinburgh City
5	T Wallace	Annan Ath

MOST BOOKINGS

7	J Leitch	Stirling Albion
7	C Little	Stenhousemuir
7	C Thomson	Edinburgh City
7	J Tiffoney	Stenhousemuir
6	M Aitken	Albion Rovers
6	C Barr	Cowdenbeath
6	J Campbell	Edinburgh City
6	J McGregor	Stirling Albion
6	F Mullen	Cowdenbeath
6	M Paton	Brechin City
6	A Ryan	Stirling Albion
6	S Swinglehurst	Annan Ath
5	A Black	Edinburgh City
5	M Douglas	Annan Ath
5	L Hunter	Annan Ath
5	L Kilday	Queen's Park
5	A McDonald	Elgin City

MOST RED CARDS

2	K Millar	Stranraer
2	O Moxon	Annan Ath

ASSISTS

10	C Thomson	Edinburgh City
7	A Ryan	Stirling Albion
7	T Orr	Stranraer
6	R Dingwall	Elgin City
6	D Galt	Queen's Park
5	A Stirling	Stranraer
4	B Biabi	Stenhousemuir
4	N Flanagan	Annan Ath
4	L Connell	Queen's Park
4	T Muir	Stenhousemuir

Supporters Direct Scotland 2020/1

Supporters Direct began in 2000 to help supporters gain influence in the running and ownership of their club. They have helped members to establish 192 trusts in the UK and we have worked with supporters to purchase and develop more than 40 community owned clubs. They have supported these members in raising more than £50 million to be reinvested back into their clubs and communities including £6 million through community shares projects.

In 2017, Supporters Direct Scotland incorporated locally as a democratic Community Benefit Society, founded on cooperative principles.
Their objectives as an organisation are as follows:
+ acting as the democratic and representative voice of the supporters of Scottish football, and protecting, promoting and furthering their interests;
strengthening the bonds between Scottish football supporters and the game's governing bodies and stakeholders;
+ promoting equality and tackling prejudice within all levels of Scottish sport;
+ providing support for community and supporter organisations that seek to buy, bid, govern and influence sports clubs;
+ supplying advice and services to supporter organisations and sports clubs in relation to their affairs and development, and supporting them in delivering social and community value;
+ operating democratically, fairly, sustainably, transparently and with financial responsibility, and encouraging Scottish sport to do likewise;
+ being a positive, inclusive and representative organisation, open and accessible to all supporters regardless of their age, income, ethnicity, gender, disability, sexuality or religious or moral belief;
+ assisting in the resolution of disputes between members;
promoting sport and sports clubs as vehicles through which positive societal change can occur.

SD SCOTLAND BOARD MEMBERS—Chair—Morag McHaffie (Partick); Andrew Miller (Kilmarnock); Dougie McMahon (St Mirren); Drew Main (Dunfermline Athletic); Louise Strutt; Graeme Baxter (Raith), Ian Baird (Dundee), Jennifer Aitchison (ICT), Jon Keen (Reading).

There was no comprehensive Scottish Supporters Survey undertaken in 2020/1. However, SDS did conduct a survey on the entry of Colts teams into the SPFL. The results were reported on the SDS website:

"Overall, just ***23.2% of Scottish fans are in favour of these proposals*** – with a sharp divide between the views of Old Firm fans and fans of other clubs. **88.2% of Old Firm fans** are in favour, but only **11% of other fans** support these proposals. Support is lowest (8%) amongst fans of the other Premiership clubs, with 11.3% in favour in the Championship, 10.4% in League One, 17.6% in League Two, and 37% support from Highland and Lowland league fans.

Of those in favour of the proposals, we asked whether promotion should be possible through the divisions. Around three quarters of these survey respondents agree that promotion should be permitted, but most feel that promotion should be limited to League One (25.1%) or the Championship (34.6%). Only 14.1% of these respondents believe that B teams should be allowed to reach the top division.

Regardless of their response to previous questions, we also asked fans whether they would watch their team play against a B team. Again, the responses from Old Firm fans were starkly different from fans of other clubs – 80.3% of Rangers and Celtic fans would watch these matches, compared with just 16.2% of other fans (a combined response of 26.3% overall).

Similarly polarised responses were received when we asked whether the introduction of B teams would result in improved player development – 88.9% of Rangers and Celtic fans believe that player development would be improved, compared with 11.2% of other fans (23.4% overall)".

It has to be said that the methodology and construction of the survey made it inevitable that it would produce such polarised outcomes, simply reinforcing preconceived opinions.

SPFL ATTENDANCE FIGURES 2020/21

Sadly there can be co comparative attendance figures for SPFL clubs for season 2020/1. The vast majority of clubs played all their home fixtures behind closed doors. There was a short period just before Christmas when very limited numbers of spectators were allowed at Elgin City, Inverness CT, Ross County, Stranraer and Annan Athletic—limited to home fans only, and numbering a few hundred at most. Aberdeen also hosted a "test event" at one home match. At the very end of the season up to 500 spectators were permitted at most of the Play Off Final matches, other than Edinburgh City v Dumbarton.

TV VIEWING FIGURES 2020/21

There were more televised matches than ever before. As well as coverage from the BBC, Sky, BT and Premier Sports, almost all clubs streamed their games live. Season ticket holders were given access to these games as part of their purchase. Matches could usually also be purchased on a one-off basis by away fans and anyone else who was interested. Pricing ranged from around £7 / £8 to £20 per match. The quality of production and commentary varied greatly from club to club. Viewing figures for these club streams were seldom made public.

Aug 1	Prem	Sky	Aberdeen v Rangers	448,000
Aug 2	Prem	Sky	Celtic v Hamilton Accies	329,000
Aug 3	Prem	Sky	Ross County v Motherwell	110,000
Aug 6	UEFA EL	BT	Bayer Leverkusen v Rangers	168,600
Aug 9	Prem	Sky	Kilmarnock v Celtic	267,000
Aug 11	Prem	Sky	Dundee United v Hibernian	107,000
Aug 15	Prem	Sky	Hibernian v Motherwell	139,000
Aug 16	Prem	Sky	Livingston v Rangers	462,000
Aug 18	UEFA CL	Pre	Celtic v KR Reykjavik	41,700
Aug 20	Prem	Sky	St Johnstone v Aberdeen	105,000
Aug 22	Prem	Sky	Dundee United v Celtic	335,000
Aug 23	Prem	Sky	St Johnstone v Hibernian	197,000
Aug 26	UEFA CL	Pre	Celtic v Ferencvaros	48,000
Aug 27	UEFA EL	Pre	Aberdeen v Runavik	2,400
Aug 27	UEFA EL	Pre	Motherwell v Glentoran	n/a
Aug 29	Prem	Sky	Hamilton Accies v Rangers	236,485
Aug 30	Prem	Sky	Hibernian v Aberdeen	158,246
Sep 4	Int	Sky	Scotland v Israel	277,514
Sep 7	Int	Sky	Scotland v Czech Republic	267,183
Sep 17	UEFA EL	Pre	Lincoln RI v Rangers	46,700
Sep 17	UEFA EL	BBC	Coleraine v Motherwell	n/a
Sep 20	Prem	Sky	Hibernian v Rangers	440,159
Sep 24	UEFA EL	Pre	Skonto Riga v Celtic	n/a
Sep 27	Prem	Sky	Motherwell v Rangers	228,694
Oct 2	Prem	Sky	St Johnstone v Celtic	137,556
Oct 6	LC	Pre	Hearts v Inverness CT	10,500
Oct 8	Int	Sky	Scotland v Israel	406,171
Oct 9	LC	Pre	Dunfermline A v Falkirk	1,800
Oct 10	LC	Pre	Cove Rangers v Hibernian	1,800
Oct 11	Int	Sky	Scotland v Slovakia`	422,636
Oct 13	LC	Pre	Hearts v Raith Rovers	23,700
Oct 14	Int	Sky	Scotland v Czech republic	204,858
Oct 16	Cha	BBC	Hearts v Dundee	153,500
Oct 17	Prem	Sky	Celtic v Rangers	496,015
Oct 22	UEFA EL	BT	Standard Liege v Rangers	251,800
Oct 22	UEFA EL	BT	Celtic v AC Milan	254,200
Oct 23	Cha	BBC	Arbroath v Hearts	113,800
Oct 25	Prem	Sky	Aberdeen v Celtic	299,387
Oct 29	UEFA EL	BT	Lille v Celtic	180,700
Oct 29	UEFA EL	BT	Rangers v Lech Poznan	241,700
Oct 31	SCSF	BBC	Hearts v Hibernian	223,200
Nov 1	Prem	Sky	Kilmarnock v Rangers	310,953
Nov 1	SCSF	Pre	Aberdeen v Celtic	112,100
Nov 5	UEFA EL	BT	Benfica v Rangers	257,899
Nov 5	UEFA EL	BT	Celtic v Sparta Prague	170,800
Nov 6	Cha	BBC	Alloa Ath v Dundee	88,600
Nov 8	Prem	Sky	Motherwell v Celtic	297,328
Nov 10	LC	Pre	St Johnstone v Dundee Utd	14,100
Nov 11	LC	Pre	St Mirren v Morton	18,400
Nov 12	Int	Sky	Serbia v Scotland	1,480,000
Nov 15	SWPL	BBC	Glasgow City v Hibernian	1,100
Nov 15	Int	Sky	Slovakia v Scotland	398,395
Nov 15	LC	Pre	Hibernian v Dundee	8,000
Nov 18	Int	Sky	Israel v Scotland	285,125
Nov 20	Cha	BBC	Dunfermline A v Hearts	145,300
Nov 22	Prem	Sky	Rangers v Aberdeen	252,722
Nov 26	UEFA EL	BT	Sparta Prague v Celtic	255,600
Nov 26	UEFA EL	BT	Rangers v Benfica	291,600
Nov 28	LC	Pre	St Mirren v Aberdeen	23,000
Nov 29	LC	Pre	Celtic v Ross County	44,999
Nov 29	LC	Pre	Falkirk v Rangers	102,300
Dec 3	UEFA EL	BT	AC Milan v Celtic	241,700
Dec 3	UEFA EL	BT	Rangers v Standard Liege	300,100
Dec 4	Cha	BBC	QOTS v Inverness CT	103,600
Dec 6	Prem	Sky	Ross County v Rangers	183,205
Dec 10	UEFA EL	BT	Lech Poznan v Rangers	214,599
Dec 10	UEFA EL	BT	Celtic v Lille	204,600
Dec 11	Cha	BBC	Ayr United v Raith Rovers	80,300
Dec 13	Prem	Sky	Dundee United v Rangers	214, 599
Dec 15	LC	Pre	Alloa Ath v Hibernian	15,600
Dec 16	LC	Pre	St Mirren v Rangers	50,600
Dec 20	Prem	Sky	Kilmarnock v Aberdeen	82,487
Dec 20	SCF	Pre	Celtic v Hearts	31,700
Dec 20	SCF	BBC	Celtic v Hearts	n/a
Dec 26	Prem	Sky	Rangers v Hibernian	629,449
Dec 26	Prem	Sky	Hamilton Accies v Celtic	300,000
Dec 28	SC	BBC	Dundonald BB v Q Park	108,300
Jan 2	Prem	Sky	Rangers v Celtic	965,772
Jan 2	Cha	BBC	Dundee v Hearts	124,300
Jan 8	SC	BBC	Q Park v QOS	84,400
Jan 9	SC	BBC	Dundee v Bonnyrigg Rose	90,400
Jan 10	Prem	Sky	Aberdeen v Rangers	381,551
Jan 11	Prem	Sky	Celtic v Hibernian	200,438
Jan 15	Cha	BBC	Morton v Dunfermline Ath	85,300
Jan 17	Prem	Sky	Motherwell v Rangers	343, 100
Jan 20	Prem	Sky	Livingston v Celtic	n/a

Jan 22	Cha	BBC	Arbroath v Dundee	91,000
Jan 23	LCSF	Pre	St Johnstone v Hibernian	54,300
Jan 24	LCSF	Pre	St Mirren v Livingston	53,700
Jan 27	Prem	Sky	Hibernian v Rangers	298,475
Feb 2	Prem	Sky	Kilmarnock v Celtic	138,364
Feb 5	Cha	BBC	Ayr United v Hearts	113,900
Feb 7	Prem	Sky	Hamilton v Rangers	379,680
Feb 10	Prem	Sky	St Mirren v Celtic	89,032
Feb 12	Cha	BBC	QOS v Hearts	104,500
Feb 14	Prem	Sky	St Johnstone v Celtic	304,139
Feb 18	UEFA EL	BT	Royal Antwerp v Rangers	375,600
Feb 21	Prem	Sky	Ross County v Celtic	293,700
Feb 25	UEFA EL	BT	Rangers v Royal Antwerp	275,100
Feb 26	Cha	BBC	ICT v Hearts	102,400
Feb 28	LCF	Pre	St Johnstone v Livingston	49,200
Mar 3	Prem	Sky	Livingston v Rangers	233,300
Mar 7	Prem	Sky	Dundee United v Celtic	335,800
Mar 11	UEFA EL	BT	Slavia Prague v Rangers	300,700
Mar 12	Cha	BBC	ICT v Raith Rovers	92,500
Mar 18	UEFA EL	BT	Rangers v Slavia Prague	299,300
Mar 19	Cha	BBC	Alloa Ath v Dundee	58,600
Mar 21	Prem	Sky	Celtic v Rangers	600,000
Mar 25	Int	Sky	Scotland v Austria	316,176
Mar 26	Cha	BBC	Dundee v Dunfermline Ath	47,300
Mar 28	Int	Sky	Isreal v Scotland	407,688
Mar 30	Cha	BBC	Raith Rovers v Dunfermline	79,800
Mar 31	Int	Sky	Scotland v Faroe Islands	211,400
Apr 2	SC	BBC	Ross County v ICT	107,500
Apr 3	SC	BBC	Dumbarton v Aberdeen	n/a
Apr 4	SC	Pre	Rangers v Cove Rangers	82,100
Apr 5	SC	BBC	QOS v Hibernian	140,700
Apr 9	Cha	BBC	Hearts v Alloa	18,000
Apr 13	Cha	BBC	Dunfermline A v Dundee	n/a
Apr 20	Cha	BBC	Morton v Hearts	69,000
Apr 24	SC	Pre	Hibernian v Motherwell	41,900
Apr 25	SC	BBC	Aberdeen v Dundee United	n/a
Apr 25	SC	Pre	Rangers v St Johnstone	120,400
Apr 26	SC	BBC	Kilmarnock v St Mirren	227,400
Apr 30	Cha	BBC	Raith Rovers v Hearts	106,100
May 2	Prem	Sky	Rangers v Celtic	601,400
May 8	SCSF	Pre	Hibernian v Dundee United	35,100
May 9	SCSF	Pre	St Mirren v St Johnstone	23,000
May 12	PO	BBC	Raith Rovers v Dundee	52,400
May 15	Prem	Sky	Rangers v Aberdeen	357,500
May 15	PO	BBC	Dundee v Raith Rovers	84,300
May 17	PO	Alb	Edinburgh City v Dumbarton	
May 18	PO	Alb	Airdrie v Morton	
May 20	PO	Alb	Dumbarton v Edinburgh City	
May 20	PO	Sky	Dundee v Kilmarnock	145,994
May 21	PO	Alb	Morton v Airdrie	
May 22	SCF	Pre	Hibernian v St Johnstone	3,200
May 22	SCF	BBC	Hibernian v St Johnstone	
May 24	PO	Sky	Kilmarnock v Dundee	
Jun 2	Int	Sky	Netherlands v Scotland	
Jun 6	Int	Sky	Luxembourg v Scotland	
Jun 14	Int	BBC	Scotland v Czech Republic	
Jun 18	Int	STV	England v Scotland	
Jun 22	Int	STV	Scotland v Croatia	

Late season figures not yet available
Pre= Premier Sports, BBC = BBC Scotland or BBC 1 , Alb = BBC Alba

FOOTBALL BANNING ORDERS 2017-2020

Football Banning Orders issued by the Scottish Courts in the period 2017-2020 (By Club)

Rangers	285
Celtic	123
Hibernian	122
Aberdeen	41
Hearts	39
Dundee United	16
Ayr United	15
Dunfermline Athletic	13
Motherwell	13
Hamilton Accies	12
Falkirk	11
Dundee	10
Kilmarnock	9
Partick Thistle	9
Airdrieonians	7
Queen of the South	6
Spartak Moscow	6
St Mirren	6
Raith Rovers	5
Auchinleck Talbot	5
St Johnstone	5
Inverness CT	4
Cowdenbeath	3
Manchester United	3
Morton	2
Southampton	2
England	2
Newcastle United	2
Albion Rovers	1
Berwick Rangers	1
Bo'ness United	1
Carluke Hearts Ams	1
Chelsea	1
Cumnock	1
East Fife	1
Glenafton Athletic	1
Irvine Meadow	1
Kilbirnie Ladeside	1
Largs Thistle	1
Musselburgh Athletic	1
Peterhead	1
Preston Athletic	1
Stirling Albion	1
Unknown	8

CLUB TWITTER FOLLOWERS 2020/21

SPFL	Jul 2021	Jul 2020	Jul 2019	Jul 2018	Jul 2017	Jul 2016	Jul 2015
Celtic	721500	684800	631000	589000	473000	337000	287000
Rangers	627500	541900	485000	436000	338000	241000	188000
Aberdeen	108200	104100	98800	92800	78200	55600	43800
Hearts	94700	90300	83100	77700	64100	49600	40100
Hibernian	91300	86000	79700	72900	59500	45900	33500
Dundee United	60200	57100	53600	49600	43300	34200	27200
Motherwell	50500	46500	41100	37200	28200	22600	19000
Dundee	47900	45900	43300	40400	34800	25400	19300
Kilmarnock	43200	39800	35500	29700	23200	17000	12900
St Johnstone	41400	37300	34900	32100	27200	20600	16000
St Mirren	36300	33800	30900	26200	20100	16000	13400
Inverness CT	31900	30500	28700	26700	24100	19400	16200
Partick Thistle	31600	29800	26400	23600	19700	15400	12200
Hamilton Accies	30000	27900	24700	21400	17400	13000	10100
Falkirk	27500	25800	23900	21300	17700	14200	10300
Livingston	26400	22800	18800	15000	11400	9015	7265
Dunfermline Ath	25000	23100	21000	18700	15200	12300	9732
Morton	21000	19700	17700	15500	13200	10200	8089
Raith Rovers	20600	19200	17500	15800	13600	10600	8058
Ross County	18900	16500	14300	11800	9016	5488	2204
Queen of the South	18600	16800	15200	12800	10400	7820	6534
Ayr United	16900	15400	13600	11000	8441	6435	4808
Cowdenbeath	16200	15800	15400	14800	13300	11500	9723
Stenhousemuir	15500	14400	13300	12100	10800	9241	8068
Albion Rovers	15500	14200	13200	11900	10100	7666	6177
Clyde	15300	14500	13100	12200	10700	7142	5598
Queen's Park	15300	13300	11700	9884	7905	5971	4560
East Fife	14800	13900	12700	11300	9772	7924	6524
Stirling Albion	14400	13500	12500	11200	9497	7605	6146
Airdrieonians	14400	13400	12100	10500	8860	6688	5022
Montrose	13300	11600	10500	8925	6816	5118	3922
Stranraer	13200	12300	11100	9929	8429	6516	4809
Elgin City	13100	12100	11200	9971	8237	6360	4988
Kelty Hearts	12900						
Edinburgh City	12800	11800	10600	8336	9943	4869	2898
Forfar Athletic	12700	11600	10600	9102	7589	5678	4336
Dumbarton	11100	10000	8973	8688	7684	6978	5827
Arbroath	10700	9674	7592	5699	4509	3064	2210
Annan Athletic	10400	8768	7902	6569	5342	4003	2823
Cove Rangers	10200	9017	6385				
Peterhead	9942	8642	7779	6367	4918	3549	2246
Alloa Athletic	8378	7227	5995	4321	2758	1929	1371

LOWLAND LEAGUE	Jul 2021	Jul 2020	Jul 2019	Jul 2018	Jul 2017	Jul 2016	Jul 2015
Berwick Rangers	13600	13100					
Spartans	10400	10200	9691	8680	7614	6833	6150
East Stirlingshire	9459	9044	8413	7806	6771	5419	4188
East Kilbride	8389	7678	7148	6136	5369	3323	1121
Bonnyrigg Rose	7003	6306	5200				
Gretna 2008	5825	5077	4275	3068	2655	2219	1864
BSC Glasgow	5528	5052	3202	2541	2009	1403	883
Gala Fairydean Rov	5386	4877	4362	3828	3285	2595	1923
Cumbernauld Colts	5031	4611	4030	3399	2972	2336	1673
Stirling University	4374	4107	3512	2911	2436	1916	1416
Dalbeattie Star	3406	3141	2802	2380	1929	1508	1164
Civil Service Strollers	2921	2262	1679	1139	749	359	
Edinburgh University	2706	2590	2339	2030	1727	1430	1142
Bo'ness United	2611						
Edusport / Cal Braves	2200	1534	3105	2446	1575		
Vale of Leithen	1975	1663	1350	955	1629	1405	1235
Kelty Hearts		8515	7055	5196			
Whitehill Welfare			4054	3496	2898	2383	1935
Selkirk				3948	3495	3047	2535
Preston Athletic						2010	1571
Threave Rovers				1992		1282	970
Hawick Royal Albert				1588	1208	672	

HIGHLAND LEAGUE	Jul 2021	Jul 2020	Jul 2019	Jul 2018	Jul 2017	Jul 2016	Jul 2015
Fort William	20200	21000	7157	3580	3042	2600	2205
Brechin City	11300						
Formartine United	8740	9057	9505	10500	11900	12900	9791
Brora Rangers	7697	6023	5264	4839	4193	3718	3199
Inverurie Locos	5267	5211	4747	4357	3941	3400	2744
Fraserburgh	5236	5060	4453	4057	3064	2544	1956
Buckie Thistle	4310	4051	3564	3105	2596	1381	984
Huntly	4162	3959	3508	3150	2754	2214	1710
Wick Academy	4042	3927	3758	3537	3333	3045	2407
Lossiemouth	3669	3556	3080	2580	2247	1724	1375
Deveronvale	3523	3408	3006	2725	2337	1906	1495
Keith	3381	3133	2519	2065	1643	1038	494
Rothes	3366	3113	2568	2118	1622	1088	640
Nairn County	3178	2916	2090	1632	1118	366	2149
Clachnacuddin	3019	2767	2150	1577	1885	1883	1577
Turriff United	2892	2754	2416	2082	1722	1166	752
Strathspey Thistle	1228	1040	708	317	1752	1579	1204
Forres Mechanics	944	761	3334	2923	2542	2008	1554

The Managers League Club Managers Since 1970

ABERDEEN
1965-71 Eddie Turnbull
1971-75 Jimmy Bonthrone
1975-77 Ally McLeod
1977-78 Billy McNeill
1978-86 Alex Ferguson
1986-88 Ian Porterfield
1988-91 Alex Smith / Jocky Scott
1991-92 Alex Smith
1992-95 Willie Miller
1995-97 Roy Aitken
1997-98 Alex Miller
1998-99 Paul Hegarty
1999-2002 Ebbe Skovdahl
2002-04 Steve Paterson
2004-09 Jimmy Calderwood
2009-10 Mark McGhee
2010-13 Craig Brown
2013-21 Derek McInnes
2021- Stephen Glass

AIRDRIEONIANS /AIRDRIE UNITED
1967-70 Ralph Collins
1970-76 Ian McMillan
1976-78 Jackie Stewart
1978-82 Bobby Watson
1982-83 Bill Munro
1983-85 Ally McLeod
1985-86 Ian McMillan
1987-87 Derek Whiteford
1987-89 Gordon McQueen
1989-91 Jimmy Bone
1991-99 Alex McDonald
1999-2000 Gary Mackay
2000-01 Steve Archibald
2001-02 Ian McCall
2006-06 Sandy Stewart
2006-10 Kenny Black
2010-13 Jimmy Boyle
2013-2015 Gary Bollan
2015-2016 Eddie Wolecki-Black
2016 Danny Lennon (Interim)
2016 Kevin McLeish (Interim)
2016-17 Mark Wilson
2017 Gordon Dalziel (Interim)
2017 Willie Aitchison
2017-18 Stephen Findlay
2018- Ian Murray

ALBION ROVERS
1969-72 Bobby Flavell
1972-73 Frank Beattie
1973-74 Ralph Brand
1974-76 George Caldwell
1976-81 Sam Goodwin
1981 Harry Hood
1981 Joe Baker
1981-82 Derek Whiteford
1982-83 Martin Ferguson
1983-84 Billy Wilson
1984 Benny Rooney
1984 Andy Ritchie
1984-85 Joe Baker
1986-87 Tommy Gemmell
1987-91 Dave Provan
1991-92 Mick Oliver
1992-93 Billy McLaren
1993-94 Tommy Gemmell
1994-95 Tom Spence
1995 Jimmy Crease
1996-98 Vinnie Moore
1998-99 Billy McLaren
1999-00 Mark Shanks
2000-02 John McVeigh
2002-03 Peter Hetherston
2003-05 Kevin McAllister
2005 Jimmy Lindsay
2005-07 Jim Chapman
2007-08 John McCormack
2008-12 Paul Martin
2012-13 Todd Lumsden
2013-14 James Ward
2014-17 Darren Young
2017-18 Brian Kerr
2018 John Brogan
2018-20 Kevin Harper
2020- Brian Reid

ALLOA ATHLETIC
1969-71 Duncan McCallum
1971-72 Ian Crawford
1972-74 Dan McLindon
1974-80 Hugh Wilson
1980-82 Alex Totten
1982-84 Willie Garner
1984-86 Jimmy Thomson
1986-87 Dom Sullivan
1987-90 Gregor Abel
1990 Billy Little
1990-93 Hugh McCann
1993-95 Billy Lamont
1995-96 Pat McAulay
1996-98 Tom Hendrie
1999-2003 Terry Christie
2003-06 Tom Hendrie
2006-11 Alan Maitland
2011-14 Paul Hartley
2014-15 Barry Smith
2015 Danny Lennon
2015- 16 Jack Ross
2016-19 Jim Goodwin
2019-21 Peter Grant
2021- Barry Ferguson

ANNAN ATHLETIC
2006-12 Harry Cairney
2013-17 Jim Chapman
2017- Peter Murphy

ARBROATH
1962-80 Albert Henderson
1980-83 Ian Stewart
1983-85 George Fleming
1985-86 Jimmy Bone
1987-90 John Young
1990-91 Ian Gibson
1991 Walter Borthwick
1991-92 Michael Lawson
1992-94 Danny McGrain
1994 Jocky Scott
1994 Donald Park / George Mackie
1995-96 John Brogan
1996-97 Tommy Campbell
1997-2000 Dave Baikie
2000-03 John Brownlie
2003-04 Stevie Kirk
2004-05 Harry Cairney
2005-09 John McGlashan
2009-10 Jim Weir
2010-14 Paul Sheerin
2014-15 Allan Moore
2015-16 Todd Lumsden
2016- Dick Campbell

AYR UNITED
1966-75 Ally McLeod
1975-78 Alex Stuart
1978 Ally McLeod
1979-83 Willie McLean
1983-85 George Caldwell
1985-90 Ally McLeod
1991-93 George Burley
1993-95 Simon Stainrod
1995-2002 Gordon Dalziel
2002-04 Campbell Money
2004-05 Mark Shanks
2005-07 Robert Connor
2007 Neil Watt
2007-12 Brian Reid
2012-14 Mark Roberts
2015-19 Ian McCall
2019-21 Mark Kerr
2021- David Hopkin

BRECHIN CITY
1962-70 John Gilmartin
1970-71 Frank Sandeman
1971-72 Bobby Methven
1972-73 Kenny Dick
1973-77 Charlie Dunn
1977-80 Ian Stewart
1980-82 Doug Houston
1982-86 Ian Fleming
1987-93 John Ritchie
1993-94 Ian Redford
1994-2000 John Young
2000-05 Dick Campbell
2005-06 Ian Campbell
2006-08 Michael O'Neill
2009-10 Jim Duffy
2010-12 Jim Weir
2012-15 Ray McKinnon
2015-18 Darren Dods
2018-19 Barry Smith
2019-20 Mark Wilson
2020-21 Michael Paton

CELTIC
1965-78 Jock Stein
1978-83 Billy McNeill
1983-87 Davie Hay
1987-91 Billy McNeill
1991-93 Liam Brady
1993-94 Lou Macari
1994-97 Tommy Burns
1997-98 Wim Jansen
1998-99 Jozef Venglos
1999-00 John Barnes
2000-05 Martin O'Neill
2005-09 Gordon Strachan

2009-10	Tony Mowbray
2010-14	Neil Lennon
2014-16	Ronnie Deila
2016-19	Brendan Rogers
2019-21	Neil Lennon
2021	John Kennedy (Interim)
2021-	Ange Postecoglou

CLYDE

1968-73	Archie Robertson
1973-77	Stan Anderson
1977	Billy McNeill
1977-86	Craig Brown
1986-92	John Clark
1992-96	Alex Smith
1996-98	Gardner Speirs
1998-02	Alan Maitland
2002-04	Alan Kernaghan
2004-05	Billy Reid
2005-06	Graham Roberts
2006-07	Joe Miller
2007-08	Colin Hendry
2008-09	John Brown
2009-10	John McCormack
2010-11	Stuart Miller
2011-14	Jim Duffy
2014-17	Barry Ferguson
2017	JP McGovern / Peter MacDonald
2017	Jim Chapman
2017-	Danny Lennon

COVE RANGERS

2018-19	John Sheran / Graeme Mathieson
2019-	Paul Hartley

COWDENBEATH

1968-74	Andy Matthew
1974	Bert Paton
1974-75	Dan McLindon
1975-77	Frank Connor
1977-80	Paddy Wilson
1980	Pat Stanton
1980-82	Andy Rolland
1982-83	Hugh Wilson
1983-84	Willie McCulloch
1984-85	John Clark
1985-87	Joe Craig
1987	Dick Campbell
1987-88	John Blackley
1988-92	John Brownlie
1992-93	Andy Harrow
1993-94	John Reilly
1994-95	Paddy Dolan
1995-97	Tom Steven
1997	Sammy Conn
1997-2000	Craig Levein
2000	Peter Cormack
2000-02	Gary Kirk
2002-04	Keith Wright
2004-05	Dave Baikie
2005-06	Mixu Paatelainen
2006-08	Brian Welsh
2008-10	Danny Lennon
2010-11	Jimmy Nicholl
2011-13	Colin Cameron
2013-15	Jimmy Nicholl
2015-16	Colin Nish
2016-17	Liam Fox
2017	Gary Locke
2017	Billy Brown
2017-	Gary Bollan

DUMBARTON

1968-73	Jackie Stewart
1973-77	Alex Wright
1977-80	Davie Wilson
1980-81	Sean Fallon
1981-84	Billy Lamont
1984-86	Davie Wilson
1986	Derek Whiteford
1986-87	Alex Totten
1987-88	Mark Clougherty
1988	Bertie Auld
1988-90	Jim George
1990-93	Billy Lamont
1993-95	Murdo McLeod
1995-96	Jim Fallon
1996-99	Ian Wallace
1999-2000	Jimmy Brown
2000-02	Tom Carson
2002-03	David Winnie
2003-04	Brian Fairley
2004-06	Paul Martin
2006-07	Gerry McCabe
2007	John Brown
2007-2010	Jim Chapman
2010-12	Alan Adamson
2012-15	Ian Murray
2015-18	Steven Aitken
2018-21	Jim Duffy
2021-	Stephen Farrell

DUNDEE

1968-71	John Prentice
1972-77	Davie White
1977-80	Tommy Gemmell
1980-83	Donald Mackay
1983-86	Archie Knox
1986-88	Jocky Scott
1988-89	Dave Smith
1989-91	Gordon Wallace
1991-92	Ian Munro
1992-93	Simon Stainrod
1993-96	Jim Duffy
1996-98	John McCormack
1998-2000	Jocky Scott
2000-02	Ivano Bonetti
2002-05	Jim Duffy
2005-06	Alan Kernaghan
2006-08	Alex Rae
2008-10	Jocky Scott
2010	Gordon Chisholm
2010-13	Barry Smith
2013-14	John Brown
2014-17	Paul Hartley
2017-18	Neil McCann
2018-19	Jim McIntyre
2019-	James McPake

DUNDEE UNITED

1959-71	Jerry Kerr
1971-93	Jim McLean
1993-95	Ivan Golac
1995-96	Billy Kirkwood
1996-98	Tommy McLean
1998-2000	Paul Sturrock
2000-02	Alex Smith
2002-03	Paul Hegarty
2003-05	Ian McCall
2005-06	Gordon Chisholm
2006	Craig Brewster
2006-09	Craig Levein
2009-13	Peter Houston
2013-15	Jackie McNamara
2015-16	Mixu Paatelainen
2016-17	Ray McKinnon
2017-18	Csabo Laszlo
2018-20	Robbie Neilson
2020-21	Micky Mellon
2021-	Tom Courts

DUNFERMLINE ATHLETIC

1967-70	George Farm
1970-72	Alex Wright
1972-75	George Miller
1975-80	Harry Melrose
1980-82	Pat Stanton
1982-83	Tom Forsyth
1983-90	Jim Leishman
1990-91	Ian Munro
1991-93	Jocky Scott
1993-99	Bert Paton
1999	Dick Campbell
1999-2004	Jimmy Caldwerwood
2004-05	Davie Hay
2005-06	Jim Leishman
2006-07	Steven Kenny
2007-12	Jim McIntyre
2012-14	Jim Jefferies
2014-15	John Potter
2015-19	Alan Johnston
2019-21	Stevie Crawford
2021-	Peter Grant

EAST FIFE

1969-70	Bill Baxter
1970-73	Pat Quinn
1973-76	Frank Christie
1976-78	Roy Barry
1978-87	Dave Clarke
1987-93	Gavin Murray
1993-94	Alex Totten
1994-96	Steve Archibald
1996-97	Jimmy Bone
1997-99	Stevie Kirk
1999-2001	Rab Shannon
2001-02	Dave Clarke
2002-06	Jim Moffat
2006-09	David Baikie
2009-10	Stevie Crawford
2010-12	John Robertson
2012	Gordon Durie
2012-13	Billy Brown
2013	Willie Aitchison
2013-16	Gary Naysmith
2016-17	Barry Smith
2017-	Darren Young

EDINBURGH CITY

2010-17	Gary Jardine
2017-21	James McDonaugh
2021-	Gary Naysmith

ELGIN CITY

2000-02	Alex Caldwell
2002-03	Harry McFadden
2003-05	David Robertson
2006	Brian Irvine
2007-08	Robbie Williamson
2009-14	Ross Jack

2014 Barry Wilson
2014-17 Jim Weir
2017- Gavin Price

FALKIRK

1968-73 Willie Cunningham
1973-75 John Prentice
1975-77 George Miller
1977-79 Billy Little
1979-82 John Hagart
1982-83 Alex Totten
1983-84 Gregor Abel
1984-87 Billy Lamont
1987-88 Dave Clarke
1988-89 Jim Duffy
1989-90 Billy Lamont
1990-95 Jim Jefferies
1995-96 John Lambie
1996 Eamonn Bannon
1996-2002 Alex Totten
2002-03 Ian McCall
2003 John Hughes / Owen Coyle
2003-09 John Hughes
2009-10 Eddie May
2010-13 Steven Pressley
2013-14 Gary Holt
2014-17 Peter Houston
2017-18 Paul Hartley
2018-19 Ray McKinnon
2019-21 Lee Miller / David McCracken
2021 Gary Holt (Interim)
2021- Paul Sheerin

FORFAR ATHLETIC

1969-71 Ian Campbell
1971-73 Alan Kennedy
1973-74 Dave Easson
1974-76 Jerry Kerr
1976-80 Archie Knox
1980 Steve Murray
1980-82 Alex Rae
1982-86 Doug Houston
1986-89 Henry Hall
1989-90 Bobby Glennie
1990-92 Paul Hegarty
1992-96 Tommy Campbell
1996-2000 Ian McPhee
2000-2003 Neil Cooper
2003-04 Raymond Stewart
2004-05 Brian Fairley
2005-06 Ray Farningham
2006-07 George Shaw
2007-08 Jim Moffat
2008-15 Dick Campbell
2015-17 Gary Bollan
2017-19 Jim Weir
2019-21 Stuart Malcolm
2021- Gary Irvine

HAMILTON ACCIES

1969-70 Tommy Ewing
1970-71 Bobby Shearer
1971-72 Ronnie Simpson
1972-78 Eric Smith
1978-82 Davie McParland
1982-83 John Blackley
1983-84 Bertie Auld
1984-88 John Lambie
1988-89 Jim Dempsey
1989-90 John Lambie
1990-92 Billy McLaren
1992-96 Ian Munro
1996-98 Sandy Clark
1998-99 Colin Miller
1999-2002 Ally Dawson
2002-03 Chris Hillcoat
2003-05 Allan Maitland
2005-13 Billy Reid
2013-15 Alex Neil
2015-19 Martin Canning
2019- Brian Rice

HEARTS

1966-70 John Harvey
1970-74 Bobby Seith
1974-77 John Hagart
1977-80 Willie Ormond
1980-81 Bobby Moncur
1981 Tony Ford
1981-86 Alex MacDonald
1986-88 Alex MacDonald / Sandy Jardine
1988-90 Alex MacDonald
1990-93 Joe Jordan
1993-94 Sandy Clark
1994-95 Tommy McLean
1995-2000 Jim Jefferies
2000-04 Craig Levein
2004-05 John Robertson
2005 George Burley
2005-06 Graham Rix
2006-07 Valdas Ivanauskis
2007-08 Anatoly Korobochka
2008 Stephen Frail
2008-10 Csabo Laszlo
2010-11 Jim Jefferies
2011-12 Paulo Sergio
2012-13 John McGlynn
2013-14 Gary Locke
2014-16 Robbie Neilson
2016-17 Ian Cathro
2017-19 Craig Levein
2019-20 Daniel Stendel
2020- Robbie Neilson

HIBERNIAN

1969-70 Willie McFarlane
1970-71 Dave Ewing
1971-80 Eddie Turnbull
1980 Willie Ormond
1980-82 Bertie Auld
1982-84 Pat Stanton
1984-86 John Blackley
1986-96 Alex Miller
1996 Jocky Scott
1996-98 Jim Duffy
1998-2001 Alex McLeish
2001-02 Franck Sauzee
2002-04 Bobby Williamson
2004-06 Tony Mowbray
2006-07 John Collins
2008-09 Mixu Paatelainen
2009-10 John Hughes
2010-11 Colin Calderwood
2011-13 Pat Fenlon
2013-14 Terry Butcher
2014-16 Alan Stubbs
2016-19 Neil Lennon
2019 Paul Heckingbottom
2019- Jack Ross

INVERNESS CALEDONIAN THISTLE

1994-95 Sergei Baltacha
1995-2002 Steve Paterson
2002-04 John Robertson
2004-06 Craig Brewster
2006-07 Charlie Christie
2007-09 Craig Brewster
2009-13 Terry Butcher
2013-16 John Hughes
2016-17 Richie Foran
2017-21 John Robertson
2021 Neil McCann (Interim)
2021- Billy Dodds

KELTY HEARTS

2021 Barry Ferguson
2021- Kevin Thomson

KILMARNOCK

1968-73 Walter McCrae
1973-77 Willie Fernie
1977-81 Davie Sneddon
1981-84 Jim Clunie
1984-88 Eddie Morrison
1988-92 Jim Fleeting
1992-94 Tommy Burns
1994-96 Alex Totten
1996-2002 Bobby Williamson
2002-10 Jim Jefferies
2010 Jimmy Caldwerwood
2010-11 Mixu Paatelainen
2011-13 Kenny Shiels
2013-15 Alan Johnston
2015-16 Gary Locke
2016-17 Lee Clark
2017 Lee McCulloch
2017-19 Steve Clarke
2019 Angelo Alessio
2019-21 Alex Dyer
2021- Tommy Wright

LIVINGSTON / MEADOWBANK THISTLE

1974-75 John Bain
1976-77 Alec Ness
1977-80 Willie McFarlane
1980-92 Terry Christie
1992-93 Donald Park
1993-94 John Brownlie
1994-95 Michael Lawson
1995-98 Jim Leishman
1998-2000 Raymond Stewart
2000-03 David Hay / Jim Leishman
2003 Marcio Maximo Barcellos
2003-04 David Hay
2004 Allan Preston
2004-05 Richard Gough
2005-06 Paul Lambert
2006-07 John Robertson
2007-08 Mark Proctor
2008 Roberto Landi
2008-09 Paul Hegarty
2009 John Murphy
2009-12 Gary Bollan
2012 John Hughes
2012-13 Gareth Evans
2013 Richie Burke
2013-14 John McGlynn
2014-15 Mark Burchill
2015-18 David Hopkin

2018 Kenny Miller
2018-20 Gary Holt
2020- David Martindale

MONTROSE
1969/75 Alex Stuart
1975-79 Kenny Cameron
1979-82 Bobby Livingstone
1982-83 Steve Murray
1983 Denis D'Arcy
1983-90 Ian Stewart
1990-91 Doug Rougvie / Chic McClelland
1992-93 Jim Leishman
1993-95 John Holt
1995-96 Andy Dornan
1996-97 David Smith
1997-98 Tommy Campbell
1998-2000 Kevin Drinkell
2000-03 John Sheran
2003-05 Henry Hall
2005-06 Eddie Wolecki
2006 Eddie Wolecki / David Robertson
2006-07 David Robertson
2007-08 Jim Weir
2009-11 Steven Tweed
2011-12 Ray Farningham
2012-14 Stuart Garden
2014-15 George Shields
2015-16 Paul Hegarty
2016- Stuart Petrie

MORTON
1961-72 Hal Stewart
1972 Eric Smith
1972-74 Hal Stewart
1974-75 Erik Sorensen
1975-76 Joe Gilroy
1976-83 Benny Rooney
1983 Alex Miller
1983-84 Tommy McLean
1984-85 Willie McLean
1985-97 Allan McGraw
1997-2000 Billy Stark
2000 Ian McCall
2000-01 Allan Evans
2001 Ally Maxwell
2001-02 Peter Cormack
2002 Dave McPherson
2002-04 John McCormack
2004-08 Jim McInally
2008-09 David Irons
2009-10 James Grady
2010-13 Allan Moore
2013-14 Kenny Shiels
2014-18 Jim Duffy
2018 Ray McKinnon
2018-19 Jonatan Johansson
2019- 20 David Hopkin
2020-21 Anton McElhone
2021- Gus MacPherson

MOTHERWELL
1965-73 Bobby Howitt
1973-74 Ian St John
1974-77 Willie McLean
1977-78 Roger Hynd
1978-81 Ally McLeod
1981-82 David Hay
1982-83 Jock Wallace
1983-84 Bobby Watson
1984-94 Tommy McLean
1994-98 Alex McLeish
1998 Harry Kampman
1998-2001 Billy Davies
2001-02 Eric Black
2002-06 Terry Butcher
2006-07 Maurice Malpas
2007-09 Mark McGhee
2009 Jim Gannon
2009-10 Craig Brown
2010-14 Stuart McCall
2014-15 Ian Barraclough
2015-17 Mark McGhee
2017-20 Stephen Robinson
2021- Graham Alexander

PARTICK THISTLE
1968-70 Scot Symon
1970-74 Davie McParland
1974-80 Bertie Auld
1980-84 Peter Cormack
1984-86 Benny Rooney
1986 Bertie Auld
1986-87 Derek Johnstone
1987-88 Billy Lamont
1988-89 John Lambie
1989-90 Sandy Clark
1990-95 John Lambie
1995-97 Murdo McLeod
1997-98 John McVeigh
1998-99 Tommy Bryce
1999-2003 John Lambie
2003-04 Derek Whyte / Gerry Britton
2005-07 Dick Campbell
2007-11 Ian McCall
2011-13 Jackie McNamara
2013-18 Alan Archibald
2018-19 Gary Caldwell
2019- Ian McCall

PETERHEAD
2000-03 Ian Wilson
2004-06 Iain Stewart / Paul Mathers
2006-08 Steve Paterson
2008-11 Neale Cooper
2011 John Sheran
2011- Jim McInally

QUEEN OF THE SOUTH
1970 Harold Davis
1971-73 Jim Easton
1973-74 Willie McLean
1975-78 Mike Jackson
1978 Willie Hunter
1979-80 Billy Little
1980 George Herd
1982 Harry Hood
1982-84 Drew Busby
1984-86 Nobby Clark
1986-87 Mike Jackson
1987-88 Davie Wilson
1988-89 Tom McGinn
1989-90 Billy McLaren
1990-91 Frank McGarvey
1991-92 Ally McLeod
1992-93 Derek Frye
1993-96 Billy McLaren
1996-98 Mark Shanks / Rowan Alexander
1998-99 Rowan Alexander
1999-00 George Rowe / Ken Eadie
2000-04 John Connolly
2004-05 Iain Scott
2005-07 Ian McCall
2007-10 Gordon Chisholm
2010-11 Kenny Brannigan
2011-12 Gus McPherson
2012-13 Allan Johnston
2013-14 Jim McIntyre
2014-16 James Fowler
2016 Gavin Skelton
2016-19 Gary Naysmith
2019- Allan Johnston

QUEEN'S PARK
1969-74 Tommy Duncan
1074-76 Davie McParland
1976-79 Joe Gilroy
1979-94 Eddie Hunter
1995-97 Hugh McCann
1997-98 Graeme Elder
1998-2002 John McCormack
2003-04 Kenny Brannigan
2004-08 Billy Stark
2008-13 Garner Speirs
2014-18 Gus McPherson
2018-19 Mark Roberts
2020-21 Ray McKinnon
2021- Laurie Ellis

RAITH ROVERS
1969-70 Jimmy Millar
1970-71 Bill Baxter
1971-74 George Farm
1974-75 Bert Paton
1975-78 Andy Matthew
1978-79 Willie McLean
1979-83 Gordon Wallace
1983-86 Bobby Wilson
1986-90 Frank Connor
1990-96 Jimmy Nicholl
1996 Jimmy Thomson
1996 Tommy McLean
1996-97 Iain Munro
1997-99 Jimmy Nicholl
1999 John McVeigh
1999-2001 Peter Hetherston
2001-02 Jocky Scott
2002-04 Antonio Calderon
2004 Claude Anelka
2004-06 Gordon Dalziel
2006 Craig Levein
2006-12 John McGlynn
2012-15 Grant Murray
2015-16 Ray McKinnon
2016-17 Gary Locke
2017 John Hughes
2017-18 Barry Smith
2018- John McGlynn

RANGERS
1969-72 Willie Waddell
1972-78 Jock Wallace
1978-83 John Greig
1983-86 Jock Wallace
1986-91 Graeme Souness
1991-98 Walter Smith
1998-2001 Dick Advocaat
2001-06 Alex McLeish
2006-07 Paul Le Guen
2007-11 Walter Smith

2011-14 Ally McCoist
2014-15 Kenny McDowall
2015 Stuart McCall
2015-17 Mark Warburton
2017 Pedro Caixinha
2017-18 Graham Murty
2018- Steven Gerrard

ROSS COUNTY
1994-96 Bobby Wilson
1996-2002 Neale Cooper
2002-2005 Alex Smith
2005 John Robertson
2005-06 Gardner Speirs
2006-07 Scott Leitch
2007 Dick Campbell
2007-10 Derek Adams
2010-11 Willie McStay
2011 Jimmy Calderwood
2011-14 Derek Adams
2014-17 Jim McIntyre
2017-18 Owen Coyle
2018-20 Stuart Kettlewell / Steven Ferguson
2020 Stuart Kettlewell
2020-21 John Hughes
2021- Malky Mackay

ST JOHNSTONE
1967-73 Willie Ormond
1973-76 Jackie Stewart
1976-78 Jim Storrie
1978-80 Alex Stuart
1980-85 Alex Rennie
1985-87 Ian Gibson
1987-92 Alex Totten
1992-93 John McClelland
1993-98 Paul Sturrock
1998-2001 Sandy Clark
2001-04 Billy Stark
2004-05 John Connolly
2005-07 Owen Coyle
2007-11 Derek McInnes
2011-13 Steve Lomas
2013-20 Tommy Wright
2020- Callum Davidson

ST MIRREN
1966-70 Alex Wright
1970-72 Wilson Humphries
1972-73 Tommy Bryceland
1973-74 Willie Cunningham
1974-78 Alex Ferguson
1978-80 Jim Clunie
1980-83 Ricky McFarlane
1983-86 Alex Miller
1986-88 Alex Smith
1988-91 Tony Fitzpatrick
1991-92 David Hay
1992-96 Jimmy Bone
1996 Iain Munro
1996-98 Tony Fitzpatrick
1998-2002 Tom Hendrie
2002-03 John Coughlin
2003-10 Gus McPherson
2010-14 Danny Lennon
2014 Tommy Craig
2014-15 Gary Teale
2015 Ian Murray
2015-16 Alex Rae
2016-18 Jack Ross
2018 Alan Stubbs
2018-19 Oran Kearney
2019- Jim Goodwin

STENHOUSEMUIR
1969-74 Alex Smith
1974-81 Harry Glasgow
1981-84 Jim Black
1984-86 Archie Rose
1987 Billy Henderson
1987-89 Alex Rennie
1989-91 Jim Meakin
1991-92 Dennis Lawson
1992-99 Terry Christie
1999-00 Graeme Armstrong
2000-1 Brian Fairley
2001-02 Jimmy Bone
2002-04 John McVeigh
2004-05 Tony Smith / Des McKeown
2005-06 Des McKeown
2006-07 Campbell Money
2007-10 John Coughlin
2010-12 Davie Irons
2012-14 Martyn Corrigan
2014-15 Scott Booth
2015-18 Brown Ferguson
2018-19 Colin McMenamin
2019-21 Davie Irons
2021- Stephen Swift

STIRLING ALBION
1969-70 Frank Joyner
1971-73 Bob Shankly
1973-74 Frank Beattie
1974-86 Alex Smith
1986-88 George Peebles
1988 Jim Fleeting
1988-94 John Brogan
1994-98 Kevin Drinkell
1998-2000 John Philliben
2000-02 Raymond Stewart
2002-2010 Allan Moore
2010-11 John O'Neill
2011 Jocky Scott
2011-14 Greig McDonald
2014-16 Stuart McLaren
2016-18 Dave MacKay
2018- Kevin Rutkiewicz

STRANRAER
1970-71 Dan McLindon
1973-75 Eric Caldow
1975-76 John Hughes
1980-81 Neil Hood
1981 Gordon Hamilton
1982-85 Davie Sneddon
1986 John Clark
1986-87 Robert Clark
1897-96 Alex McAnespie
1996-99 Campbell Money
1999-03 Billy McLaren
2003-06 Neil Watt
2006-08 Gerry Britton
2008-09 Derek Ferguson
2009-12 Keith Knox
2012-15 Stephen Aitken
2015-17 Brian Reid
2017-21 Stephen Farrell
2021- Jamie Hamill

The Managers—as at 1/8/21, by date of appointment

	Date	Manager	Club
1	07/10/2011	Jim McInally	Peterhead
2	10/06/2015	Dick Campbell	Arbroath
3	08/06/2016	Stewart Petrie	Montrose
4	08/05/2017	Peter Murphy	Annan Athletic
5	20/05/2017	Darren Young	East Fife
6	12/10/2017	Gavin Price	Elgin City
7	12/11/2017	Danny Lennon	Clyde
8	13/11/2017	Gary Bollan	Cowdenbeath
9	04/05/2018	Steven Gerrard	Rangers
10	25/09/2018	John McGlynn	Raith Rovers
11	19/10/2018	Ian Murray	Airdrieonians
12	23/10/2018	Kevin Rutkiewicz	Stirling Albion
13	31/01/2019	Brian Rice	Hamilton Accies
14	06/05/2019	Alan Johnston	Queen of the South
15	31/05/2019	James McPake	Dundee
16	28/06/2019	Jim Goodwin	St Mirren
17	03/07/2019	Paul Hartley	Cove Rangers
18	23/09/2019	Ian McCall	Partick Thistle
19	15/11/2019	Jack Ross	Hibernian
20	05/06/2020	Brian Reid	Albion Rovers
21	18/06/2020	Callum Davidson	St Johnstone
22	21/06/2020	Robbie Neilson	Hearts
23	21/12/2020	David Martindale	Livingston
24	07/01/2021	Graham Alexander	Motherwell
25	08/02/2021	Tommy Wright	Kilmarnock
26	09/03/2021	Gary Naysmith	Edinburgh City
27	10/03/2021	Gus MacPherson	Morton
28	11/03/2021	David Hopkin	Ayr United
29	23/03/2021	Stephen Glass	Aberdeen
30	27/04/2021	Stephen Swift	Stenhousemuir
31	05/05/2021	Gary Irvine	Forfar Athletic
32	21/05/2021	Laurie Ellis	Queen's Park
33	27/05/2021	Barry Ferguson	Alloa Athletic
34	28/05/2021	Paul Sheerin	Falkirk
35	26/05/2021	Malky Mackay	Ross County
36	29/05/2021	Stephen Farrell	Dumbarton
37	28/05/1991	Peter Grant	Dunfermline Athletic
38	28/05/2021	Kevin Thomson	Kelty Hearts
39	01/06/2021	Billy Dodds	Inverness CT
40	04/06/2021	Jamie Hamill	Stranraer
41	07/06/2021	Tom Courts	Dundee United
42	10/06/2021	Ange Postecoglou	Celtic

Scottish Cup 2019/20

Attendances are those submitted by home clubs to the SFA for official purposes

Round	Date	Home	Away	F	A	Att
P1	10/08/2019	Dundonald Bluebell	Auchinleck Talbot	2	2	490
P1	10/08/2019	Hill of Beath Hawthorn	Blackburn United	6	0	104
P1	10/08/2019	Lochee United	Burntisland Shipyard	7	0	77
P1	10/08/2019	Banks o' Dee	Glasgow University	5	0	50
P1	10/08/2019	Easthouses Lily	Penicuik Athletic	1	6	141
P1	10/08/2019	Coldstream	Jeanfield Swifts	1	9	136
P1	10/08/2019	Hawick Royal Albert Utd	Threave Rovers	1	6	101
P1	10/08/2019	Camelon	Newton Stewart	4	0	213
P1	10/08/2019	Linlithgow Rose	Preston Athletic	2	1	253
P1	10/08/2019	St Cuthbert Wanderers	Girvan	1	7	66
P1	10/08/2019	Broxburn Athletic	Tynecastle	2	0	177
P1	17/08/2019	Lothian Thistle HV at Broxburn	Wigtown & Bladnoch	5	0	29
P1	18/08/2019	Colville Park at Benburb	Whitehill Welfare	0	4	59
P1R	17/08/2019	Auchinleck Talbot	Dundonald Bluebell	6	1	464
P2	07/09/2019	Jeanfield Swifts	Linlithgow Rose	2	5	340
P2	31/08/2019	Girvan	Broxburn Athletic	0	1	116
P2	31/08/2019	Banks O' Dee	Golspie Sutherland	2	0	28
P2	31/08/2019	Threave Rovers	Hill of Beath Hawthorn	0	2	83
P2	31/08/2019	Lochee United	Lothian Thistle HV	5	2	40
P2	31/08/2019	Whitehill Welfare	Penicuik Athletic	0	1	226
P2	31/08/2019	Camelon	Auchinleck Talbot	0	2	625
1	21/09/2019	Gretna	Hill of Beath Hawthorn	1	0	127
1	20/09/2019	Kelty Hearts	Auchinleck Talbot	0	3	1633
1	21/09/2019	Edinburgh University	Lochee United	1	3	168
1	21/09/2019	Forres Mechanics	Banks o' Dee	1	4	188
1	21/09/2019	Cumbernauld Colts	Penicuik Athletic	1	5	245
1	21/09/2019	Linlithgow Rose	Huntly	1	0	424
1	21/09/2019	Broxburn Athletic	East Stirlingshire	3	2	509
1	21/09/2019	Caledonian Braves	Rothes	3	4	99
1	21/09/2019	Spartans	Deveronvale	1	1	269
1	21/09/2019	Buckie Thistle	Civil Service Strollers	4	1	273
1	21/09/2019	Keith	Stirling University	2	3	117
1	21/09/2019	Strathspey Thistle	Lossiemouth	2	1	74
1	21/09/2019	Nairn County	Clachnacuddin	0	0	273
1	21/09/2019	Fort William	Vale of Leithen	5	0	263
1	21/09/2019	Fraserburgh	Bonnyrigg Rose	0	1	457
1	21/09/2019	Inverurie Loco Works	Wick Academy	3	2	310
1	21/09/2019	Dalbeattie Star	Gala Fairydean Rovers	1	3	119
1	21/09/2019	Turriff United	Formartine United	1	5	223
1R	28/09/2019	Clachnacuddin	Nairn County	2	1	270
1R	30/09/2019	Deveronvale	Spartans	1	2	209
2	18/10/2019	Edinburgh City	Banks o' Dee	3	1	166
2	18/10/2019	Bonnyrigg Rose	Buckie Thistle	2	0	1693
2	26/10/2019	Penicuik Athletic	Stenhousemuir	3	0	1249
2	19/10/2019	Cowdenbeath	Broxburn Athletic	1	1	767
2	19/10/2019	Annan Athletic	Brechin City	2	2	274
2	19/10/2019	Stirling Albion	Strathspey Thistle	2	0	411
2	19/10/2019	Elgin City	Berwick Rangers	3	1	554
2	19/10/2019	Spartans	Queen's Park	0	2	411
2	19/10/2019	Auchinleck Talbot	Cove Rangers	1	0	974
2	19/10/2019	Albion Rovers	Fort William	1	1	397
2	19/10/2019	East Kilbride	Gretna	3	1	237
2	19/10/2019	Clachnacuddin	Brora Rangers	0	7	306
2	19/10/2019	Rothes	Inverurie Loco Works	1	3	239
2	19/10/2019	Formartine United	Gala Fairydean Rovers	2	2	238
2	19/10/2019	Lochee United	BSC Glasgow	1	1	270
2	20/10/2019	Stirling University	Linlithgow Rose	0	2	455
2R	26/10/2019	Broxburn Athletic	Cowdenbeath	3	0	1049
2R	26/10/2019	Brechin City	Annan Athletic	0	2	258
2R	26/10/2019	Fort William	Albion Rovers	0	5	610
2R	26/10/2019	Gala Fairydean Rovers	Formartine United	1	2	167
2R	27/10/2019	BSC Glasgow	Lochee United	2	1	203
3	22/11/2019	Linlithgow Rose	Falkirk	1	4	1720
3	23/11/2019	Auchinleck Talbot	Arbroath	1	1	1071
3	23/11/2019	Stranraer	Dunfermline Athletic	1	0	431
3	23/11/2019	Dumbarton	Forfar Athletic	3	1	424
3	23/11/2019	Elgin City	Alloa Athletic	1	3	668
3	23/11/2019	Morton	Brora Rangers	1	1	925
3	23/11/2019	Formartine United	East Kilbride	0	4	218
3	23/11/2019	Partick Thistle	Penicuik Athletic	1	0	3165
3	23/11/2019	Albion Rovers	Airdrieonians	1	4	1127
3	23/11/2019	Queen of the South	Queen's Park	1	2	1066
3	23/11/2019	Edinburgh City	Annan Athletic	4	3	176
3	23/11/2019	Stirling Albion	Clyde	0	2	820
3	23/11/2019	East Fife	BSC Glasgow	3	4	484
3	23/11/2019	Inverurie Loco Works	Broxburn Athletic	0	1	1129
3	23/11/2019	Bonnyrigg Rose	Montrose	2	1	2017
3	23/11/2019	Raith Rovers	Peterhead	1	0	1306
3R	27/11/2019	Arbroath	Auchinleck Talbot	3	0	1022
3R	03/12/2019	Brora Rangers	Morton	1	3	497
4	17/01/2020	Rangers	Stranraer	2	0	38560
4	18/01/2020	Aberdeen	Dumbarton	1	0	10010
4	18/01/2020	Alloa Athletic	Inverness CT	2	3	590
4	18/01/2020	Arbroath	Falkirk	0	0	1733
4	18/01/2020	Ayr United	Ross County	1	0	1538
4	18/01/2020	Bonnyrigg Rose	Clyde	0	1	2213
4	18/01/2020	East Kilbride	BSC Glasgow	1	3	671
4	18/01/2020	Hamilton Accies	Edinburgh City	5	0	1040
4	18/01/2020	Hearts	Airdrieonians	5	0	14777
4	18/01/2020	Kilmarnock	Queen's Park	6	0	4198
4	18/01/2020	Livingston	Raith Rovers	3	1	1725
4	18/01/2020	St Johnstone	Morton	3	0	2397
4	18/01/2020	St Mirren	Broxburn Athletic	3	0	4327
4	18/01/2020	Partick Thistle	Celtic	1	2	9542
4	18/01/2020	Dundee	Motherwell	0	3	2407
4	18/01/2020	Dundee United	Hibernian	2	2	9400
4R	28/01/2020	Falkirk	Arbroath	2	0	2704
4R	28/01/2020	Hibernian	Dundee United	4	2	10451
5	08/02/2020	Hamilton Accies	Rangers	1	4	4050
5	08/02/2020	Ayr United	St Johnstone	1	2	2625
5	08/02/2020	St Mirren	Motherwell	1	1	4323
5	08/02/2020	Aberdeen	Kilmarnock	0	0	9430
5	08/02/2020	Falkirk	Hearts	0	1	5976
5	08/02/2020	Inverness CT	Livingston	1	0	1512
5	09/02/2020	BSC Glasgow	Hibernian	1	4	2120
5	09/02/2020	Clyde	Celtic	0	3	7647
5R	18/02/2020	Motherwell	St Mirren	4	4 AET, 2-3p	4534
5R	19/02/2020	Kilmarnock	Aberdeen	3	4 AET, 2-3p	5658
6	28/02/2020	Hibernian	Inverness CT	5	2	9937
6	29/02/2020	Hearts	Rangers	1	0	11428
6	29/02/2020	St Mirren	Aberdeen	0	2	4479
6	01/03/2020	St Johnstone	Celtic	0	1	8181

Competition suspended , completed 2020/1

Round	Date	Home	Away	F	A	Att
SF	31/10/2020	Hearts	Hibernian	2	1 AET	BCD
SF	01/11/2020	Celtic	Aberdeen	2	0	BCD
	(both games at Hampden)					
F	20/12/2020	Hearts	Celtic	3	3 AET, 3-4p	BCD
	(at Hampden)					

Scottish Cup 2020/21

Round	Date	Home	Away	F	A	Pens etc	Att
P1	28/11/20	Lothian Thistle HV	St Cuthbert Wanderers	2	1	AET	BCD
P1	28/11/20	Penicuik Athletic	Musselburgh Athletic	2	3	AET	BCD
P2	12/12/20	Banks o' Dee	Vale of Leithen	6	1		BCD
P2	12/12/20	Blackburn United	Civil Service Strollers	1	1	AET, 2-4p	BCD
P2	12/12/20	BSC Glasgow	Haddington Athletic	2	3		BCD
P2	12/12/20	Clachnacuddin	Caledonian Braves	1	2		
P2	12/12/20	Deveronvale	Camelon	1	4		BCD
P2	12/12/20	Dundonald Bluebell (at Raith Rovers)	Easthouses Lily MW	4	2		BCD
P2	12/12/20	Dunipace	Berwick Rangers	1	3		BCD
P2	12/12/20	East Stirlingshire	Inverurie Locos	5	0		BCD
P2	12/12/20	Edinburgh University	Tranent	1	2		BCD
P2	12/12/20	Gala Fairydean Rovers	Wigtown & Bladnoch	6	0		BCD
P2	12/12/20	Hill of Beath Hawthorn	Whitehill Welfare	2	1		BCD
P2	12/12/20	Huntly	Dalbeattie Star	3	0		BCD
P2	12/12/20	Jeanfield Swifts	Stirling University	3	1		BCD
P2	12/12/20	Keith	Fort William	5	1		75
P2	12/12/20	Lothian Thistle HV (at Livingston)	Lossiemouth	4	4	AET, 4-2p	BCD
P2	12/12/20	Nairn County	Threave Rovers	4	0		250
P2	12/12/20	Newton Stewart	Broxburn Athloetic	0	3		BCD
P2	12/12/20	Newtongrange Star	Rothes	0	4		BCD
P2	12/12/20	Spartans	East Kilbride	2	1		BCD
P2	12/12/20	Strathspey Thistle	Buckie Thistle	0	4		60
P2	12/12/20	Tynecastle	Cumbernauld Colts	2	3		BCD
P2	13/12/20	Glasgow University (at Airdrie)	Linlithgow Rose	1	2		BCD
P2	21/12/20	Wick Academy	Musselburgh Athletic	3	1	AET	250
P2	16/12/20	Preston Athletic	Hawick RAU	3	2		BCD
P2	16/12/20	Coldstream	Bo'ness United	0	2		BCD
P2	21/12/20	Formartine United (at Keith)	Turriff United	2	1		BCD
1	26/12/20	Albion Rovers	Buckie Thistle	0	3		BCD
1	26/12/20	Berwick Rangers	Stirling Albion	0	3		BCD
1	1/1/21	Bonnyrigg Rose	Bo'ness United	5	2		BCD
1	26/12/20	Brechin City	Linlithgow Rose	2	3		BCD
1	26/12/20	Camelon	Brora Rangers	0	0	ABD	BCD
1	26/12/20	Cowdenbeath	Wick Academy	2	0		BCD
1	28/12/20	Dundonald Bluebell (at Kelty)	Queen's Park	1	3	AET	BCD
1	26/12/20	Edinburgh City	Caledonian Braves	3	1		BCD
1	26/12/20	Elgin City	Civil Service Strollers	4	0		BCD
1	26/12/20	Gala Fairydean Rovers	Annan Athletic	1	2		BCD
1	26/12/20	Haddington Athletic	Formartine United	1	2		BCD
1	6/1/21	Huntly	Cumbernauld Colts	3	1		BCD
1	26/12/20	Keith	Hill of Beath Hawthorn	4	2	AET	BCD
1	26/12/20	Kelty Hearts	Jeanfield Swifts	2	1		BCD
1	26/12/20	Lothian Thistle HV (at Livingston)	Banks o' Dee	0	3		BCD
1	26/12/20	Nairn County	Broxburn Athletic	0	0	AET, 4-3p	BCD
1	26/12/20	Rothes	Fraserburgh	1	3		BCD
1	26/12/20	Stenhousemuir	Preston Athletic	4	1		BCD
1	26/12/20	Stranraer	Spartans	5	0		BCD
1	26/12/20	Tranent	East Stirlingshire	4	1		BCD
1R	11/1/21	Camelon (at Dunipace)	Brora Rangers	1	2		BCD
2	8/1/21	Queen's Park	Queen of the South	0	3		BCD
2	9/1/21	Forfar Athletic	Linlithgow Rose	4	1	AET	BCD
2	9/1/21	East Fife	Tranent	5	1		BCD
2	9/1/21	Alloa Athletic	Cove Rangers	2	3		BCD
2	9/1/21	Fraserburgh	Banks o' Dee	2	1		BCD
2	9/1/21	Kelty Hearts (at Raith Rovers)	Stranraer	2	3		BCD
2	9/1/21	Dundee	Bonnyrigg Rose	3	2	AET	BCD
2	10/1/21	Airdrieonians	Edinburgh City	0	1		BCD
2	23/3/21	Nairn County	Montrose	1	7		BCD
2	23/3/21	Keith	Clyde	0	2		BCD
2	23/3/21	Arbroath	Falkirk	1	2		BCD
2	23/3/21	Elgin City	Ayr United	0	4		BCD
2	23/3/21	Formartine United	Annan Athletic	1	1	AET, 3-1p	BCD
2	23/3/21	Morton	Dunfermline Athletic	0	0	AET, 6-5p	BCD
2	23/3/21	Dumbarton	Huntly	4	0		BCD
2	23/3/21	Peterhead	Stenhousemuir	0	1		BCD
2	23/3/21	Stirling Albion	Raith Rovers	0	2		BCD
2	23/3/21	Partick Thistle	Cowdenbeath	3	0		BCD
2	23/3/21	Brora Rangers	Hearts	2	1		BCD
2	23/3/21	Buckie Thistle	Inverness CT	2	3		BCD
3	2/4/21	Ross County	Inverness CT	1	3		BCD
3	3/4/21	Dumbarton	Aberdeen	0	1		BCD
3	3/4/21	Forfar Athletic	Edinburgh City	2	2	AET, 5-3p	BCD
3	3/4/21	Dundee United	Partick Thistle	2	1		BCD
3	3/4/21	Livingston	Raith Rovers	2	1	AET	BCD
3	3/4/21	Brora Rangers	Stranraer	1	3	AET	BCD
3	3/4/21	Stenhousemuir	Kilmarnock	0	4		BCD
3	3/4/21	East Fife	Morton	1	2	AET	BCD
3	3/4/21	Hamilton Accies	St Mirren	0	3		BCD
3	3/4/21	Dundee	St Johnstone	0	1		BCD
3	3/4/21	Ayr United	Clyde	0	1		BCD
3	3/4/21	Formartine United	Motherwell	0	5		BCD
3	3/4/21	Fraserburgh	Montrose	2	4		BCD
3	3/4/21	Celtic	Falkirk	3	0		BCD
3	4/4/21	Rangers	Cove Rangers	4	0		BCD
3	5/4/21	Queen of the South	Hibernian	1	3		BCD
4	16/4/21	St Mirren	Inverness CT	2	1		BCD
4	16/4/21	Motherwell	Morton	1	1	AET, 5-3p	BCD
4	16/4/21	Forfar Athletic	Dundee United	0	1		BCD
4	17/4/21	Kilmarnock	Montrose	3	1		BCD
4	17/4/21	Aberdeen	Livingston	2	2	AET, 5-3p	BCD
4	17/4/21	St Johnstone	Clyde	2	0		BCD
4	18/4/21	Stranraer	Hibernian	0	4		BCD
4	18/4/21	Rangers	Celtic	2	0		BCD
5	24/4/21	Hibernian	Motherwell	2	2	AET, 4-2p	BCD
5	25/4/21	Aberdeen	Dundee United	0	3		BCD
5	25/4/21	Rangers	St Johnstone	1	1	AET, 2-4p	BCD
5	26/4/21	Kilmarnock	St Mirren	3	3	AET, 4-5p	BCD
SF	8/5/21	Dundee United	Hibernian	0	2		BCD
SF	9/5/21	St Mirren (both games at Hampden)	St Johnstone	1	2		BCD
F	22/5/21	Hibernian (at Hampden)	St Johnstone	0	1		BCD

Appearances etc. for Non SPFL teams in Scottish Cup 2020/21

Appearances and scorers for SPFL clubs can be found in their relevant club section.

Qualifying Competition Round 1

Lothian Thistle v St Cuthbert Wanderers, 2-1, AET, F.T. 1-1 H.T. 0-0,
Scorers: LTHV Mbewe, Ross; STC: Own Goal
LTHV: Jamie Henderson, Dylan Moore, Michael Deland, Paul Crawford, Sean Lally, Louis Signorini (Sub Michael Mbewe), Sean Cumming (Sub David Ross), Darren Smith, Sean Wringe, Scott Donald (Sub Liam Kelly), Iain Laver (Sub Jordan Elliot). Unused subs Neil Smeaton, Adam Brogan, Thomas Penker
STC: Jake Gemmell, John Renwick, Cameron Taylor, Jack Currie, Luke McMurtrie, Ross Hunter (Sub Sam McConaghie), Elliot Harris (Sub Campbell Black), Luke Currie (Sub Zachary Hannay), Gregor Patterson, Alistair McMillan (Sub Russell Williamson), Scott Dunn. Subs Dale Milligan, Owen Hall, Kenneth Davis
Ref: Connor Ashwood

Penicuik Athletic v Musselburgh Athletic, 2-3 AET, F.T. 2-2, H.T. 1-1,
Scorers: PA: Somerville 2; MA: Moffat, King, Downie
PA: Mark Tait, Ryan Baptie, Darrell Young (Sub Daniel Edwards), Callum Connolly, Kieran Watson, Jamie Devlin, Aaron Somerville (Sub Lumbert Kataleza), Paul Tansey (Sub Nicholas Reid), Gregor Lamb (Sub Greg Page), Paul Thomson, Craig Stevenson
Subs Robert Watt, Joe Viola, Lewis Collins
MA: Ryan McGurk, Michael Moffat (Sub John Myles), Calum Donaldson, Bradley Donaldson, Liam Reid, Jordan Orru, Declan O'Kane (Sub John McManus), Bradley Whyte, Darren Downie (Sub Lewis White), Mathu King (Sub Conor Thomson), Nathan Evans. Subs Michael Robinson, Josh Jeffries, Dean Ballantyne
Ref: Chris Gentles

Qualifying Competition Round 2

Wick Academy v Musselburgh Athletic, 3-1AET, H.T. 1-0, F.T. 1-1
Scorers: WA: Gunn 2, M Macadie; MA: King
WA: Graeme Williamson, Alan Hughes (Sub Danny Mackay), Ross Allan, Alan Farquhar, Ryan Campbell, Jack Henry, Richard Macadie (Sub Ben Sinclair), Sean Campbell, Craig Gunn, David Allan (Sub Mark Macadie), Gordon McNab (Sub Brandon Sinclair). Subs not used: Gary Manson
MA: Ryan McGurk, Callum Donaldson, Jordan Orru, John McManus, Michael Moffat (Sub Ethan Wynne), Conor Thomson, Mathu King, Lloyd Fiddler (Sub Scott McNaughton), Bradley Donaldson, Dean Ballantyne (Sub Ross McRae), Darren Downie.
Ref: Lee Robertson

Formartine United v Turriff United, 2-1, H.T. 2-0
Scorers FU: Smith, McKeown; TU: Ward
FU: Kevin Main, Jonathan Crawford, Stuart Smith, Stuart Anderson, Craig McKeown, Darryn Kelly, Graeme Rodger, Kieran Lawrence (Sub Conor Gethins), Garry Wood, Jonathan Smith (Sub Aaron Norris), Daniel Park. Unused subs: Cole Anderson, Michael Clark, Andrew Greig, Scott Lisle, Ewan MacDonald
TU: Fraser Hobday, Conor Power, Murray Esson (Sub Adam Cross), Callan Gray, Etan Smith, Luke Turner, Dylan Stuart (Sub Murray Cormack), Tyler Mykyta (Formerly Alexander), Robert Ward, Matthew McDonald (Sub Rory brown), Luke Kinsella. Unused subs Kyle Buxton, Lewis Ingram, Keir Smith, Tim Findlay
Ref: Dan McFarlane

Preston Athletic v Hawick Royal Albert United, 3-2, H.T. 0-1
Scorers: PA: Murray, Jack, Williams; HRAU Gillie, Steele
PA: David Livie, Kai Austin, Craig Innes, Matthew O'Connor, Rory Young, Dale Pennycuick, Kieran Jack, Ben Bathgate (Sub Ethan Williams), Jonathon Edmond, Joe Murray (Sub Jack Jardine), Marc Molloy (Sub Mikey Hamilton). Unused subs Jamie Chapman, Steven McCole, Nathan Stokes, Brandon Bain
HRAU: Sam Scott, Kevin Strathdee, John Shankie, David Strathdee, Daniel Chandler, Ashley Lanford, Greg Ford, Lewis Swaney, Nathan Gillie (Sub Calum Hope, Sub Ross Scott), Jordan Steele, Jordan Yardley. Unused subs: Adamo Antonnici, Ryan Shepherd, Sam Burton, Dean Fry, Steven King
Ref: Chris McNab

Coldstream v Bo'ness United, 0-2, H.T.0-1
Scorers: BU: Locke, Stevenson
C: Elliot Turnbull, Max Fox, Ross Straughan, Shane Bonnington, Greg McCrudden, Gary Windram, Benjamin Wright, Kieran Lee, Matt Corfield (Sub Bailey Paterson), Jonathan Simpson, Kristian Lee Dixon (Sub Cameron Beasley). Unused subs: Evan Smith, Tommy Malcolm, Thomas Hume, Darren McBay
BU: Andrew Murphy, Bryan Wharton, Chris Donnelly (Sub Stuart McFarlane), Michael Gemmell, Nicholas Locke, Kyle Bell, Tom Grant, Ross Campbell, Ryan Stevenson, Daniel McKenzie, Kieran Anderson. Unused subs: Zander Miller, Ryan Adamson
Ref: Jonathan Gall

Glasgow University v Linlithgow Rose, 1-2, H.T. 1-0
Scorers: GU: Baxter; LR: Coyle 2
GU: Ben Fulton, Keelan Adams, Robbie Smith, Scott Granger, Colin Granger, Lewis Gourlay, Jonathan Baxter (Sub Robbie Stirling), Calum Davidson, Donald Thomson, John Mackinnon (Sub Calum Strang), Lewis Dibble (Sub Mackenzie) Unused subs: Anthony Pilkington, Adam Duffy, Gregor Sandford, Zachary Lubin
LR: Brian Schwake, Scott Stevenson, Jay Sandison (Sub Tommy Coyne), Gary Thom, David Brownlie (Sub Daniel Nimmo), Aiden Wilson, Owen Ronald, Ruari MacLennan, Kyle Wilson, Dean Cairns, Arnault Bembo (Sub Daryl Meikle). Unused subs: Myles Hogarth, Colin Strickland, Willis Hare, Sean Slaven
Ref: Alastair Grieve

Jeanfield Swifts 3 University of Stirling 1, H.T. 3-0
Scorers JS: Whitehead, Scott, Reid; UOS: Brown
JS: Mark Mitchell, Jamie Reid, Aaron Whitehead, Jake Dolzanski, Keiran Stewart, Connor McLaren (Sub Jamie McKenzie), Fraser Smith, Chris Mcleish (Sub Chris Dodd), Paul Simpson, Gary Fergus (Sub Mark Smith), Christopher Scott. Unused subs: Shaun Struthers, Ewan Loudon, Sam Townsley, Regan McLaren
UOS: Ben Fry, Matthew Burrows, Ben Quigley, Conor Doan, Callum Downie (Sub Marcus Lavery), James Berry, Craig Brown, Calum Heath, Jamie Penker (Sub Euan Baird), Jason Jarvis, Robbie McGale (Sub Kieran Hall) Unused subs: Louis Kennedy, Callum Bremner, Ben Davidson, Joel Taylor
Ref: Gary Hanvidge

Dundonald Bluebell 4 Easthouses Lily 2, H.T. 2-0
Scorers DB: Wedderburn, Durie, Cargill, McKenzie; EL: Hunter, McDermott
DB: Darren Sommerville, Scott Durie, Aiden Hendry, Colin Wilson, Craig Wedderburn, Lewis McKenzie (Sub Liam Craig), Barry Sibanda (Sub Jed Crowe), Stuart Cargill, Derek Wallace, Chris Gay, Kieran Dall (Sub Callum Strang). Subs not used: Jason McLaren, Darren Gribbin
EL: Liam Amos, Shaun Murray, Mark Brown, Ryan McQueenie, Grant Gavin, Michael Linton (Sub Paul McDermott), Jason Young (Sub Jack Steven), Neil Janczyk, Alexander Elliot, Michael Hunter, Lewis Russell (Sub Cameron McBeth). Unused subs: James Guy, Blair Short, Jordan Dunsmore
Ref: Andrew Bryson

Hill of Beath Hawthorn 2 Whitehill Welfare 1, H.T. 2-1

Scorers HOB: Connelly, Mitchell; WW: Hornig
HOB: Stuart Hall, Russell Grierson, Lyle Kellichan, Kevin Conners (Sub Rory Harrower), Bradley Grieve, Shaun Leishman, Calum Adamson (Sub Joe Kinninmonth), Jake Mitchell, Daniel Watt, Joe Kirby (Sub Mark Wilkie), Ryan Connelly. Unused subs: Rory Marshall, Jason Finlay, Brandon Luke, Robert McFarlane
WW: Ross Gilpin, Chris Cairney, Kevin-Lee Keane, Jordan Caddow, Matthew McCormack, Dean Cunningham, Michael Hornig (Sub Scott Millar), Murray Hand (Sub Finlay Connor), Wayne McIntosh, Connor Spowart, Robert McKenzie. Subs not used: Tyler O'Neill, Jack Murray, Louis Maguire, Ross Coats
Ref: Keiran Trayner

BSC Glasgow v Haddington Athletic, 2-3, H.T. 1-0
Scorers BSC: Geggan, Hughes; HA: Harris, Lyon og, Auriemma
BSC: David Wilson, Ross Lyon (Sub Jamie McCormack), James Mills, Declan Fitzpatrick (Sub Ross McMillan), Craig McCracken, Andy Geggan, Jamie Hamilton, Declan Hughes, Michael Anderson (Sub Ryan Tierney), Darren Christie, Jamie Glasgow. Unused subs: Alfie Agyeman, Ross Lindsay, Lewis Bell, Stephen Barr
HA: Dale Cornet, Ross King, Guy McGarry, Aaron Congalton, Seamus Russell (Sub Robbie King), Gordon Harris, Ryan Hutchison (Sub Alasdair Simpson), Joe Hamill, Anes Subasic (Sub Keith Lough), Gabriele Auriemma, Shaun Hall. Unused subs: Andrew McNeill, Jack Neilson, Stewart O'Neil, Robbie Stirling
Ref: Calum Haswell

Banks o' Dee v Vale of Leithen, 6-1, H.T. 2-0
Scorers: Henderson, H MacLeod 2, L MacLeod 2, Gilmour; VOL: Robertson
BOD: Lee Sweeney, Kacper Lewecki (Sub Mark Hamilton), Greg Alexander, Neale Allan, Matthew Robertson, Stuart Duff, Lachie MacLeod, Mark Gilmour, Jack Henderson, Michael Philipson (Sub Richard Binnie), Hamish MacLeod (Sub Robert Armstrong). Unused subs: Craig Duguid, Dean Lawrie, Vitali Sahhalevlts
VOL: Ben McGinley, Andrew Martin (Sub Robbie Neave), James Frain, Martin Brogan, Brad Rixon (Sub Stan Swain), Ger Rossi, Jonny Grotlin, Chris Anderson, Levi Kinchant (Sub Arran Laidlaw), Ryan Higgins, Michael Robertson. Subs not used Jack Temple, Nicholas Weir, Graeme Campbell, David McGinley
Ref: Ryan Lee

Blackburn United v Civil Service Strollers, 1-1, H.T. 1-0, F.T. 1-1, Pens 2-4
Scorers BU: Redfern; CSS: Moffat
BU: Gavin King, Richard Hutton, Martin Lawrie, John Drummond, James Mildren, Stuart MacLeod (Sub Jordan Devine), Daniel Campbell (Sub David Howe), Marc Smith (Sub Dominic Kane), Laurie Devine, Brian Ross, Marley Redfern. Unused subs: Matthew Kinross, Justin Watson, John Queen, Craig Saunders
CSS: Lewis Budinauckas, Kyle Fee, Euan Bauld, Jonathan Moffat (Sub Ross Guthrie), Matthew Cunningham (Sub David Churchill), Mark McConnell, Alieu Faye, Jordan Hopkinson (Sub Connor Young), Matthew Shaw (Sub Andrew Johnston), Craig Newall, Domenico Gibson. Subs not used: Ross Young, Lewis Duffy, Fraser Napier
Ref: Steven MacDonald

Clachnacuddin v Caledonian Braves, 1-2, H.T. 0-1
Scorers Clach: Callum; CB: Forrester, McNeil
C: David Aitchison, Ryan MacKintosh, Douglas Bruce (Sub Blair Lawrie), Michael Finnis, Eachainn Miller, Shaun Sutherland, Martin Callum, James Anderson (Sub James Fraser), Allan McPhee, Ross Logan, Connor Bunce (Sub Scott Morrison) Unused subs: Martin Laing, James McLaren, Stephen Kelly, Daniel Rae
CB: Kieran Hughes, John Guthrie, Jamie Walker, Andrew Dowie, Scott Forrester, Gavin Lachlan, Derek Esplin, David Sinclair, Ross McNeil, Neil McLaughlin (Sub Jack Smith), Blair Docherty. Subs not used Yohann Chardon, Jack McDowall, Dom Slattery, Corey Pearson, Jamie Watson, David Winters
Ref: Craig Wilson

Deveronvale v Camelon, 1-4, H.T. 0-2
Scorers D: G Noble; C: McMullan 2, Stowe, Docherty
D: Gavin Still, Kyle Gauld (Sub Scott Dunn), Harry Noble, Ross Aitken, Aaron Hamilton, Ryan Farquhar, Dane Ballard, Kevin Adams, Greg Buchan (Sub Grant Noble), Max Stewart (Sub Robert Allan), Courtney Cooper. Subs not used: Robert Scott, Ben Allan, Sam Robertson, James Blanchard
C: Scott Law, Greg MacPherson, Keir MacAulay, Greg Skinner, Connor McMullan (Sub Mitchell McDonald), Mark Stowe (Sub Andrew Kay), Conor McKenzie, Ryan Kane, David Morrison, Alan Docherty, Ross Allum. Subs not used Jack Sharples, Calum Gray
Ref: Colin Whyte

Dunipace v Berwick Rangers, 1-3, H.T. 1-1
Scorers D: Davidson; BR: Nelson, Waugh, Allan
D: David Kane, Liam McCrory, Jeff Fergus, Danny Ashe, Morgan Galloway, Gary Wright, Liam Craig, Paul Nash, Sam Colley (Sub Alan McFadden), Martine France (Sub Aidan Stevenson), Lee Davidson. Subs not used: Chris Zok, Keir Stevenson, Wilson Romanis, Ryan Shanks, Jordan Livingstone
BR: Dougie Horne, John Ward, David Ferguson, Ryan Finnie (Sub Kevin Waugh), Jack Wright (Sub Jordan Sinclair), Calum Smith (Sub Mackenzie Lawler), Lewis Allan, Alistair Forster, Kieran Somerville, Euan Smith, Grant Nelson. Subs not used: Andrew McNeil, Jordan Purves, Daniel Purves, Darren Smith
Ref: John Stewart

East Stirlingshire v Inverurie Loco Works, 5-0, H.T. 1-0
Scorers ES: Dishington, Brown 2, Low, Tapping
ES: Ross Connelly, Martin Orr, Adam Murray, Jordan Tapping (Sub Greg McColm), Eddie Malone, Kieran Gibbons, Jamie Dishington, Reis Peggie (Sub Andrew Shirra), Sean Brown, Nicky Low, Andy Rodgers (Sub Dean Watson) Subs not used: Craig Henderson, Robbie Young, Ronan Kearney, Iain Ure
IL: Morgan Cook, Thomas Reid, Greg Mitchell, Sam Burnett (Sub Calum Dingwall), Mark Souter, Ryan Broadhurst, Neil McLean, Neil Gauld (Sub Kyle Gordon), Kieran Shanks, Hamish Ritchie, Nathan Meres. Subs not used Andrew Hunter, Jordan Cooper, Craig Gill, John Farquhar
Ref: Liam Duncan

Edinburgh University v Tranent, 1-2, H.T. 0-0
Scorers EU: Anderson; T: Ponton, Lander
EU: Nicolas Buxton, Ross McGuire, Isaac Watson, Louis Squires, Alex Hamilton, Matthew Dick, Jamie Matthews (Sub Isaac Bonisteel), Aidan Kemp (Sub Robbie Sinclair), David Maskrey (Sub Vincent Anderson), Patrick Baird, Louis Maurice. Subs not used Andrew Marshall, Calum McDonald, Conor Barnes
T: Ally Adams, Jack Chesser (Sub Adam Watson), Shaun Rutherford (Sub Arran Ponton), Dean Whitson, Euan Greig, Rickard Miller, Rhys Craigie, Ben Miller, Kayne Paterson, Sean Murphy (Sub Steven Thomson), Kyle Lander. Subs not used: Lewis Hawkins, Owen Renton, Gary Hamilton, Ian Moffat
Ref: Duncan Nicolson

Gala Fairydean Rovers v Wigtown & Bladnoch, 6-0, H.T. 3-0
Scorers GFR: Campbell 2, Galbraith, Addison, Herdman, Walsh
GFR: Fraser Morton, Lewis Grant, Calum Hall, Craig McBride, Gareth Rodger, Ben Herdman, Leeroy Makovora (Sub Marc Berry), Archue Roue, Philip Addison, Daniel Galbraith (Sub Aiden Walsh), Jacob Campbell (Sub Liam Campbell). Subs not used Ross Aitchison, Sean Ward, Jamie Shiel
W&B: Dale Leith, Liam O'Shaughnessy, William Cloy, Darrel Wilson (Sub Aaron Campbell), Scott McCulloch, James McColm, Gordon Forbes, Alistair McColm (Sub Jake Hannigan), Thomas Garrett (Sub Robert Garrett), David Nish, Mark Hoskins. Subs not used Ross Inger, Michael Dougan
Ref: Ross Hardie

Huntly v Dalbeattie Star, 3-0, H.T. 2-0
Scorers H: McGowan, McKeown 2
H: Euan Storrier, Cameron Bowden, Logan Johnstone, Glenn Murison, Ross Still, Gary McGowan, Reece McKeown (Sub Daniel Critchard), Gavin Elphinstone (Sub Alexander Thoirs), Joe Gauld, Rhys Thomas, Cai Matthew (Sub Bradley Manson) Subs not used Keith Robertshaw, Christopher Hay, Cameron Booth, Jamie Boylan
DS: Charlie Cowie, Liam Park, Greig Thorburn (Sub Aiden Kerr), Owen Bell, Liam Douglas, Jack Dickinson, Connor Graham (Sub Dean Brotherston), Steven Degnan, Ross Irving (Sub James Cowie), Lewis Sloan, Dan Orsi. Subs not used: Ryan McChesney, Connor Potts, Richard Maxwell
Ref: Iain Snedden

Keith v Fort William, 5-1, H.T. 2-1
Scorers K: Keith 2, Brownie, Watt, Duncan; FW: McConnell
K: David Dey, Stewart Hutcheon, Andrew Smith, Demilade Yunus (Sub Liam Duncan), Ryan Spink, Ryan Robertson, Craig McAskill (Sub Logan Watt), Liam Strachan, Cammy Keith (Sub Scott Gray), Michael Selfridge, James Brownie. Subs not used Callum Porteous, Andy Stewart, Kieran Yates, Greg Simpson
FW: Mayeusz Kulbacki, Iain Foggo, Gabriel Veringa, Lennon Clark, Paul Coutts (Sub Alexander White), Jamie McConnell (Sub Stephen McGhie), Kevin Mackinnon (Sub Mark McKenzie), Joe McBride, John Treasurer, Connor Moore, Aiden Taylor. Subs not used Ruaridh Munro, Ronan Cameron, Alfie Duncan, Robbie Rydings
Ref: Ross Birrell

Lothian Thistle Hutchison Vale v Lossiemouth, 4-4, H.T. 2-1, F.T. 3-3, Pens 4-2
Scorers LTHV: Cunningham, Cumming, Wringe, Mbewe; L: Sewell, Stuart, Charlesworth, MacAuley
LTHV: Jamie Henderson, Michael Deland, Sean Lally, Sandy Cunningham (Sub Scott Donald), Sean Cumming (Sub Michael Mbewe), Darren Smith, Sean Wringe, Liam Kelly (Sub Jordan Elliot), Sam Daniel, Niall Doherty (Sub Paul Crawford), Thomas Penker. Subs not used Neil Smeaton, Adam Brogan, Iain Laver
L: Logan Ross, Michael Weir, Ally Bellingham, Fergus Edwards, Thomas Palmer, Liam Archibald, James Leslie (Sub Connor McAulay), Ryan Sewell, Brodie Allan (Sub Ryan Sy=tuart), Martin Charlesworth (Sub Ross Archibald), Ross Elliot (Sub Fraser Forbes). Subs not used Stewart Black, Jack McArthur
Ref: Euan Birch

Nairn County 4 Threave Rovers 0, H.T. 2-0
Scorers NC: Dingwall, Davidson, McKenzie, Shewan
NC: Dylan MacLean, Callum McLean, Cohen Ramsay, Adam Porritt, Fraser Dingwall, Calum Howarth, Max Ewan, Tom McLennan (Sub Adam Naismith), Liam Shewan, Scott Davidson (Sub Kenneth McKenzie), Gordon McNab. Subs not used Callum Ednie, Angus Dey, Seams McConaghy, Jack McLean, Will Counsell
TR: Graham Wright, Hugh Cameron, Ewan Gourlay, Adam Uphill, Liam Patterson, Callum Williams, Ryan Coates, Philip Middlemiss (Sub Alisdair Mason), Scott Milligan (Sub Kieran McKie), Ryan Adamson (Sub Aiden McBurnie), Daniel Thom. Subs not used Daniel Carmichael, Corey Thomson, Adam Maxwell
Ref: Daniel Graves

Newton Stewart v Broxburn Athletic, 0-3, H.T. 0-1
Scorers BA: Greenhill 2, Binnie
NS: Euan Drysdale, Arran McKie, Jake Service, Jordan Magee, Fraser Anderson, Robbie Thomson, Matthew Deazeley, Marc Whyte (Sub Ross Landers), Robert Middleton (Sub Euan Sneddon), Robert Hughan, Ryan McKie (Sub Jack Marshall). Subs not used Aaron Drysdale, Euan Brown, MacCauley Rennie, Rhuri Paton
BA: Connor Wallace, Andrew Gillen (Sub Luke Murray), Ross Hutchison, Shaun Harrison, Chris Townsley, Greg Nicol, Greg Binnie (Sub Craig Turnbull), David Greenhill, Gary Brass, Cameron Ross, Liam Ireland (Sub Conor Kelly). Subs not used Jordan Wright, Andrew Grant, Jack Beesley, Shaun Donoghue
Ref: Alex Shepherd

Newtongrange Star v Rothes, 0-4, H.T. 0-2
Scorers R: Harkness, Linden, Sutherland 2
NS: Liam McCathie, Jordan Mungall, Steven Tait, Evan Glendinning, Ryan Ferguson, Ryan Porteous, Daniel McBay (Sub David Rennie), Adam Nelson, Jack Gillan (Sub Muir), Liam McIntosh (Sub Tom Davies), Craig O'Reilly. Subs not used Sean Brennan, Ross Larner, Chris Moffat, Callum Murray
R: Sean McCarthy, Alasdair Stark, Ben Johnston e, Jack Brown, Bruce Milne, Fraser Robertson, Craig Cormack, Shane Harkness (Sub Paul McLeod), Sean Linden (Sub Lewis Hyde), Alisdair Sutherland (Sub Ryan Ritchie), Ross Gunn. Subs not used Ewan Neil, Charlie Christie
Ref: Greg Soutar

Spartans v East Kilbride, 2-1, H.T. 1-1
Scorers S: McCrory-Irving, Maxwell; EK: Healy
S: Matthew Baines, Jamie Watson, Scott Maxwell, Adam Corbett, Michael Bolochoweckyj, Gregor Woods, Blair Atkinson (Sub Daniel Baur), Samuel Jones, John Grant (Sub Keir Russell), Scott McCrory-Irving, Archie Meekison (Sub Aaron Murrell) Subs not used Joe Tait, Cameron Dawson, Michael Allan, Christopher Peden
EK: Conor Brennan, Lewis Kidd (Sub Kyle Wilkie), Tom Leighton, Steven Bell, Steven Old, Kyle Hutton, Paul Woods (Sub Chris McLaughlin), Anthony Brady, Craig Malcolm, Chris Erskine, Daryl Healy (Sub Darren Lee Smith). Subs not used Richard Kirwan, Jordan Armstrong, Greig Stewart, Matthew McGinley
Ref: Paul Timmons

Strathspey Thistle v Buckie Thistle, 0-4, H.T. 0-2
Scorers BT: Fraser, McLeod, MacAskill, McCabe
ST: Michael McCallum, Andrew McLean (Sub Martin Duncan), Liam McDade, Ashley Ballam, Gabriel Hastings, James McShane (Sub Cameron Lisle), Craig McKenzie, Roderick Kennedy, Liam Taylor, Kris Duncan (Sub Joe Cuthbert), Stephen Rennie. Subs not used Adam Crichton
BT: Lee Herbert, Jack Murray, McLauchlan (Sub Callum Murray), Sam Morrison, Craig Cowie, Joe McCabe, Kevin Fraser (Sub Sam Urquhart), Kyle MacLeod, Sam Pugh, Scott Adams (Sub Hamish Munro), Andrew MacAskill. Subs not used Darren Strong, Lewis Mackinnon, Lucas Davidson
Ref: Stewart Luke

Tynecastle v Cumbernauld Colts, 2-3, H.T. 1-2
Scorers T: Hendry, Beaumont; CC: Team, Murray, MacPherson
T: Kyle Leiper, Ryan Stevenson, Blake Wales, Scott Jardine, Sean Melvin, Matthew Combe, Oban Anderson, Jack Beaumont, Fletcher Hendry (Sub Kenneth Fisher), Taylor Hendry, Ryan Cameron (Sub Matthew Dillon) Subs not used Stephane Murray, Lee Dawson, Jamie Rae, Jonathan Steel, Joseph Evenden
CC: Jonathan Grier, James Grant, Scott Gibson, Scott Davidson, Craig Murray, Ewan MacPherson (Sub Lewis Warnock), Fraser Team, Sam Davidson, Dominic McLaren, Lee Whitmore, William Mortimer. Subs not used Jordan Marshall, Martin Wright, Zander Gilchrist, Cameron Dickson, Luke Main, Cameron Foy
Ref: Scott Leslie

Round One

Camelon v Brora Rangers, 1-2
Scorers C: Morrison; BR: J McRae, Nicolson
C: Scott Law, Greg MacPherson, Keir MacAulay, Greg Skinner, Connor McMullan (Andrew Kay), Mark Stowe, Stephen Docherty, Ryan Kane, David Morrison (Sub Jordan Herron), Alan Docherty, Ross Allum (Sub Ryan Lockie). Subs not used Alan Sneddon, Jack Denham, Mitchell McDonald, Calum Gray
BR: Steven Martin, Miller Gamble (Sub Paul Brindle), Alistair MacDonald, Colin Williamson, Mark Nicolson, Dale Gillespie, Tom Kelly, Martin McLean, Andrew McRae, Jordan McRae, Bjorn Wagenaar (Sub Gregor MacDonald). Subs not used Craig Campbell, Neil MacDonald, Jamie Stephen

Ref: George Calder

Huntly v Cumbernauld Colts, 3-1, H.T. 1-1
Scorers H: Murison, McGowan, Elphinstone; CC: Team
H: Euan Storrier, Cameron Bowden, Logan, Johnstone, Glenn Murison, Ross Still, Cameron Booth, Gary McGowan (Sub Bradley Manson), Reece McKeown (Sub Kai Matthew), Gavin Elphinstone, Joe Gauld, Rhys Thomas, Subs not used Keith Robertshaw, Christopher Hay, Max McGinley, Liam McDonald, Jamie Boylan
CC: Jonathan Grier, James Grant, Scott Davidson, Stephen O'Neill, Craig Murray (Sub Ewan MacPherson), Martin Wright (Sub Lewis Bonar), Fraser Team, Luke Main (Sub Lee Whitmore), Cameron Foy, Dominic McLaren, William Mortimer. Subs not used Jordan Marshall, Zander Gilchrist, Lewis Warnock, Sam Davidson
Ref: Filipo Mazzoni

Bonnyrigg Rose v Bo'ness United, 5-2, H.T. 0-1
Scorers: BR: Hunter 2, L Currie 3; BU: Miller, Stevenson
BR: Mark Weir, Dean Brett, George Hunter, Kerr Young (Sub Robert Wilson), Dean Hoskins, Alan Horne, Scott Gray (Sub Ross Gray), Jonathan Stewart, Kieran McGachie (Sub Bradley Barrett), Lee Currie, Neil Martyniuk. Subs not used Lewis Turner, Leon Watson, Andrew Mair, Michael Andrews
BU: Andrew Murphy, Stuart McFarlane, Ross Campbell (Sub Will Snowdon), Bryan Wharton, Devon Jacobs (Sub Chris Donnelly), Daniel McKenzie, , Chris Donnelly (Sub Stuart McFarlane), Ryan Stevenson, Michael Gemmell, Zander Miller, Nicholas Locke, Thomas Grant. Unused subs Kieran Anderson, Kyle Bell, Stuart Hunter, Ryan Adamson
Ref: Ross Menzies

Dundonald Bluebell v Queen's Park, 1-3, AET H.T. 0-0, F.T. 1-1
DBB: James Lennox, Scott Durie, Aiden Hendry, Colin Wilson (Sub James MacKie), Craig Wedderburn, Billy Rogerson (Sub Callum Strang), Derek Wallace, Lewis McKenzie (Sub Jamie Allan), Barry Sibanda, Stuart Cargill (Sub Brodie Gray), Chris Gay. Subs not used Liam Craig, Darren Gribbin, Jed Crowe
Ref: Scott Lambie

Albion Rovers v Buckie Thistle, 0-3, H.T. 0-2
Scorers BT: McAskill 2, Glover og
BT: Martin McKinnon, Sam Morrison, Joe McCabe, Kevin Fraser, Kyle MacLeod (Sub Callum Murray), Andrew McAskill, Craig Cowie, McLauchlan, Sam Pugh, Jack Murray, Scott Adams (Sub Sam Urquhart) Unused subs: Shaun Wood, Lewis MacKinnon, Lee Herbert, Hamish Munro, Marcus Goodall
Ref: Lorraine Watson

Berwick Rangers v Stirling Albion, 0-3, H.T. 0-2
BR: Douglas Horne, Kevin Waugh, David Ferguson, Ryan Finnie, Jordan Sinclair (Sub Daniel Purves), Calum Smith, John Ward (Sub Jordan Purves), Alistair Forster, Kieran Somerville (Sub Jack Wright), Grant Nelson, Lewis Allan. Unused subs Andrew McNeil, Mackenzie Lawler, Darren Smith, Liall Smith
Ref: Mike Roncone

Brechin City v Linlithgow Rose, 2-3, H.T. 1-1
Scorers LR: Coyne, Ruari Mclennan, Stevenson
LR: Brian Schwake, Scott Stevenson, Gary Thom, David Brownlie, Owen Ronald, Ruari MacLennan, Tommy Coyne, Kyle Wilson, Dean Cairns, Aiden Wilson, Arnault Bembo. Unused subs Myles Hogarth, Daniel Nimmo, Colin Strickland, Willis Hare, Luke Watt, Daryl Meikle, Sean Slaven
Ref: David Dickinson

Cowdenbeath v Wick Academy, 2-0, H.T. 1-0
WA: Graeme Williamson, Jack Hendry, Craig Gunn (Sub Joe Anderson), Ben Sinclair (Sub Conor Farquhar), Richard MacAdie, David Allan, Sean Campbell, Mark MacAdie, Alan Hughes (Sub Brandon Sinclair), Ross Allan, Ryan Campbell. Subs not used Gary Manson, James More
Ref: Craig Napier

Edinburgh City v Caledonian Braves, 3-1, H.T. 1-1
Scorers CB: McNeil
CB: Yohann Chardon, John Guthrie (Sub Jack Smith), Alan Reid, Andrew Dowie, Scott Forrester, Gavin Lachlan, Derek Esplin, David Sinclair (Sub David Winters), Ross McNeil, Neil McLaughlin, Blair Docherty (Sub Corey Pearson) Subs not used Jack McDowell, Dom Slattery, Jamie Watson, Kieran Hughes
Ref: Barry Cook

Elgin City v Civil Service Strollers, 4-0, H.T. 1-0
CSS: Lewis Budinauckas, Euan Bauld, Jonathan Moffat, Jack Brydon, Alieu Faye (Sub Connor Young), Matthew Cunningham, Mark McConnell, Ross Guthrie (Sub David Churchill), Steven Froude, John Dunn, Domenico Gibson (Sub Euan Valentine). Subs not used: Scott Clapperton, Ross Young, Matthew Shaw, Fraser Napier
Ref: Dan McFarlane

Gala Fairydean Rovers v Annan Athletic, 1-2, H.T. 0-1
Scorer GFR: McBride
GFR: Fraser Morton, Lewis Grant, Calum Hall, Craig McBride, Gareth Rodger, Ben Herdman, Archie Roue (Sub Jacob Campbell), Scott Taylor-McKenzie (Sub Ross Aitchison), Philip Addison, Daniel Galbraith, Marc Berry (Sub Aiden Walsh). Subs not used Sean Ward, Liam Campbell, Jamie Shiel
Ref: Stewart Luke

Haddington Athletic v Formartine United, 1-2, H. 0-0
Scorers: HA: O'Neil, FU: Smith, Lisle
HA: Dale Cornet, Aaron Congalton, Seamus Russell, Ross King, Gordon Harris, Ben Finnan (Sub Andrew McNeill), Shaun Hill, Gabriele Auriemma, Ryan Hutchison (Sub Robbie King), Alasdair Simpson, Keith Lough (Sub Stewart O'Neil) Unused subs Jack Neilson, Harvey Thomson, Anes Subasic, Robbie Stirling
FU: Kevin Main, Jonathan Crawford, Stuart Smith, Stuart Anderson, Craig McKeown, Darryn Kelly, Graeme Rodger, Kieran Lawrence (Sub Aaron Norris), Garry Wood (Sub Scott Lisle), Jonathan Smith (Sub Conor Gethins), Daniel Park. Unused subs: Cole Anderson, Michael Clark, Andrew Greig, Ewen MacDonald
Ref: Daniel Graves

Keith v Hill of Beath Hawthorn, 4-2 AET, H.T. 1-2, F.T. 2-2
Scorers K: Keith, Gray, McAskill, Selfridge; HOB: Luke, Connelly
K: Greg Simpson, Stewart Hutcheon, Andrew Smith, Demilade Yunus (Sub Craig McAskill), Ryan Spink (Sub Marc Young), Ryan Robertson, James Brownie, Liam Strachan, Cammy Keith, Michael Selfridge, Logan Watt (Sub Scott Gray) Subs not used Andy Stewart, Liam Duncan, Callum Porteous, David Dey
HOB: Stuart Hall, Russell Grierson (Sub Joe Kinninmonth), Lyle Kellichan, Bradley Grieve, Kevin Conners (Sub Rory Marshall), Rory Harrower, Shaun Leishman (Sub Mark Wilkie), Jake Mitchell, Ryan Connelly, Brandon Luke (Sub Joe Kirby), Calum Adamson. Unused subs Michael Watt, Ross Maclachlan, Declan Morgan
Ref: Duncan Nicolson

Kelty Hearts v Jeanfield Swifts, 2-1, H.T. 1-0
Scorers KH: Ryan Shanley, Dylan Easton; JS: Chris McLeish
KH: Darren Jamieson, Jamie Stevenson, Paddy Boyle, Scott Hooper, Dougie Hill (Sub Craig Reid), Thomas Reilly, Kallum Higginbotham, Michael Tidser, Nathan Austin, Dylan Easton, Ryan Shanley (Sub Ross Philp) Unused subs Nathan Cooney, Grant Anderson, Josh Donaldson
JS: Mark Mitchell, Jamie Reid, Aaron Whitehead, Jake Dolzanski, Keiran Stewart, Connor McLaren, Fraser Smith (Sub Mark Smith), Chris McLeish, Paul Simpson, Gary Fergus (Sub Chris Dodd),

Christopher Scott. Subs not used Gregor Donald, Jamie McKenzie, Shaun Struthers, Fraser Cumming, Regan McLaren

Lothian Thistle Hutchison Vale v Banks o' Dee, 0-3, H.T. 0-0
Scorers BOD: Buglass, Armstrong, Beattie
LTHV: Kevin Swain, Michael Deland, Sean Lally, Sandy Cunningham (Sub Dylan Moore), Sean Cumming (Sub Liam Kelly), Darren Smith, Louis Signorini, Michael Mbewe (Sub Ruaridh Adams), Sam Daniel, Niall Doherty, Thomas Penker. Subs not used David Ross, Neil Smeaton, Scott Donald, Iain Laver
BOD: Lee Sweeney, Neale Allan, Dean Lawrie, Stuart Duff, Greg Alexander (Sub Craig Duguid), Mark Gilmour, Jamie Buglass (Sub Cameron Beattie), Kane Winton, Lachie McLeod, Michael Philipson, Hamish McLeod (Sub Robert Armstrong) Unused subs: Jack Henderson, Vitali Sahhalevits, Matthew Robertson, Kacper Lewecki
Ref: Alex Shepherd

Nairn County v Broxburn Athletic 0-0 AET, 4-3 pens
NC: Dylan McLean, Callum McLean, Cohen Ramsay (Sub Kenneth McKenzie), Adam Porritt, Fraser Dingwall, Callum Howarth, Max Ewan (Sub Angus Dey), Tom MacLennan, Liam Shewan (Sub Glenn Main), Scott Davidson, Gordon McNab. Subs not used Callum Ednie, Jack McLean, Seamus McConaghy, Will Counsell
BA: Connor Wallace (Sub Shaun Donoghue), Andrew Gillen, Ross Hutchison, Shaun Harrison, Chris Townsley (Sub Gordon Donaldson), Jordan Wright, Greg Binnie, David Greenhill, Gary Brass (Sub Conor Kelly), Cameron Ross, Liam Ireland (Sub Jack Beesley). Subs not used: Greg Redmond, Craig Turnbull, Rory Cosgrove
Ref: Lee Robertson

Rothes v Fraserburgh, 1-3, H.T. 1-2
Scorers R: Cormack; F: Harris, Barbour 2
R: Sean McCarthy, Alasdair Stark (Sub Ross Gunn), Ben Johnstone, Jack Brown, Bruce Milne, Fraser Robertson, Craig Cormack (Sub Sean Liden), Alisdair Sutherland, Ryan McRitchie, Lewis Hyde, Shane Harkness (Sub Gary Kerr). Unused subs Ewan Neil, Charlie Christie, Paul McLeod
F: Paul Leask, Owen Cairns, Bryan Hay, Ryan Cowie, Kieran Simpson, Grant Campbell, Paul Young, William West, Gary Harris (Sub Scott Henry), Sean Butcher (Sub Lewis Davidson), Scott Barbour (Sub Lewis Duncan). Subs not used Ryan Christie, Connor Grant, Edward Flinn
Ref: Harry Bruce

Stenhousemuir v Preston Athletic, 4-1, H.T. 2-0
Scorer PA: Edmond
PA: David Livie, Kai Austin, Craig Innes, Rory Young, Matthew O'Connor, Marc Forsyth, Dale Pennycuick, Ethan Williams, Jonathan Edmond, Ben Bathgate (Sub Nathan Stokes), Joe Murray (Sub Marc Molloy) Unused subs Brandon Bain, Kieran Jack, Mikey Hamilton, Jack Jardine
Ref: Kevin Graham

Stranraer v Spartans, 5-0, H.T. 3-0
Sp: Matthew Baines, Jamie Watson, Scott Maxwell, Adam Corbett, Keir Russell, Gregor Woods (Sub Cammy Dawson), Blair Atkinson (Sub Joe Tait), Samuel Hones, Scott McCrory-Irving, Alan Brown, Archie Meekison (Sub Aaron Murrell) Unused subs: Steve Ellison
Ref: Lloyd Wilson

Tranent v East Stirlingshire, 4-1, H.T. 4-0
Scorers T: Watson, Paterson, Hawkins, Miller; ES: Dishington
T: Ally Adams, Lewis Hawkins, Arran Ponton, Ciaran McKenzie, Richard Miller, Ben Miller, Adam Watson (Sub Owen Renton), Rhys Craigie, Kayne Paterson (Sub Kyle Lander), Sean Murphy, Steven Thomson (Sub Euan Greig) Unused subs: Gary Hamilton, Ben Reilly, Ian Moffat
ES: Ross Connelly, Martin Orr, Gregg Wylde, Jordan Tapping, Eddie Malone, Kieran Gibbons, Jamie Dishington, Nicky Low, Sean Brown, Dean Watson (Sub Craig Henderson), Scott Gray (Sub Robbie Young) Subs not used: Greg McColm, Adam Murray, Andrew Shirra, Ronan Kearney, Iain Ure
Ref: Alastair Grieve

Round Two

Dumbarton v Huntly, 4-0
H: Euan Storrier, Cameron Bowden, Logan Johnstone, Glenn Murison, Ross Still, Cameron Booth (Sub Gavin Elphinstone), Gary McGowan, Joe Gauld, Rhys Thomas, Alexander Thoirs (Sub Reece McKeown), Cai Matthew (Sub Liam McDonald) Unused subs Keith Robertshaw, Christopher Hay, Fergus Alberts, Max McGinlay, Bradley Manson, Jamie Boylan
Ref: Matthew MacDermid

Keith v Clyde, 0-2, H.T. 0-2
K: Greg Simpson, Marc Young, Andrew Smith, Demilade Yunus, Ryan Spink, Ryan Robertson, James Brownie, Liam Strachan, Cameron Keith (Sub Logan Watt), Michael Selfridge (Sub Scott Gray), Liam Duncan. Unused subs Craig McAskill, Andy Stewart, Grant Thomson, Stewart Hutcheon, Kieran Yates, Callum Porteous, David Dey
Ref: Steven Kirkland

Formartine United v Annan Athletic, 1-1 AET, H.T. 1-1, 3-1 pens
Scorer FU: Smith
FU: Kevin Main, Jonathan Crawford (Sub Conor Gethins), Stuart Smith, Stuart Anderson, Craig McKeown, Darryn Kelly, Graeme Rodger, Jonathan Smith, Garry Wood, Aaron Norris (Sub Andrew Greig), Daniel Park (Sub Scott Lisle). Unused subs Ruari Fraser, Paul Lawson, Kieran Lawrence, Cole Anderson, Ewen MacDonald
Ref: Calum Scott

Brora Rangers v Hearts, 2-1, H.T. 1-0
Scorers BR: J MacRae, Maclean
BR: Joe Malin, Tom Kelly, Alistair MacDonald, Colin Williamson, Mark Nicolson, Dale Gillespie, Bjorn Wagenaar (Sub Gregor MacDonald), Martin Maclean, Jordan MacRae (Sub Paul Brindle), Andrew MacRae (Sub Greg Morrison), Millar Gamble. Unused subs Jamie Stephen
Ref: Peter Stuart

Buckie Thistle v Inverness Caledonian Thistle, 2-3, H.T. 1-2
Scorers BT: J Murray, C Murray
BT: Daniel Bell, Lewis MacKinnon (Sub Sam Morrison), Kevin Fraser, Kyle MacLeod (Sub Callum Murray), Sam Urquhart, Craig Cowie, Mclauchlan, Sam Pugh, Max Barry, Jack Murray, Hamish Munro. Subs not used Lee Herbert, Shaun Wood, Marcus Goodall, Lucas Davidson
Ref: Steven Reid

Nairn County v Montrose, 1-7, H.T. 0-4
Scorer NC: MacLennan
NC: Dylan MacLean, Callum MacLean, Kenneth Mackenzie, Adam Porritt, Fraser Dingwall, Cohen Ramsay, Max Ewan, Tom MacLennan, Liam Shewan (Sub Dylan McKenzie), Scott Davidson (Sub Seamus McConaghy), Gordon McNab (Sub Glenn Main). Subs not used Angus Dey, Jack McLean, Will Counsell
Ref: Gavin Ross

East Fife v Tranent, 5-1, H.T. 2-1
Scorer T: Thomson
T: Ally Adams, Dean Whitson, Euan Greig, Ciaran McKenzie, Richard Miller, Ben Miller (Sub Kyle Lander), Adam Watson (Sub Owen

Renton), Rhys Craigie, Kayne Paterson (Sub Arran Ponton), Sean Murphy, Steven Thomson. Subs not used Ian Moffat, Ben Reilly, Jack Chesser
Ref: Barry Cook

Forfar Athletic v Linlithgow Rose, 4-1 AET, H.T. 1-1, F.T. 1-1
Scorer LR: Wilson
LR: Brian Schweke, Scott Stevenson, Gary Thom (Sub David Nimmo), David Brownlie, Owen Ronald, Ruari MacLennan, Tommy Coyne, Kyle Wilson (Sub Willis Hare), Dean Cairns, Aiden Wilson, Arnault Bembo (Sub Luke Watt). Subs not used Myles Hogarth, Colin Strickland, Brodie Strang, Lewis Crawford
Ref: Kevin Graham

Fraserburgh v Banks o' Dee 2-1, H.T. 0-0
Scorers F: Barbour, Beagrie; BOD Philipson
F: Paul Leask, Owen Cairns, Bryan Hay, Ryan Cowie, Grant Campbell, Paul Young, Jamie Beagrie, William West (Sub Gary Harris), Paul Campbell (Sub Sean Butcher), Lewis Duncan (Sub Aidan Combe), Scott Barbour. Subs not used Lewis Davidson, Kieran Simpson, Scott Henry, Edward Flinn
BOD: Lee Sweeney, Neale Allan, Dean Lawrie, Stuart Duff (Sub Robert Armstrong), Greg Alexander, Craig Duguid (Sub Jamie Buglass), Mark Gilmour, Kane Winton, Jack Henderson, Lachie MacLeod (Sub Hamish MacLeod), Michael Philipson. Subs not used Kacper Lewecki, Vitla Sahhalevits, Cameron Beattie, Josh Winton
Ref: Chris Graham

Kelty Hearts v Stranraer, 2-3, H.T. 2-0
Scorers KH: Austin, Higginbotham
KH: Darren Jamieson, Jamie Stevenson, Paddy Boyle, Scott Hooper, Dougie Hill, Thomas Reilly, Kallum Higginbotham, Michael Tidser, Nathan Austin, Dylan Easton, Ross Philp (Sub Grant Anderson)
Unused subs: Nathan Cooney, Ryan Shanley, Craig Reid, Josh Donaldson
Ref: Lorraine Watson

Dundee v Bonnyrigg Rose, 3-2 AET, H.T. 0-1, FT 1-1
BR Scorers: L Currie 2
BR: Mark Weir, Dean Brett, Kerr Young, Dean Hoskins, Alan Horne, Jonathan Stewart (Sub Lewis Turner), Keiran McGachie (Sub Robert Wilson), lee Currie, Neil Martyniuk, George Hunter (Sub Ross Gray), Scott Gray (Sub Bradley Barrett). Subs not used Jamie Docherty, Andrew Mair, Michael Andrews
Ref: Gavin Duncan

Round Three

Brora Rangers v Stranraer, 1-3 AET, H.T. 1-0, F.T. 1-1
Scorer BR: Gillespie
BR: Joe Malin, Tom Kelly, Alistair MacDonald, Colin Williamson, Mark Nicolson, Dale Gillespie, Bjorn Wagenaar (Sub Gregor MacDonald), Martin Maclean, Jordan MacRae, Andrew MacRae (Sub Paul Brindle), Greg Morrison (Sub John Pickles). Unused subs Jamie Stephen, Millar Gamble
Ref: Scott Lambie

Formartine United v Motherwell, 0-5, H.T. 0-2
FU: Kevin Main, Jonathan Crawford, Stuart Smith, Stuart Anderson, Craig McKeown, Darryn Kelly, Graeme Rodger, Jonathan Smith (Sub Andrew Greig), Garry Wood, Daniel Park (Sub Kieran Lawrence), Cole Anderson (Sub Aaron Norris). Unused subs Ruari Fraser, Paul Lawson, Ewen MacDonald, Scott Lisle, Conor Gethins
Ref: Mike Roncone

Fraserburgh v Montrose, 2-4, H.T. 2-2
Scorers F: Harris, Barbour
F: Paul Leask, Owen Cairns, Bryan Hay, Ryan Cowie, Grant Campbell (Sub Sean Butcher), Paul Young, Jamie Beagrie, William West , Gary Harris (Sub Paul Campbell), Kieran Simpson (Sub Lewis Duncan), Scott Barbour. Subs not used Scott Henry, Edward Flinn, Connor Grant, Ryan Sargent, Lewis Davidson, Aidan Combe
Ref: Grant Irvine

Scottish Cup Qualifiers 1957/8-2006/7

Between 1957/8 and 2006/7 eight "Non League" teams qualified for the Scottish Cup each season. Four came from the North Qualifying Cup and four from the South.

The qualifiers during that period were:
`

NORTH

57/8 Buckie Thistle, Caledonian, Fraserburgh, Lossiemouth
58/9 Buckie Thistle, Forres Mechanics, Fraserburgh, Ross County
59/0 Caledonian, Elgin City, Keith, Rothes
60/1 Buckie Thistle, Deveronvale, Elgin City, Keith
61/2 Caledonian, Elgin City, Peterhead, Ross County
62/3 Caledonian, Inverness Thistle, Keith, Nairn County
63/4 Buckie Thistle, Forres Mechanics, Fraserburgh, Inverness Thistle
64/5 Caledonian, Clachnacuddin, Elgin City, Keith
65/6 Caledonian, Elgin City, Fraserburgh, Ross County
66/7 Caledonian, Elgin City, Nairn County, Rothes
67/8 Elgin City, Fraserburgh, Keith, Nairn County
68/9 Elgin City, Fraserburgh, Nairn County, Ross County
69/0 Caledonian, Forres Mechanics, Peterhead, Ross County
70/1 Clachnacuddin, Elgin City, Nairn County, Ross County
71/2 Caledonian, Elgin City, Huntly, Inverness Thistle
72/3 Brora Rangers, Elgin City, Inverness Thistle, Ross County
73/4 Clachnacuddin, Fraserburgh, Lossiemouth, Ross County
74/5 Caledonian, Clachnacuddin, Inverness Thistle, Ross County
75/6 Elgin City, Forres Mechanics, Keith, Peterhead
76/7 Caledonian, Clachnacuddin, Elgin City, Inverness Thistle
77/8 Buckie Thistle, Caledonian, Inverness Thistle, Peterhead
78/9 Caledonian, Inverness Thistle, Keith, Peterhead
79/0 Brora Rangers, Buckie Thistle, Keith, Peterhead
80/1 Buckie Thistle, Inverness Thistle, Keith, Rothes
81/2 Caledonian, Clachnacuddin, Elgin City, Fraserburgh
82/3 Brora Rangers, Caledonian, Elgin City, Peterhead
83/4 Caledonian, Elgin City, Fraserburgh, Peterhead
84/5 Brora Rangers, Caledonian, Inverness Thistle, Keith
85/6 Buckie Thistle, Fort William, Nairn County, Peterhead
86/7 Caledonian, Forres Mechanics, Peterhead, Rothes
87/8 Buckie Thistle, Caledonian, Fraserburgh, Keith
88/9 Caledonian, Elgin City, Forres Mechanics, Inverness Thistle
89/0 Caledonian, Cove Rangers, Elgin City, Ross County
90/1 Cove Rangers, Fraserburgh, Inverness Thistle, Ross County
91/2 Caledonian, Huntly, Peterhead, Ross County
92/3 Cove Rangers, Huntly, Inverness Thistle, Peterhead
93/4 Cove Rangers, Huntly, Ross County, Rothes
94/5 Buckie Thistle, Cove Rangers, Huntly, Keith
95/6 Deveronvale, Fraserburgh, Keith, Lossiemouth
96/7 Brora Rangers, Elgin City, Huntly, Peterhead
97/8 Deveronvale, Fraserburgh, Lossiemouth, Peterhead
98/9 Clachnacuddin, Huntly, Keith, Peterhead
99/0 Clachnacuddin, Fraserburgh, Huntly, Peterhead
00/1 Buckie Thistle, Cove Rangers, Deveronvale, Keith
01/2 Buckie Thistle, Deveronvale, Forres Mechanics, Wick Academy
02/3 Cove Rangers, Deveronvale, Huntly, Keith
03/4 Buckie Thistle, Clachnacuddin, Huntly, Inverurie Loco Works
04/5 Cove Rangers, Huntly, Inverurie Loco Works, Keith
05/6 Cove Rangers, Forres Mechanics, Inverurie Loco Works, Lossiemouth
06/7 Buckie Thistle, Deveronvale, Fraserburgh, Keith

SOUTH

57/8 Chirnside United, Eyemouth United, Peebles Rovers, Vale of L eithen
58/9 Babcock & Wilcox, Coldstream, Eyemouth United, Peebles Rovers
59/0 Eyemouth United, Glasgow University, Peebles Rovers, Tarff Rovers
60/1 Duns, Gala Fairydean, Peebles Rovers, Tarff Rovers
61/2 Eyemouth United, Gala Fairydean, Wigtown & Bladnoch, Vale of Leithen
62/3 Duns, Edinburgh University, Eyemouth United, Gala Fairydean
63/4 Duns, Eyemouth United, Gala Fairydean, St Cuthbert Wanderers
64/5 Coldstream, Edinburgh University, Peebles Rovers, Vale of Leithen
65/6 Gala Fairydean, Glasgow University, Peebles Rovers, Selkirk
66/7 Chirnside United, Gala Fairydean, Hawick Royal Albert, Vale of Leithen
67/8 Hawick Royal Albert, St Cuthbert Wanderers, Tarff Rovers, Vale of Leithen
68/9 Civil Service Strollers, Glasgow University, St Cuthbert Wanderers, Vale of Leithen
69/0 Gala Fairydean, St Cuthbert Wanderers, Tarff Rovers, Vale of Leithen
70/1 Gala Fairydean, Glasgow Corporation Transport, Glasgow University, St Cuthbert Wanderers
71/2 Burntisland Shipyard, Coldstream, Gala Fairydean, St Cuthbert Wanderers
72/3 Babcock & Wilcox, Duns, Ferranti Thistle, Vale of Leithen
73/4 Civil Service Strollers, Edinburgh University, Ferranti Thistle, Hawick Royal Albert
74/5 Gala Fairydean, St Cuthbert Wanderers, Selkirk, Vale of Leithen
75/6 Civil Service Strollers, Glasgow University, Hawick Royal Albert, Selkirk
76/7 Girvan Amateurs, St Cuthbert Wanderers, Selkirk, Vale of Leithen
77/8 Burntisland Shipyard, Civil Service Strollers, Selkirk, Vale of Leithen
78/9 Gala Fairydean, Spartans, Threave Rovers, Vale of Leithen
79/0 Annan Athletic, Coldstream, Spartans, Threave Rovers
80/1 Civil Service Strollers, Hawick Royal Albert, Spartans, Whitehill Welfare
81/2 Civil Service Strollers, Coldstream, Gala Fairydean, Hawick Royal Albert
82/3 Gala Fairydean, Hawick Royal Albert, Selkirk, Vale of Leithen
83/4 Dalbeattie Star, Gala Fairydean, Spartans, Vale of Leithen
84/5 Gala Fairydean, Selkirk, Spartans, Whitehill Welfare
85/6 Gala Fairydean, Hawick Royal Albert, Threave Rovers, Whitehill Welfare
86/7 Annan Athletic, Spartans, Vale of Leithen, Whitehill Welfare
87/8 Civil Service Strollers, Gala Fairydean, Threave Rovers, Vale of Leithen
88/9 Annan Athletic, Coldstream, Gala Fairydean, Spartans
89/0 Coldstream, Gala Fairydean, Vale of Leithen, Whitehill Welfare
90/1 Spartans, Threave Rovers, Vale of Leithen, Whitehill Welfare
91/2 Civil Service Strollers, Gala Fairydean, Hawick Royal Albert, Vale of Leithen
92/3 Civil Service Strollers, Gala Fairydean, Spartans, Vale of Leithen
93/4 Gala Fairydean, St Cuthbert Wanderers, Selkirk, Whitehill Welfare
94/5 Burntisland Shipyard, Gala Fairydean, St Cuthbert Wanderers, Whitehill Welfare
95/6 Annan Athletic, Glasgow University, Spartans, Whitehill Welfare
96/7 Gala Fairydean, Hawick Royal Albert, Spartans, Whitehill Welfare
97/8 Annan Athletic, Edinburgh City, Vale of Leithen, Whitehill Welfare
98/9 Civil Service Strollers, Dalbeattie Star, Spartans, Whitehill Welfare
99/0 Annan Athletic, Dalbeattie Star, Threave Rovers, Whitehill Welfare
00/1 Coldstream, Edinburgh City, Spartans, Whitehill Welfare
01/2 Gala Fairydean, Tarff Rovers, Threave Rovers, Spartans
02/3 Preston Athletic, Selkirk, Threave Rovers, Whitehill Welfare
03/4 Edinburgh City, Spartans, Threave Rovers, Vale of Leithen
04/5 Dalbeattie Star, Edinburgh City, Girvan, Whitehill Welfare
05/6 Preston Athletic, Selkirk, Spartans, Threave Rovers
06/7 Annan Athletic, Edinburgh City, Edinburgh University, Preston Athletic

Scottish Cup Format 2021/22

Round One takes place on the weekend of 18 September, with Scottish Premiership sides entering the competition in the Fourth Round, taking place on the weekend of 22 January, 2022.

This season's final will be played on Saturday, 21 May, 2022.

There will be no replays for drawn matches in Round Four onwards, with extra-time and penalties, if required, to determine the outcome of a match.

For matches up to and including Round Three which end in a draw, a replay will be required. If the outcome of the match is still not determined after a replay, there will be **no extra-time**, with the winner determined by penalties.

The full schedule and entry point of clubs is as follows:

PRELIMINARY ROUND – Saturday 28 August 2020

37 Clubs (11 ties and 15 byes):

Auchinleck Talbot
Banks O'Dee
Blackburn United
Broxburn Athletic
Burntisland Shipyard
Camelon
Clydebank
Coldstream
Cumnock
Dalkeith Thistle
Darvel
Dunbar United
Dundonald Bluebell
Dunipace
Easthouses Lily MWFC
Girvan
Glasgow University
Golspie Sutherland
Haddington Athletic
Hawick Royal Albert United
Hill of Beath Hawthorn
Irvine Meadow XI
Jeanfield Swifts
Linlithgow Rose
Lothian Thistle Hutchison Vale
Musselburgh Athletic
Newtongrange Star
Newton Stewart
Penicuik Athletic
Preston Athletic
Sauchie Juniors
Cuthbert Wanderers
Threave Rovers
Tranent Juniors
Tynecastle
Whitehill Welfare
Wigtown & Bladnoch

ROUND ONE – Saturday 18 September 2021

60 Clubs (30 ties)
11 Preliminary Round Winners
15 Preliminary Round Byes

18 Clubs from the **Scottish Highland Football League**:
Brechin City
Brora Rangers
Buckie Thistle
Clachnacuddin
Deveronvale
Formartine United
Forres Mechanics
Fort William
Fraserburgh
Huntly
Inverurie Loco Works
Keith
Lossiemouth
Nairn County
Rothes
Strathspey Thistle
Turriff United
Wick Academy

16 Clubs from the **Scottish Lowland Football League**:
Berwick Rangers
Bo'ness United
Bonnyrigg Rose Athletic
BSC Glasgow
Caledonian Braves
Civil Service Strollers
Cumbernauld Colts
Dalbeattie Star
East Kilbride
East Stirlingshire
Edinburgh University
Gala Fairydean Rovers
Gretna 2008
Spartans
University of Stirling
Vale of Leithen

ROUND TWO – Saturday 23 October 2021

40 Clubs (20 ties)

30 Round One Winners
10 Clubs from **SPFL League 2**:
Albion Rovers
Annan Athletic
Cowdenbeath
Edinburgh City
Elgin City
Forfar Athletic
Kelty Hearts
Stenhousemuir
Stirling Albion
Stranraer

ROUND THREE – Saturday 27 November 2021

40 Clubs (20 ties)

20 Round Two Winners
10 Clubs from the **SPFL League 1:**
Airdrieonians
Alloa Athletic
Clyde
Cove Rangers
Dumbarton
East Fife
Falkirk
Montrose
Peterhead
Queen's Park

10 Clubs from the **SPFL Championship:**
Arbroath
Ayr United
Dunfermline Athletic
Greenock Morton
Hamilton Academical
Inverness Caledonian Thistle
Kilmarnock
Partick Thistle
Queen of the South
Raith Rovers

ROUND FOUR – Saturday 22 January 2022

32 Clubs (16 ties)

20 Round Three Winners
12 Clubs from the **SPFL Premiership:**
Aberdeen
Celtic
Dundee
Dundee United
Heart of Midlothian
Hibernian
Livingston
Motherwell
Rangers
Ross County
St Johnstone
St Mirren

ROUND FIVE - Saturday 12 February 2022
16 Round Four Winners (8 ties)

QUARTER-FINAL TIES – Saturday 12 March 2022
8 Round Five Winners (4 ties)

SEMI-FINAL TIES – Saturday 16 & Sunday 17 April 2022

SCOTTISH CUP FINAL TIE – Saturday 21 May 2022

Scottish Cup Finals 1873-2019

Season	Winner	Score	Runner-up	Venue	Attendance
1873–74	Queen's Park (1)	2–0	Clydesdale	Hampden Park (original)	2,500
1874–75	Queen's Park (2)	3–0	Renton	Hampden Park (original)	7,000
1875–76	Queen's Park	1–1	3rd Lanark RV	Hamilton Crescent	6,000
(R)	Queen's Park (3)	2–0	3rd Lanark RV	Hampden Park (original)	10,000
1876–77	Vale of Leven	1–1	Rangers	Hamilton Crescent	8,000
(R)	Vale of Leven	1–1	Rangers	Hamilton Crescent	15,000
(SR)	Vale of Leven (1)	3–2	Rangers	Hampden Park (original)	12,000
1877–78	Vale of Leven (2)	1–0	3rd Lanark RV	Hampden Park (original)	5,000
1878–79	Vale of Leven	1–1	Rangers	Hampden Park (original)	9,000
(R)	Vale of Leven (3)	wo	Rangers	Hampden Park (original)	
1879–80	Queen's Park (4)	3–0	Thornliebank	Hampden Park (original)	4,000
1880–81	Queen's Park	2–1 *	Dumbarton	Kinning Park	15,000
(R)	Queen's Park (5)	3–1	Dumbarton	Kinning Park	10,000
1881–82	Queen's Park	2–2	Dumbarton	Cathkin Park (first)	12,500
(R)	Queen's Park (6)	4–1	Dumbarton	Cathkin Park (first)	14,000
1882–83	Dumbarton	2–2	Vale of Leven	Hampden Park (original)	15,000
(R)	Dumbarton (1)	2–1	Vale of Leven	Hampden Park (original)	12,000
1883–84	Queen's Park (7)	wo	Vale of Leven	Cathkin Park (first)	
1884–85	Renton	0–0	Vale of Leven	Hampden Park (second)	3,000
(R)	Renton (1)	3–1	Vale of Leven	Hampden Park (second)	5,500
1885–86	Queen's Park (8)	3–1	Renton	Cathkin Park (first)	7,000
1886–87	Hibernian (1)	2–1	Dumbarton	Hampden Park (second)	15,000
1887–88	Renton (2)	6–1	Cambuslang	Hampden Park (second)	10,000
1888–89	3rd Lanark RV	3–0 *	Celtic	Hampden Park (second)	17,000
(R)	3rd Lanark RV (1)	2–1	Celtic	Hampden Park (second)	13,000
1889–90	Queen's Park	1–1	Vale of Leven	Ibrox Park (first)	11,000
(R)	Queen's Park (9)	2–1	Vale of Leven	Ibrox Park (first)	13,000
1890–91	Heart of Midlothian (1)	1–0	Dumbarton	Hampden Park (second)	10,836
1891–92	Celtic	1–0 *	Queen's Park	Ibrox Park (first)	40,000
(R)	Celtic (1)	5–1	Queen's Park	Ibrox Park (first)	26,000
1892–93	Queen's Park	0–1 *	Celtic	Ibrox Park (first)	18,771
(R)	Queen's Park (10)	2–1	Celtic	Ibrox Park (first)	13,239
1893–94	Rangers (1)	3–1	Celtic	Hampden Park (second)	17,000
1894–95	St Bernard's (1)	2–1	Renton	Ibrox Park (first)	10,000
1895–96	Heart of Midlothian (2)	3–1	Hibernian	Logie Green	17,034
1896–97	Rangers (2)	5–1	Dumbarton	Hampden Park (second)	14,000
1897–98	Rangers (3)	2–0	Kilmarnock	Hampden Park (second)	13,000
1898–99	Celtic (2)	2–0	Rangers	Hampden Park (second)	25,000
1899–1900	Celtic (3)	4–3	Queen's Park	Ibrox Park	15,000
1900–01	Heart of Midlothian (3)	4–3	Celtic	Ibrox Park	15,000
1901–02	Hibernian (2)	1–0	Celtic	Celtic Park	16,000
1902–03	Rangers	1–1	Heart of Midlothian	Celtic Park	13,000
(R)	Rangers	0–0	Heart of Midlothian	Celtic Park	35,000
(SR)	Rangers (5)	2–0	Heart of Midlothian	Celtic Park	30,000
1903–04	Celtic (4)	3–2	Rangers	Hampden Park	64,472
1904–05	Third Lanark	0–0	Rangers	Hampden Park	54,000
(R)	Third Lanark (2)	3–1	Rangers	Hampden Park	55,000
1905–06	Heart of Midlothian (4)	1–0	Third Lanark	Ibrox Park	30,000
1906–07	Celtic (5)	3–0	Heart of Midlothian	Hampden Park	50,000
1907–08	Celtic (6)	5–1	St. Mirren	Hampden Park	58,000
1909–10	Dundee	2–2	Clyde	Ibrox Park	60,000
(R)	Dundee	0–0 AET	Clyde	Ibrox Park	25,000
(SR)	Dundee (1)	2–1	Clyde	Ibrox Park	25,000
1910–11	Celtic	0–0	Hamilton Academical	Ibrox Park	45,000

Season	Winner	Score	Runner-up	Venue	Attendance
(R)	Celtic (7)	2–0	Hamilton Academical	Ibrox Park	25,000
1911–12	Celtic (8)	2–0	Clyde	Ibrox Park	45,000
1912–13	Falkirk (1)	2–0	Raith Rovers	Celtic Park	45,000
1913–14	Celtic	0–0	Hibernian	Ibrox Park	56,000
(R)	Celtic (9)	4–1	Hibernian	Ibrox Park	40,000
1919–20	Kilmarnock (1)	3–2	Albion Rovers	Celtic Park	95,000
1920–21	Partick Thistle (1)	1–0	Rangers	Celtic Park	28,294
1921–22	Morton (1)	1–0	Rangers	Hampden Park	70,000
1922–23	Celtic (10)	1–0	Hibernian	Hampden Park	82,000
1923–24	Airdrieonians (1)	2–0	Hibernian	Ibrox Park	65,000
1924–25	Celtic (11)	2–1	Dundee	Hampden Park	75,317
1925–26	St. Mirren (1)	2–0	Celtic	Hampden Park	98,000
1926–27	Celtic (12)	3–1	East Fife	Hampden Park	80,070
1927–28	Rangers (6)	4–0	Celtic	Hampden Park	118,115
1928–29	Kilmarnock (2)	1–0	Rangers	Hampden Park	114,780
1929–30	Rangers	0–0	Partick Thistle	Hampden Park	107,475
(R)	Rangers (7)	2–1	Partick Thistle	Hampden Park	103,688
1930–31	Celtic	2–2	Motherwell	Hampden Park	104,863
(R)	Celtic (13)	4–2	Motherwell	Hampden Park	98,509
1931–32	Rangers	1–1	Kilmarnock	Hampden Park	112,000
(R)	Rangers (8)	3–0	Kilmarnock	Hampden Park	104,600
1932–33	Celtic (14)	1–0	Motherwell	Hampden Park	102,339
1933–34	Rangers (9)	5–0	St. Mirren	Hampden Park	113,430
1934–35	Rangers (10)	2–1	Hamilton Academical	Hampden Park	87,740
1935–36	Rangers (11)	1–0	Third Lanark	Hampden Park	88,859
1936–37	Celtic (15)	2–1	Aberdeen	Hampden Park	147,365
1937–38	East Fife	1–1	Kilmarnock	Hampden Park	80,091
(R)	East Fife (1)	4–2 AET	Kilmarnock	Hampden Park	92,716
1938–39	Clyde (1)	4–0	Motherwell	Hampden Park	94,000
1946–47	Aberdeen (1)	2–1	Hibernian	Hampden Park	82,140
1947–48	Rangers	1–1 AET	Morton	Hampden Park	129,176
(R)	Rangers (11)	1–0 AET	Morton	Hampden Park	133,750
1948–49	Rangers (12)	4–1	Clyde	Hampden Park	108,435
1949–50	Rangers (13)	3–0	East Fife	Hampden Park	118,262
1950–51	Celtic (16)	1–0	Motherwell	Hampden Park	131,943
1951–52	Motherwell (1)	4–0	Dundee	Hampden Park	136,274
1952–53	Rangers	1–1	Aberdeen	Hampden Park	129,761
(R)	Rangers (14)	1–0	Aberdeen	Hampden Park	113,700
1953–54	Celtic (17)	2–1	Aberdeen	Hampden Park	130,060
1954–55	Clyde	1–1	Celtic	Hampden Park	106,234
(R)	Clyde (2)	1–0	Celtic	Hampden Park	68,831
1955–56	Heart of Midlothian (5)	3–1	Celtic	Hampden Park	132,840
1956–57	Falkirk	1–1	Kilmarnock	Hampden Park	83,000
(R)	Falkirk (2)	2–1 AET	Kilmarnock	Hampden Park	79,785
1957–58	Clyde (3)	1–0	Hibernian	Hampden Park	95,123
1958–59	St. Mirren (2)	3–1	Aberdeen	Hampden Park	108,591
1959–60	Rangers (15)	2–0	Kilmarnock	Hampden Park	108,017
1960–61	Dunfermline Athletic	0–0	Celtic	Hampden Park	113,618
(R)	Dunfermline Athletic (1)	2–0	Celtic	Hampden Park	87,866
1961–62	Rangers (16)	2–0	St. Mirren	Hampden Park	127,940
1962–63	Rangers	1–1	Celtic	Hampden Park	129,643
(R)	Rangers (17)	3–0	Celtic	Hampden Park	120,273
1963–64	Rangers (18)	3–1	Dundee	Hampden Park	120,982
1964–65	Celtic (18)	3–2	Dunfermline Athletic	Hampden Park	108,800

1965–66	Rangers	0–0	Celtic	Hampden Park	126,552
(R)	Rangers (19)	1–0	Celtic	Hampden Park	98,202
1966–67	Celtic (19)	2–0	Aberdeen	Hampden Park	126,102
1967–68	Dunfermline Athletic (3)	3–1	Heart of Midlothian	Hampden Park	56,365
1968–69	Celtic (20)	4–0	Rangers	Hampden Park	132,000
1969–70	Aberdeen (2)	3–1	Celtic	Hampden Park	108,434
1970–71	Celtic	1–1	Rangers	Hampden Park	120,092
(R)	Celtic (21)	2–1	Rangers	Hampden Park	103,332
1971–72	Celtic (22)	6–1	Hibernian	Hampden Park	106,102
1972–73	Rangers (20)	3–2	Celtic	Hampden Park	122,714
1973–74	Celtic (23)	3–0	Dundee United	Hampden Park	75,959
1974–75	Celtic (24)	3–1	Airdrieonians	Hampden Park	75,457
1975–76	Rangers (21)	3–1	Heart of Midlothian	Hampden Park	85,354
1976–77	Celtic (25)	1–0	Rangers	Hampden Park	54,252
1977–78	Rangers (22)	2–1	Aberdeen	Hampden Park	61,563
1978–79	Rangers	0–0	Hibernian	Hampden Park	50,610
(R)	Rangers	0–0 AET	Hibernian	Hampden Park	33,504
(SR)	Rangers (23)	3–2 AET	Hibernian	Hampden Park	30,602
1979–80	Celtic (26)	1–0	Rangers	Hampden Park	70,303
1980–81	Rangers	0–0AET	Dundee United	Hampden Park	53,000
(R)	Rangers (24)	4–1	Dundee United	Hampden Park	43,099
1981–82	Aberdeen (3)	4–1 AET	Rangers	Hampden Park	53,788
1982–83	Aberdeen (4)	1–0 AET	Rangers	Hampden Park	62,979
1983–84	Aberdeen (5)	2–1 AET	Celtic	Hampden Park	58,900
1984–85	Celtic (27)	2–1	Dundee United	Hampden Park	60,346
1985–86	Aberdeen (6)	3–0	Heart of Midlothian	Hampden Park	62,841
1986–87	St. Mirren (3)	1–0 AET	Dundee United	Hampden Park	51,782
1987–88	Celtic (28)	2–1	Dundee United	Hampden Park	74,000
1988–89	Celtic (29)	1–0	Rangers	Hampden Park	72,069
1989–90	Aberdeen (7)	0–0 AET, 9-8p	Celtic	Hampden Park	60,493
1990–91	Motherwell (2)	4–3 AET	Dundee United	Hampden Park	57,319
1991–92	Rangers (25)	2–1	Airdrieonians	Hampden Park	44,045
1992–93	Rangers (26)	2–1	Aberdeen	Celtic Park	50,715
1993–94	Dundee United (1)	1–0	Rangers	Hampden Park	37,450
1994–95	Celtic (30)	1–0	Airdrieonians	Hampden Park	36,915
1995–96	Rangers (27)	5–1	Heart of Midlothian	Hampden Park	37,730
1996–97	Kilmarnock (3)	1–0	Falkirk	Ibrox Stadium	48,953
1997–98	Heart of Midlothian (6)	2–1	Rangers	Celtic Park	48,946
1998–99	Rangers (28)	1–0	Celtic	Hampden Park	52,670
1999–00	Rangers (29)	4–0	Aberdeen	Hampden Park	50,865
2000–01	Celtic (31)	3–0	Hibernian	Hampden Park	51,824
2001–02	Rangers (30)	3–2	Celtic	Hampden Park	51,138
2002–03	Rangers (31)	1–0	Dundee	Hampden Park	47,136
2003–04	Celtic (32)	3–1	Dunfermline Athletic	Hampden Park	50,846
2004–05	Celtic (33)	1–0	Dundee United	Hampden Park	50,635
2005–06	Heart of Midlothian (7)	1–1 AET, 4-2p	Gretna	Hampden Park	51,232
2006–07	Celtic (34)	1–0	Dunfermline Athletic	Hampden Park	49,600
2007–08	Rangers (32)	3–2	Queen of the South	Hampden Park	48,821
2008–09	Rangers (33)	1–0	Falkirk	Hampden Park	50,956
2009–10	Dundee United (2)	3–0	Ross County	Hampden Park	47,122
2010–11	Celtic (35)	3–0	Motherwell	Hampden Park	49,618
2011–12	Heart of Midlothian (8)	5–1	Hibernian	Hampden Park	51,041
2012–13	Celtic (36)	3–0	Hibernian	Hampden Park	51,254
2013-14	St Johnstone (1)	2-0	Dundee United	Celtic Park	47,545
2014-15	Inverness CT (1)	2-1	Falkirk	Hampden Park	37,149
2015-16	Hibernian (3)	3-2	Rangers	Hampden Park	50,701
2016-17	Celtic (37)	2-1	Aberdeen	Hampden Park	48,713
2017-18	Celtic (38)	2-0	Motherwell	Hampden Park	49,967
2018-19	Celtic (39)	2-1	Heart of Midlothian	Hampden Park	49,434
2019-20	Celtic (40)	3-3AET, 4-3p	Heart of Midlothian	Hampden Park	BCD
2020-21	St Johnstone (2)	1-0	Hibernian	Hampden Park	BCD
* Match Void					

Scottish Cup Winning Teams 1874-2021

1873/4 Queen's Park
Dickson, Taylor, Neill, Thomson, Campbell, Weir, Leckie, W McKinnon, Lawrie, McNeill, A McKinnon

1874/5 Queen's Park
Neill, Taylor, Phillips, Campbell, Dickson, McNeill, Highet, W McKinnon, A McKinnon, Lawrie, Weir

1875/6 Queen's Park
Dickson, Taylor, Neill, Campbell, Phillips, Lawrie, McGill, Highet, W McKinnon, A McKinnon, McNeil
Replay: Hillcote and Smith replaced Lawrie and A McKinnon

1876/7 Vale of Leven
Wood, McIntyre, Michie, Jamieson, McLintock, Ferguson, Paton, McGregor, McDougall, Baird, Lindsay
Same team played in both replays

1877/8 Vale of Leven
Parlane, McLintock, McIntyre, McPherson, Jamieson, Ferguson, McFarlane, McGregor, James Baird, McDougall, John Baird

1878/9 Vale of Leven
Parlane, McLintock, A McIntyre, J McIntyre, McPherson, McFarlane, Ferguson, James Baird, McGregor, John Baird, McDougall

1879/80 Queen's Park
Graham, Somers, Neil, Campbell, Davidson, Richmond, Weir, Highet, Ker, Kay, McNeill

1880/1 Queen's Park
McCallum, Watson, Holm, Campbell, Davidson, Anderson, Fraser, Kerr, Smith, Allan, Kay

1881/2 Queen's Park
McCallum, Watson, A Holm, Davidson, J Holm, Fraser, Anderson, Kerr, Harrower, Richmond, Kay
Replay: Campbell replaced J Holm

1882/3 Dumbarton
McAuley, Hutchison, Paton, P Miller, Lang, Keir, R Brown, (1), R Brown (2), J Miller, Lindsay, McArthur.
Replay: Anderson replaced Lang

1883/4 Queen's Park
Walk over. Selected team was: McCallum, Arnott, Holm, Campbell, Gow, Christie, Allan, Smith, Harrower, Anderson, Watt

1884/5 Renton
Lindsay, Hannah, A McCall, Kelso, McKechnie, Barbour, Kelly, McIntyre, J McCall, Thomson, Grant
Replay – unchanged

1885/6 Queen's Park
Gillespie, Arnot, Watson, Campbell, Gow, Christie, Somerville, Hamilton, Allan, Harrower, Lambie

1886/7 Hibernian
Tobin, Lundy, Fagan, McGhee, McGinn, McLaren, Lafferty, Groves, Montgomery, Clark, Smith

1887/8 Renton
Lindsay, Hannah, A McCall, Kelso, Kelly, McKechnie, McCallum, J Campbell, D Campbell, J McCall, McNee

1888/9 Third Lanark
Downie, Thomson, Rae, Lochead, Auld, McFarlane, Marshall, Oswald (Minor), Oswald (Major), Hannah, Johnstone

1889/90 Queen's Park
Gillespie, Arnott, Smellie, McAra, Stewart, Robertson, Berry, Gulliland, Hamilton, Sellar, Allan
Replay: unchanged

1890/1 Heart of Midlothian
Fairbairn, Adams, Goodfellow, Begbie, McPherson, Hill, Taylor, Mason, Russell, Scott, Baird

1891/2 Celtic
Cullen, Reynolds, Doyle, Gallacher, Kelly, Maley, Campbell, Dowds, McCallum, McMahon, Brady

1892/3 Queen's Park
Baird, Sillars, Smellie, Gillespie, McFarlane, Stewart, Gulliland, Waddell, Hamilton, Lambie, Sellar

1893/4 Rangers
Haddow, Smith, Drummond, Marshall, A McCredie, Mitchell, Steel, H McCreadie, Gray, McPherson, Barker

1894/5 St Bernards
Sneddon, Hall, Foyers, McManus, Robertson, Murdoch, Laing, Paton, Oswald, Crossan, Clelland

1895/6 Hearts
Fairbairn, McCartney, Mirk, Begbie, Russell, Hogg, McLaren, Baird, Michael, King, Walker.

1896/7 Rangers
Dickie, N Smith, Drummond, Gibson, McCreadie, Mitchell, Low, McPherson, Miller, Hyslop, A Smith

1897/8 Rangers
Dickie, N Smith, Drummond, Gibson, Neil, Mitchell, Miller, McPherson, Hamilton, Hyslop, A Smith

1898/9 Celtic
McArthur, Welford, Storrier, Battles, Marshall, King, Hodge, Campbell, Divers, McMahon, Bell

1899/0 Celtic
McArthur, Storrier, Battles, Russell, Marshall, Orr, Hodge, Campbell, Divers, McMahon, Bell

1900/1 Hearts
Philip, Allan, Baird, Key, Buick, Hogg, Porteous, Walker, Thomson, Houston, Bell

1901/2 Hibernian
Rennie, Gray, Glen, Breslin, Harrower, Robertson, McCall, McGeachen, Divers, Callaghan, Atherton

1902/3 Rangers
Dickie, Fraser, Drummond, Gibson, Stark, Robertson, McDonald, Speedie, Hamilton, Walker, Smith
Replay Unchanged. Second replay Henderson and Mackie for Gibson and Walker

1903/4 Celtic
Adams, McLeod, Orr, Young, Loney, Hay, Muir, McMenemy, Quinn, Somers, Hamilton

1904/5 Third Lanark
Raeside, Barr, McIntosh, Comrie, Sloan, Neilson, Johnstone, Kidd, McKenzie, Wilson, Munro
Replay: Unchanged

1905/6 Hearts
G Philip, McNaught, D Philip, McLaren, Thomson, Dickson, Cooper, Walker, Menzies, D Wilson, G Wilson

1906/7 Celtic
Adams, McLeod, Orr, Young, McNair, Hay, Bennett, McMenemy, Quinn,

Somers, Templeton

1907/8 Celtic
Adams, McNair, Weir, Young, Loney, Hay, Bennett, McMenemy, Quinn, Somers, Hamilton

1908/9 Celtic
Adams, McNair, Weir, Young, Dodds, Hay, Munro, McMenemy, Quinn, Somers, Hamilton
Replay: Kivlichan for Munro
CUP WITHHELD DUE TO RIOT

1909/0 Dundee
Crumley, Lawson, Chaplin, Lee, Dainty, Comrie, Bellamy, Langlands, Hunter, McFarlane, Fraser
Replay: Neal for Lawson; Second Replay: McEwan for Chaplin

1910/1 Celtic
Adams, McNairn Dodds, Young, McAteer, Hay, Kivlichan, McMenemy, Quinn, Hastie, Hamilton
Replay: McAtee for Hastie

1911/2 Celtic
Mulrooney, McNair, Dodds, Young, Loney, Johnstone, McAtee, Gallacher, Quinn, McMenemy, Brown

1912/3 Falkirk
Stewart, Orrock, Donaldson, McDonald, Logan, McMillan, McNaught, Gibbons, Robertson, Croal, Terris

1913/4 Celtic
Shaw, McNair, Dodds, Young, Johnstone, McMaster, McAtee, Gallacher, Owers, McMenemy, Browning
Replay McColl for Owers

1919/0 Kilmarnock
Blair, Hamilton, Gibson, Bagan, Shortt, Neave, McNaught, M Smith, J Smith, Culley, McPhail

1920/1 Partick Thistle
Campbell, Crichton, Bulloch, Harris, Wilson, Borthwick, Blair, Kinloch, Johnston, McMenemy, Salisbury

1921/2 Morton
Edwards, McIntyre, R Brown, Gourlay, Wright, McGregor, McNab, McKay, Buchanan, A Brown, McMinn

1922/3 Celtic
Shaw, McNair, W McStay, J McStay, Cringan, McFarlane, McAtee, Gallacher, Cassidy, Mclean, Connolly

1923/4 Airdrieonians
Ewart, Dick, McQueen, Preston, McDougall, Bennie, Reid, Russell, Gallacher, McPhail, Sommerville

1924/5 Celtic
Shevlin, W McStay, Hilley, Wilson, J MCStay, McFarlane, Connolly, Gallacher, McGrory, Thomson, McLeam

1925/6 St Mirren
Bradford, Findlay, Newbiggin, Morrison, Summers, McDonald, Morgan, Gebbie, McCrae, Howieson, Thomson

1926/7 Celtic
J Thomson, W McStay, Hilley, Wilson, J McStay, McFarlane, Connolly, A Thomson, McInally, McMenemy, McLean

1927/8 Rangers
T Hamilton, Gray, R Hamilton, Buchanan, Meiklejohn, Craig, Archibald, Cunningham, Fleming, McPhail, Morton

1928/9 Kilmarnock
Clemie, Robertson, Nibloe, Morton, McLaren, McEwan, Connell, Smith, Cunningham, Williamson, Aitken

1929/0 Rangers
T Hamilton, Gray, R Hamilton, Buchanan, Meiklejohn, Craig, Archibald, Marshall, Fleming, McPhail, Nicholson
Replay: McDonald and Morton for Buchanan and Nicholson

1930/1 Celtic
J Thomson, Cook, McGonagle, Wilson, McStay, Geatons, R Thomson, A Thomson, McGrory, Scarff, Napier
Replay: unchanged

1931/2 Rangers
Hamilton, Gray, McAuley, Meiklejohn, Simpson, Brown, Archibald, Marshall, English, McPhail, Morton
Replay: Fleming for Morton

1932/3 Celtic
Kennaway, Hogg, McGonagle, Wilson, McStay, Geatons, R Thomson, A Thomson, McGrory, Napier, O'Donnell

1933/4 Rangers
Hamilton, Gray, McDonald, Meiklejohn, Simpson, brown, Main, Marshall, Smith, McPhail, Nicholson

1934/5 Rangers
Dawson, Gray, McDonald, Kennedy, Simpson, Brown, Main, Venters, Smith, McPhail, Gillick

1935/6 Rangers
Dawson, Gray, Cheyne, Meiklejohn, Simpson, brown, Fiddes, Venters, Smith, McPhail, Turnbull

1936/7 Celtic
Kennaway, Hogg, Morrison, Geatons, Lyon, Paterson, Delaney, Buchan, McGrory, Crum, Murphy

1937/8 East Fife
Milton, Laird, Tait, Russell, Sneddon, Herd, Adams, McLeod, McCartney, Miller, McKerrell
Replay: Harvey for Herd

1938/9 Clyde
Brown, Kirk, Hickie, Beaton, Falloon, Weir, Robertson, Noble, Martin, Wallace, Gillies

1946/7 Aberdeen
Johnstone, McKenna, Taylor, McLaughlin, Dunlop, Waddell, Harris, Hamilton, Williams, Baird, McCall

1947/8 Rangers
Brown, Shaw, Young, McColl, Woodburn, Cox, Rutherford, Gillick, Thornton, Findlay, Duncanson
Replay: Williamson for Findlay

1948/9 Rangers
Brown, Young, Shaw, McColl, Woodburn, Cox, Waddell, Duncanson, Thornton, Williamson, Rutherford

1949/0 Rangers
Brown, Young, Shaw, McColl, Woodburn, Cox, Rutherford, Findlay, Thornton, Duncanson, Rae

1950/1 Celtic
Hunter, Fallon, Rollo, Evans, Boden, Baillie, Weir, Collins, McPhail, Peacock, Tully

1951/2 Motherwell
Johnstone, Kilmarnock, Shaw, Cox, Paton, Redpath, Sloan, Humphries, Kelly, Watson, Aitkenhead

1952/3 Rangers
Niven, Young, Little, McColl, Stanners, Prude, Waddell, Grierson, Paton,

Prentice, Hubbard
Replay: Woodburn and Simpson for Stanners and Prentice

1953/4 Celtic
Bonnar, Haughney, Meechan, Evans, Stein, peacock, Higgins, Fernie, Fallon, Tully, Mochan

1954/5 Clyde
Hewkins, Murphy, Haddock, Granville, Anderson, Laing, Divers, Robertson, Hill, Brown, Ring
Replay: Unchanged

1955/6 Hearts
Duff, Kirk, McKenzie, Mackay, Glidden, Cumming, Young, Conn, Bauld, Wardhaugh, Crawford

1956/7 Falkirk
Slater, Parker, Rae, Wright, Irvine, Prentice, Murray, Grierson, Merchant, Moran, O'Hara
Replay: unchanged

1957/8 Clyde
McCulloch, Murphy, Haddock, Walters, Findlay, Clinton, Herd, Currie, Coyle, Robertson, Ring

1958/9 St Mirren
Walker, Lapsley, Wilson, Neilson, McGugan, Leishman, Ridger, Bryceland, Baker, Gemmell, Miller

1959/0 Rangers
Niven, Caldow, Little, McColl, Paterson, Stevenson, Scott, McMillan, Millar, Brand, Wilson

1960/1 Dunfermline Athletic
Connachan, Fraser, Cunningham, Mailer, Williamson, Miller, Peebles, Smith, Dickson, McAlindon, Melrose
Replay: Sweeney and Thomson for Williamson and McAlindon

1961/2 Rangers
Ritchie, Shearer, Caldow, Davis, McKinnon, Baxter, Henderson, McMillan, Millar, Brand, Wilson

1962/3 Rangers
Ritchie, Shearer, Caldow, Greig, McKinnon, Baxter, Henderson, McLean, Miller, Brand, Wilson
Replay McMillan for McLean

1963/4 Rangers
Ritchie, Shearer, Caldow, Greig, McKinnon, Baxter, Henderson, McLean, Miller, Brand, Wilson

1964/5 Celtic
Fallon, Young, Gemmell, Murdoch, McNeill, Clark, Chalmers, Gallagher, Hughes, Lennox, Auld

1965/6 Rangers
Ritchie, Johansen, Provan, Greig, McKinnon, Millar, Henderson, Watson, Forrest, Johnston, Wilson
Replay: Mclean for Forrest

1966/7 Celtic
Simpson, Craig, Gemmell, Murdoch, McNeill, Clark, Johnstone, Wallace, Chalmers, Auld, Lennox

1967/8 Dunfermline Athletic
Martin, W Callaghan, Lunn, McGarty, Barry, T Callaghan, Lister, Paton, Gardner, Robertson, Edwards

1968/9 Celtic
Fallon, Craig, Gemmell, Murdoch, McNeill, Brogan (Sub Clark), Connelly, Chalmers, Wallace, Lennix, Auld

1969/0 Aberdeen
Clark, Boel, Murray, Hermiston, McMillan, Buchan, McKay, Robb, Forrest, Harper, Graham

1970/1 Celtic
Williams, Craig, Brogan, Connelly, McNeill, Hay, Johnstone, Lennox, Wallace, Callaghan, Hood.
Replay: Macari for Wallace, Wallace sub for Hood

1971/2 Celtic
Williams, Craig, Brogan, Murdoch, McNeill, Connelly, Johnstone, Deans, Macari, Dalglish, Callaghan

1972/3 Rangers
McCloy, Jardine, Mathieson, Greig, Johnstone, McDonald, McLean, Forsyth, Parlane, Conn, Young

1973/4 Celtic
Connaghan, McGrain (Sub Callaghan), Brogan, Murray, McNeill, McCluskey, Johnstone, Hood, Deans, Hay, Dalglish

1974/5 Celtic
Latchford, McGrain, Lynch, Murray, McNeill, McCluskey, Hood, Glavin, Dalglish, Lennox, Wilson

1975/6 Rangers
McCloy, Miller, Greig, Forsyth, Jackson, MacDonald, McKean, Hamilton (Sub Jardine), Henderson, McLean, Johnstone

1976/7 Celtic
Latchford, McGrain, Lynch, Stanton, McDonald, Aitken, Dalglish, EDvaldsson, Craig, Conn, Wilson

1977/8 Rangers
McCloy, Jardine, Greig, Forsyth, Jackson, MacDonald, McLean, Russell, Johnstone, Smith, Cooper (Sub Watson)

1978/9 Rangers
McCloy, Jardine, Dawson, Johnstone, Jackson, MacDonald (Sub Miller), McLean, Russell, Parlane, Smith, Cooper.
Replay: Miller sub on for McLean; Second Replay: Watson for Smith, Miller and Smith subbed on for Watson and Mclean

1979/0 Celtic
Latchford, Sneddon, McGrain, Aitken, Conroy, MacLeod, Provan, Doyle (Sub Lennox), McCluskey, Burns, McGarvey

1980/1 Rangers
Stewart, Jardine, Dawson, Stevens, Forsyth, Bett, Mclean, Russell, McAdam (Sub Cooper), Redford, W Johnston
Replay: Cooper, D Johnstone and MacDonald for Mclean, McAdam and W Johnston

1981/2 Aberdeen
Leighton, Kennedy, Rougvie, McMaster (Sub Bell), McLeish, Miller, Strachan, Cooper, McGhee, Simpson, Hewitt (Sub Black)

1982/3 Aberdeen
Leighton, Rougvie (Sub Watson), McMaster, Cooper, McLeish, Miller, Strachan, Simpson, McGhee, Black, Weir.

1983/4 Aberdeen
Leighton, McKimmie, Rougvie (Sub Stark), Cooper, McLeish, Miller, Strachan, Simpson, McGhee, Black, Weir (Sub Bell)

1984/5 Celtic
Bonner, W McStay, McGrain, Aitken, McAdam, MacLeod, Provan, P McStay (Sub O'Leary), Johnston, Burns (Sub McClair), McGarvey

1985/6 Aberdeen
Leighton, McKimmie, McQueen, McMaster (Sub Stark), McLeish, W Miller, Hewitt (Sub J Miller), Cooper, McDougall, Bett, Weir

1986/7 St Mirren
Money, Wilson, D Hamilton, Abercomby, Winnie, Cooper, McGarvey, Ferguson, McDowall (Sub Cameron), B Hamilton, Lambert (Sub

Fitzpatrick)

1987/8 Celtic
McKnight, Morris, Rogan, Aitken, McCart5hy, Whyte (Sub Stark), Miller, McStay, McAvennie, Walker (Sub McGhee), Burns

1988/9 Celtic
Bonner, Morris, Rogan, Aitken, McCart6hy, Whyte, Grant, McStay, Miller, McGhee, Burns

1989/90 Aberdeen
Snelders, McKimmie, Robertson, Grant, McLeish, Irvine, Nicholas, Bett, Mason (Sub Watson), Connor, Gilhaus

1990/1 Motherwell
Maxwell, Nijholt, Boyd, Griffin, Paterson, McCart, Arnott, Angus, Ferguson (Sub Kirk), O'Donnell, Cooper (Sub O'Neill)

1991/2 Rangers
Goram, Stevens, Robertson, Gough, Spackman, Brown, Durrant (Sub Gordon), McCall, McCoist, Hateley, Mikhaitchenko

1992/3 Rangers
Goram, McCall, Robertson, Gough, McPherson, Brown, Murray, Ferguson, Durrant, Hateley, Huistra (Sub Pressley)

1993/4 Dundee United
Van de Kamp, Cleland, Malpas, McInally, Petric, Welsh, Bowman, Hannah, McLaren (Sub Nixon), Brewster, Dailly.

1994/5 Celtic
Bonner, Boyd, McKinlay, Vata, McNally, Grant, McLaughlin, McStay, Van Hooijdonk (Sub Falconer), Donnelly (Sub O'Donnell), Collins

1995/6 Rangers
Goram, Cleland, Robertson, Gough, McLaren, Brown, Durie, Gascoigne, Ferguson (Sub Durrant), McCall, Laudrup

1996/7 Kilmarnock
Lekovic, MacPherson, Kerr, Montgmoerie, McGowne, Reilly, Bagen (Sub Mitchell), Burke, Wright (Sub Henry), McIntyre (Sub Brown), Holt

1997/8 Hearts
Rousset, McPherson, Naysmith, Weir, Salvatori, Ritchie, McCann, Fulton, Adam (Sub Hamilton), Cameron, Flogel

1998/9 Rangers
Klos, Porrini (Sub Kanchelskis), Amoruso, Hendry, Vidmar, McCann (Sub Ferguson), McInnes, Van Bronckhorst, Wallace, Amato (Sub Wilson), Albertz

1999/0 Rangers
Klos, Reyna, Moore (Sub Porrini), Vidmar, Numan, Kanchelskis, Ferguson, Albertz, Van Bronckhorst (Sub Tugay), Wallace (Sub McCann), Dodds

2000/1 Celtic
Douglas, Mjalby, Valgaeren, Vega, Thompson (Sub Johnson), Agathe, Lennon, Lambert (Sub Boyd), Moravcik (Sub McNamara), Larsson, Sutton

2001/2 Rangers
Klos, Ricksen, Amoruso, Moore, Numan, Ross, Ferguson, Lovenkrands, De Boer, Caniggia (Sub Arveladze), McCann

2002/3 Rangers
Klos, Ricksen, Moore, Amoruso, Numan (Sub Muscat), Malcolm, Ferguson, McCann, De Boer, Mols (Sub Ross), Arveladze (Sub Thompson)

2003/4 Celtic
Marshall, Varga, Balde, McNamara, Agathe, Lennon, Petrov, Pearson (Sub Wallace), Thompson, Larsson, Sutton

2004/5 Celtic
Douglas, Agathe, Varga, Balde, McNamara, Petrov, Lennon, Thompson (Sub McGeady), Sutton, Hartson (Sub Valgaeren), Bellamy

2005/6 Hearts
Gordon, Neilson, Pressley, Tall, Fyssas, Cesnauskas (Sub Mikolounas), Aguilar (Sub Brellier), Hartley, Skacel (Sub Popsisil), Jankauskas

2006/7 Celtic
Boruc, Perrier-Doumbe, McManus, Pressley, Naylor, Nakamura, Lennon (Sub Caldwell), Harley, McGeady, Vennegoor of Hesselink, Miller (Sub Beattie)

2007/8 Rangers
Alexander, Whittaker, Cuellar, Weir, Papac, McCulloch, Ferguson, Thomson, Beasley (Sub Davis), Boyd, Darcheville (Sub Fleck)

2008/9 Rangers
Alexander, Whittaker, Bougherra, Weir, Papac, Davis, Ferguson, McCulloch, Lafferty (Sub Dailly), Boyd (Sub Novo), Miller (Sub Naismith)

2009/0 Dundee United
Pernis, Dillon, Webster, Kenneth, Kovacevic (Sub Watson), Conway, Swanson (Sub S Robertson), Buaben, Gomis, Daly, Goodwillie (Sub D Robertson)

2010/1 Celtic
Forster, Wilson, Loovens, Majstorovic, Izaguirre, Commons (Sub Forrest), Brown, Ki, Mulgrew, Samaras (Sub Stokes), Hooper (Sub McCourt)

2011/2 Hearts
MacDonald, McGowan, Webster, Zaliukas, Grainger, Black (Sub Robinson), Barr, Santana (Sub Beattie), Skacel, Driver (Sub Taouil), Elliot

2012/3 Celtic
Forster, Lustig, Wilson, Mulgrew, Izaguirre, Commons (Sub Samaras), brown (Sub Ambrose), Ledley, Forrest (Sub McCourt), Hooper, Stokes

2013/4 St Johnstone
Mannus, Mackay, Easton, Wotherspoon (Sub McDonald), Wright, Anderson, Millar, Dunne, May, MacLean, O'Halloran (Sub Croft)

2014/5 Inverness Caledonian Thistle
Esson, Shinnie, Devine, Meekings, Tremarco, Tansey, Draper, Watkins (Sub Ross), Doran (Sub Williams), Christie (Sub Vincent), Ofere.

2015/6 Hibernian
Logan, Gray, McGregor, Hanlon (Sub Gunnarsson), Fontaine (Sub Henderson), Stevenson, Fyvie, McGeouch, McGinn, Stokes, Cummings (Sub Keatings)

2016/7 Celtic
Gordon, Lustig, Simunovic, Boyata, Tierney (Sub Rogic), McGregor, Brown, Armstrong, Roberts (Sub Sviatchenko), Griffiths, Sinclair

2017/8 Celtic
Gordon, Lustig, Boyata, Ajer (Sub Simunovic), Tierney, Brown, Ntcham, Forrest (Sub Sinclair), Rogic (Sub Armstrong), McGregor, Dembele

2018/9 Celtic
Bain, Lustig, Simunovic, Ajer, Hayes (Sub Bitton), Brown, McGregor, Forrest, Rogic (Sub Ntcham), Johnston (Sub Sinclair), Edouard

2019/0 Celtic
Hazard, Ajer, Julien, Duffy (Sub Johnston), Taylor (Sub Laxalt), Brown (Sub Soro), McGregor, Christie, Turnbull (Sub Rogic), Elyounoussi (Sub Frimpong), Edouard (Sub Griffiths)

2020/1 St Johnstone
Clark, Kerr, Gordon, McCart, Booth, Rooney (Sub Brown), McCann, Bryson (Sub Davidson), Middleton (Sub O'Halloran), Wotherspoon, Kane.

Scottish Cup Early Round Attendances 2007/8-2017/18

Attendances published in previous editions of the Almanac for these years have been a mixture of official figures from clubs, estimates from clubs and guesstimates from other media sources. We have now been able to obtain more official figures from the SFA and these are published here. Thanks to Jock Gardiner for his help with this.

2007/8

1st round

Brora Rangers v Cove Rangers	0-5	60
Golspie Sutherland v Preston Athletic	3-1	69
Coldstream v Dalbeattie Star	0-4	
Glasgow University v Buckie Thistle	1-2	229
Wigtown & Bladnoch v Burntisland Shipyard	3-5	
Civil Service Strollers v Selkirk	1-2	
Fort William v Spartans	0-6	117
Newton Stewart v Linlithgow Rose	0-6	574
Vale of Leithen v Gala Fairydean	3-1	113
Wick Academy v Deveronvale	0-5	270
Culter v Hawick Royal Albert	7-0	383
Rothes v Nairn County	1-4	108
St Cuthbert Wanderers v Pollok	2-0	
Fraserburgh v Huntly	1-1	
Girvan v Forres Mechanics	2-0	
Lossiemouth v Whitehill Welfare	1-3	81
Clachnacuddin v Edinburgh City	2-2	153
Bye - Edinburgh University		

1st round replays

Huntly v Fraserburgh	2-0	361
Edinburgh City v Clachnacuddin	1-0	126

2nd round

Whitehill Welfare v Golspie Sutherland	6-1	186
Buckie Thistle v Nairn County	4-1	394
Edinburgh City v East Stirlingshire	1-2	188
Cove Rangers v Keith	3-0	188
Edinburgh University v Deveronvale	3-1	348
Linlithgow Rose v Spartans	4-1	1683
Montrose v Pollok	2-2	945
Forfar Athletic v Dumbarton	1-1	382
Inverurie Loco Works v East Fife	0-2	770
Selkirk v Dalbeattie Star	0-2	135
Albion Rovers v Burntisland Shipyard	8-0	265
Culter v Vale of Leithen	2-1	365
Girvan v Stranraer	1-2	487
Arbroath v Elgin City	5-0	583
Threave Rovers v Stenhousemuir	1-0	330
Annan Athletic v Huntly	2-5	243

2nd round replays

Pollok v Montrose	0-1	2200
Dumbarton v Forfar	3-0	310

3rd round

Albion Rovers v East Stirlingshire	1-5	425
Dumbarton v Berwick Rangers	2-0	526
Culter v Huntly	1-3	975
Brechin City v East Fife	1-1	652
Stranraer v Stirling Albion	0-6	326
Clyde v Montrose	2-0	821
Cove Rangers v Edinburgh University	1-0	480
Partick Thistle v Ayr United	2-1	2260
Threave Rovers v Raith Rovers	0-5	629
Greenock Morton v Buckie Thistle	3-2	1833
Linlithgow Rose v Dalbeattie Star	1-0	1519
Arbroath v Cowdenbeath	0-1	595
Ross County v Whitehill Welfare	4-0	1208
Livingston v Alloa Athletic	4-0	819
Peterhead v Queen of the South	0-5	695
Airdrie United v Queen's Park	1-1	1013

3rd round replays

Queens Park v Airdrie	2-4 aet	579
East Fife v Brechin	1-2	659

2008/9

1st Round

Rothes v Buckie Thistle	1-4	249
Golspie Sutherland v Threave Rovers	0-3	50
Banks O Dee v Fort William	10-0	175
Lochee United v Bathgate Thistle	3-1	406
Selkirk v Coldstream	1-1	95
St Cuthbert Wanderers v Wick Academy	0-3	170
Fraserburgh v Hawick Royal Albert	6-3	261
Newton Stewart v Brora Rangers	1-1	65
Huntly v Girvan	1-0	198
Pollok v Spartans	1-1	1170
Edinburgh City v Nairn County	2-0	130
Inverurie Loco Works v Deveronvale	5-2	711
Dalbeattie Star v Lossiemouth	5-1	184
Edinburgh University v Civil Service Strollers	1-2	99
Preston Athletic v Gala Fairydean	3-1	126
Wigtown & Bladnoch v Forres Mechanics	2-2	81
Clachnacuddin v Burntisland Shipyard	4-0	143
Glasgow University v Vale of Leithen	0-1	156

replays

Coldstream v Selkirk*	2-2	61
Brora Rangers v Newton Stewart	2-1 aet	49
Spartans v Pollok	1-0	487
Forres Mechanics v Wigtown & Bladnoch	2-0	204

2nd Round

Clachnacuddin v Crichton	1-0	120
Edinburgh City v Wick Academy	0-0	250
Cove Rangers v Whitehill Welfare	1-0	250
Dalbeattie Star v Selkirk	6-0	90
Montrose v Huntly	2-0	523
East Stirling v Preston Athletic	4-2	382
Fraserburgh v Dumbarton	0-1	517
Berwick Rangers v Albion Rovers	1-2	259
Civil Service Strollers v Vale of Leithen	0-1	386
Inverurie Locos v Banks O Dee	5-1	751
Stenhousemuir v Threave Rovers	5-0	247
Annan Athletic v Spartans	1-2	652
Brora Rangers v Forfar Athletic	1-3	200
Lochee United v Buckie Thistle	3-0	202
Cowdenbeath V Elgin City	1-2	328
Forres Mechanics v Keith	1-1	233

replays

Wick Academy v Edinburgh City	1-4	550
Keith v Forres Mechanics*	1-1	325

3rd Round

Stirling Albion v Partick Thistle	2-3	1472
Forfar Athletic v Stranraer	2-0	305
Lochee United v Ayr United	1-1	1223
Forres Mechanics v Dalbeattie Star	2-2	378
Inverurie Locos v Vale of Leithen	4-0	608
Elgin City v Spartans	1-2	551
East Stirling v Livingston	2-1	563
Edinburgh City v Brechin City	0-3	333
Albion Rovers v Queens Park	1-2	619
East Fife v Arbroath	2-0	729
Peterhead v Greenock Morton	2-1	817
Clyde v Montrose	2-0	677
Airdrie United v Cove Rangers	3-0	821
Raith Rovers v Alloa Athletic	0-0	1493
Clachnacuddin v Stenhousemuir	0-5	354
Ross County v Dumbarton	2-2	1200

replays

Alloa Athletic v Raith Rovers	2-1	860
Dumbarton v Ross County	1-2	557
Dalbeattie Star v Forres Mechanics	2-4 aet	402
Ayr United v Lochee United	3-1	2049

2009/10

1st round

Selkirk v Preston Athletic	3-0	83
Clachnacuddin v Wick Academy	2-2	181
Auchinleck Talbot v Fort William	7-0	549
Nairn County v Golspie Sutherland	5-2	106
Inverurie Locos v St Cuthbert Wanderers	5-0	439
Brora Rangers v Irvine Meadow	0-2	
Coldstream v Edinburgh City	1-5	90
Buckie Thistle v Forres Mechanics	0-0	362
Whitehill Welfare v Wigtown & Bladnoch	1-1	96
Fraserburgh v Bonnyrigg Rose	1-1	
Edinburgh University v Girvan	0-3	122
Glasgow University v Vale of Leithen	1-4	151
Lossiemouth v Newton Stewart	4-1	140
Rothes v Banks O Dee	1-5	
Civil Service Strollers v Gala Fairydean	1-0	62
Hawick Royal Albert v Huntly	0-7	182
Dalbeattie Star v Keith	2-4	138

replays

Wick Academy v Clachnacuddin	2-1	257
Forres Mechanics v Buckie Thistle*	0-0	404
Wigtown & Bladnoch v Whitehill Welfare	0-3	142
Bonnyrigg Rose v Fraserburgh	1-2	

2nd round

Queens Park v Livingston	1-3	678
Nairn County v Elgin City	2-4	600
Fraserburgh v Spartans	1-4	389
Deveronvale v Buckie Thistle	2-2	1025
Whitehill Welfare v Threave Rovers	1-1	215
Inverurie Loco Works v Stranraer	2-1	410
Vale of Leithen v Keith	1-3	73
Forfar Athletic v East Stirling	4-2	396
Cove Rangers v Annan Athletic	2-1	278/300
Selkirk v Irvine Meadow	0-3	238
Girvan v Wick Academy	1-4	180
Lossiemouth v Albion Rovers	0-2	235
Edinburgh City v Burntisland Shipyard	5-1	123
Banks o Dee v Montrose	0-3	190/400
Huntly v Auchinleck Talbot	1-1	488
Civil Service Strollers v Berwick Rangers	1-2	387

2nd round replays

Buckie Thistle v Deveronvale	1-3	1100
Threave Rovers v Whitehill Welfare	1-0	269
Auchinleck Talbot v Huntly	4-3	498

3rd Round

Airdrie United v Queen of the South	4-0	1141
Ross County v Berwick Rangers	5-1	819
threave Rovers v Inverurie Loco Works	1-2	520
Deveronvale v Ayr United	0-1	1100
Cowdenbeath v Alloa Athletic	0-0	377
Albion Rovers v Elgin City	1-0	275
Stirling Albion v Auchinleck Talbot	2-1	1185
Clyde v Livingston	1-1	538
Irvine Meadow v Arbroath	1-0	1216
Edinburgh City v Keith	3-1	177
Wick Academy v Brechin City	4-4	1217
Stenhousemuir v Cove Rangers	5-0	409
Greenock Morton v Dumbarton	0-0	1882
Montrose v East Fife	2-1	509
Raith Rovers v Peterhead	0-0	1418
Spartans v Forfar Athletic	0-1	723

3rd rd replays

Alloa Athletic v Cowedenbeath	1-0	432
Dumbarton v Greenock Morton	0-1	1495
Peterhead v Raith Rovers	1-4	537
Brechin City v Wick Academy	4-2	402
Livingston v Clyde	7-1	690

2010/11

1st round

Golspie Sutherland v Fort William	2-2	45
Rothes v Nairn County	2-2	114
Civil Service Strollers v Wigtown & Bladnoch	1-2	
Edinburgh City v Clachnacuddin	1-0	137
Glasgow University v Burntisland Shipyard	1-0	227
Beith v Linlithgow Rose	2-0	1079
Coldstream v Forres Mechanics	1-3	84
Fraserburgh v St Cuthbery Wanderers	3-3	272
Hawick Royal Albert v Dalbeattie Star	0-3	95
Newton Stewart v Preston Athletic	1-1	143
Edinburgh University v Brora Rangers	2-2	228
Deveronvale v Inverurie Loco Works	0-0	445
Lossiemouth v Whitehill Welfare	0-2	147
Vale of Leithen v Keith	1-3	93
Huntly v Girvan	2-2	252
Selkirk v Bo'ness United	1-6	477
Gala Fairydean v Sunnybank	1-6	196

replays

Inverurie Loco Works v Deveronvale	0-5	714
Brora Rangers v Edinburgh University	2-1	139
St Cuthbert Wanderers v Fraserburgh	3-1	202
Fort William v Golspie Sutherland	2-3	80
Girvan v Huntly	2-1	
Preston Athletic v Newton Stewart	3-0	117
Nairn County v Rothes	4-1	126

2nd round

Deveronvale v Dalbeattie Star	1-0	361
Forres Mechanics v East Stirling	0-0	374
Preston Athletic v Annan Athletic	0-0	344
Clyde v Berwick Rangers	1-2	534
Wigtown & Bladnoch v Buckie Thistle	1-7	158
Beith v Glasgow University	8-1	649
Nairn County v Cove Rangers	0-1	161
Keith v Spartans	0-3	184
Stranraer v St Cuthberts Wanderers	9-0	401
Bo'ness United v Queens Park	2-1	1448
Whitehill Welfare v Wick Academy	4-3	263
Golspie Sutherland v Girvan	2-2	75
Montrose v Arbroath	1-1	994
Edinburgh City v Threave Rovers	2-4	278
Albion Rovers v Sunnybank	0-1	357
Elgin City v Brora Rangers	5-3	723

2nd round replays

East Stirling v Forres Mechanics	4-0	326
Annan Athletic v Preston Athletic	5-0	426
Girvan v Golspie Sutherland	4-0	129
Arbroath v Montrose	2-3 aet	838

3rd Round

Peterhead v Cowdenbeath	2-0	510
Ross County v Deveronvale	4-1	1170
East Fife v Forfar Athletic	3-1	695
Bo'ness United v Buckie Thistle	0-2	1301
Spartans v East Stirling	1-2	601
Stirling Albion v Partick Thistle	1-3	1146
Cove Rangers v Berwick Rangers	0-3	250
Stenhousemuir v Threave Rovers	2-2	429
Brechin City v Annan Athletic	2-2	402
Airdrie United v Beith	2-2	1412
Dumbarton v Greenock Morton	1-2	936
Alloa Athletic v Raith Rovers	4-2	1039
Montrose v Whitehill Welfare	3-1	435
Ayr United v Sunnybank	5-0	1069
Elgin City v Livingston	2-1	802
Stranraer v Girvan	4-2	840

3rd rd replays

Beith v Airdrie United	3-4	1809
Annan Athletic v Brechin City	2-5	512
Threave Rovers v Stenhousemuir	1-5	240

2011/12

1st round

Rothes v Clachnacuddin	0-3	133
Fort William v Boness United	0-4	241
Edinburgh City v Brora Rangers	3-0	157
Nairn County v Selkirk	2-1	222
Fraserburgh v Civil Service Strollers	4-3	324
Wigtown & Bladnoch v Preston Athletic	2-0	110
Lossiemouth v Auchinleck Talbot	1-2	472
Huntly v Newton Stewart	6-1	205
Forres Mechanics v Irvine Meadow	2-2	382
Dalbeattie Star v Inverurie Locos	1-6	186
Wick Academy v Coldstream	9-1	333
Glasgow University v Cove Rangers	0-4	258
Vale of Leithen v Girvan	1-0	76
Gala Fairydean v Hawick Royal Albert	8-1	180
Culter v Burntisland Shipyard	4-0	269
Edinburgh University v Whitehill Welfare	0-3	166
St Cuthbert Wanderers v Keith	0-2	138

replays

Irvine Meadow v Forres Mechanics	6-3	444

2nd round

Clachnacuddin v Inverurie Locos	1-1	219
Vale of Leithen v Cove Rangers	3-2	193
Gala Fairydean v Golspie Sutherland	5-2	115
Bo'ness United v Whitehill Welfare	2-1	736
Fraserburgh v Elgin City	0-0	663
Wigtown & Bladnoch v Stranraer	0-9	506
Peterhead v Nairn County	2-0	625
Wick Academy v Keith	0-1	322
Culter** v Spartans	0-2	352
Alloa Athletic v Annan Athletic	2-2	490
Deveronvale v Berwick Rangers	4-0	497
Auchinleck Talbot v Threave Rovers	8-1	659
East Stirling v Buckie Thistle	1-1	372
Huntly v Queens Park	0-3	464
Montrose v Clyde	2-1	446
Edinburgh City v Irvine Meadow	0-1	775

2nd round replays

Inverurie Locos v Clachnacuddin	3-2	335
Elgin City v Fraserburgh	5-2	742
Annan Athletic v Alloa Athletic	2-0	502
Buckie Thistle v East Stirling	2-4	395

3rd Round

Culter V Partick Thistle	1-1	1050
Ayr v Montrose	2-2	962
Irvine Meadow v Livingston	0-6	1586
Stirling Albion v Dundee	1-2	1473
Stenhousemuir v Annan Athletic	4-0	602
Greenock Morton v Deveronvale	5-1	1406
Airdrie United v Gala Fairydean	11-0	732
Keith v Arbroath	0-1	327
Elgin v Queens Park	1-1	799
Stranraer v Forfar	1-1	308
Inverurie Locos v Peterhead	2-4	908
Ross County v Albion Rovers	4-0	1353
Bo'ness United v Cowdenbeath	0-3	1244
Auchinleck Talbot v Vale of Leithen	3-1	705
Brechin v Dumbarton	3-0	447
East Fife v East Stirling	5-0	585

3rd rd replays

Montrose v Ayr United	1-2	575
Partick v Culter	4-0	1864
Queens Park v Elgin	3-1	513
Forfar v Stranraer	3-0	423

2012/13

Preliminary round

Fort William v Preston Athletic	1-3	82
Keith v St Cuthbert Wanderers	0-1	79

1st round

Threave Rovers v Vale of Leithen	0-1	129
Bonnyrigg rose v Girvan	2-1	383
Huntly v Wigtown & Bladnoch	2-2	180
Shotts bon Accord v Edinburgh City	1-1	304
Irvine Meadow v Gala Fairydean	4-0	431
Edinburgh university v St Cuthberts	1-2	74
Formartine v Brora	3-2	177
Civil Service Strollers v Newton Stewart	4-0	31
Spartans v Wick Academy	0-2	226
Glasgow University v Selkirk	0-2	60
Clachnacuddin v Lossiemouth	2-1	178
Hawick Royal Albert v golspie Sutherland	2-4	63
Fraserburgh v Coldstream	4-0	242
Whitehill Welfare v Inverurie Locos	2-4	182
Buckie thistle v Rothes	0-0	244
Hermes v Deveronvale	1-4	203
Preston Athletic v Nairn County	0-2	157
Turriff Utd v Burntisland Shipyard	6-1	295

1st round replays

Wigtown & Bladnoch v Huntly	0-2	114
Edinburgh City v Shotts Bon Accord	4-1	232
Rothes v Buckie Thistle	0-4	238

2nd round

Cove rangers v Golspie Sutherland	7-0	250
Fraserburgh v East Stirling	1-2	389
Forres Mechanics v Rangers	0-1	3001
Clachnacuddin v Formartine	4-2	168
Civil Service Strollers v Turriff Utd	1-2	132
Montrose v Edinburgh City	1-3	273
Buckie Thistle v Annan Athletic	0-0	241
Berwick rangers v Wick Academy	1-0	423
Selkirk v Vale of Leithen	1-1	102
Inverurie Locos v Huntly	4-3	509
Deveronvale v Peterhead	3-2	510
elgin City v St Cuthbert Wanderers	3-1	482
Dalbeattie Star v Stirling Albion	0-5	231
Queen's Park v Irvine Meadow	3-0	1142
Stirling University v Bonnyrigg Rose	0-1	589
Clyde v Nairn County	3-3	537

2nd round replays

Annan Athleic v Buckie Thistle	1-2	404
Vale of Leithen v Selkirk	5-1	142
Nairn County v Clyde	3-2	495

3rd round

Rangers V Alloa Atheltic	7-0	25478
Elgin City v East fife	5-1	748
Buckie Thistle v Turriff United	0-1	800
Dumbarton v East Stirlingshire	4-1	446
Airdrie United v Raith Rovers	2-2	854
Stranraer v Queens Park	1-1	344
Partick Thistle V Cove Rangers	2-1	1957
Forfar Athletic v Nairn County	3-3	546
Albion Rovers v Morton	1-1	656
Cowdenbeath v Vale of Leithen	8-1	309
Edinburgh City v Queen of the South	0-2	1038
Stirling Albion v Deveronvale	0-1	688
Inverurie Loco Works v Arbroath	3-3	732
Ayr United v Clachnacuddin	2-1	1032
Stenhousemuir v Berwick Rangers	1-1	439
Brechin City v Bonnyrigg Rose	2-2	602

3rd round replays

Raith Rovers v Airdrie United	4-3	935
Queens Park v Stranraer	0-4	551
Nairn County v Forfar Athletic	2-3	578
Morton v Albion Rovers	3-0	746
Arbroath v Inverurie Loco Works	3-1	1108
Berwick Rangers v Stenhousemuir	2-5	402
Bonnyrigg Rose v Brechin City	0-6	1082

2013/14

1st round

Edinburgh Univ v Spartans	0-2	213
Threave Rovers v Rothes	3-0	120
Golspie Sutherland v Edinburgh City	0-4	26
Huntly v Preston Athletic	3-4	186
Coldstream v Wick Academy	0-6	228
Girvan v Auchinleck Talbot	1-5	568
Selkirk v Turriff Utd	1-3	65
Fort William v Newton Stewart	0-0	50
Forres Mechanics v Keith	4-5	205
Fraserburgh v Civil Service Strollers	4-0	269
Gala Fairydean Rovers v Glasgow University	3-1	152
Wigtown and Bladnoch v Buckie thistle	3-4	151
Brora Rangers v Vale of Leithen	1-0	195
Deveronvale v Clachnacuddin	5-0	250
Inverurie Locos v Burntisland Shipyard	3-0	366
Hawick Royal Albert v St Cuthbert Wanderers	0-1	90
Lossiemouth v Culter	0-0	181
Linlithgow Rose v Nairn County	2-0	844

1st round replays

Newton Stewart v Fort William	3-1	92
Culter v Lossiemouth	3-1	230

2nd round

Gala Fairydean Rovers v Clyde	0-3	705
Turriff Utd v Wick Academy	4-2	354
Albion Rovers v Spartans	1-0	437
Queens Park v Preston Athletic	2-2	593
Brora Rangers v Cove Rangers	1-1	173
Dalbeattie Star v Montrose	0-1	165
Edinburgh City v Fraserburgh	4-4	252
Berwick Rangers v Peterhead	2-1	356
Keith v Elgin City	0-4	556
East Stirling v Threave Rovers	6-0	289
Stirling Albion v Whitehill Welfare	2-2	399
Auchinleck Talbot v St Cuthberts Wanderers	4-0	500
Formartine Utd v Inverurie Loco Works	0-2	529
Newton Stewart v Culter	0-6	115
Buckie Thistle v Annan Athletic	0-0	266
Deveronvale v Linlithgow Rose	2-2	512

2nd round replays

Preston Athletic v Queens Park	1-2	806
Cove Rangers v Brora Rangers	0-3	372
Fraserburgh v Edinburgh City	2-0	442
Whitehill Welfare v Stirling Albion	1-2	512
Annan Athletic v Buckie Thistle	4-0	242
Linlithgow Rose v Deveronvale	1-3	1215

3rd round

Forfar v East Fife	2-1	485
Culter v Berwick Rangers	1-1	638
Elgin City v Dunfermline Athletic	3-5	1108
Stranraer v Auchinleck Talbot	2-2	1170
Alloa Athletic v Inverurie Loco Works	3-0	403
Ayr United v Queens Park	3-2	917
Rangers v Airdrieonians	3-0	22533
Dumbarton v Cowdenbeath	2-1	450
Arbroath v Brechin City	0-2	623
Stenhousemuir v Annan Athletic	2-2	309
Fraserburgh v Montrose	2-1	565
Turriff United v Stirling Albion	0-3	473
East Stirlingshire v Raith Rovers	0-2	790
Albion Rovers v Deveronvale	1-0	484
Clyde v Brora Rangers	2-1	575
Queen of the South v Hamilton Accies	1-0	1324

3rd round replays

Annan Athletic v Stenhousemuir	2-4	302
Auchinleck Talbot v Stranraer	2-3	1466
Berwick Rangers v Culter	3-1	411

2014/15

preliminary round

Lothian Thistle Hutcheson Vale v Burntisland Shipyward	3-0	92
Auchinleck talbot v St Cuthbert Wanderers	5-1	403
Hurlford United v Edinburgh University	2-2	214
Glasgow University v Cove Rangers	1-9	70
Vale of Leithen v Gala Fairydean Rovers	0-1	83
Newton Stewart v Hawick Royal Albert	2-2	66
Edinburgh City v Fort William	5-0	152
Wigtown & Bladnoch v Civil Service Strollers	1-2	74

preliminary round replays

Edinburgh University v Hurlford United	0-5	91
Hawick Royal Albert v Newton Stewart	3-0	82

1st round

Lossiemouth v Turriff United	0-4	172
Deveronvale v Nairn County	0-1	223
Selkirk v Bo'ness United	0-4	369
Gretna 2008 v Gala Fairydean Rovers	2-1	218
Culter v Strathspey Thistle	4-2	195
Clachnacuddin v Hurlford United	1-7	164
Rothes vs Banks O'Dee	0-4	53
Preston Athletic v Threave Rovers	1-2	108
Forres Mechanics v Civil Service Strollers	4-1	221
Huntly v Wick Academy	2-1	173
Cove Rangers v Hawick Royal Albert	9-0	121
Keith v Formartine United	1-3	111
Edinburgh City v Coldstream	2-1	138
Fraserburgh v Linlithgow Rose	0-0	499
Lothian Thistle Hutchison Vale v East Kilbride	0-1	125
Golspie Sutherland v Dalbeattie Star	1-4	44
Auchinleck Talbot v Buckie Thistle	5-0	575
Whitehill Welfare v Girvan	3-1	94

1st round replay

Linlithgow Rose v Fraserburgh	2-1	741

2nd Round

Stirling University v Albion Rovers	1-4	302
Whitehill Welfare v East Stirling	0-1	266
Inverurie Locos v Hurlford United	0-3	385
Gretna 2008 v Queens Park	0-1	380
Turriff United v Clyde	0-3	481
Berwick Rangers v Formartine United	2-0	347
Brora Rangers v Banks o Dee	5-0	207
Cove Rangers v Annan Athletic	1-2	190
Elgin City v Forres Mechanics	0-0	1025
Nairn County v Huntly	2-1	210
Arbroath v Montrose	2-2	902
East Fife v Threave Rovers	7-0	417
Spartans v East Kilbride	3-3	285
Bo'ness United v Culter	7-1	635
Linlithgow Rose v Dalbeattie Star	5-1	645
Edinburgh City v Auchinleck Talbot	2-1	573

2nd round replays

Forres Mechanics v Elgin City	1-3	895
Montrose v Arbroath	1-3	785
East Kilbride v Spartan	1-5	446

3rd round

East Fife v Berwick Rangers	2-3	477
Arbroath v Nairn County	2-1	682
Elgin City v Bo'ness United	4-4	858
Stenhousemuir v Brechin City	1-2	451
Hurlford United v Stirling Albion	1-1	551
Forfar Athletic v Cowdenbeath	1-3	592
Edinburgh City v Brora Rangers	2-3	601
Ayr United v Alloa Athletic	1-1	784
Spartans v Clyde	2-0	611
Peterhead v Stranraer	0-1	430
Dumbarton v rangers	0-1	1878
Queens Park v Albion rovers	1-2	438
Greenock Morton v Airdrieonians	0-0	1420
Annan Athletic v Livingston	3-2	560
East Stirlingshire v Dunfermline Athletic	1-4	991
Linlithgow Rose v Raith Rovers	0-2	2250

3rd round replays

Bo'ness United v Elgin City	5-4	1280
Stirling Albion* v Hurlford United	2-2	567
Alloa Athletic v Ayr United	4-0	420
Airdrieonians v Greenock Morton	0-2	668

2015/16

2015/16 - 1st preliminary round

Wigtown & Bladnoch v Vale of Leithen	1-0	52
Golspie Sutherland v Cove Rangers	1-6	34
St Cuthberts Wanderers v Burntisland Shipyard	3-1	132
Harestanes v Girvan	0-3	245
Civil Service Strollers v Newton Stewart	3-0	50

2nd Preliminary Round

Cove Rangers v St Cuthberts Wanderers	7-2	123
Lothian Thistle Hutcheson Vale v Girvan	2-2	66
Wigtown & Bladnoch v Hawick Royal Albert	2-3	66
Hermes v Auchinleck Talbot	0-4	272
Civil Service Strollers v Kelty Hearts	0-4	175

2nd Preliminary Round replay

Girvan v Lothian Thistle Hutcheson Vale	2-5	48

1st round

Banks O'Dee v Cove Rangers	2-3	290
BSC Glasgow v Auchinleck Talbot	2-2	417
Strathspey Thistle v Edinburgh University	1-2	89
Lothian Thistle HV v Kelty Hearts	3-0	154
Preston Athletic v Fort William	2-3	61
Lossiemouth v Forres Mechanics	1-4	247
Keith v Inverurie Loco Works	1-5	
Spartans v Coldsteam	5-1	189
Hawick RA v Huntly	0-3	106
Deveronvale v Clachnacuddin	0-5	231
Threave Rovers v Stirling University	1-3	92
Gala Fairydean Rovers v Linlithgow Rose	0-2	452
Cumbernauld Colts v Glasgow University	3-0	224
Nairn County v Selkirk	5-1	166
Buckie Tihstle v Rothes	7-0	147
Fraserburgh v Dalbeattie Star	3-2	273
Wick Academy v Whitehill Welfare	2-2	469
Formartine United v Gretna 2008	3-1	158

1st round replays

Auchinleck Talbot v BSC Glasgow	5-0	509
Whitehill Welfare v Wick Academy	2-3	228

2nd round

Inverurie Loco Works v Edinburgh University	2-1	239
Nairn County v Wick Academy	2-2	240
Cumbernauld Colts v Auchinleck Talbot	2-0	525
University of Stirling v Queen's Park	0-2	394
Turriff Utd v Fraserburgh	2-3	399
Edinburgh City v Buckie Thistle	1-2	221
Formartine Utd v Clyde	2-0	341
Elgin City v Spartans	1-0	563
East Kilbride v Forres Mechanics	1-1	329
Brora Rangers v Arbroath	1-2	413
Annan Athletic v Berwick Rangers	4-1	404
East Fife v Stirling Albion	0-0	504
Huntly v East Stirlingshire	2-1	187
Lothian Thistle HV v Montrose	1-1	212
Clachnacuddin v Linlithgow Rose	1-3	323
Fort William v Cove Rangers	0-4	96

2nd round replays

Wick Academy v Nairn County	5-1	356
Forres Mechanics v East Kilbride	2-3	270
Stirling Albion v East Fife	1-0	488
Montrose v Lothian Thistle HV	1-2	512

3rd round

Stranraer v Buckie Thistle	3-1	415
Queen's Park v Forfar Athletic	1-1	418
Formartine United v Cove Rangers	1-1	376
Dumbarton v Alloa Athletic	5-0	274
Stirling Albion v Cumbernauld Colts	6-0	425
Albion Rovers v Greenock Morton	0-2	505
Falkirk v Fraserburgh	4-1	1825
Wick Academy v Linlithgow Rose	2-2	615
Peterhead v Livingston	1-3	587
Huntly v Lothian Thistle Hutchison Vale	1-1	239
Elgin City v Raith Rovers	1-2	853
Airdrieonians v Brechin City	3-1	532
Ayr United v Dunfermline Athletic	0-1	1582
Inverurie Loco Works v Annan Athletic	4-4	355
Stenhousemuir v East Kilbride	2-2	502
Cowdenbeath v Arbroath	1-1	409

3rd round replays

Forfar Athletic v Queens Park	1-0	520
Cove Rangers v Formartine United	4-1	450
Lothian Thistle Hutcheson Vale v Huntly	3-0	333
Annan Athletic v Inverurie Loco Works	1-0	287
East Kilbride v Stenhousemuir	2-1	488
Arbroath v Cowdenbeath	2-4	500
Linlithgow Rose v Wick Academy	5-1	1562

2016/17

1st preliminary round

Edusport Academy v Colville Park	2-2	27
Newton Stewart v Beith	0-4	191
Wigtown & Bladnoch v Auchinleck Talbot	0-4	167
Glasgow Uni v Bonnyrigg Rose	2-8	70
St Cuthberts Wanderers v Leith Athletic	0-3	57

1st preliminary round replays

Colville Park v Edusport Academy	1-0	41

2nd preliminary round

Leith Athletic v Coldstream	1-0	73
Bonnyrigg Rose v Burntisland Shipyard	14-0	387
Colville Park v Girvan	0-1	77
Beith v Auchinleck Talbot	2-2	692
Threave Rovers v Linlithgow Rose	1-2	278
Banks O'Dee v Golspie Sutherland	4-0	68

2nd preliminary round replays

Auchinleck Talbot v Beith	0-3	563

1st Round

Turriff United v Bonnyrigg Rose	1-1	304
Leith Athletic v Cumbernauld Colts	0-0	174
Forres Mechanics v Lossiemouth	2-2	244
Ft William v Brora Rangers	1-4	45
East Kilbride v Vale of Leithen	9-1	154
BSC Glasgow v Rothes	3-1	70
Edinburgh University v Whitehill Welfare	0-1	108
Deveronvale v Gretna 2008	0-3	198
Gala Fairydean Rovers v Fraserburgh	3-1	160
Keith v Banks o'Dee	0-1	107
Civil Service Strollers v Hawick Royal Albert	1-1	43
Nairn County v Preston Athletic	2-3	121
Inverurie Loco Works v Buckie Thistle	0-6	553
Dalbeattie Star v Wick Academy	1-3	105
Beith v Strathspey Thistle	6-0	373
Inverness Clachnacuddin v Stirling University	1-2	129
Selkirk v Linlithgow Rose	0-3	177
Girvan v Huntly	1-2	68

1st Round replays

Bonnyirgg Rose v Turriff United	4-1	676
Cumbernauld Colts v Leith Athletic	1-0	167
Lossiemouth v Forres Mechanics	0-4	245
Hawick Royal Albert v Civil Service Strollers	6-2	75

2nd round

Annan Athletic v East Stirlingshire	0-0	302
Banks o'Dee v Formartine United	2-2	199
Brora Rangers v Clyde	0-2	291
BSC Glasgow v Beith	0-1	270
Bonnyrigg Rose v Cove Rangers	2-1	657
Berwick Rangers v Hawick Royal Albert	2-3	477
Linlithgow Rose v Stirling Albion	0-3	1063
Wick Academy v Whitehill Welfare	4-1	403
Preston Athletic v Montrose	0-3	257
Huntly v Spartans	0-2	181
Edinburgh City v Forfar Athletic	0-0	328
Cowdenbeath v East Kilbride	0-1	286
Cumbernauld Colts v Forres Mechanics	2-2	187
Arbroath v Stirling University	3-1	412
Gala Fairydean Rovers v Elgin City	0-4	275
Buckie Thistle v Gretna 2008	1-1	586

2nd round replays

East Stirlingshire v Annan Athletic	1-2	114
Formartine United v Banks O'Dee	7-2	136
Forfar Athletic v Edinburgh City	0-1	388
Forres Mechanics v Cumbernauld Colts	4-0	268
Gretna 2008 v Buckie Thistle	2-6	174

3rd Round

Elgin City vs. Hawick Royal Albert	8-1	549
Airdrieonians vs. Livingston	1-2	780
Buckie Thistle vs. Dunfermline Athletic	3-5	1441
Stirling Albion vs. Wick Academy	2-0	572
St Mirren vs. Spartans	5-1	1147
Stranraer vs. East Kilbride	2-1	331
Forres Mechanics vs. Stenhousemuir	2-2	369
East Fife vs. Edinburgh City	1-1	339
Albion Rovers vs. Queen of the South	2-1	387
Clyde vs. Arbroath	5-0	368
Formartine United vs. Annan Athletic	4-0	124
Beith Juniors vs. Greenock Morton	0-6	1693
Brechin City vs. Ayr United	0-1	308
Bonnyrigg Rose vs. Dumbarton	0-0	1552
Peterhead vs. Alloa Athletic	0-1	563
Queen's Park vs. Montrose	2-0	348

3rd round replays

Stenhousemuir v Forres Mechanics	3-1	291
Dumbarton v Bonnyrigg Rose	0-1	632
Edinburgh City v East Fife	0-1	397

2017/18		
1st preliminary round		
Kelty Hearts v Lothian Thistle Hutcheson Vale	0-1	222
Glenafton Athletic v Newton Stewart	6-0	211
Burntisland Shipyard v Colville Park	0-7	98
2nd preliminary round		
Banks o'Dee v Linlithgow Rose	2-1	216
Glasgow University v Threave Rovers	1-1	50
Colville Park v Preston Athletic	5-0	53
Lothian Thistle Hutcheson Vale v Coldstream	4-0	83
Glenafton Athletic v Golspie Sutherland	6-1	214
St Cuthbert Wanderers v Girvan	3-5	86
2nd preliminary round replays		
Threave Rovers v Glasgow University	2-1	80
1st Round		
Wick Academy v Stirling Uni	2-2	314
Selkirk v Gretna 2008	4-0	66
Edusport Academy v Rothes	1-1	35
Banks o Dee v Huntly	4-0	227
Spartans v Vale of Leithen	3-0	197
Gala Fairydean Rovers v Keith	0-2	92
Fraserburgh v Forres Mechanics	2-1	240
Lothian Thistle Hutcheson Vale v Inverurie Locos	3-2	123
Edinburgh Uni v Lossiemouth	2-1	54
Clachnacuddin v Fort William	8-0	117
Glenafton Athletic v Threave Rovers	4-0	240
Brora Rangers v Girvan	5-0	114
Nairn County v Whitehill Welfare	1-0	269
Colville Park v Cumbernauld Colts	2-1	98
Deveronvale v Hawick Royal Albert	3-1	220
Formartine United v Turriff United	2-1	174
Civil Service Strollers v Strathspey Thistle	2-1	85
BSC Glasgow v Dalbeattie Star	1-0	126
1st Round replays		
Stirling University v Wick Academy	1-0	106
Rothes v Edusport Academy	1-3	95
2nd round		
Banks o' Dee v Selkirk	2-0	137
Berwick Rangers v Annan Athletic	1-0	397
Buckie Thistle v BSC Glasgow	6-2	223
Civil Service Strollers v Brora Rangers	0-5	159
Cowdenbeath v East Kilbride	0-1	251
Deveronvale v Glenafton Athletic	0-2	294
Edinburgh City v Stenhousemuir	0-1	286
Edinburgh University v Fraserburgh	0-2	148
Elgin City v Edusport Academy	3-1	552
Formartine United v East Stirlingshire	4-0	177
Keith v Clyde	0-3	159
Montrose v Stirling University	4-1	476
Nairn County v Cove Rangers	1-2	170
Peterhead v Colville Park	9-0	484
Spartans v Clachnacuddin	5-0	209
Stirling Albion v Lothian Thistle Hutcheson Vale	3-5	521
3rd round		
Airdrieonians v Cove Rangers	2-3	395
Arbroath v Berwick Rangers	3-0	536
Banks o' Dee v Ayr United	2-6	469
Buckie Thistle v Brechin City	2-3	257
Clyde v East Fife	0-2	497
Dumbarton v Elgin City	1-0	490
East Kilbride v Albion Rovers	3-4	287
Formartine United v Forfar Athletic	1-0	242
Livingston v Glenafton Athletic	2-0	828
Lothian Thistle Hutcheson Vale v St Mirren	1-7	1172
Montrose v Queen of the South	0-0	530
Peterhead v Raith Rovers	3-0	671
Queens Park v Dunfermline Athletic	1-4	1179
Spartans v Fraserburgh	1-2	335
Stenhousemuir v Alloa Athletic	1-2	444
Stranraer v Brora Rangers	0-1	443
3rd round replays		
Queen of the South v Montrose	2-1	794

* Won on pens

** default, Spartans fielded inelgible player

Scottish League (Premier Sports) Cup 2021/2

Premier Sports Scottish League Cup Draw 2021/22

NORTH

Group A

Cove Rangers, Hearts, Inverness CT, Peterhead, Stirling Albion

Group B

Arbroath, Dundee United, East Fife, Elgin City, Kelty Hearts

Group C

Brora Rangers, Dundee, Forfar Athletic, Montrose, Ross County

Group D

Alloa Athletic, Brechin City, Cowdenbeath, Livingston, Raith Rovers

SOUTH

Group E

Albion Rovers, Ayr United, Edinburgh City, Falkirk, Hamilton Accies

Group F

Airdrieonians, Annan Athletic, Motherwell, Queen of the South, Queen's Park

Group G

Clyde, East Kilbride, Morton, Kilmarnock, Stranraer

Group H

Dumbarton, Dunfermline Athletic, Partick Thistle, St Mirren, Stenhousemuir

The explanation for anomalies in the North / South allocation is seeding. Teams are divided into the following groups:

Pot 1 - Premier League (7) + Champions of Championship

Pot 2 - 9 Championship plus 7 League One

Pot 3 - 3 League One plus 10 League Two plus 3 Non League

East Kilbride were the third Non league entrant after drawing lots with Fraserburgh - the two clubs finished second in the Lowland and Highland Leagues respectively.

Scottish League (Betfred) Cup 2020/1

The four clubs competing in Europe were exempted from the group stages. The remaining 38 clubs, plus Berwick Rangers and East Kilbride, were drawn into 8 groups of 5. The draw was regionalised and seeded. Teams met each other once. Drawn matches went to a penalty kicks, with 2 points to the winners and 1 to the losers of the shoot-out. The 8 Group winners and the 4 best runners-up qualified for the First Round, with the 4 European entrants joining at that stage.

Details of team-line ups, dates, attendances etc are within the relevant club grids earlier in this book.

GROUP A

Pos		P	W	PW	PL	L	GF	GA	GD	PTS
1	Hearts	4	4	0	0	0	8	3	5	12
2	Raith Rovers	4	2	1	0	1	7	7	0	8
3	Inverness CT	4	1	1	1	1	4	4	0	6
4	East Fife	4	1	0	0	3	5	6	-1	3
5	Cowdenbeath	4	0	0	1	3	0	4	-4	1

HEA	RAI	ICT	EAS	COW
	3-1	1-0		
		3-3, 3-2p	2-1	
			1-0	0-0, 4-2p
2-3				2-0
0-1*	0-1			

* at East Fife

GROUP B

Pos		P	W	PW	PL	L	GF	GA	GD	PTS
1	Hibernian	4	4	0	0	0	10	3	7	12
2	Dundee (X)	4	3	0	0	1	9	4	5	9
3	Cove Rangers	4	1	1	0	2	4	7	-3	5
4	Brora Rangers	4	0	0	2	2	6	10	-4	2
5	Forfar Athletic	4	0	1	0	3	3	8	-5	2

HIB	DUN	COV	BRO	FOR
	4-1		3-1	
		3-0		3-0wo
1-2				1-0
	0-2	2-2, 5-6p		
0-1			3-3, 4-3p	

GROUP C

Pos		P	W	PW	PL	L	GF	GA	GD	PTS
1	St Johnstone	4	3	0	1	0	12	2	10	10
2	Dundee United	4	2	1	0	1	7	3	4	8
3	Peterhead	4	2	1	0	1	6	5	1	8
4	Kelty Hearts	4	1	0	1	2	4	4	0	4
5	Brechin City	4	0	0	0	4	3	18	-15	0

STJ	DUT	PET	KEL	BRE
	0-0			7-0
		0-1	1-0	
1-3				3-1
1-2		1-1, 3-5p		
	2-6		0-2	

GROUP D

Pos		P	W	PW	PL	L	GF	GA	GD	PTS
1	Ross County	4	3	1	0	0	12	5	7	11
2	Arbroath (X)	4	3	0	0	1	9	4	5	9
3	Elgin City	4	2	0	0	2	5	7	-2	6
4	Stirling Albion	4	1	0	0	3	3	8	-5	3
5	Montrose	4	0	0	1	3	5	10	-5	1

ROS	ARB	ELG	STI	MON
	2-1		3-0	
		3-0		3-1
1-4			2-0	
	1-2			2-1
3-3, 4-5p		0-2		

GROUP E

Pos		P	W	PW	PL	L	GF	GA	GD	PTS
1	Dunfermline Athletic	4	4	0	0	0	9	2	7	12
2	Falkirk (X)	4	3	0	0	1	9	3	6	9
3	Kilmarnock	4	2	0	0	2	4	6	-2	6
4	Clyde	4	1	0	0	3	6	9	-3	3
5	Dumbarton	4	0	0	0	4	2	10	-8	0

DUN	FAL	KIL	CLY	DTN
	2-0		3-2	
		3-0wo	2-1	
0-3				2-0
		0-2		3-2
0-1	0-4			

GROUP F

Pos		P	W	PW	PL	L	GF	GA	GD	PTS
1	Ayr United	4	2	1	0	1	8	5	3	8
2	Annan Athletic	4	2	0	1	1	9	4	5	7
3	Stranraer	4	1	1	2	0	6	5	1	7
4	Hamilton Accies	4	2	0	0	2	7	6	1	6
5	Albion Rovers	4	0	1	0	3	5	15	-10	2

AYR	ANN	STR	HAM	ALB
	1-0	1-1, 5-6p		
		1-1,4-5p	3-1	
			2-1	2-2, 15-14P
2-1				3-0wo
2-5	1-5			

KELTY HEARTS

Date	Comp	H/A	Opponents	F	A		HT		Referee	Crowd	Scorers	1	2	3	4	5	6	7	8	9	10	11	12	13	14	15	16	17	18
07/10/2020	LC	H	St Johnstone	1	2		0	1	A Newlands	BCD	Tidser	Jamieson	Boyle	Reid	Hooper	Stevenson	Tidser	Philp	Reilly	Higginbotham	Easton+	Russell*	Flynn*	McNab+	*Scobbie*	*McKenzie*	*Donaldson*	*Bembo*	
13/10/2020	LC	A	Dundee United	0	1		0	1	D Robertson	BCD		Jamieson	Boyle	Reid*	Hooper	Stevenson	Tidser	Philp&	Reilly	Higginbotham	Easton	McNab+	Scobbie*	Flynn+	Russell&	*McKenzie*	*Bembo*	*Donaldson*	
10/11/2020	LC	H	Peterhead	1	1	3-5p	0	0	G Ross	BCD	Stevenson	Jamieson	Boyle	Hill	Hooper	Stevenson	Tidser	Philp	Reilly	Higginbotham	Easton	Flynn*	McNab*	*Reid*	*Scobbie*	*Bembo*	*Cooney*	*Donaldson*	
14/11/2020	LC	A	Brechin City	2	0		1	0	G Grainger	BCD	Easton, McNab	Jamieson	Boyle	Hill*	Hooper	Stevenson	Tidser	Philp+	Reid>	Higginbotham	Easton	Flynn&	Cooney*	McNab+	Austin&	Scobbie>	*Bembo*	*Donaldson*	

BRORA RANGERS

Date	Comp	H/A	Opponents	F	A		HT		Referee	Crowd	Scorers	1	2	3	4	5	6	7	8	9	10	11	12	13	14	15	16	17	18
07/10/2020	LC	A	Hibernian	1	3		0	2	A Muir	BCD	Gillespie	Malin	Nicholson	Williamson>	Pickles<	T Kelly	Gillespie&	A Macdonald	Martin MacLean	A Macrae+	Morrison*	J Macrae	Brindle*	Wagenaar+	G McDonald&	Gamble>	N Macdonald<	*C Macrae*	
10/10/2020	LC	H	Dundee	0	2		0	2	B Cook	BCD		Malin	Nicholson	Williamson>	Pickles<	T Kelly	Gillespie&	A Macdonald	Martin MacLean	A Macrae	Morrison*	J Macrae+	Brindle*	Wagenaar+	G McDonald&	*Gamble*	*N Macdonald*	*C Macrae*	*Stephen*
13/10/2020	LC	H	Cove Rangers	2	2	5-6p	1	2	D Williams	BCD	M Maclean, Wagenaar	Malin	Nicholson	Williamson	Pickles	Brindle	Gillespie*	A Macdonald	Martin MacLean	A Macrae	Wagenaar	G MacDonald+	J MacRae*	Gamble+	*N Macdonald*	*C Macrae*	*Stephen*		
10/11/2020	LC	A	Forfar Athletic	3	3	2-3p	1	1	G Irvine	BCD	Irvine og, M MacLean, J MacRae	Beattie	Nicholson	Gamble	Morrison	T Kelly	Gillespie+	A Macdonald	Martin MacLean	A Macrae	Wagenaar*	J Macrae	Brindle*	G MacDonald+	*N Macdonald*				

GROUP G

Pos										
1	St Mirren	4	2	2	0	0	8	4	4	10
2	Queen of the South	4	1	1	2	0	7	5	2	7
3	Partick Thistle	4	1	2	0	1	3	4	-1	7
4	Morton	4	1	0	3	0	4	3	1	6
5	Queen's Park	4	0	0	0	4	1	7	-6	0

STM	QOS	PAR	MOR	QP
		4-1	1-1, 6-5p	
2-2, 2-4p		0-0, 2-3p		
			0-0,4-2p	2-0
	2-2			1-0
0-1	1-3			

GROUP H

Pos										
1	Livingston	4	4	0	0	0	15	3	12	12
2	Alloa Athletic (X)	4	3	0	0	1	9	5	4	9
3	Edinburgh City	4	1	0	1	2	5	9	-4	4
4	Airdrieonians	4	1	0	0	3	3	7	-4	3
5	Stenhousemuir	4	0	1	0	3	4	12	-8	2

LIV	ALL	EDC	AIR	STE
	2-1		4-1	
		2-1		4-2
1-5				2-2, 2-4p
	0-2	0-1		
0-4			0-2	

X = Qualified as one of best four runners-up
PW = Penalty shoot outs won, 2 points
PL = Penalty shoot outs lost, 1 point
wo = walkover, 3-0 win awarded due to Covid postponement

KO STAGES

Rd	Date	H	A	F	A		Att
1	28/11/2020	Alloa Athletic	Hearts	1	0	AET	BCD
1	28/11/2020	Arbroath	Dunfermline Athl	1	3		BCD
1	28/11/2020	Hibernian	Dundee	1	0		BCD
1	28/11/2020	Livingston	Ayr United	4	0		BCD
1	28/11/2020	Motherwell	St Johnstone	1	2		BCD
1	28/11/2020	St Mirren	Aberdeen	2	1		BCD
1	29/11/2020	Celtic	Ross County	0	2		BCD
1	29/11/2020	Falkirk	Rangers	0	4		BCD
2	15/12/2020	Dunfermline Athletic	St Johnstone	1	1		BCD
2	15/12/2020	Alloa Athletic	Hibernian	1	2		BCD
2	16/12/2020	Livingston	Ross County	2	0		BCD
2	16/12/2020	St Mirren	Rangers	3	2		BCD
SF	23/01/2021	St Johnstone (at Hampden)	Hibernian	3	0		BCD
SF	24/01/2021	Livingston (at Hampden)	St Mirren	1	0		BCD
F	28/02/2021	Livingston (at Hampden)	St Johnstone	0	1		BCD

Premier Sports Scottish League Cup Dates 2021/22

Group stage
MD1: Weekend of July 10/11
MD2: Midweek of July 13/14
MD3: Weekend of July 17/18
MD4: Midweek of July 20/21
MD5: Weekend of July 24/25

Second round
Weekend of August 14/15

Quarter-finals
Midweek of September 21-23

Semi-finals
Weekend of November 20/21

Final
Sunday December 19

Premier Sports Scottish League Cup Format 2021/22

Format

The group stage involves 40 clubs - the 37 SPFL clubs from 2020/21 who did not qualify for Europe plus Brora Rangers (Highland League champions), Kelty Hearts (Lowland League champions) and East Kilbride (Lowland League runners-up).Teams are drawn into eight groups of five - split into four north groups and four south groups. Each group contains one seeded club, one second seed and three unseeded clubs.

Group matches

Clubs are awarded the usual three points for a win but all drawn games in the group stage go straight to penalties - the shoot-out winners receive a bonus point. i.e. three points for a win, two points for a shoot-out win and one point for losing on penalties.

If clubs are level on points at the end of the group stage, the criteria for separating them is 1) goal difference, 2) goals scored, 3) away goals scored, 4) matches won, 5) away matches won, 6) drawing of lots.

Knock-out rounds

The eight group winners and three best runners-up progress to the second round, where they are joined by the five clubs competing in European competitions - Rangers, Celtic, Hibernian, Aberdeen and St Johnstone, who are also the cup holders. The seeded teams in the last 16 will be the five European entrants and the three group winners with the best records. The tournament reverts to a traditional knock-out format from the second round onwards, with ties decided by extra time and penalties if the scores are level after 90 minutes.

Scottish League Cup Finals 1947-2021

Season	Winner	Score	Runner-up	Venue	Attendance	Losing SF	
1946–47	Rangers	4 – 0	Aberdeen	Hampden Park	82,700	Hearts	Hibernian
1947–48	East Fife	0 – 0 AET	Falkirk	Hampden Park	53,785	Aberdeen	Rangers
1947–48 (R)	East Fife	4 – 1	Falkirk	Hampden Park	31,000		
1948–49	Rangers	2 – 0	Raith Rovers	Hampden Park	57,450	Hamilton Accies	Dundee
1949–50	East Fife	3 – 0	Dunfermline Athletic	Hampden Park	39,744	Rangers	Hibernian
1950–51	Motherwell	3 – 0	Hibernian	Hampden Park	64,074	Ayr United	QOS
1951–52	Dundee	3 – 2	Rangers	Hampden Park	92,325	Celtic	Motherwell
1952–53	Dundee	2 – 0	Kilmarnock	Hampden Park	51,830	Rangers	Hibernian
1953–54	East Fife	3 – 2	Partick Thistle	Hampden Park	38,529	Rangers	Hibernian
1954–55	Heart of Midlothian	4 – 2	Motherwell	Hampden Park	55,640	East Fife	Airdrie
1955–56	Aberdeen	2 – 1	St. Mirren	Hampden Park	44,106	Rangers	Motherwell
1956–57	Celtic	0 – 0 AET	Partick Thistle	Hampden Park	58,794	Dundee	Clyde
1956–57 (R)	Celtic	3 – 0	Partick Thistle	Hampden Park	31,156		
1957–58	Celtic	7 – 1	Rangers	Hampden Park	82,293	Brechin City	Clyde
1958–59	Heart of Midlothian	5 – 1	Partick Thistle	Hampden Park	59,690	Kilmarnock	Celtic
1959–60	Heart of Midlothian	2 – 1	Third Lanark	Hampden Park	57,994	Cowdenbeath	Arbroath
1960–61	Rangers	2 – 0	Kilmarnock	Hampden Park	82,063	Hamilton Accies	QOS
1961–62	Rangers	1 – 1 AET	Heart of Midlothian	Hampden Park	88,000	Stirling Albion	St Johnstone
1961–62 (R)	Rangers	3 – 1	Heart of Midlothian	Hampden Park	47,500		
1962–63	Heart of Midlothian	1 – 0	Kilmarnock	Hampden Park	51,000	Rangers	St Johnstone
1963–64	Rangers	5 – 0	Morton	Hampden Park	105,907	Berwick Rangers	Hibernian
1964–65	Rangers	2 – 1	Celtic	Hampden Park	91,423	Dundee United	Morton
1965–66	Celtic	2 – 1	Rangers	Hampden Park	107,609	Kilmarnock	Hibernian
1966–67	Celtic	1 – 0	Rangers	Hampden Park	94,532	Aberdeen	Airdrie
1967–68	Celtic	5 – 3	Dundee	Hampden Park	66,660	St Johnstone	Morton
1968–69	Celtic	6 – 2	Hibernian	Hampden Park	74,240	Dundee	Clyde
1969–70	Celtic	1 – 0	St. Johnstone	Hampden Park	73,067	Ayr United	Motherwell
1970–71	Rangers	1 – 0	Celtic	Hampden Park	106,263	Cowdenbeath	Dumbarton
1971–72	Partick Thistle	4 – 1	Celtic	Hampden Park	62,740	St Mirren	Falkirk
1972–73	Hibernian	2 – 1	Celtic	Hampden Park	71,696	Aberdeen	Rangers
1973–74	Dundee	1 – 0	Celtic	Hampden Park	27,924	Kilmarnock	Rangers
1974–75	Celtic	6 – 3	Hibernian	Hampden Park	53,848	Falkirk	Airdrie
1975–76	Rangers	1 – 0	Celtic	Hampden Park	58,806	Partick Thistle	Montrose
1976–77	Aberdeen	2 – 1 AET	Celtic	Hampden Park	69,707	Rangers	Hearts
1977–78	Rangers	2 – 1 AET	Celtic	Hampden Park	60,168	Forfar Athletic	Hearts
1978–79	Rangers	2 – 1	Aberdeen	Hampden Park	54,000	Hibernian	Celtic
1979–80	Dundee United	0 – 0 AET	Aberdeen	Hampden Park	27,173	Hamilton Accies	Morton
1979–80 (R)	Dundee United	3 – 0	Aberdeen	Dens Park	28,933		
1980–81	Dundee United	3 – 0	Dundee	Dens Park	24,466	Ayr United	Celtic
1981–82	Rangers	2 – 1	Dundee United	Hampden Park	53,777	Aberdeen	St Mirren
1982–83	Celtic	2 – 1	Rangers	Hampden Park	55,572	Dundee United	Hearts
1983–84	Rangers	3 – 2 AET	Celtic	Hampden Park	66,369	Dundee United	Aberdeen
1984–85	Rangers	1 – 0	Dundee United	Hampden Park	44,698	Meadowbank Th	Hearts
1985–86	Aberdeen	3 – 0	Hibernian	Hampden Park	40,061	Dundee United	Rangers
1986–87	Rangers	2 – 1	Celtic	Hampden Park	74,219	Dundee United	Motherwell
1987–88	Rangers	3 – 3 AET + pk	Aberdeen	Hampden Park	71,961	Dundee	Motherwell
1988–89	Rangers	3 – 2	Aberdeen	Hampden Park	72,122	Dundee United	Hearts
1989–90	Aberdeen	2 – 1 AET	Rangers	Hampden Park	61,190	Dunfermline Ath	Celtic
1990–91	Rangers	2 – 1 AET	Celtic	Hampden Park	62,817	Dundee United	Aberdeen
1991–92	Hibernian	2 – 0	Dunfermline Athletic	Hampden Park	40,377	Airdrie	Rangers
1992–93	Rangers	2 – 1 AET	Aberdeen	Hampden Park	54,298	St Johnstone	Celtic
1993–94	Rangers	2 – 1	Hibernian	Celtic Park	47,632	Dundee United	Celtic
1994–95	Raith Rovers	2 – 2 AET + pk	Celtic	Ibrox Stadium	45,384	Aberdeen	Airdrie
1995–96	Aberdeen	2 – 0	Dundee	Hampden Park	33,096	Rangers	Airdrie
1996–97	Rangers	4 – 3	Heart of Midlothian	Celtic Park	48,559	Dunfermline Ath	Dundee
1997–98	Celtic	3 – 0	Dundee United	Ibrox Stadium	49,305	Dunfermline Ath	Aberdeen
1998–99	Rangers	2 – 1	St. Johnstone	Celtic Park	45,533	Hearts	Airdrie
1999–00	Celtic	2 – 0	Aberdeen	Hampden Park	50,073	Dundee United	Kilmarnock
2000–01	Celtic	3 – 0	Kilmarnock	Hampden Park	48,830	St Mirren	Rangers
2001–02	Rangers	4 – 0	Ayr United	Hampden Park	50,076	Hibernian	Celtic
2002–03	Rangers	2 – 1	Celtic	Hampden Park	52,000	Dundee United	Hearts
2003–04	Livingston	2 – 0	Hibernian	Hampden Park	45,500	Dundee	Rangers
2004–05	Rangers	5 – 1	Motherwell	Hampden Park	50,182	Dundee United	Hearts

2005–06	Celtic	3 – 0	Dunfermline Athletic	Hampden Park	50,090	Motherwell	Livingston
2006–07	Hibernian	5 – 1	Kilmarnock	Hampden Park	52,000	St Johnstone	Falkirk
2007–08	Rangers	2 – 2 AET + pk	Dundee United	Hampden Park	50,019	Aberdeen	Hearts
2008–09	Celtic	2 – 0 AET	Rangers	Hampden Park	51,193	Dundee United	Falkirk
2009–10	Rangers	1 – 0	St. Mirren	Hampden Park	44,538	St Johnstone	Hearts
2010–11	Rangers	2 – 1 AET	Celtic	Hampden Park	51,181	Motherwell	Aberdeen
2011–12	Kilmarnock	1 – 0	Celtic	Hampden Park	49,572	Ayr United	Falkirk
2012–13	St. Mirren	3 – 2	Heart of Midlothian	Hampden Park	44,036	Inverness CT	Celtic
2013–14	Aberdeen	0 – 0 AET + pk	Inverness CT	Celtic Park	51,143	St Johnstone	Hearts
2014-15	Celtic	2-0	Dundee United	Hampden Park	49,259	Aberdeen	Rangers
2015-16	Ross County	2-1	Hibernian	Hampden Park	38,796	St Johnstone	Celtic
2016-17	Celtic	3-0	Aberdeen	Hampden Park	49,629	Rangers	Morton
2017-18	Celtic	2-0	Motherwell	Hampden Park	49,483	Rangers	Hibernian
2018-19	Celtic	1-0	Aberdeen	Hampden Park	50,936	Rangers	Hearts
2019-20	Celtic	1-0	Rangers	Hampden Park	51,117	Hibernian	Hearts
2020-21	St Johnstone	1-0	Livingston	Hampden Park	BCD	Hibernian	St Mirren

Season	Winner	Score	Runner-up	Venue	Attendance	Losing SF	
1940-41	Rangers	1-1	Hearts	Hampden Park	75,000	St Mirren	Celtic
1940-41 (R)	Rangers	4-2	Hearts	Hampden Park	70,000		
1941-42	Rangers	1-0	Morton	Hampden Park	43,000	Partick Thistle	Celtic
1942-43	Rangers	1-1 + corners	Falkirk	Hampden Park	20,000	Hamilton Accies	Third Lanark
1943-44	Hibernian	0-0 + corners	Rangers	Hampden Park	63,000	Celtic	Clyde
1944-45	Rangers	2-1	Motherwell	Hampden Park	80,000	Queen's Park	Motherwell
1945-46	Aberdeen	3-2	Rangers	Hampden Park	135,000	Airdrie	Hearts

Some sources include the War Time versions of the League Cup in the records. It is certainly true that the format of the competition (Groups, followed by knock out) was established during the War. However, War Time games are not normally included in football records and are regarded as "unofficial".

Alternative names / sponsors for the League Cup have been:

1979-81	Bell's Scottish League Cup
1983-84	Final only, sponsored by Telejector
1984-92	Skol Cup
1994-97	Coca Cola Cup
1999-2008	CIS Insurance Cup
2008-11	Co-operative Insurance Cup
2011-13	Scottish Communities League Cup
2014-15	Semi Finals and Final only, The Scottish League Cup presented by QTS
2015-16	The Scottish League Cup, presented by Utilita
2016-19	Betfred Cup

Winners (Not including war-time seasons)

Rangers	27	Motherwell	1
Celtic	19	Partick Thistle	1
Aberdeen	6	Raith Rovers	1
Hearts	4	Livingston	1
Hibernian	3	Kilmarnock	1
Dundee	3	St Mirren	1
East Fife	3	Ross County	1
Dundee United	2	St Johnstone	1

Scottish League Cup Winning Teams 1947-2021

1946/7 Rangers (Manager Bill Struth)
Brown, Young, Shaw, McColl, Woodburn, Rae, Rutherford, Gillick, Williamson, Thornton, Duncanson

1947/8 East Fife (Manager Scot Symon)
Niven, Laird, Stewart, Philip, Finlay, Aitken, Adams, D Davidson, Norris, J Davidson, Duncan
Replay – unchanged

1948/9 Rangers (Manager Bill Struth)
Brown, Young, Shaw, McColl, Woodburn, Cox, Gillick, Paton, Thornton, Duncanson, Rutherford

1949/50 East Fife (Manager Scot Symon)
McGarrity, Laird, Stewart, Philip, Finlay, Aitken, Black, Fleming, Morris, Brown, Duncan

1950/1 Motherwell (Manager George Stevenson)
Johnstone, Kilmarnock, Shaw, McLeod, Paton, Redpath, Watters, Forrest, Kelly, Watson, Aitkenhead

1951/2 Dundee (Manager George Anderson)
Brown, Fallon, Cowan, Gallacher, Cowie, Boyd, Toner, Pattillo, Flavell, Steel, Christie

1952/3 Dundee (Manager George Anderson)
R Henderson, Fallon, Frew, Zeising, Boyd, Cowie, Toner, A Henderson, Flavell, Steel, Christie

1953/4 East Fife (Manager Jerry Dawson)
Curran, Emery, S Stewart, Christie, Finlay, McLennan, J Stewart, Fleming, Bonthrone, Gardiner, Matthew

1954/5 Heart of Midlothian (Manager Tommy Walker)
Duff, Parker, McKenzie, Mackay, Glidden, Cumming, Souness, Conn, Bauld, Wardhaugh, Urquhart

1955/6 Aberdeen (Manager Davie Shaw)
Martin, Mitchell, Caldwell, Wilson, Clunie, Glen, Leggat, Yorston, Buckley, Wishart, Hather

1956/7 Celtic (Manager Jimmy McGrory)
Beattie, Haughney, Fallon, Evans, Jack, Peacock, Walsh, Collins, McPhail, Tully, Fernie
Replay: Mochan replaced Walsh

1957/8 Celtic (Manager Jimmy McGrory)
Beattie, Donnelly, Fallon, Fernie, Evans, Peacock, Tully, Collins, McPhail, Wilson, Mochan

1958/9 Heart of Midlothian (Manager)
Marshall, Kirk, Thomson, Mackay, Glidden, Cumming, Hamilton, Murray, Bauld, Wardhaugh, Crawford

1959/60 Hearts (Manager Tommy Walker)
Marshall, Kirk, Thomson, Bowman, Cumming, Higgins, Smith, Crawford, Young, Blackwood, Hamilton

1960/1 Rangers (Manager Scot Symon)
Niven, Shearer, Caldow, Davis, Paterson, Baxter, Scott, McMillan, Millar, Brand, Wilson

1961/2 Rangers (Manager Scot Symon)
Ritchie, Shearer, Caldow, Davis, Paterson, Baxter, Scott, McMillan, Millar, Brand, Wilson
Replay: Baillie replaced Paterson

1962/3 Heart of Midlothian (Manager Tommy Walker)
Marshall, Polland, Holt, Cumming, Barry, Higgins, Wallace, Paton, Davidson, W Hamilton, J Hamilton

1963/4 Rangers (Manager Scot Symon)
Ritchie, Shearer, Provan, Greig, McKinnon, Baxter, Henderson, Willoughby, Forrest, Brand, Watson

1964/5 Rangers (Manager Scot Symon)
Ritchie, Provan, Caldow, Greig, McKinnon, Wood, Brand, Millar, Forrest, Baxter, Johnston

1965/6 Celtic (Manager Jock Stein)
Simpson, Young, Gemmell, Murdoch, McNeill, Clark, Johnstone, Gallagher, McBride, Lennox, Hughes

1966/7 Celtic (Manager Jock Stein)
Simpson, Gemmell, O'Neill, Murdoch, McNeill, Clark, Johnstone, Lennox, McBride, Auld, Hughes. Sub Chalmers

1967/8 Celtic (Manager Jock Stein)
Simpson, Craig, Gemmell, Murdoch, McNeill, Clark, Chalmers, Lennox, Wallace, Auld, Hughes. Sub O'Neill

1968/9 Celtic (Manager Jock Stein)
Fallon, Craig, Gemmell, Murdoch, McNeill, Brogan, Johnstone, Wallace, Chalmers, Sauld, Lennox. Sub Clark

1969/70 Celtic (Manager Jock Stein)
Fallon, Craig, Hay, Murdoch, McNeill, Brogan, Callaghan, Hood, Hughes, Chalmers, Auld. Sub Johnstone

1970/1 Rangers (Manager Willie Waddell)
McCloy, Jardine, Miller, Conn, McKinnon, Jackson, Henderson, McDonald, D Johnstone, Stein, W Johnston

1971/2 Partick Thistle (Manager David McParland)
Rough, Hansen, Forsyth, Glavin, Campbell, Strachan, McQuade, Coulston, Bone, Rae, Lawrie. Sub Gibson

1972/3 Hibernian (Manager Eddie Turnbull)
Herriot, Brownlie, Schaedler, Blackley, Black, Stanton, Edwards, O'Rourke, Gordon, Cropley, Duncan

1973/4 Dundee (Manager David White)
Allan, Wilson, Gemmell, Ford, Stewart, Philip, Duncan, Robinson, Wallace, Scott, Lambie

1974/5 Celtic (Manager Jock Stein)
Hunter, McGrain, Brogan, Murray, McNeill, McCluskey, Johnstone, Dalglish, Deans, Hood, Wilson

1975/6 Rangers (Manager Jock Wallace)
Kennedy, Jardine, Greig, Forsyth, Jackson, McDonald, Mclean, Stein, Parlane, Johnstone, Young.

1976/7 Aberdeen (Manager Ally McLeod)
Clark, Kennedy, Williamson, Smith, Garner, Miller, Sullivan, Scott, Harper, Jarvie, Graham, Sub Robb

1977/8 Rangers (Manager Jock Wallace)
Kennedy, Jardine, Forsyth, Jackson, Greig, Hamilton, McDonald, Smith, McLean, Johnstone, Cooper. Subs Miller and Parlane

1978/9 Rangers (Manager John Greig)
McCloy, Jardine, Dawson, Johnstone, Jackson, McDonald, McLean, Russell, Urquhart, Smith, Cooper. Subs Miller and Parlane

1979/80 Dundee United (Manager Jim McLean)
McAlpine, Stark, Kopel, Philip, Hegarty, Narey, Bannon, Sturrock, Pettigrew, Holt, Payne. Subs Fleming and Murray
Replay: Fleming and Kirkwood replaced Philip and Payne

1980/1 Dundee United (Manager Jim McLean)
McAlpine, Holt, Kopel, Philip, Hegarty, Narey, Bannon, Payne, Pettigrew, Sturrock, Dodds

1981/2 Rangers (Manager John Greig)
Stewart, Jardine, Miller, Stevens, Jackson, Bett, Cooper, Johnstone, Russell, McDonald, Dalziel. Sub Redford

1982/3 Celtic (Manager Billy McNeill)
Bonner, McGrain, Sinclair, Aitken, McAdam, McLeod, Provan, McStay, McGarvey, Burns, Nicholas. Sub Reid

1983/4 Rangers (Manager Jock Wallace)
McCloy, Nicholl, Dawson, McClelland, Paterson, McPherson, Russell, McCoist, Clark, MacDonald, Cooper. Subs Burns and McAdam

1984/5 Rangers (Manager Jock Wallace)
McCloy, Dawson, McClelland, Fraser, Paterson, McPherson, Russell, McCoist, Ferguson, Redford, Cooper. Subs Mitchell and Prytz

1985/6 Aberdeen (Manager Alex Ferguson)
Leighton, McKimmie, Mitchell, Stark, McLeish, Miller, Black, Simpson, McDougall, Cooper, Hewitt. Sub Gray

1986/7 Rangers (Manager Graeme Souness)
Woods, Nicholl, Munro, Fraser, Dawson, Butcher, Ferguson, McMinn, McCoist, Durrant, Cooper. Subs Fleck and McFarlane

1987/8 Rangers (Manager Graeme Souness)
Walker, Nicholl, Munro, Roberts, Ferguson, Gough, McGregor, Fleck, McCoist, Durrant, Cooper. Subs Francis and Cohen

1988/9 Rangers (Manager Graeme Souness)
Woods, Stevens, Brown, Gough, Wilkins, Butcher, Drinkell, Ferguson, McCoist, Cooper, Walters

1989/90 Aberdeen (Manager Alex Smith / Jocky Scott)
Snelders, McKimmie, Robertson, Grant, McLeish, Miller, Nicholas,

Bett, Mason, Connor, Jess. Subs Van der Ark and Irvine

1990/1 Rangers (Manager Graeme Souness)
Woods, Stevens, Munro, Gough, Spackman, Brown, Steven, Hurlock, McCoist, Hateley, Walters. Subs Huistra and Ferguson

1991/2 Hibernian (Manager Alex Miller)
Burridge, Miller, Mitchell, Hunter, McIntyre, MacLeod, Weir, Hamilton, Wright, Evans, McGinlay

1992/3 Rangers (Manager Walter Smith)
Goram, McCall, Robertson, Gough, McPherson, Brown, Steven, Ferguson, McCoist, Hateley, Durrant. Subs Gordon and Mikhailitchenko

1993/4 Rangers (Manager Walter Smith)
Maxwell, Stevens, Robertson, Gough, McPherson, McCall, Steven, Ferguson, Durrant, Hateley, Huistra. Sub McCoist

1994/5 Raith Rovers (Manager Jimmy Nicholl)
Thomson, McAnespie, Broddle, Narey, Dennis, Sinclair, Crawford, Dalziel, Graham, Cameron, Dair. Subs Rowbotham and Redford

1995/6 Aberdeen (Manager Roy Aitken)
Watt, McKimmie, Glass, Grant, Inglis, Smith, Miller, Shearer, Bernard, Dodds, Jess. Subs Hetherston and Robertson

1996/7 Rangers (Manager Walter Smith)
Goram, Cleland, Moore, Gough, Petric, Bjorklund, Miller, Gascoigne, McCoist, Albertz, Laudrup. Sub Robertson

1997/8 Celtic (Manager Wim Jansen)
Gould, Boyd, Mahe, McNamara, Rieper, Stubbs, Larsson, Burley, Thom, Wieghorst, Blinker. Subs Lambert and Annoni

1998/9 Rangers (Manager Dick Advocaat)
Niemi, Porrini, Numan, Amoruso, Hendry, Albertz, B Ferguson, Van Bronkhorst, Kanchelskis, Wallace, Gui'vrach. Subs Durie and I Ferguson

1999/00 Celtic (Manager John Barnes)
Gould, Boyd, Roseth, Mjalby, Mahe, McNamara, Wieghorst, Petrov, Moravcik, Johnson, Viduka. Subs Stubbs and Berkovic

2000/1 Celtic (Manager Martin O'Neill)
Gould, Mjalby, Valgaeren, Vega, Petta, Healy, Lennon, Lambert, Moravcik, Larsson, Sutton. Subs Crainey, Boyd and Smith

2001/2 Rangers (Manager Alex McLeish)
Klos, Ricksen, Vidmar, Amoruso, Numan, Konterman, Ferguson, Latapy, Cannigia, Flo, Lovenmkrands. Subs McCann, Dodds, Hughes

2002/3 Rangers (Manager Alex McLeish)
Klos, Ricksen, Moore, Amoruso, Bonnisel, Arteta, Ferguson, Cannigia, De Boer, Mols, Lovenkrands. Subs Arveladze, Konterman and Ross

2003/4 Livingston (Manager David Hay)
McKenzie, McNamee, McAllister, Rubio, Andrews, Dorado, Makel, O'Brien, Lovell, Fernandez, Lilley. Subs Pasquinelli, McLaughlin, McGovern

2004/5 Rangers (Manager Alex McLeish)
Watterus, Ross, Malcolm, Kyrgiakos, Ball, Ricksen, Ferguson, Vignal, Buffel, Novo, Prso. Subs Thompson and Rae

2005/6 Celtic (Manager Gordon Strachan)
Boruc, Telfer, Balde, McManus, Wallace, Nakamura, Keane, Lennon, Maloney, Zurawski, Petrov. Sub Dublin

2006/7 Hibernian (Manager John Collins)
McNeil, Whittaker, Hogg, Jones, Murphy, Sproule, Brown, Beuzelin, Stevenson, Benjelloun, Fletcher. Subs Zemmama, Martis

2007/8 Rangers (Manager Walter Smith)
McGregor, Broadfoot, Cuellar, Weir, Papac, Hemdani, Dailly, Burke, Ferguson, Davis, McCulloch. Subs Darcheville, Whittaker, Boyd

2008/9 Celtic (Manager Gordon Strachan)
Boruc, Hinkel, Loovens, McManus, O'Dea, Caldwell, Nakamura, S Brown, Hartley, McGeady, McDonald. Subs Wilson, Samaras, Vennegoor of Hesselink

2009/10 Rangers (Manager Walter Smith)
Alexander, Whittaker, Wilson, Weir, Papac, Davis, K Thomson, McCulloch, Novo, Miller, Boyd. Subs Naismith, Smith, Edu

2010/11 Rangers (Manager Walter Smith)
Alexander, Whittaker, Bougherra, Weir, Papac, Lafferty, Davis, Edu, Wylde, Naismith, Jelavic. Subs Diouf, Weiss and Hutton

2011/12 Kilmarnock (Manager Kenny Shiels)
Bell, Hay, Fowler, Nelson, Gordon, Sissoko, Kelly, Bujis, Harkins, Shiels, Heffernan. Subs Kroca, Johnson, Van Torhout

2012/13 St Mirren (Manager Danny Lennon)
Samson, Van Zanten, Goodwin, McAusland, Dummett, Newton, McGinn, Teale, McGowan, Goncalves, Thompson. Subs Parkin, Mair and Carey

2013/14 Aberdeen (Manager Derek McInnes)
Langfield, Logan, Anderson, Reynolds, Considine, Jack, Flood, Robson, McGinn, Rooney, Hayes. Subs Smith, Low, Vernon

2014/15 Celtic (Manager Ronnie Deila)
Gordon, Ambrose, Denayer, Van Dijk, Izaguirre, Brown, Bitton, Commons, Johansen, Stokes, Griffiths. Subs Guidetti, Forrest and Henderson

2015/16 Ross County (Manager Jim McIntyre)
Woods, Fraser, Quinn, Davies, Foster, Gardyne, Irvine, Woods, McShane, Boyce, Schalk. Subs Franks, Murdoch and Graham

2016/17 Celtic (Manager Brendan Rodgers)
Gordon, Lustig, Simunovic, Sviatchenko, Izaguirre, Brown, Armstrong, Rogic, Roberts, Forrest, Dembele. Subs Bitton, Griffiths and McGregor

2017/18 Celtic (Manager Brendan Rodgers)
Gordon, Lustig, Simunovic, Boyata, Tierney, Brown, Armstrong, Forrest, McGregor, Sinclair, Dembele. Subs Roberts, Griffiths and Rogic

2018/19 Celtic (Manager Brendan Rodgers)
Bain, Lustig, Boyata, Benkovic, Tierney, Rogic, McGregor, Christie, Forrest, Sinclair, Edouard. Subs Simunovic, brown and Ntcham

2019/20 Celtic (Manager Neil Lennon)
Forster, Frimpong, Julien, Ajer, Hayes, Brown, McGregor, Forrest, Christie, Elyounoussi, Morgan. Subs Bitton, Johnston, Edouard

2020/21 St Johnstone (Manager Callum Davidson)
Clark, Kerr, Gordon, McCart, Rooney, McCann, Craig, Booth, Conway, Wotherspoon, Kane. Sub May

League Challenge Cup 2019/20

The 2019/20 Final between Inverness Caledonian Thistle and Raith Rovers remained unplayed at the end of 2020/1. It was decided to share the trophy between the two clubs.

League Challenge Cup 2020/21

The competition was not played in 2020/1. The SPFL announced in October 2020 that after a consultation process involving all 42 clubs, 34 wanted to cancel the 2020-21 staging. It was disappointing to then read a tweet from Bonnyrigg Rose complaining about the decision and that they had not been consulted.

Scottish League Challenge Cup Finals 1991-2019

Season	Winner	Score	Runner-up	Venue	Att	Losing Semi Finalists	
1990–91	Dundee (1)	3–2 AET	Ayr United	Fir Park	11,506	Clyde	Kilmarnock
1991–92	Hamilton Academical (1)	1–0	Ayr United	Fir Park	9,663	QOS	Raith Rovers
1992–93	Hamilton Academical (2)	3–2	Morton	Love Street	7,391	Montrose	Meadowbank Th
1993–94	Falkirk (1)	3–0	St. Mirren	Fir Park	13,763	Ayr United	Meadowbank Th
1994–95	Airdrieonians (1)	3–2 AET	Dundee	McDiarmid Park	8,844	Clydebank	Dunfermline Ath
1995–96	Stenhousemuir (1)	0–0 aet + pens	Dundee United	McDiarmid Park	7,856	Stirling Albion	Dunfermline Ath
1996–97	Stranraer (1)	1–0	St. Johnstone	Broadwood	5,222	Montrose	Morton
1997–98	Falkirk (2)	1–0	Queen of the South	Fir Park	9,735	Hamilton Accies	Morton
1998–99	No competition						
1999–2000	Alloa Athletic (1)	4–4 aet + pens	Inverness Caledonian Thistle	Excelsior Stadium	4,043	Stirling Albion	Livingston
2000–01	Airdrieonians (2)	2–2 aet + pens	Livingston	Broadwood	5,623	Stranraer	East Stirlingshire
2001–02	Airdrieonians (3)	2–1	Alloa Athletic	Broadwood	4,548	Clyde	Brechin City
2002–03	Queen of the South (1)	2–0	Brechin City	Broadwood	6,428	Queen's Park	St Mirren
2003–04	Inverness Caledonian Thistle (1)	2–0	Airdrie United	McDiarmid Park	5,428	Raith Rovers	Brechin City
2004–05	Falkirk (3)	2–1	Ross County	McDiarmid Park	7,471	Forfar Athletic	St Johnstone
2005–06	St. Mirren (1)	2–1	Hamilton Academical	Excelsior Stadium	9,613	Morton	St Johnstone
2006–07	Ross County (1)	1–1 aet + pens	Clyde	McDiarmid Park	4,062	Morton	Albion Rovers
2007–08	St. Johnstone (1)	3–2	Dunfermline Athletic	Dens Park	6,446	Morton	Ayr United
2008–09	Airdrie United (1)	2–2 aet + pens	Ross County	McDiarmid Park	4,091	Morton	Partick Thistle
2009–10	Dundee (2)	3–2	Inverness Caledonian Thistle	McDiarmid Park	8,031	Ross County	Annan Athletic
2010–11	Ross County (2)	2–0	Queen of the South	McDiarmid Park	5,124	Partick Thistle	Peterhead
2011–12	Falkirk (4)	1–0	Hamilton Academical	Almondvale	5,210	Livingston	Annan Athletic
2012–13	Queen of the South (2)	1–1 aet + pens	Partick Thistle	Almondvale	9,452	Cowdenbeath	Arbroath
2013-14	Raith Rovers (1)	1-0 aet	Rangers	Easter Road	19,983	Stenhousemuir	Annan Athletic
2014-15	Livingston (1)	4-0	Alloa Athletic	McDiarmid Park	2,869	Stranraer	Rangers
2015-16	Rangers (1)	4-0	Peterhead	Hampden Park	48,133	Queen's Park	St Mirren
2016-17	Dundee United (1)	2-1	St Mirren	Fir Park	8,089	QOS	TNS
2017-18	Inverness Caledonian Thistle (2)	1-0	Dumbarton	McDiarmid Park	4,602	Crusaders	TNS
2018-19	Ross County (3)	3-1	Connah's Quay Nomads	Caledonian Stadium	3,057	Edinburgh City	East Fife
2019-20	Final Inverness CT v Raith Rovers (unplayed)			McDiarmid Park		Partick Thistle	Rangers Colts
2020-21	No competition						

WINNERS (25)

4	Falkirk
3	Airdrieonians, Ross County
2	Hamilton Accies, Queen of the South, Dundee, Inverness CT
1	Livingston, Raith Rovers, Airdrie United, St Johnstone, St Mirren, Alloa Athletic, Stranraer, Stenhousemuir, Rangers, Dundee United

Alternative Names / Sponsors for the Challenge Cup have been:

1990/1	B and Q Centenary Cup	2006/7-2007/8	Scottish League Challenge Cup
1991/2-1994/5	B and Q Cup	2008/9-2020/11	ALBA Challenge Cup
1995/6-1997/8	Scottish League Challenge Cup	2011/12-2013/14	Ramsdens Cup
1998/9	No competition	2014/15-2015/16	Petrofac Training Cup
1999/00-2001/2	Bells Challenge Cup	2016/17-2018/19	Irn Bru Cup
2002/3-2005/6	Bells Cup	2019/20	Tunnocks Caramel Wafer Cup

League Challenge Cup Winning Teams

1990/1 Dundee (Manager Gordon Wallace)
Tom Carson, Alan Dinnie, Rab Shannon, Gordon Chisholm, Willie Jamieson, Mark Craib, Colin West, Stewart Forsyth, Keith Wright, Billy Dodds, Gordon McLeod. Subs used Joe McBride, Stephen Frail

1991/2 Hamilton Accies (Manager Billy McLaren)
Rab McCulloch, Kevin McKee, Colin Miller, Andy Millen, Jim Weir, Paul McKenzie, Colin Harris, Billy Reid, George McCluskey, Gary Clark, Paul McDonald.

1992/3 Hamilton Accies (Manager Iain Munro)
Allan Ferguson, Chris Hillcoat, Colin Miller, Andy Millen, Jim Weir, Craig Napier, Michael Waters, Colin Harris, Colin Cramb, Gary Clark, Paul McDonald. Subs Used Paul McKenzie and Kenny Ward

1993/4 Falkirk (Manager Jim Jefferies)
Tony Parks, Joe McLaughlin, John Hughes, David Weir, Tommy McQueen, Eddie May, Ian McCall, Brian Rice, Neil Duffy, Kevin Drinkell, Richard Cadette. Subs used Neil Oliver and Greg Shaw

1994/5 Airdrieonians (Manager Alex MacDonald)
John Martin, Sandy Stewart, Paul Jack, Jimmy Sandison, Graham Hay, Kenny Black, Jimmy Boyle, John Davies, Steve Cooper, Paul Harvey, Alan Lawrence. Subs used Tony Smith, Andy Smith

1995/6 Stenhousemuir (Manager Terry Christie)
Roddy McKenzie, Eamonn Bannon, Lloyd Haddow, Graeme Armstrong, George McGeachie, Adrian Sprott, Paul Hunter, Jimmy Fisher, Miller Mathieson, Gareth Hutchison, Ian Little. Sub used Tom Steel

1996/7 Stranraer (Manager Campbell Money)
Barney Duffy, Graham Duncan, Tom Black, Jim Hughes, Tony Gallagher, John McCaffrey, Tommy Sloan, Alan Lansdowne, Gordon Young, Ian McAuley, Robert Docherty. Subs used Derek Crawford, John McMillan, John Robertson

1997/8 Falkirk (Manager Alex Totten)
Paul Mathers, Martin Corrigan, Jamie McGowan, Scott MacKenzie, Kevin James, Neil Berry, Kevin McAllister, Albert Craig, Paul McGrillen, David Moss, David Hagen. Sub used Marino Keith

1998/9 No Competition

1999/00 Alloa Athletic (Manager Terry Christie)
Mark Cairns, Craig Valentine, Paul McAneny, David Beaton, Jimmy Boyle, Derek Clark, Ian Little, Willie Irvine, Gary Clark, Mark Wilson, Martin Cameron. Subs used Max Christie, Gregor McKechnie

2000/1 Airdrieonians (Manager Steve Archibald)
Javier Sanchez Broto, Paul Armstrong, Austin McCann, Darren Brady, Eddie Forrest, Craig Ireland, John Elliot, Fabrice Moreau, Martin Prest, Antonion Calderon, David Fernandez. Subs used David McGuire, Jesus Garcia Sanjan, Salvador Capin

2001/2 Airdrieonians (Manager Ian McCall)
Allan Ferguson, Paul Armstrong, Craig McPherson, Sandy Stewart, Allan McManus, Kevin James, Lee Gardner, Neil McFarlane, Owen Coyle, Stuart Taylor, Mark Roberts. Sub used Robert Dunn

2002/3 Queen of the South (Manager John Connolly)
Andy Goram, Robbie Neilson, Derek Anderson, Brian McColligan, Andy Aitken, Jim Thomson, John O'Neill, Steve Bowey, Peter Weatherson, Derek Lyle, Joe McAlpine. Subs used Sean O'Connor, Brian McLaughlin

2003/4 Inverness Caledonian Thistle (Manager John Robertson)
Mark Brown, Ross Tokeley, Stuart Golabek, Bobby Mann, Stuart McCaffrey, Russell Duncan, Barry Wilson, Richie Hart, Paul Ritchie, Roy McBain, David Bingham. Subs used Darren Thomson, Steven Hislop, Liam Keogh

2004/5 Falkirk (Manager John Hughes)
Allan Ferguson, Andy Lawrie, Craig McPherson, Scott McKenzie, Mark Campbell, Kevin James, John O'Neill, David Nicholls, Andy Thomson, Russell Latapy, Darryl Duffy. Subs used Pedro Moutinho, Neil Scally, Daniel McBreen

2005/6 St Mirren (Manager Gus MacPherson)
Chris Smith, David van Zanten, Kirk Broadfoot, Andy Millen, Kevin McGowne, John Potter, Hugh Murray, Charlie Adam, Stewart Kean, John Sutton, Simon Lappin. Subs used Billy Mehmet, Mark Reilly

2006/7 Ross County (Manager Scott Leitch)
Craig Samson, Gary Irvine, Alex Keddie, Andy Dowie, Kevin McKinlay, Craig Gunn, Michael Gardyne, Derek Adams, Amick Ciani, Don Cowie, Martin "Jimmy" Scott. Subs used Hugh Robertson, Stuart Anderson, Jason Crooks

2007/8 St Johnstone (Caretaker Manager Sandy Stewart)
Alan Main, Gary Irvine, Allan McManus, Steven Anderson, Goran Stanic, Rocco Quinn, Derek McInnes, Paul Sheerin, Peter MacDonald, Kenny Deuchar, Andy Jackson. Subs used Kevin Rutkiewicz, Martin Hardie, Steven Milne

2008/9 Airdrie United (Manager Kenny Black)
Stephen Robertson, Marc Smyth, Paul Lovering, Kevin McDonald, Bobby Donnelly, David Nixon, Steven McDougall, Stephen McKenna, Paul di Giacomo, Scott McLaughlin, Joe Cardle. Subs used Darren Smith, Matthew Hazley, Simon Lynch

2009/10 Dundee (Manager Jocky Scott)
Rab Douglas, Eric Paton, Jim Lauchlan, Gary McKenzie, Eddie Malone, Richie Hart, Brian Kerr, Gary Harkins, Craig Forsyth, Sean Higgins, Leigh Griffiths. Subs used Kyle Benedictus, Pat Clarke, Colin McMenamin

2010/11 Ross County (Manager Jimmy Calderwood)
Michael McGovern, Gary Miller, Marc Fitzpatrick, Paul Lawson, Scott Boyd, Johnny Flynn, Michael Gardyne, Stuart Kettlewell, Andrew Barrowman, Richard Brittain, Iain Vigurs. Subs used Steven Milne, Gary Wood, Scott Morrison

2011/12 Falkirk (Manager Steven Pressley)
Michael McGovern, Kieran Duffie, Tam Scobbie, Darren Dods, Murray Wallace, Jay Fulton, Craig Sibbald, Mark Millar, Farid El Alagui, Willie Gibson, David Weatherston. Sub used Blair Alston

2012/13 Queen of the South (Manager Allan Johnston)
Lee Robinson, Chris Mitchell, Marc Fitzpatrick, Mark Durnan, Chris Higgins, Derek Young, Stephen McKenna, Nicky Clark, Daniel Carmichael, Derek Lyle, Michael Paton. Subs used Steven Black, Gavin Reilly, Kevin Smith

2013/14 Raith Rovers (Manager Grant Murray)
Lee Robinson, Jason Thomson, Paul Watson, Dougie Hill, Callum Booth, Joe Cardle, Kevin Moon, Liam Fox, Grant Anderson, John Baird, Calum Elliot. Subs used Fraser Mullen, Gordon Smith, Greig Spence

2014/15 Livingston (Manager Mark Burchill)
Darren Jamieson, Darren Cole, Declan Gallagher, Callum Fordyce, Jason Talbot, Danny Mullen, Keaghan Jacobs, Kyle Jacobs, Burton O'Brien, Myles Hippolyte, Scott Pittman. Subs used Jordan White, Jack Beaumont, Gary Glen

2015/16 Rangers (Manager Mark Warburton)
Wes Foderingham, James Tavernier, Danny Wilson, Rob Kiernan, Lee Wallace, Dominic Ball, Jason Holt, Andy Halliday, Barrie Mackay, Kenny Miller, Harry Forrester. Subs used Billy King, Dean Shiels, Michael O'Halloran

2016/17 Dundee United (Manager Ray McKinnon)
Cammy Bell, Stewart Murdoch, William Edjeungele, Mark Durnan, Jamie Robson, Charlie Telfer, Willo Flood, Ali Coote, Tony Andreu, Nick van der Velden, Simon Murray. Subs used Coll Donaldson, Alex Nicholls, Thomas Mikkelsen

2017/18 Inverness Caledonian Thistle (Manager John Robertson)
Mark Ridgers, Collin Seedorf, Gary Warren, Coll Donaldson, Carl Tremarco, Liam Polworth, Iain Vigurs, Joe Chalmers, George Oakley, Connor Bell, Jake Mulraney. Subs used Aaron Doran, Daniel Mackay

2018/19 Ross County (Co Managers Stuart Kettlewell and Steven Ferguson)
Ross Munro, Marcus Fraser, Keith Watson, Andy Boyle, Kenny van der Weg, Declan McManus, Jamie Lindsay, Don Cowie, Michael Gardyne, Ross Stewart, Brian Graham. Subs used Josh Mullin, Lewis Spence, Daniel Armstrong

League Challenge Cup Format 2021/2—known as the SPFL Trust Trophy

Round 1	Aug 10-11	6 teams from SPFL Div 1, 10 teams from SPFL Div 2, 4 teams from Lowland League, 4 teams from Highland League, 12 U21 teams from SPFL Premiership (36 teams)
Round 2	Sep 4-5	10 teams from SPFL Championship, 4 teams from SPFL Div 1, + 18 Round 1 winners (32 teams)
Round 3	Oct 9-10	16 Round 2 winners
Round 4	Nov 30-Dec 1	8 Round 3 winners
SF	Mar 1-2	
Final	April 2 or 3	

Due to uncertainties regarding the pandemic it was decided NOT to invite clubs from outside Scotland to play in the Tournament. That position will be reconsidered for 2022/3.

First round - North Section
Brechin City v Buckie Thistle
Dundee B v Peterhead
East Fife v St Johnstone B
Hibernian B v Elgin City
Brora Rangers v Aberdeen B
Fraserburgh v Cowdenbeath
Forfar Athletic v Formartine United
Ross County B v Stirling Albion (L-W)
Stenhousemuir v Dundee United B

NB - Ross County B withdrew

First round - South Section
Dumbarton v Rangers B
Livingston B v Albion Rovers (L-W)
Edinburgh City v Heart of Midlothian B
Celtic B v Annan Athletic
Queen's Park v Bonnyrigg Rose Athletic
Broomhill FC v Clyde
Falkirk v East Kilbride
St Mirren B v Kelty Hearts
Stranraer v Motherwell B

NB - Livingston B withdrew

Second round - North section
Montrose v Ross County B or Stirling Albion
Brora Rangers or Aberdeen B v Arbroath
Cove Rangers v Stenhousemuir or Dundee United B
Fraserburgh or Cowdenbeath v Alloa Athletic
Raith Rovers v Forfar Athletic or Formartine United
Hibernian B or Elgin City v Dunfermline Athletic
Inverness Caledonian Thistle v Brechin City or Buckie Thistle
Dundee B or Peterhead v East Fife or St Johnstone B

Second round - South section
Airdrieonians v Queen's Park or Bonnyrigg Rose Athletic
Celtic B or Annan Athletic v Morton
Hamilton Academical v Edinburgh City or Heart of Midlothian B
Dumbarton or Rangers B v Ayr United
Kilmarnock v Falkirk or East Kilbride
Stranraer or Motherwell B v Partick Thistle
Queen of the South v Broomhill FC or Clyde
Livingston B or Albion Rovers v St Mirren B or Kelty Hearts

First-round ties are scheduled for the midweek of August 10/11, with second-round games due to be played on the weekend of September 4/5

Fife Cup 2020/21

The Fife Cup is the only one of the Senior County Cup competitions still being played. The Ayrshire, Stirlingshire, Renfrewshire, Lanarkshire and Forfarshire Cups, as well as the East of Scotland Shield, have disappeared from the football calendar.

There was no competition in 2020/1 and the 2019/20 tournament was not completed.

Currently 8 clubs participate:

Burntisland Shipyard
Cowdenbeath
Dundonald Bluebell
Dunfermline Athletic
East Fife
Hill of Beath Hawthorn
Kelty Hearts
Raith Rovers

East of Scotland City Cup

The 2018/19 competition was not completed. Spartans beat Berwick Rangers in one Semi Final but the other game between Edinburgh City and Camelon was not played.

The 2019/20 and 2020/1 competitions have not been played.

Presumably the Tournament, if it restarts, will revert to the format of a single game between Edinburgh City and the winners of the East of Scotland Qualifying Cup.

Aberdeenshire Cup

The draw for the 2020/1 Aberdeenshire Cup was made on July 23rd 2020 and resulted:

Round 1
Dyce v Deveronvale 2-1 (at Deveronvale)
Inverurie Loco Works v Turriff United 2-1
Banks O' Dee v Buckie Thistle 1-2

Round 2
Buckie Thistle v Aberdeen 0-1**
Dyce v Formartine United 0-3 (at Formartine)
Keith v Huntly 3-1
Fraserburgh v Inverurie Loco Works 2-1

Semi Finals
Keith v Fraserburgh 1-4**
Formartine v Buckie 0-0, 7-6 p

This was the first time that Dyce had played in the competition. Further details in the Highland League section of the Almanac.

**The Buckie Thistle v Aberdeen match was played on 10/7/21, resulting in a 1-0 win for Buckie.

**The Semi Finals were played
14/7/21, Formartine United v Buckie Thistle, 0-0, 7-6pens
18/7/21, Keith v Fraserburgh, 1-4

**Final:
28/7/21, Formartine United v Fraserburgh at Inverurie
Full details in next year's Almanac

Glasgow Cup

During 2020/1 an attempt was made to complete the 2019/20 competition which had been suspended due to COVID.

The standings as of Summer 2020 were:

	Pld	W	D	L	F	A	GD	Pts
Partick Thistle	7	3	2	2	17	9	8	11
Celtic	6	3	2	1	12	6	6	11
Rangers	4	2	1	1	6	6	0	7
Clyde	6	2	1	3	11	19	-8	7
Queen's Park	5	0	2	3	3	9	-6	2

Full details of these games, including team line-ups, were included in the 2020/1 Almanac.

Queen's Park v Rangers was awarded to Rangers by 3-0 as Queen's Park were unable to fulfil the game.

Further matches were played:

2/11/2020
Rangers v Queen's Park, 0-0 (at Murray Park)
Rangers: N.Hogarth, Devine, Butterworth (Fraser, 60), McKinnon (Lowry, 60), O'Connor, McClelland, McCausland (Lyall, 87), Williamson, Young-Coombes (Lindsay, 87), McKee (Balde, 77), Mebude. Subs: J. Hogarth.
Queen's Park: Bell, McDonald (Rodger, 80), Morrison, Trialist, MacLean, Paterson, Gilles, McGlinchey, Biggar, Quitongo, Carroll. Subs not used: Bannon, Caffrey, Heraghty.

24/11/20
Partick Thistle v Celtic, 0-4 (at Firhill)
Partick: Luke Scullion, Calum Wilson, Oliver Black, Joe McDonald, Bradley Renfrew, James Lyon, Billy Owens, Charlie Reilly, Ewan Cameron, Blair Lyons and Gospel Ocholi. Subs Mason McCready, Lorenzo Giovanazzi, Chris Bell and Matthew Collins.
Celtic: n/a
SCORERS: Connell, Harper 2, Moffat

1/12/20
Celtic v Rangers, 3-0 (at Dumbarton FC)
Celtic: Olewayemi, Otoo, Montgomery, Murray, Welsh (McPherson), Connell, Harper, Coffey, Okoflex, Dembele, Johnstone (Moffat). Unused substitutes: Angelini, Wylie, Carse, Brooks, Davidson. SCORERS: Armstrong 2, Okoflex
Rangers: Firth, Devine, Shiels (Henderson), Barjonas, McClelland (O'Connor), King, Middleton, Dickson, Young-Coombes, McKee (McKinnon), Mebude (McCausland).
Unused substitutes: Hogarth, Miller, Lindsay.

22/12/20
Clyde v Rangers, 0-2 (at Broadwood)
Clyde: Vajs, McNiff, Rumsby, Robertson, Palmer, Henderson, Jack, Nicoll, Trialist 1, Trialist 2, Lamont.
Substitutes: Mitchell, Bain, Syvertsen, Goodwillie, Love.
Rangers: Kinnear, Devine, Henderson, Thomson, O'Connor, King, Middleton, Dickson, McKee, Barjonas, Young-Coombes.
Substitutes: Hogarth, McCausland, Miller, Fraser, McKinnon, Lindsay, Weston. SCORERS - Middleton 2

FINAL STANDINGS

	P	W	D	L	F	A	GD	Pts
Celtic	8	5	2	1	19	6	13	17
Rangers	8	4	2	2	11	9	2	14
Partick Thistle	8	3	2	3	17	13	4	11
Clyde	7	2	1	4	11	21	-10	7
Queen's Park	7	0	3	4	3	12	-9	3

Clyde V QP not played. Celtic and Rangers should play in the Final.

The 2019/20 City of Glasgow Cup saw the introduction of a further revised format. This season's competition was played by the 'Colts' (Under-21) sides of Rangers and Celtic, and the first teams of the other member clubs, Clyde, Partick Thistle, and Queen's Park. Clyde made a welcome return to the competition after a few years' absence. The participating teams were due to play each other twice in a round-robin league. The final league placings would determine the line-up for the City of Glasgow Cup Final (1st v 2nd).

Player eligibility rules:

In the case of 1st Teams participating in the City of Glasgow Cup, teams must field a minimum of 6 recognised 1 1st Team players in the starting line-up.

In the case of Colt Teams participating in the City of Glasgow Cup, players who qualify as U21 players (born on or after 1st January 1999), are eligible to play in the competition.

A Colt Team shall be permitted to play a maximum of two overage players in any match.

No more than two Trialists may play for a club in any one match, as long as they are eligible to do so. An individual trialist may play a maximum of three matches in the competition in any one season for any one club.

A maximum of five substitutes can be used from a total of seven players named on the team lines, within a maximum number of 3 stoppages, excluding the halftime period. A Player who has been substituted may not play in that match again .

North of Scotland FA Cup

Not played in 2020/1. Elgin City, Ross County and Inverness Caledonian Thistle participate along with Wick Academy, Brora Rangers, Clachnacuddin, Fort William, Strathspey Thistle, Nairn County, Forres Mechanics and Lossiemouth.

FROM THE GLASGOW FA WEBSITE

The Glasgow Football Association Cup, now more often referred to as 'the Glasgow Cup', was first contested in 1887-88. It was in its time an important competition and had the status of a first class tournament. It was contested as fiercely as the League Championship or the Scottish Cup by Glasgow FA member clubs who were all senior clubs in the Glasgow area. The winners received a magnificent silver trophy, one of the oldest in world football, which is still competed for today.

Not surprisingly the competition has been dominated by the two Glasgow giants, Rangers and Celtic, but the other Glasgow FA member clubs, Partick Thistle, Clyde, Queen's Park and the now defunct Third Lanark, Cambuslang, and Cowlairs had their day too. After the Second World War, the Glasgow Cup diminished in status, mainly due to the more cosmopolitan fare provided by the developing European Competitions. Traditionally the Glasgow Cup had always been played early in the season, with the Glasgow Merchants' Charity Cup concluding the season after the completion of the Scottish League and Scottish Cup. Following the demise of the Charity Cup in 1960, Glasgow Cup fixtures were fitted into the fixture list at any convenient point, with the Final being played at the end of the season, if at all.

After the 1971 competition, the Glasgow Cup was not contested for three years. It was resurrected for the 1974-75 season but its appeal was limited and interest was luke-warm at best. Sometimes the competition would be left incomplete, and on some occasions, the Final was held over until the beginning of the following season. However, when it came to an Old Firm Final, Rangers and Celtic would usually put out pretty much their full first teams. This was the case as late as 1986 when, on the Friday evening before the Scottish Cup Final, a capacity crowd of over 40,000 saw Rangers take the trophy with a 3-2 win over the Scottish Champions, Celtic, courtesy of an Ally McCoist hat-trick to give Manager Graeme Souness his first trophy, just days after taking charge at Ibrox!

This however was essentially the swan-song of the tournament as a first team tournament. Rangers retained the trophy the following season in another Old Firm Final, this time at Parkhead, but only 15,000 were there to see what were effectively the Reserve teams compete. The following season's tournament, 1987-88, was never completed; officially there were no suitable dates available to fit ties in, but in reality the competition was long past it's sell-by-date and as the days of the UEFA Champions' League rapidly approached, its significance had reduced.

For season 1988-89, the competition was relaunched as a tournament for member clubs' Under-19 sides, and the 1989 Final remarkably saw neither of the Old Firm clubs represented, Partick Thistle beating Clyde 2-0 on this occasion.

Unfortunately, from the end of this season until 2007, there is a gap in our records and only the result of each season's Final is available. From season 2007-08, the Glasgow Cup was relaunched, as a youth tournament, and was competed for by member clubs' Under-17 teams. This format extended through to the completion of the 2017-18 competition.

For 2018-19, the City of Glasgow Cup was contested by member clubs' Under-20 teams. In 2019/20 the rules were changed again—see previous page.

SPFL Reserve Football 2020/1

No formal Reserve football or Development League was played in 2020/1. At the time of going to press it was unclear what plans were in place for 2021/2.

Reserve Football—Historical Data

In the absence of current information, we have decided to include some historical data on Reserve football on an one-off basis.

Structure of Scottish Reserve Football

1945/6
A single Scottish Reserve League operated.

1946/7-1948/9
A Scottish Reserve League operated. The SFL also operated a "C Division" which included a mix of first teams and reserve teams.

1949/50-1954/5
The "C Division" was split into NE and SW sections. All reserve teams and a few first teams participated.

1955/6 – 1974/5
A Scottish Reserve League ran for First Division clubs. Fixtures were basically a mirror-image of the first team schedule.

1958/9-1974/5
A Combined Reserve League operated from reserve teams of Division Two clubs, a few Non-League club first teams, and some Colts teams from First Division clubs. This was usually played in 2 series, one in the Autumn and one in the Spring. In later years it was frequently not completed.

1975/6-1977/8
The Premier Reserve League was a "mirror image" of the first team fixtures. Another league operated for non-Premier sides, called the Combined Reserve League in 1975/6 and then just the Scottish Reserve League in 1977/8. No other competition in 1976/7.

1978/9-1979/80
Premier Reserve League continued. Other clubs played in Reserve League (East) and Reserve League (West) with a Play-Off for the Championship.

1980/1-1981/2
No Premier Reserve League. All clubs in Reserve League (East) and (West) with Play Off for overall Champions.

1982/3-1997/8
Premier Reserve League restored. Reserve League (east) and (West) continued.

1998/9-2003/4
SPL formed an U21 League rather than a Reserve League. SFL continued to run Reserve Leagues (East and West).

2004/5
SPL changed from U21 League to Reserve League. SFL continued to run Reserve Leagues (East and West). Reserve League (East) scrapped at end of season.

2005/6
SPL Reserve League and SFL Reserve League (West) operated

2006/7-2008/9
SPL Reserve League operated. Non SPL clubs focussed on youth football with no Reserve leagues.

2009/10-2011/12
SPL scrapped Reserve League and introduced U19 League.

2012/13-2013/14
SPL changed U19 League to U20 League. SFL re-started a single Scottish Reserve League. SPFL retained arrangements for 2013/14.

2014/15-2017/18
SPFL ran a Development League, Development League (West) and Development League (East). Basically U20 but with many over-age players

2018/19-2019/20
Development Leagues re-named as Reserve Leagues.

2020/1
No competitions.

	RESERVE CHAMPIONS	RESERVE LGE CUP WINNERS
1945/6	Hibernian	Rangers
1946/7	Hibernian	Hibernian
1947/8	Hibernian	Hibernian
1948/9	Hibernian	Hibernian
1949/50-1954/5 Teams Played in C Division		
1955/6	Aberdeen	Falkirk
1956/7	Rangers	Aberdeen
1957/8	Hearts	Aberdeen
1958/9	Celtic	Falkirk
1959/60	Celtic	Celtic
1960/1	Celtic	Rangers
1961/2	Rangers	Rangers
1962/3	Celtic	Rangers
1963/4	Rangers	Dundee United
1964/5	Celtic	Kilmarnock
1965/6	Celtic	Hibernian
1966/7	Rangers	Celtic
1967/8	Rangers	Rangers
1968/9	Rangers	Celtic
1969/70	Celtic	Celtic
1970/1	Celtic	Celtic
1971/2	Ayr United	Hearts
1972/3	Aberdeen	Aberdeen
1973/4	Rangers	Partick Thistle
1974/5	Rangers	Rangers
1975/6	Rangers	Rangers
1976/7	Rangers	Rangers
1977/8	Rangers	St Mirren
1978/9	Rangers	Aberdeen
1979/80	Celtic	Celtic
1980/1	Celtic	Celtic
1981/2	Aberdeen	Ayr United
1982/3	Rangers	Dundee United
1983/4	Rangers	Hamilton Accies
1984/5	Celtic	Aberdeen
1985/6	Rangers	Celtic
1986/7	Aberdeen	Dundee
1987/8	Dundee United	Motherwell
1988/9	Dundee United	Hearts
1989/90	Dundee United	Celtic
1990/1	Celtic	Dundee United
1991/2	Rangers	Celtic
1992/3	Hearts	Rangers
1993/4	Celtic	Celtic
1994/5	Celtic	Celtic
1995/6	Rangers	Celtic
1996/7	Hearts	Aberdeen
1997/8	Rangers	Rangers
1998/9	St Johnstone	Livingston
1999/00	Hearts	Dunfermline Athletic
2000/1	Rangers	Livingston
2001/2	Celtic	Arbroath
2002/3	Celtic	St Johnstone
2003/4	Celtic	St Johnstone
2004/5	Celtic	Gretna
2005/6	Celtic	St Mirren
2006/7	Celtic	St Johnstone
2007/8	Celtic	Clyde
2008/9	Celtic	Ross County
2009/10	Celtic	Dunfermline Athletic
2010/1	Celtic	Raith Rovers
2011/2	Celtic	Hamilton Accies
2012/3	Celtic	
2013/4	Celtic	
2014/5	Aberdeen	
2015/6	Celtic	
2016/7	Ross County	
2017/8	Hibernian	
2018/9	Rangers	
2019/20	Hamilton Accies	

REGIONAL RESERVE LEAGUES

	West	East
1978/9	Hamilton Accies	Stirling Albion
1979/80	Hamilton Accies	Falkirk
1980/1	Celtic	Dundee United
1981/2	Rangers	Aberdeen
1982/3		Dundee United
1983/4	Celtic	Aberdeen
1984/5	Motherwell	Stenhousemuir
1985/6	Airdrieonians	Stenhousemuir
1986/7	Airdrieonians	Dunfermline Athletic
1987/8	Clyde	Raith Rovers
1988/9	Celtic B	Forfar Athletic
1989/90	Ayr United	St Johnstone
1990/1	Rangers B	Dundee
1991/2	Clydebank	Dundee United
1992/3	Rangers B	Dunfermline Athletic
1993/4	Rangers B	Falkirk
1994/5	Rangers B	Raith Rovers
1995/6	St Mirren	St Johnstone
1996/7	Airdrieonians	St Johnstone
1997/8	Hamilton Accies	Forfar Athletic
1998/9	Morton	Raith Rovers
1999/00	Ayr United	Dunfermline Athletic
2000/1	Livingston	Ross County
2001/2	Ayr United	No competition
2002/3	Falkirk	Brechin City
2003/4	Gretna	St Johnstone
2004/5	Falkirk	St Johnstone
2005/6	Gretna	
2006/7		
2007/8		
2008/9		
2009/10		
2010/1		
2011/2		
2012/3		
2013/4		
2014/5	Airdrieonians	Forfar Athletic
2015/6	Morton	Stirling Albion
2016/7	QOTS	Raith Rovers
2017/8	Morton	Raith Rovers
2018/9		
2019/20		

SECOND LEVEL RESERVE LEAGUES

	Series 1	Series 2
1958/9	Dumbarton	Dumbarton
1959/60	East Fife	Dundee United
1960/1	Celtic B	No competition
1961/2	Celtic B	Celtic B
1962/3	Stirling Albion	Celtic B
1963/4	Celtic B	Morton
1964/5	Arbroath	Raith Rovers
1965/6	Clydebank	Celtic B
1966/7	Hearts B	Queen's Park
1967/8	Hearts B	Unfinished
1968/9	Motherwell	Rangers B
1969/70	Rangers B	Unfinished
1970/1	Partick Thistle	Partick Thistle
1971/2	Unfinished	No competition
1972/3	No competition	
1973/4	Unfinished	
1974/5	Unfinished	
1975/6		
1976/7		
1977/8		
1978/9		

Scottish Second XI Cup 1881/2-1987/8

1881/2	Dumbarton	Vale of Leven	3-0	Millburn Park, Alexandria
1882/3	Kilmarnock Athletic	Vale of Leven	2-0	Boghead Park, Dumbarton
	(after protested game, 2-2)			
1883/4	Killmarnock Athletic	Dumbarton	4-2	Agg
1884/5	Hibernian	Hearts	3-1	Easter Road, Edinburgh
1885/6	Abercorn	Rangers	2-0	Westmarch, Paisley
1886/7	Abercorn	Dumbarton	6-4	Agg
1887/8	Ayr	Hearts	3-1	Easter Road, Edinburgh
1888/9	Cambuslang	St Mirren	2-1	Thistle Park, Paisley
1889/90	Rangers	Dumbarton	1-0	Whitefield Park, Glasgow
1890/1	Celtic	St Mirren	13-1	Beechwood Park, Glasgow
1891/2	Leith Athletic	Annbank	5-4	Hawkhill, Leith
1892/3	Leith Athletic	Queen's Park	4-3	Easter Road, Edinburgh
1893/4	Hearts	St Mirren	3-0	Logie Green, Edinburgh
1894/5	Hearts	Queen's Park	3-1	Cathkin Park, Glasgow
1895/6	Queen's Park	Leith Athletic	5-1	Easter Road, Edinburgh
1896/7	Hearts	Clyde	4-0	Easter Road, Edinburgh
1897/8	Rangers	Partick Thistle	6-0	Govandale Park, Glasgow
1898/9	Rangers	St Mirren	6-2	Underwood Park, Paisley
	(abandoned after 82 mins due to crowd trouble, result stood)			
1899/00	Third Lanark	Queen's Park	3-2	Cathkin Park, Glasgow
1900/1	Hearts	Partick Thistle	8-2	Powderhall, Edinburgh
1901/2	Queen's Park	Ayr Parkhouse	2-2	Exhibition Ground, Glasgow
(R)	Queen's Park	Ayr Parkhouse	5-0	
1902/3	Queen's Park	Ayr	3-1	Somerset Park, Ayr
1903/4	Queen's Park	Renton	5-0	Ibrox, Glasgow
1904/5	Third Lanark	Queen's Park	1-0	Hampden Park, Glasgow
1905/6	Hearts	Partick Thistle	4-0	Tynecastle Park, Edinburgh
1906/7	Rangers	St Mirren	2-2	Love Street, Paisley
(R)	Rangers	St Mirren	2-0	
1907/8	Dundee	Rangers	2-0	Dens Park, Dundee
1908/9	Falkirk	St Mirren	2-1	Love Street, Paisley
1909/10	Falkirk	Queen's Park	2-0	Hampden Park, Glasgow
	(Abandoned, bad light)			
(R)	Falkirk	Queen's Park	2-2	Hampden Park, Glasgow
(R)	Falkirk	Queen's Park	2-0	Brockville Park, Falkirk
1910/11	Hearts	Third Lanark	2-1	Cathkin Park, Glasgow
1911/2	Rangers	Partick Thistle	5-2	Agg
1912/3	Rangers	Kilmarnock	4-0	Agg
1913/4	Clyde	St Mirren	4-2	Agg
1914/5	Clyde	Falkirk	4-3	Agg
1919/20	Queen's Park	Aberdeen	2-2	Agg
(R)	Queen's Park	Aberdeen	3-0	Hampden Park, Glasgow
1920/1	Rangers	Hearts	2-1	Agg
1921/2	Airdrie	Albion Rovers	3-0	Broomfield Park, Airdrie
1922/3	Airdrie	Hearts	6-1	Agg
1923/4	Airdrie	Rangers	4-1	Agg
1924/5	Rangers	Queen's Park	5-0	Agg
1925/6	Rangers	Clydebank	6-3	Agg
1926/7	St Mirren	Aberdeen	4-1	Agg
1927/8	Rangers	Ayr United	3-1	Agg
1928/9	Rangers	Third Lanark	4-1	Agg
1929/30	Rangers	Kilmarnock	3-2	Agg
1930/1	Rangers	Airdrie	6-2	Agg
1931/2	Hearts	Hibernian	3-3	Agg
(R)	Hearts	Hibernian	1-0	Tynecastle Park, Edinburgh
1932/3	Rangers	Celtic	4-3	Agg
1933/4	Hamilton Accies	Motherwell	4-1	Agg
1934/5	Celtic	St Johnstone	6-5	Agg
1935/6	Celtic	Motherwell	7-4	Agg
1936/7	Rangers	St Mirren	3-2	Agg
1937/8	Rangers	Clyde	9-1	Agg
1938/9	Hibernian	Clyde	4-3	Agg
1939/40	Ayr United	Aberdeen	3-2	Agg
1940/1	Rangers	Hamilton Accies	4-3	Agg
1941/2	Clyde	Hibernian	5-3	Agg
1942/3	Motherwell	Hibernian	3-2	Fir Park, Motherwell
1943/4	Hearts	St Mirren	7-1	Agg
1944/5	Hearts	Celtic	7-3	Agg
1945/6	Hibernian	Clyde	7-1	Agg
1946/7	Hibernian	Rangers	3-0	Agg
1947/8	Airdrie	Hearts	5-4`	Agg
1948/9	Motherwell	Dundee	3-2	Agg
1949/50	Falkirk	Dundee	6-5	Agg
1950/1	Hearts	Hibernian	2-1	Agg
1951/2	Rangers	Aberdeen	2-0	Agg
1952/3	Dundee	Raith Rovers	4-3	Agg
1953/4	Hearts	Hibernian	4-3	Agg
1954/5	Aberdeen	Hibernian	5-4	Agg
1955/6	Aberdeen	Partick Thistle	6-2	Agg
1956/7	Motherwell	Celtic	2-1	Agg
1957/8	Celtic	Rangers	8-2	Agg
1958/9	St Mirren	Motherwell	3-2	Agg
1959/60	Trophy witheld			
1960/1	St Johnstone	Falkirk	5-3	Agg
1961/2	Rangers	Hibernian	3-2	Agg
1962/3	Dundee United	Hearts	3-2	Agg
1963/4	Rangers	Partick Thistle	4-1	Agg
1964/5	Rangers	Dundee	6-1	Agg
1965/6	Celtic	Motherwell	8-3	Agg
1966/7	Dundee	Rangers	5-2	Agg
1967/8	Rangers	Hearts	4-1	Agg
1968/9	Aberdeen	Celtic	4-1	Agg
1969/70	Rangers	Aberdeen	3-1	Agg
1970/1	Celtic	Falkirk	6-1	Agg
1971/2	Partick Thistle	Dunfermline Ath	3-0	Agg
1972/3	Hearts	Dundee United	6-1	Agg
1973/4	Celtic	Dundee	4-1	
1974/5	Partick Thistle	Dundee	2-1	
1975/6	Aberdeen	Dundee	5-1	
1976/7	Rangers	Hibernian	6-3	
1977/8	Aberdeen	Rangers	3-1	
1978/9	Rangers	Aberdeen	4-3	
1979/80	Kilmarnock Athletic	Hearts	3-2	
1980/1	Dundee United	Hearts	4-1	
1981/2	Aberdeen	Celtic	4-2	
1982/3	Dundee United	Dundee	3-2	Dens Park, Dundee
1983/4	Airdrie	Dundee	4-0	
1984/5	Celtic	Hibernian	3-0	
1985/6	No competition			
1986/7	No competition			
1987/8	Dundee United	Rangers	2-0	Tannadice Park, Dundee

The Scottish Second Eleven Football Association was an independent organisation. It's main function was to run the Scottish Second Eleven Cup which was a prestigious trophy in it's day.

Played in a KO format, with replays if necessary, it became a problem for fixture scheduling and the member clubs voted to cease playing in the late 1980s. The Association was eventually wound-up around 2003.

In the early days of Under 23 Internationals the Second Eleven FA was charged with organising the Scotland team. The Association had played occasional representative matches but none as high profile as the late 1950s U23 games. The last representative match played was against a Highland League Select in the 1980s.

Club Academy Scotland

Club Academy Scotland (CAS) is the Scottish FA's structure that defines, operates and partially funds the Academy system in this country, alongside a games programme. It governs the development of players from the age of 11 to 17, rising to Under-18 level from August 2018. Clubs are assessed against set criteria and a set of Measurable Performance Outcomes (MPOs), which take into account performance in areas like domestic and international appearances for home-grown players, coaching qualifications, facilities, talent identification and sports science and medicine set-ups.

Following the auditing process, the clubs have been streamed into the following categories:

Elite Level
Aberdeen, Celtic, Hamilton Academical, Heart of Midlothian, Hibernian, Kilmarnock, Motherwell, Rangers
Performance (Progressive) Level
Ayr United, Dundee United, Greenock Morton, Inverness Caledonian Thistle, Partick Thistle, Ross County, St Johnstone, St Mirren
Performance Level
Dundee, Fife Elite Football Academy, Queen's Park

Beneath that the following clubs are classified as **Advanced Youth** level:
Airdrieonians, Alloa Athletic, Elgin City, Livingston, Montrose, Queen of the South and Stirling Albion

Under 18 Elite League

The impact of COVID on youth football was massive. The usual Leagues did not start in the Autumn of 2020. Clubs played some ad hoc friendlies and participated in tournaments when the regulations allowed them to. A short League Competition was played in April / May. The primary purpose of this was to enable the SFA to declare a Champion for participation in the 2021/2 UEFA Youth Champions League. Rangers won the mini-league and therefore go forward to European competition for the third successive year. The Youth Champions League for 2020/1 was not played.

Performance Schools

The seven performance schools across Scotland each run a programme in partnership with the Scottish FA for boys and girls within the S1 to S4 age groups. Every year, each school will select a number of the most talented under-12 players to join the programme. Over a four-year period, this will provide the most talented young footballers throughout the country with an extra 800 hours of coaching.

Each school has a full-time elite youth coach who has overall responsibility for the delivery of the programmes. Each coach in turn is supported by a range of national team and club coaches, sport scientists and other specialist experts. The schools are:

Hazlehead Academy – Aberdeen
St John's RC High School – Dundee
Broughton High School – Edinburgh
Graeme High School – Falkirk
Holyrood Secondary School – Glasgow
Grange Academy – Kilmarnock
Braidhurst High School – Motherwell

Coaching takes place during regular school hours within an appropriate timetable that compliments their academic studies and their club football team. Although the primary focus is on developing elite young players it is important to understand that the programme is also about the young person and player. The sessions delivered by the coach will assist with the development of Curriculum for Excellence outcomes, including developing pupils' ability to communicate effectively, be responsible for their actions, contribute to their own and others' learning experiences and become more confident people.

Reserve / Development Staff at SPFL Clubs 2021

ABERDEEN	
Academy Director	Gavin Levey
Manager	Paul Sheerin (until May 2021)
Manager U18 / U17	Barry Robson
Pathways Manager	Neil Simpson
ALBION ROVERS	
Reserve Team Manager	Graeme Livingston
Reserve Team Coach	Graeme Liveston
	Lewis Wilson
ALLOA ATHLETIC	
Head of Youth	Derek Nicholson
AYR UNITED	
Youth Chair	Allan Gunning
Head of Academy	David White
CELTIC	
Head of Youth Academy	Chris McCart
Reserve Team Manager	Tommy McIntyre
Reserve Team Coach	Stephen McManus
	George McCluskey
U18 Manager	Darren O'Dea
Head of Youth Recruitment	Willie McStay
DUNDEE	
Head of Academy	Stephen Wright
DUNDEE UNITED	
Academy Director	Andy Goldie
Head of Academy Operations	Michael McPake
Head Scademy Coach	Adam Ashgar
Pathways / Loans Manager	Brian Grant
EAST FIFE	
Head Coach	Stephen Batty
Head of Football Development	Dave Heddle
Coach	Brian Cooper
EDINBURGH CITY	
Coach	Callum Jeffrey
	Stevie Thomson
	Jamie Hawkins
ELGIN CITY	
Youth Academy Manager	Robbie Hope
HAMILTON ACCIES	
Head of Academy	George Cairns
Head of Youth Football	Allan Maitland
HEARTS	
U18 Coach	John Rankin
Youth Coach	Angus Beith
Academy Manager	Roger Arnott
HIBERNIAN	
Lead Coach, Emerging Talent	Eddie May
Assistant Coach	Gareth Evans
KILMARNOCK	
Academy Director	Paul McDonald
U 18 Coach	Craig Clark
	Andy Black
MONTROSE	
Development Manager	Scott Bridgewater
Development Coach	Colin Gibson
	Paul Hunt
MORTON	
Head of Youth	Derek Anderson
MOTHERWELL	
Academy Director	Steven Hammell
Reserve Team manager	Diarmuid O'Carroll
U18 Manager	Brian Kerr
Head of Intermediate Academy	David Clarkson
PARTICK THISTLE	
Youth Academy Director	Scott Allison
QUEEN'S PARK	
U18 Coach	Charley King
QUEEN OF THE SOUTH	
Head of Youth Development	Andy Irving
Youth Coach	Scott Douglas
	Darren Malin
	David Mathieson
	Neil Murray
	Ross Newlands
	Speedy Byers
RANGERS	
Head of Academy	Craig Mulholland
Head of Elite Academy	Graeme Murty
Head of Recruitment	David Stevenson
B team Coach	Brian Gilmour
Head of Professional Dev Phase	David McCallum
Loans Manager	Billy Kirkwood
ST JOHNSTONE	
Head of Youth	Alistair Stevenson
ST MIRREN	
Head of Youth	Allan McManus
U20 Coach	Andy Webster
Assistant Head of Youth	Ross Paterson
STIRLING ALBION	
Head of Youth (Coaching)	Niall Marshall
Head of Youth (Admin)	David Brown
U18 Coach	Shaun Conlon
	Aurelien Mazel

Scottish FA Youth Cup 2019/20 and 2020/1

The 2019/20 competition was not completed and the 2020/1 competition was not started.

ALL TIME SFA YOUTH CUP FINALS

YEAR	WINNERS	RUNNERS-UP	RES		VENUE
1983–84	Celtic	Rangers	2-0	AET	Celtic Park
1984–85	Aberdeen	Celtic	5-3		Pittodrie Stadium
1985–86	Aberdeen	Queen of the South	2-0		Palmerston Park
1986–87	Celtic	Motherwell	2-1		Fir Park
1987–88	Dunfermline Athletic	Dundee	2-1		East End Park
1988–89	Celtic	Dundee United	1-0		Tannadice Park
1989–90	Dundee United	Hibernian	0-0	AET, pens	Easter Road
1990–91	Dundee United	Hibernian	2-0		Tannadice Park
1991–92	Hibernian	Ayr United	2-0		Easter Road
1992–93	Heart of Midlothian	Rangers	3-1		Ibrox Stadium
1993–94	Rangers	Airdrieonians	5-3		Broomfield Park
1994–95	Rangers	St Johnstone	2-0		Hampden Park
1995–96	Celtic	Dundee	4-1		Hampden Park
1996–97	Celtic	Rangers	3-2		Broadwood Stadium
1997–98	Heart of Midlothian	Dundee United	2-0		Tynecastle Stadium
1998–99	Celtic	Dundee	4-0		Celtic Park
1999–00	Heart of Midlothian	Rangers	5-3		Hampden Park
2000–01	Aberdeen	Celtic	2-0		Hampden Park
2001–02	Rangers	Ayr United	4-2		New Douglas Park
2002–03	Celtic	Aberdeen	3-1	AET	McDiarmid Park
2003–04	Kilmarnock	Rangers	1-0		Rugby Park
2004–05	Celtic	St Mirren	2-0		Hampden Park
2005–06	Celtic	Heart of Midlothian	3-1		Celtic Park
2006–07	Rangers	Celtic	5-0		Hampden Park
2007–08	Rangers	Celtic	3-1	AET	Hampden Park
2008–09	Hibernian	Rangers	2-1	AET	Hampden Park
2009–10	Celtic	Rangers	2-0		Hampden Park
2010–11	Celtic	Rangers	2-1	AET	Hampden Park
2011–12	Celtic	Queen of the South	8-0		Hampden Park
2012–13	Celtic	Dunfermline Athletic	3-1		Hampden Park
2013–14	Rangers	Heart of Midlothian	2-2	AET, pens	St Mirren Park
2014–15	Celtic	Rangers	5-2		Hampden Park
2015–16	Motherwell	Heart of Midlothian	5-2		Hampden Park
2016-17	Celtic	Rangers	3-0		Hampden Park
2017-18	Hibernian	Aberdeen	3-1		Hampden Park
2018-19	Rangers	Celtic	3-2		Hampden Park

WINNERS

15 Celtic
7 Rangers
3 Hearts, Aberdeen, Hibernian
2 Dundee United
1 Dunfermline Athletic, Kilmarnock, Motherwell

RUNNERS UP

10 Rangers
5 Celtic
3 Hearts, Dundee
2 Hibernian, Dundee United, Queen of the South, Ayr United, Aberdeen
1 Dunfermline Athletic, Motherwell, St Mirren, St Johnstone, Airdrieonians

UEFA Youth Champions League 2020/1

The draw for this competition was made but none of the ties took place.

Round 1 (scheduled for March 2nd and 3rd)

Champions League Path

Olympiakos v Manchester City
Internazionale v Bayern Munich
Sevilla v Paris St Germain
Shakthar Donetsk v Porto
Ajax Amsterdam v Krasnodar
Manchester United v Real Madrid
Istanbul Basaksehir v Club Brugge
Atalanta Bergamo v RB Leipzig
Zenit Saint Petersbourg v Rennes
Juventus v Borussia Dortmund
Midtylland v Atletico Madrid
Chelsea v Red Bull Salzburg
Liverpool v Marseille
Dynamo Kyiv v CF Barcelona
Lokomotiv Moscow v Ferencvaros
Borussia Moenchengladbach v Lazio

Domestic Champions Path

Gornik Zabrze v PAOK Salonika
Olimpia Ljubljana v Celta Vigo
APOEL Nicosia v Viitorul Constanta
Apolonia Fier v Gyori ETO
Dinamo Zagreb v Rosenborg Trondheim
Hammarby v Waterford
Galatasaray v AZ 67 Alkmaar
Rangers v 1FC Koln
Angers v Red Star Belgrade
Genk v Zilina
Sparta Prague v Benfica
Basel v Odense BK
Sheriff Tiraspol v Kairat Almaty
Chertanovo Moscow v Maccabi Haifa
Dinamo Minsk v Ludgorets Razgrad
Shkendija v Gabala

SCOTTISH CLUBS—ALL TIME RECORD

2013/14		
Group	AC Milan v Celtic	3-1
Group	Celtic v CF Barcelona	1-2
Group	Celtic v Ajax Amsterdam	4-1
Group	Ajax Amsterdam v Celtic	2-1
Group	Celtic v AC Milan	1-1
Group	CF Barcelona v Celtic	3-0
2015/16		
Rd 1	HJK Helsinki v Celtic	0-5
	Celtic v HJK Helsinki	1-1
Rd 2	Puskas Akademia v Celtic	1-0
	Celtic v Puskas Academia	3-0
PO	Celtic v Valencia	1-1, 3-4p
2016/17		
Group	Celtic v CF Barcelona	1-4
Group	Manchester City v Celtic	3-2
Group	Borussia Moenchengladbach v Celtic	4-1

Group	Celtic v Manchester City	0-4
Group	Celtic v Borussia Moenchengladbach	1-1
Group	CF Barcelona v Celtic	2-1
2017/18		
Group	Celtic v Bayern Munchen	1-2
Group	Paris St Germain v Celtic	2-0
Group	Celtic v RSC Anderlecht	3-1
Group	Bayern Munchen v Celtic	6-2
Group	Celtic v Paris St Germain	2-3
Group	RSC Anderlecht v Celtic	1-2
2018/19		
Rd 1	FC Basel v Hamilton Accies	2-2
Rd 1	Hamilton Accies v FC Basel	2-2, 3-2p
Rd 2	Midtylland v Hamilton Accies	2-0
Rd 2	Hamilton Accies v Midtylland	1-2
2019/20		
Rd 1	Young Boys Berne v Rangers	3-3
Rd 1	Rangers v Young Boys Berne	2-2
Rd 2	Rangers v Slovan Bratislava	2-0
Rd 2	Slovan Bratislava v Rangers	1-2
PO	Rangers v Atletico Madrid	0-4

UEFA Youth Champions League 2021/2

The UEFA Youth League will return in 2021/22, with 64 teams competing for a title last won by Real Madrid in August 2020. The contenders are split into two paths in the autumn, the UEFA Champions League path and domestic champions path, both of which will be drawn in August and begin in September. They come together for the knockout phase, running from the play-offs on 8 and 9 February to the four-team final tournament in Nyon between 22 and 25 April. The full list of contenders in both paths will be confirmed after the UEFA Champions League play-offs end on 25 August.

Format
The 32 clubs that compete in the UEFA Champions League path will be those that take part in the group stage of the senior competition. They are joined by the 32 domestic youth champions from the highest-ranked associations whose senior side does not compete in the UEFA Champions League group stage, taking part in the domestic champions path.

The UEFA Champions League path groups will be the same as those for the senior competition. The group winners will progress directly to the round of 16, with the runners-up going into the play -offs.

The domestic champions path teams compete in two rounds of two-legged knockout ties. The eventual eight second-round winners progress to the play-offs.

The knockout phase consists of one-off ties starting with the play-offs, where the eight domestic champions path winners will each be at home to one of the eight UEFA Champions League path group runners-up.

The eight play-off winners then join the eight UEFA Champions League path group winners in the round of 16. The semi-finals and final are, as always, played at Colovray Stadium in UEFA's Swiss home town of Nyon.

UEFA Champions League path: group stage
Draw: 26 August, Istanbul
Matchday 1: 14/15 September
Matchday 2: 28/29 September
Matchday 3: 19/20 October
Matchday 4: 2/3 November
Matchday 5: 23/24 November
Matchday 6: 7/8 December

Domestic champions path
Draw: 31 August, Nyon
Round 1 first leg: 29 September
Round 1 second leg: 20 October
Round 2 first leg: 3 November
Round 2 second leg: 24 November

Knockout phase
Play-off draw: 14 December, Nyon
Play-offs: 8/9 February
Knockout draw (round of 16 onwards): 14 February, Nyon
Round of 16: 1/2 March
Quarter-finals: 15/16 March
Semi-finals: 22 April, Colovray Stadium, Nyon
Final: 25 April, Colovray Stadium, Nyon

Provisional entries
UEFA Champions League path
Real Madrid (ESP, holders)
Atlético de Madrid (ESP)
Barcelona (ESP)
Sevilla (ESP)
Villarreal (ESP)
Manchester City (ENG)
Manchester United (ENG)
Liverpool (ENG)
Chelsea (ENG)
Bayern München (GER)
Leipzig (GER)
Borussia Dortmund (GER)
Wolfsburg (GER)
Internazionale Milano (ITA)
AC Milan (ITA)
Atalanta (ITA)
Juventus (ITA)
LOSC Lille (FRA)
Paris Saint-Germain (FRA)
Sporting CP (POR)
Porto (POR)
Zenit (RUS)
Club Brugge (BEL)
Dynamo Kyiv (UKR)
Ajax (NED)
Beşiktaş (TUR)
The remaining six places will be filled by the winners of the UEFA Champions League play-offs.

Domestic champions path
Deportivo La Coruña (ESP)
Köln (GER)
Empoli (ITA)
Angers (FRA)
Benfica (POR)*
Genk (BEL)*
Shakhtar Donetsk (UKR)*
AZ Alkmaar (NED)
Trabzonspor (TUR)
Salzburg (AUT)*
Midtjylland (DEN)*
Rangers (SCO)*
Sparta Praha (CZE)*
APOEL (CYP)
Young Boys (SUI)*
PAOK (GER)
Crvena zvezda (SRB)*
Hajduk Split (CRO)
Hammarby (SWE)
Rosenborg (NOR)
Maccabi Haifa (ISR)
Kairat Almaty (KAZ)
Minsk (BLR)
Gabala (AZE)
Septemvri Sofia (BUL)
Csikszereda Miercurea Ciuc (ROU)
Pogoń Szczecin (POL)
Žilina (SVK)
Domžale (SVN)
MTK Budapest (HUN)
Žalgiris (LTU)
Academy-04 (ARM)

SFA Referees 2020/21

CATEGORY 1 REFEREES
Greg Aitken
Euan Anderson
Graham Beaton
John Beaton
Kevin Clancy
William Collum
Barry Cook
Andrew Dallas
David Dickinson
Gavin Duncan
Chris Fordyce
Chris Graham
Kevin Graham
Graham Grainger
Grant Irvine
Steven Kirkland
Scott Lambie
David Lowe
Matthew MacDermid
Bobby Madden
Steven McLean
Alan Muir
David Munro
Craig Napier
Alan Newlands
Steven Reid
Don Robertson
Mike Roncone
Gavin Ross
Calum Scott
Colin Steven
Peter Stuart
Nick Walsh
Duncan Williams
Lloyd Wilson

CATEGORY 1 DEVELOPMENT REFEREES
Stewart Luke
Dan McFarlane
Lorraine Watson

CATEGORY 2 REFEREES
George Calder
Jordan Curran
Kyle Hall
Ross Hardie
Chris McNab
Alex Shepherd
Iain Snedden
Colin Whyte
William Wilson

CATEGORY 2 DEVELOPMENT REFEREES
Connor Ashwood
Liam Duncan
Chris Gentles
Daniel Graves
Alastair Grieve
Calum Haswell
Ryan Lee
Jordan Paterson
Greg Soutar
Paul Timmons
Craig Wilson

CATEGORY 3 SPECIALIST ASSISTANT REFEREES
Michael Banks
Sean Carr
Graham Chambers
Frank Connor
Anthony Cooper
Gordon Crawford
David Doig
Craig Ferguson
Ralph Gordon
Gary Hilland
Stuart Hodge
Drew Kirkland
Joseph Lawson
Graeme Leslie
Ross MacLeod
Alastair Mather
John McCrossan
Daniel McFarlane
David McGeachie
Kylie McMullan
Graham McNeillie
Andrew McWilliam
Andy Milne
Alan Mulvanny
Paul O'Neill
Dougie Potter
David Roome
Douglas Ross
Calum Spence
Stuart Stevenson
Graeme Stewart

CATEGORY 3 SPECIALIST ASSISTANT REFEREE DEVELOPMENT
Scott Anderson
Jonathan Bell
Calum Doyle
Colin Drummond
David Dunne
George King
Colin McAlpine
Kevin McElhinney
David McKniff
Chris Phillips
Chris Rae
Steven Traynor

CATEGORY 3 REFEREES
Michael Addy
Ross Anderson
Billy Baxter
Euan Birch
Ross Birrell
Harry Bruce
Andrew Bryson
Alan Budd
Frazer Bushell
Brian Christie
Ross Clark
Blair Comerford
Jordan Cousland
Andrew Craven
Barry Dickson
Brent Falconer
Willie Ferguson
Blair Fraser
Tony Fullerton
Jonathan Gall
Andy Gamble
Stephen Gill
Alan Grainger
Gary Hanvidge
Mark Harris
Ian Hart
Ross Haswell
Greig Haynes
Sean Henderson
Chris Hobbs
Chris Hughes
Elliott Husband Powton
David Ingram
Joel Kennedy
Ryan Kennedy
Scott Leslie
Kevin Lindsay
Michael MacDermid
Steven MacDonald
Simon MacLean
Craig Macrae
Filippo Mazzoni
Paul McAvinue
Gordon McCabe
Michael McCart
Steven McKay
Chris McTiernan
Ross Menzies
David Milton
Bart Misiak
Gordon Morrison
Darren Munro
Richard Murray
Ross Nelson
Chris Newman
Duncan Nicolson
Mat Northcroft
Terry Ormiston
Robert Peacock
Alan Proctor
Barry Reid
Lee Robertson
Gordon Seago
Thomas Shaw
Will Smith
John Stewart
Andy Taylor
Robin Taylor
Cameron Telfer
Brian Templeton
Robert Thomson
Gary Train
Keiran Trayner
Regan Wallace
Michael Williamson
Steven Wilson

CATEGORY 3 DEVELOPMENT REFEREES
Kenneth Allen
Jamie Andrews
Chris Ashley
Jack Bell
Michael Bonner
Robert Bowie
Stuart Broadfoot
Kenny Brown
Jordan Bruce
Clyde Buchan
Kevin Buchanan
Scott Bunting
Evan Cairns
Nathan Clac-Mansfield
Steven Clark
Ross Cooper
Arran Cruickshank
Chris de Sykes
Thomas Denholm
Ross Donaldson
Scott Donohoe
Scott Douglas
Scott Downie
Sean Duff
James Duffy
Barry Feery
Dawid Galazka
Kian Gallacher
Liam Gallagher
Keiran Gibson
Zachery Gill
Conor Greenan
Jamie Guyan
Josh Hay
Abbie Hendry
Calum I MacDonald
Kieran Kennedy
Tommi Kerr
Owen Lawrence
Alastair Leghorn
Fraser MacAra
Danny MacKinnon
Neil Matheson
William McAleese
James McCluskey
Scott McGregor
Chris McLaughlin
Duncan McLullich
Sean Murdoch
Kevin Murray
Kieran O'Reilly
Will Pare
Lee Pirie
Yaser Razouk
Liam Redpath
Steven Spence
Ryan Stewart
Rhys Struthers
Alastair Taylor
Daniel Taylor
Ellis Walls
Sean Welsh
Kieran Whalen
Lauren Whitehead
Jamie Wilkie
Tim Woodcock

CATEGORY 4 REFEREES
Molly Alexander
Boise Allan
Duncan Anderson
George Anderson
Anton Brown
Jason Brown
Ally Bruce
Jim Burns

Stephen Clark
Billy Cooper
Paul Cummings
Finlay Currie
Derek Davidson
Gavin Dearie
Graham Elder
Stephen Foggin
Iain Gallacher
Paul Hanlon
Scott Jamieson
Graham John
Scott Love
Richard Macartney
George MacDonald
Laurie Mackinnon
Gary MacLean
Rodney Marshall
Keith Maskell
Stephen McDade
Andrew McGachan
Mike McIlvenny
John McKendrick
Dave McLaren
Eddie Nichol
John Nicolson
Caryl Potten
Mark Rennie
Stewart Riddoch
Jamie Shepherd
Graeme Smith
Andrew Strang
Sean Sutherland
Gary Toland
Mike Tumilty

REFEREE OBSERVERS
Graeme Alison
Iain Brines
Jim Bruce
Brian Cassidy
Kenny Clark
Martin Clark
George Clyde
Gerry Corrie
Gerry Evans
Stephen Finnie
Alan Freeland
Ian Fyfe
Douglas Hope
Bill Machray
Craig MacKay
Calum Murray
Billy Murray
Euan Norris
Mike Pocock
Sandy Roy
Dougie Smith
Craig Thomson
Louis Thow
Kevin Toner
Paul Watson
Neil Watters
Brian Winter
Douglas Yeats
Willie Young
John Young

ASSISTANT REFEREE OBSERVERS
Martin Cryans
Willie Conquer
Alan Cunningham
Mark Doyle
George Drummond
Gavin Harris
Stuart Macaulay

Scottish Referees on FIFA / UEFA List 2021

Referees
John Beaton
Kevin Clancy
William Collum
Bobby Madden
David Munro
Don Robertson
Nick Walsh

Assistant Referees
Sean Carr
Frank Connor
Daniel McFarlane
David McGeachie
Alan Mulvanny
Dougie Potter
David Roome
Douglas Ross
Calum Spence
Graeme Stewart

Video Match Officials
William Collum
Robert Madden

Women Referees
Lorraine Watson

Women Assistant Referees
Vikki Allan
Kylie Cockburn
Vikki Robertson

Futsal Referees
Gordon McCabe

BECOME A REFEREE

Refereeing can be a highly rewarding challenge, encouraging a healthy and active lifestyle as well as significantly contributing to the development of the game. Referees operate at all levels– from grassroots football right through to the Scottish Professional Football League and international matches.

INTRODUCTORY REFEREE COURSE
The Introductory Referee Course is delivered on behalf of the Scottish FA by the 12 Referees' Associations throughout the country.

Course fee
£35 (includes the first season's membership fee)
£15 for concessions (students and unemployed persons)

The course length is generally between eight and 10 weeks for two hours per night. The courses are held twice a year in the January to March and September to December periods. Other courses may be held outside this schedule depending on local circumstances and demand.
There are two parts to the Introductory Course. The first is classroom-based learning on the Laws of the Game with an exam in the final week. The exam is conducted on computers at the course venue and involves multiple choice questions, report writing and assessing match incidents on video. The second part involves officiating a match under the guidance of a more experienced referee. Once part two is completed, candidates are able to join the local Referees' Association and become a Scottish FA registered referee.
Support is given to new referees by their Referees' Association and a mentor will be arranged to provide guidance in the early stages of their refereeing careers. Direction will also be given on suitable leagues to commence refereeing.

Referees - Severity Index - 2020/21

	2020/21				2019/20				2018/19				2017/18				2016/17				2015/16				2014/15			
SEVERE	G	Y	R	PPG	G	Y	R	PPG	G	Y	R	PPG	G	Y	R	PPG	G	Y	R	PPG	G	Y	R	PPG	G	Y	R	PPG
Gavin Ross	14	56	8	5.7	19	77	9	5.47	27	100	9	4.7	23	93	11	5.48	25	148	13	7.48	25	106	9	5.32	26	102	6	4.61
Duncan Williams	17	79	6	5.7	14	64	1	4.79	11	32	0	2.91	7	22	0	3.14												
Dan McFarlane	3	13	1	5.3																								
Darren Munro	1	5	0	5					1	4	0	4																
Steven Kirkland	17	63	7	4.9	13	41	2	3.62	19	120	6	4.76	20	66	4	3.90	26	103	13	5.46	23	69	5	3.65	17	43	4	3.23
Stewart Luke	4	19	0	4.75	2	6	0	3																				
Craig Napier	20	82	4	4.7	18	59	4	3.94	28	79	5	3.36	20	75	3	4.20	25	81	12	4.68	12	33	1	3				
Lorraine Watson	13	14	0	4.7	Maternity Leave								5	15	2	4.20												
Mike Roncone	8	25	4	4.6	13	32	5	3.62	27	79	3	3.26	27	120	4	4.89	27	96	7	4.33	26	102	10	5.08	6	27	2	5.5
Barry Cook	16	57	5	4.5	19	82	1	4.47	42	122	6	3.33	28	92	4	3.71	25	114	4	5.04	30	119	7	4.67	27	97	3	3.93
Graham Grainger	12	45	3	4.5	9	29	1	3.56																				
Calum Scott	11	41	2	4.3	4	21	1	6	1	3	0	3																
Peter Stuart	17	58	4	4.1	15	56	8	5.33	11	49	4	5.55	8	38	0	4.75												
John Beaton	25	90	4	4.1	20	70	2	3.8	37	126	7	3.97	36	137	5	4.22	39	142	6	4.1	40	144	9	4.27	33	14	4	3.82
Alan Muir	19	65	4	4.1	21	62	3	3.38	30	68	5	2.77	32	119	4	4.09	32	120	3	4.03	35	108	5	3.51	31	113	7	4.32
David Lowe	15	62	0	4.1	17	54	1	3.35	32	101	4	3.53	21	43	1	2.19	27	74	4	3.19	26	71	2	2.96	6	18	0	3
Chris Graham	15	48	4	4	18	93	5	4.33	10	32	1	3.5	6	19	1	3.67												
Graeme Beaton	6	21	1	4	16	56	1	3.69	24	82	3	3.79	19	71	7	4.84	22	79	6	4.41					4	14	0	3.5
Colin Steven	19	59	5	3.9	17	64	4	4.47	31	112	2	3.81	31	76	6	3.03	3.03	80	7	5.05	24	102	7	5.12	26	89	5	4
Euan Anderson	19	65	3	3.9	22	67	2	3.32	32	112	7	4.16	32	105	5	3.75	29	95	2	3.48	32	89	5	3.25	33	129	4	4.27
Steven McLean	21	64	4	3.6	18	57	0	3.17	35	124	9	4.31	26	85	7	4.08	32	134	9	5.03	40	143	5	3.95	38	126	7	3.87
David Munro	17	50	3	3.5	21	86	2	4.38	23	70	2	3.26	18	59	3	3.78	21	77	8	4.81	26	69	4	3.11	19	55	2	3
Nick Walsh	25	66	7	3.5	16	56	3	4.06	37	131	5	3.95	30	117	6	4.50	35	142	9	4.83	31	122	12	5.1	28	83	4	3.39
Alan Newlands	15	43	3	3.5	20	64	0	3.2	37	118	6	3.68	26	85	7	4.08	26	97	6	4.42	27	93	4	3.89	40	3	3	4.67
Scott Lambie	15	42	3	3.4	15	64	3	4.87	10	31	4	4.3	7	18	2	3.43												
Matthew McDermid	14	41	2	3.4	6	22	2	4.67																				
David Dickinson	16	55	0	3.4	18	69	1	4	22	78	3	3.95	8	22	1	3.13	3	12	0	4								
Steven Reid	15	42	3	3.4	20	63	5	3.9	25	71	5	3.44	21	68	4	3.81	25	59	2	2.6	12	42	1	3.75				
Gavin Duncan	17	53	1	3.3	17	73	3	4.82	25	79	4	3.64	30	120	5	4.50	28	117	3	4.5	24	103	5	4.92	21	76	6	4.48
Kevin Clancy	20	60	2	3.3	20	76	6	4.7	34	145	8	4.87	32	140	2	4.56	32	139	3	4.34	38	145	7	4.37	35	124	4	3.89
William Collum	30	81	6	3.3	23	61	4	3.17	42	119	9	3.48	43	151	12	4.35	43	134	8	3.67	46	142	7	3.54	48	142	17	4.02
Don Robertson	25	76	1	3.2	20	68	7	4.45	34	109	4	3.56	32	122	3	4.09	33	111	7	4	39	105	8	3.31	25	101	6	3.4
Greg Aitken	19	47	4	3.1	19	75	9	5.37	33	106	5	3.67	29	111	12	5.07	30	97	3	3.53	27	95	12	4.85	34	88	13	3.73
Kevin Graham	13	37	1	3.1	12	28	0	2.33	6	11	0	1.83	22	68	1	3.23	3.23	85	4	4.04	28	109	8	4.75	29	103	7	4.28
Andrew Dallas	8	24	1	3	17	45	3	3.18	16	119	8	8.94	34	139	8	4.79	30	117	6	4.5	26	106	3	4.42	32	119	7	4.37
Bobby Madden	21	49	3	2.8	17	48	5	3.71	36	100	11	3.69	39	137	7	4.05	39	82	2	2.93	37	130	11	4.41	41	135	11	4.1
Grant Irvine	21	56	1	2.8	14	32	1	2.5	25	49	2	2.2	23	71	1	3.22	24	76	3	3.54	11	35	3	4	15	38	1	2.73
LENIENT																												
RETIRED / DEMOTED																												
Brian Colvin																					15	49	3	3.87	29	100	7	4.17
George Salmond																					27	91	6	4.04	30	77	4	2.97
Peter Newlands																									10	40	3	4.9
Calum Murray																									36	21	8	4.03
Des Roache																									13	48	0	3.69
Crawford Allan																	31	96	3	3.39	31	97	5	3.61	34	83	4	2.79
Mike Taylor																	3	6	1	3	7	18	1	3	3	7	2	4.33
Stephen Finnie													32	128	6	4.56	32	135	5	4.69	37	155	8	4.84	33	133	3	4.3
Craig Charleston													27	76	6	3.48	28	118	8	5.07	30	119	5	4.47	34	7	15	4.47
Ryan Milne													8	19	0	2.38	8	30	1	4.13	4	12	2	4.5	7	15	2	3
Mat Northcroft													24	91	5	4.42	24	74	3	3.46	21	75	3	4	25	75	5	3.6
Stephen Graham									1	0	0	0																
Connor Ashwood									1	2	0	2																
Scott Millar									15	43	4	3.67	20	68	3	3.85	23	79	6	4.22	9	30	4	4.67				
Craig Thomson									29	97	4	3.76	38	134	12	4.47	38	133	7	4.05	43	183	7	4.74	45	1269	7	4.22
Stephen Brown									10	28	3	3.7	6	16	0	2.67												
Ryan Lee									1	4	0	4																
Duncan Smith									4	16	1	4.75																
John McKendrick					13	36	0	2.77	24	65	2	2.96	22	51	1	2.45	2.45	51	2	2.38	32	71	0	2.21	35	84	2	2.57
Chris Fordyce					12	49	1	4.33	8	37	0	4.63																

The table below is provided for a little bit of fun - not for any ulterior purpose. It shows the total number of SPFL, Scottish Cup and League Cup games handled (G), total Yellow (Y) and Red (R) cards issued during 2017/18 and the four previous seasons. Yellow Cards are given 1 point each, red cards are given three points each to reach a total, and the total is then divided by the number of games to give the (PPG) - the severity index.

Of course the fewer games a referee handles the less likely they are to be representative of all games therefore figures for those with a low games total must be treated with particular caution.

A further note of caution—a referee in the middle of the list may be very good or they could be erratic with some lenient games and some severe games.

SFA DISCIPLINARY HEARINGS SEASON 2020/21

KEY TO DISCIPLINARY OFFENCES

A1-A4 Claim against unfair dismissal
B1-B4 Claim against unfair caution
AoA Breaching Articles of Association of SFA
24 Disciplinary Rule 24 – No complying with SFA rules and procedures
22 Disciplinary Rule 22 / 33 / 31 - Betting on football
26 Disciplinary Rule 26 - Clubs in full membership may not be involved in a friendly match without the prior written approval of the Board.
27 Disciplinary Rule 27: Playing a match against an uncrecognised opponent
65 Disciplinary Rule 65 - Match officials failing to comply with the SFA, Rules and Articles
71 Disciplinary Rule 71 – Bringing game into disrepute
72 Discipliary Rule 72 - Criticising decisions of match officials
76 Disciplinary Rule 76 - Harrassment of match officials
77 Disciplinary Rule 77 - Use of violent Conduct, serious foul play, threatening, abusive, indecent or insulting words or behaviour.
78 Disciplinary Rule 78 - No member or Associated Person shall take a dispute which is referable to arbitration in terms of Article 99 to a court of law except as expressly permitted by the terms of Article 99.
200 Disciplinary Rule 200 - When a Sending Off offence is missed by the match officials
202 Disciplinary Rule 202 - No player shall commit excessive misconduct
203 Disciplinary Rule 203 - No member of team staff / official shall commit misconduct
208 Disciplinary Rule 208 - No player or member of Team Staff shall breach a suspension
COVID Breaches of specific COVID rules

Date	Party			Rule	Hearing Date	Outcome
06/08/2020			Hearts	78	06/08/2020	£2500 fine
06/08/2020			Partick Thistle	78	06/08/2020	£2500 fine
14/08/2020	Jonny Hayes	Player	Aberdeen	24, 71	28/08/2020	3 match suspension (suspended)
14/08/2020	Scott McKenna	Player	Aberdeen	24, 71	28/08/2020	3 match suspension (suspended)
14/08/2020	Sam Cosgrove	Player	Aberdeen	24, 71	28/08/2020	3 match suspension (suspended)
14/08/2020	Craig Bryson	Player	Aberdeen	24, 71	28/08/2020	3 match suspension (suspended)
14/08/2020	Bruce Anderson	Player	Aberdeen	24, 71	28/08/2020	3 match suspension (suspended)
14/08/2020	Dylan McGeouch	Player	Aberdeen	24, 71	28/08/2020	3 match suspension (suspended)
14/08/2020	Matty Kennedy	Player	Aberdeen	24, 71	28/08/2020	3 match suspension (suspended)
14/08/2020	Michael Devlin	Player	Aberdeen	24, 71	28/08/2020	3 match suspension (suspended)
14/08/2020	Boli Bolingoli	Player	Celtic	24, 71	28/08/2020	5 Match Suspension (2 suspended)
24/09/2020	Fraser Murray	Player	Hibernian	202	24/09/2020	2 match Suspension (suspended)
30/09/2020	Stuart Kettlewell	Manager	Ross County	203, 72	30/09/2020	5 Match Suspension (2 suspended)
01/10/2020	Mark Connolly	Player	Dundee United	77, 24	01/10/2020	2 match Suspension (Suspended)
12/10/2020	David Murray	Player	Alness United	202	12/10/2020	6 Match Suspension (2 suspended)
12/10/2020	Steven Gerrard	Manager	Rangers	72	12/10/2020	Case not proven
23/10/2020	Michael Wilson	Manager	Peebles Rovers	203	05/11/2020	Accepted 1 match suspension
23/10/2020	Michael Houston	Manager	Heston Rovers	203	05/11/2020	Accepted 1 match suspension
26/10/2020	Gordon Herd	Head Coach	Camelon	203	05/11/2020	
26/10/2020	Gary Sutherland	Team Staff	Ormiston	203	05/11/2020	3 match suspension
26/10/2020	John Martin	Manager	Glenrothes	203	05/11/2020	2 match suspension
26/10/2020	Nathan Gillie	Player	Hawick RAU	208	05/11/2020	Accepted 1 match suspension
26/10/2020	Daniel Chandler	Player	Hawick RAU	208	05/11/2020	Accepted 1 match suspension
26/10/2020	Dean Fry	Player	Hawick RAU	208	05/11/2020	Accepted 1 match suspension
27/10/2020	Stuart Innes	Coach	Burntisland Shipyard	203	12/11/2020	4 match suspension (1 suspended)
28/10/2020	Daniel Galbraith	Player	Gala Fairydean Rovers	A2	30/10/2020	Claim of unfair dismissal upheld
28/10/2020	Neil Hassan	Team Staff	Edinburgh South	203	05/11/2020	Accepted 1 match suspension
29/10/2020	Andy Bryan	Team Staff	Dundee United	208	29/10/2020	2 Match Suspension
29/10/2020	Dale Pennycuick	Player	Preston Athletic	202	29/10/2020	6 Match Suspension (3 suspended)
29/10/2020	Andrew Wilson	Official	Motherwell	72	29/10/2020	£750 Fine
03/11/2020	Donald Morrison	Player	Dumbarton	208	10/11/2020	Accepted 1 match suspension
03/11/2020	Shelley Campbell	Player	Kilmarnock Women	208	03/11/2020	Accepted 1 match suspension
10/11/2020	Darren Affleck	Coach	Craigroyston	203	10/11/2020	Accepted 1 match suspension
11/11/2020	Sean Cummings	Player	Lothian Thistle HV	A2	11/11/2020	Claim upheld, red card rescinded
11/11/2020	Jim McAllister	Player	Morton	A1	11/11/2020	Claim Dismissed
13/11/2020	Gary MacMillan	Manager	Dunipace	203	07/11/2020	1 match suspension
13/11/2020	Gary Bollan	Manager	Cowdenbeath	203	07/11/2020	Accepted 1 match suspension
18/11/2020	Frazer Wright	Coach	BSC Glasgow	203	18/11/2020	Accepted 1 match suspension
19/11/2020	Jordan Jones	Player	Rangers	24, 77	19/11/2020	7 match suspension
19/11/2020	George Edmundson	Player	Rangers	24, 77	19/11/2020	7 match suspension
25/11/2020	Stuart Findlay	Player	Kilmarnock	A4	25/11/2020	Clain dismissed
25/11/2020	Jason Holt	Player	Livingston	200	26/11/2020	Admitted, 2 match suspension
25/11/2020	Kevin Lindsay	Referee		24, 65, 77, AoA 5, 95	11/02/2021	8 match suspension, Quashed on appeal and replaced with £150 fine
26/11/2020	Jordan Sinclair	Player	Berwick Rangers	76	26/11/2020	2 match suspension
26/11/2020	Richard Foster	Team Staff	Partick Thistle Women	203	26/11/2020	2 Match suspension (1 suspended)
03/12/2020	David Wilson	Kit Manager	BSC Glasgow	76	03/12/2020	12 match suspension (4 suspended)
03/12/2020	David Gillies	Coach	Irvine Meadow	203	03/12/2020	5 Match Suspension (2 suspended)
03/12/2020			St Mirren	COVID	03/12/2020	2 x 3-0 defeats awarded, £40,000 fine (suspended)
03/12/2020			Kilmarnock	COVID	03/12/2020	3-0 defeat awarded, £40,000 fine (suspended)
04/12/2020	Chris King	Manager	Newtongrange Star	203	10/12/2020	Accepted 1 match suspension
04/12/2020	Steven Woodward	Assistant Manager	Lochar Thistle	203	10/12/2020	Accepted 1 match suspension
04/12/2020	Stewart Kenny	Manager	Oakley United	203	10/12/2020	Accepted 1 match suspension
04/12/2020	Dale Richardson	Assistant Manager	Edinburgh South	203	10/12/2020	Accepted 1 match suspension
09/12/2020	Ryan Finnie	Player	Berwick Rangers	A4	09/12/2020	Claim dismissed
10/12/2020	Mark McCallum	Player	Forfar Athletic	22, 33, 31	10/12/2020	Censure
10/12/2020	Anthony McMinn	Assistant Manager	East Fife	203	10/12/2020	3 match suspension (1 suspended)
15/12/2020	Alfredo Morelos	Player	Rangers	200	15/12/2020	Accepted 2 match suspension
15/12/2020	Charlie Always	Manager	Orkney FC	203	07/01/2021	Fixed suspension accepted
15/12/2020	Stuart Duthie	Coach	Crossgates Primrose	203	07/01/2021	Accepted 1 match suspension
16/12/2020	Gary Fraser	Player	Peterhead	A2	16/12/2020	Claim of wrongful dismissal partially upheld, educed to caution
18/12/2020			Hill of Beath Hawthorn	208	18/12/2020	£2000 Fine (Suspended) + censure

18/12/2020			Hill of Beath Hawthorn	303	18/12/2020	combined with above
18/12/2020	Daniel Watt	Player	Hill of Beath Hawthorn	203	07/01/2001	Accepted 1 match suspension
22/12/2020	Wille Harvey	Manager	Rutherglen Glencairn	203	07/01/2021	Accepted 1 match suspension
23/12/2020	Alistair Park	Player	Beith	A2	23/12/2020	Partially upheld, dismissal reduced to caution
31/12/2020	Tony Fraser	Coach	Rutherglen Glencairn	203	15/01/2021	Accepted 1 match suspension
31/12/2020	Michael Gardyne	Player	Ross County	77		Charge withdrawn
31/12/2020	Gordon Moffat	Manager	Clydebank	203	11/02/2021	2 match suspension
07/01/2021	Simon Ferry	Player	Peterhead	A2	07/01/2001	Claim dismissed
08/01/2021	Stuart Malcolm	Manager	Forfar Athletic	203	07/01/2021	5 match suspension
08/01/2021	David Simmonds	Coach	Haddington Athletic	203	07/01/2021	4 match suspension (2 suspended)
08/01/2021			Haddington Athletic	204	07/01/2021	£250 fine (Suspended)
08/01/2021			BSC Glasgow	204	07/01/2021	£500 fine
15/01/2021			Kilmarnock		15/01/2021	Original sanctions overturned
15/01/2021			St Mirren		15/01/2021	Original sanctions overturned
16/01/2021	Gary McMenamin	Coach	Wigtown & Bladnoch	203	15/01/2021	2 match suspension
16/01/2021	Gabriel Veringa	Player	Fort William	202	15/01/2021	9 match suspension
29/01/2021	Alfredo Morelos	Player	Rangers	200 A2	02/02/2021	Accepted 2 match suspension
29/01/2021	Robbie Neilson	Manager	Hearts	203	18/02/2021	
03/02/2021			Edinburgh United		03/02/2021	Case referred back to EOSL
09/02/2021	Albian Ajeti	Player	Celtic	201	09/02/2021	Not proved
09/02/2021			Sauchie		09/02/2021	Appellate Tribunal upheld decision of EOSL
11/02/2021	Kemar Roofe	Player	Rangers	200	11/02/2021	Proved - 2 match suspension
17/02/2021	Jack Fitzwater	Player	Livingston	A4	17/02/2021	Claim for wrongful dismissal - rejected
17/02/2021	Peter Pawlett	Player	Dundee United	A1	17/02/2021	Claim for wrongful dismissal - rejected
19/02/2021	Robbie Neilson	Manager	Hearts	203	18/02/2021	4 match suspension (2 suspended)
24/02/2021	Jamie Hamilton	Player	Hamilton Accies	A1	24/02/2021	Claim partially upheld, red card reduced to yellow
03/03/2021	Steven Gerrard	Manager	Rangers	203	25/03/2021	Accepted 1 match suspension
05/03/2021	Alfredo Morelos	Player	Rangers	B1k	05/03/2021	Claim upheld, Caution rescinded
09/03/2021	Calvin Bassey	Player	Rangers	27, 77	25/03/2021	6 match suspension, 2 uspended
09/03/2021	Brian Kinnear	Player	Rangers	27, 77	25/03/2021	6 match suspension, 2 uspended
09/03/2021	Dapo Mebude	Player	Rangers	27, 77	25/03/2021	6 match suspension, 2 uspended
09/03/2021	Nathan Patterson	Player	Rangers	27, 77	25/03/2021	6 match suspension, 2 uspended
09/03/2021	Bingani Zungu	Player	Rangers	27, 77	25/03/2021	6 match suspension, 2 uspended
15/03/2021	Rhys McCabe	Player	Queen of the South	A2	17/03/2021	Claim of wrongful dismissal, partially upheld, reduced to caution
15/03/2021	Stephen Obileye	Player	Queen of the South	A1	17/03/2021	Claim of wrongful dismissal, partially upheld, reduced to caution
18/03/2021	Allan Johnston	Manager	Queen of the South	203	01/04/2021	Accepted 1 match suspension
23/03/2021	Lewis Ferguson	Player	Aberdeen	B1k	24/03/2021	Claim of wrongful caution. Upheld
23/03/2021	Kyle Turner	Player	Airdrieonians	A1	24/03/2021	Claim of wrongful dismissal. Dismissed.
09/04/2021	David Irons	Manager	Stenhousemuir	203	22/04/2021	Accepted 1 match suspension
13/04/2021	Nikolay Todorov	Player	Inverness CT	202	27/05/2021	Rule breach not proven
13/04/2021		Club	Morton	26, 27	08/04/2021	£750 fine (Suspeded)
15/04/2021	Iain Davidson	Player	Raith Rovers	202	15/04/2021	4 match suspension, 2 suspended
15/04/2021	Jim Goodwin	Manager	St Mirren	203	15/04/2021	3 match suspension, 1 suspneded
21/04/2021	Neil Parry	Player	Alloa Athletic	A4	21/04/2021	Claim of wrongful dismissal, partially upheld, reduced to caution
23/04/2021	Scott Allardice	Player	Inverness CT	A1	24/04/2021	Claim of wrongful dismissal, Upheld
23/04/2021	Brad McKay	Player	Inverness CT	A1	23/04/2021	Claim of wrongful dismissal, Dismissed
24/04/2021	Neil McCann	Manager	Inverness CT	203	20/05/2021	Accepted 1 match suspension
26/04/2021	Owen Moxon	Player	Annan Athletic	A1	27/04/2021	Claim of wrongful dismissal, Dismissed
28/04/2021	Barry Robson	Team Staff	Aberdeem (u18)	203	20/05/2021	Accepted 1 match suspension
29/04/2021	Adam Ashgar	Team Staff	Dundee United (u18)	203	29/04/2021	5 match suspension, 2 suspended
29/04/2021	Gavin Price	Manager	Elgin City	203	13/05/2021	Accepted 1 match suspension
29/04/2021	Brian Rice	Manager	Hamilton Accies	72, 77	29/04/2021	4 match suspension, 2 suspended
05/05/2021	Iain Davidson	Player	Raith Rovers	A4	06/05/2001	Claim of wrongful dismissal, Upheld
06/05/2021	John Hughes	Manager	Ross County	72, 77	06/05/2021	4 match suspension, 2 suspended
12/05/2021	Jamie Robson	Player	Dundee United	A1	19/05/2021	Claim of wrongful dismissal
12/05/2021	Charlotte Parker-Smi	Player	Hearts Ladies	A1	12/05/2021	Claim of wrongful dismissal, partially upheld, reduced to caution
18/05/2021	Paul Hartley	Manager	Cove Rangers	203	03/06/2021	Accepted 1 match suspension
19/05/2021	Jonathan Tiffoney	Player	Stenhousemuir	202, 77	24/06/2021	
19/05/2021	Jamie Robson	Player	Dundee United	A1	19/05/2021	Claim of wrongful dismissal dismissed
27/05/2021	StewartBell	Manager	Kilwinning FC	203	17/06/2021	Offered 1 game suspension
27/05/2021	Andy Kirk	Manager	Hearts Women	203	17/06/2021	Accepted 1 match suspension
07/06/2021	Jack MacIver	Player	Aberdeen	202	17/06/2021	

Scots Abroad 2021

England

Stuart Armstrong	Premier League		Southampton
Andy Robertson	Premier League		Liverpool
Harrison Ashby	Premier League		West Ham United
Che Adams	Premier League		Southampton
Matt Ritchie	Premier League		Newcastle United
Alan Irvine	Premier League	C	West Ham United
Matt Phillips	Premier League		West Bromwich Albion
Ryan Fraser	Premier League		Newcastle United
John Fleck	Premier League		Sheffield United
Robert Snodgrass	Premier League		West Bromwich Albion
John McGinn	Premier League		Aston Villa
Oli McBurnie	Premier League		Sheffield United
Kieran Tierney	Premier League		Arsenal
James McArthur	Premier League		Crystal Palace
Tom Cairney	Premier League		Fulham
Oli Burke	Premier League		Sheffield United
Brian Gilmour	Premier League		Chelsea
Liam Cooper	Premier League		Leeds United
Kevin McDonald	Premier League		Fulham
Phil Bardsley	Premier League		Burnley
Scott McTominay	Premier League		Manchester United
David Moyes	Premier League	M	West Ham United
Graeme Shinnie	Championship		Derby County
Jon McCracken	Championship		Norwich City
Aaron Pressley	Championship		Brentford
Liam Lindsay	Championship		Preston North End
Jordan Archer	Championship		Middlesbrough
Kai Naismith	Championship		Luton Town
Liam Kelly	Championship		Coventry City
David Marshall	Championship		Derby County
Reece McAlear	Championship		Norwich City
Lewis Gordon	Championship		Brentford
Frankie McAvoy	Championship		Preston North End
Barry Douglas	Championship		Blackburn Rovers
Liam Palmer	Championship		Sheffield Wednesday
Michael Rose	Championship		Coventry City
Lee Wallace	Championship		Queens Park Rangers
Tom Dickson-Peters	Championship		Norwich City
Cameron Yates	Championship		Wycombe Wanderers
Scott McKenna	Championship		Nottingham Forest
Charlie Mulgrew	Championship		Blackburn Rovers
Barry Bannan	Championship		Sheffield Wednesday
Jack Burroughs	Championship		Coventry City
Lyndon Dykes	Championship		Queens Park Rangers
Thomas Mcintyre	Championship		Reading
Jack Grimmer	Championship		Wycombe Wanderers
Clark Robertson	Championship		Rotherham United
Connor McBride	Championship		Blackburn Rovers
Jordan Rhodes	Championship		Sheffield Wednesday
Josh Reid	Championship		Coventry City
Liam Kelly	Championship		Queens Park Rangers
Murray Wallace	Championship		Millwall
Jamie Lindsay	Championship		Rotherham United
Grant Hanley	Championship		Norwich City
Callum Paterson	Championship		Sheffield Wednesday
Paul Gallagher	Championship		Preston North End
Chris Martin	Championship		Bristol City
Steven Fletcher	Championship		Stoke City
Craig Forsyth	Championship		Derby County
Kenny McLean	Championship		Norwich City
Kane O'Conner	Championship		Brentford
Lewis Coulton	Championship		Preston North End
Paul Coutts	Championship		Bristol City
Dom Hyam	Championship		Coventry City
Sturt Taylor	League One		Ipswich Town
Siriki Dembélé	League One		Peterborough United
Jon Ruddy	League One		Plymouth Argyle
Theo Archibald	League One		Lincoln City
Kyle Joseph	League One		Wigan Athletic
Darren Ferguson	League One	M	Peterborough United
Russell Martin	League One		Milton Keynes Dons
James Jones	League One		Lincoln City
Luke Robinson	League One		Wigan Athletic
Ethan Hamilton	League One		Peterborough United
Andrew Shinnie	League One		Charlton Athletic
Daniel Harvie	League One		Milton Keynes Dons
Sam Nicholson	League One		Bristol Rovers
Steve Evans	League One	M	Gillingham
James Scott	League One		Hull City
Craig MacGillivray	League One		Portsmouth
Scott Fraser	League One		Milton Keynes Dons
Jim McNulty	League One		Rochdale
Alex MacDonald	League One		Gillingham
Greg Docherty	League One		Hull City
George Byers	League One		Portsmouth
Zak Jules	League One		Milton Keynes Dons
Ryan Hardie	League One		Plymouth Argyle
Liam Bridcutt	League One		Lincoln City
Ross Stewart	League One		Sunderland
Tommy Wright	League One	C	Swindon Town
Liam MacLeod	League One		Plymouth Argyle
Conor McGrandles	League One		Lincoln City
Sam Lavelle	League Two		Morecambe
Calum MacDonald	League Two		Tranmere Rovers
George Boyd	League Two		Salford City
Derek Adams	League Two	M	Morecambe
Ali Crawford	League Two		Tranmere Rovers
Steven Hendrie	League Two		Morecambe
Willie Boyle	League Two		Cheltenham Town
Scott Cuthbert	League Two		Stevenage
Andy Dallas	League Two		Cambridge United
Nicky Cadden	League Two		Forest Green Rovers
Lewis Spence	League Two		Scunthorpe United
Matt Gilks	League Two		Bolton Wanderers
Jack Aitchison	League Two		Forest Green Rovers
Jack Armer	League Two		Carlisle United
Elliot Watt	League Two		Bradford City
Mark Beck	League Two		Harrogate Town
Calvin Miller	National League		Notts County
Ben House	National League		Eastleigh
Alex McBurnie	National League		Barnet
Cameron King	National League		King's Lynn Town
Ross McCormack	National League		Aldershot Town
Fraser Kerr	National League		Chesterfield
Archie Mair	National League		King's Lynn Town
Taylor Thain	National League		Aldershot Town
Jack McKay	National League		Chesterfield
Martin Woods	National League		Halifax Town
Kyle Cameron	National League		Torquay United

Cameron Murray	National League		Weymouth
Jim O'Brien	National League		Notts County
Brennan Camp	National League		Weymouth
Jake Sheppard	National Lea...		Hampton & Richmond
Luke Lyons	National Lea...		Bradford (Park Avenue)
Jonathan Henly	National Lea...		Tonbridge Angels
Callum Gunner	National Lea...		Chippenham Town
Ruben Sammutt	National Lea...		Dulwich Hamlet
Jordan Young	National Lea...		Gloucester City
Harry Cardwell	National Lea...		Chorley
Jordan Preston	National Lea...		Gateshead
Fraser Preston	National Lea...		Boston United
Tom Bonner	National Lea...		Dartford
Callum Harrison	National Lea...		Chelmsford City
David Noble	National Lea...		St Albans City
Dan Meredith	National Lea...		Leamington
Ruaridh Donaldson	National Lea...		Hampton & Richmond
George McLennan	National Lea...		Havant & Waterlooville
Scott McLean	National Lea...		Spennymoor Town
Craig King	Non League P...		Matlock Town
Dominic Brown-Hill	Non League P...		Barwell
Kieran Weledji	Non League P...		Whitby Town
William Davies	Non League P...		Leiston
Alex White	Non League P...		Whitby Town
Jamie Henry	Non League P...		Wimborne Town
William Hoare	Non League P...		Horsham
Martin McIntosh	Non League P...	C	Buxton
Steve Burr	Non League P...	C	Stalybridge Celtic
Craig McAllister	Non League P...		Gosport Borough
Callum Bagshaw	Non League P...		Stalybridge Celtic
Scott McGowan	Non League P...		Nantwich Town
Craig Mackail-Smith	Non League D...		Bedford Town
Cammy Clark	Non League D...		Belper Town
Chris Budrys	Non League D...		Kidsgrove Athletic
Kieran McGee	Non League D...		Chertsey Town
Sean Paterson	Non League D...		Workington
Callum Donnelly	Non League D...		Bedford Town
Steven Craig	Counties Leagues		Worcester City
Spain			
Jordan Holsgrove	La Liga		Celta Vigo
Jordan Holsgrove	Primera Divi...		Celta de Vigo II
Jack Harper	Primera Divi...		Villarreal II
Italy			
Aaron Hickey	Serie A		Bologna
Liam Henderson	Serie B		Lecce
Harvey St Clair	Serie B		Venezia
France			
Thomas Garnier	National 3		Le Mans II
Netherlands			
Geroge Johnston	Eredivisie		Feyenoord
Frank Ross	Eredivisie		Go Ahead Eagles
Lewis Fiorini	Eerste Divisie		NAC Breda
Ciaran Summers	Derde Divisie		DOVO
Scott Calderwood	Derde Divisie	C	DOVO
Australia			
Graeme Dorrans	A-League		Western Sydney Wanderers
Kenny Miller	A-League		Western Sydney Wanderers
Stvee Kean	A-League	C	Melbourne Victory
Tom Aldred	A-League		Brisbane Roar
Ziggy Gordon	A-League		Western Sydney Wanderers
Michael McGowan	Queensland NPL		Peninsula Power
Nathan Shepherd	Queensland NPL		Lions
Matt Henvey	Queensland NPL		Gold Coast Knights
Scott Ferries	Queensland P...		Sunshine Coast
Sean Ellis	Victoria NPL		Heidelberg United
Chris Duggan	Victoria NPL		Port Melbourne
Jon McShane	Victoria NPL		Altona Magic
David Thomson	Victoria NPL		Green Gully
Dan McLennan	Victoria NPL 2		Bulleen Lions
Chris McStay	New South Wa...		Sutherland Sharks
Gavin Rae	New South Wa...	C	Hakoah Sydney City
Daryll Nicoll	Western Aust...		Bayswater City
Gordon Smith	Western Aust...		Bayswater City
John Chalmers	Western Aust...		Western Knights
Graham Wright	Tasmania NPL		South Hobart
Daniel Smith	Northern Ter...		Hellenic Athletic
Belgium			
Jack Hendry	First Division A		KV Oostende
David Bates	First Division A		Cercle Brugge
Bulgaria			
Danail Dimov	Third League		Chernomorets Balchik
Cambodia			
Chris Grant	C-League		Svay Rieng
Cyprus			
Kevin Holt	1. Division		Ermis
Alistair Reynolds	1. Division		Karmiotissa
Finland			
David Dangana	Kakkonen		Kraft
Brian Page	Kakkonen	C	SJK Akatemia
Gibraltar			
John Stewart	Premier Division		Europa Point
Cavan Burns	Premier Division		Boca Juniors
Hong Kong			
Robert Scott	HKFA 1st Div...		Hong Kong
Steven McGurgan	HKFA 1st Div...		Hong Kong
Iceland			
Alex Davey	Úrvalsdeild		ÍA
Steven Lennon	Úrvalsdeild		FH
Harley Willard	1. Deild		Víkingur Ólafsvík
Nathan Ward	3. Deild		Vídir
India			
Stuart Baxter	Indian Supe...	C	Odisha
Danny Fox	Indian Supe...		East Bengal
Mason Robertson	I-League		Real Kashmir
David Robertson	I-League	C	Real Kashmir
Jonathan Craig	I-League		Real Kashmir
James Lindsay	I-League		Real Kashmir
Danny Fox	Calcutta Pre...		East Bengal
Malaysia			
Ian Gillan	Liga M3	C	Sarawak FA
Northern Ireland			
Aidan Wilson	Premiership		Crusaders
Joseph Thomson	Premier Division		Derry City
Jamal Tavares	Premiership		Dungannon Swifts
John Herron	Premiership		Larne
Rohan Ferguson	Premiership		Larne
Matthew Knox	Premiership		Warrenpoint Town
Ryan Carmichael	Premiership		Portadown
Darren Cole	Premier Division		Derry City
Elliot McKim	Championship		Ballyclare Comrades

David Graham	Championship		H&W Welders
Nathan O'Neill	Championship		Ballyclare Comrades
Norway			
Kyle Spence	2. Division		Øygarden
Portugal			
Ryan Gauld	Primeira Liga		Farense
Republic of Ireland			
Sam Stanton	Premier Division		Dundalk
Peter Cherrie	Premier Division		Dundalk
Billy King	Premier Division		St Patrick's Athletic
Matty Smith	Premier Division		St Patrick's Athletic
Kyle Ferguson	Premier Division		Waterford
Alex Cooper	Premier Division		Sligo Rovers
Ali Coote	Premier Division		Bohemians
ark. Russell	Premier Division		Finn Harps
Liam Burt	Premier Division		Bohemians
Ryan Shanley	Premier Division		Finn Harps
Alex Gilchrist	First Division		Shelbourne
Russia			
Peter Leven	FNL	C	Orenburg
Sweden			
Ciaran Brian	Division 2		Ytterhogdal
Turkey			
Stevie Mallan	Süper Lig		Yeni Malatyaspor
USA			
Jonny Russell	MLS		Sporting KC
Danny Wilson	MLS		Colorado Rapids
Stuart Findlay	MLS		Philadelphia Union
Lewis Morgan	MLS		Inter Miami
Rhys Breen	USL Championship		Orange County SC
Martin Rennie	USL Championship	C	Indy Eleven
Cammy Smith	USL Championship		Indy Eleven
Paul Dalglish	USL Championship	C	Miami FC
Robbie Crawford	USL Championship		Charleston Battery
Nick Ross	USL Championship		El Paso Locomotive
Neil Collins	USL Championship		Tampa Bay Rowdies
Jack Blake	USL Championship		San Diego Loyal
Jack Thomson	USL Championship		Orange County SC
Ian Cameron	USL League One	C	Tormenta
Craig McCall	USL League One		Tormenta
Greg Hurst	USL League One		Union Omaha
Harvey Moyes	NISA		Detroit City
Mark McKeever	USL League Two		Des Moines Menace
Adam Asghar	USL League Two		North Carolina Fusion
Ben Andoh	USL League Two		Wichita
Jordan Bell	USL League Two		Des Moines Menace
Owen Connelly	NPSL		Erie Commodores
Rhys Wallace	NPSL		Erie Commodores
Kyle McLeod	NPSL		Midland-Odessa
Wales			
Chris Hughes	Premier League		Newtown
Barry Sheehan	Premier League		Cefn Druids
Steven Leslie	Premier League		Bala Town
Jay Fulton	Championship		Swansea City

Pyramid Developments

2020/21 saw yet more progress than expected towards a working Scottish Football Pyramid. Essentially a full Pyramid Structure is now in place - something that seemed highly unlikely only a couple of years ago.

The reason for the rapid development must be put down to a "changing of the guard" at the Scottish Junior FA. Although publicly "pro pyramid" the SJFA Officials seemed to obstruct and obfuscate at every opportunity. The mass defection of the West of Scotland clubs in 2020 cut the feet from under them. The much-reduced Junior FA is now placed within the pyramid structure.

Scotland is divided into two - the Lowland and Highland regions. The Lowland League has three feeder divisions - the East, West and South of Scotland Leagues. The East is an amalgamation of the old Fife and Lothians Juniors and the East of Scotland League. The West is basically the West Region of the SJFA re-badged. The South has remained unchanged throughout the whole process. The winners of each compete in a play off for a place in the Lowland League.

In the Highland Region the Highland League now has three feeder divisions - the Midlands League, the North Junior League and the North Caledonian League. The Midlands League is the old Tayside clubs from East Juniors. The North Caledonian and North Juniors are unchanged other than re-branding as part of the pyramid. The three champions, if licensed, would meet for the chance to contest a play off with the bottom side from the Highland League.

The biggest anomaly in the system now is the Lowland League. It was formed by clubs applying. The big Junior clubs did not apply. The result is that the Lowland League is probably weaker overall in standard than the Premier Divisions of the East and West of Scotland Leagues. There are half a dozen clubs in the Lowland League that would struggle to avoid relegation from the level below. That will change through time but with only one club promoted to the Lowland League each year that will take time.

There was considerable anger when the Lowland League extended an invitation to Rangers and Celtic to enter B teams in the Lowland League. Clubs in the lower divisions felt that if the Lowland League was to be extended it should be from their ranks, not by parachuting in those two in return for a £50,000 sweetener. The Lowland League has complained about the lack of automatic relegation from the SPFL - yet it operates as a "closed shop" just as much as the SPFL does.

In the North the challenge is to get more clubs licensed. In the Summer of 20-21 only Banks I' Dee and Golspie Sutherland from outside the Highland League held licenses. Several clubs from the Dundee area are likely to push hard to get licensed which will create a whole new dynamic for the Highland League.

Calling the structure that w enow have a pyramid is slightly misleading - a pyramid gets wider as you go down the levels. At present the East of Scotland and West of Scotland Leagues seem determined to move to a "tower" structure of four divisions, top to bottom. If the lower tiers were regionalised, perhaps with a 1-1-2 structure, then it might encourage even more of the ambitious Amateur and Youth sides to apply.

Rangers and Celtic B teams

This bombshell news broke with a Press Release by the Lowland League on May 5th 2021:

"The Scottish Lowland Football League (SLFL) can today confirm that it has entered into discussions to invite Rangers and Celtic 'B' teams to enter the league for next season (2021/22) on a one-season basis.

The discussions, which are at an early stage, have come following an invite to open talks from the Lowland League to both clubs to help solve the gap which exists in the player development pathway in Scotland, helping some of the countries best young players for a year, and also bringing significant benefit to the Lowland League and our clubs. Discussions have been productive and will continue over the coming days. We share a common consensus with Rangers and Celtic that player development and the importance of the pyramid system need to be priorities for the game in Scotland.
The SLFL Board made it clear at the outset that no current member club would be adversely affected in any way by the proposal, in fact the opposite, and ultimately as a member's organisation the clubs would need to vote in favour of this. All of our clubs have the exciting proposal and consultation will be with them first and foremost.

League chairperson, George Fraser, said:
"It is clear from the discussions we have had that both Celtic and Rangers are looking for a league to put their 'B' teams into where they can develop as players. Having been on the PGB sub group tasked with further developing the well-publicised

'Scottish Football Innovation' paper, a project which is still on-going and may well be implemented for season 22/23, it was absolutely clear to me that there is a major gap in the player pathway which would, if not addressed, impact a generation of our best young talent. That is why the Lowland League, as a modern progressive organisation, have identified an opportunity, and are open to embracing positive change which will have massive benefit for our own clubs and league but importantly also for the wider Scottish game.
"Over the last few years the Lowland League has proved to be a well-run professional league and both these clubs feel their teams and players will develop by being part of it, while importantly for us we will be able to generate new revenues and shine a spotlight on the aspirational and ambitious clubs we have within our ranks. As always league integrity and the importance of the pyramid will be paramount and this will be unaffected by this plan and this was also a priority for both Rangers and Celtic who fully respect this.
"We will continue to have discussions with various parties over the next week or so and see how they progress. Hopefully this will result in an exciting outcome which is a clear demonstration of the Lowland League leading the way in how to modernise our football structures for the benefit of all."

A further Press Release from May 10th confirmed:

The Scottish Lowland Football League can confirm that member clubs have voted in favour of a proposal allowing Rangers and Celtic 'B' teams to take part in next season's competition – for one season only. The meeting of clubs was called following discussions between the SLFL Board to consider the proposal. Work will now be undertaken to make the required rule changes to allow this to happen.

League Chairman, George Fraser, said: "With all proposals of this type everyone has an opinion on it, and rightly so.
"The SLFL Board discussed this proposal last week and, as we are a members organisation, it was entirely correct that this was put to the members to vote on. As a league we have allowed our clubs to decide based on facts, and not several pieces of misinformation being actively disseminated across many social media platforms. Our league is fully committed to the integrity of the pyramid and we have shown this time and time again, so any suggestion we are not is ill-judged and misplaced. The majority of our clubs have voted in favour of this proposal, and we need to respect that, therefore we will progress this and have further discussions with all parties in the coming days."

"Since the start of this pandemic the SLFL has operated with a view that no club should be adversely affected by the decisions we make, and we believe that this is the case with this proposal. With all the tier 6 leagues opting to go 'null and void' this meant there was no champion club put forward to join the SLFL. If there was then the champion club would be taking part in the SLFL league next season. We have made Rangers and Celtic aware of the outcome of the vote".

There has not been absolute clarity on how the final Lowland League table for 2021/2 will look.

Our understanding is that Rangers and Celtic B will both complete a full League programme. This will produce an 18 team final table. However, Celtic and Rangers will be struck from the table but their results will still be included in the final placings for other clubs.

If either Rangers or Celtic finish top, then the best placed non Old Firm B club would be declared Champions. The Lowland League are confident that this will not be an issue in access to the Play Off for an SPFL League Two place. Sources from SPFL clubs are not so sure about that.

One can expect a further round of controversy as the end of the season approaches.

Club Licencing

Club Licensing Status as at June 2021 is shown below. (source SFA website)

SPFL Prem	AWARD	Last Review	Next Review	Ground	First Team	Youth	Legal / Admin	UEFA
Aberdeen	Silver	Apr-21	2022	Silver	Gold	Gold	Gold	Granted
Celtic	Platinum	Apr-21	2022	Gold	Gold	Gold	Gold	Granted
Dundee United	Silver	Apr-21	2022	Silver	Silver	Gold	Silver	Granted
Hamilton Accies	Silver	Apr-21	Jun-21	Silver	Gold	Gold	Gold	Refused
Hibernian	Gold	Apr-21	Sep-21	Gold	Gold	Gold	Gold	Granted
Kilmarnock	Silver	Apr-21	2022	Silver	Silver	Gold	Gold	Granted
Livingston	Bronze	Apr-21	Jun-21	Bronze	Bronze	N/A	Bronze	Refused
Motherwell	Silver	Apr-21	2022	Silver	Gold	Gold	Gold	Granted
Rangers	Silver	Apr-21	2022	Gold	Gold	Gold	Silver	Granted
Ross County	Silver	Apr-21	2022	Silver	Silver	Silver	Gold	Refused
St Johnstone	Gold	Apr-21	2022	Gold	Gold	Silver	Gold	Granted
St Mirren	Gold	Apr-21	2022	Gold	Gold	Silver	Gold	Granted
SPFL Champ								
Alloa Ath	Bronze	Jul-20	2021	Bronze	Bronze	Bronze	Bronze	N/A
Arbroath	Bronze	Feb-21	2022	Bronze	Bronze	N/A	Bronze	N/A
Ayr Utd	Bronze	Dec-20	2021	Bronze	Bronze	Silver	Bronze	N/A
Dundee	Bronze	Sep-20	2021	Bronze	Brone	Bronze	Bronze	N/A
Dunfermline Ath	Silver	Dec-20	2021	Silver	Silver	Fife Elite	Silver	N/A
Greenock Morton	Bronze	Dec-20	2021	Bronze	Silver	Silver	Bronze	N/A
Hearts	Silver	May-20	2021	Silver	Gold	Gold	Gold	N/A
Inverness CT	Silver	Nov-20	2021	Silver	Silver	Silver	Silver	N/A
Raith Rovers	Bronze	Dec-20	2021	Bronze	Bronze	Fife Elite	Bronze	N/A
QOTS	Bronze	Jul-20	2021	Bronze	Bronze	Bronze	Gold	N/A
SPFL Lge 1								
Airdrieonians	Bronze	Dec-20	2021	Bronze	Bronze	N/A	Bronze	N/A
Cove Rangers	Entry	Dec-20	2021	Entry	Entry	N/A	Entry	N/A
Clyde	Silver	Nov-20	2021	Silver	Silver	N/A	Silver	N/A
Dumbarton	Bronze	Dec-20	2021	Bronze	Silver	N/A	Bronze	N/A
East Fife	Bronze	Jul-20	2021	Bronze	Bronze	Fife Elite	Bronze	N/A
Falkirk	Silver	Dec-20	2021	Silver	Silver	N/A	Gold	N/A
Forfar Athletic	Bronze	Feb-21	2022	Bronze	Bronze	N/At	Bronze	N/A
Montrose	Bronze	Nov-20	2021	Bronze	Bronze	Bronze	Bronze	N/A
Partick Thistle	Silver	Jul-20	2021	Silver	Silver	Silver	Gold	N/A
Peterhead	Bronze	Jul-20	2021	Bronze	Bronze	N/A	Bronze	N/A
SPFL Lge 2								
Albion Rovers	Entry	Sep-20	2021	Entry	Entry	N/A	Entry	N/A
Annan Ath	Bronze	Dec-20	2021	Bronze	Bronze	N/A	Bronze	N/A
Brechin City	Entry	Jul-20	2021	Bronze	Bronze	N/A	Bronze	N/A
Cowdenbeath	Bronze	Jul-20	2021	Bronze	Bronze	Fife Elite	Bronze	N/A
Edinburgh City	Entry	Dec-20	2021	Bronze	Entry	N/A	Entry	N/A
Elgin City	Bronze	Sep-20	2021	Bronze	Bronze	Bronze	Gold	N/A
Queen's Park	Silver	Sep-20	2021	Gold	Silver	Bronze	Silver	N/A
Stenhousemuir	Bronze	Sep-20	2021	Bronze	Bronze	N/A	Silver	N/A
Stirling Albion	Bronze	Sep-20	2021	Bronze	Bronze	Bronze	Bronze	N/A
Stranraer	Bronze	Jul-20	2021	Bronze	Bronze	N/A	Bronze	N/A
Highland Lge								
Brora Rangers	Entry	Nov-20	2021	Entry	Entry	Entry	Entry	N/A
Buckie Thistle	Entry	Nov-20	2021	Entry	Entry	Entry	Entry	N/A
Clachnacuddin	Entry	Dec-20	2021	Entry	Entry	Entry	Entry	N/A
Deveronvale	Entry	Sep-20	2021	Entry	Entry	Entry	Entry	N/A
Formartine Utd	Entry	Sep-20	2021	Entry	Entry	Entry	Entry	N/A
Forres Mech	Entry	Sep-20	2021	Entry	Entry	Entry	Entry	N/A
Fort William	Entry	Dec-20	2021	Entry	Entry	Entry	Entry	N/A
Fraserburgh	Entry	Sep-20	2021	Entry	Entry	Entry	Entry	N/A
Huntly	Entry	Nov-20	2021	Entry	Entry	Entry	Entry	N/A
Inverurie Locos	Entry	Sep-20	2021	Entry	Entry	Entry	Entry	N/A
Keith	Entry	Dec-20	2021	Entry	Entry	Entry	Entry	N/A
Lossiemouth	Entry	Sep-20	2021	Entry	Entry	Entry	Entry	N/A
Nairn County	Entry	Dec-20	2021	Entry	Entry	Entry	Entry	N/A
Rothes	Entry	Sep-20	2021	Entry	Entry	Entry	Entry	N/A
Strathspey Th	Entry	Nov-20	2021	Entry	Entry	N/A	Entry	N/A
Turriff Utd	Entry	Jul-20	2021	Entry	Entry	Entry	Entry	N/A
Wick Acad	Entry	Nov-20	2021	Entry	Entry	Entry	Entry	N/A

Lowland League	AWARD	Last Review	Next Review	Ground	First Team	Youth	Legal / Admin	UEFA
Berwick Rangers	Entry	Jul-20	2021	Bronze	Entry	N/A	Bronze	N/A
Bonnyrigg Rose	Entry	Dec-20	2021	Entry	Entry	N/A	Entry	N/A
Bo'ness Utd	Entry	Feb-21	2022	Entry	Entry	N/A	Entry	N/A
BSC Glasgow*	Entry	Dec-20	2021	Entry	Entry	N/A	Entry	N/A
Civil SS	Entry	Sep-20	2021	Entry	Entry	N/A	Entry	N/A
Cumbernauld Colts	Bronze	Dec-20	2021	Bronze	Bronze	N/A	Bronze	N/A
Dalbeattie Star	Entry	Dec-20	2021	Entry	Entry	N/A	Entry	N/A
East Kilbride	Entry	Nov-20	2021	Entry	Entry	N/A	Entry	N/A
East Stirlingshire	Entry	Dec-20	2021	Entry	Entry	N/A	Entry	N/A
Edinburgh Univ	Entry	Jul-20	2021	Entry	Entry	N/A	Entry	N/A
Caledonian Braves	Entry	Sep-20	2021	Entry	Entry	N/A	Entry	N/A
Gala FR	Entry	Dec-20	2021	Entry	Entry	N/A	Entry	N/A
Gretna 2008	Entry	Nov-20	2021	Entry	Entry	N/A	Entry	N/A
Kelty Hearts	Entry	Sep-20	2021	Entry	Entry	N/A	Entry	N/A
The Spartans	Bronze	Dec-20	2021	Bronze	Bronze	N/A	Bronze	N/A
University of Stirling	Entry	Nov-20	2021	Entry	Entry	N/A	Entry	N/A
Vale of Leithen	Entry	Feb-21	2021	Entry	Entry	N/A	Entry	N/A
* Now Broomhill FC								
East of S League								
Blackburn Utd	Entry	Feb-21	2022	Entry	Entry	N/A	Entry	N/A
Broxburn Ath	Entry	Nov-20	2021	Entry	Entry	N/A	Entry	N/A
Burntisland SY	Entry	Dec-20	2021	Entry	Entry	N/A	Entry	N/A
Camelon	Entry	Feb-21	Jun-21	Entry	Entry	N/A	Entry	N/A
Coldstream	Entry	Nov-20	2021	Entry	Entry	N/A	Entry	N/A
Dundonald BB	Entry	Feb-21	2022	Entry	Entry	N/A	Entry	N/A
Dunipace	Entry	Jul-20	2021	Entry	Entry	N/A	Entry	N/A
Easthouses Lily	Entry	Feb-21	2022	Entry	Entry	N/A	Entry	N/A
Haddington Ath	Entry	Feb-21	2022	Entry	Entry	N/A	Entry	N/A
Hawick RAU	Entry	Nov-20	2021	Entry	Entry	N/A	Entry	N/A
Hill of Beath H	Entry	Feb-21	2022	Entry	Entry	N/A	Entry	N/A
Jeanfield S	Entry	Nov-20	2021	Entry	Entry	N/A	Entry	N/A
Linlithgow Rose	Entry	Nov-20	2021	Entry	Entry	N/A	Entry	N/A
Lothian THV	Entry	Jul-20	2021	Entry	Entry	N/A	Entry	N/A
Newtongrange S	Entry	Feb-21	2022	Entry	Entry	N/A	Entry	N/A
Penicuik Ath	Entry	Feb-20	2021	Entry	Entry	N/A	Entry	N/A
Preston Ath	Entry	Nov-20	2021	Entry	Entry	N/A	Entry	N/A
Tranent Jun	Entry	Jul-20	2021	Entry	Entry	N/A	Entry	N/A
Tynecastle	Entry	Dec-20	2021	Entry	Entry	Entry	Entry	N/A
Whitehill	Entry	Dec-20	2021	Entry	Entry	N/A	Entry	N/A
South of S Lge								
Newton Stewart	Entry	Dec-20	2021	Entry	Entry	N/A	Entry	N/A
St Cuthbert W	Entry	Nov-20	2021	Entry	Entry	N/A	Entry	N/A
Threave Rov	Entry	Dec-20	2021	Entry	Entry	N/A	Entry	N/A
Wigtown & B	Entry	Dec-20	2021	Entry	Entry	N/A	Entry	N/A
Others								
Banks o' Dee	Entry	Nov-20	2021	Entry	Entry	Entry	Entry	N/A
Girvan	Entry	Dec-20	2021	Entry	Entry	N/A	Entry	N/A
Glasgow Uni	Entry	Jul-20	2021	Entry	Entry	N/A	Entry	N/A
Golspie Suth	Entry	Dec-20	2021	Entry	Entry	N/A	Entry	N/A

In addition to the clubs listed in the SFA's table, the following clubs were granted licenses in July 2021:

West of Scotland League
Auchinleck Talbot
Clydebank
Cumnock
Darvel
Irvine Meadow

East of Scotland League
Dalkeith Thistle
Dunbar United
Musselburgh Athletic
Sauchie Juniors

Clubs known to be working towards Licensing include:

St Andrews United
Oakley United
Inverkeithing Hillfield Swifts
Lochee United
Broughty Athletic
Carnoustie Panmure
Tayport
Dyce
Petershill
Gartcairn
Kilwinning Rangers
Edinburgh United

Quality Mark Clubs—Future Seniors?

The SFA runs a "Quality Mark" system for clubs with five different levels. To achieve Standard Level clubs must satisfy various criteria regarding qualifications of staff / Volunteers, club policies etc. These become more stringent at the higher levels where clubs are also required to run larger numbers of teams for different age groups, genders etc.

There are now four levels of Quality Mark Award:

Bronze
Silver
Gold
Platinum

Over recent years several Youth clubs have progressed to Senior status. East Kilbride, Cumbernauld Colts, Edinburgh South, St Cadoc's, Drumchapel United, BSC Glasgow, Inverkeithing Hillfield Swifts, Gartcairn, Rossvale, Bonnyton Thistle etc have taken that path. Might the future Senior clubs be on this list?

PLATINUM CLUBS LIST (2020)

CENTRAL REGION
Bo'ness United CFC
Cumbernauld Colts
Dunblane Soccer Club
Falkirk FC Community Foundation
Gartcairn Football Academy (Airdrie)
Holytown Colts
Milngavie FC
Milton FC (Stirling)
Motherwell FC Community
Stenhousemuir Fc Community
Syngenta Juveniles (Grangemouth)
Tullibody Community FC
Wasp Community Football Club (Alloa)

EAST REGION
AM Soccer (Cupar)
Breadalbane (Aberfeldy)
Broughty United
Carnoustie Panmure
Dundee West
Dundee United SC
East Fife Community FC
Glenrothes Strollers
Inverkeithing Hillfield Swifts
Monifieth Athletic
Montrose Community FC

NORTH REGION
Banchory CFC
Colony Park (Inverurie)
Cove YC
Deveronvale CFC
Dyce CST
Stonehaven Youth FC
Thistle YFC
Westdyke Community Club (Westhill)

SOUTH EAST REGION
Blackburn United Community FC
Bonnyrigg Rose Community FC
Broxburn United SC
Dalkeith CFC
Hibernian Community Foundation
Linlithgow Rose Community FC
Murieston United CFC (Livingston)
Penicuik Athletic Youth FC
Spartans FC (Edinburgh)
Tranent & District Community SC

SOUTH WEST REGION
Annan Athletic
Blantyre Soccer Academy
Bonnyton Thistle (Kilmarnock)
Claremont AFC (East Kilbride)
Cumnock Juniors
Glenburn Miners Welfare (Ayr)
Kilbirnie Community FC
Kilwinning Sports Club
Strathaven Dynamos FC

WEST REGION
Ardencaple FC 1968
Barrhead YFC
Drumchapel United (Glasgow)
Giffnock SC (Glasgow)
Glasgow Girls and Boys
Greenock Morton Community Trust
Pollok United Soccer Academy (Glasgow)
Port Glasgow Juniors CFC
St Peters FC

Friendly Matches July 2020-July 2021

In the not so distant past it used to be relatively easy to identify and record Friendly matches. Senior clubs were restricted to two weeks of Friendlies from the last Saturday in July - that situation pertained until the late 1990s. In fact, as recently as the 1960s clubs were only allowed to play one pre-season friendly.

Nowadays the situation is much more fluid and all sorts of games are reported on social media. Some may be "unofficial", I.e. played without formal approval from the SFA. During the COVID pandemic various closed doors games were played.

The following is an attempt to record the results of as many of these matches as possible.

10/07/2020					
Fr	Rangers	Hamilton Accies	2	1	Murray Park
11/07/2020					
Fr	Hibernian	St Mirren	1	1	HTC
Fr	Motherwell	Dundee United	1	0	Dalziel Park
Fr	Aberdeen	Ross County	2	2	Cormack Park
14/07/2020					
Fr	St Johnstone	Hibernian	0	0	McDiarmid Park
16/07/2020					
Tnt	OGC Nice	Celtic	1	1	Lyon
Tnt	Olympique Lyonnais	Rangers	0	2	Lyon
17/07/2020					
Fr	Motherwell	Kilmarnock	2	3	Fir Park
18/07/2020					
Tnt	Olympique Lyonnais	Celtic	2	1	Lyon
Tnt	OGC Nice	Rangers	0	2	Lyon
Fr	Hamilton Accies	St Mirren	2	1	NDP
21/07/2020					
Fr	Aberdeen	St Johnstone	1	2	Pittodrie
Fr	Paris St Germain	Celtic	4	0	Parc des Princes
Fr	Hibernian	Hamilton Accies	2	1	Easter Road
22/07/2020					
Fr	Kilmarnock	Livingston	1	2	Rugby Park
Fr	Rangers	Motherwell	4	0	Ibrox
25/07/2020					
Fr	Aberdeen	Hibernian	1	1	Pittodrie
Fr	Dundee United	Kilmarnock	1	1	Tannadice
Fr	Motherwell	Hamilton Accies	2	2	Fir Park
Fr	Livingston	Ross County	2	2	Almondvale
Fr	Rangers	Coventry City	2	0	Ibrox
26/07/2020					
Fr	Celtic	Ross County	2	0	Celtic Park
27/07/2020					
Fr	Celtic	Hibernian	3	1	Celtic Park
28/08/2020					
Fr	Hearts	Sheffield United	0	1	Riccarton
25/08/2020					
Fr	Dundee United	Sheffield United	0	1	Tannadice
	ABD HT, Rain				
02/09/2020					
Fr	St Mirren	Hearts	1	2	New St Mirren Park
05/09/2020					
Fr	Burnley	Hearts	4	1	Burnley TC
12/09/2020					
Fr	Annbank United	Auchinleck Talbot	0	5	
Fr	Arbroath	Civil Service Strollers	4	0	
Fr	Ashfield	Maryhill	4	2	
Fr	Beith	Beith U20	8	0	
Fr	Benburb	Drumchapel United	0	1	
Fr	Berwick Rangers	Heriot Watt University	1	2	
Fr	Blackburn United	Bathgate Thistle	4	1	
Fr	Blantyre Vics	East Kilbride Thistle	3	0	
Fr	Bowhill Rovers	Lochore Welfare	3	3	
Fr	Caledonian Braves	Caledonian Braves XI			
Fr	Camelon	East Stirlingshire	2	2	
Fr	Clydebank	Clydebank U20	8	0	
Fr	Craigroyston	Edinburgh United Vale	3	2	
Fr	Cruden Bay	Inverurie Locos U19			
Fr	Culter	Deveronvale	3	1	
Fr	Cumnock	Lugar Boswell Thistle	7	0	
Fr	Darvel	Irvine Meadow	2	1	
Fr	Edinburgh University	Tollcross Thistle	0	2	
Fr	Elgin City	Lossiemouth	9	1	
Fr	Fauldhouse United	Carluke Rovers			
Fr	Forfar West End	Barnhill	2	0	
Fr	Formartine United	Banks o' Dee			
Fr	Gala Fairydean Rovers	Lothian Thistle HV	1	1	
Fr	Girvan	Bonnyton Thistle	0	2	
Fr	Glenafton Athletic	Muirkirk	2	1	

Fr	Glenrothes	Tayport	2	5	
Fr	Hawick Royal Albert United	Hawick United	0	0	
Fr	Hermes	Newtonhill			
Fr	Highfields United	Eyemouth United	0	4	
Fr	Hurlford United	Maybole	3	0	
Fr	Johnstone Burgh	Harmony Row	0	1	
Fr	Kelty Hearts	Tynecastle	6	1	
Fr	Kennoway Star Hearts	Kirkcaldy & Dysart	1	3	
Fr	Kilbirnie Ladeside	Port Glasgow	1	0	
Fr	Kilwinning Rangers	Irvine Vics	13	0	
Fr	Largs Thistle	Greenock	5	0	
Fr	Luncarty	Dundee North End	0	0	
Fr	Musselburgh Athletic	Preston Athletic	5	2	
Fr	Newburgh	Kinnoull	1	4	
Fr	Newtongrange Star	Edinburgh South	1	0	
Fr	Rangers B	BSC Glasgo	5	1	
Fr	Rothie Rovers	Dyce	0	0	
Fr	Sauchie Juniors CFC	Edinburgh United	1	1	
Fr	Shettleston	Vale of Clyde	3	1	
Fr	St Andrews United	Dundonald Bluebell	2	4	
Fr	Stranraer	Stranraer Reserves	7	0	
Fr	Thorniewood United	Wishaw	0	2	
Fr	Vale of Leithen	Linton Hotspur	3	0	
Fr	Vale of Leven	Vale of Leven U20			
Fr	Whitburn	Rosyth	2	0	
Fr	Clyde	Cumbernauld Colts	0	0	
Fr	Inverkeithing Hillfield Swifts	Kinross Colts	3	2	
14/09/2020					
Fr	Cumbernauld Colts	Kilsyth Rangers	5	0	
Fr	Ardrossan Winton Rovers	Beith	1	2	
Fr	Neilston	Neilston U20	5	3	
Fr	Wishaw	Wishaw HSFP	1	4	
Fr	St Rochs	Vale of Clyde	0	1	
15/09/2020					
Fr	Dundee United	Raith Rovers	1	2	St Andrews Uni
Fr	Whitehill Welfare	Berwick Rangers	1	3	
Fr	Edinburgh United	Peebles Rovers	3	2	
Fr	Bonnyrigg Rose	Broxburn Athletic	3	2	
Fr	Kelty Hearts	Musselburgh Athletic	3	0	
Fr	Falkirk	East Stirlingshire	0	1	
Fr	Dundee United	Peterhead	1	0	
Fr	Civil Service Strollers	Edinburgh City			
Fr	Clyde	Cumbernauld United	4	0	
Fr	Rossvale	St Cadocs	2	2	
Fr	Hermes	Rothie Rovers			
Fr	Newtongrange Star	Pentland Athletic	6	0	
Fr	Tranent	Heriot Watt University			
Fr	Caledonian Braves XI	Gartcairn	1	0	
Fr	Broughty Athletic	St Andrews United	8	2	
Fr	Culter	Fraserburgh United	4	0	
Fr	Dundonald Bluebell	Thornton Hibs	4	0	
Fr	Sunnybank	Dyce			
Fr	Clydebank	Dumbarton	0	4	
Fr	Penicuik Athletic	Haddington Athletic	2	1	
Fr	Brechin City	Cove Rangers	2	4	
Fr	Stenhousemuir	East Fife	1	5	
Fr	Blairgowrie	Dundee Utd SC	0	2	
Fr	Hill of Beath Hawthorn	Lochgelly United	4	2	
16/09/2020					
Fr	Craigmark Burntonians	Troon	1	1	
Fr	Drumchapel United	Maryhill			
Fr	Formartine United	Banks o' Dee	2	5	
Fr	Newmains United	Carluke Thistle			
Fr	Shotts Bon Accord	Fauldhouse United			
Fr	Mid Annandale	Ruthwell Rovers	2	2	
Fr	Newmains United	Carluke Thistle			
Fr	Nithsdale Wanderers	Glenafton Amateurs	4	2	
Fr	Irvine Vics	Irvine Meadow	1	6	
Fr	Syngenta	Camelon	0	2	

17/09/2020				
	Albion Rovers	East Kilbride		
18/09/2020				
Fr	Hearts	East Fife	5	1
19/09/2020				
Fr	Elgin City	Brora Rangers	2	3
Fr	Partick Thistle	BSC Glasgow	3	0
Fr	Ayr United	Stirling Albion	0	2
Fr	Peterhead	Fraserburgh United	0	2
Fr	Newtongrange Star	St Andrews United	1	0
Fr	Blackburn United	Stoneyburn	0	2
Fr	Clydebank	Kilwinning Rangers	1	2
Fr	Gala Fairydean Rovers	Pumpherston	4	0
Fr	Glenrothes	Dundonald Bluebell	2	0
Fr	Edinburgh University	Leith Athletic	4	0
Fr	Duns	Dunbar United	2	3
Fr	Penicuik Athletic	Edinburgh City	0	3
Fr	Burntisland Shipyard	Sauchie Comm JFC	3	3
Fr	Haddington Athletic	Whitehill Welfare	1	1
Fr	Syngenta	Sauchie	2	0
Fr	Kennoway Star Hearts	Kennoway Star Hearts U20	5	0
Fr	Craigroyston	Broxburn Athletic	1	3
Fr	Tayport	Fauldhouse United	9	2
Fr	Abbey Vale	Upper Annandale	9	0
Fr	Alness United	Tain St Duthus	3	4
Fr	Annbank United	`	2	3
Fr	Ashfield	Rossvale	0	6
Fr	Benburb	Shettleston	1	3
Fr	Berwick Rangers	Tweedmouth Rangers	7	0
Fr	Caledonian Braves	Albion Rovers	1	1
Fr	Creetown	Wigtown & Bladnoch	3	3
Fr	Cumbernauld United	Kirkintilloch Rob Roy	1	2
Fr	Cumbernauld Colts	Petershill	2	0
Fr	Cumnock	Cumnock Amateurs	3	2
Fr	Aberdeen East End	Buchanhaven Hearts	2	0
Fr	Banchory St Ternan	Culter	2	2
Fr	Forfar Athletic	Carnoustie Panmure	5	2
Fr	Glasgow University	Cambria	4	1
Fr	Glentanar	Tolbooth	2	2
Fr	Goldenhill	Vale of Leven U20	2	0
Fr	Huntly	Hermes	1	5
Fr	Hurlford United	Ardrossan Winton Rovers	1	0
Fr	Inverkeithing Hillfield Swifts	Kinnoull	0	0
Fr	Keith	Banks o' Dee	4	4
Fr	Kello Rovers	Heston Rovers	0	0
Fr	Kelty Hearts	Airdrieonians	1	1
Fr	Kilbirnie Ladeside	Greenock	0	1
Fr	Lanark United	Blantyre Vics	1	5
Fr	Linlithgow Rose	East Stirlingshire	1	2
Fr	Maybole	Troon	1	2
Fr	Montrose	Dundee	2	2
Fr	Montrose Roselea	Forfar West End	1	0
Fr	Nairn St Ninian	Forres Mechanics	5	3
Fr	Neilston	Arthurlie	1	1
Fr	Peebles Rovers	Vale of Leithen	2	3
Fr	Pollok	Maryhill	5	2
Fr	Raith Rovers	Falkirk	2	6
Fr	Rothie Rovers	Stonehaven	3	4
Fr	Rutherglen Glencairn	Carluke Rovers	9	3
Fr	St Anthonys	St Cadocs	0	4
Fr	Saltcoats Vics	Port Glasgow	1	9
Fr	Scone Thistle	Newburgh	1	2
Fr	Stirling University	Lothian Thistle HV	3	2
Fr	Threave Rovers	Gretna	0	0
Fr	Vale of Clyde	Vale of Clyde Sunday	4	5
Fr	Vale of Leven	Vale of Leven Ams	5	1
Fr	Whitletts Vics	Newton Stewart	7	0
Fr	Wishaw	Thorniewood United	0	5
Fr	Ardeer Thistle	new Farm Loch	3	2
Fr	Shotts Bon Accord	Gartcairn	2	3
Fr	Edinburgh South	Easthouses Lily	3	1

Fr	Darvel	Dalry Thistle	1	1	
Fr	Cambuslang Rangers	Cabuslang r U21	2	0	
Fr	Irvine Meadow	Auchinleck Talbot	3	2	
Fr	Edinburgh United	Tollcross Thistle	3	2	
Fr	jeanfield Swifts	Brechin Vics	2	0	
Fr	Crossgates Primrose	Rosyth	8	2	
Fr	Beith	Largs Thistle	2	1	
Fr	East Kilbride	Stranraer	3	2	
Fr	Kilsyth Rangers	Shotts AFC	5	0	
Fr	St Rochs	Armadale Thistle	3	1	
Fr	Dundee North End	Cowdenbeath	1	4	
Fr	Johnstone Burgh	St Mirren Reserves	0	3	
Fr	Ardeer Thistle	new Farm Loch	3	2	
21/09/2020					
Fr	Arthurlie	Rossvale	4	0	
Fr	Mid Annandale	Upper Annandale	1	2	
Fr	Lanark United	Larkhall Thistle	4	1	
22/09/2020					
Fr	Airdrieonians	Albion Rovers	3	2	
Fr	Cowdenbeath	Montrose	0	1	
Fr	Alloa Athletic	Stranraer	3	1	
Fr	Livingston U20	Berwick Rangers	2	1	
Fr	Hearts	Falkirk	3	0	Riccarton
Fr	Cove Rangers	Dundee	0	1	
Fr	Bonnyrigg Rose	Penicuik Athletic	2	0	
Fr	Forfar Athletic	Broughty United	2	0	
Fr	Rossvale	Drumchapel United	3	4	
Fr	Spartans	Dunfermline Athletic	0	3	
Fr	Dunbar United	Eyemouth United	10	0	
Fr	Hill of Beath Hawthorn	Kirkcaldy & Dysart	6	1	
Fr	Sauchie	East Fife	1	4	
Fr	Civil Service Strollers	Crossgates Primrose	1	1	
Fr	Newtongrange Star	Leith Athletic	0	2	
Fr	Keith	Elgin City	0	5	
Fr	Raith Rovers	Stenhousemuir	5	2	
23/09/2020					
Fr	Troon	Ardeer Thistle			Kilwinning SC
Fr	Buckie Thistle	Dyce			
Fr	Musselburgh Athletic	Civil Service Strollers	0	2	
Fr	Bonnyton Thistle	Ardrossan Winton Rovers	2	1	
Fr	Albion Rovers	Dumbarton	2	3	
Fr	Whitehill Welfare	Edinburgh South	1	2	
Fr	Lothian Thistle HV	Vale of Leithen	4	1	
Fr	Formartine United	Hermes			
Fr	Longside	Fraserburgh	1	4	
Fr	Dalbeattie Star	Abbey Vale	1	0	
Fr	BSC Glasgow	Gartcairn	2	1	Airdrie
Fr	Rutherglen Glencairn	Cambuslang Rangers	4	1	
Fr	Ashfield	Finnart	1	3	
Fr	St Antonys	St Anthonys U20	5	0	
24/09/2020					
Fr	Carluke Rovers	Lesmahagow	1	1	
Fr	Drumchapel United	Maryhill	1	1	
Fr	Stranraer Reserves	Creetown	5	4	
Fr	Lochar Thistle	Normandy Star	7	0	
Fr	East Kilbride	Blantyre Vics	1	2	
25/09/2020					
Fr	Hearts	Edinburgh City			
Fr	Cambuslang Rangers	Rutherglen Glencairn			
26/09/2020					
Fr	Airdrieonians	Queen of the South	1	0	
Fr	Annan Athletic	Dalbeattie Star	3	1	
Fr	Arbroath	Forfar Athletic	3	0	
Fr	Arniston Rangers	Greenlaw	4	3	
Fr	Bellshill Athletic	Dalziel HSFP	2	1	
Fr	Benburb	Partick Thistle XI	0	1	
Fr	Bonnyrigg Rose	Whitehill Welfare	3	0	
Fr	Bonnyton Thistle	Stranraer Reserves	3	1	
Fr	Brora Rangers	Orkney	2	0	
Fr	Broughty Athletic	Cowdenbeath	1	2	

Fr	Broxburn Athletic	Leith Athletic	5	4
Fr	Buchanhaven Hearts	Banff Rovers	1	2
Fr	Caledonian Braves	Kirkintilloch Rob Roy	4	0
Fr	Cambuslang Rangers	Rutherglen Glencairn	1	1
Fr	Camelon	Stirling University	3	2
Fr	Coldstream	Lothian Thistle HV	1	4
Fr	Colony Park	Keith	0	6
Fr	Coupar Angus	Forfar United	3	3
Fr	Craigroyston	Edinburgh United U20	7	4
Fr	Crossgates Primrose	Thornton Hibs	0	1
Fr	Culter	Formartine United	1	5
Fr	Cumbernauld United	Gartcairn	1	4
Fr	Drumchapel United	Arthurlie	7	1
Fr	Dufftown	Strathspey Thistle	0	6
Fr	Dunbar United	Edinburgh South	3	0
Fr	Dundee	Cove Rangers	1	1
Fr	Dundee Violet	Newburgh	2	0
Fr	Dunipace	Kilsyth Rangers	2	3
Fr	East Fife	Dunfermline Athletic	0	1
Fr	East Kilbride	Beith	2	1
Fr	Edinburgh United	Tynecastle	2	3
Fr	Elgin City	Inverness CT	3	7
Fr	Falkirk	Ayr United	3	2
Fr	Falkirk Athletic	Stirling Uni EOS	3	2
Fr	Fallin	Bo'ness United JFC	3	4
Fr	Fauldhouse United	Sauchie	1	2
Fr	Forfar West End	Kinnoull	1	2
Fr	Forth Wanderers	Blantyre Vics	2	3
Fr	Fraserburgh	Bridge of Don Thistle	0	0
Fr	Gartcosh	Harthill Royal	0	0
Fr	Glenafton Athletic	Craigmark Burntonians	3	2
Fr	Golspie Sutherland	Alness United	2	6
Fr	Gretna	Abbey Vale	4	1
Fr	Hawick Royal Albert United	Melrose	8	0
Fr	Hearts	Partick Thistle	2	0
Fr	Heston Rovers	Lochmaben	3	2
Fr	Hemes	Deveronvale	2	4
Fr	Heriot Watt University	West Calder United	3	0
Fr	Hill of Beath Hawthorn	Burntisland Shipyard	5	2
Fr	Huntly	Fraserburgh United	1	4
Fr	Inverness Athletic	Tain St Duthus	1	0
Fr	Inverurie Loco Works	Peterhead	0	3
Fr	Inverurie U19	Rothie Rovers	1	6
Fr	Irvine Vics	Troon	2	10
Fr	jeanfield Swifts	Blairgowrie	1	2
Fr	Johnstone Burgh	Renfrew	4	1
Fr	Kennowar Star Hearts	Cupar Hearts	1	4
Fr	Kilwinning Rangers	Darvel	2	0
Fr	Livingston United	Ormiston	1	0
Fr	Lochore Welfare	Tayport	2	3
Fr	Lossiemouth	Loch Ness	7	0
Fr	Lugar Boswell Thistle	Kello Rovers	0	9
Fr	Maud	Ellon Amateurs	5	1
Fr	Maybole	Threave Rovers		
Fr	Montrose	Brechin City	1	1
Fr	Musselburgh Athletic	Spartans	0	1
Fr	Nairn St Ninian	Buckie Thistle	0	10
Fr	Neilston	Kilbirnie Ladeside	1	1
Fr	New Elgin	Rothes	0	4
Fr	Newtongrange Star	Preston Athletic	2	2
Fr	Oakley United	Armadale Thistle	5	4
Fr	Pencaitland	Preston Athletic	2	1
Fr	Penicuik Athletic	Gala Fairydean Rovers	2	1
Fr	Pollok	Ashfield	2	1
Fr	Pumpherston	Blackburn United	1	2
Fr	Raith Rovers	Berwick Rangers	4	0
Fr	St Cadocs	Hurlford United	2	4
Fr	St Cuthbert Wanderers	Wigtown & Bladnoch		
Fr	St Rochs	St Anthonys	5	1
Fr	Shettleston	Rossvale	1	1

Fr	Shotts Bon Accord	Thorniewood United	2	1	
Fr	Stenhousemuir	Kelty Hearts	2	1	
Fr	Stoneyburn	Wishaw HSFP	2	4	
Fr	Stoneywood Parkvale	newmachar United	2	2	
Fr	Vale of Leithen	Upper Annandale	6	0	
Fr	Vale of Leven	Port Glasgow	3	4	
Fr	Whitburn	Civil Service Strollers	3	4	
Fr	Whitletts Vics	Creetown	6	3	
Fr	Ardrossan Winton Rovers	Ardeer Thistle	2	1	
Fr	Wishaw	Syngenta	4	1	
Fr	Clyde	St Mirren U20	3	0 Tnt	
Fr	Cumbernauld Colts	Stirling Albion	0	1 Tnt	
28/09/2020					
Fr	Queen of the South	Threave Rovers	3	0	
Fr	Sauchie Community JFC	Inverkeithing HS	0	1	
29/09/2020					
Fr	Airdrieonians	Albion Rovers	1	1	
Fr	Bo'ness United	Crossgates Primrose	5	0	
Fr	Caledonian Braves	Shotts Bon Accord	0	2	
Fr	Camelon	Thornton Hibs	3	6	
Fr	Cowdenbeath	Civil Service Strollers	1	0	
Fr	Dalbeattie Star	Stranraer	3	1	
Fr	Dunbar United	Gala Fairydean Rovers	5	1	
Fr	Dundee	Peterhead	4	0	
Fr	Forfar Athletic	Brechin City	2	3	
Fr	Forres mechanics	Loch Ness	4	0	
Fr	Hermes	Stoneywood Parkvale			
Fr	Hill of Beath Hawthorn	Glenrothes	5	1	
Fr	Inverurie Loco Works	Dyce			
Fr	Johnstone Burgh	Ashfield	4	1	
Fr	Lochar Thistle	Lochmaben	2	2	
Fr	Longside	Culter	0	3	
Fr	Lossiemouth	Forres Thistle	7	2	
Fr	Musselburgh Athletic	Bonnyrigg Rose	2	2	
Fr	Nairn County	Inverness CT	0	7	
Fr	Newtongrange Star	Livingston United	4	1	
Fr	Penicuik Athletic	Vale of Leithen	0	1	
Fr	Preston Athletic	Tranent Amateurs	3	1	
Fr	Queen's Park	St Johnstone U20	1	0	
Fr	Tranent	Edinburgh United	3	0	
Fr	Whitehill Welfare	Whitburn	2	0	
30/09/2020					
Fr	Lothian Thistle HV	Craigroyston	4	3	
Fr	Heston Rovers	Abbey Vale	4	0	
Fr	Drumchapel United	Kirkintilloch Rob Roy	1	5	
Fr	Bonnyton Thistle	Troon	0	3	
Fr	Newton Stewart	Wigtown & Bladnoch	2	1	
Fr	Banks O' Dee	Stonehaven	3	1	
Fr	Port Glasgow	Beith	4	4	
Fr	Arthurlie	Vale of Clyde	2	0	
Fr	Rutherglen Glencairn	BSC Glasgow	3	1	
Fr	Coupar Angus	Bridge of Earn Ams	4	7	
Fr	Partick Thistle	Ayr United	2	2	
01/10/2020					
Fr	Caledonian Braves	East Fife	4	3	
Fr	Queen of the South	Stranraer	4	1	
Fr	St Cuthbert Wanderers	Normandy Star	6	2	
02/10/2020					
Fr	Dunfermline Athletic	Stirling Albion	0	0	Alloa
Fr	Hill of Beath Hawthorn	Bo'ness United	3	0	
Fr	Clachnacuddin	Inverness CT	0	2	
Fr	Arbroath	Formartine United	4	0	
Fr	Blackburn United	Carluke Rovers	3	3	
Fr	Partick Thistle	Hearts	0	2	
03/10/2020					
Fr	Airdrieonians	Queen's Park	1	0	
Fr	Alness United	Loch Ness	5	1	
Fr	Ardeer Thistle	Neilston Amateurs	3	0	
Fr	Ashfield	Vale of Clyde	3	1	
Fr	Beith	Threave Rovers	3	1	

Fr	Benburb	Albion Rovers XI	4	2
Fr	Bonnyton Thistle	Kilmarnock U19	1	2
Fr	Brechin City	Raith Rovers	0	5
Fr	Broxburn Athletic	Gala Fairydean Rovers	2	2
Fr	Cambuslang Rangers	Bellshill Athletic	2	0
Fr	Camelon	Bathgate Thistle	7	3
Fr	Carluke Rovers	Petershill	3	5
Fr	Cove Rangers	Banks o' Dee	4	1
Fr	Craigmark Burntonians	St Cuthbert Wanderers	1	3
Fr	Cumbernauld Colts	Blantyre Vics	3	2
Fr	Cumnock	Stranraer	0	4
Fr	Darvel	Muirkirk	5	2
Fr	Drumchapel United	East Kilbride Thistle	4	1
Fr	East Kilbride	Rutherglen Glencairn	1	2
Fr	East Stirlingshire	Musselburgh Athletic	1	0
Fr	Edinburgh United	Lothian Thistle HV	1	4
Fr	Gartcairn	Kirkintilloch Rob Roy	1	2
Fr	Girvan	Creetown	1	1
Fr	Glasgow Perthshire	Albion Rovers U21	11	0
Fr	Glasgow University	Clydebank	0	3
Fr	Gretna	Lochar Thistle	5	0
Fr	Halkirk	Bonar Bridge	4	2
Fr	Hurlford United	Neilston	4	1
Fr	Inverkeithing Hillfield Swifts	Duloch	3	1
Fr	Inverness Athletic	Nairn County	0	5
Fr	Inverness Caledonian Thistle	Elgin City	1	1
Fr	Johnstone Burgh	St Rochs	1	1
Fr	Kello Rovers	Abbey Vale	2	4
Fr	Kilbirnie Ladeside	Dalry Thistle	1	0
Fr	Kilsyth Rangers	Cumbernauld United	1	4
Fr	Kinnoull	Lochee United	2	3
Fr	Leith Athletic	Vale of Leithen	7	4
Fr	Lochmaben	Heston Rovers	2	2
Fr	Lossiemouth	Dufftown	2	1
Fr	Maryhill	Kilwinning Rangers	2	4
Fr	Maybole	Stranraer Reserves	6	6
Fr	Nairn St Ninian	Rothes	1	1
Fr	Newburgh	Kennoway Star Hearts	3	2
Fr	Newtongrange Star	Dalkeith Thistle	7	1
Fr	Newton Stewart	Wigtown & Bladnoch	6	1
Fr	Pollok	Shettleston	6	1
Fr	Sauchie	Caledonian Braves	0	1
Fr	Spartans	Penicuik Athletic	1	0
Fr	Stenhousemuir	Berwick Rangers	4	1
Fr	Stirling University	Jeanfield Swifts	1	3
Fr	Tayport	Syngenta	3	2
Fr	Thorniewood United	Calderbraues U21	7	1
Fr	Tranent	Thornton Hibs	3	4
Fr	Vale of Leven	Goldenhill	4	2
Fr	Wick Academy	Orkney	3	2
Fr	Wishaw	Shotts Bon Accord	1	3
04/10/2020				
Fr	Dunbar United	Hearts XI	1	2
07/10/2020				
Fr	Deveronvale	Elgin City XI	2	2
14/10/2020				
Fr	Largs Thistle	Johnstone Burgh	4	2
15/10/2020				
Fr	Clydebank	Port Glasgow	6	1
Fr	Rutherglen Glencairn	Shotts Bon Accord	3	0
Fr	Lanark United	Lesmahagow	5	0
Fr	Larkhall Thistle	Newmains United	3	4
24/10/2020				
Fr	Rangers XI	East Stirlingshire	5	1
17/05/2021				
Fr	Fallin AFC	Bo'ness Athletic	2	3
Fr	Loch Ness	Alness United	1	1
Fr	Point	Harris AFC	6	1

22/05/2021

Fr	Arbroath Vics	Arbroath HSFP		
Fr	Brechin Vics	St Laurence		
Fr	Coupar Angus	Barnhill		
Fr	East Kilbride U20	Bo'ness Athletic		
Fr	Forfar United	Forfar Albion U19		
Fr	Invergowrie	Blairgowrie		
Fr	Johnstone Burgh	Kirkintilloch Rob Roy	0	0
Fr	St Peters Afc	St Peters WOS		

26/05/2021

Fr	Alness United	Maryburgh		
Fr	Arthurlie	Arthurlie U20		
Fr	Johnstone Burgh	Irvine Victoria	4	0
Fr	Lesmahagow	Forth Wanderers	3	2

27/05/2021

Fr	Leven United	Kirkcaldy YM		

01/06/2021

Fr	Forfar West End	Burrelton Rovers	4	0

02/06/2021

Fr	Downfield	Dundee United SC		
Fr	Johnstone Burgh	Johnstone Burgh U20	5	1

04/06/2021

Fr	Arthurlie U20	St Anthonys U20	5	2
Fr	Blackburn United U20	Fauldhouse United U20		
Fr	Blantyre Vics U20	Glebe Hibernian	5	1
Fr	Civil Service Strollers U20	Gala Fairydean Rovers U20	5	4
Fr	Dalkeith Thistle U20	Heriot Watt University	0	3
Fr	Edinburgh United U20	Tynecastle U20	0	0
Fr	Gartcairn U20	BSC Glasgow U20		
Fr	Hawick Royal Albert United	Hawick United	5	0
Fr	Kirkintilloch RR U20	Cumbernauld Colts U20		
Fr	Kinnoull	Kirrie Thistle	2	5
Fr	Largs Thistle U20	Irvine Meadow U20	1	1
Fr	Renfrew U20	St Peters U20	1	4

05/06/2021

Fr	Ardeer Thistle	AS Airdrie	5	3
Fr	Ardrossan Winton Rovers	Muirkirk	1	3
Fr	Arniston Rangers	Whitehill Welfare	1	2
Fr	Arthurlie	East Kilbride Thistle	7	0
Fr	Bellshill Athletic	Newmains United	4	3
Fr	Blairgowrie	Kirkton	9	1
Fr	Bo'ness Athletic	Kennoway Star Hearts	3	2
Fr	Brechin Vics	Barnhill	2	1
Fr	Carnoustie Panmure	Arbroath HSFP	3	1
Fr	Creetown	Crosshill Thistle	5	2
Fr	Cumbernauld Colts	Musselburgh Athletic	2	2
Fr	Darvel	Strathclyde University	5	0
Fr	Dunipace	Sauchie	2	4
Fr	Fallin AFC	Camelon	2	0
Fr	Forfar United	Downfield		
Fr	Forfar West End	Criden Bay	4	1
Fr	Forth Wanderers	Albion Rovers U20	0	2
Fr	Greenlaw	Tranent	0	9
Fr	Haddington Athletic	Tollcross Thistle	1	1
Fr	Kello Rovers	Auchinleck Talbot	1	1
Fr	Kilbirnie Ladeside	Craigmark Burntonians	1	1
Fr	Lesmahagow	Larkhall Thistle	1	1
Fr	Livingston United	Burntisland Shipyard	1	1
Fr	Lochore Welfare	Benarty Astros	3	0
Fr	Lugar Boswell Thistle	Auchinleck Talbot U20	6	2
Fr	Maryhill	Ashfield	0	3
Fr	Neilston	Glenvale	4	0
Fr	Newton Stewart	Stranraer Reserves	3	3
Fr	Royal Albert	Carluke Rovers	1	5

Fr	St Anthonys	Rossvale	0	3
Fr	St Cuthbert Wanderers	Wigtown & Bladnoch	6	1
Fr	St Rochs	Kirkintilloch Rob Roy	2	2
Fr	Thorniewood United	Shotts Bon Accord	2	3
Fr	West Park United	St Peters	6	2
Fr	Whitburn	Vale of Clyde	6	2
07/06/2021				
Fr	Ardeer Thistle	Whitletts Vics	1	3
Fr	Downfield	Dundee U18		
Fr	Syngenta	Sauchie	2	2
08/06/2021				
Fr	Ashfield	St Peters U20		
Fr	Bellfield	Ardrossan WR U20		
Fr	Broughty Athletic	Fintry		
Fr	Caledonian Braves U20	St Rochs U20	2	0
Fr	Kilsyth Rangers	Rossvale	1	4
Fr	Newtongrange Star	Arniston Rangers	3	1
Fr	Whitburn	Royal Albert	2	2
09/06/2021				
Fr	Ashfield	St Peters	7	2
Fr	Darvel U20	Rossvale U20	10	2
Fr	Forfar West End	Kinnoull	0	2
Fr	Johnstone Burgh U20	Renfrew U20	5	0
Fr	Maryhill	Irvine Victoria	2	0
Fr	Maryhill U20	Glasgow United U20	5	0
Fr	Sauchie U20	Beechwood Albion	0	4
10/06/2021				
Fr	Annan Athletic	Start Sports Management		
Fr	Blairgowrie	Monifieth U19	8	1
Fr	Stranraer Reserves	Creetown	1	1
11/06/2021				
Fr	Longside	Aberdeen East End		
Fr	Tranent	Edinburgh United	4	1
Fr	Arthurlie U20	Pollok U20		
Fr	Auchinleck Talbot U20	Maybole Y20	3	2
Fr	Blackburn United U20	Newtongrange Star U20	2	0
Fr	Edinburgh United U20	Craigroyston U20		
Fr	Edinburgh South U20	Tynecastle U20		
Fr	Glasgow United U20	Yoker Athletic U20	2	3
Fr	Irvine Meadow U20	Albion Rovers U20	10	0
Fr	Penicuik Athletic U20	Bonnyrigg Rose U20	2	0
Fr	St Anthonys U20	Troon U20	2	1
Fr	St Peters U20	Johnstone Burgh U20	1	2
Fr	St Rochs U20	Dunipace U20	0	4
Fr	Vale of Leven U20	Ardeer Thistle U20	4	1
12/06/2021				
Fr	Ashfield	St Anthonys U20	2	3
Fr	Beith	Lugar Boswell Thistle	8	0
Fr	Bellshill Athletic	Lesmahagow	2	0
Fr	Blairgowrie	Coupar Angus	3	1
Fr	Bo'ness Athletic	Lochore Welfare	3	2
Fr	Brechin Vics	Arbroath Harp	4	2
Fr	Carluke Rovers	Forth Wanderers	2	2
Fr	Clydebank	Clydebank U20	5	0
Fr	Coldstream	Tranent	2	4
Fr	Culter	Banchory St Ternan	6	3
Fr	Cumbernauld Colts	Blantyre Victoria	5	0
Fr	Cumnock	St Cadocs	2	3
Fr	Downfield	Menzieshill		
Fr	East Kilbride Thistle	Duncanrig	1	0
Fr	Fauldhouse United	Leith Athletic	3	2
Fr	Finnart	Glasgow Perthshire	6	3
Fr	Forfar United	Newburgh	1	1
Fr	Forfar West End	Arbroath HSFP	2	0

Fr	Fraserburgh United	Formartine United U20			
Fr	Glenafton Athletic	Kello Rovers	3	1	
Fr	Glenrothes	Thornton Hibs	1	3	
Fr	Haddington Athletic	Musselburgh Athletic	0	1	
Fr	Heriot Watt University	Tweeddame Rovers	7	0	
Fr	Heston Rovers	QOTS U18	5	5	
Fr	Hurlford United	Craigmark Burntonians	2	4	
Fr	Inverkeith Hillfield S	Duloch			
Fr	Johnstone Burgh	Auchinleck Talbot	0	3	
Fr	Kilbirnie Ladeside	Renfrew	1	2	
Fr	Kilsyth Rangers	Petershill			
Fr	Kirkcaldy & Dysart	Benarty Astros			
Fr	Kirkintilloch RR	Maryhill	1	2	
Fr	Largs Thistle	Ardrossan Winton R	2	1	
Fr	Larkhall Thistle	Tannochside United	4	2	
Fr	Livingston United	Scone Thistle	6	0	
Fr	Nairn St Ninian	Elgin City U20	4	1	
Fr	Neilston	Arthurlie	4	3	
Fr	Newmains United	Royal Albert	6	0	
Fr	Nithsdale Wanderers	Ardeer Thistle			
Fr	Ormiston	Gala Fairydean Rovers U20			
Fr	Pumpherston	Edinburgh United	4	2	
Fr	Rosyth	Kinnoull	2	3	
Fr	Saltcoats Vics	Troon U19	5	0	
Fr	Sauchie	Darvel	4	5	
Fr	Spartans	Lothian Thistle HV			
Fr	St Andrews United	Newtongrange Star	0	3	
Fr	St Rochs	Rossvale	1	0	
Fr	Sunnybank	Hermes			
Fr	Syngenta	Gartcairn	4	3	
Fr	Tayport	Tayport Ams	14	0	
Fr	Threave Rovers	Whitehill Welfare	0	2	
Fr	Vale of Leven	Greenock	0	6	
Fr	West Calder United	Thorniewood United	2	5	
Fr	Whitburn	Camelon	A	A	
Fr	Wishaw	Cambuslang Rangers	2	2	
Fr	Yoker Athletic	Glenvale			
13/06/2021					
Fr	Cumbernauld Colts U20	Blantyre Vics U20	2	1	
14/06/2021					
Fr	Kilwinning Rangers	Whitletts Vics	1	1	
Fr	Livingston United	Dalkeith Thistle	3	4	
15/06/2021					
Fr	Arbroath Victoria	Barnhill	7	1	
Fr	Bathgate Thistle	Kilsyth Rangers	0	6	
Fr	Bo'ness Athletic	Dundonald Bluebell	2	3	Little Kerse
Fr	Brechin Victoria	Newmachar United	5	3	Brechin CC
Fr	Broxburn Athletic	Easthouses Lily	3	1	
Fr	Carnoustie Panmure	Dundee XI	1	0	
Fr	Clyde	Dalkeith Thistle			
Fr	Coldstream	Chirnside United	14	2	
Fr	Dundee North End	Downfield	4	2	
Fr	Dunipace	Kirkintilloch Rob Roy	3	3	
Fr	Edinburgh South	Edinburgh South CFC	5	0	
Fr	Gala Fairydean Rovers	Peebles Rovers	2	2	
Fr	Hill of Beath Hawthorn U20	Kelty Hearts U20	3	2	
Fr	Leven United	Glenrothes	1	2	
Fr	Mid Annandale	Hole I' The Wa			
Fr	Newburgh	Tayport	0	3	
Fr	Preston Athletic	Edinburgh United	2	1	
Fr	Stonehaven	Banks o' Dee	0	4	
Fr	Stoneyburn	Shotts Bon Accord	1	3	
Fr	West Calder United	Heriot Watt University	2	1	
Fr	Whitburn	Linlithgow Rose	1	3	
16/06/2021					
Fr	Annan Town	Heston Rovers	2	4	

Fr	Ardrossan Winton Rovers	Hurlford United	3	2	
Fr	Blantyre Vics	Ashfield	2	1	
Fr	Bonnyton Thistle	Girvan			
Fr	Cruden Bay	Hermes			
Fr	Culter	Formartine United			
Fr	Darvel	St Cadocs	1	0	Lochinch
Fr	Forth Wanderers	Royal Albert	5	1	
Fr	Fraserburgh United	Deveronside			
Fr	Kilwinning Rangers	Troon	4	0	
Fr	Kirkcaldy & Dysart	Burntisland Shipyard	5	5	
Fr	Largs Thistle U20	St Peters	0	4	
Fr	Lugar Boswell Thistle	Kello Rovers	2	3	
Fr	Musselburgh Athletic	Arniston Rangers	1	0	
Fr	St Cuthbert Wanderers	Creetown	2	2 5-6p	
Fr	Syngenta	Oakley United	3	1	Little Kerse
Fr	Yoker Athletic	Maryhill	6	3	
Fr	Glasgow United U20	Rossvale U20	4	3	
Fr	Greenlaw	Edinburgh United	5	2	
Fr	Neilston U20	Troon U20			
Fr	Newtongrange Star4 U20	Penicuik Athletic U20	1	5	
17/06/2021					
Fr	Dunbar United	Leith Athletic	1	2	
Fr	Carluke Rovers	Bellshill Athletic	1	4	
Fr	Gala Fairydean Rovers	Lothian Thistle HV			
Fr	Greenock	Largs Thistle	3	3	
Fr	Montrose Roselea	Violet	0	1	
Fr	Normandy Star	Lochar Thistle	0	5	
Fr	Sunnybank	Dyce			
Fr	St Mungos AFC	St Rochs U20	5	0	
19/06/2021					
Fr	Abbey Vale	Dalbeattie Star	1	3	
Fr	Arthurlie	Neilston	1	1	
Fr	Blantyre Vics	St Cadocs	3	5	
Fr	Bonnyton Thistle	Maybole	2	3	
Fr	Buchanhaven Hearts	Aberdeen East End	2	0	
Fr	Clydebank	St Peters	11	1	
Fr	Darvel	Stranraer	2	3	Lochinch Lochinch
Fr	Fauldhouse United	Irvine Meadow	3	4	
Fr	Glasgow United	East Stirlingshire	2	0	
Fr	Gartcairn	Irvine Victoria			
Fr	Glenafton Athletic	Girvan	2	0	
Fr	Haddington Athletic	Newtongrange Star	2	1	
Fr	Lesmahagow	Newmains United	6	2	
Fr	Lochore Welfare	Lochore Castle	w	l	
Fr	Livingston United	Camelon	1	2	
Fr	Maryhill	St Anthonys	0	1	Springburn Park
Fr	Mid Annandale	Dalbeattie Star			
Fr	Nithsdale Wanderers	Muirkirk	1	3	
Fr	New Elgin	Strathspey Thistle			
Fr	Pollok	Auchinleck Talbot	1	4	
Fr	Rothes	Islavale			
Fr	St Rochs	Ashfield	5	4	Springburn Poark
Fr	Threave Rovers	Carlisle City	1	2	
Fr	Wishaw	Thorniewood United	6	0	
20/06/2021					
Fr	Lochore Welfare	Lochgelly United	4	0	
Fr	Oakley United	Oakley United U20			
Fr	St Anthonys U20	Maryhill U20	4	3	
21/06/2021					
Fr	Arniston Rangers	Vale of Leithen	2	2	
Fr	Benburb	Greenock	2	3	
Fr	Blackburn United	Leith Athletic	1	3	
Fr	Buckie Thistle	Banks o' Dee	1	4	
Fr	Easthouses Lily	Bonnyrigg Rose U20			
Fr	Forres Thistle	Clachnacuddin	2	3	
Fr	Kilsyth Rangers	Armadale Thistle	3	0	

Fr	Kilwinning Rangers	Stranraer	1	1	
Fr	Kinnoull	Downfield			
Fr	Kirkcaldy & Dysart	East Fife U20	5	3	
Fr	Larkhall Thistle	Albion Rovers U20	1	2	
Fr	Lothian Thistle HV	Edinburgh South CFC			
Fr	Newburgh	Hill of Beath Hawthorn	1	3	
Fr	Newtongrange Star	Kelty Hearts	0	2	
Fr	Stonehaven	Montrose Roselea	1	2	
Fr	Cumnock U20	Auchinleck Talbot U20	5	1	
Fr	Hill of Beath Hawthorn U20	Keanfield Swifts R20	4	1	
Fr	Kennoway Star Hearts U20	Kettle United	3	0	
Fr	Preston Athletic U20	Newtongrange Star U20	2	0	

22/06/2021

Fr	East Kilbride	Dumbarton	2	1	
Fr	Keith	Elgin City U20			

23/06/2021

Fr	Annan Athletic	Dalbeattie Star			
Fr	Buckie Thistle	Banchory St Ternan			
Fr	Burghead Thistle	Lossiemouth			
Fr	Camelon	Oakley United	3	2	Little Kerse
Fr	Coldstream	Alnwick Town			
Fr	Dailly	Newton Stewart			
Fr	Dalkeith Thistle	West Calder United	2	4	Dalkeith Campus
Fr	Dalry Thistle	Lesmahagow	4	5	
Fr	Dunipace	Inverkeithing Hillfield Swifts	7	3	
Fr	East Fife	The New Saints	1	1	
Fr	Fauldhouse United	Blantyre Vics U20	3	2	
Fr	Forfar West End	Arbroath HSFP			
Fr	Fraserburgh United	Newmachar United	2	4	
Fr	Harthill Royal	Kilwinning Rangers	0	5	
Fr	Johnstone Burgh	Clydebank	0	1	
Fr	Lochgelly Albert	Tayport	1	6	
Fr	Maybole	Troon			
Fr	Neilston	Neilston U20	2	0	
Fr	Ormiston	Dunbar United	0	3	
Fr	Pollok	Linlithgow Rose	1	0	
Fr	Port Glasgow	Beith			
Fr	Preston Athletic	Penicuik Athletic	1	4	
Fr	Renfrew	West Park United	1	2	
Fr	Rutherglen Glencairn	Cambuslang Rangers	1	3	
Fr	Sauchie	Cumbernauld United	3	3	
Fr	Spartans	Dunfermline Athletic	2	2	
Fr	St Cuthbert Wanderers	Newton Stewart	1	2	
Fr	Stoneywood Parkvale	Aberdeen East End			
Fr	Tweedmouth Rangers	Berwick Town	5	0	
Fr	Whitehills	Deveronvale			
Fr	Dalkeith Thistle U20	Easthouses AFC	7	1	Abbeylands Park
Fr	Edinburgh United U20	Heriot Watt University	0	1	

24/06/2021

Fr	Glenrothes	Rosyth	2	3	
Fr	Brechin City	Brechin Victoria			
Fr	Burghead Thistle	Strathspey Thistle			
Fr	East Fife	St Andrews United	3	0	
Fr	Greenock	Drumchapel United	0	3	
Fr	Irvine Meadow	Whitletts Vics	1	0	
Fr	Lochar Thistle	Queen of the South XI			
Fr	Stenhousemuir	Syngenta	8	0	
Fr	Cardross AFC	Vale of Leven U20	2	4	
Fr	Leven United	Kennoway Star Hearts U20			

25/06/2021

Fr	Ayr United	TNS	1	0	Cumnock
Fr	Ardeer Thistle U20	Benburn U17	1	2	
Fr	Arthurlie U20	Maryhill U20			
Fr	Benburn U20	Beith U20	6	1	
Fr	Blackburn United U20	Harthill Royal U20	5	0	
Fr	Carluke Rovers U20	Larkhall Thistle U20			

Fr	Dalkeith Thistle U20	Newtongrange Star U20	4	2	
Fr	Kelty Hearts U20	Glenrothes Strollers	3	2	
Fr	Kilwinning Rangers U20	Ashfield U20	8	0	
Fr	Largs Thistle U20	Johnstone Burgh U20			
Fr	Irvine Meadow U20	Gartcairn U20			
Fr	St Anthonys U20	Blantyre Vics U20	2	0	
Fr	St Peters U20	Renfrew U20			
Fr	St Rochs U20	Rossvale U18			
26/06/2021					
Fr	Ardrossan Winton Rovers	Dalry Thistle	3	2	
Fr	Arniston Rangers	West Calder United	0	2	
Fr	Ashfield	Drumchapel United	3	2	
Fr	Bathgate Thistle	Lochgelly Albert	1	1	
Fr	Beith	East Kilbride	3	2	
Fr	Bellshill Athletic	Royal Albert	3	0	
Fr	Benburb	Stenhousemuir	1	2	
Fr	Blackburn United	Harthill Royal	3	0	
Fr	Bonnyton Thistle	Renfrew	5	1	
Fr	Bonnyrigg Rose	Kilwinning Rangers	0	1	
Fr	Broughty Athletic	Sauchie	3	1	
Fr	Buchanhaven Hearts	Whitehills	4	2	
Fr	Buckie Thistle	Culter	2	0	
Fr	Carnoustie Panmure	Newburgh	10	0	
Fr	Civil Service Strollers	Dunfermline Athletic	2	2	
Fr	Clydebank	Cumbernauld Colts	2	0	
Fr	Colony Park	Keith	3	0	
Fr	Craigmark Burntonians	Port Glasgow	5	1	
Fr	Dumbarton	Motherwell	1	0	
Fr	Dunbar United	Daleith Thistle	1	1	
Fr	Dundee North End	Dunipace			
Fr	Elgin City U20	Luncarty	0	3	Aberfeldy
Fr	Falkirk	Irvine Meadow	5	0	
Fr	Forfar Athletic	Dundee	0	3	
Fr	Forfar United	Montrose Roselea	4	0	
Fr	Forfar West End	Newmachar United	1	1	
Fr	Forres Mechanics	Inverness CT	0	1	
Fr	Forth Wanderers	Armadale Thistle	0	1	
Fr	Fraserburgh United	Maud			
Fr	Gala Fairydean Rovers	Edinburgh City	3	1	
Fr	Glasgow Perthshire	Johnstone Burgh	4	2	
Fr	Glasgow United	East Kilbride Thistle	1	1	
Fr	Glasgow University	Petershill	0	2	
Fr	Glenafton Athletic	Largs Thistle	2	4	
Fr	Gentanar	Hermes			
Fr	Glenrothes	Dundonald Bluebell	1	2	
Fr	Greenock	Blantyre Victoria	3	1	
Fr	Hall Russell United	Banchory St Ternan	3	1	
Fr	Harmony Row	St Anthinys	2	3	
Fr	Heriot Watt University	Crossgates Primrose	3	0	
Fr	Hurlford United	St Cadocs	2	2	
Fr	Kello Rovers	Troon	0	5	
Fr	Kelty Hearts	Partick Thistle	2	3	
Fr	Kennoway Star Hearts	Cumbernauld United	1	2	
Fr	Kilsyth Rangers	Kilsyth Athletic	3	1	
Fr	Kirrie Thistle	Dyce	0	2	
Fr	Lesmahagow	Carluke Rovers	0	0	
Fr	Linlithgow Rose	Hearts	0	6	
Fr	Lochmaben	Saltcoats Vics	0	2	
Fr	Maybole	Stranraer Reserves	3	3	Annbank
Fr	Mid Annandale	Vale of Clyde	1	3	
Fr	Montrose	Arbroath	1	1	
Fr	Muirkiek	Larkhall Thistle	2	1	
Fr	Musselburgh Athletic	East Stirlingshire	1	3	
Fr	Neilston	Auchinleck Talbot	0	1	
Fr	Newtongrange Star	Darvel	0	2	
Fr	Newton Stewart	Whitletts Vics	0	3	
Fr	Ormiston	Peebles Rovers	1	3	
Fr	Pollok	Arthurlie	3	0	
Fr	Queen of the South	Annan Athletic	2	3	

Fr	Raith Rovers	Stranraer	4 1	
Fr	Rosyth	Lothian Thistle HV	3 3	
Fr	Rothie Rovers	Inverurie Loco Works		
Fr	Rutherglen Glencairn	Kirkintilloch Rob Roy	2 0	
Fr	Spartans	Jeanfield Swifts	1 3	
Fr	St Rochs	Cambuslang Rangers	0 7	
Fr	Stirling University	Queen's Park	2 2	
Fr	Syngenta	Tranent	1 1	
Fr	Threave Rovers	Cumnock	0 0	
Fr	Tweedmouth Rangers	Berwick Colts	10 0	
Fr	Upper Annandale	Nithsdale Wanderers	1 2	
Fr	Vale of Leithen	Hawick Royal Albert	2 1	
Fr	Vale of Leven	Maryhill	5 4	
Fr	Whitburn	Rossvale	0 0	
Fr	Wishaw	Whitehill Welfare	0 4	
Fr	Finnart	Clydebank U20		
Fr	Neilston U20	Auchinleck Talbot U20	3 1	
Fr	Stonehaven U20	Hermes U20	6 1	

27/06/2021

Fr	Strathspey Thistle	Rothes		Aviemore
Fr	Wigtown & Bladnoch	Normandy Star	3 0	

28/06/2021

Fr	Aberdeen East End	Glentanar		
Fr	Ardeer Thistle	Ardeer Thistle U20	2 0	
Fr	Bo'ness Athletic	Stirling University	2 3	
Fr	Dunipace U20	Livingston United	6 2	
Fr	FC Europa (GIB)	Livingston	0 2	Marbella
Fr	Larkhall Thistle	Glasgow United	1 3	
Fr	Lossiemouth	Elgin City U20	1 1	
Fr	Oakley United	Inverkeithing Hillfield Swifts	1 1	

29/06/2021

Fr	Alloa Athletic	Stenhousemuir	1 2	
Fr	Arniston Rangers	Lothian Thistle HV		
Fr	Armadale Thistle	Linlithgow Rose	3 1	
Fr	Bonnyrigg Rose	Edinburgh City	1 1	
Fr	Brechin City	Forfar Athletic	2 1	Brechin Vics
Fr	Caledonian Braves	Petershill		
Fr	Camelon	East Stirlingshire	3 3	
Fr	Civil Service Strollers	Hearts XI	0 4	
Fr	Colony Park	Inverurie Loco Works	1 5	
Fr	Craigroyston	Preston Athletic U20	2 2	
Fr	Dumbarton	Morton	0 0	
Fr	East Fife	Queen of the South	0 3	
Fr	Gala Fairydean Rovers	Penicuik Athletic	2 1	
Fr	Leven United	St Andrews United	1 0	
Fr	Lochgelly United	Glenrothes		
Fr	Montrose Roselea	Brechin Victoria	1 0	
Fr	Raith Rovers	Clyde	0 1	
Fr	Rossvale	Vale of Clyde	0 1	
Fr	Spartans	Hearts	0 7	
Fr	St Cadocs	Clydebank	2 3	
Fr	Steins Thistle	Cumbernauld United	1 10	
Fr	Stirling University Reserves	Bathgate Thistle		
Fr	Stranraer	Ayr United	0 2	
Fr	Vale of Leithen	Peebles Rovers	4 2	
Fr	Whitburn	Stirling Albion		
Fr	Clydebank U20	Yoker Athletic U20		

30/06/2021

Fr	Ashfield	East Kilbride Thistle	1 2	
Fr	Berwick Rangers	Dundee United XI	3 1	
Fr	Dundee United	Cowdenbeath	1 1	
Fr	Blackburn United	Edinburgh College	2 1	
Fr	Buckie Thistle	Islavale	7 0	
Fr	Burntisland Shipyard	East Fife U20		
Fr	Crossgates Primrose	Arbroath	1 3	
Fr	Culter	Stonehaven	3 1	

Fr	Darvel	Whitletts Vics			
Fr	Fauldhouse United	Kirkintilloch Rob Roy	2	1	
Fr	Forth Wanderers	Glasgow Perthshire	4	1	
Fr	Irvine Meadow	Hurlford United	2	1	
Fr	Largs Thistle	Port Glasgow	3	1	
Fr	Linfield	Kilmarnock	0	1	
Fr	Lugar Boswell Thistle	Nithsdale Wanderers	4	4	
Fr	Maryhill	Glenvale	6	1	
Fr	Maud	Turriff United	1	4	
Fr	Petershill	Petershill U20			
Fr	Rothie Rovers	Deveronvale	3	0	
Fr	Rutherglen Glencairn	Lesmahagow	1	1	
Fr	Stirling University EOS	Kilsyth Rangers			
Fr	Stoneywood Parkvale	Hermes			
Fr	St Peters	Glasgow Wellington	5	0	
Fr	Threave Rovers	Penrith	4	1	
Fr	Vale of Leven	Johnstone Burgh	1	4	
Fr	West Calder United	Edinburgh United U20	4	1	
Fr	Yoker Athletic	Pollok	1	0	
Fr	Ardeer Thistle U20	St Anthonys	1	6	
Fr	East Kilbride U20	Kirkintilloch Rob Roy	3	3	
Fr	Kilwinning Rangers U20	Glasgow United U20	4	1	
01/07/2021					
Fr	Drumchapel United	Gartcairn			
Fr	Dufftown	Deveronside			
Fr	Craigroyston	Edinburgh South	1	2	
Fr	Fallin AFC	Syngenta	0	2	
Fr	Finnart	Cumbernauld United	1	1	
Fr	Forres Thistle	Strathspey Thistle			
Fr	Kello Rovers	Abbey Vale	2	4	
Fr	Preston Athletic	Newtongrange Star	1	1	
Fr	Thornton Hibs	Hill of Beath Hawthorn	0	2	
Fr	Upper Annandale	Five Arches Bombers			
02/07/2021					
Fr	Ayr United	Hearts	1	1	at Largs
Fr	Bo'ness Athletic	Arbroath	2	2	
Fr	Civil Service Strollers	Hibernian XI	3	5	
Fr	Lochmaben	Ruthwell Rovers	5	0	
Fr	Montrose Roselea	Downfield			
Fr	Spartans U20	Tweedmouth Rangers	1	5	
Fr	Arthurlie U20	Rossvale U20			
Fr	Ashfield U20	Glenvale U20			
Fr	Benburb U20	Glasgow United U20	5	2	
Fr	Blackburn United U20	St Peters U20	0	3	
Fr	Blantyre Vics U20	Bellshill Athletic U20	5	0	
Fr	Caledonian Braves U20	Ardrossan Winton R U20	7	2	
Fr	Civil Service Strollers U20	Edinburgh City U20	4	3	
Fr	Clydebank U20	Irvine Meadow U20	3	3	
Fr	East Kilbride U20	Duncanrig AFC	8	1	
Fr	Gartcairn U20	Cambuslang Rangers U20			
Fr	Musselburgh Athletic U20	Dalkeith Thistle U20	4	2	
Fr	Neilston U20	Maryhill U20			
Fr	Penicuik Athletic U20	Kennoway Star Hearts U20	3	2	
03/07/2021					
NL Cup	Cumbernauld Colts	Airdrieonians	0	2	Broadwood
NL Cup	Clyde	Albion Rovers	3	1	Broadwood
PC	Troon	Wishaw	5	4	Portland Park
PC	Fauldhouse United	Lothian Thistle HV	2	3	
Fr	Abbey Vale	Carlisle City Reserves	10	0	
Fr	Annan Athletic	Atherton Collieries	1	0	
Fr	Ardrossan Winton Rovers	Benburb	1	0	
Fr	Berwick Rangers	North Shields	3	1	
Fr	Blairgowrie	Bridge of Earn	3	2	
Fr	Bo'ness United	Stirling Albion	3	2	
Fr	Brechin City	Dundee United	1	4	
Fr	Bridge of Don Thistle	Kennoway Star Hearts	2	3	
Fr	Broxburn Athletic	Bathgate Thistle	2	0	

Fr	Buckie Thistle	Dyce	3	0	
Fr	Carlisle City	Longridge Town	3	0	Lochmaben
Fr	Coldstream	Gala Fairydean Rovers	2	0	
Fr	Craigmark Burntonians	Vale of Clyde			
Fr	Creetown	Maryhill	1	1	
Fr	Cumnock	Glasgow United	3	1	
Fr	Deveronvale	Banks o' Dee	0	6	
Fr	Drumchapel United	Glasgow Wellington			
Fr	Dumbarton	Clydebank	1	0	
Fr	Dunbar United	Rosyth	1	2	
Fr	Dundee North End	East Fife	1	4	
Fr	Dunipace	Dundonald Bluebell	3	1	
Fr	East Fife U20	Lochore Welfare			
Fr	East Kilbride	Partick Thistle	1	2	
Fr	Edinburgh United	Ryton & Crawcrook Albion	0	1	
Fr	Elgin City	Ross County	0	5	
Fr	Falkirk	Hearts	0	4	at Largs
Fr	Forth Wanderers	Whitbburn	2	4	
Fr	Fraserburgh United	Forfar West End			
Fr	Girvan	Newton Stewart	2	2	
Fr	Glenafton Athletic	Whitletts Vics	4	0	
Fr	Greenock	Bonnyton Thistle	1	3	
Fr	Harmony Row	Milngavie Wanderers	6	2	
Fr	Heriot Watt University	Muirkirk	1	1	
Fr	Heston Rovers	Upper Annandale	0	3	
Fr	Hurlford United	Rutherglen Glencairn	1	0	
Fr	Huntly	Newmachar United	2	1	
Fr	Inverkeith Hillfield S	Glenrothes	4	1	
Fr	Inverurie Loco Works	Peterhead	1	2	Colony Park
Fr	Irvine Meadow	Rossvale	1	1	
Fr	Johnstone Burgh	Kirkintilloch Rob Roy	0	2	
Fr	Kelty Hearts	Montrose	1	1	
Fr	Kilbirnie Ladeside	Yoker Athletic	2	1	
Fr	Kilwinning Rangers	St Cadocs	2	2	
Fr	Kirkcaldy & Dysart	Preston Athletic	A	A	
Fr	Largs Thistle	Arthurlie	1	2	
Fr	Larne	Kilmarnock	2	2	
Fr	Leith Athletic	Pumpherston	4	1	
Fr	Linlithgow Rose	Bonnyrigg Rose	1	1	
Fr	Livingston	East Stirlingshire	3	0	
Fr	Lochee United	Gartcairn	0	0	
Fr	Longside	Fraserburgh	1	6	
Fr	Lossiemouth	Colony Park	3	1	
Fr	Luncarty	St Rochs	2	0	
Fr	Newtongrange Star	Stirling University	2	1	
Fr	Nithsdale Wanderers	Larkhall Thistle	4	0	
Fr	Ormiston	Blackburn United	0	7	
Fr	Penicuik Athletic	Haddington Athletic	1	2	
Fr	Petershill	Fort William	3	1	
Fr	Pollok	Cowdenbeath	1	1	
Fr	Port Glasgow	St Anthonys	3	3	
Fr	Queen of the South	Stranraer	2	1	
Fr	Raith Rovers	Queen's Park	2	2	
Fr	Rangers B	Edinburgh City	0	1	Murray Park
Fr	Renfrew	Neilston	1	3	
Fr	Rothie Rovers	Formartine United	0	0	
Fr	Sauchie	East Kilbride Thistle	3	1	
Fr	Scone Thistle	Kirrie Thistle	1	2	
Fr	Shotts Bon Accord	Cambuslang Rangers	5	1	
Fr	Spartans	Stenhousemuir	1	5	
Fr	St Andrews United	East Craigie	0	3	
Fr	St Cuthbert Wanderers	Finnart	1	2	
Fr	Stenhousemuir CFC	Letham	3	1	
Fr	Stirling Uni EOS	Glasgow University	0	1	
Fr	Stoneyburn	Bellshill Athletic	1	1	
Fr	Syngenta	Hill of Beath Hawthorn	2	2	
Fr	Threave Rovers	Maybole	3	3	
Fr	Tranent	Darvel	3	4	
Fr	Turriff United	Culter	3	2	
Fr	Vale of Leithen	Cumbernauld United	0	4	

Fr	Vale of Leven	Oakley United	3	3		
Fr	West Calder United	Easthouses Lily	1	2		
Fr	Whitehill Welfare	Hearts XI	2	2		
Fr	Vale of Leven U20	Oakley United U20	4	0		
04/07/2021						
NLC	Albion Rovers	Cumbernauld Colts	1	1	5-4p	
NLC	Airdrieonians	Clyde	0	3		
PC	Troon	Lothian Thistle HV				
Fr	Elgin City U20	Deveronvale				
05/07/2021						
Fr	Bellshill Athletic	Albion Rovers Reserves	1	4		
Fr	Kilsyth Rangers	Thorniewood United	1	0		
Fr	Livingston	Arbroath	4	0		
Fr	Partick Thistle	Rangers	0	1		
Fr	Preston Athletic	Hearts	1	3		
Fr	Rossvale	Lesmahagow	0	3		
06/07/2021						
Fr	Bo'ness United	Tranent	1	0		
Fr	Broxburn Athletic	East Stirlingshire	2	1		
Fr	BSC Glasgow	Drumchapel United	3	3		
Fr	Camelon	Armadale Thistle	1	2		
Fr	Craigroyston	Lothian Thistle HV				
Fr	Cumbernauld Colts	Morton				
Fr	Dalbeattie Star	Queen of the Soputh XI	3	1		
Fr	Dunbar United	Hibernian XI	2	2		
Fr	Dundee	Leyton Orient	3	0		
Fr	Dunipace	East Kilbride Thistle				
Fr	Dyce	Inverurie Loco Works	1	2		
Fr	East Fife	Burntisland Shipyard	15	0		
Fr	Easthouses Lily	Whitehill Welfare	3	4		
Fr	Edinburgh South	Vale of Leithen	1	1		
Fr	Forres Thistle	Nairn County				
Fr	Glenrothes	Greig Park Rangers				
Fr	Johnstone Burgh	Glasgow Perthshire	1	0		
Fr	Kennoway Star Hearts	Hill of Beath Hawthorn	1	7		
Fr	Kirkcaldy & Dysart	Kelty Hearts U20				
Fr	Mid Annandale	Five Arches Bombers	10	0		
Fr	Newmachar United	Insch	7	1		
Fr	Penicuik Athletic	Peebles Rovers	9	0		
Fr	Rangers B	Albion Rovers	3	1		Murray Park
Fr	Rothie Rovers	Colony Park	2	1		
Fr	St Andrews United	Coupar Angus				
Fr	Stirling University	Crossgates Primrose	5	3		
Fr	Strathspey Thistle	Elgin City	1	2		
Fr	Thornton Hibs	Dundonald Bluebell	3	0		
07/07/2021						
Fr	Abbey Vale	Scaur	12	0		
Fr	Ardeer Thistle	Lugar Boswell Thistle	3	1		
Fr	Arthurlie	Vale of Clyde	1	1		
Fr	Banchory St Ternan	Stoneywood Parkvale				
Fr	Blackburn United	Preston Athletic	1	0		
Fr	Blantyre Vics	Shotts Bon Accord	1	2		
Fr	Bonnyrigg Rose	Hearts	0	3		
Fr	Celtic	Sheffield Wednesday	3	1		in Wales
Fr	Cumbernauld United	Gartcairn	2	2		
Fr	Dalry Thistle	Maryhill	2	3		
Fr	Formartine United	Hermes				
Fr	Glasgow United	Pollok	0	7		
Fr	Glenafton Athletic	Matbole				
Fr	Kello Rovers	Lochar Thistle	2	0		
Fr	Largs Thistle	Irvine Victoria	4	0		
Fr	Lochee United	Dundee St James	4	1		
Fr	Maud	Deveronvale	2	3		
Fr	Monrose Roselea	East Craigie				
Fr	Newmains United	Carluke Thistle				
Fr	Rutherglen Glencairn	Petershill	1	0		

Fr	Dundonald Bluebell	Lochore Welfare	3	0
Fr	Dunipace	Armadale Thistle	3	1
Fr	Drumchapel United	Irvine Victoria	3	0
Fr	Finnart	Newmains United	5	1
Fr	Forfar West End	Montrose Roselea	2	3
Fr	Forth Wanderers	Lanark United	0	1
Fr	Gartcairn	Rossvale	0	3
Fr	Girvan	Creetpwn	2	1
Fr	Glasgow University	Cambria	5	0
Fr	Glenafton Athletic	Glenafton AFC	9	0
Fr	Glenrothes	Strathmiglo United	5	1
Fr	Hawick Royal Albert United	Civil Service Strollers U20	1	2
Fr	Hill of Beath Hawthorn	Whitburn	6	1
Fr	Inverkeithing Hillfield Swifts	Livingston United	6	1
Fr	Inverurie Loco Works	Hernes	4	1
Fr	Irvine Meadow	Kilwinning Rangers	2	4
Fr	Johnstone Burgh	Kello Rovers	4	0
Fr	Kinross Colts A	Letham	1	7
Fr	Kirrie Thistle	Turriff United	3	2
Fr	Largs Thistle	Bonnyton Thistle	3	0
Fr	Larkhall Thistle	Abbey Vale	0	2
Fr	Linlithgow Rose	Bo'ness United	1	0
Fr	Lochee Harp	Kinnoull	1	1
Fr	Lochee United	St Anthonys	2	0
Fr	Lochgelly Albert	Ormiston	2	2
Fr	Lugar Boswell Thistle	Dalry Thistle	2	0
Fr	Luncarty	Kilsyth Rangers	3	1
Fr	Maybole	Hurlford United	2	5
Fr	Mid Annandale	Carluke Rovers	1	6
Fr	Muirkirk	St Peters	5	1
Fr	Musselburgh Athletic	Edinburgh University	3	3
Fr	Nairn St Ninian	Forres Mechanics	1	4
Fr	Newmachar United	Ellon United	3	0
Fr	Newtongrange Star	Edinburgh South	1	1
Fr	Newton Stewart	Glasgow United	1	0
Fr	Oakley United	Edinburgh College	1	1
Fr	Pekney Select	Wick Academy	0	4
Fr	Peebles Rovers	Dalkeith Thistle	0	3
Fr	Ponteland United	Heriot Watt University	0	3
Fr	Preston Athletic	Tollcross Thistle	5	1
Fr	Pumpherston	Scone Thistle	2	1
Fr	Renfrew	Troon	0	0
Fr	Rothes	Steonehaven	5	1
Fr	Rosyth	Blackburn United	3	1
Fr	St Johnstone	Stenhousemuir	6	1
Fr	St Rochs	Kilbirnie Ladeside	A	A
Fr	Stoneyburn	Fort William	4	2
Fr	Syngenta	Benburb	2	4
Fr	Tayport	St Andrews United	4	0
Fr	Threave Rovers	Spartans	1	0
Fr	Tranent	East Stirlingshire	1	0
Fr	Tranmere Rovers	Rangers	1	0
Fr	Tynecastle	Tweedmouth Rangers	2	0
Fr	Vale of Leven	Kirkintilloch Rob Roy	1	0
Fr	West Calder United	Royal Albert	6	1
Fr	Whitehill Welfare	St Cuthbert Wanderers	4	3
Fr	Wishaw	Whitletts Vics	0	4
Fr	Yoker Athletic	Harmony Row	1	3
11/07/2021				
Fr	Wigtown & Bladnoch	Dumfries Athletic		
12/07/2021				
Fr	Fraserburgh	Maud	8	0
Fr	St Rochs	St Josephs AFC		
13/07/2021				
Fr	Colony Park	Banchory St Ternan	1	1
Fr	Dunbar United	Hearts	1	1
Fr	Easthouses Lily	Leith Athletic	2	5

Fr	Edinburgh United	Edinburgh United Vale	2	2	
Fr	Greig Park Rangers	Lochore Welfare			
Fr	Hall Russell United	Inverurie Loco Works	1	6	
Fr	Hermes	Echt			
Fr	Hibernian	Arsenal	2	1	
Fr	Letham	Jeanfield Swifts	1	7	
Fr	Leven United	Dundonald Bluebell	2	7	
Fr	Lochar Thistle	Terregles	3	1	
Fr	Lochmaben	Five Arches Bombers			
Fr	Longside	Deveronvale			
Fr	Montrose U18	Cruden Bay			
Fr	Nairn County	Dufftown	5	0	
Fr	Newmachar United	Bervie Caledonian	4	2	
Fr	Rothes	Strathspey Thistle	2	1	
Fr	St Johnstone	Preston North End	1	1	
Fr	Thornton Hibs	Crossgates Primrose	2	2	
Fr	Tynecastle	Bonnyrigg Rose	0	4	
Fr	Edinburgh United U20	Preston Athletic U20	4	2	
Fr	Hill of Beath Hawthorn U20	Glenrothes U20	5	1	
14/07/2021					
Fr	Banks o' Dee	Fraserburgh	1	1	
Fr	Celtic	Bristol City	0	0	in Wales
Fr	Forres Mechanics	Burghead Thistle			
Fr	Huntly	Aberdeen University			
Fr	Lochee United	Dundee XI			
Fr	Rangers B	Burnley U21	4	2	
Fr	Yoker Athletic	Yoker Athletic U20			
16/07/2021					
Fr	Raith Rovers	Hibernian	1	3	
		Ian Davidson Testimonial			
Fr	Auchinleck Talbot U20	Arthurlie U20	1	1	
Fr	Benburb u20	Largs Thistle U20	1	2	
Fr	Blackburn United U20	Bonnyrigg Rose U20	1	3	
Fr	Blantyre Vics U20	Harthill Royal U20	6	1	
Fr	Dunipace U20	Clydebank U20			
Fr	Drumchapel United U20	Yoker Athletic U20			
Fr	East Kilbride U20	Craigroyston U20	6	1	
Fr	Edinburgh United U20	Penicuik Athletic U20	1	6	
Fr	Johnstone Burgh U20	Carluke Rovers U20	2	2	
Fr	Kirkintilloch Rob Roy U20	Irvine Meadow U20			
Fr	St Cadocs U20	Broomhill U20	1	0	
Fr	St Peters U20	Darvel U20	1	2	
Fr	St Rochs U20	Cambuslang Rangers U20	2	2	
Fr	Vale of Leven U20	Singer AFC	1	1	
17/07/2021					
Fr	Armadale Thistle	Fallin			
Fr	Ayr United	Burnley U23	2	1	
Fr	Celtic	Preston North End	0	1	
Fr	Clachnacuddin	Burghead Thistle	6	0	
Fr	Craigroyston	Edinburgh United Vale			
Fr	Deveronvale	Rothes	4	5	
Fr	Elgin City	Nairn County	3	0	
Fr	Hearts	Sunderland	0	2	
Fr	Huntly	Insch	2	0	
Fr	Leven United	Thornton Hibs	0	1	
Fr	Nithsdale Wanderers	Carluke Rovers	2	3	
Fr	Rangers	Arsenal	2	2	
Fr	Spartans	Chelmsford City	5	1	
Fr	St Mirren	Annan Athletic	4	0	
Fr	Strathspey Thistle	Forres Mechanics	1	0	
Fr	Turriff United	Inverurie Loco Works	0	6	
20/07/2021					
Fr	Kilwinning Rangers U20	Dalry Thistle U20	11	1	
Fr	Rhu Amateurs	Clydebank U20	1	5	

21/07/2021

Fr	Arbroath	St Johnstone	1	4
Fr	Hill of Beath Hawthorn U20	Inverkeithing HS U20		
Fr	Irvine Meadow U20	Cambuslang Rangers U20		

23/07/2021

Fr	Ardrossan WR U20	Vale of Leven U20	3	2
Fr	Arthurlie U20	Yoker Athletic U20	8	1
Fr	Ashfield U20	Glasgow United U20	1	2
Fr	Auchinleck Talbot U20	Cambuslang Rangers U20	1	3
Fr	Civil Service Strollers U20	Dalkeith Thistle U20	3	1
Fr	Clydebank U20	Benburb U20	9	0
Fr	Darvel U20	St Rochs U20	4	2
Fr	Johnstone Burgh U20	Beith U20	4	2
Fr	Newtongrange Star U20	Lothian Thistle HV U20	4	6
Fr	Spartans U20	Edinburgh United U20	6	3
Fr	St Peters U20	Rossvale U20	2	5

24/07/2021

Fr	Celtic	West Ham United	2	6
Fr	Rangers	Brighton	0	0
Fr	St Johnstone	Fleetwood Town	0	0

25/07/2021

Fr	Rangers	Real Madrid	2	1
Fr	Nithsdale Wanderers	Abertay University	4	1

26/07/2021

Fr	Cambuslang Rangers U20	Ardeer Thistle U20		
Fr	Danderhall MW	Edinburgh United U20	5	4
Fr	Lochgelly United	Kennoway Star H U20	4	0
Fr	Newtongrange Star U20	Whitehill Welfare U20	1	2

"PYRAMID" FOOTBALL

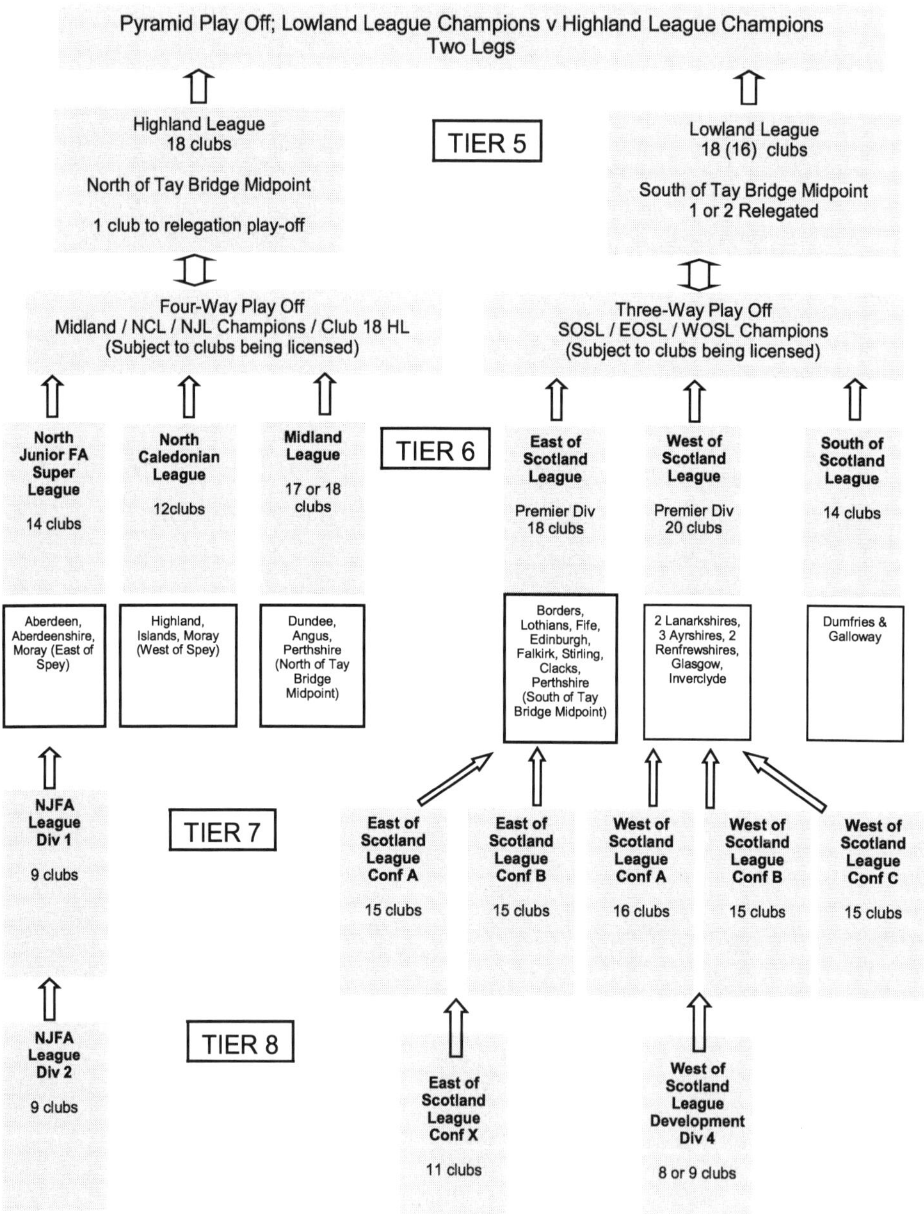

Pyramid Non League Clubs Directory 2021/22

L = Licensed Club, F = Floodlights, A = Artificial Pitch, S = Spectator Seating

Contacting Clubs

Club contacts may have changed since the Almanac was compiled. In general the best way to contact a club is via their Twitter Account or Facebook Page. Send a Direct Message – experience suggests this is by far the best way of getting a response. If telephoning please do not do so at anti-social hours and unless it is absolutely necessary.

Club Abbey Vale

League South of Scotland
Formed 1971
Ground Maryfield Park, New Abbey, DG2 8BY
Tel 07762230648 (Sec Mob)
Capacity 1000
Colours Black and Yellow
Secretary David Morton
Davidmorton362@gmail.com
Nickname Vale
Sometimes play homes games at Dumfries HS due to pitch conditions at New Abbey

Club Aberdeen East End

League North Junior
Secretary Ms Fiona Anderson Tel: (M) 07817850845
Email f.anderson3@nhs.net
Ground New Advocates Park, Aberdeen, AB24 1RG.
Capacity 1000
Tel 01224 276977
Colours Black and Yellow
Founded 1887

Club Aberdeen University (F, S)

League North Junior
Secretary Mr Daniel McKendrick Tel: (M) 07902498225
Email Daniel.s.mckendrick@gmail.com
Ground Hillhead Centre, Don Street, Old Aberdeen, AB24 1UH
Capacity 1000
Colours Blue
Founded 1889

Club Alness United (F)

League North Caledonian
Founded 1870s
Secretary Fiona Sutherland
Tel 01349 884149
Email fiona.sutherland15@gmail.com
Ground Dalmore Park, Alness
Colours Black and White

Club Annbank United

League West of Scotland
Formed 1939
Motto
Ground New Pebble Park, KA6 5EE
Tel
Capacity c 1500
Colours Black and White
Contact ANNBANKUNITED@WOSFL.CO.UK
Nickname Bankies
Annbank are taking a year in abeyance for 2021/2. A local Amateur side will use the ground and will hopefully be the basis of a revived Annbank United in the West of Scotland League for 2022/3.

Club Arbroath Victoria

League Midlands
Secretary Mr Neil Hardie Tel: (M) 07774030028
Email neilhardievics@btinternet.com
Ground Ogilvy Park, Cairnie Loan, Arbroath, DD11 4DS
Capacity 1000
Colours Black and White Stripes
Formed 1880s

Club Ardeer Thistle

League West of Scotland
Formed 1900
Motto
Ground Ardeer Stadium, KA20 3JD
Tel
Capacity c 2500
Colours Red and White
Secretary Peter McBlain (07767898818)
Contact ARDEERTHISTLE@WOSFL.CO.UK
Nickname

Club Ardrossan Winton Rovers (F, S)

League West of Scotland
Formed 1902
Motto
Ground Winton Park, KA22 8JG
Tel
Capacity c. 2500
Colours Black and White
Secretary Bobby McNamara
Contact ARDROSSANWINTONROVERS@WOSFL.CO.UK
Nickname Winton

Club Armadale Thistle (S)

League East of Scotland
Formed 1936
Motto
Ground Volunteer Park, EH48 3BQ
Tel
Capacity 2500
Colours Blue and White
Secretary Scott Watson
Tel 07421 017516
Nickname

Club Arniston Rangers

League East of Scotland
Formed 1878
Ground Newbyres Park, Gorebridge, EH23 4TP
Tel 07734924577 (Sec Mob)
Capacity c2000
Colours Maroon and White
Secretary Allan Hares
allan.hares@aol.com
Nickname Rangers, Arni

Club Arthurlie

League West of Scotland
Formed 1931
Motto
Ground Dunterlie Park, Barrhead, G78 1AA
Tel
Capacity c 3000
Colours Sky Blue and White
Secretary Jim Hannigan
Contact ARTHURLIE@WOSFL.CO.UK
Nickname Lie

Club Ashfield (F, S)

League West of Scotland
Formed 1886
Motto
Ground Peugeot Ashfield Stadium, G22 6RU
Tel 07703 759604
Capacity c 5000
Colours Black and White
Contact ASHFIELD@WOSFL.CO.UK
Nickname

Club Auchinleck Talbot (L F S)

League West of Scotland
Formed 1909
Motto
Ground Beechwood Park, KA18 2AR
Tel
Capacity 3000
Colours Black and Gold
Secretary Henry Dumigan
Contact henry.dumigan@sky.com
Nickname Bot

Club Banchory St Ternan

League North Juniors
Secretary Ms Wendy Sadler
Tel: 07817653741
Email wendysadler@hotmail.co.uk
Ground Milton Park, Crathes, AB31 5QH
Capacity 800
Colours Blue
Founded 1992
Nickname Saints

Club Banks o' Dee (L F A S)

League North Junior Super League
Formed 1902
Ground Spain Park, Aberdeen, AB12 3AB
Tel 01244 893333 (Ground)
Capacity 1500
Colours Dark Blue / Light Blue
Secretary Thomas Ewen
secretary@banksodeefc.co.uk
Nickname Rechabites
Turned down an invitation to join the Highland League for 2019/20

Club Bathgate Thistle (F S)

League East of Scotland
Formed 1937
Motto
Ground Creamery Park, EH48 2BW
Tel

Capacity 2500
Colours Blue and White
Secretary Robert Napier
Tel 07864 071506
Nickname

Club Beith
League West of Scotland
Formed 1938
Motto
Ground Bellsdale Park, KA15 2AF
Tel
Capacity 2500
Colours Black and White
Secretary Chris Irving (07787297348)
Nickname The Cabes, or The Mighty

Club Bellshill Athletic
League West of Scotland
Formed 1897
Motto Here We Go
Ground Rockburn Park, ML4 3EU
Tel
Capacity c 1000
Colours Black and Gold
Secretary Brian Closs
Nickname

Club Benburb (F A S)
League West of Scotland
Formed 1900
Motto Nihil Sine Labore
Ground New Tinto Park, Govan G51 4XG
Tel 0141 445 5148
Capacity c 1500
Colours Blue and White
Secretary Frank Lovering
Nickname Chooky Hens, Bens
Benburb are a registered Community Interest Company.

Club Berwick Rangers (L F S)
League Lowland League
Formed 1884
Ground Shielfield Park, Tweedmouth, TD15 2EF
Tel 01289 307424
Capacity 4099
Colours Black and Gold
Secretary Dennis McCleary
d.mccleary133@btinternet.com
Nicknames Rangers, Borderers

Club Blackburn United (L F A)
League East of Scotland
Formed 1978
Ground New Murrayfield Park, Blackburn, EH47 7LL
Tel 07540434899 (Sec Mob)
Capacity c1000
Colours Black and White
Secretary Paul Meechan
pgmeechan@yahoo.co.uk
Nickname Burnie
No connection with former Junior club New Blackburn Athletic

Club Blairgowrie Juniors
League Midlands
Secretary Mr Martin Mackay
Tel 07858089312
Email martin.mackay2@googlemail.com
Ground Davie Park, Rattray, Blairgowrie, PH10 7BJ
Capacity 1200
Colours Royal Blue
Formed 1946
Nickname Berrypickers, Blair

Club Blantyre Victoria (S)
League West of Scotland
Formed 1889
Motto
Ground Castle Park, Blantyre, G72 0JL Sponsor name, KG Stadium)
Tel
Capacity c 1500
Colours Blue and White
Secretary Duncan Sinclair (07831327483)
Nickname Vics

Club Bonar Bridge
League North Caledonian
Founded 1968
Secretary Carrie Vetters
Tel 07799211753
Email vetters.linside@gogglemail.com
Ground Migdale Playing Field, Bonar Bridge
Colours Green

Club Bo'ness Athletic (F A)
League East of Scotland
Formed 1985 (as Linlithgow Thistle)
Motto
Ground Newtown Park, Bo'ness, EH51 0JX
Tel
Capacity 2000
Colours Blue and White
Secretary Derek Oliver
Tel 07802 758333
Nickname

Club Bo'ness United (F A L)
League East of Scotland
Formed 1945
Ground Newtown Park, Bo'ness, EH51 0DP
Tel 01506 822313 (Ground)
07545347577 (Sec Mob)
Capacity 2000
Colours Blue
Secretary Chris Veitch
dchrisveitchbufc@gmail.com
Nickname BU

Club Bonnyrigg Rose Athletic (F L)
League Lowland League
Formed 1890
Ground New Dundas Park, Bonnyrigg, EH19 3AE
Tel 07762268986 (Sec Mob)
Capacity 2500
Colours Red and White
Secretary Robert Dickson
rob.dickson226@btinternet.com
Nickname Rose

Club Bonnyton Thistle (F A)
League West of Scotland
Formed 1912
Ground Harriet Road, Kilmarnock, KA3 1BB (Synergy Arena)
Tel 07594358268 (Sec Mob)
Capacity 500
Colours Black and Red
Secretary Neil Wilson
mrneil.wilson7@btinternet.com
Nickname

Club Brechin City (F L S)
League Highland
Ground Glebe Park, Brechin
Capacity 4083
Tel 01356 622856
Secretary TBC
E Mail secretary@brechincityfc.com
Colours Red
Nickname City

Club Brechin Victoria (S)
League Midlands
Secretary Mr Clark Crighton
Tel 07512206416
Email c.crighton1@yahoo.com
Ground Victoria Park (aka Nursery Park), Brechin, DD9 7EY
Capacity 800
Colours Red with Black trim
Formed 1917

Club Bridge of Don Thistle (F S)
League North Juniors
Secretary Ms Samantha Errington
Tel: 07931822581
Email samantha.errington@uniconn.co.uk
Ground Aberdeen Sports Village, AB24 5RU
Capacity 400
Colours Blue
Founded 1983

Club Brora Rangers (F L S)
League Highland
Formed 1878
Ground Dudgeon Park, Brora
Tel 07721 940938 (Sec Mob)
Capacity 2000
Colours Red and White
Secretary Kevin Mackay
brorarangers@highlandleague.com
Nickname Cattachs

Club Broomhill FC (F A L S)
Changed name from BSC Glasgow, Summer 2021
League Lowland
Formed 2014
Ground Recreation Park, Alloa, FK10 1RY
Tel 01259 219596 (Alloa FC)
Capacity 2500
Colours Yellow and Blue
Secretary George Fraser
Nickname
Hope to obtain a ground in the Glasgow area in the not too distant future

Broughty Athletic (F,A)
League Midlands
Secretary Mr Willie Henderson
Tel 07565477146
Email wh515191@ncr.com
Ground Whitton Park, Dundee, DD5 1LG
Capacity 1200
Colours Red
Formed 1922
Nickname The Fed

Club Broxburn Athletic (F A L)
League East of Scotland
Formed 1948
Ground Albyn Park, Broxburn, EH52 5BY
Tel 01506 858057 (Ground)
Capacity 3000
Colours Red and White
Secretary Jim Provan
jamesprovan@hotmail.com
Nickname Badgers
Broxburn renewed their artificial playing surface during the early part of 2020.

Club BSC Glasgow (Broomhill SC) (F A)
League West of Scotland
Formed
Ground Springburn Park, Glasgow, Broomfield Rd, Glasgow G21 3UQ
Tel 0141 339 3606 (Club)
0141 557 1692 (Pitch)
Capacity 500
Colours Blue and Yellow
Secretary
E Mail mail@bscglasgow.co.uk
Nickname

Club Buchanhaven Hearts
League North Juniors
Secretary Mr Graeme Mackie
Tel 07950974466
Email graeme@billmackieengltd.co.uk
Ground Raemoss Park, Peterhead, AB41 1UB
Capacity 1000
Colours Maroon
Founded 1908
Nickname Hearties

Club Buckie Rovers
League North Junior
Ground Merson Park, Buckie, AB56 1DS
Capacity 800
Colours Black and White
Founded 1889
Club in abeyance for 2021/2

Club Buckie Thistle (L F S)
League Highland
Formed 1889
Ground Victoria Park, Buckie, AB56 1BY
Tel 01542 831946
Capacity 5000
Colours Green and White
Secretary David Pirie
buckiethistle@highlandleague.com
Nickname Jags

Club Bunillidh Thistle
League North Caledonian
Founded 1970
Secretary Billy Cowie
Tel 01431 821326
Email billycowie@hotmail.co.uk
In abeyance for 2021/2

Club Burghead Thistle
League North Junior
Secretary Mr Andrew Gordon
Tel 07717478279
Email agordon314@btinternet.com
Ground Forest Park, Burghead, IV30 5YJ
Capacity 800
Colours Green
Founded 1889

Club Burntisland Shipyard (F L)
League East of Scotland
Formed 1925
Ground Shipyard Recreation Ground, KY3 0JG
Tel 07856 728634 (Sec Mob)
Capacity 2000
Colours White and Black
Secretary Andrew Beveridge
abeveridge.shipyard@sky.com
Nickname Shippy
Floodlights were expected to be installed in time for 2021/2

Club Caledonian Braves (L A F S)
League Lowland
Formed 2014
Ground Alliance Park, Bothwellhaugh, ML1 3RB
Tel (Club) 0033183757293
Capacity 800
Colours Blue and White
Secretary Chris Ewing
c.ewing@edusportacademy.com
Nickname
First team play in Lowland League, Reserve team play in South of Scotland League

Club Cambuslang Rangers
League West of Scotland
Formed 1899
Motto
Ground Somervell Park, Cambuslang, G72 7EB
Tel
Capacity c 2500
Colours Blue and White
Secretary
Nickname Lang

Club Camelon Juniors (F L S)
League East of Scotland
Formed 1920
Ground Carmuirs Park, Camelon, FK1 4NP
Tel 01324 638060 (Ground)
07739984264 (Sec Mob)
Capacity 2500
Colours Red and White
Secretary Allan Morrison
Tel 07505 354012
E Mail info@camelonjuniors.co.uk
Nickname Mariners
Camelon have applied for grant funding to install an artificial pitch

Club Campbeltown Pupils
League West of Scotland
Formed 1919
Motto
Ground Kintyre Park, PA28 6JT
Tel 01555 751384
Capacity c. 1500
Colours Blue and White
Secretary Campbell Robertson
Tel 07429000409
Nickname

Club Carluke Rovers (F A)
League West of Scotland
Formed 1887
Motto
Ground John Cumming Stadium, ML8 4EA
Tel 01555 751384
Capacity c. 1500
Colours Blue and White
Secretary Tracey Cranston
Nickname The Jam Town

Club Carnoustie Panmure
League Midlands
Secretary Mr Mark Johnson
Tel 07825993608
Email cpfcgenmanager@outlook.com
Ground Laing Park, Carnoustie, DD7 7QX
Capacity 1500
Colours Red and White
Founded 1936
Nickname The Gowfers

Club Civil Service Strollers (L F S)
League Lowland
Formed 1908
Ground Christie Gillies Park, Edinburgh, EH4 5EJ
Tel 0131 332 1175
07802 916832 (Sec Mob)
Capacity 2000
Colours Red
Secretary Keith Stewart
stewartykl@gmail.com
Nickname Strollers, Civvy

Club Clachnacuddin (L F S)
League Highland
Formed 1886
Ground Grant Street Park, Inverness, IV3 8DR
Tel 07810 798607 (Sec Mob)
Capacity 1500
Colours Black and White
Secretary Scott Dowling
clachnacuddin@highlandleague.com
Nickname Clach

Club Clydebank (L F A)
League West of Scotland
Formed 2003
Motto Labor Et Scientia
Ground Holm Park, G81 1LX
Tel
Capacity c. 2000
Colours White, Red and Black
Secretary Matt Bamford
Nickname Bankies, Paper Hankies

Club Coldstream (L F)
League East of Scotland
Formed 1895
Motto Nulli Secundus
Ground Home Park, Coldstream, TD12 4DT
Tel 01890 883085
07879 682360 (Sec Mob)
Capacity c1500
Colours Blue
Secretary Brian Balmbro
Brian.balmbro@btinternet.com
Nickname Streamers

Club Colony Park Juniors
League North Junior
Secretary Mr Douglas Benzie
Tel 07712240583
Email dbenzie14150@gmail.com
Ground Colony Park, Inverurie, AB51 4SG
Capacity 1200
Colours Red and Black
Founded 1978

Club Coupar Angus
League Midlands
Secretary Ms Gillian McColl
Tel 07874364722
Email gmccoll06@tiscali.co.uk
Ground Foxhall Park, Coupar Angus, PH13 9AN
Capacity 800
Colours Black and Red Stripes
Founded: 1935
Nickname Coupar

Club Craigmark Burntonians
League West of Scotland
Formed 1946
Motto
Ground Station Park, Dalmellington, KA6 7SJ
Tel
Capacity c. 1500
Colours Red and White
Secretary
Nickname

Club Craigroyston
League East of Scotland
Formed 1976
Motto S'Rioghal Mo Dhream
Ground St Marks Park, Edinburgh, EH7 4HN
Tel 07512176751 (Sec Mob)
Capacity 1000
Colours Blue and Yellow
Secretary Billy Reilly
craigroystonfootballclub@gmail.com
Nickname Craigie

Club Creetown (F)
League South of Scotland
Formed 1905
Ground Castle Cary Park, Creetown, DG8 7BX
Tel 07806213406 (Sec Mob)
Capacity 300
Colours Yellow and Black
Secretary Larry Stanley
Larry667stanley@btinternet.com
Nickname Ferrytoun

Club Crossgates Primrose
League East of Scotland
Formed 1926
Ground Humbug Park, Crossgates, KY4 8AT
Tel 07896 337729 (Sec Mob)
Capacity 1500
Colours Blue and Yellow
Secretary Frazer Martin
Primrose.secretary@gmail.co.uk
Nickname Primrose

Club Cruden Bay
League North Juniors
Secretary Mr Graham Heddle
Tel 07876340139
Email graham.heddle@yahoo.co.uk
Ground Watson Park, Cruden Bay, AB42 0PJ
Capacity 800
Colours Purple
Founded 1934

Club Culter JFC
League North Junior
Secretary Mr David Thomson
Tel 07902592272
Email dave.thomson@rocketmail.com
Ground Corbie Park, Peterculter, AB14 0XB
Colours Red and White
Founded 1891

Club Cumbernauld Colts (L F A S)
League Lowland
Formed 1969
Ground Broadwood Stadium, Cumbernauld, G68 9NE
Tel 07798646110
Capacity 7936
Colours Yellow and Blue
Secretary Stewart McKenzie
stewart.mckenzie@ggc.scot. nhs.uk
Nickname Colts

Club Cumbernauld United
League West of Scotland
Formed 1964
Motto
Ground Guy's Meadow, G67 2SA
Tel 07977 497605
Capacity c. 1000
Colours Maroon and Sky Blue
Chairman George Watson
Nickname

Club Cumnock (L F A)
League West of Scotland
Formed 1912
Motto
Ground Townhead Park, Cumnock
Tel 01290 426156
Capacity c. 2000
Colours Black and White
Secretary Jamie Campbell (07545 882291)
Nickname Nock

Club Dalbeattie Star (L F S)
League Lowland
Formed c1900
Ground Islecroft Stadium, Dalbeattie, DG5 4HE
Tel 07860 549444 (Match Sec Mobile)
Capacity c1500
Colours Red and Black
Secretary Robert Geddes
bob.solwaypressservices@gmail.com
Nickname Star

Club Dalkeith Thistle (L F)
League East of Scotland
Formed 1892
Ground King's Park, Dalkeith, EH22 3BA
Tel 07762550391 (Sec Mob)
Capacity 1500
Colours Black and White
Secretary Duncan Purdie
dunx1892@gmail.com
Nickname Jags

Club Dalry Thistle
League West of Scotland
Formed 1920
Motto
Ground Merksworth Park, KA24 4BA
Tel
Capacity c. 2000
Colours Blue and White
Secretary
Nickname

Club Darvel (L F S)
League West of Scotland
Formed 1889
Motto
Ground Recreation Park, KA17 0HA
Tel
Capacity c. 2500
Colours Blue and White
Secretary Lesley Gibson
Nickname Vale

Club Deveronside (F A)
League North Junior
Secretary Ms Linda Legge
Tel 07840073441
Email admin@prsct.org
Ground Myrus Centre, Macduff, AB44 1AA
Capacity 300
Colours Black and White
Founded 1977

Club Deveronvale (L F S)
League Highland
Formed 1938
Ground Princess Royal Park, Banff, AB45 1AZ
Tel 01261 818303
Capacity 5000
Colours Red
Secretary Stewart McPherson
deveronvale@highlandleague.com
Nickname Vale

Club Downfield (S)
League Midlands
Secretary Mr Ryan Marr
Tel 07584630042
Email ryanmarr12e@gmail.com
Ground Downfield Park, Dundee

Tel 01383 810594
Colours Black and White Hoops
Founded 1912
Nickname The Spiders

Club Drumchapel United (F, A)
League West of Scotland
Formed 2001
Motto
Ground Donald Dewar Centre, G15 8SX
Tel 0141 276 0774
Capacity c. 500
Colours Red and Black
Secretary Scott Bland
Nickname

Club Dufftown
League North Junior
Secretary Ms Susan Farrell
Tel 07745178435
Email farrell294@btinternet.com
Ground Westburn Park, Dufftown, AB55 4AW
Capacity 1500
Colours Green and Black
Founded 1890

Club Dunbar United (F, L)
League East of Scotland
Formed 1925
Ground New Countess Park, Dunbar, EH42 1RF
Tel 07736 211340 (Sec Mob)
Capacity 1200
Colours Black and Yellow
Secretary Pamela Munro
Tel 07970 109691
Nickname Seasiders

Club Dundee East Craigie
League Midlands
Secretary Mr Jack Stephenson
Tel 07773582908
Email jakestephenson583@yahoo.co.uk
Ground Craigie Park, Dundee, DD4 7HX
Capacity 2000
Colours Sky Blue and White
Founded 1880

Club Dundee North End (F)
League Midlands
Secretary Mr David Thomson
Tel 07759634854
Email djrs9176@gmail.com
Ground North End Park, Dundee, DD3 8HU
Capacity 2000
Colours Maroon and White
Founded 1896
Nickname The Dokens

Club Dundee St James
League Midlands
Formed
Ground Fairfield Park, Dundee, DD4 8LU
Tel
Capacity 1200
Colours Green and White
Secretary
Tel
Nickname

Club Dundee Violet JFC
League Midlands
Secretary Mr Brian Coutts
Tel (M) 07720443374
Email briancouttsdvjfc@gmail.com
Ground Glenesk Park, Dundee, DD3 6AG
Colours Royal Blue
Founded 1883
Nickname The Pansies

Club Dundonald Bluebell (F, L)
League East of Scotland
Formed 1938
Ground Moorside Park, Dundonald, KY5 0DG
Tel 07725199773 (Sec Mob)
Capacity 1000
Colours Blue
Secretary Allan Halliday
allanhal@gmx.com
Nickname Bell

Club Dunipace (F L A)
League East of Scotland
Formed 1888
Ground Westfield Park, Denny, FK6 5DW
Tel 07850142774 (Sec Mob)
Capacity 1000
Colours Black and White
Secretary John Higgins
Nickname Pace

Club Dyce
League North Junior
Secretary Mr Keith McIntosh
Tel (M) 07787127574
Email keith.mcintosh@raeburns.co.uk
Ground Ian Mair Park, Dyce, AB21 0BA
Capacity 800
Colours Blue and White
Founded 1989, amalgamation of Mugiemoss and Rosslyn Sports

Club East Kilbride (L F A S)
League Lowland
Formed 2010
Motto A Priori
Ground K Park, East Kilbride, G74 2AG
Tel 01355 279204
Capacity c1200
Colours Blue and Gold
Secretary Peter Hickey
hickeyfamily07@blueyonder.co.uk
Nickname Kilby
No connection with East Kilbride Thistle JFC

Club East Kilbride Thistle
League West of Scotland
Formed 1968
Motto Advance and Prosper
Ground Showpark, G74 4HG
Tel 07954 309949 (Peter Kelsall)
Capacity c. 2000
Colours Black and White
Secretary
Nickname EK, The Jags

Club East Stirlingshire (L F A S)
League Lowland
Formed 1881
Ground Falkirk Stadium, FK2 9EE
Tel 01324 618740
Capacity 7937
Colours Black and White
Secretary Andrew Williamson
fceaststirlingshire@gmail.com
Nickname Shire, Shirey-Pirey
LFA

Club Easthouses Lily Miners Welfare (L F S)
League East of Scotland
Formed 1950
Ground Newbattle Complex, EH22 4EW
Tel 07902 908766 (Sec Mob)
Capacity 1500
Colours Red
Secretary David Arthur
Tel 07599 462359
Nickname Hooses

Club Edinburgh College (F A S)
League East of Scotland
Formed
Motto
Ground Oriam (Outside), Heriot Watt University, EH14 4AS
Tel
Capacity 500
Colours Navy Blue
Secretary David Hiddleston
Tel 07803 277671
Nickname

Club Edinburgh South (F)
League East of Scotland
Formed 1969
Motto Vinculum Unitatis
Ground Sharing with Dalkeith Thistle
Capacity 1500
Colours Red
Secretary Neil Hassan
Tel 07525 795788
Nickname South

Club Edinburgh United (S)
League East of Scotland
Formed 1985
Ground Paties Road Stadium, EH14 1JF
Tel 07525349008 (Sec Mob)
Capacity 1200
Colours Black and White
Secretary Kevin Hanratty
juniors@edinburghunitedfc.co.uk
Nickname United
Originally formed as an off-shoot of North Merchiston BC

Club Edinburgh University (L F S)
League Lowland
Formed 1877
Ground East Peffermill, Edinburgh, EH16 5LL
Tel 07889 849577 (Sec Mobile)
Capacity c1500
Colours Dark Blue and Green
Secretary Isaac Watson
football@ed.ac.uk
Nickname Uni

Club Ellon United
League North Junior
Secretary Mr Irvine Morris
Tel 07791026406
Email r.morris645@btinternet.com
Ground The Meadows, Ellon, AB41 9QJ.
Capacity 500
Tel 01358 725162
Colours Red and Black
Founded 1890

Club Fauldhouse United (S)
League East of Scotland
Formed
Motto
Ground Park View, EH47 9JZ
Tel
Capacity 1500
Colours Red and White
Secretary David Huddlestone
Tel 07881 938534
Nickname Hoose

Club Finnart (F)
League West of Scotland
Formed 1979
Motto
Ground Springburn Park, Broomfield Rd, Glasgow G21 3UQ
Tel 0141 557 1692
Capacity 500
Colours Blue
Secretary Brian Blair
E Mail bblair10.bb@gmail.com
Nickname Star
Finnart originate from the Bridgeton area of Glasgow. They hope to develop a ground of their own on Glasgow Green.

Club Forfar United
League Midlands
Secretary Mr Jack Florence
Tel (M) 07899937340
Email jackflorence1969@gmail.com
Ground Guthrie Park, Forfar, DD8 3JD
Capacity 1500
Colours Maroon
Founded 1974 (amalgamation of Forfar EE and Forfar Celtic)

Club Forfar West End
League Midlands
Secretary Mr Jamie Hart
Tel (M) 07905261960
Email forfarwestend1892@hotmail.com
Ground Strathmore Park, Forfar, DD8 1BT
Capacity 1200
Colours Royal Blue
Founded 1903

Club Formartine United (L F S)
League Highland
Formed 1946
Motto Sans Peur
Ground North Lodge Park, Pitmedden, AB41 7PA
Tel 01651 843266
Capacity 2500
Colours Red and White
Secretary Bryan Braidwood
formartineunitedfc@highlandleague.com
Nickname United

Club Forres Mechanics (L F S)
League Highland
Formed 1884
Ground Mosset Park, Forres, IV36 1AU
Tel 01309 675096
Capacity c2000
Colours Yellow and Brown
Secretary David W Macdonald
forresmechanics@highlandleague.com
Nickname Can Cans

Club Forres Thistle
League North Junior
Secretary Mr Dutch Holland
Tel: (M) 07769041876
Email dutchinforres@btinternet.com
Ground Logie Park, ForresIV36 1PH
Capacity 1000
Colours Red
Founded 1906
Nickname Jags

Club Forth Wanderers
League West of Scotland
Formed 1904
Motto
Ground Kingshill Park, Forth, ML11 8AE
Tel
Capacity c. 2000
Colours Red and White
Secretary
Nickname

Club Fort William (L F S)
League Highland
Formed 1984
Ground Claggan Park, Fort William
Tel 01397 698003
Capacity 4000
Colours Amber and Black
Secretary Laura McMorran
fortwilliamfc@highlandleague.com
Nickname Fort

Club Fraserburgh (L F S)
League Highland
Formed 1910
Ground Bellslea Park, Fraserburgh, AB43 9BB
Tel 01346 518444
Capacity 2000
Colours Black and White
Secretary Finlay Noble
fraserburghfc@highlandleague.com
Nickname Broch

Club Fraserburgh United (S)
League North Junior
Secretary Mr Gordon Laird
Tel 07925501113
Email gordonlaird23@aol.com
Ground College Park, Fraserburgh, AB43 9GA
Capacity 1000
Colours Black and Gold
Founded 1976

Club Gala Fairydean Rovers (L F A S)
League Lowland
Formed 2013
Motto Unitas Est Fortitude
Ground Netherdale, Galashiels, TD1 3HE
Tel 07963 728562
Capacity c2500
Colours Black and Red
Secretary Paul Gray
Paul.gray@grfc.co.uk
Nickname Gala, Fairies
Main stand currently out of action due to dilapidation

Club Gartcairn (F A S)
League West of Scotland
Formed 2015
Motto
Ground New MTC Park, Airdrie, ML6 6HB
Tel
Capacity c. 400
Colours Blue and White
Secretary
Nickname Cairn

Club Girvan JFC (L S)
League West of Scotland League
Formed 1947
Motto Weave Industry With Truth
Ground Hamilton Park, Girvan, KA26 9HF
Tel 07759 753425
Capacity 4000
Colours Black and Blue
Secretary Andrew Sinclair
Andrewsinclair35@hotmail.com
Nickname Seasiders
Girvan will require to install floodlights to retain their licence. They have started fund raising and have received planning permission.

Club Glasgow Perthshire
League West of Scotland League
Formed 1890
Motto
Ground Keppoch Park, G22 5HE
Tel
Capacity c. 2000
Colours Black and White
Secretary
Nickname Shire
Although now unconnected to the club, the Glasgow Perthshire Charitable Society, founded in 1835, still provides bursaries for Perthshire students in Glasgow. It also pays grants to elderly Perthshire-born people living in Glasgow.

Club Glasgow United (S)
Formerly Shettleston FC
League West of Scotland
Formed 1903
Motto
Ground Greenfield Park, G32 7JN
Tel 0141-778-6415 (Social Club)
Capacity c. 1800
Colours White
Secretary
Nickname Town

Club Glasgow University (L F A S)
League West of Scotland League
Formed 1877
Ground Excelsior Stadium, Airdrie (for SFA matches), ML6 8QZ
Tel 01236 622000
Capacity 10101
Colours Black and Gold
Secretary Donald Fergusson
donniefergusson@aol.com
Nickname Students, Uni

Club Glenafton Athletic
League West of Scotland
Formed 1930
Motto
Ground Loch Park, New Cumnock, KA18 4AE
Tel
Capacity c. 2500
Colours Red and White
Secretary John Stewart
Twitter @johnstewart9
Nickname Glens

Club Glenrothes (S)
League East of Scotland League
Formed 1964
Ground Warout Stadium, KY7 4JY
Tel 07941074517 (Sec Mob)
Capacity 5000
Colours Red and White
Secretary Robbie Penman
Tel 07941 074517
Robbie.penman@hotmail.com
Nickname The Glens

Club Glentanar
League North Junior
Secretary Mr Finlay Ross
Tel (M) 07584960174
Email finlayross1@gmail.com
Ground Woodside Sports Complex, Aberdeen, AB24 2UL
Capacity 1000
Tel 01224 276141
Colours Blue and Yellow
Founded 1978

Club Glenvale (F A)
League West of Scotland
Formed 1967
Motto
Ground Ferguslie Park Sports Centre, Paisley
Tel
Capacity BCD at start of 2021/2
Colours Dark Blue
Secretary
Contact 07880708998
Nickname

Club Golspie Sutherland (L F)
League North Caledonian League
Formed 1877
Ground King George V Park, Golspie, KW10 6SN
Tel 07774 913946 (Sec Mob)
Capacity 1000
Colours Royal Blue
Secretary James Urquhart
email@jamesurquhart.co.uk
Nickname

Club Greenock (F S)
League West of Scotland
Formed 1956
Ground Ravenscraig Stadium
Tel
Capacity c. 4000
Colours Red
Secretary Kyle Wilson
Nickname

Club Gretna FC 2008 (L F A S)
League Lowland
Formed 2008
Ground Raydale Park, Gretna, DG16 5AP
Tel Sec Mob 07902 826124
Capacity c1500
Colours Black and White
Secretary Kevin Smith
kevinsmith@gretnafc2008.co.uk
Nickname Black and Whites
Gretna installed an artificial playing surface during the Summer of 2021

Club Haddington Athletic (F L)
League East of Scotland
Formed 1939
Ground Millfield Park, Haddington, EH41 4DB
Tel 01620 826547 (Ground)
Capacity 1200
Colours Maroon and white
Secretary Tom Thornton
Tel 07878 333586
E Mail T_Thornton_2006@yahoo.co.uk
Nickname Hi Hi

Club Halkirk United (F)
Founded 1993
Secretary William Manson
Tel 01847 831459
Email billy.manson@btopenworld.com
Ground Morrison Park, Halkirk
Colours Red and Black

Club Hall Russell United
League North Junior
Secretary Mr John V. Carroll
Tel (M) 07749673786
Email john@jvcarroll.co.uk
Ground Denmore Park, Bridge of Don, Aberdeen, AB23 8JW
Capacity 1000
Colours Navy Blue
Founded 1968

Club Harthill Royal
League West of Scotland
Formed 1992
Ground Gibbshill Park, Greenrigg, Harthill, ML7 5QQ
Tel
Capacity 1000
Colours Blue
Contact Pat Beattie
E Mail
Nickname

Club Harmony Row (A F S)
League West of Scotland
Formed 1915
Ground Sir Alex Ferguson Park, 8 Row Avenue, Braehead, Glasgow, G51 4SY
Groundsharing at Benburb early in 2021/2
Tel
Capacity
Colours Red
Contact Gary Watt: 07812 368295
Email
HarmonyRowYouthClub@btconnect.com
Nickname

Club Hawick Royal Albert United (L F S)
League East of Scotland
Formed 1947
Ground Albert Park, Hawick, TD9 8AG
Tel 01450 374231
Capacity c2000
Colours Blue and White
Secretary Douglas Purves
Tel 07862 295028
Nickname Albert, Royalists
Amalgamated with Hawick United in 2019
Played several matches at Volunteer Park during 2018/20 due to flooding

Club Heriot Watt University (F A S)
League East of Scotland
Formed 1971
Ground John Brydson Arena, Riccarton, EH14 4AS
Tel 07713283803 (Sec Mob)
Capacity c600
Colours Yellow and Blue
Secretary Aonghas Sellar
E-mail footballdevelopment@hw.ac.uk
Tel 07713 283803
Nickname Watt
Occasionally play games at the indoor ORIAM arena

Club Hermes (F)
League North Junior
Secretary Ms Deborah Wallace
Tel (M) 07814288020
Email
deborah.wallace@btinternet.com
Ground Lochside Park, Bridge of Don, Aberdeen, AB23 8JW
Capacity 1000
Colours White
Founded 1968

Club Heston Rovers (F A S)
League South of Scotland
Formed 1978
Ground Palmerston Park, Dumfries, DG2 9BA
Tel 07513969362 (Sec Mob)
Capacity 7620
Colours Black and White
Chairman Alan Watson
Alanwatson67@tiscalo.co.uk
Nickname
Heston opted to take a "year out" and will not play in 2021/2. They said this was due to lack of committee and volunteers. It is not clear if they will return for 2022/3.

Club Hill of Beath Hawthorn (F L)
League East of Scotland
Formed 1975
Motto Strength Through Unity
Ground Keirs Park, Hill of Beath, KY4 8EF
Tel 07926840020 (Sec Mob)
Capacity 2000
Colours Red and White
Secretary Scott Forrest
Tel 07826 840020
E Mail sforrest3@aol.com
Nickname Haws

Club Huntly (F L S)
League Highland
Formed 1928
Ground Christie Park, Huntly, AB54 8JE
Tel 07867 625303
Capacity 1800
Colours Black and Gold
Secretary Alex Turner
huntlyfc@highlandleague.com
Nickname

Club Hurlford United
League West of Scotland
Formed 1938
Motto Pride, Honour, Dignity, Respect
Ground Blair Park, KA1 5BN
Tel
Capacity c. 2500
Colours Red and White
Secretary Clark Nicol
Twitter @clarknicol_
Nickname Ford

Club Invergordon
League North Caledonian
Founded: 1945
Secretary Mandy MacKenzie
Tel 01862 842967
Email
mandy.mackenzie123@btinternet.com
Ground Invergordon Recreation Grounds
Colours White and Blue

Club Inverkeithing Hillfield Swifts (F A)
League East of Scotland
Formed 1996
Ground Dalgety Bay Sports Centre
Capacity 1000
Colours Blue and Yellow
Secretary Ronnie Jamieson
Tel 07976 158155
Nickname Divit, Swifts

Club Inverness Athletic
League North Caledonian
Founded 2016
Secretary Sandy Stephen
Tel 07921570058
Email invernessathleticfc@gmail.com
Ground Arderseir
Colours Royal Blue

Club Inverurie Loco Works (L F S)
League Highland
Formed 1903
Ground Harlaw Park, Inverurie
Tel 07867 625303
Capacity 2500
Colours Black and Red
Secretary Billy Thomson
inverurielocoworksfc@highlandleague.com
Nickname Locos

Club Irvine Meadow XI (L F S)
League West of Scotland
Formed 1904
Motto
Ground Meadow Park, KA12 0TW
Tel (01294) 274459
Capacity c. 4000
Colours Blue and White
Secretary Lyn McFarlane (07854767062)
Nickname Medda

Club Irvine Victoria
League West of Scotland
Formed 1904
Motto Conatus Metu
Ground Victoria Park, KA12 8PG
Tel
Capacity c. 1200
Colours Black and Orange
Secretary David Loach (07969486913)
Nickname Vics, The Westenders

Club Islavale
League North Junior
Secretary Mr David Roberts
Tel: (M) 07929444254
Email
david1955roberts@gmail.com
Ground Simpson Park, Keith, AB55 5EP
Capacity 800
Colours Red and Black
Founded 1949

Club Jeanfield Swifts (F L)
League East of Scotland
Formed 1928
Ground Riverside Stadium, Perth, PH1 3BG
Capacity 1200
Colours Black and White
Secretary Scott Cummings
Tel 07795 168931
Nickname Swifts

Club Johnstone Burgh
League West of Scotland
Formed 1956
Motto Gang Forward
Ground James Y Keanie Park, PA5 9PE
Tel
Capacity c. 5000
Colours Red and White
Secretary Ricky Cantwell (07719 323744)
Nickname Burgh

Club Keith (F L S)
League Highland
Formed 1910
Ground Kynoch Park, Keith, AB55 5EN
Tel 01542 882629
Capacity 4000
Colours Maroon and Sky Blue
Secretary Fiona Simpson
keithfc@highlandleague.com
Nickname Maroons

Club Kello Rovers
League West of Scotland
Formed 1903
Ground Nithside Park, Kirkconnel, DG4 6NB
Capacity c. 2000
Colours Black and White
Secretary
Nickname Nithsiders

Club Kennoway Star Hearts (F)
League East of Scotland
Formed 2013 (Merger of Star Hearts and Kennoway Ams)
Motto Together We Succeed
Ground Treaton Park, Star of Markinch, KY7 6LZ
Tel 07885 439172 (Sec Mob)
Capacity c.1500
Colours Blue / Maroon
Secretary Steven Black
sb010a1792@blueyounder.co.uk
Nickname Budgies

Club Kilbirnie Ladeside

League West of Scotland
Formed 1901
Motto Timor No Inimicus
Ground Valefield, KA25 6HR
Tel
Capacity 2500
Colours Black and Gold
Secretary Gordon Ronney
E Mail info@kilbirnieladesidefc.co.uk
Nickname Blasties

Club Kilsyth Athletic (A F)

League West of Scotland
Formed 1999
Motto
Ground Kilsyth Sports Field, Garrell Road, Kilsyth, G65 9JX
Tel
Capacity 300
Colours Blue
Secretary
E Mail enquiries@kilsythathletic.co.uk
Nickname

Club Kilsyth Rangers

League West of Scotland
Formed 1945
Motto
Ground Duncansfield, G65 9JX
Tel
Capacity c. 5000
Colours Blue and White
Secretary William Dunbar
Nickname

Club Kilwinning Rangers (F S)

League West of Scotland
Formed 1899
Motto
Ground Kilwinning Sports Club, KA13 6LF
Tel 01294 556 444
Capacity c. 2000
Colours Blue and White
Secretary Charlie Brown
Nickname Buffs

Club Kinnoull

League East of Scotland
Formed 1943
Ground Tulloch Park, Perth, PH
Tel 07783 809049 (Sec Mob)
Capacity c.1000
Colours Red and White
Secretary Paul Carnegie
Tel 07753 756999
E Mail secretary@kinnoullfc.co.uk
Nickname Noull

Club Kirkcaldy and Dysart

League East of Scotland
Formed 1970 (as Kirkcaldy YM)
Motto Place of the Hard Fort
Ground Alex Penman Park, Kirkcaldy (aka Denfield Park), KY1 2ER
Tel 07963 437455 (Sec Mob)
Capacity c.1200
Colours Red and Black
Secretary Stewart Wilson
Tel 07941 345179
Nickname YM

Club Kirkintilloch Rob Roy

League West of Scotland
Formed 1884
Motto
Ground Sharing with Cumbernauld United
Tel
Capacity c. 1000
Colours Black and Red
Secretary Jim Black
E Mail jimblack@robroy.org.uk
Nickname Rabs, Roy

Club Kirriemuir Thistle (S)

League Midlands
Secretary Mrs Leesa Collie
Tel 07928418347
Email stephen.collie@sky.com
Ground Westview Park, Kirriemuir, DD8 5LG, Tel 01575 572722
Capacity 1500
Colours Royal Blue
Founded 1921
Nickname Kirrie

Club Lanark United

League West of Scotland
Formed 1920
Motto
Ground Moor Park, ML11 9BG
Tel 01555 663796
Capacity c. 2500
Colours Blue and White
Secretary
Nickname Yowes

Club Largs Thistle (A S)

League West of Scotland
Formed 1890
Motto
Ground Barrfields, KA30 8NN
Tel
Capacity c. 3000
Colours Yellow and Black
Secretary David Blackwood
E Mail david94blackwood@gmail.com
Telephone: 07711764530
Nickname

Club Larkhall Thistle

League West of Scotland
Formed 1878
Motto
Ground Gasworks Park, ML9 1AJ
Tel
Capacity c. 2500
Colours Red and White
Secretary
Nickname Thistle

Club Leith Athletic (F A)

League Lowland
Formed 1996
Motto Persevere
Ground Peffermill 3G, EH16 5LL
Capacity c500
Colours Black and White
Secretary Jim Gardiner
Tel 07810 832991
E Mail jimgardiner1@sky.com
Nickname
No formal connection with earlier club of same name
In 2019/20 and 2020.1 Leith used the second (newer) artificial pitch at Peffermill. Previously they had used the main artificial pitch. They intend to play at Meadowbank Stadium from some time in 2021/2.

Club Lesmahagow

League West of Scotland
Formed 1885
Motto In Friendship
Ground Craighead Park, ML11 0HE
Tel
Capacity c. 5000
Colours Red and White
Secretary Andrew Irving
E Mail irvandr4@aol.com
Nickname Gow

Club Letham (F A)

League Midlands
Formed 1960
Ground Seven Acres Park, Perth, PH1 2JB
Capacity 300
Colours Yellow
Secretary Jon Kidd
E Mail enquiries@lethamfc.com
Nickname

Club Linlithgow Rose (L F S)

League East of Scotland
Formed 1889 (more likely 1898)
Ground Prestonfield, Linlithgow, EH49 6HF
Tel 01506 842108
Capacity 2500
Colours Maroon and White
Secretary Derek Crossan
Tel 07885 468172
E Mail derek.crossan@hotmail.co.uk
Nickname Rosey-Posey, Gallant

Club Livingston United

League East of Scotland
Formed 1970
Motto
Ground Station Park, Deans, EH54 8DT
Tel
Capacity 1500
Colours Black and White
Secretary Scott Burgess
07747 195312
Nickname Livi

Club Lochar Thistle (F A)

League South of Scotland
Formed 1969
Ground North West Community Campus, Dumfries, DG2 9LU

Tel 07828160408 (Sec Mob)
Capacity 600
Colours Red and Black
Secretary Russell Caskie
r.caskie@btinternet.com
Nickname

Club Lochee Harp (F A)
League Midlands
Secretary Mr Mark Duffy
Tel (M) 07454020098
Email markduffy.1@hotmail.com
Ground Lochee Community Sports Hub, DD2 3NY
Capacity 500
Colours Green and White
Founded 1904

Club Lochee United
League Midlands
Secretary Mr Marc Stanton
Tel 07830144788
Email Marcstanton67@hotmail.com
Ground Thomson Park, Lochee, Dundee, DD2 2SJ
Capacity 2000
Colours Royal Blue
Founded 1924
Nickname The Bluebells

Club Lochgelly Albert
League East of Scotland
Formed 1926
Motto By Industry We Prosper
Ground Gardiners Park, Lochgelly
Capacity c.3000
Colours Black and Yellow
Secretary Ian Patrick
Tel 07740 982985
E Mail Ipatrick1926@gmail.com
Nickname Berts

Club Loch Ness
League North Caledonian
Founded 1999
Secretary Shane Carling
Tel 07539 993230
Email lochnessfc@gmail.com
Ground Canal Park, Inverness / The Bught, Inverness
Colours Silver and Gold

Club Lochore Welfare
League East of Scotland
Formed 1934
Ground Central Park, Crosshill
Capacity c.1200
Colours Black and White
Secretary Tom Graham
Tel 07900 025180
E Mail Tamgraham1966@gmail.com
Nickname Welfare

Club Lochmaben
League South of Scotland
Formed 1972
Ground Whitehills Park, Lochmaben, DG11 1QP
Tel 075726249496 (Sec Mob)
Capacity 1000
Colours Black and Yellow
Secretary George Trudt
Nickname

Longside (F)
League North Junior
Secretary Mr Gavin Davidson
Tel 07748558461
Email gavin.davidson23@gmail.com
Ground Davidson Park, Longside, AB42 4GR
Capacity 1000
Colours Red and Black
Founded 1933

Club Lossiemouth (L F S)
League Highland
Formed 1945
Ground Grant Park, IV31 6JG
Tel 01343 813717
Capacity 2400
Colours Red and White
Secretary Alan McIntosh
lossiemouthfc@highlandleague.com
Nickname Lossie, Coasters

Club Lothian Thistle Hutchison Vale (L F A S)
League East of Scotland
Formed 1969
Ground Ainslie Park, Edinburgh, EH5 2HF
Tel 07730 256 783 (Sec Mobile)
Capacity 3000
Colours Black and Gold
Secretary Tom Allison
Tel 07730 256783
tom@lothianthistlefc.co.uk
Nickname Hutchie

Club Lugar Boswell Thistle
League West of Scotland
Formed 1878
Motto
Ground Rosebank Park, Lugar, KA18 3LT
Tel
Capacity c.1500
Colours Maroon
Secretary Derek Montgomery
Tel: 07824598533
Nickname Jaggy Bunnets

Club Luncarty
League East of Scotland
Formed 1886
Ground Brownlands Park, Luncarty
Tel 07921 662332 (Sec Mob)
Capacity c.1000
Colours Black and Gold
Secretary Gregor Walker
luncartfootballclub@gmail.com
Nickname Bleachers

Club Maryhill (F)
League West of Scotland
Formed 1884
Motto
Ground Lochburn Park, Glasgow, G20 9AQ
Tel 0141 946 8850 (Social Club)
Capacity c. 2500
Colours Black and Red
Secretary Jeff Holmes
Nickname Hill

Club Maud
League North Junior
Secretary Mr Graham Lawson
Tel (M) 07825585524
Email maudjfc@aol.com
Ground Maud Pleasure Park, Maud, AB42 4NP
Capacity 1000
Colours Red
Founded 1973

Club Maybole
League West of Scotland
Formed 1946
Motto Forward to Victory
Ground Ladywell Stadium, KA19 7AZ
Tel
Capacity c. 2000
Colours Maroon and White
Chairman Mr Alex Meek
Tel: (H) 01655 883419
Nickname

Club Mid Annandale (F A)
League South of Scotland
Formed 1959
Ground King Edward Park, Lockerbie, DG11 2BL
Tel 07841512287 (Sec Mob)
Capacity 1000
Colours Black and Yellow
Secretary Peter Carruthers
Nickname Mids

Montrose Roselea (F A S)
League North Junior
Secretary Mr Roy Gill
Tel 07908763219
Email: gill.fin@btinternet.com
Ground Links Park, Montrose, DD10 8QD.
Capacity 4000
Games may be played at Broomfield Park on occasions
Colours Green

Club Muirkirk
League West of Scotland
Formed 1937
Motto
Ground Burnside Park, KA18 3RE
Tel
Capacity c. 1600
Colours Royal Blue and White
Secretary Billy Tait
Twitter @TaitBilly
Nickname Kirk

Club Musselburgh Athletic (F L)
League East of Scotland
Formed 1934
Ground Olive Bank, EH21 6QA
Tel 0131 653 3319 (Ground)
Capacity 1500
Colours Blue and White
Secretary Kennie Scott
Tel 07925 188222
Email kenniescott68@aol.com
Nickname Burgh

Club Nairn County (F L S)
League Highland
Formed 1914
Ground Station Park, IV 12 5LT
Tel 01667 454298
Capacity 3000
Colours Black and Yellow
Secretary Ian Finlayson
nairncountyfc@highlandleague.com
Nickname County

Club Nairn County "A"
League North Caledonian
Secretary Graeme Macleod
Tel 07970 064235
Email
graeme.macleod@hotmail.co.uk
Ground Riverside Park, Nairn

Nairn St Ninian
League North Junior
Secretary Mr Derek Davidson
Tel 07743165525
Email
derekdavidson789@btinternet.com
Ground Showfield, Nairn IV12 4QL, may be unsuitable for some Cup ties
Capacity 1000
Colours Maroon
Founded 1968
Nickname Saints

Club Neilston
League West of Scotland
Formed 1945
Motto
Ground Brig O' Lea Stadium, G78 3LB
Tel
Capacity c. 2500
Colours Red and White
Secretary Mark Kirkland
Twitter @thekirklands51
Nickname Farmers Boys

Club Newburgh (S)
League East of Scotland League
Formed 1909
Ground East Shore Park
Tel 07516625033 (Sec Mob)
Capacity c.1600
Colours Black and White
Secretary Graham Strachan
Tel 07516 625033
E Mail secretary@newburghfc.co.uk

Club New Elgin
League North Junior
Secretary Mr George Rose
Tel 07580508190
Email gernejfc@yahoo.co.uk
Ground Nicol Togneri Park, Pinefield, Elgin, IV30 3AF
Capacity 600
Colours Black and Red
Founded 1896

Club Newmachar United
League North Junior
Secretary Mr Brian Johnston
Tel (M) 07740909531
Email n
ewmacharutdjuniorsfc@gmail.com
Ground Charlie Gordon Park, Newmachar, AB21 0QD
Capacity 800
Colours Red and Black
Founded 1987

Club Newmains United
League West of Scotland
Formed 2006
Motto
Ground Victoria Park, ML2 8HF
Tel
Capacity c. 1500
Colours Red
Secretary
E Mail info@newmainsunitedfc.com
Nickname Dahlias

Club Newton Stewart (L F A)
League South of Scotland
Formed 1884
Ground Blairmount Park, DG8 6NU
Tel 07825600725 (Sec Mobile)
Capacity c1000
Colours Black and White
Secretary Gary McKie
gary_mckie@hotmail.co.uk
Nickname Creesiders

Club Newtongrange Star (L F)
League East of Scotland
Formed 1890
Ground New Victoria Park, EH22 4NG
Tel 0131 663 3362 (Ground)
Capacity 2000
Colours Blue and White
Secretary Neil Frankland
Tel 07941 028458
E Mail
secretary@newtongrangestar.org
Nickname Star

Club Nithsdale Wanderers (F)
League South of Scotland
Formed 2001
Ground Lorimer Park, Sanquhar, DG4 6DB
Tel 07795071234
Capacity c1000
Colours Royal Blue
Secretary Bobby Moore
bsbbmoore@btinternet.com
Nickname

Club Oakley United
League East of Scotland
Formed 1964
Ground Blairwood Park, Oakley, KY12 9RA
Tel 07814 059363 (Sec Mob)
Capacity 1500
Colours Maroon and Sky Blue
Secretary Craig Cowan
Tel 07814 059363
E Mail lammymis150@gmail.com
Nickname
Club was preparing to install floodlights in 2021/2

Club Orkney (F)
League North Caledonian
Founded 2012
Secretary Inga Foubister
Tel 01856 741278
Email inga.foubister@btinternet.com
Ground The Rockworks, Holm / Pickaquoy Centre, Kirkwall
Colours Red and Blue

Club Ormiston
League East of Scotland
Formed 1890
Ground New Recreation Park, Ormiston, EH35 5LQ
Capacity c1000
Colours Maroon
Secretary Tom Cuthbert
Tel 07739 850614
E Mail tamcuthbert@blueyonder.co.uk
Nickname Ormy

Club Peebles Rovers (S)
League East of Scotland
Formed 1893
Ground Whitestone Park, Peebles, EH45 8BE
Tel 07446 825751
Capacity c1500
Colours Red and White
Secretary Ian Clark
Tel 07446 825751
E Mail ac70@btinternet.com
Nickname

Club Penicuik Athletic (L F)
League East of Scotland
Formed 1888
Ground Penicuik Park, EH26 9HU
Capacity 1500
Colours Blue and White
Secretary Neil Gordon
Tel 07936 156451
E Mail neil@johnmackayinsurance.co.uk
Nickname Cuiky

Club Petershill (F A S)
League West of Scotland
Formed 1897
Motto
Ground Petershill Park, G21 4DD
Tel 0141 276 8446
Capacity 3000
Colours Maroon and White
Secretary Peter Harding
Nickname Peasy

Club Pollok
League West of Scotland
Formed 1908
Motto
Ground Newlandsfield Park, Glasgow, G43 2XR
Tel 0141 632 4940
Capacity c. 4000
Colours Black and White
Secretary Stuart McCulloch
E Mail info@pollokfc.com
Nickname Lok

Club Port Glasgow (F A)
League West of Scotland
Formed 1899
Motto
Ground Port Glasgow Community Stadium, PA14 6TR
Tel
Capacity c. 1500
Colours Black and White
Secretary Peter Loughlin
Nickname Undertakers

Club Preston Athletic (L F S)
League East of Scotland
Formed 1945
Ground Pennypit Park, Prestonpans, EH32 9JQ
Tel 01875 815221
Capacity c3000
Colours Blue and White
Secretary Lesley Birrell
Tel 07724 091906
E Mail lesleybirrell@aol.com
Nickname Panners

Club Pumpherston
League East of Scotland
Formed 1896 (re formed 1990)
Motto
Ground Recreation Park, EH53 0PE
Tel
Capacity 2000
Colours Orange and Black
Secretary William Rogers
Tel 07786 021303
Nickname Pumphy

Club Renfrew (F A)
League West of Scotland
Formed 1911
Motto
Ground New Western Park, PA4 9EF
Tel
Capacity c. 1500
Colours Blue and White
Secretary Will Johnston
E Mail renfrew1912@hotmail.com
Nickname Frew

Club Rossvale (F A S)
League West of Scotland
Formed 1976
Motto
Ground Petershill Park, G21 4DD
Tel 0141 276 8446
Capacity 3000
Colours Red and Yellow
Secretary Andy Sandilands
E Mail andysandilands@blueyonder.co.uk
Nickname

Club Rosyth (F A)
League East of Scotland
Formed 1992 (formerly Jubilee Athletic)
Ground Fleet Grounds
Capacity c.400
Colours Red and Black
Secretary Alfie Blair
Tel 07727 188293
E Mail alfie.blair@yahoo.co.uk
Nickname Rec

Club Rothes (L F S)
League Highland
Formed 1938
Ground MacKessack Park, AB38 7AD
Tel
Capacity 1731
Colours Black and Tangerine
Secretary Gary Davies
rothesfc@highlandleague.com
Nickname Speysiders

Club Rothie Rovers
League North Junior
Formed
Motto
Ground Rothienorman Playing Field, AB51 8UE
Tel
Capacity 800
Colours Yellow and Blue
Secretary Sandy Rattan
Nickname

Club Royal Albert Athletic
League West of Scotland
Formed 1878
Motto
Ground Tileworks Park, Stonehouse, ML9 3DZ
Tel
Capacity c. 1500
Colours Black and White
Secretary Peter Higgins
Nickname Albert

Club Rutherglen Glencairn (F)
League West of Scotland
Formed 1896
Motto Ex Fumo Fama
Ground Celsius Stadium, G&3 1JH
Tel
Capacity c. 2500
Colours Black and White
Secretary Peter Ferguson
Nickname Glens

Club Saltcoats Victoria
League West of Scotland
Formed 1889
Motto Per Mare Per Terras
Ground Campbell Park, KA21 6AP
Tel
Capacity c. 1500
Colours Brown and Yellow
Secretary Donald Currie
Nickname

Club Sauchie (L F S)
League East of Scotland
Formed 1960
Ground Beechwood Park, FK10 3AX
Tel 07934900920 (Sec Mob)
Capacity 2500
Colours Red and White
Secretary Robert McAdam
rabafmcadam@gmail.com
Nickname

Club Scone Thistle
League Midlands
Secretary Mr Jon Baker Tel: (M) 07984408366
Email secretary@sconethistlefc.org
Ground Farquharson Park, Scone, Perth, PH2 6NT
Capacity 800
Colours Red and Black
Founded 1882

Club Scourie
League North Caledonian
Founded 2020
Secretary Neil Macdonald
Tel 01971 502371
Ground Achlochan Park, Scourie, IV27 4TE
Colours White and Green

Club Spartans (L F A S)
League Lowland
Formed 1951
Ground Ainslie Park, Edinburgh, EH5 2HF
Tel 0131 552 7854
Capacity 2500
Colours White and Red
Secretary John McCabe
macabiteam@hotmail.com
Nickname
A new artificial surface was laid during the Summer of 2020 to replace the one put down ten years earlier.

Club Spey Valley United JFC
League North Juniors
Secretary Mr Graeme Mackie Tel: (M) 07719777125
Email graememackie1@btinternet.com
Ground Cromdale Park, Cromdale, PH26 3LW
Capacity 300
Colours Red
Founded 2016

Club in abeyance for 2021/2

Club St Andrews United

League East of Scotland
Formed 1920
Ground Recreation Park, KY16 8BN
Tel 01334 477365 (Ground)
Capacity 1200
Colours Black and White
Secretary Donald Gellatly
Tel 07714 525489
E Mail donaldgellatly@hotmail.com
Nickname Saints
Floodlights currently being installed (July 2021)

Club St Anthony's

League West of Scotland
Formed 1902
Motto
Ground McKenna Park, Govan, G51 4HU
Tel
Capacity c. 1200
Colours Green and White
Secretary Felix McKenna
Nickname Ants

Club St Cadoc's

League West of Scotland
Formed 1987
Motto
Ground Groundshare with St Anthony's
Tel
Capacity
Colours Red and Black
Secretary
Nickname

Club St Cuthbert Wanderers (L F A)

League South of Scotland
Formed 1879
Ground St Marys Park, Kirkcudbright, DG6 4AW
Tel 07813634787 (Sec Mobile)
Capacity c1000
Colours Blue and White
Secretary Michael McGarrie
michaelmcgarrie@gmail.com
Nickname Saints

Club St Duthus

League North Caledonian
Founded 1885
Secretary Tony Farquhar
Tel 07780 995476
Email committee@stduthusfc.co.uk
Ground Grant Park, Tain, or The Links Tain
Colours Red, White and Black

Club St Peter's

League West of Scotland
Formed 1984
Motto
Ground Sharing with Renfrew FC
Tel
Capacity c. 1000
Colours Red and Black
Secretary
E Mail st.peters.fnc@gmail.com
Nickname

Club St Roch's

League West of Scotland
Formed 1920
Motto
Ground James McGrory Park, G21 4AA
Tel
Capacity c. 2000
Colours Green and White
Secretary Christopher Potter
Nickname Candy

Club Shotts Bon Accord

League West of Scotland
Formed 1950
Motto
Ground Hannah Park, Shotts
Tel 01501 821542 (Social Club)
Capacity c.5000
Colours Maroon and White
Secretary
Nickname Bonny

Club Stirling University EOS (F)

League East of Scotland
Formed 1969
Ground Gannochy Sports Centre, FK9 4LA
Tel 01786 466901
Capacity c1000
Colours Green
Secretary Murray Bushell
Tel 07903 414249
Nickname

Club Stonehaven

League North Junior
Secretary Mr Neale Scott
Tel (M) 07738293966
Email stonehavenjfc@hotmail.co.uk
Ground Glenury Park, Stonehaven, AB39 3LA
Colours Blue
Founded 1919
Nickname The Hive

Club Stoneyburn

League East of Scotland
Formed 1928 (Reformed 1983)
Motto
Ground Beechwood Park, EH47 8AZ
Tel
Capacity 2000
Colours Black and White
Secretary Steven McMillan
Tel 07824 662273
Nickname Fulshie

Club Stoneywood Parkvale

League North Junior
Secretary Mr Brian Hay
Tel (M) 07876258116
Email hayubrian@aol.com
Ground Clark Commercial Park, Dyce, Aberdeen, AB21 9JH
Colours Red and White
Founded 1898 (as Parkvale)

Club Strathspey Thistle (L F S)

League Highland
Formed 1993
Ground Seafield Park, Grantown on Spey, PH26 3HY
Tel 01479 870161
Capacity 2000
Colours Blue, Black and White
Secretary Karen Race
strathspeythistlefc@highlandleague.com
Nickname

Club Stranraer Reserves (F A)

League South of Scotland
Formed 1870
Ground Stranraer Academy
Tel 07711682819 (Contact Mobile)
Capacity
Colours Blue and White
Contact Hilde Law (Secretary)
Nickname

Club Sunnybank

League North Junior
Secretary Ms Lesley Christie
Tel (M) 07709192286
Email lesley.cochrane@hotmail.co.uk
Ground Heathryfold Park, Aberdeen, AB16 7DS
Tel 01224 696309
Capacity 1500
Colours Black and White
Founded 1946
Nickname Bank

Club Syngenta (F A S)

League East of Scotland
Formed 1960 (as ICI Juveniles)
Motto
Ground Ochilview Park, FK5 4QL
Tel
Capacity
Colours Orange and Black
Secretary Ian Hutton
Tel 07414 811249
Nickname The Dyes

Club Tayport

League Midlands
Secretary Mr John Morris
Tel (M) 07889170364
Email johnmorris37@btinternet.com
Ground The Canniepairt, Tayport, DD6 9DX
Capacity 1500
Colours Red and White
Formed 1947

Club Thorniewood United

League West of Scotland
Formed 1924
Motto
Ground Robertson Park, Viewpark, G71 6HG

Tel
Capacity c. 2000
Colours Red and White
Secretary
E Mail thorniewoodunited@gmail.com
Nickname Wood

Club Thornton Hibs
League East of Scotland League
Formed 1935
Ground Memorial Park, Thornton
Capacity c.1500
Colours Green and White
Secretary Graeme Turnbull
Tel 07745 376025
E Mail Tucco2501@gmail.com
Nickname Hibs
Floodlights were being installed at the start of 2021/2

Club Threave Rovers (L F S)
League South of Scotland
Formed 1953
Ground Meadow Park, Castle Douglas, DG7 1DJ
Tel 01556 504536
Capacity c1500
Colours Black and White
Secretary David McMath
mcmathgardenhill@aol.com
Nickname

Club Thurso
League North Caledonian
Founded 1998
Secretary Mark Boulton
Tel 01847 891707
Email markboulton.thursofc@yahoo.co.uk
Ground Sir George's Park, aka The Dammies, KW14 8HN
Colours Red

Club Tranent (L F S)
League East of Scotland
Formed 1911
Motto Lie Forrit
Ground Forresters Park, New Abbey, EH33 1HY
Tel 07765 253706 (Sec Mob)
Capacity 1200
Colours Maroon
Secretary Paul MacGregor
Tel 07765 253706
E Mail pmacgregor@jdennis.com
Nickname Belters

Club Troon
League West of Scotland
Formed 1946
Motto
Ground Portland Park, KA10 6QN
Tel
Capacity c. 2000
Colours Blue and White
Secretary Richard Henderson
Nickname Seasiders, Seagulls

Club Turriff United (L F S)
League Highland
Formed 1954
Ground The Haughs, Turriff, AB53 4ER
Tel 01888 562169
Capacity 1200
Colours Red and Blue
Secretary Philip Napier
turriffunitedfc@highlandleague.com
Nickname

Club Tweedmouth Rangers
League East of Scotland
Formed 2010
Motto Noli Caesum Credentes

Ground Old Shielfield, Tweedmouth, TD15 2EF
Tel 07803 797555 (Sec Mob)
Capacity 1000
Colours Orange and white
Secretary Colin Pike
colinpike598@gmail.com

Club Tynecastle (L F S)
League East of Scotland
Formed 1928
Ground Meggetland, Edinburgh, EH14 1XN
Tel 0131 455 8375 (Ground)
Capacity 3000
Colours Maroon
Secretary Alistair Wilkie
Tel 07889 931054
E Mail alistair@wilkielaw.co.uk
Nickname Tynie

Club University of Stirling (L F S)
League Lowland
Formed 1969
Ground Forthbank Stadium, Stirling, FK7 7UJ
Tel
Capacity 3800
Colours Green
Secretary Chris Geddes
Tel 07739 049047
E Mail Chris.geddes@stir.ac.uk
Nickname Uni

Club Upper Annandale
League South of Scotland
Formed 1966
Ground Moffat Academy, DG10 9QF
Tel 07796273488 (sec Mob)
Capacity c1000
Colours Black and White
Secretary Michael Notman
Nickname Uppers

Club Vale of Clyde
League West of Scotland
Formed 1873
Motto
Ground Fullarton Park, Tollcross, G32 8LD
Tel
Capacity c. 2000
Colours Blue
Secretary
Nickname Tin Pail

Club Vale of Leithen (L F)
League Lowland
Formed 1891
Motto Keep Faith
Ground Victoria Park, Innerleithen, EH44 6RB
Tel 07751 580665
Capacity c1500
Colours Navy and White
Secretary Rob Wilson
E Mail Wilsor84@gmail.com
Nickname Vale

Club Vale of Leven
League West of Scotland
Formed 1939
Motto
Ground Millburn Park, Alexandria, G32 8LD
Tel
Capacity c. 3000
Colours Navy Blue
Secretary Brian Brown
E Mail
brian.brown@scottishwater.co.uk
Nickname Vale

Club West Calder United
League East of Scotland
Formed 1950
Motto
Ground Hermand Park, EH55 8BG
Tel
Capacity 1000
Colours Red and Black
Secretary Robert Anthony
Tel 07881 364297
Nickname Cauther

Club Whitburn (S)
League East of Scotland
Formed 1934
Motto Onward
Ground Central Park, EH47 0RB
Tel
Capacity 2500
Colours Amber and Claret
Secretary Ann Haddow
Tel 07917 753017
Nickname Burn

Club Whitehills
League North Junior
Secretary Ms Sandie Cummings
Tel (M) 07927347072
Email secwfc@gmail.com
Ground School Park, Whitehills, Banffshire AB45 2LT
Colours Red
Founded 1999

Club Whitehill Welfare (L F S)
League Lowland

Formed 1953
Ground Ferguson Park, Roswell, EH24 9DS
Tel 07780 903768 (Sec Mob)
Capacity c1500
Colours Maroon and Sky Blue
Secretary John Quinn
Jockeq1975@gmail.com
Nickname Welfare

Club Whitletts Victoria (F S)
League West of Scotland
Formed 1944
Motto
Ground Dam Park, Ayr, KA8 0ET
Tel
Capacity c. 4000
Colours Red and Black
Secretary John Dalton
E Mail jbd@sky.com
Nickname

Club Wick Academy (L F S)
League Highland
Formed 1893
Ground Harmsworth Park, Wick, KW1 5NH
Tel 07803 667593 (Sec Mob)
Colours Black and White
Secretary Melanie Roger
wickacademyfc@highlandleague.com
Nickname Scorries

Club Wigtown and Bladnoch (L F)
League South of Scotland
Formed 1888
Ground Trammondford Park, Wigtown, DG8 9DY
Tel 07849432008 (Sec Mobile)
Capacity c2000
Colours Red and White
Secretary Kerr Inger
Nickname

Club Wishaw
League West of Scotland
Formed 1885
Motto
Ground The Beltane, ML2 0HL
Tel
Capacity c. 1500
Colours Black and Red
Secretary
Nickname

Club Yoker Athletic (F A)
League West of Scotland
Formed 1886
Motto
Ground Holm Park, G81 1LX
Tel
Capacity c. 2000
Colours Blue
Secretary Sean Roberts (07984028801)
E Mail media@yokerathletic.com
Nickname Whey Ho

PHOTOCARDS

No. 145.

YOKER ATHLETIC F.C.

Left to right, back row:—*W. McLean, W. Milne, H. Scott, A. Fulton. W. Colvin, S. Boyd (Capt.).* Front row:—*T. Ferguson. A. Howie, J. Weir, W. Forbes, R. Wilson.*

One of the most successful seasons of this club was 1930/31, when they won the Scottish Intermediate Cup, Glasgow Charity Cup, Elder Cottage Hospital Cup and were Champions of the Western Intermediate League

Expanding de Luxe Albums for Ardath Photocards on sale at Tobacconists Price 6d

ARDATH TOBACCO CO. LTD. Manufacturers of STATE EXPRESS and ARDATH CIGARETTES

D

The Lowland "Pyramid"

Lowland League 2020/21

LOWLAND LEAGUE 2020-1	BER	BU	BRO	BSC	CAL	CIV	CUM	DAL	EK	ES	EDU	GAL	GRE	KEL	SPA	STI	VAL
Berwick Rangers									Oct 24 0-1	Nov 14 1-3	Oct 27 3-1			Dec 5 0-4		Nov 10 3-2	Oct 10 1-0
Bo'ness United	Nov 7 2-1			Nov 11 4-4	Oct 24 2-0	Oct 28 1-1	Oct 10 2-1					Dec 19 1-2					Oct 14 4-0
Bonnyrigg Rose					Oct 13 2-0	Nov 10 2-0	Oct 31 1-1		Nov 28 2-1		Dec 15 3-0		Oct 17 3-0				Nov 24 5-0
BSC Glasgow	Oct 31 0-0				Jan 1 3-2		Oct 28 4-0	Oct 10 2-1		Nov 25 5-1					Nov 7 3-1	Dec 16 2-1	
Caledonian Braves	Oct 17 0-1					Dec 19 2-2		Oct 27 3-1					Nov 10 0-5	Oct 31 0-1		Nov 14 2-3	Dec 15 9-0
Civil Service Strollers	Nov 24 1-0			Oct 13 0-0							Jan 5 1-1		Nov 14 1-0	Oct 17 2-3		Oct 31 1-0	
Cumbernauld Colts	Dec 19 0-2				Nov 28 0-1	Dec 15 1-1					Oct 24 3-0	Nov 7 0-2		Nov 25 0-2	Dec 4 2-6	Oct 13 1-2	
Dalbeattie Star			Dec 5 1-3							Oct 17 0-4	Nov 14 0-0	Oct 13 2-3	Dec 22 2-2				
East Kilbride		Nov 14 1-1			Nov 24 4-1	Dec 5 2-0						Oct 17 3-0	Oct 13 6-1		Oct 31 2-0		
East Stirlingshire			Nov 7 2-1		Dec 4 3-0	Oct 10 1-0	Nov 11 2-3		Oct 28 0-0			Dec 16 2-2					
Edinburgh University		Oct 17 0-4		Nov 28 0-6	Nov 7 1-2				Dec 19 0-9	Oct 13 0-2			Oct 31 1-0		Nov 24 1-6		
Gala Fairydean Rovers			Oct 10 0-4	Nov 14 2-0		Oct 24 3-1					Nov 10 4-1			Nov 28 1-2	Oct 27 3-1		
Gretna	Nov 28 1-0			Oct 24 0-3											Oct 10 1-2		Nov 7 5-0
Kelty Hearts							Nov 21 5-0	Oct 24 2-0	Nov 7 0-1		Oct 10 4-0		Dec 12 7-0			Dec 19 2-0	Oct 27 4-0
Spartans	Oct 13 1-0		Nov 14 0-2					Nov 28 3-1						Dec 15 0-4		Oct 17 1-3	Nov 10 6-0
Stirling University		Nov 25 3-1	Oct 28 1-1					Nov 7 2-4	Oct 10 1-2	Nov 28 0-3	Dec 26 7-1	Dec 5 2-0					Oct 24 4-1
Vale of Leithen				Oct 17 4-6		Nov 28 0-3	Nov 14 0-4			Oct 31 0-7							

		P	W	D	L	F	A	GD	PT	PPG
1	Kelty Hearts	13	12	0	1	40	4	+36	36	2.77
2	East Kilbride	12	9	2	1	32	6	+26	29	2.42
3	Bonnyrigg Rose Athletic	12	9	2	1	29	6	+23	29	2.42
4	BSC Glasgow	13	9	3	1	38	16	+22	30	2.31
5	East Stirlingshire	12	8	2	2	30	12	+18	26	2.17
6	Gala Fairydean Rovers	12	7	1	4	22	20	+2	22	1.83
7	Bo'ness United	10	5	3	2	22	13	+9	18	1.80
8	The Spartans	12	6	0	6	27	22	+5	18	1.50
9	University of Stirling	15	7	1	7	31	25	+6	22	1.47
10	Berwick Rangers	13	5	1	7	12	16	-4	16	1.23
11	Civil Service Strollers	14	4	5	5	14	16	-2	17	1.21
12	Caledonian Braves	14	4	1	9	22	28	-6	13	0.93
13	Gretna 2008	11	3	1	7	15	25	-10	10	0.91
14	Cumbernauld Colts	14	3	2	9	17	30	-13	11	0.79
15	Dalbeattie Star	10	1	2	7	12	24	-12	5	0.50
16	Edinburgh University	15	1	2	12	7	54	-47	5	0.33
17	Vale of Leithen	12	0	0	12	5	58	-53	0	0.00

MEMBERSHIP 2021/2

Berwick Rangers	Shielfield Park	Tweedmouth
Bo'ness United	Newtown Park	Bo'ness
Bonnyrigg Rose	New Dundas Park	Bonnyrigg
BSC Glasgow	Recreation Park	Alloa
Caledonian Braves	Bothwellhaugh	Motherwell
Celtic "B"	Excelsior Stadium	Airdrie
Civil Service Strollers	Christie Gillies Park	Edinburgh
Cumbernauld Colts	Broadwood	Cumbernauld
Dalbeattie Star	Islecroft Stadium	Dalbeattie
East Kilbride	K Park	East Kilbride
East Stirlingshire	Falkirk Stadium	Falkirk
Edinburgh University	East Peffermill	Edinburgh
Gala Fairydean Rovers	Netherdale	Galashiels
Gretna 2008	Raydale Park	Gretna
Rangers "B"	C&G Systems Stad	Dumbarton
Spartans	Ainslie Park	Edinburgh
Stirling University	Forthbank	Stirling
Vale of Leithen	Victoria Park	Innerleithen

Lowland League - All Time Positions

	2013-14	2014-15	2015-16	2016-17	2017-18	2018/19	2019/20	2020/1
Berwick Rangers							12	10
BSC Glasgow		10	7	7	3	2	3	4
Bo'ness United								7
Bonnyrigg Rose							2	3
Civil Service Strollers				12	7	5	6	11
Cumbernauld Colts			4	6	6	7	9	14
Dalbeattie Star	3	4	9	5	14	14	15	15
East Kilbride	8	2	5	1	2	1	7	2
East Stirlingshire				2	4	6	4	5
Edinburgh City	5	1	1*					
Edinburgh University		11	6	11	11	11	14	16
Edusport Academy / Caledonian Braves					10	9	8	12
Gala Fairydean Rovers	10	8	11	10	13	8	11	6
Gretna 2008	7	3	10	9	8	12	13	13
Hawick Royal Albert				14	16~			
Kelty Hearts						3	1	1*
Preston Athletic	9	13	14	16~				
Selkirk	12	12	12	15	5	F		
Spartans	1	5	2	3	1	4	5	8
Stirling University	2	6	3	4	9	10	10	9
Threave Rovers	11	14	15~					
Vale of Leithen	6	9	13	13	15	13	16	17
Whitehill Welfare	4	7	8	8	12	15~		

F = Folded
* =Promoted
~ = Relegated

LOWLAND LEAGUE TOP SCORERS 2020/1

Player	Club	Goals
Jamie Penker	Stirling University	11
Nathan Austin	Kelty Hearts	10
Craig malcolm	East Kilbride	8
Scott Taylor-McKenzie	Gala FR	8
Andy Rodgers	East Stirlingshire	8
Kallum Higginbotham	Kelty Hearts	7
Lee Currie	Bonnyrigg Rose	7
Zander Miller	Bo'ness United	7
Jamie Glasgow	BSC Glasgow	7
Dylan Easton	Kelty Hearts	6
Ross McNeil	Caledonian Braves	6
Ross Lyon	BSC Glasgow	6
Alieu Faye	Civil Service S	5
Scott McCrory-Irving	Spartans	5
Daniel Smales	Gretna	5
Kieran McGachie	Bonnyrigg Rose	5
Darren Christie	BSC Glasgow	5
Ryan Tierney	BSC Glasgow	5
Reis Peggie	East Stirlingshire	5

Lowland League Cup

The Cup was not played for in 2020/1.

Previous Lowland League Cup Finals

Season	Winners	Runners Up	Score	Venue
2013/14	Stirling University	Preston Athletic	5-2	Netherdale, Gala
2014/15	East Kilbride	Gretna 2008	3-1	Netherdale, Gala
2015/16	East Kilbride	Gretna 2008	0-0, 4-2p	Netherdale, Gala
2016/17	Spartans	BSC Glasgow	3-0	Ainslie Park
2017/18	Cumbernauld Colts	Selkirk	3-1	Netherdale, Gala
2018/19	BSC Glasgow	East Stirlingshire	2-1	East Peffermill
2019/20	No competition			

LOWLAND LEAGUE OFFICIALS 2021/2

CHAIRMAN - George Fraser (BSC Glasgow), **VICE CHAIRMAN** - Thomas Brown (Civil Service Strollers), **TREASURER**—Andrew Waddell (Edinburgh University); **BOARD MEMBERS** - Findlay Murray (Spartans), Chris Ewing (Caledonian Braves), Graham Murie (East Kilbride)

The **SECRETARY** of the Lowland League is David Baxter.

Lowland League Club Playing Squads 2020/1

BERWICK RANGERS

			A	S	G	Signed	From	Notes	Contract
Allan	Lewis	F	8	5	2	2020	Raith Rovers	ex Hibernian, Tranent, RETIRED Juine 2021	End 2021/2
Barr	Lewis	M		2		2018	Penicuik Athletic	ex East Fife	End 2021/2
Cook	Jack	D	4			2017	Berwick Rangers Youths		End 2021/2
Daniel	Sam	D	5	3		2020	Univ of Mobile Rams	Transferred to Lothian Thistle HV Dec 2020	
Ferguson	David	D	8		1	2020	Unattached	Ex peterhead, Motherwell etc	End 2021/2
Finnie	Ryan	D	11			2020	Queen's Park	ex Hamilton, Annan etc, OL to Cowdenbeath Mar-May	End 2022/3
Forster	Ali	M	5	5		2019	Newtongrange Star		
Horne	Dougie	GK	13			2020	Whitburn	ex Hibernian, Tranent, RETIRED Juine 2021	
Lawler	Mckenzie		1	2		2020	Hearts (OL)		
McNeil	Andrew	GK				2020	Airdrieonians		End 2021/2
Nelson	Grant	M	11	2	1	2020	Tranent	ex Dundee and Rangers Youths	End 2021/2
Purves	Jo	D	5	1		2020	Edinburgh Univ		
Purves	Dan	F	5	6	2	2019	Berwick Rangers Youths		End 2021/2
Reid	Craig	D	9	1		2020	Newtongrange Star		End 2021/2
Sinclair	Jordan	M	7		2	2020	Edinburgh City	ex Hibs, Livingston, Brechin	End 2021/2
Smith	Darren	M		2		2019	Newtongrange Star	Released 2021, ex Berwick, Brechin, Raith etc	
Smith	Liall	M		3		2020	Vale of Leithen	OL to Whitehill Welfare Oct-Dec, joined Newtongrange Star May 2021	
Smith	Euan	M	13			2019	Brechin City	ex Hibs, Arbroath, Killie, Joined Spartans May 2021	
Smith	Calum	F	13		2	2020	Dundonald BB	ex Dunfermline, Brechin, Forfar	End 2021/2
Somerville	Kieran	M	10	2	1	2020	Whitehill Welfare	ex Livingston, Arniston R	End 2021/2
Ward	John		1	1		2020	St Johnstone Youths		End 2021/2
Waugh	Kevin	D	3	2		2019	Hibernian	Joined Spartans, May 2021	
Wright	Jack	M	11		1	2019	Whitehill Welfare		End 2021/2

Manager Ian Little (Until May)
Stuart Malcolm (from May)

NEW SIGNINGS

			Signed	From	Notes	Contract
Craig	Jonathan	GK	2021	Falkirk	GK Coach, ex Real Kashmir	
Pyper	Jamie	D	2021	Cowdenbeath		
Stewart	Sean	F	2021	Penicuik Athletic		
Heeps	Ciaran	M	2021	Hutchison Vale	ex Rangers Youths	
Taylor-McKenzie	Scott	M	2021	Gala Fairydean Rovers		End 2021/2
Harris	Alex	F	2021	Edinburgh City		
Swinton	Ben	GK	2021	Dunfermline Athletic		

BERWICK RANGERS F.C. — 1970-71
Back row, left to right: John Brown, John Keith, Tom Davidson, Willie Wilson, Benny McCabe, Gordon Haig, Harry Melrose (Player-Manager).
Front row, left to right: John Hamilton, Eric Tait, Mike Judge, John Stoddart, Raymond Cormack, Jock Richardson.

BO'NESS UNITED

			A	S	G	Signed	From	Notes
Adamson	Ryan	GK	1			2019	Edinburgh City	OL to Cowdenbeath Mar 2021, Released May 2021 joined Musselburgh Ath
Anderson	Kieron	F	6		3	2020	Stenhousemuir	
Bell	Kyle	M	2	3	1	2020	East Fife (OL)	Oct-Jan
Campbell	Ross	D	8		1	2014	Clydebank	Retired May 2021
Comrie	Craig	M	3	1	1	2018	Spartans	
Donnelly	Chris	M	4	1	1	2009	Camelon	Released May 2021 joined Armadale Thistle
Gemmell	Michael	M	10			2015	Hill of Beath Hawthorn	
Grant	Thomas	M	10		2	2019	Alloa Athletic	
Jacobs	Devon	D	9			2017	Kelty Hearts	
Locke	Nicky	M	9		2	2020	Broxburn Athletic	
McFarlane	Stuart	D	9	1		2020	Edinburgh Univertsity	OL to Montrose Mar-May
McKenzie	Danny	D	3			2020	Pollok (OL)	Oct-Jan
Meikle	Craig	D	2			2020	Whitehill Welfare	
Miller	Zander	F	5	1	7	2020	Broxburn Athletic	OL to Cowdenbeath Mar-May
Murphy	Andy	GK	9			2017	Queen's Park	
Nimmo	Ian	M		1		2019	Kelty Hearts	Retired Dec 2020
Ritchie	Brian	F	3	4		2019	Kelty Hearts	Released May 2021 joined Crossgates Primrose
Snowdon	Will	D	3			2007	Stranraer	Retired May 2021
Stevenson	Ryan	M	9		3	2019	Raith Rovers	
Trialist			4		1			
Wharton	Bryan	D	1			2020	Pollok (OL)	Oct-Jan
Moyes	Ewan	D				2021	Bonnyrigg Rose	Retired June 2021
Turnbull	Kyle	D				2021	Sauchie	

Manager Max Christie
Assistant Ian Black (until May 2021)

NEW SIGNINGS

			Signed	From	Notes
McCormack	Jamie	M	2021	BSC Glasgow	
Galbraith	Danny	M	2021	Gala FR	
McCormack	Darren	D	2021	Ex Brechin City	
Skinner	Greg	D	2021	Camelon	
Macauley	Keir	D	2021	Camelon	
MacPherson	Greg	D	2021	Camelon	
Hawkins	Lewis	D	2021	Tranent	
McMullan	Connor	M	2021	Camelon	
Mckenzie	Conor	M	2021	Camelon	
Herron	Jordan	M	2021	Camelon	
Flynn	Matty	F	2021	Kelty Hearts	
Cunningham	Sandy	F	2021	Lothian Thistle HV	ex Stenhousemuir

BONNYRIGG ROSE ATHLETIC

			A	S	G	Signed	From	Notes
Andrews	Michael	GK				2015	Cowdenbeath	
Balde	Joao	M	1	5	1	2020	Livingston (OL)	Nov-Jan
Barrett	Bradley	F		2		2020	Tranent	
Brett	Dean	D	10		1	2017	Cowdenbeath	
Brown	Jonathan	D	2			2014	Brechin City	Retired May 2021
Currie	Lee	M	11		7	2017	Newtongrange Star	
Docherty	Jamie	F	1	5	1	2019	Livingston	Joined Tranent May 2021
El Yamani	Sami					2020	Bonnyrigg Rose U20	Ex Tynecastle BC
Gray	Ross	M	5	5		2017	Linlithgow Rose	
Gray	Scott	M	11		3	2015	Airdrieonians	
Horne	Alan	D	3	1	1	2013	Tranent	
Hoskins	Dean	D	5	4	1	2020	Spartans	
Hunter	George	F	10	1	3	2019	Newtongrange Star	
Jones	Alassan	M		2		2020	Livingston (OL)	Nov-Jan
Laidlaw	Aaron	F						OL to Vale of Leithen Oct-Mar
Mair	Andy	D	3	2		2020	Civil Service Strollers	
Martyniuk	Neil	D	11			2017	Edinburgh City	
McGachie	Kieran	F	11		5	2015	Civil Service Strollers	
Moyes	Ewan	D				2015	Montrose	OL to Linlithgow Rose Sep-Dec, Transferred to Bo'ness U jan
Neave	Robbie	M				2019	Edinburgh City	OL to Vale of Leithen Oct-Mar
Smith	Jordan			3	1	2020	Tynecastle	Transferred to Tranent Nov 2020
Stevenson	Danny	M				2020	Bonnyrigg Rose U20	
Stewart	Jonny	M	10		1	2014	East Fife	
Trialist				3				
Turner	Lewis	M	1	3		2015	Musselburgh Athletic	
Watson	Leon	D	4	1		2020	Hearts (OL)	Nov-Jan
Weir	Nicky	M						OL to Vale of Leithen Oct-Mat, Transferred to Dunbar Utd May
Weir	Mark	GK	12			2019	FC Wichita	
Wilson	Bob	D	9	1		2020	Stenhousemuir	
Wilson	Kyle			1				
Young	Kerr	D	12		2	2016	Berwick Rangers	
Own Goals					2			
Manager	Robbie Horn							
Assistant Manager	David Burrell							
NEW SIGNINGS								
Connolly	Callum	M				2021	Penicuik Athletic	
Adams	Ally	GK				2021	Tranent	
Hall	Kieran	F				2021	Stirling University	

BROOMHILL

			A	S	G	Signed	From	Notes
Agyeman	Alfie		6	2	2	2020	Queen's Park	
Anderson	Michael		12	1	3	2019	East Kilbride	OL to Forfar Ath Mar-May, Joined Stenhousemuir June 2021
Avci	Lyle	GK	3			2020	Annan Athletic	Released November 2020
Ballantyne	Jamie	D		1		2020	Annan Athletic	Released Jan 2021
Barr	Stephen	GK	1	1		2019	Pollok	
Bell	Lewis	D	6	5		2019	Celtic	
Christie	Darren	F	11		5	2020	Pollok (OL)	Oct-Jan
Easdale	Alexander	F				2020	Morton (OL)	Sep-Nov
Fitzpatrick	Declan	D	8	1		2020	Clyde	
Galasso	Evan	F					Trialist, ex Partick Th	
Geggan	Andy	M	9	1	2	2020	Ayr United	OL to Njardvik Sep-Oct, to Partick Th Mar-May, Joined Dumbarton June 2021
Glasgow	Jamie	F	7		7	2020	Auchinleck Talbot (OL)	Nov-Jan
Grehan	Martin	F				2021	Gartcairn	Joined Drumchapel United June 2021
Hamilton	Jamie	M	9	2	2	2019	Petershill	Joined East Stirlingshire June 2021
Hughes	Declan	M	9		3	2018	East Kilbride	Joined Stenhousemuir June 2021
Leishman	Andy	GK	1			2020	Auchinleck Talbot (OL)	Dec-Jan
Lindsay	Ross	M		8		2018	Fresno FC U23	
Lyon	Ross		11	1	6	2020	Clyde	Joined Stenhousemuir June 2021
McBrearty	Conor	D		5		2020	St Mirren	Freed Jan 2021
McCormack	Jamie	D	11		2	2019	East Stirlingshire	Joined Bo'ness United June 2021
McCracken	Craig		7			2020	Auchinleck Talbot (OL)	Nov-Jan
McMillan	Ross	D	2	1		2017	Stirling Albion	
McNair	Cammy	M						OL to St Anthonys Nov-Jan
Mills	Jamie	D	11	1		2017	Stirling Albion	Joined Stenhousemuir June 2021
Monk	Andy	F	2	1	2	2020	Kilmarnock	OL to Shreveport Pilots Jan-Jun
Nicol	Ayden	M				2017	Dumbarton Youths	
Rose	Grant	F	1	1		2020	Berwick Rangers	
Smith	Ross	D		1		2018	Stirling Albion	
Tierney	Ryan	F	8	1	4	2020	Dumbarton	
Wilson	David	GK	8			2020	Clyde (OL)	Oct-Dec

Manager Steven Swift (Until May 2021)
Martin Hardie (from May 2021)
Davie Gormley (from July 2021)

NEW SIGNINGS

			Signed	From
McCalman	Jack	D	2021	Alloa Athletic Youths
Gray	Finlay	M	2021	St Mirren Youths
Stott	Owen	GK	2021	Rossvale
Fotheringham	Gregor	M	2021	Albion Rovers
Hodge	Jack	M	2021	Stenhousemuir
Sinnamon	Ryan	D	2021	Annan Athletic
Monk	Andy	M	2021	LSU Shreveport Pilots
Dunlop	Mick	D	2021	Hurlford United
Williamson	Lucas	D	2021	Alloa Athletic (OL)
Crawford	Lewis	D	2021	Linlithgow Rose
Cusick	Scott	M	2021	Dunfermline Athletic
Lavelle	Dominic	M	2021	St Mirren Youths
Slaven	Sean	F	2021	Hamilton Accies
Evans	Liam	F	2021	Alloa Athletic (OL)
Baker	Lewis	F	2021	Albion Rovers
Rose	Grant	F	2021	Berwick Rangers

CALEDONIAN BRAVES

			A	S	G	Signed	From	Notes
Bouchentouf	Ahmed	M	3	2		2020	Royal Francs Borains	
Chardon	Yoann	GK	4	1				
Daily	Ben	M		2		2019	Albion Rovers	
Docherty	Blair	F	9	2	1	2019	Morton	
Dowie	Andy	D	14		2	2020	Cumnock	
Esplin	Derek	F	8			2020	Pollok (OL)	Nov-Mar
Forrester	Scott	D	11		2	2020	Kirkintilloch Rob Roy	
Guthrie	John	M	14			2019	Albion Rovers	
Guthrie	Callum			2				
Hughes	Kieran	GK	3			2020	Cumnock (OL)	Nov-Mat
Lachlan	Gavin	M	6	2	2	2020	Queen's Park	
Marshall	Alex	GK	7			2019	Bo'ness United	Joined Cumbernauld Colts June 2021
McDowall	Jack	D	3			2019	Celtic Youths	
McKenna			1		1			
Mclaughlin	Neil	F	8	1	1	2019	Motherwell	Joined East Kilbride, June 2021
McNeill	Ross	F	7		6	2019	East Kilbride	
Pearson	Corey	M		6		2020	Auchinleck Talbot (OL)	Nov-Jan
Reid	Alan	D	11			2019	Stenhousemuir	
Sinclair	David	M	11		2	2017	Stenhousemuir	
Slattery	Dominic	D	2	1		2019	Stirling University	
Smith	Jack	F	14		3	2020	Spartans	
Walker	Jamie	D	10	1		2020	Annan Athletic	
Watson	Jamie	F	3	6	1	2020	Kirkintilloch Rob Roy	
Winters	David	F	5	5	1	2019	BSC Glasgow	retired May 2021
Own Goals					2			
Manager	Ricky Waddell							
NEW SIGNINGS								
Henry	Chris	GK				2021	Albion Rovers	
Duncan	Jack	D				2021	Livingston	
Brown	Jack	D				2021	Albion Rovers	
Lindsay	Ross	M				2021	Broomhill FC	
Main	Luke	M				2021	Cumbernauld Colts	
McLear	Lewis	M				2021	Annan Athletic	
Starrs	Cole	F				2021	Forfar Athletic	

FROM THEIR WEBSITE - What the Braves say about themselves . . .

You may think that as Scotland's youngest senior club, we don't have much of a history to speak of, though you'd be surprised. Although Caledonian Braves was formed in 2019, the club itself existed formerly as Edusport Academy. Initially created as a private football academy, Edusport Academy was founded to provide young French footballers the opportunity to combine football with education in Scotland during one year.

Created in 2011, the Edusport Academy successfully applied to join the pyramid via the South of Scotland League in 2014 and became the first club in the history of Scottish football to win promotion from the bottom of the pyramid when we won the League in 2017.

We also made history in 2015 when we won the South of Scotland League Cup. As holders of the League Cup, the trophy was displayed in the National Football Museum at Hampden Park from 2015-2017 as having 'documented contemporary football history' as the trophy was won by a team full of French nationals.

Promotion to the Lowland League along with our continued ambition meant that we had to take a look at our current model and in 2018, we launched OUR FOOTBALL CLUB. OFC was the name of the project aimed at separating the club from the academy and by doing so, creating a new club where an online community of fans took an active part in the running of the club.

With over 800 fans from 30 different countries, a series of online votes gave birth to Caledonian Braves. A new club identity, with a new badge and a new home ground, Caledonian Braves were officially born when the SFA Professional Game Board ratified the name change on 20th June 2019.

Edusport Academy continues to exist as the Academy of the Caledonian Braves FC.

CIVIL SERVICE STROLLERS

			A	S	G	Signed	From	Notes
Bauld	Euan	D				2020	Cape Breton Univ	ex Hibs, Berwick
Brydon	John	D			1	2020	Hibernian (OL)	
Budinauckas	Lewis	GK				2020	Rangers (OL)	
Churchill	David	M						Joined East Stirlingshire June 2021
Clapperton	Scott	M				2015	Spartans	
Cunningham	Matthew	M					Spartans	
Devers	Jonathan	M				2017	CSS Youths	
Duffy	Lewis	M				2019	Edinburgh City	
Dunn	John	M				2019	Edinburgh City	ex Dunfermline Ath
Faye	Alieau	F			5			
Fee	Kyle	D						
Froude	Steven	F				2020	Whitehill Welfare	
Gibson	Nico	F				2020	Broxburn Ath	ex Aberdeen, Edinburgh City etc
Guthrie	Ross				2	2018	Spartans	
Hopkinson	Jordan	M			1	2020	Broxburn Ath	ex Selkirk, Tynecastle
Irving	Daniel	M				2019	Queen of the South	
Johnston	Andrew	F					East Kilbride	
McConnell	Mark	M				2018	Bonnyrigg Rose	ex Edinburgh City
McKee	Chris	D				2019	East Stirlingshire	
Moffat	Jonathan	D				2020	Livingston (OL)	
Napier	Fraser	GK						
Newall	Craig	D			1	2013	Cowdenbeath	Joined Broxburn Ath June 2021
Shaw	Matthew	D				2020	Edinburgh City	Brother of Oli Shaw
Valentine	Euan	M				2020	Cowdenbeath	
Young	Connor	M			4	2020	Hibernian (OL)	

Manager Gary Jardine
Assistant Manager Ross McNamara (until May 2021)
Joe Mbu (from May

NEW SIGNINGS

Whyte	Macallan	GK	2021	Cowdenbeath	
Leddie	Dino	D	2021	Hibernian	
Moffat	Jonathan	D	2021	Livingston	
Galantes	Yrik	M	2021	Hibernian (OL)	Philippines International
Currie	Josh	F	2021	Hibernian (OL)	

Civil Service Strollers v Berwick Rangers in the Scottish Cup when the pitch at Muirhouse was just roped off

CUMBERNAULD COLTS

			A	S	G	Signed	From	Notes
Bonar	Lewis	F	4	5	2	2019	Stirling University	Ex Falkirk, Stirling Albion
Crawford	Craig	M		1		2020	Cambuslang Rangers#	
Davidson	Scott	D	14		2	2018	Stirling Albion	
Davidson	Sam	M	7	4		2020	Rocky Mointain College	
Dickson	Cameron	M	7	4		2020	Queen's Park	
Fergus	Jeff	D				2015		OL to Dunipace Oct-Dec
Foy	Cameron	M	8	2	2	2020	Queen's Park	
Foy	Alexander	M				2019	Moorlands YC	OL to Dunipace Oct-Dec
Gibson	Scott	D	12	2		2020	Queen's Park	
Gilchrist	Alex	GK	3			2019	Cumbernauld Colts U19	
Grant	James	D	8	2		2020	Queen's Park	
Grier	Jonathan	GK	11	1		2019	Fauldhouse United	
Johnston	Gregor	F				2019	Cumbernauld Colts U19	OL to Kilsyth R Oct-Jan
MacPherson	Ewan	F	3	7	3	2020	Queen's Park	
Main	Luke	M	10		1	2020	Queen's Park	
Marshall	Jordan	D	9	1		2020	Petershill	
McLaren	Dominic		2					
Mortimer	Willie	F	12	1	1	2020	Queen's Park	
Murray	Craig	M	10	4	1	2016	East Fife	
O'Neill	Stephen	M	12	1	1	2015	Montrose	
Renfrew	Bradley			1				
Romanis	Wilson	M		1		2019	Stirling Albion	
Scullion	Luke	M				2019	Cumbernauld Colts U19	OL to Dunipace Oct-Dec
Team	Fraser	D	5	1	1	2018	Cumbernauld United	
Warnock	Lewis	M	1	9		2019	Clyde	
Whitmore	Lee	D	5	6	1	2020	Queen's Park	
Wright	Marty	F	11	1	2	2019	Bo'ness United	
Manager	Jame Orr							
NEW SIGNINGS								
Marshall	Alex	GK				2021	Caledonian Braves	
Kirwan	Richard	D				2021	East Kilbride	
Mclaughlin	Dominic	D				2021	East Kilbride	
Winter	Sean	F				2021	St Rochs	
Forrest	Dylan	M				2021	Celtic Youths	
Murdoch	Reece	GK				2021	Airdrieonians	
Hall	Kieran	D				2021	Cumernauld Colts Youths	
Holmes	Graeme	M				2021	Forfar Athletic	
Hatfield	Daniel	F				2021	Cumernauld Colts Youths	
Davidson	Sam	F				2021		

DALBEATTIE STAR

			A	S	G	Signed	From	Notes
Bell	Owen		3			2020	Cumnock	
Black	Steven	D	4					Ex QOS, Annan, Gretna
Brotherston	Dean	F	5	2		2019	Cumnock	Ex Forfar Ath, QOS
Cowie	Calvin	M	3	3	1	2019	Edusport Academy	ex Airdrie
Degnan	Steven	F	5	3	3	2019	Cumnock	Ex QOS, Threave, Gretna etc
Dickinson	Jack	D	10			2020	Gretna	ex Carlisle United
Douglas	Liam	D	1	3		2020	QOS (OL)	
Graham	Connor	M	8			2016	Gretna	
Irving	Ross	F	8	2	2			
Kerr	Aiden	M		7				ex QOS Youths
Malley	Darren	GK	3					
Martin	Darren	GK	5			2020	Lochar Thistle	Ex Nithsdale W
McChesney	Ryan	D	4	1	1	2020	Glenafton Athletic	Rejoined Glenafton Ath June 2021
Murray	Craig	GK	1			2020	Mid Annandale (OL)	
Orsi	Dan	F	9	1	3	2020	Glenafton Athletic	Ex QOS, Annan Ath
Park	Liam	D	8			2016	Annan Athletic	
Potts	Connor	F		5		2020	QOS (OL)	
Sloan	Lewis	M	8	1	1	2011	Glenafton Athletic	
Steele	Jack	M	4	2	1			
Thomson	Ross	D		1				Ex QOS, Kello R, Lochar Th
Thorburn	Greg	D	8			2015	Gretna	
Trialist			4					
Wells	Lee	M	8			2011	Annan Athletic	

Manager Ritchie Maxwell

NEW SIGNINGS

Holy	Darren	GK	2021	Abbey Vale
Phillips	Scott	D	2021	Stranraer
Gordon	Adam	D	2021	Gretna
Dunn	Lewis	D	2021	Stranraer
Todd	Lewis	M	2021	Threave Rovers
Currie	Russell	F	2021	Annan Athletic

EAST KILBRIDE

			A	S	G	Signed	From	Notes
Adeloye				1	2			
Armstrong	Jordan	D	10			2020	Stenhousemuir	
Bell	Steven	D	10		2	2020	Ayr United	OL to Partick Th Mar-May, permanent from June
Bradley			2	3				
Brady	Anton	M	4	5	1	2018	Queen's Park	
Brennan	Connor	GK	10			2020	Dumbarton	
Erskine	Chris	F	12		3	2020	Livingston	OL to Partick Th Mar-May
Healy	Daryl	F	3	9	3	2019	Berwick Rangers	Joined Gala Fairydean Rovers June 2021
Hutton	Kyle	M	9	1		2020	Dumbarton	OL to Cowdenbeath Mar-May, permanent from June
Kidd	Lewis		6			2020	Queen of the South	Joined Edinburgh City June 2021
Kirwan	Richard	D	3	1		2020	Cumbernauld Colts	
Leighton	Tom		6	2				
Malcolm	Craig	F	10	1	8	2018	Alloa Athletic	
McGinley	Matt	GK	2			2015	Buckie Thistle	Released June 2021 joined Rutherglen Glencairn
Mclaughlin	Dom	D		2		2020	EK Youths	OL to East Kilbride Thistle Oct-Jan
Millar	Ricky	D	7	2	2	2019	Berwick Rangers	
Old	Steven	D	5	1	2	2020	Morecambe	
own goal					1			
Paton	Paul	D	10		1	2020	Dunfermline Athletic	OL to Airdrie Mar-May, joined Dumbarton June
Saunders	Steven	D	1			2020	Gartcairn	ex Partick, Motherwell etc
Smith	Darren	F	6	5	3	2020	Clyde	OL to Edinburgh City Mar 2021, Released June 2021
Stewart	Greg	F		3	1	2020	East Kilbride Youths	
Wilkie	Kyle		5	5	1	2020	Annan Athletic	
Winter	Sean	M		2		2015	Stranraer	
Woods	Paul	M	10	1	2	2018	Stranraer	Joined Stranraer June 2021
McGrath	Keiran	F				2021	Celtic	OL to Peterhead Mar-May

Manager Stevie Aitken
Coaches Chris Aitken, Ian Durrant

NEW SIGNINGS

Malcolm	Blair	M	2021	Alloa Athletic
Wylde	Gregg	D	2021	East Stirlingshire
Millar	Chris	M	2021	Morton
Stevenson	Jamie	M	2021	Kelty Hearts
McLaughlin	Neil	F	2021	Caledonian Braves
Miller	Lee	F	2021	Falkirk
Victoria	Joao	F	2021	Stranraer
Elliot	Cammy	F	2021	Stranraer
kenny	Luke	D	2021	St Mirren (OL)
Millar	Chris	M	2021	Morton
Rodgers	Shaun	M	2021	Morton

EAST STIRLINGSHIRE

			A	S	G	Signed	From	Notes
Brown	Sean	F	3	2	3	2019	Cumbernauld Colts	
Connelly	Ross	GK	12					
Dishingtoı	Jamie	M	12		4	2020	Spartans	
Gibbons	Kieran	M	12			2020	East Kilbride	
Henderso	Craig	M	8	3	2	2020	Livingston	
Kearney	Ronan	F	1	6	1			
Low	Nicky	M	4	2	2	2019	Queen of the South	
Hadden	Lee	M		6	1	2020	Wishaw HSFP	
Malone	Eddie	D	7	1		2019	Forfar Athletic	
McColm	Greg	D	7	3				
Murray	Adam	D	8	1		2015	E Stirling Youths	
Orr	Martin	D	12			2019	Largs Thistle	
Peggie	Reis	M	12		5	2019	Alloa Athletic	
Rodgers	Andy	F	8	3	8	2016	Peterhead	
Shirra	Andy	M		5		2019	Bo'ness United	
Tapping	Jordan	D	4	2		2019	Brechin City	
Ure	Iain	GK				2017	Camelon	
Ure	Derek	M		2		2017	Unattached	
Wylde	Gregg	D	12		3	2020	Clyde	
Young	Robbie	F	5	1				
Watson			4	2	1			
Young	Craig		1	1				
Trialist				2				

Manager: Derek Ure

NEW SIGNINGS

			Signed	From	Notes
Greene	Connor	D	2021	Darvel	Ex Shire
Hamilton	Jamie	M	2021	Broomhill FC	
Churchill	David	M	2021	Civil Service S	
Watson	Dean	F	2021	Partick Thistle	
Rodden	Andrew	D	2021	Partick Thistle	
Turner	Kevin		2021	Vale of Clyde	
Crooks	Cameron	D	2021	Queen of the South	
Fulton	Tyler	D	2021	Annan Athletic	
Barr	Kenny	D	2021	Livingston	
Renfrew	Bradley	D	2021	Partick Thistle	
Kay	Andy	M	2021	Camelon	
Duncan	Jordan	F	2021	Bellshill Ath	

EDINBURGH UNIVERSITY

			A	S	G	Signed	From	Notes
Anderson			2	2				
Baird	Patrick		14		1			
Barnes	Connor	GK	12					
Bonisteel	Isaac		5	1				
Buxton	Nicholas	GK	1					
Condie	Max		8	2	1			
Dick	Matthew		14		1			
Hamilton	Alex		13					
Kemp	Aidan		4	1		2020	Stenhousemuir	
Kulvalainen	Santeri		5	1	1	2020	Southern United (NZ)	Joined IF Gnistan (FIN) Jan 2021
Lawton	James		2	2				
Marshall			1	1				
Maskrey	David		13		2	2020	Musselburgh Athletic	
Matthews			2	1				
Maurice	Louis		7	1	1			
McBeath	Daniel		6	1				
McDonald	Calum		6	1		2019	Stirling Albion	
McGuire	Ross		13					
Motlin			1					
Rawlinson			1					
Ross	Stefen		3	1				
Sinclair	Robbie		6	1				
Squires	Louis		6	1				
Torres			1					
Watson	Isaac		5	2				
Watters	Ross		1	3				
Manager	Dorian Ogunro							

GALA FAIRYDEAN ROVERS

			A	S	G	Signed	From
Addison	Phil		8	2	4	2018	Selkirk
Aitchison	Ross	F	10		2	2019	Eyemouth United
Berry	Marc	M	3	8	2	2019	Vale of Leithen
Campbell	Liam	M	9	4			
Campbell	Jake	M				2019	Loyola University
Galbraith	Danny	M	12		1	2019	Edinburgh City
Grant	Lewis	D	11			2019	Brora Rangers
Hall	Calum	D	12			2020	Edinburgh City
Herdman	Ben	D	9	2	2	2015	Kelso United
Makavora	Leroy		2	1		2020	Hearts (OL)
McBride	Craig	D	8	1		2019	Vale of Leithen
McRitchie	Kit	GK				2019	Hibernian
Morton	Fraser	GK	12			2019	Edinburgh City
Murray	Zander	F	4		1		
Patterson	Tommy	M				2019	Vale of Leithen
Rodger	Gareth	D	12			2020	Stirling Albion
Roue	Archie	M	8	2	1		
Sheerin	Jordyn			1		2020	Craigroyston
Tait	Joe	M					
Taylor-Mackenzie	Scott	M	11		8	2019	Kelty Hearts
Temple	Jack	D					
Walsh				3			
Ward	Sean	F		9	1		

Manager: Neil Hastings

NEW SIGNINGS

Healy	Daryl	F	2021	East Kilbride
Scott	Martin "Jimmy"	M	2021	Forfar Athletic
Beveridge	Dean	GK	2021	Edinburgh City
Miller	Ricky	D	2021	Tranent
Beaumont	Jack	M	2021	Tynecastle
Hall	Lewis	M	2021	Vale of Leithen
Gray	Liam	F	2021	Armadale Thistle

GRETNA 2008

			A	S	G	Signed	From	Notes
Bell	Colin	GK				2020	Gretna Youths	
Cairnie	Dylan	F	11		1	2020	Abbey Vale	
Galasso	Evan	F	2					
Gilfillan	Bryan	D	1			2019	Lochar Thistle	Ex Cowdenbeath, Gretna etc
Gordon	Adam	D	1	1		2020	QOS	
Harvey	Daniel	D	9		1	2020	Tow Law Town	
Hogg	Robbie			1		2020	Lochar Thistle	
Hynes	Darren		8			2020	Morton (OL)	
Irving	Jordan		4	3	2	2020	Carlisle City	
Ivison	Robbie	M	10			2020	Tow Law Town	
Jackson	Joe	D	7	3	1	2019	Unattached	ex Drogheda United
Liddell	Connor	F		3		2019	Threave Rovers	
McGrattan	Lewis		10		3	2020	Morton (OL)	
Muir	Ryan	D	9	2		2020	Rangers Youths	
Muir	Sam		5	2	1	2020	Motherwell (OL)	
O'Sullivan	Farrell	D	10			2020	Dalbeattie Star	
Patrick	Jack	D	5	2				
Rodgers	Shaun		9	1	1	2020	Morton (OL)	
Smailes	Daniel		9	1	5	2020	Morton (OL)	
Taylor	Aaron	GK	11			2019	Annan Athletic	

Manager Rowan Alexander

NEW SIGNINGS

			Signed	From
Kelly	Jay	D	2021	Workington
Griffiths	Euan	D	2021	Kirkintilloch RR
Duffy	Aidan	F	2021	Morton (OL)
McCready	Mason	GK	2021	Partick Thistle (OL)
Holt	Luke	GK	2021	Falkirk (OL)
Sneddon	Blair	D	2021	Falkirk (OL)
Swailes	Ryan	M	2021	Carlisle United
Kemoe	Jordan	F	2021	Craigmark Burntonians

SPARTANS

			A	S	G	Signed	From
Allan	Michael	D	6	2			
Atkinson	Blair	F	5	2	4	2016	Spartans Youths
Baines			3				
Baur	Daniel	D	5	3		2020	Hearts
Bolochoweckyj	Michael	D	8	1		2019	Montrose
Brown	Alan	M	9	2		2013	Whitehill Welfare
Caddow	Jordan	D		3		2019	Penicuik Athletic
Carswell	Blair	GK	2			2015	Spartans EOS
Corbett	Adam	D	11		2	2017	Spartans Youths
Dawson	Cammy	M	3	3	4	2019	Spartans Youths
Grant	John		3	2			
Jones	Sam		12			2020	Penicuik Athletic
Maxwell	Scott	M	11	1		2015	Berwick Rangers
McCrory-Irving	Scott		9	3	5		
McFarland	Ian	M	2			2017	Edinburgh City
Meekison	Archie		8	4	4	2020	Dundee United (OL)
Murrell	Aaron	F	5	6	4	2019	Bonnyrigg Rose
Own Goals					1		
Russell			3	6			
Stone	Harry	GK	5			2020	Hearts (OL)
Tait	Joe	F		8	2	2020	Spartans Youths
Trialist			2	1			
Watson			9				
Woods			11	1	1		

Manager: Dougie Samuel

NEW SIGNINGS

			Signed	From
Herd	Michael	M	2021	Cowdenbeath
Dishington	Jamie	F	2021	East Stirlingshire
Henderson	Blair	F	2021	Edinburgh City
Smith	Euan	M	2021	Berwick Rangers
Waugh	Kevin	D	2021	Berwick Rangers
Inglis	Chris	M	2021	Tranent

STIRLING UNIVERSITY

			A	S	G	Signed	From	Notes
Baird	Euan	F		9	3			Joined Camelon June 2021
Berry	James	M	14			2019	Raith Rovers	
Bremner	Callum	M	1	6				Joined Newtongrange Star June 2021
Brown	Craig	M	12	1		2017	Ayr United Youths	OL to Elgin C Mar-May, Joined Montrose June
Burrows	Matthew	D	14	1		2018	Ossett Albion	
Bushall	Murray	GK	1					
Davidson	Ben	M	2	3		2020	Stirling Uni U20	
Doan	Conor	M	14		4			
Downie	Callum	M	15		2			
Fry	Ben	GK	14			2019	Ballyclare Comrades	
Hall	Kieran	F	2	11	2	2017	Carlisle United	
Heath	Callum	D	3	11	1	2017	Broxburn Athletic	Joined Tranent June 2021
Jarvis	Jason	M	14	1	4	2019	Falkirk	
Kennedy	Louis	F	3	7	1	2019	Alloa Athletic	
Lavery	Marcus	D	12			2020	Glenvale AFC	
McGale	Robbie		12	2	2	2018	Queen of the South	OL to Montrose Mar-May
McIver				1				
Penker	Jamie	F	14	1	11			
Quigley	Ben	D	14			2019	St Johnstone	
Taylor	Joel			1		2020	Stirling Uni U20	
Webb	Alex	D	2			2017	Morecambe	
Mirzasalimov	Buronbek	F				2020	Bunyodkor-Farm Tashkent	
MANAGER	Chris Geddes							
NEW SIGNINGS								
Gromov	Yan							
De Zoeten	Lucas							
Mirazasalimov	Buronbek							

VALE OF LEITHEN

			A	S	G	Signed	From
Anderson	Chris	F	4	1		2016	Spartans
Brogan	Martin		6				
Campbell			1	2			
Grotlin	Jonny	F	10		1	2020	Preston Athletic
Hall			12				
Higgins	Ryan	D	4	4		2019	Heriot Watt University
Imlah	Alex	D	2			2017	Peebles Rovers
Kinchant	Levi	D	9	1		2020	Gala Fairydean Rovers
Laidlaw	Aaron		8		3	2020	Bonnyrigg Rose (OL)
Martin				1			
McGinley	Ben	GK	11			2020	Leith Athletic
McQueen	Andrew	GK	1			2014	Haddington Ath
Ndweni	Donovan		4			2020	Preston Athletic
Neave	Robbie		9			2020	Bonnyrigg Rose (OL)
O'Neill	Calum			1		2019	Spartans Youths
Rixon	Brad		8	1	1		
Robertson	Michael		10			2019	Tweeddale Rovers
Rossi	Ger	M	8			2016	Spartans
Swain			1	3			
Temple	Jack		9				
Trialist			4	1			
Weir	Nicky		11				
Whylie				2			

Manager: Chris Anderson

NEW SIGNINGS

Kerr	Guy	D	2021	Dalkeith Thistle
Brown	Ben			
Blaikie	Jack	D	2021	Civil Service Strollers
Dickson	Paul	D	2021	Craigroyston

Lowland League Fixtures 2021/22

Saturday, July 17
Berwick Rangers - Caledonian Braves
Bonnyrigg Rose - Celtic B
Dalbeattie Star - Civil Service Strollers
Edinburgh University - Broomhill FC
Gala FR - East Stirlingshire
Rangers B - Bo'ness United
Stirling University - Gretna 2008
Vale of Leithen - Cumbernauld Colts
East Kilbride playing in Premier Sports Cup, Spartans free

Tuesday, July 20
Caledonian Braves - Dalbeattie Star
Civil Service Strollers - Edinburgh University
Spartans - Rangers B

Wednesday, July 21
Bo'ness United - Gala FR
Broomhill FC - Stirling University
Celtic B - Berwick Rangers
Cumbernauld Colts - Bonnyrigg Rose
East Stirlingshire - Vale of Leithen

Saturday, July 24
Berwick Rangers - Gretna 2008
Bo'ness United - Dalbeattie Star
Broomhill FC - Vale of Leithen
Caledonian Braves - Stirling University
Celtic B - East Kilbride
Civil Service Strollers - Bonnyrigg Rose
Cumbernauld Colts - Gala FR
East Stirlingshire - Rangers B
Spartans - Edinburgh University

Tuesday, July 27
Berwick Rangers - East Stirlingshire
East Kilbride - Caledonian Braves
Edinburgh University - Bo'ness United
Gala FR - Spartans
Rangers B - Civil Service Strollers

Wednesday, July 28
Bonnyrigg Rose - Broomhill FC
Dalbeattie Star - Cumbernauld Colts
Stirling University - Celtic B
Vale of Leithen - Gretna 2008

Saturday, July 31
Vale of Leithen - Bo'ness United
Bonnyrigg Rose - Gretna 2008
Broomhill FC - Caledonian Braves
Celtic B - Rangers B
Dalbeattie Star - Edinburgh University
East Kilbride - Civil Service Strollers
East Stirlingshire - Cumbernauld Colts
Gala FR - Berwick Rangers
Stirling University - Spartans

Friday, August 6
Cumbernauld Colts - Stirling University

Saturday, August 7
Berwick Rangers - Dalbeattie Star
Bo'ness United - Celtic B
Caledonian Braves - Bonnyrigg Rose
Civil Service Strollers - Vale of Leithen
Edinburgh University - Gala FR
Gretna 2008 - East Stirlingshire
Spartans - Broomhill FC

Sunday, August 8
Rangers B - East Kilbride

Saturday, August 14
Bonnyrigg Rose - Edinburgh University
Dalbeattie Star - Spartans
East Kilbride - Bo'ness United
East Stirlingshire - Civil Service Strollers
Gala FR - Caledonian Braves
Rangers B - Gretna 2008
Stirling University - Berwick Rangers
Vale of Leithen - Celtic B

Tuesday, August 17
Civil Service Strollers - Celtic B
Edinburgh University - Caledonian Braves
Gala FR - Dalbeattie Star
Rangers B - Stirling University

Wednesday, August 18
Bo'ness United - Spartans
Broomhill FC - Berwick Rangers
Cumbernauld Colts - Gretna 2008
East Stirlingshire - Bonnyrigg Rose
Vale of Leithen - East Kilbride

Saturday, August 21
Berwick Rangers - East Kilbride
Bo'ness United - Bonnyrigg Rose
Caledonian Braves - Vale of Leithen
Celtic B - Dalbeattie Star
Civil Service Strollers - Cumbernauld Colts
Edinburgh University - Rangers B
Gretna 2008 - Broomhill FC
Spartans - East Stirlingshire
Stirling University - Gala FR

Saturday, August 28
Berwick Rangers - Cumbernauld Colts
Bonnyrigg Rose - University of Stirling
Broomhill FC - Civil Service Strollers
Dalbeattie Star - East Stirlingshire
Edinburgh University - Celtic B
Gala FR - East Kilbride
Gretna 2008 - Bo'ness United
Rangers B - Vale of Leithen
Spartans - Caledonian Braves

Tuesday, August 31
Berwick Rangers - Bo'ness United
Caledonian Braves - East Stirlingshire
Dalbeattie Star - Vale of Leithen
East Kilbride - Broomhill FC
Gretna 2008 - Edinburgh University
Spartans - Cumbernauld Colts

Saturday, September 4
Broomhill FC - Rangers B
Bo'ness United - East Stirlingshire
Bonnyrigg Rose - Berwick Rangers
Caledonian Braves - Celtic B
Dalbeattie Star - Gretna 2008
East Kilbride - Cumbernauld Colts
Edinburgh University - Stirling University
Vale of Leithen - Gala FR

Wednesday, September 8
Celtic B - Gala FR
Stirling University - Civil Service Strollers

Saturday, September 11
East Kilbride - Spartans
Cumbernauld Colts - Broomhill FC
Bonnyrigg Rose - Rangers B

Saturday, September 18
Scottish Cup, First Round

Wednesday, September 22
Gretna 2008 - East Kilbride

Saturday, September 25
Bo'ness United - Caledonian Braves
Bonnyrigg Rose - East Kilbride
Civil Service Strollers - Gretna 2008
Cumbernauld Colts - Celtic B
Dalbeattie Star - Stirling University
East Stirlingshire - Broomhill FC
Edinburgh University - Vale of Leithen
Gala FR - Rangers B
Spartans - Berwick Rangers

Friday, October 1
Bo'ness United - Civil Service Strollers - groundhop game
Broomhill FC - Gala FR

Saturday, October 2
Bonnyrigg Rose - Dalbeattie Star (2pm) - groundhop game
Berwick Rangers - Rangers B
Caledonian Braves - Cumbernauld Colts
East Kilbride - Edinburgh University
Gretna 2008 - Spartans
Vale of Leithen - Stirling University

Sunday, October 3
Celtic B - East Stirlingshire

Tuesday, October 5
Bo'ness United - Broomhill FC
Civil Service Strollers - Caledonian Braves
East Kilbride - Dalbeattie Star
Edinburgh University - Berwick Rangers
Rangers B - Cumbernauld Colts

Wednesday, October 6
Celtic B - Spartans
Gretna 2008 - Gala FR
Stirling University - East Stirlingshire
Vale of Leithen - Bonnyrigg Rose

Saturday, October 9
Berwick Rangers - Vale of Leithen
Broomhill FC - Dalbeattie Star
Celtic B - Gretna 2008
Cumbernauld Colts - Bo'ness United
East Stirlingshire - Edinburgh University
Gala FR - Civil Service Strollers
Spartans - Bonnyrigg Rose
Rangers B - Caledonian Braves
Stirling University - East Kilbride

Saturday, October 16
South Challenge Cup, Second Round

Saturday, October 23

Scottish Cup, Second Round

Saturday, October 30
Bonnyrigg Rose - Civil Service Strollers
Caledonian Braves - Spartans
Celtic B - Cumbernauld Colts
Dalbeattie Star - Bo'ness United
East Stirlingshire - Gala FR
Edinburgh University - East Kilbride
Gretna 2008 - Vale of Leithen
Rangers B - Berwick Rangers
Stirling University - Broomhill FC

Saturday, November 6
Berwick Rangers - Celtic B
Bo'ness United - Rangers B
Broomhill FC - Bonnyrigg Rose
Civil Service Strollers - Dalbeattie Star
Cumbernauld Colts - Caledonian Braves
East Kilbride - Gretna 2008
Gala FR - Edinburgh University
Spartans - Stirling University
Vale of Leithen - East Stirlingshire

Tuesday, November 9
Berwick Rangers - Edinburgh University
Caledonian Braves - Civil Service Strollers
Gala FR - Gretna 2008
Spartans - Celtic B

Wednesday, November 10
Bonnyrigg Rose - Vale of Leithen
Broomhill FC - Bo'ness United
Cumbernauld Colts - Rangers B
Dalbeattie Star - East Kilbride
East Stirlingshire - Stirling University

Saturday, November 13
Bo'ness United - Stirling University
Bonnyrigg Rose - Gala FR
Celtic B - Broomhill FC
Civil Service Strollers - Berwick Rangers
Dalbeattie Star - Rangers B
East Kilbride - East Stirlingshire
Edinburgh University - Cumbernauld Colts
Gretna 2008 - Caledonian Braves
Vale of Leithen - Spartans

Saturday, November 20
South Challenge Cup, Third Round

Saturday, November 27
Scottish Cup, Third Round

Saturday, December 4
Bonnyrigg Rose - Cumbernauld Colts
Caledonian Braves - East Kilbride
Celtic B - Edinburgh University
Civil Service Strollers - Broomhill FC
East Stirlingshire - Dalbeattie Star
Gala FR - Bo'ness United
Gretna 2008 - Berwick Rangers
Rangers B - Spartans
Stirling University - Vale of Leithen

Friday, December 9
East Stirlingshire - Celtic B

Saturday, December 10
Berwick Rangers - Broomhill FC
Bo'ness United - Vale of Leithen
Caledonian Braves - Gala FR
Cumbernauld Colts - Civil Service Strollers
East Kilbride - Rangers B
Edinburgh University - Gretna 2008
Spartans - Dalbeattie Star
Stirling University - Bonnyrigg Rose

Friday, December 17
Cumbernauld Colts - Spartans

Saturday, December 18
Broomhill FC - East Kilbride
Celtic B - Bo'ness United
Dalbeattie Star - Berwick Rangers
East Stirlingshire - Caledonian Braves
Gala FR - Stirling University
Gretna 2008 - Bonnyrigg Rose
Vale of Leithen - Civil Service Strollers

Sunday, December 19
Rangers B - Edinburgh University

Sunday, December 26
Berwick Rangers - Gala FR
Bo'ness United - Gretna 2008
Bonnyrigg Rose - Caledonian Braves
Broomhill FC - Cumbernauld Colts
Civil Service Strollers - East Stirlingshire
East Kilbride - Celtic B
Edinburgh University - Spartans
Stirling University - Dalbeattie Star
Vale of Leithen - Rangers B

Saturday, January 1
Berwick Rangers - Bonnyrigg Rose
Caledonian Braves - Broomhill FC
Cumbernauld Colts - East Kilbride
East Stirlingshire - Bo'ness United
Gala FR - Vale of Leithen
Gretna 2008 - Dalbeattie Star
Rangers B - Celtic B
Spartans - Civil Service Strollers
Stirling University - Edinburgh University

Saturday, January 8
Bo'ness United - Cumbernauld Colts
Bonnyrigg Rose - Spartans
Broomhill FC - Gretna 2008
Civil Service Strollers - Gala FR
East Kilbride - Stirling University
Edinburgh University - East Stirlingshire
Rangers B - Dalbeattie Star
Vale of Leithen - Berwick Rangers

Sunday, January 9
Celtic B - Caledonian Braves

Saturday, January 15
Berwick Rangers - Civil Service Strollers
Caledonian Braves - Rangers B
Cumbernauld Colts - Edinburgh University
Dalbeattie Star - Broomhill FC
East Stirlingshire - East Kilbride
Gala FR - Bonnyrigg Rose
Gretna 2008 - Celtic B
Spartans - Vale of Leithen
Stirling University - Bo'ness United

Saturday, January 22
Scottish Cup, Fourth Round

Saturday, January 29
Bo'ness United - Edinburgh University
Broomhill FC - Spartans
Caledonian Braves - Berwick Rangers
Celtic B - Bonnyrigg Rose
Civil Service Strollers - Rangers B
Dalbeattie Star - Gala FR
East Kilbride - Vale of Leithen
East Stirlingshire - Gretna 2008
Stirling University - Cumbernauld Colts

Saturday, February 5
South Challenge Cup, Fourth Round

Saturday, February 12
Bo'ness United - Berwick Rangers
Broomhill FC - Edinburgh University
Celtic B - Vale of Leithen
Civil Service Strollers - East Kilbride
Dalbeattie Star - Bonnyrigg Rose
Gala FR - Cumbernauld Colts
Rangers B - East Stirlingshire
Spartans - Gretna 2008
Stirling University - Caledonian Braves

Saturday, February 19
Berwick Rangers - Stirling University
Bonnyrigg Rose - Bo'ness United
Broomhill FC - East Stirlingshire
Cumbernauld Colts - Dalbeattie Star
Edinburgh University - Civil Service Strollers
Gala FR - Celtic B
Gretna 2008 - Rangers B
Spartans - East Kilbride
Vale of Leithen - Caledonian Braves

Friday, February 25
East Stirlingshire - Spartans

Saturday, February 26
Caledonian Braves - Bo'ness United
Cumbernauld Colts - Berwick Rangers
East Kilbride - Gala FR
Edinburgh University - Bonnyrigg Rose
Gretna 2008 - Civil Service Strollers
Rangers B - Broomhill FC
Vale of Leithen - Dalbeattie Star

Sunday, February 27
Celtic B - Stirling University

Saturday, March 5

Saturday, March 12

Friday, March 18
Caledonian Braves - Edinburgh University

Saturday, March 19

Saturday, March 26

Friday, April 1
Cumbernauld Colts - East Stirlingshire

Saturday, April 2
Civil Service Strollers - Bo'ness United
Dalbeattie Star - Celtic B
East Kilbride - Berwick Rangers
Gretna 2008 - Stirling University
Rangers B - Bonnyrigg Rose
Spartans - Gala FR
Vale of Leithen - Broomhill FC

Saturday, April 9
Berwick Rangers - Spartans
Bo'ness United - East Kilbride
Bonnyrigg Rose - East Stirlingshire
Caledonian Braves - Gretna 2008
Celtic B - Civil Service Strollers
Cumbernauld Colts - Vale of Leithen
Edinburgh University - Dalbeattie Star
Gala FR - Broomhill FC
Stirling University - Rangers B

Saturday, April 16
Broomhill FC - Celtic B
Civil Service Strollers - Stirling University
Dalbeattie Star - Caledonian Braves
East Kilbride - Bonnyrigg Rose
East Stirlingshire - Berwick Rangers
Gretna 2008 - Cumbernauld Colts
Rangers B - Gala FR
Spartans - Bo'ness United
Vale of Leithen - Edinburgh University

Saturday, April 23
Pyramid Play Off – Semi Final 1st Leg

Saturday, April 30
Pyramid Play Off – Semi Final 2nd Leg

Saturday, May 7
League Two Play Off – Final 1st Leg

Saturday, May 14
League Two Play Off– 2nd Leg

SFA South Region Challenge Cup 2019/20

When the Scottish Qualifying Cups (North and South) were scrapped in favour of an all-in Scottish Cup draw from 2007/8, the SFA sponsored tournaments to replace the Qualifying Cups in the fixture lists. The North Challenge Cup was dropped from the fixture list after a couple of years but the South competition carries on. It is open to all members of the Lowland, East and South of Scotland Leagues, as well as the 'odd' SFA member from the South—Glasgow University. Girvan are also eligible but have opted not to play in the competition in recent years.

Rd	Date	Home	Away			Att	
1	24/08/2019	Berwick Rangers	Newtongrange Star	4	0	291	
1	24/08/2019	Broxburn Athletic	Tynecastle	4	0	109	
1	24/08/2019	Coldstream	Dunipace	1	3	83	
1	24/08/2019	Lothian Thistle HV	Dalkeith Thistle	4	0	49	
1	24/08/2019	Oakley United	Easthouses Lily	4	4 3-4p		
1	24/08/2019	Ormiston	Dumfries YMCA	6	1	40	
2	13/09/2019	Cumbernauld Colts	Dalbeattie Star	1	0	93	
2	14/09/2019	Blackburn United	St Cuthbert Wanderers	8	1	59	
2	14/09/2019	Bo'ness United	BSC Glasgow	1	2	275	at Camelon
2	14/09/2019	Bonnyton Thistle	Lothian Thistle HV	5	2	20	
2	14/09/2019	Broxburn Athletic	Edinburgh University	3	1	96	
2	14/09/2019	Burntisland Shipyard	Threave Rovers	1	2	69	
2	14/09/2019	Caledonian Braves	Crossgates Primrose	4	0	50	
2	14/09/2019	Creetown	Craigroyston	1	5	40	
2	14/09/2019	Dunbar United	Abbey Vale	1	0 aet	110	
2	14/09/2019	Edinburgh United	Dunipace	1	2	37	
2	14/09/2019	Gala Fairydean Rovers	Newton Stewart	2	1	73	
2	14/09/2019	Glasgow University	Bonnyrigg Rose	0	5	75	at Airdrie
2	14/09/2019	Glenrothes	Lochmaben	3	0	105	
2	14/09/2019	Haddington Athletic	Camelon	0	5	94	
2	14/09/2019	Hawick Royal Albert United	Easthouses Lily MW	1	2	52	
2	14/09/2019	Hill of Beath Hawthorn	Whitehill Welfare	2	1	133	
2	14/09/2019	Kinnoull	Spartans	0	3	65	
2	14/09/2019	Leith Athletic	East Kilbride	1	5	68	
2	14/09/2019	Linlithgow Rose	Gretna	5	1	283	
2	14/09/2019	Lochar Thistle	East Stirlingshire	0	5	78	
2	14/09/2019	Musselburgh Athletic	Mid Annandale	5	0	183	
2	14/09/2019	Peebles Rovers	Nithsdale Wanderers	2	3	66	
2	14/09/2019	Penicuik Athletic	Dundonald Bluebell	5	2	177	
2	14/09/2019	Preston Athletic	Inverkeithing HS	3	2	43	
2	14/09/2019	Sauchie	Civil Service Strollers	1	2	126	
2	14/09/2019	St Andrews United	Jeanfield Swifts	2	3	90	
2	14/09/2019	Tranent	Berwick Rangers	2	1	303	
2	14/09/2019	Tweedmouth Rangers	Upper Annandale	1	2	45	
2	14/09/2019	Vale of Leithen	Kelty Hearts	1	6	105	
2	14/09/2019	Wigtown & Bladnoch	Heriot Watt University	0	2	26	
2	15/09/2019	Heston Rovers	Ormiston	4	0	62	
2		Stirling University	Arniston Rangers	wo	scr		
3	12/10/2019	Blackburn United	East Stirlingshire	1	2	170	
3	12/10/2019	Bonnyrigg Rose	Threave Rovers	3	0	436	
3	12/10/2019	BSC Glasgow	Gala Fairydean Rovers	3	1	82	
3	12/10/2019	Caledonian Braves	Musselburgh Athletic	5	3	104	
3	12/10/2019	Civil Service Strollers	Kelty Hearts	1	2 aet	237	
3	12/10/2019	Craigroyston	Preston Athletic	1	6	55	
3	12/10/2019	Cumbernauld Colts	Jeanfield Swifts	1	0	88	
3	12/10/2019	Dunbar United	Broxburn Athletic	1	2	196	
3	12/10/2019	Dunipace	Glenrothes	3	1	100	
3	12/10/2019	Easthouses Lily	East Kilbride	0	4	84	
3	12/10/2019	Heston Rovers	Linlithgow Rose	0	6	166	
3	12/10/2019	Nithsdale Wanderers	Bonnyton Thistle	1	4	75	
3	12/10/2019	Spartans	Stirling University	2	3	181	
3	12/10/2019	Penicuik Athletic	Hill of Beath Hawthorn	2	3	230	
3	12/10/2019	Upper Annandale	Tranent	0	3	83	
3	12/10/2019	Camelon	Heriot Watt University	4	1	130	
4	09/11/2019	Broxburn Athletic	Tranent	2	4	204	
4	09/11/2019	Hill of Beath Hawthorn	Cumbernauld Colts	1	1 4-2p	110	
4	09/11/2019	East Kilbride	East Stirlingshire	1	0	150	
4	09/11/2019	Camelon	Linlithgow Rose	2	1	372	
4	09/11/2019	Dunipace	Bonnyrigg Rose	1	0	209	
4	09/11/2019	Kelty Hearts	Stirling University	2	0	303	
4	09/11/2019	Caledonian Braves	Bonnyton Thistle	3	0		
4	08/11/2019	BSC Glasgow	Preston Athletic	6	1	75	
5	07/03/2020	East Kilbride	Camelon	5	0		
5	07/03/2020	Hill of Beath Hawthorn	Tranent	5	1	172	
5	07/03/2020	Caledonian Braves	Dunipace	0	1		
5	06/03/2020	BSC Glasgow	Kelty Hearts	1	1 6-5p	212	

SOUTH CHALLENGE CUP ALL-TIME FINALS

Year	Winners	Runners Up	Score		Venue
2007/8	Annan Athletic	Edinburgh City	3-2		Netherdale
2008/9	Spartans	Edinburgh University	6-0		Meadowbank
2009/10	Spartans	Gretna 2008	3-1		Tynecastle
2010/1	Spartans	Edinburgh City	3-0		Tynecastle
2011/2	Stirling University	Duns	4-2		Netherdale
2012/3	Whitehill Welfare	Dalbeattie Star	3-1		Galabank
2013/4	East Kilbride	Dalbeattie Star	2-0		Palmerston
2014/5	BSC Glasgow	Civil Service Strollers	2-0		Ferguson Park
2015/6	Whitehill Welfare	Edinburgh City	2-2	AET, 3-2p	Peffermill
2016/7	East Kilbride	Cumbernauld Colts	4-2		Falkirk Stadium
2017/8	Civil Service Strollers	BSC Glasgow	2-1	AET	Musselburgh
2018/9	East Kilbride	Bonnyrigg Rose	2-1		Meggetland
2019/20	Not completed				

All time winners:

3	Spartans, East Kilbride
2	Whitehill Welfare
1	Annan Athletic, Stirling University, BSC Glasgow, Civil Service Strollers

SOUTH CHALLENGE CUP SUSPENDED

The competition was suspended following the Quarter Final stage. The four remaining teams were:

BSC Glasgow (Lowland League)
Hill of Beath Hawthorn (East of Scotland League Prem)
East Kilbride (Lowland League)
Dunipace (East of Scotland League Conference)

One further game was played during 2020/1

SF 27/12/20 BSC Glasgow v East Kilbride 1-0 BCD

The other Semi Final and Final were scheduled to be played at the start of 2021/22.

SF Hill of Beath Hawthorn v Dunipace

F BSC Glasgow v Hill of Beath Hawthorn or Dunipace (at Linlithgow)

SFA South Region Challenge Cup 2020/21

Arniston Rangers and Cumbernauld Colts excluded due to fielding inelgibile players in 2019/20

Rd	Date	H	A	F	A		
1		Pollok	Tranent	scr	wo		
1	24/10/20	Threave Rovers	Ormiston	7	2		
1	24/10/20	Irvine Victoria	St Anthonys	3	3	3-5p	
1	24/10/20	Jeanfield Swifts	Lochgelly Albert	5	0		
1	4/11/20	Sauchie	Kilwinning Rangers	2	1		
1	24/10/20	Bonnyrigg Rose	Newtongranmge Star	2	0		
1	24/10/20	Broxburn Athletic	Creetown	6	0		
1	23/10/19	Spartans	Kinnoull	4	0		
1	21/11/20	Thornton Hibs	Rutherglen Glencairn	1	0		at East Fife
1		Dunbar United	Drumchapel United	scr	wo		
1	24/10/20	Vale of Clyde	East Kilbride Thistle	4	1	AET	
1	24/10/20	Maybole	Vale of Leven	2	3		
1	24/10/20	Easthouses Lily	Larkhall Thistle	5	3		
1		Carluke Rovers	Kilbirnie Ladeside	wo	scr		
2		Annbank United	Vale of Leven	2	3		at Dam Park
2	21/11/20	Ardeer Thistle	Tranent	0	12		
2		Ardrossan Winton Rovers	University of Stirling	scr	wo		
2	28/11/20	Beith	Clydebank	0	3	AET	
2	21/11/20	Bellshill Athletic	Cumbernauld United	2	3	AET	
2	21/11/20	Blackburn United	Newburgh	3	1		
2	21/11/20	Bo'ness United	Burntisland Shipyard	4	1		
2	21/11/20	Broxburn Athletic	Irvine Meadow	0	3		
2		Cambuslang Rangers	Girvan	scr	scr		
2	21/11/20	Coldstream	Crossgates Primrose	2	0		
2	21/11/20	Craigmark Burntonians	Bonnyton Thistle	2	2	AET, 4-3p	
2		Cumnock	Wishaw	scr	wo		
2	21/11/20	Dalkeith Thistle	BSC Glasgow	0	6		
2	21/11/20	Darvel	Easthouses Lily	3	2		
2		Dundonald Bluebell	Kirkintilloch Rob Roy				
2	21/11/20	Dunipace	Mid Annandale	5	3		
2	20/11/20	East Stirlingshire	Spartans	3	4	AET	
2	22/11/20	Edinburgh South	Blantyre Vics	4	5	AET	
2		Edinburgh United	Arthurlie	wo	scr		
2	21/11/20	Eyemouth United	Muirkirk	1	3		
2	21/11/20	Forth Wanderers	Threave Rovers	4	2		
2	21/11/20	Gala Fairydean Rovers	Sauchie	2	1		
2	21/11/20	Gartcairn	Inverkeithing HS	6	3		
2		Glasgow Perthshire	Petershill	wo	scr		
2	21/11/20	Glasgow University	Hill of Beath Hawthorn	0	1		
2		Glenafton Athletic	Neilston	scr	wo		
2	21/11/20	Glenrothes	St Cadocs	1	5		at Raith R
2	21/11/20	Greenock	Vale of Clyde	3	0		
2		Gretna	Penicuik Athletic				
2	21/11/20	Haddington Athletic	Abbey Vale	3	1		
2	21/11/20	Heriot Watt University	Drumchapel United	3	2		
2	21/11/20	Hurlford United	Civil Service Strollers	4	1		
2	21/11/20	Jeanfield Swifts	Caledonian Braves	3	1		
2	21/11/20	Johnstone Burgh	Maryhill	2	1		
2		Kelty Hearts	Auchinleck Talbot	wo	scr		
2	21/11/20	Kennoway Star Hearts	St Rochs	0	3		
2	21/11/20	Kilsyth Rangers	Rossvale	2	2	AET,4-5p	
2		Lanark United	Ashfield	scr	wo		
2	21/11/20	Largs Thistle	Dalbeattie Star	2	1		
2	21/11/20	Leith Athletic	Tweedmouth Rangers	3	0		
2		Lesmahagow	Port Glasgow	scr	wo		
2	21/11/20	Linlithgow Rose	Kello Rovers	2	1		
2	21/11/20	Lochmaben	Kirkcaldy & Dysart	3	6		
2		Lothian Thistle HV	Dalry Thistle	wo	scr		
2		Lugar Boswell Thistle	Lochar Thistle	scr	wo		
2		Luncarty	Whitletts Vics	wo	scr		
2		Musselburgh Athletic	Benburb	wo	scr		
2		Newmains United	Edinburgh University				
2	21/11/20	Newton Stewart	Yoker Athletic	1	3		
2		Peebles Rovers	Oakley United				
2	21/11/20	Renfrew	Bonnyrigg Rose	3	0		
2	21/11/20	Rosyth	Camelon	3	5		
2		Royal Albert	Wigtown & Bladnoch	scr	wo		
2		Saltcoats Victoria	Lochore Welfare	scr	wo		
2		Shettleston	Shotts Bon Accord	scr	scr		
2	21/11/20	St Andrews United	Hawick RAU	2	3		
2	21/11/20	St Anthonys	East Kilbride Thistle	1	3		
2	21/11/20	St Cuthbert Wanderers	Tynecastle	0	3		
2		Thorniewood United	Craigroyston				
2		Thornton Hibs	Nithsdale Wanderers				
2	21/11/20	Troon	Preston Athletic	3	4	AET	
2	21/11/20	Upper Annandale	Berwick Rangers	1	4		
2	21/11/20	Vale of Leithen	Heston Rovers	5	1	ABD 75 mins, rain	
2	21/11/20	Whitehill Welfare	Carluke Rovers	2	0		

Following the draw, a number of teams scratched from the competition. It was agreed to proceed with the tournament, giving teams walkovers where appropriate.

Round 1 was completed. Most Round 2 games were played but some were postponed due to weather. Subsequently football below the SPFL was stopped die to COVID restrictions.

It was agreed to declare the competition unfinished for season 2020/1.

SFA South Region Challenge Cup 2021/2

Due to the large number of entrants it was agreed to have a four-way regional split in the draw for the first two rounds.

Round	Home	Away	
1NW	Maryhill	Arthurlie	1
1NW	Kilbirnie Ladeside	Ardeer Thistle	2
1NW	St Rochs	Largs Thistle	3
1NW	Glenvale*	Petershill	4
1NW	Ashfield	Greenock	5
1NW	Glasgow United	Dalry Thistle	6
1NW	Kilwinning Rangers	Ardrossan WR	7
1NW	Beith	Neilston	8
1SW	Troon	Mid Annandale	9
1SW	Dalbeattie Star	Whitletts Vics	10
1SW	Lugar BT	Wigtown & Bladnoch	11
1SW	Glenafton Athletic	Craigmark Burntonians	12
1SW	Royal Albert	Wishaw	13
1SW	Nithsdale Wanderers	Hurlford United	14
1SW	Upper Annandale	Lesmahagow	15
1SW	Carluke Rovers	Cambuslang Rangers	16
1SE	Edinburgh University	Heriot Watt University	17
1SE	Craigroyston	Armadale Thistle	18
1SE	Tranent	Livingston United	19
1SE	Haddington Athletic	Dunbar United	20
1SE	Musselburgh Athletic	Tynecastle	21
1SE	Pumpherston	Vale of Leithen	22
1SE	Whitehill Welfare	Coldstream	23
1SE	Edinburgh South	Whitburn	24
1SE	Preston Athletic	Fauldhouse United	25
1NE	Bellshill Athletic	Dundonald Bluebell	26
1NE	Caledonian Braves	Shotts Bon Accord	27
1NE	Syngenta	Newburgh	28
1NE	East Stirlingshire	Linlithgow Rose	29
1NE	Hill of Beath Hawthorr	Sauchie	30
1NE	Kilsyth Athletic*	Oakley United	31
1NE	Camelon	Kirkintilloch RR	32
1NE	Kinnoull	Lochgelly Albert	33

Round	Home	Away	
2SE	Lothian Thistle HV	Civil Service Strollers	
2SE	Berwick Rangers	Broxburn Athletic	
2SE	17	Dalkeith Thistle	
2SE	21	18	
2SE	24	Gala Fairydean Rovers	
2SE	Edinburgh College	Penicuik Athletic	
2SE	25	Peebles Rovers	
2SE	Newtongrange Star	19	
2SE	23	Tweedmouth Rangers	
2SE	Easthouses Lily	Spartans	
2SE	20	Leith Athletic	
2SE	Bonnyrigg Rose	Arniston Rangers	
2SE	West Calder United	Bathgate Thistle	
2SE	22	Edinburgh United	
2SE	Blackburn United	Stoneyburn	
2SE	Ormiston	Hawick RA United	
2NE	28	31	
2NE	Thornton Hibs	Lochore Welfare	
2NE	29	32	
2NE	33	Harthill Royal	
2NE	Bo'ness United	Kirkcaldy & Dysart	
2NE	Glasgow University	Luncarty	
2NE	Cumbernauld United	Inverkeithing HS	
2NE	Glenrothes	St Andrews United	
2NE	27	Kennoway Star Hearts	
2NE	Kilsyth Rangers	Thorniewood United	
2NE	Dunipace	30	
2NE	Jeanfield Swifts	BSC Glasgow	
2NE	Bo'ness Athletic	Gartcairn	
2NE	Burntisland Shipyard	University of Stirling	
2NE	26	Crossgates Primrose	
2NE	Cumbernauld Colts	Rosyth	
2NW	3	Glasgow Perthshire	
2NW	1	Benburb	
2NW	Finnart*	Broomhill Sports Club	
2NW	St Anthonys	Rutherglen Glencairn	
2NW	Johnstone Burgh	5	
2NW	Saltcoats Victoria	6	
2NW	Harmony Row*	Clydebank	
2NW	Irvine Meadow	7	
2NW	Irvine Victoria	Vale of Leven	
2NW	Vale of Clyde	Pollok	
2NW	Renfrew	Westerton United	wo scr
2NW	St Cadocs	4	
2NW	St Peters	8	
2NW	Rossvale	Campbeltown Pupils	
2NW	2	Port Glasgow	
2NW	Yoker Athletic	Drumchapel United	
2SW	Darvel	Gretna 2008	
2SW	East Kilbride Thistle	Newton Stewart	
2SW	Bonnyton Thistle	St Cuthbert Wanderers	
2SW	Blantyre Victoroa	Cumnock	
2SW	Abbey Vale	Newmains United	
2SW	Girvan	Maybole	
2SW	Larkhall Thistle	East Kilbride	
2SW	Auchinleck Talbot	Forth Wanderers	
2SW	11	Heston Rovers	
2SW	16	Lochmaben	
2SW	Lochar Thistle	Threave Rovers	
2SW	15	Creetown	
2SW	9	Lanark United	
2SW	12	Kello Rovers	
2SW	Muirkirk	10	
2SW	14	13	

Dates

Rd 1	11/9/21
Rd 2	16/10/21
Rd 3	20/11/21
Rd 4	5/2/22
Rd 5	5/3/22
QF	2/4/22
SF	30/4/22
F	22/5/22

* Game may be reversed or moved to neutral venue due to ground issues

EAST SENIORS

The East of Scotland League played a number of games between October and January 2020/1. The League was declared Null and Void. From the Evening News:

"With concerns over the timeframe available for teams to complete 50 per cent of fixtures, the East of Scotland Football League Board recommended nulling-and-voiding the season. Some teams had managed to complete 13 fixtures while others had managed just seven and with 17 matches the halfway point, there was understandable concern over all clubs' ability to complete half of their scheduled games.
League chiefs last week requested permission to resume activities in accordance with updated guidance permitting outdoor professional sport and those involved to travel across local authority boundaries for the purposes of training or competing. But the Scottish FA indicated that Holyrood was signing off which levels of football were cleared to resume and the East of Scotland was not included.
Clubs were instructed to cast their vote by 4pm on Sunday April 11 with a final result of 73 per cent to 27 per cent backing the null-and-void option".

East of Scotland League Premier Division 2020/21

EOS LEAGUE PREM 2020/21	BLA	BROX	CAM	CRO	DBAR	BLUE	HOB	INV	JEA	LIN	LTHV	MUS	NEW	PEN	SAU	TRA	TYN	WHI
Blackburn United				Nov 11 0-1		Nov 28 1-2			Oct 10 0-6	Nov 14 2-3	Oct 13 1-4	Oct 24 2-4						
Broxburn Athletic	Nov 7 4-2		Oct 13 2-0	Dec 5 4-5									Oct 17 3-0				Nov 10 0-3	Oct 31 3-1
Camelon					Oct 17 6-0			Dec 5 6-2				Nov 7 1-2		Oct 31 1-0			Dec 19 8-0	
Crossgates Primrose			Nov 28 1-4			Nov 7 0-0					Oct 31 0-3				Dec 19 1-2	Oct 17 2-3		
Dunbar United		Nov 24 1-4								Dec 5 0-3	Nov 21 5-0				Oct 10 2-0	Nov 7 1-1		Dec 29 1-1
Dundonald Bluebell							Nov 14 3-2				Oct 17 0-2							
Hill of Beath Hawthorn	Oct 17 2-1				Oct 13 3-0			Nov 7 0-4	Nov 11 0-3						Oct 28 2-1		Oct 31 4-2	Nov 28 2-0
Inverkeithing Hillfield S					Nov 28 0-1				Dec 19 1-3				Nov 14 0-2	Oct 17 0-3		Oct 31 1-5		
Jeanfield Swifts		Nov 14 3-1		Oct 13 1-1	Oct 31 3-0													Oct 17 6-3
Linlithgow Rose				Oct 10 1-1				Oct 24 3-0	Nov 7 0-0		Nov 11 2-3		Nov 28 2-1				Oct 13 2-0	
Lothian Thistle HV		Dec 2 3-3					Oct 24 2-0								Nov 7 1-3			
Musselburgh Athletic	Dec 26 4-2				Nov 14 3-1					Oct 31 3-3	Oct 9 2-3		Oct 27 2-5				Oct 17 5-3	
Newtongrange Star			Oct 10 1-1		Nov 10 2-0	Oct 31 1-5			Nov 25 1-2			Nov 21 1-2		Dec 23 3-2		Oct 13 2-3		Nov 7 5-0
Penicuik Athletic		Oct 10 4-1		Oct 24 4-0								Dec 1 3-2				Nov 10 2-2	Nov 7 2-1	
Sauchie	Oct 31 1-2	Nov 28 2-0	Nov 14 4-4			Oct 13 1-2		Nov 11 5-0		Oct 17 1-1								
Tranent	Dec 19 3-1				Oct 24 4-0		Oct 10 2-1				Nov 14 4-1				Nov 24 3-3			Oct 28 6-1
Tynecastle	Oct 27 5-1			Nov 14 3-3		Oct 24 2-0		Oct 10 6-0								Nov 28 0-0		
Whitehill Welfare			Oct 24 1-2			Oct 10 0-1				Dec 19 2-3		Oct 21 1-3						

	Club	P	W	D	L	F	A	GD	Pts	Adj
1	Tranent Juniors	12	8	4	0	36	15	21	28	
2	Jeanfield Swifts	9	7	2	0	27	7	20	23	
3	Linlithgow Rose	11	6	4	1	23	13	10	22	
4	Musselburgh Athletic	11	7	1	3	32	25	7	22	
5	Lothian Thistle HV *	10	6	1	3	22	20	2	22	+3
6	Camelon Juniors	10	6	2	2	33	13	20	20	
7	Penicuik Athletic	8	5	1	2	20	10	10	16	
8	Dundonald Bluebell	8	5	1	2	13	9	4	16	
9	Newtongrange Star	12	5	1	6	24	22	2	16	
10	Broxburn Athletic	11	5	1	5	25	24	1	16	
11	Hill of Beath Hawthorn	10	5	0	5	16	18	-2	15	
12	Tynecastle	11	4	2	5	25	25	0	14	
13	Sauchie Juniors *	11	4	3	4	23	18	5	12	-3
14	Dunbar United	13	3	2	8	12	30	-18	11	
15	Crossgates Primrose	11	2	4	5	15	25	-10	10	
16	Blackburn United	12	1	0	11	15	39	-24	3	
17	Inverkeithing Hillfield S	10	1	0	9	8	34	-26	3	
18	Whitehill Welfare	10	0	1	9	10	32	-22	1	

East of Scotland League All-Time Champions

Season	Champions
1923/4	Coldstream
1924/5	Vale of Leithen
1925/6	Civil Service Strollers
1926/7	Civil Service Strollers
1927/8	Berwick Rangers
1928/9	Peebles Rovers
1929/30	Bathgate
1930/1	Bathgate
1931/2	Penicuik Athletic
1932/3	Peebles Rovers
1933/4	Peebles Rovers
1934/5	Peebles Rovers
1935/6	Peebles Rovers
1936/7	Jedburgh Artisans
1937/8	Penicuik Athletic
1938/9	Bo'ness
1945/6	Peebles Rovers
1946/7	Berwick Rangers
1947/8	Hibernian Colts
1948/9	Hibernian Colts
1949/50	Hearts Colts
1950/1	Hibernian Colts
1951/2	Hibernian Colts
1952/3	Hibernian Colts
1953/4	Not completed
1954/5	Eyemouth United
1955/6	Eyemouth United
1956/7	Eyemouth United
1957/8	Not completed
1958/9	Not completed
1959/60	Not completed
1960/1	Gala Fairydean
1961/2	Gala Fairydean
1962/3	Not completed
1963/4	Gala Fairydean
1964/5	Gala Fairydean
1965/6	Gala Fairydean
1966/7	Hawick Royal Albert
1967/8	Hawick Royal Albert
1968/9	Gala Fairydean
1969/70	Cowdebeath Reserves
1970/1	Eyemouth United
1971/2	Spartans
1972/3	Civil Service Strollers
1973/4	Hawick Royal Albert
1974/5	Selkirk
1975/6	Selkirk
1976/7	Selkirk
1977/8	Vale of Leithen
1978/9	Vale of Leithen
1979/80	Whitehill Welfare
1980/1	Whitehill Welfare
1981/2	Whitehill Welfare
1982/3	Whitehill Welfare
1983/4	Spartans
1984/5	Whitehill Welfare
1985/6	Whitehill Welfare
1986/7	Vale of Leithen
1987/8	Whitehill Welfare
1988/9	Gala Fairydean
1989/90	Annan Athletic
1990/1	Gala Fairydean
1991/2	Easthouses Lily
1992/3	Whitehill Welfare
1993/4	Whitehill Welfare
1994/5	Whitehill Welfare
1995/6	Whitehill Welfare
1996/7	Spartans
1997/8	Whitehill Welfare
1998/9	Whitehill Welfare
1999/00	Annan Athletic
2000/1	Annan Athletic
2001/2	Spartans
2002/3	Whitehill Welfare
2003/4	Spartans
2004/5	Spartans
2005/6	Edinburgh City
2006/7	Annan Athletic
2007/8	Whitehill Welfare
2008/9	Spartans
2009/10	Spartans
2010/1	Spartans
2011/2	Stirling University
2012/3	Whitehill Welfare
2013/14	Lothian Thistle HV
2014/15	Lothian Thistle HV
2015/16	Leith Athletic
2016/17	Lothian Thistle HV
2017-18	Kelty Hearts
2018/19	Bonnyrigg Rose
2019/20	Bo'ness United*
2020/1	Unfinished

LEVEL TWO CHAMPIONS

Season	Champions
1987/8	Annan Athletic
1988/9	Peebles Rovers
1989/90	Coldstream
1990/1	Easthouses Lily
1991/2	Manor Thistle
1992/3	Civil Service Strollers
1993/4	Tollcross United
1994/5	Pencaitland
1995/6	Edinburgh City
1996/7	Lothian Thistle
1997/8	Peebles Rovers
1998/9	Easthouses Lily
1999/00	Threave Rovers
2000/1	Pencaitland & Ormiston
2001/2	Preston Athletic
2002/3	Edinburgh University
2003/4	Kelso United
2004/5	Easthouses Lily
2005/6	Craigroyston
2006/7	Dalbeattie Star
2007/8	Heriot-Watt Uni
2008/9	Tynecastle
2009/10	Stirling University
2010/1	Gretna 2008
2011/2	Heriot-Watt Uni
2012/3	Craigroyston
2013/14	Hibernian Colts
2014/15	Peebles Rovers
2019/20	Lothian Thistle HV* Tynecastle*
2020/1	Unfinished

* Decided on Points Per Game

Central Taxis East of Scotland League 2020/21 —Conference A

EOS LEAGUE DIV 1 CONF A	ARN	COL	CRA	DAL	DUN	ESOU	EUTD	HAD	KEN	KIR	LEI	ORM	ROS	STA	THO	TWE
Arniston Rangers								Oct 17 1-5								
Coldstream	Oct 28 1-2		Oct 31 3-1	Oct 17 2-1			Oct 13 1-2					Nov 14 3-0				
Craigroyston	Oct 24 1-1					Nov 7 2-3							Dec 12 2-0		Nov 28 2-6	Oct 10 6-0
Dalkeith Thistle					Nov 7 2-1		Oct 10 1-2					Oct 27 3-0	Nov 14 2-2		Oct 13 0-2	Oct 24 5-1
Dunipace	Nov 14 2-3									Oct 13 4-1	Oct 17 1-2	Dec 5 3-0		Oct 31 6-0	Oct 27 1-1	
Edinburgh South	Nov 10 2-1	Nov 28 3-4		Oct 31 1-0						Oct 28 5-1				Oct 17 2-0		Dec 19 4-0
Edinburgh United	Nov 21 4-1		Nov 14 1-2						Oct 17 1-0			Nov 28 5-0			Oct 31 4-1	
Haddington Athletic			Oct 13 1-1		Oct 10 2-0	Oct 24 2-1	Oct 28 2-2					Nov 7 2-1	Dec 5 3-1			Nov 14 4-0
Kennoway Star Hearts	Oct 10 3-0			Dec 19 2-0				Nov 28 0-2		Nov 7 2-0						
Kirkcaldy & Dysart	Dec 19 2-1		Oct 17 0-2	Nov 28 2-1				Oct 31 0-6								
Leith Athletic		Oct 10 6-2		Dec 5 7-0		Nov 14 5-0	Nov 7 2-0			Oct 24 6-1					Dec 12 3-2	
Ormiston									Oct 31 0-3				Oct 17 2-1			
Rosyth	Nov 7 7-0	Oct 24 6-1							Oct 13 3-7	Oct 10 4-2	Nov 28 1-2			Oct 28 5-2		
St Andrews United				Dec 12 2-1			Oct 24 2-1			Nov 14 1-1	Dec 19 2-7	Oct 10 2-0			Nov 7 1-2	
Thornton Hibs						Oct 10 3-0			Nov 14 1-5							
Tweedmouth Rangers					Nov 28 1-8								Oct 31 2-3		Oct 17 0-5*	

* at Shielfield Park

Central Taxis East of Scotland League 2020/21—Conference B

EOS LEAGUE DIV 1 CONF B	BSY	EAS	EYE	GLE	HAW	HER	KIN	ALB	WEL	LUN	NEW	OAK	PEE	PRE	STI
Burntisland Shipyard									Nov 14 3-1		Oct 17 2-4		Oct 31 2-1	Dec 19 4-1	
Easthouses Lily			Oct 10 8-0		Nov 25 2-2			Nov 11 5-0				Oct 28 1-3			Nov 14 1-1
Eyemouth United	Nov 28 0-6					Oct 17 2-11			Dec 19 0-5			Oct 31 1-5			Dec 12 1-4
Glenrothes		Oct 31 4-2							Nov 7 2-2		Dec 19 6-0		Nov 28 1-3		
Hawick Royal Albert United				Oct 10 2-1~		Nov 28 2-5			Oct 24 1-1				Nov 7 4-4		
Heriot Watt University	Nov 24 1-3	Nov 7 2-3		Oct 27 2-0				Oct 13 3-1	Dec 5 2-0	Oct 24 0-1	Dec 12 2-0			Nov 14 2-0	
Kinnoull		Oct 17 3-0			Dec 19 5-1	Oct 31 2-4		Nov 28 5-1							
Lochgelly Albert	Nov 7 3-3			Nov 14 1-1	Oct 17 3-2						Oct 31 1-2				
Lochore Welfare													Oct 17 2-5		
Luncarty				Dec 5 1-2							Nov 14 6-0			Oct 17 1-0	
Newburgh			Oct 24 11-0				Nov 7 3-0		Oct 10 3-0						
Oakley United	Oct 24 3-2						Nov 14 1-1	Oct 10 3-0		Nov 7 1-3					
Peebles Rovers			Nov 14 7-1							Oct 10 2-9					Oct 24 0-2
Preston Athletic			Nov 10 7-0				Oct 10 0-5					Nov 28 1-1	Oct 13 0-0		Nov 7 1-1
Stirling University EOS					Oct 31 5-3		Nov 21 0-4		Oct 28 2-2	Nov 28 0-2	Oct 14 5-3	Oct 17 0-3			

~ Points awarded to Glenrothes, Hawick fielded an ineligible player

VOIDED GAME
10/10/20, Heriot Watt v Burntisland SY, 2-0, Confusion over substitution rules

Final League Tables

Conference A

	Club	P	W	D	L	F	A	GD	Pts	Adj
1	Leith Athletic	9	9	0	0	40	9	31	27	
2	Haddington Athletic	10	8	2	0	29	7	22	26	
3	Kennoway Star Hearts	8	6	0	2	22	7	15	18	
4	Edinburgh South	10	6	0	4	21	18	3	18	
5	Edinburgh United *	10	6	1	3	22	12	10	16	-3
6	Rosyth	11	5	1	5	33	25	8	16	
7	Thornton Hibs	9	5	1	3	23	16	7	16	
8	Craigroyston	9	4	2	3	19	15	4	14	
9	Dunipace	9	4	1	4	26	12	14	13	
10	Coldstream	8	4	0	4	17	21	-4	12	
11	Dalkeith Thistle	12	3	1	8	16	24	-8	10	
12	St Andrews United	9	3	1	5	12	25	-13	10	
13	Arniston Rangers	9	2	1	6	10	27	-17	7	
14	Kirkcaldy & Dysart	10	2	1	7	10	32	-22	7	
15	Ormiston	8	1	0	7	3	22	-19	3	
16	Tweedmouth Rangers	7	0	0	7	4	35	-31	0	

Conference B

	Club	P	W	D	L	F	A	GD	Pts	Adj
1	Heriot Watt University	11	8	0	3	34	14	20	24	
2	Luncarty	7	6	0	1	23	5	18	18	
3	Oakley United	8	5	2	1	20	9	11	17	
4	Kinnoull FC	8	5	1	2	25	10	15	16	
5	Burntisland Shipyard	8	5	1	2	25	14	11	16	
6	Newburgh Juniors	9	5	0	4	26	22	4	15	
7	Stirling University (EOSFL)	10	4	3	3	20	20	0	15	
8	Glenrothes *	8	3	2	3	17	13	4	14	+3
9	Easthouses Lily MW	8	3	2	3	22	15	7	11	
10	Peebles Rovers	8	3	2	3	22	21	1	11	
11	Preston Athletic	8	1	3	4	10	14	-4	6	
12	Lochore Welfare	8	1	3	4	13	18	-5	6	
13	Lochgelly Albert	8	1	2	5	10	24	-14	5	
14	Hawick Royal Albert United *	8	1	3	4	17	26	-9	3	-3
15	Eyemouth United	9	0	0	9	5	64	-59	0	

Lowland League Play Off 2020/21

Due to the season being incomplete, no Play Off was played.

PREVIOUS RESULTS

2016/17	Not played, Lothian Thistle HV not eligible, Edusport Academy promoted		
2017/18	Threave Rovers v Kelty Hearts	0-4, 0-6	Agg 0-10
2018/19	Not played, Stranraer Reserves not eligible, Bonnyrigg Rose promoted		
2019/20	Not played, South of Scotland League declared null and void		

East of Scotland League 2021/2

PREMIER DIVISION (18)
Blackburn United*
Broxburn Athletic*
Camelon*
Crossgates Primrose
Dunbar United*
Dundonald Bluebell*
Hill of Beath Hawthorn*
Inverkeithing Hillfield Swifts
Jeanfield Swifts*
Linlithgow Rose*
Lothian Thistle HV*
Musselburgh Athletic
Newtongrange Star*
Penicuik Athletic*
Sauchie
Tranent*
Tynecastle*
Whitehill Welfare*

CONFERENCE A (15)
Arniston Rangers
Coldstream*
Craigroyston
Dalkeith Thistle
Dunipace*
Edinburgh United
Haddington Athletic*
Kennoway Star Hearts
Kirkcaldy & Dysart
Leith Athletic
Ormiston
Rosyth
St Andrews United
Thornton Hibs
Tweedmouth Rangers

CONFERENCE B (15)
Burntisland Shipyard*
Easthouses Lily MW*
Edinburgh South
Glenrothes
Hawick Royal Albert United*
Heriot Watt University
Kinnoull
Lochgelly Albert
Lochore Welfare
Luncarty
Newburgh
Oakley United
Peebles Rovers
Preston Athletic*
Stirling University Reserves

CONFERENCE X (11)
Armadale Thistle
Bathgate Thistle
Bo'ness Athletic
Edinburgh College
Fauldhouse United
Livingston United
Pumpherston
Stoneyburn
Syngenta
West Calder United
Whitburn

* Indicates SFA Licensed Club

FORMAT FOR 2021/2

Premier Division
Champions (if licensed) go forward to Play Off for promotion to Lowland League

Minimum of 4 teams relegated. Would 5 be 5 if EoS Premier gains a team from the Lowland League

Conferences A and B
Champions of each promoted to Premier Division

Clubs in Places 2-7 qualify for First Division

Other clubs go to Division 2

Conference X
Top two teams qualify for Second Division

Other clubs go to Division 3

Format for 2022/3

Premier Division
16 clubs

First Division
16 teams

Second Division
18 teams

Third Division
9 teams from 2021/2, + new members

The format for Division 2 / 3 could be revised depending on numbers

East of Scotland League Cup 2020/21

The competition did not take place in 2020/1

Complete East of Scotland League Cup Finals

Season	Winners	Runners Up	Score	Venue
1987/8	Whitehill Welfare	Spartans	1-0	Tynecastle
1988/9	Whitehill Welfare	Spartans	1-0	Easter Road
1989/90	Berwick Rangers Reserves	Gala Fairydean	2-1 aet	Netherdale
1990/1	Whitehill Welfare	Spartans	1-0	Muirhouse
1991/2	Whitehill Welfare	Manor Thistle	4-1	Muirhouse
1992/3	Edinburgh City	Civil Service Strollers	1-0	Ferguson Park
1993/4	Gala Fairydean	Whitehill Welfare	0-0, 4-2pens	Whitestone Park
1994/5	Whitehill Welfare	Civil Service Strollers	2-0	Pennypit Park
1995/6	Whitehill Welfare	Annan Athletic	3-2 aet	Netherdale
1996/7	Whitehill Welfare	Vale of Leithen	2-0	Pennypit Park
1997/8	Whitehill Welfare	Craigroyston	3-0	Pennypit Park
1998/9	Whitehill Welfare	Threave Rovers	1-1, 5-4 pens	Netherdale
1999/00	Annan Athletic	Coldstream	2-1	Netherdale
2000/1	Civil Service Strollers	Edinburgh City	3-1	Ferguson Park
2001/2	Edinburgh City	Spartans	1-0	Ferguson Park
2002/3	Whitehill Welfare	Craigroyston	2-0	Saughton Enclosure
2003/4	Spartans	Edinburgh City	4-1	Saughton Enclosure
2004/5	Spartans	Edinburgh City	2-0	Ferguson Park
2005/6	Heriot Watt University	Easthouses Lily	2-0	Ferguson Park
2006/7	Whitehill Welfare	Annan Athletic	1-0	Islecroft Stadium
2007/8	Spartans	Whitehill Welfare	1-0	Pennypit Park
2008/9	Dalbeattie Star	Preston Athletic	2-0	Yarrow Park
2009/10	Spartans	Lothian Thistle	2-1	St Marks Park
2010/1	Spartans	Edinburgh University	4-2	Pennypit Park
2011/2	Whitehill Welfare	Edinburgh City	2-0	St Marks Park
2012/3	Edinburgh City	Spartans	2-0	Muirhouse
2013/4	Hibernian U20	Craigroyston	4-1	Muirhouse
2014/5	Leith Athletic	Spartans EOS	2-0	St Marks Park
2015/6	Spartans EOS	Leith Athletic	2-1	St Marks Park
2016/7	Leith Athletic	Tynecastle	2-1	Muirhouse
2017/8	Lothian Thistle HV	Leith Athletic	3-2 AET	Easthouses
2018/9	Bo'ness United	Musselburgh Athletic	1-0	Penicuik
2019/20	Not completed			
2020/1	No competition			

All Time Winners

12	Whitehill Welfare			
5	Spartans			
3	Edinburgh City			
2	Leith Athletic			
1	Berwick Rangers Reserves	Gala Fairydean	Annan Ath	Civil Service S
	Heriot Watt University	Dalbeattie Star	Hibernian U20	Spartans EOS
	Lothian Thistle HV	Bo'ness United		

Alex Jack Cup 2020/1

The Alex Jack Cup was not contested in 1920/1.

This competition, named after former League Secretary Alex 'Sandy' Jack, is for clubs which are not full members of the Scottish Football Association, and therefore do not play in the Scottish Cup. It was introduced to provide a parallel competition for the old Scottish Qualifying Cup (South). In 2016 the South of Scotland Association introduced a similar competition. The winners of the Alex Jack and the South Alternate Cup Play Off with a place in the following season's Scottish Cup at stake. It is expected that from 2021/2 a similar Cup will operate in the West of Scotland League, requiring a three-way Play Off for the Scottish Cup place.

Complete Alex Jack Cup Finals

Season	Winners	Runners Up	Score	Venue
1988/9	Kelso United	Craigroyston	2-1	Netherdale, Galashiels
1989/90	Edinburgh City	Berwick Rangers 'A'	4-2	Ferguson Park, Rosewell
1990/1	Easthouses Lily	Pencaitland	2-1 aet	Ferguson Park, Rosewell
1991/2	Edinburgh City	Easthouses Lily	2-1	Ferguson Park, Rosewell
1992/3	Manor Thistle	Edinburgh City	1-0	Ferguson Park, Rosewell
1993/4	Craigroyston	Tollcross	1-0	Marine Drive, Edinburgh
1994/5	Preston Athletic	Craigroyston	2-0	Ferguson Park, Rosewell
1995/6	Manor Thistle	Lothian Thistle	2-0	Ferguson Park, Rosewell
1996/7	Edinburgh Athletic	Pencaitland	1-0	Ferguson Park, Rosewell
1997/8	Tollcross	Lothian Thistle	2-1 aet	Ferguson Park, Rosewell
1998/9	Easthouses Lily	Craigroyston	3-1	Ferguson Park, Rosewell
1999/00	Peebles Rovers	Easthouses Lily	1-1, 5-4 pens	Ferguson Park, Rosewell
2000/1	Lothian Thistle	Craigroyston	2-0	Ferguson Park, Rosewell
2001/2	Kelso United	Easthouses Lily	2-1	Victoria Park, Innerleithen
2002/3	Edinburgh Athletic	Lothian THistle	2-1	Ferguson Park, Rosewell
2003/4	Lothian THistle	Edinburgh Athletic	1-0	Ferguson Park, Rosewell
2004/5	Easthouses Lily	Lothian Thistle	1-1, 5-4 pens	Ferguson Park, Rosewell
2005/6	Lothian Thistle	Kelso United	2-1	Pennypit, Prestonpans
2006/7	Easthouses Lily	Tynecastle	2-0	Ferguson Park, Rosewell
2007/8	Lothian Thistle	Peebles Rovers	3-0	Victoria Park, Innerleithen
2008/9	Gretna	Tynecastle	4-2	Netherdale, Galashiels
2009/10	Leith Athletic	Eyemouth United	2-0	Pennypit, Prestonpans
2010/1	Stirling University	Lothian Thistle	8-0	Falkirk Stadium
2011/2	Stirling University	Gretna	3-0	Pennypit, Prestonpans
2012/3	Leith Athletic	Craigroyston	1-0	Ainslie Park, Edinburgh
2013/4	Leith Athletic	Lothian Thistle	2-1	Marine Drive, Edinburgh
2014/5	Leith Athletic	Peebles Rovers	4-1	Victoria Park, Innerleithen
2015/6	Leith Athletic	Eyemouth United	6-0	Home Park, Coldstream
2016/7	Lothian Thistle HV	Tynecastle	3-1	Riccarton, Edinburgh
2017/8	Tynecastle	Leith Athletic	3-0	Pennypit, Prestonpans
2018/9	Camelon	Bo'ness United	wo	
2019/20	Musselburgh Athletic	Oakley United	4-2	New Victoria Park, Newtongrange

ALL TIME WINNERS

9 Manor Th / Edinburgh Ath / Leith Ath
5 Lothian Thistle / LTHV
4 Easthouses Lily
2 Kelso United, Edinburgh City, Stirling University,
Tollcross / Tynecastle
1 Craigroyston, Peebles Rovers, Preston Athletic, Gretna, Camelon, Musselburgh Athletic

East of Scotland Qualifying Cup 2020/21

This competition was not played for in 2020/1.

ALL TIME WINNERS

11 - Peebles Rovers,
10 - Gala Fairydean, Whitehill Welfare, Spartans,
6 - Vale of Leithen,
5 - Berwick Rangers, Duns,
Eyemouth United,
4 - Hawick Royal Albert,
Murrayfield Amateurs,
3 - Broxburn, Edinburgh University, Raith Rovers, Edinburgh City / Postal United,
2 - Bathgate, Bo'ness, Civil Service Strollers, Coldstream, Cowdenbeath, Gretna, Lothian Thistle / HV, East Kilbride,
1 - Armadale, Chirnside United, Corstorphine, Edinburgh Civil Service, Ferranti Thistle, Kelso United, Manor Thistle, Penicuik Athletic, Preston Athletic, Selkirk, West Calder, West Lothian Albion

Current Sponsors - Football Nation

Previous Sponsors - Image Printers

Recent East of Scotland Qualifying Cup Finals

Season	Winners	Runners Up	Score	Venue
1988/9	Civil Service Strollers	Spartans	3-1	Ferguson Park, Rosewell
1989/90	Spartans	Edinburgh City	3-0	Tynecastle Park, Edinburgh
1990/1	Gala Fairydean	Whitehill Welfare	1-0	Victoria Park, Innerleithen
1991/2	Whitehill Welfare	Vale of Leithen	4-0	Netherdale, Galashiels
1992/3	Manor Thistle	Kelso United	2-2, 4-2 pens	Victoria Park, Innerleithen
1993/4	Whitehill Welfare	Selkirk	2-0	Netherdale, Galashiels
1994/5	Gala Fairydean	Kelso United	2-1	Netherdale, Galashiels
1995/6	Spartans	Edinburgh City	3-1	Pennypit Park, Prestonpans
1996/7	Lothian Thistle	Whitehill Welfare	2-1	Pennypit Park, Prestonpans
1997/8	Spartans	Gala Fairydean	2-0	Victoria Park, Innerleithen
1998/9	Whitehill Welfare	Lothian Thistle	2-0	Pennypit Park, Prestonpans
1999/00	Whitehill Welfare	Coldstream	4-2	Victoria Park, Innerleithen
2000/1	Whitehill Welfare	Lothian Thistle	2-0	Pennypit Park, Prestonpans
2001/2	Spartans	Whitehill Welfare	2-1 aet	Saughton Enclosure, Edinburgh
2002/3	Edinburgh City	Edinburgh University	2-1	Pennypit Park, Prestonpans
2003/4	Preston Athletic	Edinburgh City	2-1	Saughton Enclosure, Edinburgh
2004/5	Edinburgh University	Spartans	2-1 aet	Riccarton, Currie
2005/6	Spartans	Preston Athletic	6-4	Marine Drive, Edinburgh
2006/7	Spartans	Kelso United	3-0	Riccarton, Currie
2007/8	Selkirk	Lothian Thistle	3-1	Victoria Park, Innerleithen
2008/9	Whitehill Welfare	Edinburgh City	3-2	Pennypit Park, Prestonpans
2009/10	Gretna	Vale of Leithen	2-0	Albert Park, Hawick
2010/1	Spartans	Tynecastle	2-1 aet	St Marks Park, Edinburgh
2011/2	Edinburgh City	Whitehill Welfare	3-2	Ainslie Park, Edinburgh
2012/3	Gretna	Stirling University	2-1	Albert Park, Hawick
2013/4	Whitehill Welfare	Spartans	2-2 aet, 5-4 pens	St Marks Park, Edinburgh
2014/15	Lothian Thistle	Leith Athletic	3-2aet	St Marks Park, Edinburgh
2015/16	East Kilbride	Spartans	4-1	Albyn Park, Broxburn
2016/17	Spartans	Lothian Thistle HV	2-1	ORIAM, Edinburgh
2017/18	East Kilbride	Lothian Thistle HV	4-1	New Murrayfield, Blackburn
2018/19	Spartans	Camelon	2-0	Forresters Park, Tranent
2019/20	Not completed			
2020/1	No competition			

King Cup 2020/1

The draw for the King Cup was made but no matches were played.

Rd		H	A	F	A
1	6/3/21	Arniston Rangers	Glenrothes	A	
1		Burntisland Shipyard	Thornton Hibs	B	
1		Coldstream	Eyemouth United	C	
1		Haddington Athletic	Tweedmouth Rangers	D	
1		Hawick RAU	Heriot Watt University	E	
1		Kinnoull	St Andrews United	F	
1		Kirkcaldy & Dysart	Dunipace	G	
1		Leith Athletic	Edinburgh United	H	
1		Lochgelly Albert	Dalkeith Thistle	I	
1		Lochore Welfare	Newburgh	J	
1		Luncarty	Rosyth	K	
1		Ormiston	Oakley United	L	
1		Peebles Rovers	Easthouses Lily	M	
1		Preston Athletic	Edinburgh South	N	
2	3/4/21	B	G		
2		A	M		
2		I	E		
2		Kennoway Star Hearts	F		
2		H	C		
2		N	L		
2		J	K		
2		D	Stirling University		

KING CUP - ALL TIME WINNERS

12 - Spartans
9 - Gala Fairydean
7 - Vale of Leithen
6 - Peebles Rovers, Whitehill Welfare
5 - Berwick Rangers, Hearts "B" / Colts
4 - Mossend Swifts, Penicuik Athletic, Duns
3 - Broxburn, Raith Rovers, Cowdenbeath, Hibernian "B" / Colts, Edinburgh University, Hawick Royal Albert, Postal United / Edinburgh City, Civil Service Strollers
2 - Bo'ness, Bathgate FC, Leith Athletic (new club), Selkirk, Berwick Rangers Reserves
1 - Armadale, Bathgate Rovers, Polton Vale, St Bernards, Lochgelly United, Hearts of Beath, West Lothian Albion, West Calder Swifts, Edinburgh Civil Service, Leith Athletic (old club), Clerwood Amateurs, Eyemouth United, Hawick Royal Albert, Coldstream, Craigroyston, Heriot Watt University, Lothian Thistle, Stirling University, Kelty Hearts

Recent King Cup Finals

Season	Winners	Runners Up	Score	Venue
1989/90	Berwick Rangers Reserves	Civil Service Strollers	2-1	Rosewell
1990/1	Civil Service Strollers	Edinburgh University	3-0	Rosewell
1991/2	Vale of Leithen	Spartans	1-0	Rosewell
1992/3	Whitehill Welfare	Spartans	1-0	Muirhouse
1993/4	Whitehill Welfare	Craigroyston	3-1	Muirhouse
1994/5	Whitehill Welfare	Spartans	2-0 aet	Prestonpans
1995/6	Whitehill Welfare	Civil Service Strollers	3-0	Tynecastle Park, Hearts FC
1996/7	Craigroyston	Edinburgh Athletic	2-0	Prestonpans
1997/8	Whitehill Welfare	Civil Service Strollers	3-2	Rosewell
1998/9	Edinburgh City	Edinburgh University	3-1	Rosewell
1999/00	Edinburgh City	Whitehill Welfare	2-1	Rosewell
2000/1	Spartans	Vale of Leithen	2-0	Rosewell
2001/2	Spartans	Gala Fairydean	4-2	Prestonpans
2002/3	Spartans	Ormiston	2-0	Rosewell
2003/4	Lothian Thistle	Heriot Watt University	1-1 aet, 4-1 pens	Muirhouse
2004/5	Spartans	Edinburgh City	4-0	Muirhouse
2005/6	Spartans	Edinburgh City	6-1	Rosewell
2006/7	Edinburgh University	Lothian Thistle	2-0	Selkirk
2007/8	Spartans	Vale of Leithen	7-2	Rosewell
2008/9	Heriot Watt University	Vale of Leithen	1-0	Rosewell
2009/10	Spartans	Stirling University	2-0	Rosewell
2010/1	Spartans	Stirling University	2-1	Falkirk Stadium
2011/2	Stirling University	Spartans	2-1	Rosewell
2012/3	Spartans	Berwick Rangers Reserves	3-1	St Marks Park, Edinburgh
2013/14	Edinburgh University	Whitehill Welfare	1-0	Prestonpans
2014/15	Peebles Rovers	Spartans EOS	2-0	Muirhouse
2015/16	Leith Athletic	Lothian Thistle HV	4-2 aet	Musselburgh
2016/17	Leith Athletic	Lothian Thistle HV	4-2 aet	Rosewell
2017/18	Kelty Hearts	Preston Athletic	1-1 aet, 7-6 pens	Dalkeith
2018/19	Tranent	Bonnyrigg Rose	2-1	Linlithgow
2019/20	Not completed			
2020/1	Nor completed			

KING CUP - ALL PREVIOUS WINNERS

1886/7	Mossend Swifts
1887/8	Mossend Swifts
1888/9	Mossend Swifts
1889/90	Broxburn
1890/1	Armadale
1891/2	Raith Rovers
1892/3	Bathgate Rovers
1893/4	Bo'ness
1894/5	Cowdenbeath
1895/6	Polton Vale
1896/7	Mossend Swifts
1897/8	St Bernards
1898/9	Cowdenbeath
1899/00	Raith Rovers
1900/1	Cowdenbeath
1901/2	Raith Rovers
1902/3	Lochgelly United
1903/4	Hearts of Beath
1904/5	Bathgate
1905/6	Broxburn
1906/7	Broxburn
1907/8	West Lothian Albion
1908/9	Peebles Rovers
1909/10	Berwick Rangers
1910/11	West Calder Swifts
1911/12	Gala Fairydean
1912/13	Gala Fairydean
1913/14	No competition
1914/15	Gala Fairydean
1915/20	No competition
1920/1	Bo'ness
1921/2	Edinburgh Civil Service
1922/3	Vale of Leithen
1923/4	Leith Athletic
1924/5	Berwick Rangers
1925/6	Civil Service Strollers
1926/7	Berwick Rangers
1927/8	Civil Service Strollers
1928/9	Berwick Rangers
1929/30	Gala Fairydean
1930/1	Bathgate
1931/2	Penicuik Athletic
1932/3	Penicuik Athletic
1933/4	Berwick Rangers
1934/5	Clerwood Amateurs
1935/6	Duns
1936/7	Penicuik Athletic
1937/8	Vale of Leithen
1938/9	Penicuik Athletic
1939/40	Duns
1940/6	No competition
1946/7	Gala Fairydean
1947/8	Hibernian "B"
1958/9	Hibernian "B"
1949/50	Hearts "B"
1950/1	Hearts "B"
1951/2	Hearts "B"
1952/3	Peebles Rovers
1953/4	Peebles Rovers
1954/5	Not completed
1955/6	Vale of Leithen
1956/7	Not completed
1957/8	Duns
1958/9	Eyemouth United
1959/60	Vale of Leithen
1960/1	Gala Fairydean
1961/2	Peebles Rovers
1962/3	Peebles Rovers
1963/4	Duns
1964/5	Gala Fairydean
1965/6	Gala Fairydean
1966/7	Hawick Royal Albert
1967/8	Coldstream
1968/9	Gala Fairydean
1969/70	Hearts Colts
1970/1	Hearts Colts
1971/2	Gala Fairydean
1972/3	Hibernian Colts
1973/4	Spartans
1974/5	Selkirk
1975/6	Selkirk
1976/7	Edinburgh University
1977/8	Spartans
1978/9	No competition
1979/80	Kelso United
1980/1	Berwick Rangers Reserves
1981/2	Hawick Royal Albert
1982/3	Whitehill Welfare
1983/4	Hawick Royal Albert
1984/5	Postal United
1985/6	Vale of Leithen
1986/7	Vale of Leithen
1987/8	Spartans
1988/9	Gala Fairydean
1989/90	Berwick Rangers Reserves
1990/1	Civil Service Strollers
1991/2	Vale of Leithen
1992/3	Whitehill Welfare
1993/4	Whitehill Welfare
1994/5	Whitehill Welfare
1995/6	Whitehill Welfare
1996/7	Craigroyston
1997/8	Whitehill Welfare
1998/9	Edinburgh City
1999/00	Edinburgh City
2000/1	Spartans
2001/2	Spartans
2002/3	Spartans
2003/4	Lothian Thistle
2004/5	Spartans
2005/6	Spartans
2006/7	Edinburgh University
2007/8	Spartans
2008/9	Heriot Watt University
2009/10	Spartans
2010/1	Spartans
2011/2	Stirling University
2012/3	Spartans
2013/4	Edinburgh University
2014/5	Peebles Rovers
2015/6	Leith Athletic
2016/7	Leith Athletic
2017/18	Kelty Hearts

South-East Challenge Shield 2020/21

Introduced for 2016/17, this is a match played between the winners of the Alex Jack Cup (East) and Alternate (Alba) Cup South. These are competitions for East and South of Scotland League clubs respectively, who do not have licences or who have not otherwise qualified for the Scottish FA Cup. From 2017/18 the winners qualified for the following season's Scottish Cup.

There was no competition in 2020/1 as neither the Alex Jack nor the Alba Cup were contested.

ALL TIME FINALS

Season	Final	Score	Venue	Attendance
2016/17	Lothian Thistle v Lochar Thistle	6-1	at King Edward Park, Lockerbie	
2017/18	Tynecastle v Mid-Annandale	3-0	at ORIAM Outdoors Astro	
2018/19	Camelon v Bonnyton Thistle	4-0	at King Edward Park, Lockerbie	
2019/20	Musselburgh Athletic v Mid Annandale	7-0	at New Murrayfield, Blackburn	242
2020/1	No competition			

East of Scotland City Cup

The City Cup is now played between East of Scotland FA members who are SPFL members but outwith the top flight, plus the finalists of the East of Scotland Qualifying Cup. In practice this has meant, until 2016, a single tie between Berwick Rangers and the Qualifying Cup winners. With Edinburgh City's promotion to the SPFL, Semi Finals were re-started for 2016/17.

The 2018/19 Semi Finals were:

2018/19 SF 29/10/19 Berwick Rangers v Spartans 1-2 Shielfield Park
2018/19 SF 13/11/19 Camelon v Edinburgh City P-P Carmuirs Park
The referee deemed that the floodlights were not good enough for the match.
2018/19 SF 8/1/20 Edinburgh City v Camelon P-P Ainslie Park
Postponed due to snow
2018/19 SF 11/3/20 Camelon v Edinburgh City P-P Carmuirs Park
Postponed due to waterlogging

For 2019/10 the Cup was due to return to a single game format, with Edinburgh City facing the winners of the Football Nation Cup. The latter was not completed. Presumably the 2018/19, 2019/20 and 2020/1 City Cup competitions have been abandoned. Kelty Hearts are included in the 2021/2 competition, meaning two semi finals and a final again.

RECENT CITY CUP FINALS

	WINNERS	LOSERS			VENUE
1959/60	Duns	Berwick Rangers	1-1	2-1 rep	Shielfield
1960/1	Berwick Rangers	Duns	2-1		Shielfield
1961/2	Gala Fairydean	Berwick Rangers	2-1		Shielfield
1962/3	Berwick Rangers	Peebles Rovers			Shielfield
1963/4	Berwick Rangers	Ferranti Thistle	4-0		Powderhall
1964/5	Hawick Royal Albert	Berwick Rangers	3-1		Shielfield
1965/6	Berwick Rangers	Gala Fairydean	4-1		Shielfield
1966/7	Berwick Rangers	Coldstream	5-1		Shielfield
1967/8	Berwick Rangers	Kelso United	1-0		Shielfield
1968/9	Berwick Rangers	Hawick Royal Albert	3-1		Shielfield
1969/70	Berwick Rangers	Gala Fairydean	3-0		Shielfield
1970/1	Berwick Rangers	Gala Fairydean	3-1		Shielfield
1971/2	Berwick Rangers	Eyemouth United	5-2		Shielfield
1972/3	Berwick Rangers	Edinburgh University	2-1		Shielfield
1973/4	Berwick Rangers	Selkirk	4-0		Shielfield
1974/5	Berwick Rangers	Meadowbank Thistle	1-0		Meadowbank
1975/6	Berwick Rangers	Meadowbank Thistle	2-1		Shielfield
1976/7	Berwick Rangers	Edinburgh University	2-0		Shielfield
1977/8	Berwick Rangers	Hawick Royal Albert	3-1		Shielfield
1978/9	Berwick Rangers	Meadowbank Thistle			
1979/80	Berwick Rangers	Meadowbank Thistle	4-3		Rosewell
1980/1	Meadowbank Thistle	Berwick Rangers	1-1	9-8 pens	Meadowbank
1981/2	Berwick Rangers	Meadowbank Thistle	1-1	pens	Shielfield
1982/3	Berwick Rangers	Postal United	3-0		Shielfield
1983/4	Berwick Rangers	Meadowbank Thistle	2-1		Shielfield
1984/5	Berwick Rangers	Meadowbank Thistle			
1985/6	Meadowbank Thistle	Gala Fairydean	3-1		Netherdale
1986/7	Meadowbank Thistle	Berwick Rangers	0-1		Meadowbank
1987/8	Gala Fairydean	Berwick Rangers	1-1	4-2 pens	Shielfield
1988/9	Meadowbank Thistle	Berwick Rangers	2-1		Shielfield
1989/90	Meadowbank Thistle	Berwick Rangers	1-1	5-4 pens	Meadowbank
1990/1	Berwick Rangers	Meadowbank Thistle	2-1		Shielfield
1991/2	Vale of Leithen	Whitehill Welfare	4-1		Innerleithen
1992/3	Berwick Rangers	Meadowbank Thistle	2-1		Shielfield
1993/4	Whitehill Welfare	Berwick Rangers	2-2	6-5 pens	Shielfield
1994/5	Meadowbank Thistle	Kelso United	7-1		Netherdale
1995/6	Berwick Rangers	Livingston	5-2		Almondvale
1996/7	Livingston	Whitehill Welfare	2-1		Almondvale
1997/8	Spartans	Livingston	2-1		Almondvale
1998/9	Whitehill Welfare	Lothian Thistle	5-0		Rosewell
1999/00	Whitehill Welfare	Livingston	1-0		Rosewell
2000/1	Livingston	Lothian Thistle	3-0		Rosewell
2001/2	Berwick Rangers	Spartans	2-1		Rosewell
2002/3	Berwick Rangers	Edinburgh City	3-1		Shielfield
2003/4	Preston Athletic	Berwick Rangers	3-2		Prestonpans
2004/5	Spartans	Berwick Rangers	4-1		Shielfield
2005/6	Spartans	Berwick Rangers	2-1		Shielfield
2006/7	Spartans	Berwick Rangers	3-2		Shielfield
2007/8	Berwick Rangers	Lothian Thistle	2-0		Saughton
2008/9	Berwick Rangers	Whitehill Welfare	3-1		Shielfield
2009/10	Berwick Rangers	Gretna	2-0		Shielfield
2010/11	Berwick Rangers	Spartans	2-1		Shielfield
2011/12	Berwick Rangers	Edinburgh City	2-0		Shielfield
2012/13	Gretna	Berwick Rangers	4-2		Gretna
2013/14	Whitehill Welfare	Berwick Rangers	2-1		Shielfield
2014/15	Berwick Rangers	Lothian Thistle HV	0-0	4-3p	Shielfield
2015/16	East Kilbride	Berwick Rangers	2-0		Shielfield
2016/17	Lothian Thistle HV	Edinburgh City	2-1		Meadowbank
2017/18	Edinburgh City	East Kilbride	5-2		ORIAM (O)
2018/19	Not completed				
2019/20	No competition				
2020/1	No competition				

East of Scotland Shield

The East of Scotland Shield, played for by Hearts and Hibernian, has not been contested since 2015/16.

East of Scotland Cup Draws 2021/2

EAST OF SCOTLAND QUALIFYING CUP

First Round
Bo'ness Athletic – Livingston United (Aug 10)
Gala Fairydean Rovers – Rosyth (Aug 10)
Whitehill Welfare – Broxburn Athletic (Aug 10)
Lothian Thistle HV – Hill of Beath Hawthorn (Aug 11)

Second Round
Whitburn Juniors 0-2 Camelon Juniors (Jul 31)
Bathgate Thistle – Craigroyston (Aug 10)
Dunbar United – Leith Athletic (Aug 10)
Musselburgh Athletic – Stoneyburn (Aug 10)
Oakley United – Thornton Hibs (Aug 10)
Peebles Rovers – Fauldhouse United (Aug 10)
Preston Athletic – Burntisland Shipyard (Aug 10)
Pumpherston Juniors – Blackburn United (Aug 10)
Sauchie Juniors – Crossgates Primrose (Aug 10)
Spartans – Linlithgow Rose (Aug 10)
Armadale Thistle – Easthouses Lily MW (Aug 11)
Haddington Athletic – Heriot Watt University (Aug 11)
Inverkeithing Hillfield Swifts – Edinburgh University (Aug 11)
Jeanfield Swifts – Vale of Leithen (Aug 11)
Luncarty – Dundonald Bluebell (Aug 11)
Syngenta – Glenrothes (Aug 11)
Arniston Rangers – Kirkcaldy & Dysart (Sep 11)
Dunipace – Edinburgh United (Sep 11)
Edinburgh College – Dalkeith Thistle (Sep 11)
Gretna 2008 – Bo'ness United (Sep 11)
Kennoway Star Hearts – Lochore Welfare (Sep 11)
Lothian Thistle HV or Hill of Beath Hawthorn – Ormiston (Sep 11 if LTHV, Sep 21 if HoB)
Newtongrange Star – Civil Service Strollers (Sep 11)
Penicuik Athletic – Hawick Royal Albert United (Sep 11)
St Andrews United – Stirling University (Sep 11)
Tweedmouth Rangers – Gala Fairydean Rovers or Rosyth (Sep 11)
West Calder United – Berwick Rangers (Sep 11)
Bo'ness Athletic or Livingston United – Lochgelly Albert (Sep 21 if Bo'ness)
Tynecastle – Bonnyrigg Rose (Sep 21)
Edinburgh South – Tranent Juniors
Kinnoull – Coldstream
Newburgh – Whitehill Welfare or Broxburn Athletic

ALEX JACK CUP

First Round (Aug 7)
Arniston Rangers – Edinburgh United
Craigroyston – Luncarty
Crossgates Primrose – Kirkcaldy & Dysart
Edinburgh South – Ormiston
Heriot Watt University – Thornton Hibs
Kinnoull – Newburgh
Leith Athletic – Lochore Welfare
Lochgelly Albert – Inverkeithing Hillfield Swifts
Oakley United – Pumpherston Juniors
Rosyth – Glenrothes
St Andrews United – Bo'ness Athletic

Second Round (Aug 28)
Arniston Rangers or Edinburgh United – Craigroyston or Luncarty
Kennoway Star Hearts – Edinburgh College
Kinnoull or Newburgh – Crossgates Primrose or Kirkcaldy & Dysart
Lochgelly Albert or Inverkeithing Hillfield Swifts – Peebles Rovers
Rosyth or Glenrothes – Leith Athletic or Lochore Welfare
St Andrews United or Bo'ness Athletic – Oakley United or Pumpherston Juniors
Tweedmouth Rangers – Heriot-Watt University or Thornton Hibs
Whitburn Juniors – Edinburgh South or Ormiston

KING CUP

First Round
Easthouses Lily 2-2(3-4p) Haddington Athletic (Jul 24)
Preston Athletic – Burntisland Shipyard (Aug 7)
Armadale Thistle – Bathgate Thistle (Aug 28)
Lochore Welfare – Kennoway Star Hearts (Oct 2)
Luncarty – Dunipace (Nov 6)
Edinburgh United – Leith Athletic
Lochgelly Albert – Syngenta
Pumpherston Juniors – Stirling University EOS
Tweedmouth Rangers – Edinburgh South

Second Round
Coldstream – Livingston United (Aug 14)
Peebles Rovers – West Calder United (Aug 21)
Kirkcaldy & Dysart – Fauldhouse United (Sep 28)
Edinburgh United or Leith Athletic – Hawick Royal Albert United (Oct 30, if Edin Utd)
Bo'ness Athletic – Tweedmouth Rangers or Edinburgh South (Nov 9)
Rosyth – Luncarty or Dunipace (Nov 9)
Pumpherston Juniors or Stirling University EOS – Whitburn Juniors (Nov 10, if Stir Uni)
Thornton Hibs – Newburgh (Dec 4)
Haddington Athletic – Glenrothes (Dec 11)
Lochore Welfare or Kennoway Star Hearts – Lochgelly Albert or Syngenta (Dec 18 if KSH v Albert)
Armadale Thistle or Bathgate Thistle – Edinburgh College
Arniston Rangers – Oakley United
Craigroyston – Heriot Watt University
Kinnoull – Preston Athletic or Burntisland Shipyard
Ormiston – St Andrews United
Stoneyburn Juniors – Dalkeith Thistle

EAST OF SCOTLAND CITY CUP

Semi Finals (March 30 2022)
Edinburgh City v East of Scotland Qualifying Cup Finalist
Kelty Hearts v East of Scotland Qualifying Cup Finalist

Final (April 12 or 13)

East of Scotland League Club Playing Squads 2020/21

NB These are not comprehensive lists of players used - there will be some omissions. However, all players listed were associated with the club concerned during 2020/21.

New signings listed are for 2021/2.

ARNISTON RANGERS

Manager: Jimmy McCusker / Darren Black (until December 2020), Phil Alexander / Scott Steele (2021/2)
Anton McKillop
Ben Pritchett
Cameron Reynolds
Connor Dyet
David Livie
Drew Horsburgh
Euan Watson
Faron Gribben
Frazer Ewart
Gary Nicholson (OL)
Greg Hogarth
J McQueen
L Gallacher
Laurie Jones
Marc Scott
Nathan Williamson
P Suddaby
Scott Ritchie
Sean Elliot
Stephen Anderson
Steven Milne (OL from Tollcross Thistle)
Jordan Easton
Gordon Ramsay
Steven Nethery (ex Easthouses, Dalkeith Th)
Kevin Dyet
Willie Linton
Barry Hogg (ex Musselburgh Ath)
Gary Shearer (ex Dunbar United)

NEW SIGNINGS 2021/2
Jai Whyte (ex Dalkeith Th, Lothian Vale)
Scott Waterston (ex Edinburgh South Vics, Dalkeith Th)
Connor McLeod
James Peggie (ex Tranent, Haddington, Lothian Vale)
Dean Apicella
Steven Philp
Ben Kettrick
Ali Adams
Bradley Geddes (ex Dunbar United)

BLACKBURN UNITED

Manager: Mark Campbell
Gavin King (2016 Broxburn Athletic)
Richard Hutton (2017 Bathgate Th, ex Edinburgh City, E Fife Youths)
Martin Lawrie (2018 Whitletts Vics, 2nd spell at Blackburn, ex Bathgate Th, Fauldhouse Utd)
John Drummond (ex Harthill Royal, Livingston United)
James Mildren (2015 Amateur Football)
Stuart McLeod (2019 Bathgate Th, ex West Calder U, Armadale Th, Raith Rovers Youths)
Danny Campbell (2010 Blackburn Youths, son of the Manager)
Marc Smith (OL from Livingston, ex BSC Glasgow St Mirren Youths)
Laurie Devine (2019 Tynecastle, ex Airdrie and Livingston Youths)
Brian Ross (2020 Wishaw HSFP, ex Cowdenbeath, Dundonald BB, Albion Rovers)
Marley Redfern (OL from Hamilton Accies)
Matthew Kinross
David Howe (ex Hibernian Youths, Broxburn Ath)
Justin Watson (OL from Livingston, ex Stirling Albion)
John Queen
Dominic Kane (ex Stirling University)
Craig Saunders (2019 Hawick RA, ex Heriot Watt Uni)
Jordan Devine (ex Stoneyburn, West Calder United)

BROXBURN ATHLETIC

Manager: Chris Townsley;
Assistant: Jack Beesley
Jack Beesley (ex Spartans)
Greg Binnie
Stuart Burnside
Gary Brass (ex Whitburn, Camelon, Stirling Albion)
Tom Cowley (2020 Stirling University)
Gordon Donaldson (2017 Edinburgh City)
Shaun Donoghue (2017 Cowdenbeath)
Saul Duffy (OL to Pumpherston for part of season)
Andy Gillen (2016 Stirling University)
Andrew Grant (2020 East Stirlingshire, joining Dunipace for 2021/2)
David Greenhill (ex Berwick R, Spartans etc)
Aaron Hamilton (OL to Pumpherston for part of season)
Shaun Harrison (2018 Edinburgh City)
Jordan Hopkinson
Ross Hutchison (2020 Linlithgow Rose)
Liam Ireland (2020 Vale of Leithen)
Connor Kelly (2018 Sauchie)
Luke Murray (2020 Edinburgh University)
Greg Nicol
Ross Nimmo
Scott Richards
Cameron Ross (2018 Leith Athletic)
Craig Scott (2015 Bo'ness United)
Chris Townsley (2017 Spartans)
Craig Turnbull
Connor Wallace (2015 Bo'ness United)
Jordan Wright (2020 Sauchie)
Rory Cosgrove

NEW SIGNINGS 2020/1
Joe Tait (OL from Spartans)
Craig Newall (2021 Civil Service Strollers)
John Grant (2020 Spartans)
Jackson Barker (2021 Heriot Watt Uni)
Ross Allum (ex Edinburgh City, Spartans, Linlithgow Rose etc)

BURNTISLAND SHIPYARD

Manager: Stuart Innes
Ben Anthony
Darrell Anthony
Dean Hunter
Dale Allan
Gavin Ross (2020 Crossgates P, ex Lochgelly Albert, Steelend Vics)
Iain Millar
Jay Bridgeford (Oct 2020 OL from Kelty Hearts)
Jordan Galloway
Jordan McKenzie (OL from East Fife)
Matty Miller
Michael Gibb
Nathan Laird (OL from East Fife)
Peter Bell (ex Steelend Vics etc)
Raymond "Mondo" Crichton
Reece Brown
Robbie Crawford
Ross Gallagher (2021 Lochgelly Albert, ex Q Park, Kirkintilloch RR)
Ryan O'Donnell
Sam Glancy
Sandy Strang
Scott Costello (ex Brechin C, Spartans, Hill of Beath H etc)
Scott Orrock
Shaun Keatings
Tyler McKenzie (Oct 2020 OL from Kelty Hearts)

NEW SIGNINGS
Nathan Feeley (2021 Lochgelly Albert, ex Kirkcaldy & Dysart, Thornton Hibs)

CAMELON

Manager: Gordon Herd (until Mar 2021), Andy Colley (from Mar 2021)
Assistant: David Strathie (from Mar 2021)
Alan Docherty (2017 Stenhousemuir, OL to Stenhousemuir Mar-May 2021, joined Linlithgow Rose July 2021)
Alan Sneddon
Andrew Kay (2016 East Stirlingshire, joined E Stirling June 2021)
Calum Gray
Connor McMullan (2018 Stirling Albion)
Conor McKenzie
Dean Shaw
David Morrison (2019 Dunipace, joined Dunipace Jul 2021)
Don Morrison
McCrory
Finlay Mckay
Greg MacPherson (2020 Dunipace
Greg Skinner
Jack Denham (joined Dunipace Jul 2021)
Jack Sharples (2020 Lothian Thistle HV)
Jordan Herron (2016 Stirling Albion)
Keir MacAulay (2020 Kelty Hearts)
Mark Stowe (2019 Falkirk, joined Linlithgow Rose July 2021)
Mitchell McDonald (OL from Alloa Athletic)
Ross Allum (2020 Linlithgow Rose, Joined Broxburn Ath for 2021/2)

Ryan Duffy
Ryan Kane (joined Dunipace Jul 2021)
Ryan Lockie (2018 Stirling Albion)
Scott Law (OL from Petershill)

NEW SIGNINGS 2021/2
Jamie Canavan (2021 ex Westerton United, Darvel, Morton)
Jacob Welna (ex Livingston, West Calder Utd, Bathgate Th)
Aaron Reid (2021 Bathgate Th, ex Albion R, Rangers, Stenhousemuir Youths)
Cole Cattanach
Darren McIsaac (2021 Bathgate Th)
Greg Forrest (2021 Whitburn)
Jay Sandison (2021 Cowdenbeath, ex Hearts)
Reece Boyle 2021, ex Bo'ness U, Blackburn Utd, Bathgate Th, Whitburn)
Ryan Duffy
Jack Simpson (ex Eroe Commodores, CBU Capers, Hearts and Hamilton Accies Youths)
Jackson Cowan (2021 West Calder United)
Kyle Mowatt (2021 Bo'ness United)
Lewis McArthur (2021 Bathgate Th, ex Hearts, Dundee Utd, Livingston, West Calder Utd)
Mitchell McDonald (2021, Alloa Ath, ex Stirling Albion)
Sean Stewart (2021 ex Dumbarton, Clydebank, Celtic Youths)
Euan Baird (2021 Stirling University)
Kris Goss (ex Hebburn Town, Whitley Bay, West Auckland Town, Seaham Red Star)
Michael Gould (2021 LC Aris FC (USA), ex Linlithgow Rose)
Mitchell Taylor (ex BSC Glasgow, Kilsyth Rangers)

COLDSTREAM
Manager: Kieran Ainslie
Ejay Gay
Craig Heugh
Greg McCrudden
Shane Bonnington
Matt Corfield
Ben Wright
Calum Helm
Elliot Turnbull
Max Fox
Owen Renton
Ross Straughan
Tommy Malcolm
Jonny Simpson
Kris Dixon
Thomas Hume
Evan Smith
Bailey Paterson
Darren McBay
Tom Kerr
Sam Dawson
Kieran Ainslie
Cameron Beasley

Kieran Lee
Gary Windram
Martyn Tait
Ben Fairbairn
Christian Briggs

CRAIGROYSTON
Manager: Ryan Dinse
Brad Raiker (2020 Spartans, ex Vale of Leithen)
Bradley Anderson
Dean Horribine (ex Hibernian, Berwick R, Spartans)
Dylan Tait
Euan Gilhooley
Gavin Pettigrew (ex Tynecastle)
James Hainey (2020 ex Leith Ath, Civil Service S, Lothian Thistle HV)
Jamie Newman (ex E Stirlingshire, Berwick R, Tynecastle, Newtongrange Star, Edinburgh Utd)
John Paul McLennan (ex Arniston R, Dalkeith Th, Edinburgh Utd)
John Robertson (2020 Dalkeith Th)
Kai Wilson (2020, Australian football)
Louis Swanson (2020 Whitehill W, ex Tynecastle, Bonnyrigg Rose)
Luke Leiper (ex Edinburgh Utd)
Matty Hunter (2020 ex Dalkeith Th)
Paul Dickson (ex Spartans, Vale of Leithen)
Paul Dunlop (2020, ex Edinburgh Rose, St Bernards, Salvesen)
Rees Allan (2020, ex Salvesen, St Bernards, Tollcross Th)
Rees Smith
Ross Nisbet (2020 Leith Ath, ex Whitehill W, Craigroyston)
Ryan Currie (2020 Leith Ath, ex Livingston, E Kilbride, Vale of Leithen)
Ryan Mack
Ryan Moore (2020, ex Preston Ath)
Ryan Robertson (2020 Laurieston Thistle)
Scott Wilson (2020 Leith Ath, ex Livingston, St Johnstone, Spartans, Vale of Leithen)
Shaun Turnbull (2020 Civil Service Strollers, ex Craigroyston)

CROSSGATES PRIMROSE
Manager: Alan Campbell
Adam Moffat (ex Cowdenbeath)
Ally Campbell
Archie Campbell (ex Rangers, Morton etc)
Cammy Lumsden
Ciaran Chalmers
Craig Burt
Darren Aitken
Dougie Swan
Garry Leighton (ex Kelty H, son of Stevie Leighton)
Johnny Galloway (ex Dunfermline, Burntisland SY)
Lewis Sawers (ex Dunfermline Ath)
Mark Forbes
Mark McKenzie
Reece Sawers
Regan Lumsden (ex Edinburgh City, HOB Haws)
Rhory Mooney
Robbie Gilmour

DALKEITH THISTLE
Manager: Jock Landells
Shea Dowie
Ross Aitchison
Guy Kerr
Ronan Clelland
Darren Leslie
Michael Fairnie
Michael Bennett
Jack Burrows
Chris Roxburgh
Matthew Johnston
Greig Callaghan
Mattie Dillon
Cameron Leslie
Andrew Wilson
Norani Vuna
James McPartlin

DUNBAR UNITED
Manager: Geoff Jones, John Coughlin (Interim), Kevin Haynes (from July 2021)
Daniel Laing
Grant Thomson
Liam Peden
Mark McGovern
Andy Jones
James Harle
Kieran Ingram
Darren McTernan
Ian Black
Fraser McLaren
Darren Handling
Fraser Neave
John Johnstone (ex Banks o' Dee)
Cropley
Zach Szemis
Chris Robertson
Matt Brady
Hamish Law

Jack Duncan
Gary Shearer
Neil Smeaton
Michael McFarlane
Keith Tait

DUNDONALD BLUEBELL
Manager: Kevin Fotheringham
Liam Craig
Jed Crowe
Aiden Hendry
Lewis McKenzie
John Cameron (ex Ross County, Nairn County, Clach)
Barry Sibanda (2020 Cupar Hearts, 2nd spell with club)
Ross Drummond
Billy Rogerson
James Mackie
Keiran Dall
Callum Strang
Mikey Ness (to Rosyth Nov 2020)
Kyle Bell (OL from East Fife Jan 2021)
Stuart Cargill
Chris Gay
Campbell Durie
Jason McLaren
Darren Gribbin (ex Berwick, Hamilton, Stirling etc)
Greg Halliday (2020 Bowhill Rovers, released Nov 2020)
Colin Wilson
Derek Wallace
Craig Wedderburn
James Lennox
Jamie Allan (Dec 2020 OL from E Fife)
Brodie Gray (ex St Johnstone, E Fife)
Darren Somerville

NEW SIGNINGS 2021/2
Murray Carstairs (2021 Glenrothes, 3rd spell with club)
Kyle Marley (2021 Irvine Meadow, ex Stenhousemuir, Kelty Hearts)
Elliot Ford (2021 Thornton Hibs, ex Kelty H, Brechin City)
Jack Smith (2021 Raith Rovers)
Ross Brown (2021 Brechin City, ex Airdrie, East Fife etc)
Scott Gilfillan (2021 Rosyth)

DUNIPACE
Manager: Danny Smith; Assistant: Allan Moffat
David Kane (2018 ex Camelon, Kilsyth R, Steins Th)
Liam McCroary (2019 Camelon, ex Cumbernauld Colts, Kilsyth R, Raith Rovers Youths)
Jeff Fergus
Danny Ashe (2019 Kelty Hearts, ex Stirling Alb, E Stirling, Sauchie etc)
Morgan Galloway (2018 Milton

Ams, ex Stirling Albion Youths)
Paul Nash
Sam Colley (2019 Camelon, ex Falkirk Youths)
Alan McFadden
Martin France
Gary Wright (ex Camelon, Kilsyth R, Dunipace)
Liam Craig
Aidan Stevenson
Lee Davidson
Chris Zok
Keir Stevenson (2018 Stenhousemuir)
Wilson Romanis (OL from Cumbernauld Colts)
Ryan Shanks
Jordan Livingstone

NEW SIGNINGS 2021/2
Jack Denham (2021 Camelon)
Marty Wright (2021 Cumbernauld Colts)
Scott Taylor (2021 Bannockburn Ams)
David Morrison 92021 Camelon)
Wilson Romanis (2021 Cumbernauld Colts)
Ryan Kane (2021 Camelon)
David Grant (2021 Darvel)
David Donaldson (2021 Bannockburn Ams)
Andy Grant (2021 Broxburn Ath)

EASTHOUSES LILY

Manager: David McQueenie (19th season as Manager)
Liam Amos
Shaun Murray
Mark Brown
Ryan McQueenie
Grant Gavin
Michael Linton
Paul McDermott
Jason Young
Jack Steven
Neil Janczyk
Alexander Elliot
Michael Hunter
Lewis Russell
Cameron McBeth
James Guy
Blair Short
Jordan Dunsmore

EDINBURGH SOUTH

Manager: John O'Hara
Darren Walker
Matthew Lynch
Blair Tolmie
Jim Young
Ian Ballantyne
Ainslie Hunter
Sean Jamieson
Stephen Manson
Charles McAleavy
Stuart Martin
Mark Tennant
John Kerr
Dale O'Hara
Conan Murie
Taylor Aitchison
Daniel Mcleavy
Greg Fisher
Kris Mitchell

EDINBURGH UNITED

Manager: Ian Flynn
Andrew Swinney 2020 Australian football, ex Whitehill W, Edinburgh University)
Andy Smith (2020 Glasgow University)
Calum Henderson
Cameron Coppola
Cameron Young
Cammy Hanratty (ex Shotts Victoria)
Corey Robertson (2018 Whitehill Welfare)
Daniel McKinlay (2017 Whitehill Welfare)
Darren McCraw (2020 Dunbar United)
Declan Morrison
Euan Lee (2020 Edinburgh Utd U20)
James Flynn (2017)
Jordan Brown
Kyle Brockie
Kyle Scott (2020 Newtongrange Star, Stephen's twin)
Liam Robertson
Robert Downie (2020 Whitehill W)
Robbie Walker
Ryan Sclater (ex Edinburgh Utd, Newtongrange Star, Lothian Thistle, Selkirk)
Scott Hay (ex Edinburgh Utd Youths)
Sean Guiney (2018)
Shaun Miller
Sonny Swanson Ex Leith Ath, Whitehill W)
Stephen Scott (Kyle's twin)
Stevie Clark (2020 Lesmahagow)
Taylor Black (2020 Vale of Leithen, ex Leith Athletic, Newtongrange S)

EYEMOUTH UNITED

Manager: Kevan Wright
Jay Baverstock
Callum Borowski
Reece Bowling
Alexander Chapman
Ryan Chapman
Kyle College
Kieran Grant
Andrew Henderson
David Hendry
Robbie King
James MacDougall
Roderick MacDougall
Dean McKenzie
Khasim Mdalasini
James Moore
Connor Muir
Tadiwanashe Muzambi
Joseph Ngoa
Coner Purvis
Melvin Sebastian
Dennis Smolenskij
Brian Tait
Dylan Thomas
Joao Vieira

GLENROTHES

Co Managers: John Martin / Kevin Smith
Murray Carstairs (2020 Kelty H)
Scott Russell
Graeme Walker
Craig Richardson
Charlie Denton
Blair Smart
Andy McDonald
Stephen King
Fionn McLeod-Kay
Shaw
Callum Kinnes
Blair Smart
Grant Skinner
Lewis Grierson
Conor Schiavone
Craig Watt
Paul McManus (2021 Brechin C, ex East Fife etc)
Frazer Robinson
Stuart Walton
Michael Perrie
Lee Schiavone
Ross Wortley
Roberts
Stephen King

NEW SIGNINGS 2021/2
Kyle Bell
Ryan McInnes (2021 St Andrews United)
Dylan Honeyman
Cammy Lumsden (2021 Crossgates Primrose)

HADDINGTON ATHLETIC

Manager: Joe Hamill
Dale Cornet
Ross King
Guy McGarry
Aaron Congalton
Seamus Russell
Robbie King
Gordon Harris
Ryan Hutchison
Alasdair Simpson
Joe Hamill
Anes Subasic
Gabriele Auriemma
Shaun Hall
Andrew McNeill
Jack Neilson
Stewart O'Neil
Robbie Stirling

HAWICK ROYAL ALBERT UNITED

Manager: George Shepherd
Sam Scott
Kevin Strathdee
John Shankie
David Strathdee
Daniel Chandler
Ashley Lanford
Greg Ford
Lewis Swaney
Nathan Gillie
Calum Hope
Ross Scott
Jordan Steele
Jordan Yardley
Adamo Antonnici
Ryan Shepherd
Sam Burton
Dean Fry
Steven King

HERIOT WATT UNIVERSITY

Manager: Banji Koya
C Reid
J Hogg
T Teviotdale
L Morton
J Wishart
N Kelly
J Barker
R Cairns
C Donnelly
G MacDonald
C Stewart
A McMahon
Calvin Muttitt
A McCreadie
J Kennedy
A Singh
J Thomson
C Smith

HILL OF BEATH HAWTHORN

Manager: John Mitchell
Stuart Hall
Russell Grierson
Lyle Kellichan
Kevin Conners
Rory Harrower
Bradley Grieve
Shaun Leishman
Calum Adamson
Joe Kinninmonth
Jake Mitchell
Daniel Watt
Joe Kirby
Mark Wilkie

Ryan Connelly
Rory Marshall
Jason Finlay
Brandon Luke
Robert McFarlane
Michael Watt
Declan Morgan
Ross Maclachlan

New Signings 2021/2
Lee Wilson (ex Linlithgow Rose, St Andrews United)
Johnny Galloway (Crossgates P)

INVERKEITHING HILLFIELD SWIFTS

Manager: Grant Brough
Coaches: Pat Scullion, Tam Graham, Mark Leslie
Kyle Bow (OL from Raith Rovers)
Macaulay Jarrett
Kieran Annandale
Blair Duff
Shay brough
Johnny Pennel
Reece Pentleton
Callum Deas
Pat Scullion (ex Cowdenbeath, Dunfermline Ath etc)
Dean Anderson
Ynyr Liddell
Steven Slimmings
Josh Morris (ex Berwick R, Cowdenbeath etc)
Finn Graham (2020 Stirling Lions, ex Dunfermline Ath, Arbroath etc)
Gavin Smith
Ronan McMurchie
Hamilton
Cammy Liddell
Reece Bernard
Cai MacDonald
Ryan Mauchlan
Scott Houston
Michael Paterson
Ryan Maclean
Liam Jackson

New Signings 2021/2
Greg Spence (2021 Stenhousemuir)

KENNOWAY STAR HEARTS

Manager: Lee Richardson, Assistant: John Steel
Adam Mansouri (2020 Dundee OL)
Ally Griffin (2020 Inverkeithing HS, ex Falkirk Juniors, Sauchie, Livingston Utd)
Anthony Couper (ex Methil Star)
Calum Brodie (ex Dundee, Arbroath, East Craigie, USA College football)
Brooklyn Mair (2019 Stirling Albion)
Callum Hughes (2020 Kennoway Ams, Abertay Univ)
Craig Brand (2020 Eastern New Mexico Greyhounds, ex St Andrews Utd, Dundee Youths, Cowdenbeath)
Craig Doctor
Craig Wallace (2019, ex Dundee, Kelty Hearts, Bo'ness U, Dundonald BB, Glenrothes)
Dylan Harrison (2020)
Dylan Walker (2019 Kennoway SH Youths)
Gavin McMillan (ex Oakley United, Dunfermline Ath, E Stirlingshire, Berwick R)
Harris Kay (2020 OL from Hill of Beath H)
James Collins
Jason Watson (2019, Youths)
Lee Bryce (2017 ex East Fife, Arbroath etc)
Lewis Payne (2020 Crossgates P, ex Hill of Beath H)
Liam Hogg
Luis O'Rourke (ex AM Soccer, Alloa Athletic U19)
Robbie Hall
Ross Balmer (ex Dunipace, Bo'ness United)
Willie Thomson

JEANFIELD SWIFTS

Manager: Ross Gunnion
Mark Mitchell
Jamie Reid
Aaron Whitehead
Jake Dolzanski
Keiran Stewart
Connor McLaren
Jamie McKenzie
Fraser Smith
Chris McLeish
Chris Dodd
Paul Simpson
Gary Fergus
Mark Smith
Christopher Scott
Shaun Struthers
Ewan Loudon
Sam Townsley
Regan McLaren

KINNOULL

Manager: Alan Cameron
Lukasz Osinski
Patrick Brown
Kyle Woolley
David Gray
Andrew McKenzie
Dale Smart
Shaun Simpson
Cammy Robertson
Ben Ragan
Paul Anderson
Scott Finlay
Liam Woolley
Keiron Dott
Darren Spence
Jordi Duncan
Alan Cunningham
Darren Gray

KIRKCALDY & DYSART

Manager: Craig Ness
Robert Wilson
Steve Jeffries (2019 Glenrothes Strollers)
Chris Ireland (2020 Thornton Hibs, ex Kirkcaldy YM and Ballingry R))
Todd Arthur (2020 Lochore Welfare, ex Raith Rovers Youths, Burntisland Shipyard)
Ryan McEwan
Connor Kirton
Morgan Miller (ex St Johnstone Youths)
Lewis Ross (2020 Dundonald BB)
Chris Price (2018 Greig Park Rangers)
Ricki Cooper (ex Glenrothes, Lochgelly Albert, Thornton H)
Ronnie Martin
Ryan McGowan (2019 ex Raith Rovers Youths)
Steven Page (ex St Andrews Utd, Newburgh, Dundonald BB, Lochgelly Albert)
John Smith (2020 Dundonald BB, ex Dundee)
Lee Duffy (ex Rochdale, Halifax T, Glenrothes, Bo'ness U, Dundonald BB, Oakley Utd, Inverkeithing HS)
Sam Buchan (ex St Andrews Utd, Glenrothes, Dundonald BB)
John Soutar (2019 Dundonald BB)
Nathan Feeley
Calum Geddes
Kyle Fenton
Jason Nouri (2018 Dysart Ans)
Kieran Johnston (2019 Dundonald BB)
Ewan Henderson (ex Thornton Hibs)
Scott Warrender
Callum Doran

LEITH ATHLETIC

Manager: Steven Chalmers
Campbell McLellan
James Redpath (2019 Edinburgh United)
Michael Shaw (ex Leith U19)
Craig Hume (2020 Tranent, ex Berwick R, Newtongrange S, Penicuik Ath, Haddington Ath)
Kerr Allan (2019 Civil Service S, ex Vale of Leithen, Newtongrange S)
Euan Morrice
Andrew Dempster (ex Berwick R)
Ryan Mayer (2020 Gala FR)
Wayne Sproule (2020 Whitehill W, ex Penicuik Ath)
Brodie McKenzie
Martin Maughan (2020 Edinburgh United)
Jay Watson
Rhys Kerr
Gregg Veitch (ex Edinburgh South)
Callum Mein
Gavin Kneeshaw (ex Leith Athletic Youths)
Daniel Simpson (2020 St Kilda (Australia))
Ryan Day (2019 Edinburgh City)
Lewis Tracey
Cameron Stewart
Daryl Williamson (ex Hibs U18)
Kyle Rankin

LINLITHGOW ROSE

Manager: Brown Ferguson
Lee Wilson
Jay Sandison (OL from Hearts)
Brian Schwake (2020 OL from Livingston)
Gary Thom (ex Stenhousemuir, Stirling Albion etc)
Dan Nimmo
Scott Stevenson (2020 E Kilbride)
David Brownlie (2020 E Kilbride)
Liam Allison (2020 Clyde)
Lewis Crawford (2020 Dumbarton)
Ruari McLennan
Roddy McLennan
Owen Ronald
Pat Scullion (Released Nov 2020)
Willis Hare (ex Kelty Hearts)
Sean Dickson (2020 Hurlford United, Released Nov 2020)
Craig Donaldson (2020 Sauchie)
Dean Cairns (2020 E Kilbride)
Daryl Meikle (2020 OL from Hamilton Accies)
Paul Willis (2020 Stirling Albion, ex Berwick R, Dunfermline etc)
Tommy Coyne
Ross Allum
Colin Strickland
Sean Slaven (2020 OL from Hamilton Accies)
Jonny Court (2020 Edinburgh City, Released Nov 2020)
Arnault Bembo (2020 Kelty Hearts)
Myles Hogarth (ex Hearts, Falkirk etc)

New Signings
Mark Stowe (2021 Camelon)

Cammy Thomson (2021 Stirling Albion)

LOCHORE WELFARE

Manager: James Adam
Gary Inglis
Stuart Gillespie
Matthew Christie
Ethan Anderson
Lewis Thomson
Greig Denton
Scott Small
Logan Donaldson
Joe Dawson
Peter Thomson
Ewan Sutherland
Liam Carruthers
Scott Renton
Dylan Gilmour
Adam Doig
Sean Cusick
Kellar Harris
Nathan Harley
Aaron Wood

New Signings
Joe Kirby (2021 Hill of Beath Haws)

LOTHIAN THISTLE HUTCHISON VALE

Manager: Ryan Harding
Kevin Swain
Dylan Moore
Michael Deland
Paul Crawford
Neil Smeaton
Sandy Cunningham (ex Stirling Albion etc)
Darren Smith
Sean Wringe
Liam Kelly
Michael Mbewe
Jamie Henderson
Scott Donald
Louis Signorini
Iain Laver
Adam Brogan
Niall Doherty
Sam Daniel
Thomas Penker
Sean Cumming
David Ross
Sean Lally
Jordan Elliot

MUSSELBURGH ATHLETIC

Manager: Kevin MacDonald (until May 2021), then Kevin Milne
Ryan McGurk
Callum Donaldson
Jordan Orru
Liam Reid
Bradley Donaldson
Declan O'Kane
Nathan Evans
Josh Jeffries
Dean Ballantyne (ex Dunbar United)
Conor Thomson
Bradley Whyte
Paul Grant
Jackie Mylles
Jonjo McManus
Mathu King
Lewis White
Liam Gregory
Darren Downie
Michael Moffat
Ethan Wynne
Lloyd Fiddler
Brian Martin
Scott McNaughton
Ross McRae
Kyle Somers

NEWBURGH

Manager: Scott Hudson, Coaches: Scott Lawson, Rikkie Melville, Willie Hutchison
Aaron Leadbetter (ex Cupar Hearts)
Aidan Edwards (2019 Abernethy U19)
Aman Johal (2018 Strathmiglo United)
Andy Cameron
Ben English (ex Abernethy U19, Kinnoull)
Ben Scarborough (ex Abernethy U19)
Brandon Wright (ex Leven U19)
Calum Sutherland (2018 Strathmiglo United)
Connor Findlay
Connor Murdoch (2020 Bowhill Rovers, ex Strathmiglo United, Cupar Hearts)
Craig Begg (ex Cupar Hearts)
Craig Robinson
Gordon Clark (ex Strathmiglo United)
Harry Galloway
Jack Hutchison (ex Abernethy U19)
Jack Parr (2020 ex Kinnoull, Jeanfield Swifts)
Jamie Gay
Jordan Annandale (ex Bridge of Earn Ams)
Josh Robertson (ex Fife Elite FA, Dunfermline Athletic, Civil Service Strollers)
Kyle Fraser
Kyle Meany
Reece Redpath
Sam Kirkham
Scott Sutherland
Sean Hastie
Tijan Nyass (2020 Kinnoull)

NEWTONGRANGE STAR

Manager: Chris King
Adam Nelson
Dean Apicella
Chris Moffat
Callum Murray
Craig O'Reilly
Dan Garvey (Oct 2020 Leith Athletic)
Dan Garvie
Daniel McBay
David Rennie
Evan Glendinning
Ryan Ferguson
Jack Gillan
Jordan Mungall
Kevin Bracks
Kyle Mitchell
Liam McCathie (ex Dunbar United)
Liam McIntosh
Ross Larner
Ryan Porteous
Sean Brennan
Steven Tait (ex Dunbar United)
Tom Davies
Andrew Muir (OL from Edinburgh City)

OAKLEY UNITED

Manager: Stewart Kenny; Coach: Mark Johnston; Assistant: Peter Kelly
Sean Robertson
Daniel Kelly (2018, ex Sauchie, Tullibody Ams)
Ryan McGill (ex Heston Rovers, South Yarra SC, Victoria United NZ)
Mark Mooney
Craig Martin
Callum Runciman
Bruce McAdam (ex E Stirling, Scone Thistle, Newburgh, Sauchie, Tullibody Ams)
Ross Gunn (ex Tullibody Ams, Whitburn)
James McAteer (ex Bonnybridge YC, Kilsyth Rangers)
Mark Allan
Stuart Love (ex Stenhousemuir, E Stirling, Sauchie, Tullibody Ams)
Johnny Harrison
Ross Gruar
Josh Urquhart
Cameron Shaw
Keir Young
Colin Sanchez
C Neilson
Reece Bernard (2020 Inverkeithing HS)
Ally Burns

ORMISTON

Manager: Richie Weir
Adam Dougan
Brandon McGill
Cameron Burt
Chris Hogg
Conner Scott
Craig Sutherland
Daniel Nichol
Fraser Bell
Jack O'Connor
James Neill
Jonathan Crutcher
Juwon Abubakar
Kacper Korpalski
Kieran Beveridge
Matthew Underhill (ex Spartans, Vale of Leithen son of ref John Underhill)
Olajuwon Abubakar
Reece Cochrane
Reece Hope
Richard Fairnie
Scott Hunter
Scott Siegel
Sean Ballard
Taylor Stepney
Thomas Prior
Tinashe Ruwona
Zac Scally

PEEBLES ROVERS

Manager: Michael Wilson
Jack Stewart
Craig Spalding
Calum Henderson
Liam Andrew
Kern Hutchison
Cameron Coppola
Jack Chessar
David Brown
Grant Doyle
Liam Andrew (2020 Tynecastle)
Dale Skinner
Luke McLean (2019 Tweeddale Rovers, ex Airdrieonians)
David Lindsay
Harry McGill
Ross Lamb (2018 ex Livingston, Gala FR)
Jamie Mackay
Liam Taylor (2020 Danderhall MW)
Euan Anderson
James Dodds
Gary Tickle (OL from Penicuik Ath, permanent for 201/2)

New Signings 2021/2
Connor Muir (2021 Eyemouth United)
Robbie Renwick (2021 Stonehaven, ex Peebles Rovers)
Kieran Weighland (2021, ex Dalkeith Th)
Callum Mitchell (2021 Royal Penicuik)
Scott Latto (2021 Tweeddale Rovers)

PENICUIK ATHLETIC

Manager: Tony Begg (Until July 2021)
Mark Tait
Ryan Baptie
Darrell Young

Daniel Edwards
Callum Connolly
Kieran Watson
Jamie Devlin
Aaron Somerville
Lumbert Kataleza
Paul Tansey
Nicholas Reid
Gregor Lamb
Greg Page
Paul Thomson
Craig Stevenson
Robert Watt
Joe Viola
Lewis Collins

PRESTON ATHLETIC

Manager: Jack Lynch (ex Spartans etc)
David Livie
Kai Austin
Craig Innes
Matthew O'Connor
Rory Young
Dale Pennycuick
Kieran Jack
Ben Bathgate
Ethan Williams
Jonathon Edmond
Joe Murray
Jack Jardine
Marc Molloy
Mikey Hamilton
Jamie Chapman
Steven McCole
Nathan Stokes
Brandon Bain

ROSYTH

Manager: Jamie Cannon
Blair Clark
Blair Penman (ex Cowdenbeath, Crossgates P)
Cammie Lambie
Colin Paterson
Craig Anderson
Gregg Page
Iain Griffin
Jack Henderson
Jarek Butryn
Jason Keith
Kyle Walls
Liam Queen
Martin Woods
Michael Cameron
Michael McMillan
Ruaridh McPhate
Ryan McDonald
Sean Johnstone
Stephen Young
Tom Hampson

SAUCHIE

Manager: Fraser Duncan; Assistant: David Beaton; Coaches: Darren Petrie, Darren Cummings, Greg Maitland
Chic Bell
Iain Syme
Mark Finlayson
Brian Morgan (2020 Bo'ness United, ex Sauchie)
Ross Crawford
Ant McTaggart
Sam Collumbine
Jon Tully
Mark Sharp
Darren Carroll
Lewis Turnbull
Aaron Bryson
David McCaughie (Ex E Stirling, completing a PhD in Architectural Preservation)
Donaldson
Ross Wilson
Danny Smith
David Cross
Gary Carroll
Ross Crawford
Stewart Houston
Adam Green
Chris Brown
Craig Donaldson
Darren Carr
Mark Sharp
Brett Young
Jack Docherty
Oliver Fleming (Released Oct 2020)

ST ANDREWS UNITED

Manager: Charlie King; Coaches: Paul Quinn, Drew Fleming, Darren Tennant
Connor Shaw (ex Pumpherston)
Michael Fleming (ex Oakley United)
Nik Rendall n(ex Pumpherston)
Willie Campbell (ex Fauldhouse United)
Ryan O'Connor (ex Inverkeithing HS, Steelend Vics etc)
Ryan McInnes (ex Leven United)
Dylan Honeyman (ex Glenrothes)
Jason Penman (ex Dundonald BB)
Kyle Wilson (ex Dundonald BB, joined Linlithgow Rose Nov 2020)
Graeme Hart (ex Forfar WE)
Ross Cunningham (ex Newburgh)
Douglas Crowe (ex Spartans)
Kyle Moran (ex Dundonald BB)
Daryl Falconer (ex Glenrothes)
Scott Cunningham (ex St Andrews Colts)
Jake Grady (ex Fairmuir BC)
Charlie King (ex Tayport, Brechin Vcs, St Johnstone, Brechin C etc)
Michael Potter (ex Tayport)
Owen Andrew (ex Kelty Hearts, son of Benny Andrew)
Drew Fleming (ex Broughty Athletic)
Kyle Sneddon (Nov 2020 OL from Cowdenbeath)
Jack Healy (Nov 2020 OL from East Fife)
Alistair Wilkinson (Nov 2020 OL from East Fife)

STIRLING UNIVERSITY (EOS)

Cammy McKinley
Finlay Bainbridge
Jack Docherty
Fraser Binnie
Archie Perris
Murray Bushell

THORNTON HIBS

Manager: Craig Gilbert, Assistant: Charles Dignan, Coach: Peter Simpson, Jack Martin
Adam Drummond (2017 Ex Glenrothes, Linlithgow Rose & Greig Park Rangers, plus 3 previous spells with Thornton)
Andrew Adam (ex Raith Rovers, Kettle United, Lomond Vics, Greig Park Rangers, Thornton H)
Daniel McNab (2013 Unattached, ex Dunfermline Ath, St johns)
Darren Ormiston (2020 ex Glenrothes, Lochgelly Albert and Lothian Thistle Hutchison Vale)
Dean McMillan (2016 Lochore Welfare, Ex Ballingry Rovers, Oakley United, Rosyth, East Fife, Dunfermline Ath)
Elliot Ford (2019 Kelty Hearts, ex Rangers, Hearts, Raith Rovers, Brechin City)
Fergus Mackie (2018 Thornton Hibs U19)
Garry Thomson (2009 Raith Rovers)
Ian Hepburn (3rd spell with Thornton)
Ian Shanks
Jack Hoskisson (2019 Thornton Hibs U19)
Jack Wilson (2019 St Andrews United, ex Bo'ness United (Loan), Lochgelly Albert (Loan), Kelty Hearts, Thornton Hibs)
Jamie McNeish (2020 Lochore Welfare, ex Kirkcaldy YMCA, St Andrews United, Crossgates Primrose)
Jimmy Shields (2014 Dundonald BB, exHill of Beath H, Glenrothes, Thornton H
Jordan Millar (2020 Kelty Hearts, ex Hearts, St Johnstone, Montrose, Lochee United)
Liam Rolland (2020 Greig Park Rangers, ex Dundonald Bluebell, St Andrews United, Kennoway Star Hearts, Grandson of Andy Rolland)
Matthew Robertson (2016 Rosyth, ex East Fife Youths, Eastvale)
Max Coleman (2016 Balgonie Scotia)
Michael Lee (2020 ex Dundee United, Glenrothes, Hill of Beath Hawthorn, Thornton Hibs, Kennoway Star Hearts, Kennoway Amateurs
Ross Hain (2020 Thornton Hibs U19)
Ryan Linton (2016 Denbeath)
Stuart Drummond (2015 Eastvale, nephew of Adam)

TRANENT

Manager: Calum Elliot (ex Hearts, Raith Rovers etc)
Adam Watson
Ally Adams
Arran Ponton
Bradley Barrett
Ben Miller
Ciaran McKenzie
Dean Whitson
Euan Greig
Gary Hamilton
Ian Moffat
Jack Chesser
Andy Jones
Kayne Paterson
Kyle Lander
Lewis Hawkins
Ciaran McKenzie
Owen Renton
Ben Reilly
Rhys Craigie
Richard Miller
Sean Murphy
Shaun Rutherford
Steven Thomson

TWEEDMOUTH RANGERS

Manager: Neil Oliver (ex Berwick R, Falkirk etc);
Assistant: David Brown
Stuart Allan
Craig Bell
Conor Brian
Craig Heath
Sean Campbell
Jordan Crombie
Drew Cummings
Rhys Dixon
Yassine Essalhi
Danny Fletcher
Jack Forster
Miguel Freire
Regan Graham
Ciaran Hatsell

Craig Heath
Ben Jackson
Lee Lambert
Leiper
Adam Mutch
Niall Richards
Jake Rutherford
Simpson
Lennon Stewart
Jack Strangeways

TYNECASTLE

Manager: Stephen McLeish
Kyle Leiper
Ryan Stevenson
Blake Wales
Scott Jardine
Sean Melvin
Matthew Combe
Oban Anderson
Jack Beaumont
Fletcher Hendry
Kenneth Fisher
Taylor Hendry
Ryan Cameron
Matthew Dillon
Stephane Murray
Lee Dawson
Jamie Rae
Jonathan Steel
Joseph Evenden

WHITEHILL WELFARE

Manager: Neil Janczyk, then Andrew Kidd
Andrew Kidd (2020 Sandys)
Bryan Wilson (2020 Preston Athletic)
C McGregor
Chris Cairney
Chris Cairney
Connor Spowart
Darren McGlashan (2020 Dalkeith Thistle_)
Dean Cunningham
Finlay Connor
G Twaddle
Jordan Lister (2019 Dalkeith Thistle)
Jack Murray
James Scobie
Jordan Caddow
K Lough
K Stewart
Kevin-Lee Keane (2018 Newtongrange Star)
L McCormack
Liam McKenna (2020 Sandys)
L Smith
Louis Maguire
M Ramos
Matthew McCormack
Michael Barfoot (2020 Tynecastle)
Michael Hornig
Murray Hand (2020 Spartans, joined Leith Athletic July 2021)
Neil Janczyk (ex Hearts etc)
O Hetherington
R Connell
Robert McKenzie
Ross Coats
Ross Gilpin
Ross Gilpin (2020 Vale of Leithen)
S Millar
S Thomson
Scott Millar
Stephen Anderson (2021)
Tyler O'Neill
Wayne McIntosh

East of Scotland League Fixtures 2021/22

PREMIER DIVISION

Friday, July 16
Lothian Thistle HV 2-2 Musselburgh Athletic

Saturday, July 17
Broxburn Athletic 1-4 Penicuik Athletic
Camelon Juniors 4-1 Newtongrange Star
Crossgates Primrose 1-1 Linlithgow Rose
Dundonald Bluebell 4-1 Whitehill Welfare
Hill of Beath Hawthorn 2-3 Tranent Juniors
Inverkeithing Hillfield Swifts 1-1 Tynecastle
Jeanfield Swifts 0-4 Blackburn United
Sauchie Juniors 1-3 Dunbar United

Tuesday, July 20
Dunbar United 2-1 Broxburn Athletic
Linlithgow Rose 6-1 Hill of Beath Hawthorn
Musselburgh Athletic 2-0 Sauchie Juniors
Newtongrange Star 1-1 Inverkeithing Hillfield Swifts
Penicuik Athletic 1-0 Crossgates Primrose
Tranent Juniors 3-0 Lothian Thistle HV
Tynecastle 2-2 Jeanfield Swifts
Whitehill Welfare 3-4 Camelon Juniors

Wednesday, July 21
Blackburn United 0-2 Dundonald Bluebell

Saturday, July 24
Blackburn United 3-1 Hill of Beath Hawthorn
Dunbar United 0-1 Camelon Juniors
Linlithgow Rose 4-0 Inverkeithing Hillfield Swifts
Musselburgh Athletic 2-2 Crossgates Primrose
Newtongrange Star 0-1 Jeanfield Swifts
Penicuik Athletic 3-1 Lothian Thistle HV
Tranent Juniors 2-0 Dundonald Bluebell
Tynecastle 3-2 Sauchie Juniors
Whitehill Welfare 0-2 Broxburn Athletic

Tuesday, July 27
Broxburn Athletic 1-3 Tranent Juniors
Hill of Beath Hawthorn 1-6 Tynecastle
Camelon Juniors A-A(0-0) Musselburgh Athletic – abandoned 28 mins, pitch waterlogged
Sauchie Juniors A-A(3-2) Blackburn United – abandoned 83 mins, pitch waterlogged

Wednesday, July 28
Crossgates Primrose – Newtongrange Star
Dundonald Bluebell – Linlithgow Rose
Inverkeithing Hillfield Sw. – Penicuik Athletic
Jeanfield Swifts – Whitehill Welfare
Lothian Thistle HV – Dunbar United
Saturday, July 31
Blackburn United – Whitehill Welfare
Broxburn Athletic – Newtongrange Star
Crossgates Primrose – Tranent Juniors
Dundonald Bluebell – Musselburgh Athletic
Jeanfield Swifts – Dunbar United
Lothian Thistle HV – Inverkeithing Hillfield Sw
Penicuik Athletic – Tynecastle
Sauchie Juniors – Linlithgow Rose

Saturday, August 7
Camelon Juniors – Dundonald Bluebell
Dunbar United – Hill of Beath Hawthorn
Linlithgow Rose – Penicuik Athletic
Musselburgh Athletic – Jeanfield Swifts
Newtongrange Star – Blackburn United
Tranent Juniors – Sauchie Juniors
Tynecastle – Broxburn Athletic
Whitehill Welfare – Lothian Thistle HV

Saturday, August 14
Blackburn United – Broxburn Athletic
Crossgates Primrose – Tynecastle
Dunbar United – Musselburgh Athletic
Hill of Beath Hawthorn – Dundonald Bluebell
Inverkeithing Hillfield Swifts – Camelon Juniors
Jeanfield Swifts – Tranent Juniors
Lothian Thistle HV – Linlithgow Rose
Sauchie Juniors – Penicuik Athletic
Whitehill Welfare – Newtongrange Star

Tuesday, August 17
Linlithgow Rose – Musselburgh Athletic
Penicuik Athletic – Jeanfield Swifts
Sauchie Juniors – Newtongrange Star
Tynecastle – Tranent Juniors
Whitehill Welfare – Inverkeithing Hillfield Swifts

Wednesday, August 18
Blackburn United – Dunbar United
Broxburn Athletic – Hill of Beath Hawthorn
Crossgates Primrose – Camelon Juniors
Dundonald Bluebell – Lothian Thistle HV

Saturday, August 21
Broxburn Athletic – Crossgates Primrose
Dundonald Bluebell – Sauchie Juniors
Inverkeithing Hillfield Swifts – Jeanfield Swifts
Linlithgow Rose – Dunbar United
Musselburgh Athletic – Hill of Beath Hawthorn
Newtongrange Star – Lothian Thistle HV
Penicuik Athletic – Camelon Juniors
Tranent Juniors – Blackburn United
Tynecastle – Whitehill Welfare

Tuesday, August 31
Camelon Juniors – Sauchie Juniors
Dunbar United – Tynecastle
Hill of Beath Hawthorn – Whitehill Welfare
Musselburgh Athletic – Penicuik Athletic
Newtongrange Star – Dundonald Bluebell
Tranent Juniors – Linlithgow Rose

Saturday, September 4
Camelon Juniors – Blackburn United
Crossgates Primrose – Hill of Beath Hawthorn
Inverkeithing Hillfield Swifts – Dundonald Bluebell
Jeanfield Swifts – Sauchie Juniors
Linlithgow Rose – Broxburn Athletic
Lothian Thistle HV – Tynecastle
Newtongrange Star – Penicuik Athletic
Tranent Juniors – Musselburgh Athletic
Whitehill Welfare – Dunbar United

Wednesday, September 8
Inverkeithing Hillfield Swifts – Blackburn United
Jeanfield Swifts – Broxburn Athletic
Lothian Thistle HV – Crossgates Primrose

Saturday, September 11
Crossgates Primrose – Jeanfield Swifts
Inverkeithing Hillfield Swifts – Broxburn Athletic

Saturday, September 25
Blackburn United – Crossgates Primrose
Camelon Juniors – Tranent Juniors
Dunbar United – Inverkeithing Hillfield Swifts
Dundonald Bluebell – Penicuik Athletic
Hill of Beath Hawthorn – Newtongrange Star
Jeanfield Swifts – Lothian Thistle HV
Musselburgh Athletic – Tynecastle
Sauchie Juniors – Broxburn Athletic
Whitehill Welfare – Linlithgow Rose

Tuesday, September 28
Hill of Beath Hawthorn – Camelon Juniors

Saturday, October 2
Camelon Juniors – Jeanfield Swifts
Crossgates Primrose – Dunbar United
Inverkeithing Hillfield Swifts – Musselburgh Athletic
Linlithgow Rose – Lothian Thistle HV
Newtongrange Star – Tranent Juniors
Penicuik Athletic – Hill of Beath Hawthorn
Tynecastle – Blackburn United
Whitehill Welfare – Sauchie Juniors

Sunday, October 3
Broxburn Athletic – Dundonald Bluebell

Tuesday, October 5
Dunbar United – Penicuik Athletic
Hill of Beath Hawthorn – Sauchie Juniors
Newtongrange Star – Linlithgow Rose
Tranent Juniors – Whitehill Welfare

Wednesday, October 6
Blackburn United – Musselburgh Athletic
Broxburn Athletic – Inverkeithing Hillfield Swifts
Dundonald Bluebell – Tynecastle
Jeanfield Swifts – Crossgates Primrose
Lothian Thistle HV – Camelon Juniors

Saturday, October 9
Blackburn United – Linlithgow Rose
Broxburn Athletic – Lothian Thistle HV
Dunbar United – Tranent Juniors
Dundonald Bluebell – Jeanfield Swifts
Hill of Beath Hawthorn – Inverkeithing Hillfield Swifts
Musselburgh Athletic – Newtongrange Star
Penicuik Athletic – Whitehill Welfare
Sauchie Juniors – Crossgates Primrose
Tynecastle – Camelon Juniors

Saturday, October 30
Crossgates Primrose – Whitehill Welfare
Dunbar United – Dundonald Bluebell
Linlithgow Rose – Jeanfield Swifts
Lothian Thistle HV – Hill of Beath Hawthorn
Musselburgh Athletic – Broxburn Athletic
Penicuik Athletic – Blackburn United
Sauchie Juniors – Camelon Juniors

Tranent Juniors – Inverkeithing Hillfield Swifts
Tynecastle – Newtongrange Star

Saturday, November 6
Blackburn United – Tranent Juniors
Broxburn Athletic – Whitehill Welfare
Camelon Juniors – Linlithgow Rose
Dundonald Bluebell – Dunbar United
Hill of Beath Hawthorn – Musselburgh Athletic
Jeanfield Swifts – Inverkeithing Hillfield Swifts
Newtongrange Star – Crossgates Primrose
Sauchie Juniors – Lothian Thistle HV
Tynecastle – Penicuik Athletic

Tuesday, November 9
Camelon Juniors – Lothian Thistle HV
Linlithgow Rose – Newtongrange Star
Musselburgh Athletic – Blackburn United
Penicuik Athletic – Dunbar United
Sauchie Juniors – Hill of Beath Hawthorn
Tynecastle – Dundonald Bluebell
Whitehill Welfare – Tranent Juniors

Wednesday, November 10
Inverkeithing Hillfield Swifts – Crossgates Primrose

Saturday, November 13
Camelon Juniors – Broxburn Athletic
Crossgates Primrose – Dundonald Bluebell
Inverkeithing Hillfield Swifts – Sauchie Juniors
Jeanfield Swifts – Hill of Beath Hawthorn
Linlithgow Rose – Tynecastle
Lothian Thistle HV – Blackburn United
Newtongrange Star – Dunbar United
Tranent Juniors – Penicuik Athletic
Whitehill Welfare – Musselburgh Athletic

Saturday, December 4
Blackburn United – Newtongrange Star
Broxburn Athletic – Jeanfield Swifts
Dunbar United – Linlithgow Rose
Dundonald Bluebell – Camelon Juniors
Lothian Thistle HV – Whitehill Welfare
Musselburgh Athletic – Inverkeithing Hillfield Swifts
Penicuik Athletic – Sauchie Juniors
Tranent Juniors – Crossgates Primrose
Tynecastle – Hill of Beath Hawthorn

Saturday, December 11
Camelon Juniors – Dunbar United
Crossgates Primrose – Musselburgh Athletic
Hill of Beath Hawthorn – Broxburn Athletic
Inverkeithing Hillfield Swifts – Lothian Thistle HV
Jeanfield Swifts – Penicuik Athletic
Linlithgow Rose – Dundonald Bluebell
Newtongrange Star – Tynecastle
Sauchie Juniors – Tranent Juniors
Whitehill Welfare – Blackburn United

Saturday, December 18
Blackburn United – Jeanfield Swifts
Broxburn Athletic – Tynecastle
Camelon Juniors – Crossgates Primrose
Dunbar United – Sauchie Juniors
Lothian Thistle HV – Dundonald Bluebell
Musselburgh Athletic – Linlithgow Rose
Penicuik Athletic – Inverkeithing Hillfield Swifts
Tranent Juniors – Newtongrange Star
Whitehill Welfare – Hill of Beath Hawthorn

CONFERENCE A

Saturday, July 17
Arniston Rangers 0-5 Kennoway Star Hearts
Coldstream 0-4 Leith Athletic
Dunipace 0-0 Haddington Athletic
Edinburgh United 0-0 Dalkeith Thistle
Kirkcaldy & Dysart 2-1 Rosyth
Ormiston 0-2 St Andrews United
Craigroyston P-P Tweedmouth Rangers

Tuesday, July 20
Dalkeith Thistle 1-2 Ormiston
Kennoway Star Hearts 2-1 Craigroyston
Kirkcaldy & Dysart 0-2 Leith Athletic – fixture reversed
Rosyth 2-2 Coldstream

Wednesday, July 21
Haddington Athletic 4-1 Arniston Rangers
Thornton Hibs 2-4 Dunipace
Tweedmouth Rangers 1-4 Edinburgh United

Saturday, July 24
Dalkeith Thistle 2-1 Dunipace
Kennoway Star Hearts 5-0 Coldstream
Kirkcaldy & Dysart 3-2 Tweedmouth Rangers – fixture reversed
Leith Athletic 7-1 Arniston Rangers
Rosyth 3-1 Edinburgh United
St Andrews United 1-2 Craigroyston
Thornton Hibs 0-2 Ormiston

Tuesday, July 27
Coldstream 3-0 Dalkeith Thistle
Craigroyston 3-5 Rosyth
Dunipace 7-0 St Andrews United
Edinburgh United 1-1 Kennoway Star Hearts
Ormiston 0-2 Leith Athletic

Wednesday, July 28
Arniston Rangers 0-4 Thornton Hibs
Kirkcaldy & Dysart 0-3 Haddington Athletic

Saturday, July 31
Arniston Rangers – Tweedmouth Rangers
Coldstream – Kirkcaldy & Dysart
Craigroyston – Thornton Hibs
Haddington Athletic – Dalkeith Thistle
Ormiston – Kennoway Star Hearts
Rosyth – Leith Athletic
Edinburgh United P-P St Andrews United

Saturday, August 7
Dalkeith Thistle – St Andrews United
Dunipace – Coldstream

Saturday, August 14
Arniston Rangers – Craigroyston
Kennoway Star Hearts – Dunipace
Kirkcaldy & Dysart – Ormiston
Leith Athletic – Dalkeith Thistle
St Andrews United – Haddington Athletic
Thornton Hibs – Edinburgh United
Tweedmouth Rangers – Rosyth

Tuesday, August 17
Edinburgh United – Haddington Athletic

Saturday, August 21
Coldstream – Arniston Rangers
Craigroyston – Kirkcaldy & Dysart
Dalkeith Thistle – Thornton Hibs
Edinburgh United – Ormiston
Haddington Athletic – Kennoway Star Hearts
Rosyth – Dunipace
St Andrews United – Tweedmouth Rangers

Tuesday, August 31
Coldstream – Edinburgh United
Haddington Athletic – Craigroyston

Saturday, September 4
Arniston Rangers – Dalkeith Thistle
Craigroyston – Leith Athletic
Edinburgh United – Dunipace
Kennoway Star Hearts – St Andrews United
Kirkcaldy & Dysart – Thornton Hibs
Ormiston – Haddington Athletic
Tweedmouth Rangers – Coldstream
Rosyth idle

Saturday, September 11
Ormiston – Rosyth
Thornton Hibs – Leith Athletic

Saturday, September 25
Coldstream – St Andrews United
Craigroyston – Dalkeith Thistle
Dunipace – Ormiston
Edinburgh United – Arniston Rangers
Haddington Athletic – Leith Athletic
Kennoway Star Hearts – Rosyth
Tweedmouth Rangers – Thornton Hibs

Saturday, October 2
Arniston Rangers – Dunipace
Dalkeith Thistle – Tweedmouth Rangers
Kirkcaldy & Dysart – Edinburgh United
Leith Athletic – St Andrews United
Ormiston – Craigroyston
Rosyth – Haddington Athletic
Thornton Hibs – Coldstream

Saturday, October 9
Coldstream – Ormiston
Dalkeith Thistle – Rosyth
Dunipace – Craigroyston
Haddington Athletic – Tweedmouth Rangers
Leith Athletic – Edinburgh United
St Andrews United – Kirkcaldy & Dysart
Thornton Hibs – Kennoway Star Hearts
Arniston Rangers idle

Saturday, October 30
Arniston Rangers – Ormiston
Coldstream – Craigroyston
Haddington Athletic – Thornton Hibs
Leith Athletic – Kennoway Star Hearts
Kirkcaldy & Dysart – Dalkeith Thistle
St Andrews United – Rosyth
Tweedmouth Rangers – Dunipace

Saturday, November 6
Dalkeith Thistle – Leith Athletic
Edinburgh United – Coldstream
Kennoway Star Hearts – Tweedmouth

Rangers
Kirkcaldy & Dysart – Craigroyston
Ormiston – Arniston Rangers
Rosyth – St Andrews United
Thornton Hibs – Haddington Athletic

Saturday, November 13
Craigroyston – Edinburgh United
Dunipace – Leith Athletic
Haddington Athletic – Coldstream
Kennoway Star Hearts – Kirkcaldy & Dysart
Rosyth – Arniston Rangers
Thornton Hibs – St Andrews United
Tweedmouth Rangers – Ormiston
Dalkeith Thistle idle

Saturday, December 4
Dalkeith Thistle – Edinburgh United
Haddington Athletic – Dunipace
Kennoway Star Hearts – Arniston Rangers
Leith Athletic – Coldstream
Rosyth – Kirkcaldy & Dysart
St Andrews United – Ormiston
Tweedmouth Rangers – Craigroyston

Saturday, December 11
Arniston Rangers – Leith Athletic
Coldstream – Kennoway Star Hearts
Craigroyston – St Andrews United
Dunipace – Dalkeith Thistle
Edinburgh United – Rosyth
Ormiston – Thornton Hibs
Tweedmouth Rangers – Kirkcaldy & Dysart

Saturday, December 18
Arniston Rangers – Coldstream
Dalkeith Thistle – Haddington Athletic
Kirkcaldy & Dysart – Dunipace
Rosyth – Ormiston
St Andrews United – Edinburgh United
Thornton Hibs – Craigroyston
Tweedmouth Rangers – Leith Athletic

CONFERENCE B

Saturday, July 17
Burntisland Shipyard 2-2 Heriot-Watt University
Edinburgh South 3-4 Easthouses Lily
Glenrothes 9-1 Hawick Royal Albert United
Kinnoull 1-3 Preston Athletic
Lochgelly Albert 0-3 Oakley United
Peebles Rovers 2-4 Luncarty
Stirling University EOS 2-3 Lochore Welfare

Tuesday, July 20
Easthouses Lily 2-4 Kinnoull
Heriot-Watt University 3-1 Newburgh
Oakley United 4-4 Burntisland Shipyard
Preston Athletic 1-0 Lochore Welfare
Wednesday, July 21

Hawick Royal Albert United 1-2 Edinburgh South
Luncarty 8-0 Lochgelly Albert
Stirling University EOS 3-2 Peebles Rovers

Saturday, July 24
Hawick Royal Albert United 0-6 Kinnoull
Heriot-Watt University 2-0 Lochgelly Albert
Luncarty 2-0 Lochore Welfare
Newburgh 2-1 Edinburgh South – fixture reversed
Oakley United 5-1 Peebles Rovers
Preston Athletic 0-0 Glenrothes
Stirling University EOS 0-0 Burntisland Shipyard

Tuesday, July 27
Edinburgh South 1-0 Luncarty
Lochore Welfare 3-1 Oakley United
Peebles Rovers 0-3 Glenrothes
Preston Athletic 1-0 Heriot-Watt University

Wednesday, July 28
Burntisland Shipyard 6-0 Hawick Royal Albert United
Lochgelly Albert 1-4 Easthouses Lily
Newburgh 1-3 Stirling University EOS

Saturday, July 31
Easthouses Lily – Luncarty
Edinburgh South – Burntisland Shipyard
Glenrothes – Oakley United
Kinnoull – Lochore Welfare
Newburgh – Hawick Royal Albert United
Peebles Rovers – Heriot-Watt University
Stirling University EOS – Lochgelly Albert
Preston Athletic idle

Friday, August 6
Easthouses Lily – Peebles Rovers

Saturday, August 7
Hawick Royal Albert United – Stirling University EOS

Saturday, August 14
Burntisland Shipyard – Easthouses Lily
Heriot-Watt University – Glenrothes
Lochgelly Albert – Edinburgh South
Lochore Welfare – Hawick Royal Albert United
Newburgh – Peebles Rovers
Oakley United – Preston Athletic
Stirling University EOS – Kinnoull
Luncarty idle

Tuesday, August 17
Lochore Welfare – Newburgh
Preston Athletic – Edinburgh South

Wednesday, August 18
Burntisland Shipyard – Luncarty
Hawick Royal Albert United – Heriot-Watt University
Kinnoull – Glenrothes

Saturday, August 21
Burntisland Shipyard – Preston Athletic
Easthouses Lily – Newburgh
Glenrothes – Stirling University EOS
Hawick Royal Albert United – Lochgelly Albert
Lochore Welfare – Kinnoull
Luncarty – Heriot-Watt University
Oakley United – Edinburgh South

Saturday, September 4
Glenrothes – Burntisland Shipyard
Kinnoull – Luncarty
Lochore Welfare – Lochgelly Albert
Newburgh – Oakley United
Peebles Rovers – Hawick Royal Albert United
Preston Athletic – Easthouses Lily
Stirling University EOS – Heriot-Watt University
Edinburgh South idle

Saturday, September 11
Burntisland Shipyard – Peebles Rovers
Luncarty – Glenrothes
Stirling University EOS – Easthouses Lily

Saturday, September 25
Easthouses Lily – Heriot-Watt University
Edinburgh South – Kinnoull
Glenrothes – Newburgh
Lochgelly Albert – Preston Athletic
Luncarty – Stirling University EOS
Oakley United – Hawick Royal Albert United
Peebles Rovers – Lochore Welfare
Burntisland Shipyard idle

Saturday, October 2
Easthouses Lily – Glenrothes
Hawick Royal Albert United – Luncarty
Heriot-Watt University – Oakley United
Kinnoull – Burntisland Shipyard
Newburgh – Lochgelly Albert
Peebles Rovers – Edinburgh South
Preston Athletic – Stirling University EOS
Saturday, October 9
Burntisland Shipyard – Lochore Welfare
Easthouses Lily – Peebles Rovers
Hawick Royal Albert United – Preston Athletic
Heriot-Watt University – Edinburgh South
Lochgelly Albert – Glenrothes
Luncarty – Newburgh
Oakley United – Kinnoull
Stirling University EOS idle

Saturday, October 30
Glenrothes – Edinburgh South
Kinnoull – Heriot-Watt University
Lochore Welfare – Easthouses Lily
Newburgh – Burntisland Shipyard
Oakley United – Stirling University EOS
Peebles Rovers – Lochgelly Albert
Preston Athletic – Luncarty

Saturday, November 6
Burntisland Shipyard – Newburgh
Easthouses Lily – Lochore Welfare
Hawick Royal Albert United – Oakley United
Heriot-Watt University – Peebles Rovers
Kinnoull – Lochgelly Albert
Stirling University EOS – Preston Athletic

Sunday, November 7
Edinburgh South – Glenrothes

Saturday, November 13
Easthouses Lily – Hawick Royal Albert United
Edinburgh South – Stirling University EOS
Glenrothes – Lochore Welfare
Lochgelly Albert – Burntisland Shipyard
Luncarty – Oakley United
Newburgh – Kinnoull
Peebles Rovers – Preston Athletic
Heriot-Watt University idle

Saturday, December 4

Easthouses Lily – Edinburgh South
Hawick Royal Albert United – Glenrothes
Heriot-Watt University – Burntisland Shipyard
Lochore Welfare – Stirling University EOS
Luncarty – Peebles Rovers
Oakley United – Lochgelly Albert
Preston Athletic – Kinnoull

Saturday, December 11

Burntisland Shipyard – Oakley United
Edinburgh South – Hawick Royal Albert United
Kinnoull – Easthouses Lily
Lochgelly Albert – Luncarty
Lochore Welfare – Preston Athletic
Newburgh – Heriot-Watt University
Peebles Rovers – Stirling University EOS

Saturday, December 18
Glenrothes – Luncarty
Heriot-Watt University – Hawick Royal Albert United
Lochore Welfare – Edinburgh South
Newburgh – Easthouses Lily
Peebles Rovers – Kinnoull
Preston Athletic – Burntisland Shipyard
Stirling University EOS – Oakley United

CONFERENCE X

Saturday, July 17
Bathgate Thistle 1-3 Syngenta
Bo'ness Athletic 0-1 West Calder United
Edinburgh College 1-4 Pumpherston Juniors – behind closed doors
Fauldhouse United 2-1 Stoneyburn Juniors
Livingston United 0-2 Whitburn Juniors

Tuesday, July 20
Bo'ness Athletic 7-2 Whitburn Juniors
Livingston United 4-1 Bathgate Thistle
Stoneyburn Juniors 1-2 Edinburgh College

Wednesday, July 21
Armadale Thistle 2-0 West Calder United
Syngenta 5-0 Pumpherston Juniors

Friday, July 23
Bo'ness Athletic 7-4 Fauldhouse United

Saturday, July 24
Armadale Thistle 2-3 Livingston United
Pumpherston Juniors 2-0 Bathgate Thistle
West Calder United 0-4 Syngenta
Whitburn Juniors 4-0 Edinburgh College
Stoneyburn Juniors idle

Tuesday, July 27
Edinburgh College 0-1 Livingston United
Fauldhouse United 0-1 Syngenta
Stoneyburn Juniors 0-4 Bo'ness Athletic
Whitburn Juniors 3-3 West Calder United

Wednesday, July 28
Armadale Thistle 8-0 Pumpherston Juniors

Saturday, July 31
Bathgate Thistle – West Calder United
Edinburgh College – Fauldhouse United
Livingston United – Bo'ness Athletic
Pumpherston Juniors – Syngenta
Stoneyburn Juniors – Armadale Thistle

Saturday, August 7
Stoneyburn Juniors – Fauldhouse United
Syngenta – Bathgate Thistle
West Calder United – Armadale Thistle

Saturday, August 14
Bathgate Thistle – Edinburgh College
Fauldhouse United – West Calder United
Pumpherston Juniors – Bo'ness Athletic
Syngenta – Armadale Thistle
Whitburn Juniors – Stoneyburn Juniors

Tuesday, August 17
Armadale Thistle – Bo'ness Athletic
Pumpherston Juniors – Fauldhouse United

Wednesday, August 18
Syngenta – Livingston United
West Calder United – Edinburgh College

Friday, August 20
Bo'ness Athletic – Bathgate Thistle
Syngenta – Stoneyburn Juniors

Saturday, August 21
Edinburgh College – Armadale Thistle
Livingston United – Fauldhouse United
Pumpherston Juniors – Whitburn Juniors

Tuesday, August 31
Bo'ness Athletic – Pumpherston

Saturday, September 4
Bathgate Thistle – Armadale Thistle
Fauldhouse United – Whitburn Juniors
Pumpherston Juniors – Livingston United
Syngenta – Edinburgh College
West Calder United – Stoneyburn Juniors
Bo'ness Athletic idle
Saturday, September 11

Bathgate Thistle – Stoneyburn

Tuesday, September 21
Edinburgh College – Whitburn

Friday, September 24
Bo'ness Athletic – Armadale Thistle

Saturday, September 25
Bathgate Thistle – Pumpherston Juniors
Edinburgh College – West Calder United
Livingston United – Syngenta
Stoneyburn Juniors – Whitburn Juniors

Saturday, October 2
Armadale Thistle – Stoneyburn Juniors
Bathgate Thistle – Livingston United
Fauldhouse United – Edinburgh College
West Calder United – Bo'ness Athletic
Whitburn Juniors – Syngenta
Pumpherston Juniors idle

Saturday, October 9
Armadale Thistle – Fauldhouse United
Bo'ness Athletic – Syngenta
Livingston United – West Calder United
Stoneyburn Juniors – Pumpherston Juniors
Whitburn Juniors – Bathgate Thistle
Edinburgh College idle

Saturday, October 23
Armadale Thistle – Edinburgh College
Fauldhouse United – Livingston United
Stoneyburn Juniors – Bathgate Thistle
Syngenta – West Calder United
Whitburn Juniors – Bo'ness Athletic
Pumpherston Juniors idle

Saturday, October 30
Edinburgh College – Bathgate Thistle
Fauldhouse United – Bo'ness Athletic
Pumpherston Juniors – Armadale Thistle
Stoneyburn Juniors – Syngenta
Whitburn Juniors – Livingston United
West Calder United idle

Saturday, November 6
Bathgate Thistle – Bo'ness Athletic
Livingston United – Armadale Thistle
Pumpherston Juniors – Edinburgh College
Syngenta – Whitburn Juniors
West Calder United – Fauldhouse United
Stoneyburn Juniors idle

Saturday, November 13
Armadale Thistle – Whitburn Juniors
Edinburgh College – Bo'ness Athletic
Fauldhouse United – Bathgate Thistle
Stoneyburn Juniors – Livingston United
West Calder United – Pumpherston Juniors
Syngenta idle

Saturday, December 4
Armadale Thistle – Syngenta
Bo'ness Athletic – Stoneyburn Juniors
Fauldhouse United – Pumpherston Juniors
Livingston United – Edinburgh College
West Calder United – Whitburn Juniors
Bathgate Thistle idle

Saturday, December 11
Armadale Thistle – Livingston United
Bathgate Thistle – West Calder United
Edinburgh College – Bo'ness Athletic
Fauldhouse United – Stoneyburn Juniors
Whitburn Juniors – Syngenta
Pumpherston Juniors idle

Saturday, December 18
Bo'ness Athletic – Fauldhouse United
Livingston United – Whitburn Juniors
Pumpherston Juniors – Bathgate Thistle
Syngenta – Edinburgh College
West Calder United – Armadale Thistle
Stoneyburn Juniors idle

WEST SENIORS

West of Scotland League

West of Scotland League 2020/1

The new Senior West of Scotland League could not have started in more difficult circumstances. In normal times the new 67-team structure would have been one of the most exciting developments in Scottish football for years. However, the intervention of COVID meant that some teams decided not to participate in 2020/1. The Premier Division began with 15 clubs rather than 20. The 3 Conference Divisions had to be re-allocated due to teams withdrawing leaving them unbalanced. The Leagues began belatedly and then had to close down again. Ultimately the West of Scotland League were left with no option but to declare the Leagues "Null and Void" for 2020/1.

PREMIER DIVISION (15 + 5 withdrawn pre season and 1 withdrawn mid season)

Auchinleck Talbot (W)
Beith
Benburb (W - Nov)
Blantyre Victoria
Bonnyton Thistle
Clydebank
Cumbernauld United
Cumnock (W)
Darvel
Glenafton Athletic (W)
Hurlford United
Irvine Meadow XI
Kilbirnie Ladeside (W)
Kilwinning Rangers
Kirkintilloch Rob Roy
Largs Thistle
Pollok (W)
Rossvale
Rutherglen Glencairn
Troon

CONFERENCE A (12)

Annbank United
Ardeer Thistle
Ashfield
Bellshill Athletic
Craigmark Burntonians
Glasgow University
Kello Rovers
Maryhill
Maybole
Muirkirk
Renfrew
St Rochs

CONFERENCE B (13)

Carluke Rovers
Forth Wanderers
Gartcairn
Greenock
Irvine Vics
Johnstone Burgh
Lugar Boswell Thistle
Neilston
Port Glasgow
St Cadoc's
Vale of Clyde
Vale of Leven
Wishaw

CONFERENCE C (9)

Drumchapel United
East Kilbride Thistle
Glasgow Perthshire
Kilsyth Rangers
Lanark United
Newmains United
St Anthony's
Thorniewood United
Yoker Athletic

CONFERENCE NON-PARTICIPANTS (13)

Ardrossan Winton Rovers
Arthurlie
Cambuslang Rangers
Dalry Thistle
Girvan
Larkhall Thistle
Lesmahagow
Petershill
Royal Albert
Saltcoats Victoria
Shettleston
Shotts Bon Accord
Whitletts Victoria

West of Scotland League 2021/2

For 2021/2 there were a large number of new applicants. Rather than fitting them into the existing Conferences it was agreed to create a new "Development Conference". This would give these newcomers the chance to bring their facilities up to scratch within a two-year time frame.

Structure for 2021/2

PREMIER DIVISION (20)

1 qualifier for Lowland League Play off (if licensed)
7 or 8 relegated

Auchinleck Talbot
Beith
Benburb
Blantyre Victoria
Bonnyton Thistle
Clydebank
Cumbernauld United
Cumnock
Darvel
Glenafton Athletic
Hurlford United
Irvine Meadow
Kilbirnie Ladeside
Kilwinning Rangers
Kirkintilloch Rob Roy
Largs Thistle
Pollok
Rossvale
Rutherglen Glencairn
Troon

CONFERENCE A (16)

1 promoted to Premier League
3 qualify for Division 1
Remainder to Division 2 / Conferences (tbc)

Arthurlie
Bellshill Athletic
Craigmark Burntonians
Forth Wanderers
Girvan
Glasgow University
Irvine Victoria
Johnstone Burgh
Lesmahagow
Lugar Boswell Thistle
Maryhill Maybole
Muirkirk
Saltcoats Victoria
Shotts Bon Accord
Whitletts Victoria

CONFERENCE B(15)

1 promoted to Premier League
3 qualify for Division 1
Remainder to Division 2 / Conferences (tbc)

Ardeer Thistle
Ashfield
Cambuslang Rangers
Carluke Rovers
Dalry Thistle
Gartcairn
Glasgow United
Greenock
Kello Rovers
Newmains United
Port Glasgow
Renfrew
Royal Albert
St Cadoc's
Thorniewood United

CONFERENCE C 15)

1 promoted to Premier League
3 qualify for Division 1
Remainder to Division 2 / Conferences (tbc)

Ardrossan Winton Rovers
Drumchapel United
East Kilbride Thistle
Glasgow Perthshire
Kilsyth Rangers
Lanark United
Larkhall Thistle
Neilston
Petershill
St Anthonys
St Rochs
Vale of Clyde
Vale of Leven
Wishaw
Yoker Athletic

DIVISION 4 (8)

Depending on facilities may qualify for Division 2 / Conferences (tbc)

Broomhill Sports Club
Campbeltown Pupils
Finnart
Glenvale
Harmony Row
Harthill Royal
Kilsyth Athletic
St Peter's

Teams will play each other 4 times

Withdrew pre-season:
Westerton United

CUP COMPETITIONS

A **West of Scotland League Cup** will be played later in the season.

The **Strathclyde Demolition Cup** is the West equivalent of the Alex Jack / Alba Cups, for clubs who are not SFA members. Clubs have the choice of playing in this or in the Scottish Junior Cup but cannot play in both, as each offers a qualification route to the 2022/3 Scottish Cup.

Preliminary Round
Kilsyth Athletic 3-3(7-8p) St Cadoc's (@ McKenna Park)
Rutherglen Glencairn 3-0 Forth Wanderers

First Round
Bellshill Athletic – Bonnyton Thistle
Campbeltown Pupils – Harmony Row
Glenvale – Royal Albert
Kilwinning Rangers – St Cadoc's
Port Glasgow Juniors – Neilston
Rutherglen Glencairn – Finnart
St Peter's – Drumchapel United
Vale of Clyde – BSC Glasgow

West of Scotland League 2020/1

PREMIERSHIP	BEI	BEN	BLA	BON	CLY	CUM	DAR	HUR	IRV	KIL	KIR	LAR	ROS	RUT	TRO
Beith									Dec 12 0-0		Oct 31 2-1		Oct 24 1-1		Nov 14 2-2
Benburb	Nov 7 0-5					Oct 24 1-3									
Blantyre Victoria							Nov 14 0-4					Dec 12 1-3			
Bonnyton Thistle			Dec 5 1-6		Nov 7 1-2	Dec 19 2-1									Oct 24 0-3
Clydebank						Dec 29 4-1		Oct 31 4-0					Dec 19 1-1	Dec 5 4-0	
Cumbernauld United							Nov 28 0-3				Nov 7 1-4				
Darvel		Oct 31 2-0								Nov 7 0-1	Oct 24 3-0				Dec 27 3-2*
Hurlford United			Oct 24 2-2	Dec 26 1-2							Nov 28 2-1			Nov 7 2-1	
Irvine Meadow			Dec 27 3-2	Nov 28 2-0				Nov 14 1-2		Dec 19 1-2					
Kilwinning Rangers			Oct 31 1-2			Dec 5 4-2		Dec 12 3-1				Nov 28 1-2	Nov 14 2-1		
Kirkintilloch Rob Roy				Dec 12 4-2	Nov 14 0-4										
Largs Thistle	Dec 19 2-2				Oct 24 0-1	Nov 14 4-1			Nov 7 0-1				Dec 5 0-0		
Rossvale			Nov 28 3-4			Dec 12 3-2			Oct 31 1-2					Dec 22 3-1	
Rutherglen Glencairn				Nov 14 2-1											Nov 28 1-2
Troon											Dec 5 2-0		Nov 7 2-1	Dec 12 1-0	

* at Cumnock

CONFERENCE A	ANN	ARD	ASH	BEL	CRA	GLA	KEL	MAR	MAY	MUI	REN	STR
Annbank United			Dec 5 6-4	Oct 31 2-2			Nov 14 3-1			Dec 12 1-0		
Ardeer Thistle								Nov 14 1-2		Oct 31 1-5		
Ashfield											Nov 28 2-5	
Bellshill Athletic	Dec 19 1-3	Nov 7 7-2			Dec 12 4-2				Nov 28 2-1		Oct 24** 3-3	
Craigmark Burntonians		Oct 24 7-2						Dec 19 1-1	Nov 7 3-2			Nov 28 0-3
Glasgow University			Dec 19 3-3	Nov 14 1-3	Oct 31*** 1-1		Dec 5 1-0					Nov 7 3-1***
Kello Rovers		Nov 28 5-1									Nov 7 1-1	
Maryhill	Nov 7 0-2					Nov 28 3-1						
Maybole			Nov 14 1-4					Dec 5 1-0		Dec 19 7-0		Oct 31* 0-2
Muirkirk	Nov 28 0-0	Dec 5 7-0	Nov 7 2-1									
Renfrew								Oct 31 3-0		Nov 14 0-0		
St Rochs					Nov 14 2-2		Dec 19 3-4					

* at Cambusdoon
** at Matt Busby Centre
*** at Garscube

Premier Division

Pos	Team	Pld	W	D	L	GF	GA	GD	Pts
1	Clydebank	7	6	1	0	20	3	+17	19
2	Troon	7	5	1	1	14	9	+5	16
3	Kilwinning Rangers	7	5	0	2	14	9	+5	15
4	Irvine Meadow XI	7	4	1	2	10	7	+3	13
5	Darvel	5	4	0	1	15	3	+12	12
6	Largs Thistle	7	3	2	2	11	7	+4	11
7	Blantyre Victoria	7	3	1	3	17	17	0	10
8	Hurlford United	7	3	1	3	10	14	-4	10
9	Rossvale	9	2	3	4	14	15	-1	9
10	Beith Juniors	5	1	4	0	7	6	+1	7
11	Kirkintilloch Rob Roy	7	2	0	5	10	16	-6	6
12	Bonnyton Thistle	8	2	0	6	9	21	-12	6
13	Rutherglen Glencairn	6	1	0	5	5	13	-8	3
14	Cumbernauld United	7	0	0	7	8	24	-16	0
15	Benburb	0	0	0	0	0	0	0	0

Conference A

Pos	Team	Pld	W	D	L	GF	GA	GD	Pts
1	Annbank United	7	5	2	0	17	8	+9	17
2	Bellshill Athletic	7	4	2	1	22	14	+8	14
3	Muirkirk Juniors	7	3	2	2	14	10	+4	11
4	Renfrew	5	2	3	0	12	6	+6	9
5	Craigmark Burntonians	7	2	3	2	16	15	+1	9
6	Glasgow University	6	2	2	2	10	11	-1	8
7	Kello Rovers	5	2	1	2	11	9	+2	7
8	St Roch's	5	2	1	2	11	9	+2	7
9	Maryhill	6	2	1	3	6	9	-3	7
10	Maybole Juniors	6	2	0	4	12	11	+1	6
11	Ashfield	5	1	1	3	14	17	-3	4
12	Ardeer Thistle	6	0	0	6	7	33	-26	0

CONFERENCE B	CAR	FOR	GAR	GRE	IRV	JOH	LUG	NEI	POR	STC	VOC	VOL	WIS
Carluke Rovers									Nov 28 0-4	Dec 12 0-7		Nov 7 6-0	Oct 24 1-2
Forth Wanderers	Nov 14 2-2					Dec 5 0-2							
Gartcairn				Dec 19 1-4	Dec 5 5-3				Oct 24 3-4	Nov 7 0-3			
Greenock		Nov 7 4-1				Oct 24 0-0	Nov 28 4-2	Dec 12 0-1					
Irvine Vics							Nov 7 2-1	Nov 28 1-5	Nov 21 3-4		Dec 19 0-2		
Johnstone Burgh	Oct 31 6-1								Dec 12 2-1				
Lugar Boswell T			Oct 31 1-2			Dec 19 1-3					Nov 14 2-2		
Neilston	Dec 19 4-2		Nov 14 4-1				Oct 24 6-0				Dec 5 5-1		Nov 21 4-1
Port Glasgow				Nov 14 2-5	Oct 31 5-1							Dec 19 2-0	Dec 5 1-2
St Cadoc's		Oct 24 3-2		Dec 5 0-1	Nov 14 5-0			Oct 31 0-2					Dec 19 1-0
Vale of Clyde		Oct 31 2-3	Dec 12 4-4						Nov 7 2-5	Nov 28 0-3			
Vale of Leven		Dec 12 1-3		Oct 31 1-5		Nov 28 1-3							Nov 14 1-2
Wishaw		Nov 28 2-5				Nov 7 0-2	Dec 12 2-2						

CONFERENCE C	DAL	DRU	EKT	GLA	KIL	LAN	LAR	NEW	SHE	STA	THO	YOK
Dalry Thistle												
Drumchapel United			Nov 14 3-1								Dec 19 1-3	
East Kilbride Thistle								Dec 12 1-0				
Glasgow Perthshire		Dec 12 2-3		Nov 21 4-8		Nov 21 4-8		Nov 7 6-0				
Kilsyth Rangers		Oct 24 4-0	Dec 19 6-1	Nov 14 2-1								
Lanark United		Nov 28 4-2		Dec 5 1-1	Nov 7 0-2					Nov 14 2-1	Oct 24 0-3	
Larkhall Thistle												
Newmains United												Oct 31 2-4
Shettleston												
St Anthony's		Oct 31 0-4	Nov 7 2-2		Dec 12 1-5						Nov 28 1-1	
Thorniewood United												Nov 14 3-1
Yoker Athletic		WO 0-3$	Nov 4 3-1		Dec 4 2-2			Nov 28 0-2			Dec 12 1-0	

$ Yoker unable to field team, Covid

Conference B

Pos	Team	Pld	W	D	L	GF	GA	GD	Pts
1	Neilston	8	8	0	0	31	6	+25	24
2	Greenock Juniors	8	6	1	1	23	8	+15	19
3	Johnstone Burgh	7	6	1	0	18	4	+14	19
4	St Cadoc's	8	6	0	2	22	5	+17	18
5	Port Glasgow	9	6	0	3	28	18	+10	18
6	Forth Wanderers	7	3	1	3	16	16	0	10
7	Wishaw	8	3	1	4	11	17	-6	10
8	Gartcairn	7	2	1	4	16	23	-7	7
9	Vale of Clyde	7	1	2	4	13	22	-9	5
10	Carluke Rovers	7	1	1	5	12	25	-13	4
11	Irvine Victoria	7	1	0	6	10	27	-17	3
12	Lugar Boswell Thistle	7	0	2	5	9	21	-12	2
13	Vale of Leven	6	0	0	6	4	21	-17	0

Conference C

Pos	Team	Pld	W	D	L	GF	GA	GD	Pts
1	Kilsyth Rangers	6	5	1	0	21	5	+16	16
2	Drumchapel United	7	4	0	3	16	14	+2	12
3	Thorniewood United	5	3	1	1	10	4	+6	10
4	Lanark United	6	3	1	2	15	13	+2	10
5	Yoker Athletic	7	3	1	3	11	13	-2	10
6	Glasgow Perthshire	5	1	1	3	14	14	0	4
7	East Kilbride Thistle	5	1	1	3	6	14	-8	4
8	Newmains United	4	1	0	3	4	11	-7	3
9	St Anthony's	5	0	2	3	5	14	-9	2

West of Scotland League Club Playing Squads 2020/21

NB These are not comprehensive lists of players used - there will be some omissions. However, all players listed were associated with the club concerned during 2020/1 New signings refer to players signed after games came to a halt.

Annbank United

Clun in abeyance for 2021/2
Manager: Matt Maley;
Assistant: Robert Love
Robert Love (ex Stenhousemuir, Stranraer, Cumnock, Auchinleck T)
Joe White
David Anderson (2020 Ex Stranraer, Irvine Meadow)
Alan Orr
Jordan Ryan
Martyn Brown (2020 Ardrossan WR, ex Hurlford United)
David Markey (ex Kilwinning Rangers, Darvel)
Grant Richmond
Mitchell Ewing
Marc Dyer
Steven McLelland
Steven Currie
Lee Sloan
Tommy Sloan
Jack Taylor
John Dunlop
Mark Gilmour
Lewis Kirkwood
Scott Bates
Declan Murphy (ex Kilmarnock, Airdrie, Stranraer SOS)
Lewis Kerr
Mitchell Ewing
Steven Currie (2020 Hurlford United, OL)
Christian Nade (2020 ex Hearts, Annan Athletic etc)

Ardeer Thistle

Figures refer to League apps and goals 2020/1
Manager: Craig Johnston;
Assistant: Blair Gilmour;
Coaches: Alan Morrison, Stuart Smith.
Dave Barrett (6)
Kane Howarth (6, 3)
Jordan Philbin (6)
Jamie Morgan (5)
Jonny Duff (3+1)
Jackson Stevenson (3+1)
Dylan Howarth (2+2, 1)
Andrew Martin (2+2)
Jonathan Duncan (3)
Patrick Woods (3)
Marcus Worrall (3)
Robbie Laurie (2+1)
Paul McKay (2+1)
Calum Hamilton (1+2)
Kyle McCulloch (2)
Aaron Shanley (2)
Declan Hughes (1+1)
Miguel McIntosh (1+1, 2)
Aiden McMurray (1+1)
Ross Steele (1+1)
Damien Bloy (1)
Mark Cuthbertson (1)
Jamie Donnelly (1)
Dillan Dunn (1, 1) 2020 Lugar BT
David Ewing (1)
Darren Frye (1)
William Hall (1)
David Hillier (1)
Logan Stevenson (1)
Aaron Tait (1)
Ryan Wilson (1)
Cameron Blair (0+1)
Paul Dawson (0+1)
Alexander Sommerville (0+1)
Eoin Waite (0+1)
Kyle McCulloch, 2019 Maybole
Nduati Kabutha, 2020, Kenyan Internationalist

Ardrossan Winton Rovers

No matches played during 2020/1
Manager: Steven Wilson
Ross Higgins
Blair Lochhead (2019, ex Queens Park / Albion Rovers / Glenafton Athletic / Dalry Thistle
David Donald (2020 Ardeer West Recreation AFC)
John McFarland (2019 ex Ardeer Thistle / Dalry Thistle)
Andy McGregor (2016 ex Beith / Dalry Thistle (Loan))
David Ewing (2020, ex Largs Thistle / Greenock / Bonnyton Thistle)
Michael Lennox (2017 Bonnyton Thistle)
Reece Lapham (2020, ex Ayr United / Bonnyton Thistle)
Andy Hunter (2018 ex Glenafton Athletic / Dalry Thistle (Loan) / Girvan)
Kyle Lochhead (ex Partick Thistle / Kirkintilloch Rob Roy / Bellshill Athletic (Loan) / Girvan / Maryhill / Glasgow Perthshire / Shettleston / Blantyre Vics / Neilston / Ashfield / Dalry Thistle)
Jordan Bruce (2018 ex Ardeer Thistle / Craigmark Burntonians)
Rory Campbell (2018 ex Hurlford Thistle / Ardeer Thistle / Irvine Vics)
Kyle Cumming (2020 ex Dalry Thistle / Clydebank / Kilwinning Rangers / Neilston)
Lewis Harvey (2019 ex Ayr United / Bonnyton Thistle (Loan))
Ryan Morrow (2020 ex Dalry Thistle / Ardeer Thistle / Irvine Vics)
Kyle Samson
Patrick Woods (2020 ex Irvine Meadow / Ardeer Thistle (Loan))
Kyle Black (2019 Renfrew)
Thomas Donovan (2020 ex Ardeer Thistle / Saltcoats Vics / Whitletts Vics)
Ryan Singleton (2020 ex Bonnyton Thistle / Dalry Thistle (Loan) / Irvine Vics)
Peter Haggarty (2019 ex Queens Park / Arthurlie / Beith Juniors)
Calum McDade (2020 ex Saltcoats Vics / Maybole / Girvan / Irvine Vics)
Jamie McKenna (2020 ex Port Glasgow / Greenock / Largs Thistle)
David Sawyers

Arthurlie

Manager: Andy McFadyen;
Assistant: George Fotheringham
No competitive matches played during 2020/1
Arthurlie released all their players from their contracts on October 20th 2020.

Squad 2021/2
Aiden Green
Andrew McLaughlin
Calum Nolan
Conor Bradley
Dale Simeon
Darren Ramsey (2021 Beith)
David Mackay
Gary Carroll
Gary Smith
James Scott (2021 Drumchapel)
Jamie MacLeod
Jordan Leydon
Kris Gebbie
Kyle McLachlan
Kyle Pirie
Lance Pearce (2021 Darvel)
Lee Roulston
Lewis Hobbs
Michael MacNeil
Nad Zeb (2021 Blantyre Vics)
Tam McGaughey

Auchinleck Talbot

Manager: Tommy Sloan; Assistant: Allan McCluckie
No matches played during 2020/1
Retained Players:
Andy Leishman (2010 Lugar BT, ex Kello R), OL to BSC Glasgow 2020/1
Brian Hewitt (2016 Dalry Thistle, ex Beith Juniors, Dalry Thistle, Irvine Meadow, Neilston)
William Lyle (2012 Stenhousemuir, ex Ayr United)
Gordon Pope (2014 Ayr United, ex Dundee United, Montrose, Auchinleck T). Retired Oct 2020.
Dylan Young (2019 Kirkintilloch RR, ex Stirling Albion, Wishaw OL)
Craig McCracken (2016 Ayr United) OL to BSC Glasgow 2020/1
Neil McPherson (2016 Darvel), OL to Maybole 2020/1
Aiden Wilson (2019 Caledonian Braves, ex Kilmarnock), OL to Linlithgow Rose 2020/1
Kieran Healy (2019 Renfrew)
Gareth Armstrong (2017 Troon, ex Ayr United)
Stephen Wilson (2015 Troon)
Dwayne Hyslop (2012 Annbank United)
Steven White (2006, ex Annbank United, Craigmark B)
Jack McDowell (2018 Girvan, ex Annbank United), OL to Maybole 2020/1
Corey Pearson (2019 Petershill, ex Dumbarton, Kilsyth R, Blantyre Vics, BSC Glasgow), OL to Caledonian Braves 2020/1
Hamish McKinlay (2019 Irvine Vics, ex Stranraer Youths)
Jamie Glasgow (2017 East Stirling, ex Camelon) OL to BSC Glasgow 2020/1
Mark Shankland (2014 Ayr United, ex Albion Rovers OL)
Graham Wilson (ex Cumnock, Dumbarton)
Brian Boylan (2019 Kilwinning Rangers, ex KSC Wolves)
Keir Samson (Oct 2018 Cumnock, ex Ayr United, Kilmarnock, Stranraer Youths)

New Signings:
William Boyd (2021 Lostock St Gerards, ex Auchinleck T, Largs Th)

Beith

Player Manager: Bryan Young;
Assistant: Chris Friel; Coaches: John Sherry, Alan Kerr
Figures refer to League apps and goals
Dale Burgess (7) (2020 Stranraer, ex Renfrew, Dalry

Thistle)
Paul Frize (7, 2) (2013 Glasgow Perthshire, ex Harmony Row)
Conner McGlinchey (6, 2) (2016 Arthurlie, ex Rangers (youth), Hamilton Accies, Berwick (loan), Peterhead)
Lawrence McMahon (6) (2019 ex Kilbirnie L, Largs T, Ardrossan WR, Albion Rovers)
Nicky Docherty (5+1) (2012 Drumchapel United, ex Livingston, Westerton Utd, Blantyre Vics)
Jordan Hood (5+1) (2920 Pollok United)
Alistair Park (5+1, 1) (2020 Glenafton Athletic, ex Auchinleck T, Clyde, Hibs, Rangers)
Jay Shields (5+1)
Kevin Watt (4+2,1) (2020 Linlithgow Rose, ex Kirkintilloch RR, Clyde Bo'ness Utd, Cumbernauld Utd, E Stirling, Albion Rovers)
Steven Noble (5) (2018 ex Stirling Albion, Peterhead, Stranraer, Berwick Rangers, Albion Rovers(loan), Kilmarnock (youth))
Daniel O'Neill (5) (2020 Harmony Row U21)
Callum Watt (5, 2) (2020 Hurlford U, ex Bonnyton Th, Beith)
Darren Jones (1+3)
Jordan Duffy (3, 1)
Callum Imrie (1+2) (2020 Pollok United)
Ross McKenzie (1+2)
Jamie Conn (0+3) (OL from Cumnock 2020/1)
Odhran Markey (2, 1)
Darren Ramsay (2) (2019 Cambuslang Rangers, ex Clyde, Annan Ath, East Kilbride, Arbroath, Rangers Youths)
Derek Hepburn (1+1, 1) (2020 Clydebank, ex Pollok, Vale of Clyde, Harmony Row, Partick Thistle U19)
Kenny McLean (1+1) (2007 Maryhill, ex Queen's Park, Morton)
Michael McCabe (0+2)
Ryan Docherty (2017 Q Park, ex Lanark U, Lesmahagow, Rutherglen G)
Iain Gray (2020 Linlithgow Rose, ex Kilbirnie L, Clyde, St Mirren)
Bryan Young (2020 Pollok, ex Auchinleck T, Ross County)
Sean McIlroy (2019 ex Irvine Vics, Neilston, Auchinleck T)

Bellshill Athletic

Bellshill played their home games at the Matt Busby Centre due to fire damage to the pavilion at Rockburn Park.
Manager: Derek Wilson;
Assistant: David Menelaws;
Coach : Colin Reilly)
Andrew Lindsay
Ben McDougall
Callum Bradford
Campbell Gray (Oct 2020 Cambuslang Rangers)
Ciaran Lafferty (2019 Cambuslang R, ex Clydebank, Celtic, Dunfermline Ath)
Daniel Haskim (Dec 2020 Cambuslang Rangers)
Danny McHugh
David Menelaws
Dylan McGuigan (Oct 2020 Shotts BA)
Euan Scott
Jonathan Cookman
Jonny Rawlings (2020 ex Johnstone Burgh, Muirkirk)
Jordan Duncan (2020 Bathgate Thistle)
Jordan Moore
Kevin "KP" McAllister
Mark Doran (Oct 2020 Albion Rovers On Loan)
Martin Hannaway
Matthew Clarke (July 2020 Wishaw)
Matthew Grant (Oct 2020 St Mirren)
Michael Brunton (Dec 2020 Larkhall Th)
Neil Schoneville (Oct 2020 Lesmahagow)
Patrick Cullen
Paul McCaulay
Ryan Cherrie
Ryan Renwick (2020 Airdrieonians Youths)
Scott Robson (Oct 2020 St Anthonys)
Sean McKenna (2020 Shotts BA, ex Queen's Park, Clyde, Camelon, Brechin City, Bellshill Ath, Girvan, Bellshill Ath, Petershill, Beith, Troon, Wishaw)
Shaun Rouse (Dec 2020 Larkhall Th)

Benburb

Benburb withdrew from the 2020/1 season in mid November 2020.
Manager: Paul Lovering
Ryan McWilliams (2018 Largs Th, ex Morton, Ayr United, Albion Rovers, East Stirling)
Lewis Lovering (2020 Albion Rovers, ex Benburb, Neilston, Caley Braves)
Liam Mushet (2020 Arthurlie)
Jamie Waddell (2020 Yoker Ath)
Andrew Rankin
Stephen Waddell (2020 ex Pollok, Yoker Ath, Benburb)
Michael McMullin (2020 Petershill, ex Partick Th, E Stirling, Petershill, Albion Rovers, Pollok, Bo'ness Utd, Ytterhogdal FF, Clyde)
Jamie McKenna
Andrew Muir
Alan Frizzell (2020 Kilbirnie Ladeside, ex Morton, Port Glasgow, Dumbarton, Largs Th, Clydebank, Neilston, Greenock)
Jordan Bow
Liam O'Kane
Scott Jarvie
Daniel McKay (2020 Arthurlie, ex Kilmarnock, Arbroath, Ayr United, Brechin City, Albion Rovers, Beith, Neilston, Irvine Meadow, Troon)
John Sheridan (2020 St Cadocs, ex Beith)
Conor Cullen
Scott Lewis
David Murray (2020 Houston United)
David Taylor (2020 Queen's Park)

Blantyre Vics

Manager: John Gibson (ex Hamilton Acc, Alloa, Stirling Albion, Morton),
Assistant: Paul McAneny (ex Kilmarnock, Stirling Albion, Alloa etc)
Alan Dunsmuir
Andy Sinclair (ex St Rochs, Cumbernauld United)
Brodie Flanagan
Con Boyle (ex Irvine M, Shettleston, EK Thistle, Lanark Utd)
Connor McGuinness (ex Rutherglen Glencairn)
Craig Kerr (ex Rangers)
Dale Jones (ex Q Park)
Fraser Allan
Fraser Allan (ex Kilmarnock, Mill United)
Gary Campbell (ex Clyde, Shotts BA)
John Cunningham (ex Clydebank, Albion Rovers, Annan Athletic, Cumbernauld Utd)
Lewis MacDonald
Liam Campbell (ex Clydebank, Yoker Athletic)
Liam McLaughlin
Martin Smith (2020 Albion Rovers)
Martin Smith (ex Albion Rovers, Lanark United, Gartcairn)
McLeish
Mike Archer (ex Kilsyth R, St Anthonys, Royal Albert)
Nadeem Zeb (ex Rutherglen Glencairn, Newtonvale)
Sam McKenzie (ex Queen's Park, Kirkintilloch RR)
Simon Eeles (ex Gretna, Glenafton Ath, Auchinleck T, Irvine M, Royal Albert, Hurlford Utd)
Stefan Law

Bonnyton Thistle

Manager: Alan Robertson (ex Kilmarnock, 607 apps for Killie);
Assistant: Paul Wright (ex Aberdeen, QPR, Hibs, St Johnstone, Kilmarnock etc)
Gordon Young
David Stevenson
Kris Brown
Jackson Sivewright
Chris Kelly
Sandy Robertson
Kris Kerr
Adam Houston
Kyle Gilroy
Chris Gardiner
Greig Connor
Dylan Stevenson (2020, e Troon, Largs Th, Auchinleck T, Berwick Rangers, Morton)
Eddie Ablohr (2020 ex Irvine Vics, Hurlford Th)
Callum Walsh (ex Darvel, Whitletts Vics, Bonnyton Th Youth)
Thomas Dempsie (2020 Girvan, ex Bonnyton Th)
Logan Smith (2020 Bonnyton Th Youth)
Andrew Tremble (2020 Bonnyton Th U20)

Cambuslang Rangers

No competitive matches played in 2020/1
Co-Managers: Billy Campbell, Paul McColl
Iain Stewart (ex BSC Glasgow)
Craig Crawford
Kevin Ross (2020, Gartcairn, ex Stirling Albion, Harthill Royal, Stoneyburn, Fauldhouse United)
Scott Faulds
Paul Murphy 2020 Gartcairn, ex Celtic BC, Stenhousemuir, Stirling Albion, Stranraer, Glenafton Ath, Bo'ness Utd, Cumnock, Petershill, Cumbernauld Utd)
Callum Mclean (2018 EK Thistle, ex St Cuthbert W)
Scott Jarvie
Thomas Sinclair (ex Pollok)
Gary Campbell (ex Clyde)
Willie McLaren (ex Airdrie, St Johnstone etc)
Scott Williamson
Ryan Stewart (2020 Fauldhouse Utd, ex Hearts, Brechin C, E Fife)
Scott McManus (2020 Cumbernauld Utd, ex Motherwell, Stenhousemuir, Stranraer, Vale of Clyde Clyde, Q Park, Petershill)
Fermin Jiminez (ex UDX Txantrea, UD Mutilvera, CD Odoya, CD Huarte)
Andy Duffy (to Wishaw Oct 2020)
Kevin McFarlane
Gary McMullan

Campbell Gray
Dean Richardson (2020, ex Celtic, Bohemians Dublin, E Stirling, Larkhall Th, Peterhead, Pollok)
Lee McClelland (2020 Albion Rovers, ex Alloa Ath, Maryhill)
Barry McGeechan
Nicky Fraser
Scott McKean (to EK Thistle Oct 2020)
Paul McAulay (2020 Colville Park, ex Alloa Ath)
Taylor Scott

Carluke Rovers

Manager: Mark Weir
Adam Brown
David Kennedy
Dean Wilson
Dillan Duddy
Dominik Chiedu
Eddie Hayley
Evan Kane
Gary Livingstone (2019 Thorniewood U, ex Linlithgow R, Kilsyth R, Arthurlie, Bathgate Th)
James Frame
Greg Kane
James Miller
Jamie Dickson
Jordan Conlon
Jordan Lithgow
Josh Kane
Jonny Wilson
Kwaku Nyame
Maxime Neossi
Jamie Dickson
Jamie Murphy (2020 Carluke R U20)
Liam Sneddon (2020 Carluke R U20)
Mark O'Reilly
Jordan Conlon
James Miller (ex Colville Park, Castlemilk Dynamo)
Kwaku Nyame
Nicky Aitchison (Jul 2020 Muirkirk)
Dominic Chiedu (Nov 2020 Larkhall Th, ex Carluke R)
Garry Fleming (Dec 2020 Greenock, ex Kilwinning R, ex Dumbarton, Alloa Ath)
Lewis Hill (Dec 2020, Lanark United, ex Carluke R)

Clydebank

Manager: Gordon Moffat; Assistant: Gary McMenamin (ex Rossvale, Kirkntilloch RR, Cumnock); Coaches: Kirk Forbes, Drew Marshall
Ben Cameron (2020 Clydebank U20)
Christopher Black
Ciaran Mulcahy
Frazer Johnstone (2020 Rossvale, ex Motherwell, Airdrie, East Kilbride)
Jamie Darroch
Jamie Donnelly
Jamie Stevenson (2020 Clydebank U20)
Joe Slattery (2020 Rossvale, ex Kilmarnock, Gretna, Dalbeattie Star)
Lee Gallacher (2020 Glenafton Ath, ex Partick Th, Stenhousemuir, Kirkintilloch RR)
Liam Harris (OL from Hamilton Accies 2020/1)
Liam McGonigle
Matt Niven (2020 Rossvale, ex BSC Glasgow)
Matthew McLean
Michael Bailey (2019 ex Queen's Park, Yoker Ath)
Nicky Little (2018 Pollok, ex Largs Th)
Oisin McHugh
Ross McPherson (2020 Darvel, ex Airdrie, Knightswood U21, Clydebank, Q Park, Irvine M, Beith, Pollok)

Craigmark Burntonians

Manager: Graeme Neil; Assistant: Jason Stewart; Coach: Scott Gilmour, Scott Dinwoodie
Adam Lowe (left Dec 2020)
Alistair Boyle
Daniel Graham (2020 ex Ayr United)
David Cunningham
David Richardson (Jul 2020, ex Ayr United, Stranraer, Saltcoats Vics)
David Smith (Sep 2020 ex Irvine Vics, Ardrossan WR, Kilwinning R, Cumnock)
Fraser Smith (Aug 2020 ex Kilmarnock Youths, Bonnyton Th, Ardrossan WR)
Graeme Whittaker
Grant Kirkwood
James Lamont
Jamie Newton (Jul 2020 Armadale Th)
Jordan Cherrie
Jordan Kermoe (Sep 2020 ex Lesmahagow, Cumnock, Partick Th)
Kieran McCrum (Nov 2020 OL from Kilbirnie Ladeside)
Liam Caddis (Dec 2020, OL from Darvel, ex St Johnstone, Arbroath, Cowdenbeath, Alloa, Ardrossan WR, Stirling Albion, Hurlford Utd, Cumnock)
Robert Boyd
Rhys Russell
Ryan Caddis (Nov 2020 OL from Cumnock)
Ryan Connelly
Ryan McKay
Scott Dempster (Left Dec 2020)
Scott Dinwoodie
Stephen Cargill (Nov 2020 Hurlford Thistle, ex Maybole, Girvan.
Steven Hill (Jul. 2020 ex Kilwinning R, Bonnyton Th)
Steven Tan Aug 2020, ex Saltcoats Vics, Ardrossan WR, Darvel, Kilwinning R)

Cumbernauld United

Manager: Kieran McAnespie (2019 Clydebank, ex St Johnstone, Fulham, Ayr United etc)
Aidan McIlduff (ex Stenhousemuir, Celtic)
Alan Benton
Willie Greenhorn (OL from Stirling Albion Oct-Jan)
Cameron Crooks (OL from QOS Oct-Jan)
Colin McMenamin (2020 Hurlford U, ex QOS, Annan Ath, Newcastle Utd, Livingston, Falkirk, Shrewsbury T, Gretna, Dundee, QOS, Ross Com Morton, Celtic Nation, Stenhousemuir)
Conor Stevenson (2018 Petershill, ex Clyde, Vale of Clyde, Albion Rovers)
Dale Fulton (2020 Eastfield, Grandson of Norrie)
Darren Hill (2019 Arbroath, ex Falkirk, E Stirling, Linlithgow Rose etc)
Dylan Henry (Jul 2020 ex Hamilton Accies, Clyde, East Kilbride)
Eddie Ferns (Jul 2020 Darvel, ex Alloa, Albion R, Stirling Albion, Arbroath, Stenhousemuir, Clyde, St Rochs)
Jack Breslin (2020 Petershill, season -long loan)
Jack Harrison (2019 Kilsyth R, ex Hamilton Accies, St Mirren, E Kilbride, Clyde)
John Boyle
John Paul McGovern (ex Celtic, Swindon T, Carlisle U, Sheffield Wed, Elgin City etc)
Jordan Kennedy (Jun 2020 ex Petershill, Pollok)
Josh Flood (Jul 2020 Sauchie, ex Stirling Albion, Shotts BA)
Kane Paton
Kieran McAnespie
Klark Thomson
Lee Duncanson (2020 Brechin City, ex Partick Thistle)
Michael McGee (Oct 2020 OL from Clyde), ex Airdrie Youths)
Paddy McCabe
Ryan Murney
Sandy Carey (OL from Stirling Albion 2020/1)
Scott Morrison (ex Arbroath, Stirling Albion, East Stirling etc)
Scott Thomson (2019 Airdrieonians)
Tom Neil (July 2020 Kilsyth R)

Cumnock

No matches played during 2020/1
Manager: Tony McInally; Coaches: Mark Cameron and Brian Whelan
Alan Murdoch (2019 Albion Rovers, ex Ayr United, Lanark Utd, Arthurlie, Shotts BA, Blantyre Vics etc)
Alistair Miller (2019 Queen's Park)
Ally Semple (2017 Troon, ex St Mirren, Glenafton Ath)
Christopher Campbell
Darren McGill (2020, ex Rangers, Ayr United, Glenafton Ath)
Finlay Frye (2020 Glenafton Ath, ex Ardrossan WR, Kirkintilloch RR, Irvine M, Pollok, Kilwinning R)
Grant Thorburn (2020 Ayr United, ex Celtic Youths, Troon)
Greg Ferry (2018 Girvan)
Jamie Conn (2019 Troon, ex Lugar BT)
Keiran Hughes (2020 Kilbirnie L, ex Q Park, St Mirren, Albion R. Clyde, Caley Braves)
Kyle Faulds (2018 Auchinleck T, ex St Mirren, Arbroath, Girvan, Stirling Univ)
Kyle McAusland (2020 Glenafton Ath, ex Rangers, Ayr United, Brechin C, Dunfermline Ath, Alloa)
Owen Bell (2019 Workington, ex QOS, transferred to Dalbeattie Star Jul 2020)
Paul Burns (2015 QOS, ex Dunfermline Ath)
Ruaridh McIntyre
Ryan Caddis (2019 Hurlford U, ex Ayr Utd, Stranraer, Alloa Ath, Girvan, Irvine M, Ardrossan WR)

Dalry Thistle

No matches played during 2020/1

Squad 2021/2
Manager: Chris Wilson; Assistant: Stuart McLean
Brian Ashe (2021 Maryhill)
Logan Anderson
Ryan Bell
Adam Bridges (ex Beith)
Burns
Aidan Chisholm
Evan Currie
Dawson
Kevin Gallagher
Cammy King
Love
Sam McNeil (ex Maryhill)
Roan Miller
Tinashe Mugwanda (ex Beith)

Vinny Newlands (2021 Gartcairn)
Ciaran O'Donohue (ex Maryhill)
Gillies O'Hanlon
Euan Ross
Billy Wilson (2021 Larkhall Thistle)
Cole Wilson

Darvel

Chairman: John Gall (Owner of Brownings Bakeries); Manager: Michael Kennedy (Owner of Black Rooster Peri-Peri Chain); Assistant: Kevin MacDonald, Coach: Brian Miller, Willie Torrance, Barry Phill
Cameron Eadie (2020 Peterhead,ex Falkirk, Elgin C, OL to Stirling Albion Mar-May 2021)
Jordan Kirkpatrick (2020 Forfar Ath, ex Alloa, Hamilton, Dumbarton etc ,OL to Stirling Albion Mar-May 2021)
Jordan Allan (2020 Stranraer, ex Morton, Montrose, Elgin C, Coleraine, Stirling Albion, OL to Stirling Albion Mar-May 2021)
Darryll Meggatt (2019 East Fife, ex Alloa, Dundee, Ayr Utd etc, OL to Stirling Albion Mar-May 2021)
Willie Robertson (ex Dundee United, Forfar Ath, Alloa, Stirling Albion)
Thomas McGauhey (Nov 2020 ex Maryhill, Arthurlie)
Ian McShane (2020 Falkirk, ex QOS, Ross Co, St Mirren)
Connor Greene (2020 East Stirling, ex Falkirk)
Jamie McKernon (2019 Stenhousemuir, ex St Mirren, Transferred to Albion Rovers Mar 2021)
Ross Perry (2019 Dumbarton, ex Rangers, Oxford U, Falkirk, Raith R, Northampton T, Brechin C, Clyde, Albion R)
Liam Caddis (2020 Hurlford United, ex St Johnstone, Stirling Albion etc – OL to Craigmark 2020/1)
Scott McLean (Aug 2020 Annan Ath, ex Kilmarnock, Albion Rovers, Q Park)
Chris Truesdale (ex Troon, Celtic, Hamilton Acc, Rutherglen G)
Andy Duncan (2020 Maryhill, ex Dumbarton, Airdrie, Pollok)
Lance Pearce (ex Partick Th, Dalry Th, Colville Park)
Kenny Marshall (ex Colville Park)
Jason Marr (ex Celtic, Falkirk, Ross Co, Clyde, Alloa, Albion R, Stirling Albion)
Gavin Mitchell (2020 Kilbirnie Ladeside, ex Q Park)
Scott Ferguson (ex Clyde, Cumbernauld Colts, Hurlford U)
Ryan Thomson (2020 Stranraer, ex Dunfermline Ath, Albion R, Dumbarton)
Aaron Black (ex Troon, Motherwell, Blantyre Vics)
David Grant (2019 Dunipace, ex Camelon, E Stirling)
Darren Miller (ex Colville Park, Albion R, Irvine M, Q {Park, Clyde etc))
Gary Muir (2019 ex Stirling Albion , Lisburn , Clyde , Ballymena , Airdrie , Floriana and Sliema Wanderers)
Ross Caldwell (Oct 2020 Blantyre Vics, ex Hibernian, Alloa etc)
Harry Monaghan (Dec 2020 Hume City (NZ), ex Hibernian, Stenhousemuir, Derry City)
Lee Hadden (Dec 2020, ex Wishaw Ams, East Stirlingshire)
Allan McKenzie (2019 Bo'ness Utd, ex Pollok, Auchinleck T, Shotts BA, Alloa)

Drumchapel United

Co Managers: Adam Hopes / John Black; Coach: Craig McPherson; Goalkeeping Coach: Jon Connolly (ex Motherwell etc)
Alex Docherty
Bradley Rodden
Ben Daly (Dec 2020 Caledonian Braves, ex Drumchapel Utd)
Chris Prior (Sep 2020 Ashfield, ex Drumchapel United)
Chris Craig
Ciaran McElroy
Dan Finnigan
Darian McKinnon (ex Hamilton Accies, Partick Thistle)
Darren McGuire
Donald McCallum (ex Dumbarton, Arbroath)
Grant Dickie (Sep 2020 Kilbirnie Ladeside)
Harry Granger
James Scott
Jamie Gilmartin
Joe Coleman (ex Dumbarton)
Josh Kelly
Jordan Scott
Kevin Fell
Kyle Lochhead
Kris Lafferty
Nathan Fell
Ryan Hynes
Shaun Bowers (Oct 2020, ex Celtic, Motherwell, BSC Glasgow_
William Plommer
Willie Dyer (ex St Johnstone, Dundee, Morton)

New Signings
Ryan Deas (April 2021 Kilsyth R, ex Clydebank, Irvine M, Kirkintilloch RR)

East Kilbride Thistle

Manager: Iain Diack (ex Stenhousemuir etc); Assistant Manager: Kevin Coyle; Goalkeeping Coach: Allan Creer (ex Alloa etc)
Ally Morgan
Alexander Riddock
Anderson
Blair McDonald
Craig Scott
David McKean
Dean Quinn (2020 OL from Livingston)
Dean Trainor (Nov 2020 Kilbirnie L)
Dom McLaughlin (2020 OL from East Kilbride)
Dougie Ryan
Dylan Taylor (2020 Sauchie)
Johnny Diack
Kevin McLean
Kieran Brennan (2020 Wishaw, Ex Celtic, Spartak Trnava, Arbroath, Armadale Th, Arthurlie, Scotland U19 Caps)
Lewis Miller
Liam Barclay
M McLaughlin (Freed Nov 2020)
Matt Gray
Michael Collinder (Oct 2020 ex Lesmahagow, Fauldhouse Utd, Wishaw)
Robbie Peebles (2020 Colville Park)
Scott Davidson Oct 2020 (Cambuslang R, ex Stirling Albion, Irvine M, Rossvale etc2020 Wishaw,)
Scott Gillespie
Scott Hadden
Scott McKean (2020 Cambuslang R)
Tony Kerr
Taylor

New Signings
Tony Kerr (April 2020, EK Thistle Colts)
Zander Riddock (April 2020, Royal Albert)
Robbie Peebles

Forth Wanderers

Manager: Tom Devine
Mark McHendry (2020 Bellshill Athletic)
Sandro Savarese (2020 Bellshill Athletic)
Billy Stevenson
Paul McCambley
Johnny Brown
Firmen Jiminez
Nathan Cassidy
David Donnelly
Fraser McDuff
Andrew Murray
Jamies Stewart
Brandon Hutchison
Scott Anderson
Jonathan Branks
Craig Murdoch
Josh McDonald
David Lamond
Johnny Banks
Colm Lafferty
Willie McLaren (ex St Johnstone, Airdrie etc)
Connor McDonald

Gartcairn

Manager: Willie Kinniburgh
Martin Grehan (ex Stirling, Motherwell, Stranraer etc)
Danny Burns (2020 Thorniewood United)
Josh Moore
Derek Armstrong
Danny Boyle (ex Darvel, Auchinleck T, Pollok)
Jordan Love
Steven Saunders (ex Motherwell, Partick Th etc, Full Scotland Cap)
Stewart Hall (ex Rutherglen Glencairn, Dumbarton)
Graeme Murphy (ex Cumbernauld United)
JC Hutchison
Ben Cappie (ex Cumbernauld Utd, Albion Rovers)
Jamie Van Nuil
Jordan Moore
Jordan Duncan (ex Q Park, Airdrie)
Liam Crichton
Fraser Scott (ex Royal Albert, Stirling Albion Youth)

Girvan

Club did not play any matches in 2020/1
Manager: Matt Maley (2021/2)

Squad 2021/2
Ross Clark
Alan Orr
Lewis Clark (2021, ex Kilmarnock, Troon)
Jackson Biggar

Glasgow Perthshire

Manager: Billy Adams

Squad 2021/2
Darren Malley
Connor Gaffney
Cameron Murray
Logan McIntyre
Jordan Fraser
Jordan Kinnaird
Mo Gabir
Mark Thompson
Brogan Murphy
Ryan Gemmell
David Quinn
Jordan Simpson

Conor Clarke
Paul Butler
Fraser Malcolm
David Kirkwood
Andy Gibson (ex Partick Th, Stirling Albion, Stranraer etc)

Glasgow University

Manager: Phil Storrier
Ben Fulton
Kieran Adams
Robbie Smith
Scott Granger
Colin Granger
Lewis Gourlay
Jonathan Baxter
Calum Davidson
Donald Thomson
John McKinnon
Lewis Dibble
Robbie Stirling
Calum Strang
Mackenzie
Anthony Pilkington
Adam Duffy
Gregor Sandford
Zachary Lubin

Glenafton Athletic
Did not play competitive football in 2020/1, all players released
Manager: Mick McCann (from Feb 2021)

Squad 2021/2
Justin Devenny (2021 Kilmarnock)
Scott Johnson (2021 Bonnyton Thistle)
Daniel Sloan (2021 Valspar)
Alan Cairns (2021 St Cadocs , ex Glenafton Ath)
Ross Fisher (2021 Hurlford United)
Craig Pettigrew (2021 St Cadocs, ex Glenafton)
Ryan McChesney (2021 Dalbeattie Star, ex Glenafton)
Ian McKnight (2021 Amateurs)
Sean Bennie (2021 Kello Rovers)
Mark Gilmour (2021 Annbank United)
Cameron Marlow (2021 Maybole, ex Glenafton)
Leon Murphy (2021 St Cadocs, ex Glenafton)
Darren Curtis (2021 Lugar BT)
Scott Sherrie (2021 Lugar BT)
Calum Thomson (2021 Glenafton Youths)
Sean McIlroy (2021 Beith)
Jordan Ryan (2021 Annbank United)
David Blyth (2021 St Cadocs, ex Glenafton and Kilmarnock)
Sam McKee (2021 Ayr United U17)

Greenock

Manager: Craig Molloy
Francis Carlin
Matthew Ashe
Gary Fleming
Jamie Black
Dylan McLaughlin
James Marks
Mark Alexander
Jamie Cunningham
John Mitchell
Scott Paterson
Ben Docherty
Kane O'Neill
Derek Kennedy
Aidan Duffy
Andrew Lavelle
Stuart Higgins
Craig Brown
Shaun Wigzell

Hurlford United

Manager: Darren Henderson (ex Stranraer etc)
Chris Murchie
Adam Hodge
Sam Lidington
Richie McKillen
Chris McKnight
Paul McKenzie
Michael Wardrope
Kerr
Jack Whittaker
Callan Veitch
Lewis Morrison
Josh Rennie
Marc McKenzie
Martin McDonald
Darren Moffat
Alex Bell
Ross Fisher

New Signings 2021/2
Craig Burns
Carter Frew
Graham Muir
Liam Miller
Lewis Magee
Chris Robertson
Lewis McIntyre

Irvine Meadow

Manager: James Latta / Colin Spence
Kyle Marley
Neil Slooves
Lee McCrae
Ryan McKie
Liam Miller
Connor Boyd
Jamie Martin
Andrew McLaughlin
Jared Willet
Martin Findlay
Nathan Baird
Michael Reilly
Dylan Pooler
Jamie Henderson
Darren Miller
James Latta
Fraser McMillan
Mark McLennan

Irvine Victoria

Manager: Brian McLuckie (until July 2021), then Alan Kelly (ex Maryhill manager)
Chris Taylor
Struan Robb
Kinlay Bilham
Kevin Onanu
Daniel Martins
Chris Callander
Joy Goma
Declan McFadyen
Sam McKee
Brian Connor
Roddy Watupa
Christopher Lyon
Liam Wells
Charlie Stevenson

Johnstone Burgh

Manager: Jamie McKim
Stuart Collins
Dominic Boland
Kerian Brady
Christopher Stafford
Stuart Fyfe
Sean Fitzharris
Sam Esplin
Malcolm McDonald
Jason Hardie
Richard McArthur
Nathan Marriott
Ross McFarlane
Josh Fowler
Joseph Gillespie
Harry Pittaway
Ross Geddes
Mark McIlvaney
Christopher Burns

Kello Rovers

Manager: Scott Clelland
Ryan Dunsmuir
Kai Bell
Kieran Pagan
Lori Johnston
Andrew Struthers
Sean Bennie
Robert Hampson
Mark Armour
Josh Blackwood
Jordan Boyd
Ewan Lawrie
Paul Weir
Declan Hill
Aiden Lang
Alistair Smith
David Jardine
Jamie Kerr

Kilbirnie Ladeside

Did not play any games in 2020/1
Manager: Martin Ferry; Assistant: Des Roache

Squad 2021/2
Dean Trainor
Joe Wilton
John Kelly
David Gray
Anton McGuigan
David McNair
Andy Strachan
Roan Fitzpatrick
Greg Kean
Martin McBride
Corey Pearson
Daniel Bamford
Josh Winton
Liam Coogans
Jon Scullion
Brendan Sharpe
Kyle Girvan
Lewis Kinnaird

Kilsyth Rangers

Manager: Gary Kelly (ex East Fife, Stirling Albion, East Stirling etc)
Alex Connell
Davy Waters
Stuart Conway
Craig Hughes
Scott Simon
Martyn Shields
Franny Kelly
Gary Stewart
Andrew McNulty
Scott Upton
Gavin Mackie
David Tait
Nicky Prentice
Deas
Willie Sawyers

New Signings 2021/2
G Johnston
G Murphy
T Nash
T O'Kane
C Reid
D Welsh
G Mackie

Kilwinning Rangers

Manager: Chris Strain
Jamie Whyte
Sam McCloskey
Tommy Maitland
David Syme
Ricky Hanvey
Carlo Monti
Jordan Stewart
Ally McColm
David Syme
Ben Lewis
Liam McGuinness
Jordan Stuart
David Anderson
Alex McWaters
Chris McGowan
Adam Caldwell
Tony Coutts
Adam Strain

New Signings 2021/2
Jamie Barclay (2021 East Stirlingshire)
Craig Ross (2021 Kilmarnock)
Adam Caldwell (2021 Girvan)
David Ramsey (2021 Kilbirnie Ladeside)

Kirkintilloch Rob Roy

Manager: Stewart Maxwell; Assistant: Chris McFadyen; Coach: Craig Young
Matthew Kerr
Scott Walker
Daniel O'Halloran
Robert Griffiths
Ian Gold
Craig Truesdale
Robbie Leighton
Alexander Cassells
Ciaran McPherson
Euan Griffiths
Conor Bell
Anthony McGuigan
Kian Gilday
Scott Gold
Grant Brennan
Andrew Coyle
Jack Gordon
Sean McMonagle

Lanark United

Manager: Jamie McKenzie (Nov 2020-July 2021), then Colin Slater
Gareth Halford
Josh Grace
David Collins
Marc McGinty
Cameron Lawson
Ross Barclay
Peter O'Donnell
Kieran Brannan
Andrew Gilchrist
James Martin
Callum Anderson
Lewis Ebbs
Hugh Kerr
Jack Hamilton
Gordon Dick

Largs Thistle

Manager: Stuart Davidson
Sean McLeod
Laurie McMaster
Cory Hughes
George Sewell
Stuart Faulds
Blair McIntyre
Simo McBryde
Scott Adam
Keir Milliken
Jack Haggerty
James McGowan
Ben Black
Graham Muir
Kyle Chrystal
Craig Forbes
William Sewell
Jack Loudon
Daniel Farrell

Larkhall Thistle

Club did not play any matches in 2020/1

Squad 2021/2
Manager: Brian Crawford
Coach: Jason Scotland (ex Dundee United, St Johnstone etc)
Aaron Shanley
Connor Phairs
Gary McMullen (2021 ex Forth W, Gartcairn, Cambuslang R)
Scott Cowan
Macauley Kennedy (ex Cadzow Oak)
Warren Grenfell (ex Forth Wanderers)
Luke Clark
Ryan Carlin
Josh Lindsay (2021 Wishaw Wycombe Wanderers)
Aiden McMurray
Jack Currie
Johnny Duncan
Jonny Lindsay (ex St Johnstone, Partick Th, Dumbarton, Arbroath, Stalybridge Celtic)
Mark Cuthbertson
Kyle Stewart (ex Vale of Clyde, Fauldhouse U, Petershill)
Darren Orr
Bartez Mackiewicz
Kyle Caig (2021 E Kilbride U20)
Ben Fraser
Adam Boyle (ex Gartcairn, Cambuslang R)
Christian Kasongo (2021 Albion Rovers)

Lesmahagow

Club did not play any matches in 2020/1
Manager (from April): Neil Schoneville

Squad 2021/2
Brown
Gray
Mathieson
Jordan Whitefield
Salah
Ross Marchant
Coffey
Jonny Boal
Paterson
Paul Woodlock (ex Motherwell Thistle)
Lewis Hill
Darren Lygate
Weir
Lyndsay
Murphy
Kalvin Hill
Faugnan

Lugar Boswell Thistle

Manager: Greg Gallagher
Robbie Wilson
Grant Wallace
Montgomery
Andrew Reid
Darren Curtis
Conan Mackin
Christopher Hunter
Lewis Kerr
Bryce Reid
Hay
Scott Sherrie
Ryan Singelton
Crombie
Cole Curtis
Denver Bolland
Hall
Cole Millen
Robbie Urie
Dean Marshall
Callum Davidson
Jordan Orr
Craig McLean

Maryhill

Manager: Alan Kelly, then Ross Wilson
Garry Black
Craig McEwan
Matthew Meechan
Michael Brown
Luke Martin
Robert O'Neil
Jack Easdon
Roan Fitzpatrick
Craig Stevenson
Jay McInally
Jamie Gray
Ryan Wallace
Andrew McLaughlin
Gerald Dobbs
Ross Lyden
Darren Kennedy
Brian Turner
Lewis Sanderson

Maybole

Manager: Carlo Walker
Andy Stevenson
Blair Anderson
Cammy Marlow
Chrissy Campbell
Craig Reid
Darren Johnstone
Euan Smith
Greg Frame
Jack McDowell
Jack Peacock
Jack Smith
Jai Holland
James Cuthbertson
John Frame
Jordan Banks
Kenny Parris
Kori Howard
Mark Doolan
Neil McPherson
Paul Cameron
Robbie Hannah
Robert Paterson
Scott Johnstone
Steven Crawford

Muirkirk

Manager: Kevin Murihead; Assistant: Mark O'Neill; Coach: Craig Bingham
Nathan Bogle
Lee Cruikshanks
Craig Peck
Nathan Gordon
Aidan Ferris
Curtis Baxter
Fraser McDonald
Thomas Kelly
Gavin Goodall
Dillan McLauchlan
Ryan Cowie
Calum Bryan
Dean Patrick
Gavin Hay
Scott Steedman
Gary Nugent
Ross Gemmell
Lennon Wight
Peter Marshall
Jason McCuaig

Neilston

Squad 2021/2
Co Managers: Chris Cameron / Derek Carson
Grant Hay (2020 Rutherglen Glencairn)
Robbie Halliday (2018 Kilbirnie Ladeside)
Ross Loughlin (2020 Irvine Vics)
Paul Doyle (2019 Armadale Thistle)
Euan Clark (2016 Beith)
Daryl Convery (2017 Arthurlie)
Olly Smith (2020 Johnstone Burgh CC)
Kieran Brophy (2020 Morton)
Conor Bolger (2020 Neilston Youths)
Kai McGivern (2021 Johnstone Burgh)
Stephen Stirling (2019 Stenhousemuir)
Ross Mackinnon (2019 Linlithgow Rose)
Robbie McCutcheon (2021 Johnstone Burgh)
Dylan Fletcher (2017 Johnstone Burgh)
Darren Jones 92021 Beith)
James Digney (2019 Arthurlie)
Fraser McLaughlin (2021 Port Glasgow)
S Cochran (Goalkeeping Coach)
Cammy Haddow (2018 Yoker Athletic)
Jamie Docherty (2020 Arthurlie)

Newmains United

Co-Managers: Craig Gupwell and Paul Davies
Darren Lygate (2020

Lesmahagow)
Lee Nichol
Peter Copland

Squad 2021/2
Cammy Farquhar
Lewis Noble
Marc Howson
Dominic Cherrie
Michael Barton
James Shepard
Connor Cowan
Adem Luzha
Kris Todd (2020 Huntershill AFC)
Lee Nichol
Sean Power
Andrew Frodsha
Andrew Mackenzie
Bryden Nolan
Kris Jarvie (2020 Lesmahagow)

Petershill

Club did not play any matches in 2020/1

Squad 2021/2
Manager: Martin Lauchlan
Assistant: Carlo Girasoli
Coaches: Paul Roberts, Peter Keegan, Allan Hamilton
Scott Law
Craig McGregor
David Aubrey
Jordan Scott
Jack Breslin
Chris Ketterer
Ross McCabe
Scott Brodie
Paul Callander
Antony Eadie
Craig Quinn
Ronan Sweeney
Keiran Campbell
Stephen Docherty
Roddy Paterson
Fraser Team
Aaron Davis
Kyle Connor
Chris Hall

Pollok

Club did not play any competitive matches in 2020/1
Manager:
Jordan Longmuir (2014 Colville Park, ex Bathgate Th, Bo'ness United_
Josh Lumsden (2019 Clydebank, ex Dumbarton Youths)
Bryan Wharton (Ex Q Park etc, OL to Bo'ness United, then Albion Rovers Oct-May)
Danny McKenzie (2018 Kirkintilloch RR, ex Knightswood Juvs, Q Park Youths)
David Barron (2019 Hurlford Utd, OL to Greenock Dec 2020-June 2021, ex Partick Th, St Mirren, Stranraer)
Grant Evans (2016 Irvine Meadow, OL to Albion Rovers Jan -Mar 2021, ex Hamilton Accies, Dumbarton, Morton, Airdrie United)
Jordan McMillan (ex Cambuslang, Clyde, Dumbarton, Dunfermline Athletic, Edusport Academy, Hamilton Academical, Partick Thistle, Queen of the South, Rangers, Wrexham)
Kyle Bradley (2021 East Kilbride, ex Rangers, Clyde, Annan Ath)
Mark Sideserf (2015 Irvine Meadow, OL to Albion Rovers Oct-May. Ex Gretna, Motherwell, Maryhill, Shotts BA)
Paul Gallacher (2014 Q Park)
Alex McWaters (2021 Kilwinning Rangers, ex Huirlford U, Largs Th, Morton, Troon)
Chris Duff (2019 Rossvale, ex Cambuslang, Rob Roy, Queen's Park)
Derek Esplin (2019 Rutherglen Glencairn, OL to Caledonian Braves Nov 2020-June 2021), ex Cumnock)
Evan Horne (2020 Unattached, ex Annan Athletic, Dundee United, Dunfermline Athletic, East Stirlingshire, St. Mirren, Stirling Albion)
Gary McCann (2016 Irvine Meadow, ex Ashfield)
Ryan McGregor (2017 Arthurlie, ex Bellshill Athletic, Kilbirnie, Kilwinning, Petershill, Renfrew, Vale of Clyde)
Shaun Fraser (2018 Kirkintilloch RR, ex Ashfield, Irvine Meadow XI, Petershill, Queen's Park, Ross County
Stephen McDevitt (2020 Darvel)
Adam Forde (2017 Kilbirnie Ladeside, ex Neilston, Stranraer)
Callum Graham (2021 Ashfield)
Ian Russell (2019 Dumbarton, OL to Cowdenbeath Jan-May, Airdrieonians, Alloa Athletic, Brechin City, Dumbarton, Livingston, Morton, Motherwell, Queen of the South, Rangers, Stirling Albion, retired May 2021)
Jordan Shelvey (2019 Clydebank)
Josh Weir (2020 Barshaw AFC)
Stuart McCann (2017 Petershill, ex Irvine Meadow)

Port Glasgow

Manager: Paul Coyle / Eddie Walton
Christopher Wylie (2020 Morton OL)
Euan Campbell
Craig McCormick
Barry McLaughlin
Andrew Banks
Jamie Campbell
Liam Coogans
Mark Millar
David McNeil
Daniel Bamford
John Gallacher
Jack McLarty
Fraser McLaughlin
Macaulay McArthur
Brad Cooper
Josh Cooper
Darren Patton
Josh Winton

Renfrew

Manager:
Manager: Colin Clark
Graeme Milne (2020 Tower Hearts)
Aboubacar Karamoko (2020 Kilbirnie Ladeside)
Fraser Barbour
Danny McLeay
Gilmour
Callender
McGillion
Scott Morton
Liam McMenemy
Patrick O'Keefe
Craig Dallas
David McKenna (ex Stranraer, Shire, Stirling etc)
Ciaran Diver (ex Celtic)

New Signings 2021/2
Graeme Milne
David McCallum
Andrew Mclennan
Dominic Innes
Cameron Kerr
James McLennan
Gregor Wylie
Ryan Rutherford
Alexander Wright
Lewis Guy
David Verlaque
Jamie Benton
Adam Telford

Rossvale

Manager: David Gormley; Assistant: Sean Higgins; Coaches: Bill Raeside, Gary McGrath, Fraser Wilson
Management team left July 2021 to join Broomhill FC, replaced by Ian Diack (East Kilbride Thistle)
Jamie Smith
Peter Bradley
Stephen McDevitt
Craig Buchan
Ross Urquhart
Stephen Larkin
Chris Lennon
Mikey McWilliams
James Finlay
Regan O'Sullivan
Gary McGrath
Sean Higgins
Anthony Higgins
Paul Brennan
Craig Gordon
Kyle Prior
Lee Roulston
Euan Rodger
Robbie Torrance
Ross Kavanagh (ex Stirling Albion, Montrose)
Ross Alexander
Mclean
Baird
Welsh

New Signings 2021/2
Jonny Hogg (OL from Ayr United)
Jonny Kavanagh
Conor McDonald
Steven Bain
Dominik Chiedu
Josh Docherty
Dean Miller
Ross McKenzie
Zak Taylor
Donnie Wilson

Royal Albert

Club did not play any matches in 2020/1

Squad 2021/2
Manager: Stewart Thomson
Davie Hamilton
Rico Janetta
Connor Blades
Darren Hunter
Taylor Meharly
Mark Montgomery
Gareth Kerr

Rutherglen Glencairn

Manager: Willie Harvey
Callum Shields
Craig McGregor
Craig Quinn
Dale Simeon
Derek McNab
Drew Wingate
Garry Whyte
Harry Mitchell
Jackson Biggar
Jay McKay
Keirin Coleman
Kieran Hannaway
Kieron Maxwell
Liam Gormley
Michael Lone
Mick O'Byrne
Rikki McIntosh
Scott McLellan
Scott Schoneville
Sean McGuire
Tam Miller
Tommy Lone

St Anthonys

Manager: Danny Taylor
Anton Conway
Ciaran Smith
Danny Smith
Declan Walsh
Drew Boult

Evariste Bembo
Graeme Crawford
Jake Cowan
Jay Burns
James Penders
Kris Littler
Njabulo Ndlovu
Reagan Maliska
Robbie Ewart
Robert McKenzie
Rui Carballo
Scott Perry
Sean Brennan
Shaun Gallacher
Stephen McGarrigle
Zander Tran

St Cadocs

Manager: John Millar (ex Beith etc), then Craig McEwan / Craig Potter
Stephen Grindlay (2020 Beith, joined Drumchapel United July 2021)
Kevin Green (2020 Beith, joined Clydebank July 2021)
Craig Pettigrew (2020 Glenafton Athletic, rejoined them July 2021)
Keiran Wood (2020 Kilbirnie Ladeside)
Dylan Dykes (2020 Cumbernauld Colts)
Jamie Wilson (2020 Beith, Joined Cumnock July 2021)
Gary Muir (2020 Benburb)
Joe Bradley (2020 Beith)
Kenny McLean (2020 Beith)
Mark Stewart (2020 Unattached, ex Falkirk, Kilmarnock etc)
Chris Dallas (2020 Pollok)
Michael McKinven
Craig Menzies
Alan Cairns (2020 Glenafton Athletic, rejoined them June 2021)
Anthony McParland (2020 Glenafton Ath, ex Celtic, Livingston, QOS etc)
Dean Hawkshaw (ex Kilmarnock, Stranraer etc)
Dale "Gunner" Moore
Michael McCann
Evan Maley
Leon Murphy (2020 Glenafton Athletic, rejoined them June 2021)
Kevin Green
Michael Garrity
Aaron Millar
Cammy Marlow (2020 Glenafton Athletic, rejoined them June 2021)
David Blyth (ex Kilmarnock, 2020 Glenafton Athletic, rejoined them June 2021)

St Rochs

Manager: Paul Kelly
Assistant: Ryan McStay
Chris Calder (OL to Dumbarton for part of season)
Brian McQueen
Jason Elliot
Paul Tierney
Reece Glackin
Matty Sutherland
Connor Hughes
Pat O'Donnell
Jon Jay Reid
Jamie Longworth
Keiran Daw
Aaron Connolly
Sean Winter (Dec 2020 East Kilbride)
Barry Russell (ex east Kilbride etc)
CJ Hughes
Dean Kindlan
Liam Coogans (Joined Port Glasgow Dec 2020)
Liam McLaughlin
John Stark
Daniel Kindlan (transferred to Rossvale May 2021)

Squad 2021/2
Chris Calder
John Stark
Pat O'Donnell
Barry Russell
Paul Tierney
Jason Elliot
Brian McQueen
Luke Crerand
Liam Crichton
Kieran Daw
CJ Hughes
Kieran Martin
Liam McLaughlin
Jonjay Reid
Matty Sutherland
Connor Hughes
Jamie Longworth

Saltcoats Victoria

Did not play competitive games during 2020/1
Manager: Ian McMillan
Shaun McCormack
Scott Thomson
Ewan Farrell
Scott Watson (2020 Ardrossan WR)
Paul Young (2020 Ardrossan WR)
George Thomson (2020 Yoker Ath)
Ally Patrick
Gavin Sim
Kames Morgan
Lewis Paton
Adam Easton
Logan Stevenson
Chris Lyon
Alan McKelvie

Squad 2021/2
Logan Stevenson
Declan Walsh
Robbie Laidlaw
Jack Robertson

Shettleston / Glasgow United

Club did not play any matches in 2020/1
Manager:
Jordan McGrotty
Ross Barclay
Liam Ferguson
Steven Smith

Shotts Bon Accord

No competitive matches played in 2020/1.
Manager:
Jordan Love
Barry Eley
Adam Hunter

Squad 2021/2
Jonny Murdoch
Paul McGeough
Andrew Muir
Martin Cassells
Taylor Evans
Dean Sutherland
Chris Meikle
Craig Hastings
Ally Martin
Jordan Logan
Kyle Richford
Josh Watt
Euan Scott
Gerry Watt
Jonathan McStay
Jack McQuade
Dean Kinlan
Jay Anderson
Derek Barnes

Thorniewood United

Manager: James McKenna
Lewis Purves
Ryan Spalding
Jake Morris
Ross Gillan
Paul O'Brien
James Marr
Grant Kelly (ex St Anthonys, Johnstone Burgh)
Stevie Seaton
Andy Brown
Declan Brown
Jack Baptie (2020 Royal Albert)
Darren Bowie
McLear
Mark Fitzpatrick (2020 Lesmahagow)
Ally Small (ex Jerviston FC, Motherwell Youths)
Craig Smith
Ali Morgan
Lewis Archer
Murphy
Josh McCorry
Allan Campbell (2020 Royal Albert)
Ryan Sullivan

Troon

Manager: Jimmy Kirkwood
Ross Lundy
Jack Sherrie
James McGowan
Scott Chatham
Ramond Montgomerie
Ryan Stevenson
Todd Henderson
Dean Fulton
Jordan Morton
Josh Black
Jaime Gallagher
Ryan Nisbet
Lewis McDowall
Reece Allan
Jordan Lusk
Scott McLeod
Jack Paterson
Marty Fraser

Vale of Clyde

Manager: Ian Currie
Don Scott
Lee Morrison
Jamie McArthur
Adam Watt
Craig Garden
Kevin Fraser
Billy McKee
Martin Welsh
Marcus Fraser
Keiran Christie
Ryan Murphy
Keiran Chalmers
Scott Matthews
John McCue
Robert O'Donnell
Connor Blades
Dean Scott
Luke Kelly
Lee Martin
Harry Clift

Vale of Leven

Manager: Brian Brown;
Assistant: Alan Brown
Fraser Williams
Mark Butler
Robbie Dolan
Chris Jackson
Adam Monaghan
Richie Stewart
Fraser Forbes
Stephen Griffen
David McNaught
Cameron Smith
Darren Boyle
Lewis King
Lee McGeachy
Martin Connolly
Owen McCallum
Reece Pollock
Josh Grace
Steven Stibbs
Paul Callaghan

Alistair Shields
Niall Carslaw
Ross Cameron
Cameron Brisbane
Ryan Kerr
Paul McCormick
Daniel Paterson

Whitletts Victoria

Club did not play in competitive matches during 2020/1.
Manager: George Grierson
Scott Johnson (Released Oct 2020, joined Bonnyton Th)
Callum Ogston
Sean Stewart
Lyall Cameron (2020, Bonnyton Th, OL to Irvine Vics Oct-Jan)
Isaac Kerr (OL to Kilwinning Rangers, then OL to Troon)
Marc Dyer (Released Oct 2020, joined Annbank Utd)
Stewart Davidson (Released Oct 2020, joined Bonnyton Th)
Cameron Ross (Released November 2020)
Ross George (Released Nov 2020, joined Bonnyton Th)
Louis Kerr (OL to Hurlford United, then Troon for part of season)
Marc Walker (2020 Bonnyton Th, Released December 2020, joined Irvine Vics)
Jordan Baird (OL to Ardeer Thistle Nov-Jan)
Jordan Boyd
Stuart Hannah
Rory Tait (Released Oct 2020 ex Girvan, Annbank, Bonnyton Th)
Blair Craig
Connor Yair
Lauchlan Kirkland (2020 Ayr United Youths)
Kaylum Ferguson (2020 Ayr United Youths)
Adam Forsyth

Wishaw

Manager: Mark Daly
Andy Duffy (2020 Cambuslang R)
Matthew Craig
Ewan Herriot
Steven McGurgan
Gary Fallon
Christopher Patrick
Kerian Campbell
Aiden Ward
Stephen McDonald
James Brown
Kevin Barry Grant
William Graham
Gary Duggan
Scott Nicol
James Coffey
Christopher McIntyre
Vincent McGuire
Scott Sommerville

Yoker Athletic

Co Managers: Peter McKenna / Tommy Montgomery
Joe Wilton
Robbie Davidson
Kyle Girvan
Ryan McCreath
Andy Campbell
Jon Scullion
David Crerand
Gregor Cree
Scott Gallagher
Kyle Maxwell
Lewis Costello
Shaun Gallacher
Chris Meikle
Calum Dillon
Cameron Ferrier
David McGrath
Greig Barr
Ross McDonald
Abdul Karim

RENFREW FOOTBALL CLUB

PHOTOCARDS

No. 141.

RENFREW FOOTBALL CLUB.

Left to right, back row :—*W. Williams (Treasurer), J. Watkins (President), R. Adair (Sec.), T. Middleton (Vice-President).* 2nd row :—*W. Reid, R. Govin (Trainer), J. Leonard, J. Barclay, W. Watson, G. Simpson, J. Strang, J. Marshall.* 3rd row :—*J. Bean (Capt.), J. Govan, R. Logan, B. Cox, J. Dean, J. McQuatter, W. Scott.* Front row :—*W. Strang, A. McCallum, F. Geater, J. Mathers.*

Originally known as The Renfrew Victoria Junior F.C., changed to present name in 1911-1912. They won the Renfrewshire Junior Cup 1934/35 and were Runners-up in this competition 1935/36.

Expanding de Luxe Albums for Ardath Photocards on sale at Tobacconists Price 6d

ARDATH TOBACCO CO: LTD: Manufacturers of STATE EXPRESS and ARDATH CIGARETTES

D

PHOTOCARDS

No. 123.

SHETTLESTON JUNIORS F.C.

Left to right, back row :—*J. Mess, J. Smith, J. Ferguson, J. Forgie (Capt.), A. McGachy, D. Lorimer.* Front row :—*A. Dowdells (Trainer), S. Rennie, N. Murphy, A. McVicar, J. McGuigan, J. Kempton, H. O'Brian.*

On two occasions this team has won Championship of the Glasgow Junior League, in addition to winning the Glasgow Junior Charity Cup once. Several former players of this club have gained international honours.

Expanding de Luxe Albums for Ardath Photocards on sale at Tobacconists Price 6d

ARDATH TOBACCO CO: LTD: Manufacturers of STATE EXPRESS and ARDATH CIGARETTES

D

SHETTLESTON JUNIORS F.C

Shettleston have changed their name to Glasgow United for season 2021/2

West of Scotland League Fixtures 2021/22

West of Scotland League - Premier Division

Saturday, July 17
Auchinleck Talbot - Clydebank
Benburb - Kirkintilloch Rob Roy
Cumbernauld Utd - Rossvale
Cumnock Juniors - Beith Juniors
Darvel - Bonnyton Thistle
Hurlford Utd - Kilbirnie Ladeside
Irvine Meadow XI - Glenafton Athletic
Kilwinning Rangers - Troon
Largs Thistle - Rutherglen Glencairn
Pollok - Blantyre Victoria

Wednesday, July 21
Beith Juniors - Largs Thistle
Blantyre Victoria - Hurlford Utd
Bonnyton Thistle - Pollok
Clydebank - Cumbernauld Utd
Glenafton Athletic - Darvel
Kilbirnie Ladeside - Kilwinning Rangers
Kirkintilloch Rob Roy - Auchinleck Talbot
Rossvale - Cumnock Juniors
Rutherglen Glencairn - Irvine Meadow XI
Troon - Benburb

Saturday, July 24
Auchinleck Talbot - Troon
Benburb - Kilbirnie Ladeside
Cumnock Juniors - Cumbernauld Utd
Darvel - Rutherglen Glencairn
Hurlford Utd - Bonnyton Thistle
Irvine Meadow XI - Beith Juniors
Kilwinning Rangers - Blantyre Victoria
Kirkintilloch Rob Roy - Clydebank
Largs Thistle - Rossvale
Pollok - Glenafton Athletic

Wednesday, July 28
Beith Juniors - Darvel
Blantyre Victoria - Benburb
Bonnyton Thistle - Kilwinning Rangers
Clydebank - Cumnock Juniors
Cumbernauld Utd - Largs Thistle
Glenafton Athletic - Hurlford Utd
Kilbirnie Ladeside - Auchinleck Talbot
Rossvale - Irvine Meadow XI
Rutherglen Glencairn - Pollok
Troon - Kirkintilloch Rob Roy

Saturday, July 31
Auchinleck Talbot - Blantyre Victoria
Benburb - Bonnyton Thistle
Darvel - Rossvale
Hurlford Utd - Rutherglen Glencairn
Irvine Meadow XI - Cumbernauld Utd
Kilwinning Rangers - Glenafton Athletic
Kirkintilloch Rob Roy - Kilbirnie Ladeside
Largs Thistle - Cumnock Juniors
Pollok - Beith Juniors
Troon - Clydebank

Wednesday, August 4
Auchinleck Talbot - Largs Thistle
Blantyre Victoria - Beith Juniors
Glenafton Athletic - Clydebank
Hurlford Utd - Pollok
Kilbirnie Ladeside - Rossvale
Kilwinning Rangers - Darvel
Kirkintilloch Rob Roy - Cumnock Juniors
Troon - Cumbernauld Utd

Saturday, August 7
Beith Juniors - Hurlford Utd
Blantyre Victoria - Kirkintilloch Rob Roy
Bonnyton Thistle - Auchinleck Talbot
Clydebank - Largs Thistle
Cumbernauld Utd - Darvel
Cumnock Juniors - Irvine Meadow XI
Glenafton Athletic - Benburb
Kilbirnie Ladeside - Troon
Rossvale - Pollok
Rutherglen Glencairn - Kilwinning Rangers

Wednesday, August 11
Auchinleck Talbot - Glenafton Athletic
Benburb - Rutherglen Glencairn
Darvel - Cumnock Juniors
Hurlford Utd - Rossvale
Irvine Meadow XI - Largs Thistle
Kilbirnie Ladeside - Clydebank
Kilwinning Rangers - Beith Juniors
Kirkintilloch Rob Roy - Bonnyton Thistle
Pollok - Cumbernauld Utd
Troon - Blantyre Victoria

Saturday, August 14
Beith Juniors - Benburb
Blantyre Victoria - Kilbirnie Ladeside
Bonnyton Thistle - Troon
Clydebank - Irvine Meadow XI
Cumbernauld Utd - Hurlford Utd
Cumnock Juniors - Pollok
Glenafton Athletic - Kirkintilloch Rob Roy
Largs Thistle - Darvel
Rossvale - Kilwinning Rangers
Rutherglen Glencairn - Auchinleck Talbot

Wednesday, August 18
Auchinleck Talbot - Beith Juniors
Benburb - Rossvale
Blantyre Victoria - Clydebank
Darvel - Irvine Meadow XI
Hurlford Utd - Cumnock Juniors
Kilbirnie Ladeside - Bonnyton Thistle
Kilwinning Rangers - Cumbernauld Utd
Kirkintilloch Rob Roy - Rutherglen Glencairn
Pollok - Largs Thistle
Troon - Glenafton Athletic

Saturday, August 21
Beith Juniors - Kirkintilloch Rob Roy
Bonnyton Thistle - Blantyre Victoria
Clydebank - Darvel
Cumbernauld Utd - Benburb
Cumnock Juniors - Kilwinning Rangers
Glenafton Athletic - Kilbirnie Ladeside
Irvine Meadow XI - Pollok
Largs Thistle - Hurlford Utd
Rossvale - Auchinleck Talbot
Rutherglen Glencairn - Troon

Saturday, August 28
Auchinleck Talbot - Cumbernauld Utd
Benburb - Cumnock Juniors
Blantyre Victoria - Glenafton Athletic
Bonnyton Thistle - Clydebank
Hurlford Utd - Irvine Meadow XI
Kilbirnie Ladeside - Rutherglen Glencairn
Kilwinning Rangers - Largs Thistle
Kirkintilloch Rob Roy - Rossvale
Pollok - Darvel
Troon - Beith Juniors

Saturday, September 4
Beith Juniors - Kilbirnie Ladeside
Clydebank - Pollok
Cumnock Juniors - Auchinleck Talbot
Cumbernauld Utd - Kirkintilloch Rob Roy
Darvel - Hurlford Utd
Glenafton Athletic-v Kilwinning Rangers
Largs Thistle - Benburb
Rossvale - Troon
Rutherglen Glencairn - Blantyre Victoria

Saturday, September 11
Phase 1
Benburb - Irvine Meadow XI
Bonnyton Thistle - Rutherglen Glencairn

Phase 2
Blantyre Victoria - Auchinleck Talbot
Cumbernauld Utd - Clydebank
Cumnock Juniors - Darvel
Pollok - Rossvale

Saturday, September 18
Beith Juniors - Bonnyton Thistle
Clydebank - Hurlford Utd
Cumbernauld Utd - Kilbirnie Ladeside
Cumnock Juniors - Troon
Darvel - Benburb
Irvine Meadow XI - Auchinleck Talbot
Largs Thistle - Kirkintilloch Rob Roy
Pollok - Kilwinning Rangers
Rossvale - Blantyre Victoria
Rutherglen Glencairn - Glenafton Athletic

Saturday, September 25
Auchinleck Talbot - Darvel
Benburb - Pollok
Blantyre Victoria - Cumbernauld Utd
Bonnyton Thistle - Rossvale
Glenafton Athletic - Beith Juniors
Kilbirnie Ladeside - Cumnock Juniors
Kilwinning Rangers - Hurlford Utd
Kirkintilloch Rob Roy - Irvine Meadow XI
Rutherglen Glencairn - Clydebank
Troon - Largs Thistle

Saturday, October 2
Beith Juniors - Rutherglen Glencairn
Clydebank - Kilwinning Rangers
Cumbernauld Utd - Bonnyton Thistle
Cumnock Juniors - Blantyre Victoria
Darvel - Kirkintilloch Rob Roy
Hurlford Utd - Benburb
Irvine Meadow XI - Troon
Largs Thistle - Kilbirnie Ladeside
Pollok - Auchinleck Talbot
Rossvale - Glenafton Athletic

Saturday, October 9
Auchinleck Talbot - Hurlford Utd
Beith Juniors - Clydebank
Benburb v Kilwinning Rangers

Blantyre Victoria - Largs Thistle
Bonnyton Thistle - Cumnock Juniors
Glenafton Athletic - Cumbernauld Utd
Kilbirnie Ladeside - Irvine Meadow XI
Kirkintilloch Rob Roy - Pollok
Rutherglen Glencairn - Rossvale

Saturday, October 16

Saturday, October 23
Clydebank - Benburb
Cumbernauld Utd - Rutherglen Glencairn
Cumnock Juniors - Glenafton Athletic
Darvel - Kilbirnie Ladeside
Hurlford Utd - Kirkintilloch Rob Roy
Irvine Meadow XI - Blantyre Victoria
Kilwinning Rangers - Auchinleck Talbot
Largs Thistle - Bonnyton Thistle
Pollok - Troon
Rossvale - Beith Juniors

Saturday, October 30
Auchinleck Talbot - Benburb
Beith Juniors - Cumbernauld Utd
Blantyre Victoria - Darvel
Bonnyton Thistle - Irvine Meadow XI
Glenafton Athletic - Largs Thistle
Kilbirnie Ladeside - Pollok
Kirkintilloch Rob Roy - Kilwinning Rangers
Rossvale - Clydebank
Rutherglen Glencairn - Cumnock Juniors
Troon - Hurlford Utd

West of Scotland League - Conference A

Saturday, July 17
Arthurlie - Glasgow University
Forth Wanderers - Shotts Bon Accord
Girvan - Craigmark Burntonians
Irvine Victoria - Whitletts Victoria
Lesmahagow Juniors - Maybole Juniors
Maryhill - Bellshill Athletic
Muirkirk Juniors - Johnstone Burgh
Saltcoats Victoria - Lugar Boswell Thistle

Wednesday, July 21
Bellshill Athletic - Lesmahagow Juniors
Craigmark Burntonians - Irvine Victoria
Glasgow University - Girvan
Johnstone Burgh - Maryhill
Lugar Boswell Thistle - Muirkirk Juniors
Maybole Juniors - Forth Wanderers
Shotts Bon Accord - Arthurlie
Whitletts Victoria - Saltcoats Victoria

Saturday, July 24
Arthurlie - Forth Wanderers
Bellshill Athletic - Maybole Juniors
Girvan - Shotts Bon Accord
Irvine Victoria - Glasgow University
Lesmahagow Juniors - Johnstone Burgh
Maryhill - Lugar Boswell Thistle
Muirkirk Juniors - Whitletts Victoria
Saltcoats Victoria - Craigmark Burntonians

Wednesday, July 28
Craigmark Burntonians - Muirkirk Juniors
Forth Wanderers - Girvan
Glasgow University - Saltcoats Victoria
Johnstone Burgh - Bellshill Athletic
Lugar Boswell Thistle - Lesmahagow Juniors
Maybole Juniors - Arthurlie
Shotts Bon Accord - Irvine Victoria
Whitletts Victoria - Maryhill

Saturday, July 31
Bellshill Athletic - Lugar Boswell Thistle
Girvan - Arthurlie
Irvine Victoria - Forth Wanderers
Johnstone Burgh - Maybole Juniors
Lesmahagow Juniors - Whitletts Victoria
Maryhill - Craigmark Burntonians
Muirkirk Juniors - Glasgow University
Saltcoats Victoria - Shotts Bon Accord

Wednesday, August 4
Bellshill Athletic - Irvine Victoria
Craigmark Burntonians - Shotts Bon Accord
Lesmahagow Juniors - Saltcoats Victoria
Lugar Boswell Thistle - Arthurlie
Maryhill - Muirkirk Juniors
Whitletts Victoria - Forth Wanderers

Saturday, August 7
Arthurlie - Irvine Victoria
Craigmark Burntonians - Lesmahagow Juniors
Forth Wanderers - Saltcoats Victoria
Glasgow University - Maryhill
Lugar Boswell Thistle - Johnstone Burgh
Maybole Juniors - Girvan
Shotts Bon Accord - Muirkirk Juniors
Whitletts Victoria - Bellshill Athletic

Wednesday, August 11
Bellshill Athletic - Craigmark Burntonians
Irvine Victoria - Girvan
Johnstone Burgh - Whitletts Victoria
Lesmahagow Juniors - Glasgow University
Lugar Boswell Thistle - Maybole Juniors
Maryhill - Shotts Bon Accord
Muirkirk Juniors - Forth Wanderers
Saltcoats Victoria - Arthurlie

Saturday, August 14
Arthurlie - Muirkirk Juniors
Craigmark Burntonians - Johnstone Burgh
Forth Wanderers - Maryhill
Girvan - Saltcoats Victoria
Maybole Juniors - Irvine Victoria
Shotts Bon Accord - Lesmahagow Juniors
Whitletts Victoria - Lugar Boswell Thistle
Glasgow University - Bellshill Athletic (now Aug 25)

Wednesday, August 18
Bellshill Athletic - Shotts Bon Accord
Johnstone Burgh - Glasgow University
Lesmahagow Juniors - Forth Wanderers
Lugar Boswell Thistle - Craigmark Burntonians
Maryhill - Arthurlie
Muirkirk Juniors - Girvan
Saltcoats Victoria - Irvine Victoria
Whitletts Victoria - Maybole Juniors

Saturday, August 21
Arthurlie - Lesmahagow Juniors
Craigmark Burntonians - Whitletts Victoria
Forth Wanderers - Bellshill Athletic
Girvan - Maryhill
Glasgow University - Lugar Boswell Thistle
Irvine Victoria - Muirkirk Juniors
Maybole Juniors - Saltcoats Victoria
Shotts Bon Accord - Johnstone Burgh

Wednesday, August 25
Glasgow University - Bellshill Athletic

Saturday, August 28
Bellshill Athletic - Arthurlie
Craigmark Burntonians - Maybole Juniors
Johnstone Burgh - Forth Wanderers
Lesmahagow Juniors - Girvan
Lugar Boswell Thistle - Shotts Bon Accord
Maryhill - Irvine Victoria
Whitletts Victoria - Glasgow University
Muirkirk Juniors - Saltcoats Victoria

Saturday, September 4
Arthurlie - Johnstone Burgh
Forth Wanderers - Lugar Boswell Thistle
Girvan - Bellshill Athletic
Glasgow University - Craigmark Burntonians
Irvine Victoria - Lesmahagow Juniors
Maybole Juniors - Muirkirk Juniors
Saltcoats Victoria - Maryhill
Shotts Bon Accord - Whitletts Victoria

Saturday, September 11
Phase 1
Glasgow University - Maybole Juniors
Johnstone Burgh - Girvan

Phase 2
Irvine Victoria - Saltcoats Victoria
Forth Wanderers - Muirkirk Juniors

Saturday, September 18
Arthurlie - Whitletts Victoria
Forth Wanderers - Craigmark Burntonians
Girvan - Lugar Boswell Thistle
Irvine Victoria - Johnstone Burgh
Maybole Juniors - Maryhill
Muirkirk Juniors - Lesmahagow Juniors
Saltcoats Victoria - Bellshill Athletic
Shotts Bon Accord - Glasgow University

Saturday, September 25
Bellshill Athletic - Muirkirk Juniors
Craigmark Burntonians - Arthurlie
Glasgow University - Forth Wanderers
Johnstone Burgh - Saltcoats Victoria
Lesmahagow Juniors - Maryhill
Lugar Boswell Thistle - Irvine Victoria
Shotts Bon Accord - Maybole Juniors
Whitletts Victoria - Girvan

West of Scotland League - Conference B

Saturday, July 17
Ardeer Thistle - Thorniewood Utd
Ashfield - Glasgow Utd
Cambuslang Rangers - St Cadoc's
Dalry Thistle - Kello Rov
Greenock Juniors - Port Glasgow Juniors
Newmains Utd - Gartcairn
Renfrew - Royal Albert
Carluke Rov idle

Wednesday, July 21
Gartcairn - Carluke Rov

Glasgow Utd - Cambuslang Rangers
Kello Rov - Ardeer Thistle
Port Glasgow Juniors - Dalry Thistle
Royal Albert - Newmains Utd
St Cadoc's - Greenock Juniors
Thorniewood Utd - Renfrew
Ashfield idle

Saturday, July 24
Ardeer Thistle - Port Glasgow Juniors
Cambuslang Rangers - Ashfield
Carluke Rov - Royal Albert
Dalry Thistle - St Cadoc's
Greenock Juniors - Glasgow Utd
Newmains Utd - Thorniewood Utd
Renfrew - Kello Rov
Gartcairn idle

Wednesday, July 28
Ashfield - Greenock Juniors
Glasgow Utd - Dalry Thistle
Kello Rov - Newmains Utd
Port Glasgow Juniors - Renfrew
Royal Albert - Gartcairn
St Cadoc's - Ardeer Thistle
Thorniewood Utd - Carluke Rov
Cambuslang Rangers idle

Saturday, July 31
Ardeer Thistle - Glasgow Utd
Carluke Rov - Kello Rov
Dalry Thistle - Ashfield
Gartcairn - Thorniewood Utd
Greenock Juniors - Cambuslang Rangers
Newmains Utd - Port Glasgow Juniors
Renfrew - St Cadoc's
Royal Albert idle

Wednesday, August 4
Carluke Rov - Ardeer Thistle
Gartcairn - Dalry Thistle
Kello Rov - Ashfield
Port Glasgow Juniors - Glasgow Utd
Royal Albert - Greenock Juniors
Thorniewood Utd - Cambuslang Rangers

Saturday, August 7
Ashfield - Ardeer Thistle
Cambuslang Rangers - Dalry Thistle
Glasgow Utd - Renfrew
Kello Rov - Gartcairn
Port Glasgow Juniors - Carluke Rov
St Cadoc's - Newmains Utd
Thorniewood Utd - Royal Albert
Greenock Juniors idle

Wednesday, August 11
Ardeer Thistle - Cambuslang Rangers
Carluke Rov - St Cadoc's
Dalry Thistle - Greenock Juniors
Gartcairn - Port Glasgow Juniors
Newmains Utd - Glasgow Utd
Renfrew - Ashfield
Royal Albert - Kello Rov
Thorniewood Utd idle

Saturday, August 14
Ashfield - Newmains Utd
Cambuslang Rangers - Renfrew
Glasgow Utd - Carluke Rov
Greenock Juniors - Ardeer Thistle
Kello Rov - Thorniewood Utd
Port Glasgow Juniors - Royal Albert
St Cadoc's - Gartcairn
Dalry Thistle idle

Wednesday, August 18
Ardeer Thistle - Dalry Thistle
Carluke Rov - Ashfield
Gartcairn - Glasgow Utd
Newmains Utd - Cambuslang Rangers
Renfrew - Greenock Juniors
Royal Albert - St Cadoc's
Thorniewood Utd - Port Glasgow Juniors
Kello Rov idle

Saturday, August 21
Ashfield - Gartcairn
Cambuslang Rangers - Carluke Rov
Dalry Thistle - Renfrew
Glasgow Utd - Royal Albert
Greenock Juniors - Newmains Utd
Port Glasgow Juniors - Kello Rov
St Cadoc's - Thorniewood Utd
Ardeer Thistle idle

Saturday, August 28
Carluke Rov - Greenock Juniors
Gartcairn - Cambuslang Rangers
Kello Rov - St Cadoc's
Newmains Utd - Dalry Thistle
Renfrew - Ardeer Thistle
Royal Albert - Ashfield
Thorniewood Utd - Glasgow Utd
Port Glasgow Juniors idle

Saturday, September 4
Ardeer Thistle - Newmains Utd
Ashfield - Thorniewood Utd
Cambuslang Rangers - Royal Albert
Dalry Thistle - Carluke Rov
Glasgow Utd - Kello Rov
Greenock Juniors - Gartcairn
St Cadoc's - Port Glasgow Juniors
Renfrew idle

Saturday, September 11
Phase 1
Newmains Utd - Renfrew
Phase 2
Thorniewood Utd - Gartcairn
Kello Rov - Port Glasgow Juniors

Saturday, September 18
Ardeer Thistle - Gartcairn
Ashfield - Port Glasgow Juniors
Cambuslang Rangers - Kello Rov
Dalry Thistle - Royal Albert
Glasgow Utd - St Cadoc's
Greenock Juniors - Thorniewood Utd
Renfrew - Carluke Rov
Newmains Utd idle

Saturday, September 25
Carluke Rov - Newmains Utd
Gartcairn - Renfrew
Kello Rov - Greenock Juniors
Port Glasgow Juniors - Cambuslang Rangers
Royal Albert - Ardeer Thistle
St Cadoc's - Ashfield
Thorniewood Utd - Dalry Thistle
Glasgow Utd idle

West of Scotland League - Conference C

Saturday, July 17
Ardrossan Winton Rov - Vale of Leven
East Kilbride Thistle - Glasgow Perthshire
Lanark Utd - Larkhall Thistle
Neilston - Wishaw Juniors
Petershill - Drumchapel Utd
St Anthony's - Kilsyth Rangers
Vale of Clyde - St Roch's
Yoker Athletic idle

Wednesday, July 21
Drumchapel Utd - Yoker Athletic
Glasgow Perthshire - Lanark Utd
Kilsyth Rangers - Petershill
Larkhall Thistle - St Anthony's
St Roch's - Neilston
Vale of Leven - Vale of Clyde
Wishaw Juniors - East Kilbride Thistle
Ardrossan Winton Rov idle

Saturday, July 24
East Kilbride Thistle - St Roch's
Lanark Utd - Wishaw Juniors
Neilston - Vale of Leven
Petershill - Larkhall Thistle
St Anthony's - Glasgow Perthshire
Vale of Clyde - Ardrossan Winton Rov
Yoker Athletic - Kilsyth Rangers
Drumchapel Utd idle

Wednesday, July 28
Ardrossan Winton Rov - Neilston
Glasgow Perthshire - Petershill
Kilsyth Rangers - Drumchapel Utd
Larkhall Thistle - Yoker Athletic
St Roch's - Lanark Utd
Vale of Leven - East Kilbride Thistle
Wishaw Juniors - St Anthony's
Vale of Clyde idle

Saturday, July 31
Drumchapel Utd - Larkhall Thistle
East Kilbride Thistle - Ardrossan Winton Rov
Lanark Utd - Vale of Leven
Neilston - Vale of Clyde
Petershill - Wishaw Juniors
St Anthony's - St Roch's
Yoker Athletic - Glasgow Perthshire
Kilsyth Rangers idle

Wednesday, August 4
Glasgow Perthshire - Ardrossan Winton Rov
Kilsyth Rangers - Neilston
Petershill - St Anthony's
Wishaw Juniors - Vale of Leven

Saturday, August 7
Ardrossan Winton Rov - Lanark Utd
Glasgow Perthshire - Drumchapel Utd
Larkhall Thistle - Kilsyth Rangers
St Roch's - Petershill
Vale of Clyde - East Kilbride Thistle
Vale of Leven - St Anthony's
Wishaw Juniors - Yoker Athletic
Neilston idle

Wednesday, August 11
Drumchapel Utd - Wishaw Juniors

East Kilbride Thistle - Neilston
Kilsyth Rangers - Glasgow Perthshire
Lanark Utd - Vale of Clyde
Petershill - Vale of Leven
St Anthony's - Ardrossan Winton Rov
Yoker Athletic - St Roch's
Larkhall Thistle idle

Saturday, August 14
Ardrossan Winton Rov - Petershill
Glasgow Perthshire - Larkhall Thistle
Neilston - Lanark Utd
St Roch's - Drumchapel Utd
Vale of Clyde - St Anthony's
Vale of Leven - Yoker Athletic
Wishaw Juniors - Kilsyth Rangers
East Kilbride Thistle idle

Wednesday, August 18
Drumchapel Utd - Vale of Leven
Kilsyth Rangers - St Roch's
Lanark Utd - East Kilbride Thistle
Larkhall Thistle v Wishaw Juniors
Petershill - Vale of Clyde
St Anthony's - Neilston
Yoker Athletic - Ardrossan Winton Rov
Glasgow Perthshire idle

Saturday, August 21
Ardrossan Winton Rov - Drumchapel Utd
East Kilbride Thistle - St Anthony's
Neilston - Petershill
St Roch's - Larkhall Thistle
Vale of Clyde - Yoker Athletic
Vale of Leven - Kilsyth Rangers
Wishaw Juniors - Glasgow Perthshire
Lanark Utd idle

Saturday, August 28
Drumchapel Utd - Vale of Clyde
Glasgow Perthshire - St Roch's
Kilsyth Rangers - Ardrossan Winton Rov
Larkhall Thistle - Vale of Leven
Petershill - East Kilbride Thistle
St Anthony's - Lanark Utd
Yoker Athletic - Neilston
Wishaw Juniors idle

Saturday, September 4
Ardrossan Winton Rov - Larkhall Thistle
East Kilbride Thistle - Yoker Athletic
Lanark Utd - Petershill
Neilston - Drumchapel Utd
St Roch's - Wishaw Juniors
Vale of Clyde - Kilsyth Rangers
Vale of Leven - Glasgow Perthshire
St Anthony's idle

Saturday, September 11
Phase 1
Drumchapel Utd - East Kilbride Thistle
Larkhall Thistle - Vale of Clyde
Yoker Athletic - Lanark Utd
Phase 2
Kilsyth Rangers - St Anthony's
Glasgow Perthshire - Vale of Leven

Saturday, September 18
Ardrossan Winton Rov - Wishaw Juniors
East Kilbride Thistle - Kilsyth Rangers
Lanark Utd - Drumchapel Utd
Neilston - Larkhall Thistle
St Anthony's - Yoker Athletic
Vale of Clyde - Glasgow Perthshire
Vale of Leven - St Roch's
Petershill idle

Saturday, September 25
Drumchapel Utd - St Anthony's
Glasgow Perthshire - Neilston
Kilsyth Rangers - Lanark Utd
Larkhall Thistle - East Kilbride Thistle
St Roch's - Ardrossan Winton Rov
Wishaw Juniors - Vale of Clyde
Yoker Athletic - Petershill
Vale of Leven idle

West of Scotland League - Division 4

Saturday, July 17
Broomhill Sports Club - St Peter's
Campbeltown Pupils - Kilsyth Athletic
Glenvale - Harmony Row
Harthill Royal - Finnart

Wednesday, July 21
Finnart - Glenvale
Harmony Row - Broomhill Sports Club
Kilsyth Athletic - Harthill Royal
St Peter's - Campbeltown Pupils (8pm)

Saturday, July 24
Campbeltown Pupils - Broomhill Sports Club
Finnart - Harmony Row
Glenvale - Kilsyth Athletic
Harthill Royal - St Peter's

Wednesday, July 28
Broomhill Sports Club - Harthill Royal
Harmony Row - Campbeltown Pupils (8pm)
Kilsyth Athletic - Finnart
St Peter's - Glenvale

Saturday, July 31
Finnart - St Peter's
Glenvale - Broomhill Sports Club
Harthill Royal - Campbeltown Pupils
Kilsyth Athletic - Harmony Row

Wednesday, August 4
Finnart - Kilsyth Athletic
Glenvale - St Peter's

Saturday, August 7
Broomhill Sports Club - Finnart
Campbeltown Pupils - Glenvale
Harmony Row - Harthill Royal
St Peter's - Kilsyth Athletic

Saturday, August 14
Finnart - Campbeltown Pupils
Glenvale - Harthill Royal
Kilsyth Athletic - Broomhill Sports Club
St Peter's - Harmony Row

Saturday, August 21
Finnart - Harthill Royal
Harmony Row - Glenvale
Kilsyth Athletic - Campbeltown Pupils
St Peter's - Broomhill Sports Club

Saturday, August 28
Broomhill Sports Club - Harmony Row
Campbeltown Pupils - St Peter's
Glenvale - Finnart
Harthill Royal - Kilsyth Athletic

Saturday, September 4
Broomhill Sports Club - Campbeltown Pupils
Harmony Row - Finnart
Kilsyth Athletic - Glenvale
St Peter's - Harthill Royal

Saturday, September 11
Campbeltown Pupils - Harmony Row
Harthill Royal - Broomhill Sports Club
St Peter's - Finnart

Saturday, September 18
Broomhill Sports Club - Glenvale
Campbeltown Pupils - Harthill Royal
Harmony Row - Kilsyth Athletic

Saturday, September 25
Finnart - Broomhill Sports Club
Glenvale - Campbeltown Pupils
Harthill Royal - Harmony Row
Kilsyth Athletic - St Peter's

Saturday, October 2
Broomhill Sports Club - Kilsyth Athletic
Campbeltown Pupils - Finnart
Harmony Row - St Peter's
Harthill Royal - Glenvale

SOUTH SENIORS

The South of Scotland League managed to get games played between October 2020 and the turn of the year. However, the abrupt suspension of fixtures made it impossible to complete the season which was declared Null and Void.

For 2021/2 the South League has lost Heston Rovers from its ranks. The club shared Palmerston Park with Queen of the South. The reason given for their withdrawal was lack of committee / volunteers. Clubs required extra bodies at the start of 2021/2 to implement COVID protocols. Hopefully Heston will be in a position to return to senior football for 2022/3.

South of Scotland League 2020/21

	ABB	CAL	CRE	HES	LTHI	LMAB	MIDS	NEW	NIT	STC	STRA	THR	UPP	WIG
Abbey Vale						Oct 10 6-2					Dec 12 1-1	Nov 7 3-1	Oct 24 2-0	
Caledonian Braves Reserves			Dec 5 4-1					Nov 28 4-2	Nov 7 7-4		Nov 21 2-2			
Creetown						Dec 19 3-3						Oct 10 1-8		
Heston Rovers			Nov 14 3-0					Nov 7 1-1			Dec 19 0-3		Oct 17 0-2	
Lochar Thistle	Dec 5 0-3	Dec 12 3-1	Oct 31 2-3	Nov 28 3-1			Dec 19 4-1	Oct 24 3-3	Oct 10 2-3		Nov 14 0-2			Nov 21 2-3
Lochmaben									Nov 28 3-4	Oct 31 1-1				Nov 7 1-0
Mid Annandale						Oct 24 2-2				Oct 17 2-3	Dec 5 0-2	Nov 28 2-5	Nov 7 5-4	
Newton Stewart	Nov 14 2-2		Oct 17 3-2	Dec 5 7-1							Oct 31 1-6			Dec 19 6-0
Nithsdale Wanderers				Oct 24 6-3			Nov 14 4-1				Oct 17 2-4			Dec 5 4-1
St Cuthbert Wanderers				Dec 12 3-0	Nov 7 3-0			Oct 10 1-2						Nov 14 2-0
Stranraer Reserves	Nov 28 4-1		Nov 6 8-0							Oct 24 2-4			Oct 10 5-2	
Threave Rovers				Oct 31 5-3	Oct 17 3-1	Dec 5 8-0								
Upper Annandale		Oct 31 2-1				Nov 14 5-2			Dec 12 4-1			Dec 19 0-3		
Wigtown & Bladnoch	Oct 17 3-1			Oct 10 3-1									Nov 28 2-0	

Pos	Team	Pld	W	D	L	GF	GA	GD	Pts
1	Stranraer reserves	11	8	2	1	40	13	27	26
2	Threave Rovers	7	6	0	1	33	10	23	18
3	St Cuthbert Wanderers	7	5	1	1	17	7	10	16
4	Newton Stewart	9	4	3	2	27	20	7	15
5	Nithsdale Wanderers	8	5	0	3	28	25	3	15
6	Abbey Vale	8	4	2	2	19	13	6	14
7	Upper Annandale	9	4	0	5	19	21	-2	12
8	Wigtown & Bladnoch	8	4	0	4	12	17	-5	12
9	Caledonian Braves reserves	6	3	1	2	19	14	5	10
10	Lochar Thistle	11	3	1	7	20	26	-6	10
11	Lochmaben	8	1	3	4	14	29	-15	6
12	Mid-Annandale	7	1	1	5	13	24	-11	4
13	Heston Rovers	10	1	1	8	13	34	-21	4
14	Creetown	7	1	1	5	10	31	-21	4

South of Scotland League - Recent Placings

	1980-1	1981-2	1982-3	1983-4	1984-5	1985-6	1986-7	1987-8	1988-9	1989-90	1990-1	1991-2	1992-3	1993-4	1994-5	1995-6	1996-7	1997-8	1998-9	1999-00	2000-1	2001-2	2002-3	2003-4	2004-5	2005-6	2006-7	2007-8	2008-9	2009-10	2010-11	2011-12	2012-13	2013-14	2014-15	2015-16	2016-17	2017-18	2018-19	2019/20	2020/1*
Abbey Vale																						14	6	12	8	3	12	12	9	7	13	11	7	9	7	11	8	5	4	3	6
Annan Athletic	3	2	3	1	2	4	1	3																																	
Annan Athletic Reserves									7	7	9		10	7	8	6	12	8	5	5	8	7	13	5	3	2	6	10	6									14	16		
Blackwood Dynamoes / Crichton Royal / Crichton / Lochmaben													5	9		7	2	13	8	7	4	12	7	16	11	11	8	1	2	5	5	8	9	5	9	4	11	12	11	14	11
Bonnyton Thistle																																						6	2	4	
Creetown	8	5	9	9	3	9	10	10	5	5	11	9	12	10		12	10	4	4	8	7	4	11	3	2	5	4	6	13	11	9	13	11	11	12	10	10	13	14	15	14
Dalbeattie Star	6	3	4	2	1	1	2	5	1	3	4	3	2	5	6	10	13	6	7	2	3									2	2	1	1								
Dalbeattie Star Reserves																						8	14	14	13	10	9	4	7												
Dumfries HSFP / Dumfries / Heston Rovers															4	3	5	3	2	13	5	6	8	6	6	13	11	15	10	10	8	3	5	6	6	5	7	7	8	7	13
Dumfries YMCA																																			14	14	14	15	15		
Edusport Academy / Caledonian Braves																																			5	2	1			10	9
Fleet Star																									10	14	14	11	14	12	11	9	12	10	8	13					
Girvan Amateurs / Girvan	7	10	10	6	8	8	8	9	8	1	7	4	9	8	7	4	9	7	12	11	9	2	4	7																	
Gretna Reserves																						9	3																		
Lochar Thistle																																		7	4	7	9	3	7	11	10
Maxwelltown HSFP											1	2	7	2	3	8	8	10	3	10																					
Mid Annandale																								11	9	9	13	14	11	9	7	6	10	8	10	8	5	2	6	4	12
Newton Stewart	10	9	5	8	7	3	6	1	4	8	5	6	8	6		13	7	12	10	3	10	15	15	15	14	12	10	9	12	8	6	5	6	3	2	9	6	9	13	5	4
Nithsdale Wanderers																						11	9	10	7	7	2	7	8	13	12	12	8	4	13	12	13	11	3	6	5
Queen of the South Reserves													6				1				1			2																	
St Cuthbert Wanderers	1	7	7	7	4	6	3	6	3	4	6	7	4	3	5	1	3	5	9	4	6	3	5	8	5	6	5	5	5	3	3	4	2	2	3	1	3	4	10	9	3
Stranraer Athletic																2	4	9	11	6	13	5	1	1	1	4	3	8													
Stranraer Reserves	2	1	1	3	5	7	7	4			8													4				3	4	6	4	7						8	1	2	1
Tarff Rovers	9	8	8	10	10	10	9	8			10	8	11	11	9	11	11	1	1	1	2	1	2																		
Threave Rovers	4	4	2	4	6	2	5	2	2	2	2	5	1	1	1	9	6	2	6						4	1	1	2	1	1	1	2	4				4	1	9	1	2
Threave Rovers Reserves																				9	11	10	12	9																	
Upper Annandale																																			11	6	12	10	5	12	7
Wigtown & Bladnoch	5	6	6	5	9	5	4	7	6	6	3	1	3	4	2	5	14	11	13	12	12	13	10	13	12	8	7	13	3	4	10	10	3	1	1	3	2		12	13	8

* Season Declared Null and Void

The table on the left shows the finishing positions in the South of Scotland League back to 1980.

SOUTH OF SCOTLAND LEAGUE HISTORICAL MEMBERSHIP

Abbey Vale	2001-
Annan Athletic	1977-1987
Annan Athletic Res	1987-1991, 1992-2009, 2017-19
Ayr United 'A'	1946-48
Bonnyton Thistle	2017-20
Caledonian Braves Res	2019-
Creetown	1946-48, 1972-
Crichton Royal	1992-2015
Dalbeattie Star	1946-47, 1976-2001, 2009-2012
Dalbeattie Star Res	2001-2009
Dumfries	2000-2008
Dumfries HSFP	1994-2000
Dumfries United	1987-88
Dumfries YMCA	2014-
Edusport Academy	2014-2017
Fleet Star	2004-2016
Girvan	1951-62, 1975-2005
Glenluce	1948-50
Gretna Community	1991-92
Gretna Reserves	2001-03
Greystone Rovers	1956-58
Heathhall Athletic	1948-50
Heston Rovers	2008-
Kilmarnock 'A'	1946-48
Lincluden Swifts	1977-80
Lochar Thistle	2013-
Lochmaben	2016-
Maxwelltown HSFP	1990-2000
Mid-Annandale	2003-
Newton Stewart	1946-
Nithsdale Wanderers (1)	1946-47, 1948-50
Nithsdale Wanderers (2)	2001-
Queen of the South Res	1972-73, 1992-93, 1996-97, 2003-04
RAF West Freugh	1948-49
Solway Star	1946-47
St Cuthbert Wanderers	1946-
Stranraer	1946-1949
Stranraer Athletic	1995-2008
Stranraer reserves	1949-88, 1990-91, 2003-04. 2007-2012, 2017-
Tarff Rovers	1946-88, 1990-2003
Threave Rovers	1959-1998, 2004-2012, 2016-
Upper Annandale	2014-
Whithorn	1946-59, 1962-63, 1964-69
Wigtown & Bladnoch	1946-17, 2018-

South of Scotland Cups 2020/1

No fixtures were played in the various Cup competitions for 2020/1, other than the South Challenge Cup. ***Details of these matches can be found in the East Seniors section of the Almanac.***

Alba Cup Finals

This is the Cup for clubs who do not a full SFA licence. The winners play off against the winners of the Alex Jack Cup for a place in the next year's Scottish Cup.

ALL-TIME SOUTH ALBA CUP FINALS

Season	*Winners*	*Runners Up*	*F*	*A*	*Venue*
2016/17	Lochar Thistle	Nithsdale Wanderers	4	0	Palmerston Park
2017/18	Mid Annandale	Bonnyton Thistle	4	1	Galabank
2018/19	Bonnyton Thistle	Mid Annandale	3	1	Harriet Road
2019/20	Mid Annandale	Abbey Vale	4	2	Galabank

South of Scotland League Cup

Recent South of Scotland League Cup Finals

Season	Winners	Runners Up	Score	Venue
1988/9	Dalbeattie Star	Threave Rovers	3-2	2 legs
1989/90	Threave Rovers	Dalbeattie Star	3-2	2 legs
1990/1	Threave Rovers	Maxwelltown HSFP	3-2	2 legs
1991/2	Girvan Amateurs	Dalbeattie Star	6-1	2 legs
1992/3	Dalbeattie Star	Wigtown & Bladnoch	2-2, 4-3 pens	2 legs
1993/4	Threave Rovers	Wigtown & Bladnoch	4-1	2 legs
1994/5	Wigtown & Bladnoch	Annan Athletic	4-2	2 legs
1995/6	St Cuthbert Wanderers	Maxwelltown HSFP	4-3	2 legs
1996/7	QOS Reserves	Stranraer Athletic	5-3	2 legs
1997/8	Tarff Rovers	Threave Rovers	5-2	2 legs
1998/9	Tarff Rovers	QOS Reserves	5-4	2 legs
1999/00	Tarff Rovers	Threave Rovers	2-0	Kirkcowan
2000/1	Newton Stewart	St Cuthbert Wanderers	5-0	Newton Stewart
2001/2	Girvan	Stranraer Athletic	2-1	Girvan
2002/3	Crichton	Nithsdale Wanderers	4-1	Crichton
2003/4	Stranraer Athletic	Girvan	3-1	Girvan
2004/5	Annan Athletic Reserves	St Cuthbert Wanderers	5-0	Kirkcudbright
2005/6	Creetown	Stranraer Athletic	1-0	Creetown
2006/7	Threave Rovers	Crichton	2-1	Castle Douglas
2007/8	St Cuthbert Wanderers	Stranraer Reserves	4-2	Kirkcudbright
2008/9	St Cuthbert Wanderers	Crichton	1-0	Crichton
2009/10	Stranraer Reserves	St Cuthbert Wanderers	3-0	Stranraer
2010/1	Dalbeattie Star	Threave Rovers	1-0	Castle Douglas
2011/2	Dalbeattie Star	St Cuthbert Wanderers	4-1	Dalbeattie
2012/3	Dalbeattie Star	Threave Rovers	3-1	Palmerston Park
2013/4	Wigtown & Bladnoch	Lochar Thistle	5-1	Kirkcudbright
2014/5	Edusport Academy	St Cuthbert Wanderers	3-1	Lockerbie
2015/6	Edusport Academy	Mid Annandale	7-2	Palmerston Park
2016/7	Newton Stewart	Threave Rovers	0-0, 4-1p	Kirkcudbright
2017/8	Abbey Vale	Heston Rovers	2-1	Dumfries HS
2018/9	Upper Annandale	Bonnyton Thistle	3-3, 4-2p	Moffat Academy
2019/20	Stranraer Reserves	Threave Rovers	3-2	Newton Stewart

All Time Winners 1951-2019

10 Threave Rovers, 9 Tarff Rovers, St Cuthbert Wanderers, Stranraer Reserves, 6 Wigtown & Bladnoch, 5 Dalbeattie Star, Newton Stewart, 4 Girvan, 3 Annan Athletic, 2 Edusport Academy, Lincluden Swifts, 1 Creetown, Queen of the South Reserves, Stranraer Athletic, Abbey Vale, Upper Annandale

CUP DRAWS 2021/2

None Of the draws for Cups had been made before the Almanac went to print.

The Alba Cup and Southern Counties Challenge Cup will definitely take place. Decisions on the other Cups will be made later depending on progress with League fixtures.

Potts Cup Finals

The Potts Cup was donated to the Southern Counties FA by Mr and Mrs EW Potts, proprietors of the Theatre Royal in Dumfries.

Recent Potts Cup Finals

Season	Winners	Runners Up	Score	Venue
1988/9	St Cuthbert Wanderers	Threave Rovers	3-2	Castle Douglas
1989/90	Wigtown & Bladnoch	St Cuthbert Wanderers	3-2	Wigtown
1990/1	Threave Rovers	Dalbeattie Star	5-0	Dalbeattie
1991/2	Dalbeattie Star	Wigtown & Bladnoch	1-0 aet	Dalbeattie
1992/3	Dalbeattie Star	Newton Stewart	4-1	Dalbeattie
1993/4	Threave Rovers	Dalbeattie Star	5-2	Dalbeattie
1994/5	Threave Rovers	Dumfries HSFP	4-2	David Keswick Centre
1995/6	Stranraer Athletic	Dumfries HSFP	2-1	Stair Park
1996/7	St Cuthbert Wanderers	Maxwelltown HSFP	2-0	Maxwelltown HS
1997/8	Tarff Rovers	Newton Stewart	3-0	Newton Stewart
1998/9	Dalbeattie Star	Dumfries HSFP	1-0	Dalbeattie
1999/00	Dalbeattie Star	Creetown	5-1	Creetown
2000/1	Season abandoned			
2001/2	Tarff Rovers	St Cuthbert Wanderers	3-1	Kirkcudbright
2002/3	Annan Athletic Reserves	Tarff Rovers	3-0	Annan
2003/4	Stranraer Athletic	Creetown	4-0	Creetown
2004/5	Stranraer Athletic	Newton Stewart	3-0	Newton Stewart
2005/6	Nithsdale Wanderers	Threave Rovers	2-0	Sanquhar
2006/7	Wigtown & Bladnoch	Crichton	3-1	Crichton
2007/8	Stranraer Reserves	Creetown	1-1, 4-1 pens	Creetown
2008/9	Wigtown & Bladnoch	St Cuthbert Wanderers	3-1	Wigtown
2009/10	Stranraer Reserves	St Cuthbert Wanderers	2-0	Kirkcudbright
2010/1	Threave Rovers	Crichton	0-0, 3-0 pens	Crichton
2011/2	Dalbeattie Star	Threave Rovers	2-0	Dalbeattie
2012/3	Wigtown & Bladnoch	Newton Stewart	2-0	Stair Park
2013/4	Heston Rovers	Newton Stewart	3-1	Kirkcudbright
2014/5	Newton Stewart	Mid Annandale	4-0	Kirkcudbright
2015/6	Lochar Thistle	Creetown	2-0	Palmerston Park
2016/7	St Cuthbert Wanderers	Newton Stewart	4-3	Creetown
2017/8	Abbey Vale	Threave Rovers	2-2, 5-4 pens	Castle Douglas
2018/9	No competition			
2019/20	Not completed			

Tweedie Cup Finals

The Tweedie Cup trophy was presented to the Wigtownshire FA by Allan Tweedie of Kirkholm in 1898 and was open to all the senior clubs in the county plus other clubs based in and around Stranraer, with all the finals being played in the town. In 1912-13 it was awarded to the winners of the Stranraer Junior League. The competition lapsed in 1930 when it was believed the trophy was lost. However it was rediscovered in 1935 and for the next three seasons was played for as the end of season Wigtownshire Charity Cup. It reverted to its original title after WWII and has been played for, albeit for a time irregularly, ever since. For many years now it has been open to all Southern Counties clubs.

Recent Tweedie Cup Finals

Season	Winners	Runners Up	Score	Venue
1988/9	No competition			
1989/90	St Cuthbert Wanderers	Threave Rovers	4-2	Kirkcudbright
1990/1	No competition			
1991/2	Newton Stewart	Wigtown & Bladnoch	1-0	Newton Stewart
1992/3	No competition			
1993/4	Maxwelltown HSFP	Dalbeattie Star	2-1	Maxwelltown HS
1994/5	No competition			
1995/6	Annan Athletic	Stranraer Athletic	3-1	Annan
1996/7	Threave Rovers	Annan Athletic	3-1	Castle Douglas
1997/8	Tarff Rovers	Annan Athletic	2-0	Annan
1998/9	Tarff Rovers	Creetown	2-2, 6-5 pens	Creetown
1999/00	Dalbattie Star	Threave Rovers	3-0	Kirkcowan
2000/1	Not completed			
2001/2	St Cuthbert Wanderers	Gretna	2-1	Kirkcudbright
2002/3	Creetown	Girvan	4-0	Creetown
2003/4	Creetown	Gretna	2-0	Creetown
2004/5	Annan Athletic	Stranraer Athletic	3-1	Annan
2005/6	Abbey Vale	Wigtow & Bladnoch	2-1	Abbey Vale
2006/7	Annan Athletic	Stranraer Athletic	6-2	Annan
2007/8	Creetown	St Cuthberts Wanderers	3-1	Creetown
2008/9	St Cuthbert Wanderers	Newton Stewart	2-0	Newton Stewart
2009/10	Crichton	Threave Rovers	3-3, 4-3 pens	Crichton
2010/1	Stranraer	Heston Rovers	6-3	Heston Rovers
2011/2	Threave Rovers	Newton Stewart	1-0	Castle Douglas
2012/3	Dalbeattie Star	Threave Rovers	2-1 AET	Annan
2013/4	Wigtown & Bladnoch	Threave Rovers	4-2 AET	Newton Stewart
2014/5	Abbey Vale	Edusport Academy	1-0	Sanquhar
2015/6	Edusport Academy	Upper Annandale	4-0	Lockerbie
2016/7	Nithsdale Wanderers	Threave Rovers	2-0	Dalbeattie
2017/8	Stranraer Reserves	Threave Rovers	3-2	Castle Douglas
2018/9	No competition			
2019/20	Not completed			

Cree Lodge Cup (Wigtownshire FA)

Recent Cree Lodge Cup Finals

Season	Winners	Runners Up	Score	Venue
1988/9	St Cuthbert Wanderers	Threave Rovers	3-1	Castle Douglas
1989/90	No competition			
1990/1	Annan Athletic	Stranraer Reserves	2-1	Stair Park
1991/2	No competition			
1992/3	Threave Rovers	Girvan	2-1	Girvan
1993/4	Annan Athletic	Threave Rovers	3-0	Annan
1994/5	Annan Athletic	Threave Rovers	7-1	Annan
1995/6	Annan Athletic	Stranraer Athletic	3-2	Stair Park
1996/7	Threave Rovers	Tarff Rovers	4-0	Castle Douglas
1997/8	Tarff Rovers	Threave Rovers	1-0	Castle Douglas
1998/9	Tarff Rovers	Dumfries HSFP	1-0	David Keswick Centre
1999/00	Tarff Rovers	Creetown	3-1	Kirkcowan
2000/1	Not completed			
2001/2	Girvan	St Cuthbert Wanderers	1-0 aet	Girvan
2002/3	Annan Athletic Reserves	Dumfries	3-2	Annan
2003/4	Creetown	Annan Athletic Reserves	2-0	Annan
2004/5	Creetown	Mid Annandale	4-0	Lockerbie
2005/6	Threave Rovers	Wigtown & Bladnoch	2-1	Wigtown
2006/7	Stranraer Athletic	Creetown	1-1, 8-7 pens	Stranraer High School
2007/8	Crichton	St Cuthbert Wanderers	3-0	Crichton
2008/9	Threave Rovers	Nithsdale Wanderers	6-2	Sanquhar
2009/10	Stranraer Reserves	St Cuthbert Wanderers	1-1, 8-7 pens	Stair Park
2010/1	Threave Rovers	St Cuthbert Wanderers	5-1	Kirkcudbright
2011/2	Threave Rovers	St Cuthbert Wanderers	4-2	Castle Douglas
2012/3	St Cuthbert Wanderers	Nithsdale Wanderers	5-2	Dalbeattie
2013/4	Heston Rovers	Threave Rovers	3-2	Dalbeattie
2014/5	Wigtown & Bladnoch	Edusport Academy	2-0	Annan
2015/6	St Cuthbert Wanderers	Heston Rovers	5-3 aet	Dumfries High School
2016/7	St Cuthbert Wanderers	Heston Rovers	5-2	Castle Douglas
2017/8	Threave Rovers	Heston Rovers	2-0	Palmerston Park
2018/9	Mid Annandale	Stranraer	wo	
	(Stranraer expelled from competition)			

Originally the Cree Lodge Cup was open only to Wigtownshire and Kirkcudbrightshire clubs, but this restriction was relaxed in the 1950s. The trophy was donated to the Wigtownshire FA by John McGugan of Cree Lodge in Ayr, a former player for Newton Stewart Athletic.

ALL TIME WINNERS (1922-2019)

8 Threave Rovers
7 Newton Stewart,
Stranraer Reserves, Threave St Cuthbert Wanderers
6 Annan Athletic, 4 Tarff Rovers
3 Creetown, Stranraer
2 Dalbeattie Star, Wigtown, Wigtown & Bladnoch,
1 Crichton, Girvan,
Greystone Rovers,
Kirkcudbright, Stranraer Athletic,
Whithorn, Heston Rovers, Mid Annandale
Competition has been in abeyance at some times

Haig Gordon Memorial Trophy (SCFA)

Recent Haig Gordon Memorial Trophy Finals

Season	Winners	Runners Up	Score	Venue
1988/9	Dalbeattie Star	Annan Athletic	3-1	Dalbeattie
1989/90	Threave Rovers	Newton Stewart	4-3 aet	Castle Douglas
1990/1	Wigtown & Bladnoch	Dalbeattie Star	2-1	Wigtown
1991/2	Maxwelltown HSFP	Annan Athletic	1-0	Maxwelltown HS
1992/3	Annan Athletic	St Cuthbert Wanderers	5-2	Annan
1993/4	Annan Athletic	Wigtown & Bladnoch	0-0, 7-6 pens	Wigtown
1994/5	No competition			
1995/6	Annan Athletic	Dumfries HSFP	5-0	Glencaple
1996/7	Stranraer Athletic	Dumfries HSFP	0-0, 5-3 pens	Glencaple
1997/8	St Cuthbert Wanderers	Newton Stewart	4-1	Newton Stewart
1998/9	Tarff Rovers	Newton Stewart	1-1, 6-5 pens	Newton Stewart
1999/00	Tarff Rovers	St Cuthbert Wanderers	3-1	Castle Douglas
2000/1	Not completed			
2001/2	Tarff Rovers	Crichton	4-1	Crichton
2002/3	Gretna	Tarff Rovers	5-3	Kirkcowan
2003/4	Creetown	Dumfries	6-3	Glencaple
2004/5	Stranraer Athletic	Threave Rovers	1-0	Stair Park, Stranraer
2005/6	Annan Athletic	Wigtown & Bladnoch	3-2	Wigtown
2006/7	Stranraer Athletic	Mid Annandale	3-0	Lockerbie
2007/8	Annan Athletic	St Cuthbert Wanderrs	3-3, 4-1 pens	Kirkcudbright
2008/9	Nithsdale Wanderers	Creetown	5-5, 5-4 pens	Sanquhar
2009/10	St Cuthbert Wanderers	Dalbeattie Star	2-1	Kirkcudbright
2010/1	Queen of the South	Threave Rovers	2-2, 4-2 pens	Palmerston Park, Dumfries
2011/2	Dalbeattie Star	Threave Rovers	3-0	Dalbeattie
2012/3	Wigtown & Bladnoch	St Cuthbert Wanderers	2-1 AET	Kirkcudbright
2013/4	Wigtown & Bladnoch	Newton Stewart	2-1	Creetown
2014/5	Wigtown & Bladnoch	Newton Stewart	2-1	Creetown
2015/6	St Cuthbert Wanderers	Mid Annandale	4-3	Annan
2016/7	Wigtown & Bladnoch	Heston Rovers	4-1	Kirkcudbright
2017/8	Threave Rovers	Mid Annandale	2-0	Lockerbie
2018/9	Edusport Academy	Upper Annandale	3-2	Annan

J Haig Gordon was an SFA Councillor. The trophy was donated following his death in 1964.

ALL TIME WINNERS (1964-2019)

8 Annan athletic
7 Stranraer Reserves, Threave Rovers
6 Tarff Rovers, , St Cuthbert Wanderers
4 Dalbeattie Star, Wigtown & Bladnoch
3 Stranraer Athletic,
2 Wigtown & Bladnoch
1 Creetown, Gretna, Maxwelton HSFP, Nithsdale Wanderers, Queen of the South Reserves, Edusport Academy

Southern Counties FA Challenge Cup

Recent Southern Counties Challenge Cup Finals

Season	Winners	Runners Up	Score	Venue
1988/9	Stranraer	Queen of the South	2-1	Palmerston Park
1989/90	Annan Athletic	Threave Rovers	1-0	Galabank
1990/1	Queen of the South	Annan Athletic	2-2, 4-3 pens	Palmerston Park
1991/2	Stranraer	Dalbeattie Star	2-1	Islecroft Stadium
1992/3	Dalbeattie Star	Annan Athletic	4-2	Islecroft Stadium
1993/4	Stranraer	Wigtown & Bladnoch	3-1	Trammondford Park
1994/5	Stranraer	Annan Athletic	3-1	Galabank
1995/6	Annan Athletic	Stranraer	4-0	Galabank
1996/7	Queen of the South	Annan Athletic	2-0	Palmerston Park
1997/8	Threave Rovers	Newton Stewart	5-1	Blairmount Park
1998/9	Annan Athletic	Stranraer Athletic	4-0	Galabank
1999/00	Queen of the South	Tarff Rovers	5-2 aet	Palmerston Park
2000/1	Not completed			
2001/2	Tarff Rovers	Annan Athletic	3-0	Ballgreen Park
2002/3	Queen of the South	Stranraer Athletic	2-0	Stranraer High School
2003/4	Queen of the South	Threave Rovers	3-1	Palmerston Park
2004/5	Gretna	Stranraer	4-3	Raydale Park
2005/6	Annan Athletic	Creetown	3-1	Galabank
2006/7	Dalbeattie Star	Stranraer Athletic	4-1	Islecroft Stadium
2007/8	Threave Rovers	Mid Annandale	4-0	Meadow Park
2008/9	Dalbeattie Star	Annan Athletic	4-1	Galabank
2009/10	St Cuthbert Wanderers	Wigtown & Bladnoch	3-1	St Marys Park
2010/1	Annan Athletic	Newton Stewart	3-2	Blairmount Park
2011/2	Dalbeattie Star	Queen of the South	8-1	Galabank
2012/3	Dalbeattie Star	Nithsdale Wanderers	6-2	Annan
2013/4	Wigtown & Bladnoch	Dalbeattie Star	2-1	St Marys Park
2014/5	Queen of the South	Wigtown & Bladnoch	3-2	Blairmount Park
2015/6	Queen of the South	St Cuthbert Wanderers	5-1	Annan
2016/7	Dalbeattie Star	Queen of the South	2-1	Annan
2017/8	Dalbeattie Star	Mid Annandale	3-1	Annan
2018/9	Bonnyton Thistle	Queen of the South	1-1, 4-2p	Sanquhar

ALL TIME WINNERS (1891-2019)

18 Queen of the South Reserves
13 Stranraer Reserves
12 Dalbeattie Star
10 Nithsdale Wanderers, 8 Dumfries,
7 Stranraer
6 Newton Stewart, Tarff Rovers, Threave Rovers, St Cuthbert Wanderers
5 Annan Athletic
2 5th K.R.V., Lincluden Swifts, Maxwelltown Volunteers, Solway Star
1 Creetown, 5th KOSB, Greystone Rovers, Maxwelltown Thistle, Mid Annandale, Queen of the South, Wigtown & Bladnoch, Bonnyton Thistle

South Senior Competitions—All Time Winners

	SOS League Champions	Southern Counties Challenge Cup	Potts Cup	Haig Gordon Trophy	Cree Lodge Cup	Tweedie Cup	SOS League Cup
1891/2		5th Kirkcudbright RV					
1892/3		QOS Wanderers					
1893/4		5th Kirkcudbright RV					
1894/5		Maxwelltown Thistle					
1895/6		St Cuthbert Wanderers					
1896/7		5th Kirkcudbright RV					
1897/8		Dumfries					
1898/9		Dumfries				Newton Stewart Athletic	
1899/00		Dumfries				Stranraer	
1900/1		Dumfries				Newton Stewart Athletic	
1901/2		Dumfries	Maxwelltown Volunteers			Barholm Rovers	
1902/3		Dumfries	Nithsdale Wanderers			Stranraer	
1903/4		Nithsdale Wanderers	Maxwelltown Volunteers			Stranraer	
1904/5		Maxwelltown Volunteers	Dumfries			Stranraer	
1905/6		Dumfries	Nithsdale Wanderers			Newton Stewart	
1906/7		Nithsdale Wanderers	Dumfries			Newton Stewart	
1907/8		Maxwelltown Volunteers	Dumfries			Garlieston	
1908/9		Dalbeattie Star	Nithsdale Wanderers			Whithorn	
1909/10		Dumfries	Nithsdale Wanderers			Stranraer	
1910/11		Nithsdale Wanderers	St Cuthbert Wanderers			Stranraer	
1911/12		Nithsdale Wanderers	Dumfries			Home Office Rovers	
1912/13		Solway Star	Solway Star				
1913/14		Nithsdale Wanderers	Nithsdale Wanderers				
1914/15		5th KOSB	St Cuthbert Wanderers				
1915/16		No competition					
1916/17		No competition					
1917/18		No competition					
1918/19		No competition					
1919/20		Nithsdale Wanderers	Nithsdale Wanderers				
1920/1		QOTS	QOTS				
1921/2		Nithsdale Wanderers	Douglas Wanderers		Newton Stewart		
1922/3		Nithsdale Wanderers	Nithsdale Wanderers		Whithon		
1923/4		QOTS	Douglas Wanderers		Newton Stewart		
1924/5		Dalbeattie Star	Dalbeattie Star		Tarff Rovers		
1925/6		Stranraer	Stranraer		Stranraer		
1926/7		Stranraer	Stranraer		St Cuthbert Wanderers	Newton Stewart	
1927/8		Nithsdale Wanderers	Stranraer		Stranraer	Stranraer	
1928/9		Mid Annandale	not completed		Newton Stewart	Stranraer	
1929/30		St Cuthbert Wanderers	St Cuthbert Wanderers		Newton Stewart	Stranraer	
1930/1		Dalbeattie Star	Stranraer				
1931/2		Stranraer	Wigtown & Bladnoch				
1932/3		Stranraer	Stranraer		Wigtown & Bladnoch		
1933/4		Dalbeattie Star	Creetown		Stranraer		
1934/5		QOTS	Creetown		Wigtown & Bladnoch		
1935/6		QOTS	St Cuthbert Wanderers				
1936/7		Stranraer	St Cuthbert Wanderers		Creetown		
1937/8		Solway Star	No competition				
1938/9		Stranraer	Wigtown & Bladnoch		St Cuthbert Wanderers		
1939/40		No competition					
1940/1		No competition					
1941/2		No competition					
1942/3		No competition					
1943/4		No competition					
1944/5		No competition					
1945/6		Nithsdale Wanderers					
1946/7	Ayr United Reserves	Dalbeattie Star	Stranraer		Wigtown & Bladnoch		
1947/8	Ayr United Reserves	Stranraer	Wigtown & Bladnoch			Stranraer	
1948/9	Stranraer	Newton Stewart	Stranraer		Newton Stewart	St Cuthbert Wanderers	
1949/50	Tarff Rovers	Tarff Rovers	Tarff Rovers		Stranraer "A"	Stranraer	
1950/1	Newton Stewart	Newton Stewart	Wigtown & Bladnoch			not completed	Newton Stewart
1951/2	Wigtown & Bladnoch	Tarff Rovers	Newtown Stewart			not completed	Wigtown & Bladnoch
1952/3	Tarff Rovers	St Cuthbert Wanderers	Newtown Stewart			Stranraer "A"	Wigtown & Bladnoch
1953/4	Wigtown & Bladnoch	St Cuthbert Wanderers	Tarff Rovers		Stranraer "A"	not completed	St Cuthbert Wanderers
1954/5	St Cuthbert Wanderers	Whithorn	St Cuthbert Wanderers			St Cuthbert Wanderers	Tarff Rovers
1955/6	Newton Stewart	Newton Stewart	St Cuthbert Wanderers		Stranraer "A"	not completed	Tarff Rovers
1956/7	St Cuthbert Wanderers	Stranraer	St Cuthbert Wanderers			Tarff Rovers	Stranraer "A"
1957/8	Greystone Rovers	Greystone Rovers	Greystone Rovers		Greystone Rovers	not completed	Stranraer "A"
1958/9	St Cuthbert Wanderers	Newton Stewart	Stranraer "A"			Wigtown & Bladnoch	Newton Stewart
1959/60	Stranraer Reserves	Stranraer	QOTS "A"		Stranraer "A"	Stranraer "A"	Tarff Rovers
1960/1	Stranraer Reserves	Stranraer	QOTS "A"		Threave Rovers	not completed	Tarff Rovers
1961/2	Stranraer Reserves	QOTS	Newtown Stewart		Newton Stewart	Stranraer "A"	Stranraer "A"
1962/3	Tarff Rovers	Newton Stewart	Threave Rovers			not completed	
1963/4	Tarff Rovers	Stranraer	Stranraer "A"		Newton Stewart	Threave Rovers / St Cuthbert W	
1964/5	Threave Rovers	Threave Rovers	Tarff Rovers	Tarff Rovers		not completed	
1965/6	Stranraer Reserves	QOTS	Threave Rovers	Tarff Rovers	Stranraer "A"	not completed	
1966/7	Stranraer Reserves	Stranraer	Tarff Rovers	Threave Rovers		Stranraer "A"	
1967/8	Stranraer Reserves	Tarff Rovers	Threave Rovers	Stranraer "A"		not completed	
1968/9	Threave Rovers	Stranraer	No competition	Threave Rovers		Threave Rovers	Stranraer "A"
1969/70	Stranraer Reserves	St Cuthbert Wanderers	St Cuthbert Wanderers	St Cuthbert Wanderers		not completed	St Cuthbert Wanderers

	SOS League Champions	Southern Counties Challenge Cup	Potts Cup	Haig Gordon Trophy	Cree Lodge Cup	Tweedie Cup	SOS League Cup
1970/1	St Cuthbert Wanderers	Stranraer	Stranraer "A"	Stranraer "A"		Stranraer "A"	St Cuthbert Wanderers
1971/2	Threave Rovers	QOTS	St Cuthbert Wanderers	Stranraer "A"	St Cuthbert Wanderers	not completed	Threave Rovers
1972/3	Stranraer Reserves	Tarff Rovers	Stranraer "A"	St Cuthbert Wanderers		not completed	St Cuthbert Wanderers
1973/4	Stranraer Reserves	Stranraer	Stranraer "A"	Threave Rovers		St Cuthbert Wanderers	
1974/5	Stranraer Reserves	Tarff Rovers	St Cuthbert Wanderers	Stranraer "A"	Stranraer "A"	no competition	
1975/6	Stranraer Reserves	QOTS	Stranraer "A"	Stranraer "A"		Lincluden Swifts	Girvan Amateurs
1976/7	Stranraer Reserves	Stranraer	Stranraer "A"	Stranraer "A"		not completed	Stranraer "A"
1977/8	Girvan Amateurs	Lincluden Swifts	Stranraer "A"	Dalbeattie Star		Threave Rovers	Girvan Amateurs
1978/9	Threave Rovers	Lincluden Swifts	No competition			not completed	Lincluden Swifts
1979/80	Lincluden Swifts	Threave Rovers	No competition			Annan Athletic	Lincluden Swifts
1980/1	St Cuthbert Wanderers	Threave Rovers	Threave Rovers	Threave Rovers	Dalbeattie Star	no competition	Threave Rovers
1981/2	Stranraer Reserves	QOTS	Creetown	Threave Rovers		Threave Rovers	St Cuthbert Wanderers
1982/3	Stranraer Reserves	QOTS	Dalbeattie Star	Wigtown & Bladnoch	Annan Athletic	no competition	Annan Athletic
1983/4	Annan Athletic	Newton Stewart	Stranraer "A"	Dalbeattie Star		Annan Athletic	Wigtown & Bladnoch
1984/5	Dalbeattie Star	Creetown	St Cuthbert Wanderers	Annan Athletic	Dalbeattie Star	no competition	Annan Athletic
1985/6	Dalbeattie Star	Threave Rovers	Dalbeattie Star	Stranraer "A"		Threave Rovers	Newton Stewart
1986/7	Annan Athletic	QOTS	St Cuthbert Wanderers	Annan Athletic	St Cuthbert Wanderers	no competition	Wigtown & Bladnoch
1987/8	Newton Stewart	QOTS	Newtown Stewart	Annan Athletic		Threave Rovers	Threave Rovers
1988/9	Dalbeattie Star	Stranraer	St Cuthbert Wanderers	Dalbeattie Star	St Cuthbert Wanderers	no competition	Dalbeattie Star
1989/90	Girvan	Annan Athletic	Wigtown & Bladnoch	Threave Rovers		St Cuthbert Wanderers	Threave Rovers
1990/1	Maxwelltown HSFP	QOTS	Threave Rovers	Wigtown & Bladnoch	Annan Athletic	no competition	Threave Rovers
1991/2	Wigtown & Bladnoch	Stranraer	Dalbeattie Star	Maxwelltown HSFP		Newton Stewart	Girvan
1992/3	Threave Rovers	Dalbeattie Star	Dalbeattie Star	Annan Athletic	Threave Rovers	no competition	Dalbeattie Star
1993/4	Threave Rovers	Stranraer	Threave Rovers	Annan Athletic	Annan Athletic	Maxwelltown HSFP	Threave Rovers
1994/5	Threave Rovers	Stranraer	Threave Rovers	Annan Athletic	Annan Athletic	no competition	Wigtown & Bladnoch
1995/6	St Cuthbert Wanderers	Annan Athletic	Stranraer Athletic	Annan Athletic	Annan Athletic	Annan Athletic	St Cuthbert Wanderers
1996/7	QOTS Reserves	QOTS	St Cuthbert Wanderers	Stranraer Athletic	Threave Rovers	Threave Rovers	QOS Reserves
1997/8	Tarff Rovers	Threave Rovers	Tarff Rovers	St Cuthbert Wanderers	Tarff Rovers	Tarff Rovers	Tarff Rovers
1998/9	Tarff Rovers	Annan Athletic	Dalbeattie Star	Tarff Rovers	Tarff Rovers	Tarff Rovers	Tarff Rovers
1999/00	Tarff Rovers	QOTS	Dalbeattie Star	Tarff Rovers	Tarff Rovers	Dalbeattie Star	Tarff Rovers
2000/1	Season abandoned	not completed	Season abandoned	Not completed	Not completed	not completed	Newton Stewart
2001/2	Tarff Rovers	Tarff Rovers	Tarff Rovers	Tarff Rovers	Girvan	St Cuthbert Wanderers	Girvan
2002/3	Stranraer Athletic	QOTS	Annan Athletic Reserves	Gretna	Annan Athletic Reserves	Creetown	Crichton
2003/4	Stranraer Athletic	QOTS	Stranraer Athletic	Creetown	Creetown	Creetown	Stranraer Athletic
2004/5	Stranraer Athletic	Gretna	Stranraer Athletic	Stranraer Athletic	Creetown	Annan Athletic	Annan Athletic Reserves
2005/6	Threave Rovers	Annan Athletic	Nithsdale Wanderers	Annan Athletic	Threave Rovers	Abbey Vale	Creetown
2006/7	Threave Rovers	Dalbeattie Star	Wigtown & Bladnoch	Stranraer Athletic	Stranraer Athletic	Annan Athletic	Threave Rovers
2007/8	Crichton	Threave Rovers	Stranraer Reserves	Annan Athletic	Crichton	Creetown	St Cuthbert Wanderers
2008/9	Threave Rovers	Dalbeattie Star	Wigtown & Bladnoch	Nithsdale Wanderers	Threave Rovers	St Cuthbert Wanderers	St Cuthbert Wanderers
2009/10	Threave Rovers	St Cuthbert Wanderers	Stranraer Reserves	St Cuthbert Wanderers	Stranraer Reserves	Crichton	Stranraer Reserves
2010/1	Threave Rovers	Annan Athletic	Threave Rovers	Queen of the South	Threave Rovers	Stranraer "A"	Dalbeattie Star
2011/2	Dalbeattie Star	Dalbeattie Star	Dalbeattie Star	Dalbeattie Star	Threave Rovers	Threave Rovers	Dalbeattie Star
2012/3	Dalbeattie Star	Dalbeattie Star	Wigtown & Bladnoch	Wigtown & Bladnoch	St Cuthbert Wanderers	Dalbeattie Star	Dalbeattie Star
2013/4	Wigtown & Bladnoch	Wigtown & Bladnoch	Heston Rovers	Wigtown & Bladnoch	Heston Rovers	Wigtown & Bladnoch	Wigtown & Bladnoch
2014/5	Wigtown & Bladnoch	QOTS	Newton Stewart	Wigtown & Bladnoch	Wigtown & Bladnoch	Abbey Vale	Edusport Academy
2015/6	St Cuthbert Wanderers	QOTS	Lochar Thistle	St Cuthbert Wanderers	St Cuthbert Wanderers	Edusport Academy	Edusport Academy
2016/7	Edusport Academy	Dalbeattie Star	St Cuthbert Wanderers	Wigtown & Bladnoch	St Cuthbert Wanderers	Nithsdale Wanderers	Newton Stewart
2017/18	Threave Rovers	Dalbeattie Star	Abbey Vale	Threave Rovers	Threave Rovers	Stranraer "A"	Abbey Vale
2018/19	Stranraer Reserves	Bonnyton Thistle	No competition	Edusport Academy	Mid Annandale	no competition	Bonnyton Thistle
2019/20	Null and Void	not completed	Not completed	Not completed	No competition	not completed	Stranraer Reserves
2020/1	Null and Void	No competition	No competition	No competition	No competition	No competition	No competition

Sadly demolished - the magnificent old stand at St Cuthbert Wanderers

South of Scotland League Club Playing Squads 2020/1

NB These are not comprehensive lists of players used - there will be some omissions. However, all players listed were associated with the club concerned during 2020/21. New signings refer to 2021/2.

ABBEY VALE

Manager: Frazer Brolls
Sam Hughes (2020 Heston Rovers, ex Abbey Vale)
Robbie Ferguson
Adam Kirk
Greig Corbett
Ben Irving
Ross Wilson
Craig Kerr
Andy Forsyth
Lewis McKenna (2020 Heston Youths)
Taylor Hall
Curtiss Wilson (2020 Dalbeattie Star)
Rory Copland (2020 ex QOS Youths, Lochar Youths)
Keiran Pirrie
Michael Swan
Steven Couper
Struan Parker
Aidan Dobie (2020 QOS Youths)
Aidan Moffat (OL from Queen of the South Sep-Jan)
Jordan Muirhead
David Kennedy
Denver Milligan (2020 Lochmaben)

CALEDONIAN BRAVES RESERVES

Manager: Simon Mensing
Yohann Chardon
Enzo Martinet
Raphaelle Veillerette
Jeremy Mazzilli
Rodrique Dupre
Lilian Dupuis
Axel Duhoux
Simon Ferhoun
Axel Weinachter
Theo nestor
Thomas Merle
Jillali Touis
Mathieu Yago-Roisot
Nicolas Certaux
Silver Smith
William Blanch
Clement Thiery
Florian Buffat
Mamadou Tangara
Matei Cavallucci
Mathis Lande
Ibrahim Youyate
Gregoire Lezin
Valentin Reynaud
Yanis Sanghour
Tristan Barbaray
Melih Sallabas
Mathieu Bref
Theo Tomas Silva
Yoav Sender
Alan Raboteur
Ryan Vert
Yanis Feze
Mohamed Kara
Matthieu Gonzalez
Jules Bourmaut
Elijah Danso
Noah Godard
Pablo Gonzalez
Morhand Gaci
Abdoulaye Sow
Said El Omari
Karim Nlamu
Medie Tussevo
Jovanny Nsonga
Romeo Naili
Yacine Boualem
Mohamed Amine Samri

CREETOWN

Manager: Colin Wilson
Alistair Birse
Arran Thomson (2020 Newton Stewart)
Ben Herries
Bobby Landers
Callum McDonald
Callum Murray
Craig McCulloch
David Hughes
Euan Brown
Hanlin
Ian Miller
Jamie Adams (ex Kilmarnock etc)
Jamie McHarrie (ex Wigtown & B, Dalbeattie Star)
Kenny McKenzie
Kiltie
Liam Clive
Mark Whorlow
Matthew Robertson
Nathan McKay
Richard Jones
Robert Bruce
Rogers
Tyler Rennie
William White

NEW SIGNINGS
Stuart McColm (ex Clyde, Annan Athletic, Stranraer)
Lewis Richardson
Blair Dougan
John Lowe (2021 Stranraer Reserves)

HESTON ROVERS

Heston withdrew from the League for 2021/2
Manager: Michael Houston
T Wilson
Liam Crosbie
M Hughes
C Adamson
Thomas Bowden
T Coles
C Docherty
Alex Henderson
R Jardine
C Jamieson
B Mullen
K McCulloch
T Smith
Jamie Struthers
C Stewart
Gary Tweedie
B Wilson

LOCHAR THISTLE

Manager: Scott Wilby
Ryan Cochrane
Bez Stevenson
Liam Robertson
Kieran Krause
Tom Wright
Ross Woodward
Brodie Turner
Steven Scott
Ben Jaekel
Ben Loudon
Islam Kadyrov
Dev Nicholson
Greig Goodwin
Alex Maxwell
Joe McMillan
Sandy Kennedy

LOCHMABEN

Manager: Jim Thompson
Logan Galloway
Conor Murray
Benjamin Wagner
Laurie Maxwell
Ben English
Bailey White
Danny Graham
Andy Gilston
Danny Collins
Shayne Watson
Alan Birdsall

MID ANNANDALE

NEWTON STEWART

Manager:
Euan Drysdale
Arran McKie
Jake Service
Jordan Magee
Fraser Anderson
Robbie Thomson
Matthew Deazeley
Marc Whyte
Ross Landers
Robert Middleton
Euan Sneddon
Robert Hughan
Ryan McKie
Jack Marshall
Aaron Drysdale
Euan Brown
MacCauley Rennie
Rhuri Paton

NEW SIGNINGS
Robbie Blair (2021 Stranraer Reserves)
Lewis Blain (2021 Stranraer Reserves)
Kyle MacDonald (2021 St Cuthbert Wanderers)
Alistair Collins (2021 Ayr United Youths)

NITHSDALE WANDERERS

Manager: Dougie Taylor
Coaches: Billy Gracie, Darren Johnstone, Shaka Hyslop
Sean McKenzie (2020 Cumnock, ex Nithsdale W)
Declan Farrow
Cameron McKenzie
Jordan Telfer
Owen Welsh
Ress Brown (ex Gretna)
Jamie Rae
Jack Loudon
Lewis Lang
Scott Montgomery
Jerzy Grzebieniak
Danny Naismith
Arthur McAdam (2020 St Cuthbert W)
Robert McColl
Sam Wilson
Mitchell Black
Steven Hyslop
Stuart Bell
Callum Falconer
Dale West
Robbie Simpson

ST CUTHBERT WANDERERS

Manager: Jordan Williamson
Jake Gemmell
John Renwick
Cameron Taylor
Jack Currie
Luke McMurtrie
Ross Hunter
Sam McConaghie
Elliot Harris
Campbell Black
Luke Currie

Zachary Hannay
Gregor Patterson
Alistair McMillan
Russell Williamson
Scott Dunn
Dale Milligan
Owen Hall
Kenneth Davis

STRANRAER RESERVES

Alexander
Downie
Robbie Murray
Palmer
Robert Adair
C Phillips
Scott Phillips
Smith
Wilde
D Agnew
McKane
Reece Agnew
Marshall
Dunn
Dean Fyfe
R McIntyre
Lowe
Harry Mitchell
Andrew Donlay

THREAVE ROVERS

Manager: Vinnie Parker
Dan Carmichael
Graham Wright
Hugh Cameron
Ewan Gourlay
Adam Uphill
Liam Patterson
Callum Williams
Ryan Coates
Philip Middlemiss
Alisdair Mason
Scott Milligan
Kieran McKie
Ryan Adamson
Aiden McBurnie
Corey Thomson
Adam Maxwell

UPPER ANNANDALE

Manager: Darren Ferbie
Oliver Tobin
Kyle McAvoy
Graeme Maxwell
Curtis Telfer
D Campbell
McAvoy
Reid
Oliver Tobin
Justin Borthwick
Turner
Dixon
Bruce
Black
Luke McMullan
Robert Shaw
Pagan
Johnstone
Logan Turner

WIGTOWN AND BLADNOCH

Manager: Michael Dougan (Until June 2021), John Kiltie (from June 2021)
Dale Leith
Liam O'Shaughnessy
William Cloy
Darrel Wilson
Scott McCulloch
James McColm
Gordon Forbes
Alistair McColm
Thomas Garrett
David Nish
Mark Hoskins
Ross Inger
Michael Dougan

NEW SIGNINGS
Scott Forrester

Islecroft Stadium, home of Dalbeattie Star, currently hosting Lowland League football

Lowland Under 20s 2020/1

68 clubs applied for membership in 2020/1. Conferences were allocated but no games were played.

EAST CONFERENCE (30) - 2 divisions
Blackburn United
Bonnyrigg Rose
Camelon
Civil Service Strollers
Dalkeith Thistle
Dunipace
East Fife
Edinburgh City
Edinburgh South
Edinburgh United
Edinburgh University
Gala Fairydean Rovers
Glenrothes
Heriot Watt University
Hill of Beath Hawthorn
Inverkeithing Hillfield Swifts
Jeanfield Swifts
Kelty Hearts
Kennoway Star Hearts
Kirkcaldy & Dysart
Leith Athletic
Lothian Thistle Hutchison Vale
Musselburgh Athletic
Penicuik Athletic
Preston Athletic
Sauchie
Spartans
Stirling University
Tynecastle
Whitehill Welfare

WEST CONFERENCE (38) - 2 divisions
Ardrossan Winton Rovers
Arthurlie
Beith
Bellshill Athletic
Benburb
Blantyre Victoria
Bonnyton Thistle
BSC Glasgow
Caledonian Braves
Carluke Rovers
Clydebank
Cumbernauld Colts
Cumnock
Darvel
Drumchapel United
East Kilbride
Forth Wanderers
Irvine Meadow
Johnstone Burgh
Kilwinning Rangers
Kirkintilloch Rob Roy
Largs Thistle
Maryhill
Maybole
Mid Annandale
Neilston
Newmains United
Pollok
Renfrew
Rossvale
Shettleston
St Anthony's
St Rochs
Troon
Vale of Leven
Whitletts Victoria
Yoker Athletic

EAST LOWLAND U20 PREVIOUS WINNERS

	League Champions	Challenge Cup	KO Cup	League Cup
2014/15	Spartans	Spartans	East Kilbride	Spartans
2015/16	Preston Athletic	Preston Athletic	Lothian Thistle HV	Cumbernauld Colts
2016/17	East Kilbride	Spartans	East Kilbride	East Kilbride
2017/18	Heriot Watt Univers	Stirling University	Cumbernauld Colts	Edinburgh City
2018/19	Spartans	Kelty Hearts	Spartans	Spartans

Lowland Under 20s 2021/2

FORMAT 2021/2

Conference A (14 teams)

Bonnyrigg Rose
Bonnyton Thistle
BSC Glasgow
Caledonian Braves
Civil Service Strollers
Cumbernauld Colts
East Fife
East Kilbride
Edinburgh City
Gala Fairydean Rovers
Kelty Hearts
Spartans
Stirling Albion
University of Stirling

Conference B (14 teams)

Kennoway Hearts
Armadale
Camelon
Edinburgh College
Edinburgh South
Edinburgh United
Edinburgh University
Glenrothes
Heriot Watt University
Musselburgh Athletic
Penicuik Athletic
Preston Athletic
Sauchie
Whitehill Welfare

Conference C (15 teams)

Blackburn United
Craigroyston
Dalkeith Thistle
Dunipace
Fauldhouse United
Hill of Beath Hawthorn
Inverkeithing Hillfield Swifts
Jeanfield Swifts
Leith Athletic
Livingston United
Lothian Thistle Hutchison Vale
Newtongrange Star
Oakley United
Tynecastle
West Calder

Conference D (16 teams)

Bellshill
Blantyre Victoria
Cambuslang Rangers
Carluke Rovers
East Kilbride Thistle
Forth Wanderers
Gartcairn
Glasgow United
Glenvale
Harthill Royal
Kirkintilloch Rob Roy
Mid Annandale
Petershill
Shotts Bon Accord
St Peters
St Roch's

Conference E (14 teams)

Ashfield
Benburb
BSC Glasgow (WOSL)
Clydebank
Drumchapel United
Johnstone Burgh
Maryhill
Pollok
Renfrew
Rossvale
St Anthonys
St Cadocs
Vale of Leven
Yoker Athletic

Conference F (15 teams)

Ardeer Thistle
Ardrossan Winton Rovers
Arthurlie
Auchinleck Talbot
Beith
Cumnock
Darvel
Irvine Meadow
Kilwinning Rangers
Largs Thistle
Maybole
Neilston
Port Glasgow
Troon
Whittlets Victoria

The Highland Pyramid

HIGHLAND LEAGUE MEMBERSHIP

1st Batallion Highland Light Infantry	1949-50
30th Training Batallion	1946-47
93rd Highlanders	1912-14
Aberdeen "A"	1912-15, 1924-25
Black Watch	1904-06, 1926-29
Brora Rangers	1963-date
Buckie Thistle	1909-date
Caledonian	1893-1994
Cameron Highlanders	1893-94, 1897-98, 1903-04, 1919-20
Clachnacuddin	1893-date
Cove Rangers	1986-2019
Deveronvale	1938-date
Elgin Caledonian	1900-01
Elgin City	1895-96, 1897-1900, 1903-2000
Elgin City United	1902-03
Formartine United	2009-date
Forres Mechanics	1893-95, 1897-1901, 1902-
Fort William	1985-date
Fraserburgh	1922-26, 1928-
HG Training Batallion	1948-49
Highland Light Infantry	1907-09
Huntly	1928-date
Inverness Celtic	1897-99
Inverness Citadel	1893-1914, 1919-35
Inverness Thistle	1893-1994
Inverness Union	1893-96, 1897-99
Inverurie Loco Works	2001-date
Keith	1924-date
King's Own Scottish Borderers	1931-34
Lossiemouth	1946-47
Nairn County	1919-date
Peterhead	1931-2000
RAF Kinloss	1939-40
Ross County	1929-94
Rothes	1938-date
Royal Air Force	1947-48
Seaforth Highlanders	1909-11, 1919-20
Strathspey Thistle	2009-date
Turriff United	2009-date
Wick Academy	1994-date

The Highland League is the pre-eminent competition in football in the North of Scotland. The League also runs a Cup for member clubs. The North Caledonian League, formerly known as the North Reserve League, is the only other Senior Saturday winter league competition and serves the area north of Inverness.

The Aberdeenshire FA and North of Scotland FA run their own Cup competitions, contested by Highland league sides and some others.

Cove Rangers won the Highland League title for the second year running. Having failed in the promotion Play off in 2018, they went one better in 2018/19, defeating East Kilbride then Berwick Rangers to claim a place in the Scottish Professional Football League.

The League operated with 17 teams In 2019/20. Banks o' Dee Juniors were sounded out about joining but were not interested at the time. The member clubs considered making an invitation to Inverness Caledonian Thistle to enter a reserve side but this was rejected.

In 2020/1 Brechin City were relegated to the Highland League, taking membership to 18.

Agreement was also reached on a Pyramid type structure with 3 Leagues potentially feeding into the Highland league from 2021/2. These were the North Caledonian League (West of the Spey), North Junior League (between Spey and Montrose) and the Midlands League (between Tay and Montrose).

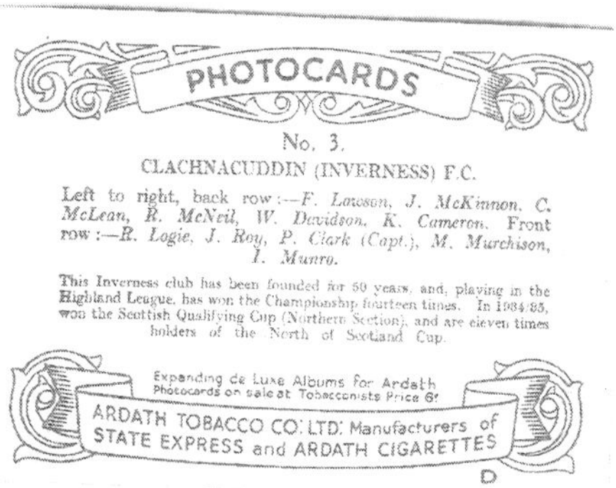
PHOTOCARDS

No. 3.

CLACHNACUDDIN (INVERNESS) F.C.

Left to right, back row:—*F. Lawson, J. McKinnon, C. McLean, R. McNeil, W. Davidson, K. Cameron.* Front row:—*R. Logie, J. Roy, P. Clark (Capt.), M. Murchison, I. Munro.*

This Inverness club has been founded for 50 years, and, playing in the Highland League, has won the Championship fourteen times. In 1934/35, won the Scottish Qualifying Cup (Northern Section), and are eleven times holders of the North of Scotland Cup.

Expanding de Luxe Albums for Ardath Photocards on sale at Tobacconists Price 6d

ARDATH TOBACCO CO. LTD. Manufacturers of STATE EXPRESS and ARDATH CIGARETTES

D

Press & Journal Highland League 2020/21

	BRO	BUC	CLA	DEV	FMT	FWI	FRA	HUN	INV	KEI	LOS	NAI	ROT	STR	TUR	WIC
Brora Rangers						Dec 19 10-0										Dec 5 5-1
Buckie Thistle																
Clachnacuddin									Jan 2 2-4							
Deveronvale	Nov 28 0-5									Dec 19 1-2						
Formartine United												Jan 2 2-1				
Fort William																
Fraserburgh															Jan 2 13-1	
Huntly				Dec 5 1-1												
Inverurie Locos										Nov 28 2-0						
Keith																
Lossiemouth							Nov 28 0-2	Dec 19 2-2								
Nairn County							Dec 19 0-1									
Rothes		Dec 19 1-5						Nov 28 1-0								
Strathspey Thistle																
Turriff United					Nov 28 1-5											
Wick Academy		Nov 28 2-3														

		P	W	D	L	F	A	GD	PTS	PPG
1	Brora Rangers	3	3	0	0	20	1	19	9	3
2	Fraserburgh	3	3	0	0	16	1	15	9	3
3	Buckie Thistle	2	2	0	0	8	3	5	6	3
4	Formartine United	2	2	0	0	7	2	5	6	3
5	Inverurie Loco Works	2	2	0	0	6	2	4	6	3
6	Keith	2	1	0	1	2	3	-1	3	1.5
7	Rothes	2	1	0	1	2	5	-3	3	1.5
8	Huntly	3	0	2	1	3	4	-1	2	0.67
9	Lossiemouth	2	0	1	1	2	4	-2	1	0.5
10	Deveronvale	3	0	1	2	2	8	-6	1	0.33
11	Strathspey Thistle	0	0	0	0	0	0	0	0	
12	Clachnacuddin	1	0	0	1	1	4	-2	0	0
13	Nairn County	2	0	0	2	2	3	-2	0	0
14	Wick Academy	2	0	0	2	2	8	-5	0	0
15	Fort William	1	0	0	1	1	10	-10	0	0
16	Turriff United	2	0	0	2	2	18	-16	0	0

Forres Mechanics did not take part.

The decision to award the Championship to Brora Rangers on the basis of having played just three games was controversial. Buckie with 2 away wins over decent opposition must have felt they had a strong case for consideration—had they enjoyed a match against Fort William or Turriff then their goal difference might well have matched that of Brora and Fraserburgh. A mathematician would also tell you that Strathspey should have been champions as anything divided by zero equals infinity!

Of course given the previous season's results there was no real debate about Brora's worthiness but the whole process of declaring a winner when a League is incomplete should be clarified to avoid any repetition of circumstances such as this.

Brora went on to contest the Play Off against Kelty Hearts but were soundly beaten.

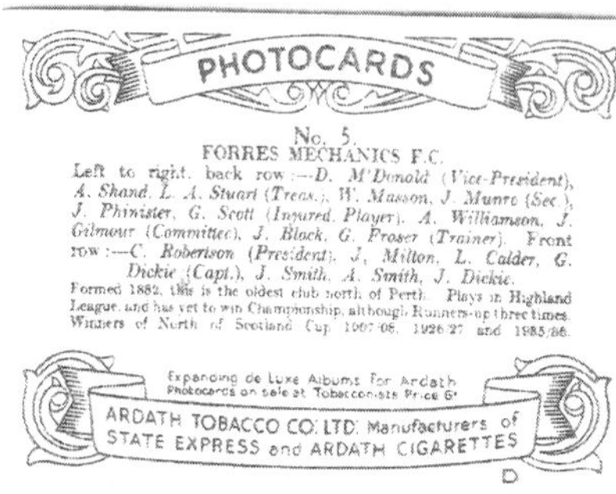
PHOTOCARDS

No. 5.

FORRES MECHANICS F.C.

Left to right, back row:—*D. M'Donald (Vice-President), A. Shand, L. A. Stuart (Treas.), W. Masson, J. Munro (Sec.), J. Phinister, G. Scott (Injured Player), A. Williamson, J. Gilmour (Committee), J. Black, G. Fraser (Trainer).* Front row:—*C. Robertson (President), J. Milton, L. Calder, G. Dickie (Capt.), J. Smith, A. Smith, J. Dickie.*

Formed 1882, this is the oldest club north of Perth. Plays in Highland League, and has yet to win Championship, although Runners-up three times. Winners of North of Scotland Cup 1907-08, 1926/27 and 1935/36.

Expanding de Luxe Albums for Ardath Photocards on sale at Tobacconists Price 6d

ARDATH TOBACCO CO. LTD. Manufacturers of STATE EXPRESS and ARDATH CIGARETTES

Highland League - Recent Positions

	1980-1	1981-2	1982-3	1983-4	1984-5	1985-6	1986-7	1987-8	1988-9	1989-90	1990-1	1991-2	1992-3	1993-4	1994-5	1995-6	1996-7	1997-8	1998-9	1999-00	2000-1	2001-2	2002-3	2003-4	2004-5	2005-6	2006-7	2007-8	2008-9	2009-10	2010-11	2011-12	2012-13	2013-14	2014-15	2015-16	2016-17	2017-18	2018-19	2019-20	2020/1*
Brora Rangers	10	5	3	7	3	16	15	12	14	14	9	14	13	10	5	8	14	11	9	12	13	8	14	12	15	14	13	14	14	15	11	16	8	1	1	3	3	6	2	1	1
Buckie Thistle	5	14	13	5	5	7	5	2	9	10	11	7	9	8	10	12	13	10	12	3	3	3	4	2	6	3	3	4	6	1	1	5	12	10	10	7	1	7	8	5	3
Caledonian	9	1	1	1	2	4	2	1	10	2	2	2	4	2																											
Clachnacuddin	4	12	8	11	12	13	16	14	16	18	16	12	7	12	13	11	5	8	6	7	4	4	7	1	7	9	9	10	11	12	15	10	5	11	11	14	11	13	16	15	12
Cove Rangers							8	10	2	6	3	4	2	4	2	2	7	4	7	8	1	6	3	10	5	8	6	1	1	2	2	2	1	7	3	1	2	1	1		
Deveronvale	13	11	14	14	14	17	17	11	13	16	15	13	11	14	9	9	8	9	10	11	6	2	1	4	4	1	4	3	2	3	4	7	7	6	12	13	15	8	12	11	10
Elgin City	3	4	2	4	7	2	3	7	5	1	7	8	1	6	8	7	9	5	4	9																					
Formartine United																														6	9	11	2	4	6	2	4	2	4	6	4
Forres Mechanics	16	13	11	9	4	1	6	6	6	5	4	11	17	13	11	13	12	7	8	6	7	10	11	8	9	4	12	8	9	5	6	1	9	9	9	11	6	5	6	7	A
Fort William						12	11	17	18	13	12	16	16	16	12	14	16	15	16	16	14	13	15	15	13	15	15	15	15	17	18	18	18	18	13	17	17	18	18	17	15
Fraserburgh	2	7	6	8	13	14	13	13	11	7	13	15	10	9	7	5	6	2	5	2	8	1	6	3	3	7	8	5	7	4	13	6	6	5	5	9	5	4	3	3	2
Huntly	12	9	12	10	9	6	9	9	3	8	6	3	6	1	1	1	1	1	2	5	2	9	8	6	1	6	5	7	8	7	10	13	13	13	16	15	14	11	9	12	8
Inverness Thistle	8	8	7	6	11	8	1	4	4	4	5	10	8	15																											
Inverurie Locos																						7	9	7	2	2	2	6	3	10	7	4	10	2	7	6	9	3	5	2	5
Keith	1	3	4	2	1	5	4	5	7	12	14	5	12	7	4	6	2	6	3	1	5	5	2	5	8	5	1	2	4	8	3	9	14	14	14	10	10	15	13	9	6
Lossiemouth	15	16	16	16	16	15	10	16	12	9	10	6	3	5	3	3	4	12	13	10	12	11	10	13	11	13	14	13	12	14	12	12	17	15	15	12	12	16	17	16	9
Nairn County	14	15	10	12	10	9	12	18	15	15	17	18	18	17	16	16	15	16	15	15	9	12	5	9	10	10	7	9	10	11	5	3	4	3	8	8	13	9	11	8	13
Peterhead	6	2	5	3	8	3	7	3	1	3	8	9	14	11	6	4	3	3	1	4																					
Ross County	11	6	9	13	6	10	18	8	8	11	1	1	5	3																											
Rothes	7	10	15	15	15	11	14	15	17	17	18	17	15	18	15	15	11	13	11	13	11	15	12	14	14	11	10	12	13	16	16	15	16	17	18	18	16	10	10	4	7
Strathspey Thistle																														18	17	17	15	16	17	16	18	17	14	13	11
Turriff United																														13	8	14	11	12	2	4	7	14	15	14	16
Wick Academy															14	10	10	14	14	14	10	14	13	11	12	12	11	11	5	9	14	8	3	8	4	5	8	12	7	10	14

A = Abeyance
* = Decided on PPG with teams having played 0-3 matches

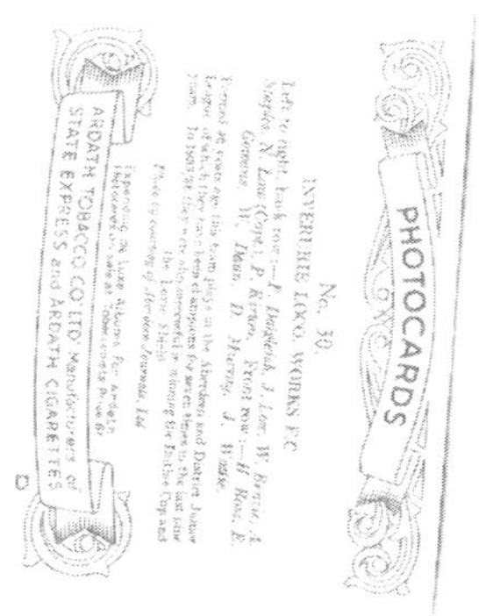

ALL TIME HIGHLAND LEAGUE CHAMPIONS

1893/4	Inverness Thistle	1936/7	Buckie Thistle	1979/80	Keith
1894/5	Clachnacuddin	1937/8	Fraserburgh	1980/1	Keith
1895/6	Caledonian	1938/9	Clachnacuddin	1981/2	Caledonian
1896/7	Clachnacuddin	1939/40	No competition	1982/3	Caledonian
1897/8	Clachnacuddin	1950/1	No competition	1983/4	Caledonian
1898/9	Caledonian	1941/2	No competition	1984/5	Keith
1899/00	Caledonian	1942/3	No competition	1985/6	Forres Mechanics
1900/1	Clachnacuddin	1943/4	No competition	1986/7	Inverness Thistle
1901/2	Caledonian	1944/5	No competition	1987/8	Caledonian
1902/3	Clachnacuddin	1945/6	No competition	1988/9	Peterhead
1903/4	Clachnacuddin	1946/7	Peterhead	1989/90	Elgin City
1904/5	Clachnacuddin	1947/8	Clachnacuddin	1990/1	Ross County
1905/6	Clachnacuddin	1958/9	Peterhead	1991/2	Ross County
1906/7	Inverness Thistle	1949/50	Peterhead	1992/3	Trophy witheld
1907/8	Clachnacuddin	1950/1	Caledonian	1993/4	Huntly
1908/9	Inverness Citadel	1951/2	Caledonian	1994/5	Huntly
1909/10	Inverness Thistle	1952/3	Elgin City	1995/6	Huntly
1910/11	Caledonian	1953/4	Buckie Thistle	1996/7	Huntly
1911/12	Clachnacuddin	1954/5	Not completed	1997/8	Huntly
1912/13	Aberdeen "A"	1955/6	Elgin City	1998/9	Peterhead
1913/14	Caledonian	1956/7	Buckie Thistle	1999/00	Keith
1914/15	Not completed	1957/8	Buckie Thistle	2000/1	Cove Rangers
1915/16	No competition	1958/9	Rothes	2001/2	Fraserburgh
1916/17	No competition	1959/60	Elgin City	2002/3	Deveronvale
1917/18	No competition	1960/1	Elgin City	2003/4	Clachnacuddin
1918/19	No competition	1961/2	Keith	2004/5	Huntly
1919/20	Buckie Thistle	1962/3	Elgin City	2005/6	Deveronvale
1920/1	Clachnacuddin	1963/4	Caledonian	2006/7	Keith
1921/2	Clachnacuddin	1964/5	Elgin City	2007/8	Cove Rangers
1922/3	Clachnacuddin	1965/6	Elgin City	2008/9	Cove Rangers
1923/4	Clachnacuddin	1966/7	Ross County	2009/10	Buckie Thistle
1924/5	Aberdeen "A"	1967/8	Elgin City	2010/1	Buckie Thistle
1925/6	Caledonian	1968/9	Elgin City	2011/2	Forres Mechanics
1926/7	Buckie Thistle	1969/70	Elgin City	2012/3	Cove Rangers
1927/8	Buckie Thistle	1970/1	Caledonian	2013/4	Brora Rangers
1928/9	Inverness Thistle	1971/2	Inverness Thistle	2014/5	Brora Rangers
1929/30	Huntly	1972/3	Inverness Thistle	2015/6	Cove Rangers
1930/1	Caledonian	1973/4	Elgin City	2016/7	Buckie Thistle
1931/2	Elgin City	1974/5	Clachnacuddin	2017/8	Cove Rangers
1932/3	Fraserburgh	1975/6	Nairn County	2018/19	Cove Rangers
1933/4	Buckie Thistle	1976/7	Caledonian	2019/20	Brora Rangers
1934/5	Elgin City	1977/8	Caledonian	2020/1	Brora Rangers
1935/6	Inverness Thistle	1978/9	Keith		

Evening Express Aberdeenshire Cup 2020/21

The competition was not completed until the start of 2021/2.

1	14/11/20	Banks o' Dee	Buckie Thistle	1 2
1	17/11/20	Deveronvale	Dyce	1 2
1	17/11/20	Inverurie Locos	Turriff United	2 1
2	21/11/20	Formartine United	Dyce	3 0
2	21/11/20	Fraserburgh	Inverurie Locos	2 1
2	25/11/20	Buckie Thistle	Aberdeen	
2	2/12/20	Keith	Huntly	3 1
SF		Keith	Fraserburgh	
SF		Formartine United	Buckie Th / Aberdeen	

ALL TIME WINNERS
35 Aberdeen (1903)
20 Peterhead
13 Buckie Thistle
11 Fraserburgh
8 Deveronvale
7 Keith, Huntly
6 Victoria United
5 Orion, Aberdeen (1881)
3 Cove Rangers,
2 Formartine United
1 Aberdeen University

Recent Aberdeenshire Cup Finals

Season	Winners	Runners Up	Score	Venue
1989/90	Aberdeen	Peterhead	3-0	Recreation Park, Peterhead
1990/1	Aberdeen	Huntly	1-0	Pittodrie, Aberdeen
1991/2	Huntly	Aberdeen	2-1	Christie Park, Huntly
1992/3	Aberdeen	Cove Rangers	1-0	Allan Park, Cove
1993/4	Huntly	Peterhead	1-0	Kynoch Park, Keith
1994/5	Huntly	Cove Rangers	3-0	Kynoch Park, Keith
1995/6	Huntly	Deveronvale	2-1	Kynoch Park, Keith
1996/7	Fraserburgh	Peterhead	3-2	Recreation Park, Peterhead
1997/8	Aberdeen	Deveronvale	5-1	Kynoch Park, Keith
1998/9	Peterhead	Aberdeen	3-1	Balmoor Stadium, Peterhead
1999/00	Huntly	Deveronvale	2-0	Christie Park, Huntly
2000/1	Deveronvale	Fraserburgh	2-1	Christie Park, Huntly
2001/2	Cove Rangers	Deveronvale	1-1. 5-4 pens	Christie Park, Huntly
2002/3	Aberdeen	Deveronvale	3-0	Harlaw Park, Inverurie
2003/4	Aberdeen	Inverurie Locos	4-0	Harlaw Park, Inverurie
2004/5	Aberdeen	Fraserburgh	4-1 aet	Bellslea Park, Fraserburgh
2005/6	Buckie Thistle	Deveronvale	2-2, 3-2 pens	Christie Park, Huntly
2006/7	Deveronvale	Inverurie Locos	1-0	Kynoch Park, Keith
2007/8	Buckie Thistle	Keith	1-0	Christie Park, Huntly
2008/9	Keith	Huntly	5-2	Harlaw Park, Inverurie
2009/10	Buckie Thistle	Cove Rangers	2-0	The Haughs, Turriff
2010/1	Cove Rangers	Buckie Thistle	3-0	Harlaw Park, Inverurie
2011/2	Deveronvale	Keith	5-4	Christie Park, Huntly
2012/3	Fraserburgh	Formartine United	2-2 aet, 3-1 pens	Victoria Park, Buckie
2013/4	Formartine United	Inverurie Locos	3-2	Bellslea Park, Fraserburgh
2014/5	Fraserburgh	Buckie Thistle	3-2	Kynoch Park, Keith
2015/6	Fraserburgh	Inverurie Locos	2-0	Christie Park, Huntly
2016/7	Buckie Thistle	Cove Rangers	2-2 aet, 5-4 pens	The Haughs, Turriff
2017/8	Formartine United	Cove Rangers	1-0	Balmoor Stadium, Peterhead
2018/9	Cove Rangers	Banks o' Dee	4-1	Harlaw Park, Inverurie
2019/20	Fraserburgh	Formartine United	2-1	Balmoral Stadium, Cove

ABERDEENSHIRE CUP DRAW 2021/2

First Round (Aug 4)
Banks o' Dee 6-1 Keith
Dyce Juniors 2-2(w-l pens) Hermes
Turriff United 1-4 Inverurie Loco Works
Buckie Thistle 1-2 Formartine United

Quarter Finals
Banks o' Dee – Inverurie Loco Works
Formartine United – Huntly
Deveronvale – Dyce Juniors
Fraserburgh – Aberdeen University

Semi Finals
Formartine United or Huntly – Deveronvale or Dyce Juniors
Fraserburgh or Aberdeen University – Banks o' Dee or Inverurie Loco Works

Morrison Motors Aberdeenshire Shield 2020/21

The competition was not held.

Recent Aberdeenshire Shield Finals

Season	Winners	Runners Up	Score	Venue
1990/1	Cove Rangers	Fraserburgh	1-0	Peterhead
1991/2	Fraserburgh	Deveronvale	2-2, 4-3 pens	Huntly
1992/3	Buckie Thistle	Huntly	3-2	Keith
1993/4	Fraserburgh	Keith	4-2	Huntly
1994/5	Deveronvale	Cove Rangers	1-0	Keith
1995/6	Fraserburgh	Peterhead	2-1	Huntly
1996/7	Fraserburgh	Peterhead	6-3 aet	Cove
1997/8	Keith	Peterhead	3-2	Banff
1998/9	Peterhead	Keith	3-1	Keith
1999/00	Fraserburgh	Keith	2-1	Keith
2000/1	Cove Rangers	Buckie Thistle	2-1	Peterhead
2001/2	Keith	Fraserburgh	3-2	Inverurie
2002/3	Deveronvale	Inverurie Locos	3-2	Keith
2003/4	Inverurie Locos	Deveronvale	5-1	Banff
2004/5	Keith	Inverurie Locos	3-1 aet	Inverurie
2005/6	Keith	Inverurie Locos	2-1	Banff
2006/7	Keith	Fraserburgh	3-0	Inverurie
2007/8	Buckie Thistle	Inverurie Locos	3-0	Huntly
2008/9	Cove Rangers	Banks o' Dee	2-0	Pittodrie
2009/10	Peterhead	Inverurie Locos	3-0	Peterhead
2010/11	Turriff United	Aberdeen	2-0	Peterhead
2011/12	Fraserburgh	Banks o' Dee	5-0	Peterhead
2012/13	Turriff United	Cove Rangers	6-1	Inverurie
2013/14	Inverurie Locos	Turriff United	5-0	Huntly
2014/15	Turriff United	Fraserburgh	4-3	Banff
2015/16	Fraserburgh	Cove Rangers	1-0	Inverurie
2016/17	Inverurie Locos	Banks o' Dee	5-2	Huntly
2017/18	Cove Rangers	Banks o' Dee	5-2	Inverurie
2018/19	Formartine United	Banks o' Dee	4-1	Balmoral Stadium
2019/20	Fraserburgh	Inverurie Locos	3-1	Balmoral Stadium

Aberdeenshire Shield

The Shield is open to all Aberdeen and District FA clubs that have senior status. This includes the Highland League clubs from Aberdeenshire and Banffshire, plus Banks o' Dee and Aberdeen University - although the Senior status of the latter is debatable. Aberdeen FC are excluded from the modern version of the competition.

Originally known as the Fleming Charity Shield, the competition was held from 1899 until 1929. It was resurrected in 1990 as the Aberdeenshire Shield.

The following clubs have won the Shield:

Aberdeen	12
Fraserburgh	9
Keith	5
Cove Rangers	4
Inverurie Locos	3
Turriff United	3
Buckie Thistle	2
Deveronvale	2
Peterhead	2
Victoria United	2
Aberdeen "A"	2
Dundee United	1
Formartine United	1

North of Scotland Cup 2020/21

Recent North of Scotland Cup Finals

Season	Winners	Runners Up	Score	Venue
1988/9	Elgin City	Brora Rangers	3-1	Kingsmills
1989/90	Elgin City	Inverness Thistle	0-0, 4-0 rep	Forres
1990/1	Brora Rangers	Forres Mechanics	2-1	Dingwall
1991/2	Ross County	Lossiemouth	0-0, 1-0 rep	Kingsmills
1992/3	Clachnacuddin	Inverness Thistle	4-2 aet	Caley
1993/4	Caledonian	Forres Mechanics	1-0	Kingsmills
1994/5	Lossiemouth	Fort William	4-0	Forres
1995/6	Lossiemouth	Clachnacuddin	1-0	Forres
1996/7	Lossiemouth	Forres Mechanics	4-1	Elgin
1997/8	Elgin City	Inverness CT	3-1	ICT
1998/9	Elgin City	Rothes	2-0	Forres
1999/00	Inverness CT	Lossiemouth	3-0	Forres
2000/1	Lossiemouth	Forres Mechanics	3-1	Forres
2001/2	Clachnacuddin	Inverness CT	2-0	ICT
2002/3	Lossiemouth	Rothes	3-1	Forres
2003/4	Elgin City	Inverness CT	1-0	Forres
2004/5	Forres Mechanics	Clachnacuddin	2-0	Dingwall
2005/6	Nairn County	Forres Mechanics	3-1	Clachnacuddin
2006/7	Ross County	Nairn County	3-0	Clachnacuddin
2007/8	Inverness CT	Elgin City	3-2	Forres
2008/9	Nairn County	Inverness CT	2-0	Clachnacuddin
2009/10	Inverness CT	Nairn County	3-2	Forres
2010/1	Forres Mechanics	Wick Academy	3-2	Brora
2011/2	Inverness CT	Forres Mechanics	4-3	Forres
2012/3	Nairn County	Wick Academy	2-1	Clachnacuddin
2013/4	Brora Rangers	Nairn County	3-0	Clachnacuddin
2014/5	Brora Rangers	Elgin City	3-1	Clachnacuddin
2015/6	Wick Academy	Nairn County	6-2	Brora
2016/7	Brora Rangers	Fort William	4-1	Rothes
2017/8	Brora Rangers	Lossiemouth	2-0	Clachnacuddin
2018/9	Ross County	Inverness CT	3-2	Clachnacuddin
2019/20	Brora Rangers	Inverness CT	3-2	Forres

The North of Scotland Cup was not contested in 2020/1.

ALL TIME WINNERS

22- Clachnacuddin
20- Caledonian
18 - Elgin City
13 - Inverness Thistle
8 - Forres Mechanics
7 - Inverness Citadel, Nairn County, Brora Rangers
6 - Ross County
5- Lossiemouth
4 - Inverness Caledonian Thistle
2 - Rothes
1 - Cameronians, Crown, Wick Academy

NORTH OF SCOTLAND CUP DRAW 2021/2

First Round
Nairn County 2-4 Lossiemouth (Jul 28)
Forres Mechanics 0-3 Rothes (Aug 4)
Strathspey Thistle wo-scr Golspie Sutherland

Quarter Final (Aug 18)
Clachnacuddin – Strathspey Thistle
Lossiemouth – Fort William
Rothes – Elgin City
Wick Academy – Brora Rangers

Semi Finals (Sept 1)
Clachnacuddin or Strathspey Thistle – Rothes or Elgin City
Wick Academy or Brora Rangers – Lossiemouth or Fort William

Utilita Highland League Cup 2019/20

P	02/11/2019	Strathspey Thistle	Clachnacuddin	4 1	100
1	20/11/2019	Buckie Thistle	Deveronvale	2 1	
1	20/11/2019	Keith	Lossiemouth	3 2	65
1	04/12/2019	Rothes	Nairn County	4 1	67
1	16/11/2019	Formartine United	Inverurie Locos	1 0	
1	16/11/2019	Fort William	Fraserburgh	1 3	
1	16/11/2019	Strathspey Thistle	Forres Mechanics	0 2	
1	16/11/2019	Turriff United	Brora Rangers	0 7	
1	16/11/2019	Wick Academy	Huntly	1 3	
2	07/12/2019	Huntly	Brora Rangers	0 6	
2	05/02/2020	Buckie Thistle	Fraserburgh	1 1 5-4p	
2	25/01/2020	Forres Mechanics	Formartine United	1 3	
2	05/02/2020	Rothes	Keith	3 1	

COMPETITION SUSPENDED

The competition was suspended but was completed at the start of the aborted 2020/1 season.

SF	17/10/20	Formartine United	Rothes	1 2 AET	
SF	18/10/20	Brora Rangers	Buckie Thistle	2 2 3-4p	
F	31/10/20	Rothes (postponed 24/10/20, waterlogged)	Buckie Thistle	1 2	at Huntly

FINAL DETAILS

Rothes: Sean McCarthy, Paul MacLeod, Ben Johnstone, Jack Brown, Bruce Milne, Fraser Robertson, Craig Cormack, Allan Pollock, Gary Kerr, Alisdair Sutherland, Allen McKenzie. Subs Danny McCarthy, Ross Gunn, Ewan Neil, Gregg Main, Sean Linden, Scott Anderson, Jack Maley.
Buckie: Daniel Bell, Sam Morrison, Joe McCabe, Kevin Fraser, Steven Ross, Andrew Macaskill, Sam Urquhart, Mark McLauchlan, Sam Pugh, Callum Murray, Jack Murray. Subs Lee Herbert, Shaun Wood, Lewis Mackinnon, kyle MacLeod, Craig Cowie, Marcus Goodall, Scott Adams

0-1	McCabe	8 mins
1-1	McKenzie	28 mins
	Cormack (Rothes) Sent Off	63 mins
1-2	Macleod`	94 mins

HIGHLAND LEAGUE CUP

The competition is often known as the Morganti Cup. It was first contested in 1946/7.
Past winners are:
10 times - Keith; 8 times - Buckie Thistle; 7 times - Forres Mechanics; 6 times—Cove Rangers, 5 times - Peterhead, Caledonian, Elgin City, Clachnacuddin and Huntly; 4 times - Ross County; 3 times - Inverness Thistle; 2 times - Nairn County, Lossiemouth, Fraserburgh and Inverurie Locos; 1 time - Brora Rangers, Formartine United, Rothes
Deveronvale, Wick Academy, Formartine United, Turriff United and Strathspey Thistle, of the current HFL members, have never won the Cup.

Recent Highland League Cup Finals

Season	Winners	Runners Up	Score	Venue
1988/9	Keith	Caledonian	1-1, Replay3-2	Boroughbriggs, Elgin
1989/90	Peterhead	Forres Mechanics	2-1	Boroughbriggs, Elgin
1990/1	Elgin City	Cove Rangers	2-1	Kynoch Park, Keith
1991/2	Ross County	Fraserburgh	3-1	Boroughbriggs, Elgin
1992/3	Huntly	Cove Rangers	1-1, 5-4 pens	Boroughbriggs, Elgin
1993/4	Huntly	Fraserburgh	4-1	Boroughbriggs, Elgin
1994/5	Cove Rangers	Lossiemouth	2-2, 5-3 pens	Christie Park, Huntly
1995/6	Huntly	Cove Rangers	2-1 aet	Kynoch Park, Keith
1996/7	Lossiemouth	Fraserburgh	2-1	Christie Park, Huntly
1997/8	Elgin City	Cove Rangers	1-0	Christie Park, Huntly
1998/9	Forres Mechanics	Keith	1-0	Boroughbriggs, Elgin
1999/00	Cove Rangers	Elgin City	4-3	Kynoch Park, Keith
2000/1	Forres Mechanics	Deveronvale	2-1	Christie Park, Huntly
2001/2	Forres Mechanics	Deveronvale	1-1, 4-3 pens	Kynoch Park, Keith
2002/3	Keith	Deveronvale	3-2	Harlaw Park, Inverurie
2003/4	Clachnacuddin	Forres Mechanics	3-0	Kynoch Park, Keith
2004/5	Cove Rangers	Deveronvale	2-0	Kynoch Park, Keith
2005/6	Fraserburgh	Cove Rangers	4-1	Kynoch Park, Keith
2006/7	Keith	Buckie Thistle	5-0	Princess Royal Park, Banff
2007/8	Inverurie LW	Cove Rangers	3-1	Christie Park, Huntly
2008/9	Inverurie LW	Fraserburgh	2-1 aet	Kynoch Park, Keith
2009/10	Forres Mechanics	Rothes	2-0	Victoria Park, Buckie
2010/1	Nairn County	Fraserburgh	4-0	Princess Royal Park, Banff
2011/2	Buckie Thistle	Cove Rangers	2-0	Princess Royal Park, Banff
2012/3	Keith	Inverurie LW	2-1	Princess Royal Park, Banff
2013/4	Clachnacuddin	Buckie Thistle	3-3, 4-3 pens	Kynoch Park, Keith
2014/5	Cove Rangers	Wick Academy	4-0	Grant Street Park, Inverness
2015/6	Brora Rangers	Nairn County	0-0, 5-4p	Grant Street Park, Inverness
2016/7	Cove Rangers	Formartine United	2-1	Bellslea Park, Fraserburgh
2017/8	Formartine United	Fraserburgh	2-1	McKessack Park, Rothes
2018/9	Cove Rangers	Formartine United	2-0	Harlaw Park, Inverurie
2019/20	Rothes	Buckie Thistle	2-1	Christie Park, Huntly
2020/1	No competition			

Highland League Under 20 / Under 17 Competitions 2020/1

The competitions were not contested in 2020/1.

Aberdeenshire & District League 2021/2

Eleven teams have entered for 2021/2:

Buckie Thistle
Deveronvale
Dyce
Formartine United
Fraserburgh
Hermes
Huntly
Inverurie Loco Works
Keith
Stonehaven
Turriff United

They are scheduled to meet each other once for a ten match season.

Highland League Club Playing Squads 2020/21

NB These are not comprehensive lists of players used - there will be some omissions. However, all players listed were associated with the club concerned during 2020/21

BRORA RANGERS

Manager Steven Mackay

Surname	**First Name**	**Apps**	**Subs**	**Goals**		**Signed**	**From**	
Brindle	Paul	2		3	F	2015	Clach	Ex Muir of Ord, NOW Nairn County
Campbell	Craig				F	2012	Alloa Athletic	Ex Vikingur, Nairn Co, Elgin C, Ross Co, Forres M, OL to Invergordon Oct-Nov
Gamble	Miller	3			D	2020	Inverness CT	
Gillespie	Dale	3			M	2018	Rothes	Ex ICT, Elgin C, Nairn Co, Forres M
Kelly	Tom	1		1	D	2020	Ross County	
Macdonald	Ally	3		1	D	2012	Huntly	Ex USA Soccer, Balintore, ICT, Elgin C
MacDonald	Gregor	1	1	1	F	2020	Ross County	
Macdonald	Neil				M	2018	Invergordon	Ex Ross Co, Nairn, Elgin C, Clach
Mackay	Steven			1	F	2012	Nairn County	OL to Invergordon Oct-Nov
MacLean	Martin	3		1	M	2012	Back FC	
MacRae	Jordan	3		5	F	2019	Cove Rangers	
MacRae	Andrew	3		2	F	2019	Forres Mechanics	
MacRae	Colin					2015	Bunillidh Thistle	Transferred to Golspie S Oct 2020
Malin	Joe	3			GK	2013	Elgin City	Ex Celtic, Ross Co
Martin	Steven					2019	Clach	Transferred to Tain Jul 2020
Morrison	Greg	1			F	2019	Ross County	NOW ROTHES
Nicolson	Mark	3		1	D	2017	Elgin City	Ex Ross Co
Pickles	John	3			D	2015	Wick Academy	
Stephen	Jamie				GK	2020	Ross County	
Wagenaar	Bjorn	1		4	M	2019	SVV Scheveningen	
Williamson	Colin		1		D	2014	Clach	Ex ICT, Tain Th, Bonar bridge, Alness, Strathspey Th etc
NEW SIGNINGS								
Sutherland	Ali				F	2021	Rothes	
Meekings	Josh				D	2021	Dundee	
Wallace	James				F	2021	Morton	Ex Brora R

BUCKIE THISTLE

Manager Graeme Stewart

Surname	**First Name**	**Apps**	**Subs**	**Goals**		**Signed**	**From**	
Adams	Scott	2			M	2018	Peterhead	
Barry	Max				M	2021	Aberdeen	
Bell	Daniel				GK	2016	Keith	
Cowie	Craig	2			M	2017	Deveronvale	
Davidson	Lucas				M	2018	Ross County	
Fraser	Kevin	2			M	2015	Northern Fury	
Goodall	Marcus				F	2020	Ross County	
Herbert	Lee	1			GK	2018	Ross County	
Mackinnon	Lewis				D	2006	Elgin City	Had a spell in Australian football
Macleod	Kyle	2		3	F	2019	Brora Rangers	
McAskill	Andrew	2		1	M	2017	Holland Park Hawks	
McCabe	Joe	2		1	M	2020	Inverurie Locos	
McKinnon	Martin	1			D	2006	Elgin City	
McLauchlan	Mark	2			D	2019	Aberdeen	
McLeod	John				F	2016	Brora Rangers	
Morrison	Sam	2		1	D	2018	Ross County	
Munro	Hamish	1			D	2016	Formartine United	
Murray	Jack	2		1	D	2019	Ross County	
Murray	Callum		1		D	2016	Buckie Rovers	
Pugh	Sam	1	1		D	2020	Grand View Vikings	
Ross	Steven		1		F	2017	Brora Rangers	
Strong	Darren				GK	2006	Rothes	
Urquhart	Sam		1	1	F	2016	Nairn County	
Wood	Shaun				D	2012	Buckie Rovers	
NEW SIGNINGS								
Barry	Max					2021	Aberdeen	Short term contract
MacLeod	Adam					2021	Strathspey Thistle	

CLACHNACUDDIN

Manager	Jordan MacDonald						
Surname	**First Name**	**Apps**	**Subs**	**Goals**		**Signed From**	
Aitchison	David	1			GK	2020 IRN Security	
Anderson	James	1		1	F	2019 Clach Youths	
Bruce	Douglas	1			D	2017 Clach Youths	
Bunce	Connor				F	2019 Clach Youths	
Callum	Martin	1		1	M	2011 Muir of Ord Rovers	
Finnis	Michael	1			D	2009 Inverness CT	NOW ROTHES
Fraser	James				M	2020 Burghead Thistle	
Fyfe	Ryan	1			D	2020 Inverness CT (OL)	Dec-Jan
Kelly	Stephen				D	2020 Clach Youths	
Laing	Martin				M	2020 Inverurie Locos	
Lawrie	Blair	1			F	2012 Elgin City	
Logan	Ross				M	2019 Clach Youths	
MacKintosh	Ryan	1			D	2015 Forres Mechanics	
MacPhee	Allan	1			F	2020 Forres Mechanics (OL)	Nov-Mar
McBride	Ronan				M	2019 Clach Youths	
McLaren	James				F	2020 Lossiemouth	
Miller	Eachainn				D	2019 Stirling University	
Morrison	Scott	1			F	2020 Strathspey Thistle	
Rae	Daniel				GK	2020 Inverness Athletic	
Sutherland	Shaun	1			M	2019 Clach Youths	
NEW SIGNINGS							
Taylor	Liam						
McRobert	Michael					2021 Loch Ness	
Black	Calum						

DEVERONVALE

Manager	Craig Stewart						
Surname	**First Name**	**Apps**	**Subs**	**Goals**		**Signed From**	
Adams	Kevin	2			D	2019 Inverness CT	
Aitken	Ross	2			D	2013 Inverness CT	
Allan	Robbie	1			M	2018 Turriff United	
Allan	Ben				M	2020 Rochester Lancers	
Ballard	Dane	2			F	2016 Buchanhaven Hearts	
Blanchard	James				GK	2016 Aberdeen	
Buchan	Greg	2				2020 Fraserburgh (OL)	Dec-Mar
Cooper	Courtney	1			M	2019 Maud	
Dunn	Scott	1	1		F	2019 Clachnacuddin	
Farquhar	Ryan	2			M	2020 Fraserburgh (OL)	Dec-Mar
Gauld	Kyle	1			D	2017 Buckie Thistle	
Hamilton	Aaron	2			D	2020 Forres Mechanics	
Munro	Jody				F	2017 Deveronvale Youths	OL to Deveronside for part of season
Noble	Harry	2			D	2018 Lossiemouth	
Noble	Grant		1		F	2016 Fraserburgh	
Robertson	Sam	1			M	2018 Keith	
Sargent	Ryan	1				2019 Fraserburgh (OL)	Dec-Mar
Scott	Robert		1	1	F	2017 Buckie Thistle	
Stewart	Max				M	2020 Deveronvale Youths	
Still	Gavin	2			GK	2020 Deveronside	
Williamson	Jamie				GK	2020 Deveronvale Youths	
NEW SIGNINGS							
Tinnock	Jamie					2021 Elgin City (OL)	
Hay	Charlie					2021 Elgin City (OL)	
Jamieson	Matty					2021 Elgin City (OL)	
Connelly	James					2021 Inverurie Locos (OL)	
McIntosh	Sean					2021 Dufftown	
Watson	Michael					2021 Dufftown	
Davidson	Rory					2021 Deveronside	
Mackay	Innes					2021 Deveronside	

FORMARTINE UNITED

Manager	Paul Lawson							
Surname	**First Name**	**Apps**	**Subs**	**Goals**		**Signed**	**From**	
Anderson	Stuart	1		1	M	2014	Brechin City	
Anderson	Cole	1			M	2020	Formartine Utd Youths	
Clark	Michael				D	2018	Huntly	
Crawford	Jonathan	1			D	2015	Montrose	
Ellis	Zack				GK	2020	Cove Rangers	
Fraser	Ruari				D	2020	Ross County	
Gethins	Conor				F	2016	Nairn County	NOW NAIRN COUNTY
Greig	Andrew				F	2017	Brora Rangers	
Kelly	Darryn	1			D	2019	Cove Rangers	
Lawson	Paul				M	2015	Motherwell	Player Manager
Lisle	Scott				F	2019	Strathspey Thistle	
MacDonald	Ewen				GK	2018	Peterhead	
MacPhee	Archie				D	2017	Elgin City	OL to Elgin City Mar-May
Main	Kevin	1			GK	2018	Turriff United	
McKeown	Craig	1			D	2015	Brora Rangers	
Norris	Aaron	1			M	2019	Peterhead	
Park	Daniel	1			F	2019	Cove Rangers	
Rodger	Graeme	1			M	2015	Deveronvale	
Smith	Stuart	1			D	2011	Peterhead	
Smith	Jonathan	1		1	F	2020	Inverurie Locos	
Strachan	Liam				M	2019	Turriff United	
Wood	Gary				F	2015	Montrose	Joined Brechin City June 2021
NEW SIGNINGS								
Demus	Balint					2021	Peterhead (OL)	
Paterson	Andy					2021		Ex Aberdeen and Dundee Youths
Mykyta	Tyler					2021	Aberdeen (OL)	
Hanratty	Kevin					2021	Aberdeen (OL)	
Spink	Ryan					2021	Keith	

FORRES MECHANICS

Manager	Charlie Rowley		
No games played in 2020/1			
2021/2 Players			
Wood	Dale		
Fraser	Graham		
Soane	Stuart		
McNab	Gordon		
Fraser	Ruari	2021	Formartine United
Brindle	Paul	2021	Brora Rangers

FORT WILLIAM

Manager	Ashley Hollyer						
Surname	First Name	Apps	Subs	Goals		Signed From	
Cameron	Ronan				D	2018 Fort William Youths	
Clark	Lennon	1			M	2020 Edinburgh United	
Coutts	Paul				D	2020 NMM Sams	
Duncan	Alfie						
Foggo	Ian				D	2020 Clachnacuddin	
Kulbacki	Matheusz				GK	Unattached	
McBride	Sean	1			D		
McBride	Joe	1			M	2020 East Dunbarton Ams	
McConnell	Jamie	1			M	2020 ICT Youths	
McGhie	Stephen				F		
Mckenzie	Mark	1			D	2020 Bunillidh Thistle	OL to Bonar Bridge Oct-Nov
McKinnon	Kevin		1		M	2018 Bunillidh Thistle	
Miller	Greg		1		M	Amateurs	
Moore	Connor	1			F	2020 Fort William Youths	
Munro	Ruaridh						
Rothnie	Lewis	1			GK		
Rydings	Robbie				M	2020 Fort William Youths	
Taylor	Aiden	1			M	2019 Keith	
Treasurer	John	1			F	2017 Strathspey Thistle	
Veringa	Gabriel	1			D	2020 NMM Sams	
Wallace	Josh				M		
White	Alexander	1			D		

NEW SIGNINGS

Brew	Darren	2021 North Greenford United
Scott	Brandon	
Avraam	Marcos	2021 Billinge
Wallace	Josh	
Rydings	Robbie	
Adisi	Cameron	2021 Boreham Wood Youths
Caulker	Junior	2021 Farnham Town

FRASERBURGH

Manager	Mark Cowie						
Surname	**First Name**	**Apps**	**Subs**	**Goals**		**Signed From**	
Barbour	Scott	3		4	F	2018 Formartine United	
Beagrie	James	1			M	2016 Turriff United	
Buchan	Greg		1		M	2016 Deveronvale	
Butcher	Sean	2		1	F	2018 Longside	
Cairns	Owen	3			D	2019 Turriff United	
Campbell	Paul	1	1		F	2016 Maud	
Campbell	Grant	3		1	M	2020 Cove Rangers	
Combe	Aiden		3		F	2015 Fraserburgh Youths	
Cowie	Ryan	3		1	D	2012 Turriff United	
Davidson	Lewis				D	2017 Turriff United	
Duncan	Lewis	2		3	M	2020 Aberdeen	
Flinn	Edward				GK	2016 Fraserburgh Youths	
Grant	Connor						
Harris	Gary	1	2	4	F	2016 Deveronvale	
Hay	Bryan	3		1	D	2007 Fraserburgh Youths	
Henry	Scott	1		1	D	2020 Formartine United	
Leask	Paul	3			GK	2017 Keith	
Sargent	Ryan					2019 Fraserburgh Youths	OL to Deveronvale Dec-Mar
Simpson	Kieran	2			D	2019 Fraserburgh Youths	
West	William	2			M	2004 Fraserburgh Youths	
Young	Paul	3			M	2017 Turriff United	
Barbour	Joe				GK	2014 Maud	

HUNTLY								
Manager	Allan Hale							
Surname	**First Name**	**Apps**	**Subs**	**Goals**		**Signed**	**From**	
Booth	Cameron		1		M	2018	Turriff United	
Bowden	Cameron	2			D	2020	Turriff United	
Boylan	Jamie				M	2020	CBC Hilton United	
Critchard	Daniel				F	2020	Cove Rangers U20	
Elphinstone	Gavin	1			M	2020	Turriff United	
Gauld	Joe	2			D	2020	Forres Mechanics (OL)	Dec-Apr
Hay	Chris				D	2016	Inverurie Locos	
Johnston	Logan	2			D	2019	Inverness CT	
Manson	Bradley	1	1		M	2019	Keith	
Matthew	Cai	1			M	2019	Formartine United	
McDonald	Liam				M	2019	Peterhead	
McGinlay	Max	1			F	2020	Formartine United (OL)	Nov-Mar
McGowan	Gary	2		2	F	2020	Banks o' Dee (OL)	Nov-Mar
McKeown	Reece	2			F	2019	Turriff United	
Murison	Glen	2			M	2020	Shepparton South	2nd spell at Huntly
Robertshaw	Keith				GK	2017	Huntly Youths	
Still	Ross	2			M	2016	Inverurie Locos	
Storrier	Euan	2			GK	2019	Dufftown	
Thoirs	Alexander		1		M	2011	Dyce	
Thomas	Ryan	2			D	2020	Cove Rangers U20 (OL)	Nov-Mar
Trialist			1					
NEW SIGNINGS								
Clark	Michael					2021	Formartine United	
Buchan	Greg					2021	Fraserburgh	
Grant	Angus					2021	Turriff United	
Imbert-Thomas	Caiden					2021	Hullbridge Sports	Brother of Jay-Emmanuel Thomas
Dalling	Kyle					2021	Forfar Athletic	
McCormick	Jack					2021		

INVERURIE LOCOS								
Manager	Andy Low							
Surname	**First Name**	**Apps**	**Subs**	**Goals**		**Signed**	**From**	
Broadhurst	Ryan	2			D	2009	Stourbridge	
Burnett	Sam	2		1	M	2020	Cove Rangers	
Cook	Morgan	2			GK	2016	Inverurie Locos Youths	
Cooper	Jordan		1		M	2018	Inverurie Locos Youths	
Dingwall	Calum	1			M	2019	Formartine United	
Farquhar	John				GK	2020	Huntly	
Gauld	Neil	1		2	F	2017	Formartine United	
Gill	Craig	2			M	2019	Inverurie Locos Youths	
Gordon	Kyle					2016	Inverurie Locos Youths	Transferred to Turriff United Feb 2021
Henderson	Kai				F	2020	Montrose	
Hinks	Harrison				D	2020	Inverurie Locos Youths	
Hunter	Andrew		1				Banks o' Dee	
McLean	Neil	2			M	2004	Elgin City	
Meres	Nathan	2		1	F	2020	Cove Rangers	
Mitchell	Greg	2		1	D	2013	St Johnstone	
Reid	Thomas	1	1		D	2018	Inverurie Locos Youths	
Ritchie	Hamish	1			M	2020	Seattle Redhawks	OL to Peterhead Mar-May
Shanks	Kieran	2		1	F	2020	Aberdeen	
Souter	Mark	2			D	2020	Inverurie Locos Youths	
NEW SIGNINGS								
Adams	Kieran					2021	Bridge of Don Thistle	
Connolly	James					2021	Montrose	

KEITH

Manager Andy Roddie

Surname	First Name	Apps	Subs	Goals		Signed	From	
Brownie	James	2			M	2010	Turriff United	
Dey	David				GK	2019	Keith Youths	Now Turriff United
Duncan	Liam	1			M	2020	Cove Rangers	
Gray	Scott				M	2018	Keith Youths	
Hutcheon	Stewart	1			D	2012	Keith Youths	
Keith	Cameron	2		1	F	2017	Formartine United	Retired July 2021, scored 263 goals for Keith
McAskill	Craig	1			M	2018	Turriff United	
Olumofe	James				F	2020	OAU Giants (NIG)	
Porteous	Callum				D	2019	Flying Knights	
Robertson	Ryan	2			D	2016	Deveronvale	
Selfridge	Michael	2		1	F	2018	Inverurie Locos	
Simpson	Greg	2			GK	2018	Hall Russell United	
Smith	Andrew	2			D	2017	Turriff United	
Spink	Ryan	2			D	2016	Cove Rangers	
Stewart	Andrew				F			
Strachan	Liam	2						
Watt	Logan	1						
Yeats	Kieran				D	2019	Keith Youths	
Young	Mark	1			D	2018	Colony Park	
Yunus	Demilade	1			M	2020	Cove Rangers	
Scott	Lee				M	2020	Elgin City	

NEW SIGNINGS

Emmett	Luke
Andrews	Tom
Ironside	Michael
Reid	Craig

LOSSIEMOUTH

Manager Joe Russell

Surname	First Name	Apps	Subs	Goals		Signed	From	
Allan	Brodie	1	1		F	2016	Lossiemouth Youths	
Archibald	Liam	2			M	2018	Deveronvale	
Archibald	Ross				F	2020	Deveronvale	
Bellingham	Ally	1			D	2015	Lossiemouth United	
Black	Stuart		1		GK	2017	Strathspey Thistle	
Campbell	Baylee				M	2019	Lossiemouth Youths	
Charlesworth	Martin	2			F	2020	Unattached	
Edwards	Fergus	1			M	2020	Buckie Thistle	
Elliot	Ross	2			F	2018	Elgin City	
Forbes	Fraser		2		F	2018	Forres Mechanics	
Kennedy	Jared	1	1		D	2020	Burghead Thistle	
Leslie	James	2			M	2020	Lossiemouth Youths	
Macauley	Connor	1			M	2015	Elgin City	
McArthur	Jack				D	2018	Lossiemouth Youths	
Palmer	Tom	2			D	2019	RAF Lossiemouth	
Ross	Logan	2			GK	2020	Ross County (OL)	Nov-Jan
Sewell	Ryan	2		1	M	2018	Lossiemouth Youths	
Stuart	Ryan	1	1	1	M	2018	Forres Mechanics	
Weir	Michael	2			D	2019	New Elgin	

NAIRN COUNTY

Manager	Ronnie Sharp							
Surname	**First Name**	**Apps**	**Subs**	**Goals**		**Signed**	**From**	
Counsell	Will				GK	2020	Brora Rangers	
Davidson	Scott	2			F	2019	Brora Rangers	
Dey	Angus	1			F	2018	Stirling University	
Dingwall	Fraser	2			D	2018	Invergordon	
Ednie	Callum				M	2016	Clachnacuddin	
Ewan	Max	2			F	2017	Inverness CT	
Howarth	Calumn	2			D	2020	Forres Mechanics	
Mackenzie	Kenneth				M	2015	Fort William	
MacLean	Dylan	2			GK	2015	Inverness CT	
MacLean	Callum	2		1	D	2015	Fort William	
Main	Glen				D	2007	Nairn St Ninian	
McConaghy	Seamus				F	2018	Nairn County Youths	
McKenzie	Dylan				F	2016	Clachnacuddin	
McLean	Jack				D	2018	Nairn County Youths	
McLennan	Tom	2			M	2018	Ross County	
McNab	Gordon	1			M	2019	Clachnacuddin	
Naismith	Adam				D	2017	Huntly	Retired 2021
Porritt	Adam	2			D	2017	Fort William	
Ramsay	Cohen	2			D	2017	Ross County	
Shewan	Liam	2			F	2019	Clachnacuddin	
NEW SIGNINGS								
Gethins	Conor					2021	Formartine United	
Treasurer	John					2021	Fort William	

ROTHES

Manager	Ross Jack							
Surname	**First Name**	**Apps**	**Subs**	**Goals**		**Signed**	**From**	
Anderson	Scott				D	2020	Rothes Youths	
Brown	Jack	2			M	2020	Inverness CT	
Christie	Charlie				GK	2020	Rothes Youths	
Cormack	Craig	2			M	2015	Keith	
Gunn	Ross	2			M	2020	Inverness CT	
Harkness	Shane	1		1	F	2020	Inverness CT (OL)	Dec-Jan
Hyde	Lewis		1		M	2020	Inverness CT (OL)	Dec-Jan
Johnstone	Ben	2			D	2019	Ross County	
Kerr	Gary	1	1		F	2018	Nairn County	
Linden	Sean	1			M	2020	Aberdeen	
MacLeod	Paul				D	2017	Nairn County	
Main	Greg	1	1		M	2019	Nairn County	
Maley	Jack				M	2017	Strathspey Thistle	
McCarthy	Sean	2			GK	2020	Wick Academy	
McCarthy	Daniel				GK	2020	Tain St Duthus	
McRitchie	Ryan		1		D	2019	Inverness CT	
McRitchie	Mark							
Milne	Bruce	2			D	2017	Keith	
Neil	Ewan				D	2020	Rothes Youths	
Robertson	Fraser	2		1	M	2019	Clachnacuddin	
Stark	Alisdair	2			D	2018	Inverness CT	
Sutherland	Alisdair	2			F	2019	Elgin City	Joined Brora Rangers Mar 2021
NEW SIGNINGS								
Morrison	Greg					2021	Brora Rangers	
Mackintosh	Wayne					2021	Formartine United	ex nairn County
Finnis	Michael					2021	Clachnacuddin	
Harkness	Shane					2021	Inverness CT	

STRATHSPEY THISTLE

Manager	Charlie Brown						
Surname	**First Name**	**Apps**	**Subs**	**Goals**		**Signed**	**From**
Ballam	Ashley				D	2020	Elgin City
Crichton	Adam				GK	2020	Forres Mechanics
Cuthbert	Joe				M	2020	Nairn County
Duncan	Kris				F	2020	Lossiemouth
Duncan	Martin				D	2018	Inverness City
Hastings	Gabriel				D	2020	Inverness CT
Kennedy	Roderick				F	2020	Inverness CT
Lisle	Cameron				M	2018	Brora Rangers
MacLean	Andrew				D		Burghead Thistle
McCallum	Michael				GK	2015	Nairn County
McDade	Liam				D	2020	Elgin City
McKenzie	Craig				M	2020	Ross County
McShane	James				M	2013	Strathspey Thistle Youth
Rennie	Stephen				M	2019	Rothes
Taylor	Liam				F	2019	Forres Mechanics
NEW SIGNINGS							
Thomson	Jake					2021	Elgin City (OL)
Donaldson	Robert					2021	Rothes

TURRIFF UNITED

Surname	**First Name**	**Apps**	**Subs**	**Goals**		**Signed**	**From**	
Brown	Rory	1	1		<	2018	Inverurie Locos	
Buxton	Kyle		2		F	2019	Peterhead	
Cormack	Murray		1		M	2020	Turriff United Youths	
Cross	Adam	2			M	2017	Fraserburgh	
Esson	Murray	2			D	2019	Glentanar	
Findlay	Tim				GK	2020	Turriff United Youths	
Gray	Callan	2			M	2020	Banks o' Dee	
Hobday	Fraser	2			GK	2018	Peterhead	
Ingram	Lewis				M	2019	Huntly	
Kinsella	Owen	2			D	2018	Turriff United Youths	
Kinsella	Luke	1	1		D	2019	Turriff United Youths	
McDonald	Matthew	2		1	F	2019	Huntly	
Mykyta	Tyler	2			M	2020	Aberdeen (OL)	Sep-Feb
Power	Conor	1			D	2020	Aberdeen (OL)	Sep-Feb
Smith	Ethan	1			D	2019	Dundee	
Smith	Keir				M	2018	Inverness CT	
Stuart	Dylan	2			M	2019	Turriff United Youths	
Turner	Luke	2			D	2020	Aberdeen (OL)	Sep-Feb
Ward	Robert	2		1	F	2019	Dundee United	Transferred to Inverurie Locos Feb 2021
NEW SIGNINGS								
Clark	Rhys					2021	Montrose	
Gordon	Kyle					2021	Inverurie Locos (OL)	
Cooper	Jordan					2021	Inverurie Locos (OL)	
dey	David					2021	Keith	

WICK ACADEMY

Surname	**First Name**	**Apps**	**Subs**	**Goals**		**Signed**	**From**	
Allan	Ross	2			M	2010	Ross County	
Allan	David	2			F	2008	Elgin City	
Anderson	Joe							
Bain	Liam							
Campbell	Sean		2		D	2020	Thurso	
Campbell	Ryan	2	1		M	2019	Wick Academy Youths	
Clark	Gordon				GK	2018	Golspie Sutherland	
Farquhar	Alan	2			D	2009	Halkirk United	
Gunn	Craig	2	1		F	2017	Brora Rangers	
Hardwick	Andrew	2			D	2020	Strathspey Thistle	
Henry	Jack	2	1		M	2017	Wick Groats	
Hughes	Alan	2			F	2012	Halkirk United	
Macadie	Richard	2			M	2006	Ross County	
Macadie	Mark	1			M	2019	Wick Acad Youths	
Mackay	Danny	1			D	2015	Brora Rangers	
Manson	Gary					2000	Wick Acad Youths	
McNab	Gordon		1		F	2017	Halkirk United	
More	James				GK	2004	Wick Acad Youths	
Sinclair	Ben				M	2019	Wick Academy Youths	OL to Golspie Sutherland Aug-Dec
Sinclair	Brandon				D	2020	Salem University Tigers	
Williamson	Graeme	2			GK	2020	Golspie Sutherland	
NEW SIGNINGS								
Anderson	Steven					2021	Rothes	

North Caledonian League 2021/2

NORTH CALEDONIAN CUP COMPETITIONS 21-22

FOOTBALL TIMES CUP
Orkney not entered
First Round
Golspie Sutherland – Inverness Athletic (Sep 11)
Invergordon – Alness United (Sep 11)
Tain St Duthus – Halkirk United (Sep 11)
Thurso – Bonar Bridge (Sep 11)

Quarter Finals
Scourie – Nairn County 'A' (Sep 11)
Invergordon or Alness United – Tain St Duthus or Halkirk United
Lewis & Harris FA – Thurso or Bonar Bridge
Loch Ness – Golspie Sutherland or Inverness Athletic

NORTH CALEDONIAN CUP
First Round
Bonar Bridge – Thurso
Halkirk United – Invergordon
Inverness Athletic – Tain St Duthus
Scourie – Golspie Sutherland

Quarter Finals
Bonar Bridge or Thurso – Nairn County 'A'
Halkirk United or Invergordon – Alness United
Inverness Athletic or Tain St Duthus – Orkney
Scourie or Golspie Sutherland – Loch Ness

Details of the 2020/1 North Caledonian League season can be found later in the Almanac

North Junior Leagues 2021/2

Details of the 2020/1 North Junior season can be found later in the Almanac

LEAGUE STRUCTURE FOR 2021/22

Superleague (14 - play each other twice)
Banchory Thistle
Banks o' Dee
Bridge of Don Thistle
Colony Park
Culter
Deveronside
Dyce
East End
Ellon United
Hall Russell United
Hermes
Maud
Montrose Roselea
Nairn St Ninian

1st Division (8 - play each other 4 times)
Aberdeen University
Buchanhaven Hearts
Dufftown
Fraserburgh United
Longside
Stonehaven
Stoneywood Parkvale
Sunnybank

2nd Division (9 - play each other 3 times)
Burghead Thistle
Cruden Bay
Forres Thistle
Glentanar
Islavale
New Elgin
Newmachar United
Rothie Rovers
Whitehills

In abeyance
Buckie Rovers
Spey Valley United

Cup Draws 2021/2

Grill League Cup 2021/22

Group 1
Dufftown
Buckie Rovers
Whitehills
New Elgin
Forres Thistle

Group 2
Islavale
Deveronside
Burghead Thistle
Nairn St Ninian

Group 3
Rothie Rovers
Maud
Cruden Bay
Fraserburgh United

Group 4
Colony Park
Ellon United
Longside
Buchanhaven Hearts

Group 5
Newmachar United
Aberdeen East End
Dyce Juniors
Banks o' Dee

Group 6
Banchory St Ternan
Culter
Stoneywood Parkvale
Glentanar

Group 7
Bridge of Don Thistle
Montrose Roselea
Aberdeen University
Stonehaven

Group 8
Hall Russell United
Hermes
Sunnybank

The draw was then made for the quarter finals, which resulted in the following;

Winner of Group 4 v Winner of Group 3
Winner of Group 5 v Winner of Group 2
Winner of Group 7 v Winner of Group 8
Winner of Group 6 v Winner of Group 1

North Region Cup 2021/22

Whitehills v Deveronside
Maud v Stoneywood Parkvale
Hermes v Montrose Roselea
Dyce Juniors v Culter
Longside v Ellon United
Cruden Bay v Colony Park
Banchory St Ternan v Sunnybank
Buckie Rovers v Dufftown
Rothie Rovers v Aberdeen University
Stonehaven v New Elgin
Nairn St Ninian v Bridge of Don Thistle
Newmachar United v Hall Russell United
Banks o' Dee v Islavale
Buchanhaven Hearts v Forres Thistle
Aberdeen East End v Burghead Thistle
Fraserburgh United v Glentanar

Inter Regional Cup 2021/22

Bridge of Don Thistle v Stonehaven
Forres Thistle v Colony Park
Cruden Bay v Ellon United
Stoneywood Parkvale v Banchory St Ternan
Dufftown v Fraserburgh United
Rothie Rovers v Culter
Deveronside v Newmachar United
Maud v Buchanhaven Hearts
Longside v Aberdeen East End
Hall Russell United v Buckie Rovers
Glentanar v Islavale
Sunnybank v Montrose Roselea
New Elgin v Hermes
Aberdeen University v Burghead Thistle
Whitehills v Banks o' Dee
Bye - Dyce Juniors

Opted Out- Nairn St Ninian

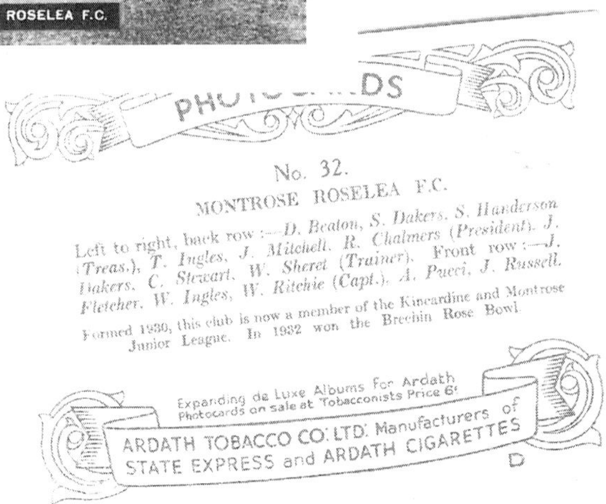

PHOTO...DS

No. 32.

MONTROSE ROSELEA F.C.

Left to right, back row :—*D. Beaton, S. Dakers, S. Handerson (Treas.), T. Ingles, J. Mitchell, R. Chalmers (President), J. Dakers, C. Stewart, W. Sheret (Trainer).* Front row :—*J. Fletcher, W. Ingles, W. Ritchie (Capt.), A. Pucci, J. Russell.*

Formed 1930, this club is now a member of the Kincardine and Montrose Junior League. In 1932 won the Brechin Rose Bowl.

Expanding de Luxe Albums For Ardath Photocards on sale at Tobacconists Price 6d

ARDATH TOBACCO CO. LTD. Manufacturers of STATE EXPRESS and ARDATH CIGARETTES

D

Midlands Junior League 2021/2

The "Tayside Question" was one of the final imponderables in the Scottish Pyramid saga. Since 2002 the Tayside clubs had bene part of the SJFA East Region competing with clubs from the Lothians and Fife. By 2021, with the last remaining Lothians sides all moving to the East of Scotland League, the only part of the East Juniors remaining was Tayside. It became clear that they would form their own League but it was not initially clear of this would be self-standing, or part of the Lowland or North pyramid structure.

Ultimately it was agreed that the East Juniors (i.e. Tayside) would be one of the three feeder leagues for the Highland League. The new league would be called the Midlands League and would still be run under the auspices of the Scottish Junior FA.

All the current clubs joined up along with two newcomers. Fintry Amateurs became Dundee St James and moved into St Joseph's old ground at Fairfield Park. Letham FC, from Perth, initially applied to join the East of Scotland League but were knocked back. However, they then applied to the Midlands League and were accepted - arriving in the Pyramid one tier higher than they would have been in the East!

Midlands Junior League Fixtures 2021/2

Saturday, July 17
Arbroath Victoria - East Craigie
Broughty Athletic - Dundee St James
Carnoustie Panmure - Forfar United
Coupar Angus - Letham
Dundee Violet - Brechin Victoria
Forfar West End - Kirriemuir Thistle
Lochee United - Blairgowrie
Scone Thistle - Lochee Harp
Tayport - Dundee North End
Downfield idle

Wednesday, July 21
Blairgowrie - Broughty Athletic
Dundee North End - Dundee Violet
Dundee St James - Coupar Angus
East Craigie - Carnoustie Panmure
Forfar United - Tayport
Kirriemuir Thistle - Arbroath Victoria
Letham - Forfar West End
Lochee Harp - Downfield
Scone Thistle - Brechin Victoria
Lochee United idle

Saturday, July 24
Blairgowrie - Forfar West End
Brechin Victoria - Lochee United
Carnoustie Panmure - Dundee Violet
Dundee North End - Downfield
Dundee St James - Arbroath Victoria
East Craigie - Tayport
Forfar United - Scone Thistle
Letham - Kirriemuir Thistle
Lochee Harp - Broughty Athletic
Coupar Angus idle

Wednesday, July 28
Arbroath Victoria - Letham
Coupar Angus - Blairgowrie
Downfield - Brechin Victoria
Dundee Violet - Forfar United
Forfar West End - Dundee St James
Kirriemuir Thistle - East Craigie
Lochee United - Lochee Harp
Scone Thistle - Dundee North End
Tayport - Carnoustie Panmure
Broughty Athletic idle

Saturday, July 31
Arbroath Victoria - Blairgowrie
Broughty Athletic - Brechin Victoria
Coupar Angus - Lochee Harp
Downfield - Forfar United
Dundee Violet - Tayport
Kirriemuir Thistle - Dundee St James
Letham - East Craigie
Lochee United - Dundee North End
Scone Thistle - Carnoustie Panmure
Forfar West End idle

Wednesday, August 4
Blairgowrie - Kirriemuir Thistle
Brechin Victoria - Coupar Angus
Carnoustie Panmure - Downfield
Dundee North End - Broughty Athletic
Dundee St James - Letham
East Craigie - Dundee Violet
Forfar United - Lochee United
Lochee Harp - Forfar West End
Tayport - Scone Thistle
Arbroath Victoria idle

Saturday, August 7
Blairgowrie - Dundee St James
Brechin Victoria - Arbroath Victoria
Carnoustie Panmure - Broughty Athletic
Dundee North End - Forfar West End
Dundee Violet - Downfield
East Craigie - Scone Thistle
Forfar United - Coupar Angus
Lochee Harp - Kirriemuir Thistle
Tayport - Lochee United
Letham idle

Wednesday, August 11
Arbroath Victoria - Lochee Harp
Broughty Athletic - Forfar United
Coupar Angus - Dundee North End
Downfield - Tayport
Dundee St James - East Craigie
Forfar West End - Brechin Victoria
Letham - Blairgowrie
Lochee United - Carnoustie Panmure
Scone Thistle - Dundee Violet
Kirriemuir Thistle idle

Saturday, August 14
Arbroath Victoria - Dundee North End
Blairgowrie - East Craigie
Broughty Athletic - Tayport
Coupar Angus - Carnoustie Panmure
Downfield - Scone Thistle
Forfar West End - Forfar United
Kirriemuir Thistle - Brechin Victoria
Letham - Lochee Harp
Lochee United - Dundee Violet
Dundee St James idle

Wednesday, August 18
Brechin Victoria - Letham
Carnoustie Panmure - Forfar West End
Dundee North End - Kirriemuir Thistle
Dundee Violet - Broughty Athletic
East Craigie - Downfield
Forfar United - Arbroath Victoria
Lochee Harp - Dundee St James
Scone Thistle - Lochee United
Tayport - Coupar Angus
Blairgowrie idle

Saturday, August 21
Scottish Junior Cup, First Round

Wednesday, August 25
Arbroath Victoria - Carnoustie Panmure
Blairgowrie - Lochee Harp
Broughty Athletic - Scone Thistle
Coupar Angus - Dundee Violet
Dundee St James - Brechin Victoria
Forfar West End - Tayport
Kirriemuir Thistle - Forfar United
Letham - Dundee North End
Lochee United - Downfield
East Craigie idle

Saturday, August 28
Brechin Victoria - Blairgowrie
Carnoustie Panmure - Kirriemuir Thistle
Downfield - Broughty Athletic
Dundee North End - Dundee St James
Dundee Violet - Forfar West End
East Craigie - Lochee United
Forfar United - Letham
Scone Thistle - Coupar Angus

Tayport - Arbroath Victoria
Lochee Harp idle

Saturday, September 4
Arbroath Victoria - Dundee Violet
Blairgowrie - Dundee North End
Broughty Athletic - Lochee United
Coupar Angus - Downfield
Dundee St James - Forfar United
Forfar West End - Scone Thistle
Kirriemuir Thistle - Tayport
Letham - Carnoustie Panmure
Lochee Harp - East Craigie
Brechin Victoria idle

Saturday, September 11
North & Tayside Cup, First Round

Saturday, September 18
Brechin Victoria - Lochee Harp
Downfield - Forfar West End
Dundee St James - Carnoustie Panmure
Dundee Violet - Kirriemuir Thistle
East Craigie - Broughty Athletic
Forfar United - Blairgowrie
Lochee United - Coupar Angus
Scone Thistle - Arbroath Victoria
Tayport - Letham
Dundee North End idle

Saturday, September 25
Scottish Junior Cup, Second Round

Saturday, October 2
Arbroath Victoria - Downfield
Blairgowrie - Carnoustie Panmure
Brechin Victoria - East Craigie
Coupar Angus - Broughty Athletic
Dundee St James - Tayport
Forfar West End - Lochee United
Kirriemuir Thistle - Scone Thistle
Letham - Dundee Violet
Lochee Harp - Dundee North End
Forfar United idle

Saturday, October 9
Broughty Athletic - Forfar West End
Downfield - Kirriemuir Thistle
Dundee North End - Brechin Victoria
Dundee Violet - Dundee St James
East Craigie - Coupar Angus
Forfar United - Lochee Harp
Lochee United - Arbroath Victoria
Scone Thistle - Letham
Tayport - Blairgowrie
Carnoustie Panmure idle

Saturday, October 16
Arbroath Victoria - Broughty Athletic
Blairgowrie - Dundee Violet
Brechin Victoria - Forfar United
Dundee North End - East Craigie
Dundee St James - Scone Thistle
Forfar West End - Coupar Angus
Kirriemuir Thistle - Lochee United
Letham - Downfield
Lochee Harp - Carnoustie Panmure
Tayport idle

Saturday, October 23
Scottish Junior Cup, Third Round

Saturday, October 30
Broughty Athletic - Kirriemuir Thistle
Carnoustie Panmure - Brechin Victoria
Coupar Angus - Arbroath Victoria
Downfield - Dundee St James
East Craigie - Forfar West End
Forfar United - Dundee North End
Lochee United - Letham
Scone Thistle - Blairgowrie
Tayport - Lochee Harp
Dundee Violet idle

Saturday, November 6
Arbroath Victoria - Forfar West End
Blairgowrie - Downfield
Brechin Victoria - Tayport
Dundee North End - Carnoustie Panmure
Dundee St James - Lochee United
Forfar United - East Craigie
Kirriemuir Thistle - Coupar Angus
Letham - Broughty Athletic
Lochee Harp - Dundee Violet
Scone Thistle idle

Saturday, November 13
Blairgowrie - Lochee United
Brechin Victoria - Dundee Violet
Dundee North End - Tayport
Dundee St James - Broughty Athletic
East Craigie - Arbroath Victoria
Forfar United - Carnoustie Panmure
Kirriemuir Thistle - Forfar West End
Letham - Coupar Angus
Lochee Harp - Scone Thistle
Downfield - idle

Saturday, November 20
North & Tayside Cup, Second Round

Saturday, November 27
Scottish Junior Cup, Fourth Round

Saturday, December 4
Arbroath Victoria - Kirriemuir Thistle
Broughty Athletic - Blairgowrie
Carnoustie Panmure - East Craigie
Coupar Angus - Dundee St James
Dundee Violet - Dundee North End
Downfield - Lochee Harp
Forfar West End - Letham
Scone Thistle - Brechin Victoria
Tayport - Forfar United
Lochee United idle

Saturday, December 11
Blairgowrie - Coupar Angus
Brechin Victoria - Downfield
Carnoustie Panmure - Tayport
Dundee North End - Scone Thistle
Dundee St James - Forfar West End
East Craigie - Kirriemuir Thistle
Forfar United - Dundee Violet
Letham - Arbroath Victoria
Lochee Harp - Lochee United
Broughty Athletic idle

Saturday, December 18
Arbroath Victoria - Dundee St James
Broughty Athletic - Lochee Harp
Downfield - Dundee North End
Dundee Violet - Carnoustie Panmure
Forfar West End - Blairgowrie
Kirriemuir Thistle - Letham
Lochee United - Brechin Victoria
Scone Thistle - Forfar United
Tayport - East Craigie
Coupar Angus - idle

Saturday, January 8
Blairgowrie - Arbroath Victoria
Brechin Victoria - Broughty Athletic
Carnoustie Panmure - Scone Thistle
Dundee North End - Lochee United
Dundee St James - Kirriemuir Thistle
East Craigie - Letham
Forfar United - Downfield
Lochee Harp - Coupar Angus
Tayport - Dundee Violet
Forfar West End idle

Saturday, January 15
Broughty Athletic - Dundee North End
Coupar Angus - Brechin Victoria
Downfield - Carnoustie Panmure
Dundee Violet - East Craigie
Forfar West End - Lochee Harp
Kirriemuir Thistle - Blairgowrie
Letham - Dundee St James
Lochee United - Forfar United
Scone Thistle - Tayport
Arbroath Victoria idle

Saturday, January 22
Blairgowrie - Letham
Brechin Victoria - Forfar West End
Carnoustie Panmure - Lochee United
Dundee North End - Coupar Angus
Dundee Violet - Scone Thistle
East Craigie - Dundee St James
Forfar United - Broughty Athletic
Lochee Harp - Arbroath Victoria
Tayport - Downfield
Kirriemuir Thistle idle

Saturday, January 29
North & Tayside Cup, Third Round

Saturday, February 5
Arbroath Victoria - Brechin Victoria
Broughty Athletic - Carnoustie Panmure
Coupar Angus - Forfar United
Downfield - Dundee Violet
Dundee St James - Blairgowrie
Forfar West End - Dundee North End
Kirriemuir Thistle - Lochee Harp
Lochee United - Tayport
Scone Thistle - East Craigie
Letham idle

Saturday, February 12
Dundee North End - Arbroath Victoria
Brechin Victoria - Kirriemuir Thistle
Carnoustie Panmure - Coupar Angus
Dundee Violet - Lochee United
East Craigie - Blairgowrie
Forfar United - Forfar West End
Lochee Harp - Letham
Scone Thistle - Downfield
Tayport - Broughty Athletic
Dundee St James idle

Saturday, February 19
Arbroath Victoria - Forfar United
Broughty Athletic - Dundee Violet

Coupar Angus - Tayport
Downfield - East Craigie
Dundee St James - Lochee Harp
Forfar West End - Carnoustie Panmure
Kirriemuir Thistle - Dundee North End
Letham - Brechin Victoria
Lochee United - Scone Thistle
Blairgowrie idle

Saturday, February 26
Brechin Victoria - Dundee St James
Carnoustie Panmure - Arbroath Victoria
Downfield - Lochee United
Dundee North End - Letham
Dundee Violet - Coupar Angus
Forfar United - Kirriemuir Thistle
Lochee Harp - Blairgowrie
Scone Thistle - Broughty Athletic
Tayport - Forfar West End
East Craigie idle

Saturday, March 5
Arbroath Victoria - Tayport
Blairgowrie - Brechin Victoria
Broughty Athletic - Downfield
Coupar Angus - Scone Thistle
Dundee St James - Dundee North End
Forfar West End - Dundee Violet
Kirriemuir Thistle - Carnoustie Panmure
Letham - Forfar United
Lochee United - East Craigie
Lochee Harp idle

Saturday, March 12
Carnoustie Panmure - Letham
Downfield - Coupar Angus
Dundee North End - Blairgowrie
Dundee Violet - Arbroath Victoria
East Craigie - Lochee Harp
Forfar United - Dundee St James
Lochee United - Broughty Athletic
Scone Thistle - Forfar West End
Tayport - Kirriemuir Thistle
Brechin Victoria idle

Saturday, March 19
Arbroath Victoria - Scone Thistle
Blairgowrie - Forfar United
Broughty Athletic - East Craigie
Coupar Angus - Lochee United
Dundee St James - Carnoustie Panmure
Forfar West End - Downfield
Kirriemuir Thistle - Dundee Violet
Letham - Tayport
Lochee Harp - Brechin Victoria
Dundee North End idle

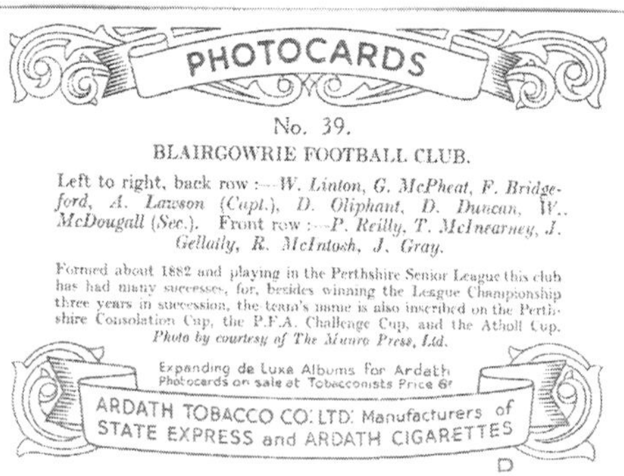
PHOTOCARDS

No. 39.

BLAIRGOWRIE FOOTBALL CLUB.

Left to right, back row :—*W. Linton, G. McPheat, F. Bridgeford, A. Lawson (Capt.), D. Oliphant, D. Duncan, W. McDougall (Sec.).* Front row :—*P. Reilly, T. McInearney, J. Gellatly, R. McIntosh, J. Gray.*

Formed about 1882 and playing in the Perthshire Senior League this club has had many successes, for, besides winning the League Championship three years in succession, the team's name is also inscribed on the Perthshire Consolation Cup, the P.F.A. Challenge Cup, and the Atholl Cup.

Photo by courtesy of The Munro Press, Ltd.

Expanding de Luxe Albums for Ardath Photocards on sale at Tobacconists Price 6d

ARDATH TOBACCO CO. LTD. Manufacturers of STATE EXPRESS and ARDATH CIGARETTES

D

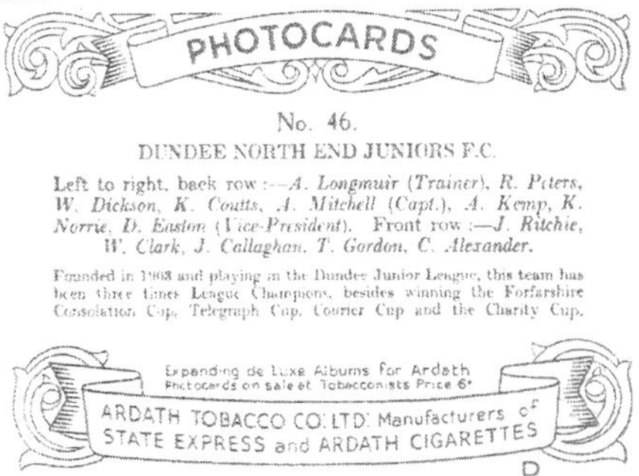
PHOTOCARDS

No. 46.

DUNDEE NORTH END JUNIORS F.C.

Left to right, back row :—*A. Longmuir (Trainer), R. Peters, W. Dickson, K. Coutts, A. Mitchell (Capt.), A. Kemp, K. Norrie, D. Easton (Vice-President).* Front row :—*J. Ritchie, W. Clark, J. Callaghan, T. Gordon, C. Alexander.*

Founded in 1908 and playing in the Dundee Junior League, this team has been three times League Champions, besides winning the Forfarshire Consolation Cup, Telegraph Cup, Courier Cup and the Charity Cup.

Expanding de Luxe Albums for Ardath Photocards on sale at Tobacconists Price 6d

ARDATH TOBACCO CO. LTD. Manufacturers of STATE EXPRESS and ARDATH CIGARETTES

D

North Junior League Fixtures 2021/2

North Super League

Saturday, July 17
Aberdeen East End - Nairn St Ninian
Banchory St Ternan - Montrose Roselea
Banks o' Dee - Maud
Bridge of Don Thistle - Hermes
Colony Park - Hall Russell United
Culter - Ellon United
Deveronside - Dyce Juniors

Tuesday, July 20
Dyce Juniors - Culter
Ellon United - Colony Park
Hall Russell United - Bridge of Don Thistle
Hermes - Banks o' Dee
Maud - Banchory St Ternan
Montrose Roselea - Aberdeen East End
Nairn St Ninian - Deveronside

Saturday, July 24
Banchory St Ternan - Nairn St Ninian
Banks o' Dee - Aberdeen East End
Bridge of Don Thistle - Montrose Roselea
Colony Park - Maud
Culter - Hermes
Dyce Juniors - Ellon United
Hall Russell United - Deveronside

Tuesday, July 27
Aberdeen East End - Banchory St Ternan
Culter - Hall Russell United
Deveronside - Ellon United
Hermes - Colony Park
Maud - Bridge of Don Thistle
Montrose Roselea - Banks o' Dee

Saturday, July 31
Banchory St Ternan - Banks o' Dee
Bridge of Don Thistle - Aberdeen East End
Ellon United - Nairn St Ninian
Hall Russell United - Dyce Juniors
Hermes - Deveronside
Maud - Culter
Montrose Roselea - Colony Park

Tuesday, August 3
Banchory St Ternan - Bridge of Don Thistle
Colony Park - Aberdeen East End
Culter - Montrose Roselea
Deveronside - Maud
Dyce Juniors - Hermes
Ellon United - Hall Russell United

Saturday, August 7
Nairn St Ninian - Dyce Juniors
Inter Regional Cup, First Round

Tuesday, August 10
Aberdeen East End - Culter
Colony Park - Banchory St Ternan
Hermes - Ellon United

Wednesday, August 11
Banks o' Dee - Bridge of Don Thistle

Saturday, August 14
Bridge of Don Thistle - Nairn St Ninian
Banks o' Dee - Colony Park
Culter - Banchory St Ternan
Deveronside - Aberdeen East End
Dyce Juniors - Montrose Roselea
Ellon United - Maud
Hall Russell United - Hermes

Saturday, August 21
Scottish Junior Cup, First Round

Saturday, August 28
Aberdeen East End - Dyce Juniors
Banchory St Ternan - Deveronside
Bridge of Don Thistle - Colony Park
Culter - Banks o' Dee
Maud - Hall Russell United
Montrose Roselea - Ellon United
Nairn St Ninian - Hermes

Saturday, September 4
Aberdeen East End - Hall Russell United
Banks o' Dee - Dyce Juniors
Colony Park - Culter
Deveronside - Bridge of Don Thistle
Ellon United - Banchory St Ternan
Nairn St Ninian - Maud
Hermes - Montrose Roselea

Saturday, September 11
North Regional Cup, First Round

Saturday, September 18
Bridge of Don Thistle - Culter
Colony Park - Nairn St Ninian
Deveronside - Banks o' Dee
Dyce Juniors - Banchory St Ternan
Ellon United - Aberdeen East End
Hall Russell United - Montrose Roselea
Maud - Hermes

Saturday, September 25
Scottish Junior Cup, Second Round

Saturday, October 2
Aberdeen East End - Maud
Banchory St Ternan - Hermes
Banks o' Dee - Hall Russell United
Bridge of Don Thistle - Ellon United
Culter - Deveronside
Dyce Juniors - Colony Park
Montrose Roselea - Nairn St Ninian

Saturday, October 9
Inter Regional Cup, First Round

Saturday, October 16
Maud - Dyce Juniors
Montrose Roselea - Deveronside
Nairn St Ninian - Hall Russell United

Saturday, October 23
Scottish Junior Cup, Third Round

Saturday, October 30
Deveronside - Colony Park
Dyce Juniors - Bridge of Don Thistle
Ellon United - Banks o' Dee
Hall Russell United - Banchory St Ternan
Hermes - Aberdeen East End
Maud - Montrose Roselea
Nairn St Ninian - Culter

Saturday, November 6
Banks o' Dee - Culter
Colony Park - Bridge of Don Thistle
Deveronside - Banchory St Ternan
Dyce Juniors - Aberdeen East End
Ellon United - Montrose Roselea
Hall Russell United - Maud
Hermes - Nairn St Ninian

Saturday, November 13
Aberdeen East End - Hermes
Banchory St Ternan - Hall Russell United
Banks o' Dee - Ellon United
Bridge of Don Thistle - Dyce Juniors
Colony Park - Deveronside
Culter - Nairn St Ninian
Montrose Roselea - Maud

Saturday, November 20
Aberdeen East End - Colony Park
Bridge of Don Thistle - Banchory St Ternan
Hall Russell United - Ellon United
Hermes - Dyce Juniors
Maud - Deveronside
Montrose Roselea - Culter
Nairn St Ninian - Banks o' Dee

Saturday, November 27
Scottish Junior Cup, Fourth Round

Saturday, December 4
Banks o' Dee - Nairn St Ninian
Deveronside - Hall Russell United
Ellon United - Hermes

Saturday, December 11
Banks o' Dee - Montrose Roselea
Banchory St Ternan - Maud
Dyce Juniors - Deveronside
Ellon United - Culter
Hall Russell United - Colony Park
Hermes - Bridge of Don Thistle
Nairn St Ninian - Aberdeen East End

Saturday, December 18
Aberdeen East End - Deveronside
Banchory St Ternan - Culter
Colony Park - Banks o' Dee
Hermes - Hall Russell United
Maud - Ellon United
Montrose Roselea - Dyce Juniors
Nairn St Ninian - Bridge of Don Thistle

North SJFA McBookie.com First Division

Saturday, July 17
Aberdeen University - Buchanhaven Hearts
Fraserburgh United - Longside
Stonehaven - Stoneywood Parkvale
Sunnybank - Dufftown

Saturday, July 24
Aberdeen University - Sunnybank
Buchanhaven Hearts - Longside
Dufftown - Stonehaven
Stoneywood Parkvale - Fraserburgh United

Tuesday, July 27
Longside - Stoneywood Parkvale
Stonehaven - Aberdeen University
Sunnybank - Buchanhaven Hearts

Saturday, July 31
Buchanhaven Hearts - Stoneywood Parkvale
Fraserburgh United - Aberdeen University
Longside - Dufftown
Sunnybank - Stonehaven

Tuesday, August 3
Aberdeen University - Longside
Stonehaven - Buchanhaven Hearts
Stoneywood Parkvale - Sunnybank

Saturday, August 7
Inter Regional Cup, First Round

Tuesday, August 10
Aberdeen University - Dufftown
Fraserburgh United - Buchanhaven Hearts

Friday, August 13
Longside - Sunnybank

Saturday, August 14
Buchanhaven Hearts - Aberdeen University
Dufftown - Stoneywood Parkvale
Stonehaven - Fraserburgh United

Saturday, August 21
Scottish Junior Cup, First Round

Saturday, August 28
Buchanhaven Hearts - Dufftown
Longside - Stonehaven
Stoneywood Parkvale - Aberdeen University
Sunnybank - Fraserburgh United

Saturday, September 4
Aberdeen University - Stonehaven
Dufftown - Longside
Fraserburgh United - Sunnybank
Stoneywood Parkvale - Buchanhaven Hearts

Saturday, September 11
Fraserburgh United - Dufftown
North Regional Cup, First Round

Saturday, September 18
Aberdeen University - Stoneywood Parkvale
Dufftown - Buchanhaven Hearts
Longside - Fraserburgh United
Stonehaven - Sunnybank

Saturday, September 25
Scottish Junior Cup, Second Round

Saturday, October 2
Buchanhaven Hearts - Stonehaven
Dufftown - Fraserburgh United
Stoneywood Parkvale - Longside
Sunnybank - Aberdeen University

Saturday, October 9
Inter Regional Cup, First Round

Saturday, October 16
Fraserburgh United - Stoneywood Parkvale
Stonehaven - Dufftown

Saturday, October 23
Scottish Junior Cup, Third Round

Saturday, October 30
Buchanhaven Hearts - Fraserburgh United
Dufftown - Aberdeen University
Stonehaven - Longside
Sunnybank - Stoneywood Parkvale

Saturday, November 6
Aberdeen University - Fraserburgh United
Dufftown - Sunnybank
Longside - Buchanhaven Hearts
Stoneywood Parkvale - Stonehaven

Saturday, November 13
Buchanhaven Hearts - Sunnybank
Fraserburgh United - Stonehaven
Longside - Aberdeen University
Stoneywood Parkvale - Dufftown

Saturday, November 20
Buchanhaven Hearts - Stoneywood Parkvale
Dufftown - Aberdeen University
Stonehaven - Fraserburgh United
Sunnybank - Longside

Saturday, November 27
Scottish Junior Cup, Fourth Round

Saturday, December 4
Aberdeen University - Sunnybank
Dufftown - Stonehaven
Fraserburgh United - Longside

Saturday, December 11
Fraserburgh United - Sunnybank
Longside - Dufftown
Stonehaven - Buchanhaven Hearts
Stoneywood Parkvale - Aberdeen University

Saturday, December 18
Aberdeen University - Fraserburgh United
Buchanhaven Hearts - Dufftown
Stoneywood Parkvale - Longside
Sunnybank - Stonehaven

North SJFA McBookie.com Second Division

Saturday, July 17
Forres Thistle - Rothie Rovers
Islavale - Glentanar
New Elgin - Cruden Bay
Whitehills - Newmachar United

Tuesday, July 20
Rothie Rovers - Newmachar United

Saturday, July 24
Cruden Bay - Glentanar
Islavale - Rothie Rovers
New Elgin - Whitehills
Newmachar United - Burghead Thistle

Tuesday, July 27
Glentanar - Newmachar United

Saturday, July 31
Burghead Thistle - Islavale
Newmachar United - Forres Thistle
Rothie Rovers - New Elgin
Whitehills - Cruden Bay

Saturday, August 7
Inter Regional Cup, First Round

Tuesday, August 10
Forres Thistle - Burghead Thistle
Glentanar - Rothie Rovers

Wednesday, August 11
Whitehills - Islavale

Saturday, August 14
Burghead Thistle - Glentanar
Forres Thistle - Cruden Bay
New Elgin - Newmachar United
Rothie Rovers - Whitehills

Saturday, August 21
Scottish Junior Cup, First Round

Saturday, August 28
Burghead Thistle - New Elgin
Cruden Bay - Rothie Rovers
Glentanar - Whitehills
Islavale - Forres Thistle

Saturday, September 4
Forres Thistle - Glentanar
Islavale - New Elgin
Newmachar United - Cruden Bay
Whitehills - Burghead Thistle

Saturday, September 11
North Regional Cup, First Round

Saturday, September 18
New Elgin - Glentanar
Newmachar United - Islavale
Rothie Rovers - Burghead Thistle
Whitehills - Forres Thistle

Saturday, September 25
Scottish Junior Cup, Second Round

Saturday, October 2
Burghead Thistle - Newmachar United
Forres Thistle - New Elgin
Glentanar - Islavale
Rothie Rovers - Cruden Bay

Saturday, October 9
Inter Regional Cup, First Round

Saturday, October 16
Cruden Bay - Burghead Thistle
Glentanar - Forres Thistle
Islavale - Whitehills
Newmachar United - Rothie Rovers

Saturday, October 23
Scottish Junior Cup, Third Round

Saturday, October 30
Cruden Bay - Islavale
New Elgin - Burghead Thistle
Rothie Rovers - Forres Thistle
Whitehills - Glentanar

Saturday, November 6
Forres Thistle - Newmachar United
Glentanar - New Elgin
Islavale - Cruden Bay
Whitehills - Rothie Rovers

Saturday, November 13
Burghead Thistle - Whitehills
Cruden Bay - New Elgin
Newmachar United - Glentanar
Rothie Rovers - Islavale

Saturday, November 20
Burghead Thistle - Cruden Bay
New Elgin - Forres Thistle
Newmachar United - Whitehills
Rothie Rovers - Glentanar

Saturday, November 27
Scottish Junior Cup, Fourth Round

Saturday, December 4
Cruden Bay - Forres Thistle
Islavale - Burghead Thistle
Whitehills - New Elgin

Saturday, December 11
Cruden Bay - Newmachar United
Forres Thistle - Islavale
Glentanar - Burghead Thistle
New Elgin - Rothie Rovers

Saturday, December 18
Burghead Thistle - Rothie Rovers
Forres Thistle - Whitehills
Glentanar - Cruden Bay
Islavale - Newmachar United

North Caledonian League Fixtures 2021/2

Saturday, August 21
Alness United – Invergordon
Golspie Sutherland – Inverness Athletic
Nairn County 'A' – Tain St Duthus
Scourie – Bonar Bridge

Wednesday, August 25
Halkirk United – Thurso
Nairn County 'A' – Loch Ness

Saturday, August 28
Bonar Bridge – Alness United
Invergordon – Scourie
Inverness Athletic – Orkney
Tain St Duthus – Halkirk United
Thurso – Golspie Sutherland

Saturday, September 4
Bonar Bridge – Tain St Duthus
Golspie Sutherland – Invergordon
Halkirk United – Nairn County 'A'
Loch Ness – Inverness Athletic
Orkney – Alness United
Scourie – Thurso

Saturday, September 11
Loch Ness – Orkney
+ Football Times Cup, First Round

Saturday, September 18
Alness United – Thurso
Golspie Sutherland – Bonar Bridge
Halkirk United – Scourie
Invergordon – Loch Ness
Orkney – Nairn County 'A'
Tain St Duthus – Inverness Athletic

Saturday, September 25
Bonar Bridge – Invergordon
Halkirk United – Alness United
Inverness Athletic – Thurso
Loch Ness – Tain St Duthus
Nairn County 'A' – Scourie
Orkney – Golspie Sutherland

Saturday, October 2
Football Times Cup, Quarter Finals

Saturday, October 9
Bonar Bridge – Halkirk United
Golspie Sutherland – Nairn County 'A'
Inverness Athletic – Invergordon
Scourie – Loch Ness
Tain St Duthus – Alness United
Thurso – Orkney

Saturday, October 16
Alness United – Inverness Athletic
Halkirk United – Golspie Sutherland
Invergordon – Nairn County 'A'
Loch Ness – Thurso
Orkney – Bonar Bridge
Scourie – Tain St Duthus

Saturday, October 23
Football Times Cup, Semi Finals

Saturday, October 30
Alness United – Golspie Sutherland
Loch Ness – Halkirk United
Nairn County 'A' – Bonar Bridge
Tain St Duthus – Orkney
Thurso – Invergordon
Scourie – Inverness Athletic

Saturday, November 6
Alness United – Nairn County 'A'
Bonar Bridge – Loch Ness
Golspie Sutherland – Scourie
Invergordon – Orkney
Inverness Athletic – Halkirk United
Thurso – Tain St Duthus

Saturday, November 13
Halkirk United – Orkney
Inverness Athletic – Bonar Bridge
Loch Ness – Golspie Sutherland
Nairn County 'A' – Thurso
Scourie – Alness United
Tain St Duthus – Invergordon

Saturday, November 20
Alness United – Loch Ness
Bonar Bridge – Thurso
Invergordon – Halkirk United
Nairn County 'A' – Inverness Athletic
Orkney – Scourie
Tain St Duthus – Golspie Sutherland

Saturday, November 27
Bonar Bridge – Scourie
Invergordon – Alness United
Inverness Athletic – Golspie Sutherland
Orkney – Loch Ness
Tain St Duthus – Nairn County 'A'
Thurso – Halkirk United

Saturday, December 4
Alness United – Bonar Bridge
Golspie Sutherland – Thurso
Halkirk United – Tain St Duthus
Loch Ness – Nairn County 'A'
Orkney – Inverness Athletic
Scourie – Invergordon

Saturday, December 11
Alness United – Orkney
Invergordon – Golspie Sutherland
Inverness Athletic – Loch Ness
Nairn County 'A' – Halkirk United
Tain St Duthus – Bonar Bridge
Thurso – Scourie

Saturday, December 18
Bonar Bridge – Golspie Sutherland
Inverness Athletic – Tain St Duthus
Loch Ness – Invergordon
Nairn County 'A' – Orkney
Scourie – Halkirk United
Thurso – Alness United

Junior Football

The SJFA has communicated very little information in recent years. The West Junior League ceased to function in 2020/1 and was replaced with the West of Scotland (Senior) League.

Some of the former West Region clubs have retained SJFA membership which permits them to take part in the Scottish Junior Cup.

In 2020/1 the East Region consisted of two separate leagues. The South League was made up of clubs mainly from West Lothian. The North League included the teams from Dundee, Angus and Perthshire, plus Tayport from Fife. At the end of 2020/1 the South clubs all transferred to the East of Scotland League. The North League was renamed as the Midlands League. It is still part of the SJFA and will feed into the Highland League as part of the pyramid.

The North Region of the SJFA remains unchanged except that it will also feed into the Highland League pyramid system.

The SJFA AGM took place in July 2021. No formal announcements have been made regarding what was discussed or concluded, other than to confirm that Mark Stanton of Lochee United is the new President.

The SJFA had intended to conclude the 2019/20 Scottish Junior Cup and play a 2020/1 competition. However, neither was possible and both competitions have been terminated.

SCOTTISH JUNIOR FOOTBALL ASSOCIATION
2020/21

HON. PRESIDENT
Peter Gardiner, Ex President SFA

HON. VICE-PRESIDENTS
David Roy, Past President
Matt Spiers, Ayrshire Region
Ron Ross, Fife Region
J. Gordon Law, Past President
Jack Whitehead, North Region
John Reilly, Past President
Joseph P. Black, Assistant Secretary
John Brodie, Former Treasurer
Robert Smith, Past President
J.Scott Robertson, Secretary, West Region
George Rose, Past President
Tom Anderson, Past President
George Morton, Past President
Harry Lawrie, Past president

PRESIDENT
Felix McKenna (St Anthonys)

VICE PRESIDENT
Marc Stanton (Lochee United)

CHIEF OPERATING OFFICER
Alex McDowall

ASST. SECRETARY / TREASURER
John Fyfe

S.J.F.A. OFFICES
HAMPDEN PARK, GLASGOW G42 9DD
TELEPHONE: 0141 620 4560
FAX: 0141 620 4561
email: scottishjuniorfa@scottish-football.com

AUDITORS
Peter Deans Chartered Accountants, Denny

MANAGEMENT COMMITTEE

WEST OF SCOTLAND LEAGUE
Gordon Ronney, (Kilbirnie Ladeside)
Bobby McNamara (Ardrossan Winton Rovers)

EAST REGION
Mark Johnson (Carnoustie Panmure)
Steven McMillan (Stoneyburn)

NORTH REGION
Norman Mackay, (Dyce Juniors)
George Rose, (New Elgin)

REGIONAL SECRETARIES

EAST REGION
SECRETARY
John Reilly,
email: rjohnreilly18@yahoo.co.uk

ASSISTANT SECRETARY
Syd McAlpine
email: sydmcalpine@hotmail.co.uk

NORTH REGION
SECRETARY
Richard Easton
email: richardeaston5@aol.com

ASSISTANT SECRETARY
Angela Cumming
email: angelacumming@hotmail.co.uk

SCOTTISH JUNIOR CUP 2021/2

The Scottish Junior Cup will continue in season 2021/2. The North and Tayside areas continue to have Junior Leagues and all their teams can participate. Many former Junior clubs from the West of Scotland have retained SJFA membership and will compete. The SJFA has also said they will be happy to accept any team from the "Pyramid" that wishes to enter the competition in future years.

ROUND ONE (August 21st)

Ashfield – Islavale
Auchinleck Talbot – Montrose Roselea
Banks o' Dee – Harthill Royal
Bathgate Thistle – Vale of Leven
Beith Juniors – Maud
Bridge of Don Thistle – Lochee United
Burghead Thistle – Ardrossan Winton Rovers
Cambuslang Rangers – Fauldhouse United
Carluke Rovers – Sunnybank
Colony Park – Hurlford Utd
Coupar Angus – Yoker Athletic
Cruden Bay – Lanark United
Culter – Hermes
Cumbernauld United – Kilbirnie Ladeside
Downfield – Blantyre Victoria
Dufftown – Letham
Dundee Violet – Thorniewood United
Dyce Juniors – Buchanhaven Hearts
East Craigie – St Rochs
East Kilbride Thistle – Broughty Athletic
Ellon United – Dundee St James
Forfar United – Muirkirk
Forres Thistle – Tayport
Gartcairn – Aberdeen east End
Glasgow Perthshire – Ardeer Thistle
Greenock Juniors – Kirkintilloch Rob Roy
Hall Russell United – Renfrew
Irvine Meadow XI – Deveronside
Johnstone Burgh – Forfar West End
Kirriemuir Thistle – Petershill
Largs Thistle – Glasgow United
Lesmahagow Juniors – Dundee North End
Livingston United – Stoneyburn Juniors
Lochee Harp – Glenafton Athletic
Longside – Fraserburgh United
Lugar Boswell Thistle – Craigmark Burntonians
Nairn St Ninian – Shotts Bon Accord
Newmains United – Dalry Thistle
Pollok – Maybole Juniors
Rothie Rovers – Kilsyth Rangers
Saltcoats Victoria – West Calder United
Scone Thistle – New Elgin
Stonehaven – Syngenta
Stoneywood Parkvale – Wishaw Juniors
Troon – Benburb
Whitehills – Arthurlie

ROUND TWO (September 25th)

Aberdeen University – Bridge of Don United or Lochee United
Armadale Thistle – Dyce Juniors or Buchanhaven Hearts
Banks o' Dee or Harthill Royal – Stonehaven or Syngenta
Blairgowrie – Troon or Benburb
Brechin Victoria – Newmachar United
Burghead Thistle or Ardrossan Winton Rovers – Larkhall Thistle
Carluke Rovers or Sunnybank – Auchinleck Talbot or Montrose Roselea
Carnoustie Panmure – Longside or Fraserburgh United
Cumnock Juniors – Lochee Harp or Glenafton Athletic
Cruden Bay or Lanark United – East Kilbride Thistle or Broughty Athletic
Culter or Hermes – Beith Juniors or Maud
Downfield or Blantyre Victoria – Saltcoats Victoria or West Calder United
Dufftown or Letham – Forfar United or Muirkirk
Dundee Violet or Thorniewood United – Whitletts Victoria
East Craigie or St Roch's – Banchory St Ternan
Ellon United or Dundee St James – Johnstone Burgh or Forfar West End
Gartcairn or Aberdeen East End – Forres Thistle or Tayport
Girvan – Greenock Juniors or Kirkintilloch Rob Roy
Glasgow Perthshire or Ardeer Thistle – Scone Thistle or New Elgin
Glentanar – Pollok or Maybole
Hall Russell United or Renfrew – Lugar Boswell Thistle or Craigmark Burntonians
Irvine Meadow XI or Deveronside – Arbroath Victoria
Kirriemuir Thistle or Petershill – Stoneywood Parkvale or Wishaw Juniors
Largs Thistle or Glasgow United – Kello Rovers
Lesmahagow Juniors or Dundee North End – Colony Park or Hurlford United
Livingston United or Stoneyburn Juniors – Cumbernauld United or Kilbirnie Ladeside
Maryhill – Coupar Angus or Yoker Athletic
Nairn St Ninian or Shotts Bon Accord – Irvine Victoria
Newmains United or Dalry Thistle – Bathgate Thistle or Vale of Leven
Rossvale – Cambuslang Rangers or Fauldhouse United
Rothie Rovers or Kilsyth Rangers – Whitehills or Arthurlie
St Anthony's – Ashfield or Islavale

Round Three October 23rd

Round Four November 27th

Subsequent Rounds, dates to be confirmed

TEAMS IN LAST 16 OF THE SCOTTISH JUNIOR CUP (Round 5)

	2006/7	2007/8	2008/9	2009/10	2010/11	201/12	2012/13	2013/14	2014/15	2015/16	2016/17	2017/18	2018/19	2019/20
Ardrossan Winton Rovers					5									
Arthurlie	SF		QF			5			5	QF		5		
Ashfield			5			5								
Auchinleck Talbot		QF	W	5	W	F	W		W	QF	F	W	W	QF*
Ballingry Rovers		5												
Bathgate Thistle		W		QF										
Beith			5		5					W		QF		SF*
Bo'ness United				5	SF	QF	QF	QF				QF		
Bonnyrigg Rose					QF	SF			5	5	SF	5		
Broughty Athletic														QF*
Cambuslang Rangers													5	
Camelon	5	5	5				QF	SF	5	QF				
Carluke Rovers											5			
Carnoustie Panmure			5							5		QF		
Clydebank		QF	F	SF									QF	
Craigmark Burntonians													5	
Cumnock		F					QF	QF						
Dalry Thistle					SF			5						
Darvel										5				QF*
Dunbar United											5			
Dundonald Bluebell							5	QF						
East Kilbride Thist	5													
Fauldhouse United									5					5
Gartcairn											QF			5
Girvan													5	
Glenafton Athletic		QF						F			W			
Glenrothes			5		5									
Haddington Athletic					5									
Hermes										5				
Hill of Beath Hawthorn				QF										
Hurlford United								W	SF	SF		F	SF	QF*
Irvine Meadow	5		QF	QF	QF	QF	5	SF				5		5
Jeanfield Swifts							5							
Kello Rovers														QF
Kelty Hearts	F					5	QF			5	5			
Kilbirnie Ladeside					QF	5			5	QF		5		
Kilsyth Rangers	5						5	5						
Kilwinning Rangers	SF					QF				SF	QF		QF	
Kinnoull						5								
Kirkintilloch Rob Roy			SF	5	QF		5				QF	QF		5
Lanark United	QF	QF	5											
Largs Thistle				F		SF							F	
Larkhall Thistle						5								
Lesmahagow									5					
Linlithgow Rose	W			W			F		SF	5	SF	5		
Lochee United	5	5		SF		5	5					SF	SF	
Luncarty											5			
Maryhill				5							5			
Maybole		5												
Montrose Roselea			5											
Musselburgh Athletic	5	5			F				F					
Neilston	QF	5												QF
Newtongrange Star		5	QF	5					5					
Penicuik Athletic								5	QF		5			
Petershill	5		QF		5					5	5			5
Pollok	QF	SF	SF				5		QF	F		5	QF	SF*
Pumpherston							5							
Renfrew					5						5			
Rossvale										5			5	
Rosyth													5	
Rutherglen Glencairn				5			SF	5					5	
Sauchie					5			5			QF	5		
Shettleston					5				QF					
Shotts Bon Accord		5		5		W	SF	5						
St Andrews United						QF			5					
St Rochs						5							5	5
Stoneywood Parkvale														5
Tayport				QF				5						5
Thorniewood United			5											
Thornton Hibs		SF											5	
Tranent	5													
Troon													QF	
Whitletts Vics				5				QF						
Wishaw												SF		
Yoker Athletic	QF							5	QF			5		

JUNIOR CLUBS IN THE SCOTTISH CUP

Since 2007/8 the 3 Regional Champions and the Scottish Junior Cup winners have been eligible to play in the Scottish Cup. They join Girvan who are "legacy members" of the SFA from their days as a Senior clubs, and Linlithgow Rose and Banks o' Dee who achieved club licenses in recent seasons.

The Junior clubs participating have been:

Auchinleck Talbot
2009/10, 2011/12, 2013/14, 2014/15, 2015/16, 2016/17, 2018/19, 2019/20
Banks o' Dee
2008/9, 2009/10, 2014/15-2020/21 inclusive
Bathgate Thistle
2008/9
Beith
2010/11, 2016/17, 2018/19
Bo'ness United
2010/11, 2011/12, 2014/15
Bonnyrigg Rose
2009/10, 2012/13. 2016/17
Culter
2007/8, 2011/12, 2013/14, 2014/15
Girvan
2007/8-2019/20 inclusive
Glenafton Ath
2017/18
Hermes
2012/13, 2015/16
Hurlford United
2014/15
Irvine Meadow
2009/10, 2011/12, 2012/13
Kelty Hearts
2015/16, 2017/18
Lochee United
2008/9, 2019/20
Linlithgow Rose
2007/8, 2010/11, 2013/14, 2014/15-2017/18 inclusive
Pollok
2007/8, 2008/9
Shotts Bon Accord
2012/13
Sunnybank
2010/11

There were no Junior Champions involved in the 2020/1 Cup. Banks o' Dee (North) already qualified as full SFA members, the East did not declare a Champion in 2019/20 and West Champions Auchinleck Talbot were in abeyance for the season.

SCOTTISH JUNIOR CUP FINALS and SEMI FINALISTS

Season	Winners	Runners Up		LOSING SEMI FINALISTS	
1886/87	Fairfield Govan	Edinburgh Woodburn	3 1 after protest	Westburn	Burnbank Swifts
1887/88	Wishaw Thistle	Maryhill	3 1 after 2 protests	Hamilton West End	Carluke Milton Rovers
1888/89	Burnbank Swifts	West Benhar Violet	4 1	Hamilton West End	Edinburgh Woodburn
1889/90	Burnbank Swifts	Benburb	3 1 after protest	Kilmarnock Shawbank	Carluke Milton Rovers
1890/91	Vale of Clyde	Chrytson Athletic	2 0 after 1-1 draw	Leith Rangers	Newton Thistle
1891/92	Minerva	West Benhar Violet	5 2	Vale of Clyde	Darvel
1892/93	Vale of Clyde	Dumbarton Fern	3 2 after 1-1 draw	Crown Athletic	Haywood Wanderers
1893/94	Ashfield	Renfrew Victoria	3 0 after 1-1 draw	Broxburn Athletic	Blantyre Vics
1894/95	Ashfield	West Calder Wanderers	2 1 after 1-1 draw	Lenzie	Glasgow Perthshire
1895/96	Cambuslang Hibs	Parkhead	2 1	Broxburn Athletic	Strathclyde
1896/97	Strathclyde	Dunfermline Juniors	2 0	Captain Colt's Rovers	Ashfield
1897/98	Dalziel Rovers	Parkhead	2 1	Captain Colt's Rovers	Glenbuck Cherrypickers
1898/99	Parkhead	Westmarch XI	4 1	Dalziel Rovers	Duntocher Hibs
1899/00	Maryhill	Rugby XI	3 2	Holytown Thistle	Cambuslang Hibs
1900/01	Burnbank Athletic	Maryhill	2 0	Parkhead Athletic	Renfrew Vics
1901/02	Glencairn	Maryhill	1 0	Dunipace	Strathclyde
1902/03	Parkhead	Larkhall Thistle	3 0	Ardeer Thistle	Burnbank Athletic
1903/04	Vale of Clyde	Parkhead	3 0	Maryhill	Darvel
1904/05	Ashfield	Renfrew Victoria	2 1	Maryhill	Arniston Rangers
1905/06	Dunipace	Rob Roy	1 0 after 2-2 draw	Maryhill	Kirkintilloch Rob Roy
1906/07	Strathclyde	Maryhill	1 0 after two 1-1 draws	St Ninian's Thistle	Clydebank
1907/08	Larkhall Thistle	Queen's Park Hampden XI	1 0	St Ninian's Thistle	Cowie Wanderers
1908/09	Kilwinning Rangers	Strathclyde	1 0 ater 0-0 draw	Penicuik	Yoker Athletic
1909/10	Ashfield	Kilwinning Rangers	3 0 after protest	Port Glasgow	Arniston Rangers#
1910/11	Burnbank Athletic	Petershill	1 0 after 2-2 draw	Cambuslang Rangers	Ardrossan Winton Rovers
1911/12	Petershill	Denny Hibs	5 0	Cambuslang Rangers	Kilbirnie Ladeside
1912/13	Inverkeithing United	Dunipace	1 0	Kilbirnie Ladeside	Larkhall Thistle
1913/14	Larkhall Thistle	Ashfield	1 0 after draws 0-0, 1-1	Renfrew	Yoker Athletic
1914/15	Parkhead	Port Glasgow	2 0	Ashfield	Petershill
1915/16	Petershill	Parkhead	2 0	Cambuslang Rangers	Larkhall Thistle
1916/17	St Mirren Juniors	Renfrew	1 0 after 0-0 draw	Cambuslang Rangers	Bellshill Athletic
1917/18	Petershill awarded cup			St Mirren Juniors	Parkhead / Renfrew
1918/19	Glencairn	St Anthonys	1 0 after 1-1 draw	Kilsyth Emmet	Parkhead
1919/20	Parkhead	Cambuslang Rangers	2 0	Cumnock	Burnbank
1920/21	Rob Roy	Ashfield	1 0	Cambuslang Rangers	Parkhead
1921/22	St Rochs	Kilwinning Rangers	2 1 after protest	Cambuslang Rangers	Rutherglen Glencairn
1922/23	Musselburgh Bruntonians	Arniston Rangers	2 0	Carluke Rovers	Port Glasgow Ath Juniors
1923/24	Parkhead	Baillieston	3 1 after 1-1 draw	Auchinleck Talbot	Blantyre Celtic
1924/25	Saltcoats Victoria	St Anthonys	2 1 after draws 1-1, 3-3	Shettleston	Shieldmuir Celtic
1925/26	Strathclyde	Bridgeton Waverley	2 0 after 1-1 draw	Parkhead Athletic	St Rochs
1926/27	Glencairn	Cambuslang Rangers	2 1	Tranent	Darvel
1927/28	Maryhill Hibs	Burnbank Athletic	6 2	Coalburn	Saltcoats Vics
1928/29	Dundee Violet	Denny Hibs	4 0 after protest and 2-2 draw	Coalburn	Burnbank Athletic
1929/30	Newtongrange Star	Hall Russell	3 0	Croy Celtic	Larkhall Royal Albert
1930/31	Denny Hibs	Burnbank Athletic	1 0	Rothesay Royal Vivs	Lochee Harp
1931/32	Glasgow Perthshire	Rob Roy	2 1	Larkhall Thistle	Rosslyn Juniors
1932/33	Yoker Athletic	Tranent	4 2 after 0-0 draw	Renfrew	Bonnyrigg Rose
1933/34	Benburb	Bridgeton Waverley	3 1	Lochee Harp	Ardrossan Winton Rovers
1934/35	Tranent	Petershill	6 1	Shawfield	Wishaw
1935/36	Benburb	Yoker Athletic	1 0 after 1-1 draw	Renfrew	St Anthonys
1936/37	Arthurlie	Rob Roy	5 1	Morton Juniors	Glasgow Perthshire
1937/38	Cambuslang Rangers`	Benburb	3 2	Dunipace	Blantyre Celtic
1938/39	Glencairn	Shawfield	2 1	Benburb	Cambuslang Rangers
1939/40	Maryhill	Morton Juniors	1 0	Larkhall Royal Albert	Arthurlie
1940/41	Glasgow Perthshire	Armadale Thistle	3 1 after draws 2-2, 0-0	Petershill	Winchburgh Albion
1941/42	Clydebank	Vale of Clyde	4 2	Polkemmet	St Anthonys
1942/43	Rob Roy	Benburb	3 1 after draws 1-1, 0-0	Bedlay	Petershill
1943/44	Glasgow Perthshire	Blantyre Vics	1 0	Ardeer Recreation	Maryhill
1944/45	Burnbank Athletic	Cambuslang Rangers	3 1 after protest	St Rochs	Pollok
1945/46	Fauldhouse United	Arthurlie	2 0	Polkemmet	Blantyre Celtic

1946/47	Shawfield	Bo'ness United	2 1 after 1-1 draw	Irvine Meadow	Renfrew
1947/48	Bo'ness United	Irvine Meadow	2 1	Bathgate Thistle	Shawfield
1948/49	Auchinleck Talbot	Petershill	3 2	Benburb	Newtongrange Star
1949/50	Blantyre Vics	Cumnock	3 0	Ardeer Recreation	Stoneyburn
1950/51	Petershill	Irvine Meadow	1 0	Broxburn Athletic	Armadale Thistle
1951/52	Kilbirnie Ladeside	Camelon	1 0	Lugat Boswell Thistle	Carnoustie Panmure
1952/53	Vale of Leven	Annbank United	1 0	Arniston Rangers	Ashfield
1953/54	Sunnybank	Lochee Harp	2 1	Clydebank	Baillieston
1954/55	Kilsyth Rangers	Duntocher Hibs	4 1 after 1-1 draw	Ashfield	Armadale Thistle
1955/56	Petershill	Lugar Boswell Thitle	4 1	Whitletts Vics	Broxburn Athletic
1956/57	Banks o' Dee	Kilsyth Rangers	1 0	Loanhead Mayflower	Duntocher Hibs
1957/58	Shotts Bon Accord	Pumpherston	2 0	Baillieston	Irvine Meadow
1958/59	Irvine Meadow	Shettleston	2 1	Carluke Rovers	Johnstone Burgh
1959/60	St Andrews United	Greenock	3 1	Thornton Hibs	Ardeer Thistle
1960/61	Dunbar United	Cambuslang Rangers	2 0 after 2-2 draw	Ashfield	Dundee St Josephs
1961/62	Rob Roy	Renfrew	1 0 after 1-1 draw	Glenafton Athletic	Newburgh
1962/63	Irvine Meadow	Glenafton Athletic	2 1	Bonnyrigg Rose	Craigmark Burntonians
1963/64	Johnstone Burgh	Cambuslang Rangers	3 0 after 1-1 draw	Irvine Meadow	Kirkintilloch Rob Roy
1964/65	Linlithgow Rose	Baillieston	4 1	Aberdeen Rosemount	Kilsyth Rangers
1965/66	Bonnyrigg Rose	Whitburn	6 1 after 1-1 draw	Penicuik Athletic	Shettleston
1966/67	Kilsyth Rangers	Glencairn	3 1 after 1-1 draw	Carluke Rovers	Johnstone Burgh
1967/68	Johnstone Burgh	Glenrothes	4 3 after 2-2 draw	Larkhall Thistle	Lochee Harp
1968/69	Cambuslang Rangers`	Rob Roy	1 0	Irvine Meadow	Linlithgow Rose
1969/70	Blantyre Vics	Penicuik Athletic	1 0 after 2-2 draw	Ardrossan Winton Rovers	Ashfield
1970/71	Cambuslang Rangers`	Newtongrange Star	2 1	Dalkeith Thistle	Broxburn Athletic
1971/72	Cambuslang Rangers`	Bonnyrigg Rose	3 2 after 1-1 draw	Newtongrange Star	Johnstone Burgh
1972/73	Irvine Meadow	Cambuslang Rangers	1 0 after draws 3-3, 2-2	East Kilbride Thistle	Newburgh
1973/74	Cambuslang Rangers`	Linlithgow Rose	3 1	Glasgow Perthshire	Blantyre Vics
1974/75	Glenrothes	Glencairn	1 0	Kilbirnie Ladeside	Ashfield
1975/76	Bo'ness United	Darvel	3 0	Lanark United	Kilbirnie Ladeside
1976/77	Kilbirnie Ladeside	Rob Roy	3 1	Shettleston	Lesmahagow
1977/78	Bonnyrigg Rose	Stonehouse Violet	1 0	Carnoustie Panmure	Renfrew
1978/79	Cumnock	Bo'ness United	1 0	Pollok	Glenafton Athletic
1979/80	Baillieston	Benburb	2 0 AET and 2-2 draw	Dunipace	Lochee United
1980/81	Pollok	Arthurlie	1 0	Bo'ness United	Forth Wanderers
1981/82	Blantyre Vics	Baillieston	1 0	Bonnyrigg Rose	Kirkintilloch Rob Roy
1982/83	East Kilbride Thistle	Bo'ness United	2 0	Auchinleck Talbot	Pollok
1983/84	Bo'ness United	Baillieston	2 0	Auchinleck Talbot	Darvel
1984/85	Pollok	Petershill	3 1 after 1-1 draw	Darvel	Downfield
1985/86	Auchinleck Talbot	Pollok	3 2	Cumnock	Kilbirnie Ladeside
1986/87	Auchinleck Talbot	Kilbirnie Ladeside	1 0 after 1-1 draw	Irvine Meadow	Arthurlie
1987/88	Auchinleck Talbot	Petershill	1 0	Newtongrange Star	Whitburn
1988/89	Cumnock	Ormiston Primrose	1 0	Shotts Bon Accord	Lesmahagow
1989/90	Hill of Beath Hawthorn	Lesmahagow	1 0	Linlithgow Rose	Whitburn
1990/91	Auchinleck Talbot	Newtongrange Star	1 0	Arthurlie	Glenafton Athletic
1991/92	Auchinleck Talbot	Glenafton Athletic	4 0	Beith	Whitburn
1992/93	Glenafton Athletic	Tayport	1 0	Auchinleck Talbot	Lesmahagow
1993/94	Largs Thistle	Glenafton Athletic	1 0	Arthurlie	Kilwinning Rangers
1994/95	Camelon	Whitburn	2 0 AET	Lochee United	Glenafton Athletic
1995/96	Tayport	Camelon	2 1	Auchinleck Talbot	Pollok
1996/97	Pollok	Tayport	3 1	Blantyre Vics	Arthurlie
1997/98	Arthurlie	Pollok	4 0	Maryhill	Kilwinning Rangers
1998/99	Kilwinning Rangers	Kelty Hearts	1 0	Petershill	Arthurlie
1999/00	Whitburn	Johnstone Burgh	2 2 AET, 4-3 pens	Benburb	Shotts Bon Accord
2000/1	Renfrew	Carnoustie Panmure	0 0 AET, 6-5 pens	Auchinleck Talbot	Shettleston
2001/2	Linlithgow Rose	Auchinleck Talbot	1 0	Kilwinning Rangers	Tayport
2002/3	Tayport	Linlithgow Rose	1 0	Bo'ness United	Maryhill
2003/4	Carnoustie Panmure	Tayport	0 0 AET, 6-5 pens	Glenrothes	Hill of Beath Hawthorn
2004/5	Tayport	Lochee United	2 0	Maryhill	Renfrew
2005/6	Auchinleck Talbot	Bathgate Thistle	2 1	Irvine Meadow	Tayport
2006/7	Linlithgow Rose	Kelty Hearts	2 1 AET	Kilwinning Rangers	Arthurlie
2007/8	Bathgate Thistle	Cumnock	2 1	Pollok	Thornton Hibs
2008/9	Auchinleck Talbot	Clydebank	2 1	Pollok	Kirkintilloch Rob Roy
2009/10	Linlithgow Rose	Largs Thistle	1 0	Lochee United	Clydebank
2010/11	Auchinleck Talbot	Musselburgh Athletic	2 1 AET	Bo'ness United	Dalry Thistle
2011/12	Shotts Bon Accord	Auchinleck Talbot	2 1	Largs Thistle	Bonnyrigg Rose
2012/13	Auchinleck Talbot	Linlithgow Rose	1 0	Rutherglen Glencairn	Shotts Bon Accord
2013/14	Hurlford United	Glenafton Athletic	3 0	Irvine Meadow	Camelon
2014/15	Auchinleck Talbot	Musselburgh Athletic	2 1	Linlithgow Rose	Hurlford United
2015/16	Beith	Pollok	1 1 4-3p	Hurlford United	Kilwinning Rangers
2016/17	Glenafton Athletic	Auchinleck Talbot	2 1	Bonnyrigg Rose	Linlithgow Rose
2017/18	Auchinleck Talbot	Hurlford United	3 2	Lochee United	Wishaw
2018/19	Auchinleck Talbot	Largs Thistle	2 0	Lochee United	Hurlford United

EAST REGION JUNIORS

Traditionally the East Region of Scottish Junior football included the counties of Angus, Perthshire, Fife, East, Mid and West Lothian, Clackmannanshire, parts of Stirlingshire as well as the cities of Dundee and Edinburgh.

At the end of 2017/18 the majority of the clubs from the Lothians and Fife resigned in order to join the East of Scotland Senior League. The remaining Fife clubs all resigned at the end of 2019/20. Consequently , the East Region now comprises two distinct geographic groupings - Tayside and West Lothian.

LEAGUE STRUCTURE 2020/1

NORTH LEAGUE (17)	SOUTH LEAGUE (12)
Arbroath Victoria	Armadale Thistle
Blairgowrie	Bathgate Thistle
Brechin Victoria	Bo'ness United Juniors
Broughty Athletic	Harthill Royal
Carnoustie Panmure	Linlithgow Rose Community
Coupar Angus	Livingston United
Downfield	Pumpherston
Dundee North End	Sauchie Community
East Craigie	Stoneyburn
Forfar Albion	Syngenta
Forfar West End	West Calder United
Kirriemuir Thistle	Whitburn
Lochee Harp	
Lochee United	
Scone Thistle	
Tayport	
Violet	

At the end of the 2020/1 season the South League clubs all applied to join the East of Scotland League.

The North League sides formed a new league, the Midlands League. This is still under the auspices of the Scottish Junior FA but now feeds into the Highland League section of the Scottish pyramid.

LOCHEE HARP JUNIORS (DUNDEE) F.C.

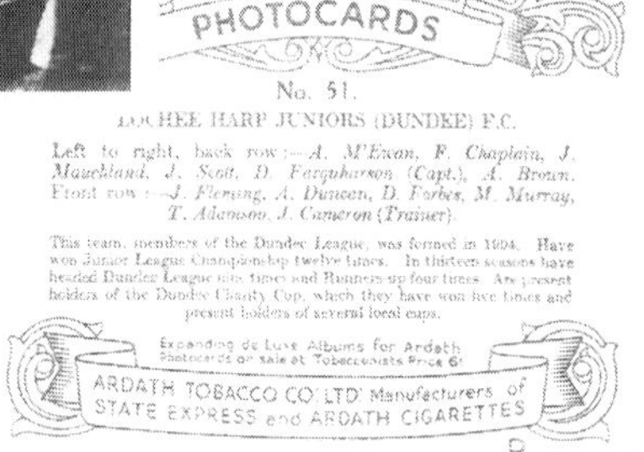

PHOTOCARDS

No. 51.

LOCHEE HARP JUNIORS (DUNDEE) F.C.

Left to right, back row :—*A. M'Ewan, F. Chaplain, J. Mauchland, J. Scott, D. Farquharson (Capt.), A. Brown.* Front row :—*J. Fleming, A. Duncan, D. Forbes, M. Murray, T. Adamson, J. Cameron (Trainer).*

This team, members of the Dundee League, was formed in 1904. Have won Junior League Championship twelve times. In thirteen seasons have headed Dundee League nine times and Runners-up four times. Are present holders of the Dundee Charity Cup, which they have won five times and present holders of several local cups.

Expanding de Luxe Albums for Ardath Photocards on sale at Tobacconists Price 6d

ARDATH TOBACCO CO. LTD. Manufacturers of STATE EXPRESS and ARDATH CIGARETTES

D

McBookie.com East Super League North 2020/21

	ARB	BLA	BRE	BRO	CAR	COU	DOW	NEND	EAS	FUTD	FWEN	KIR	HARP	LOCU	SCO	TAY	VIO
Arbroath Victoria												Dec 5 4-1	Dec 19 5-0				
Blairgowrie							Dec 5 0-1									Nov 21 0-1	
Brechin Victoria		Dec 19 5-2		Dec 5 0-3				Nov 21 2-2									
Broughty Athletic		Nov 28 3-1					Nov 21 1-3										Dec 12 2-0
Carnoustie Panmure										Dec 19 2-5					Nov 21 10-0		
Coupar Angus														Nov 28 0-11			
Downfield			Dec 12 1-1														
Dundee North End																	Nov 28 1-1
East Craigie						Nov 21 12-0				Dec 5 4-0						Dec 19 1-3	
Forfar United											Nov 28 1-1			Dec 12 0-3			
Forfar West End				Dec 19 2-5									Nov 21 1-0				
Kirrie Thistle					Nov 28 1-2										Dec 12 3-0		
Lochee Harp					Dec 12 1-6				Nov 28 1-7								
Lochee United								Dec 19 3-1				Nov 21 2-1	Dec 5 3-0				
Scone Thistle	Nov 28 1-3																
Tayport			Nov 28 7-0								Dec 12 3-1						
Violet										Nov 21 3-2							

McBookie.com East Super League South 2020/21

	ARM	BAT	BON	FAU	HAR	LIV	PUM	SAU	STO	SYN	WES	WHI
Armadale Thistle					Nov 28 6-1							
Bathgate Thistle				Dec 19 1-2								
Bo'ness United CFC		Nov 28 2-0										Dec 12 3-1
Fauldhouse United												
Harthill Royal												
Livingston United								Dec 19 3-2				
Pumpherston										Nov 28 1-6		
Sauchie CFC												Nov 28 1-3
Stoneyburn						Nov 28 1-1	Dec 19 3-3					
Syngenta	Dec 12 1-2		Dec 5 1-1					Nov 21 6-0			Dec 19 5-3	
West Calder United		Dec 12 5-0		Nov 28 1-2								
Whitburn												

	EAST SUPER LEAGUE NORTH	GP	W	D	L	GF	GA	GD	PTS
1	Lochee United	5	5	0	0	22	2	20	15
2	Tayport	4	4	0	0	14	2	12	12
3	Broughty Athletic	5	4	0	1	14	6	8	12
4	Dundee East Craigie	4	3	0	1	24	4	20	9
5	Carnoustie Panmure	4	3	0	1	20	7	13	9
6	Arbroath Victoria	3	3	0	0	12	2	10	9
7	Downfield	3	2	1	0	5	2	3	7
8	Brechin Victoria	5	1	2	2	8	15	-7	5
9	Dundee Violet	3	1	1	1	4	5	-1	4
10	Forfar West End	4	1	1	2	5	9	-4	4
11	Forfar United	5	1	1	3	8	13	-5	4
12	Kirriemuir Thistle	4	1	0	3	6	8	-2	3
13	Dundee North End	3	0	2	1	4	6	-2	2
14	Blairgowrie Juniors	4	0	0	4	3	10	-7	0
15	Scone Thistle	3	0	0	3	1	16	-15	0
16	Lochee Harp	5	0	0	5	2	22	-20	0
17	Coupar Angus	2	0	0	2	0	23	-23	0

	EAST SUPER LEAGUE SOUTH	GP	W	D	L	GF	GA	GD	PTS
1	Syngenta	5	3	1	1	19	7	12	10
2	Bo'ness United Junior	3	2	1	0	6	2	4	7
3	Armadale Thistle	2	2	0	0	8	2	6	6
4	Fauldhouse United	2	2	0	0	4	2	2	6
5	Livingston United	2	1	1	0	4	3	1	4
6	West Calder United	3	1	0	2	9	7	2	3
7	Whitburn Juniors	2	1	0	1	4	4	0	3
8	Stoneyburn	2	0	2	0	4	4	0	2
9	Pumpherston	2	0	1	1	4	9	-5	1
10	Harthill Royal	1	0	0	1	1	6	-5	0
11	Bathgate Thistle	3	0	0	3	1	9	-8	0
12	Sauchie Juniors Community	3	0	0	3	3	12	-9	0

PHOTOCARDS

No. 49.

DUNDEE VIOLET JUNIORS F.C.

Left to right, back row:—*W. M'Ewan, H. M'Kenzie, D. Cargill, A. Ireland, J. Calder (Capt.), J. Mudie.* Front row:—*R. Brown, D. M'Gurk, D. M'Naughton, P. Finnegan, D. Wilson.*

Formed in 1888, this is the only club north of the Firth to win the Scottish Cup (1928/29). By winning the Forfarshire Cup seven times, the club has established a record which will not easily be broken.

EAST JUNIOR SUPER LEAGUE - ALL TIME POSITIONS	2002-3	2003-4	2004-5	2005-6	2006-7	2007-8	2008-9	2009-10	2010-11	2011-12	2012-13	2013-14	2014-15	2015-16	2016-17	2017-18	2018/19
Armadale Thistle												11	14				
Arniston Rangers	4	5	9	11													
Ballingry Rovers												13	Res				
Bathgate Thistle	3	7	7	2	7	8	8	3	8	11							
Bo'ness United		6	5	7	11		10	1	1	4	4	1	2	4	3	8	
Bonnyrigg Rose	6	3	4	6	2	4	1	10	4	1	2	3	7	1	2	1	
Broughty Athletic														10	7	10	2
Broxburn Athletic											6	7	8	6	8	5	
Camelon			11		10	3	2	6	10	6	3	5	12	11	12	9	
Carnoustie Panmure	10		8	8	4	11				10	9	12	13	12	11	12	7
Downfield																	11
Dundee North End	9	12		12													
Dundee Violet	12																
Dundonald Bluebell															6	4	
Edinburgh United	11																
Fauldhouse United													10	13	16		10
Forfar West End							11		6	Res						16	6
Glenrothes	8	8	6	10		9	7	12									12
Hill of Beath Haws	2	11		3	6	10	6	8	2	2	8	6	9	8	10	7	
Jeanfield Swifts															13	14	
Kelty Hearts		10				7	5	9	9	5	5	14	1	2	1		
Kennoway Star Hearts																15	8
Kinnoull					12												
Kirrie Thistle																	9
Linlithgow Rose	5	1	3	5	1	5	3	2	3	3	1	2	3	3	9	2	
Lochee United		4	1	9	5	1	9	5	5	7	10	10	15		5	6	1
Musselburgh Athletic								7	7	8	7	8	11	7	15		
Newtongrange Star								4	12			4	4	5	14	11	
Oakley United	7	9	10		9	12											
Penicuik Athletic													6	9	4	3	
Sauchie											11	9	5	14		13	
St Andrews United										9	12	16		15			
Tayport	1	2	2	1	8	6	12		11			15		16			5
Thornton Hibs			12														3
Whitburn				4	3	2	4	11									4

East Region Officials 2020-21

HONORARY PRESIDENT
John Wilson (Carlsberg)

PRESIDENT
Robert Napier (Bathgate Thistle)

VICE-PRESIDENT
Mark Stanton (Lochee United)

GENERAL SECRETARY
John Reilly

ASSISTANT SECRETARY
Syd McAlpine

ACCOUNTANT
J.(Chic) Spence,

DISCIPLINE/APPEALS COMMITTEE
Steven McMillan, (Stoneyburn), Dave Don (Broughty Athletic), Neil Hardie (Arbroath Vics), Ian Patrick (Lochgelly Albert), Mark Johnson (Carnoustie Panmure), Scott Watson (Armadale Thistle)

DELEGATES TO SJFA
Robert Napier and Marc Stanton

East Juniors Central Division - All Time Positions	2006-7	2007-8	2008-9	2009-10	2010-11	2011-12	2012-13
Ballingry Rovers	3	1					
Bankfoot Athletic	12	10	7	7	6	5	12
Crossgates Primrose	10	6	8	10	9	9	10
Dundonald Bluebell	1			5	2	2	3
Jeanfield Swifts	7	5	4	4	4	1	
Kinnoull						3	1
Kirkcaldy YM	2	Ab	3	3	3	7	2
Lochgelly Albert	4	3	9	11	5	4	8
Lochore Welfare	5	7	6	6	7	11	5
Luncarty	6	11	13	14	13	13	13
Newburgh	11	9	12	12	11	6	4
Oakley United				2	1		
Rosyth			2	8	12	10	6
Scone Thistle		8	11	13	10	Ab	11
St Andrews United		2	1				
Steelend Vics	8	12	10	9	8	12	9
Thornton Hibs	9	4	5	1		8	7

From 2006 until 2013 the third tier of the East Region operated with three Divisions. The Perth area clubs were transferred from Tayside and grouped with the Fife clubs to form a Central Division. In 2013 a two-division set-up was established with the Central Division clubs split between the North and South Leagues. Fife clubs were vulnerable to being switched between divisions without consultation.

JUNIOR LEAGUE CHAMPIONS Pre 2002/3

	Lothians	Fife	Tayside
1968/9	Bo'ness United	Thornton Hibs	
1969/70	Arniston Rangers	Glenrothes	Blairgowrie
1970/1	Musselburgh Ath	Glenrothes	Blairgowrie
1971/2	Arniston Rangers	Oakley United	Blairgowrie
1972/3	Broxburn Athletic	Newburgh	Jeanfield Swifts
1973/4	Broxburn Athletic	Lochgelly Albert	Kirrie Thistle
1974/5	Linlithgow Rose	Glenrothes	Blairgowrie
1975/6	Bonnyrigg Rose	Glenrothes	Carnoustie P
1976/7	Bonnyrigg Rose	Newburgh	Carnoustie P
1977/8	Linlithgow Rose	Glenrothes	Carnoustie P
1978/9	Penicuik Athletic	Oakley United	Carnoustie P
1979/80	Camelon	Oakley United	Lochee Utd
1980/1	Penicuik Athletic	Halbeath	Carnoustie P
1981/2	Linlithgow Rose	Leven	Lochee Utd
1982/3	Fauldhouse Utd	Dindonald Bluebell	Kinnoull
1983/4	Linlithgow Rose	Glenrothes	Kinnoull
1984/5	Bonnyrigg Rose	Glenrothes	Lochee Harp
1985/6	Whitburn	Oakley United	Lochee Harp
1986/7	Whitburn	Hill of Beath H	Lochee Utd
1987/8	Linlithgow Rose	Oakley United	Downfield
1988/9	Whitburn	Hill of Beath H	Downfield
1989/90	Whitburn	St Andrews Utd	Downfield
1990/1	Newtongrange Star	Kelty Hearts	Forfar West End
1991/2	Newtongrange Star	Kelty Hearts	Tayport
1992/3	Fauldhouse Utd	Kelty Hearts	Tayport
1993/4	Camelon	Hill of Beath H	Tayport
1994/5	Camelon	Hill of Beath H	Tayport
1995/6	Whitburn	Hill of Beath H	Tayport
1996/7	Linlithgow Rose	Kelty Hearts	St Josephs
1997/8	Whitburn	Hill of Beath H	Dundee NE
1998/9	Linlithgow Rose	Kelty Hearts	Tayport
1999/00	Linlithgow Rose	Hill of Beath H	Tayport
2000/1	Whitburn	Oakley United	Tayport
2001/2	Linlithgow Rose	Hill of Beath H	Tayport

EAST PREMIER LEAGUE ALL-TIME POSITIONS	2006-7	2007-8	2008-9	2009-10	2010-11	2011-12	2012-13	2013-14	2014-15	2015-16	2016-17	2017/18
Armadale Thistle	5	11		9	7	10	4			13	15	
Arniston Rangers	8	8	6	4	9	12		9	6	4	6	12
Ballingry Rovers			7	6	6	7	2					
Bathgate Thistle							6	8	13	6	8	13
Blackburn United												5
Blairgowrie			8	11								
Bo'ness United		1										
Broughty Athletic					8	9	12	7	3			
Broxburn Athletic					3	2						
Carnoustie Panmure			3	5	2							
Dalkeith Thistle							7	3	4	7	7	14
Downfield						11					10	10
Dunbar United												7
Dundee North End	6	5	12						15	12		
Dundee Violet							10	11	8		14	
Dundonald Bluebell		9	11						5	2		
Edinburgh United									9	15		
Falkirk										10		
Fauldhouse United			9	10				2				2
Forfar West End		2		2					10	8	3	
Glenrothes	1				4	8	11	5	14		11	9
Haddington Athletic										5	9	3
Jeanfield Swifts							8	4	7	1		
Kelty Hearts	2											
Kennoway Star Hearts										9	2	
Kinnoull		7	5	3	10			10	16			
Kirkcaldy YM								13				
Kirrie Thistle								15				16
Livingston United								14				
Lochee Harp	11											
Lochee United										3		
Montrose Roselea	7	10		12				12	11	11		
Musselburgh Athletic	4	4	1									1
Newtongrange Star		3	2			6	1					
Oakley United			10			5	9	6	12	16		
Penicuik Athletic	9	6	4	7	5	4	5	1				
Pumpherston								16				
Rosyth	3	12										
Sauchie						1					1	
Scone Thistle	12											
St Andrews United	10			8	1	3	3		2		13	11
Tayport				1					1		5	4
Thornton Hibs					12					14		6
Tranent											4	8
Whitburn					11						12	15

The East Premier League was dissolved when a number of clubs left to join the Seniors in 2018.

East Juniors Playing Squads 2020/21

NB These are not comprehensive lists of players used - there will be some omissions. However, all players listed were associated with the club concerned during 2020/21 New signings refer to 2021/2.

Arbroath Victoria

Manager: Eddie Gray
Assistant: David Sturrock
Ryan Stirton
Max Reid
Sam Clark
Gary Grant (2020 Brechin Vics)
John Dye
Connor Gray
Matty Keogh
Ben Starkey
Jonathan Bastow
Marc Walker
Craig Tosh
Andi Manolache
Josh Chalmers
Zac Archer
Ben Fraser
Lewis Quinn
Struan Christie
Ross Fraser
Jack Whitton
Dean Hardie
Luke O'Brien
Michael Fotheringham

Armadale Thistle

Manager:
Colin "Scifo" Allison (ex Linlithgow Rose, retired at end of 2020/1)
Liam Gray
Ally McInnes
Robert Sloan
Liam Kane
Sammy Watson
Robbie Feeney
Tomas Murphy
Callum Rodger
Kyle Sampson
Stephen Horn
Ryan Slessor
Colin Leiper
Fraser Keast
Jonathan Clements
John James Henderson
Scott Dalziel

New Signings
Conor Shaw (ex Pumpherston, St Andrews United)

Bathgate Thistle

Manager: Andrew Colley (until March 2021), Stewart Devine (from March 2021, ex Stirling Albion, Stranraer etc)
Assistant: Sean Roycroft (ex Stirling Albion, Broxburn Ath)
Fraser Cormack
Stewart Devine
Laurie Cunningham
Grant Ferguson
Kenny Knox
Paul McCarthy
Willie Rodger
Ross Mackay
Kieran Sweeney
Jordan Thomson
Jakub Weina
Grant Plenderleith
Chris Rooney
Mike Zaleski
Darrel Adams
Lewis McArthur
Aaron Reid (ex Hearts, Scotland Youths)
Brayden Docherty

Blairgowrie

Manager: Mark Brash
Matty Adam
Gary Axworthy
Ryan Beedie
Rudi Brown
Steven Findlay
Corey Gray
Robbie Hood
Cammy Johnstone (2020 ex Montrose, Forfar WE,)
Sean Kelly
Drew Madoc-Jones
Greg McDonald
Callan McKenzie (2020 ex North End)
Cammy McManus
Liam McPherson
Ben Middleton
Darren Neave
Gordon O'Brien
Andy Pattullo (2020 ex Dundee Violet, Forfar Albion)
Gordon Pirie
Ian Plenderleith
James Simpson
Kai Whytock
Paul Scott

Bo'ness United Juniors

Changed name to Bo'ness Athletic, Summer 2021
Manager: Willie Irvine (ex Stirling Albion, Airdrie, Hibernian, Dunfermline etc)
Dylan Paterson (to Arbroath June 2021)
Darren Gribben (ex Hamilton, Forfar etc)
Stuart McIntyre
Dylan Robb
Chris Snedden
Aidan Curran
Ryan Lemetti
Sean Brown
Robbie Taylor
Jason Mackay
Scott Sinclair
Aidan McKeown
Warren Paterson
Craig Snedden
Brett Ward
Grant Forrester
Gregor Dryden (to Bathgate Th Dec 2020)
Robbie McCafferty
Reece Boyle (2020 Blackburn United)
Tiwi Daramola (ex Stenhousemuir, Bo'ness United)
Mati Zata (ex Rangers, Dundee United)
Fraser Currid (2020 OL from Alloa Ath)

New Signings
Jonny Mitchell (2021Stirling Albion, ex Falkirk, Brentford)
Fraser Currid 92021 OL from Dunfermline Ath)

Brechin Victoria

Manager:
Aaron Stephen
AJ Govier
Cameron Fraser
Campbell Bruce
Charlie Wilson
Colin Lawson
David Cargill
Elliot Burns
Euan Duff
Greg Sturrock
Jack Gribben
Jordan Will
Kieran Longmuir
Kyle Brown
Lawrie Mitchell
Lewis Greig
Lewis Stracey (2020, OL from Montrose)
Matthew Solomons
Morgan Smith
Robbie Ferries
Sam Rogerson
Tyler Webley
Kyle Buik
Lee Hutcheson

New signings
Lewis Stracey (2021 Montrose)

Broughty Athletic

Manager: Jamie McCunnie; Assistant: Ralph Henderson (until May 2021)
Brad Smith (OL to Cowdenbeath Oct-Nov)
Jamie Reid
Connor McLeod
Daryl McKenzie (Released at end of 2020/1)
Andy Walls (ex Lochee United, East Craigie, Raith Rovers)
Josh Skelly
John Roberts (Released at end of 2020/1)
Paul Sludden (ex East Stirlingshire etc)
Ross McDonald (Released at end of 2020/1)
Sean Diamond
Greig McNaughton
Greg Warwick
Gregor Anderson
Marc Scott
Kieran Conway (Released at end of 2020/1)
Ryan Ferguson
Graham Hay (OL to Cowdenbeath Oct-Nov)
Ryan McCord
Bryan Duell (Released at end of 2020/1)
Ross McCord (Released at end of 2020/1)
Stewart McConnachie (Released at end of 2020/1)

Carnoustie Panmure

Manager: Phil McGuire (ex Aberdeen etc)
Bailey Steel
Brian Clark
Bruce Hearn
Cameron McMahon
Gordon McDonald
Jake Mair
Jamie Robbie
Jamie Winter
Pat Martin
Paul McLellan
Ryan Dignan
Ryan Roche
Ryan Suttie
Sam Simpson
Steven McPhee
Robert Smith (2020 Kirrie Thistle)

New Signings (2021/2)
Dale Reid (2021 Kirrie Thistle)
Bradley Bately
Finn Kemlo (2021 Dundee FC Youths)
Connor Coupe (2021 Brechin City)

Coupar Angus

Manager: Gordon Hennessy
Allan Cruikshank (ex Blairgowrie, Kirrie Th, Rattray, St Johnstone Youths)
Lewis Gemine
Tai McCluskey
Jamie Fyfe (ex Luncarty, Craigie, E Fife, Burntisland Utd)
Owen Kerrigan
Jamie Duncan
Ruiaridh Smith
Lee Davidson
Dylan Higgins
Sam King (ex E Fife, Berwick R, E

Stirling, Civil Service Strollers, Kirrie Thistle)
David Cattanach
Andrew Smith
Lewis McNaughton (ex Dundee Youths, Blairgowrie, Coupar Angus Ams)
Jamie Selfridge (ex Pitfour, Jeanfield S)
Cammy Henderson
Mark Pattullo
Cole Arnold
John Black

Downfield

Manager: Lewis Toshney
Ryan Blair (Died December 2020)
Sean Tucker
David Rae
John Farquharson
Lee Cameron
Andrew Walls
Connor McLeod (transferred to Broughty Ath Dec 2020)

Club Statement March 2021
"At a meeting of the management committee of Downfield JFC yesterday the current office bearers Peter Marr President, Dougie Morton Vice President and Ryan Marr Secretary/Treasurer resigned and were replaced by new office bearers Danny Martin President, Barry Cooney Vice President, Billy Buchanan Secretary and Jamie Thomson Treasurer".

Dundee North End

Manager: Tony McAulay (until Dec 2020), Ross Lunan (from Dec 2020)
Coach: Lee Wilkie (ex Dundee, Dundee United etc)
Greg Fairweather
Kieran Sturrock (2020 Carnoustie Panmure)
Ryan Smith
Owen McCabe
Jamie Gibb
Mark Stewart
Jordan Timmons
Ross Jamieson
Callum Petrie
Neal Ferrie
Jack Allan
Brian Rice
Frankie Devine
Cameron Black
Gary Sutherland (ex St Andrews, Lochore W, Dunfermline Ath)
Liam Montgomery
McKenzie Lemon (2020 Dundee United On Loan)

East Craigie

Manager:
Finlay Baird
Scott Brannan
Adam Brown
Cameron Christie
Liam Dunn
Lewis Fraser
Conen Howett
Fraser MacLeod
James Malone
Grady McGrath
Ross McNaughton
Paul Moran
Chris Mudie
Grant Paterson
Ian Ross
David Salisbury

Fauldhouse United

Manager: Chris Mackie
Darren Gribben (ex Hamilton, Berwick, Forfar Ath etc)
Kieran McDougall (ex Q Park, Hamilton Accies)
Liam Scullion (ex Stenhousemuir, Hamilton Accies)
Jacob Jackson (Ex Livingston Utd, Dunipace)
Liam Baillie (ex Harthill Royal, Clyde)
Jordan Critchley (ex Dundee Utd, Rangers)
Graeme Weir (ex Hearts, Raith Rovers etc)
Jake Hughes (ex Blantyre Vics)
Jordan Craig (Ex Petershill Arthurlie)
Declan McDonald (ex Hearts, Albion Rovers, Alloa)
Steven Weir (ex Stirling Albion, East Fife etc)
Conor Scullion (ex E Kilbride, Dumbarton, Albion Rovers)
Gary O'Hara (ex Livingston Utd, E Stirlingshire)
Steven Tart (ex Cumbernauld Colts, Arthurlie)
Scott Edgar (ex Maryhill, Benburb)
Lewis Collins (ex Dalry Thistle)

Squad 2021/2
Dan Tobin
Jacob Wetherby
Steven Weir
Liam Baillie
Steven Tart
Ally Morgan
Chris Lennon
Reece Lowdon
Chris Mackie Jnr
Josh Moore
Jack Breen
Connor Scullion
Nathan Khanna
Euan Moffat
Cameron Stokes
Dec McDonald
Craig Johnson
Jordan Moore

Forfar United

Manager:
Kyle Clark
Louis Starkey
Kyle Millar
Jamie Timmons
Jack Shaw
Liam Godfrey
Fraser Sturrock
Dean Fletcher
Dylan Stephen
Finlay Campbell
Liam Healy
Kieran Crighton
Cammy Howie
Callum Boath
Callum Rennie
Zack Williams
Conner Birse

Forfar West End

Manager: Derek Lawson
Assistant: Kevin Longmuir
Aaron Morrison
Rikkie Gillespie
Matthew Reynolds
Lee Maloney
Robbie Davidson
Ben Ranstead
Ross Matthews
Blair Stephen
Cameron Fleming
Dale Riddell
Barrie Gourlay
Abdourahman Njie
Nick Fletcher
Andrew Webster
Ross McClearey
Aiden Benvie

New Signings:
Guy Fisher (2021 Montrose)
Ryan Cormack (2021 Kirrie Th)
Ethan Samson (2021 Fairmuir BC)
Robbie McLauchlan (2021 Forfar Athletic CC U19)

Harthill Royal

Co-Managers: Ali Grier / Steven Barclay
William Gardner
Gary Bonnes
Jamie Barclay
Luke Barclay
Scott Gill
David Thomson
Broghin Taylor
Kiegan Thomas
Lewis McKee
Josh Redpath
Matthew Hamilton
Ewan MacNeil
Billy Dunlop
Kieran McParland
Scott Macgregor
Kieran Mckee

Kirriemuir Thistle

Manager: Daz Scott (until June 2021); Steven McNally (from June 2021)
Fraser Anderson
Steven Barclay
Darryl Burns
Ryan Cormack
Greg Fairweather
Robbie George
Ross Grant
Kamil Kadela
Ryan Kerrigan
Stuart McKenna
Dale Reid
Duncan Reid
Gary Robertson
Stewart Russell
Robert Smith
Ryan Winter

Livingston United

Manager: Andrew Malone
Graham Baird
George Bonnar
Mark Brown
Daniel Clancy
James Davidson
Jason Gregory
Scott Hay
Calum MacMillan
Andy McQuillan
Nicholas Mullen
David Murphy
Hassan Nyang
Chris O'Kane
William Pearson
Calum Polland
Harry Purves
Keron Welsh

New Signings 2021/2
Jeremiah Otonti
Danny Kleinman
Seb Tinning
Steve Dolan
Scott Bruce

Lochee Harp

Manager:
Ryan Mitchell
Brian Harris
Marc Kelly
Joe Kidd
David Buchan
Martin McCabe
Cameron McCormack
Sam McDonald
Sean McVicar
Kai Flynn
Jackson Dobbie
Michael McBrearty
Stephen Martin
Daniel Smith
Darren Brown
Paul Stewart

Lochee United

Manager: George Shields
Alan Tulleth
Bryan Deasley
Connor Birse
Craig Smith
Danny Cavanagh
Danny Millar
Dougie Cameron
Gary Kenneth
Grant Lawson
Greg Kirk
James Thomson

Jordan Millar
Josh McConville (2020 OL from East Fife)
Kevin Buchan
Kieran McWalter
Logan Davie
Mark Stewart
Reece Ritchie
Ross McDonald
Scott McComiskie
Scott Webster
Stephen McNally (left July 2021 to become Kirrie Th Manager)

New Signings
Grant Adam (ex Glasgow Rangers, St Mirren, Dundee, Airdrie, Cowdenbeath, Forfar Athletic, Morton and Dumbarton)
Kerr Hay (2021 Downfield, ex Lochee Utd)
Josh McConville (2021 East Fife)

Pumpherston

Manager: Craig Martin
Jamie Bowman
Aaron Hamilton
Adam Forrest
Dean Hunter
Steven Fyffe
Kieran Swanson
Craig Robertson
Brandan Murray
Mikey Adams
Adam Kennedy
Barry Nicholson
Ben Magee
John Batt
Ally McInnis
Craig Sneddon
Jordan Rodgers
Luke Mathieson
David Henderson
Alan Higgins
Greig Rae
Greg Redmond
Liam Magee

Sauchie Community

Manager: Darrel Drew
Zander Ryan
Jason Atkins
Dylan Taylor
Peter Maxwell
Jerry Ontont
Nicolas Rosenzweig
Peter Brown
Reece Docherty
Danny Kleinman
Roan Fulton
Sean Preston
Scott McInnes
Ryan Convery
Ryan Mack
Scott Bruce
Ross Wilson
Josh Carroll
Corin Stone
Aedan Houston
Arron Bryson
Brian McAdam

Scone Thistle

Manager: Paul Martin (until May 2021), Willie Laing (from June 2021)

Stoneyburn

Manager: Steven Sharp; Coaches: Gary Calvey, Keith Paton
Colin Gallagher
Cameron Donaldson
Matthew Craig
Joe Brady
Calum Wilson
David Hendry
Kyle Mooney
Ryan Robertson
Callan Stone
Tony Guatella
Dean McConnell
Euan Scott
Liam Young
Nick Wood
John Wood
Scott Dickson
Barry Craig
Daniel Wolfe
Evan Drew
Gavin McQuillan
Stephen McLay
Scott Hislop

NEW SIGNINGS
Jamie Stanaird

Syngenta

Manager: Allan Walker
Coach: Martin Mooney (ex Falkirk, Dumbarton etc)
Dean Shaw (2020 Camelon, ex Stenhousemuir)
Steven Jackson
Andy Jackson
Greg McGuinness
Scott Anson (2020 Petershill, ex Kilmarnock, Hamilton accies, Montrose, Clyde, Bo'ness Utd, Cumnock).
David Wilson (2020 Pumpherston, ex Hearts and Livingston youths)
Callum Reid
Bryan bell (ex Camelon)
Blair Hastings (ex E Stirlingshire)
Ruaridh Macdonald (ex East Stirlingshire)
Gregor Gwynne
Simon White (2020 BSC Glasgow, ex St Johnstone, East Stirling)
Kevin Fotheringham
Ryan Miller
David Smith (2020 Stranraer, ex Hearts, Falkirk, Raith R, Dumbarton)
Finn Graham
Ryan Russell (ex Pennies AFC)
Jason Walton
Liam Taggart (ex Alloa Ath etc)
Michael Wallace (ex Arbroath, East Stirling etc)
Iain Smith
Aaron McMillan (2020 Dunipace U20)
Callum Rodger (2020 Gartcairn U21)
Marc-Anthony Byrne (2020 Dunipace)
Andrew Mochan
Jay McMahon (2020 ex Pennies)
Ryan Millar(2020 Bannockburn Ams, ex Sauchie)
Ian Smith (ex Dundee, Stranraer)

New Signings
Andy Rodgers (2021 Kelty Hearts, ex Falkirk, Shire, Peterhead etc)
Josh Grigor (2021 OL from Stenhousemuir)
Darren Hill (2021 ex Falkirk, Arbroath etc)
Dave Mackay (2021 Brechin City, ex Celtic)
Declan Fitzpatrick (2021 ex BSC Glasgow, Clyde, Falkirk Youths)
Danny Armstrong (2021Campsie FC, ex Campsie Minerva, Yoker Ath, Stenhousemuir)
Adam Kettings (2021, ex Motherwell Youths)

Tayport

Manager: Chris MacPherson
Brad Ness
Bradie Heggie
Craig Sturrock
Dayle Robertson
Fraser Butter
Fraser Wilson
Gary Thain
Gordon Norrie
Greg Breen
Greg White
Jack Shaw
Jamie Gill
Jamie Hume
Jamie McCabe
Kris Rollo
Liam McCartney
Lyall Shaw
Logan Irvine
Louis Joyce
Zak Wilson

Violet

Manager: Andy Heggie
Coaches: Stuart McAra, Scott Kinnear
Ryan Kinnear
Calum Kinnear
Michael Edgar
Barry Wilson
Lewis Coutts
James Connelly
Andy Kelly
Kieran McWilliam
Jay Taylor
Ryan Bannon
Derek Johnston
Jason Hill
Allan Leith
John Hughes
Scott Cameron
Cammy Ross
Fraser Burnett

West Calder United

Manager:
Andrew Kennedy
Kallum McAulay
Lee Gillespie
Gordon Wilson
Gary Shanks
Jamie Booth
Jackson Cowan
Sid Easton
Paul McCracken
Craig Russell
Ross Lindsay
Gary White
Mark Wilkins
David Swan
Bryan King
Ally McRitchie

New Signings
James Miller
Kieran McDougall
Gary Livingston
Gary Fallon
Graham Baird
Ryan Stevenson (ex Tynecastle)
Rory Cosgrove
Dane Johnston

Whitburn

Manager: Jamie Sandilands; Coach: Darren Wilson
Declyn Cumming
Darren Liddell
Campbell Young (OL from QOS)
Taylor Evans (ex Shotts BA)
Reece Duncan (ex Camelon Juniors, Dunfermline, Rangers)
Martin Russell
Martin Hughes
Dewi Taylor
Greg Forrest
Chris Kelly
Grant Hamilton
Andy Thomson
Lewis Milton
Kieran Mitchell (OL from Dunfermline Ath)
Daniel Potts (ex Albion Rovers)
Darren Tomaszewski
Alistair Martin
Michael McGarahan (ex Wishaw, St Rochs)

NEW SIGNINGS
Jack Henderson (2021 Rosyth)
Stuart McIntyre (2021 Bo'ness United)
Louis Maguire (2021 Whitehill Welfare)

East Region League Cup Competitions

These competitions were discontinued from 2013/14 until 2017/18 due to the increased number of League fixtures. A different format of league Cup, covering the whole region, was brought in from 2018/19 when the number of league fixtures decreased.

Recent East (Central) Sectional League Cup Finals

Season	Winners	Runners Up	Score	Venue
2003/4	Rosyth Recreation	Thornton Hibs	2-1	Keir's Park, Hill of Beath
2004/5	Hill of Beath Hawthorn	Kircaldy YM	4-0	Ore Park, Glencraig
2005/6	Oakley United	Kelty Hearts	1-1, 4-3 pens	Recreation Park, Rosyth
2006/7	Kelty Hearts	Glenrothes	3-1	Recreation Park, Rosyth
2007/8	Hill of Beath Hawthorn	Glenrothes	2-1	Ore Park, Glencraig
2008/9	Hill of Beath Hawthorn	Glenrothes	1-1, 7-6 pens	Ore Park, Glencraig
2009/10	Glenrothes	Hill of Beath Hawthorn	1-1, 5-4 pens	Moorside Park, Dundonald
2010/1	Hill of Beath Hawthorn	Glenrothes	2-1	Central Park, Kelty
2011/2	Hill of Beath Hawthorn	Dundonald Bluebell	4-0	Keir's Park, Hill of Beath
2012/3	Jeanfield Swifts	Kelty Hearts	1-0	Blairwood Park, Oakley

Recent East (South) Sectional League Cup Finals

Season	Winners	Runners Up	Score	Venue
2004/5	Harthill Royal	Broxburn Athletic	2-0	Prestonfield, Linlithgow
2005/6	Musselburgh Athletic	Penicuik Athletic	1-0	New Victoria Park, Newtongrange
2006/7	Linlithgow Rose	Armadale Thistle	4-3	Carmuirs Park, Camelon
2007/8	Linlithgow Rose	Newtongrange Star	3-1	Prestonfield, Linlithgow
2008/9	Newtongrange Star	Camelon	1-1, 2-1 pens	Creamery Park, Bathgate
2009/10	Camelon	Linlithgow Rose	2-1	Prestonfield, Linlithgow
2010/1	Linlithgow Rose	Camelon	2-1	Creamery Park, Bathgate
2011/2	Linlithgow Rose	Newtongrange Star	3-0	Albyn Park, Broxburn
2012/3	Linlithgow Rose	Newtongrange Star	3-0	Albyn Park, Broxburn

Recent East (North) Sectional League Cup Finals

Season	Winners	Runners Up	Score	Venue
2000/1	Tayport	Dundee North End	2-0	Westfield Park, Carnoustie
2002/3	Montrose Roselea	Forfar West End	4-2	Westfield Park, Carnoustie
2003/4	Montrose Roselea	Carnoustie Panmure	3-0	Strathmore Park, Forfar
2004/5	Dundee North End	Scone Thistle	3-0	Westfield Park, Carnoustie
2005/6	Scone Thistle	Violet	4-1	Laing Park, Carnoustie
2006/7	Lochee United	Tayport	3-1	Laing Park, Carnoustie
2007/8	Lochee United	Tayport	2-2, 5-3 pens	Laing Park, Carnoustie
2008/9	Forfar West End	Lochee United	1-0	Laing Park, Carnoustie
2009/10	Montrose Roselea	Lochee United	0-0, 4-3 pens	Laing Park, Carnoustie
2010/1	Forfar West End	Tayport	2-2, 4-3 pens	Laing Park, Carnoustie
2011/2	Lochee United	Carnoustie Panmure	1-0	North End Park, Dundee
2012/3	Kirrie Thistle	Lochee United	2-1	Laing Park, Carnoustie

All-Time Fife and Lothians Cup Finals

Season	Winners	Runners Up	Score	Venue
1934/5	Kirkford Juniors	West Calder United	3-1	Tynecastle Park
1935/6	Bowhill Rovers	Dunbar United	3-1	Tynecastle Park
1936/7	Lochgelly Albert	Tranent	6-2	Central Park, Cowdenbeath
1937/8	Arniston Rangers	Blairhall Colliery	6-4	Central Park, Cowdenbeath
1938/9	Tranent	Armadale Thistle	3-1	Tynecastle Park
1939/40	Haddington Athletic	Tranent	4-2	Tynecastle Park
1968/9	Linlithgow Rose	Lochore Welfare	3-1	Newtown Park, Bo'ness
1969/70	Whitburn	Bo'ness United	2-0	Prestonfield, Linlithgow
1970/1	Camelon	Glenrothes	3-2	Newtown Park, Bo'ness
1971/2	Glenrothes	Armadale Thistle	4-1	Prestonfield, Linlithgow
1972/3	Linlithgow Rose	Dalkeith Thistle	2-0	Newtown Park, Bo'ness
1973/4	Linlithgow Rose	Fauldhouse United	2-1	Central Park, Whitburn
1974/5	Linlithgow Rose	Glenrothes	2-2, 4-3p	Central Park, Lochore
1975/6	Arniston Rangers	Linlithgow Rose	4-1	Newtown Park, Bo'ness
1976/7	Penicuik Athletic	Glenrothes	3-0	Central Park, Lochore
1977/8	Newtongrange Star	Glenrothes	4-2	Prestonfield, Linlithgow
1978/9	Linlithgow Rose	Broxburn Athletic	2-0	Central Park, Whitburn
1979/80	Linlithgow Rose	Newtongrange Star	2-1	Newbyres Park, Gorebridge
1980/1	Penicuik Athletic	Arniston Rangers	1-0	King's Park, Dalkeith
1981/2	Bonnyrigg Rose	Broxburn Athletic	1-0 AET	Victoria Park, Newtongrange
1982/3	Oakley United	Fauldhouse United	3-1	Warout Stadium, Glenrothes
1983/4	Linlithgow Rose	Fauldhouse United	2-1	Central Park, Whitburn
1984/5	Linlithgow Rose	Newtongrange Star	3-0	Central Park, Whitburn
1985/6	Linlithgow Rose	Newtongrange Star	2-1	Prestonfield, Linlithgow
1986/7	Whitburn	Oakley United	3-0 AET	Prestonfield, Linlithgow
1987/8	Newtongrange Star	Kelty Hearts	1-0	Prestonfield, Linlithgow
1988/9	Edinburgh United	Camelon	1-1, 3-1 pens	Prestonfield, Linlithgow
1989/90	Newtongrange Star	Bo'ness United	2-0	Prestonfield, Linlithgow
1990/1	Newtongrange Star	Linlithgow Rose	2-1 aet	Newtown Park, Bo'ness
1991/2	Whitburn	Livingston United	2-1	Albyn Park, Broxburn
1992/3	Fauldhouse United	Bathgate Thistle	1-0	Volunteer Park, Armadale
1993/4	Bo'ness United	Hill of Beath Hawthorn	2-1	Carmuirs Park, Camelon
1994/5	St Andrews United	Hill of Beath Hawthorn	4-3	Warout Stadium, Glenrothes
1995/6	Hill of Beath Hawthorn	Whitburn	1-0	Prestonfield, Linlithgow
1996/7	Bo'ness United	Bonnybridge	3-1	Carmuirs Park, Camelon
1997/8	Arniston Rangers	Haddington Athletic	1-0	New Dundas Park, Bonnyrigg
1998/9	Whitburn	Bo'ness United	3-2 aet	Prestonfield, Linlithgow
1999/00	Linlithgow Rose	Stoneyburn	4-1	Carmuirs Park, Camelon
2000/1	Linlithgow Rose	Whitburn	5-1	Carmuirs Park, Camelon
2001/2	Linlithgow Rose	Hill of Beath Hawthorn	6-5	Carmuirs Park, Camelon
2002/3	Sauchie	Glenrothes	5-3	Carmuirs Park, Camelon
2003/4	Sauchie	Linlithgow Rose	4-0	Central Park, Whitburn
2004/5	Bonnyrigg Rose	St Andrews United	1-0	Central Park, Whitburn
2005/6	Camelon	Kelty Hearts	2-1 aet	Prestonfield, Linlithgow
2006/7	Bonnyrigg Rose	Musselburgh Athletic	2-0	Prestonfield, Linlithgow
2007/8	Camelon	Hill of Beath Hawthorn	5-0	Prestonfield, Linlithgow
2008/9	Linlithgow Rose	Thornton Hibs	1-0	Keir's Park, Hill of Beath
2009/10	Bathgate Thistle	Musselburgh Athletic	1-0	New Victoria Park, Newtongrange
2010/1	Linlithgow Rose	Bo'ness United	2-1	Prestonfield, Linlithgow
2011/2	Linlithgow Rose	Broxburn Athletic	3-1	Newtown Park, Bo'ness
2012/3	Linlithgow Rose	Camelon	5-3	Creamery Park, Bathgate
2013/4	Linlithgow Rose	Bo'ness United	2-1	Newtown Park, Bo'ness
2014/5	Camelon	Sauchie	1-0	Creamery Park, Bathgate
2015/6	Penicuik Athletic	Bonnyrigg Rose	3-1	Olive Bank, Musselburgh
2016/7	Tranent	Broxburn Athletic	1-0	New Victoria Park, Newtongrange
2017/8	Bonnyrigg Rose	Newtongrange Star	5-1	Penicuik Park, Penicuik
2018/9	Thornton Hibs	Livingston United	3-2	Creamery Park, Bathgate

All Time East of Scotland Cup Finals

Season	Winners	Runners Up	Score	Venue
1885/6	North Western	Hawthorn	3-2	Drum Park, Leith
1886/7	Leith Emerald	Cardinals	7-1	Olive Park, Musselburgh
1887/8	Woodburn	Leith Craighall	5-4	Drum Park, Leith
1888/9	Woodburn	Bathgate Harp	1-0	Boghall, Linlithgow
1889/90	Broxburn Athletic	Uphall Athletic	6-0	Newton Park, Bo'ness
1890/1	Hawthorn	Dalry Primrose	8-2	Powderhall, Edinburgh
1891/2	Hawthorn	Broxburn Emmet	6-5	Powderhall, Edinburgh
1892/3	Niddrie Bluebell	East Benhar Heatherbell	1-0	Bogshole Park, Bathgate
1894/5	Leith Celtic	Hawthorn	3-2	Powderhall, Edinburgh
1895/6	Hawthorn	Balmoral	6-0	Easter Road, Edinburgh
1896/7	Broxburn Athletic	Hearts of Beath	wo	
1897/8	Bonnyrigg Rose	Broxburn Athleic	1-0	Bogshole Park, Bathgate
1898/9	Leith Ivanhoe	Dundee Violet	2-1	Carolina Port, Dundee
1899/00	Niddrie Bluebell	Leith Renton	1-0	Tynecastle Park, Edinburgh
1900/1	Vale of Grange	Leith Craighall	4-3	Bogshole Park, Bathgate
1901/2	Leith Ivanhoe	Lochgelly Rangers	2-1	Brucefield, Dunfermline
1902/3	Vale of Grange	Broxburn Athletic	2-1	Volunteer Park, Armadale
1903/4	Broxburn Athletic	Brechin Harp	2-2, 4-2	Gayfield Park, Arbroath
1904/5	Vale of Grange	Lochgelly Rangers	7-1	East End Park, Dunfermline
1905/6	Alva Albion Rangers	Bowhill Thistle	1-1, 2-1	East End Park, Dunfermline
1906/7	Newtongrange Star	Bonnyrigg Rose	2-0	Mains Park, Tranent
1907/8	Alva Albion Rangers	Arniston Rangers	2-2, 3-0	Easter Road / Forthbank Park, Stirling
1908/9	Penicuik Juniors	Newtongrange Star	1-1, 1-0	Royal Gymnasium, Edinburgh
1909/10	Arniston Rangers	Bowhill Thistle	1-1, 2-0	East End Park, Dunfermline
1910/11	Penicuik Juniors	Kelty Rangers	2-0	Prestonfield, Linlithgow
1911/2	Wemyss Athletic	Penicuik Juniors	2-0	Easter Road, Edinburgh
1912/3	Arniston Rangers	Vale of Grange	1-0	Royal Gymnasium, Edinburgh
1913/4	Tranent	Inverkeithing United	2-1	Royal Gymnasium, Edinburgh
1914/5	Denbeath Star	Loanhead Mayflower	2-1	Newton Park, Bo'ness
1915/6	Loanhead Mayflower	Broxburn Athletic	4-0	Tynecastle Park, Edinburgh
1916/7	Denbeath Star	Winchburgh Violet	4-0	East End Park, Dunfermline
1917/8	Winchburgh Violet	Leith Benburb	1-0	Tynecastle Park, Edinburgh
1918/9	Winchburgh Violet	Broxburn Athletic	1-0	Easter Road, Edinburgh
1919/20	Tranent	Hearts of Beath	1-1, 3-0	Easter Road, Edinburgh
1920/1	Musselburgh Bruntonians	Tranent	1-0	Tynecastle Park, Edinburgh
1921/2	Arniston Rangers	Bonnyrigg Rose	3-1	King's Park, Dalkeith
1922/3	Arniston Rangers	West Calder	0-0, 1-0	Chancelot Park, Edinburgh / Royal Gymnasium
1923/4	Musselburgh Bruntonians	Wallyford Bluebell	2-0	Tynecastle Park, Edinburgh
1924/5	Edinburgh Emmet	West Calder	3-0	Easter Road, Edinburgh
1925/6	Newtongrange Star	Dalkeith Thistle	4-0	New Logie Green, Edinburgh
1926/7	Portobello Thistle	Duns Juniors	3-1	Easter Road, Edinburgh
1927/8	Portobello Thistle	Dalkeith Thistle	2-1	Tynecastle Park, Edinburgh
1928/9	Edinburgh Emmet	Wallyford Bluebell	1-0	Tynecastle Park, Edinburgh
1929/30	Newtongrange Star	Wallyford Bluebell	1-1, 1-0	Tynecastle Park, Edinburgh
1930/1	Tranent	Dunbar United	3-1	Tynecastle Park, Edinburgh
1931/2	Tranent	Ormiston Primrose	3-1	Tynecastle Park, Edinburgh
1932/3	Rosewell Rosedale	Tranent	4-2	Tynecastle Park, Edinburgh
1933/4	Tranent	Rosewell Rosedale	1-0	Tynecastle Park, Edinburgh
1934/5	Thorntree United	Tranent	2-0	Tynecastle Park, Edinburgh
1935/6	Tranent	West Calder United	5-1	Tynecastle Park, Edinburgh
1936/7	Musselburgh Athletic	Thorntree United	3-2	Easter Road, Edinburgh
1937/8	Tranent	Thorntree United	2-0	Easter Road, Edinburgh
1938/9	Stoneyburn	Portobello Renton	3-1	Tynecastle Park, Edinburgh
1939/40	Polkemmet	Whitburn	2-2, 4-2	Easter Road, Edinburgh
1940/1	Haddington Athletic	Polkemmet	4-1	Tynecastle Park, Edinburgh
1941/2	Bathgate Thistle	Armadale Thistle	4-3	Easter Road, Edinburgh
1942/3	Burnbank Athletic	Wishaw	2-2, 4-2	Fir Park, Motherwell
1943/4	Armadale Thistle	Bathgate Thistle	3-1	Tynecastle Park, Edinburgh
1944/5	Fauldhouse United	Burnbank Athletic	2-1	Easter Road, Edinburgh
1945/6	Fauldhouse United	Bo'ness United	2-0	Tynecastle Park, Edinburgh
1946/7	Stoneyburn	Bo'ness United	2-1	Tynecastle Park, Edinburgh
1947/8	Arniston Rangers	Haddington Athletic	1-0	Easter Road, Edinburgh
1948/9	Armadale Thistle	Stoneyburn	1-1, 3-0	Albyn Park, Broxburn
1949/50	Stoneyburn	Newtongrange Star	3-0	Tynecastle Park, Edinburgh
1950/1	Broxburn Athletic	Thorntree United	2-0	Easter Road, Edinburgh
1951/2	Bo'ness United	Arniston Rangers	2-0	Tynecastle Park, Edinburgh

1952/3	Armadale Thistle	Bathgate Thistle	3-1	Easter Road, Edinburgh
1953/4	Linlithgow Rose	Fauldhouse United	1-1, 4-0	Volunteer Park, Armadale
1954/5	Bo'ness United	Arniston Rangers	3-2	Tynecastle Park, Edinburgh
1955/6	Loanhead Mayflower	Haddington Athletic	2-1	Tynecastle Park, Edinburgh
1956/7	Haddington Athletic	Newtongrange Star	2-0	Easter Road, Edinburgh
1957/8	Newtongrange Star	Arniston Rangers	2-0	Tynecastle Park, Edinburgh
1958/9	Newtongrange Star	Musselburgh Athletic	5-3	Easter Road, Edinburgh
1959/60	Tranent	Broxburn Athletic	1-0	Tynecastle Park, Edinburgh
1960/1	Dunbar United	Bo'ness United	2-0	Easter Road, Edinburgh
1961/2	Armadale Thistle	Arniston Rangers	2-1	Tynecastle Park, Edinburgh
1962/3	Bonnyrigg Rose	Tranent	3-3, 3-1	Easter Road, Edinburgh
1963/4	Dunbar United	Bo'ness United	2-2, 2-2, 6-1	Olive Bank, Musselburgh
1964/5	Linlithgow Rose	Armadale Thistle	3-1	Tynecastle Park, Edinburgh
1965/6	Whitburn	Tranent	3-1	Easter Road, Edinburgh
1966/7	Dalkeith Thistle	Newtongrange Star	2-0	Tynecastle Park, Edinburgh
1967/8	Linlithgow Rose	Arniston Rangers	4-1	Tynecastle Park, Edinburgh
1968/9	Whitburn	Bo'ness United	1-0	Tynecastle Park, Edinburgh
1969/70	Whitburn	Newtongrange Star	1-1, 3-0	Prestonfield, Linlithgow
1970/1	Arniston Rangers	Camelon	6-2	Meadowbank Stadium, Edinburgh
1971/2	Dalkeith Thistle	Musselburgh Athletic	1-1, 1-0	Newbyres Park, Gorebridge
1972/3	Haddington Athletic	Linlithgow Rose	1-0	Tynecastle Park, Edinburgh
1973/4	Whitburn	Sauchie	2-1	Firs Park, Falkirk
1974/5	Newtongrange Star	Broxburn Athletic	2-2, 3-1	Olive Bank, Musselburgh
1975/6	Linlithgow Rose	Newtongrange Star	4-1	Tynecastle Park, Edinburgh
1976/7	Newtongrange Star	Bonnyrigg Rose	1-0	Olive Bank, Musselburgh
1977/8	Linlithgow Rose	Bonnyrigg Rose	1-1, 3-2	Newbyres Park, Gorebridge
1978/9	Tranent	Camelon	3-1	Prestonfield, Linlithgow
1979/80	Newtongrange Star	Penicuik Athletic	1-0	Newbyres Park, Gorebridge
1980/1	Arniston Rangers	Newtongrange Star	3-2	New Dunas Park, Bonnyrigg
1981/2	Newtongrange Star	Camelon	2-0	Prestonfield, Linlithgow
1982/3	Sauchie	Camelon	2-1	Prestonfield, Linlithgow
1983/4	Ormiston Primrose	Bo'ness United	1-1, 4-1	Prestonfield, Linlithgow
1984/5	Bo'ness United	Linlithgow Rose	2-2, 3-1	Newtown Park, Bo'ness
1985/6	Bonnyrigg Rose	Linlithgow Rose	3-1	Forresters Park, Tranent
1986/7	Bonnyrigg Rose	Whitburn	2-1 AET	Prestonfield, Linlithgow
1987/8	Broxburn Athletic	Linlithgow Rose	1-1, 2-1 AET	Central Park Whitburn
1988/9	Linlithgow Rose	Broxburn Athletic	3-0	Central Park, Whitburn
1989/90	Dunbar United	Whitburn	2-1	Forresters Park, Tranent
1990/1	Linlithgow Rose	Bo'ness United	4-3	Central Park, Whitburn
1991/2	Newtongrange Star	Whitburn	2-0	Newbyres Park, Gorebridge
1992/3	Linlithgow Rose	Fauldhouse United	2-0	Volunteer Park, Armadale
1993/4	Camelon	Livingston United	2-1	Prestonfield, Linlithgow
1994/5	Ormiston Primrose	Dunbar United	2-1	Newbyres Park, Gorebridge
1995/6	Linlithgow Rose	Camelon	3-0	Newtown Park, Bo'ness
1996/7	Newtongrange Star	Bo'ness United	3-3, 3-1 pens	Recreation Park, Pumpherston
1997/8	Whitburn	Bonnybridge	2-0	Prestonfield, Linlithgow
1998/9	Bo'ness United	Whitburn	2-0	Prestonfield, Linlithgow
1999/00	Linlithgow Rose	Bo'ness United	2-1	Carmuirs Park, Camelon
2000/1	Linlithgow Rose	Harthill Royal	5-0	Station Park, Livingston
2001/2	Whitburn	Musselburgh Athletic	2-1	Newbyres Park, Gorebridge
2002/3	Bonnyrigg Rose	Musselburgh Athletic	5-3	Newbyres Park, Gorebridge
2003/4	Linlithgow Rose	Whitburn	1-0	Albyn Park, Broxburn
2004/5	Linlithgow Rose	Newtongrange Star	1-0	Carmuirs Park, Camelon
2005/6	Bonnyrigg Rose	Hill of Beath Hawthorn	2-1	Volunteer Park, Armadale
2006/7	Bathgate Thistle	Rosyth	3-0	Recreation Park, Rosyth
2007/8	Camelon	Bonnyrigg Rose	4-0	Prestonfield, Linlithgow
2008/9	Lochee United	Glenrothes	3-0	Canniepairt, Tayport
2009/10	Linlithgow Rose	Musselburgh Athletic	2-1	Creamery Park, Bathgate
2010/1	Newtongrange Star	Dundee North End	2-0	Central Park, Kelty
2011/2	St Andrews United	Kinnoull	2-1	Keir's Park, Hill of Beath
2012/3	Bonnyrigg Rose	Linlithgow Rose	3-0	Creamery Park, Bathgate
2013/4	Sauchie	Arniston Rangers	4-1	Prestonfield, Linlithgow
2014/5	Hill of Beath Hawthorn	Bo'ness United	0-0, 4-2p	Beechwood Park, Sauchie
2015/6	Bo'ness United	Dundonald Bluebell	5-1	Creamery Park, Bathgate
2016/7	Tranent	Bonnyrigg Rose	1-1, 4-1p	Creamery Park, Bathgate
2017/8	Penicuik Athletic	Tranent	2-0	Prestonfield, Linlithgow
2018/9	Broughty Athletic	Carnoustie Panmure	2-2, 4-2p	Thomson Park, Lochee

NORTH JUNIORS

The North Region of the Scottish Junior FA was created in 1968. Prior to that there were several County and Local Associations, mainly in the North East of Scotland. An Inverness Junior League existed in the 1950s.

The North Region now encompasses teams from Moray, Strathspey, Banffshire, Aberdeenshire, the City of Aberdeen and as far south as Montrose. The League structure has changed several times over the years.

In 2017/18 the structure had a region-wide Super League with two parallel First Divisions, East and West. It was agreed that for 2018/19 the structure would be changed to 3 region-wide Leagues in a vertical structure.

The 2019/20 season was declared null and void. The league composition for 2020/1 was to be unchanged, with the addition of one new member club, Rothie Rovers, from Rothienorman.

The start of the season was suspended due to COVID. Many clubs opted to sit out the entire season. Some played a mini-tournament mid season but that was never completed.

NORTH JUNIOR LEAGUE CHAMPIONS 1968-2001

	East Div 1	East Div 2	North
1968/9	Banks o' Dee		Formartine Utd
1969/70	Banks o' Dee		Buckie Rovers
1970/1	Banks o' Dee		Islavale
1971/2	Sunnybank		Forres Thistle
1972/3	Banks o' Dee		Burghead Thistle
1973/4	Parkvale	Mugiemoss	Burghead Thistle
1974/5	Sunnybank	Stoneywood Works	Buckie Rovers
1975/6	Sunnybank	Lads Club	Nairn St Ninian
1976/7	Banks o' Dee	Mugiemoss	Burghead Thistle
1977/8	east End	Cuminestown	Nairn St Ninian
1978/9	Banks o' Dee	Rosemount	Nairn St Ninian
1979/80	Fraserburgh Utd	Buchanhaven H	Forres Thistle
1980/1	Banks o' Dee	Rosemount	Bishopmill Utd
1981/2	Banks o' Dee	FC Stoneywood	Nairn St Ninian
1982/3	Sunnybank	Parkvale	Buckie Rovers
1983/4	Banks o' Dee	Ellon United	Deveronside
1984/5	FC Stoneywood	East End	Fochabers
1985/6	Banks o' Dee	Cove Rangers	Deveronside
1986/7	Banks o' Dee	East End	Cabarfeidh
1987/8	Rosslyn Sports	Bon Accord	Deveronside
1988/9	Bon Accord	Stonehaven	Deveronside
1989/90	Stonehaven	Hall Russell Utd	Deveronside
1990/1	FC Stoneywood	Fraserburgh Utd	Deveronside
1991/2	FC Stoneywood	Buchanhaven H	Lossiemouth Utd
1992/3	Inverurie Locos	East End	Buckie Rovers
1993/4	Stonehaven	Longside	Deveronside
1994/5	FC Stoneywood	Hermes	Lossiemouth Utd
1995/6	Inverurie Locos	Banks o' Dee	Deveronside
1996/7	Sunnybank	Lewis United	Islavale
1997/8	Inverurie Locos	Cruden Bay	Islavale
1998/9	Sunnybank	Banks o' Dee	New Elgin
1999/00	Longside	Cruden Bay	Deveronside
2000/1	Longside	Culter	Deveronside

NORTH JUNIOR LEAGUE CHAMPIONS 2002-date

	Super Lge	East Div 1	West Div 1	Division 1	Division 2
2001/2	Formartine United	Lads Club	Strathspey Thistle		
2002/3	Sunnybank	Turriff United	Forres Thistle		
2003/4	Culter			Maud	Islavale
2004/5	Culter			Parkvale	New Elgin
2005/6	Culter			Dyce	New Elgin
2006/7	Culter			East End	Fochabers
2007/8	Banks o' Dee			Banchory St Ternan	Bishopmill Utd
2008/9	Banks o' Dee			Buchanhaven Hearts	Inverness City
2009/10	Sunnybank			Fraserburgh Utd	Burghead Th
2010/1	Culter			Inverness City	Parkvale
2011/2	Hermes			Inverness City	Portgordon Vics
2012/3	Culter			New Elgin	Colony Park
2013/4	Culter	Cruden Bay	Inverness City		
2014/5	Hermes	Bridge of Don	Grantown		
2015/6	Banks o' Dee	Colony Park	Buckie Rovers		
2016/7	Banks o' Dee	Ellon United	Spey Valley Utd		
2017/8	Banks o' Dee	East End	Nairn St Ninian		
2018/9	Banks o' Dee			Banchory St Ternan	Buchanhaven Hearts
2019/20	N/A			N/A	N/A

North Junior Mini Leagues 2020/1

NORTH REGION WEST GROUP 1

	BUR	DUF	ISL	NAI
Burghead Thistle		Dec 5 0-3	Dec 12 2-3	Nov 28 2-0
Dufftown			Nov 28 1-3	
Islavale	Nov 21 1-1	Dec 19 1-3		
Nairn St Ninian	Dec 19 4-0	Nov 21 2-2		

	P	W	D	L	F	F	GD	P
Dufftown	4	2	1	1	9	6	3	7
Islavale	4	2	1	1	8	7	1	7
Nairn St Ninian	3	1	1	1	6	4	2	4
Burghead Thistle	5	1	1	3	5	11	-6	4

NORTH REGION WEST GROUP 2

	DEV	FOR	NEW	WHI
Deveronside		Dec 12 1-1		Nov 28 4-0
Forres Thistle	Nov 21 3-2		Dec 19 1-0	
New Elgin	Dec 5 1-4	Nov 28 1-1		Dec 12 2-3
Whitehills	Dec 19 1-4		Nov 21 2-3	

	P	W	D	L	F	F	GD	P
Deveronside	5	3	1	1	15	6	9	10
Forres Thistle	4	2	2	0	6	4	2	8
New Elgin	5	1	1	3	7	11	-4	4
Whitehills	4	1	0	3	6	13	-7	3

NORTH REGION BANFF AND BUCHAN GROUP 1

	BUC	COL	CRU	MAU
Buchanhaven Hearts		Dec 12 0-4		Nov 28 0-2
Colony Park	Nov 21 0-2		Dec 19 2-0	
Cruden Bay	Dec 5 3-2	Nov 28 2-2		
Maud			Nov 21 1-0	

	P	W	D	L	F	F	GD	P
Colony Park	4	2	1	1	8	4	4	7
Maud	2	2	0	0	3	0	3	6
Cruden Bay	4	1	1	2	5	7	-2	4
Buchanhaven Hearts	4	1	0	3	4	9	-5	3

NORTH REGION BANFF AND BUCHAN GROUP 2

	ELL	FRA	LON	ROT
Ellon United		Nov 21 2-3	Dec 19 1-1	
Fraserburgh United			Dec 12 1-2	Nov 28 0-3
Longside	Nov 28 4-0			Dec 23 0-3
Rothie Rovers		Dec 19 2-0	Nov 21 5-4	

	P	W	D	L	F	F	GD	P
Rothie Rovers	4	4	0	0	13	4	9	12
Longside	5	2	1	2	11	10	1	7
Fraserburgh United	4	1	0	3	4	9	-5	3
Ellon United	3	0	1	2	3	8	-5	1

NORTH REGION ABERDEEN GROUP 1

	ABE	HAL	HER	STO
Aberdeen University		Nov 28 3-4	Dec 12 0-4	
Hall Russell United	Dec 19 3-1			Nov 21 2-2
Hermes	Nov 21 6-1			Dec 19 1-1
Stonehaven	Dec 5 4-3		Nov 28 1-2	

	P	W	D	L	F	F	GD	P
Hermes	4	3	1	0	13	3	10	10
Hall Russell United	3	2	1	0	9	6	3	7
Stonehaven	4	1	2	1	8	8	0	5
Aberdeen Uni	5	0	0	5	8	21	-13	0

NORTH REGION ABERDEEN GROUP 2

	ABE	BOD	NEW	SUN
Aberdeen East End		Nov 21 2-4	Dec 19 0-1	Dec 5 2-2
Banks o' Dee	Dec 16 4-2		Dec 5 10-0	Nov 28 5-0
Newmachar United				
Sunnybank		Dec 19 2-3	Nov 21 4-1	

	P	W	D	L	F	F	GD	P
Banks o' Dee	5	5	0	0	26	6	20	15
Aberdeen East End	4	0	1	3	6	11	-5	1
Sunnybank	4	1	1	2	8	11	-3	4
Newmachar Utd	3	1	0	2	2	14	-12	3

NORTH REGION ABERDEEN GROUP 3

	BDT	CUL	STO
Bridge of Don Thistle		Dec 19 2-1	Dec 5 5-0
Culter			Dec 12 8-0
Stoneywood Parkvale		Nov 21 1-3	

	P	W	D	L	F	F	GD	P
Culter	3	2	0	1	12	3	9	6
Bridge of Don Thistle	2	2	0	0	7	1	6	6
Stoneywood Parkvale	3	0	0	3	1	16	-15	0

NORTH REGION ABERDEEN GROUP 3

	BST	DYC	GLE
Banchory St Ternan		Nov 28 3-5	
Dyce	Dec 19 7-0		Dec 5 7-0
Glentanar	Nov 21 0-3		

	P	W	D	L	F	F	GD	P
Dyce	3	3	0	0	19	3	16	9
Banchory St Ternan	3	1	0	2	6	12	-6	3
Glentanar	2	0	0	2	0	10	-10	0

North Junior Autumn "Friendly" League 2020/1

	BST	BDT	CUL	DYC	HER	SUN
Banchory St Ternan		Oct 17 0-4			Nov 7 0-3	
Bridge of Don Thistle			Oct 24 2-2	Nov 14 5-3		Nov 7 6-1
Culter				Nov 7 5-1		Oct 17 3-1
Dyce	Oct 24 2-1					Oct 10 5-2
Hermes		Nov 10 3-2	Nov 14 1-2	Oct 20 2-4		
Sunnybank	Nov 14 4-3				Oct 24 1-3	

	P	W	D	L	F	A	GD	P
Bridge of Don T	5	3	1	1	19	9	10	10
Culter	4	3	1	0	12	5	7	10
Dyce	5	3	0	2	15	15	0	9
Hermes	5	2	0	3	12	9	3	6
Sunnybank	5	1	0	4	9	20	-11	3
Banchory St T	4	0	0	4	4	13	-9	0

6 clubs played a semi-official League competition in the Autumn. One game, Culter v Banchory St Ternan, appears to have been unplayed.

NORTH JUNIOR SUPER LEAGUE ALL TIME POSITIONS	2001-2	2002-3	2003-4	2004-5	2005-6	2006-7	2007-8	2008-9	2009-10	2010-11	2011-12	2012-13	2013-14	2014-15	2015-16	2016-17	2017/18	2018/19	*2019/20*
Banchory St Ternan								5	3	6	7	10	11	10	12	9	13		*11*
Banks o' Dee	5	8	6	6	3	3	1	1	5	4	5	4	2	3	1	1	1	1	*1*
Buchanhaven Hearts	14								13										
Buckie Rovers																13			
Colony Park																7	11	9	*9*
Cruden Bay	10	12	13											13					
Culter	2	2	1	1	1	1	3	3	2	1	4	1	1	4	5	3	4	5	*2*
Deveronside	13	14										5	6	5	10	14			*8*
Dufftown															8	12	8	13	
Dyce						6	6	4	4	5	3	2	3	8	4	2	3	8	*6*
East End	6	4	11	12			9	9	14				13					11	*10*
Ellon United				13	7	12	5	10	10	11	8	9	10	12	13		5	12	*13*
FC Stoneywood	3	5	12	8	14				12	12	6	6	12	6	14				
Formartine United	1	6	7	4	2	7	13												
Forres Thistle											13								
Fraserburgh United					13					14		14							
Glentanar	12	10	3	2	9	14													
Hall Russell United									11	2	10	12	9	11	6	5	10	10	*12*
Hermes	7	11	8	9	6	9	12	7	6	3	1	3	4	1	2	8	2	4	*3*
Inverness City														7	7	10	14		
Islavale						13													
Lads Club		9	14																
Lewis United								11	8	8	11	13							
Longside	9	3	10	5	11	8	11	6	9	13	9	11	14						
Maud				14			4	8	7	9	12	8	5	2	9	11	6	6	*14*
Montrose Roselea																	7	3	*7*
Nairn St Ninian																		7	*4*
New Elgin													8	14					
Parkvale					12	10	14												
Stonehaven	8	7	4	11	10	4	8	14		10	2	7	7	9	3	4	9	14	
Sunnybank	4	1	2	7	5	2	2	2	1	7	14								
Turriff United			5	3	8	5	7	12											
Wilsons XI / Hillhead / Newburgh Th / Bridge of Don Thistle	11	13	9	10	4	11	10	13							11	6	12	2	*5*

Between 2013 and 2018 there were East and West Divisions operating below the Super League.

EAST DIVISION Since Reconstruction					
	2013/14	2014/15	2015/16	2016/17	2017/18
Aberdeen East End		10	4	3	1
Aberdeen University		8	9	8	7
Bridge of Don Thistle / Newburgh Th	2	1			
Buchanhaven Hearts	9	4	3	6	8
Colony Park	3	3	1		
Cruden Bay	1		12	11	11
Ellon United				1	
Fraserburgh United	7	4	2	7	4
Glentanar	4	11	11	10	6
Lewis United	5	6	5	9	10
Longside		9	7	5	3
Newmachar United	10	12	8		9
Parkvale / Stoneywood-Parkvale	6	2	6	4	5
Sunnybank	8	7	10	2	2

WEST DIVISION Since Reconstruction					
	2013/14	2014/15	2015/16	2016/17	2017/18
Buckie Rovers	7	4	1		4
Burghead Thistle	4	7	9	6	5
Deveronside					2
Dufftown	2	1			
Fochabers	10	Ab	8	10	
Forres Thistle	6	6	2	5	3
Grantown		2	7		
Inverness City	1				
Islavale	3	3	4	4	6
Lossiemouth United		9	res		
Montrose Roselea				2	
Nairn St Ninian	8	5	3	3	1
New Elgin			6	7	7
Newmachar United				9	
Portgordon Victoria	5	10	5		
Spey Valley (United)		8	5	1	8
Whitehills	9	11	Ab	8	9

Recent finishing positions in Divisions One and Two up to 2013 are included below:

North Juniors First Division 2003-2013

	2003-4	2004-5	2005-6	2006-7	2007-8	2008-9	2009-10	2010-11	2011-12	2012-13
Banchory St Ternan	6	4	6	3	1					
Bishopmill United							9	14		
Buchanhaven Hearts	8	9	12	5	4	1		5	11	13
Buckie Rovers	9					12	7	13	14	
Burghead Thistle	12	11	14					12	13	11
Cruden Bay		13	8	13	13	14				
Deveronside	3	6	10				5	9	3	
Dufftown	13	12	11	10	10	13	13	11	12	
Dyce	10	7	1							
East End			5	1				10	5	2
Ellon United	2									
FC Stoneywood				11	12	4				
Formartine United						2				
Forres Thistle				7	9	8	11	2		10
Fraserburgh United	5	2		9	11	6	1		2	
Glentanar					7	11	4	3	4	4
Hall Russell United	4	10	13	12	8	5				
Hillhead / Bridge of Don Thistle							10	8	8	12
Inverness City							2	1	1	3
Islavale		3	2		6	9	12	6	9	5
Lads Club		8	7	6	3					
Lewis United	11	5	4	4	2					
Lossiemouth United						7	6	7	10	14
Maud	1		3	2						
Nairn St Ninian					14					9
New Elgin							8	4	6	1
Parkvale	7	1				10	14		7	6
Portgordon Vics										7
Stonehaven							3			
Strathspey Thistle			9	8	5	3				
Sunnybank										8
Whitehills	14									

North Juniors Second Division 2003-2013

	2003-4	2004-5	2005-6	2006-7	2007-8	2008-9	2009-10	2010-11	2011-12	2012-13
Bishopmill United	9	6	7	5	1	4			7	
Buckie Rovers			5	3	3					2
Burghead Thistle				8	5	5	1			
Colony Park									4	1
Cruden Bay							5	7	5	4
Deveronside					6	3				
Fochabers	7	3	3	1	Ab	6	3	5	9	5
Forres Thistle	3	2	2							
Inverness City						1				
Islavale	1									
Kinloss	10	9	9							
Lossiemouth United	5	7	6	4	2					
Nairn St Ninian	6	5	4	2		7	2	4	2	
New Elgin	4	1	1	6	4	2				
Newmachar United								2	3	3
Parkvale								1		
Portgordon Victoria									1	
RAF Lossiemouth	8	8	8	9	7	8	4	6	8	
Strathspey Thistle	2	4								
Whitehills		10	10	7	8	9	6	3	6	6

North Juniors Cups 2020/1

None of the North Region Junior Cups were played during 2020/1.

Recent North Sectional League Cup Finals

Season	Winners	Runners Up	Score	Venue
1999/00	Sunnybank	Formartine United	4-3	Harlaw Park, Inverurie
2000/1	Sunnybank	Formartine United	2-0	Harlaw Park, Inverurie
2001/2	Sunnybank	Glentanar	1-0 aet	Keith Park, Aberdeen*
2002/3	Strathspey Thistle	Banks o' Dee	2-2, 4-3 pens	Keith Park, Aberdeen*
2003/4	Hermes	Glentanar	0-0, 4-3 pens	Heathryfold Park, Aberdeen
2004/5	Glentanar	Stonehaven	4-2	Heathryfold Park, Aberdeen
2005/6	Culter	Formartine United	2-0	Heathryfold Park, Aberdeen
2006/7	Turriff United	Hillhead	3-0	Heathryfold Park, Aberdeen
2007/8	Sunnybank	Culter	2-2, 5-4 pens	Hillhead Sports Centre, Aberdeen*
2008/9	Dyce	East End	0-0, 4-2 pens	Spain Park, Aberdeen
2009/10	Sunnybank	Longside	3-1	New Advocates Park, Aberdeen
2010/1	Culter	Inverness City	1-0	Merson Park, Buckie
2011/2	Maud	Inverness City	3-2	Simpson Park, Keith
2012/3	FC Stoneywood	Dyce	2-0	Hillhead Sports Centre, Aberdeen*
2013/4	Banks o' Dee	Culter	0-0, 4-2 pens	Hillhead Sports Centre, Aberdeen*
2014/5	Hermes	Maud	3-1	Davidson Park, Longside
2015/6	Dyce	Culter	3-1	Heathryfold Park, Aberdeen
2016/7	Banks o' Dee	Maud	2-0	Ian Mair Park, Dyce
2017/8	Dyce	Maud	1-1, 4-2 pens	Davidson Park, Longside
2018/9	Banks o' Dee	Hermes	4-0	Heathryfold Park, Aberdeen

* Keith Park was later renamed Hillhead Sports Centre

Recent North Region Cup Finals

Season	Winners	Runners Up	Score	Venue
1988/9	Bon Accord	Culter	2-1 aet	Spain Park, Aberdeen
1989/90	Culter	Stonehaven	2-1	Spain Park, Aberdeen
1990/1	Stonehaven	FC Stoneywood	2-1	Spain Park, Aberdeen
1991/2	FC Stoneywood	Aberdeen East End	3-0	Heathryfold Park, Aberdeen
1992/3	Hall Russell United	Stonehaven	3-2	Heathryfold Park, Aberdeen
1993/4	Sunnybank	FC Stoneywood	0-0, 2-0 pens	Spain Park, Aberdeen
1994/5	FC Stoneywood	Sunnybank	2-1	Spain Park, Aberdeen
1995/6	Inverurie Locos	Bon Accord	3-1	Spain Park, Aberdeen
1996/7	Sunnybank	Bon Accord	3-1	New Advocates Park, Aberdeen
1997/8	Hermes	Cruden Bay	2-1	The Meadows, Ellon
1998/9	FC Stoneywood	Stonehaven	1-0	Heathryfold Park, Aberdeen
1999/00	Culter	Formartine United	2-1	Heathryfold Park, Aberdeen
2000/1	Inverurie Locos	Forres Thistle	3-1	The Haughs, Turriff
2001/2	Sunnybank	Culter	3-0	Pittodrie Stadium, Aberdeen
2002/3	Islavale	Banks o' Dee	3-2	Pittodrie Stadium, Aberdeen
2003/4	Hermes	Aberdeen East End	2-1	Pittodrie Stadium, Aberdeen
2004/5	Islavale	Banchory St Ternan	7-1	North Lodge Park, Pitmedden
2005/6	Islavale	Longside	3-1	The Haughs, Turriff
2006/7	Turriff United	Forres Thistle	2-1	Simpson Park, Keith
2007/8	Dyce	Turriff United	2-0	Pleasure Grounds, Maud
2008/9	Dyce	Formartine United	4-1	Heathryfold Park, Aberdeen
2009/10	FC Stoneywood	Hermes	5-3	Heathryfold Park, Aberdeen
2010/1	Banks o' Dee	Sunnybank	7-1	Crombie Park, Culter
2011/2	Culter	Inverness City	2-0	Kynoch Park, Keith
2012/3	Stonehaven	Maud	3-1	Ian Mair Park, Dyce
2013/4	Culter	Banks o' Dee	0-0, 4-2 pens	Ian Mair Park, Dyce
2014/5	Hermes	Dyce	4-1	Crombie Park, Culter
2015/6	Islavale	Dyce	2-0	Colony Park, Inverurie
2016/7	Aberdeen East End	Colony Park	2-0	Ian Mair Park, Dyce
2017/8	Banks o' Dee	Stonehaven	1-0	Ian Mair Park, Dyce
2018/9	Banks o' Dee	Hermes	6-2	Crombie Park, Culter

Earlier Winners

1968/9	Inverurie Locos
1969/70	Banks o' Dee
1970/1	Banks o' Dee
1971/2	Formartine United
1972/3	Forres Thistle
1973/4	Banks o' Dee
1974/5	Lewis United
1975/6	Sunnybank
1976/7	Banks o' Dee
1977/8	St Machar
1978/9	Banks o' Dee
1979/80	Sunnybank
1980/1	Banks o' Dee
1981/2	Banks o' Dee
1982/3	Sunnybank
1983/4	Banks o' Dee
1984/5	Banks o' Dee
1985/6	Deveronside
1986/7	Turrif United
1987/8	Bon Accord

Recent Elginshire Cup Finals

Season	Winners	Runners Up	Score	Venue
1988/9	Bishopmill United	Deveronside	2-0	Forest Park, Burghead
1989/90	Islavale	Deveronside	2-1	Forest Park, Burghead
1990/1	Islavale	Forres Thistle	3-1	Merson Park, Buckie
1991/2	Nairn St Ninian	RAF Kinloss	2-1	Forest Park, Burghead
1992/3	Islavale	Nairn St Ninian	3-1	Logie Park, Forres
1993/4	Kinloss	Lossiemouth United	3-2	Logie Park, Forres
1994/5	New Elgin	Strathspey Thistle	2-1	Mosset Park, Forres
1995/6	Deveronside	Islavale	1-0	Gordon Park, Portgordon
1996/7	Deveronside	Islavale	2-2 aet, 4-3 pens	Mosset Park, Forres
1997/8	Deveronside	Lossiemouth United	5-2	Logie Park, Forres
1998/9	Islavale	Bishopmill United	2-1	Logie Park, Forres
1999/00	Nairn St Ninian	Islavale	1-0	Mosset Park, Forres
2000/1	Deveronside	Whitehills	3-2	Canal Park, Banff
2001/2	Strathspey Thistle	Islavale	3-2	Mosset Park, Forres
2002/3	Forres Thistle	Islavale	1-0	Merson Park, Buckie
2003/4	New Elgin	Lossiemouth United	2-0	Mosset Park, Forres
2004/5	Forres Thistle	New Elgin	4-3 aet	Mosset Park, Forres
2005/6	New Elgin	RAF Lossiemouth	1-1	Mosset Park, Forres
2006/7	Nairn St Ninian	Fochabers	1-1, 5-3 pens	Fochabers
2007/8	Burghead Thistle		wo	
2008/9	Inverness City	Bishopmill United	3-0	Logie Park, Forres
2009/10	Burghead Thistle	Cruden Bay	1-0	Merson Park, Buckie
2010/1	Newmachar United	Nairn St Ninian	1-0	Kynoch Park, Keith
2011/2	Nairn St Ninian	Portgordon Victoria	3-0	Logie Park, Forres
2012/3	Colony Park	Buckie Rovers	1-0	Boroughbriggs, Elgin
2013/4	Forres Thistle	Buckie Rovers	3-1	Boroughbriggs, Elgin
2014/5	Buckie Rovers	Dufftown	1-1, 3-1 pens	Boroughbriggs, Elgin
2015/6	Forres Thistle	Buckie Rovers	6-2	Boroughbriggs, Elgin
2016/7	Islavale	Nairn St Ninian	2-0	Boroughbriggs, Elgin
2017/8	Nairn St Ninian	Islavale	0-0, 5-4 pens	Boroughbriggs, Elgin
2018/9	Deveronside	Buckie Rovers	4-2	Boroughbriggs, Elgin

Recent Morrison Cup Finals

Season	Winners	Runners Up	Score	Venue
1988/9	Buchanhaven Hearts	Banks o' Dee	2-1	North Lodge Park
1989/90	Longside	Turriff United	2-1	North Lodge Park
1990/1	FC Stoneywood	Banks o' Dee	1-0	Heathryfold Park
1991/2	Lewis United	Dyce	3-1	New Advocates Park
1992/3	Lewis United	Hall Russell United	1-0	Keith Park
1993/4	Hermes	Banchory St Ternan	1-0	New Advocates Park
1994/5	Banchory St Ternan	Hermes	1-0	Crombie Park, Culter
1995/6	Banchory St Ternan	Buchanhaven Hearts	2-1	Denmore Park
1996/7	Hermes	Lewis United	2-1	Denmore Park
1997/8	Cruden Bay	East End	1-1, 4-3 pens	The Meadows, Ellon
1998/9	East End	Patkvale	2-1	Spain Park
1999/00	Cruden Bay	Buchanhaven Hearts	4-1	Davidson Park, Longside
2000/1	Lads Club	Glentanar	3-2	Ian Mair Park, Dyce
2001/2	Dyce	Lewis United	2-1	Woodside
2002/3	Lewis United	Parkvale	2-1	Ian Mair Park, Dyce
2003/4	Fraserburgh United	Banchory St Ternan	2-1	Ian Mair Park, Dyce
2004/5	Banchory St Ternan	Parkvale	2-1	Ian Mair Park, Dyce
2005/6	Banchory St Ternan	Lewis United	2-1	Ian Mair Park, Dyce
2006/7	East End	Maud	5-0	Ian Mair Park, Dyce
2007/8	Islavale	Hall Russell United	1-0	Pleasure Park, Maud
2008/9	Formartine United	Buckie Rovers	2-2, 5-4 pens	The Haughs, Turriff
2009/10	Stonehaven	Inverness City	2-2, 5-4 pens	Simpson Park, Keith
2010/1	Glentanar	Lossiemouth United	4-2	Pleasure Park, Maud
2011/2	New Elgin	Fraserburgh United	4-4, 4-3 pens	Colony Park, Inverurie
2012/3	East End	Inverness City	1-1, 5-4 pens	Simpson Park, Keith
2013/14	Sunnybank	Buchanhaven Hearts	1-1, 4-3 pens	The Meadows, Ellon
2014/15	Longside	Buchanhaven Hearts	3-2	Balmoor Stadium, Peterhead
2016/16	Fraserburgh United	Buchanhaven Hearts	3-1	Davidson Park, Longside
2016/17	Aberdeen East End	Longside	1-1, 4-3 pens	The Meadows, Ellon
2017/18	Aberdeen East End	Fraserburgh United	3-1	Colony Park, Inverurie
2018/19	Banchory St Ternan	Buchanhaven Hearts	1-0	New Advocates Park

Until 91/2	played for by all North (East) clubs
1991/2 - 2012/3	played for by tier 2 clubs
2013/4-	played for by all North (East) clubs

ALL TIME WINNERS 1971/2 -date

6 Parkvale, East End
5 Banchory St Ternan
3 Lewis United, Stonehaven, Fraserburgh United,
2 Cruden Bay, FC Stoneywood, Longside, Sunnybank, Formartine United
1 Banks o' Dee, Buchanhaven Hearts, Dyce, Ellon United, Hermes, Islavale, Lads Club, Mugiemoss, Rosslyn Sports, Glentanar, New Elgin, Sunnybank, Longside

Recent North / Tayside Region Cup Finals

Season	Winners	Runners Up	Score	Venue
1988/9	Deveronside	Downfield	1-0	North End Park, Dundee
1989/90	Downfield	Banks o' Dee	2-1	Heathryfold Park, Aberdeen
1990/1	Downfield	Bon Accord	2-0	North End Park, Dundee
1991/2	Tayport	Forfar West End	2-0	North End Park, Dundee
1992/3	Forfar West End	Islavale	4-2	The Haughs, Turriff
1993/4	St Josephs	Downfield	3-1	North End Park, Dundee
1994/5	Tayport	Violet	4-2	North End Park, Dundee
1995/6	St Josephs	Downfield	2-1	North End Park, Dundee
1996/7	St Josephs	Tayport	2-1	North End Park, Dundee
1997/8	St Josephs	Dundee North End	0-0, 5-4 pens	Glenesk Park, Dundee
1998/9	Kirrie Thistle	Inverurie Locos	3-2	Heathryfold Park, Aberdeen
1999/00	Tayport	Lochee United	1-0	North End Park, Dundee
2000/1	Dundee North End	Broughty Athletic	2-2, 3-0 pens	Strathmore Park, Forfar
2001/2	Tayport	Sunnybank	5-1	Keith Park, Aberdeen
2002/3	Tayport	Dundee North End	3-0	Glenesk Park, Dundee
2003/4	Tayport	Lochee United	3-1 aet	North End Park, Dundee
2004/5	Tayport	Carnoustie Panmure	3-1	North End Park, Dundee
2005/6	Lochee United	Montrose Roselea	3-2	North End Park, Dundee
2006/7	Montrose Roselea	Forfar West End	1-1, 10-9 pens	Station Park, Forfar
2007/8	Forfar West End	Carnoustie Panmure	3-2	Westview Park, Kirriemuir
2008/9	Sunnybank	Blairgowrie	2-2, 4-3 pens	Hillhead, Aberdeen
2009/10	Sunnybank	Broughty Athletic	4-0	North End Park, Dundee
2010/1	Dundee North End	Broughty Athletic	3-2	Downfield Park, Dundee
2011/2	Jeanfield Swifts	Culter	3-0	Heathryfold Park, Aberdeen
2012/3	Jeanfield Swifts	Montrose Roselea	3-0	Whitton Park, Broughty Ferry
2013/4	Lochee United	Luncarty	1-1, 4-3 pens	Tannadice Park, Dundee
2014/5	Tayport	Dundee North End	4-1	Tannadice Park, Dundee
2015/6	Lochee United	Jeanfield Swifts	1-1, 4-2 pens	Tannadice Park, Dundee
2016/7	Broughty Athletic	Tayport	5-1	Tannadice Park, Dundee
2017/8	Carnoustie Panmure	East Craigie	0-0, 3-1 pens	Tannadice Park, Dundee
2018/9	Broughty Athletic	Dundee North End	3-0	Tannadice Park, Dundee

ALL TIME WINNERS
1920/1-Date

16 Banks o' Dee,
14 Sunnybank
9 Culter
8 Hall Russells
5 FC Stoneywood / Stoneywood W
4 East End, Lewis United, Mugiemoss, Parkvale, Richmond, Stonehaven
3 Inverurie Locos, Formartine Utd
2 A Hall & Co, Hawthorn, Rosemount / Rosslyn Sports, Woodside
1 Aberdeen Juniors, Bon Accord, Caledonian, Ellon United, ITC, St Clements, Turriff United, Glentanar, Ellon United, Hermes, Newburgh Thistle

Recent McLeman Cup Finals

Season	Winners	Runners Up	Score	Venue
1988/9	Culter	Inverurie Loco Works	2-1	Heathryfold Park
1989/90	Bon Accord	East End	1-0	Spain Park
1990/1	Banks o' Dee	Crombie Sports	1-0	Heathryfold Park
1991/2	Lewis United	Sunnybank	2-1	Spain Park
1992/3	Culter	Longside	4-3	North Lodge Park
1993/4	FC Stoneywood	Culter	3-3, 3-2 pens	Spain Park
1994/5	Stonehaven	Hermes	3-1	Heathryfold Park
1995/6	Sunnybank	Banks o' Dee	3-1	New Advocates Park
1996/7	Sunnybank	Lads Club	4-0	New Advocates Park
1997/8	Sunnybank	Formartine United	3-2	New Advocates Park
1998/9	Formartine United	Stonehaven	1-0	Denmore Park
1999/00	Sunnybank	East End	2-1	Pittodrie
2000/1	Culter	Longside	4-1	Lochside Park
2001/2	Formartine United	Culter	1-0	Heathryfold Park
2002/3	Culter	Longside	1-0	Heathryfold Park
2003/4	Glentanar	Formartine United	2-1	Lochside Park
2004/5	Culter	Sunnybank	1-0	Lochside Park
2005/6	Formartine United	Parkvale	3-0	Heathryfold Park
2006/7	Sunnybank	Stonehaven	1-1, 4-3 pens	Keith Park
2007/8	Ellon United	Sunnybank	3-2	Lochside Park
2008/9	Hermes	Banks o' Dee	1-0	New Advocates Park
2009/10	Culter	Hermes	2-1	Keith Park
2010/1	Culter	Fraserburgh United	2-1	Longside
2011/2	Stonehaven	Hermes	1-1, 5-4 pens	Keith Park
2012/3	Culter	FC Stoneywood	3-1	Pittodrie
2013/4	Culter	Maud	2-1	Colony Park
2014/5	FC Stoneywood	Hall Russell United	4-2	Heathryfold Park
2015/6	Banks o' Dee	Inverness City	3-0	Merson Park, Buckie
2016/7	Banks o' Dee	Hermes	5-1	Heathryfold Park
2017/8	Newburgh Thistle	Stonehaven	4-3	Heathryfold Park
2018/9	Banks o' Dee	Bridge of Don Thistle	8-0	Ian Mair Park, Dyce

aka Gordon Campbell Construction Trophy 1991-2001
Acorn Heating Trophy 2002-2006
ATR Group Cup 2006-7

North Region Juniors Playing Squads 2020/21

These are not necessarily comprehensive lists of players used - there will be some omissions. However, all players listed were associated with the club concerned during 2020/21. new signings refer to 2021/2.

Aberdeen East End

Manager: Stuart Whicher

Aberdeen University

Coaches: Dan McKendrick, Darren Stephenson, Steven Brownlie
Ian Blackhouse
Charlie Unsworth
Robert Mallinder
Daniel Cotton
Riyadh Nacef
Gregor Morgan
Alex Clark
Ross Clark
Fareid Yassein
Kurtis Turek
Euan McLuckie
Adam Crawford
Adrian Gassama
Nduoma Chilaka
Oscar Forbes
Robert Jones
Brandon Donnelly
Matthew Watson
Kieran Mooney
Glen Mackay
Nathan Brown
Owen McColgan
Cameron Angus
Eli Musepelo
Murray Addison
Nizam Abdulkarim

Banchory St Ternan

Manager: Anton Lennox
Lewis Johnston (2020 Dyce)
Sandy Wood
Rian Wilson
Rhys Gray
Josh Robertson
Jordan Robertson
Calum Reid (2020 OL from Huntly)
Craig Peter
Mikey Bruce
Jordan Clark
Lewis Buxton Nov 2020 Turriff United)
Craig Mackie
Eric Edgar
Dean Henderson
Kyle Harker (2020 Newmachar United)
Ryan Wheelan
Matthew Fleming
Ross Salmon
Trevor Glansbeek
Marc Morrison
Sandy Wood

Banks o' Dee

Manager: Jamie Watt / Tommy Forbes
Greg Alexander
Vitali Sahhalevsit
Neale Allan
Robert Armstrong
Cameron Beattie
Richard Binnie
Jamie Buglass
Stuart Duff
Craig Duguid
Mark Gilmour
Mark Hamilton
Jack Henderson
Dean Lawrie
Kacper Lewecki
Hamish McLeod
Lachie McLeod
Michael Philipson
Matthew Robertson
Max Scoular
Lee Sweeney
Josh Winton
Kane Winton

Bridge of Don Thistle

Manager: Lewis Muirhead
Andy Shearer
Nikolas Wozniak
Ross Forsyth
Chris Angus
Gary Clark
Liam Burnett
Ian Cruickshank
Nicky Gordon
Adam Wilson
Lewi Kidd
Sam Muirhead
Luke Emmett (2020 OL from Formartine United)
Stephen Jeffrey
Lee McKenzie
Max Alexander
Fyfe
Forsyth
Adams
Todd
Rennie

Buchanhaven Hearts

Manager: Anton Lennox / Andrew Wyness (both resigned August 2020), Pat McPherson, Assistant Stuart Whyte (both joined from New Deer, Sep 2020)
Mowat
Grant Reid
Jordan Abolghassem
L Lovell
Mackay
Dean Marr
Beagrie
Ross Cow (2020 OL from Fraserburgh)
M Lovell
Matthew
Glennie
Ritchie
Joe Pedrosa
Dean Donald
Lee Adams
Nick Shewan
Walker
Callum Watson (2020 OL from Fraserburgh)
Stuart Kemp
R Duncan
Zane Laird (2020 OL from Fraserburgh)
Jamie Shewan
Adam McKenzie (2020 OL from Fraserburgh)
Stuart Elphinstone
Pirie
Nathan Gatt
Lee Hulse
Mark Duncan

Burghead Thistle

Manager:
Lewis Grant
James Fraser
Kelvin Mackenzie
Finlay Nicol
James Dingwall
Jack Lingard
Matthew McLeod
Euan Docherty
Dylan Davidson
Lewis Taylor

Colony Park

Manager: Richard Davidson
Ross Durno
David Clark
Barry Peden
Stuart Mackay
Jamie Lind
Adam Morrison
Mike McTavish
Kai Henderson
Conor Strachan
Andy Mitchell
Graeme Cochrane
Martin Crisp
Greg Dorrat
Harrison Hinks
Stuart Gray

Cruden Bay

Manager:
Elihah Ogunwale (2020 Woodside Dons)
Mark Foley
Brodie Ross
Ross Mitchell
Adam Carter
Matty Buckham
Ross Mitchell
Jadon Robb
LJ Stephen
Neil Robb
John Milne
Angus Calder
Owen Silvers
Ross MacKenzie
Ross Young
Shawn Bruce
James Reid
Jamie Butler

Culter

Manager: Lee Youngson
Ritchie Petrie
Gordon Russell
Ryan Stewart
Peter Tait
Ryan Smart
Andrew Youngson
Mark Adam
Jay Cheyne
Elliot Duff
Lenny Johnson
William Mathers
Ben McGregor
Graeme Wilson
Max Berton
Neal McTavish
Jordan Cromar
Lewis Jopp
Shaun Carroll
Kai Ross

Deveronside

Co Managers: Mike Duncan / Ernie Milne
Jordan Russell
Ethan Murray
James Duguid (ex Fraserburgh, Turriff Utd, Deveronvale, Huntly)
Ryan Matheson
Jody Munro (2020 Deveronvale)
Michael Wood
Colin Legge
Mikey Ironside (2020 Turriff United)
Nathan Ross
Rory Davidson
Joel Watt
Ryan Matheson
Callum McIntosh (ex Rothes, Dufftown)
Innes McKay (2020 Buckie Rovers)
Shaun Sopel
Gregor Whyte (2020 OL from Formartine United)

Dufftown

Manager: Jim Stables

Sean McIntosh
Andrew Milton
Michael Simpson
Finlay Stables
James Stables
Scott Thompson
Michael Watson
Cameron Grant
Darren Street
Mark Thomson
Callum Clark
Scott Bowie
Karl Harris
Kelvin Main
Blair MacDonald
Caiol Provan

Dyce
Manager: Alfie Youngson
Sam Anderson
Mark Bartlet
Ben Dalgleish
Glen Donald
Gordon Forsyth
Nicky Gray
Blair Johnston
Lyall Keir
Ian Leith
Jordan Leyden
Gary Livingstone
Craig Mackie
Dean McDonald
Adam McNamee
Andy Pennycook
C Reid
Darren Reid
Sam Robertson
Dean Still
Ryan Wallace

Ellon United
Manager: Mark Kerr (until May 2021), Keith McHarrie (from June 2021)
Scott Baldwin
Sam Barrett
Jay Biggerstaff
Bradley Buckle
Hamish Burr
Kyle Johnston
Neil Law
Andrew Leonard
Grant Anderson
Scott Fraser
Callum Irvine
Callum Tremaine
Neil Irvine
David Coutts
Alexander Blair
Andreas Misacas
Greg Johnston
Stuart Gilmour
Josh Duncan
Lewis Smith
Louis Smith
Fraser Thomson

Forres Thistle
Manager: Tony Ross
Ross Paterson
Neil Moir
Danny Black
Rian Wilson
Matty Milne
Stewart Hunter
Matty Rascal
Charlie Beck
Neil Moir
Dan McLeod
Owen Paterson

Fraserburgh United
Manager:
Michael Lumsden
Steven Lawrence
Bruce Patterson
Tyler Chicken (2020 IL from Fraserburgh)
Zak Conway
William Pauline
James Gibb

Glentanar
Manager: Graham MacBeath

Hall Russell United
Manager: John Carroll

Hermes
Manager: Neil Dawson
Jack Tait
Callum Youngson (ex Sunnybank)
Barbour
Joe Burr
Mitchell
Jack Craig (2020 Bridge of Don Thistle)
Jacob Otto
Grant Mitchell
Cairns
Begg
Stevenson
Hunter
Jack Dawson
McKenzie
Jordan Reid
Ross Gibbon
Jack Sim (ex Ellon United)
Chris Courage

Islavale
Manager: Paul Winton; Assistant: Paul Lamberton (ex Buckie Thistle player)
Lee Alexander
Cameron Chyla
Aaron McPherson
Bruce Morrison
Matthew Nicol
Craig Smith
Michael Gauld
Elliot Gordon
Gary Morrison
Owen Christie
Ricky Henderson
Liam Wood
Craig Simpson
Stuart Thomson
Scott Barron
Scott Riddoch
Lewis Massie

Longside
Manager: Charles West
Buchan
James Bain
Jason Bain
Marshall
Dale McCouaig
McLellan
McLeod
Milne
Mowat.
Murison
Murray
Noble,
Ritchie
Robertson
Taylor
Owen Tocher

Maud
Manager:
Ryan Christie (Dec 2020 OL from Fraserburgh)
Liam Hay
Jordan Smith
Jamie Masson
Jack Walker
Liam Norris (Nov 2020 OL from Turriff United)
George Mead (ex Buchanhaven Hearts)
Austin McLennan
Joe Barbour (Nov 2020 OL from Fraserburgh)
Craig Lowden

Montrose Roselea
Squad 2021/2
Player Manager: Eric Watson (ex Cove Rangers)
McCormack
McDonald
Soutar
Joe Reoch
Taylor
Stephen
Greig
Dave Beedie
Keiran Thomson
Airens
Fergus Alberts (OL from Huntly)
Jamieson
Bailey
Davidson
Gill
Tweed
Callum Watson
Callum Rae
Conlan Robertson
Jordan Harrison

Nairn St Ninian
Manager: K Mason
Kyle Whyte
Keith Mason
Colin Mason
Sean McWilliams
Cameron Angus
Calum Neil
Craig Munro
Marc McDonald
Sam Walker
Ryan MacLeod
Adam MacLeod
J Bell
Lee Haines
Matty Grant
Charlie Fonweban
Ross McKenzie
R Slaney
J Anderson
P Smith
N Grant
C McDonald
C MacPhee
Michael Mulligan
M Brown
Angus Davidson

New Elgin
Manager:
Robert Forsyth
Stephen Dey
David McNamara
Ross Morrison
Dean Stewart

Newmachar United
Manager:
Rhys Bain
Bruce Dryburgh
Lewis Robertson
Dave Black
Murray Dawson
Stevo Young
Steven Travers
Callum Saunders
Chris Hardie
Natty Tough
Connor Walton
Dylan Forsyth
Riley Cooper
Greg Wood
Josh Reynolds
Stewart Gerrie
Craig Mackie
Euan Dryburgh
Kyle Harker
Calum McDonald
Conor Watt
Cameron Cook
Wallace Rodger
Paul Davidson

Rothie Rovers
Manager:
Milne

Scott Chalmers
Gray
Jamie McKinnon (2020 Deveronside)
Graffin
Scott Moir (2020 Maud)
Keith Walker
Wood
Matthew Tewnion
Kenny Mair (2020 Turriff United)
Stuart Hodge
Jake Stewart
Thomson
Andy Bremner
S.Bremner
Ewan Clark (2020 Turriff Thistle)
Jack Brown

Stonehaven

Manager:
Assistant: Paul Mitchell
Chris Jolly
Blair McLennan
Ryan Fenby
Keith Horne (2020 Culter, ex Stonehaven)
Findlay Masson
James Robson (2020 Turriff United)
Adam McLennan
Robbie Fenwick
Curtis Kane
Blair McLennan
David Baillie
Clark Robertson
Alan Lloyd
Danny Anderson
Wayne Barron
Ronan Masson
Cameron Pashley
Josh Peters
Derek Boylan
Curtis Kane
Reece Duncan
Blair Duthie (Dec 2020 Aberdeen University)

Stoneywood Parkvale

Manager:
Kurtis Kane (Dec 2020 Stonehaven, ex Buchanhaven H, Hall Russell Utd))

Sunnybank

Manager: Paul Leahy
2021/2 Squad
Keller Emslie
Matthew Connell
Brian Docherty
Cameron Elphinstone
Andy Mutch
Clark Petrie
Connor Rae Jason Stewart
Aiden Taylor
Jack Burnett
Sean Mackie
Chris Davidson
Edward Fuller
Lewis Kidd
Josh Petrie
Scott Burnett
Dominic Rae
Kevin Robertson
Craig Michie
Jack Craigie

Whitehills

Manager: Ross McAuslin
Assistant: Craig Young
Grant Bryceland (2020 Buckie Rovers)
Stuart Davidson
James MacKintosh
Connor Merson
Matthew Henderson
Keith Cruickshank
Kieran Geddes
Callum Findlay
Rory McKinnon
Ahmed Many
Ritchie Gibb (2020 Deveronside)
Brodie Christie (2020 Buckie Rovers)
Jamie Wood
Kyle Stewart
Ross Coull
Euan Simpson
Matty Henderson (2020 Buckie Rovers)
Kieran Geddes
Buist
King
Golebiewski

WEST JUNIORS

The West Region existed in its present format since 2002 when the Ayrshire and Central Regions were merged. For 2018/19 a new League structure was introduced with four vertical divisions. This meant that the distinction between Ayrshire and Central was effectively ended. Each League operated on a simple "three up three down" basis with no play offs.

2018/19 also saw streamlining of the Cup competitions. The Ayrshire and Central Sectional League Cups were amalgamated. The Ayrshire and Central Knock Out cups were discontinued. Therefore the only knock put competition at Regional level was the West of Scotland Cup.

Towards the end of 2019/20 all member clubs resigned to move to the new Senior West of Scotland League. The West Region of the Scottish Junior FA is no more.

The historical details are included in this year's Almanac for the last time.

West Super League Placings 2002-2020

	2002-3	2003-4	2004-5	2005-6	2006-7	2007-8	2008-9	2009-10	2010-11	2011-12	2012-13	2013-14	2014-15	2015-16	2016-17	2017-18	2018-19	2019-20 (ppg)
Arthurlie		2	2	10	3	7	7	2	2	7	6	9	9	9	7	12		
Ashfield										6	10							
Auchinleck Talbot	10	8	3	1	2	4	4	3	3	3	1	1	1	1	4	2	1	1
Beith						5	3	1	7	5	11		6	7	3	1	4	6
Bellshill Athletic			6	9	9	9	9	11										
Benburb	12																	13
Cambuslang Rangers																	16	
Clydebank										4	3	4	12			10	8	9
Cumnock	9	4	7	5	6	10	11		9	9	9	5	11		6	9	10	10
Girvan																11		
Glenafton Athletic	3	5	9	8	10	6	10				4	6	4	6	1	7	5	4
Hurlford United												3	2	2	5	8	2	7
Irvine Meadow	11					2	1	4	1	1	5	2	3	12			6	5
Johnstone Burgh	5	9	10	11														
Kilbirnie Ladeside	6	12						6	8	12		7	8	3	9	5	13	8
Kilsyth Rangers				7	8	12												
Kilwinning Rangers	4	1	11												10	4	9	2
Kirkintilloch Rob Roy							6	8	6	8	7	10		8	2	6	11	16
Lanark United								10	11									
Largs Thistle								7	5	11		12			11		7	12
Larkhall Thistle	7	10	5	12														
Maryhill	8	6	4	6	11													
Neilston	2	11			4	8	12											
Petershill					7	3	5	9	10	2	2	8	5	11			15	
Pollok	1	3	1	3	1	1	2	5	4	19	8	11		5	8	3	3	3
Renfrew			8	2	12												14	
Rossvale																		11
Rutherglen Glencairn									12									15
Shettleston														10				
Shotts Bon Accord				4	5	11					12		10					
Troon		7	12										7	4	12		12	14
Vale of Clyde							8	12										

	2002-3	2003-4	2004-5	2005-6	2006-7	2007-8	2008-9	2009-10	2010-11	2011-12	2012-13	2013-14	2014-15	2015-16	2016-17	2017-18	2018-19	2019-20 (ppg)
Arthurlie		2	2	10	3	7	7	2	2	7	6	9	9	9	7	12		
Ashfield										6	10							
Auchinleck Talbot	10	8	3	1	2	4	4	3	3	3	1	1	1	1	4	2	1	1
Beith						5	3	1	7	5	11		6	7	3	1	4	6
Bellshill Athletic			6	9	9	9	9	11										
Benburb	12																	13
Cambuslang Rangers																	16	
Clydebank										4	3	4	12			10	8	9
Cumnock	9	4	7	5	6	10	11		9	9	9	5	11		6	9	10	10
Girvan																11		
Glenafton Athletic	3	5	9	8	10	6	10				4	6	4	6	1	7	5	4
Hurlford United												3	2	2	5	8	2	7
Irvine Meadow	11					2	1	4	1	1	5	2	3	12			6	5
Johnstone Burgh	5	9	10	11														
Kilbirnie Ladeside	6	12						6	8	12		7	8	3	9	5	13	8
Kilsyth Rangers				7	8	12												
Kilwinning Rangers	4	1	11												10	4	9	2
Kirkintilloch Rob Roy							6	8	6	8	7	10		8	2	6	11	16
Lanark United								10	11									
Largs Thistle								7	5	11		12			11		7	12
Larkhall Thistle	7	10	5	12														
Maryhill	8	6	4	6	11													
Neilston	2	11			4	8	12											
Petershill					7	3	5	9	10	2	2	8	5	11			15	
Pollok	1	3	1	3	1	1	2	5	4	19	8	11		5	8	3	3	3
Renfrew			8	2	12												14	
Rossvale																		11
Rutherglen Glencairn									12									15
Shettleston														10				
Shotts Bon Accord				4	5	11					12		10					
Troon		7	12										7	4	12		12	14
Vale of Clyde							8	12										

AYRSHIRE DISTRICT LEAGUE - All Time Positions	2002-3	2003-4	2004-5	2005-6	2006-7	2007-8	2008-9	2009-10	2010-11	2011-12	2012-13	2013-14	2014-15	2015-16	2016-17	2017/18
Annbank United	10	4	2							5	8	10	8	9	5	11
Ardeer Thistle	11	12	11	5	5	9	12	12	8	9	4	2		11	9	10
Ardrossan Winton Rovers	9	9	3	9	6	5	4	4	1			5	1		3	6
Craigmark Burntonians	8	8	7	4	7	6	9	6	12	11	11	13	10	7	8	3
Dalry Thistle	5	13	10	8	3	4	1		2		10	8	9	8	6	1
Darvel	13	7	9	12	12	11	7	9	5	10	9	6	3	3	1	
Girvan			4	2		2					7	7	11	1		
Hurlford United						1		1								
Irvine Meadow				1												
Irvine Victoria	6	3	5	10	9	7	8	8	9	6	5	1		2		2
Kello Rovers	4	5	6	6	8	10	6	5	11	2		11	6	6	2	
Kilbirnie Ladeside				3	1											
Kilwinning Rangers								2		4	1		2			
Largs Thistle		6	1									4				
Lugar Boswell Thistle	1					8	3	3	7	7	12	3	5	5	11	5
Maybole	2	1			2				4	1					7	7
Muirkirk	3	11	8	13	11	13	10	11	10	8	12	12	12	10	12	8
Saltcoats Victoria	7	2		11	10	12	11	10	3	7	6	9	7	12	10	9
Troon							5	7	6	3	2					
Whitletts Victoria	12	10	12	7	4	3	2					3	4	4	4	4

WEST SUPER FIRST DIVISION / CHAMPIONSHIP ALL TIME PLACES	2002-3	2003-4	2004-5	2005-6	2006-7	2007-8	2008-9	2009-10	2010-11	2011-12	2012-13	2013-14	2014-15	2015-16	2016-17	2017/18	2018/19	2019/20 (PPG)
Annbank United				10	8	9	9	9	14									
Ardeer Thistle													13					
Ardrossan Winton Rovers										8	13			12				
Arthurlie	1																5	8
Ashfield								8	1			11						
Beith	4	5	4	4	2							2						
Bellshill Athletic	3	1							12					13				
Benburb		11															2	
Blantyre Vics														5	13			1
Cambuslang Rangers	11		10	14												2		14
Clydebank						8	5	3	2					4	2			
Craigmark Burntonians																	13	15
Cumbernauld United	10	10	13						9	7	8	5	4	8	9	8	4	3
Cumnock								2						1				
Dalry Thistle								11		14							11	9
Darvel																9	7	2
Dunipace				13														
East Kilbride Thistle					9	7	8	6	6	11								
Gartcairn																		12
Girvan					14		4	5	4	13					1		14	
Glasgow Perthshire											11							
Glenafton Athletic								7	3	1								
Greenock												9	8	11				
Hurlford United	9	8	6	8	11		14		10	10	1							
Irvine Meadow		7	11		1										6			
Irvine Vics													11		14	5	12	16
Johnstone Burgh					10	14												
Kello Rovers											12					12	15	
Kilbirnie Ladeside			12			4	2				2							
Kilsyth Rangers		4	1				10	13		4	9	10	7	6	3	10	6	7
Kilwinning Rangers				7	3	3	13		11			13		3				
Kirkintilloch Rob Roy			8	11		1							3					
Lanark United							3			12								
Largs Thistle	12			3	6	5	1				3		9	2		3		
Larkhall Thistle					12											11	15	
Lesmahagow					7	13						14						
Lugar Boswell T		9	7	9	13													
Maryhill						11									10	13		
Maybole			9	12		6	6	12			10	4	6	14				
Neilston			5	1				14					12				8	6
Petershill	6	6	3	2											4	1		13
Pollok													1					
Port Glasgow							11											
Renfrew	8	2				10	7	4	8	3	7	12			8	4		5
Rossvale																	3	
Rutherglen Glencairn								1		6	6	7	5	7	5	7	1	
Saltcoats Victoria			14															
Shettleston	5	12											2		7	14		
Shotts Bon Accord	7	3	2				12		7	2		3		9	12			4
St Rochs																	10	11
Thorniewood United										5	4	6	14					
Troon	2			5	5	12						1				6		
Vale of Clyde				6	4	2			13									
Whitletts Victoria								10	5	9	14						9	10
Yoker Athletic											5	8	10	10	11			

League Positions in the Discontinued West Junior Leagues

West Region Central Division One - All Time Positions	2002-3	2003-4	2004-5	2005-6	2006-7	2007-8	2008-9	2009-10	2010-11	2011-12	2012-13	2013-14	2014-15	2015-16	2016-17	2017-18
Ashfield						3	2						14			
Bellshill Athletic										10	9	4	2		13	
Benburb			11			8	11			5	8	3	12		8	3
Blantyre Victoria	12				9	10		7	13				1			5
Cambuslang Rangers		1			11		5	4	5	12		11			1	
Carluke Rovers			12								7	5	5	12		
Clydebank			2	8	2											
Cumbernauld United				5	3	5	6	1								
Dunipace		6	3		10	11		8	9	8	10	7	4	14		
East Kilbride Thistle	6	5	6	2							14					11
Forth Wanderers															10	13
Glasgow Perthshire	8	12			13			10	6	1		13				7
Greenock	3	3	9	10					10	3	1				9	12
Johnstone Burgh							12		12			12		7	14	
Kilsyth Rangers	1								1							
Kirkintilloch Rob Roy	7	2			1											
Lanark United	5	11		6	7	2					6	10	13			
Larkhall Thistle						7	8	12		6	3	6	8	6	2	
Lesmahagow	11			1			9	11			2		6	9	11	15
Maryhill							4	13				9	3	2		
Neilston									4	4	11	1		11	7	4
Port Glasgow		10			4	1		9	8	7	12					8
Renfrew													7	1		
Rossvale														4	5	1
Rutherglen Glencairn	2	9	8	3	5	4	1									
Shettleston			7	12					11	9	4	2				
Shotts Bon Accord								2								9
St Anthonys		8	5	9	8	9	7	3	3	11	5	8	11	13		
St Rochs	10					12					13			5	3	2
Thorniewood United				11			3	6	2					10	4	14
Vale of Clyde	9	7	1							14			9	8	12	
Vale of Leven	4	4	10	7	12		10	5	7	13						
Wishaw													10	3	6	6
Yoker Athletic			4	4	6	6				2						10

West Region Central Division Two - All Time Positions	2002-3	2003-4	2004-5	2005-6	2006-7	2007-8	2008-9	2009-10	2010-11	2011-12	2012-13	2013-14	2014-15	2015-16	2016-17	2017-18
Ashfield	4	7	5	4	1									11	9	5
Baillieston	5															
Bellshill Athletic																3
Benburb				8	3			4	3					2		
Blantyre Vics		5	8	1			1			9	8	1				
Cambuslang Rangers						3					1		5	3		
Carluke Rovers	12	2		7	5	4	4	6	7	1					5	10
Clydebank		1														
Coltness United / Newmains United	11	13	13	W	9	Ab	10	11	12	10	11	11	11	9	12	12
Cumbernauld United																
Dunipace	3						2								8	11
East Kilbride Thistle												10	8	7	3	
Forth Wanderers	6	6	10	9	7	5	8	9	11	3	9	4	7	1		
Gartcairn														5	7	2
Glasgow Perthshire			12	3			3						4	8	1	
Greenock					4	6	7	3								
Johnstone Burgh								1		6	3		2			9
Lanark United			1											6	4	6
Larkhall Thistle									2							
Lesmahagow		4	3						9	4						
Maryhill									6	5	2					
Port Glasgow	2		4	2								8	6	4	2	
Rossvale										8	5	7	1			
Royal Albert	13	9	11	10	11	10	6	10	10	11	10	5	10	12	10	1
Shettleston					6	7	5	2								
St Anthonys	1														11	4
St Rochs		8	7	5	2		9	7	4	2		9	3			
Stonehouse Violet	10	12	6	6	10	8	Ab	Ab	5							
Thorniewood United	9	10	2		8	2										
Vale of Clyde											6	2				7
Vale of Leven						1					7	6	9	10	6	8
Wishaw	7	11	9	11	12	9	11	8	8	7	4	3				
Yoker Athletic	8	3						5	1							
Ab = In abeyance																
W= withdrew																

The West of Scotland Sectional League Cup was the replacement for the separate Central and Ayrshire Sectional Cups. These were discontinued due to the additional League fixtures in the revamped divisional structure. For 2019/20 the sectional fixtures are the reverse of 2018/19. Groups will be re-drawn for 2020/1 but still with some geographic structure.

Recent Ayrshire Sectional League Cup Finals

Season	Winners	Runners Up	Score	Venue
1989/90	Auchinleck Talbot	Irvine Meadow	1-1, 5-3 pens	Rugby Park, Kilmarnock
1990/1	Auchinleck Talbot	Beith	2-1	Rugby Park, Kilmarnock
1991/2	Beith	Glenafton Athletic	2-1	Rugby Park, Kilmarnock
1992/3	Auchinleck Talbot	Irvine Meadow	1-1, 4-3 pens	Winton Park, Ardrossan
1993/4	Beith	Auchinleck Talbot	0-0, 4-3 pens	Somerset Park, Ayr
1994/5	Kilbirnie Ladeside	Auchinleck Talbot	0-0, 4-2 pens	Somerset Park, Ayr
1995/6	Cumnock	Ardeer Thistle	3-1	Somerset Park, Ayr
1996/7	Cumnock	Kilwinning Rangers	1-0	Somerset Park, Ayr
1997/8	Auchinleck Talbot	Beith	2-1	Somerset Park, Ayr
1998/9	Kilwinning Rangers	Auchinleck Talbot	2-1	Somerset Park, Ayr
1999/00	Glenafton Athletic	Kilwinning Rangers	4-1	Somerset Park, Ayr
2000/1	Cumnock	Kilwinning Rangers	2-2, 5-3 pens	Somerset Park, Ayr
2001/2	Cumnock	Irvine Meadow	3-2	Somerset Park, Ayr
2002/3	Auchinleck Talbot	Irvine Meadow	3-1	Somerset Park, Ayr
2003/4	Irvine Meadow	Auchinleck Talbot	2-0	Somerset Park, Ayr
2004/5	Beith	Auchinleck Talbot	1-1, 4-2 pens	Somerset Park, Ayr
2005/6	Glenafton Athletic	Cumnock	4-3	Somerset Park, Ayr
2006/7	Auchinleck Talbot	Cumnock	2-1	Somerset Park, Ayr
2007/8	Auchinleck Talbot	Irvine Meadow	2-1	Somerset Park, Ayr
2008/9	Irvine Meadow	Lugar Boswall Thistle	3-0	Meadow Park, Irvine
2009/10	Kilbirnie Ladeside	Cumnock	3-0	Meadow Park, Irvine
2010/1	Auchinleck Talbot	Irvine Meadow	1-1, 8-7 pens	Bellsdale Park, Beith
2011/2	Auchinleck Talbot	Irvine Meadow	3-0	Bellsdale Park, Beith
2012/3	Irvine Meadow	Auchinleck Talbot	4-4, 4-2 pens	Bellsdale Park, Beith
2013/4	Cumnock	Beith	1-1, 9-8 pens	Portland Park, Troon
2014/5	Glenafton Athletic	Auchinleck Talbot	2-0	Portland Park, Troon
2015/6	Hurlford United	Troon	4-2	Meadow Park, Irvine
2016/7	Kilbirnie Ladeside	Auchinleck Talbot	1-0	Meadow Park, Irvine
2017/8	Auchinleck Talbot	Glenafton Athletic	1-0	Meadow Park, Irvine

Earlier Winners

1968/9	Kello Rovers	1979/80	Glenafton Athletic
1969/70	Kello Rovers	1980/1	Craigmark Burntonians
1970/1	Cumnock	1981/2	Beith
1971/2	Hurlford United	1982/3	Irvine Meadow
1972/3	Kello Rovers	1983/4	Cumnock
1973/4	Irvine Victoria	1984/5	Cumnock
1974/5	Kello Rovers	1985/6	Cumnock
1975/6	Hurlford United	1986/7	Cumnock
1976/7	Cumnock	1987/8	Annbank United
1977/8	Auchinleck Talbot	1988/9	Kilbirnie Ladeside
1978/9	Cumnock		

The Ayrshire Sectional League Cup was introduced in 1968/9 following the establishment of the 6 Junior Regions.

All-Time Winners (50)
12- Cumnock
11- Auchinleck Talbot
4 - Glenafton Athletic, Beith, Irvine Meadow, Kilbirnie Ladeside, Kello Rovers
3 - Hurlford United
1 - Irvine Victoria, Craigmark Burntonians, Annbank United, Kilwinning Rangers

Recent Central Sectional League Cup Finals

Season	Winners	Runners Up	Score	Venue
1978/9	Arthurlie	East Kilbride Thistle	3-1	New Kilbowie Park, Clydebank
1979/80	Shettleston	Blantyre Vics	2-1	Fir Park, Motherwell
1980/1	Larkhall Thistle	Shotts Bon Accord	2-1	Fir Park, Motherwell
1981/2	Petershill	Blantyre Celtic	2-0	Fir Park, Motherwell
1982/3	East Kilbride Thistle	Kirkintilloch Rob Roy	2-1	Fir Park, Motherwell
1983/4	Pollok	Larkhall Thistle	1-0	Fir Park, Motherwell
1984/5	Shotts Bon Accord	Ashfield	3-0	Fir Park, Motherwell
1985/6	Yoker Athletic	Arthurlie	3-2	Fir Park, Motherwell
1986/7	Arthurlie	Pollok	2-1	Fir Park, Motherwell
1987/8	Larkhall Thistle	Pollok	2-1	Douglas Park, Hamilton
1988/9	Shotts Bon Accord	Renfrew	2-1	Fir Park, Motherwell
1989/90	Dunipace	Arthurlie	2-2, 7-6 pens	Fir Park, Motherwell
1990/1	Pollok	Arthurlie	0-0, 4-3 pens	Fir Park, Motherwell
1991/2	Rutherglen Glencairn	Arthurlie	4-1	Hannah Park, Shotts
1992/3	Pollok	Rutherglen Glencairn	3-1	Douglas Park, Hamilton
1993/4	Lesmahagow	Petershill	2-1	Kilbowie Park, Clydebank
1994/5	Petershill	Larkhall Thistle	2-1	Fir Park, Motherwell
1995/6	Blantyre Vics	Pollok	1-0	Fir Park, Motherwell
1996/7	Pollok	Shettleston	4-2	Fir Park, Motherwell
1997/8	Shotts Bon Accord	Arthurlie	0-0, 4-1 pens	Fir Park, Motherwell
1998/9	Neilston	Baillieston	5-0	Fir Park, Motherwell
1999/00	Pollok	Shotts Bon Accord	4-1	Firhill Stadium, Glasgow
2000/1	Cambuslang Rangers	Shotts Bon Accord	1-0	Firhill Stadium, Glasgow
2001/2	Bellshill Athletic	Larkhall Thistle	3-0	Firhill Stadium, Glasgow
2002/3	East Kilbride Thistle	Bellshill Athletic	2-0	Firhill Stadium, Glasgow
2003/4	Pollok	Kilsyth Rangers	1-1, 5-3 pens	Firhill Stadium, Glasgow
2004/5	Maryhill	Shotts Bon Accord	2-0	Firhill Stadium, Glasgow
2005/6	Neilston	East Kilbirde Thistle	0-0, 4-3 pens	Firhill Stadium, Glasgow
2006/7	Pollok	Clydebank	2-1	Lochburn Park, Glasgow
2007/8	Rutherglen Glencairn	Port Glasgow	2-1	Lochburn Park, Glasgow
2008/9	Arthurlie	Shotts Bon Accord	3-2	Lochburn Park, Glasgow
2009/10	Arthurlie	Shotts Bon Accord	1-0	Lochburn Park, Glasgow
2010/1	Shotts Bon Accord	Lanark United	1-0	New Southcroft, Rutherglen
2011/2	Petershill	Shotts Bon Accord	3-2	Lochburn Park, Glasgow
2012/3	Pollok	Renfrew	3-0	Lochburn Park, Glasgow
2013/4	Clydebank	Pollok	2-0	Lochburn Park, Glasgow
2014/5	Blantyre Vics	Cumbernauld United	3-3, 4-2p	Gasworks Park, Larkhall
2015/6	Petershill	Vale of Clyde	1-1, 4-2p	Somervell Park, Cambuslang
2016/7	Kirkintilloch Rob Roy	Shettleston	0-0, 4-2p	Somervell Park, Cambuslang
2017/8	Clydebank	Pollok	2-0	Somervell Park, Cambuslang

Earlier Winners

1968/9	Benburb
1969/70	Shettleston
1970/1	Cambuslang Rangers
1971/2	Kirkintilloch Rob Roy
1972/3	Benburb
1973/4	Kirkintilloch Rob Roy
1974/5	East Klilbride Thistle
1975/6	Lanark United
1976/7	Shettleston
1977/8	Petershill

From 2018/19 the Central and Ayrshire League Cups were amalgamated

2018/9	Auchinleck Talbot	Lesmahagow	6-1	Newlandsfield Park, Glasgow
2019/20	Auchinleck Talbot	Lanark United	6-1	Beechwood Park, Auchinleck

All Time West of Scotland Cup Finals

Season	Winners	Runners Up	Score	Venue
1931/2	Irvine Meadow	Kirkintilloch Rob Roy	2-0	
1932/3	Strathclyde	Kirkintilloch Rob Roy	3-1	
1933/4	Wishaw	Kirkintilloch Rob Roy	3-1	
1934/5	Ardrossan Winton Rove	Arthurlie	2-2, 4-0	
1935/6	Bridgeton Waverley	Vale of Clyde	1-1, 3-2	
1936/7	Parkhead	Petershill	2-0	
1937/8	St Anthonys	Shieldmuir Celtic	3-0	
1938/9	Shawfield	Clydebank	2-0	
1939/40	Glasgow Perthshire	Morton juniors	2-1	
1940/1	Benburb	Blantyre Victoria	3-1	
1941/2	Benburb	Glasgow Perthshire	2-0	
1942/3	Arthurlie	Maryhill	3-0	
1943/4	Blantyre Victoria	Yoker Athletic	3-1	
1944/5	Pollok	Glasgow Perthshire	3-3, 6-1	
1945/6	Saltcoats Victoria	Cambuslang Rangers	3-1	
1946/7	Saltcoats Victoria	Kilbirnie Ladeside	4-1	
1947/8	Auchinleck Talbot	Blantyre Celtic	1-1, 1-0	
1958/9	Newarthill Hearts	Auchinleck Talbot	2-1	
1949/50	Clydebank	Dunipace	3-1	
1950/1	Irvine Meadow	Wishaw	2-1	
1951/2	Petershill	Irvine Victoria	2-0	
1952/3	Baillieston	Wishaw	2-1	
1953/4	Kilsyth Rangers	Duntocher Hibs	1-0	
1954/5	Douglas Water Thistle	Maryhill Harp	3-3, 3-2	
1955/6	Irvine Meadow	Clydebank	4-1	
1956/7	Lesmahagow	Baillieston	2-1	
1957/8	Petershill	Beith	3-1	
1958/9	Johnstone Burgh	Kilsyth Rangers	1-0	
1959/60	Cambuslang Rangers	Thorniewood United	2-0	
1960/1	Kirkintilloch Rob Roy	Cambuslang Rangers	0-0, 6-4	
1961/2	Irvine Meadow	Greenock	2-2, 4-0	
1962/3	Kirkintilloch Rob Roy	Neilston	7-2 Agg	
1963/4	Shotts Bon Accord	Cambuslang Rangers	5-4 Agg	
1964/5	Johnstone Burgh	Beith	5-5 Agg, 1-0	
1965/6	Beith	Cambuslang Rangers	6-4 A	
1966/7	Beith	Greenock	5-3 Agg AET	
1967/8	Kilsyth Rangers	Kilbirnie Ladeside	5-3 A gg	
1968/9	Petershill	Irvine Meadow	4-1	
1969/70	Irvine Meadow	Greenock	1-0	
1970/1	Irvine Meadow	Cambuslang Rangers	0-0, 2-1	
1971/2	Cambuslang Rangers	Kilbirnie Ladeside	2-1	
1972/3	Cambuslang Rangers	Irvine Meadow	4-2	
1973/4	East Kilbride Thistle	Cambuslang Rangers	3-1	
1974/5	Shettleston	Lesmahagow	3-2	
1975/6	Arthurlie	East Kilbride Thistle	1-1, 1-0	
1976/7	Lanark United	Petershill	2-0	
1977/8	Arthurlie	Kirkintilloch Rob Roy	1-0	
1978/9	Auchinleck Talbot	Cumnock	4-0	
1979/80	Auchinleck Talbot	Kirkintilloch Rob Roy	2-1	
1980/1	Auchinleck Talbot	Cumnock	1-1, 1-0	
1981/2	Auchinleck Talbot	Rutherglen Glencairn	3-0	
1982/3	Benburb	Port Glasgow	2-2, 4-2 pens	
1983/4	Auchinleck Talbot	Cumnock	3-2	
1984/5	Auchinleck Talbot	Glenafton Athletic	3-2	
1985/6	Auchinleck Talbot	Pollok	3-2	
1986/7	Pollok	Auchinleck Talbot	3-2	
1987/8	Auchinleck Talbot	Annbank United	2-1	
1988/9	Auchinleck Talbot	Shotts Bon Accord	1-0 aet	Rugby Park, Kilmarnock
1989/90	Irvine Meadow	Larkhall Thistle	4-1	Newlandsfield, Glasgow
1990/1	Largs Thistle	Renfrew	1-0	Somervell Park, Cambuslang
1991/2	Pollok	Beith	1-0	Somervell Park, Cambuslang
1992/3	Shettleston	Lesmahagow	2-0	Somervell Park, Cambuslang

1993/4	Kilwinning Rangers	Shettleston	2-0	Somervell Park, Cambuslang
1994/5	Shettleston	Pollok	1-1, 4-2 pens	Somervell Park, Cambuslang
1995/6	Petershill	Maryhill	2-0	Somervell Park, Cambuslang
1996/7	Arthurlie	Irvine Meadow	5-0	Somervell Park, Cambuslang
1997/8	Pollok	Petershill	3-1	Somervell Park, Cambuslang
1998/9	Kilwinning Rangers	Arthurlie	2-1	Newlandsfield, Glasgow
1999/00	Pollok	Glenafton Athletic	2-1	Somervell Park, Cambuslang
2000/1	Maryhill	Pollok	1-0	Somervell Park, Cambuslang
2001/2	Benburb	Johnstone Burgh	3-2	Newlandsfield, Glasgow
2002/3	Glenafton Athletic	Bellshill Athletic	4-2	Meadow Park, Irvine
2003/4	Maryhill	Bellshill Athletic	3-1	Newlandsfield, Glasgow
2004/5	Troon	Arthurlie	4-3	Newlandsfield, Glasgow
2005/6	Glenafton Athletic	Maryhill	1-1, 4-3 pens	Newlandsfield, Glasgow
2006/7	Petershill	Kilbirnie Ladeside	2-1	Newlandsfield, Glasgow
2007/8	Kilbirnie Ladeside	Pollok	5-1	Lochburn Park, Glasgow
2008/9	Beith	Auchinleck Talbot	2-1	Newlandsfield, Glasgow
2009/10	Irvine Meadow	Kirkintilloch Rob Roy	1-0	Newlandsfield, Glasgow
2010/1	Arthurlie	Pollok	1-0	Newlandsfield, Glasgow
2011/2	Irvine Meadow	Ashfield	2-0	Newlandsfield, Glasgow
2012/3	Glenafton Athletic	Glasgow Perthshire	2-2, 4-3 pens	Newlandsfield, Glasgow
2013/14	Auchinleck Talbot	Troon	2-0	Newlandsfield, Glasgow
2014/15	Arthurlie	Kilwinning Rangers	4-2	Newlandsfield, Glasgow
2015/16	Auchinleck Talbot	Hurlford United	2-0	Newlandsfield, Glasgow
2016/17	Pollok	Cumnock	2-2, 5-4 pens	Newlandsfield, Glasgow
2017-18	Hurlford United	Beith	2-2, 3-1p	Meadow Park, Irvine
2018-19	Beith	Kirkintilloch Rob Roy	1-1, 4-2p	Meadow Park, Irvine
2019-20	Not completed			

Recent Ayrshire Cup Finals

Season	Winners	Runners Up	Score	Venue
1988/9	Glenafton Athletic	Dalry Thistle	3-1	Meadow Park, Irvine
1989/90	Cumnock	Saltcoats Vics	3-0	Meadow Park, Irvine
1990/1	Beith	Largs Thistle	3-2 aet	Valefield, Kilbirnie
1991/2	Beith	Irvine Meadow	3-0	Valefield, Kilbirnie
1992/3	Glenafton Athletic	Cumnock	2-1	Townhead Park, Cumnock
1993/4	Auchinleck Talbot	Irvine Meadow	2-0	Abbey Park, Kilwinning
1994/5	Kilwinning Rangers	Largs Thistle	3-1	Meadow Park, Irvine
1995/6	Auchinleck Talbot	Cumnock	3-1	Beechwood Park, Auchinleck
1996/7	Auchinleck Talbot	Kilwinning Rangers	2-1	Meadow Park, Irvine
1997/8	Kilwinning Rangers	Troon	3-2 aet	Meadow Park, Irvine
1998/9	Kilwinning Rangers	Irvine Meadow	2-1	Meadow Park, Irvine
1999/00	Kilwinning Rangers	Auchinleck Talbot	3-2	Beechwood Park, Auchinleck
2000/1	Glenafton Athletic	Kilwinning Rangers	1-0	Meadow Park, Irvine
2001/2	Kilwinning Rangers	Lugar Boswall Thistle	2-0	Blair Park, Hurlford
2002/3	Beith	Kilwinning Rangers	3-1	Meadow Park, Irvine
2003/4	Beith	Lugar Boswall Thistle	2-0	Townhead Park, Cumnock
2004/5	Auchinleck Talbot	Kilbirnie Ladeside	5-0	Rosebank Park, Lugar
2005/6	Irvine Meadow	Kilwinning Rangers	2-1	Townhead Park, Cumnock
2006/7	Irvine Meadow	Dalry Thistle	7-0	Meadow Park, Irvine
2007/8	Cumnock	Kilwinning Rangers	5-0	Townhead Park, Cumnock
2008/9	Irvine Meadow	Auchinleck Talbot	2-1	Townhead Park, Cumnock
2009/10	Cumnock	Girvan	4-3	Beechwood Park, Auchinleck
2010/1	Auchinleck Talbot	Irvine Meadow	4-0	Beechwood Park, Auchinleck
2011/2	Auchinleck Talbot	Troon	5-1	Portland Park, Troon
2012/3	Largs Thistle	Cumnock	3-0	Bellsdale Park, Beith
2013/4	Troon	Hurlford United	2-0	Beechwood Park, Auchinleck
2014/5	Hurlford United	Auchinleck Talbot	2-0	Meadow Park, Irvine
2015/6	Beith	Irvine Meadow	5-1	Abbey Park, Kilwinning
2016/7	Auchinleck Talbot	Cumnock	5-1	Meadow Park, Irvine
2017/8	Kilwinning Rangers	Largs Thistle	1-0	Meadow Park, Irvine

All Time Winners 1889/90—2017/18

14 Irvine Meadow
15 Auchinleck Talbot
11 Beith, Kilwinning Rangers
8 Kilbirnie Ladeside
7 Cumnock
6 Glenafton Athletic
4 Ardeer Recreation, ArdeerThistle Glenbuck Cherrypickers, Newmilns Saltcoats Victoria, Hurlford United, Largs Thistle
3 Annbank United, Ardrossan Winton Rovers, Lugar Boswell Thistle
2 Darvel, Kello Rovers, Vale of Garnock Strollers
1 Benquhat Heatherbell, Cronberry Eglinton, Dalry Thistle, Dreghorn, Glenburn Rovers, Hurlford Thistle, Irvine Rangers, Irvine Victoria, Kilmarnock Winton, Muirkirk Ath, Shawbank, Stevenston Thistle, Stewarton, Troon Athletic, Troon Juniors

Recent Central District KO Cup Finals

Season	Winners	Runners Up	Score	Venue
1988/9	Pollok	Glasgow Perthshire	2-1	Greenfield Park, Glasgow
1989/90	Vale of Clyde	Shotts Bon Accord	5-1	Newlandsfield, Glasgow
1990/1	Arthurlie	Cambuslang Rangers	3-2	Newlandsfield, Glasgow
1991/2	Petershill	Shotts Bon Accord	1-0	Newlandsfield, Glasgow
1992/3	Lesmahagow	Bellshill Athletic	3-1	Newlandsfield, Glasgow
1993/4	Shotts Bon Accord	Shettleston	0-0, 4-2 pens	Newlandsfield, Glasgow
1994/5	not completed			
1995/6	Maryhill	Pollok	1-0	Somervell Park, Cambuslang
1996/7	Arthurlie	Pollok	2-1 aet	Somervell Park, Cambuslang
1997/8	Arthurlie	Shettleston	4-0	Newlandsfield, Glasgow
1998/9	Rutherglen Glencairn	Shettleston	4-1	Newlandsfield, Glasgow
1999/00	Benburb	Shettleston	2-1	Newlandsfield, Glasgow
2000/1	Bellshill Athletic	Pollok	0-0, 3-2 pens	Somervell Park, Cambuslang
2001/2	Shettleston	Johnstone Burgh	4-1	Petershill Park, Glasgow
2002/3	Arthurlie	Larkhall Thistle	2-1	Petershill Park, Glasgow
2003/4	Petershill	Maryhill	2-0	Adamslie Park, Kirkintilloch
2004/5	Pollok	Arthurlie	2-0	Petershill Park, Glasgow
2005/6	Maryhill	Greenock	2-1	Newlandsfield, Glasgow
2006/7	Lanark United	Kirkintilloch Rob Roy	2-1	Somervell Park, Cambuslang
2007/8	Arthurlie	Renfrew	3-0	Dunterlie Park, Barrhead
2008/9	Pollok	Kilsyth Rangers	1-1, 4-3 pens	Newlandsfield, Glasgow
2009/10	Clydebank	Ashfield	2-0	Newlandsfield, Glasgow
2010/1	Pollok	Shotts Bon Accord	7-3	Newlandsfield, Glasgow
2011/2	Clydebank	Shotts Bon Accord	3-0	Newlandsfield, Glasgow
2012/3	Pollok	Ashfield	3-0	Newlandsfield, Glasgow
2013/4	Clydebank	Cumbernauld United	3-0	Newlandsfield, Glasgow
2014/5	Thorniewood United	Blantyre Vics	2-2, 4-3 pens	Newlandsfield, Glasgow
2015/6	Pollok	Greenock	7-1	Somervell Park, Cambuslang
2016/7	Petershill	Yoker Athletic	2-0	Somervell Park, Cambuslang
2017/8	Pollok	Cumbernauld United	3-1	Greenfield Park, Glasgow

All Time Winners 1921/2—2017/18

14 Pollok
9 Petershill
7 Arthurlie, Maryhill
6 Clydebank
5 Ashfield, St Rochs
4 Renfrew
3 Benburb, Greenock, Kirkintilloch Rob Roy, Shettleston Strathclyde
2 Bellshill Athletic, Cambuslang Rangers, Kilsyth Rangers, Lanark United, Larkhall Thistle, Rutherglen Glencairn, Vale of Clyde
1 Blantyre Vics, Duntocher Hibs, Forth Wanderers, Johnstone Burgh, Lesmahagow, Morton Juniors Port Glasgow, Shawfield, Yoker Athletic, Thorniewood United

Evening Times Cup Winners Cup / Champions Cup - Recent Finals

Year	*Winners*	*Runners Up*	*Score*	*Venue*
1988/9	Arthurlie	Lesmahagow	2-1	Somervell Park, Cambuslang
1989/90	Vale of Clyde	Dunipace	1-0	Greenfield Park, Shettleston
1990/1	Cambuslang Rangers	Pollok	2-0 AET	Greenfield Park, Shettleston
1991/2	Petershill	Johnstone Burgh	3-1 AET	Somervell Park, Cambuslang
1992/3	Lesmahagow	Pollok	4-1	Somervell Park, Cambuslang
1993/4	Arthurlie	Shotts Bon Accord	3-1	Somervell Park, Cambuslang
1994/5	Arthurlie	Petershill	3-1	Newlandsfield, Pollok
1995/6	Maryhill	Blantyre Vics	3-0	Somervell Park, Cambuslang
1996/7	Maryhill	Pollok	2-1	Somervell Park, Cambuslang
1997/8	Maryhill	Greenock	5-1	Lochburn Park, Maryhill
1998/9	Dunipace	Rutherglen Glencairn	3-0	Somervell Park, Cambuslang
1999/00	Port Glasgow	Shettleston	3-1	Somervell Park, Cambuslang
2000/1	Arthurlie	Bellshill Athletic	2-0	Adamslie Park, Kirkintilloch
2001/2	Johnstone Burgh	Bellshill Athletic	3-1	Adamslie Park, Kirkintilloch
2002/3	Kilsyth Rangers	Larkhall Thistle	1-0	Petershill Park, Glasgow
2003/4	Pollok	Petershill	3-1	Lochburn Park, Maryhill
2004/5	Lanark United	Beith	2-0	Petershill Park, Glasgow
2005/6	Irvine Meadow	Maryhill	1-0	Newlandsfield, Pollok
2006/7	Pollok	Irvine Meadow	3-1	Somervell Park, Cambuslang
2007/8	Pollok	Cumnock	3-1	Lochburn Park, Maryhill
2008/9	Irvine Meadow	Pollok	1-0	Newlandsfield, Pollok
2009/10	Irvine Meadow	Kilbirnie Ladeside	4-0	Newlandsfield, Pollok
2010/11	Arthurlie	Shotts Bon Accord	1-0	Newlandsfield, Pollok
2011/2	Ashfield	Irvine Meadow	1-0	Newlandsfield, Pollok
2012/3	Auchinleck Talbot	Hurlford United	3-0	Newlandsfield, Pollok
2013/4	Auchinleck Talbot	Neilston	7-1	Newlandsfield, Pollok
2014/5	Pollok	Blantyre Vics	3-1	Newlandsfield, Pollok
2015/6	Auchinleck Talbot	Renfrew	5-2	Newlandsfield, Pollok
2016/7	Glenafton Athletic	Glasgow Perthshire	2-0	New Tinto Park, Govan
2017/8	Beith	Petershill	4-1	New Tinto Park, Govan

MISCELLANEOUS FOOTBALL

North Caledonian League 2020/21

RECENT LEAGUE CHAMPIONS

1970/1	Dingwall Thistle
1971/2	Dingwall Thistle
1972/3	Alness
1973/4	Alness
1974/5	Golspie Sutherland
1975/6	Golspie Sutherland
1976/7	Invergordon
1977/8	Dingwall Thistle
1978/9	Wick Academy
1979/80	Wick Academy
1980/1	Wick Academy
1981/2	Wick Academy
1982/3	Bunillidh Thistle
1983/4	Muir of Ord
1984/5	Fort William
1985/6	Muir of Ord
1986/7	Wick Academy
1987/8	Invergordon
1988/9	Bunillidh Thistle
1989/90	Balintore
1990/1	Balintore
1991/2	Clachnacuddin Reserves
1992/3	Golspie Sutherland
1993/4	Halkirk United
1994/5	ICT Reserves
1995/6	Fearn Thistle
1996/7	Ross County Reserves
1997/8	ICT Reserves
1998/9	Golspie Sutherland
1999/00	Thurso
2000/1	Alness United
2001/2	Invergordon
2002/3	Thurso
2003/4	Golspie Sutherland
2004/5	Thurso
2005/6	Balintore
2006/7	Golspie Sutherland
2007/8	Golspie Sutherland
2008/9	Golspie Sutherland
2009/10	Thurso
2010/1	Halkirk United
2011/2	Halkirk United
2012/3	Thurso
2013/4	Halkirk United
2014/5	Golspie Sutherland
2015/6	Halkirk United
2016/7	Invergordon
2017/18	Orkney
2018/19	Golspie Sutherland

LEAGUE ONE

	GOL	HAL	INV	ORK	TAI	THU
Golspie Sutherland		Dec 12 5-1	Oct 24 0-4	NOT PLAYED	Nov 28 4-0	Nov 7 1-3
Halkirk United	May 29 0-3		Nov 14 0-0	Nov 28 1-0	Nov 7 0-2	Oct 24 4-0
Invergordon	Jun 5 0-0	Oct 31 3-2		Nov 7 2-0	Oct 17 3-2	NOT PLAYED
Orkney	June 12 0-1	Jun 5 2-3	May 22 1-1*		Dec 12 1-2	May 29 2-2*
Tain St Duthus	Oct 31 1-2	Dec 5 4-1	May 29 2-0	Oct 24 5-5		Nov 14 2-2
Thurso	Oct 17 0-3	May 22 2-1	Jun 12 3-1	Dec 5 3-1	Jun 5 1-1	

* at Holm

LEAGUE TWO

	ALN	BON	INV	LOC	NAI	SCO
Alness		Jun 5 4-1	Dec 19 2-1	Nov 14 1-1	Dec 5 6-1	May 29 W-L**
Bonar Bridge	Oct 24 0-9		Nov 14 1-2	Dec 5 1-0	Nov 28 1-4	Nov 21 5-0
Inverness Athletic	Jun 2 2-3	Nov 7 4-0		Oct 31 1-1	Oct 17 1-3	Dec 5 4-0
Loch Ness		May 29 7-0	Nov 28 0-0		Nov 6 3-5	Oct 17 11-1
Nairn County Reserves	Jun 12 4-2	Oct 31 7-3	Dec 12 0-1	Oct 24 2-3		Jun 5 W-L**
Scourie	Nov 7 0-13	Dec 12 0-2	Oct 24 0-4	May 22 1-3	Nov 14 1-5	

** Scourie scratched

LEAGUE ONE

Pos	Team	Pld	W	D	L	GF	GA	GD	Pts	ADJ
1	Golspie Sutherland	9	6	1	2	19	9	+10	19	
2	Invergordon	9	4	3	2	14	10	+4	15	
3	St Duthus	10	4	3	3	21	19	+2	15	
4	Thurso	9	4	3	2	16	16	0	11	(-4)
5	Orkney	9	0	3	6	12	20	-8	8	(+5)
6	Halkirk United	10	3	1	6	13	21	-8	7	(-3)

LEAGUE TWO

Pos	Team	Pld	W	D	L	GF	GA	GD	Pts
1	Alness United	10	8	1	1	46	11	+35	25
2	Nairn County A	10	7	0	3	32	21	+11	21
3	Inverness Athletic	10	5	2	3	20	10	+10	17
4	Loch Ness	10	4	3	3	30	17	+13	15
5	Bonar Bridge	10	3	0	7	14	37	-23	9
6	Scourie	10	0	0	10	3	49	-46	0

NORTH CALEDONIAN CUP

1	Thurso	Alness United	1	1	3-0p
1	Loch Ness	Tain St Duthus	3	2	
1	Golspie Sutherland	Nairn County Reserves	6	0	
1	Bunillidh Thistle	Orkney	D		
1	Invergorodon	Inverness Athletic	4	1	
2	Bonar Bridge	Halkirk	1	2	
2	Thurso	Loch Ness	G		
2	Golspie Sutherland	D	H		
2	Invergordon	Scourie	wo	scr	
SF	H	Halkirk			
SF	G	Invergordon			
F					

Due to their very short League season, the NCAL were able to complete the season in June following a six-month lay off.

The North Caledonian Cup competition was not completed and the other Cups never started.

For season 2021/2 the League returns to a single division. It now sits below the Highland League in the northern portion of the "Pyramid". If the NCAL Champions have an SFA License they will be eligible to enter a Play Off with the Champions of the North Juniors and the Midlands League. The winners would then play the bottom team in the Highland League.

At present only Golspie Sutherland are licensed.

University Football 2020/1

Over many years the biggest prize in Scottish University football was the Queen's Park Shield, competed for on Wednesday afternoon's by the Scottish seats of learning. Nowadays the top Scottish sides compete in the various divisions of the UK-wide British Universities and Colleges Sport (BUCS) tournaments. The Queen's Park Shield is still played for but it is now a knock out competition rather than a League. All University football is played on Wednesday afternoons from September through until April. The BUCS website provides admirable detail.

No University football was played during 2020/1. Arrangements for 2021/2 were not made when the Almanac went to press.

AMATEUR FOOTBALL

SCOTTISH AMATEUR FA

PAST OFFICE BEARERS

PRESIDENTS
1909-21 Robert A. Lambie (Glasgow F.P.AFL)
1921-23 James M. Fullarton (Scottish AFL)
1923-24 John T. Robson (Moorpark AFC)
1924-28 Peter Buchanan (Whitehill F.P.AFC)
1928-30 James A. McArthur (Murrayfield Amateurs)
1930-33 James Taylor (Glasgow F.P.AFL)
1933-36 Robert W. Milne (Falkirk Amateurs F.C.)
1936-38 Peter Wallace (Bankvilla AFC)
1938-46 William W. Terris (Warrender AFC)
1946-48 John S. Welsh (7th Home Guard O.C.)
1948-53 Thomas M. Paterson (Mearns AFC)
1953-59 George H. Keith (Windsor AFC)
1959-64 George Bowman (Whitehill F.P.AFC)
1964-69 George W. Dallas (Bankvilla AFC)
1969-74 William Jarrett (Angus AFA.)
1974-78 Alex. M. Campbell (Babcock & Wilcox AFC)
1978-83 John Robertson (Fenwick Thistle AFC)
1983-87 Thomas A. Wilkie (Ashdale AFC)
1987-90 Robert Hay (Ashvale Victoria AFC)
1990-94 Alan Gordon (Barr & Stroud AFC)
1994-98 Robert Lamberton (Springfield United AFC)
1998-02 George Wilson (Milngavie Wanderers AFC)
2002-05 Jack Keating (Scottish Amateur F.L.)
2005-10 Angus Mackay (Symington Tinto AFC)
2010-13 Graham Harkness (Dumfries Sunday AFL)
2013-14 Hugh Knapp (Life Member)
2014-18 Charles R Gallacher (Lothian & Edinburgh AFA)
2018- Stuart Urquhart (Troon Dundonald AFC)

VICE PRESIDENTS
1922-24 George H. Mitchell (Scottish AFL)
1924-25 John Paterson (Glasgow University AFC)
1925-26 F.W.M. Keith (Scottish AFL)
1928-30 James Taylor (Glasgow F.P.AFL)
1930-33 Robert W. Milne (Falkirk Amateurs F.C.)
1933-36 Peter Wallace (Bankvilla AFC)
1936-38 William W. Terris (Warrender AFC)
1938-46 John S. Welsh (L.M.S. Rovers AFC)
1946-48 Thomas M. Paterson (Mearns AFC)
1948-49 A.M. Thomson (Killermont AFC)
1949-53 George H. Keith (Windsor AFC)
1953-58 Jack G. Orr (Eaglesham AFC)
1958-59 George Bowman (Whitehill F.P.AFC)
1959-64 George W. Dallas (Bankvilla AFC)
1964-69 William Jarrett (Angus AFA.)
1969-74 Alex. M. Campbell (Babcock & Wilcox AFC)
1974-78 John Robertson (Fenwick Thistle AFC)
1978-79 Alan J. Mochrie (Cambria AFC)
1979-83 Thomas A. Wilkie (Ashdale AFC)
1983-87 Robert Hay (Ashvale Victoria AFC)
1987-90 Alan Gordon (Barr & Stroud AFC)
1990-94 Robert Lamberton (Springfield United AFC)
1994-98 George Wilson (Milngavie Wanderers AFC)
1998-02 Jack Keating (Scottish Amateur F.L.)
2002-10 Stuart Urquhart, Hon. Senior (Troon AFC)
2010-14 Alex McDowall, Hon. Junior (Sunday Central AFL)
2014-18 Stuart Urquhart (Troon Dundonald AFC)
2018- Iain Cowden (Caledonian AFL)

SECRETARIES
1909-15 James W. Millen (Hamilton Crescent F.P.AFC)
1919-21 J. Gardner Guthrie C.A.
1929-37 R.A.D. Sinclair C.A.
1937-49 Norman H. Chapman (Bellahouston Academy F.P.AFC)
1949-69 A. Murray McNab (Queen's Park F.P.AFC)
1969-74 W. M. Leslie Michie (Neilsonians AFC)
1974-76 J. A. Barbour Esq., F.R.I.C.S.
1976-92 Iain McTweed M.B.I.M., D.M.S.
1992-94 No Secretary
1994-94 Arthur Duncan
1994-12 Hugh Knapp
2012-13 Martin Bell
2013- Thomas McKeown M.C.I.B.S.

TREASURERS
1909-15 Walter M. Crow (Bellahouston Academy F.P.AFC)
1919-21 Walter M. Crow (Bellahouston Academy F.P.AFC)
1929-30 James Taylor (Glasgow F.P.AFL)
1930-33 Norman H. Chapman (Bellahouston Acad. F.P.AFC)
1933-34 James Taylor (Glasgow F.P.AFL)
1934-48 A. M. Thomson (Killermont AFC)
1948-49 A. Murray McNab (Queen's Park F.P.AFC)
1949-50 Norman H. Chapman (Bellahouston Acad. F.P.AFC)
1950-58 James Weir (Dalziel H.S.F.P.AFC)
1958-69 James Brown (City Chamberlains AFC)
1969-75 Alexander Sloan & Co C.A.
1975-81 Thomas S. Churchill C.A.
1981-83 Alexander Sloan & Co C.A.
1983-92 Iain McTweed M.B.I.M., D.M.S.
1992-94 Hugh Knapp (Lanarkshire AFA.)
1994-98 Jack Keating (Scottish Amateur F.L.)
1998- George Dingwall (Central Scottish A.F.L)

MATCH SECRETARIES
J. Jamieson (John Neilson F.P.AFC)
1946-54 A. R. Drummond (West of Scotland AFL)
1954-58 James W. Allan (Scottish AFL)
1958-88 Andrew S. Laird (Woodside F.P.AFC)
1988-90 James Robertson (Stirling & District AFA)
1987-12 George Watson, (Stirling & District AFA)

ASSISTANT MATCH SECRETARIES
1979-88 James Robertson (Stirling & District AFA.)
1988-90 George Watson (Stirling & District AFL)
1990-94 George Steele (Doune Castle AFC)
1994-99 T. W. Allison (Lothian AFA.)

MATCH SECRETARIES (Sunday Trophy)
1987-90 George Steel (Doune Castle AFC)
1990-92 David Blair (Kirkcaldy & District AFL)
1992-95 Rex Gallagher (Maybury AFA)
1995-99 George Butler (Muirend AFC)
1999-12 Robert W. McGechie (Lothian & Edin. AFA)

PRESIDENTS AWARD
T. F. Harding - West of Scotland AFL (1998)
J. G. McQuade - West of Scotland AFL (1998)
P. M. Omand - Kirkcaldy & District AFA. (1999)
H. Morrison – North West Sutherland AFA. (1999)
H. Murphy - Central Scottish AFL (1999)
P. Hills - Mid Annandale AFC (2002)
G. Harkness - Dumfries Sunday AFL (2003)
R. Ferrol - Ayrshire AFA. (2005)
J. F. Keron – Perthshire AFA (2009)
G. F. R. Japp – Stirling & District AFA (2013)
R. Torrance – Stirling & District AFA (2013)
D. Tosh - Midlands AFA. (2013)
J. Clarke - Lothian & Edinburgh AFA (2014)
S. McSwiggan - Dundee Saturday Morning AFL (2015)
K. McIvor - Lewis and Harris AFA (2016)
J. Thomson – Perthshire AFA (2016)
A. Denny – Fife AFA (2017)

Amateur football was severely impacted by COVID during 2020/1. The impact varied slightly from area to area depending on the level of restrictions applied there by the Scottish Government.

A few Leagues in the North and East of the country did make a start to the 2020/1 season. However, these were all quickly abandoned. When restrictions eased in May 2021 some Leagues opted to run "Summer Cups" for interested clubs. In many ways these were more like Friendly tournaments and some were not played to a conclusion.

None of the Scottish Amateur FA Cups, national or regional, took place in 2020/1.

SUMMER LEAGUES

CAITHNESS AMATEUR FA 2020

Season Cancelled.

CAITHNESS AMATEUR FA 2021

In June 2021 the Caithness AFA announced a reduced format for the 2021 season. The clubs were split into two divisions as follows:

EAST LEAGUE	WEST LEAGUE
John O'Groats	Castletown
Keiss	Halkirk
Lybster	High Ormlie Hotspurs
Staxigoe United	Pentland United
Watten	Thurso Academicals
Wick Groats	Thurso Pentland
Wick Thistle	Top Joes

Due to further COVID cases it was decided in July 2021 NOT to go ahead with the season meaning a second year of no competition.

Club	Formed	Ground		Postcode
Castletown	1900	Murrayfield Park	Castletown	KW14 8TY
Halkirk	1928	Morrison Park	Halkirk	KW12 6XF
High Ormlie Hotspur	2011	Ormlie Park	Thurso	KW14 7LD
John o' Groats	1982	Folke Park	John o' Groats	KW1 4YH
Keiss	1927	Bayview Park	Keiss	KW1 4UY
Lybster	1887	Cow Park	Lybster	KW3 6BJ
Pentland United	1948	Ham Park	Dunnett	KW14 8XE
Staxigoe United	2006	Bignold Park	Wick	KW1 5NH
Thurso Acks	1898	The Dammies	Thurso	KW14 8HN
Thurso Pentland	1918	The Dammies	Thurso	KW14 8HN
Thurso Swifts	1897	The Dammies	Thurso	KW14 8HN
Top Joes		Ormlie Park	Thurso	KW14 7LD
Watten		Watten Park	Watten	KW1 5YW
Wick Groats	1893	Bignold Park	Wick	KW1 5NH
Wick Thistle	1889	Bignold Park	Wick	KW1 5NH
		Naver 3G	Thurso	KW14 7HF

INVERNESS & DISTRICT A.F.A. 2020

Season Cancelled.

INVERNESS & DISTRICT A.F.A. 2021

The 2021 season did go ahead.

Participating Clubs:

INVERNESS AND DISTRICT FA

Premier Division	Home Ground	POSTCODE
Ardersier	Ardersier Park	IV2 7SL
Avoch	Coronation Park, Avoch	IV9 8RW
Contin	Munro Park, Contin	IV14 9ES
ICM Electrical	Culloden	IN2 7NY
IRN Security	Bught Pitches	IV3 5SP
Loch Ness	Bught Pitches	IV3 5SP
Maryburgh	Maryburgh Playing Field	IV7 8BE
NMM Sam's	Bught Pitches	IV3 5SP
Tomatin	Bught Pitches	IV3 5SP
Division One		
Black Rock Rovers	Culcairn Park, Evanton	IV16 9YT
Balloan Compass	Culloden, Bught	q.v.
Charlestelona	Culloden, Bught	q.v.
Culloden Blacksmiths	Bught Pitches	IV3 5SP
Drakies PDG	Culloden, Bught	q.v.
Highland Hospice	Bught Pitches	IV3 5SP
Hill Rovers	Bught Pitches	IV3 5SP
Innes CI	Bught Pitches	IV3 5SP
Muir of Ord Rovers	Pavilion Park, Muir of Ord	IV6 7RR
Division Two		
AFC River Ness	Bught Pitches	IV3 5SP
Black Isle United	Culbokie	IV7 8GZ
Citadel	Bught Pitches	IV3 5SP
Conon Bridge	Conon Bridge	IV7 8AZ
Gellions Hotel		
Highland Athletic	Bught Pitches	IV3 5SP
Invergordon Soc Club	Riverside Park, Nairn	IV12 5EL
Inverness Athletic	Bught Pitches	IV3 5SP
NT Highland Airways		
Tomatin United	Bught Pitches / Raigbeg School	q.v. / IV13 7XY

LEWIS AND HARRIS A.F.A. 2020

Season Cancelled.

LEWIS AND HARRIS A.F.A. 2021

The season began in June 2021, with eight teams participating:

Athletic	Goathill Park, Stornoway	HS1 2NY
Back	Coal Uarah, Back	HS2 0LS
Carloway	Cnoc a' Choilich, Carloway	HS2 9AG
Harris	Reilly Park, Tarbert	HS3 3BH
Lochs	Creaghan Dubh, Lochs	HS2 9NU
Ness	Fivepenny, Ness	HS2 0XG
Point	Garrabost, Knock	HS2 0PD
United	Goathill Park, Stornoway	HS1 2NY
Westside	Barvas Hall, Barvas	HS2 0RA

LEWIS AND HARRIS LEAGUE HONOURS

Year	Champions	Runners-up	Third place
1980	Ness	Point	Stornoway Rovers
1981	Point	Ness	Stornoway Athletic
1982	Ness	Stornoway Athletic	Tolsta
1983	Harris	Point	Ness
1984	Ness	Back	Stornoway Athletic
1985	Ness	Point	Stornoway Athletic
1986	Ness	Point	Stornoway Athletic
1987	Ness	Stornoway Athletic	Lochs
1988	Stornoway Athletic	Ness	Lochs
1989	Ness	Lochs	Stornoway Athletic
1990	Ness	Stornoway Athletic	Stornoway Rovers
1991	Ness	Stornoway Athletic	Lochs
1992	Ness	Point	Stornoway Athletic
1993	Point	Ness	Harris
1994	Ness	Back	Point
1995	Lochs	Back	Ness
1996	Point	Ness	Harris
1997	Point	Stornoway Athletic	Harris
1998	Point	Stornoway Athletic	Harris
1999	Ness	Point	Harris
2000	Back	Harris	Point
2001	Harris	Ness	Lochs
2002	Point	Harris	Back
2003	Lochs	Back	Point
2004	Point	Back	Lochs
2005	Lochs	Stornoway Athletic	Back
2006	Stornoway Athletic	Lochs	Point
2007	Lochs	Back	Stornoway Athletic
2008	Lochs	Back	Carloway
2009	Lochs	Back	Carloway
2010	Lochs	Back	West Side
2011	Back	Carloway	West Side
2012	Stornoway Athletic	Back	Lochs
2013	Carloway	Stornoway Athletic	West Side
2014	Westside	Lochs	Carloway
2015	Lochs	Point	West Side
2016	Lochs	Point	West Side
2017	Carloway	Westside	Point
2018	Point	Lochs	West Side
2019	Point	Westside	Carloway
2020	No competition		

NORTH WEST SUTHERLAND A.F.A. 2020

Season Cancelled.

NORTH WEST SUTHERLAND A.F.A. 2021

The North West Sutherland FA planned to start in July 2021. The 12 teams were to be split into four mini leagues of three on a geographical basis.

However, the season was cancelled again at the last minute due to a spike in COVID cases. The need to travel long distances in shared cars left players and officials unwilling to take the risks involved.

MEMBERSHIP 2019

Club	Home Ground	Postcode
Brora Wanderers	School Park, Brora	KW9 6PH
Embo	Back Park, Embo	IV25 3PT
Golspie Stafford	Stafford Park, Golspie	KW10 6TT
Helmsdale United	Couper Park	KW8 6HH
Inver	Inver Football Pitch	IV20 1RX
Invergordon Social Club	Recreation Ground, Invergordon	IV18 0AZ
Kinlochbervie	Scourie Football Pitch	IV27 4TF
Lairg Rovers	Ferry Croft Park, Lairg	IV27 4AZ
Lochinver	Culag Park, Lochinver	IV27 4LR
Melvich	Melvich Primary School	KW14 7YR
Tain Thistle	The Links, Tain	IV19 1EH
Tongue	Bettyhill Football Pitch	KW14 7TD

Twelve teams had intended to compete in 2021:

Brora Wanderers
Dornoch City
Golspie Stafford
Helmsdale United
Inver
Invergordon Social Club
Kinlochbervie
Lairg Rovers
Lochbroom (Ullapool)
Lochinver
Melvich

ORKNEY A.F.A. 2020

Season Cancelled.

ORKNEY A.F.A. 2021

The 2021 season is operating as normal with Division A, Division B and the Parish Cup all being contested.

ORKNEY FOOTBALL GROUNDS

Bignold Park	Kirkwall	Bignold Park Road	KW15 1PT
Burrayfield	Burray	Burray Community School	KW17 2SS
Dounby	Dounby	Dounby Community School	KW17 2HH
Firth	Firth	Firth Primary School	KW17 2ES
Harray	Harray	Harray Community Centre	KW17 2LE
Holm Rockworks	Holm	St Mary's	KW17 2RU
Hoy	Hoy	North Walls School	KW16 3NX
KGS Playing Fields	Kirkwall	Kirkwall Grammar School	KW15 1QN
Pickaquoy	Kirkwall	Pickaquoy Centre	KW15 1LR
Sanday	Sanday	Sanday Community School	KW17 2AY
South Ronaldsay	St Margaret's Hope	St Margaret's Hope Primary School	KW17 2TN
St Andrews	Tankerness	St Andrews Community Centre	KW15 1PX
Stromness Astro	Stromness	Stromness Avademy	KW16 3JS
Stromness Market Green	Stromness	North End Road	KW16 3AH
The Rockery	Norseman Village	Rendall Community Centre	KW17 2NY
Westray	Westray	Westray Community School	KW17 2DH

ORKNEY FOOTBALL 2021

Orkney Cheese A League

Accies
Dounby
Hotspurs
Isles United
Rendall
Rovers
Stromness
Thorfinn

E Fraser Electrical Limited B League

East United
Firth
Harray
Wanderers

Parish Cup Draw

Stenness vs Firth
Westray vs Flotta, Hoy & Walls
Sandwick vs Holm
Stromness vs Deerness
St Ola vs South Ronaldsay
Birsay vs St Andrews

Byes - Sanday and Rendall

SHETLAND A.F.A. 2020

Season Cancelled.

SHETLAND A.F.A. 2021

The 2021 season operated normally.

Participating clubs were:

Ocean Kinetics Premier League

Celtic
Delting
Ness United
Scalloway
Spurs
THistle
Whalsay
Whitedale

RG Construction Reserve League

Banks
Bressay
Celtic
Delting
LK Galaxy
Ness United
Scalloway
Spurs
Thistle
West Side Rebels
Whalsay
Whitedale

SHETLAND FOOTBALL VENUES

Ground	Town	Postcode
Aith Junior High School	Aith	ZE2 9NB
Boddam Sportsfield	Dunrossness	ZE2 9JG
Brae Grass Pitch	Brae	ZE2 9TY
Bressay Sports Field	Bressay	ZE2 9ET
Clickimin Leisure Complex 1	Lerwick	ZE1 0PJ
Clickimin Leisure Complex 4	Lerwick	ZE1 0PJ
Cunningsburgh Sportsfield	Cunningsburgh	ZE2 9HQ
Fraser Park	Scalloway	ZE1 0TR
Gilbertson Park	Lerwick	ZE1 0HN
Hamnavoe Playing Field	Hamnavoe	ZE2 9LA
Harbison Park	Symbister, Whalsay	ZE2 9AB
Sandwick Playing Field	Sandwick	ZE2 9NU
Seafield Park	Lerwick	ZE1 0RJ
Strom	Whiteness	ZE2 9LJ

VENUES 2021

'A' Div.
Celtic @ Clickimin / Gilbertson / Seafield.
Delting @ Brae Grass.
Ness Utd @ Boddam. (Occasionally Cunningsburgh).
Scalloway @ **Hamnavoe.** (Appear to have moved from Fraser Park)
Spurs @ Clickimin / Gilbertson / Seafield.
Thistle @ Clickimin / Gilbertson / Seafield.
Whalsay @ Harbison Park.
Whitedale @ Strom.

Reserve Div.
Banks @ Clickimin / Gilbertson / Seafield.
Bressay @ Bressay.
LK Galaxy @ Clickimin / Gilbertson / Seafield.
West Side Rebels @ Aith.

SKYE AND LOCHALSH A.F.A. 2020

Season Cancelled.

SKYE AND LOCHALSH A.F.A. 2021

Eight teams signed up for the 2021 Skye and Lochalsh season.

Glenelg
Kyle
Kyleakin
Mallaig
NW Skye
Portree
Portree Juniors
Sleat & Strath

	Club	Home Ground	Postcode
1	Mallaig	Mallaig HS Astro	PH41 4RG
2	Sleat & Strath	Broadford Primary School Park	IV49 9AG
3	Kyleakin	Kyleakin Commnunity Hall	IV41 8PQ
4	NW Skye	Uig Football Pitch	IV51 9XP
5	Gairloch & Aultbea United	Glebe Park, Gairloch	IV21 2DE
6	Portree Juniors	King George V Park	IV51 9BW
7	Glenelg	Glenelg Community Hall	IV40 8JR
8	Portree	Portree HS	IV51 9BW
9	Kyle	Douglas Park, Kyle of Lochalsh	IV40 8AB

UIST AND BARRA A.F.A. 2020

Season Cancelled.

UIST AND BARRA A.F.A. 2021

The season was operating as usual. Competing teams were:

	Ground	Postcode
Barra	Horve PF, Castlebay	HS9 5XQ
Iochdar Saints	Liniclate School / Dark Island Pitch	HS7 5PJ / HS7 5PJ
Southend	Daliburgh School	HS8 5SS
Eriskay	Eriskay	HS8 5JL
Benbecula	Liniclate School / Dark Island Pitch	HS7 5PJ / HS7 5PJ
North Uist	Paible School, Bayhead	HS6 5DX

WINTER FOOTBALL 2020/1 SEASON

ABERDEEN SUNDAY AMATEUR FA 2020/1

The season began in October but was suspended in December due to COVID restrictions.

Contact: Mr. Brian Derrett
Email: brianderre@gmail.com
Telephone: 01224 725157

None of the Cup competitions in the Aberdeen Sunday Amateurs were completed.

Games are usually played on Sunday Mornings with a 10.30am Kick Off.

	BAA	BUC	DEE	GOL	GRA	KTH	KSTRE	MAL	NSTAR	NEA	OVE	POR	SEA	SHE
Bon Accord Ams								1-1				4-3		2-1
Bucksburn Thistle				0-6			3-2					5-3	2-2	
Dee Ams		5-0					11-2						4-5	
Golden Tee			3-3					2-0			2-3			
Granite Thistle									4-0	5-1				
Kincorth Athletic				5-1	7-2			2-0		3-1		6-0	6-0	13-0
King Street Calcio	0-6					1-7								
Malibu							1-0							
Northstar Inverdee	3-3	2-3												
North East Albion			5-2				8-2				1-2			
Overhype	0-0	4-1					4-2		3-1				1-6	
Portland Milltimbers			1-5					3-1	1-4					
Seaton Forest					5-2									
Sheddocksley					0-9									

1	Kincorth Athletic	8	8	0	0	49	5	+44	100
2	Overhype	6	5	1	0	16	7	+9	93
3	Bon Accord Amateurs	6	3	3	0	16	8	+8	73
4	Dee Amateurs	6	3	1	2	30	16	+14	66
5	Seaton Forest	5	3	1	1	18	15	+3	64
6	Bucksburn Thistle	7	3	1	3	14	24	-10	66
7	Granite Thistle	5	3	0	2	22	13	+9	66
8	Golden Tee	5	2	1	2	14	11	+3	43
9	North East Albion	5	2	0	3	16	14	+2	34
10	Northstar Inverdee	5	1	1	3	10	14	-4	26
11	Malibu	5	1	1	3	3	8	-5	29
12	Portland Milltimbers	7	1	0	6	12	31	-19	18
13	Sheddocksley	3	0	0	3	1	24	-23	0
14	King Street Calcio	7	0	0	7	9	40	-31	0

ABERDEENSHIRE AMATEUR FA 2020/21

Season Cancelled.

Contact: Mr. Martin Smith
Email: martinsmith610@gmail.com
Telephone: 07413 756654

The Aberdeenshire Amateur Football Association has a membership of 66 clubs and is currently one of the largest amateur football associations in Scotland. The Association was formed in 1947 and its coverage extends to both the City of Aberdeen and Aberdeenshire. The Association is affiliated to the Scottish Amateur Football Association ("SAFA"), which celebrated its centenary in 2009, and the aims of the Association are to foster and develop the game of amateur football in the local area.

League Structure

The AAFA clubs are divided into five leagues – a Premier Division, two First Division sections (North and East) and two Second Division sections (North and East). The system of promotion and relegation allows new clubs to reach the Premier Division within two seasons.

Cup Competitions

All AAFA Clubs are eligible to enter the Scottish Amateur Cup competition. The first two rounds are drawn on a regional basis and there is a national draw from the third round onwards.

AAFA Clubs are also eligible to enter the North of Scotland Amateur Cup which is one of seven regional cup competitions run under the auspices of the Scottish Amateur Football Association.

The AAFA also organises a range of cup competitions for member clubs each season. The most prestigious of these is the Aberdeen FC Trophy, which was donated to the Association by Aberdeen Football Club in season 1947-48. The Aberdeen FC Trophy is a knock-out cup competition for all 71 member clubs. The two other main AAFA cup competitions are the Association Trophy (contested by clubs at Premier and First Division level) and the Dickie Trophy (contested by clubs at Second Division level).

In addition, there is a knockout league cup competition for each division, as follows:

Premier Division – Premier Trophy
Division One (North) – Stephen Shield
Division One (East) – White Cup
Division Two (North) – Castle Rovers Cup
Division Two (East) – Barclay Cook Cup

The Edmond Trophy is contested by the clubs who lose in the first round of the Aberdeen FC Trophy. The Bowie Cup is contested by the clubs who lose in the first round of the Association Trophy. The Hans Fyfe Trophy is contested by the clubs who lose in the first round of the Dickie Trophy.

The Ian Napier Memorial Shield is contested annually by the Division One (North) and Division One (East) champions from the previous season. The John Todd Memorial Trophy was introduced in season 2009/10 and is contested by the top two clubs from the Premier Division in the previous season.

ABERDEENSHIRE AMATEUR FA 2021/22

Premier Division

Banchory Amateurs
Bervie Caledonian
Cove Thistle
Cowie Thistle
Echt
Insch
Kincorth
Newburgh Thistle
Newtonhill
Old Aberdonians
Rattrays XI
St Laurence
Tarves
Woodside

Division One (North)

Bridge of Don
Blackburn
BSFC or Feughside *
Ellon Amateurs
FC Polska
JS XI
Lads Club Amateurs
Nicolls Amateurs
St Marnans
Stonehaven Athletic
Stoneywood Parkvale
Tolbooth
Turriff Thistle
University

Division One (East)

AC Mill Inn
Alford
Beacon Rangers
Cammachmore
Continental
Ellon Thistle
Faithlie United
Glendale
Great Western United
Halliburton
Kaimhill United
Kemnay Amateurs
Kintore
Westdyke

Division Two (North)

BSFC or Feughside *
Burghmuir
Fyvie
Glentanar Reflex
Huntly Amateurs
Kemnay Youth
Monymusk
Newmachar United
West End United
University Colts

Division Two (East)

Aboyne
AC Mill Inn Academy
Auchnagatt Barons
Bon Accord City
Ferryhill
Grammar FP's
Jesus House
Middlefield Wasps
Postal ALC
Theologians

Home Grounds from Season 2019/20 are listed below

PREMIER DIVISION	Ground	
Echt	Echt Pleasure Park	AB32 7AA
Woodside	Woodside Complex, Aberdeen	AB24 2UL
Rothie Rovers	Rothienorman	AB51 8XA
St Laurence	Memorial Park, Laurencekirk	AB30 1HD
Cove Thistle	Catto Park	AB12 3NX
Tarves	Hillhead Park, Tarves	AB41 7JY
Newtonhill	Newton Park, Newtonhill	AB39 3PX
Old Aberdonians	Balgownie	AB22 8LX
Newburgh Thistle	Gallowhills Park, Newburgh	AB41 6BY
Cowie Thistle	Mineralwell Park / Jim Glennie Park	AB39 3XY
Rattrays XI	Westdyke Community Centre	AB32 6QX
Insch	Recreation Park, Insch	AB52 6HN
Bervie Caledonian	Booth Park, Gourdon	DD10 0LX
MS United	Heathryfold Park, Aberdeen	AB16 7DS

DIVISION ONE NORTH	Ground	
Great Western United	Kaimhill, Garthdee Crescent, Aberdeen	AB10 7HP
Banchory Amateurs *	KGV Park, Banchory	AB31 5ST
Turriff Thistle	The Haughs (Astro)	AB53 4EF
Kintore	Pleasure Park, Kintore	AB51 0ZG
Stoneywood East End	New Advocates Park, Aberdeen	AB24 1RG
Faithlie United	James Ramsay Park, Fraserburgh	AB43 9TH
Bridge of Don	Westfield Park	AB22 8PE
Nicolls Amateurs *	Denmore Park	AB23 8JW
Torphins	Pleasure Park, Kincardine O'Neil	AB34 5BZ
Kemnay Amateurs	Kemnay Academy	AB51 5FW
Stonehaven Athletic	Jim Glennie Park, Stonehaven	AB39 3XY
Ellon Amateurs	The Meadows, Ellon	AB41 9QJ
JS XI	Groats Road, Aberdeen	AB15 8BE
Continental	Webster Park, Kingswells, Aberdeen	AB15 8TX

DIVISION ONE EAST	Ground	
Kincorth	Sheddocksley	AB16 6QZ
FC Polska *	Jack Wood Pavilion, Inverdee	AB12 5XA
Alford	Alford	AB33 8TY
Tolbooth	Hazlehead Pitches, Aberdeen	AB15 8BE
AC Mill Inn	Jim Glennie Park, Stonehaven	AB39 3XY
Colony Park	Colony Park, Inverurie	AB51 4SX
Ellon Thistle	The Meadows, Ellon	AB41 9QJ
St Marnans	McRobert Park, Aberchirder	AB54 7SH
Dyce ITC Hydraulics	Arjo Wiggins Stoneywood Park	AB231 9JH
Westdyke	Lawsondale Astro, Westhill	AB32 6SE
Kaimhill United	Kaimhill Grass	AB10 7HP
Cammachmore	Newton Park, Newtonhill	AB39 3PX
University	Balgownie, Aberdeen	AB22 8LX
Halliburton	Lawsondale, Westhill	AB32 6SE

DIVISION TWO NORTH	Ground	
Lads Club Amateurs	Westdyke Community Centre	AB32 6QX
Glendale	Corbie Park, Maryculter	AB12 5FX
Huntly Amateurs	The Meadows, Huntly	AB54 4SE
Grammar FP's	Rubislaw	AB14 4YS
BSFC	Hazlehead Pitches, Aberdeen	
Glendale Youth	Hazlehead Pitches, Aberdeen	AB15 8BE
Postal ALC	Webster Park, Kingswells, Aberdeen	AB15 8TX
Monymusk	Deer Park, Monymusk	AB51 7HF
Auchnagatt Barons	Auchnagatt	AB41 8TA
Glentanar Reflex	Hazlehead Pitches, Aberdeen	AB15 8BE
Theologians	Hazlehead Pitches, Aberdeen	AB15 8BE
West End United	Hazlehead Pitches, Aberdeen	AB15 8BE

DIVISION TWO EAST	Ground	
Beacon Rangers	Bucksburn Academy	AB21 9DG
Blackburn	Kinellar Play Park, Blackburn	AB21 0JQ
Feughside	Farquharson Park, Finzean	AB31 6LX
Aboyne	Charleston Green, Aboyne	AB34
Newmachar United	Charles Gordon Park, Newmachar	AB21 0QD
University Colts	Balgownie, Aberdeen	AB22 8LX
Burghmuir	Garioch SC, Strathburn Park, Inverurie	AB51 4GY
Middlefield Wasps	Beach Park, Balmedie	AB23 8SX
Kemnay Youth	Bogbeth Park, Kemnay	AB51 5RL
Jesus House	Jack Wood Pavilion, Inverdee	AB12 5XA
University Strollers	Balgownie, Aberdeen	AB22 8LX
Ferryhill	Jack Wood Pavilion, Inverdee	AB12 5XA

ABERDEENSHIRE AFA CHAMPIONS

1947-48 Cove Rangers
1948-49 Cove Rangers
1949-50 Ellon United
1950-51 Ellon United
1951-52 Millburn FC
1952-53 Millburn FC
1953-54 Cove Rangers
1954-55 Cove Rangers
1955-56 Cove Rangers
1956-57 Cove Rangers
1957-58 Cove Rangers
1958-59 Nicoll's XI
1959-60 Cove Rangers
1960-61 Cove Rangers
1961-62 Ellon United
1962-63 Ellon United
1963-64 Bon Accord FC
1964-65 Cove Rangers
1965-66 Aboyne
1966-67 Aberdeen City Police
1967-68 Aberdeen City Police
1968-69 Aberdeen City Police
1969-70 Aberdeen City Police
1970-71 Maud
1971-72 Kemnay
1972-73 Culter
1973-74 Culter
1974-75 Culter
1975-76 Culter
1976-77 Cove Rangers
1977-78 Kemnay
1978-79 Culter
1979-80 Culter
1980-81 Culter
1981-82 Grandholm Rosslyn
1982-83 Cove Rangers
1983-84 Aberdeen Shamrock
1984-85 Cove Rangers
1985-86 Crombie Sports
1986-87 Mugiemoss Amateurs
1987-88 Longside
1988-89 Hall Russell United
1989-90 Great Western United
1990-91 Kincorth
1991-92 Kincorth
1992-93 Kincorth
1993-94 Kincorth
1994-95 Dyce
1995-96 Hilton
1996-97 Echt
1997-98 Hilton
1998-99 Hilton
1999-00 Hilton
2000-01 Echt
2001-02 Echt
2002-03 Kincorth
2003-04 Kincorth
2004-05 Sunnybank Amateurs
2005-06 Sunnybank Amateurs
2006-07 Echt
2007-08 Echt
2008-09 Cove Thistle
2009-10 Bon-Accord City
2010-11 Kincorth
2011-12 Woodside
2012-13 Sportsmans Club
2013-14 Sportsmans Club
2014-15 Cove Thistle
2015-16 RGU
2016-17 Woodside
2017-18 Woodside
2018-19 Woodside

ABERDEENSHIRE AFA TROPHY

1947-48 Cove Rangers
1948-49 Cove Rangers
1949-50 Cove Rangers
1950-51 Ellon United
1951-52 Cove Rangers
1952-53 Cove Rangers
1953-54 Cove Rangers
1954-55 Banchory
1955-56 Cove Rangers
1956-57 Cleansing Department
1957-58 Cove Rangers
1958-59 Cove Rangers
1959-60 Banchory
1960-61 Bon Accord
1961-62 Cove Rangers
1962-63 Cove Rangers
1963-64 Ellon United
1964-65 Cove Rangers
1965-66 Ellon United
1966-67 Aberdeen University
1967-68 Aberdeen City Police
1968-69 A.D. Club
1969-70 Aboyne
1970-71 Maud
1971-72 Culter
1972-73 Maud
1973-74 Culter
1974-75 Cove Rangers
1975-76 Culter
1976-77 Culter
1977-78 Kemnay
1978-79 Longside
1979-80 Chattan Rovers
1980-81 Denmore Thistle
1981-82 Aboyne
1982-83 Cove Rangers
1983-84 Cove Rangers
1984-85 Cove Rangers
1985-86 Culter
1986-87 Culter
1987-88 Longside
1988-89 Kincorth
1989-90 Kincorth
1990-91 Hermes
1991-92 Kincorth
1992-93 Kincorth
1993-94 Hilton
1994-95 Dyce
1995-96 Echt
1996-97 Hilton
1997-98 Echt
1998-99 Echt
1999-00 Echt
2000-01 Cowie Thistle
2001-02 Echt
2002-03 Walker Road
2003-04 Kincorth
2004-05 Sunnybank Amateurs
2005-06 Echt
2006-07 Stoneywood SSC
2007-08 Echt
2008-09 University
2009-10 Bon-Accord City
2010-11 Woodside
2011-12 Woodside
2012-13 Sportsmans Club
2013-14 Cove Thistle
2014-15 Rothie Rovers
2015-16 Ellon Amateurs
2016-17 Cove Thistle
2017-18 Cowie Thistle
2018-19 Tolbooth

AIRDRIE & COATBRIDGE SUNDAY AMATEUR LEAGUE 2020/21

Season Cancelled.

Contact: Mr A Coleman
Email: archiec@blueyonder.co.uk
Telephone: 07961579078

The league decided to play a "Mini League" season from May to July. Latest tables were as follows:

PREMIER DIVISION A

	P	W	D	L	F	A	GD	PTS
Panther	7	6	0	1	36	4	32	18
Bellshill United	7	5	0	2	31	9	22	15
Easterhouse Phoenix	6	4	1	1	12	7	5	13
Viewpark United	7	4	1	2	17	17	0	13
Sauchie AFC	6	4	0	2	16	8	8	12
Tollcross	6	1	0	5	6	16	-10	3
Symington Tinto	7	1	0	6	6	40	-34	3
Cumbernauld Colts	6	0	0	6	4	27	-23	0

PREMIER DIVISION B

	P	W	D	L	F	A	GD	PTS
Cross Tavern	6	6	0	0	29	5	24	18
Lochgreen	7	4	1	2	28	10	18	13
Wishaw United	6	4	0	2	23	20	3	12
Newarthill Athletic	6	3	1	2	22	26	-4	10
Eastend United	5	2	1	2	14	17	-3	7
Villa Park	6	2	0	4	6	12	-6	6
DT United	7	1	1	5	7	19	-12	4
East End Heart	5	0	0	5	6	26	-20	0

DIVISION ONE A

	P	W	D	L	F	A	GD	PTS
Colts Athletic	6	6	0	0	29	6	23	18
Mill United	6	3	2	1	19	8	11	11
Stepford Thistle	6	2	2	2	12	18	-6	8
Blantyre Vics	5	2	1	2	9	8	1	7
Firhill Star	4	1	2	1	9	12	-3	5
Douglas Amateurs	6	1	0	5	12	27	-15	3
Coatbridge United	5	0	1	4	5	16	-11	1

DIVISION ONE B

	P	W	D	L	F	A	GD	PTS
Blackstar Glasgow	6	5	1	0	29	5	24	16
Salsburgh United	6	4	0	2	15	14	1	12
EastEnd Rovers	5	3	1	1	9	5	4	10
Albion Rovers	6	2	0	4	10	14	-4	6
Garrionwood	4	1	1	2	8	11	-3	4
Glasgow City Star	5	1	1	3	7	14	-7	4
Strathy West	4	0	0	4	1	16	-15	0

CUP FINALS (from 2019/20, played 18/7/2021)
Billy Harkness Memorial Trophy
Blantyre Vics v Symington Tinto, 0-1

Billy Harkness Challenge Trophy
Bellshill United v Wishaw United, 0-2

All-In Cup Final (from 2019/20, played 25/7/2021)
Lochgreen v Bellshill United, 3-2

GROUNDS
No fixed home grounds.
Venues used include:

Bothwellhaugh, Motherwell	ML1 3RB
Clyde Valley HS, Wishaw	ML2 0QS
Townhead CC, Coatbridge	ML5 2HT
Craigneuk Park, Airdrie	ML6 8DF
Dalziel Park, Motherwell	ML1 5RZ
Wishaw SC	MK2 0HQ
Langloan SC, Coatbridge	ML5 1HH
Stepford Centre, Glasgow	G33 4NU
St Ambrose HS	ML1 4TP
Symington Public Park	ML12 6LL
Keir Hardie SC, Holytown	ML1 4TP
Lochend SC, Glasgow	G34 0NZ
Ladywell Park, Motherwell	ML1 3LZ
Bathgate Academy	EH48 1LF
Greenfield 3G, Glasgow	G32 6TP

AYRSHIRE AMATEUR FA 2020/21

Contact: Mr. Neil Turner
Email: turner2@sky.com
Telephone: 01294 317105

The 2020/1 season was not contested.

Some clubs opted to play in a Mini Tournament in the Summer of 2021, sponsored by Stewarton United.

STEWARTON UNITED SUMMER TOURNAMENT

Date	Grp	Home	Away		
12/6/21	A	Ardeer West Recreation	Irvine AFC	0	3
15/6/21	A	Ardeer West Recreation	Bonnyton Thistle AFC	1	2
16/6/21	A	Irvine AFC	Kilmarnock	2	4
21/6/21	A	Kilmarnock AFC	Ardeer West Recreatic	3	3
21/6/21	A	Bonnyton Thistle	Irvine AFC	0	3
	A	Kilmarnock AFC	Bonnyton Thistle AFC	wo	scr
9/6/21	A	Irvine AFC	Bonnyton Thistle AFC	3	2
9/6/21	A	Ardeer West Recreation	Kilmarnock AFC	2	2
	A	Kilmarnock AFC	Irvine AFC	wo	scr
	A	Bonnyton Thistle	Ardeer West Recreatic	scr	wo
	A	Irvine AFC	Ardeer West Recreatic	wo	scr
	A	Bonnyton Thistle	Kilmarnock AFC	scr	wo
11/6/21	B	Tass Thistle	New Farm Loch	0	9
12/6/21	B	Stewarton United	Shortlees	2	5
16/6/21	B	Stewarton United	Tass Thistle	6	3
16/6/21	B	Shortlees	New Farm Loch	2	2
19/6/21	B	Tass Thistle	Shortlees	2	5
19/6/21	B	Stewarton Thistle	New Farm Loch	3	3
21/6/21	B	Shortlees	Tass Thistle	11	3
23/6/21	B	Shortlees	Stewarton Thistle	4	3
23/6/21	B	New Farm Loch	Tass Thistle	2	0
26/6/21	B	New Farm Loch	Shortlees	0	4
9/6/21	B	New Farm Loch	Shortlees	0	4
9/6/21	B	New Farm Loch	Stewarton United	2	0
12/6/21	C	Kilmarnock United	Crosshouse Waverley	4	1
	C	Onthank	Crosshouse Waverley	scr	wo
	C	Kilmarnock United	Onthank AFC	wo	scr
	C	Ardeer Thisle	Crosshouse Waverley	wo	scr
23/6/21	C	Onthank	Ardeer Thistle AFC	4	2
23/6/21	C	Crosshouse Waverley	Kilmarnock United	1	3
26/6/21	C	Kilmarnock United	Ardeer Thistle AFC	1	2
9/6/21	C	Crosshouse Waverley	Ardeer Thistle AFC	1	6
9/6/21	C	Onthank	Kilmarnock United	0	3
		Ardeer Thisle	Onthank AFC	wo	scr
		Ardeer Thisle	Kilmarnock United	wo	scr
26/6/21		Kilmarnock United	Ardeer Thistle AFC	1	2
12/6/21	D	Largs Thistle	West Kilbride	3	2
12/6/21	D	Gleburn MW	Minishant	2	1
15/6/21	D	Largs Thistle	Glenburn MW	1	6
16/6/21	D	West Kilbride	Minishant	0	4
	D	Glenburn MW	West Kilbride	wo	scr
	D	Largs Thistle AFC	Minishant	wo	scr
	D	West Kilbride	Largs Thistle AFC	scr	wo
	D	Minishant	Glenburn MW	scr	wo
26/6/21	D	Glenburn MW	Largs Thistle AFC	8	1
9/6/21	D	West Kilbride	Glenburn MW	0	2
9/6/21	D	Minishant	Largs AFC	1	1
		Minishant	West Kilbride	wo	scr

WINNERS

	Date	Home	Away		
SF	3/7/21	Kilmarnock AFC	Ardeer Thistle	1	2
SF	3/7/21	Shortlees	Glenburn MW	3	2
PO	10/7/21	Kilmarnock AFC	Glenburn MW	1	4
F	10/7/21	Ardeer Thistle	Shortlees	0	2

SECOND PLACED

	Date	Home	Away		
SF	3/7/21	Irvine	Largs Thistle	1	0
SF	3/7/21	New Farm Loch	Kilmarnock United	3	1
PO	10/7/21	Largs Thistle	Kilmarnock United	P	P
F	10/7/21	Irvine	New Farm Loch	P	P

THIRD PLACED

	Date	Home	Away		
SF	3/7/21	Dirrans Athletic	Stewarton United	1	4
SF	3/7/21	Ardeer West	Minishant	9	2
PO	10/7/21	Dirrans Athletic	Minishant	P	P
F	10/7/21	Stewarton United	Ardeer West	3	2

FOURTH PLACED

	Date	Home	Away		
SF	3/7/21	Crosshouse Waverley	Bonnyton Thistle	0	3
SF	3/7/21	Tass Thistle	West Kilbride	3	4
PO	10/7/21	Crosshouse Waverley (6-5 pens)	Tass Thistle	2	2
F	10/7/21	West Kilbride	Bonnyton Thistle	3	2

AYRSHIRE AMATEUR FA 2021/2

LEAGUE COMPOSITION 2021/2

Budget Blinds Premier League

Ardeer West Recreation	Ardeer Quarry, Stevenston, KA20 3AQ
Cumnock AFC	Townhead Park, Cumnock, KA18 1LZ
Dailly	Riverside Park Dailly, KA26 9SB
Dirrans Athletic	Kilwinning SC, KA13 6LF
Glenburn MW	Prestwick Acad (Grass), KA9 2LB
New Farm Loch	Dean Park, Kilmarnock, KA3 1RR
Shortlees	Burn Park, Kilmarnock, KA1 4SD
Stewarton United	Cocklebie Park, KA3 3DX
Tarbolton	Tarbolton Public Park, KA5 5PY

Budget Blinds Division One

Beith AFC	Orr's Trust Park, KA15 2AH
Catrine	Riverside Park, Catrine, KA5 6SJ
Craigie	Newlands Drive, Kilmarnock, KA3 2DZ
Crosshouse Waverley	Lindsay Park, Crosshouse, KA2 0JJ
Dalry AFC	Putyan Park, Dalry, KA24 5NB
Drongan United	Drongan Public Park, KA6 7AZ
Galston United	Loudon Acad 4G, Galston, KA4 8PD
Irvine AFC	Irvine Sports Club, KA12 8PE
Largs Thistle AFC	Barrfields, KA30 8NP
West Kilbride	Kirktonhall Glen, KA23 9HQ
Whitletts Vics	KGV Playing Field, Ayr, KA8 9ET

Budget Blinds Division 2A

Annbank AFC	New Pebble Park
Crosshill Thistle	Crosshill Public Park, KA19 7RH
Irvine Thistle	Kilwinning Acad, KA13 7HD
Irvine Victoria AFC	
Kilbirnie AFC	
Kilbride Thistle	
Kilwinning AFC	
Kilwinning Rangers AFC	
Mauchline United	Beechgrove Park, KA5 5DP
Minishant	Kewnston Park, KA19 8DL
Symington Caledonian	Shaw Park, Symington, KA1 5QZ

Budget Blinds Division 2B

Bellfield	Stuthers Park, Kilmarnock. KA1 3XG
Black's Bar	
Bonnyton Thistle AFC	Synergy Arena, Kilmarnock, KA3 1BB
Darvel Vics	Gavin Hamilton SC, KA17 0 BT
Dean Fenwick Thistle	Dean Park, Kilmarnock, KA3 1RR
Glenafton AFC	Greenhead Park, New Cumnock, KA18 4AY
Kilmarnock AFC	Dean Park, Kilmarnock, KA3 1RR
Kilmarnock United	Scott Ellis PF, KA1 3JF
Ochiltree Community AFC	Kay Park, Ochiltree, KA18 2NS
Onthank AFC	Knockentiber PP, KA2 0DB
Troon Dundonald	Marr College PF, LA10 7AB

	AYRSHIRE CUP	JAMES SCOTT MEMORIAL TROPHY	THISTLE BAR TROPHY
		(North Ayrshire)	(South Ayrshire)
1935/6	Ayr Corinthians		
1936/7	Kilmarnock Accies		
1937/8	Boswell Thistle		
1938/9	Maybole Ams		
1939/40	Glenburn Ams		
1945/6	Towholm United		
1946/7	Claremont Ams		
1947/8	Galston Ams		
1948/9	Eglinton Ams		
1949/50	Girvan Ams		
1950/1	Crosshill Thistle		Ayr British Leghion
1951/2	Star of the Sea	Eglinton Ams	Ayr British Leghion
1952/3	Dunlop Corinthians	Irvine Corinthians	Springside Ams
1953/4	Springside Ams	Eglinton Ams	Crosshill Thistle
1954/5	Crosshill Thistle	Glengarnock Thistle	Crosshill Thistle
1955/6	Star of the Sea	Shell Ams	Glenfield Welfare
1956/7	Crosshill Thistle	Shell Ams	Newmilns Ams
1957/8	Dunlop Corinthians	Star of the Sea	Minishant Ams
1958/9	Crosshill Thistle	Ardrossan Winton	Minishant Ams
1959/60	Ramblos Ams	Girdle Toll United	Crosshill Thistle
1960/1	Ayr Volants	Girdle Toll United	Barony Colliery
1961/2	Minishant Ams	Crosshouse Waverley	Crosshill Thistle
1962/3	Crosshill Thistle	Eglinton Ams	Crosshill Thistle
1963/4	Crosshill Thistle	Crosshouse Waverley	Crosshill Thistle
1964/5	Mossblown Ams	St Joseph's	Dalmellington Red Star
1965/6	Eglinton Ams	Fenwick Thistle	Dalrymple Ams
1966/7	Minishant Ams	Irviine United	Crosshill Thistle
1967/8	St Joseph's	Troon Rovers	Drongan Utd
1968/9	Knockentiber	Dirrans Ath / Fenwick Thistle	Vale of Girvan
1969/70	Eglinton Ams	Dirrans Ath	Vale of Girvan
1970/1	Crosshouse Waverley	Crosshouse Waverley	Stiebel Ams
1971/2	Dirrans Athletic	Girdle Toll United	Crosshill Thistle
1972/3	Whitletts Ams	Knockentiber	Whitletts Ams
1973/4	Newmilns Vesuvius	Winlinton Wolves	Vale of Girvan
1974/5	Knockentiber	Knockentiber	Vale of Girvan
1975/6	Crosshouse Waverley	Knockentiber	Vale of Girvan
1976/7	Crosshouse Waverley	West Kilbride	Darvel Vics
1977/8	Crosshouse Waverley	Knockentiber	Galston Ams
1978/9	Knockentiber	Crosshouse Waverley	Minishant Ams
1979/80	Crosshouse Waverley	Knockentiber	Heathside
1980/1	Knockentiber	Knockentiber	Heathside
1981/2	Darvel Vics	Ardrossan Castle Rovers	Minishant Ams
1982/3	Knockentiber	Crosshouse Waverley	Heathside
1983/4	Hysters	Knockentiber	Heathside
1984/5	Drongan Utd	Knockentiber	Drongan Utd
1985/6	Knockentiber	Crossbrae Thistle	Wallacefield
1986/7	Knockentiber	Knockentiber	Drongan Utd
1987/8	Clark Drive	Ardrossan Castle Rovers	Dalmellington Red Star
1988/9	Johnnie Walkers	Dreghorn SC	Galston United
1989/90	Clark Drive	Knockentiber	Drongan Utd
1990/1	Minishant Ams	Clark Drive	Maybole Ams
1991/2	Heathside	Johnnie Walkers	Heathside
1992/3	Shortlees	Knockentiber	Heathside
1993/4	Knockentiber	Girdle Toll United	Heathside
1994/5	Clark Drive	Knockentiber	Galston United
1995/6	West Kilbride	West Kilbride	Heathside
1996/7	Dailly Ams	Not awarded	Heathside
1997/8	Knockentiber	Bourtreehill	Heathside
1998/9	Dailly Ams	Clark Drive	Dailly Ams
1999/00	Maybole Ams	Kilwinning Ams	Mossblown
2000/1	Mossblown Ams	Clark Drive	Maybole Ams
2001/2	Maybole Ams	West Kilbride	Maybole Ams
2002/3	Galston United	Knockentiber	Hurlford Thistle
2003/4	Craigie Ams	Clark Drive	Hurlford Thistle
2004/5	Ardeer Rovers	Dean Thistle	Hurlford Thistle
2005/6	Clark Drive	Knockentiber	Broomfield Rov
2006/7	Clark Drive	Knockentiber	Broomfield Rov
2007/8	Knockentiber	Clark Drive	Hurlford Thistle
2008/9	Knockentiber	Knockentiber	Glenburn MW
2009/10	Hurlford Thistle	Clark Drive	Galston United
2010/1	Galston United	Clark Drive	Hurlford Thistle
2011/2	Hurlford Thistle	Girdle Toll United	Hurlford Thistle
2012/3	Hurlford Thistle	Stewarton United	Hurlford Thistle
2013/4	Clark Drive	Clark Drive	Hurlford Thistle
2014/5	Hurlford Thistle	Ardrossan Castle Rovers	Carrick
2015/6	Shortlees	Dirrans Athletic	Hurlford Thistle
2016/7	Hurlford Thistle	Shortlees	Hurlford Thistle
2017/8	Hurlford Thistle	Ardeer West Recreation	Hurlford Thistle
2018/9	Glenburn MW	Shortlees	Glenburn MW

AYRSHIRE SUNDAY AFA 2020/21

Season Cancelled.

Contact: Mr Edward Gibb
Email: asafasecretary@gmail.com
Telephone: 07900 665335

A Summer Challenge Tournament was organised for interested clubs. Those taking part were:
Group A
Grange, Kilbirnie United, Irvine No.1 CSC
Group B
Lawthorn, Saltcoats, Girdle Toll
Group C
Glencairn, Irvine Sports Bar, Bobbys Bar
Group D
Arran, Troon, Killie United

CONFIRMED HOME VENUES 2021/2

Bobby's Bar	St Matthew's Acad, Saltcoats	KA21 5SH
Craigie		
Girdletoll		
Glencairn	Scott Ellis Park, Kilmarnock	KA1 3JF
Grange	Grange Academy, Kilmarnock	KA1 2EN
Irvine CSC	Kilwinning SC	KA13 7HD
Irvine SB	Greenwood Academy, Dreghorn	KSA11 4HL
Isle of Arran	Ormidale Park, Brodick / Kilwinning SC	KA27 8BY / KA13 6LF
Kilbirnie United	Garnock Campus, Beith	KA14 3BJ
Lawthorn		
Saltcoats		
Troon	Hosiery Park, Troon	KA10 6PZ

The same 12 teams have signed up to play in the 2021/2 season. The League will consist of a single division.

BORDER AMATEUR FA 2020/21

Season Cancelled.

BORDER AMATEUR FA 2021/2

Contact: Mr Colin. H. Campbell
Email: colinhcam@talktalk.net
Telephone: 01450 373840

DIVISION A		
Ancrum	Bridgend Park	TD8 6SR
Chirnside Utd	Comrades Park	TD11 3UA
Duns Ams	New Hawthorn Park	TD11 3QQ
Greenlaw	Happer Park, Greenlaw	TD10 6UG
Hawick Utd	Albert Park / Volunteer Park	TD9 8AG / TD9 0EH
Hawick Waverley	Wilton Lodge Park / Volunteer Park	TD9 7LG / TD9 0EH
Langholm Legion	Castleholm	DG13 0ND
Langlee Ams	Gala Public Park / Netherdale	TD1 3DF / TD1 3HJ
Newtown	KGV Park, Newtown St Boswells	TD6 0QP
Tweeddale Rovers	Kerfield Park, Peebles	EH45 8BG

DIVISION B		
Biggar Utd	Hartree Mill	ML12 6JJ
Coldstream Ams	Home Park, Coldstream (Outside Pitch)	TD12 4DT
Earlston Rhymers	Runciman Park, Earlston	TD4 6BW
Gala Hotspur	Netherdale / Gala Public Park	TD1 3HJ / TD1 3DF
Hawick Legion	Wilton Lodge Park / Volunteer Park	TD9 7LG / TD9 0EH
Jed Legion	Elliot Park, Jedburgh	TD8 6EF
Kelso Thistle	Woodside Park, Kelso	TD5 7DG
Leithen Rovers	Victoria Park, Innerleithen (Outside Pitch)	EH44 6QT
Selkirk Victoria	Yarrow Park (Outside Pitch)	TD7 5AX
Stow	Stow Park	TD1 2SH
Tweedmouth Ams	Five Arches	TD15 2UT

DIVISION C		
Berwick Colts	Billendean. Tweedmouth	TD15 1QS
CFC Bowholm	Canonbie	DG14 0UX
Eyemouth United	Warner Park, Eyemouth	TD14 5DX
Gala Fairydean Rovers	Netherdale	TD1 3HJ
Hawick Colts		
Highfields Utd	Swan Centre, Berwick	TD15 2AS
Lauder	Woodcot Park, Lauder	TD2 6AD
Netherdale Thistle	Netherdale, Gala	TD1 3HJ
Spittal Rovers	Newfields Park, Berwick	TD15 1SW
St.Boswells	Jenny Moore's Park	TD6 0AL
Tweeddale Rovers Colts	Kerfield Park, Peebles	EH45 8BG

MAJOR POST WAR HONOURS

	LEAGUE CHAMPIONS	BORDER CUP	BEVERIDGE CUP	WADDELL CUP	WRIGHT CUP	WALLS CUP	COLLIE CUP
1946/7		Gala Fairydean					
1947/8	Hawick SC LNER	Gala Fairydean	Hawick Royal Albert				
1948/9	Hawick Royal Albert		Hawick Royal Albert				
1949/50	Gala Rovers	Penicuik Athletic	Lauder Leadervale				
1950/1	Gala Rovers	Peebles Rovers	Fairydean Ams				
1951/2		Peebles Rovers	Roxburgh United				
1952/3	Gala Rovers	Peebles Rovers	Lauder Leadervale				
1953/4	Gala Rovers	Vale of Leithen	Gala Rovers				
1954/5	Gala Rovers	Eyemouth United	Selkirk Parkvale Rovers				
1955/6	Greenlaw	Gala Fairydean	Gala Amateurs				
1956/7	Greenlaw		Ancrum				
1957/8	Greenlaw		Jedburgh Amateurs				
1958/9	Leithen Rovers		Leithen Rovers				
1959/60	Leithen Rovers		Leithen Rovers				
1960/1	Morebattle	Morebattle					
1961/2	Morebattle	Morebattle					
1962/3	Hawick Legion	Gala Rovers	Gala Hotspur		Gala Rovers		
1963/4	Gala Rovers	Kelso Thistle	Kelso United		Leithen Rovers		
1964/5	Hawick Legion		Gala Amateurs		Gala Ams		
1965/6	Hawick Legion	Hawick United	Gala Amateurs		Gala Rovers		
1966/7	Kelso United	Hawick Legion	Gala Rovers		Hawick Legion Rovers		
1967/8	Duns Amateurs	Gala Rovers	Duns Amateurs		Leithen Rovers		
1968/9	Hawick Legion		Kelso United		Duns Ams	Hawick United	
1969/70	Hawick Legion		Leithen Rovers				
1970/1	Kelso United	Hawick Legion	Hawick United		Hawick Utd Colts	Earlston Rhymers	
1971/2	Hawick United		Hawick United		Gala Hotspur	Gala Hotspur	Kelso United
1972/3	Gala Hotspur	Chirnside	Kelso United		Hawick Legion Rovers	Lauder	Hawick Legion
1973/4	Hawick United		Hawick United		Chirnside	Hawick Utd Colts	Hawick Utd
1974/5	Greenlaw		Leithen Rovers		Morebattle	Yetholm	
1975/6	Hawick Legion	Hawick United	Hawick United			Hawick YC	
1976/7	Leithen Rovers	Greenlaw	Hawick United	Greenlaw	Yetholm	Heriot	
1977/8	Gala Rovers		Gala Rovers	Greenlaw	Peebles Rovers	Peebles Rovers	
1978/9	Gala Hotspur	Peebles Rovers	Peebles Rovers	Greenlaw	Earlston Rhymers		
1979/80	Gala Hotspur		Gala Hotspur	Eyemouth Legion	St Abbs Thistle	Selkirk Vics	
1980/1	Gala Hotspur	Hawick YC	Hawick Legion	Hawick Legion	Kelso Legion Thistle		
1981/2	Hawick United		Hawick YC	St Abbs Thistle	Ancrum	Eyemouth Colts	
1982/3	Hawick United	Ancrum	Hawick Waverley	Spittal Rovers	Spittal Rovers	Spittal Rovers	
1983/4	Eyemouth Legion	Hawick United	Gala Hotspur		Selkirk Vics	Selkirk Vics	
1984/5	Hawick United	Hawick United	Hawick United	Earlston Rhymers	Gala Rovers	Grove	
1985/6	Hawick United	Hawick United	Hawick United	Hawick Waverley	Grove	St Abbs Thistle	
1986/7	Gala Rovers	Hawick Waverley	Selkirk Victoria	Hawick Waverley	Ancrum	Leithen Rovers	
1987/8	Eyemouth Legion	Eyemouth Legion	Hawick Legion	Gala Rovers	Heriot	Ancrum	
1988/9	Spittal Rovers	Duns Legion	Eyemouth Legion	Eyemouth Legion	Heriot	Heriot	
1989/90	Duns Legion	Hawick United	Duns Legion	Eyemouth Legion	Earlston Rhymers	Ancrum	
1990/1	Duns Legion	Hawick Legion	Selkirk Victoria	Spittal Rovers	Stow	Earlston Rhymers	
1991/2	Hawick Legion	Heriot	Eyemouth Legion	Chirnside	Chirnside Colts	Chirnside Colts	
1992/3	Chirnside	Duns Legion	Chirnside	Chirnside	Hawick United	Kelso Thistle	Leithen Rovers
1993/4	Hawick Waverley	Chirnside	Chirnside	Ancrum	Leithen Rovers	Hawick Legion Rovers	Chirnside Colts
1994/5	Chirnside	Chirnside	Chirnside	Chirnside	Gala Rovers	Gala Rovers	Coldstream Ams
1995/6	Gala Rovers	Gala Rovers	Gala Rovers	Earlston Rhymers	Kelso Thistle	Gala Hotspur	Coldstream Ams
1996/7	Chirnside	Lanmgholm Legion	Stow	Duns Legion	Gala Hotspur	Kelso Thistle	Hawick Legion Rovers
1997/8	Duns Legion	Hawick Legion	Duns Legion	Duns Legion	Berwick Harrow	Ayton	Cockburnspath
1998/9	Duns Legion	Duns Legion	Chirnside	Stow	Cockburnspath	Hawick United	Leithen Rovers
1999/00	Gala Rovers	Gala Rovers	Duns Legion	Earlston Rhymers	Jed Legion	Jed Legion	Selkirk Vics
2000/1	Gala Rovers	Chirnside	Hawick Waverley	Gala Rovers	Gala Hotspur	Gala Hotspur	Gala McQueen
2001/2	Gala Rovers	Gala Rovers	Leithen Rovers	Hawick Waverley	Eyemouth	Duns Legion	Gala McQueen
2002/3	Earlston Rhymers	Gala Rovers	Gala Rovers	Gala Rovers	Jed Legion	Hawick Legion	Pencaitland
2003/4	Gala Rovers	Kelso Thistle	Gala McQueen	Duns Ams	Duns Ams	Duns Ams	West Barns Star
2004/5	Hawick Waverley	Hawick Waverley	Chirnside	Hawick Waverley	West Barn Star	Ancrum	Gordon
2005/6	Pencaitland	Pencaitland	Pencaitland	Pencaitland	Selkirk Vics	Hawick United	Coldstream Ams
2006/7	Leithen Rovers	Chirnside	Leithen Rovers	Duns Ams	Jed Legion	Gordon	Winton
2007/8	Pencaitland	Hawick Waverley	Hawick Legion	Leithen Rovers	Stow	Greenlaw	Gordon
2008/9	Chirnside	Chirnside	Leithen Rovers	Newtown	Jed Legion	Hawick United	Tweeddale Rovers
2009/10	Leithen Rovers	Hawick Legion	Gala Rovers	Pencaitland	Gordon	Tweeddale Rovers	Linton Hotspur
2010/1	Duns Amateurs	Pencaitland	Pencaitland	Leithen Rovers	Tweeddale Rovers	Tweeddale Rovers	Selkirk Vics
2011/2	Pencaitland	Leithen Rovers	Hawick Waverley	Pencaitland	Ancrum	Ancrum	CFC Bowholm
2012/3	Gala Rovers	Pencaitland	Gala Rovers	Gala Rovers	Hawick Legion	Ancrum	Biggar
2013/4	Chirnside United	West Barns Star	Newtown	Greenlaw	Gordon	Gordon	Lauder
2014/5	Leithen Rovers	Gala Fairydean Rovers	Gala Fairydean Rovers	Stow	Eyemouth Ams	Hawick Legion	Tweedmouth Ams
2015/6	West Barns Star	Gordon	Gordon	Stow	Gala Hotspur	Hawick United	Newtown
2016/7	Chirnside United	Chirnside United	Chirnside United	Hawick Waverley	Hawick United	Hawick United	CFC Bowholm
2017/8	Hawick Waverley	Hawick Waverley	Hawick Waverley	Hawick Waverley	Gala Hotspur	Hawick United	Berwick Colts
2018/9	Hawick Waverley	Hawick Waverley	Hawick Waverley	Langlee Ams	Newtown	Langlee Ams	Tweedmouth Harrow

CALEDONIAN AMATEUR LEAGUE 2020/21

Contact: Mr Iain Cowden
Email: johncowden@ntlworld.com
Telephone: 0141 576 8507

The 2020/1 season started but only one week of fixtures was completed:

The Final of the 2019/20 Douglas Smith League Cup was also played:

June 25th 2021
Finnart v St Mungos, 2-3
At Duncansfield, Kilsyth Rangers FC

ALL TIME CHAMPIONS (37)

Club	Titles
Bannockburn	7
Dalziel HSFP	6
Stanley	3
Bannockburn	3
Dumbarton Academy FP	2
Glasgow Harp	2
Doune Castle	2
Drumchapel Amateurs	2
Queen's Park Hampden XI	2
Muirend	1
Milngavie Wanderers	1
Milton Ams	1
Netherton	1
Coatbridge CC	1
Strathclyde University	1
Giffnock North	1
Thorn Athletic	1
Liberton Cropley	1

PREMIER DIVISION (3/10/20)

Dalziel HSFP v Wishaw Wycombe Wanderers	2-4
Dumbarton Acad FP v Milngavie Wanderers	4-3
Eaglesham v Giffnock North	5-0
East Kilbride YM v Thorn Athletic	1-2
Glasgow Harp v Glasgow University	10-1
St Mungos v Cambria	2-1
Strathclyde Uni v Stenhousemuir C	0-3

FIRST DIVISION (3/10/20)

Cambusbarron Rovers v Dunblane Soccer A	4-1
Doune Castle v Callander Thistle	0-4
Finnart v Holytown Colts	11-0
Milton v Kilsyth AFC	4-1
Rhu v Rothesay Brandane	6-1
St Josephs v Westerlands	4-3

When football was able to restart in May, the Caledonian League opted to play the **William Turner Challenge Cup.**

Results were:

Group Stage

Date	Grp	Home	Away	Score
18/5/21	1	Holytown Colts	Glasgow Harp	0 2
19/5/21	1	Milngavie Wanderers	St Mungos	2 4
22/5/21	1	Glasgow Harp	Milngavie Wanderers	5 0
22/5/21	1	St Mungos	Holytown Colts	6 0
26/5/21	1	Glasgow Harp	St Mungos	1 1
26/5/21	1	Milngavie Wanderers	Holytown Colts	7 1
29/5/21	1	Holytown Colts	St Mungos	0 3
29/5/21	1	Milngavie Wanderers	Glasgow Harp	1 2
2/6/21	1	St Mungos	Milngavie Wanderers	1 1
5/6/21	1	Holytown Colts	Milngavie Wanderers	3 5
5/6/21	1	St Mungos	Glasgow Harp	2 2
9/6/21	1	Glasgow Harp	Holytown Colts	5 2
19/5/21	2	Dumbarton Academy FP	St Josephs	2 2
19/5/21	2	Rhu	Thorn Athletic	0 4
22/5/21	2	Dumbarton Academy FP	Thorn Athletic	0 0
22/5/21	2	St Josephs	Rhu	5 1
26/5/21	2	Dumbarton Academy FP	Rhu	4 0
26/5/21	2	Thorn Athletic	St Josephs	0 4
29/5/21	2	St Josephs	Dumbarton Aacademy FP	1 2
29/5/21	2	Thorn Athletic	Rhu	4 0
2/6/21	2	Rhu	St Josephs	1 5
2/6/21	2	Thorn Athletic	Dumbarton Aacademy FP	0 1
5/6/21	2	Rhu	Dumbarton Aacademy FP	2 5
5/6/21	2	St Josephs	Thorn Athletic	1 0
19/5/21	3	Callander Thistle	Stirling University	2 1
22/5/21	3	Stirling University	Dunblane Soccer Club	1 5
25/5/21	3	Dunblane Soccer Club	Callander Thistle	2 0
29/5/21	3	Stirling University	Callander Thistle	2 4
2/6/21	3	Callander Thistle	Dunblane Soccer Club	0 2
5/6/21	3	Dunblane Soccer Club	Stirling University	8 3
19/5/21	4	East Kilbride YM	Dalziel HSFP	1 2
22/5/21	4	Dalziel HSFP	Eaglesham	1 0
22/5/21	4	East Kilbride YM	Giffnock North	1 1
25/5/21	4	East Kilbride YM	Eaglesham	2 2
26/5/21	4	Dalziel HSFP	Giffnock North	2 3
29/5/21	4	Dalziel HSFP	East Kilbride YM	0 3
29/5/21	4	Eaglesham	Giffnock North	0 4
2/6/21	4	Eaglesham	East Kilbride YM	0 1
2/6/21	4	Giffnock North	Dalziel HSFP	1 2
5/6/21	4	Eaglesham	Dalziel HSFP	3 1
5/6/21	5	Giffnock North	East Kilbride YM	3 0
12/6/21	SF	Dumbarton Academy FP	Dunblane Soccer Club	6 0
12/6/21	SF	Glasgow Harp	Giffnock Borth	2 2 5-4p
19/6/21	F	Dumbarton Academy FP (at Duncansfield, Kilsyth)	Glasgow Harp	1 2

	LEAGUE CHAMPIONS	DIVISION ONE CHAMPIONS	DOUGLAS SMITH LEAGUE CUP	WILLIAM TURNER TROPHY
1983/4	Drumchapel Ams Queen's Park Hampden XI		Cambusbarron Rovers	Strathclyde Police
1984/5	Bannockburn	Pencaitland	Muirend	Coatbridge CC
1985/6	Muirend	Viewfield Rovers	Muirend	Giffnock North
1986/7	Stanley	Strathclyde Police	Bannockburn	Strathclyde Police
1987/8	Stanley	Queen's Park	Viewfield Rovers	Stanley
1988/9	Queen's Park Hampden XI	Liberton Cropley	Strathclyde Police	Viewfield Rovers
1989/90	Liberton Cropley	Morriston YMCA	Drumchapel	Milngavie Wanderers
1990/1	Stanley	Milngavie Wanderers	Queen's Park	Bannockburn
1991/2	Dalziel HSFP	Lothian Thistle	Stanley	Lothian Thistle
1992/3	Milngavie Wanderers	Viewfield Rovers	Bannockburn / Westerlands	Dalziel HSFP
1993/4	Dalziel HSFP	Muirend	Milngavie Wanderers	Lothian Thistle
1994/5	Dalziel HSFP	Strathclyde Police	Liberton Cropley	Dalziel HSFP
1995/6	Dalziel HSFP	East Kilbride YM	Dalziel HSFP	Bannockburn
1996/7	Bannockburn	Giffnock North / Eastwood	Milton	Milngavie Wanderers
1997/8	Dalziel HSFP	Links United	Drumchapel	East Kilbride YM
1998/9	Milton Ams	Westerlands	Dalziel HSFP	Bannockburn
1999/00	Bannockburn	Netherton	Drumchapel	Dalziel HSFP
2000/1	Bannockburn	Viewfield Rovers	Dalziel HSFP	Milton
2001/2	Drumchapel Ams	Coatbridge CC	Cambusbarron Rovers	Dalziel HSFP
2002/3	Netherton	Balmore	Milton	Balmore
2003/4	Coatbridge CC	Glasgow Harp	Drumchapel	Glasgow Harp
2004/5	Bannockburn	St Mungos	Bannockburn	Dalziel HSFP
2005/6	Dumbarton Academy FP	Links United	Cambusbarron Rovbers	Strathclyde University
2006/7	Bannockburn	Milton	Glasgow Harp	Balmore
2007/8	Bannockburn	Strathclyde University	Dumbarton Acad FP	Giffnock North
2008/9	Bannockburn	Cambusbarron Rovers	Dumbarton Acad FP	Strathclyde University
2009/10	Strathclyde University	Milton	Cambusbarron Rovers	Strathclyde University
2010/1	Bannockburn	Dalziel HSFP	Glasgow Harp	Milngavie Wanderers
2011/2	Glasgow Harp	Doune Castle	St Mungos	Bearsden
2012/3	Giffnock North	EKFC Whitehills	Glasgow University	Giffnock North
2013/4	Glasgow Harp	Dalziel HSFP	Glasgow Harp	Milton
2014/5	Doune Castle	Castlemilk	Milton	Giffnock North
2015/6	Doune Castle	Thorn Athletic	Dumbarton Acad FP	Giffnock North
2016/7	Dalziel HSFP	Broomhouse	Dumbarton Acad FP	Dalziel HSFP
2017/8	Dumbarton Academy FP	Cambria	Dalziel HSFP	Dumbarton Academy FP
2018/9	Thorn Athletic	Milngavie Wanderers / East Kilbride YM (Joint)	Giffnock North	Thorn Athletic
2019/20			St Mungos	
2020/1				Glasgow Harp

CALEDONIAN LEAGUE - ALL TIME MEMBERSHIP					
		East Kilbride YM	1995-2020	Muirhead	2007/8
Baillieston Juniors	2015-17	Eddlewood	2017-19	Myre	2014/15
Balmore	2002-19	EKFC Whitehills	2012-14	Newton Mearns Rovers	2004-07, 2008-12
Bannockburn	1983-2011	Erskine Thistle	2004-07	Overtown Thistle	2014-16
Barr & Stroud / Netherton	1983-2007	FC Dal Riata	2017-2020	Pencaitland	1984-86
Bearsden	2005/6, 2008-18	Finnart	2016-2020	Queen's Park Hampden XI	1983-94
Bo'ness Amateurs	1984-2001	Gartcosh United	2007-2017	Rannoch	2014-16
Broomhouse	2014-18	Giffnock North	1983-2020	Rhu	1988-2020
Callander Thistle	2017-20	Glasgow Harp	2003-2020	Rothesay Brandane	2004-2020
Cambria	2012-20	Glasgow University	1983-2020	St Mungos FP	1983-2020
Cambusbarron Rovers	1983-2020	Hamilton Academy FP	1999-2017	Stanley	1983-98
Castlemilk	2014-16	Holytown Colts	2017-20	Stenhousemuir Comm	2016-2020
Coatbridge CC	1984-2007	Jordanhill College	1983-	Stirling University	1983/4, 1985-88, 1989-2013, 2018-20
Corkerhill	2015-17	Kilsyth Ams	2018-20	Strathclyde Police	1983-2004
Cumbernauld Colts	2013-18	Larkhall Thistle Ams	2015-18	Strathclyde University	2007-2020
Dalziel HSFP	1990-2020	Liberton Cropley	1988-95	Symington Tinto	1987-2019
Doune Castle	2003-20	Links United	1995-2010	Thorn Athletic	2015-2020
Drumchapel Ams	1983-2008	Lothian Thistle	1991-95	Viewfield Rovers	1983-2007, 2008-20
Drumchapel FP	2010-16	Milngavie Wanderers	1988-2020	Weir Recreation	1983-2020
Dumbarton Academy FP	1998-2020	Milton Amateurs	1990-2020	Westerlands	1983-2020
Dunblane Soccer Club	2018-20	Morriston YMCA	1984-1998	Wishaw Wycombe Wanderers	2017-20
Eaglesham	2015-20	Muirend	1983-2009	Woodhall	2016-18

CALEDONIAN LEAGUE MEMBERSHIP 2021/2

PREMIER DIVISION

Cambria	Strathclyde Uni PF, Stepps	G33 6ND
Dalziel HSFP	Ravenscraig	ML1 2TZ
Dumbarton Academy FP	Dumbarton Acad PF	G82 2BG
Eaglesham	Eaglesham Public Park	G76 0LO
East Kilbride YM	Kirktonholme	G74 1EF
Giffnock North	Northolm	G46 6HU
Glasgow Harp	Allan Glens SC, Bishopbriggs	G64 2NE
Glasgow University	Garscube	G20 0SP
Milngavie Wanderers	Staney Brig Park	G62 7LN
St Mungos	Loretto PF, Bishopbriggs	G62 2PZ
Stenhousemuir Community	Ochilview Park	FK5 4QL
Strathclyde University	Strathclyde Uni PF, Stepps	G33 6ND
Thorn Athletic	McMaster SC, Johnstone	PA5 0LD
Wishaw Wycombe Wanderers	Clyde Valley GS, Wishaw	ML2 0LB

FIRST DIVISION

Callander Thistle	McLaren Leisure Centre, Callander	FK17 8JP
Cambusbarron Rovers	Mill Road Park	FK7 9LP
Doune Castle	Moray Park, Doune	FK16 6DJ
Dunblane Soccer Academy	Dunblane HS	FK15 9EW
Finnart	Glasgow Green	G40 1HB
Holytown Colts	Keir Hardie SC	ML1 4TP
Kilsyth AFC	Kilsyth Sports Field	G65 9LX
Milton	Bluebellwood Park, Bannockburn	FK7 0EN
Rhu	Ardenconnel Park, Rhu	G84 8RX
Rothesay Brandane	Rothesay Stadium	PA20 9BS
St Josephs	Scotstoun SC	G14 9HY
Stirling University 3rd XI	Garscube SC	G20 0SP
Westerlands	Science Parks	G20 0SP

CENTRAL SCOTTISH AMATEUR LEAGUE 2020/21

Contact: Mr George Dingwall
Email: georgedingwall@outlook.com
Telephone: 01698 749 044

When football was allowed to start in October 2020, the CSAL opted to complete the outstanding fixtures for 2019/20. A few games were played before football was closed down again. When it re-started again in May, they again chose to continue with the 2019/20 season, bringing it to a conclusion.

The 2020/21 season was not started.

2019/20 FINAL TABLES

PREMIER

1	ST PATRICK'S FP'S	20	15	3	2	52	19	33	48
2	HARESTANES	20	12	3	5	45	29	16	39
3	EASTFIELD	20	12	3	5	33	22	11	39
4	BANNOCKBURN	20	11	3	6	60	37	23	36
5	UDDINGSTON ANVIL	20	8	6	6	38	46	-8	30
6	FALLIN FALLIN	20	7	6	7	37	30	7	27
7	DRUMCHAPEL	20	6	7	7	41	32	9	25
8	DRUMCHAPEL UNITED PYM	20	5	7	8	45	48	-3	22
9	WISHAW HSFP'S	20	6	4	10	26	38	-12	22
10	GREENOCK HSFP'S	20	4	2	14	23	59	-36	14
11	CAMPSIE MINERVA	20	1	2	17	16	56	-40	5

DIVISION ONE A

1	CASTLEMILK DYNAMO	12	11	0	1	41	17	24	33
2	GARTCOSH UTD	12	10	1	1	37	10	27	31
3	STEINS THISTLE	12	5	3	4	36	25	11	18
4	ARTHURLIE	12	4	1	7	25	31	-6	13
5	BSC GLASGOW	12	3	2	7	28	39	-11	11
6	THIRD LANARK	12	3	1	8	23	41	-18	10
7	BEARSDEN	12	2	0	10	16	43	-27	6

DIVISION ONE B

1	OBAN SAINTS	12	10	1	1	45	12	33	31
2	LESMAHAGOW	12	7	2	3	32	13	19	23
3	BLANTYRE RGM	12	7	2	3	32	21	11	23
4	GARROWHILL THISTLE	12	4	3	5	19	23	-4	15
5	CAMBUSNETHAN TALBOT	12	2	5	5	15	32	-17	11
6	STEDFAST K	12	2	3	7	14	32	-18	9
7	CLYDEBANK	12	1	2	9	12	36	-24	5

The 2019/20 **Bunrigh League Cup Final was** also played:

July 3rd 2021 (at Dalziel Parks)

Drumchapel Amateurs v Castlemilk Dynamo, 3-2

The **Division One Play Off** resulted:

July 10th (at Dalziel Parks)

Oban Saints v Castlemilk Dynamo, 1-1 (Castlemilk won on penalties)

LEAGUE CONSTITUTION 2021/2

PREMIER DIVISION

BANNOCKBURN	Ladywell Park, Bannockburn	FK7 8LF
CASTLEMILK DYNAMO	Eastgate, Gartcosh	G69 8AT
DRUMCHAPEL	Glenhead Park, Duntocher	G81 6HH
DRUMCHAPEL UTD PYM	Mountblow SC	G81 4NX
EASTFIELD	Broadwood Stadium, Cumbernauld	G68 9NE
FALLIN	Paterson PF, Fallin	FK7 7GZ
GARTCOSH UTD	Barlia Complex, Glasgow	G45 9UH
GREENOCK HSFP	Battery Park, Greenock	PA16 7QG
HARESTANES	Merkland Park, Kirkontilloch	G66 3SN
LESMAHAGOW AFC	Glebe Park, Lesmahagow	ML11 0EQ
OBAN SAINTS	Glencruitten, Oban	PA34 4EJ
ST PATRICKS FP	Posties Park, Dumbarton	G82 4BG
UDDINGSTON ANVIL	Porters Well, Uddingston	G71 7QU
WISHAW HSFP	Dalziel Park, Motherwell	ML1 5LZ

CHAMPIONSHIP

ARTHURLIE AFC	Nethercraig PF	G52 1RR
BEARSDEN	Thorn Park, Bearsden	G61 4BS
BLANTYRE RGM	Matt Busby Complex, Bellshill	ML4 3PD
CAMBUSNETHAN TALBOT	Dalziel Park, Motherwell	ML1 5LZ
CAMPSIE MINERVA	High Park, Lennoxtown	G66 7EJ
CLYDEBANK AFC	John Brown Pitches	G81 1AA
COLVILLE PARK E.	Dalziel Park, Motherwell	ML1 5LZ
GARROWHILL THISTLE	Lochend High School, Glasgow	G34 0NZ
GOLDENHILL	Mountblow SC	G81 4NX
STEDFAST K	Scotstoun Campus, Glasgow	G14 9HY
STEINS THISTLE	Allandale Park	FK4 2HD
THIRD LANARK	Toryglen Football Centre	G42 0BY
TOWER HEARTS	St Ambrose HS, Coatbridge	ML5 2JE
WATERSIDE	Waterside Park, Kirkintilloch	G66 3PE
WESTPARK UNITED	Huntershill	G64 1RU

CSAFL HONOURS

	LEAGUE CHAMPS	DIV 1 CHAMPS	CINEMA CUP	MCAVOY McINTYRE	BUNRIGH TROPHY	ROBERT WHYTE
1988/89	Knightswood Afc	Tower Hearts Afc	Bankhall Villa Afc	Bankhall Villa Afc	St Benedict's Afc	
1989/90	Bankhall Villa Afc	Hillwood Afc	Knightswood Afc	Dumbarton Academy Fp Afc	Cumbernauld Thistle Afc	
1990/91	Bankhall Villa Afc	Denny Westpark Afc	St. Benedicts Afc	Cardross Rock Afc	Knightswood Afc	
1991/92	St. Benedict's Afc	IBM Afc	Dumbarton Academy Fp Afc	Gartcosh Utd	Vale Of Clyde Afc	
1992/93	Cardross Rock Afc	Bellshill Ymca Afc	Cardross Rock Afc	Cardross Rock Afc	Bellshill Ymca Afc	
1993/94	Cardross Rock Afc	Renfrew Ymca Afc	Bankhall Villa Afc	Gartcosh Utd	High Blantyre Utd Afc	
1994/95	Bellshill Ymca Afc	Colville Park Afc	BP Afc	Colville Park Afc	Bellshill Ymca Afc	
1995/96	Bankhall Villa Afc	Wellhouse Afc	Bellshill Carousel Afc	Cardross Rock Afc	Wellhouse Afc	
1996/97	Killermont Afc	Shettleston Afc	St Benedict's Afc	Vale Of Clyde Afc	Fauldhouse Afc	
1997/98	Harestanes Afc	Balmore Afc	BP Afc	Bellshill Ymca Afc	Vale Of Clyde Afc	
1998/99	Balmore Afc	Motherwell Mw Afc	Motherwell Mw Afc	St Benedict's Afc	Harestanes Afc	
1999/00	Harestanes Afc	Aberforth Rangers Afc	Balmore Afc	Plains Afc	Balmore Afc	
2000/01	Harestanes Afc	Spartans Afc	Aberforth Rangers Afc	Harestanes Afc	Aberforth Rangers Afc	
2001/02	Balmore Afc	Motherwell Mw Afc	Harestanes Afc	Brightons Afc	Drumchapel Utd Afc	
2002/03	Harestanes Afc	Tullibody Afc	Colville Park Afc	Harestanes Afc	Harestanes Afc	
2003/04	Kilsyth Afc	Motherwell Mw Afc	Blantyre Afc	Aberforth Rangers Afc	The Spartansafc	Redbrae Afc
2004/05	Drumchapel Utd Afc	Mearns Afc	Harestanes Afc	The Spartans Afc	Drumchapel Utd Afc	
2005/06	Redbrae Afc	Colville Park Afc		Kilsyth Afc	Motherwell Mw Afc	Waterside Afc
2006/07	Colville Park Afc	Buchanan Thistle Afc	Drumchapel Utd Afc	Colville Park Afc	Harestanes Afc	Eastfield Utd Afc
2007/08	Drumchapel Utd Afc	Eddlewood Afc	Drumchapel Utd Afc	The Spartans Afc	Colville Park Afc	Uddingston Afc
2008/09	Drumchapel Utd Afc	St Patricks Fp Afc	Harestanes Afc	The Spartans Afc	Eddlewood Afc	Stedfast Afc
2009/10	Drumchapel Utd Afc	Pollok Afc	Drumchapel Utd Afc	Steins Thistle Afc	Colville Park Afc	Wishaw Hsfp Afc
2010/11	Drumchapel Utd Afc	Ashvale Victoria Afc	Drumchapel Utd Afc	Harestanes Afc	Drumchapel Utd Afc	Ashvale Victoria Afc
2011/12	Colville Park Afc	Bannockburn Afc	Drumchapel Utd Afc	Drumchapel Utd Afc	Drumchapel Utd Afc	Drumchapel Afc
2012/13	Colville Park Afc	Drumchapel Afc	Bannockburn Afc	Bannockburn Afc	Colville Park Afc	Drumchapel Afc
2013/14	Bannockburn Afc	Aikenhead Thistle Afc	Colville Park Afc	Wellhouse Afc	Wellhouse Afc	Blantyre Celtic Afc
2014/15	Harestanes Afc		Greenock HSFP	East Kilbride	Drumchapel Ams	Steins Thistle
2015/16	Colville Park Afc		Campsie Minerva Afc	East Kilbride	Greenock HSFP	Garrowhill Thistle
2016/17	Colville Park Afc		Stirling City AFC	Colville Park Afc	Possil YMCA	
2017/18	Colville Park E AFC		Southside	Eastfield AFC	Colville Park E AFC	
2018/19	Colville Park E AFC		Eastfield AFC	Colville Park E AFC	Eastfield AFC	

DUMFRIES SUNDAY AMATEUR FA 2020/21

Season Cancelled.

Contact: Mr Richard Irving
Email:
totti14@btinternet.com
Telephone: 01387261592

League Membership 2019/20

PREMIER DIVISION	Home Ground	
Terregles Athletic	Terregles Park / North West Community Campus	DG2 9RX / DG2 9LU
Five Arches Bombers	Dumfries HS 3G	DG1 1PX
Hole in the Wa	Holm Park	DG2 7GZ
Annan Town	King Edward Park, Lockerbie	DG11 2PQ
Palmerston Colts	Holm Park	DG2 7GZ
Morton Thistle	Jock's Loaning / Holm Park	DG2 0NP / DG2 7GZ
Dumfries Athletic	Maryfield	DG1 4AA
Normandy Star	Crichton Hospital Park	DG1 4ZE
FC Annan	Everholm	DG12 5DG
Scaur	Penpont Public Park	DG3 4BY
Ruthwell Rovers	Clarencefield	DG1 4NF
AFC Gretna	Graitney Sports Field, Gretna	DG16 5BX
Riverside	Jock's Loaning	DG2 0NP

New Members 2021/2

Eastriggs
Greystone Rovers
Threave Rovers Youth Development
Lochside Club

DUNDEE SATURDAY MORNING AMATEUR LEAGUE 2020/21

Venues Used

Teams do not have specified home grounds

Fairmuir Park	DD3 8HU
Lochee Park	DD2 2HN
Drumgeith	DD4 0JX
Riverview, Monifieth	DD5 4NN
Charlotte Street	DD3 8QP
Craigie 3G	DD4 7PZ
University Grounds, Riverside	DD2 1UG
St Saviours	DD4 0JX
Baldragon Academy	DD3 0LF
Dawson Park	DD5 1PJ
Monymusk	DD4 7SX

Season 2020/1 got underway but was quickly suspended. Results of games played are below.

PREMIER LEAGUE

	BAN	CAI	CHA	DRY	DUS	FCS	FIN	NOR	OCC	POW	RIV	STO
Bank Street Athletic										3-3		
Cairdy Thistle									4-1			
Charlie Accies								6-2				
Dryburgh Athletic							2-2					
DUSC						4-0						0-3
FC Spartak				3-2								0-1
Fintry Athletic			4-0		3-2							
North End Amateurs		3-4		0-4								
Occidental	4-3		2-0									
Powrie		0-1									3-8	
Riverside	5-1											
Stobswell											2-4	

FIRST DIVISION

	CAN	CLA	DUM	DWE	FIF	KEL	KIR	LOC	PAR	TBEA	TMAI	WHI
Cannon Fodder						3-2						
Clark's					3-1							
DUMS (Medics)				5-2								4-4
Dundee West		3-2										
Fife Thistle											0-5	0-6
Kelso				1-4								
Kirkton			3-2							9-1		
Lochee Celtic		5-1							1-2	1-1		
Park Tool	6-1											
The Beat											1-6	
The Maidens							4-3					
Whitfield Tavern									4-2			

SECOND DIVISION

	ABE	ATL	CRA	DATH	DTHI	DUNI	FIN	LOC	MAC	RIV	SPO	STJ	STR	TFB
Abertay Uni						3-5								3-2
Athletico Monifieth					1-3							0-2		
Craigie				10-1									8-1	6-0
Dundee Athletic											1-5			
Dundee Thistle	8-0									0-2				
Dundee Uni		1-7												
Finlathen								6-5					3-1	
Lochee Albion											1-6			
MacAlpine														
Riverside SCIO														
Sporting Club									6-2					
St James							8-1							
Strathmartine								3-2						
Tayside Fire Brigade										1-6				

A Summer Cup, the "Adamson Cup" was played in July / August 2021. It was played in mini-leagues with the top two from each advancing to the KO stages.

Round 1 KO Draw:
Craigie v The Maidens
Fairmuir Social v Dryburgh Athletic
DUSC v Fintry Athletic
St James v Clepington Social
Riverside West End v Fife Thistle B
Bank Street Ath v Riverside CSC
Cairdy Thistle v Whitfield Tavern
Dundee West v Stobswell

Full details in the 2022/3 Almanac

Contact: Mr. Steve McSwiggan
Email: smcswiggan@nhs.net
Telephone: 07821589881

Structure for 2021/2

Premier Division
Bank Street Athletic
Cairdy Thistle
Charlie Accies
Dryburgh Athletic
DUSC
FC Spartak
Fintry Athletic
North End Amateurs
Occidental
Powrie
Riverside CSC
Stobswell

First Division
Cannon Fodder
Clarks
DUMS
Dundee West
Fife Thistle
Kelso
Kirkton
Lochee Celotic
Park Tool
The Beat
The Maidens
Whitfield Tavern

Second Division
Clepington Social
Craigie
Dolphin
Dundee Athletic
Dundee St James
Fairmuir Social
Lochee Albion
Monifieth Athletic
Riverside West End
Sporting Tayside
St Andrews Colts
St James
Strathmartine Athletic
Tayside Fire Brigade

FIFE SUNDAY AMATEUR FOOTBALL LEAGUE 2020/21

A Fife Sunday Cup competition was held in the Summer of 2021.

Group Standings were:

Group A									
Pos	Team	P	W	D	L	F	A	GD	Pts
1	Yeoman	6	6	0	0	51	2	49	18
2	Fife Arms	6	3	0	3	20	18	2	9
3	Kirkcaldy Thistle	6	3	0	3	22	24	-2	9
4	Buckhaven Utd	6	0	0	6	9	58	-49	0

Group B									
Pos	Team	P	W	D	L	F	A	GD	Pts
1	Rosyth Sundays	4	4	0	0	28	8	20	12
2	Athletico FC	4	1	1	2	11	13	-2	4
3	Kirkland Bar	4	0	1	3	6	24	-18	1

Group C									
Pos	Team	P	W	D	L	F	A	GD	Pts
1	FC Brig	6	5	1	0	31	5	26	16
2	Sky	6	4	1	1	25	9	16	13
3	Bruce Arms	6	2	0	4	12	14	-2	6
4	Cowdenbeath Colts	6	0	0	6	3	43	-40	0

Group D									
Pos	Team	P	W	D	L	F	A	GD	Pts
1	Cowdenbeath United	5	5	0	0	17	4	13	15
2	Kingdom Rovers	5	3	0	2	25	15	10	9
3	Bayview Thistle	5	1	0	4	14	15	-10	3
4	Ciswo	5	1	0	4	9	22	-13	3

Contact: Mr Craig Lindsay
Email: fife528@hotmail.co.uk
Telephone: 01337831049

The season got underway in October but was suspended after two weeks.

Results of games played:

West League	ATH	BRU	COW	DUN	LOC	ROS	SKY	YEO
Athletico								
Bruce Arms				0-2	0-4	6-2		
Cowdenbeath United	6-2			3-0				
Dunfermline Town								
Lochore Castle			1-0					
Rosyth Sundays							3-2	
Sky AFC	9-0			3-2				
Yeoman	3-1					5-3		

East League	BAY	CIS	DYN	FCB	FIF	KIN	COW	WEA	WHI	KIR
Bayview Thistle								1-4		
Ciswo	5-3									
Dynamo KB										
FC Brig					9-1					
Fife Arms						1-3			4-3	
Kingdom Rovers										4-0
Cowdenbeath United Colts		3-3							4-6	
Weavers				1-5		4-2				
White Heather										4-1
Kirkland Bar	5-1									

KO Stages - Karens Canine Summer Cup

QF Yeoman v Athletic Townhill, 1-6; Rosyth Sundays v Fife Arms, 3-1; FC Brig v Kingdom Rovers, 4-1; Cowdenbeath v Sky 1-3.
SF Yeoman v FC Brig, 3-3, 3-4p; Rosyth Sundays v Sky 3-1.
F FC Brig v Rosyth Sundays, 10-0

KO Stages - Harrys Doggycare Consolation Cup

QF Kirkcaldy Thistle Bye; Kirkland Bar v Buckhaven United 2-1; Bruce Arms v CISWO 2-0; Bayview Thistle v Cowdenbeath Colts 7-1.
SF Kirkcaldy Thistle v Bruce Arms 5-2; Kirkland Bar v Bayview Thistle 4-3.
F Kirkcaldy Thistle v Kirkland Bar 4-4, 4-3p

RECENT HONOURS						
	Premier League	Division 2	Division 3	Fife Cup	JS Anderson Cup	League Cup
2006/7	Bogarts	Wishart Abbey	Wemyss Central	The Yard, Glenrothes	Royal Scot	Sun Tavern
2007/8	White Heather	Wemyss Central	Station Buffet	Gilvenbank	Bowhill	Bogarts
2008/9	Bogarts	Prinlaws	Lochore Castle	Bogarts	Bogarts	Prinlaws
2009/10	Railway Tavern	Burns Tavern	Jokers	Jokers	Lang Toun Thistle	Railway Tavern
2010/11	St Clair Tavern	Lochore Castle	Crystal Barcelona	Railway Tavern	Dunfermline Thistle	Railway Tavern
2011/12	Railway Tavern	Dunfermline Thistle	Crown Inn	Railway Tavern	Railway Tavern	Railway Tavern
2012/13	Railway Tavern	Crown Inn	King's Arms	Brucefield	Railway Tavern	Railway Tavern
2013/14	Rosyth	Minto Lounge	Bayview Bar	Rosyth	Bayview Bar	Society
2014/15	Brucefield	Auld Hoose	Jokers	FC Brig	Auld Hoose	Auld Hoose
2015/16	FC Brig	Kennoway		FC Brig	FC Brig	Crystal Barcelona
2016/17	Lauders	McPhails		Lauders	Styx	Lauders
2017/18	Yeoman	Steadings		West End Bar	Athletico Rosyth	McPhails
2018/19	Yeoman	Cairneyhill Athletic		Minto Lounge	Wellesley	Lochore Castle

GLASGOW & DISTRICT SATURDAY MORNING A.F.L. 2020/21

Contact: Mr Gordon A. Fergusson
Email: gdsml1968@hotmail.co.uk
Telephone: 01419567371

Season 2020/1 was cancelled. Teams played Friendlies from May 2021.

The League was due to re-start in August 2021.

Clubs in membership in 2019/20 were:

PREMIER DIVISION	Ground	Postcode	DIVISION ONE		
Abronhill - Stepps	Nethercraigs, Glasgow	G52 1RR	AC Milanda	Stepfoird Centre	G33 4NU
Bishopton AFC	Top Park Pitches, Bishopton	PA7 5JP	Accies AFC	Hamilton Palace Pitches	ML3 6EF
Braehead AFC	KGV Parks, Renfrew	PA4 0SA	Bellahouston AFC	Glasgow Green SC	G40 1HB
Bridgend Amateurs	Greenfield Socer Centre	G32 6TP	Belvidere AFC	Lochend SC, Glasgow	G34 0NZ
Cleland AFC	Cleland Public Park	ML1 5RL	Cambuslang Utd	Greenfield Socer Centre	G32 6TP
Crosslands Utd AFC	Glasgow Club, Milton	G22 7QR	Dumbarton AFC	Dumbarton Common	G82 2AA
Drumchapel United	Donald Dewar Centre, Garscadden	G15 8SX	East Kilbride AFC	Ballerup 4G, E Kilbride	G75 0SD
EK Thistle Colts	Murray Pitches, E Kilbride	G75 0RT	Glenavon Thistle	Overlee Pitches	G76 8NL
Finnieston Park AFC	Nethercraigs, Glasgow	G52 1RR	Hamilton Wanderers	Hamilton Palace Pitches	ML3 6EF
Glasgow Islay	Springburn 4G, Glasgow	G21 3UH	Moorpark Athletic AFC	Drumoyne SC	G51 4AJ
Lanarkshire Forrest	Hamilton Palace Pitches	ML3 6EF	Newmains Hammers AFC	Bonkle Park	ML2 9QE
Red Star	Lochend SC, Glasgow	G34 0NZ	Renfrew Town	KGV Parks, Renfrew	PA4 0SA
Woodside AFC	Matt Busby Centre, Bellshill	ML4 3DP	Strathclyde University	Stepps Playing Fields	G33 6ND

GLASGOW AND DISTRICT SUNDAY CHAMPIONSHIP AFL 2020/21

LEAGUE STRUCTURE 2020/21

PREMIERSHIP	CHAMPIONSHIP	LEAGUE ONE
Airdrie Albion	Anchor Sociedad (Paisley)	Clyde Thistle
Atlantic Quay	Baljaffray	Dumbarton United
Barrhead Colts	Barrhead United	East End Athletic
BSC Glasgow Sunday	Clerwood Thistle	FC Dynamo Glasgow
Ferguslie Star	Clydebank SFC	DC Southside United
Glasgow Diverse	Coltness United	Finnieston
GSC United	EK United	Kelvindale
Keppochhill	Firwood United	Renfrew Rovers
Maryhill Black Star	Fernhill United	Southside Star
Maryhill Milan	Glasgow Irish	Strathclyde Thistle
Pollokshields United	Sarry Red Star	Strathclyde United
Southside Spartans	Unity FC	Woodlands

Confirmed New Clubs for 2021/2:

Abbey Athletic
Cumbernauld FC
United Glasgow FC
Springburn Thistle
Men United Glasgow (Home Ground: Science Parks)
Rozelle AFC

Contact: Nim Roy
Email: nim.roy@sky.com
Telephone: 0790974787

The GDSAFL has been running since 2008 and started off with only 6 teams. It has since grown and grown and in 2018/19 season became affiliated under the SAFA constitution/ For 2020/1 it was to have 36 members including several sides moving from other Sunday leagues.

The season was not started.

A Friendly Cup and a Friendly Trophy competition was held for interested teams in June / July 2021.

Friendly Cup QF
Maryhill Blackstar v Southside Spartans, 4-3
EK United v Maryhill Milan, 0-1
Clydebank SFC v Coltness Utd, 0-5
GSC v Firwood United, 1-3

Friendly Trophy QF
Dormy Forest v Kelvindale, 2-8
Barrhead United v Unity, 4-2
Fernhill v Woodlands, 7-2
Strathclyde United v Renfrew Rovers, 1-4

Details of later stages in next year's Almanac

GLASGOW COLLEGES A.F.A. 2020/21

Contact: Mr Donald Brooks
Email: donnie_brooks2003@hotmail.com
Telephone: 0141 578 9961

Season 2020/1 was not contested.

CONSTITUTION 2021/2

GCDA PREMIER DIVISION

	Team		
1	Clydeside Athletic	Petershill Park / Glasgow Green	G21 4DD / G40 1HB
2	Erskine AFC	Netherton / Clydebank HS / Petershill Park	G13 2RX / G81 3EJ / G21 4DD
3	Glasgow Island	Firhill Complex	G20 7HH
4	Hampden AFC	Cathkin Park / Toryglen / Glasgow Green	G42 8XG / G42 0BY / G40 1HB
5	Lokomotiv Glasgow	Greenfield SC / Palace of Arths	G32 6TP / G52 1EQ
6	Lomond Vale	Dumbarton Common / Argyle Park / Vale of Leven Academy	G82 2AA / G83 0SE / G83 0BH
7	Rosehill United	Beith Astro	KA15 1DW
8	Rossvale Kelvinbridge	Colquhoun Park / Huntershill	G61 4AL / G64 1RU

GCFA DIVISION ONE (A) TABLE

	Team		
1	Burnhill FC		
2	Cambuslang Football Academy		
3	Croftpark AFC	Scotstoun SC / Glasgow Green / Springburn Astro	G14 9HD /G40 1HB / G21 3UQ
4	Glasgow Medics	Donald Dewar centre / Toryglen	G15 8SX / G42 0BY
5	Greater Glasgow	Glasgow Green	G40 1HB
6	Kings Park United		
7	Lomond FC		
8	Newlands AFA	Bothwellhaugh / Toryglen	ML1 3RB / G42 0BY

GCFA DIVISION ONE (B) TABLE

	Team		
1	AFC Sporto	Drumoyne Astro / Peterson Park / Greenfield SC	G51 4AW / G13 4PF / G32 6TP
2	Cambuslang FA Pirates		
3	Cambuslang United		
4	Cathcart AFA	Nether Pollok / Toryglen / Milton Centre	G41 4AR / G42 0BY / G22 7QR
5	DTI AFC		
6	Glasgow Ansar	Glasgow Green / Springburn Astro	G40 1HB / G21 3UQ
7	Glasgow East	Greenfield SC / Drumoyne Astro	G32 6TP / G51 4AW
8	MSM AFC	Whifflet Park, Coatbridge	ML5 4HF

GREATER GLASGOW PREMIER A.F.L. 2020/21

Contact: Mr Iain Marshall
Email: imarshall02@msn.com
Telephone: 0141 316 6826

The season 2020/1 did not start. In the late Spring / Summer a Cup competition was played. Some groups, especially those involving Glasgow city area clubs, were badly disrupted by further COVID lockdown measures.

SPRING CUP

SECTION			
1	Oban Saints AFC	3-5	South Lochaber Thistle AFC
1	Rhu GGP AFC	2-5	Vale of Leven AFC
1	Oban Saints AFC	2-3	Vale of Leven AFC
1	Rhu GGP AFC	0-10	Oban Saints AFC
2	Westcliff AFC	9-0	The Lovat Arms AFC
2	Colquhoun Utd AFC	1-2	Westcliff AFC
3	Kilbarchan Thistle AFC	4-5	St. Patrick's FP AFC
3	Belleaire AFC	3-3	Houston Utd AFC
3	Calderglen AFC	2-1	Belleaire AFC
3	Houston Utd AFC	1-3	Kilbarchan Thistle AFC
3	Kilbarchan Thistle AFC	2-2	Calderglen AFC
3	St. Patrick's FP AFC	2-4	Houston Utd AFC
3	Belleaire AFC	2-0	Kilbarchan Thistle AFC
3	Calderglen AFC	2-3	St. Patrick's FP AFC
3	Houston Utd AFC	4-1	Calderglen AFC
3	St. Patrick's FP AFC	5-0	Belleaire AFC
4	Langcraigs AFC	2-2	Glenvale AFC
4	Ferguslie Star	3-0	Langcraigs AFC
4	Glenvale AFC	1-0	Newshot AFC
4	Ferguslie Star	2-5	Newshot AFC
4	Langcraigs AFC	0-2	Newshot AFC
4	Glenvale AFC	1-0	Ferguslie Star
7	East Kilbride Y.M. AFC	5-2	GSC Ams Red
7	Eaglesham AFC	1-6	East Kilbride Y.M. AFC
8	Craigneuk AFC	4-4	Kirkfield Utd AFC
8	Craigneuk AFC	1-1	Carluke Thistle AFC
9	Kirkfield Utd AFC	0-3	Carluke Thistle AFC
QFPO	GSC Amateurs	2-2	Houston Utd AFC
QF	East Kilbride Y.M. AFC	3-3	Carluke Thistle AFC
QF	St. Patrick's FP AFC	2-3	Newshot AFC
QF	Vale of Leven AFC	4-2	Westcliff AFC
QF	Glenvale AFC	AW	GSC Amateurs
SF	Vale of Leven AFC	1-0	Newshot AFC
SF	GSC Amateurs	0-0	Carluke Thistle AFC
F	Vale of Leven AFC	2-1	Carluke Thistle AFC

COMPOSITION 2021/2

DIVISION ONE

Calderglen AFC	Lochwinnoch Public Park	PA12 4AE
Cambria AFC	Strathclyde Uni PF, Stepps	G33 6ND
Eaglesham AFC	Eaglesham Public Park	G76 0L0
East Kilbride Y.M. AFC	Kirktonholme Park, E Kilbride	G74 1DD
Eastwood Parkmount 'A' AFC	Bogton PF, Glasgow	G44 3HQ
Erskine AFC	Inchinnan PF	PA4 9PH
Glasgow University 'A' AFC	Garscube SC	G20 0SP
Rhu GGP AFC	Hermitage Acad, Helenburgh	G84 7LA
South Lochaber Thistle AFC	Kinlochlevven Astro	PH50 4QH
St. Patrick's FP AFC	Dumbarton Common	G82 2BL
Westerlands AFC	Garscube SC	G20 0SP

DIVISION TWO

Belleaire AFC	Rankin Park, Greenock	PA16 9EU
Dynamo East Kilbride AFC	John Wright SC, E Kilbride	G74 3EU
Eastwood Parkmount 'B' AFC	Bogton PF, Glasgow	G44 3HQ
EKRR AFC	Ballerup PF, E Kilbride	G75 0SD
GSC Amateurs	Norwood PF, Glasgow	G41 4RF
GSC Jordanhill AFC	Norwood PF, Glasgow	G41 4RF
John Street AFC	Glasgow Green	G40 1HB
Langcraigs AFC	The Marshes, Paisley	PA2 6SA
Newshot AFC	Renfrew LC	PA4 8LJ
Strathclyde University AFC	Strathclyde Uni PF, Stepps	G33 6ND

DIVISION 3A

Carluke Thistle AFC	John Cumming SC	ML8 4EA
Colquhoun Utd AFC	Colquhoun Park, Bearsden	G61 4AL
Duncanrig AFC	Ballerup PF, E Kilbride	G75 0SD
GSC Ams Red	Norwood PF, Glasgow	G41 4RF
Houston Utd AFC	Beith Astro	KA15 1DW
Kilbarchan Thistle AFC	Miller Street PF, Johnstone	PA5 8HP
Mosspark Albion AFC	Hillwood	G53 6QP
Oban Saints AFC	Glencruitten / Oban HS	PA34 5DR / PA34 4BJ
Viewfield Rovers AFC	Kildale Road, Lochwinnoch	PA12 4DF
Westcliff AFC	Dumbarton Common	G82 2AA

DIVISION 3B

Antonine AFC	William Street, Clydebank	G81 6DF
Boswell AFC	Rosshall Academy, Glasgow	G52 3PD
Craigneuk AFC	Muirhouse Park	ML1 2EX
Ferguslie Star	Ferguslie Park SC, Paisley	PA3 1NR
Kirkfield Utd AFC	Lanark Race Course	ML11 9TA
Pollok AFC	Nethercraigs SC	G52 1TQ
Rannoch AFC	Netherton PF	G13 2RX
The Lovat Arms AFC	John Brown Playing Field	G81 1DE
Vale of Leven AFC	Argyle Park, Alexandria	G83 0SE
Weir AFC	Albert Park, Cathcart	G43 2HR
Westerlands G.G. AFC	Garscube SC	G20 0SP

KINGDOM OF FIFE AFA 2020/21

Contact: James Mitchell
Email: jjlpsmitch@aol.com
Telephone: 01383 414339

Season 2020/1 began in October but was suspended after only a few matches had been played.

Once COVID restrictions had been relaxed the Jon Harrison Memorial Trophy was played in May / June. This involved Group Matches followed by a KO competition.

Results were:

1	Burntisland Thistle	Fife Thistle	0	0
1	Fife Thistle	Balgonie Scotia	1	1
1	Burntisland United	Balgonie Scotia	0	6
2	Fife Star	Eastvale	0	8
2	Greig Park Rangers	Cupar Hearts	2	2
2	Cupar Hearts	Fife Star	21	0
2	Eastvale	Greig Park Rangers	3	11
2	Eastvale	Cupar Hearts		
2	Fife Star	Greig Park Rangers	0	14
3	Glenrothes Strollers	Kirkcaldy Blues	5	4
3	Lochgelly United	Kelty AFC	3	0
3	Kelty AFC	Glenrothes Strollers	5	1
3	Kirkcaldy Blues	Lochgelly United	0	4
3	Glenrothes Strollers	Lochgelly United	1	7
3	Kirkcaldy Blues	Kelty AFC	3	4
4	Bridge of Earn	Methilhill Strollers	2	1
4	Kennoway United	Kennoway Star Hearts A	5	1
4	Kennoway Star Hea	Bridge of Earn	3	5
4	Methilhill Strollers	Kennoway United	0	4
4	Kennoway Star Hea	Methilhill Strollers	2	2
4	Kennoway United	Bridge of Earn	2	2
5	Lumphinnans Unite	Leslie Hearts	3	2
5	St Andrews Colts	Blairhall Villa	3	1
5	Blairhall Villa	Leslie Hearts	5	0
5	Lumphinnans Unite	St Andrews Colts	1	2
5	Blairhall Villa	Lumphinnans United	2	1
5	St Andrews Colts	Leslie Hearts	5	0
6	Hearts of Beath	Auchtermuchty Bellevue	2	2
6	Rosyth	Strathmiglo	1	2
6	Auchtermuchty Bell	Rosyth AFC	4	3
6	Strathmiglo	Hearts of Beath	5	1
6	Auchtermuchty Bell	Strathmiglo		
6	Hearts of Beath	Rosyth AFC	6	1
7	Glenrothes AFC	Kinross Colts Ams	2	5
7	Kettle United	Kirkcaldy YM	0	2
7	Kettle United	Kinross Colts Ams	2	3
7	Glenrothes AFC	Kinross AFC	3	0
7	Glenrothes	Kirkcaldy YM	1	3
7	Glenrothes	Kettle United	2	2
7	Kinross Colts A	Kirkcaldy YM	2	3
8	Kinross Colts	Rosebank Rangers	2	2
8	Leven United	AFC Kincardine	8	0
8	AFC Kincardine	Kinross Colts Ams	3	2
8	Rosebank Rangers	Leven United	0	5
8	Kinross Colts	Leven United	0	10
8	Rosebank Rangers	AFC Kincardine	0	8

KO Stages

8/6/21	1	Auchtermuchty Bellevue	Kinross Colts	1	4	
8/6/21	1	Balgonie Scotia	Greig Park Rangers	2	1	
8/6/21	1	Cupar Hearts	Kelty	wo	scr	
8/6/21	1	Kennoway AFC	Blairhall Villa	7	0	
8/6/21	1	Kirkcaldy YM	AFC Kincardine	4	1	
8/6/21	1	Leven United	Fife Thistle	3	2	
8/6/21	1	Lochgelly United	Bridge of Earn	2	1	
8/6/21	1	St Andrews Colts	Strathmiglo	3	3	6-5p
12/6/21	QF	Balgonie Scotia	Cupar Hearts	1	6	
12/6/21	QF	Kirkcaldy YM	Leven United	2	1	
12/6/21	QF	Lochgelly United	Kennoway AFC	2	1	
12/6/21	QF	St Andrews Colts	Kinross Colts	1	9	
15/6/21	SF	Cupar Hearts	Lochgelly United	4	0	
15/6/21	SF	Kinross Colts	Kirkcaldy YM	0	1	
26/6/21	F	Cupar Hearts (at Coaltown of Balgonie)	Kirkcaldy YM	3	3	3-0p

PREMIER DIVISION

	AUC	BAL	BOW	CUP	GRE	KEL	KEN	KIN	KC	YM	LEV	YLUM	PIT	STA
Auchtermuchty Bellevue			2-3									3-0		
Balgonie Scotia								2-0					2-1	
Bowhill Rovers														
Cupar Hearts	4-0						5-2						9-0	
Greig Park Rangers	2-1										0-2			
Kelty Amateurs										1-4				
Kennoway	1-3										0-1			
Kinross												4-2		
Kinross Colts	3-0													
Kirkcaldy YMCA			0-3	0-6	3-3			3-0						
Leven United				1-2				7-2	5-1					
Lumphinnans United			0-5	2-7				2-1						
Pittenweem Rovers						1-1		1-1						
St Andrews Uni														

CHAMPIONSHIP

	BUR	DUL	EAS	FATH	FTHI	FRE	GLE	LOC	MAR	RBK	RYT	STA	STM	STR
Burntisland United				3-0		7-0						2-2		
Duloch					4-3							0-4		
Eastvale		4-1						1-5						1-4
Fife Athletic								1-1	1-6		0-2			
Fife Thistle										4-1	0-1			
Freuchie			3-1								0-5		5-1	
Glenrothes Ams	3-2			1-2	5-3	7-2								
Lochgelly United														
Markinch		5-2			1-1									2-1
Rosebank Rangers						0-3		0-6						
Rosyth Amateurs								1-2						
St Andrews Colts			4-3						1-6				4-1	
St Monans Swallows		1-6			3-3				0-2					
Strathmiglo United										4-1				

DIVISION ONE

	BLA	BOE	FIF	GLE	HOB	KSH	KET	KDN	KRO	KALB	KBLU	LES	MET	NEW	UNI
Blairhall Villa			9-0	3-0	6-2									6-1	
Bridge of Earn			14-0								20-0				
Fife Star				0-10	1-18									1-14	
Glenrothes Strollers					1-3										
Hearts of Beath															
Kennoway Star Hearts Ams					0-9				1-4	17-0					
Kettle United						4-2						4-3			
Kincardine										21-0		3-1			
Kinross Colts B	0-1										7-1				
Kirkcaldy Albion		0-22		1-2					0-9					0-8	
Kirkcaldy Blues				5-6		2-9		0-18					1-5		
Leslie Hearts		0-4			2-3				4-2						
Methilhill Strollers & EF			7-2	6-1			8-2								
Newburgh Ams		0-7				3-2									
United Colleges															

LEAGUE COMPOSITION 2021/2

Premiership	**Ground**	
Auchtermuchty Bellvue	Low Road Park, Auchtermuchty	KY14 7BB
Balgonie Scotia 1896	KGV Park, Coaltown of Balgonie	KY7 6HY
Bowhill Rovers	Wallsgreen Park, Cardenden	KY5 0BW
Cupar Hearts	Duffus Park, Cupar	KY15 4HY
Greig Park Rangers	Greig Park, Windygates	KY8 5DG
Kelty AFC	Blairadam Park, Kelty	KY4 0LT
Kennoway Ams	Cotlands Park, Kennoway	KY8 5HX
Kinross AFC	The Myre, Kinross	KY13 8DY
Kinross Colts Ams		
Kirkcaldy YMCA	Beveridge Park, Kirkcaldy	KY2 5LZ
Leven United	Premier Park, Leven (formerly KGV Park)	KY8 5BL
Lumphinnans United	Ochilview Park, Lumphinnans	KY4 9HY
Pittenweem Rovers	Recreation Park, Pittenweem	KY10 2QP
St. Andrews University AFC	University PF, St Andrew's	KY16 9DY

Championship	**Ground**	
Burntisland United AFC	Myers Park, Kinghorn	KY3 9XU
Eastvale Ams AFC	Greig Park, Windygates	KY8 5DG
Fife Athletic AFC	Dalgety Bay SC	KY11 9NA
St. Monans Swallows AFC	Recreation Park, St Monans	KY10 2DA
Fife Thistle AFC	Balmullo Park, Balmullo	KY16 0AZ
Glenrothes AFC	Quarry Park, Leslie	KY6 3DT
Rosebank Rangers AFC	Pitreavie PF, Dunfermline	KY11 8PP
Markinch AFC	John Dixon Park, Markinch	KY7 6BQ
Lochgelly United AFC	Moore Park, Lochgelly	KY5 9JJ
St. Andrews Colts AFC	Cockshaugh Park, St Andrew's	KY16 9DA
Strathmiglo United AFC	Town Green, Strathmiglo	KY14 7QD
The Swifts		

First Division		
AFC Kincardine		
Methilhill Strollers & East Fife AFA	Herd Park, Methil	KY8 2DJ
Bridge of Earn		
Kennoway Star Hearts AFC	Cotlands Park, Kennoway	KY8 5HX
Kinross Colts AFC	Loch Leven Campus, Kinross	KY13 8FQ
Hearts of Beath		
Glenrothes Strollers		
Kettle United		
Leslie Hearts		

Second Division		
Benarty Astros	Lochore Meadows	
Fife Star	KGV Pavilion, Kinglassie	
Hearts of Beath Colts		
Kinross Colts B		
Kirkcaldy Blues		
Leven AFC		
Newburgh Juveniles		
Rothes AFC		
United Colleges		

LOTHIAN & EDINBURGH A.F.A. 2020/21

Contact: Mr Chris Lowrie
Email: clowrie@yahoo.co.uk
Telephone: 07867 534736

Season 2020/1 was not played.

A Cup competition was played in the late Spring / Summer 2021 - the FN teamwear Cup. 48 teams entered: Bingham AFC, Broxburn Mornings AFC, Broughton Albion AFC, Burgh Vale AFC, Cavalry Park AFC, Carrick Athletic AFC, Corstorphine Dynamo Mornings AFC, Craigshill Thistle AFC, Carbrera AFC, Clermiston Vale AFC, Duddingston Athletic AFC, Edinburgh United 20s AFC, Edina Hibs AFC, Edinburgh Caledonia AFC, Edinburgh Harps AFC, Edinburgh United Vale AFC, Fernabaque AFC, Frederick Douglas AFC, Fauldhouse AFC, Fernieside AFC, Gorgie Vale AFC, Heriot Watt Reserves AFC, Hunterfield AFC, Kingsknowe AFC, Leith Athletic AFC, Livingston AFC, Meadowbank AFC, Meadowbank Wednesday AFC, MC2 United AFC, Maybury Star AFC, MacMillan Samba AFC, Murieston United AFC, Musselburgh AFC, Niddrie Star AFC, Newcraighall Leith Vics AFC, Pentland Athletic AFC, Preston Athletic 20s AFC, Restalig AFC, Roseburn Athletic AFC, Ratho AFC, Royal Penicuik AFC, Saughton Sounders Afternoon AFC, Saughton Sounders Morning AFC, Sandys AFC, Tollcross Thistle AFC, Tranent AFC, Vittoria AFC, and Wallyford Bluebell AFC.

After playing Sectional Games the placings were used to allocate teams into three KO Cups.

These concluded:

CHAMPIONSHIP FINAL
Sandys v Edinburgh Star, 5-0

LEAGUE CUP FINAL
Fernieside v Tranent, 2-0

CONFERENCE CUP FINAL
Saughton Sounders v Pentland Athletic, 0-1

All 3 Finals were staged at Albyn Park, Broxburn.

Some of the 2019/20 Cup competitions were due to be concluded at the start of 2021/2.

Clubs in Membership for 2021/22

SATURDAY SECTION

Premier Division		
Danderhall Miners AFC	Danderhall Recreation Park	EH22 1QG
Edinburgh Star	Saughton 3G	EH11 3BQ
Edinburgh Utd Vale	Paties Road	
Fauldhouse Ams	Eastfield Park	EH47 9LE
Meadowbank FC	Meadowbank 3G	
Murieston Utd	Murieston Pavilion	
Musselburgh Ams	Pinkie PF	EH21 7LN
New'hall Leith Vics	Newcraighall Park	EH21 8SB
Sandys	Castleview Centre	EH16 4DW
Tollcross Th	Saughton 3G	EH11 3BQ
Tranent Ams	Polson Park	EH33 1AN

Championship		
B of S Strollers	Royal High School 3G, Edinburgh	EH4 6AQ
Barca-Milton 97	The Jewel, Edinburgh	EH15 3JL
Blackridge V of C	Westrigg Park	EH48 3SX
Cavalry Park	Cavalry Park	EH15 1ND
Corstorphine Dynamo	Gyle	EH12 8LJ
Craigshill Th CFC	Craigswood SC, Livingston	
Dunbar Ath	Hallhill Complex	EH42 1RF
Edin Uni Colts	Peffermill	EH16 5LL
Edinburgh Harps	Royal High School 3G, Edinburgh	EH4 6AQ
KSQ AFC	Queensferry Sports Hub	EH30 9JN
Musselburgh Windsor	Whitecraig	EH21 8NG
Ratho Ath	Ratho Public Park	EH28 8PE

Division 1 West		
Armadale Ath	Armadale Academy 3G	
Balerno Ath	KGV Park, Balerno	EH14 5RU
Bathgate AFC	Meadow Park, Bathgate	
Bo'ness Utd	Newtown Park, Bo'ness	
Carrick Ath	Forrester HS Grass	
East Calder Utd	East Calder Park	EH53 0EW
Fauldhouse SC	Fauldhouse 3G	
Heriot Watt	ORIAM	EH14 4AS
Loganlea Utd	Recreation Park	
Mental Mechanics	Forrester HS (Grass)	EH12 9AE
Mill AFC	Victoria Park, Falkirk	FK2 7EB
Polbeth Utd	Limefield Park	EH55 8QU
Saughton Sounders	Saughton	EH11 3BQ
Whitburn AFC	KGV Park, Whitburn	

Division 1 East		
Bonnyrigg Rose Ath A	KGV Park, Bonnyrigg	EH19 2AD
Dalkeith Th	Cowden Park, Dalkeith	
East Linton	East Linton Park	
Edin University	Peffermill	EH16 5LL
Edina Hibs	Portobello HS 3G	EH15 3BY
Fernieside	Peffermill	EH16 5LL
Leith Ath	Leith Links	
Linton Hotspur	New Moor Road, West Linton	EH46 7AU
Loanhead Miners AFC	Memorial Park, Loanhead	
Longniddry Villa	Longniddry Park	
North Berwick	North Berwick 3G	
Pencaitland AFC	Park View, Pencaitland	
Penicuik AFC	Penicuik Public Park	EH26 9EP
Restalrig AFC	Seafield	EH7 6RD

SUNDAY SECTION

Sunday Morning Premier Division

Broxburn AFC	Holmes Park, Broxburn	EH52 5JP
Cabrera MC AFC	Gyle	EH12 8LJ
Corstorphine Timbers	Gyle	EH12 8LJ
Edinburgh Caledonian	Peffermill	EH16 5LL
Macmillan Samba	Broughton HS 3G	EH4 1EG
Meadowbank Wednesday	Broughton HS 3G	EH4 1EG
Morningside AFC	Broughton HS 3G	EH4 1EG
Niddrie Star	Castlebrae HS	EH16 4DP
Pentland Ath	Bilston PS	EH25 9SD
Victoria Loco Stables	Forrester HS 3G	EH12 9AE
Vittoria Group	Peffermill	EH16 5LL

Sunday Morning Championship

Burgh Vale	Gyle	EH12 8LJ
Easthouses Mornings AFC	Easthouses Park	EH22 4EG
Edinburgh City	The Jewel	EH15 3JL
Gotham City	Gyle	EH12 8LJ
Haddington Town	Knox Academy	EH41 4DT
Kingsknowe AFC	Dalkeith Campus	EH22 2PS
Oxgangs Trinity	Colinton Mains	EH13 9ED
Pumpherston Th	Gyle	EH12 8LJ
Roseburn Th	Gyle	EH12 8LJ
The Oranjetangs	Cavalry Park	EH15 1ND

Sunday Morning Division 1 (West)

Harvester AFC	Mosswood, Livingston	EH54 8JF
Boca Amateurs	Craigswood SC, Livingston	EH54 5ER
Burnside Tower AFC	A89 Station Road Park	
East Calder CFC	East Calder Park	
Livi North AFC	Inveralmond CHS	EH54 6HW
M2C United	Gyle	EH12 8LJ
Maybury Star AFC	Gyle	EH12 8LJ
Pumpherston United	Beechwood Park, Uphall	
South Gyle Rovers AFC	Gyle	EH12 8LJ
Livingston Community AFC		

Sunday Morning Division 1 (East)

Bingham Athletic	Jack Kane Centre	EH16 4ND
Bonnyrigg Rose	Poltonhall Rec Ground	EH19 2NU
Broughton Albion	Seafield	EH7 6RD
Ferniebahce AFC	Jack Kane Centre	EH16 4ND
Lochend AFC	Seafield	EH7 6RD
Newcraighall Leith Vic's	Newcraighall Park	EH21 8SB
Saughton Sounders SM AFC	Saughton 3G	EH11 3BQ
Silverknowes AFC		
Tamsons Bar AFC	Seafield	EH7 6RD
Tranent AFC	Polson Park	

SUNDAY AFTERNOON

Premier Division

Bathgate Th	Bathgate SC	EH48 1BA
Corstorphine Dynamo	Gyle	EH12 8LJ
Duddingston Ath	Cavalry Park	EH15 1ND
Easthouses CFC	Easthouses Park	EH22 4EG
Edinburgh East	Jack Kane Centre	EH16 4ND
Gorgie Hearts	Forrester HS	EH12 9AE
Saughton Sounders	Saughton 3G	EH11 3BQ
Wallyford Bluebell	Fisherrow	EH21 6JR
Westside AFC	Saughton 3G	EH11 3BQ

Division 1

Boroughmuir AFC	Gyle	EH12 8LJ
Clermiston AFC	Edinburgh Leisure	
Corstorphine Dynamo Swifts	Gyle	EH12 8LJ
Dollys AFC	Gyle	EH12 8LJ
Edinburgh South	The Inch	EH16 5UD
Frederick Douglass 1846	Seafield	EH7 6RD
Gallo AFC	Edinburgh Leisure	
Hunterfield Vale AFC	Gore Glen, Gorebridge	EH23 4AE
Musselburgh Utd	Newcraighall Park	EH21 8SB
Riccarton Young Boys	Forrester HS	EH12 9AE
Thornybank Th	Dalkeith Campus	EH22 2PS

MIDLANDS A.F.A. 2020/21

Contact: Mr Alistair Martin
Email: ally1martin@btinternet.com
Telephone: 01382477903

Season 2020/1 began but was halted after a few games.

PREMIER DIVISION

	AHA	AHS	BAR	BRE	BRO	CAR	FVN	FTY	FOR	INV	MEN	MER	MOR	NEW	WEL
Arbroath Harp															
Arbroath HSFP							5-2						2-1		
Barnhill				8-1			2-2								
Brechin City Ams		2-3													
Broughty United				10-0											
Carnoustie Panmure YM									6-1		0-7				
Finavon						3-0									
Fintry												0-0			
Forfar Athletic CC															
Invergowrie								1-5						3-1	
Menzieshill															
Merpro											0-4				6-1
Morgan Acad FP										3-3					
Newport					0-3										
Wellbank								0-7							

ALLIANCE	AHA	AHSA	AHSB	BAR	BRO	CAR	INV	MOR	NEW
Arbroath Harp A			2-0	2-4					
Arbroath HSFP A									1-1
Arbroath HSFP B	4-0								
Barnhill A									
Broughty United A	6-0						5-0		
Carnoustie Panmure YM A									
Invergowrie A		0-5							
Morgan FP A			4-0	6-4					
Newport A						1-3			

LEAGUE COMPOSITION 2021/22

PREMIER DIVISION

Arbroath Harp	McDonald Park	
Arbroath HSFP	Arbroath Sports Centre	DD11 3EW
Barnhill	Monifieth HS	DD5 4QT
Brechin	Brechin Public Park	
Broughty Utd	Dawson Park	DD5 1PJ
Carnoustie Panmure YM	Carlogie Park	DD7 6HQ
Finavon	Market Muir, Forfar	DD8 3JL
Forfar Athletic CSC	Lochside Park	
Invergowrie	Memorial Park, Invergowrie	DD2 5AY
Kirriemuir Thistle	Martin Park	DD8 5HN
Merpro	Broomfield Park, Montrose	DD10 8TZ
Morgan Academy FP	Craigie 3G	DD4 7SQ
Newport	Waterstone Crook	DD6 8HY
Wellbank	Wellbank Park	DD5 3PE

ALLIANCE

Arbroath Harp	McDonald Park
Arbroath HSFP A	Arbroath Sports Centre
Arbroath HSFP B	Arbroath Sports Centre
Barnhill	Monifieth HS
Brechin	
Broughty Utd	Esplanade
Carnoustie Panmure YM	Carlogie Park
Forfar Athletic	
Invergowrie	Memorial Park, iNvergowrie
Kirriemuir Thistle	
Morgan Academy FP	Craigie 3G
Newport	Waterstone Crook

	League Champions	Carne Trophy	Buckman Mackie Trophy	Fairfield S and L Trophy	Gray Trophy	Lunan Trophy	Mel Ross Trophy	Wallace Trophy
1926/27	Aeros							
1927/28	YM Anchorage							
1928/29	Grove Academy FP							
1929/30	Aeros							
1930/31	Aeros							
1931/32	Clifton Thistle							
1932/33	RAF Leuchars							
1933/34	YM Anchorage							
1934/35	YM Anchorage							
1935/36	YM Anchorage							
1936/37	YM Anchorage							
1937/38	YM Anchorage							
1938/39	YM Anchorage							
1939/40	YM Anchorage							
1946/47	YM Anchorage							
1947/48	YM Anchorage							
1948/49	YM Anchorage					YM Anchorage		
1949/50	YM Anchorage					YM Anchorage		
1950/51	YM Anchorage				Tayport Violet	YM Anchorage		
1951/52	YM Anchorage				Tayport Violet	YM Anchorage		
1952/53	YM Anchorage				Alyth Violet	YM Anchorage		
1953/54	Invergowrie				Wormit	YM Anchorage		
1954/55	YM Anchorage				Invergowrie	YM Anchorage		
1955/56	Wormit				RAF Leuchars	Bullionfield		
1956/57	Wormit	NCR			YM Anchorage	Bullionfield		
1957/58	YM Anchorage	YMCA			YM Anchorage	YM Anchorage		
1958/59	YM Anchorage	Broughty Hearts			Wormit Ams	Grays United		
1959/60	NCR	Harris Academy FP			Morgan Acad FP	YM Anchorage		
1960/61	NCR	Craigiebank			Grays Utd	Morgan Acad FP		
1961/62	NCR	Auchterhouse			Longforgan	Grays United		
1962/63	NCR	6th BB			No competition	No competition		
1963/64	NCR	Tayport Ams			NCR	NCR		

	League Champions	Carne Trophy	Buckman Mackie Trophy	Fairfield S and L Trophy	Gray Trophy	Lunan Trophy	Mel Ross Trophy	Wallace Trophy
1964/65	NCR	Lawside Academy FP			NCR	NCR		
1965/66	NCR	Monifieth			NCR	Grove Academy FP		
1966/67	NCR	Tayport Ams			No competition	Grove Academy FP		
1967/68	NCR	YM Anchorage			Lawside Academy FP	NCR		
1968/69	NCR	YMCA			Lawside Academy FP	Longforgan		
1969/70	Broughty United	Carnoustie YM			NCR	NCR		
1970/71	NCR	Kingsway TC			Lawside Academy FP	Wormit Ams		
1971/72	Broughty United	SMT			Grove Ams	Broughty United		
1972/73	Lawside FP	Kelso			SMT	Timex		
1973/74	Broughty United	Arbroath HSFP			Broughty United	Carnoustie YM		
1974/75	Broughty United	Barnhill			NCR	St James		
1975/76	Auchterhouse	Lochee BC			Auchterhouse	NCR		
1976/77	Auchterhouse	Kelso			SMT	Carnoustie YM B		
1977/78	Auchterhouse	Timex			Tayport Ams	Timex		
1978/79	SMT	Kelso			SMT	Carnoustie YM A		
1979/80	Harris Academy FP	YM Anchorage			Timex	Broughty United		
1980/81	Harris Academy FP	Arbroath HSFP			Harris Academy FP	Harris Academy FP		
1981/82	Tayport	PO Phones			Timex	Kingsway TC		
1982/83	Harris Academy FP	Riverside Athletic			Harris Academy FP	Kingsway TC		
1983/84	Kingsway TC	Carnoustie YM			Kingsway TC	Kingsway TC		
1984/85	Harris Academy FP	YM Anchorage			Kingsway TC	Harris Academy FP		
1985/86	Riverside Ath	Broughty Ex-Service			Riverside Ath	NCR		
1986/87	Riverside Ath	Hillside BC			Lawside Academy FP	YMCA		
1987/88	Lawside FP	St Francis			NCR	Riverside Ath		
1988/89	Riverside Ath	Broughty East End			Riverside Ath	DCFE		
1989/90	Riverside Ath	Broughty United			Riverside Ath	Riverside Ath		
1990/91	Riverside Ath	Kingsway Athletic	Lawside Academy	Riverside Athletic	Timex	Kingsway Ath		
1991/92	Riverside Ath	Letham Lads Club	Lawside Academy	Riverside Athletic	Kingsway Athletic	Riverside Ath		
1992/93	Lawside FP	Harris Academy FP	Tayside Fire Brigade	Tayside Fire Brigade	Letham LC	NCR		
1993/94	NCR	Fintry Thistle	NCR	Riverside Athletic	Dundee YMCA	NCR		
1994/95	Barnhill	Douglas Ams	SS Peter & Paul	Tayside Fire Brigade	Dundee YMCA	Riverside Ath		
1995/96	Riverside Ath	Whitfield Labour Club	Riverside Athletic	Barnhill	Broughty United	Arbroath Harp		Auchterhouse Admiral
1996/97	Riverside Ath	Lochee United	Douglas Ams	Riverside Athletic	Letham LC	Inchture Ath		St James
1997/98	NCR	Carnoustie YM / HS	Lawside Academy	Logie Harp	Fintry Thistle	Riverside Ath		Monifieth Tayside
1998/99	Riverside Ath	Lowson United	Riverside Athletic	Tayside Fire Brigade	Dee Club	Riverside Ath	Logie Harp	Dundee Shamrock
1999/00	Riverside Ath	Dundee Shamrock	Barnhill	Dundee College	Arbroath HSFP	Barnhill	Harris Acad FP	Harris Academy FP
2000/1	Riverside Ath	Fintry Thistle	Riverside Athletic	Arbroath Ams	Arbroath HSFP	NCR B	Dundee College	Arbroath Ams
2001/2	SS Peter & Paul	Carnoustie YM	Riverside Athletic	Riverside Athletic	Dee Club	NCR B	Carnouistie YM	Carnoustie YM
2002/3	Riverside Ath	Invergowrie	Riverside Athletic	Riverside Athletic	Carnoustie YM	Broughty United	Harris Acad FP	Cup witheld
2003/4	Riverside Ath	Dundee University	SS Peter & Paul	Riverside Athletic	Invergowrie	NCR	Arbroath HSFP	Morgan Acad FP
2004/5	Riverside Ath	Arfbroath Harp	Riverside Athletic	Riverside Athletic	Dundee Shamrock	Carnoustie YM	NCR	Dundee University
2005/6	Riverside Ath	St James	Riverside Athletic	SS Peter and Paul	Morgan Acad FP	NCR	Dundee College	Dundee University
2006/7	Riverside Ath	Portcullis	Carnoustie YM	Riverside Athletic	Arbroath HSFP	NCR	Invergowrie	Carnoustie YM B
2007/8	SS Peter & Paul	Douglas Sports Club	Riverside Athletic	Riverside Athletic	Menzieshill Athletic	Barnhill	Carnouistie YM B	Harris Academy FP
2008/9	Riverside Ath	FC Claypotts	Invergowrie	Riverside Athletic	Bank Street Ath	Broughty United	Riverside Ath	Michelin Ath
2009/10	Riverside Ath	Caird Park	St James	Bank Street Ath	SS Peter and Paul	Barnhill	Carnoustie YM A	Morgan Acad FP
2010/11	Bank Street Ath	Monifieth Tayside	Bank Street Athletic	Carnoustie YM	Newport	Carnoustie YM B	Broughty United A	Arbroath HSFP A
2011/12	Bank Street Ath	Inchture Ath	NCR	Bank Street Ath	Dundee College	Broughty United B	Broughty United B	Arbroath CSC A
2012/13	St James	Monfiieth Tayside	NCR	St James	Dundee City	Invergowrie	Carnoustie YM A	St James
2013/14	Riverside Ath	Menzieshill	Riverside Athletic	St James	Lowson United	Tayside Fire Brigade	Arbroath HSFP A	Monifieth Tayside
2014/15	St James	Mid Craigie	St James	St James	Portcullis	St James	NCR	Riverside Ath
2015/16	Carnoustie Panmure	Bank Street Ath	Menzieshill Rovers	Riverside Athletic	Morgan Acad FP	Arbroath HSFP A	Riverside Ath	St James
2016/17	Menzieshill AFC	No competition	Menzieshill AFC	Menzieshill AFC	Douglas AFC	Logie Harp	Morgan Acad FP	Portcullis
2017/18	Douglas Athletic	No competition	Douglas Athletic	Menzieshill AFC	Finavon	Broughty United	Lochee United	Portcullis
2018/19	Menzieshill AFC	Shotz	Menzieshill AFC	Menzieshill AFC	Shotz	Broughty United		

PERTHSHIRE A.F.A. 2020/1

Contact: Mr Keith Barclay
Email: kenithbarclay@btinternet.com
Telephone: 01738636160

Season 2020/1 began in October but was suspended within a matter of days.

FIRST DIVISION	BAL	BRI	BUR	CRA	JEA	KET	LHM	LCC	LUN	STJ	VOE
Balmoral United							0-4				1-2
Bridgeton											
Burrelton										0-0	
Craigie							1-3				
Jeanfield											
Kettins											
Letham				4-1	7-0						
Letham CC		2-2							0-2		
Luncarty ASC		9-1									
St Johns					7-2						
Vale of Earn											

SECOND DIVISION	ALY	BAL	BRE	FAI	KIN	PIT	RAT	SCO	STA	VOA	WOL
Alyth					3-1				2-0		
Ballinluig											
Breadalbane											
Fair City			5-1								
Kinrossie Caledonian											
Pitfour				2-8							
Rattray											
Scone Thistle							3-5				
Stanley		3-0									
Vale of Atholl											2-4
Wolfhill											

In Spring 2021 3 League Cup competitions were organised. These ended:

PERTH & DISTRICT CUP

	P	W	D	L	PTS
Letham CC	6	5	0	1	18
St Johns	6	5	0	1	15
Gair City	6	4	0	2	12
Letham CC	6	3	0	3	9
Jeanfield	6	2	0	4	6
Craigie	6	2	0	4	6
Scone Thistle	6	1	0	5	3

Letham defeated St Johns 5-3 in a Play Off

NORTH PERTHSHIRE CUP

	P	W	BP	L	PTS
Vale of Earn	5	5	0	0	15
Breadalbane	5	3	2	1	11
Ballinluig	5	5	1	2	10
Stanley	5	2	2	3	5
Luncarty	5	1	1	4	4
Vale of Atholl	5	0	0	5	0

MARSHALL CUP

	P	W	L	BP	PTS
Alyth	6	6	0	0	18
Burrelton	6	5	0	0	15
Kettins	6	4	0	2	12
Balmoral	6	2	2	3	8
Wolfhill	6	2	1	3	7
Rattray	6	1	0	5	3
Kinrossie	6	0	0	6	0

LEAGUE COMPOSITION 2021/2

DIVISION ONE	Ground	Postcode
Balmoral	Davie Park Pitch 2, Blairgowrie	PH10 7BJ
Bridge of Earn	Victory Park, Bridge of Earn	PH2 9DY
Bridgeton United	South Inch, Perth	PH2 8AX
Burrelton Rovers	Recreation Park, Burrelton	PH13 9NH
Coupar Angus	Larghan Park, Coupar Angus	PH13 9ER
Craigie	Huntingtower Park, Ruthvenfield	PH1 3JR
Jeanfield	Riverside Park, Perth	PH1 3BG
Kettins	Lindsay Park, Kettins	PH13 9JL
Letham	7 Acres, Perth	PH1 2JB
Letham Community	7 Acres, Perth	PH1 2JB
Luncarty ASC	Langlands Park, Luncarty / Crieff HS	PH1 3UT / PH7 3JN
St John's	Perth Grammar School / North Inch	PH1 5AZ / PH1 5BF
Vale of Earn	Market Park, Crieff	PH7 3HE
DIVISION TWO		
Alyth	Diamond Jubilee Park, Alyth	PH11 8GA
Ballinluig	Ballinluig Recreation Park	PH9 0LQ
Breadalbane	Home Street, Aberfeldy	PH15 2AZ
Dunkeld & Birnam	Dunkeld Recreation Ground, Birnam	PH8 0AD
Fair City	Huntingtower Park	
Kinrossie Caledonian afc	Recreation Park, Kinrossie	PH2 6TS
Pitfour	St Madoes Park	PH2 7LZ
Rattray	Davie Park Pitch 2, Blairgowrie	PH10 7BJ
Scone Thistle	Scone Public Park	PH2 6RT
Stanley	KGV Park, Methven / Crieff HS	PH1 3ST / PH7 3JN
Strathearn Grove	Braidhaugh Park, Crieff	PH7 4DH
Vale of Atholl	Recreation Park, Pitlochry	PH16 5DZ
Wolfhill	7 Acres, Perth	PH1 2JB

All Time Perthshire Amateur League Champions

1930 -31	Burrelton Rovers
1931 -32	Blairgowrie Amateurs
1932 -33	Central Amateurs
1933 -34	Keith Athletic
1934 -35	Black Watch AFC
1935 -36	
1936 -37	Black Watch AFC
1937 -38	Alyth Violet
1946 -47	Kinrossie AFC
1947 -48	Balbeggie Rovers
1948 -49	Kinrossie AFC
1949 -50	Kinrossie AFC
1950 -51	Kinrossie AFC
1951 -52	Coupar Angus Amateurs
1952 -53	Kinrossie AFC
1953 -54	Rait Rovers AFC
1954 -55	Burrelton Rovers
1955 -56	Dunkeld Amateurs
1956 -57	Kinrossie AFC
1957 -58	Ballinluig Amateurs
1958 -59	Kinrossie AFC
1959 -60	Breadalbane
1960 -61	Guildtown Amateurs
1961 -62	Guildtown Amateurs
1962 -63	Guildtown Amateurs
1963 -64	Guildtown Amateurs
1964 -65	Guildtown Amateurs
1965 -66	Guildtown Amateurs
1966 -67	Guildtown Amateurs
1967 -68	Guildtown Amateurs
1968 -69	Newtyle Hearts
1969 -70	Errol AFC
1970 -71	Vale of Earn FC
1971 -72	Vale of Atholl FC
1972 -73	Errol AFC
1973 -74	Glencarse AFC
1974 -75	Burrelton Rovers
1975 -76	Burrelton Rovers
1976 -77	Burrelton Rovers
1977 -78	Glenfarg AFC
1978 -79	Newtyle Hearts
1979 -80	Breadalbane
1980 -81	Newtyle Hearts
1981 -82	Auchterarder Primrose
1982 -83	Kettins
1983 -84	Tayside
1984 -85	Fair City
1985 -86	Scone
1986 -87	Fair City
1987 -88	Fair City
1988 -89	Vale of Earn FC
1989 -90	ASC
1990 -91	Stanley
1991 -92	Rattray
1992 -93	Strathmore Albion
1993 -94	Alyth
1994 -95	Letham United
1995 -96	Kettins
1996 -97	Letham United
1997 -98	Letham United
1998 -99	Rattray
1999 2000	Letham
2000 -1	Bridgeton United
2001 -2	Alyth
2002 -3	Murray Royal
2003 -4	Balmoral United
2004 -5	Letham AFC
2005 -6	Breadalbane
2006 -7	Balmoral United
2007 -8	Letham AFC
2008 -9	Letham AFC
2009 -10	Ballinluig
2010 -11	Balmoral United
2011 -12	Balmoral United
2012 -13	Letham AFC
2013 -14	Letham AFC
2014 -15	Letham AFC
2015 -16	Letham AFC
2016 -17	Letham AFC
2017 -18	Letham AFC
2018 -19	Letham AFC

All Time Perthshire Amateur Cup Winners

1930 -31	Burrelton Rovers
1931 -32	Blairgowrie Amateurs
1932 -33	Central Amateurs
1933 -34	Keith Athletic
1934 -35	Black Watch AFC
1935 -36	
1936 -37	Black Watch AFC
1937 -38	Alyth Violet
1946 -47	Kinrossie AFC
1947 -48	Balbeggie Rovers
1948 -49	Kinrossie AFC
1949 -50	Kinrossie AFC
1950 -51	Kinrossie AFC
1951 -52	Coupar Angus Amateurs
1952 -53	Kinrossie AFC
1953 -54	Rait Rovers AFC
1954 -55	Burrelton Rovers
1955 -56	Dunkeld Amateurs
1956 -57	Kinrossie AFC
1957 -58	Ballinluig Amateurs
1958 -59	Kinrossie AFC
1959 -60	Breadalbane
1960 -61	Guildtown Amateurs
1961 -62	Guildtown Amateurs
1962 -63	Guildtown Amateurs
1963 -64	Guildtown Amateurs
1964 -65	Guildtown Amateurs
1965 -66	Guildtown Amateurs
1966 -67	Guildtown Amateurs
1967 -68	Guildtown Amateurs
1968 -69	Newtyle Hearts
1969 -70	Errol AFC
1970 -71	Vale of Earn FC
1971 -72	Vale of Atholl FC
1972 -73	Errol AFC
1973 -74	Glencarse AFC
1974 -75	Burrelton Rovers
1975 -76	Burrelton Rovers
1976 -77	Burrelton Rovers
1977 -78	Glenfarg AFC
1978 -79	Newtyle Hearts
1979 -80	Breadalbane
1980 -81	Newtyle Hearts
1981 -82	Auchterarder Primrose
1982 -83	Kettins
1983 -84	Tayside
1984 -85	Fair City
1985 -86	Scone
1986 -87	Fair City
1987 -88	Fair City
1988 -89	Vale of Earn FC
1989 -90	ASC
1990 -91	Stanley
1991 -92	Rattray
1992 -93	Strathmore Albion
1993 -94	Alyth
1994 -95	Letham United
1995 -96	Kettins
1996 -97	Letham United
1997 -98	Letham United
1998 -99	Rattray
1999 2000	Letham
2000 -1	Bridgeton United
2001 -2	Alyth
2002 -3	Murray Royal
2003 -4	Balmoral United
2004 -5	Letham AFC
2005 -6	Breadalbane
2006 -7	Balmoral United
2007 -8	Letham AFC
2008 -9	Letham AFC
2009 -10	Ballinluig
2010 -11	Balmoral United
2011 -12	Balmoral United
2012 -13	Letham AFC
2013 -14	Alyth
2014 -15	Luncarty Ams
2015 -16	ASC
2016 -17	Letham AFC
2017 -18	St JohnIs
2018 -19	Letham AFC

SCOTTISH AMATEUR FOOTBALL LEAGUE 2020/21

Contact: Mr Raymond McMillan
Email: secretary@safl.co.uk
Telephone: 07950 690324

Season 2020/1 did not start. Once football was permitted from May 2021 a short "Jimmy Marshall Summer Cup" was played.

LEAGUE MEMBERSHIP 2021/2

Premier		
Busby	Overlee PF	G76 8NL
Castlemilk BC	Barlia Sports Complex, Glasgow	G45 9UD
Easthall Star	Stepford Complex, Glasgow	G33 4NU
Glynhill Moorcroft	KGV PF, Renfrew	PA4 0AP
Hillington	Penilee Community Centre, Glasgow	G52 4BD
Inverclyde	Battery Park, Greenock	PA16 7QG
Kings Park Rangers	Glasgow Green SC	G40 1HB
Motherwell Th	Ravenscraig SC	ML1 2TZ
Neilston	Kingston PF	G78 3JN
Parkhall	Singers Park, Clydebank	G81 4YA
Rutherglen	Toryglen Soccer Centre	G42 0BY
Port Glasgow Ams	Parklea PF	PA14 6TR
Division 1 Championship		
Arthurlie U21's		
Baljaffray Ams		
Cardross Ams	Station Park, Cardross	G82 5NS
Carlton YM	Kibble Complex, Paisley	PA3 2LG
Claremont	Ballerup Recreation Centre, E Kilbride	G75 0DY
Duncanrig FP	Ballerup Recreation Centre, E Kilbride	G75 0DY
Dunoon	Dunoon Stadium	PA23 7RL
Glenburn	Univ of West of Scotland, Paisley	PA2 7TR
Lochgilphead Red Star	Ropework Park	PA31 8JU
Port Glasgow OBU	Parklea PF	PA14 6TR
St.Convals	Missedgel 3G, Linwood	PA3 3HR
Strathaven Dynamo	John Hastie Pitches, Strathaven	ML10 6EB
Tarbert	Cil Andreis	PA29 6TF

SCOTTISH POLICE A.F.A. 2020/21

Season 2020/1 did not start.

STIRLING & DISTRICT A.F.A.
2020/21

Contact: Mr Gordon F. R. Japp
Email: gordon.japp@sky.com
Telephone: 01324 613135

Season 2020/1 was not started. In May / June 2021 a short Cup competition was played:

KINGDOM COATINGS TROPHY

Saturday 29th. May
Section 1
Grangemouth 0 Falkirk Athletic LK 3
Westfield Colts scr Alva w/o

Section 2
Cowie United 1 Clackmannan Community 4
Kildrum United 1 Bo'ness United 2

Wednesday 2nd. June
Section 1
Alva w/o Grangemouth scr
Falkirk Athletic LK 2 Linlithgow Rose Community 2
Linlithgow won 5-4 pen.
Section 2
Bo'ness United 11 Cowie United 1
Clackmannan Community 1 Dollar Glen 2
Westfield, Kildrum United no games

Saturday 5th. June
Section 1
Linlithgow Rose Community 1 Alva 2
Grangemouth scr Westfield Colts w/o

Section 2
Dollar Glen P Bo'ness United P
Cowie United P Kildrum United P
Falkirk LK, Clackmannan no games

Wednesday 9th. June
Section 1
Westfield Colts 0 Linlithgow Rose Community 1
Alva 1 Falkirk Athletic LK 1
4-5 Pens.
Section 2
Kildrum United 3 Dollar Glen 2
Bo'ness United 4 Clackmannan Community 2
Grangemouth, Cowie United no games

Saturday 12th. June
Section 1
Falkirk Athletic LK P Westfield Colts P
Linlithgow Rose Community w/o Grangemouth scr

Section 2
Clackmannan Community scr Kildrum United w/o
Dollar Glen 8 Cowie United 3
Alva, Bo'ness United no games

Wednesday 16th. June
Section 1
Falkirk Athletic LK w/o Westfield Colts scr

Section 2
Dollar Glen 2 Bo'ness United 0
Cowie United 2 Kildrum United 3

Wednesday 23rd. June Section 2 **Playoff**

Bo'ness United 3 Dollar Glen 2

Saturday 26th. June Trophy **SEMIFINALS**

Alva 1 Kildrum United 2
Bo'ness United 1 Falkirk Athletic LK 2

FINAL:
Little Kerse Wednesday 30/6/21 7.00pm
KO (GRASS)
KILDRUM UNITED 2 FALKIRK ATHLETIC LK 3 (AET)
ref: G Heeps assistants: K Martin & M Charles

COMPOSITION 2021/2

PREMIER DIVISION		
AFC Chryston	Carrick Park, Glenboig	ML5 2RY
Alva	Alva Academy 3G	FK12 5FE
Barrhill	Twechar SC	G65 9TA
Bo'ness Cadora	Newtown Park, Bo'ness	EH51 9HL
Braehead	Braehead Park, Stirling	FK7 7PX
Clackmannan Community	Alloa Academy 3G	FK10 2EQ
Condorrat	Merkland SC, Kirkintilloch	G66 3SN
Dunipace	Westfield Park, Dunipace / Herbertshire PF	FK6 5DX / FK6 6EE
Falkirk Athletic LK	Little Kerse	
Westfield Colts	Westfield Park, Falkirk	FK2 9DX
DIVISION ONE		
Beechwood Albion	Mayfield Centre, Stirling / Wallace HS 3G	FK7 0DB / FK9 5HW
Campsie	Battlefield Park, Milton of Campsie	G66 8EF
Cowie United	Cowie	
Dollar Glen	Alva Academy 3G	FK12 5FE
Drumpellier Thistle	Greenfaulds HS 3G, Cumbernauld / Ravenswood	G67 4AQ / G67 1LA
Grangemouth	Zetland Park, Grangemouth	FK3 9JX
Kildrum United	Cumbernauld	
Linlithgow Rose CSC	Xcite Linlithgow	
MLS Leeds	St Ambrose HS, Coatbridge	ML5 2HT
Riverside	Haws Park, Bridge of Allan	FK9 4DA

STRATHCLYDE EVANGELICAL CHURCHES A.F.L. 2020/21

Contact: Mr Raymond McMillan
Email: secretary@safl.co.uk
Telephone: 07950 690324

Season 2020/1 was not contested

LEAGUE COMPOSITION 2021/2

PREMIER DIVISION

Anniesland	Garscube Complex	G20 0SP
Auchenfoyle	Parklea PF, Port Glasgow	PA14 6TR
Avendale	Tileworks Park, Stonehouse	ML9 3LF
Coatdyke Congregational	Lochend SC, Easterhouse	G34 0NZ
Craighalbert FC	Strathclyde Uni PF, Stepps	G33 6ND
Cumbernauld Colts	Kilsyth Sportsfield	G65 9XJ
Houston and Killellan	KGV Playing Fields, Renfrew	PA4 0SA
Law Parish	Law Public Park	ML8 5HA
Machan United	Birkenshaw Park, Larkhall	ML9 2TP
Motherwell King's FC	Keir Hardie SC, Holytown	ML1 4TP
Re:Hope	Netherton PF, Glasgow	G13 2RX
South Glasgow FC	Muirend PF	G44 3HQ
United Churches of Ayr	Ayr Academy	KA8 0HN
West Glasgow	Garscube Complex	G20 0SP

DIVISION ONE

Croftfoot Parish	Toryglen Sports Centre	G42 0BY
Dennistoun Thistle	Whitehill 4G	G31 2QF
Fullarton Irvine	Quarry Road, irvine	KA12 0PX
Glasgow Elim	Kingston Park, Neilston	G78 3JQ
Glasgow Free Churches	Ballerup Parks, E Kilbride	G75 0SD
Greenbank Church of Scotland	Muirend PF, Glasgow	G44 3HQ
Homechurch		
Kings Park Baptist FC	Eaglesham Pavilion	G76 0LO
Mearns Churches	Crookfur PF	G77 6DT
Mount Kirk	Parklea PF, Port Glasgow	PA14 6TR
Tollcross AFC	Holyrood 4G / Toryglen	G42 8AU / G42 0BY
Trinity AFC	Netherburn Park	ML9 3BT
West Hamilton	Dalserf Primary School, Ashgill	ML9 3FJ

STRATHCLYDE SATURDAY MORNING A.F.L. 2020/21

Contact: Mr Paul King
Email: ssmaflsec@outlook.com
Telephone: 07881 020715

Season 2020/1 was not contested

LEAGUE COMPOSITION 2021/2

Premier Division		
As Airdrie	Bothwellhaugh, Motherwell	ML1 3RB
Bengal Lancers	Springburn	G21 3AQ
Blackthorn Rovers	Battery Park, Greenock	PA16 7QG
East Dunbartonshire	Petershill Park	G21 4DD
Glasgow South	Glasgow Green / Toryglen	G40 1HB / G42 0BY
Haghill St Rochs	Glasgow Club Haghill	
Kirkintilloch Thistle	Merkland PF	G66 2SN
Lenzie Thistle		
Maryhill Thistle	Yoker Athletic FC	
Shawbridge	Toryglen	G42 0BY
Southside	Giffnock North SC / Nethercraigs	G46 6HU
Tynecastle	Ibrox Football Centre	G51 2XP
UB United	Stepford Centre, Glasgow	G33 4NU
Uddingston	Matt Busby Centre, Bellshill / Jock Stein Centre	ML4 3DP
Westercommon Star	Glasgow Club, Scotstoun	G14 9HY
Championship A		
Balmore		
Dinamo Paisley	Mossedge, Linwood	
East Lane	Linwood, ON-X	
Gleniffer Thistle	Seedhill PF, Paisley / Ralston	PA1 1QU / PA1 3AX
PGU	Parklea PF, Port Glasgow / Darroch Park, Gourock	PA14 6TR / PA19 1YT
Royalle Madrid	Inverclyde Acad / Battery Park, Greenock / Parklea PF	PA16 0FB / PA16 7QG / PA14 6TR
Port Glasgow Celtic		
Stanley Athletic	Johnstone Hub	
Viewfield Rovers		
Championship B		
Dormy Forest	Nethercraigs	
Drumchapel United	Donald Dewar Centre	
Glasgow Wellington	Sir Alex Ferguson Park	
Huntershill	Springburn	
Knightswood		
Semsa	Toryglen	G42 0BY
Southpark	Cowan Park / Huntly Playing Fields	G78 2RN / G46 6LW
St Peters	The Marshes / Ferguslie Park, Paisley / KGV Renfrew	PA2 6SB / PA3 1EX / PA4 0AP
Vale of Clyde	Stepford Centre	
Championship C		
Kirkintilloch Rob Roy	Merkland PF	G66 2SN
Manhattan Blacks	Ravenswood, Cumbernauld	G67 1LA
Moorlands	Hamilton Palace Grounds / Bent Park	ML3 6EF
Netherton	KGV Park, Wishaw	
Overtoun Park	Stonelaw HS	G73 3PH
Plains	Plains Playing Field	
Shotts Bon Accord	Mansey Park / Lochend SC	ML7 5GA / G34 0NZ
Tannochside United	Porterswell PF	G71 7QE
Wishaw Rangers	St Ambrose HYS, Ciatbridge	
Development Section		
Blackhall	Paisley Rugby Club	
Blantyre Soccer Academy		
Carluke Hotspur	Dalziel Parks	
New Stevenston Celtic	Dalziel Parks	
North Glasgow Victory	Glasgow Club Milton	
PGA	Parklea PF / St Columbas HS, Gourock	PA14 6TR / PA19 1TP
Rutherglen Gllencairn		
Stratton Southside	Toryglen	

SUNDAY CENTRAL A.F.L. 2019/20

Season 2020/1 was cancelled

LEAGUE COMPOSITION 2021/2

DIVISION A
Argyle Wanderers
Bullwood
Carron Thistle
EK Albion
Kincardine Colts
Maddiston
Knightswood
Southside Panthers
Lanark
Todholm
Third Lanark
Polonia Glasgow
Newton Farm
Overlee Colts

DIVISION B
AFS Silverburn
Weirs
Bardykes Rovers
Bellgrove
Thorniewood
WEW
Blantyre Albion
Dinner Inn
Muirend
Greenfield
Larbert

DIVISION C
Bonamay
Kirkintilloch Harp
Brunswick
Inter Inchinnan
Budhill United
Holytown Colts
Eastwood Park
Castlemilk United
Checkbar
Duncanrig
Colquhoun United
Drumchapel United

DIVISION D
Broomfield
Carron Valley
Eastend Tower
Cranhill
Southside
Stenhousemuir
Greenbank
Nethercraigs United
EK Athletic
Kilsyth Rovers
Summerston
Cambuslang Colts

WEST LOTHIAN SUNDAY A.F.L. 2020/21

Contact: Mr Steven Lynch
Email: stevielynch77@yahoo.co.uk
Telephone: 07858 948490

Season cancelled for 2020/1

At the time of going to press no details had been issued regarding the 2021/2 season.

SCOTTISH AMATEUR CUP WINNERS

1909/10	John Neilson FP	(Paisley)	1970/71	Dumbarton Academy FP	
1910/11	Edinburgh Civil Service		1971/72	Douglas	
1911/12	Queen's Park Hampden XI		1972/73	Knockentiber	
1912/13	Leith Amateurs		1973/74	Douglas	
1913/14	Cameronians	(Stirling)	1974/75	Star Hearts	
1919/20	Queen's Park Hampden XI		1975/76	Colville Park	(Motherwell)
1920/21	Edinburgh Civil Service		1976/77	Morriston YMCA	(Cambuslang)
1921/22	Greenock HSFP		1977/78	Cambusbarron Rovers	
1922/23	Falkirk Amateurs		1978/79	Crosshouse Waverley	
1923/24	Moorpark	(Renfrew)	1979/80	Newarthill Hearts	
1924/25	Coldstream		1980/81	Knockentiber	
1925/26	Murrayfield Amateurs	(Edinburgh)	1981/82	Avon Villa	(Hamilton)
1926/27	Glasgow University		1982/83	Strathclyde Police	
1927/28	Queen's Park Hampden XI		1983/84	Pencaitland	
1928/29	Murrayfield Amateurs	(Edinburgh)	1984/85	Drongan United	
1929/30	Murrayfield Amateurs	(Edinburgh)	1985/86	Coatbridge CC	
1930/31	Murrayfield Amateurs	(Edinburgh)	1986/87	Bannockburn	
1931/32	Glasgow Corporation Transport		1987/88	Coatbridge CC	
1932/33	Queen's Park Hampden XI		1988/89	Norton House	(Leven)
1933/34	Queen's Park Hampden XI		1989/90	St Patricks FP	(Dumbarton)
1934/35	Camphill Secondary FP	(Paisley)	1990/91	Bannockburn	
1935/36	Queen's Park Hampden XI		1991/92	Heathside	
1936/37	Gogarburn	(Edinburgh)	1992/93	Bankhall Villa	
1937/38	Coats	(Paisley)	1993/94	Bannockburn	
1938/39	Murrayfield Amateurs	(Edinburgh)	1994/95	Heathside	
1945/46	Craigton Athletic	(Glasgow)	1995/96	Bellshill YMCA	
1946/47	Queen's Park Hampden XI		1996/97	Knockentiber	
1947/48	Mearns		1997/98	Dalziel HSFP	(Motherwell)
1948/49	Greenock HSFP		1998/99	St Patricks FP	(Dumbarton)
1949/50	Queen's Park Hampden XI		1999/00	Liberton Royal Mail	(Edinburgh)
1950/51	Queen's Park Hampden XI		2000/1	Dalziel HSFP	(Motherwell)
1951/52	Port Glasgow Hibernian		2001/2	Harestanes	(Kirkintilloch)
1952/53	Mearns		2002/3	Harestanes	(Kirkintilloch)
1953/54	Royal Technical College	(Glasgow)	2003/4	Viewfield Rovers	(Lochwinnoch)
1954/55	Eglinton Ams	(Glasgow)	2004/5	Drumchapel	
1955/56	Milanda	(Glasgow)	2005/6	St Patricks FP	(Dumbarton)
1956/57	Giffnock North		2006/7	Drumchapel United	
1957/58	Weir Recreation	(Glasgow)	2007/8	Eddlewood	(Hamilton)
1958/59	Crosshill Athletic	(Glasgow)	2008/9	Queen's Park Hampden XI	
1959/60	Minishant		2009/10	Eddlewood	(Hamilton)
1960/61	Glenavon		2010/11	Wishaw HSFP	
1961/62	Bearsden Ams		2011/12	Hurlford Thistle	
1962/63	Queen's Park Hampden XI		2012/13	Wellhouse	(Glasgow)
1963/64	Queen's Park Hampden XI		2013/14	Hurlford Thistle	
1964/65	NCR	(Dundee)	2014/15	Harestanes	(Kirkintilloch)
1965/66	Jordanhill TC	(Glasgow)	2015/16	Colville Park	(Motherwell)
1966/67	Rhu		2016/17	Colville Park	(Motherwell)
1967/68	Cambusbarron Rovers		2017/18	Shortlees	(Kilmarnock)
1968/69	Cambusbarron Rovers		2018/19	Colville Park E	(Motherwell)
1969/70	Douglas				

SCOTTISH AMATEUR FA - PREVIOUS CUP WINNERS

	West	East	North of Tay	Fife
1923/24	Moorpark Ams			
1924/25	Greenock HSFP			
1925/26	Moorpark Ams			
1926/27	Whitehall Athletic			
1927/28	Castings Ams			
1928/29	Greenock HSFP		YMCA Anchorage	
1929/30	Greenock HSFP		Hillcrest	
1930/31	Pointhouse		Aeros (Leuchars)	
1931/32	Glasgow University		Woodside Rangers	Burntisland Shipyard
1932/33	Queen's Park		Pittenweem Rangers	Bishopshire Swifts
1933/34	Mavor's XI		YMCA Anchorage	Glencraig Victoria
1934/35	Camphill Sec School FP		Pittenweem Rovers	St Andrews University
1935/36	Glasgow Corporation Transport		St Monance Swifts	Crail
1936/37	Greenock HSFP		Pittenweem Rovers	Pittenweem Rovers
1937/38	Coats Ams		RAF Leuchars	Freuchie Rovers
1938/39	Cartha Athletic		Harris Academy FP	Pittenweem Rovers
1945/46	Queen's Park		Lochee Ams	Burntisland Shipyard
1946/47	Queen's Park		YMCA Anchorage	Gallatown
1947/48	Rothesay Brandane	Edinburgh University	Ashdale	Milton Violet
1948/49	Laidlaw Ams	Civil Service Strollers	YMCA Anchorage	Victoria Swifts
1949/50	Queen's Park	Torphichen Ams	YMCA Anchorage	Boreland
1950/51	Govan Ams	Eastern Ams	YMCA Anchorage	Ladybank Violet
1951/52	Gartsherrie United	Dalkeith Ams	YMCA Anchorage	Ladybank Violet
1952/53	Babcock & Wilcox	Cobbinshaw Rovers	Kinrossie	Boreland
1953/54	Albion Motors	Cobbinshaw Rovers	Windsor	Thornton Loco
1954/55	Albion Motors	Cobbinshaw Rovers	Invergowrie	Thornton Loco
1955/56	Queen's Park	Lorwood AFC	YMCA Anchorage	Boreland
1956/57	Shell Amateurs	Pathead AFC	Windsor	Thornton Loco
1957/58	Muirend Ams	Orphan Hospital AFC	YMCA Anchorage	St Andrews University
1958/59	Kilmacolm AFC	Lorwood AFC	YMCA Anchorage	Cupar YM
1959/60	Crosshill Thistle	Pathead AFC	Ballinluig	Westwood Wanderers
1960/61	Queen's Park	Grangemouth Refinery	NCR	Nairn Star
1961/62	Glenavon	Winchburgh Albion	NCR	Westwood Wanderers
1962/63	Lincluden Swifts	West Lothian Steel Foundry	Ballinluig	Nairn Star
1963/64	Fenwick Thistle	Lorwood AFC	NCR	St Monance Swallows
1964/65	Lincluden Swifts	Edinburgh Albion	NCR	St Monance Swallows
1965/66	Minishant	Blackrodge Welfare	Withheld	Cambusbarron Rovers
1966/67	Vale of Girvan	Lorwood AFC	NCR	Cambusbarron Rovers
1967/68	Vale of Girvan	Lorwood AFC	Westgrove Albion	Star Hearts
1968/69	Bishopton AFC	Lorwood AFC	NCR	Star Hearts
1969/70	Fenwick Thistle	Bilston AFC	Broughty United	Star Hearts
1970/71	Douglas Ams	Cambusbarron Rovers	Newtyle Hearts	Star Hearts
1971/72	Morriston YMCA	Pathead AFC	Errol	St Monance Swallows
1972/73	Clyde United	Links United	Hillside BC	Methil United
1973/74	Knockentiber	Whitson Star	Auchterhouse	Star Hearts
1974/75	Morriston YMCA	Whitson Star	Auchterhouse	Star Hearts
1975/76	Nithsdale	Bilston MW	Auchterhouse	Star Hearts

	West	East	North of Tay	Fife
1976/77	Weir Recreation	Pencaitland	Auchterhouse	Hill of Beath Hawthorn
1977/78	Morriston YMCA	Pencaitland	Auchterhouse	Windygates
1978/79	Newarthill Hearts	Pencaitland	Riverside Athletic	Star Hearts
1979/80	Muirend Ams	Windsor AFC	Harris Academy FP	Windygates
1980/81	Cambusbarron Rovers	Telman Star	SMT	Norton House
1981/82	Westerlands	Bilston Colliery	Harris Academy FP	Strathmiglo United
1982/83	Bannockburn Ams	Milton Ams	Fintry	Star Hearts
1983/84	Initial Star	Cropley AFC	Harris Academy FP	Norton House
1984/85	Hyster	Bilston Cropley	Harris Academy FP	Ballingry Rovers
1985/86	Muirend Ams	Bilston Cropley	Riverside Athletic	Strathmiglo United
1986/87	Drumchapel AFC	Lothian Thistle	Lawside FP	Norton House
1987/88	Coatbridge CC	Liberton Cropley	Lawside FP	Hill of Beath Ramblers
1988/89	Knightswood AFC	Telman Star	Riverside Athletic	Norton House
1989/90	Clark Drive	Liberton Cropley	Riverside Athletic	Burntisland Shipyard
1990/91	Bellshill YMCA	Fallin MW	Riverside Athletic	Star Hearts
1991/92	Clark Drive	Bentswood Inn	Kingsway Athletic	Burntisland Shipyard
1992/93	Milngavie Wanderers	Craigmillar AFC	Lawside FP	Norton House
1993/94	Heathside	Cambusbarron Rovers	Alyth	Benarty
1994/95	Dalziel HSFP	Fallin MW	SS Peter and Paul	Benarty
1995/96	Dalziel HSFP	Cambusbarron Rovers	Riverside Athletic	Kettle United
1996/97	Knockentiber	AVU	Riverside Athletic	Burntisland Shipyard
1997/98	Newmilns Vesuvius	Fallin MW	Fair City Athletic	Lomond Victoria
1998/99	West Kilbride	Royburn AFC	Riverside Athletic	Leven United
1999/00	Dalziel HSFP	Manfort AFC	Fair City Athletic	Norton House
2000/1	Bannockburn Ams	Spartans	Riverside Athletic	Norton House
2001/2	Bannockburn Ams	Aberforth Rangers	Fair City Athletic	Norton House
2002/3	Drumchapel AFC	Aberforth Rangers	Fair City Athletic	Norton House
2003/4	Wellhouse AFC	Tullibody	Tayside Fire Brigade	Valleyfield
2004/5	Drumchapel United	Falkirk Amateurs	Riverside Athletic	Kettle United
2005/6	Drumchapel United	Stenhouse Athletic	Riverside Athletic	Kirkland
2006/7	St Patricks FPs	Doune Castle	NCR	Cupar Hearts
2007/8	Drumchapel United	Links United	Carnoustie YMCA	Cupar Hearts
2008/9	Bannockburn Ams	Cambusbarron Rovers	Vale of Earn	Strathmiglo United
2009/10	Harestanes	Bluebell	Breadalbane	Cupar Hearts
2010/11	Drumchapel United	Falkirk Amateurs	Riverside Athletic	Cupar Hearts
2011/12	Dumbarton Academy FP	Doune Castle	Burrelton Rovers	Kennoway
2012/13	Colville Park	Edinburgh Rose	Arbroath CSC	Leven United
2013/14	Hurlford Thistle	Steins Thistle	St James	Bowhill Rovers
2014/15	Greenock HSFP	Steins Thistle	St James	Pittenweem Rovers
2015/16	Shortlees	Craigshill Thistle	Menzieshill	Pittenweem Rovers
2016/17	Cambria	Salvesen	Letham	Leven United
2017/18	Colville Park	St Bernards	Menzieshill	Strathmiglo United
2018/19	Bannockburn Ams	Pennies	Kinross	Cupar Hearts

	North of S	South	Highland	Sunday Trophy
1949/50	Dyce			
1950/51	Aberdeen University			
1951/52	Invercairn United	Eyemouth Swifts		
1952/53	Millburn	Peebles YMCA		
1953/54	Cove Rangers	Gala Rovers		
1954/55	Invercairn United	Greenlaw		
1955/56	Fraserburgh Toolworks	Greenlaw		
1956/57	Fraserburgh Toolworks	Gordon Westruther		
1957/58	Fraserburgh Toolworks	Broughton United		
1958/59	Aberdeen University	Selkirk Thistle		
1959/60	Formartine United	Gordon Westruther		
1960/61	Bon Accord	Tweeddale Rovers		
1961/62	Old Meldrum	Morebattle		
1962/63	Bon Accord	Gala Rovers		
1963/64	Aberdeen Dockers	Gala Rovers		
1964/65	Ellon United	Gala Ams		
1965/66	Bon Accord	Tweeddale Rovers		
1966/67	Cove Rangers	Tweeddale Rovers		
1967/68	Aberdeen University	Tweeddale Rovers		
1968/69	Kemnay	Symington		
1969/70	Maud	Lauder		
1970/71	Culter	Symington		
1971/72	Kemnay	Hawick United		
1972/73	Culter	Kelso United		
1973/74	Kemnay	Tweeddale Rovers		
1974/75	Culter	Tweeddale Rovers		
1975/76	Culter	Tweeddale Rovers		
1976/77	Banchory	Dunbar Blue Circle		
1977/78	Newtonhall	Dunbar Blue Circle	Blackmuir	
1978/79	Kemnay	Lanark Thistle	South Ronaldsay	Liberton Cropley
1979/80	Chatton Rovers	Lanark Thistle	Thurso Pentland	GJs
1980/81	Mugiemoss	Shotts MD	Thurso Pentland	Elphinston / Hillburn
1981/82	Shamrock	Monteith	Halkirk	Cambridge United
1982/83	Cove Rangers	Monteith	Thurso Pentland	Duncraig
1983/84	Longside	Tweeddale Rovers	Ness	Cambridge United
1984/85	Shamrock	Douglas Thistle	Halkirk	CISWO
1985/86	Chatton Rovers	Monteith	Maryburgh	Cambridge United
1986/87	Culter	Hawick Legion	Pentland United	Househill
1987/88	Kemnay Youth	Maxwelltown HSFP	Kirkwall Thorfinn	Dolphin
1988/89	Kincorth	Chirnside	Dingwall Thistle	Linden 30 Club
1989/90	Glentanar	Rigside	Marybugh	Cambridge United
1990/91	Great Western United	Monteith	Ness	St Lawrence
1991/92	Kincorth	Duns Legion	Ness	FJR
1992/93	Wilsons XI	Shotts YM	Pentland United	Jolly Farmer
1993/94	Hilton	Monteith	Point	Gauntlet
1994/95	Echt	Shotts YM	Ness	Tower
1995/96	Echt	Kirk United	Dingwall Thistle	Finnart
1996/97	Hilton	Duns Legion	Kirkwall Rovers	Finnart
1997/98	Hilton	Duns Legion	Pentland United	Cathkin

	North of S	South	Highland	Sunday Trophy
1998/99	Hilton	Upper Annandale	Contin	Railway Hotel
1999/00	Wilsons XI	Coldstream	Pentland United	Finnart
2000/1	Echt	Symington Tinto	Wick Thistle	Centaur
2001/2	Great Western United	Kirkconnel	Pentland United	The Braes
2002/3	Mintlaw	Symington Tinto	Lochs	Cavendish
2003/4	Aberdeen SC	Monteith	Back	Harvester
2004/5	Mintlaw	Chirnside	Lochs	Cavendish
2005/6	Dyce	Hawick W	Avoch	Rowantree
2006/7	Echt	Leithen Rovers	Avoch	Finnart
2007/8	Cove Thistle	Gala Rovers	Pentland United	Finnart
2008/9	Hazlehead United	Chirnside	Kirkwall THorfinn	Gantry
2009/10	Sportsmans Club	Newtongrange Star A	Pentland United	Finnart
2010/11	Kincorth	Leithen Rovers	Avoch	Tower
2011/12	Cove Thistle	Leithen Rovers	Avoch	Finnart
2012/13	Cove Thistle	Pencaitland	Wick Groats	Rutherglen Vogue
2013/14	Cove Thistle	Leithen Rovers	Wick Groats	Harvester
2014/15	Cove Thistle	Shotts Victoria	Avoch	Cranhill United
2015/16	Cove Thistle	Danderhall MW	Wick Groats	Dundee Argyle
2016/17	Newburgh Thistle	Danderhall MW	Wick Groats	Harvester
2017/18	Sportsmans Club	Hawick Waverley	Avoch	Drumchapel United
2018/19	Rothie Rovers	Carluke Hearts	Pentland United	Castlemilk Dynamo

WELFARE FOOTBALL

WINTER SEASON 2020/21

GREENOCK WELFARE F.A. 2020/21

The 2020/1 season was cancelled.

The Association ran a **Summer Cup** competition in June / July 2021.

The clubs were drawn in sections:

Section A
Digit-Al
Mount Kirk
St Francis
Vic Suite

Section B
Braezil
Gourock
Maukenhill United
Willareal

Section C
Blackthorn Rovers
Broomhill
Greenock Athletic
InterClyde

Section D
Bellaire
OC United
Port Glasgow
Renfrewshire Rovers

Matches were played at Battery Park, Notre Dame HS and Darroch Park.

Also played were two other Cup competitions:

RidgeDoc Cup
Group A
Willareal 7pts
Athletic FC 6pts
OC United 4
Mount Kirk 0

Group B
Bellaire 6
Maukinhill United 4
Gourock FC 4
Blackthorn United 0

Semi Finals
Willareal v Bellaire
Maukinhill U v Greenock Ath

Final
Bellaire v Maukinhill U

And the **McShane Builders Cup**

Group A
Vic Suite 10pts
Digit-Al 6
Port Glasgow 3
Broomhill 0

Group B
AFC Clyde 6pts
InterClyde 0
Renfrewshire 0

Semi Finals
Vic Suite v InterClyde
AFC Clyde v Digit-Al

Final
AFC Clyde v InterClyde

MONTROSE AND DISTRICT WELFARE F.A. 2020/21

Season 2020/21 was suspended after just one league game had been played.

FC 1320 v St Tams's, 8-1

Other clubs due to take part were:

Fisgies
Hillside
Johnshaven Athletic
Lochside
Luthermuir
Results Gym
Stables
The Legion.

A League Cup was held in May / June 2021.

The score in the Final was:

FC1320 v Hillside, 3-1

SUMMER SEASON 2020

FORRES AND NAIRN WELFARE F.A. 2020

Season not contested

FORTH AND ENDRICK WELFARE F.A. 2020

Season not contested

MORAY WELFARE F.A. 2020

Season not contested

NORTH EAST SCOTLAND WELFARE F.A. 2020

Season not contested

STRATHSPEY AND BADENOCH WELFARE F.A. 2020

Season not contested

MID DEESIDE SUMMER WELFARE F.A. 2020

Season not contested

DONALD McNAIR Scottish Cup 2020/21

not contested

Tom Hunter Highland Welfare Cup 2020

not contested

SCOTTISH WELFARE F.A. ALL TIME NATIONAL CUP WINNERS

Season	Templeton Cup / Donald McNair Cup	Daily Record Cup / Jack Bryson Cup
1919/20	Beardmore Mossend	
1920/21	Coats Juniors	
1921/22	Coats Juniors	
1922/23	Coats Juniors	
1923/24	Cleansing	
1924/25	Coats Juniors	
1925/26	Clark Anchor	
1926/27	Coats Juniors	
1927/28	Phoenix	
1928/29	Seafield	
1929/30	Westfield	Renton Thistle
1930/31	Hydepark Loco Works	St Martins Guild
1931/32	Anniesland	Camelot Welfare
1932/33	Napier House	Withheld
1933/34	Napier House	Shawfield Chemicals
1934/35	St Pauls	Shawfield Chemicals
1935/36	Templeton Albert	Smith & McLean
1936/37	Templeton Albert	Carwadric
1937/38	Kelvindale	Kerse
1938/39	Clyde Alloy	Scotia
1939/40		Vulcan
1940/41		Queen's Society
1941/42		Forth and Clyde
1942/43		Ardnance
1943/44		Scottish Cables
1944/45		Phoenix
1945/46	Harland & Wolff Ordnance	RNAS
1946/47	Milton Welfare	Carron Primrose
1947/48	ICI Welfare	Cadder Welfare
1948/49	Loco	Seafield Athletic
1949/50	Singers	Germiston Works
1950/51	Dalmarnock Power	Dalmarnock Power
1951/52	Singers Athletic	Templeton Albert
1952/53	Templeton Albert	Provan Gas / Ferranti Thistle
1953/54	Dalmarnock Power	Singer Athletic
1954/55	Rolls Royce (Hillington)	Rolls Royce (Hillington)
1955/56	Metro Vics	Howdens Athletic
1956/57	Singers	British Legion Polmont
1957/58	Rolls Royce (Hillington)	St Bernards
1958/59	Clyde Trust	St Bernards
1959/60	Dalmarnock Power	Clyde Trust
1960/61	J and T Boyds	Shanks Welfare
1961/62	Dalmarnock Power	Quay United
1962/63	Burroughs (Cumbernauld)	Grangemouth Dockers
1963/64	Grangemouth Dockers	Shanks Welfare
1964/65	Grangemouth Dockers	Quay United
1965/66	Clyde Port Authority	Grangemouth Dockers
1966/67	British Hydro Chemicals	Shanks Welfare
1967/68	Rolls Royce (Hillington)	Brown Land Boilers
1968/69	British Aluminium	Shanks Welfare
1969/70	British Aluminium	Hoods
1970/71	Waverly Thistle	British Aluminium
1971/72	Winchburgh	Waverly Thistle
1972/73	Waverly Thistle	Dukes Head
1973/74	Plean Welfare	Waverly Thistle
1974/75	Tennents Caledonia	Tennents Caledonina
1975/76	200 FC	Tennents
1976/77	Singers	Clyde Blowers
1977/78	Singers	Singers
1978/79	Grangemouth Dockers	Singers
1979/80	Tennents	GSL
1980/81	East Stirlingshire Social Club	200 FC
1981/82	John Brown Engineering	Tennents
1982/83	200 FC	Malvern Star
1983/84	Malvern Star	Possil
1984/85	Withheld	Westquarter Violet
1985/86	Springfield	Commercial
1986/87	Glen Star	Westquarter Violet
1987/88	Westquarter Violet	Withheld
1988/89	Gordon Athletic	Tennents
1989/90	Robert Rae FC	Westquarter Violet
1990/91	Concord Metals	John Brown Engineering
1991/92	Withheld	Robert Rae
1992/93	Aldbury	Kelty Villa
1993/94	Aldbury	Aldbury
1994/95	John Brown Engineering	Jamestown
1995/96	Templeton Albert	Valley Bar
1996/97	Summerhill	Summerhill
1997/98	St Peters	Summerhill
1998/99	Rosyth Ex Service Club	St Ninians
1999/00	Peppes	Valley Bar
2000/1	St Peters	Tullibody WMC
2001/2	Calton Athletic	Kelty Villa
2002/3	Clydeshore	Peppes
2003/4	Invercairn United	Jokers
2004/5	Lauders FC	Oakwood
2005/6	Valley Bar	Braehead
2006/7	Blairhall	St Ninians Borestone
2007/8	Linlithgow Rose B	Star Inn
2008/9	Oakwood	Valley Bar
2009/10	Peppes	Oakwood
2010/11	Oakwood	Blairhall
2011/12	Castleview	Treetops
2012/13	Horseshoe	MISC
2013/14	Bank	Maukenhill United
2014/15	Clinton Thistle	Dollar Glen
2015/16	Invercairn United	
2016/17	Invercairn United	
2017/18	Montrose Golfy Thistle	
2018/9	Montrose Golfy Thistle	

UNOFFICIAL FOOTBALL

ISLE OF ARRAN LEAGUE 2020

Season not contested

ISLAY LEAGUE 2020

Season not contested

YOUTH FOOTBALL

This grade of football might best be termed as "Age Group Football". The Scottish Youth FA organises national cups for teams at age groups up to Under 21. The SYFA is a comparatively recent creation, having bene formed in 1999 to rationalise the various age group football associations that existed.

The Scottish Juvenile FA dated back to Victorian times. In 1921 it split into two organisations - the Scottish Juvenile FA (First Class Juveniles) and the Scottish Secondary Juvenile FA. The difference was age groups - First Class Juveniles went up to "Under 27" and Secondary Juveniles to "Under 21".

Other age group football existed, organised by the Scottish Amateur FA, the Boys Brigade, the Churches FA and the Boys Guilds, amongst others.

By the 1980s much had changed. The First Class Juveniles were confined mainly to the Dundee area. The Scottish Juvenile FA began to run Under 21 and other age group competitions as well as Under 27s. The Secondary Juveniles became the Association of Scottish Youth Football Clubs and were dominant in the Edinburgh area, the Forth Valley and Ayrshire.

There was much confusion about different rules, eligibility and so on. It made eminent sense to bring all age group under one umbrella and this was achieved in 1999 through the creation of the Scottish Juvenile FA.

The Scottish Juvenile Cup (Under 27s) was a very prestigious tournament in its heyday and winners are shown below. Several teams progressed to the Junior grade after success in the Juveniles:

The various Scottish Cup competitions were not contested during 2020/1 due to COVID restrictions. Some local leagues played small competitions at different times in the year, depending on restrictions in force in the area at the time.

SCOTTISH JUVENILE UNDER 27 CUP

1899-00 Granton Oak Vale
1900-01 Dumbarton Corinthians
1901-02 Airdriehill Shamrock
1902-03 Vale of Garnock Strollers
1903-04 Orbiston Star
1904-05 Burnbank Oakvale
1905-06 Dunipace Juveniles
1906-07 Benvue
1907-08 Anderston Benburb
1908-09 Motherwell Hearts
1909-10 Fern Thistle
1910-11 Fern Thistle
1911-12 Govan Hibernian
1912-13 Clydebank Corinthians
1913-14 Old Kilpatrick
1914-15 Old Kilpatrick
1915-16 Parkhead White Rose
1916-17 Blantyre Caledonian
1917-18 Mosshill United
1918-19 Cadzow St Anne's
1919-20 Parkhead White Rose
1920-21 Vale of Bannock
1921-22 Bridgeton Waverley
1922-23 Bridgeton Waverley
1923-24 Bridgeton Waverley
1924-25 Regent Star
1925-26 Springburn United
1926-27 Greenhead Thistle
1927-28 Niddrie Thistle
1928-29 Cowie
1929-30 Blairhall
1930-31 Blairhall
1931-32 St Mungo
1932-33 Shieldhill Thistle
1933-34 Park United
1934-35 Holytown United
1935-36 Holytown United
1936-37 Cleland St Mary's
1937-38 Partick Dolphins
1938-39 St Mungo
1939-40 Park United
1940-41 Mossend Boys Guild
1941-42 Mossend Boys Guild
1942-43 Lumphinnans Wanderers
1943-44 Thorniewood United
1944-45 Dundonald Bluebell
1945-46 Dundonald Bluebell
1946-47 Kilbowie Union
1947-48 Banknock United
1948-49 St Mungo
1949-50 Coylton
1950-51 Kirkmuirhill
1951-52 Sauchie
1952-53 Cowie
1953-54 Cowie
1954-55 Germiston Star
1955-56 Burnbank Swifts
1956-57 Sauchie
1957-58 Sauchie
1958-59 Burnbank Swifts
1959-60 Sauchie
1960-61 Burnbank Swifts
1961-62 Lochend Hearts
1962-63 Tradeston Holmlea
1963-64 Rosebery
1964-65 Lochee Renton
1965-66 Glencairn
1966-67 Lochee Renton
1967-68 Maryfield United
1968-69 Provanside Hibernian
1969-70 Burnbank Swifts
1970-71 Germiston Star
1971-72 Inverurie Locos 'A'
1972-73 Germiston Star
1973-74 Coatbridge
1974-75 Mount Ellen
1975-76 Newburgh
1976-77 Fairfield
1977-78 ALC Spurs
1978-79 Fairfield
1979-80 Woodacon
1980-81 Newburgh
1981-82 Stanley
1982-83 Scone Thistle
1983-84 Dee Club
1984-85 Blue Star BC
1985-86 Royals
1986-87 Royals
1987-88 Dundee United SC
1988-89 Dundee United SC
1989-90 Royals
1990-91 Fintry

SCHOOLS FOOTBALL

The Scottish Schools FA runs National Cup competitions for Boys and Girls in age groups from Under 13 through to Under 18. The early rounds are regionalised. Entrants range from the Nicolson Institute from the Western Isles, to schools in the Borders and Dumfries & Galloway. Some private schools enter, as well as local authority schools. Readers from outwith Scotland should note that the terminology of a school name (e.g. HS or Academy) gives no indication of its status.

HS = HS, GS = Grammar School, Acad = Academy, Sec = Secondary

Scottish Schools Cup Competitions 2019/20

Some of the 2019/20 Cup competitions were concluded at the end of 2020/1.

Details to add to those in last year's Almanac:

Senior Shield				
SF	Woodmill HS	St Ninians HS Gifnock	3-3	6-7p
SF	Bearsden Academy	St John's HS	wo	scr
F	Bearsden Academy	St Ninians HS Gifnock	0-1	
Under 16 Boys				
Grange Academy and Broughton HS declared joint winners				
Under 15 Boys				
SF	St Maurice's HS	St John's HS	1-1	5-4p
SF	Preston Lodge HS	Notre Dame HS	3-1	
F	St Maurice's HS	Preston Lodge HS	1-1	3-4p
Under 14 Boys				
Not completed				
Under 13 Boys				
Not completed				
Girls Senior Shield				
SF	Braidhurst HS	St Ninians HS Giffnock	0-2	
SF	St John's HS	George Watson / George Heriots	0-4	
F	St Ninians HS	George Watson / George Heriots	1-1	3-4p
Girls U15				
SF	Kilmarnock Acad	Lasswade HS	1-2	
SF	Perths HS	St Johns HS	7-6	
F	Lasswade HS	Perth HS	2-3	

Scottish Schools Under 18 Shield Previous Winners

1904 Paisley Grammar
1905 Morrison's Academy, Crieff
1906 Hutcheson's Grammar, Glasgow
1907 Hutcheson's Grammar, Glasgow
1908 Hutcheson's Grammar, Glasgow
1909 Allan Glen's School, Glasgow
1910 Hamilton Academy
1911 Falkirk High School
1912 Whitehill Secondary School, Glasgow
1913 John Street Secondary School, Glasgow
1914 Clydebank High School
1915 St.Mungo's Academy, Glasgow
1916 St.Mungo's Academy, Glasgow
1917 Dumbarton Academy
1918 Queen's Park Secondary School, Glasgow
1919 Hamilton Academy
1920 Hamilton Academy
1921 St.Mungo's Academy, Glasgow
1922 Allan Glen's School, Glasgow
1923 St.Mungo's Academy, Glasgow
1924 Irvine Royal Academy
1925 Hamilton Academy
1926 Hamilton Academy
1927 St.Aloysius' College, Glasgow
1928 St.Mungo's Academy, Glasgow
1929 Falkirk High School
1930 Hamilton Academy
1931 Greenock High School
1932 Clydebank High School
1933 Whitehill Secondary School, Glasgow
1934 Queen's Park Secondary School, Glasgow
1935 Govan Secondary School, Glasgow
1936 Dalziel High School, Motherwell
1937 St.Mungo's Academy, Glasgow
1938 Our Lady's High School, Motherwell
1939 Dalziel High School, Motherwell
1940 Dalziel High School, Motherwell
1941 St.Mungo's Academy, Glasgow
1942 Our Lady's High School, Motherwell
1943 Our Lady's High School, Motherwell
1944 Dumbarton Academy
1945 Falkirk High School
1946 Falkirk High School
1947 Queen's Park Secondary School, Glasgow
1948 St.Mungo's Academy, Glasgow
1949 Our Lady's High School, Motherwell
1950 Our Lady's High School, Motherwell
1951 Wishaw High School
1952 Hamilton Academy
1953 Irvine Royal Academy
1954 St.Gerard's Secondary School, Glasgow
1955 Bellahouston Academy, Glasgow
1956 Dumfries Academy
1957 Not Awarded
1958 Bellahouston Academy, Glasgow
1959 Lanark Grammar School
1960 Our Lady's High School, Motherwell
1961 St.Mungo's Academy, Glasgow
1962 Holyrood Secondary School, Glasgow
1963 Hamilton Academy
1964 Dalziel High School, Motherwell
1965 St.Patrick's High School, Coatbridge
1966 Liberton Secondary School, Edinburgh
1967 Airdrie Academy
1968 Liberton Secondary School, Edinburgh
1969 Cumnock Academy
1970 Dalziel High School, Motherwell
1971 Our Lady's High School, Motherwell
1972 Dalziel High School, Motherwell
1973 Holy Cross High School, Hamilton
1974 St.Patrick's High School, Coatbridge
1975 Holy Cross High School, Hamilton
1976 Harris Academy, Dundee
1977 Holy Cross High School, Hamilton
1978 Ardrossan Academy
1979 St.Roch's Secondary School, Glasgow
1980 Coatbridge High School
1981 Dumfries Academy / Kirkcaldy High - jointwinners
1982 Holyrood Secondary School, Glasgow
1983 St.Columba's High School, Gourock
1984 Dumfries Academy
1985 St.Bride's High School, East Kilbride
1986 Braidhurst High School, Motherwell
1987 Holyrood Secondary School, Glasgow
1988 Holyrood Secondary School, Glasgow
1989 Kyle Academy, Ayr
1990 St.Mungo's Academy, Glasgow
1991 Columba High School, Coatbridge
1992 Cardinal Newman High School, Bellshill
1993 Brannock High School, Newarthill
1994 Dingwall Academy
1995 Aberdeen Grammar School
1996 Lornshill Academy, Alloa
1997 Renfrew High School
1998 Larbert High School
1999 Uddingston Grammar School
2000 Our Lady's High School, Motherwell
2001 Perth High School
2002 St.Augustine's High School, Edinburgh
2003 Craigmount High School, Edinburgh
2004 Johnstone High School
2005 Inverkeithing High School
2006 Knightswood Secondary School, Glasgow
2007 Knightswood Secondary School, Glasgow
2008 Our Lady's High School, Cumbernauld
2009 Bishopbriggs Academy
2010 Largs Academy
2011 Larbert High School
2012 St.Mungo's High School, Falkirk
2013 Bishopbriggs Academy
2014 St.Ambrose High School, Coatbridge
2015 Penicuik High School
2016 St John's RC HS, Dundee
2017 Braidhurst HS, Motherwell
2018 Cathkin HS, Glasgow
2019 St John's RC HS, Dundee

Scottish Schools Under 16 Shield Previous Winners

1922 Queen's Park Secondary School, Glasgow
1923 Queen's Park Secondary School, Glasgow
1924 Whitehill Secondary School, Glasgow
1925 Uddingston Secondary School
1926 Wishaw High School
1927 Clydebank High School
1928 Queen's Park Secondary School, Glasgow
1929 Dumbarton Academy
1930 Greenock High School
1931 Queen's Park Secondary School, Glasgow
1932 Wishaw High School
1933 John Street Secondary School, Glasgow
1934 St.Aloysius' College, Glasgow
1935 Clydebank High School
1936 Queen's Park Secondary School, Glasgow
1937 Queen's Park Secondary School, Glasgow
1938 Dalziel High School, Motherwell
1939 St.Mungo's Academy, Glasgow
1940 Falkirk Technical
1941 Falkirk High School
1942 Wishaw High School
1943 St.Mungo's Academy, Glasgow
1944 Falkirk High School
1945 Coatbridge Technical
1946 Shawlands Secondary School, Glasgow
1947 St.John's Grammar School, Hamilton
1948 Our Lady's High School, Motherwell
1949 Carrickvale Secondary School, Edinburgh
1950 Larkhall Academy
1951 St.Anthony's Secondary School, Edinburgh
1952 St.Gerard's Secondary School, Glasgow
1953 Our Lady's High School, Motherwell
1954 Larbert High School
1955 St.Gerard's Secondary School, Glasgow
1956 Musselburgh Grammar School
1957 St.Patrick's High School, Dumbarton
1958 Tynecastle Secondary School, Edinburgh
1959 St.Mary's Secondary School, Bathgate
1960 St.Mungo's Academy, Glasgow
1961 Bo'ness Academy
1962 Camphill Secondary School, Paisley
1963 John Street Secondary School, Glasgow
1964 Camphill Sec., Paisley / St.Michael's College,Irvine*
1965 Liberton Secondary School, Edinburgh
1966 Dalkeith High School
1967 St.Pius Secondary School, Glasgow
1968 Lawside Academy, Dundee
1969 St.Anthony's Secondary School, Edinburgh
1970 Kingsridge Secondary School, Glasgow
1971 Bathgate Academy
1972 CaldervaleHigh School, Airdrie
1973 Douglas Academy, Milngavie
1974 Our Lady's High School, Motherwell
1975 Graeme High School, Falkirk
1976 All Saints Secondary School, Glasgow
1977 Whitburn Academy
1978 Trinity High School, Cambuslang
1979 Holy Cross High School, Hamilton
1980 Cardinal Newman High School, Bellshill
1981 St.Ambrose High School, Coatbridge
1982 St.Aelred's High School, Paisley
1983 St.Modan's High School, Stirling
1984 Linwood High School
1985 St.Andrew's Academy, Saltcoats
1986 St.Ninian's High School, Kirkintilloch
1987 St.Ambrose High School, Coatbridge
1988 Larbert High School
1989 St.Patrick's High School, Dumbarton
1990 Trinity High School, Cambuslang
1991 Cardinal Newman High School, Bellshill
1992 St.Ambrose High School, Coatbridge
1993 Cardinal Newman High School, Bellshill
1994 St.Margaret's High School, Airdrie
1995 Lasswade High School, Bonnyrigg
1996 Holyrood Secondary School, Glasgow
1997 Our Lady & St.Patrick's High School, Dumbarton
1998 John Ogilvie High School, Hamilton
1999 Bearsden Academy
2000 St.Andrew's Secondary School, Glasgow
2001 Our Lady & St.Patrick's High School, Dumbarton
2002 Johnstone High School
2003 St.Aidan's High School, Wishaw
2004 Oban High School
2005 Bellahouston Academy, Glasgow
2006 Auchinleck Academy
2007 Mintlaw Academy
2008 St.Margaret's High School, Airdrie
2009 Dumfries Academy
2010 St.Peter the Apostle High School, Clydebank
2011 Holyrood Secondary School, Glasgow
2012 Springburn Academy, Glasgow
2013 St.Margaret's High School, Airdrie
2014 Holyrood Secondary School, Glasgow
2015 Boclair Academy, Bearsden
2016 St Ninian's HS, Giffnock
2017 Braidhurst HS, Motherwell
2918 Holyrood Secondary, Glasgow
2019 St John's RC HS, Dundee

Under 15 Shield

1957 Crookston Castle Secondary School, Glasgow
1958 Clydebank High School
1959 Onslow Secondary School, Glasgow
1960 Penilee Secondary School, Glasgow
1961 Our Lady's High School, Motherwell
1962 Graeme High School, Falkirk
1963 St.Mungo's Academy, Glasgow
1964 St.Mungo's Academy, Glasgow
1965 Holy Cross High School, Hamilton
1966 Liberton Secondary School, Edinburgh
1967 St.Margaret Mary's Secondary School, Glasgow
1968 St.Anthony's Secondary School, Edinburgh
1969 Broxburn Academy
1970 Crookston Castle Secondary School, Glasgow
1971 Caldervale High School, Airdrie
1972 Camphill High School, Paisley
1973 Holy Cross High School, Hamilton
1974 Graeme High School, Falkirk
1975 All Saints Secondary School, Glasgow
1976 Holy Cross High School, Hamilton
1977 St.Ambrose High School, Coatbridge
1978 Larbert High School
1979 Cardinal Newman High School, Bellshill
1980 Liberton High School, Edinburgh
1981 James Hamilton Academy, Kilmarnock
1982 Gracemount High School, Edinburgh
1983 Kincorth Academy, Aberdeen
1984 Lesmahagow High School
1985 Braidhurst High School, Motherwell
1986 Cathkin High School, Cambuslang
1987 St.Patrick's High School, Dumbarton
1988 St.Patrick's High School, Coatbridge
1989 Auchmuty High School, Glenrothes
1990 Taylor High School, New Stevenston
1991 Dalkeith High School
1992 King's Park Secondary School, Glasgow
1993 Madras College, St.Andrews
1994 St.Columba's High School, Dunfermline
1995 Holyrood Secondary School, Glasgow
1996 Lourdes Secondary School, Glasgow
1997 John Ogilvie High School, Blantyre
1998 St.Margaret's High School, Airdrie
1999 Whitburn Academy
2000 Holyrood Secondary School, Glasgow
2001 Johnstone High School
2002 Holy Cross High School, Hamilton
2003 Oban High School
2004 Ardrossan Academy
2005 St.Ambrose High School, Coatbridge
2006 Greenwood Academy, Irvine
2007 Nicolson Institute, Stornoway
2008 Dumfries Academy
2009 Bishopbriggs Academy
2010 St.Ambrose High School, Coatbridge
2011 Musselburgh Grammar School
2012 Dunfermline High School
2013 Bannerman High School, Glasgow
2014 Braidhurst High School, Motherwell
2015 Braidhurst High School, Motherwell
2016 Broughton HS, Edinburgh
2017 Gryffe HS, Houston
2918 Grange Academy, Kilmarnock
2019 St Ninians HS (Giffnock)

Under 14 Shield

1980 St.Andrew's High School, Kirkcaldy
1981 Holyrood Secondary School, Glasgow
1982 St.Bride's High School, East Kilbride
1983 Holyrood Secondary School, Glasgow
1984 Bellshill Academy
1985 St.Patrick's High School, Dumbarton
1986 Caldervale High School, Airdrie
1987 Cathkin High School, Cambuslang
1988 Queensferry High School
1989 Lasswade High School, Bonnyrigg
1990 Beath High School, Cowdenbeath
1991 Holyrood Secondary School, Glasgow
1992 Uddingston Grammar
1993 Holy Cross High School, Hamilton
1994 Holyrood Secondary School, Glasgow
1995 Lourdes Secondary School, Glasgow
1996 John Ogilvie High School, Hamilton
1997 Holy Cross High School, Hamilton
1998 St.Patrick's High School, Coatbridge
1999 Our Lady & St.Patrick's High School, Dumbarton
2000 Johnstone High School
2001 Holy Cross High School, Hamilton
2002 Aberdeen Grammar School
2003 Our Lady & St.Patrick's High School, Dumbarton
2004 Greenwood Academy, Irvine
2005 Harris Academy, Dundee
2006 Peterhead Academy
2007 St.Andrew's & St.Bride's High School, East Kilbride
2008 St.Andrew's & St.Bride's High School, East Kilbride
2009 St.Ambrose High School, Coatbridge
2010 Portlethen Academy
2011 St.Peter the Apostle High School, Clydebank
2012 St.Andrew's High School, Coatbridge
2013 Braidhurst High School, Motherwell
2014 St.Ninian's High School, Giffnock
2015 Grange Academy, Kilmarnock
2016 St Ninian's High School, Giffnock
2017 St Ninian's High School, Giffnock
2018 Grange Academy, Kilmarnock
2019 Boclair Academy, Bearsden

Under 13 Shield

1998 Musselburgh Grammar School
1999 Queen Anne High School, Dunfermline
2000 Holy Cross High School, Hamilton
2001 Craigmount High School, Edinburgh
2002 St.Aidan's High School, Wishaw
2003 St.Machar Academy, Aberdeen
2004 Currie High School
2005 Craigmount High School, Edinburgh
2006 Holyrood Secondary School, Glasgow
2007 St.Andrew's & St.Bride's High School, East Kilbride
2008 Hazlehead Academy, Aberdeen
2009 Lockerbie Academy
2010 Braidhurst High School, Motherwell
2011 Paisley Grammar School
2012 Braidhurst High School, Motherwell
2013 Broughton High School, Edinburgh
2014 Broughton High School, Edinburgh
2015 Broughton High School, Edinburgh
2016 Graeme HS, Falkirk
2017 Lourdes Sec, Glasgow
2018 Boclair Academy, Bearsden
2019 St Andrews Secondary, Glasgow

Girls U18 Shield

1999 Kirkland High School, Leven
2000 Kirkland High School, Leven
2001 Kirkland High School, Leven
2002 St.Augustine's High School, Edinburgh
2003 St.Augustine's High School, Edinburgh
2004 St.Andrew's Academy, Paisley
2005 St.Augustine's High School, Edinburgh
2006 Mintlaw Academy
2007 Mintlaw Academy
2008 Mintlaw Academy
2009 Mintlaw Academy
2010 Mintlaw Academy
2011 St.Mungo's High School, Falkirk
2012 St.Mungo's High School, Falkirk
2013 Boroughmuir High School, Edinburgh
2014 Nicolson Institute, Stornoway
2015 Graeme High School, Falkirk
2016 Lasswade HS, Bonnyrigg
2017 St Peter the Apostle HS, Glasgow
2018 Linlithgow Academy
2019 Broxburn Academy

Girls U15 Shield

1998 Torry Academy, Aberdeen
1999 St.Augustine's High School, Edinburgh
2000 Inverurie Academy
2001 St.Augustine's High School, Edinburgh
2002 St.Andrew's Secondary School, Glasgow
2003 Perth High School
2004 Mintlaw Academy
2005 Mintlaw Academy
2006 Mintlaw Academy
2007 Perth Grammar School
2008 Calderglen High School, East Kilbride
2009 Arbroath High School
2010 Webster's High School, Kirriemuir
2011 Hawick High School
2012 Nicolson Institute, Stornoway
2013 Woodmill High School, Dunfermline
2014 Lasswade High School, Bonnyrigg
2015 St.John's High School, Dundee
2016 Lasswade HS, Bonnyrigg
2017 Broxburn Academy
2018 Boroughmuir HS, Edinburgh
2019 Boroughmuir HS, Edinburgh

SCOTTISH SCHOOLS FA

Management Committee

ANDY ENGLISH – President
ROBERT ALLAN – Vice-President/Assistant to Treasurer
JOHN C. WATSON – General Secretary
ALEX B. McMENEMY – Treasurer/S.F.A. Congress Delegate
W. LES DONALDSON – International Teams Secretary/SAFIB Delegate
ALASTAIR T. BORTHWICK – Assistant General Secretary
STEWART TAYLOR – Assistant to International Teams Secretary
GRENVILLE DAWSON – Assistant Secretary
DAVID GILCHRIST – Assistant to General Secretary
RONNIE HAMILTON – Assistant Secretary
GILLIAN DUFFY – Assistant Secretary
GEORGE MACKIE – Assistant Secretary/Child Protection Officer
IAN CAIRNS – Assistant Secretary

Steering Committee

ANDY ENGLISH – President
ROBERT ALLAN – Vice-President
JOE HARKINS – Past President
JOHN GOLD – S.F.A. Delegate
ALEX B. McMENEMY – Treasurer/S.F.A. Congress Delegate
W. LES DONALDSON – International Teams Secretary/SAFIB Delegate
ROBERT DOCHERTY – Hon Vice President
ROD HOUSTON – Hon Vice President
GORDON PATE – Hon Vice President
ALISON GOLD – Non-Executive Member
JIM EDGAR – Non-Executive Member
BILL MCMILLAN – Non-Executive Member
GEORGE MACKIE – Assistant Secretary/Child Protection Officer
ALASTAIR T. BORTHWICK – Secretary

Executive Committee
ABERDEEN
Delegate: Walter Craig
Alternate: Craig Cowie

ABERDEENSHIRE
Delegate: TBC
Alternate: TBC

NORTH OF SCOTLAND
Delegate: TBC
Alternate: TBC

ANGUS
Delegate: TBC
Alternate: TBC

DUNDEE
Delegate: Alan Gallazzi
Alternate: Mark Duffy

PERTH & KINROSS
Delegate: TBC
Alternate: TBC

FIFE
Delegate: Kenny Findlay
Alternate: Gary Cunningham

FORTH VALLEY
Delegate: David Eccles
Alternate: Craig Johnstone

LANARKSHIRE
Delegate: Jim Bettley
Alternate: David Thomson

EDINBURGH SECONDARY
Delegate: Peter Clark
Alternate: Bill Barclay

LOTHIAN
Delegate: Pete Clark
Alternate: Bill Barclay

WEST LOTHIAN
Delegate: TBC
Alternate: TBC

INDEPENDENT SCHOOLS
Delegate: TBC
Alternate: TBC

GLASGOW
Delegate: Ian Burns
Alternate: Stewart McLachlan

PAISLEY
Delegate: Gerry O'Hare
Alternate: TBC

AYRSHIRE
Delegate: Stephen Gilmour
Alternate: Martin Robertson

DUMFRIES & GALLOWAY
Delegate: Michael Downie
Alternate: Laurie Kirk

CO-OPTED MEMBERS
Alastair Macpherson
Jamie Baxter
Rhys Donaldson

MEMBER SCHOOLS ACTIVE IN LOCAL FOOTBALL 2019/20

ABERDEEN GRAMMAR SCHOOL
ABOYNE ACADEMY
AIRDRIE ACADEMY
ALBYN SCHOOL (Aberdeen)
ALFORD ACADEMY
ALLOA ACADEMY
ALL SAINTS SECONDARY SCHOOL (Glasgow)
ALNESS ACADEMY
ALVA ACADEMY
ANNAN ACADEMY
ARBROATH ACADEMY
ARBROATH HS
ARDROSSAN ACADEMY
ARMADALE ACADEMY
AUCHINLECK ACADEMY
AUCHMUTY HS (Glenrothes)

BALERNO HS (Edinburgh)
BALFRON HS
BALWEARIE HS (Kirkcaldy)
BANCHORY ACADEMY
BANFF ACADEMY
BANNERMAN HS (Glasgow)
BANNOCKBURN HS
BARRHEAD HS
BATHGATE ACADEMY
BEARSDEN ACADEMY
BEATH HS (Cowdenbeath)
BEESLACK HS (Penicuik)
BELLAHOUSTON ACADEMY (Glasgow)
BERTHA PARK HIGH (Perth)
BISHOPBRIGGS ACADEMY
BLAIRGOWRIE HS
BOCLAIR ACADEMY (Bearsden)
BO'NESS ACADEMY

BOROUGHMUIR HS (Edinburgh)
BRAES HS (Falkirk)
BRAIDHURST HS (Motherwell)
BREADALBANE ACADEMY (Aberfeldy)
BROUGHTON HS (Edinburgh)
BROXBURN ACADEMY
BUCKIE HS
BUCKSBURN ACADEMY (Aberdeen)

CALDERGLEN HS (East Kilbride)
CALDERVALE HS (Airdrie)
CAMPBELTOWN GRAMMAR SCHOOL
CARDINAL NEWMAN HS (Bellshill)
CARLUKE HS
CARNOUSTIE HS
CARRICK ACADEMY (Maybole)
CASTLEMILK HS (Glasgow)
CATHKIN HS (Cambuslang)
CHRYSTON HS (Glasgow)
CLYDEBANK HS
CLYDE VALLEY HS (Wishaw)
CLYDEVIEW ACADEMY (Gourock)
COATBRIDGE HS
COLTNESS HS (Wishaw)
CRAIGMOUNT HS (Edinburgh)
CRIEFF HS
CULTS ACADEMY (Aberdeen)
CURRIE COMMUNITY HS (Edinburgh)

DALZIEL HS (Motherwell)
DEANS COMMUNITY HS (Livingston)
DENNY HS
DOUGLAS ACADEMY (Milngavie)
DOUGLAS EWART HS (Newton Stewart)
DRUMCHAPEL HS (Glasgow)
DUMFRIES ACADEMY
DUMFRIES HS
DUNBAR GRAMMAR SCHOOL
DUNBLANE HS
DUNCANRIG SECONDARY SCHOOL (East Kilbride)
DUNFERMLINE HS

EASTBANK ACADEMY (Glasgow)
EASTWOOD HS (Newton Mearns)
ELGIN ACADEMY
ELLON ACADEMY

FALKIRK HS
FIRRHILL HS (Edinburgh)
FORFAR ACADEMY
FORTROSE ACADEMY
FRASERBURGH ACADEMY

GARNOCK COMMUNITY CAMPUS (Kilbirnie)
GEORGE HERIOT'S SCHOOL (Edinburgh)
GEORGE WATSON'S COLLEGE (Edinburgh)
GIRVAN ACADEMY
GLASGOW ACADEMY
GLASGOW GAELIC SCHOOL
GLENIFFER HS (Paisley)
GLENROTHES HS
GORDONSTOUN SCHOOL (Elgin)
GRACEMOUNT HS (Edinburgh)
GRAEME HS (Falkirk)
GRANGE ACADEMY (Kilmarnock)
GRANGEMOUTH HS
GRANTOWN GRAMMAR SCHOOL
GREENFAULDS HS (Cumbernauld)
GREENWOOD ACADEMY (Irvine)
GROVE ACADEMY (Broughty Ferry, Dundee)

GRYFFE HS (Houston)

HAMILTON COLLEGE
HARLAW ACADEMY (Aberdeen)
HARRIS ACADEMY (Dundee)
HAZLEHEAD ACADEMY (Aberdeen)
HERMITAGE ACADEMY (Helensburgh)
HILLHEAD HS (Glasgow)
HILLPARK SECONDARY SCHOOL (Glasgow)
HOLY ROOD HS (Edinburgh)
HOLYROOD SECONDARY SCHOOL (Glasgow)
HUTCHESONS' GRAMMAR SCHOOL (Glasgow)
HYNDLAND SECONDARY SCHOOL (Glasgow)

INVERCLYDE ACADEMY (Greenock)
INVERKEITHING HS
INVERNESS HS
INVERNESS ROYAL ACADEMY
INVERURIE ACADEMY
IRVINE ROYAL ACADEMY

JAMES GILLESPIE'S HS (Edinburgh)
JAMES YOUNG HS (Livingston)
JOHN PAUL ACADEMY (Glasgow)
JOHNSTONE HS
JORDANHILL SCHOOL (Glasgow)

KEMNAY ACADEMY
KILMARNOCK ACADEMY
KILSYTH ACADEMY
KILWINNING ACADEMY
KING'S PARK SECONDARY SCHOOL (Glasgow)
KINROSS HS
KIRKCALDY HS
KIRKWALL GRAMMAR SCHOOL
KNIGHTSWOOD SECONDARY SCHOOL (Glasgow)

LANARK GRAMMAR SCHOOL
LARBERT HS
LARGS ACADEMY
LASSWADE HS (Bonnyrigg)
LEITH ACADEMY (Edinburgh)
LENZIE ACADEMY
LEVENMOUTH ACADEMY (Buckhaven)
LIBERTON HS (Edinburgh)
LINLITHGOW ACADEMY
LINWOOD HS
LOCHEND COMMUNITY HS (Glasgow)
LOCHGILPHEAD HS
LOCHSIDE ACADEMY, (Aberdeen)
LOCKERBIE ACADEMY
LORNSHILL ACADEMY (Alloa)
LOUDOUN ACADEMY (Galston)
LOURDES SECONDARY SCHOOL (Glasgow)

MACKIE ACADEMY (Stonehaven)
MEARNS ACADEMY (Laurencekirk)
MEARNS CASTLE HS (Newton Mearns)
MELDRUM ACADEMY
MILLBURN ACADEMY (Inverness)
MINTLAW ACADEMY
MONIFIETH HS
MONTROSE ACADEMY
MORGAN ACADEMY (Dundee)

MUSSELBURGH GRAMMAR SCHOOL

NEWBATTLE COMMUNITY HS (Dalkeith)
NORTH BERWICK HS
NORTH WEST COMMUNITY CAMPUS, Dumfries
NOTRE DAME HS (Greenock)

OBAN HS
OUR LADY & ST. PATRICK'S HS (Dumbarton)
OUR LADY'S HS (Cumbernauld)
OUR LADY'S HS (Motherwell)

PAISLEY GRAMMAR SCHOOL
PARK MAINS HS (Erskine)
PEEBLES HS
PENICUIK HS
PERTH GRAMMAR SCHOOL
PERTH HS
PETERHEAD ACADEMY
PORTLETHEN ACADEMY
PORTOBELLO HS (Edinburgh)
PRESTWICK ACADEMY

QUEEN ANNE HS (Dunfermline)
QUEEN MARGARET ACADEMY (Ayr)
QUEENSFERRY HS (South Queensferry)

RENFREW HS
ROBERT GORDON'S COLLEGE (Aberdeen)
ROSS HS (Tranent)
ROTHESAY ACADEMY
ROYAL HS (Edinburgh)

SHAWLANDS ACADEMY (Glasgow)
SMITHYCROFT SECONDARY SCHOOL (Glasgow)
SPRINGBURN ACADEMY (Glasgow)
ST. AIDAN'S HS (Wishaw)
ST. ALOYSIUS COLLEGE (Glasgow)
ST. AMBROSE HS (Coatbridge)
ST. ANDREW'S ACADEMY (Paisley)
ST. ANDREW'S AND ST. BRIDE'S HS (East Kilbride)
ST. ANDREW'S HS (Coatbridge)
ST. ANDREW'S HS (Kirkcaldy)
ST. ANDREW'S SECONDARY SCHOOL (Glasgow)
ST. AUGUSTINE'S HS (Edinburgh)
ST. COLUMBA'S HS (Dunfermline)
ST. COLUMBA'S HS (Gourock)
ST. COLUMBA'S SCHOOL (Kilmacolm)
ST. DAVID'S HS (Dalkeith)
ST. JOHN'S HS (Dundee)
ST. JOSEPH'S ACADEMY (Kilmarnock)
ST. JOSEPH'S COLLEGE (Dumfries)
ST. KENTIGERN'S ACADEMY (Blackburn, West Lothian)
ST. LUKE'S HS (Barrhead)
ST. MARGARET MARY'S SECONDARY SCHOOL (Glasgow)
ST. MARGARET'S ACADEMY (Livingston)
ST. MARGARET'S HS (Airdrie)
ST. MATTHEW'S ACADEMY (Saltcoats)
ST. MAURICE'S HS (Cumbernauld)
ST. MODAN'S HS (Stirling)
ST. MUNGO'S ACADEMY (Glasgow)
ST. MUNGO'S HS (Falkirk)
ST. NINIAN'S HS (Giffnock)
ST. NINIAN'S HS (Kirkintilloch)
ST. PAUL'S ACADEMY (Dundee)
ST. PAUL'S HS (Glasgow)
ST. PETER THE APOSTLE HS (Clydebank)

ST. ROCH'S SECONDARY SCHOOL (Glasgow)
ST. THOMAS OF AQUIN'S HS (Edinburgh)
STEWARTON ACADEMY
STEWART'S MELVILLE COLLEGE (Edinburgh)
STIRLING HS
STONELAW HS (Rutherglen)
STRANRAER ACADEMY
STRATHAVEN ACADEMY

TAIN ROYAL ACADEMY
TARBERT ACADEMY
TAYLOR HS (New Stevenston)
THE MARY ERSKINE SCHOOL (Edinburgh)
THE NICOLSON INSTITUTE (Stornoway)
THURSO HS
TRINITY ACADEMY (Edinburgh)
TRINITY HS (Rutherglen)
TURNBULL HS (Bishopbriggs)
TURRIFF ACADEMY
TYNECASTLE HS (Edinburgh)

UDDINGSTON GRAMMAR SCHOOL

VALE OF LEVEN ACADEMY (Alexandria)
VIEWFORTH HS (Kirkcaldy)

WALLACE HS (Stirling)
WEBSTER'S HS (Kirriemuir)
WESTHILL ACADEMY
WHITBURN ACADEMY
WHITEHILL SECONDARY SCHOOL (Glasgow)

WILLIAMWOOD HS (Clarkston)
WOODMILL HS (Dunfermline)

WOMEN'S FOOTBALL 2020

The season started on 21 February 2020 and was scheduled to end in November 2020, but was interrupted by the coronavirus pandemic. In July 2020, the 2020 season was declared null and void. A new season was due to start in October 2020 and end in June 2021, with the league reverting to a winter season format.

SCOTTISH WOMEN'S PREMIER LEAGUE ONE 2020

Only 4 matches were played:

Celtic v Glasgow City	2-1
Forfar F v Motherwell	0-1
Hibernian v Spartans	1-0
Rangers v Hearts	3-0

SCOTTISH WOMEN'S PREMIER LEAGUE TWO 2020

Only 5 matches were played:

Aberdeen v Kilmarnock	1-1
Dundee United v Boroughmuir	8-4
Hamilton Accies v Stirling Univ	5-0
Partick Thistle v Glasgow Women	2-0

SCOTTISH WOMEN'S PREMIER LEAGUE ONE 2020/1

Team	Coach	Home Ground
Celtic	Fran Alonso	K Park, East Kilbride
Forfar Farmington	Ryan McConville	Station Park, Forfar
Glasgow City	Scott Booth	Broadwood Stadium, Cumbernauld
Hearts	Andy Kirk	ORIAM, Edinburgh
Hibernian	Dean Gibson	Ainslie Park, Edinburgh
Motherwell	Eddie Wolecki Black	Excelsior Stadium, Airdrie
Rangers	Malky Thomson	Rangers Training Centre, Glasgow
Spartans	Debbi McCulloch	Ainslie Park, Edinburgh

Matches 1 to 14

	CEL	FOR	GLA	HOM	HIB	MOT	RAN	SPA
Celtic		2–2	0–3	3–0	3–1	3–0	1–0	1–0
Forfar Farmington	0–8		0–7	3–0	0–5	4–2	1–3	1–2
Glasgow City	2–0	8–1		5–0	3–2	8–0	0–5	3–1
Heart of Midlothian	0–10	1–1	0–4		1–0	0–3	0–6	1–2
Hibernian	2–6	3–0	1–2	6–0		3–2	0–1	2–1
Motherwell	0–5	2–3	0–3	2–1	0–6		0–6	0–2
Rangers	0–1	11–0	0–2	5–1	1–0	9–0		5–0
Spartans	1–5	1–0	1–3	3–0	2–0	3–1	0–1	

Matches 15-21

	CEL	FOR	GLA	HOM	HIB	MOT	RAN	SPA
Celtic		10–0	0–0					4–0
Forfar Farmington				1–2		0–1	0–4	
Glasgow City		8–0		4–1	0–0		2–0	
Heart of Midlothian	0–3				0–2	0–1		1–1
Hibernian	0–1	7–0					0–3	1–1
Motherwell	0–8		2–4		0–1			2–3
Rangers	1–2			4–0		6–0		
Spartans		3–0	2–6				0–5	

Pos	Team	Pld	W	D	L	GF	GA	GD	Pts
1	Glasgow City	21	18	2	1	77	16	+61	56
2	Celtic	21	17	2	2	76	12	+64	53
3	Rangers	21	16	0	5	76	10	+66	48
4	Hibernian	21	9	2	10	42	27	+15	29
5	Spartans	21	9	2	10	29	42	-13	29
6	Motherwell	21	4	0	17	18	78	-60	12
7	Forfar Farmington	21	3	2	16	17	90	-73	11
8	Heart of Midlothian	21	2	2	17	9	69	-60	8

SCOTTISH WOMEN'S PREMIER LEAGUE TWO 2020/1

Team	Coach	Home Ground
Aberdeen	Emma Hunter / Stuart Bathgate	Cormack Park
Boroughmuir Thistle	Suzy Shepherd	Meggetland 3G
Dundee United	Gavin Beith	Regional Performance Centre
Glasgow Women	Craig Joyce	New Tinto Park
Hamilton Accies	Gary Doctor	New Douglas Park
Kilmarnock	Andy Gardner	Rugby Park
Partick Thistle	Brian Graham	Lochinch
Queen's Park	Mark Kirk	New Lesser Hampden
St Johnstone	Jason McCrindle	McDiarmid Park Astro
Stirling University	Craig Beveridge	Gannochy Sports Centre

Pos	Team	Pld	W	D	L	GF	GA	GD	Pts
1	Aberdeen	12	11	0	1	53	10	+43	33
2	Hamilton Academical	12	8	1	3	34	11	+23	25
3	Partick Thistle	12	8	1	3	29	14	+15	25
4	Dundee United	12	7	3	2	30	17	+13	24
5	St Johnstone	11	5	1	5	21	23	-2	16
6	Glasgow Women	11	4	1	6	15	16	-1	13
7	Queen's Park	12	4	1	7	14	29	-15	13
8	Kilmarnock	12	4	1	7	10	26	-16	13
9	Boroughmuir Thistle	12	3	0	9	13	33	-20	9
10	Stirling University	12	0	1	11	10	50	-40	1

	ABE	BOR	DUN	GLW	HAM	KIL	PAR	QPA	STJ	STI
Aberdeen			4–3			3–0		5–1	8–1	7–0
Boroughmuir Thistle	0–9		1–2			0–1	1–0	1–3	3–2	
Dundee United		4–1		2–2	2–1	2–2				3–1
Glasgow Women	0–1	3–1			0–2		1–4			4–0
Hamilton Academical	0–1	3–1		1–2				5–0		8–0
Kilmarnock	0–5	3–1	0–4	1–0	0–3[a]		1–2			2–1
Partick Thistle	5–1	3–1	1–1	1–0	1–3				2–3	
Queen's Park	0–3		3–1	2–0	0–2	2–0	0–3		0–3	
St Johnstone			0–1	1–3	2–2	3–0	1–3	3–0		
Stirling University	0–6	0–2	1–5	3–3	2–4		1–4		1–2	

SCOTTISH WOMEN'S FOOTBALL 2021/2 KEY DATES

August 2021
8th : SWPL Cup – Group Stage, Matchday 1
8th : SWF Highlands & Islands League Cup – Quarter-Final
8th : 2021/22 Championship South season kick-off
14th : 2021/22 SHAAP National Performance League 16's season kick-off
15th : SWPL Cup – Group Stage, Matchday 2
15th : 2021/22 Championship North season kick-off
15th : 2021/22 SHAAP National Performance League 19's season kick-off
17th/18th : UEFA Women's Champions League – Round 1, Semi-Finals
20th/21st : UEFA Women's Champions League – Round 1, Final/Third-place play-off
22nd : SWPL Cup – Group Stage, Matchday 3
25th : SWPL Cup – Group Stage, Matchday 4
29th : SWPL Cup – Group Stage, Matchday 5
29th : SWFL Cup – Quarter-Final
29th : SWFL Plate – Quarter-Final
29th : SWF Championship Cup 1st Round
31st : UEFA Women's Champions League – Round 2, First leg

September 2021
1st : UEFA Women's Champions League – Round 2, First leg
5th : 2021/22 SWPL 1 season kick-off
5th : 2021/22 SWPL 2 season kick-off
5th : SWF Highlands & Islands League Cup – Semi-Final
8th/9th : UEFA Women's Champions League – Round 2, Second leg
19th : SWF Championship Cup 2nd Round
26th : SWFL Cup – Semi-Final
26th : SWFL Plate – Semi-Final

October 2021
3rd : 2021 SWF Highlands & Islands League Cup Final
5th/6th : UEFA Women's Champions League – Group Stage, Matchday 1
10th : Final day of SWF Highlands and Islands League
10th : SWF Championship Cup – Quarter-Final
13th/14th : UEFA Women's Champions League – Group Stage, Matchday 2
24th : Scottish Cup 1st Round
31st : SWPL Cup – Quarter-Final

November 2021
7th : SWF Championship Cup – Semi-Final
9th/10th : UEFA Women's Champions League – Group Stage, Matchday 3
14th : SWPL Cup – Semi-Final
17th/18th : UEFA Women's Champions League – Group Stage, Matchday 4
21st : 2021 SWFL Cup Final
21st : 2021 SWFL Plate Final
28th : Final day of SWFL Central/South East League.
28th : 2021 SWF Championship Cup Final

December 2021
5th : 2021 SWPL Cup Final
5th : Final day of SWFL North/East League
8th/9th : UEFA Women's Champions League – Group Stage, Matchday 5
12th : Final day of SWFL West/South West League
15th/16th : UEFA Women's Champions League – Group Stage, Matchday 6

January 2022
9th : Scottish Cup 2nd Round
29th : 16's SHAAP NPL Cup – Semi-Final
30th : 19's SHAAP NPL Cup – Semi-Final

February 2022
13th : Scottish Cup 3rd Round

March 2022
5th : 16's SHAAP NPL Cup Final
6th : 19's SHAAP NPL Cup Final
22nd/23rd : UEFA Women's Champions League – Quarter-Final, First leg
30th/31st : UEFA Women's Champions League – Quarter-Final, Second leg

April 2022
3rd : Scottish Cup – Quarter-Final
23rd/24th : UEFA Women's Champions League – Semi-Final, First leg
24th : Final day of SWF Championship North
24th : Final day of SWF Championship South
30th : UEFA Women's Champions League – Semi-Final, Second leg

May 2022
1st : Scottish Cup – Semi-Final
1st : UEFA Women's Champions League – Semi-Final, Second leg
8th : SWPL 2 Promotion Play-off Final
15th : Final day of SWPL 1
15th : Final day of SWPL 2
15th : Final day of 19's SHAAP National Performance League
21st : Final day of 16's SHAAP National Performance League
22nd : SWPL 1 Promotion Play-off Final
22nd : UEFA Women's Champions League – Final
29th : 2021/22 Scottish Cup Final

SCOTTISH WOMEN'S FOOTBALL HISTORICAL DATA

Scottish Women's Premier League

	Champ	RU
2002/3	Kilmarnock Ladies	Hibernian
2003/4	Hibernian	Glasgow City
2004/5	Glasgow City	Hibernian
2005/6	Hibernian	Glasgow City
2006/7	Hibernian	Glasgow City
2007/8	Glasgow City	Hibernian
2008/9	Glasgow City	Spartans
2009	Glasgow City	Celtic
2010	Glasgow City	Celtic
2011	Glasgow City	Spartans
2012	Glasgow City	Forfar Farmington
2013	Glasgow City	Hibernian
2014	Glasgow City	Rangers
2015	Glasgow City	Hibernian
2016	Glasgow City	Hibernian
2017	Glasgow City	Hibernian
2018	Glasgow City	Hibernian
2019	Glasgow City	Hibernian

Scottish Women's Cup Final

1995/6	Cove Rangers	Aberdeen	5 1
1996/7	Cove Rangers	Ayr United	5 4
1997/8	Cumbernauld United	Giuliano	3 1
1998/9	Cumbernauld United	Ayr United	1 0
1999/00	Stenhousemuir	Clyde	9 0
2000/1	Kilmarnock	Ayr United	3 3 3-2p
2001/2	Kilmarnock	Glasgow City	5 0
2002/3	Hibernian	Kilmarnock	2 2 5-4p
2003/4	Glasgow City	Queen's Park	3 0
2004/5	Hibernian	Cove Rangers	8 0
2005/6	Glasgow City	Aberdeen	5 1
2006/7	Hibernian	Glasgow City	5 1
2007/8	Hibernian	Celtic	3 1 AET
2008/9	Glasgow City	Rangers	5 0
2010	Hibernian	Rangers	2 1
2011	Glasgow City	Hibernian	3 0
2012	Glasgow City	Forfar Farmington	1 0
2013	Glasgow City	Hibernian	1 0
2014	Glasgow City	Spartans	5 0
2015	Glasgow City	Hibernian	3 0
2016	Hibernian	Glasgow City	1 1 AET, 6-5p
2017	Hibernian	Glasgow City	3 0
2018	Hibernian	`Motherwell	8 0
2019	Glasgow City	Hibernian	4 3

Scottish Womens Premier League Cup Final

2002/3	Kilmarnock	Glasgow City	2 0
2003/4	Kilmarnock	Glasgow City	3 1
2004/5	Hibernian	Raith Rovers	6 1
2005/6	Kilmarnock	Glasgow City	3 2
2006/7	Edinburgh Ladies	Hibernian	4 1
2007/8	Hibernian	Queen's Park	4 0
2008/9	Glasgow City	Spartans	3 0
2009	Glasgow City	Hibernian	3 1
2010	Celtic	Spartans	4 1
2011	Hibernian	Spartans	5 2
2012	Glasgow City	Spartans	5 1
2013	Glasgow City	Spartans	5 0
2014	Glasgow City	Hibernian	3 0
2015	Glasgow City	Hibernian	2 1 aet
2016	Hibernian	Glasgow City	2 1
2017	Hibernian	Celtic	4 1
2018	Hibernian	Celtic	9 0
2019	Hibernian	Glasgow City	0 0 4-2p

SCOTTISH WOMEN'S FOOTBALL AWARDS 2020/1

Scottish Building Society SWPL 1 Top Scorer
Lizzie Arnot (Rangers)

Scottish Building Society SWPL 2 Top Scorer
Bayley Hutchison (Aberdeen)

Recognition Express Lockdown Hero
Sarah Herd (East Fife GWFC)

Sportscotland Youth Player of the Year
Eilidh Adams (Hibernian Women)

Kat Lindner Award for Outstanding Academic & Athletic Achievement
Kirsten Reilly (Rangers)

SWPL Coach of the Year
Scott Booth (Glasgow City)

MG Alba International Player of the Year
Caroline Weir (Manchester City)

Save of the Season
Charlotte Parker-Smith (Hearts)

Goal of the Season
Amy Bulloch (Partick Thistle)

SWPL 2 Player of the Year
Bayley Hutchison (Aberdeen)

SWPL 1 Player of the Year
Lisa Robertson (Celtic)

SWPL Team of the Year
Glasgow City

2020/1 Services to Girls and Women's Football
Julie Fleeting

Stadia / Grounds Update

Aberdeen
Aberdeen's plans for a new stadium at Kingsford seem to be dead in the water. The club's training base was completed at the site but work on the stadium itself never began. Aberdeen are now in talks with Aberdeen City Council about developing a new stadium on the Beach Front. This would be a much more palatable plan for many Dons fans who were unhappy at the "out of town" aspect of the Kingsford development. City chiefs want any new stadium to include other community facilities too, such as a new home for extreme sports centre Transition and a replacement for the ageing Beach Leisure Centre. It would be included as part of the council's revised city centre masterplan, which includes £150 million of investment in transport infrastructure and regeneration of the beach area. Douglas Lumsden, co-leader of the Council said: "I still believe it would be much better for the club and the city as a whole if we could find a way for the club to remain in the beach area," Mr Lumsden said.

Airdrieonians
The Penny Car Stadium is to become home to the Celtic B side in the Lowland League for 2021/2. Where this leaves Glasgow University AFC is unclear. They required a licensed standard stadium for their Scottish Cup and Challenge Cup ties and had been submitting Airdrie as their designated home ground.

Armadale Thistle
There has been a huge amount of tidying up done at Volunteer Park to bring it up to scratch. They were also one of the clubs to benefit from Motherwell's largesse in offering free seats to clubs as they did some replacement at Fir Park. These have been installed under the covered enclosure to give Armadale a seated stand. The club have also built new changing rooms for match officials, suggesting that they may be exploring licensing in the not too distant future.

Arbroath
The Red Lichties have replaced the roofing on the three covered enclosures at Gayfield. There is no material alteration meaning that Gayfield still remains in the same configuration as it had in the 1960s.

Auchinleck Talbot
The installation of floodlights at Beechwood Park is now complete.

Ayr United
The chances of Ayr United leaving Somerset Park look ever less likely. In April 2021 the club bought land in their car park area to develop as the "Somerset Hub", a fanzone type area.

Bathgate Thistle
The Creamery Park side are one of many to have benefited from a donation of old seating from Motherwell FC. Some of these seats have now been installed in the covered enclosure.

Bellshill Athletic
Following a fire at their Rockburn Park pavilion in early 2020, Bellshill were offered an old pavilion by English side Bridlington Town. The building was dismantled and transported and has now been re-installed at the Lanarkshire ground.

Blackburn United
Blackburn have plans to improve the covered enclosure at New Murray field Park by installing stepped terracing in it and possibly adding seats.

Blantyre Victoria
Vics have undertaken a great deal of improvement works at Castle Park. These include installing several covered seated areas and replacing the seats to the front of the pavilion. Much of the work was undertaken by their energetic sponsor George Fulston, of Hamilton Accies and Falkirk fame.

Bonnyrigg Rose
Some seating was installed adjacent to the pavilion at new Dundas Park. It was not clear whether this was available to the general public or for officials only.

Bridge of Don Thistle
Bridge of Don Thistle are hopeful of getting a new ground as part of a housing development at Cloverhill. It's just across the A90 from the Hermes and Hall Russell parks. This would allow them to pursue long-term ambitions of becoming licensed.

Burntisland Shipyard
Work on installing floodlights at Kirkton Park (aka Recreation Park) was close to completion in August 2021.

Camelon
Having completed the installation of proper floodlights, Camelon are now seeking funding to lay an artificial pitch at Carmuirs Park. They have fitted seats into the pavilion side enclosure turning it into a grandstand.

Clyde
Now that the football club and North Lanarkshire Council have a better relationship a great deal of work has been done to improve the seating at Broadwood. Old broken and faded seats have been replaced.

Clydebank
A new covered enclosure has been completed at Holm Park, bringing the ground up to SFA Licensing requirements.

Coldstream
The Home Park side played their first home game under floodlights in October 2020 with a friendly against Chirnside United.

Cowdenbeath
The stand and facilities at Central Park suffered extensive water damage during a rain storm in late August 2020. Damage ran to many tens of thousands of pounds.

Creetown
Creetown have completed the installation of floodlights at their neat ground on the outskirts of the village.

Crossgates Primrose
Humbug Park has been spruced up with a new walkway created to the far side of the ground. In the longer term the club have ambitious plans to redevelop the ground completely. This would involve rotating the pitch by 90 degrees and laying an artificial playing surface with floodlights etc.

Dalkeith Thistle
The club have completed all the interior work that was necessary to bring the changing room area up to licensing standards.

Darvel
A great deal of work has taken place at Recreation Park. The pitch has been levelled, new drainage installed and re-laid. Floodlights were completed in March 2021.

Downfield
Permanent seating has been installed in the covered enclosure at Downfield Park.

Drumchapel United
The club are continuing to work towards bringing their pitch at the Donald Dewar Centre up to standard for SFA Licensing.

Dumbarton
Uncertainties continue at Dumbarton. Establishing a clear picture of the ownership of the club is difficult. Regardless, the land at the ground is still coveted for future housing development and the club could be on the move at some point. A previous scheme at Young's farm could be revived or another site might be explored.

Dunbar United
The Seasiders moved to Hallhill in 2001. Initially the ground had no cover but some years later a number of sections of cover were added. In the Summer of 2021 it was announced that a 200-seater grandstand will be built at the ground.

Dundee
Dundee's American owners still plan to move Dundee from their Dens Park home into a 15,000-seater stadium at Camperdown Park. Though the project has been ongoing since 2017, Chief Exec John Nelms insists it is getting nearer to fruition. In April 2021 he confirmed that the club had hired a project manager to oversee the development.

Dundee St James
The former Fintry Amateurs have joined the Midlands League and taken over the old Dundee St Josephs ground at Fairfield Park, also known as Midmill Park. They have repaired the pitch railings and revamped the pavilion area.

Dundonald Bluebell
As well as upgrading the floodlights at Moorside Park, Bluebell have completely renewed two of the three covered enclosures.

East Kilbride Thistle
The pitch at The Showground was re-laid over the Summer of 2021 meaning that they had to play home games elsewhere at the start of the 2021/2 season.

Edinburgh City
City have been ground-sharing with Spartans since 2017. Early in 2021 they announced that they would be returning to Meadowbank for 2021/2. It was initially thought that the new stadium there would be unsuitable for SPFL football due to limited capacity on a small stand on the south side of the ground. City came to an agreement with the Council to build another larger stand on the north (Marionville Road) side of the ground, which would house City's facilities. Having lost City as tenants, Spartans quickly agreed to ground share with Lothian Thistle HV for 2021/2. Then it became clear that Meadowbank would not be ready for the start of the season. City were effectively homeless. They have now agreed to return to Ainslie Park but playing all their home games on Friday evenings. If they do get access to Meadowbank in the course of the season then they will continue to play home games on Fridays.

Fort William
In July 2021 the Highland League ordered Fort William to play all their League games away from home throughout 2021/2. This was due to the poor condition of the pitch at Claggan Park.

Gartcairn
A grandstand has been built at the club's ground at Rawyards Sports Centre in Airdrie.

Girvan
A grant of £25,000 awarded to Girvan Football Club from the Carrick Futures Trust will contribute to the cost of installing cost effective low energy LED floodlights around the pitch and running track at Hamilton Park. This will allow the club to retain SFA membership.

Glasgow United
Formerly Shettleston Juniors, the club have long-term plans to sell Greenfield Park and move to the nearby Greenfield Soccer Centre.

Gretna
During the close season on 2021 Gretna began work on installing an artificial pitch at Raydale Park.

Hamilton Accies
The floodlighting system at New Douglas Park was replaced in the Summer of 2021.

Hill of Beath Hawthorn
The Haws have had to make improvements to their floodlights to keep up with the required standards. Their initial plan was to extend the current system. However, this was deemed to be unsuitable and the club have now installed a brand new set of lights.

Inverkeithing Hillfield Swifts
The Divit club have taken over the running of the artificial pitch and grass pitches at Dalgety Bay Leisure Centre. While still to be confirmed publicly, it seems that first team games will be played on the floodlit Astro at Dalgety Bay from 2021/2.

Irvine Meadow
Floodlights have been installed at Meadow Park.

Kilwinning Rangers
The Buffs continue to develop the facilities at their ground at Kilwinning Sports Centre, now known as Buffs Park.

Kirkcaldy & Dysart
The club have improved the perimeter barricade at Denfield Park to prevent cheapskates from watching the game for free from outside.

Kirkintilloch Rob Roy
Seven years after leaving Adamslie Park, work had still not started on their new ground by the Summer of 2021. The scheme, run by east Dunbartonshire Council, has been slimmed down to a very basic ground but in the meantime Rob Roy continue to ground share at Cumbernauld.

Kirriemuir Thistle
Kirrie were another club to get a delivery of seats for their grandstand from the ones going spare after redevelopment at Motherwell's Fir Park.

Leith Athletic
The club will share the main pitch at Meadowbank with Edinburgh City once the stadium is opened, sometime in 2021/2. In the meantime they continue on the Astro at Peffermill.

Lesmahagow
A replacement shelter has been provided on the side of the pitch for the one declared unsafe a couple of years ago.

Lochee Harp
The Harp are now resident at their new ground, close to the site of their old home at Beechwood Park. There is spectator access on two sides and some elevated banking. The club have had an injection of enthusiasm from the players and officials of Menzieshill Amateurs, who moved en masse to Harp in the Summer after their own bid to join the Midlands League was knocked back.

Lochee United
The Bluebells are striving to eb the first Midlands League side to achieve licensing standards. The major development will be the addition of floodlights at Thomson Park.

Lothian Thistle Hutchison Vale
The club have left Saughton Enclosure to share with Spartans at Ainslie Park. They do hope to return to Saughton at some point but only after issues about sharing withy athletics and pitch maintenance have been sorted out.

Newburgh
Fife Council, the owners of East Shire Park, have agreed to pass it to Newburgh Community Trust (NCT) who will manage it on behalf of the people of the town. The East of Scotland League football club will continue to use the park with the NCT hoping its management, and the plans it has for it, will strengthen and further develop the bond between Newburgh Juniors and the people of the town. Funding for the venture has been made available by the Scottish Land Fund.

Queen's Park
Having sold Hampden Park to the SFA, Queen's Park were planning to upgrade New Lesser Hampden as their new home ground. Some work did begin but then halted with no full explanation given. Queen's used the Falkirk Stadium as their home ground for the latter part of 2020/1 and will be "lodgers" at Partick Thistle for at least the early part if not all of 2021/2.

Rangers
The addition of a grandstand to the main pitch at their Murray Park / Auchenhowie Training Ground has been a welcome development.

Rossvale
After a period of ground sharing at Benburb, Rossvale have moved back to Petershill Park in the North of the city, closer to their home area of Bishopbriggs.

Rosyth
The saga of Rosyth's new ground continues. They left Recreation Park in 2018 on the basis that the site was to be developed for housing and a supermarket. The developers would fund a replacement sports facility when work began on their supermarket. Rosyth moved to the caged 3G at the Fleet Grounds. The proposed supermarket has not happened so far with the developers arguing that there is no need for a replacement ground as a suitable alternative facility has been made available to Rosyth. The land earmarked for a new Rosyth ground has now been chosen as the site of a replacement High School. The latest twist concerns the disused Rosyth Civil Service Sports Ground. This has been suggested as a home for Rosyth FC and as a new training base / academy for Dunfermline Athletic – the two purposes possibly being combined into a single development. Meanwhile Rosyth plough on at the Fleet Grounds cage.

Spartans
At the start of the 2021/2 season a new area of covered terracing was under construction at the west side of Ainslie Park.

St Andrews United
Saints are another club to have gone ahead with the installation of floodlights with a view to obtaining an SFA Licence.

Syngenta
Having had a peripatetic existence during their short time in the Juniors, Syngenta's move to the Seniors coincides with them coming to a ground-sharing and player pathway arrangement with Stenhousemuir FC at Ochilview Park.

Tayport
The Canniepairt club are keen to move on with SFA Licensing. This will involve floodlighting and fund-raising is now underway.

Thornton Hibs
Memorial Park in Thornton used to be "infamous" as the ground in a public park. Public no more – the club have built a substantial perimeter barricade to keep the public out. They have also installed floodlights – a great achievement for a village club.

Tweedmouth Rangers
The East of Scotland League side have completed the transformation of Old Shielfield. The ground now has a pavilion and covered accommodation for spectators which will allow Tweedmouth to move forward with plans for obtaining an SFA Licence.

Whitburn
Another club to benefit from "free seats" from Motherwell – part of the large covered enclosure has been transformed into an excellent grandstand.

Whitehill Welfare
Welfare have completed the installation of a floodlighting system at Ferguson Park meaning that they can maintain their SFA Licence.

Wigtown and Bladnoch
Like Whitehill Welfare, Wigtown had to install floodlights to keep their place at the SFA table. The work has now been completed.

OBITUARIES

John "Jock" Aird
Born 18 December 1926, Died June 2021
A native of Glencraig in Fife, Jock made his name playing for the successful Jeanfield Swifts side of the immediate post-war years. In 1948 he was transferred to Burnley. Originally a forward, he was converted into a full back at Turf Moor and his career took off. His consistent displays attracted the international selectors and he was capped four times by Scotland, including in the 1954 World Cup Finals in Switzerland. In 1955 Jock emigrated to New Zealand. He played there for eastern union and was also capped by New Zealand, playing twice of them in 1958. He moved to Australia and settled there becoming a coach with prominent Sydney club Hakoah FC.

Alastair MacPherson Alexander
Born 15 November 1937 in Port Glasgow, Died 7 March 2021
Alexander was a familiar voice to all Scottish football fans in the 1970s and 1980s as he commentated on matches for the BBC. He had got into commentating as a youngster – his father was blind and the young Alexander commentated for the "Blind Party" at St Mirren home games. He joined the BBC in 1965, spending 20 years on tv, then 20 on radio. Away from football he was an architect, an expert on naval history, and rose to high office in Freemasonry.

Eddie Beaton
Born 27 January 1932, Died July 2020
Eddie was a busting centre forward who had a long and varied career. He was capped by Junior Scotland while with Clydebank in 1949/50 and Aberdeen signed him up. He didn't make the first team and moved on to Dumbarton in 1951. He then did his National Service, playing for Hartlepools United Reserves and Nairn County during postings at various parts of the country. In 1955 he joined Arbroath before he went back Junior with Clydebank. In 1956 he stepped up again for four years at Morton where he had a phenomenal scoring record. Spells at Berwick Rangers and Stranraer drew the curtain down on a career in which he scored 132 Senior goals.

David Bell
Died August 29 2020
Anyone attending Junior games in Lanarkshire in recent years would be familiar with David Bell. He often spent 20 minutes watching part of two or three games on a Saturday afternoon with his notebook and camera in hand. In retirement he was contributing reports and pictures to the Hamilton Advertiser. The lifelong Motherwell supporter worked for several newspapers in the Lanarkshire area in the late 1960s and 70s before becoming a Press Officer with Glasgow District Council in 1975. In the 1990s he set up his own media agency, Bell Media. He was often duty journalist for national newspapers and agencies at Motherwell and Hamilton Accies games. David's other interest was in football programmes – he was Editor of the Motherwell, Clyde and Airdrie programmes at various times. David was awarded a Life Membership of the NUJ in 2010 and was also prominent in Church and Masonic affairs in Lanarkshire.

Gordon Bennett
Died 17 September 2020
Bennett was Aberdeen's first-ever Chief Executive when he was appointed in 1999. He had previous experience in similar roles with Bristol Rovers, West Bromwich Albion and Norwich City. Illness curtailed his spell in charge of the Dons but he later returned to football as Academy Director at Stoke City and Plymouth Argyle. In retirement he found a new interest as a football programme dealer.

Ryan Blair
Died December 21 2020, Aged 25
Downfield Juniors defender Ryan Blair was found dead on Hogmanay 2020. His previous clubs included Lochee United and Broughty Athletic.

John "Jack" McCaig Bolton
Born 26 October 1941 in Lesmahagow, Died 22 February 2021 in Larbert
Son of a miner who moved from Lanarkshire to Stirlingshire, Bolton joined Junior side Alva Albion Rangers and then crack Juveniles Sauchie. His talent was recognised by senior clubs and he joined Raith Rovers in February 1961. He was farmed out to Nairn Thistle Juniors where his displays attracted a bid of £3000 from Rangers for his services. Raith rejected it. His displays in the first team generated more interest with both Rangers and Stoke City making offers but it was Ipswich Town who signed him in 1963. Bolton played 77 times for Ipswich, half of them in the First Division. In 1967 he joined Morton but returned to Raith after a single season despite scoring 12 goals in 18 games for the Cappielow side. In 1970 Bolton moved to Dumbarton, helping them to promotion in 1971/2 and to avoid relegation in 1972/3. At the end of his career he played for home-town team Sauchie Juniors for a couple of years.

Walter Borthwick
Born 4 April 1948, Died 24 April 2021
A product of Tynecastle Boys Club, Borthwick was a familiar figure in Scottish football as a player in the 1970s and later as a coach. He had first signed for Morton in 1965 and then had a season with Brighton before making the breakthough at East Fife. He was at Bayview from 1967 until 1974 – a spell that saw the Methil team promoted to the top division and keep their place for three seasons. After that he moved on to St Mirren, St Johnstone and finally Dunfermline Athletic before retiring from playing in 1981. Always interested in the technical side of the game, he coached at Hearts for much of the 1980s. Walter had a short spell as Arbroath Manager and then worked for the SFA as a Football Development Manager in East Lothian. He was universally liked and highly regarded as a Coach for his ability to communicate with

and improve young players.

Russell Brebner

Born 29 July 1960 in Dunfermline; Died 14 February 2021.

Russell joined Hill of Beath Hawthorn in 1984 and went on to be a magnificent servant to the club. He gave them 13 years of service as a full back, 12 of them as club captain. He played 549 competitive games and lifted 26 trophies as captain of the Haws – a record that would be hard to match. He was the type of player who was happy to play Junior – he could have stepped up had he wanted to but he just enjoyed it too much at Hill of Beath.

Frank Anthony Brogan

Born 3 August 1942, Died 29 April 2021

Playing as a winger, Frank was signed up by Celtic from St Rochs in 1960. He was a schoolboy internationalist and sought after by several clubs. He had the distinction of scoring Celtic's 5000th League goal during the 1962/3 season. Despite a good record with Celtic (13 goals in 37 games) he was allowed to leave in 1964, joining Ipswich Town. Over a 7 year spell he was a regular for the Portman Road side, scoring 69 times in 223 League appearances before injuries blighted his later years. A move to Morton failed after just two appearances. After that he had a couple of seasons with Halifax Town before retiring. Frank was a qualified Chartered Accountant. His brother Jim Brogan was probably better known in Scotland having a long career at Celtic. The two brothers played together in the Celtic team on a few occasions in 1963/4.

George Jenkins Brown

Born 3 February 1948, Died 11 January 2021 in Sauchie

George was a great servant to Alloa in the late 1960s and early 1970s. He played 317 League and Cup games for them. A solid defender, his scoring contribution amounted to 4 goals. In 1974 he was signed by St Mirren. He was Willie Cunningham's last signing for the Buddies and his replacement as boss, Alex Ferguson, released Brown at the end of the season. He then spent eight seasons with home town team Sauchie.

Thomas McIntyre Brown

Born 29 March 1941 in Kilmaurs, Died March 2021 Aged 79

Brown joined Kilmarnock from Stewarton United in 1958 after an impressive scoring record in youth football. He signed a "back stop" form with Dreghorn in case he failed to make the grade. Tom was an example of a player that you never see now – a long term reserve team man. He made his debut for Killie's first team in March 1959. He played just four first team games yet remained at the club until the end of season 1965/6. He was part of the reserve side that won the Reserve League Cup and Championship in 1964/5 – the same year that the first team won the Scottish League. Brown moved to Queen of the South in 1966, then Newton Stewart in 1967/8. By 1969 he was with Troon. His son Andrew played for Kilmarnock and Stranraer in the 1980s.

Alex Byrne

Born 4 June 1933 in Greenock, Died November 2020

Byrne's football career began while on National Service with the Royal Engineers. He played for Cheltenham Town whilst based down south then signed for Gourock Juniors when he returned to civilian life. Celtic signed him in 1954 and after several years in the reserves he made his first team debut in March 1957. A left-sided forward, Byrne was in an out of the Celtic side over the next few years but played in both the Scottish Cup Final and Replay in 1961. He was a part-timer throughout his Celtic career, working in the |Greenock shipyards. Celtic freed him in 1963 and he moved to Morton and on to Queen of the South eight months later. Byrne then emigrated to Australia where he was a player / coach with Hellas and Juventus.

Donald Clark

Died December 13 2020 in Windygates, aged 86.

Donald was full back in the Cowdenbeath team that reached the Semi Final of the League Cup in 1959. His career had taken him from Kelty Hearts Juveniles to Nairn Thistle, Lochgelly Albert and Forres Mechanics. His Highland League stint was during National Service at RAF Kinloss and he played for the Mechanics against Celtic in the Scottish Cup. He signed for Cowden in 1957 after trial spells at Queen's Park and Dunfermline.

Hugh Cochrane

Born 9 February 1943 in Glasgow, Died 17 August 2020

Cochrane stepped up from Dundee Junior football to Dundee United in 1961. He was released two years later without having played in the first team and joined Barnsley. After a few games in the first team he dropped to non-league football and turned out for Wimbledon, Ashford Town and Margate. In 1972 he returned to Barnsley to live and became Player Manager at Wombwell.

Tommy Coggill

Born 21 March 1948, Died June 2021

As a player Tommy joined Kilmarnock in 1967 from Fauldhouse United. His career had begun at the age of 14 with Blantyre Celtic in the Lanarkshire Juniors. He was transferred to Cambuslang Rangers but then went back to Amateur football with Low Waters Miners Welfare. After just three months at Fauldhouse United he was snapped up by Killie. Spells with Queen of the South, Stranraer and Hamilton Accies followed. Tommy was a grafting inside forward who loved the game. After stepping down to the Juniors he played for Shotts Bon Accord, Carluke Rovers and finally Blantyre Vics. He was capped by Junior Scotland in 1981/2 and 1982/3 and won the Junior Cup with Vics in 1982. Two years later Tommy was made Vics Manager, a post he held from 1984 until 1988. He was then a Coach at both Lesmahagow and Cumnock before returning for a second spell as Blantyre Vics Manager.

Edward Devlin Connachan

Born 27 August 1935 in Prestonpans, Died 28 January 2021 in East London, South Africa

Eddie was a miner at Prestongrange Colliery in East Lothian and playing for Dalkeith Thistle when he was signed by Dunfermline Athletic in 1957. After an apprenticeship in the reserves he stablished himself as the number one goalkeeper at East End Park. He played in the team that won the Scottish Cup Final against Celtic in 1961. His form was recognised with Scottish League international caps. He was capped at full level for Scotland – the first coming in a World Cup Play Off against Czechoslovakia in Brussels. By the start of 1963/4 he was being challenged for his place at Dunfermline by Jim Herriot. The Pars greed to sell him to Middlesbrough where he was Player of the Year in 1964/5. Eddie returned to Scotland with Falkirk for a short while at the end of his domestic career. Like many pros of that era he was able to carry on playing in South Africa. He joined Port Elizabeth City and then East London Celtic, managing the latter for a spell from 1972. He settled in South Africa and was involved in the plumbing business.

Robert Connelly

Died May 2021

Bobby Connelly was the goalkeeper for Johnstone Burgh when they won the Scottish Junior Cup in 1968. He had joined them from Renfrew and was a key player on the long road to Hampden that year. He made a single appearance for East Fife as a trialist during the 1964/5 season.

Thomas Connery

Born 25 August 1930 Edinburgh, Died 31 October 2020 Bahamas

After leaving school "Tam" worked as a milkman for the Coop and played football for Grove Vale and Oxgangs Rovers. After two years National Service in the Navy he returned to Edinburgh and played for Fet-Lor, a club set up by Fettes and Loretto Public Schools for less privileged youngsters. In 1952 he was signed by Bonnyrigg Rose for whom he played up front. He reportedly had trials with East Fife but by this time was looking at a change of career – acting. Whilst on Tour with a production of South Pacific he played in a bounce game in Manchester and was offered a trial with Manchester United. He declined. Now calling himself "Sean", he went on to have stellar career in the film industry.

Jim Cousin

Died December 2020

Jim Cousin, brother of Alan (ex Hibs and Dundee) was an inspirational player and administrator for Sauchie. He played for the hugely successful Sauchie Juveniles side of the mid 1950s and then had three seasons senior with Stenhousemuir and Stirling Albion. After that he played for Sauchie after they moved up to the Juniors. In later years he was club Secretary and President. Like his brother Alan, Jim was a school teacher and spent many years as Depute Head of Graeme High School in Falkirk. He was also prominent in schools football as President of the Central Scotland schools FA for many years.

Justin Crowe

Died 2021, Aged 48

Justin was a reserve team player at Hamilton Accies in 1990 and 1991. He had been an S Form signing with Motherwell. After Hamilton he joined Glenafton Athletic and played in the Scottish Junior Cup Final for them. Partick gave him a second chance in the Seniors but he then moved to Hong Kong Rangers where he won the HK league Championship. On his return to Scotland in the late 90s he played Junior for a spell then switched to rugby for Hamilton's Second XV. He ran his own engineering firm and died tragically from COVID in April 2021.

Robert Davidson

Died 2 February 2021, Aged 81

"Sconie" Davidson was Manager of Kilbirnie Ladeside for 27 years from 1965 until 1992. When he arrived the club were on their uppers and he brought in a squad from his old Amateur side to revive their fortunes. Twelve years later, in 1977, Kilbirnie won the Scottish Junior Cup at Hampden. He led them to another Final appearance in 1987,, this time losing to Auchinleck.

Alexander Downie Dawson

Born 21 February 1940 in Aberdeen, Died 17 July 2020 in Edinburgh

The son of a Grimsby trawlerman, Dawson was born in Aberdeen but his family moved to Hull when he was still at school. He played for England Schoolboys against Scotland. A stocky inside forward, Dawson signed for Manchester United and played in two FA Youth Cup winning sides in 1956 and 1957. He was a reserve in 1957/8 but was pressed into first team action in the wake of the Munich Air Disaster. He scored five times as United advanced to the FA Cup Final including a hat trick in the Semi Final replay against Fulham. In 1961 Dawson was sold to Preston North End and he scored for them in the 1964 FA Cup Final against West Ham United. In total he scored 114 goals in 197 games for Preston before moving on to Bury and then Brighton and Brentford. His playing days ended with a spell at Corby Town.

Johnny Divers

Died 21 December 2020, aged 87

There were four players called Johnny Divers active in Scottish football in the 1950s and 60s. This Johnny Divers joined Hamilton Accies from Thorniewood United in 1959. His scoring record was impressive over several seasons encouraging Clyde to sign him in 1961. His 13 goals helped them win the Second Division Championship in 1963. He returned to Hamilton in 1963 but a bad leg injury brought bis playing career to a premature end. He worked for British Rail and was a coach at St Charles Juveniles for a spell.

Thomas Henderson Docherty

Born 24 August 1928 in Glasgow, Died 31 December 2020, aged 92

Tommy Docherty was a household name in football during the 1960s and 70s. He had played for St Paul's Boys Guild and joined Shettleston in April 1946. Almost immediately he was called up for National Service, serving with the Highland Light Infantry in Palestine. His management skills saw him promoted to Sergeant. He had shone in Services football and on his return he signed for

Celtic. Docherty couldn't earn a regular berth at Parkhead and in 1949 he moved on to Preston North End. His Coach in the Reserves at Deepdale was Bill Shankly. Over the next eight years he seldom missed a game for Preston as they finished as high as second in the Football League on two occasions and reached the FA Cup Final. He made his Scotland debut in 1951 and played in the 1954 World Cup. His 25th and final Cap for Scotland was against England at Wembley in 1959. By then he was an Arsenal player with a fee of £28,000 paid for his services. A broken leg brought a premature end to his playing days. He moved to Chelsea as a Coach and within months had taken over as Manager. From 1961 to 1967 Chelsea were the most stylish team in England playing great football but with few honours to show for it. Docherty resigned in 1967 and surprised everyone by taking over at Rotherham a few weeks later. That move was not successful and he was soon back in London as Manager of QPR. That lasted just a month – Docherty's abrasive manner did not endear him to Chairmen.

He was soon back with Aston Villa where he failed again. Docherty tried his luck in Portugal with FC Porto. In his season there they finished runners up to Benfica. In 1971 he came back to Britain as Assistant Manager of Hull City and part-time Manager of Scotland. The SFA were desperate. Scotland had scored just twice in ten games and attendances at Hampden plummeted. Docherty injected some life into the game bringing in young players like Kenny Dalglish and Martin Buchan. Scotland were well on the road to qualification for the 1974 World Cup when Docherty resigned to take over at Manchester United. They were relegated in his first season in charge, as had been Rotherham and Aston Villa. Surprisingly United persevered and they won the Second Division in style with Docherty at the helm. They competed for honours over the next couple of years until Docherty was sacked in July 1977 as news of his affair with the club physio's wife broke. From there he was manager at Derby, QPR, Sydney Olympic, Preston North End, South Melbourne, Wolves and Altrincham, all without success. From the mid-80s he focused on after-dinner speaking and PR work. His son Michael played for Burnley and Sunderland.

John Donnelly
Died 13 November 2020
"JD" was a well-known figure in Scottish football from the 1970s through to the late 1990s. He worked in various roles for Clyde but was most prominent as Commercial Manager and Kitman.

Robert Donnelly
Born 30 July 1961, Died 16 July 2020
Rab Donnelly was a consistent defender for Clyde between 1987 and 1989. He later played for Lesmahagow.

Willie Drew
Died 1 September 2020, Aged 75
Willie Drew was a long-serving committee member at Glenrothes Juniors. He had been involved in the formation of the club in the mid-1960s and remained with them until his death in 2020. He was club Secretary over several decades and reported on their matches for the local press.

Johannes Edvaldsson
Born 3 September 1950 in Reykjavik, Died 24 January 2021 in Glasgow
"Shuggie" joined Celtic in 1975 from Danish side Holbaek. Foreign players were a novelty in Scottish football at the time but Edvaldsson proved to be a formidable player. He had bags of experience from time at Valur, Cape Town City and Metz as well as in Denmark. He could play as a centre half or in midfield and had a good degree of skill for a big man. He made a total of just under 200 appearances for Celtic, contributing an impressive 36 goals. In 1981/2 he joined Hannover 96 in Germany but returned to Scotland a year later with Motherwell. Following a spell as Manager of Throttur in Iceland, he returned to settle in Glasgow. He won 34 caps for Iceland. His younger brother Atli was a prominent Icelandic player and international manager. Their father, Edvald, was an Estonian international in the 1930s and deputy head of police in Tallinn. He fled the country to escape the Nazis and settled in Iceland. In modern times Edvaldsson would therefore have been eligible to play for Estonia in the same way as his predecessor as Celtic centre half, Billy McNeill would have been eligible for Lithuania.

John Herbert Norton Fitzpatrick
Born 18 August 1946 in Aberdeen, Died 21 December 2020
Collectors of football cards and stickers in the late 60s and early 709s all knew the face of John Fitzpatrick. He looked like one of the Beatles with long hair at a time when most of his team-mates sported short back and sides or less than elegant comb-overs. He joined Manchester United straight from school in Aberdeen as a 15 year old. He could play right-back or right half. He was seldom a first pick but often stood in for Nobby Stiles or Shay Brennan. His hopes of a more permanent place in the side were dashed by a knee injury which ended his career at the age of 26. By that time he had played 141 times for United which was no mean achievement in the company of the likes of Law, best and Charlton. He returned to his native Aberdeen and became a wine importer and had spells as Manager at both Huntly and Buckie Thistle.

Duncan Falconer
Born 21 April 1941 in Leith, Died January 2021
Falconer graduated from Edinburgh Norton to Hibs in 1959 and was quickly drafted into the first team. He was hard working right half who liked to push forward. In 1961/2 he grabbed 12 goals in just 18 games. By 1964 he was unable to claim a place in the team and he moved to Australia. By the late 60s he was back in the UK and playing for the Kent Police football team.

James Paterson Fleming
Born 7 January 1942, Died 10 December 2020
Jim was a product of the top Juvenile side in Sauchie who went on to become Sauchie Juniors. He was signed by Partick Thistle in 1958 and quickly established himself on the wing for the Firhill side. In October 1960 he was transferred to Luton Town in exchange for striker Joe McBride. He was a reserve for the Scotland U23 side before returning north to rejoin Thistle in December 1962. From there he

moved on to Dunfermline and featured in some memorable European nights for the club. In 1967 he moved on again, this time to Hearts, where he played at the same time as his namesake George. Jim's career then took him south to Wigan Athletic where he scored 57 goals in 175 games in the Northern Premier League. Wigan Manager Ian McNeill moved to Ross County and took Fleming with him. He had four good years with County before spending 1977/8 as Player / Manager of Clachnacuddin.

Robert Campbell Forsyth

Born 5 May 1934 in Plean, Died November 2020

Goalkeeper Campbell first played with Gairdoch United and was signed by Shettleston in 1954. After less than a season he was snapped up by St Mirren and in January 1957 he was capped at Under 23 level for Scotland. He lost his place at Love Street and was sold to Kilmarnock where his career took off. During the title season of 1964/5 he vied for the jersey with Bobby Ferguson – Forsyth played more games but Ferguson was in goal for the title clincher against Hearts. By this time Forsyth was a full Scotland and Scottish League internationalist, having won his first Cap against England. Ferguson was also capped in 1965 and Killie were in the difficult position of having the best two goalies in Scotland. Forsyth was sold to Southampton whom he helped to promotion. Ferguson soon joined West Ham. Campbell suffered a broken leg playing for Southampton against Liverpool and never fully recovered. He retired in 1968 and worked for Watney's as their Scottish rep for 28 years. He scouted for Southampton and his home in Falkirk was called "The Dell".

Tom Forsyth

Born 23 January 1949, Died 14 August 2020

"Jaws" was often characterised as a "stopper" type defender, that is a bit unfair on a fine footballer who gave great service to Motherwell, Rangers and Scotland. He joined Motherwell in 1967 from Stonehouse Thistle and quickly settled into the first team. He helped them to promotion in 1969 and was outstanding when they returned to the top division. Rangers signed him in October 1972 and that season ended with him scoring the winner in the Centenary Scottish Cup Final against Celtic. By that time he was a full internationalist having been capped while at Motherwell. He won 22 caps in all – the last of them in Argentina in that 3-2 win over the Netherlands. Forsyth was a hugely popular player at Ibrox over a difficult period for the club. His last four years were spent under the management of John Greig when Rangers were investing funds in their stadium rather than the team. He retired at the end of 1981/2 and moved into management with Dunfermline a few months later. It was not a great success but he worked as Assistant to Tommy McLean for many years at both Motherwell and Hearts.

Gordon Frew

Born South Africa in 1927, Died in South Africa January 2021

Gordon was one of several South African born players to try their luck in Scotland in the years following World War Two. He had played with Wanderers and Marist Brothers and had won 4 caps for South Africa before moving to Dundee in August 1950. Over the next few years he was in and out of the Dundee side but he toured his homeland with them in 1953. After returning to South Africa Dundee retained his professional registration but allowed him to play as an Amateur for Maris brothers. The Dens Park eventually released him in 1959, five years after he had left the club. He became player manager of Highlands Park in the new South African Pro League. He retired in 1960 to concentre on his accountancy career.

Joe Frickleton

Died December 20

Frickleton starred with Armadale Thistle in the mid-1950s and was signed by Rangers in 1955. He didn't play in the first team and he went back to Junior football with Clydebank. In 1959 he signed for East Stirlingshire at the start of a fine spell in their history. He helped them to promotion in 1962.3 and was an important player for them in Division One in 1963/4. At the end of that season he moved to South Africa and signed for Highlands Park, winning many trophies with them. Joe moved into coaching and became manager of Lusitano, Highlands Park and then Kaiser Chiefs, again winning several trophies. After coaching he moved into football administration – he had two years as Chief Executive of the FA of Boputhatswana, one of the quasi-homelands established by the Apartheid government to deny basic rights to migrant workers in South Africa. Spells as an advisor to Adidas followed and he was Technical Advisor to Orlando Pirates when they won the African Champions Cup. Joe's brother Jim, known always as "Sammy" played with Falkirk, East Fife and Stenhousemuir.

Andy Gemmell

Born 27 April 1945, Died

Andy joined Morton in 1965 from Rankin Park United. He was released after a year at Cappielow and moved to Bradford Park Avenue. He went into business and became a Director of home town team Morton for many years. He later assisted clubs in financial difficulty such as Clydebank, Airdrie, Dumbarton and finally Livingston, where Andy was a founder / director of the company which bought Livingston out of administration in 2009. The "Livingston 5" company also involved Neil Rankine and Gordon McDougall, amongst others. He was a director of Livingston until 2017 and also had a spell on the Board of Dumbarton. Neil Rankine described him as "the life and soul of lower league club boardrooms for over 40 years always with a bottle he donated to the home team bar. A character and a half who will be sadly missed with even the most disgruntled fans who claimed you could not give Gemmell a red neck with a blow torch!"

Johnny Glover

Died 11 February 2021, Aged 85

John won the Scottish Junior Cup both as a player and as a coach with Kilsyth Rangers. A native of Twechar, he joined them in 1952 and was left half as they lifted the Cup at Hampden three years alter. In 1956 he went Senior at Dumbarton but failed to make much impact. Glover returned to Kilsyth then played for Johnstone Burgh. In 1967 when Kilsyth won the Cup for the second time, Glover was their Coach.

Stuart Gordon

Born 18 January 1947 in Glasgow, Died 9 April 2021 in St Andrews

Gordon learned his football at Possil YM in Glasgow and stepped up to Kilsyth Rangers where he won a Scottish Junior Cup medal in

1967. He had played a first team trial for Dumbarton but it was Dunfermline who won the race for his signature. After a promising start he sustained a bad leg break in a reserve game and he was released in 1970. He was reinstated to the Juniors and had a spell with Petershill. In later life he moved to St Andrews where he ran the Cross Keys Bar.

Stephen Graham
Born 29 May 1957 in Dundee, Died 14 February 2021 in Derby
Educated at Kirkton HS in Dundee, Stevie signed for Forfar Athletic as a teenager. He couldn't hold down a regular place and was freed in 1979, joining Stobswell in the Juniors. Brechin City gave him a second crack at Senior football between 190 and 1983 then he re-joined Forfar Athletic for a season. His Senior career ended with a short spell at Cowdenbeath before he signed for Carnoustie Pan-mure. Stevie moved to Derby to live and work in the late 1980s.

John Grant
Born 16 June 1931, Died 28 January 2021
Edinburgh Juvenile football was a hotbed of talent in the late 1940s. Many players went on to have top careers and one such as John Grant, signed by Hibernian from Merchiston Thistle in 1949. He worked his way up through Hibs East of Scotland and Reserve teams but like so many players of that era his career was interrupted by National Service. He made his first team debut in December 1954. Nicknamed "The Duke", Grant was a versatile defender who played both centre half and right back to good effect. In 1958 Grant was called up to the national team and he made his debut in the same game as Denis Law in October of that year. John left Hibs in 1964 when John McNamee was signed and he lost his first team place. He had one season with Raith Rovers before retiring and later settled in Bramhall, Cheshire.

George Gray
Born 27 September 1930 in Glencraig, Died 4 February 2021, aged 90
Goalkeeper George joined Raith Rovers in 1851 from Balgonie Scotia. He was quickly pitched into the first team for the St Mungo Quaich games against Queen of the South and Celtic, the latter in front of nearly 50,000 at Hampden. He played for more first team games but was otherwise confined to the Reserves until he was released in April 1953.

David Hagen
Born 5 May 1973 in Edinburgh, Died 24 July 2020 aged 47.
Rangers snapped him up from Falkirk-based Grahamston BC in 1989. He played for Scotland at U16, U18, U19 and U21 before making his first team debut. He found it hard to win a regular place at Ibrox at a time when home-grown talent was discarded in favour of big money imports. David moved to Hearts in 1994 and then to Falkirk in 1995. A strong midfield player, Hagen did well with Falkirk. He moved to Livingston in 2000, then to Clyde and finally Peterhead. He spent 2006/7 with Bo'ness United before being diagnosed with Motor Neurone Disease.

Derek "Dodger" Haston
Born June 18 1960, Died June 1 2021
Derek was a product of schools and youth football in Falkirk. He signed for local team Falkirk in 1978 but was released in 1980. The Tamfourhill-lad went on to have a hugely successful career in Junior football with Dunipace, Whitburn and Camelon. A lorry driver by trade, Derek's proudest footballing moment was being part of the Camelon Juniors side that won the Scottish Junior Cup in 1995. He was a tireless midfield player – the sort of player who did the dirty work for his team without always getting the credit he deserved.

Gary Holden
Died December 25 2020, Aged 51
Dalbeattie Star Assistant Manager Gary Holden lost his battle with cancer on Christmas Day 2020, just weeks after marrying his long-term partner. He started out with Blue Bell Amateurs and then spent 30 years at Threave Rovers as kitman, coach, manager and player. In 2013 he moved to Creetown as Manager then to Dalbeattie Star.

Robert M Hopkins
Died 2 May 2021
Referees were always associated with their home time – RM "Bert" Hopkins (Markinch) was a Grade 1 referee for several seasons in the late 1970s and a linesman for many more. He worked for Haig's in his home town of Markinch.

Willie Hunter
Born 14 February 1940 in Edinburgh, Died 2 August 2020
A product of Edinburgh Norton, Willie joined Motherwell in 1957 having been registered with Burnbank Athletic as a "back stop" measure. He quickly broke into the first team was capped by the Scottish League and Under 23s whilst still a teenager. The "Ancell Babes" Motherwell team were a joy to behold. Hunter earned his first international cap in 1960 and scored against Hungary. He remained with Motherwell through the first half of the 1960s. In 1967/8 he moved to the USA with Detroit Cougars but returned to join Hibs in 1968. He was hindered by injuries and made little impact at Easter Road. He was Assistant to fellow Ancell Babe Ian St john at Portsmouth for a spell and had a shot at management himself for a short and unsuccessful stint at Queen of the South in 1978/9.

Brian John Howie
Born 13 April 1955, Died June 2020
Goalkeeper Brian Howie joined Stirling Albion min 1973 from Dunipace. He played only a few first team games due to the consistency of George Young and moved back to the Juniors in 1977 with Bo'ness United. In 1979 he joined Stenhousemuir for whom he was the regular keeper for four seasons. He later played for Linlithgow Rose and Kilsyth Rangers.

Archie Irvine
Born 25 June 1946 in Coatbridge, Died September 2020

Archie was signed by Airdrie from Armadale Thistle in 1965. A creative midfield player, his promise saw Sheffield Wednesday pay £15,000 for his transfer in 1968. Three weeks later he was making his debut in the English First Division. Now playing on the wing he was a first team regular for a spell before losing his place to fellow Scot Jackie Sinclair. In late 1969 he moved to Doncaster Rovers where he played 247 games and scored 19 goals. He ended his professional career with Scunthorpe but continued to play Sunday football for many years in the Sheffield area.

George Johnston
Died 14 August 2020 in Dundee
George was 25 years as Secretary of Brechin City and a well-known figure around the Scottish football scene.

Alexander Anderson Kiddie
Born Dundee 28 April 1927, Died 27 March 2021, Aged 93
Kiddie was an old-style right winger who played for Ashdale BC and Stobswell in his native Dundee. Celtic signed him on a provisional form in 1944 but he was never called up to Celtic Park. Instead he joined Aberdeen in August 1945. He had a couple of seasons in the first team but remained a part-time player which probably hindered his long term prospects. Alex graduates with a BSc in Maths and Physics from St Andrews University and became a teacher at Lawside Academy in Dundee, then head of Maths at St John's RC Secondary. The Dons moved him on to Falkirk in 1950 which was followed by a short spell with Dundee in 1952/3. He then played the four Angus clubs – Arbroath, Brechin, Montrose and Forfar between 1953 and 1958.

Allan Kilpatrick
Born 1959, Died 7 December 2020
Allan Kilpatrick was one of the most important figures in the reborn Edinburgh City club. After time with Eyemouth United, Allan was playing for Postal United when they changed their name to Edinburgh City. A forward, he played for seven seasons and netted on 39 occasions. Ex Motherwell goalkeeper Stuart Rennie, who was Allan's manager for many years whilst at City summed up his value to the team: "If fit (and sometimes when he wasn't fully) Allan's name was always on the team sheet because I knew exactly what he was going to give to the team – skill, determination and a wonderful team player. For a guy small in stature, Allan had the heart of a lion."

Peter Patrick Lorimer
Born 14 December 1946, Dundee; Died 20 March 2021, Aged 74
Every schoolboy of the 1970s wanted to be Peter Lorimer. We all aspired to replicate his thunderous shooting power and audacious goal celebrations for the talented Leeds United side of the day. Lorimer never played in Scotland having left Dundee in 1962 to join Leeds, making his first team debut at just 15 years and 289 days. Back home he had played for Stobswell HS and Broughty YM. He was capped by Scotland at Schools, Amateur and Youth level – his Amateur caps coming after his Leeds debut as he was too young to sign pro forms. Later he would add Under 23 and Full caps to his CV. It was surprising that he won just 21 full caps but they included playing and scoring in the 1974 World Cup Finals. Lorimer was an absolute legend at Leeds United and a model of consistency. He left in 1978/9 to play in Canada but returned to Elland Road in 1983. He added another 18 goals to his Leeds total, making it 705 games and 238 goals. Spells as Manager of Whitby Town and Hapoel Haifa followed but he returned to Leeds in 1987. He ran a pub there and was on the Board of Directors at Elland Road for a while and then worked as an ambassador and matchday host for the club he had grown to love.

Malcolm Manley
Born 1 December 1949 in Johnstone, Died 16 August 2000
Malcolm was a schools internationalist and was on the books of Johnstone Burgh. However, his entire senior career was spent south of the border with Leicester City and Portsmouth. He was a valued member of the Leicester squad over 7 seasons and was substitute in the 1969 FA Cup Final. Following his transfer to Portsmouth he suffered a career-ending knee injury after only 11 games.

Brian Lynas "Gunter" Marr
Died 18 August 2020, aged 69
"Gunter" was a well-known figure in Fife and beyond. He played for Lochgelly Albert, managed at Crossgates Primrose and coached at Kelty Hearts over many years. John McGlynn took him to Raith Rovers as kit man in 2006 and he then moved to Hearts, working with their youth teams. His daughter Sophie was a physio with Cowdenbeath.

Les Massie
Born 20 July 1935 in Aberdeen, Died 11 November 2020
Les learned his football with Banks o'Dee but was destined to play his entire senior career in England. He signed for Huddersfield Town in 1956. Over ten years he played 335 League games and scored 100 goals for the Terriers. Initially he was paired up front with fellow Aberdonian Denis Law. . Subsequently he played for Darlington, Halifax, Bradford Park Avenue and Workington. His total Football League stats show 520 games and 160 goals. Les spent a short time in Ireland with Drogheda before retiring. He went into the haulage business and settled in the Huddersfield area.

Tom Matthews
Died 9 April 2021, aged 72.
Tom was a well-known figure in Fife refereeing circles. In his 20 years as a senior official his biggest day was running the line at the 1979 UEFA Cup Final between Red Star Belgrade and Borussia Moenchengladbach. Tom was a member of the Fife Referees Association for 53 years and its' President for part of that time.

Kevin McCann
Born 10 June 1953, Died May 2021
Kevin McCann, a talented wide player, was best known for his spell with Airdrie between 1972 and 1979. He scored their goal in the 1975 Scottish Cup Final when they lost 1-3 to Celtic. He was inducted to the club's Hall of Fame. He had joined the club from Carluke Rovers

and was outstanding as they won promotion back to the top flight after relegation in 1973. He later played for Queen of the South and Stenhousemuir before ending his senior career with a short spell at Workington in 1984/5.

Ronnie McCall

Born 9 July 1949, Died 16 April 2021, Aged 71

Ayr United were impressed with young McCall's displays for Irvine Vics and Ally McLeod took him to Somerset Park in March 1969. He helped Ayr to promotion that season but seldom featured in the first team during 1969/70. In June `1970 he moved to Stranraer for whom he would play for eight seasons. It was unusual for a non-local player to spend that long at Stair Parkin those days. In 1978 he returned to Irvine Vics for a further six seasons.

Kevin McCarra

Born 1 February 1958, Died 24 October 2020

McCarra was one of a new generation of journalists to emerge in Scottish football in the 1980s and 1990s. He did not fir the stereo-type of chain-smoking, whisky-drinking reporters. A graduate of Glasgow University, he was a tutor in their Scottish Literature Department and co-editor of Glasgow Magazine when he was appointed to research a major exhibition on the history of Scottish Football in 1983. From that came an excellent nook on the history of Scottish football. He joined Scotland on Sunday when it opened in 1988. Later he moved to the Times and Sunday Times before becoming Chief Football Correspondent of the Guardian. A lifelong Celtic fan he co-authored several books about the club.

Pat McCluskey

Born 13 April 1952 in Kilsyth, Died 24 August 2020

Pat was much sought after with Glasgow United in 1967. After trials for various clubs he joined Maryhill Juniors and signed provisional forms for Celtic. The Parkhead side sent him on loan to Sligo Rovers for a spell in 1970. By 1971/2 he was on the fringe of the first team and actually played in both legs of the European Cup Semi Final against Inter Milan. From 1972 until 1976 he was a first team regular in a successful Celtic side. He was capped for Scotland at Under 23 level. In 1975 he was banned for life by the SFA from international football as one of the "Copenhagen Five" following a nightclub incident. In 1977 Pat moved to Dumbarton for £15,000 and for three seasons he was a mainstay there as the Sons challenged for promotion to the Premier Division. Spells with Clyde and Airdrie followed before a move to the USA with Pittsburgh Spirit in 1982/3. Pat ended his playing career at Queen of the South. Never a showy player, he was very dependable and could defend effectively. He also packed a powerful shot and was Celtic's designated penalty taker at times.

Brian McConnell

Born 1951, Died May 2021

Born in 1951, McConnell, nicknamed the Bear, began making a name for himself locally as a centre-forward in the late 1960s and continued playing right up until the end of the 1990s. He played for three teams in his home-town of Hawick – Hawick United, Hawick Royal Albert, as they were known then, and Hawick Legion – as well as Gala Fairydean, albeit only very fleetingly, but he is probably best remembered for his time at Selkirk in the 1970s. Selkirk were a top side at the time and Brian was a key player in their team. He was still playing for Hawick Legion at the age of 48. Brian was an all-round sportsman and represented Scotland at water polo. His brother David was a player with St Mirren and Berwick Rangers.

John McCormack

Born 18 October 1933 in Fallin, Died 23 May 2020

After leaving school at 14 to work in Polmaise Colliery, McCormack was playing for Cowie Juveniles when he was spotted by Falkirk boss Bob Shankly. He was signed in 1954 and spent six seasons at Brockville. He was seldom a first pick but was always a valued member of the squad. In 1959/60 he moved on to play for Alloa for a short spell. John was Chairman of Polmaise Colliery Branch of the N UM. Polmaise was the first pit to come out on strike in 1984 and the last to return to work in 1986 and McCormack was a familiar figure from tv interviews at the time.

Peter McGauley

Died May 2021

In 1962 Whitehill Welfare's committee resigned when they found themselves with no funds and in debt. It was at that point a young Peter McGauley formed a new committee and the rest as they say is history. In 2012 Peter McGauley received a special award from the East of Scotland League for 50 years of service to Whitehill Welfare. During his early years with the club Whitehill were a top Under 21 Juvenile side. Peter was the driving force behind them and wanted to see the club progress – so they applied to join the East of Scotland League in 1979. Over the next thirty years they were one of the most successful clubs in the League. Peter worked tirelessly to improve the ground, prepare the pitch, work in the bar etc. as well as having the more formal role of Club Secretary. His proudest m moment may have been when Welfare played Celtic in the Scottish Cup in the 1990s. His dedication to the club was legendary, as was his tendency to call a spade a spade. In recent years he fell out with the new committee at Whitehill which was very sad. His funeral cortege stopped outside his beloved Ferguson Park which he visited almost every day of life over nearly 60 years.

Eddie McGavigan

Born 7 December 1963 in Glasgow, Died 9 December 2020 in New Zealand

Morton picked up McGavigan from Celtic Boys Club in March 1980. He was a member of the first team squad for a couple of seasons. In 1983 he accepted the offer of a contract with Mount Wellington of New Zealand. The move worked out well for him with a successful football career and a business career in the food industry, latterly as Chief Executive of Foodfirst, a major New Zealand food company.

John McGuinness

Born 21 April 1937, Died 21 January 2021

John was a very effective defender for Albion Rovers, Stirling Albion and the Shire over a 15 year career in the late 1950s and 1960s. He joined Albion Rovers in 1956 from Espieside Thistle. In 1960 he was transferred to Stirling Albion for whom he played in the top division and in a League Cup Semi Final. The club were relegated in 1968 and shortly afterwards McGuinness moved on to East Stirlingshire. In a career of 424 League and Cup games he scored just three goals. Unusually he was awarded a Testimonial by Stirling Albion after five years service – a match against Hibs was played.

David McIlroy
Born 25 September 1951, Died 22 December 2020
McIlroy was a well-known figure in Ayrshire Junior football between 1968 and 1989. Apart from a brief spell with Hamilton Accies in 1971/2. An old-style outside left, he played and or managed Ardrossan Winton Rovers, Beith, Kilbirnie Ladeside, Irvine Meadow, Dalry Thistle, Troon, Maybole and Saltcoats Vics

George McKenzie (Cambuslang Rangers)
Died 14 November 2020
Maryhill-boy George played for Victoria Thistle and signed for Rutherglen Glencairn at a young age. After one season at the Glens he moved to Queen's Park. George then played Army football on National Service alongside Alan Gilzean and he skipped the British Army team in Hong Kong. He returned to play with Kirkintilloch Rob Roy in 1959/60. His last games for them were memorable – on the afternoon of June 30 1960 they drew 0-0 at Shawfield in the West of Scotland Final, watched by 6000. The replay took place the same evening with Rob Roy winning 5-4 with 8000 there. George signed for Cambuslang soon afterwards. In 1964 he signed for Bloemfontein City where he played for the next three years. Returning home in 1967 he became player-coach at Cambuslang. He was Coach during their amazing Cup successes of the early 70s. After a spell as Coach with Hamilton Accies he was offered a similar role at Rangers, but turned it down as the wage for a full time post was not as much as he could earn through his career as a pharmacist.

Columb McKinley
Born 24 August 1950, Died 6 April 2021
The tall wing half stood out in Junior football with Vale of Leven and Airdrie snapped him up in 1969. During his first two seasons at Airdrie he featured regularly in the team but his appearances became less frequent after that. He was looking for more consistent first team football and moved to Dumbarton in 1975. Colum had a couple of decent seasons with the Sons before returning to Vale of Leven. He played briefly in Hong Kong in 1981.

Hugh McLaughlin
Born 28 May 1945, Died 21 July 2020 in Larkhall
While playing with Denny BC in 1962, the young Hugh was picked for a Scottish Youth trial game. However, it emerged he had not been born in Scotland and he was left out. He joined Dunipace Juniors and then Stirling Albion. The midfield player struggled in a poor Albion side and was freed in 1964. After a short spell at Alloa he joined Larkhall Thistle, before being handed another senior chance with Third Lanark in 1965. He was an ever-present in Third's final two seasons. St Mirren took on his registration after Thirds folded. Mclaughlin's best days were spent with St Mirren and he played in a League Cup Semi Final for them in 1971. He moved on to Queen of the South and then Cambuslang Rangers. He ended with senior career stats of 24 goals in 264 games.

Eddie McLaren
Born 8 September 1929, Died 23 December 2020
Eddie was a wing half in Perthshire Amateur football when he was signed by Blackpool in 1948. After several years in the reserve side he moved on to Reading where he quickly established himself in the first team. He played 184 League games for the Biscuitmen before ending his career with Guildford City.

Jim McLean
Born 2 August 1937, Ashgill, Died 26 December 20
Had he been born 30 years later there is no doubt that Jim Mclean would have been bracketed with Mancini, Mourinho, Guardiola and the other icons of the present day. He was a Manager who was ahead of his time and took Dundee United to heights they could never have dreamt of. The Semi Finals of the European Cup, the UEFA Cup Final . . .victories over Barcelona and the likes. Jim was the middle brother of three who all played professionally. Willie and Tommy also became managers but without the success achieved by Jim. As a player he was a model of consistency, clocking up nearly 500 games for Hamilton Accies, Clyde, Dundee and Kilmarnock. In 1970 he gave up playing to concentrate on coaching with Dundee. When Dundee Manager Davie White left the Directors apparently though Mclean wasn't management material. A few months later he crossed the street to join Dundee United as their Manager. He was a student of the game. He'd watch a game every night of the week if he could. Before satellite tv was commonplace he had a dish the size of Joddrell Bank is his back garden so that he could watch games from Europe and South America. Trophy success came in 1979/80 with the League Cup but the pinnacle was becoming Scottish Champions in 1982/3. United and Aberdeen, the "New Firm", dominated Scottish football with McLean and Alex Ferguson at the helm. He stood down as Dundee United Manager in 1993. He had built up a large shareholding in the club and became managing Director, then Chairman in 1994. Throughout his career he had a reputation for being quick tempered and he was a frequent visitor to Park Gardens for a slap on the wrists from the SFA. His time with Dundee United ended when in a live tv interview he was asked about the future of club manager Alex Smith. McLean took exception to the question and banjoed the reporter.

Charles "Chic" McLelland
Born 24 March 1963 in Glasgow, Died 26 December 2020
Aberdeen's Glasgow-based Scout Bobby Calder took many fine players to Pittodrie in the 1960s and 1970s. One such was Charles "Chic" McLelland, signed from Eastercraigs in 1969. Aberdeen farmed him out to Banks o' Dee "A" for a while but his promise was evident from selection for the Scotland Youth side. It took until 1974 for him to break into the first team. He kept his place until 1978 and won Scotland Under 23 caps in 1976. As Alex Ferguson re-moulded the squad McLelland was transferred to Motherwell and then

to Dundee. In 1982 he ended up at Montrose where he was a great success. In July 1990 he was appointed as co-manager of the club with old Dons team mate Doug Rougvie. They were sacked in the middle of 1991/2. McLelland became an SFA Community Coach and then Youth Development Manager at Aberdeen FC.

John Haddon McSeveney

Born 8 February 1931 in Shotts; Died 12 December 2020

John had a lengthy career North and South of the Border, as well as coaching abroad. He joined Hamilton Accies in 1948 from Carluke Rovers. Playing on the left side of the forward line, his style and finishing attracted interest and in 1951 he was sold to Sunderland for £5000. His time at Roker Park was spent mainly in the reserves, playing 38 first team games over four seasons. From there McSeveney was transferred to Cardiff City where he enjoyed more first team football. In 1957 he joined Newport County where he hit 53 goals in 172 appearances. Hull City was his next port of call and he proved a bargain buy for just £1000. He netted 70 goals in 183 appearances for the Boothferry Park side. One season he was top scorer with 22 goals from his left wing berth. John retired from playing in 1965 but remained at Hull as a Coach. He became Barnsley Manager in 1971 then had a spell in charge of Home Farm in Dublin. A spell as Assistant Manager of Nottingham Forest followed then it was back to Ireland with Waterford before taking coaching roles in Guyana and Oman. During the 1980s he was Assistant Manager at Rotherham and Sheffield United under Ian Porterfield and Coach at Coventry City. His brother Willie played for Motherwell and Dunfermline Athletic.

Jock McVicar

Died 3 April 2021, Glasgow, aged 83

Jock was a well-known journalist with the Scottish Daily Express back in the days when it was a best-selling Scottish-produced title. Gold was his first love, but the Motherwell fan covered football for the Express for many years.

Alan Miller

Born 29 March 1970, Died 3 June 2021, Aged 51

Alan was a much travelled goalkeeper who played 18 games for St Johnstone in 2001/2 whilst on loan from Blackburn Rovers. Prior to that he had played for Arsenal, Plymouth Argyle, West Bromwich Albion (3 spells), Birmingham City, Middlesbrough, Huddersfield Town, Grimsby Town, Bristol City and Coventry City. Alan played over 200 games in the English League and changed hands for transfer fees that totalled well over one million pounds. He won FA Cup, League Cup and European Cup Winners Cup medals as an unused substitute with Arsenal in the early 1990s. He was capped 4 times by England at Under 21 level. Alan died suddenly at the young age of 51. At the time of his death he was Executive Events Manager at Holkham Hall in Norfolk.

Barrie Horace Mitchell

Born 15 March 1947 in Aberdeen, Died 24 January 2021

Barrie was playing Junior with Banks o' Dee when Arbroath signed him on a provisional form. He was called up to Gayfield in 1967 and was outstanding in the League Cup group games. Before he had even made his League debut George Farm signed him for Dunfermline for £13,000, a then record for a Second Division player let alone one who had never played a Second Division game! He played European football for the Pars although he had to serve a three game ban for being sent off in a tempestuous clash in Athens against Olympiakos. In modern parlance he's be a "false 9" or such nonsense – a striker who wasn't the main target man. Mitchell fell out with Dunfermline manager George Farm – not an unusual occurrence – and he was sold to Aberdeen. Injuries curtailed his appearances and he moved on to Tranmere Rovers in 1974. Spells with Preston North End, Vancouver Whitecaps, York City and Morton brought his career to an end in 1978/ he became a publican in the Wirral.

Frank Mooney

Born 1 January 1932 in Fauldhouse, Died May 23 2021 in Fauldhouse

Frank was a talented young footballer who represented Scotland at Youth level. Playing against England at Aberdeen in 1948, he was directly up against Brian Close, who later became a Test cricketer. He joined Manchester United as an 18 year old in `1950. He found it difficult to break into the first team and National Service in Rhodesia kept him out for two years. He went on to have a fine career with Blackburn Rovers, Carlisle United and Berwick Rangers, before retiring in 1960. He played mainly on the wing but had a good scoring record. After retiring from football Frank trained as a teacher and taught at Harrysmuir Primary in Livingston. His elder brother John was also a professional footballer and two played against each other when John was with Doncaster Rovers.

Conan Murie

Died January 4 2021, Aged 18

Young Edinburgh South football Conan Murie was found dead close to Arthur's Seat in Edinburgh on January 4th.

Robert Reekie Nee

Born 22 October 1932, Died 23 June 2020

Raith Rovers picked him up from St Monance Swifts and quickly farmed him out to Dalkeith Thistle. In five seasons with Raith he made just one first team appearance. His career was interrupted by National Service in Japan.

Craig Neeson

Died August 2020

Craig was part of the Cowdenbeath team that won promotion from the Scottish Third Division in 2001. He was on loan from Hearts whom he had helped to win the SFA Youth Cup. Craig's body was found at his home in Port Glasgow.

David John "Jack" Nimmo

Died November 2020, aged 97

David Nimmo was a former Hamilton Accies player and a lifelong supporter of the club. He joined the club in 1946 and then played Junior with New Stevenston Thistle and Royal Albert. During the War he had served in Burma. As a supporter he held his season ticket until into his 90s and was thought to be the last surviving Accies supporter to have seen his team in the 1935 Scottish Cup Final.

Frank O'Callaghan
Died 15 July 2020, Aged 80
Frank was a Director of Celtic from February 1999 until June 2000. He was chairman of the McDonald Hotels Group.

James O'Donnell
Died December 24 2020, Aged 29
James was a long-term player of Lochs FC on the island of Harris. He died a road traffic accident on Christmas Eve 2020.

Tom O'Malley OBE
Died 28 August 2020
Tom O'Malley was a Director of his beloved Hibernian FC in the 1990s and Chairman for a spell towards the of that decade. He helped stabilise the club after a traumatic spell when they nearly went bust and were the subject of take-over talk from rivals Hearts. Away from football O'Malley was Head Teacher of St David's High School in Dalkeith and he was awarded an OBE for services to education.

Martin O'Neill MP, Baron O'Neill of Clackmannan
Died 26 August 2020, aged 75
Martin was a Director of Hibernian between 2004 and 2007. As a Labour MP for Clackmannan and East Stirlingshire he served as Shadow Defence Secretary and Chair of the Trade and Industry Select Committee.

Archie Page
Born 21 April 1946, Died 25 March 2021
A product of Fife Junior club Thornton Hibs, Archie joined Montrose in 1967. He was first choice keeper at Links Park for several seasons and respected as an agile and athletic player. He was reinstated to the Juniors with Glenrothes.

Alan Quilietti
Born 25 March 1960, Died
From a Scots-Italian family in Falkirk, Alan played Juvenile football in the Falkirk area for Gairdoch United and signed for Hibs in 1978. Confined to the reserves, he still thought it a great honour to play for the team he supported. He had short spell with Broxburn. Away from football Alan was employed by British Rail for many years.

Billy Reid
Died November 2020
Billy was capped for Junior Scotland whilst with Kirkintilloch Rob Roy. He joined Stirling Albion in 1964 and went on to play over 100 games for the Annfield club, mainly in the old First Division. He had one season with East Stirling. He was Trainer for Rob Roy when they reached the Junior Cup Final in 1977.

Brian Reid
Died September 2020
Brian enjoyed great success as a player with rival clubs Rutherglen Glencairn and Cambuslang Rangers in the 1970s. he played in two successive Junior Cup Finals, winning the Cup with Cambuslang in 1974 and being in the losing Rutherglen side in the 1975 Final. A cultured defender, Brian ended his playing days with East Kilbride YM.

Andrew Shaw
Died October 2020, Aged 33
Perth-man Shaw was a youth signing with Hearts and a Scotland U16 international. He failed to make the grade and was released. He subsequently joined the Army and served in Afghanistan. He suffered from PTSD and was jailed in 2016 for a series of drug-related thefts. He was found dead in his Perth flat shortly after his release from an apparent drugs overdose.

Ebbe Skovdahl
Born 5 July 1945 in Copenhagen, Died 23 October 2020 in Karlslunde
A journeyman player for Vanlose and Brondby, Ebbe turned to coaching in the mid 1970s. His first major success was with Bronshoj who he led to successive promotions to the Danish top tier. He then managed Brondby (three spells) and Benfica, as well as Vejle BK. He was a surprise appointment as Aberdeen Manager in June 1999. Skovdahl was up against the weight of expectation from Dons fans used to success under Alex Ferguson and he resigned in 2002. His last appointment was Manager of Frem. Ebbe was an uncle of Brian and Michael Laudrup.

John Sludden
Born 29 December 1964, Died 7 May 2021, Aged 56
Every Scottish football fan of a certain age remembers a Schoolboy international at Wembley in 1980 when Scotland defeated England 5-4. Two of the goals that day were scored by Falkirk-lad John Sludden. He had signed for Celtic on the same days as one of his teammates from Wembley, Paul McStay. The young Sludden showed great promise at Celtic but was never really given a chance. In 1983 he moved on to St Johnstone. Two years later he signed for Airdrie but it was at Ayr between 1985 and 1989 that he fully realised his potential.

Sludden scored 78 goals in 140 League games for Ayr before moving on to further successful spells at Kilmarnock, East Fife, Clyde and Stenhousemuir. He was Player Manager of Bo'ness United between 1995 and 2001 and then worked in Youth Development for Celtic. Between 2014 and 2018 he had two-year spells as Manager at both Camelon Juniors and East Stirlingshire.

Archie Smith

Died August 2020

Smith was a full back who joined the highly successful East Fife team in 1951 from Bayview BC. He found it hard to get game time in a side that finished third in the top division. He moved on to Dundee United and then Arbroath before a knee injury ended his playing days in 1954.

Davie Snedden M.B.E.

Born 24 April 1936, Died 24 December 2020

The young Davie was capped by Scottish Schools in 1951 and the following year he signed for Kilwinning Rangers. He was training as a telephone engineer when he was signed by Dundee in 1954. The Dens Park side had to wait two years to see their man in action as he completed his National Service with the Royal Signals Corps. A crafty inside forward, Sneddon was admired by many other clubs and Preston North End signed him for £12,000. Snedden was by then an Under 23 internationalist. After several productive years at Deepdale he was signed by Kilmarnock who were building a decent team at the time. Snedden slotted in and was one of the mainstays of their title winning team in 1964/5 – he scored the first goal in their 2-0 win at Tynecastle to secure the title. After playing for Killie against the likes of Real Madrid his next move was to Stark's Park and a struggling Raith Rovers side. By 1971 he was back in Junior football with Hurlford United. Davie moved into coaching and went back to Killie to take the reserves in 1972. In 1977 he became Killie Manager and led them to promotion in 1979. Sacked in 1981 he returned to management with Stranraer where he did much to improve a struggling side. Afterward he worked as a scout and matchday host for Killie and in 2014 he was awarded an MBE for his services to football in the community in Kilmarnock.

Jimmy Stevenson

Born Bellshill 4 August 1946, Died March 2021

Jimmy joined Hibs in 1963 from Edina Hearts and became a regular in the reserves and was capped by Scotland Youths. After a promising start to his first team career he fell out of favour and couldn't command a regular place. In 1967 he joined Southend United and later played for Brentwood Town and Chelmsford City, winning the Southern League with them in 1971/2. He moved to Dover FC for two seasons and settled in the Kent town where he went on to be a referee in local football.

Ian St John

Born 7 June 1938 in Motherwell, Died 2 March 2021 in the Wirral

For one generation of fans St John was a busting and talented striker and for another he was a tv personality and pundit. Regardless of which sphere he was operating in, St John certainly never lacked confidence in his own ability. A native of Motherwell, he joined his home town team after a short spell with Douglas Water Thistle in the Juniors. One of the "Ancell Babes" who lit up Fir Park with some scintillating football without winning major honours, St john was called up for his first Scotland cap in 1959, against West Germany at Hampden. He scored 105 goals in 144 games for Motherwell. It was no surprise when he moved to England in 1961 but his destination was a shock – struggling Second Division outfit Liverpool. That was all about to change under Bill Shankly and St john was a key player in Liverpool's emergence as a football power. His 21st and last cap for Scotland came in 1966 – he blamed his lack of selection after that on some sort of dispute with the selectors. By 1970/1 St john had lost his place in the Liverpool side and he left to join Hellenic in South Africa after 425 games and 118 goals for the Anfield side. He returned to the UK with Coventry in 1971 and then played for Tranmere. Motherwell brought him "home" as Manager in 1973. St John said that he had been promised the Leeds United job in succession to Don revie but it was given to Brian Clough instead. St John did head south to take charge of lowly Portsmouth who were in financial difficulty at the time. He left when they narrowly avoided a second successive relegation. Instead m he moved into football punditry, eventually having his own Saturday lunchtime show with Jimmy Greaves on ITV. He also started the "Ian St John Soccer Camps", Summer schools for young players.

David FT Syme

Died 27 October 2020

David Syme of Rutherglen came from a refereeing family – his father Willie was a Grade One official. Davie joined the SFA list of referees in 1968 and reached Grade One in 1972. He retired in 1994. He refereed several Scottish Cup and League Cup Finals. As a FIFA list official he was awarded the 1985 World Youth Cup Final between Brazil and Spain. Other appointments included five World Cup Qualifiers , a European Cup Semi Final and a UEFA Cup Semi Final. Davie also officiated in the USA during the Summer of 1979 in the BASL. He worked as a rep for a watch company.

Matt Tees

Born 13 October 1939 in Johnstone, Died 4 November 2020

The goalscoring exploits of the young Matt Tees had senior scouts watching him at Cambuslang Rangers in the late 1950s. He signed a provisional form for Airdrie but remained with Cambuslang until their Junior Cup run was over. Tees slotted into Airdrie's side very quickly. In 1963 he was sold to Grimsby Town of the Second Division for £5,000. Although not tall for a striker, his athleticism and tenacity made up for any lack of bulk physique. Charlton Athletic shelled out £23,000 to sign him in 1967. They recouped that fee and a little more when he moved on to Luton Town in 1969 where he partnered a young Malcolm Macdonald up front. He later returned to Grimsby for a second spell where he had a fine scoring record. His career ended with a spell at Boston United. Tees trained as an HGV drive rand settled in Cleethorpes.

James Clabby Townsend

Born 2 February 1945 in Greenock, Died 19 October 2020 in Canada

Jim Townsend was one of the best midfielder in Scottish football in the mid-1960s and early 1970s. Had he ever joined one of the big two Glasgow clubs there is little doubt he would have won many international caps. As it was he was restricted to eight appearances in unofficial internationals during Scotland's World Tour of 1967. He had gone senior to St Johnstone in 1961 as a 16 year old from Port Glasgow Juniors. In 1964 Middlesbrough paid £20,000 for him. His skill and vision were a delight to watch but injuries blighted his time with Boro. He returned to St Johnstone and by the time he went on tour with Scotland he was a Hearts player. Once again his skills were evident at Tynecastle but he lost his place in 1972 and moved on to Morton. He was de facto Manager of Morton for two years although Hal Stewart gave him the title Head Coach. In 1977 he moved to Canada and settled there becoming Manager of a team called Windsor Wheels.

Alexander "Sandy" Veitch

Born 3 June 1935 in Peebles, Died March 30 2021 in Melrose

Alexander Veitch CEng, C MarEng, FIMarEST was an all-round sportsman who had a successful spell with Peebles Rovers in the early 1950s, helping them to win the Border Cup in 1951/2. He moved away from the Borders to become a Marine Engineer, eventually becoming Chief Superintendent for the Canadian Pacific company. He retired to the Borders in 2000, settling back in his native Peebles.

Josef Venglos

Born 18 February 1936 in Ruzomberok, Died 26 January 2021 in Bratislava

Dr Venglos enjoyed a lengthy playing career with Slovan Bratislava. He studied for a PhD in Philosophy and Physical Education. When his playing career was ended up hepatitis he moved into coaching, firstly with Australian side Sydney Prague. He was manager of the Australian National team that played a Scottish touring side in 1967. Venglos returned to Czechoslovakia in 1969 and managed VSS Kosice as well as being assistant national team boss. By the time he helped the Czechoslovaks become European Champions in 1976 he was manager of Slovan Bratislava. His coaching career then took him to being in charge of the national team, manager of Sporting Lisbon, manager of Malaysia and then a second stint in charge of Czechoslovakia. His lengthy and varied track record led to him being appointed Aston Villa manager, the first non-British Isles national to manage in the English League. After that he was manager of Fenerbahce, the new Slovakia national team and the Oman national team. It was a surprise when Fergus McCann appointed him as the man to turn Celtic around. His Celtic team played good football and he signed players like Lubo Moravcik and Johan Mjallby. However, a lack of trophies saw him looking for another job. His final management role was at JEF United in Japan.

Derek Waterson

Died 27 December 2020

A newsagent by trade, Derek was Chairman and Treasurer of Whitehill for many years. Along with Peter McGauley and Andrew Renwick, they were the driving force behind Welfare's rise from Juvenile football to a spell as one of the best teams in Scotland outside the Scottish League.

Frankie Watt

Died 19 November 2020 in Tenerife, aged 62

Watt was an Inverness Caley player in the 1970s. He joined them in 1975 and remained until 1977. He then had a distinguished career in the Fire Service, ending as Assistant Chief Officer in Derbyshire then working at the Fire Service College at Moreton in the Marsh.

John Watson

Died July 1 2020

John was physio at Clyde from March 1973 until September 2001. He also helped out with numerous Scotland age group teams over the years. He was an NHS Superintendent Physio in his professional life.

Alan Welsh

Born 9 July 1947 in Edinburgh, Died 16 August 2020

An orthodox winger, Welsh went south from Bonnyrigg Rose to Millwall in 1965. He subsequently played for Torquay United, Plymouth Argyle and Bournemouth before returning for a second spell at Millwall. His Football League stats show 261 games and 63 goals. A short spell with Maidstone and month's trial with Hearts followed but he ended his playing career in South Africa with cape Town City. His brother in law was another Millwall-Scot, defender Billy Neill.

William Murdoch Whigham

Born Airdrie 9 October 1939, Died Airdrie 3 March 2021

Whigham was a living embodiment of the adage that "goalkeepers are crazy". He was loved by the fans at all his clubs, at times as much for his eccentricity as for his shot stopping qualities. He can't have been that mad or bad – he played 472 League and Cup matches in his long career. Willie began with Strathclyde Juniors in the shadow of Celtic Park then moved on to Shotts Bon Accord. Senior clubs began to take an interest. After playing atrial for Albion Rovers he was snapped up by Falkirk in 1960. He had six years at Brockville before Middlesbrough moved in to sign him for £10k. He helped them move from the Third Division to a place challenging for promotion to the First Division. He lost his place at Middlesbrough to Jim Platt in 1971 and moved on for a short spell at Dumbarton. After a few games with Darlington in 1974 he retired. After moving back to Airdrie he worked for a ground investigation company.

Charles Edward "Ward" White

Born October 12 1946, Died December 2020

Ward White's football career was long and varied. It took him from Celtic to Clydebank, Beith, Irvine Meadow, Dalbeattie Star, Hurlford and Maybole, where he was Manager for 10 years and played a game aged 50. His time at Celtic was in the reserves alongside the likes of Lou Macari and Kenny Dalglish. He had actually been playing in the Ayrshire Juniors for four seasons before getting the switch to Parkhead. Ward won Scotland Amateur Youth and Junior caps before he joined Celtic.

Arthur Williamson

Born 26 July 1930 in Bankfoot, Died 26 June 2020 in Perth

Williamson starred for Jeanfield Swifts and Blairgowrie in the Perthshire Juniors before signing for Clyde in 1952. He played just two first team games for the Shawfield side before joining Southend United in 1955. The right back was a great success at Southend he played 230 consecutive League and Cup games for them between 1955 and 1960. He lost his place in the team in 1961 and returned to nis native Perthshire to run the family butchery business.

John Mackie "Jackie" Wren

Born 26 April 1936 in Bonnybridge, Died 13 August 2020 in South Africa
As a young goalkeeper with Gairdoch United, Wren already displayed the agility that served him so well. He moved to Bo'ness United and the all-conquering Sauchie Juveniles before joining Hibs in 1956. Jackie was seen as the replacement for Tommy Younger but National Service intervened. Whilst serving around the country Hibs brought in Lawrie Leslie and Wren couldn't reclaim the first team jersey. In 1960 he signed for Rotherham but a year later was back in Scotland with Stirling Albion whom he helped to a League Cup Semi Final. Short spells at Falkirk, Dundee United and Berwick followed before he emigrated to South Africa and had seven years in goals for Hellenic.

Robert Whyte "Bobby" Wishart

Born 10 March 1933 Edinburgh, Died 3 December 2020
Wishart attended the rugby-playing George Heriot's School in Edinburgh but also played football for crack Juvenile side Merchiston Thistle. Aberdeen signed him in 1951 and he played for three years in their reserves. Part of time he was loaned to Portadown due to National Service in Northern Ireland. By 1954/5 he was a first team regular at inside left for the Dons as they won the Scottish League Championship for the first time. He was picked for the Scottish League but bever for the full international side. He lost his place in the Dons team in 1961 to young Charlie Cooke and was sold to Dundee. He slotted in at left half and was instrumental in helping Dundee win the League in 1961/2. He then played in all eight European Cup ties for the club as they reached the Semi Final in 1963. At the end of his career he played a few matches for Airdrie and Raith Rovers. In later life he was Scottish Secretary of the National Farmers Union and a manager with the Britannia Building Society.

Marius Zaliukas

Born 10 August 1983 in Kaunas, Died 31 October 2020
The Lithuanian defender joined Hearts in July 2006 and he captained the side to victory in the 2012 Scottish Cup Final against Hibernian, sealing a place in the history books. He was the longest-serving of the many Lithuanians who came to Hearts at that time and played under a bewildering succession of managers and coaches. When Hearts went into administration Zaliukas became a free agent and he signed for Leeds United. From there he moved to Rangers and played 25 games as the Ibrox side failed to secure promotion from the Championship. He returned to Lithuania and signed for Zalgiris Vilnius. "Zal" was already living with the diagnosis of Motor Neurone Disease which claimed his life at the age of 36. He won 25 caps for Lithuania between 2005 and 2016.

The Most Complete Record of Scottish Football available
Covers internationals at all levels, SPFL, Highland and Lowland Leagues, other Seniors, Juniors, Amateurs, Welfare, Schools, Youth and Womens Football

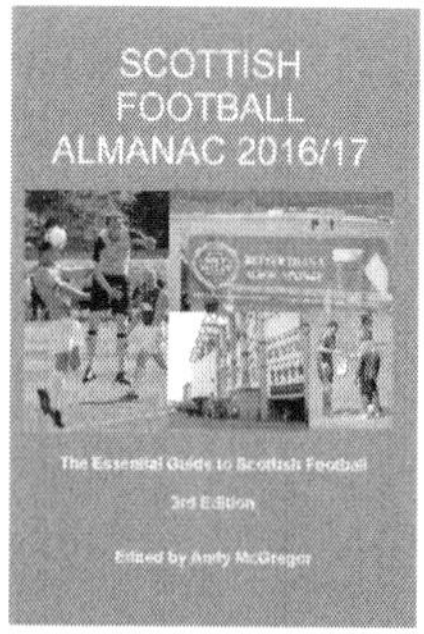

Previous editions still available at the website or from Amazon

2014/15 £14.99
2015/16 £19.99
2016/17 £19.99
2017/18 £19.99
2018/19 £19.99
2019/20 £24.99
2020/21 £24.99

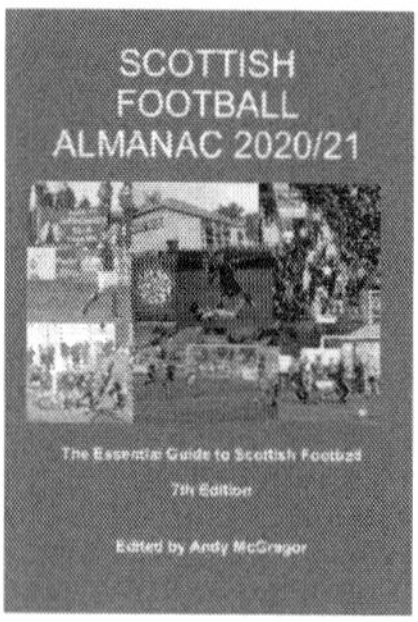

www.rel8mediapublishing.weebly.com